Essentials of Understanding
PSYCHOLOGY
FIRST CANADIAN EDITION

Robert S. Feldman
University of Massachusetts–Amherst

Joan E. Collins
Sheridan College

Judy M. Green
Sheridan College

Expert Consultant
Catharine Rankin
University of British Columbia

 **McGraw-Hill
Ryerson**

Toronto   Montréal   Boston   Burr Ridge, IL   Dubuque, IA   Madison, WI   New York   San Francisco
St. Louis   Bangkok   Bogotá   Caracas   Kuala Lumpur   Lisbon   London   Madrid
Mexico City   Milan   New Delhi   Santiago   Seoul   Singapore   Sydney   Taipei

McGraw-Hill
Ryerson Limited
A Subsidiary of The **McGraw·Hill** Companies

ESSENTIALS OF UNDERSTANDING PSYCHOLOGY
Canadian Edition

ISBN: 0-07-087468-9

1 2 3 4 5 6 7 8 9 10   QD   0 9 8 7 6 5 4 3 2 1

Care has been taken to trace ownership of copyright material contained in this text; however, the publisher will welcome any information that enables them to rectify any reference or credit for subsequent editions.

Vice President and Editorial Director: Pat Ferrier
Senior Sponsoring Editor: Veronica Visentin
Associate Sponsoring Editor: Marianne Minaker
Senior Developmental Editor: Lesley Mann
Marketing Manager: Ralph Courtney
Senior Supervising Editor: Margaret Henderson
Copy Editor: Karen Hunter, The Last Word
Production Coordinator: Brad Madill
Composition: Bookman Typesetting Co.
Cover Design: Greg Devitt
Photo Research: LouAnn K. Wilson, Lesley Mann, Elaine Freedman
Printer: Quebecor Printing, Dubuque, Inc.

Canadian Cataloguing in Publication Data

Feldman, Robert S. (Robert Stephen), 1947–
    Essentials of understanding psychology

Canadian ed.
Includes bibliographical references and index.
ISBN 0-07-087468-9

1. Psychology.   I. Collins, Joan E.   II. Green, Judy, 1958–   .   III. Title.

BF121.F338 2001   150   C00-932976-5

About the Authors

Robert S. Feldman is Professor of Psychology at the University of Massachusetts at Amherst, where he is Director of Undergraduate Studies and recipient of the College Outstanding Teacher Award. As Director of Undergraduate Studies, he initiated the Minority Mentoring Program, and he teaches in the Talent Advancement Program. His introductory psychology classes, which he teaches every term, range in size from 20 to 300 students.

A graduate of Wesleyan University and the University of Wisconsin–Madison, Professor Feldman is a Fellow of both the American Psychological Association and the American Psychological Society. He has written some 100 scientific articles, book chapters, and books. His books, several of which have been translated into languages other than English, include *Fundamentals of Nonverbal Behavior*, *Development of Nonverbal Behavior in Children*, *Essentials of Understanding Psychology*, *Social Psychology*, and *Development Across the Life Span*. His research interests encompass the development of nonverbal behaviour in children and the social psychology of education. Professor Feldman's spare time is most often devoted to serious cooking and earnest, but unpolished, piano playing. He lives with his wife, also a psychologist, and has three children.

Joan Collins has spent most of her life in school. Her commitment to education has been inspired by the inscription above the front door of the college she attended at the University of Toronto, which reads "The Truth shall make you free." As a secondary school teacher teaching English, the most significant event she experienced was the discovery that a young student who sat at the front of the classroom could not read. Her awareness of student reading problems led her to develop a remedial reading program and later to write a thesis and a dissertation on reading.

Since 1988, Joan Collins has taught psychology at Sheridan College in Oakville, Ontario, at first to students in different daytime programs (Library Techniques, Computer Studies, Advertising, Applied Research, General Arts and Science) as well as to mature students in Continuing Education. Currently, she teaches a variety of psychology courses to General Arts and Science students. Joan Collins finds it very rewarding to introduce students to psychology and to see them discover that the subject matter is interesting, exciting, and relevant to everyday life.

Judy Green grew up in Montreal, Quebec, and graduated from Concordia University in that city. For more than ten years now, Judy Green has taught introductory psychology, social psychology and human development at Sheridan College in Oakville, Ontario. She has also taught at the American School in London (England). She and her colleague Joan Collins previously collaborated on the writing of *A Textbook of Social Psychology*, Brief Edition, with James Alcock, Bill Carment, and Stan Sadava.

Judy Green writes, "Working on this project has been most rewarding. With Robert Feldman's excellent book as a starting point, we expanded the representation of Canadian research, which has reinforced for me the knowledge that while psychology in Canada is unique in some respects, it has a great deal to offer on the world stage. Connecting with the very talented people who agreed to be featured in our 'Pathways' and 'Prologue' sections was a wonderful experience. We asked them to tell us about their journey . . . and we have been truly inspired by their achievements and their generosity of spirit."

Brief Contents

Contents

CHAPTER 6
Memory

CHAPTER 7
Cognition and Language

CHAPTER 8
Intelligence

Preface to the First Canadian Edition

People everywhere, both young and old, try to make sense of the world they live in. Understanding and explaining our own behaviour and the behaviour of others is vitally important to everyday living. However, the complexities and contradictions we see in human behaviour are not easily explained. We see behaviour that is good and bad, conduct that is rational and illogical. We see love and hate, dedication and indifference, cooperation and conflict.

Psychologists have taken up the challenge to comprehend and explain human behaviour, using the tools and methods that science has to offer. They ask many of the questions about life that we all do, but the answers they offer reflect the rigour of the scientific method.

Essentials of Understanding Psychology is designed to offer Canadian students an introduction to what psychologists have learned in their quest to understand human behaviour. While providing a broad introduction to the field of psychology, it also makes clear the relevance of psychological findings to our everyday lives.

In developing the First Canadian Edition of *Essentials of Understanding Psychology* we had four main goals:

1. To provide broad coverage of the field of psychology, introducing the major theories, research and applications that constitute the discipline; and to include inspiring examples of significant Canadian research achievements, without reducing American coverage and other international research that has shaped the discipline.

2. To stimulate critical thinking about psychological phenomena, particularly those that impact on everyday life and those that deal with controversial issues; to explore how psychological findings and theories relate to a number of Canadian issues; and to enhance critical thinking skills through a consideration of these issues.

3. To illustrate the substantial diversity both within the field of psychology and in society as a whole by presenting material that reflects the discipline's increasing concern with gender, cultural, and ethnic issues; and to provide examples of diversity within Canadian society, as they relate to language, education, values, and cultural practices.

4. To arouse intellectual curiosity and build an appreciation of how psychology can increase students' understanding of the world around them; and to apply psychology to specific Canadian issues in order to demonstrate the relevance of psychological findings and the scientific approach for dealing with everyday situations.

WHAT'S NEW IN THE FIRST CANADIAN EDITION?

While previous editions of *Essentials of Understanding Psychology* included references to important research by Canadian scholars, the First Canadian Edition of the text contains a significant amount of new Canadian content. More than 200 new citations to Canadian research have been added, enhancing the discussion in the text and informing students of the exciting work being done by Canadian researchers.

Canadian content is integrated seamlessly within the text and added to or featured in the text's special boxes—Applying Psychology in the 21ˢᵗ Century, Pathways Through Psychology, Exploring Diversity, and The Informed Consumer of Psychology. Students will find the following examples of new Canadian content particularly relevant and interesting:

- Details of Canadian registration requirements for psychologists are discussed in Chapters 1 and 13 (pages 12 and 506). It is important for students to be aware of the level of education and experience required for registration, whether they plan to work in psychology or to be consumers of psychological services.

- Chapter 1 introduces the pioneering contributions of Canadian women (page 15), focusing attention on psychologists such as Mary J. Wright and Brenda Milner.

- Various kinds of addictions are discussed, enabling students to understand how these behaviours create a variety of problems for those engaging in them and for society as a whole. In Chapter 4 (pages 150–162), we introduce information on the extent and patterns of alcohol and drug use in Canada. Of particular significance is the finding that heavy drinking is highest in young adults aged 20 to 24, making this topic particularly relevant for students. The Applying Psychology box in Chapter 13 (page 488) focuses on gambling, which has become a significant problem with the opening of casinos in many parts of the country.

- For Canadians, the problem of post-traumatic stress disorder (PTSD) among military personnel has particular significance. Until the summer of 2000, the Canadian Forces have been involved in every United Nations peacekeeping mission. However, the role of peacekeeper has changed dramatically in recent years, making it significantly more stressful. In Chapter 12 (page 473) the discussion of General Roméo Dallaire's public acknowledgement of his experience with PTSD emphasizes the need for more public awareness of the disorder.

Diversity and multiculturalism are significant themes in contemporary psychology, and the First Canadian Edition of *Essentials of Understanding Psychology* explores gender and ethnic differences, as well as cultural issues. The discussion is both integrated within the existing text and highlighted in selected Exploring Diversity boxes. For example, we comment on educational systems that are appropriate (Chapter 5, page 194) and inappropriate (Chapter 9, page 326) in relation to learning styles and aboriginal culture. We discuss the use of standardized tests with aboriginal children (Chapter 8, page 294). We examine the problem of suicide in young aboriginals and other young Canadians (Chapter 13, page 498). How people understand and relate to diversity is a major theme in our presentation of all these issues.

Canadian statistics have been added at various points in the text. For instance, we note the proportion of Canadians who suffer from chronic pain (Chapter 3, page 107) and insomnia (Chapter 4, page 143). We give statistics for the prevalence of Alzheimer's at various ages during the senior years (Chapter 6, page 230). We identify the portion of Canadians who develop psychological disorders, such as major depression (Chapter 12, page 459) and schizophrenia (page 463). And we discuss the results of a World Health Organization study that provides information about mental health in Canada, the United States, and other parts of the world (page 472). These statistics, which focus on the occurrence and prevalence of various physical and psychological problems, draw attention to the relative seriousness of these problems in Canadian society.

Research by Canadian scholars at universities from Memorial University of Newfoundland to the University of British Columbia is integrated throughout the text. What is especially exciting about this content is the fact that no research has been included simply because it is Canadian, or to replace important international studies that students must understand. On the contrary, the studies we report demonstrate the major contributions of Canadian scholars to the discussion of key issues in psychology today. Consider, for example, the following:

- Chapter 6: Endel Tulving's view of memory (semantic, episodic, and procedural systems) is described. This view is important because it has been supported by some recent neuropsychological research, thus bringing together cognitive and biological approaches to memory.

- Chapter 9: Norman Endler's multidimensional interaction model of stress is introduced (page 345). This model is consistent with the systems approach that currently predominates in health psychology.

- Chapter 10: We introduce Albert Kozma's work on the psychosocial aspects of development. His emphasis on happiness and life satisfaction in seniors extends the discussion in the direction of well-being, a recurring theme in contemporary psychology, especially within the field of health psychology.

- Chapter 14: we have extended the discussion of prejudice by including the work of Mark Zanna (page 533). His distinctions among different types of prejudice (affect prejudice, symbolic belief prejudice, and stereotype prejudice) lead to a much richer conceptualization of this phenomenon. We also introduced the work of John Berry of Queen's University and his colleagues, who examine the significance of ethnicity for psychological research.

Profiles of Canadians working with psychology are featured in the Pathways Through Psychology boxes, all of which have been newly created for the First Canadian Edition. Most of these profiles are about psychologists working at universities, but we have also included a profile of a psychological associate working for a school board, and a psychologist working in private practice. Each person featured has written his or her own profile, making it a truly personal and accessible portrait. These profiles inform students about the exciting work being done by Canadians from coast to coast, and they also portray the individual's motivation and commitment to this work. They illustrate what psychology in Canada is really all about.

SCOPE AND STRUCTURE OF THE FIRST CANADIAN EDITION

Like the American Fourth Edition of *Essentials of Understanding Psychology,* the First Canadian Edition includes coverage of the **traditional topical areas** of psychology, including the biological foundations of behaviour, sensation and perception, learning, cognition, development, personality, abnormal behaviour, and the social psychological foundations of behaviour. It focuses on the essence of psychology, providing a broad introduction to the field. The book also shows how the field's theories and research have an impact on readers' everyday lives by emphasizing the applications of psychology.

The text's **organizational structure** offers considerable flexibility. Each chapter is divided into three or four manageable, self-contained units, allowing instructors to choose and omit sections in accordance with their course outlines, and providing review questions to ensure students understand the content before moving on. In addition, material on applying psychology is well integrated throughout. As a result, the book reflects a combination of traditional core topics and contemporary applied subjects, providing a broad, eclectic, and current view of the field of psychology.

Special boxes in every chapter provide in-depth coverage of important topics and issues, as well as discussions of issues of the future and profiles of practitioners in psychology today. The four kinds of boxes presented in the text include:

Applying Psychology in the 21st Century

These boxes illustrate applications of current psychological theory and research findings to real-world problems, focusing on current advances and future possibilities likely to occur in the new century. For example, these discussions include research on the development of artificial sense organs, drugs to reduce forgetting, and post-traumatic stress disorder.

Exploring Diversity

In addition to a substantial amount of material relevant to diversity integrated throughout the text discussions, every chapter also devotes at least one special section to an aspect of diversity. These sections highlight the way in which psychology informs (and is informed by) issues relating to the increasing multiculturalism of world society. Among the Exploring Diversity sections are those on cross-cultural differences in memory, learning styles, educational achievements, linguistic variety, and cultural perspectives on female circumcision.

The Informed Consumer of Psychology

Every chapter includes material designed to make readers more informed consumers of psychological information by giving them the ability to critically evaluate what the field of psychology offers. For example, these sections discuss ways of assessing research claims, managing pain, identifying drug and alcohol problems, memory improvement, critical thinking strategies, losing weight successfully, ending sexual harassment, adjusting to death, assessing personality assessments, and choosing a therapist. These unique sections illustrate the applications built on psychological research while also providing sound, useful guidance regarding common problems.

Pathways Through Psychology

Every chapter provides a biographical sketch of someone working in psychology in Canada. For example, there are profiles of a sleep researcher, a pain researcher, and a clinical psychologist with a special interest in Alzheimer's disease. There are profiles of psychologists whose research concerns bilingualism and mutlilingualism, neural functioning, parapsychology, learning, and adolescent development. And there are profiles about people interested in self-concept and self-esteem, motivation, family therapy, the treatment of depression in women, education, and the problem of violence.

A number of other pedagogical devices have been designed to help students to master the field of psychology. These features occur in every chapter:

- **Prologue.** Each chapter starts with an account of a real-life situation that demonstrates the relevance of the basic principles and concepts of psychology to pertinent issues and problems. These prologues often depict well-known people (such as Olympic rower Emma Robinson and children's writer Jean Little) and events (such as the striking public reaction to the death of former Prime Minister Pierre Trudeau).

- **Looking Ahead.** A chapter overview follows the Prologue, articulating the key themes and issues covered within the chapter.

- **Guiding Questions.** Each major section of the chapter begins with several broad questions, providing a framework for understanding and mastering the material that is to come. These questions appear in the margin next to the Section Reading.

- **Section Reading:** An extract from an illustrative study or article appears at the beginning of each major section of the chapter, inviting the student to think about the real-life application of issues discussed in the section.

- Margin icons indicate Internet resources for further study and research accessible from the *Essentials of Understanding Psychology* Online Learning Centre at http://www.mcgrawhill.ca/college/feldmanPsych

- **Recap, Review, and Rethink.** Every chapter is divided into three or four sections, each of which concludes with a Recap, Review, and Rethink section. The Recap summarizes key points of the previous section. The Review tests initial recall of the material (answers are provided at the bottom of the next page). The Rethink provides thought-provoking, critical-thinking questions.

- **Running Glossary.** Key terms are highlighted in **bold** when they are introduced in the text and defined in the margin of the page. Pronunciation guides are provided for difficult words. All key terms are reproduced in the end-of-book Glossary, which can also be consulted in a searchable version in the Online Learning Centre at http://www.mcgrawhill.ca/college/feldmanPsych

- **Looking Back.** To facilitate both the review and synthesis of the information covered, two end-of-chapter features reinforce student learning. First, a *numbered chapter summary* emphasizes the key points of the chapter and is organized according to the orienting questions posed at the beginning of every major section. Second, a list of *key terms and concepts*, including the page number on which each is introduced, is provided at the end of each chapter.

- **Epilogue.** Each chapter ends with an epilogue that incorporates critical-thinking questions relating to the prologue at the opening of the chapter. The thought-provoking questions in the epilogue provide a way of tying the chapter together and illustrating how the concepts addressed in the chapter apply to the real-world situation presented in the prologue.

SUPPLEMENTS PACKAGE

A complete, integrated multimedia package supports the First Canadian Edition of *Essentials of Understanding Psychology*. Please contact your local McGraw-Hill Ryerson sales representative for details concerning policies, prices, and availability, as some restrictions may apply.

Instructor's Manual (ISBN 0-07-087729-7), prepared by Sandy Ciccarelli of Gulf Coast Community College and Joan E. Collins and Judy M. Green, both of Sheridan College and the Canadian adapters of the text. For every chapter the following materials are provided to assist instructors in using the text and other resources to maximum advantage: Detailed Outline, Chapter Map, Learning Objectives (with accompanying overhead masters or handout masters), Lecture Leads, Classroom Activities and Demonstrations, suggested Multimedia activities, and suggestions for Independent Projects.

Test Bank (0-07-087731-9), prepared by Jeff Kaufmann of Muscatine Community College and Joan E. Collins and Judy M. Green, both of Sheridan College and the Canadian adapters of the text. The Test Bank contains more than 2,500 multiple-choice questions, classified by cognitive type (factual or conceptual) and level of difficulty (basic, moderate, challenging). Correct answers with page references to the text are provided, as well as the Learning Objective or title of the box to which the content of the question relates. In addition, at least 10 suggested Essay questions are included at the end of each chapter.

Computerized Test Bank (0-07-087728-9). This Windows-based supplement contains all the multiple choice and essay questions developed for the print Test Bank (described above). The flexible Brownstone format allows instructors to select, edit, and/or write their own questions, print exams, administer network based tests, collect grades, compile curve averages, generate reports, and more.

Online Learning Centre. The Online Learning Centre for *Essentials of Understanding Psychology*, First Canadian Edition, consists of three sections, each designed with a special function.

- The **Information Centre** provides a general overview of the text, with Author Biographies, the Table of Contents, a downloadable Preface and sample chapter, and details about the supplements.

- The **Instructor Centre** is a password-protected area that includes downloadable supplements and PowerPoint presentations. It also links instructors to Robert S. Feldman's *Psych Week* newsletter, which provides instructors with current and informative features including a Research Report, Psychology at Work, News Briefs, Website of the Week, Questions for Critical Thinking, and the weekly Pysch Calendar. The link to McGraw-Hill's **PageOut** site enables instructors who have adopted this text to create a custom course Web site that matches their syllabus. By following PageOut's template-driven instructions, you can easily develop a sophisticated, feature-rich Web site in minutes, without needing any special technical expertise. Or you may utilize our **PageOut Library,** which provides a course Web site for use with this text, based on representative course syllabi from schools across Canada that have been reviewed by an experienced instructor to ensure effective content coverage and flexibility. (Online Learning Centre content is also available in WebCT and Blackboard course management cartridges. Contact your McGraw-Hill Ryerson sales representative for details.)

- The **Student Centre** provides Chapter Outlines, Learning Objectives, hyperlinks for all the PsychLinks Internet resources flagged in the margins of the text, and a searchable Glossary of Key Terms. Other valuable study aids include additional Activities and Projects, Suggested Answers to Epilogue Questions, content reviews in the forms of Crossword Puzzles, an in-depth look at the meaning of common Cultural Idioms, international perspectives on psychology in Around the Globe, Suggested Readings, presentations in Microsoft® PowerPoint®, and answers to Frequently Asked Questions. Online Primers for Statistics, Careers, and the Internet help students develop further knowledge of research techniques and career opportunities. Finally, students will especially appreciate the review opportunities offered by interactive multiple-choice Quiz Questions, Essay Questions, and Interactive Exercises. Visit http://www.mcgrawhill.ca/college/feldmanPsych to explore the wealth of support material available!

Interactive e-Source. Based on the Canadian edition of the textbook, the interactive e-Source combines print, media, and Web-based study materials into one easy-to-use resource. The complete text is provided on CD-ROM, with numerous media enhancements including **Interactive Exercises**, quizzes, and games, sound bites, and additional photos and art. Special features of the e-Source include seamless connections to the text's **PsychLinks** to encourage focused Internet research, a powerful **Search Engine** for finding specific content, an **Annotation** function so that students may add (and share) notes and comments, **Highlighting** capabilities that allow students to flag important concepts, an **Audio** option that enables students to hear as well as read the text, and a **Media Gallery** that organizes figures, photos, sound bites, and interactive exercises for easy access and review. (Contact your McGraw-Hill Ryerson sales representative for details.)

Canadian instructors may also make use of the following supplements, prepared for the fourth American edition of *Essentials of Understanding Psychology*:

- **Presentation Manager** to accompany *Essentials of Understanding Psychology*, Fourth Edition (ISBN 0-07-228545-1)

- **Student PRISM** Interactive exercises on CD-ROM for use with *Understanding Psychology*, Fifth Edition, and *Essentials of Understanding Psychology*, Fourth Edition (ISBN 0-07-229774-3)

- **Student Survival Guide** to accompany *Understanding Psychology*, Fifth Edition, and *Essentials of Understanding Psychology*, Fourth Edition, by Robert S. Feldman and Sara Pollak Levine (ISBN 0-07-232521-6)

Robert S. Feldman
Joan E. Collins
Judy M. Green

ACKNOWLEDGEMENTS FOR THE FIRST CANADIAN EDITION

The creation of the First Canadian Edition of *Essentials of Understanding Psychology* has involved a well-coordinated team. We would like to thank Veronica Visentin, Senior Sponsoring Editor at McGraw-Hill Ryerson, for inviting us to be part of this team, and for her enthusiastic involvement at every stage of the project.

As research consultant for this project, Catharine Rankin of the University of British Columbia was an essential member of the team. Catharine read our proposal to review the changes we planned to make and discussed them with us. She helped us identify Canadian psychologists who are doing important work within the biological and neuropsychological fields and contributed a profile of her own work for Chapter 5. We very much appreciate the help she gave us.

We want to give special thanks to the outstanding psychologists who contributed their profiles for the Pathways Through Psychology boxes. We greatly appreciate the generosity and enthusiasm with which all of these people contributed to the book. In order of appearance in the text, they are:

Wendy Josephson, *University of Winnipeg*
Julien Doyon, *University of Montreal*
Patrick McGrath, *Dalhousie University*
Robert Ogilvie, *Brock University*
Catharine Rankin, *University of British Columbia*
Holly Tuokko, *University of Victoria*
Fred Genesee, *McGill University*
Jo-Anne Trigg, *Halton District School Board*
Tara MacDonald, *Queen's University*
Lorrie Sippola, *University of Saskatchewan*
Romin Tafarodi, *University of Toronto*
Sylvia Geist, *Geist Family Centre*
Janet Stoppard, *University of New Brunswick*
James Alcock, *York University*

Jean Little and Emma Robinson talked to us at length, providing first-hand information for the Prologues to Chapters 5 and 9. We thank them for their interest and participation in this project. We appreciate the help provided by Judy E. Green. Her information on the current guidelines for the education of exceptional students in Canada was invaluable. We are also grateful to our colleague Kathryn Duguid for her contribution to the discussion of the endocrine system.

The preparation of the First Canadian Edition of *Essentials of Understanding Psychology* has benefitted from the contribution of numerous psychology instructors across the country. We would like to thank the following for their thoughtful reviews:

Peter Bender, *John Abbott College*
Gregory Bird, *Lethbridge Community College*
Gary Bonczak, *Sir Sanford Fleming College of Applied Arts and Technology*
Tom Busnarda, *Niagara College of Applied Arts and Technology*
Neil McGrenaghan, *Humber College of Applied Arts and Technology*
Lorraine Mockford, *Nova Scotia Community College*
and others who preferred to remain anonymous

Other important members of our team include everyone at McGraw-Hill Ryerson who contributed to the development of the book. Lesley Mann, Senior Developmental Editor, was always there when we needed her. Her resourcefulness and encouragement helped enormously. Karen Hunter, our Copy Editor, went over the manuscript with great care in preparing it for typesetting. We appreciate the patient and cheerful manner with which she tackled this job. We would also like to acknowledge the work of Greg Devitt, Designer, in creating the cover for the book. Margaret Henderson, Senior Supervising Editor, did an amazing job in coordinating everything so that the book went through production smoothly. And thanks also to Ralph Courtney, Marketing Manager, and Shane Osborne, our McGraw-Hill Ryerson sales representative.

Finally, we would like to thank our families for their support and encouragement.

Joan E. Collins
Judy M. Green

ACKNOWLEDGMENTS FOR THE FOURTH EDITION

One of the most important features of *Essentials of Understanding Psychology* is the involvement of both professionals and students in the review process. The fourth edition of *Essentials of Understanding Psychology* has relied heavily on—and profited substantially from—the advice of instructors and students from a wide range of backgrounds.

First, the manuscript was evaluated by traditional academic reviewers, who served in their capacity as content experts and teachers of psychology. These reviewers helped ensure that the coverage and presentation was accurate, incorporated state-of-the-art research findings, and remained focused on the diverse needs of introductory psychology courses. They include the following:

Mike Aamodt, *Radford University*
Susan K. Beck, *Wallace State College*
Therison Bradshaw, *Macomb Community College*
Andrew R. Eisen, *Fairleigh Dickinson University*
Steve Ellyson, *Youngstown State University*
Gary King, *Rose State College*
Jeff Kaufmann, *Muscatine Community College*
Dave G. McDonald, *University of Missouri*
Tom Moye, *Coe College*
Brenda Nantz, *Vincennes University*
Robert F. Schultz, *Fulton-Montgomery Community College*
Joanne Stephenson, *Union University*
George T. Taylor, *University of Missouri–St. Louis*

Several people also gave us their input in reviews and interviews about the ancillary package. I am grateful to the following teachers of psychology:

Mike Aamodt, *Radford University*
Craig Beauman, *California State–Fullerton*
Don Brodeaur, *Sacred Heart University*
Cindy Dulaney, *Xavier University*
Jeff Kaufman, *Muscatine Community College*
George T. Taylor, *University of Missouri–St. Louis.*

Another group of reviewers consisted of a panel of three students who had used the previous edition of *Understanding Psychology* in their introductory psychology class. Over the course of a subsequent semester, they reviewed the entire manuscript, literally line-by-line. Their insights, suggestions, and sometimes all-too-enthusiastic criticism were invaluable to me as I prepared this revision. The student review panel consisted of Petra Doyle, Benjamin Happ, and Jean Pacifico.

Finally, dozens of students read parts of the manuscript to ensure that the material was clear and engaging. Their suggestions are incorporated throughout the text.

I am grateful to all of these reviewers who provided their time and expertise to help ensure that *Essentials of Understanding Psychology* reflects the best that psychology has to offer.

Robert S. Feldman
Amherst, Massachusetts

To the Student

USING *ESSENTIALS OF UNDERSTANDING PSYCHOLOGY:* A GUIDE FOR STUDENTS

Essentials of Understanding Psychology has been written with you, the reader, in mind. At every step in the development of the book, we have consulted students and instructors, seeking to identify the combination of learning features that would maximize readers' ability to learn and retain the subject matter of psychology. The result is a book that contains features that will not only help you to understand psychology, but also make it a discipline that is part of your life.

Now it's your turn; take the following steps to maximize the effectiveness of the learning tools in this book. These steps include familiarizing yourself with the arrangement of the book, using the built-in learning aids, and employing a systematic study strategy.

Familiarize Yourself with the Arrangement of *Essentials of Understanding Psychology*

Begin by reading the list of chapters and skimming the detailed table of contents. It provides an overview of the topics that will be covered and gives a sense of the way in which the various topics are interrelated. Note that every chapter follows the same diamond-shaped pattern: The heart of each chapter consists of three or four self-contained units that provide logical starting and stopping points for reading and studying. You can use these sections of each chapter to plan your studying. For instance, if your instructor assigns a chapter to read over the course of a week, you might plan to read and study one major section each day, using later days in the week to review the material.

Use the Built-in Learning Aids

Once you have acquired a broad overview of *Essentials of Understanding Psychology,* you're ready to begin reading and learning about psychology. Each chapter contains the same set of features that will help you master the material (see p. xxi–xxiii).

Because every chapter contains these features, the book provides a set of familiar landmarks to help you chart your way through new material. This structure will help you in organizing each chapter's content, as well as learning and remembering the material.

One final note: You should be aware that psychologists use a style of writing approved by the American Psychological Association. The only out-of-the-ordinary aspect of this style is in terms of citations to previous research. These citations are indicated by a name and date, typically set off in parentheses at the end of a sentence specifying the author and the year of publication (e.g., Kirsch & Lynn, 1998). Each of these names and dates refers to a book or article included in the References at the end of this book.

Prologue

Each chapter begins with a Prologue. The Prologue sets the stage for the content of the chapter, providing a relevant, real-life scenario.

Looking Ahead

The Looking Ahead sections raise the key themes and issues addressed in the chapter. They alert you to what you'll have learned after reading and studying the chapter.

Guiding Questions

Several broad questions are found at the start of every major section. These questions help focus your thinking about the chapter content. The same questions organize the chapter summary at the end of the chapter. Use these questions (which psychologists refer to as "advance organizers") to help organize what you will need to learn.

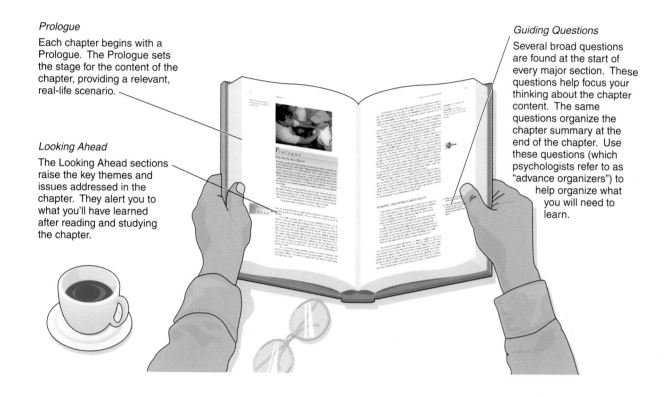

Applying Psychology in the 21st Century

This box in each chapter describes psychological research issues, applied to everyday problems. It focuses on the applications of psychology relevant to the next century. Read it to understand the very real ways that psychology promises to improve the human condition.

PsychLinks

The *PsychLinks* logo, shown here, indicates that a World Wide Web site is associated with the material being discussed. To find the site, go to the *Essentials of Understanding Psychology* site for this book, located at http://www.mcgrawhill.ca/feldmanPsych. Look for the page number from this book on which the logo is located, and you'll find a link to relevant material.

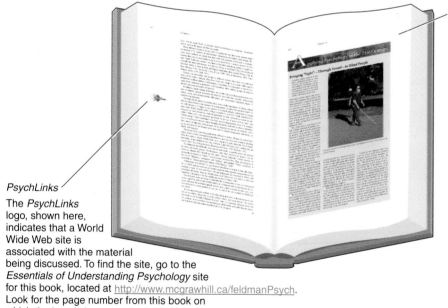

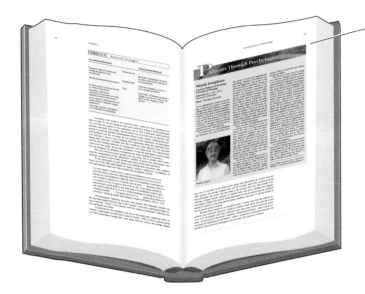

Pathways Through Psychology
This feature presents interviews with individuals whose professions and daily work are affected by the findings from the field of psychology. These biographical sketches show you the ways that the study of psychology is related to a broad range of issues. They can help answer your questions about how you could use your knowledge of psychology once you graduate.

Exploring Diversity
Every chapter includes at least one section devoted to an aspect of racial, ethnic, gender, or cultural diversity. These discussions show you many similarities between psychology and the multi-cultural issues that are so central to our increasingly diverse global society.

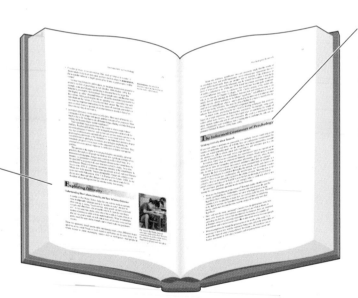

The Informed Consumer of Psychology
A major goal of *Essentials of Understanding Psychology* is to make readers more informed, critical consumers of psychological information. This feature, found in every chapter, gives you the tools to evaluate information relating to human behaviour and will help make you a more informed consumer of that information.

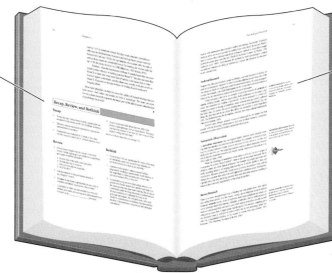

Recap, Review, and Rethink

Every main section of a chapter ends with a Recap, Review, and Rethink section. The **Recap** is a short, bulleted list that states the main points addressed in that section. The **Review** provides a series of questions that ask for concrete information, in a multiple choice, fill-in, or true-false format. The answers to these questions appear at the bottom of the pages that follow the questions. Finally, **Rethink** questions are designed to evoke critical thinking; they are thought-provoking questions that often have more than one correct answer.

Answer these questions! Your responses will indicate both your degree of mastery of the material and the depth of your knowledge. Use questions with which you have difficulty to guide your future studying.

Running Glossary

When a key term or concept appears in the text, it appears either in italics or bold type. Italicized words are of secondary importance; boldfaced words are of primary importance. Terms in bold are also printed and defined in the margins and in the end-of-book Glossary. Pronunciations are given for the difficult terms. In addition, bold-faced terms are included in the list of Key Terms and Concepts at the end of every chapter. You might want to highlight the difficult definitions with a marker or highlighter. A searchable version of the Key Terms and Glossary is provided in the Online Learning Centre at http://www.mcgrawhill.ca/college/feldmanPsych.

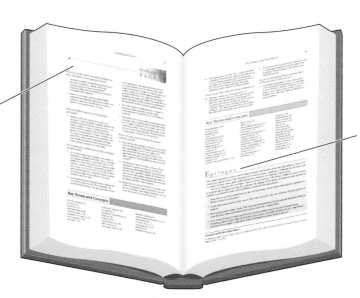

Looking Back

These end-of-chapter sections include two important parts: The numbered summary is organized around the guiding questions asked earlier in the chapter. The key terms and concepts list includes a page number where the term is first introduced in the chapter. To find its definition, you have two choices: turn to the margin of the page where the term is first introduced, or consult the end-of-book Glossary, which contains every key term and concept.

Epilogue

The Epilogue refers back to the Prologue scenario, which opened the chapter. The Epilogue helps you to place this scenario in the context of the chapter material, asking questions designed to get you thinking critically about the information.

Use a Proven Strategy for Effective Study and Critical Thinking

Now that you are acquainted with the special features of *Essentials of Understanding Psychology* that are designed to help you learn the content and thinking of psychology, you should consider using a general study strategy. It is ironic that although we are expected to study and ultimately learn a wide range of material throughout our schooling, we are rarely taught any systematic strategies that permit us to study more effectively. Yet, just as we wouldn't expect a physician to learn human anatomy by trial and error, it is the unusual student who is able to stumble upon a truly effective studying strategy.

Psychologists, however, have devised several excellent (and proven) techniques for improving study skills, two of which are described here. By employing one of these procedures—known by the initials "SQ3R" and "MURDER"—you can increase your ability to learn and retain information and to think critically, not just in psychology classes but in all academic subjects.

The SQ3R method includes a series of five steps, designated by the initials S-Q-R-R-R. The first step is to *survey* the material by reading the chapter outlines, chapter headings, figure captions, recaps, and Looking Ahead and Looking Back sections, providing yourself with an overview of the major points of the chapter. The next step—the "Q" in SQ3R—is to *question*. Formulate questions—either aloud or in writing—prior to actually reading a section of the material. For instance, if you had first surveyed this section of the book, you might jot down in the margin, "What do "SQ3R" and "MURDER" stand for?" The queries posed in the marginal guiding questions and the reviews that end each part of the chapter are also a good source of questions. But it is important not to rely on them entirely; making up your own questions is critical. *Essentials of Understanding Psychology* has wide margins in which you can write your own questions. This process helps you to focus on the key points of the chapter, while at the same time putting you in an inquisitive frame of mind.

It is now time for the next, and most crucial, step: to *read* the material. Read carefully and, even more importantly, read actively and critically. For instance, while you are reading, answer the questions you have asked yourself. You may find yourself coming up with new questions as you read along; that's fine, since it shows you are reading inquisitively and paying attention to the material. Critically evaluate material by considering the implications of what you are reading, thinking about possible exceptions and contradictions, and examining the assumptions that lie behind the assertions made by the author.

The next step—the second "R"—is the most unusual. This "R" stands for *recite*, in which you look up from the book and describe and explain to yourself, or to a friend, the material you have just read and answer the questions you have posed earlier. Do it aloud; this is one time when talking to yourself is nothing to be embarrassed about. The recitation process helps you to clearly identify your degree of understanding of the material you have just read. Moreover, psychological research has shown that communicating material to others, or reciting it aloud to yourself, assists you in learning it in a different—and deeper—way than material which you do not intend to communicate. Hence, your recitation of the material is a crucial link in the studying process.

The final "R" refers to *review*. As we discuss in Chapter 6, reviewing is a prerequisite to fully learning and remembering material you have studied. Look over the information; reread the Recaps and Looking Back summaries; answer in-text review questions; and use any ancillary materials you may have available. Reviewing should be an active process, in which you consider how different pieces of information fit together and develop a sense of the overall picture.

An alternative approach to studying—although not altogether dissimilar to SQ3R—is provided by the MURDER system (Dansereau, 1978). Despite the deadly connotations of its title, the MURDER system is a useful study strategy.

In MURDER, the first step is to establish an appropriate *mood* for studying by setting goals for a study session and choosing a time and place in which you will not be distracted. Next comes reading for ***understanding***, in which careful attention is paid to the meaning of the material being studied. ***Recall*** is an immediate attempt to recall the material from memory, without referring to the text. ***Digesting*** the material comes next; you should correct any recall errors, and attempt to organize and store newly learned material in memory.

You should work next on ***expanding*** (analyzing and evaluating) new material, and try to apply it to situations that go beyond the applications discussed in the text. By incorporating what you have learned into a larger information network in memory, you will be able to recall it more easily in the future. Finally, the last step is ***review***. Just as with the SQ3R system, MURDER suggests that the systematic review of material is a necessary condition for successful studying.

Both the SQ3R and MURDER systems provide a proven means of increasing your study effectiveness. It is not necessary, though, to feel tied to a particular strategy; you might want to combine other elements into your own study system. For example, learning tips and strategies for critical thinking will be presented throughout *Essentials of Understanding Psychology,* such as in Chapter 6 when the use of mnemonics (memory techniques for organizing material to help its recall) are discussed. If these tactics help you to successfully master new material, stick with them. The last aspect of studying that warrants mention is that *when* and *where* you study are in some ways as important as *how* you study. One of the truisms of the psychological literature is that we learn things better, and are able to recall them longer, when we study material in small chunks over several study sessions, rather than massing our studying into one lengthy session. This implies that all-night studying just prior to a test is going to be less effective—and a lot more tiring—then employing a series of steady, regular study sessions.

In addition to carefully timing your studying, you should seek out a special location to study. It doesn't really matter where it is, as long as it has minimal distractions and is a place that you use *only* for studying. Identifying a special "territory" allows you get in the right mood for study as soon as you begin.

Table I	Study Skills Techniques

SQ3R	MURDER
Survey	Mood
Question	Understanding
Read	Recall
Recite	Digesting
Review	Expanding
	Review

A Final Comment

By using these proven study strategies, as well as by making use of the learning tools integrated in the text, you will maximize your understanding of the material in this book and will master techniques that will help you learn and think critically in all of your academic endeavours. More importantly, you will optimize your understanding of the field of psychology. It is worth the effort: the excitement, challenge, and promise that psychology holds for you are significant.

For the Student

ONLINE QUIZ QUESTIONS

Do you understand the material? You'll know after taking an Online Quiz! Try the Multiple Choice questions for each chapter. They're auto-graded with feedback and you have the option to send results directly to faculty. Essay Questions and Interactive Exercises offer additional challenges.

PSYCH LINKS

This section links you to various Web sites, including all Web Psych Links from the text.

ONLINE GLOSSARY

All definitions in the text are included in the searchable glossary.

ADDITIONAL RESOURCES

Online Primers on statistics, careers, and the Internet will help you expand your research knowledge. Around the Globe (international studies) and Suggested Readings are also available.

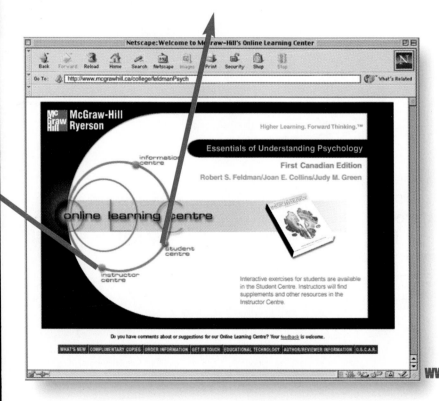

Your Internet companion to the most exciting educational tools on the Web!

The Online Learning Centre can be found at:
www.mcgrawhill.ca/college/feldmanPsych

Mourners comfort each other at a memorial service for students gunned down at Columbine High School in Colorado. The shootings raise numerous psychological issues.

Prologue

Countdown to Violence

On an April day in 1999, the world watched as a terrible tragedy unfolded at Columbine High School in Littleton, Colorado. When it was over, 15 people were dead including the two student gunmen who had gone on a killing rampage. They had targeted for death, athletes and minorities, among others. Amid the tragedy, acts of great courage were evident as students, teachers, police, and rescue workers risked death to help others.

A year later, in memory of the victims, citizens of Colorado observed a minute of silence. In Littleton, a bell tolled 13 times.

As the remembrance was being observed, a 15-year-old student at a high school in Orleans, Ontario, stabbed four fellow students and a faculty member, injuring himself as well. No lives were lost and the principal, who is lauded as a hero, talked the student into surrendering his knife. Unlike Columbine, the attacks appeared to be random in nature. However, like the assailants at Columbine who were said to be loners, this boy was reported to have been isolated from the other students and made fun of, by them, because of his looks and behaviour. In the aftermath, a crisis team supported traumatized students.

Was this a "copycat" act of violence by the Ontario student? Authorities are not sure; however he is reported to have been overheard counting down the days to the anniversary of Columbine.

looking
AHEAD

Tragic and traumatic events, like those described above, highlight a range of human behaviours from aggression and violence to acts of courage and heroism. These behaviours raise many issues of a psychological nature. Consider, for example, the ways in which different kinds of psychologists would look at these incidents:

- Psychologists studying biological factors might examine heredity or hormonal factors underlying such behaviours.

- Those psychologists who study learning and memory might examine what people remember of the incident afterward.

- Psychologists who study thinking processes might consider how people calculated what action to take during the crisis.

- Psychologists who focus on motivation would seek to explain the reasons behind the assailants' actions.

- Developmental psychologists, who study growth and change throughout the life span, might look at peer relationships and adolescent social development and the effect on students' lives in the future.

- Health psychologists would examine present stress reactions and future illness that might result from the experience.

- Clinical and counselling psychologists would try and identify the most effective ways of helping the people involved cope.

- Social psychologists would attempt to explain the causes of aggressive and helping behaviours.

Although the approaches that different types of psychologists would take in the Columbine and Orleans cases are diverse, there is a common link: Each represents a specialty area within the general field of study called psychology. **Psychology** is the scientific study of behaviour and mental processes.

psychology: The scientific study of behaviour and mental processes

This definition seems straightforward, but its simplicity is deceptive. In fact, since the first stirrings of the discipline, psychologists have debated just what should constitute the appropriate scope of the field. Should psychologists limit themselves to the study of outward, observable behaviour? Is it possible to study internal thinking scientifically? Should the field encompass the study of such diverse topics as physical and mental health, perception, dreaming, and motivation? Is it appropriate to focus solely on human behaviour, or should the behaviour of nonhumans be included?

Psychological Associations

Most psychologists have answered these questions by taking a broad view, arguing that the field should be receptive to a variety of viewpoints and approaches. Consequently, the phrase "behaviour and mental processes" in the definition must be understood to mean many things: It encompasses not just what people do but also their thoughts, feelings, perceptions, reasoning processes, memories, and even the biological activities that maintain bodily functioning.

When psychologists speak of "studying" behaviour and mental processes, their perspective is equally broad. To psychologists, it is not enough simply to describe behaviour. As with any science, psychology attempts to explain, predict, modify, and ultimately improve the lives of people and the world in which they live.

By using scientific methods, psychologists are able to find answers to questions about the nature of human behaviour and thought processes that are far more valid and legitimate than those resulting from mere intuition and speculation. And what a variety and range of questions psychologists pose. Consider these examples: How do we distinguish between colours? What is intelligence? Can abnormal behaviour be altered? How long can we go without sleep? Can aging be delayed? How does stress affect us? What is the best way to study? What is normal sexual behaviour? How do we reduce violence?

These questions—which will be addressed in this book—provide just a hint of the various topics that we will encounter as we explore the field of psychology. Our discussions will take us across the spectrum of what is known about behaviour and mental processes. At times, we will leave the realm of human beings to explore animal behaviour, because many psychologists study nonhuman animals in order to determine general laws of behaviour that pertain to *all* organisms. Behaviour of other animals thus provides important clues to answering questions about human behaviour. But we will always return to a consideration of the usefulness of psychology in helping to solve the everyday problems that confront all human beings.

In sum, this book will not only cover the breadth of the field of psychology, it will also try to convey its content in a way that arouses your interest and continuing curiosity about psychology. To that end, this text is intended to provide as close a facsimile to two people sitting down and discussing psychology as we can convey with the written word.

The book also incorporates several features meant to illustrate how psychology can have an impact on each of our lives. You will find how psychologists are applying what they have learned to resolve practical problems that people encounter (Applying Psychology in the 21st Century boxes). You will meet people who use psychology in their professional lives (Pathways Through Psychology boxes). You will learn about the contributions that psychology can make to enhancing our understanding of our differences (Exploring Diversity sections). You will also find material in each chapter that is intended to make you a more knowledgeable consumer of psychological information. These Informed Consumer of Psychology sections discuss concrete recommendations for incorporating psychology into your life. They are meant to enhance your ability to evaluate critically the contributions that psychologists can offer society. Finally, links to World Wide Web pages are indicated by the "PsychLinks" symbol in the margins. When a PsychLinks symbol appears, it alerts you to related material on Web sites that can be reached through the *Essentials of Understanding Psychology* Web site at www.mcgrawhill.ca/feldmanPsych.

The book itself has been designed to make it easier for you to learn the material we discuss. Based on principles developed by psychologists who specialize in learning and memory, information is presented in relatively small chunks, with each chapter containing three or four major segments. Each segment starts with a few broad questions and concludes with a Recap, Review, and Rethink section that lists the key points and poses questions for you to consider. Some questions ("Review") provide a quick test of recall, with answers provided immediately following the review. Others, designated "Rethink," are broader in scope and are designed to elicit critical analysis of the information you have read. These self tests will help you in learning, and later recalling, the material in each segment. To further reinforce your understanding of important terms and concepts, each chapter ends with a comprehensive summary, a list of key terms, and a brief epilogue, which asks you to return to the opening prologue and consider a few additional questions about it.

The framework of the book (explained in detail on pages xv to xxvi of the Preface) is embodied in this introductory chapter, which presents several topics that are central to an understanding of psychology. We begin by describing the different types of psychologists and the various roles they play. Next, we examine the major perspectives used to guide the work psychologists do. Finally, we identify the major issues that underlie psychologists' views of the world and human behavior.

PSYCHOLOGISTS AT WORK

▶ **What is psychology, and why is it a science?**

▶ **What are the different branches of the field of psychology?**

▶ **Where do psychologists work?**

One month after losing his left arm in a car accident, Victor Quintero sat with his eyes closed in a brain-research laboratory as a scientist poked his cheek with a cotton swab.

"Where do you feel that?" asked Dr. Vilayanur S. Ramachandran, a psychologist at the University of California in San Diego.

"On my left cheek and on the back of my missing hand," said the 17-year-old high school student.

Dr. Ramachandran touched a spot under Mr. Quintero's left nostril. "And where do you feel that?"

"On my left pinky. It tingles."

Eventually Dr. Ramachandran found points all over the young man's left face and jaw that evoked sensations in his amputated hand and arm. . . .

Finally, Dr. Ramachandran dribbled warm water down Mr. Quintero's left cheek. Both were amazed. "I feel it running down my arm," said Mr. Quintero, blinking his eyes to check that the limb was still gone (Blakeslee, 1992b, p. C1).

***

The middle-aged woman welcomes the participants in the study, who, more often than not, enter the room in pairs. This is hardly surprising since the point of the study is to examine twins. They have come to a testing site to meet with researchers studying similarities in the behavioural and personality traits of twins. By comparing twins who have lived together virtually all their lives with those who have been separated from birth, researchers are seeking to determine the relative influence of heredity and experience on human behaviour.

***

A graduate-school student in China shows a group of university students a list of short proverbs, some of which contain two contradictory ideas ("too humble is half proud"), while others are more "linear" ("as the twig is bent, so grows the tree"). After learning which proverbs the Chinese students prefer, she then repeats the same study at a university in the United States. She finds that Chinese students prefer proverbs that contain two contradictory ideas, while U.S. students have the opposite preference (Peng & Nisbett, 1997).

***

Four King pigeons are provided with a choice of four pecking keys. All of these keys can potentially trigger the release of food. On any given trial, only one of these keys will actually trigger the release of food. Over a number of trials, the pigeons demonstrate that they know which key produces the food and concentrate their attention on that key. They also demonstrate memory that lasts up to 96 hours for which key had last produced food and would return to that key first, on the next trial (Willson & Wilkie, 1993).

***

Methodically—and painfully—retracing events of years before, the college student discloses a childhood secret that he has revealed previously to no one. The listener responds with support, suggesting to him that his concern is in fact shared by many people.

Although the last scene may be the only one that fits your image of what a psychologist does, each of these episodes describes work carried out by contemporary psychologists. The range and scope of psychology is remarkably broad.

The Branches of Psychology: Psychology's Family Tree

Psychology can be likened to a large extended family, with assorted nieces and nephews, aunts and uncles, and cousins who may not interact on a day-to-day basis, but who are related to one another in fundamental ways.

We will examine psychology's family tree by considering each of the major specialty areas of the field, describing them in the general order in which they are discussed in subsequent chapters of this book.

The Biological Foundations of Behaviour

In the most fundamental sense, people are biological organisms. Some psychologists investigate the ways in which the physiological functions and structures of our body work together to influence our behaviour. *Biopsychology* is the branch of psychology that specializes in the biological bases of behaviour. Studying a broad range of topics, biopsychologists focus on the operation of the brain and nervous system. For example, they may examine the ways in which specific sites in the brain are related to the muscular tremors found in Parkinson's disease (discussed in Chapter 2), or they may attempt to determine how our body's sensations are related to our emotions (Chapter 9).

Biological Bases of Behaviour

Sensing, Perceiving, Learning, and Thinking

If you have ever wondered how acute your vision is, how you sense pain, or how you can most effectively study, you have raised a question that is most appropriately answered by an experimental psychologist. *Experimental psychology* is the branch of psychology that studies the processes of sensing, perceiving, learning, and thinking about the world.

The work of experimental psychologists overlaps that of biopsychologists, as well as other types of psychologists. For this reason, the term "experimental psychologist" is somewhat misleading; psychologists in every specialty area use experimental techniques, and experimental psychologists do not limit themselves solely to experimental methods.

Several subspecialties have grown out of experimental psychology to become central branches of the field in their own right. One example is *cognitive psychology*, which focuses on the study of higher mental processes, including thinking, language, memory, problem solving, knowing, reasoning, judging, and decision making. Covering a wide range of human behaviour, cognitive psychologists have, for instance, identified more efficient ways of remembering and better strategies for solving problems involving logic (as we will discuss in Chapters 6 and 7).

Understanding Change and Individual Differences

A baby producing her first smile . . . taking her first step . . . saying her first word. These events, which can be characterized as universal milestones in development, are also singularly special and unique for each person. Developmental psychologists, whose work we will discuss in Chapter 10, trace the physical, cognitive, social, and emotional changes that occur throughout life.

Developmental psychology, then, is the branch of psychology that studies how people grow and change from the moment of conception through death. Another branch, *personality psychology*, attempts to explain both consistency and change in a person's behaviour over time, as well as the individual traits that differentiate the behaviour of one person from another when they confront the same situation. The major issues relating to the study of personality will be considered in Chapter 11.

Physical and Mental Health

If you suffer from constant stress, are frequently depressed, or seek to overcome a fear that prevents you from carrying out your normal activities, your problems would be addressed by one of the psychologists who devote their energies to the study of physical or mental health: health psychologists, clinical psychologists, and counselling psychologists.

Health psychology explores the relationship between psychological factors and physical ailments or disease. For instance, health psychologists are interested in how long-term stress (a psychological factor) can affect physical health. They are also concerned with identifying ways of promoting behaviour related to good health (such as increased exercise) or discouraging unhealthy behaviour such as smoking.

Clinical psychology is the branch of psychology that deals with the study, diagnosis, and treatment of abnormal behaviour. Clinical psychologists are trained to diagnose and treat problems ranging from the everyday crises of life, such as grief due to the death of a loved one, to more extreme conditions, such as losing touch with reality. Some clinical psychologists also conduct research, investigating issues that range from identifying the early signs of psychological disturbance to studying the relationship between family communication patterns and psychological disorders.

As we will see in Chapters 12 and 13, the kinds of activities carried out by clinical psychologists are varied indeed. It is clinical psychologists who administer and score psychological tests and who provide psychological services in community mental health centres. Even sexual problems are often treated by clinical psychologists.

Like clinical psychologists, counselling psychologists deal with people's psychological problems, but the problems they deal with are of a particular sort. *Counselling psychology* is the branch of psychology that focuses primarily on educational, social, and career adjustment problems. Almost every college has a centre staffed with counselling psychologists. This is where students can get advice on the kinds of jobs they might be best suited for, methods of studying effectively, and strategies for resolving everyday difficulties, such as problems with roommates and concerns about a

Health Psychology

Counselling psychologists who staff college centres advise students on career choices, methods of study, and strategies for coping with everyday problems.

specific professor's grading practices. Many large business organizations also employ counseling psychologists to help employees with work-related problems.

Two close relatives of counselling psychology are educational psychology and school psychology. *Educational psychology* is concerned with teaching and learning processes. It is, for example, concerned with ways of understanding intelligence, developing better teaching techniques, and understanding teacher-student interaction. *School psychology,* in contrast, is the specialty area devoted to assessing children in elementary and secondary schools who have academic or emotional problems and developing solutions to such problems.

Understanding Our Social Networks

None of us lives in isolation; rather, we are all part of a complex network of social interrelationships. These networks with other people and with society as a whole are the focus of study for many different kinds of psychologists.

Social psychology, as we will see in Chapter 14, is the study of how people's thoughts, feelings, and actions are affected by others. Social psychologists focus on such diverse topics as human aggression, liking and loving, persuasion, and conformity. For instance, social psychologists ask, "Does observation of televised violence make people more aggressive?" "What is the role of physical attractiveness in choosing a spouse?" and "How are we influenced by salespeople?"

The study of the *psychology of women* concentrates on psychological factors relating to women's behaviour and development. It focuses on a broad range of issues, such as discrimination against women, the possibility that structural differences exist in men's and women's brains, the effects of hormones on behaviour, and the causes of violence against women (Greenglass, 1991; Chrisler, Golden, & Rozee, 1996; Matlin, 1996; Kimura, 1999).

Industrial-organizational psychology is concerned with the psychology of the workplace. Specifically, it considers issues such as productivity, job satisfaction, and decision-making (Cascio, 1995; Riggio & Porter, 1996; Spector, 1996; Aamodt, 1996). A related branch is *consumer psychology,* which analyzes people's buying habits and the effects of advertising on buyer behaviour. An industrial-organizational psychologist might ask a question such as "How do you influence workers to improve the quality of products they produce," while a consumer psychologist might ask "How does product quality enter into decisions to purchase a specific product?"

Finally, *cross-cultural psychology* investigates the similarities and differences in psychological functioning in various cultures and ethnic groups. As we discuss throughout this book, psychologists specializing in cross-cultural issues investigate such questions as the following (Shweder & Sullivan, 1993; Goldberger & Veroff, 1995; Gergen et al., 1996): What are the social and psychological issues related to multiculturalism (Berry, 1998)? How do child-rearing practices, which differ substantially among various cultures, affect subsequent adult values and attitudes? and Why do cultures vary in their interpretation of what constitutes physical attractiveness?

Newer Speciality Areas

As the field of psychology matures, the number of specialty areas continues to increase (Bower, 1993; Koch, 1993). For example, *evolutionary psychology,* an increasingly influential area, seeks to identify behaviour patterns that are a result of our genetic inheritance from our ancestors. Evolutionary psychology is rooted in the work of Charles Darwin, whose *On the Origin of Species* in 1859 argued that a process of natural selection produces traits in a species that are adaptive to their environment. Following Darwin's perspective, evolutionary psychology examines whether our genetic inheritance not only determines such traits as hair colour and race, but also holds the key to understanding certain behaviours. As we'll see in future chapters, recent evidence suggests that a surprising array of behaviours, such as the degree to which we are outgoing or introverted, may well be influenced by genetic factors (Plomin & McClearn, 1993; Crawford & Krebs, 1997).

Some more recent additions to the field of psychology are clinical neuropsychology and environmental psychology. *Clinical neuropsychology* unites the areas of biopsychology and clinical psychology. It focuses on the relationship between biological factors, such as brain dysfunctions, and psychological disorders. *Environmental psychology* considers the relationship between people and their physical environment. Environmental psychologists have made significant progress in understanding how our physical environment affects our emotions, the way we behave toward others, and the amount of stress we experience in a particular setting. *Forensic psychology* focuses on legal issues, such as deciding on criteria for determining whether a person is legally insane, and whether larger or smaller juries make fairer decisions (Stern, 1992; Palermo & Knudten, 1994; Davies et al., 1995; Gudjonsson, 1996).

"Is there a home court advantage?" "Are there personality differences between people who participate in sports and exercise programs and those who don't?" "Does participation in sports reduce aggressive behaviour?" "How can we motivate ourselves to perform at an optimal level?" Questions of this sort are addressed by *sport and exercise psychology,* the branch of the field that investigates the applications of psychology to athletic activity and exercise. It considers the role of motivation, the social aspects of sports, and even such physiological issues as the impact of training on muscle development. The growing influence of the field is suggested by the fact that no fewer than twenty sport and exercise psychologists were on site at the Olympics in Atlanta (Murray, 1996).

Psychologists interested in *program evaluation* also constitute a growing body. They focus on assessing large-scale programs, usually managed by the government, to determine whether they are effective in meeting their goals. For example, such psychologists have examined the effectiveness of such governmental social services as the Head Start preschool program and the Healthy Relationships dating violence prevention curriculm (Rossi & Freeman, 1993; Sisk et al., 1996; Josephson et al., 1999).

The Demographics of the Discipline

Help Wanted: Professor at a college of arts, science, and technology. Teach undergraduate courses in introductory psychology and courses in specialty areas of cognitive psychology, perception, and learning. Strong commitment to quality teaching and student advising necessary. The candidate must also provide evidence of scholarship and research productivity or potential.

Help Wanted: Industrial-organizational consulting psychologist. International firm is seeking psychologists for full-time career positions as consultants to management. Candidates must have the ability to establish a rapport with senior business executives and to assist them with innovative, practical, and psychologically sound solutions to problems concerning people and organizations.

Help Wanted: Clinical psychologist. Ph.D., internship experience, and license required. Comprehensive clinic seeks psychologist to work with children and adults providing individual and group therapy, psychological evaluations, crisis intervention, and development of behaviour treatment plans on multidisciplinary team. Broad experience with substance abuse problems is desirable.

Psychology's Workplace

Given the diversity of roles that psychologists play, it is not surprising that they are employed in a variety of settings. Many doctoral-level psychologists are employed by institutions of higher learning (universities and colleges) or are self-employed, usually working as private practitioners treating clients. The next-most-frequent employment settings are private for-profit and non-profit organizations, such as hospitals, clinics, mental-health centres, and counselling centres. Other settings include government human-services organizations and schools (APA, 1996).

Why are so many psychologists found in academic settings? The answer is that the three major roles played by psychologists in society—teacher, scientist, and clinical practitioner—are easily carried out in such an environment. Very often psychology professors are also actively involved in research or in serving clients. Whatever their particular job site, however, psychologists share a commitment to improving individual lives as well as society in general (Peterson, 1991; Coie et al., 1993; Rheingold, 1994; Robertson, 1994; Gautier & Phillips, 1997).

The Education of a Psychologist

How do people become psychologists? The most common route is a long one. Most psychologists have a doctoral graduate degree in the form of a Ph.D. This degree typically takes four or five years of work past the bachelor level (H. C. Ellis, 1992).

Education in Psychology

Some fields of psychology involve education beyond the doctorate. For instance, doctoral-level clinical psychologists, who deal with people with psychological disorders, typically spend an additional year on a supervised internship at a health or mental health agency or facility accredited by the Canadian Psychological Association and/or the American Psychological Association. The profession of psychologist is regulated in Canada and psychologists must be licensed by a provincial or territorial board (Dobson & Breault, 1998). Although many psychologists work in a clinical setting, others may teach, or work in specialized programs in government or industry.

An undergraduate major in psychology provides worthwhile preparation for a variety of occupations, although it does not allow professional work in psychology per se. For instance, many people in business, nursing, law, social work, and other professions report that an undergraduate background in psychology has proven invaluable in their careers. Undergraduates who specialize in psychology typically have good analytical, higher-order thinking abilities, and they are able to synthesize and evaluate information well—skills that are held in high regard by employers in business and industry and the government.

People other than psychologists also deal with psychological issues, but their training tends to differ in significant ways from that of psychologists. For instance, although psychiatrists treat people with psychological disorders, they have medical degrees and can prescribe medicine. Trained initially as physicians, they often focus on the physical causes of psychological disorders. Consequently, they may be more apt to employ treatments involving medications than to focus on psychological causes of disorders. In addition, people in allied fields such as social work, marriage counselling, and school counselling often deal with psychological issues. However, their direct training in psychology is more limited than that attained by psychologists.

Psychology in Canada and the United States

As a student of psychology in Canada, you might ask the question: is Canadian psychology the same as American psychology? The answer is yes it is and no it isn't.

In many ways they are the same. They share the same early history, starting with Wilhelm Wundt in 1879 (see The Roots of Psychology later in the chapter). They both share the same branches on the family tree, the same major areas of specialization, and they both use the same perspectives (see Today's Perspectives). The psychological communities in both countries are interested in many of the same issues. They both have professional associations that support and regulate the work of psychology: The American Psychological Association (APA) in the United States (founded in 1892) and The Canadian Psychological Association (CPA) in Canada (founded in 1939) are the largest but not the only ones.

In the beginning there was little to distinguish Canadian from American psychology. Sometimes the same person is significant in the history of both academic communities. For example, an American, James Baldwin, teaching at the University of

Toronto in the late 1800s and called "the first modern psychologist in Canada," was a founding member of the APA (Wright and Myers, 1982; Ferguson, 1993). Although research and practice, in both countries, have much in common there are some significant differences between them.

They differ in scale. The much larger population in the United States provides a larger research base. With many more universities, more research can be generated. Academic credentials differ. In Canada, most psychologists with a doctoral-level degree will have a Ph.D. In the U.S., psychologists may have a Ph.D. (for those whose focus is on research with original investigation) or a Psy.D. (for those who wish to focus on the treatment of psychological disorders).

As both countries moved towards more applied psychology in the 1940s they faced a division in their ranks between those psychologists who favoured academic (pure) psychology and those who were interested in applied research. In Canada, the emerging applied psychology remained rooted in the experimental, university, thesis-based model (Ph.D.) In the United States, there were more financial incentives to develop private teaching programs and the larger population could support such initiatives (Dobson, 1995; Goodman, 2000). This tradition, in Canada, of a strong experimental and empirical focus translates into a tendency for Canadian clinical psychologists more than their American counterparts to work from a behavioural or cognitive behavioural model (Hunsley and Lefebvre, 1990; Warner, 1991).

In both countries, because of their different historical, social, and cultural experiences, there are areas of special concern. In social psychology, as an example, both will study violence, but the experience of it may differ. Canada's universal health care system makes issues of health and well-being different from those in the United States. Canada's federal multicultural policy creates a potentially different experience around issues of ethnic diversity. Therefore studies in these areas will produce a unique body of research. This knowledge is essential for those psychologists who are involved in program planning or evaluation.

In conclusion, it seems fair to say that, although their roots are the same and much research is easily transferable, psychology in Canada and the United States has evolved each in its own unique way. This is primarily as a result of a difference in population size and a different historical and social experience.

Recap, Review, and Rethink

Recap

- Psychology is the scientific study of behaviour and mental processes.

- Among the major branches of psychology are biopsychology; experimental and cognitive psychology; developmental and personality psychology; health, clinical, and counselling psychology; educational and school psychology; social psychology; psychology of women; industrial-organizational psychology; consumer psychology; and cross-cultural psychology. Many new specialty areas are also springing up.

- Many psychologists are employed by institutions of higher learning, and the balance are employed by hospitals, clinics, community health centres, human-service organizations, and schools or are engaged in private practice.

Review

1. The foundation of psychology today lies in
   a. intuition.
   b. observation and experimentation.
   c. trial and error.
   d. metaphysics.

2. Match each branch of psychology with the issues or questions posed below.
   a. Biopsychology
   b. Experimental psychology
   c. Cognitive psychology
   d. Developmental psychology
   e. Personality psychology
   f. Health psychology
   g. Clinical psychology
   h. Counselling psychology
   i. Educational psychology
   j. School psychology
   k. Social psychology
   l. Industrial psychology
   m. Consumer psychology

   1. Joan, a college freshman, is panicking. She needs to learn better organizational skills and study habits to cope with the demands of college.
   2. At what age do children generally begin to acquire an emotional attachment to their fathers?
   3. It is thought that pornographic films that depict violence against women may prompt aggressive behaviour in some men.

4. What chemicals are released in the human body as a result of a stressful event? What are their effects on behaviour?
5. John is unique in his manner of responding to crisis situations, with an even temperament and a positive outlook.
6. The general public is more apt to buy products that are promoted by attractive and successful actors.
7. The teachers of eight-year-old Jack are concerned that he has recently begun to withdraw socially and to show little interest in school work.
8. Janet's job is demanding and stressful. She wonders if her lifestyle is making her more prone to certain illnesses such as cancer and heart disease.
9. A psychologist is intrigued by the fact that some people are much more sensitive to painful stimuli than others.
10. A strong fear of crowds leads a young woman to seek treatment for her problem.
11. What mental strategies are involved in solving complex word problems?
12. What teaching methods most effectively motivate elementary school students to successfully accomplish academic tasks?

13. Jessica is asked to develop a management strategy that will encourage safer work practices in an assembly plant.

Answers to Review Questions are on page 14.

Rethink

1. Why might the study of twins who were raised together and twins who were not be helpful in distinguishing the effects of heredity and environment?

2. Imagine you had a seven-year-old child who was having problems learning to read. Imagine further that you could consult as many psychologists as you wanted. How might each type of psychologist approach the problem?

3. Are intuition and common sense sufficient for understanding why people act the way they do? Why is a scientific approach appropriate for studying human behaviour?

A SCIENCE EVOLVES: THE PAST, THE PRESENT, AND THE FUTURE

Some half-million years ago, people assumed that psychological problems were caused by the presence of evil spirits. To allow these spirits to escape, ancient healers performed an operation called trephining. Trephining consisted of chipping away at a patient's skull with crude stone instruments until a hole was cut through the bone. Because archaeologists have found skulls with signs of healing around the opening, we can assume that patients sometimes managed to survive the cure.

***

The famous Greek physician Hippocrates thought that personality was made up of four temperaments: sanguine (cheerful and active), melancholic (sad), choleric (angry and aggressive), and phlegmatic (calm and passive). These temperaments were influenced by the presence of "humours," or fluids, in the body. If one humour was out of balance, a physician would seek to either increase the deficient humour (through a medicinal potion) or decrease the excess (often through bloodletting).

***

According to the philosopher Descartes, nerves were hollow tubes through which "animal spirits" conducted impulses in the same way that water is transmitted through a pipe. When a person put a finger too close to the fire, the heat was transmitted via the spirits through the tube, directly into the brain.

***

Franz Josef Gall, an eighteenth-century physician, argued that a trained observer could discern intelligence, moral character, and other basic personality characteristics from the shape and number of bumps on a person's skull. His theory gave rise to the "science" of phrenology, employed by hundreds of devoted practitioners in the nineteenth century.

While these "scientific" explanations may sound far-fetched, at one time they represented the most advanced thinking regarding what might be called the psychology of the era. Even without knowing much about modern-day psychology, you can surmise that our understanding of behaviour has advanced tremendously since these

▶ **What are the historical roots of the field of psychology?**

▶ **What approaches are used by contemporary psychologists?**

Classical Studies in Psychology

earlier views were formulated. Yet most of the advances have been recent, for, as sciences go, psychology is one of the new kids on the block.

Although psychology's roots can be traced back to the ancient Greeks and Romans, and although philosophers have argued for several hundred years about some of the same sorts of questions that psychologists grapple with today, the formal beginning of psychology is generally set at 1879. In that year, Wilhelm Wundt established the first laboratory devoted to the experimental study of psychological phenomena in Leipzig, Germany. At about the same time, William James was setting up his laboratory in Cambridge, Massachusetts.

Throughout its almost twelve decades of formal existence, psychology has led an active and dynamic life, gradually developing into a true science. As part of this evolution, it has produced a number of conceptual perspectives, or *models*. These perspectives represent organized systems of interrelated ideas and concepts used to explain phenomena. Some of these perspectives have been discarded—as have the views of Hippocrates and Descartes—but others have been elaborated and provide a set of pathways for psychologists to follow (Wright & Myers, 1982; Hilgard, Leary, & McGuire, 1991; Robinson, 1995; Benjafield, 1996; Benjamin, 1997).

Each of the perspectives offers a distinctive outlook, emphasizing different factors. Just as we may employ not one but many maps to find our way around a particular geographical area—one map to show the roads, one the major landmarks, and one the topography of the hills and valleys—psychologists also find more than one approach useful in understanding behaviour. Given the range and complexity of behaviour, no single perspective or model will invariably provide an optimal explanation. Together, though, the differing perspectives provide us with a means to explain the extraordinary breadth of behaviour.

The Roots of Psychology

When Wilhelm Wundt set up the first psychology laboratory in 1879, his aim was to study the building blocks of the mind. Considering psychology to be the study of conscious experience, he developed a model that came to be known as structuralism. **Structuralism** focused on the fundamental elements that form the foundation of thinking, consciousness, emotions, and other kinds of mental states and activities.

To come to an understanding of how basic sensations combined to produce our awareness of the world, Wundt and other structuralists used a procedure called **introspection** to study the structure of the mind. In introspection, people were presented with a stimulus—such as a bright green object or a sentence printed on a card—and asked to describe, in their own words and in as much detail as they could manage, what they were experiencing. Wundt argued that psychologists could come to understand the structure of the mind through the reports that people offered of their reactions (Bjork, 1997).

Wundt's structuralism did not stand the test of time, however. Psychologists became increasingly dissatisfied with the assumption that introspection could unlock the fundamental elements of the mind. For one thing, people had difficulty describing some kinds of inner experiences, such as emotional responses. (Try to analyze and explain the primary elements of what you are feeling the next time you experience anger, for instance.)

Moreover, breaking down objects into their most basic mental units sometimes seemed to be a most peculiar undertaking. A book, for example, could not be described by a structuralist as merely a book, but instead had to be broken down into its various components, such as the material on the cover, the colours, the shapes of the letters, and so on. Finally, introspection was not a truly scientific technique. There

structuralism: Wundt's model that focuses on the fundamental elements that form the foundation of thinking, consciousness, emotions, and other kinds of mental states and activities

introspection: A procedure used to study the structure of the mind, in which subjects are asked to describe in detail what they are experiencing when they are exposed to a stimulus

---

Answers to Review Questions:

1. b 2. a-4, b-9, c-11, d-2, e-5, f-8, g-10, h-1, i-12, j-7, k-3, l-13, m-6

were few ways in which an outside observer could verify the accuracy of the introspections that people did make. Such drawbacks led to the evolution of new models, which largely supplanted structuralism.

Interestingly, however, important remnants of structuralism still exist. As we shall see in Chapter 7, the past twenty years have seen a resurgence of interest in people's descriptions of their inner experience. Cognitive psychologists, who focus on higher mental processes such as thinking, memory, and problem solving, have developed innovative techniques for understanding people's conscious experience that overcome many of the difficulties inherent in introspection.

The model that largely replaced structuralism in the evolution of psychology was known as functionalism. Rather than focusing on the mind's components, **functionalism** concentrated on what the mind *does*—the functions of mental activity—as well as the functions of behavior in general. Functionalists, whose model rose to prominence in the early 1900s, asked what roles behaviour played in allowing people to better adapt to their environments. Led by the American psychologist William James, the functionalists examined the ways in which behaviour allows people to satisfy their needs (Johnson & Henley, 1990). By using functionalism, the famous American educator John Dewey developed the field of school psychology, proposing ways that students' educational needs could best be met.

Another reaction to structuralism was the development of gestalt psychology in the early 1900s. **Gestalt psychology** is a model focusing on the study of how perception is organized. Instead of considering the individual parts that make up thinking, gestalt psychologists took the opposite tack, concentrating on how people consider individual elements together as units or wholes. Their credo was "The whole is different from the sum of its parts," meaning that, when considered together, the basic elements that compose our perception of objects produce something greater and more meaningful than those individual elements alone. As we shall see when we examine sensation and perception in Chapter 3, the contributions of gestalt psychologists to the understanding of perception are substantial.

functionalism: An early approach to psychology that concentrated on what the mind does—the functions of mental activity—and the role of behaviour in allowing people to adapt to their environments

gestalt *(geh SHTALLT)* **psychology:** An approach to psychology that focuses on the organization of perception and thinking in a "whole" sense, rather than on the individual elements of perception

Women in Psychology: Pioneering Contributions

Despite societal constraints that limited women's participation in many professions, including psychology, women made major contributions in the early years of psychology (Russo & Denmark, 1987; Bohan, 1992). In the United States for example, Leta Stetter Hollingworth coined the term "gifted" in reference to unusually bright children, and she wrote a book on adolescence that became a classic (Hollingworth, 1928).

Another influential figure was Karen Horney (1937) (pronounced "HORN-eye"), who focused on the social and cultural factors behind personality. She was one of the earliest psychologists to advocate for women's issues.

The 1930s and 40s were years that saw women, in increasing numbers, take their places in teaching positions at Canadian universities. Mary Salter Ainsworth began teaching at the University of Toronto in 1939. In 1950 she left for England, then on to Uganda and the United States. A truly international scholar, her academic interests focused on developmental psychology.

Reva Gerstein, who taught at the University of Toronto in the early 1940s, was to use her education in a career of service to Canada. Her work in the field of mental health won her a national award in 1987. Among her many accomplishments was the Gerstein Report, which provided a plan for deinstitutionalized psychiatric patients (Wright, 1992).

A distinguished lecturer and pioneer in the field of neuropsychology, Brenda Milner began teaching psychology in the 1940s. Her research at the Montreal Neurological Institute, and McGill University has contributed substantially to our knowledge of learning, memory, and speech functions of the brain. Awarded many honours, she was inducted into the Canadian Medical Hall of Fame in 1997 (Montreal Neurological Institute, 1997).

Mary Wright, whose career in psychology has spanned 50 years, became the first woman president of the CPA in 1969. Her research interests are in the areas of

Brenda Milner

Mary J. Wright

biological perspective: The psychological model that views behaviour from the perspective of biological functioning

psychodynamic perspective: The psychological model based on the belief that behaviour is motivated by inner forces over which the individual has little control

Sigmund Freud

cognitive perspective: The psychological model that focuses on how people know, understand, and think about the world

child development and education. She has written extensively on the history of psychology in Canada (Wright & Myers, 1982; Wright, 1993).

Despite the contributions of such women, psychology was largely a male dominated field in its early years. However, the number of women has been increasing rapidly in recent years. Consequently, when future historians of science write about psychology they will be recording a history of men and women (Denmark, 1994).

Today's Perspectives

The early roots of psychology are complex and varied. It is not surprising, then, that the field is so diverse today. However, it is possible to encompass the breadth of psychology by using just a few basic perspectives: the biological, psychodynamic, cognitive, behavioural, and humanistic perspectives. Each of these broad perspectives, which continue to evolve, emphasizes different aspects of behaviour and mental processes and steers the thinking of psychologists in a somewhat different direction.

The Biological Perspective: Blood, Sweat, and Fears

When we get down to the basics, behaviour is carried out by living creatures made of skin and guts. The **biological perspective** considers the behaviour of both people and animals in terms of biological functioning: how the individual nerve cells are joined together, how the inheritance of certain characteristics from parents and other ancestors influences behaviour, how the functioning of the body affects hopes and fears, which behaviours are due to instincts, and so forth. Even more complex kinds of behaviours, such as a baby's response to strangers, are viewed as having critical biological components by psychologists using the biological perspective. The biological perspective also takes into account how heredity and evolution not only shape such traits as height and hair colour, but also may influence behaviour.

Because every behaviour can at some level be broken down into its biological components, the biological perspective has broad appeal. Psychologists who subscribe to this perspective have made major contributions to the understanding and betterment of human life, ranging from developing cures for certain types of deafness to identifying medications to treat people with severe mental disorders.

The Psychodynamic Perspective: Understanding the Inner Person

To many people who have never taken a psychology course, psychology begins and ends with the psychodynamic perspective. Proponents of the **psychodynamic perspective** believe that behaviour is motivated by inner forces and conflicts over which the individual has little awareness and control. Dreams and slips of the tongue are viewed as indications of what a person is truly feeling within a seething cauldron of unconscious psychic activity.

The psychodynamic view is intimately linked with one individual: Sigmund Freud. Freud was a Viennese physician in the early 1900s whose ideas about unconscious determinants of behaviour had a revolutionary effect on twentieth-century thinking, not just in psychology but in related fields as well. Although many of the basic principles of psychodynamic thinking have been roundly criticized, the perspective that has grown out of Freud's work has provided a means of not only treating mental disorders, but also understanding everyday phenomena such as prejudice and aggression.

The Cognitive Perspective: Comprehending the Roots of Understanding

The route to understanding behaviour leads some psychologists straight into the mind. Evolving in part from structuralism, the **cognitive perspective** focuses on how people know, understand, and think about the world. The emphasis is on learning how people comprehend and represent the outside world within themselves. Cognitive psychologists seek to explain how we process information and how our ways of thinking about the world influence our behaviour.

Psychologists relying on this perspective ask questions ranging from whether a person can watch television and study at the same time (the answer is "probably not") to how people figure out for themselves the causes of others' behaviour. The common elements that link cognitive approaches are an emphasis on how people understand and think about the world and a concern about describing the patterns and regularities of the operation of our minds.

The Behavioural Perspective: Observing the Outer Person

While the biological, psychodynamic, and cognitive approaches look inside the organism to determine the causes of its behaviour, the behavioural perspective takes a very different approach. The **behavioural perspective** grew out of a rejection of psychology's early emphasis on the inner workings of the mind, suggesting instead that observable behaviour should be the focus of the field.

behavioural perspective: The psychological model that suggests that observable behaviour should be the focus of study

John B. Watson was the first major American psychologist to advocate a behavioural approach. Working in the 1920s, Watson was adamant in his view that one could gain a complete understanding of behaviour by studying and modifying the environment in which people operated. In fact, he believed rather optimistically that by controlling a person's environment, it was possible to elicit any desired sort of behaviour. His own words make this philosophy clear: "Give me a dozen healthy infants, well-formed, and my own specified world to bring them up in and I'll guarantee to take any one at random and train him to become any type of specialist I might select— doctor, lawyer, artist, merchant-chief, and yes, even beggar-man and thief, regardless of his talents, penchants, tendencies, abilities, vocations and race of his ancestors" (Watson, 1924). In more recent times, the behavioural perspective was championed by B. F. Skinner, who, until his death in 1990, was the best-known contemporary psychologist. Much of our understanding of how people learn new behaviours is based on the behavioural perspective.

John B. Watson

As we will see, the behavioural perspective crops up along every byway of psychology. Along with the influence it has had in the area of learning processes, this perspective has also made contributions in such diverse areas as the treatment of mental disorders, the curbing of aggression, the resolution of sexual problems, and even the halting of drug addiction.

The Humanistic Perspective: The Unique Qualities of Homo Sapiens

Rejecting the views that behaviour is determined largely by automatic, biological forces, by unconscious processes, or solely by the environment, the **humanistic perspective** instead suggests that people are naturally endowed with the capacity to make decisions about their lives and to control their behaviour. Humanistic psychologists maintain that everyone has the power to develop higher levels of maturity and fulfillment. In their view, people will strive to reach their full potential if given the opportunity. The emphasis, then, is on **free will,** the human ability to make decisions about one's life.

humanistic perspective: The psychological model that suggests that people are in control of their lives

The humanistic perspective assumes that people have the ability to make their own choices about their behaviour, rather than relying on societal standards. In this view, it is not a person's role or status that is important, but whether they live up to their full potential.

free will: The human ability to make decisions about one's life

More than any other approach, the humanistic perspective stresses the role of psychology in enriching people's lives and helping them to achieve self-fulfillment. While somewhat more limited than the other perspectives, the humanistic perspective has had an important influence on psychologists, reminding them of their commitment to the individual person and society.

It is important not to let the abstract qualities of the humanistic perspective, or of the other broad approaches we have discussed, lull you into thinking that they are purely theoretical. These perspectives underlie ongoing work of a practical nature, as we will discuss throughout this book. As a start, consider the Applying Pscyhology in the 21st Century box.

Applying Psychology in the 21st Century

Psychology and the Reduction of Violence

A bomb explodes during the 1996 Olympics in Atlanta, killing one person and injuring dozens more. A terrible tragedy plays itself out at Columbine High School in Colorado. Violence is the reality we live with. No country, in fact no community, is unaffected. It invades our homes: Two young sisters are murdered in their suburban Toronto home. It invades our streets: A 14-year-old girl in British Columbia is viciously beaten and then drowned by youths her own age. It invades our schools: One student is killed and another injured when an Alberta boy takes a gun to school.

In the aftermath of these events, we may feel disgusted, sad, or angry. We become fearful for ourselves and for our children. On the anniversary of Columbine dozens of Toronto schools were patrolled by uniformed police officers and parents kept children home because of fears of violence.

Yet violence is not going unchallenged, and the field of psychology is playing a key role in efforts to reduce this social ill. Psychologists specializing in diverse areas and employing the major perspectives of the field are making a concerted effort to understand and reduce violence as well as to deal with its aftermath (Pepler & Slaby, 1994; Human Capital Initiative, 1997; Osofsky, 1997; Jaffe, 1999). Their work is reflected in several key areas:

- *Examining the notion that a "cycle of violence" perpetuates violent behaviour across generations.* According to the "cycle of violence" explanation, abuse and neglect during childhood make people more likely to abuse and neglect their own children (Widom, 1989). Research in developmental psychopathology by Muller and Diamond at York University (1999) found a relationship between physical maltreatment by both fathers and mothers and elevated levels of aggression in both sons and daughters, as early as preschool. They also found a consistence in these patterns across generations.

  Developmental psychologists have found a considerable amount of evidence to support the "cycle of violence" notion. However, the evidence does not tell the full story: Being abused does not inevitably lead to the abuse of one's own children. Only one-third of people who have been abused or neglected as children go on to abuse their own children (Kaufman & Zigler, 1987). Current research is aimed at determining when a childhood history of abuse is most likely to result in adult violence, and how the cycle can be broken.

- *Examining the effects of media violence.* Violence on television is common. One survey found that of 94 prime time programs examined, 48 showed at least one act of violence, including 57 people killed and 99 assaulted (Hansom & Knopes, 1993).

  Although they cannot be fully certain, most social and developmental psychologists agree that observation of media aggression enhances the likelihood that viewers will act aggressively. In an extensive study done for the Department of Canadian Heritage, and Health Canada, Wendy Josephson (1995) examined the effects of television violence on children of different ages. She found that although all ages are affected, preschoolers are particularly vulnerable. She and others have also found that observing media aggression serves to desensitize viewers to displays of aggression, leading them to react with passivity to actual incidents of aggression (Molitor & Hirsch, 1994; Josephson, 1995; Palermo, 1995).

  Although television receives a lot of attention in this regard, the Internet is another media source that increasingly provides interactive violence, allowing people not only to observe violence but also to participate in it. One of the more popular games has players hitting, teasing, and abusing each other until they are driven sobbing out of the game. It has 25,000 registered users (Spencer, 2000).

- *Considering the role of biological factors in aggression.* Several psychologists have considered the issue of whether biological factors are linked to aggression. For instance, psychologist James Dabbs, Jr., believes that there is a link between hormones and aggressive behaviour, based on research in the areas of biopsychology and social

Violence occurs in many forms, such as the bomb blast that shook the Olympic Games in Atlanta.

psychology. Examination of a large group of prisoners found that males with higher testosterone levels were more likely to have committed personal crimes of sex and violence, while those with lower levels of testosterone were more apt to have committed property crimes involving burglary, theft, and drugs. If this work, which is controversial, is supported by other studies, the future may hold the controversial possibility of medical treatments designed to reduce violence in perpetrators (Dabbs, 1993; Dabbs et al., 1995).

- *Identifying methods for reducing youth violence.* The rate of young people, in Canada, charged with violent crimes is 77 percent higher than it was a decade ago. Of significant concern is the increasing violence reported for female youths. Since 1988 the increase in violent crime rates for female youth is 127 percent for males it is 65 percent (Juristat report on Youth violent crime, December 21, 1999).

Psychologist Ervin Staub argues that a combination of factors such as a lack of nurturance, neglect, and harsh treatment; frequent observation of violence; difficult life conditions; and poverty, prejudice, and discrimination result in higher rates of violence. He also suggests ways of reducing violence. For example, he has developed a training program for inner-city students. Through a combination of role playing, videotaping, and structured discussion, these students are taught to respond to provoca-tive situations in ways that do not involve aggression (Staub, 1996a, 1996b; Loeber & Hay, 1997).

In Winnipeg, a three-year study on violence prevention is being evaluated (see Pathways Through Psychology). The

program taught students to deal with anger, to be assertive not aggressive, and to recognize the effect of media on behaviour as well as other issues related to dating relationships. Preliminary results suggest that students in the program did demonstrate a decrease in violent behaviour by the end of the program (Josephson et al., 1999).

Bullying is an ongoing area of concern for many psychologists and educators. Debra Pepler and colleagues at the LaMarsh Centre for Research on Violence and Conflict Resolution at York University investigate issues related to youth violence, bullying, and intervention (Pepler et al., 1995; Craig & Pepler, 1996).

In Coquitlam, B.C., a school-based, anti-bullying program called Bully B'ware was developed by a team of educators and counsellors. Workshops targeted at teachers, parents and students, are designed to raise awareness, about bullies and victims. Developers believe that it is critical to educate and mobilize the 60 percent of students who are neither victim nor bully not to tolerate the bullying of others. (Bully B'ware Productions)

- *Reducing sexual aggression.* In 1998 there were over 21,000 reported cases of sexual assaults against Canadian women (Tremblay, 1999). Psychologists from several different branches of the field—including specialists in clinical psychology, developmental psychology, and the psychology of women—have been working to devise ways of reducing sexually aggressive behaviour. Objectives of a program for young male offenders accused of sexual and physical assault, include developing an understanding of their hurtful behaviour as well as developing

remorse for their behaviour and empathy for their victims. They are also taught to identify the situations that might lead them to repeat their aggressive behaviour (Mamabolo, 1996).

- *Helping children who are the victims of violence.* More than 225,000 Canadian children are abused in their communities each year (Carney, 1999). The belief that children who are abused directly or who are witness to violence may have similar adjustment problems has prompted Peter Jaffee and colleagues to focus on prevention. They believe there should be more early intervention for high-risk children. Two models developed for the National Crime Prevention Council included initiatives such as home visitation programs for high-risk parents. Programs that involve schools and community agencies are also important. One such program developed in London, Ontario, has shown positive results.

This is an area of research where Canadian and American studies can help each other. A program called Multisystemic Therapy (MST), developed by Scott Henggler and his associates in South Carolina, is being tried in five Ontario communities. The program provides youth with intensive intervention in the home, school, and community (Jaffee & Baker, 1999).

As we can see, psychologists are playing important and quite varied roles in combating violence. And violence is not the only societal problem to which psychologists are contributing their ex-pertise in an effort to alleviate human suffering. As we will explore in Apply-ing Psychology in the 21st Century boxes in every chapter, the basic principles of psychology are being used, as we move into the new century, to address a wide range of social problems.

CONNECTIONS: PSYCHOLOGY'S UNIFYING THEMES

▶ What is the future of psychology likely to hold?

As you consider the many topical areas and perspectives that make up the field of psychology, you may find yourself thinking that you've embarked on a journey into a fragmented discipline that lacks cohesion. You may fear that psychology consists merely of a series of unrelated, separate subject areas, no closer to one another than physics is to chemistry. In fact, such a conclusion is not unreasonable, given that psychology covers so many diverse areas, ranging from a narrow focus on the minute biochemical influences on behaviour to a broad focus on social behaviour in its most encompassing sense.

Yet despite the seeming disparity among the various topics and perspectives, the differences in some ways are only skin deep. The field is actually more unified than a first glimpse might imply, in terms of both the links between psychology's branches and perspectives and the key issues that psychologists address.

The Links Between Psychology's Branches and Perspectives

The field's five major perspectives play an important role in integrating the various branches of the discipline. Specifically, a psychologist from any given branch might choose to employ any one, or more, of the major perspectives.

For example, a developmental psychologist might subscribe to the psychodynamic perspective *or* the behavioural perspective *or* any of the other perspectives. Similarly, a clinical psychologist might use the behavioural perspective *or* the cognitive perspective *or* one of the other perspectives. The perspectives may be used in different ways by various psychologists, but the assumptions of a given perspective are similar regardless of the subfield to which it is applied.

Of course, not every branch of psychology is equally likely to employ a particular perspective. Historically, some kinds of psychologists have been more apt to rely on certain perspectives, and some perspectives have proven more useful than others to psychologists attempting to deal with a particular topical area.

For example, biopsychologists studying the brain are most likely to employ the biological perspective, given its emphasis on the biological foundations of behaviour. At the same time, most biopsychologists reject the psychodynamic perspective's reliance on unconscious determinants of behaviour. Similarly, social psychologists who are interested in explaining the roots of prejudice are more likely to find the cognitive perspective of use than the biological perspective.

Psychology's Future

We have examined the foundations from which the field of psychology has evolved. But what does the future hold for the discipline? Although the course of scientific development is notoriously difficult to predict, several trends do seem likely to emerge in the not-so-distant future:

- Psychology will become increasingly specialized. In a field in which practitioners must be experts on such diverse topics as the intricacies of the transmission of electrochemical impulses across nerve endings and the communication patterns of employees in large organizations, no one individual can be expected to master the field. Thus, it is likely that specialization will increase as psychologists delve into new areas (Bower, 1993; Koch, 1993; Plomin, 1995).

- New perspectives will evolve. As a growing, maturing science, psychology will develop new perspectives to supplant current approaches. Moreover, older perspectives may merge to form new ones. We can be certain, then, that as psychologists accumulate more knowledge they will become increasingly sophisticated in their understanding of behaviour and mental processes (Boneau, 1992; Gibson, 1994; Andreasen, 1997).

- Explanations for behaviour will simultaneously consider genetic and environmental factors, as well as biological and social influences. For instance, it is clear that phenomena such as memory cannot be fully understood without reference to the biological mechanisms that allow memories to be stored as well as the situational influences regarding what information is attended to in the first place (Eichenbaum, 1997; Veitch & Gifford, 1997; Segal, Weisfeld, & Weisfeld, 1997).

- Psychological treatment will become more accessible and socially acceptable as the number of psychologists increases. More psychologists will focus on prevention of psychological disturbance, rather than just on its treatment. In addition, they will act as consultants to the growing number of volunteer and self-help groups as can be seen in Pathways Through Psychology in Chapter 12 (Jacobs & Goodman, 1989; R. E. Fox, 1994; Pepler et al., 1995; Gautier & Philips, 1997).

- Psychology's influence on issues in the public interest will grow. Each of the major problems of our time—such as the threat of terrorism, racial and ethnic prejudice, poverty, and environmental and technological disasters—has important psychological ramifications (Archer, Pettigrew, & Aronson, 1992; Calkins, 1993; Cialdini, 1997). While psychology alone will not solve these problems, its major accomplishments in the past (many of which are documented in other chapters of this book) foretell that psychologists will make important practical contributions toward their resolution.

- Psychology will take the growing diversity of the country's population into account. As the population of Canada becomes more diverse, the consideration of racial, ethnic, linguistic, and cultural factors will become more critical to psychologists providing psychological services and conducting research. The result will be a field that can provide an understanding of *human* behaviour in its broadest sense (Goodchilds, 1991; Brislin, 1993; Berry & Laponce, 1994; Fowers & Richardson, 1996; Gautier & Philips, 1997).

Cross-cultural Psychology

Recap, Review, and Rethink

Recap

- Traces of the early perspectives of structuralism, functionalism, and gestalt psychology can be seen in the major perspectives used by psychologists today.

- The dominant psychological perspectives encompass biological, psychodynamic, cognitive, behavioural, and humanistic approaches.

- In the future, the field of psychology is likely to become more specialized; to consider both biological and environmental factors; to take the increasing diversity of the country's population into account more fully; and to become increasingly concerned with the public interest. Psychological treatment is also likely to become more accessible.

Review

1. The statement "In order to study human behaviour, we must consider the whole of perception rather than its component parts" is one that might be made by a person subscribing to which perspective of psychology?

2. Identify the perspective that suggests that abnormal behaviour may be the result of largely unconscious forces.

3. "Psychologists should worry only about behaviour that is directly observable." This statement would most likely be made by a person using which psychological perspective?

4. Psychology is currently moving toward increased specialization. True or false?

Answers to Review Questions are on page 22.

Rethink

1. How are today's major perspectives of psychology related to the earlier models of structuralism, functionalism, and gestalt psychology?

2. Consider some event that has recently been well-publicized in the news. How might the different perspectives of psychology be used to explain the event?

While we may notice that someone is in trouble, we may not provide help. The concept of diffusion of responsibility helps explain why individuals in a crowd are not likely to assist strangers in distress—each bystander assumes that others will take the responsibility for helping.

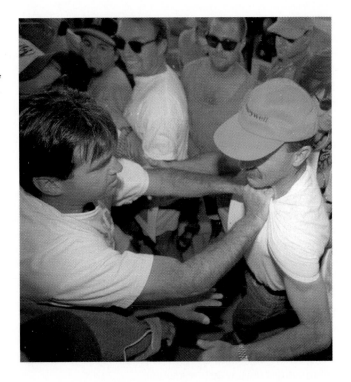

RESEARCH IN PSYCHOLOGY

▶ **What is the scientific method, and how do psychologists use theory and research to answer questions of interest?**

▶ **What are the different research methods employed by psychologists?**

▶ **How do psychologists establish cause-and-effect relationships in research studies?**

Imagine that you are on a busy street and a fight breaks out. Nearby a young man is being beaten. Do you stop and help? Do you call the police? Do you walk right by? Do you watch and do nothing to intervene? Can you remember a situation where you saw someone in trouble and did nothing? Do you remember what you thought at the time?

If you did nothing you are not alone. Bystander inaction is all too common.

Possibly the best known case of bystander inaction involved a woman named Kitty Genovese who was attacked by a man near an apartment building in New York City in the mid-1960s. At one point during the assault, which lasted thirty minutes, she managed to free herself and screamed, "Oh, my God, he stabbed me. Please help me!" In the stillness of the night, no fewer than thirty-eight neighbors heard her screams. Windows opened and lights went on. One couple pulled chairs up to the window and turned off the lights so they could see better. Someone called out, "Let that girl alone." But shouts were not enough to scare off the killer. He chased her, stabbing her eight more times, and sexually molested her before leaving her to die. And how many of those thirty-eight witnesses came to her aid? Not one person helped (Rogers & Eftimiades, 1995).

In *A Textbook of Social Psychology,* Alcock, Carment and Sadava (2000) tell a story about a young woman from Scarborough, Ontario. She died in very similar circumstances to Kitty Genovese, crying for her life while no one helped.

Both of these cases remain dismaying—and puzzling—examples of "bad Samaritanism." The general public, as well as psychologists, found it difficult to explain how so many people could stand by without coming to the aid of the victims.

One easy explanation, supplied by many editorial writers, was that the incidents could be attributed to the basic shortcomings of "human nature." But such a supposition is woefully inadequate. For one thing, there are numerous examples of people who have placed their own lives at risk to help others in dangerous situations.

Answers to Review Questions:

1. gesalt   2. psychodynamic   3. behavioral   4. true

Clearly, then, "human nature" encompasses a wide range of both negative and positive responses. Consequently it does not provide a very satisfying explanation for the bystanders' unhelpful behaviour. The mystery, then, of the lack of bystander intervention in both incidents remained unsolved.

Psychologists in particular puzzled over the problem and after much research finally reached an unexpected conclusion: The two women might well have been better off had there been just a few people who heard their cries for help rather than the many that did. In fact, had there been just one bystander present in each instance, the chances of that person intervening might have been fairly high. For it turns out that the *fewer* witnesses present in a situation such as the two in question, the better the victim's chances of getting help.

How did psychologists come to such a curious conclusion? After all, logic and common sense clearly suggest that the presence of more bystanders would produce a greater likelihood that someone would help a person in need. This seeming contradiction—and the way psychologists resolved it—illustrates a central task for the field of psychology: the challenge of asking and answering questions of interest.

Posing Questions: The Scientific Method

The challenge of appropriately framing those questions of interest to psychologists and properly answering them has been met through reliance on the scientific method. The **scientific method** is the approach used by psychologists to systematically acquire knowledge and understanding about behaviour and other phenomena of interest (Hazen & Trefil, 1991; Leong & Austin, 1996). It consists of three main steps: (1) identifying questions of interest, (2) formulating an explanation, and (3) carrying out research designed to lend support to or refute the explanation.

scientific method: The approach used by psychologists to systematically acquire knowledge and understanding about behaviour and other phenomena of interest

Theories: Specifying Broad Explanations

In using the scientific method, psychologists start with the kinds of observations about behaviour with which we are all familiar. If you have ever asked yourself why a particular teacher is so easily annoyed, why a friend is always late for appointments, or how your dog understands your commands, you have been formulating questions about behaviour. Psychologists, too, ask questions about the nature and causes of behaviour, although their questions are typically more precise.

Once a question has been formulated, the next step in the scientific method involves developing theories to explain the phenomenon that has been observed. **Theories** are broad explanations and predictions concerning phenomena of interest. They provide a framework for understanding the relationships among a set of otherwise unorganized facts or principles.

Growing out of the diverse models of psychology described earlier, theories vary both in their breadth and in the level of detail they employ. For example, one theory might seek to explain and predict as broad a phenomenon as emotional experience in general. A narrower theory might purport to predict how people display the emotion of fear nonverbally after receiving a threat. An even more specific theory might attempt to explain how the muscles of the face work together to produce expressions of fear.

theories: Broad explanations and predictions concerning phenomena of interest

All of us have developed our own informal theories of human behaviour, such as "People are basically good" or "People's behaviour is usually motivated by self-interest" (Sternberg, 1985a; Sternberg, 1990; Sternberg & Beall, 1991). However, psychologists' theories are more formal and focused. They are established on the basis of a careful study of the psychological literature to identify relevant research conducted and theories formulated previously, as well as psychologists' general knowledge of the field (McGuire, 1997).

In an ambiguous situation, the presence of others behaving as if there is no emergency will indicate to the observer that help is not required.

Psychologists Bibb Latané and John Darley, responding specifically to the Kitty Genovese case, developed a theory based on a phenomenon they called *diffusion of responsibility* (Latané & Darley, 1970). According to their theory, the greater the number of bystanders or witnesses to an event that calls for helping behaviour, the more the responsibility for helping is perceived to be shared by all the bystanders. Because of this sense of shared responsibility, then, the more people present in an emergency situation, the less personally responsible each person feels—and the less likely it is that any single person will come forward to help.

Hypotheses: Crafting Testable Predictions

While such a theory makes sense, it represented only the beginning phase of Latané and Darley's investigative process. Their next step was to devise a way of testing their theory. To do this, they needed to derive a hypothesis. A **hypothesis** is a prediction stated in a way that allows it to be tested. Hypotheses stem from theories; they help to test the underlying validity of theories.

hypothesis: A prediction, stemming from a theory, stated in a way that allows it to be tested

Just as we have our own broad theories about the world, so do we develop hypotheses about events and behaviour (ranging from trivialities, such as why a particular professor is such an eccentric, to more meaningful matters, such as what is the best way for people to study). Although we rarely test them systematically, we do try to determine whether or not they are right. Perhaps we try cramming for one exam but studying over a longer period of time for another. By assessing the results, we have created a way to compare the two strategies.

Latané and Darley's hypothesis was a straightforward derivation from their more general theory of diffusion of responsibility: The more people who witness an emergency situation, the less likely it is that help will be given to a victim. They could, of course, have chosen another hypothesis (for instance, that people with greater skills related to emergency situations will not be affected by the presence of others), but their initial formulation seemed to offer the most direct test of the theory.

Psychologists rely on formal theories and hypotheses for many reasons. For one thing, theories and hypotheses allow psychologists to make sense of unorganized, separate observations and bits of information by permitting them to place the pieces within a structured and coherent framework. In addition, theories and hypotheses offer psychologists the opportunity to move beyond already known facts and principles and to make deductions about as yet unexplained phenomena. In this way, theories and hypotheses provide a reasoned guide to the direction that future investigation ought to take.

In sum, then, theories and hypotheses help psychologists pose appropriate questions. But how are such questions answered? As we shall see, the answers come from research.

Finding Answers: Psychological Research

Research, systematic inquiry aimed at the discovery of new knowledge, is a central ingredient of the scientific method in psychology. It provides the key to understanding the degree to which theories and hypotheses are accurate.

Just as we can develop several theories and hypotheses to explain particular phenomena, so we can use a considerable number of alternative means to carry out research. First, though, the hypothesis must be restated in a way that will allow it to be tested, a procedure known as operationalization. **Operationalization** is the process of translating a hypothesis into specific, testable procedures that can be measured and observed.

operationalization: The process of translating a hypothesis into specific, testable procedures that can be measured and observed

There is no single way to go about operationalizing a hypothesis; it depends on logic, the equipment and facilities available, the psychological model being employed, and ultimately the ingenuity of the researcher (Creswell, 1994). For example, one researcher might develop a hypothesis in which she operationalizes "fear" as an increase in heart rate. In contrast, another psychologist might operationalize "fear" as a written response to the question, "How much fear are you experiencing at this moment?"

We will consider several of the major tools in the psychologist's research kit. As we discuss these research methods, keep in mind that their relevance extends beyond testing and evaluating theories and hypotheses in psychology. Even people who do not have degrees in psychology, for instance, often carry out rudimentary forms of research on their own. For example, a supervisor may need to evaluate an employee's performance. A physician might systematically test the effects of different dosages of a drug on a patient. A salesperson may compare different persuasive strategies. Each of these situations calls for the use of the research practices we are about to discuss (Breakwell, Hammond, & Fife-Schaw, 1995; Shaughnessy & Zechmeister, 1997; Graziano & Raulin, 1997).

Furthermore, a knowledge of the research methods used by psychologists permits us to better evaluate the research that others conduct. The media constantly bombard us with information about research studies and findings. Knowledge of research methods allows us to sort out what is credible from what should be ignored. Finally, there is evidence that studying some kinds of research methods in depth allows people to learn to reason more critically and effectively (Lehman, Lempert, & Nisbett, 1988; Leshowitz et al., 1993). Understanding the methods by which psychologists conduct research may enhance our ability to analyze and evaluate the situations we encounter in our everyday lives.

Archival Research

Suppose that, like psychologists Latané and Darley, you were interested in finding out more about emergency situations in which bystanders did not provide help. One of the first places to which you might turn would be historical accounts. By using newspaper records, for example, you might find support for the notion that a decrease in helping behavior has accompanied an increase in the number of bystanders.

Using newspaper articles is an example of archival research. In **archival research,** existing records, such as census data, birth certificates, or newspaper clippings, are examined to confirm a hypothesis. Archival research is a relatively inexpensive means of testing a hypothesis, since someone else has already collected the basic data. Of course, the use of existing data has several drawbacks. For one thing, the data may not be in a form that allows the researcher to test a hypothesis fully. The information may be incomplete, or it may have been collected haphazardly (Stewart & Kamins, 1993).

archival research: Research in which existing records, such as census data, birth certificates, or newspaper clippings, are examined to confirm a hypothesis

In most cases, though, archival research is hampered by the simple fact that records with the necessary information do not exist. In these instances, researchers often turn to another research method: naturalistic observation.

Close to election time, surveys may be done, following a debate by party leaders to monitor people's attitudes in an attempt to predict who may win.

Naturalistic Observation

naturalistic observation: Research in which an investigator simply observes some naturally occurring behaviour and does not intervene in the situation

In **naturalistic observation,** the investigator simply observes some naturally occurring behaviour and does not intervene in the situation. For example, a researcher investigating helping behaviour might observe the kind of help given to victims in a high-crime area of a city. The important point to remember about naturalistic observation is that the researcher is passive and simply records what occurs (Erlandson et al., 1993; Adler & Adler, 1994).

While the advantage of naturalistic observation is obvious—we get a sample of what people do in their "natural habitat"—there is also an important drawback: the inability to control any of the factors of interest. For example, we might find so few naturally occurring instances of helping behaviour that we would be unable to draw any conclusions. Because naturalistic observation prevents researchers from making changes in a situation, they must wait until appropriate conditions occur. Furthermore, if people know that they are being watched, they may alter their reactions, resulting in behaviour that is not truly representative of the group in question.

Survey Research

survey research: Research in which people chosen to represent some larger population are asked a series of questions about their behaviour, thoughts, or attitudes

There is no more straightforward way of finding out what people think, feel, and do than asking them directly. For this reason, surveys are an important research method. In **survey research,** people chosen to represent some larger population are asked a series of questions about their behaviour, thoughts, or attitudes. Survey methods have become so sophisticated that even with a very small sample researchers are able to infer with great accuracy how a larger group would respond. For instance, sampling just a few thousand voters is sufficient to predict within one or two percentage points who will win a Federal election—if the sample is chosen with care (Fowler, 1995; Schuman & Presser, 1996; Weisberg, Krosnick, & Bowen, 1996).

Researchers investigating helping behaviour might conduct a survey asking people to indicate their reasons for not wanting to come forward to help another individual. Similarly, researchers interested in learning about sexual practices have carried out surveys to learn which practices are common and which are not, and to chart changing notions of sexual morality over the past several decades.

While asking people directly about their behaviour seems in some ways the most straightforward approach to understanding what people do, survey research has several potential drawbacks. For one thing, people may give inaccurate information because of memory lapses or because they don't want to let the researcher know what they really believe about a particular issue. Moreover, people sometimes offer responses they think the researcher wants to hear—or, in just the opposite instance, responses they assume the researcher *doesn't* want to hear. In some cases, unscrupulous pollsters ask biased questions deliberately designed to yield a particular result, for either commercial or political purposes.

"This is the New York 'Times' Business Poll again, Mr. Landau. Do you feel better or worse about the economy than you did twenty minutes ago?"

Drawing by Handelsman; © 1993 The New Yorker Magazine, Inc.

The Case Study

What is it that makes violent video games so appealing? Is there something in the personality or background of players that leads to the choice to play? Does playing them increase aggressive behaviour? In order to answer these questions, psychologists might conduct a case study. In contrast to a survey, in which many people are studied, a **case study** is an in-depth, intensive investigation of an individual or small group of people. Case studies often include psychological testing, a procedure in which a carefully designed set of questions is used to gain some insight into the personality of the individual or group being studied (Stake, 1995; Kvale, 1996).

case study: An in-depth, intensive investigation of an individual or small group of people

When case studies are used as a research technique, the goal is often not only to learn about the few individuals being examined, but to use the insights gained from the study to improve our understanding of people in general. However, generalizations must be made cautiously. For instance, the degree to which a small group of participants are representative of the general population is certainly open to question.

Correlational Research

In using the research methods that we have described, researchers often wish to determine the relationship between two behaviours or between responses to two questions on a questionnaire. For example, we might want to find out if people who report that they attend religious services regularly also report that they are more helpful to strangers in emergency situations. If we did find such a relationship, we could say that there was an association—or correlation—between attendance at religious services and being helpful in emergencies.

In **correlational research,** the relationship between two sets of factors is examined to determine whether they are associated, or "correlated." The strength and direction of the relationship between the two factors is represented by a mathematical score, known as a *correlation,* that can range from +1.0 to –1.0.

correlational research: The relationship between two sets of factors is examined to determine whether they are associated, or "correlated"

A positive correlation indicates that as the value of one factor increases, we can predict that the value of the other factor will also increase. For example, if we predict that the *more* students study for a test, the *higher* their subsequent grades on the test, and that the *less* they study, the *lower* their test scores, we are expecting to find a positive correlation. (Higher values of the factor "amount of study time" would be associated with higher values of the factor "test score," and lower values of "amount of study time" would be associated with lower values of "test score.") The correlation, then, would be indicated by a positive number, and the stronger the association between studying and test scores, the closer the number would be to +1.0.

On the other hand, a correlation with a negative value tells us that as the value of one factor increases, the value of the other decreases. For instance, we might predict that as the number of hours spent studying *increases,* the number of hours spent in recreational activities will *decline.* Here, we are expecting a negative correlation, ranging between 0 and –1. More studying is associated with less recreation, and less studying is associated with more recreation. The stronger the association between study and play, the closer to –1.0 would be the correlation. For instance, a correlation of –.15 would indicate that there is little association between the two factors; a correlation of –.45 would indicate a moderate negative relationship; and a correlation of –.80 would indicate a strong negative association.

Of course, it's quite possible that no relationship exists between two factors. For instance, we would probably not expect to find a relationship between number of study hours and height. Lack of a relationship would be indicated by a correlation close to 0; knowing how much someone studies does not tell us anything about how tall he or she is.

When we find that two variables are strongly correlated with one another, it is tempting to presume that one factor causes the other. For example, if we find that more study time is associated with higher grades, we might guess that more studying *causes* higher grades. While not a bad guess, it remains just a guess—because finding that two factors are correlated does not mean that there is a causal relationship. Although the strong correlation suggests that knowing how much a person studies can help us predict how he or she will do on a test, it does not mean that the studying caused the test performance. It might be, for instance, that people who are interested in the subject matter tend to study more than those who are less interested, and that it is the amount of interest that actually causes test performance, not the number of hours spent studying. The mere fact that two factors occur together does not mean that one causes the other.

Another example illustrates the critical point that correlations tell us nothing about cause and effect but only provide a measure of the strength of a relationship between two factors. We might find that children who watch a lot of television programs featuring high levels of aggression are apt to demonstrate a relatively high degree of aggressive behaviour, while those who watch few television shows that portray aggression are apt to exhibit a relatively low degree of such behaviour (see Figure 1-2). But we cannot say that the aggression is *caused* by the TV viewing, because several other explanations are possible.

For instance, it may be that children who have an unusually high level of energy seek out programs with aggressive content *and* are more aggressive. The children's energy level, then, may be the true cause of the children's higher incidence of aggression. Finally, it is also possible that people who are already highly aggressive choose to watch shows with high aggressive content *because* they are aggressive. Clearly, then, any number of causal sequences are possible—none of which can be ruled out by correlational research.

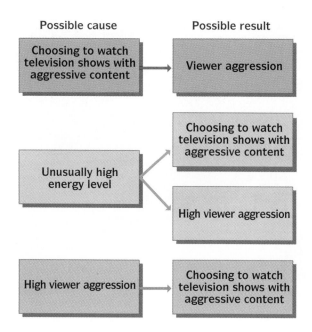

Possible cause

Possible result

Choosing to watch television shows with aggressive content → Viewer aggression

Unusually high energy level → Choosing to watch television shows with aggressive content

Unusually high energy level → High viewer aggression

High viewer aggression → Choosing to watch television shows with aggressive content

FIGURE 1-1 *If we find that frequent viewing of television programs having aggressive content is associated with high levels of aggressive behaviour, we might cite several plausible causes, as suggested in this figure. Correlational findings, then, do not permit us to determine causality.*

The inability of correlational research to demonstrate cause-and-effect relationships is a crucial drawback to its use. There is, however, an alternative technique that does establish causality: the experiment.

Experimental Research

The *only* way that psychologists can establish cause-and-effect relationships through research is by carrying out an experiment. In a formal **experiment,** the relationship between two (or more) factors is investigated by deliberately producing a change in one factor in a situation and observing the effects of that change on other aspects of the situation. In an experiment, then, the conditions required to study a question of interest are created by an experimenter, who deliberately makes a change in those conditions in order to observe the effects of that change.

The change that an experimenter deliberately produces in a situation is called the **experimental manipulation.** Experimental manipulations are used to detect relationships between **variables,** which are behaviours, events, or other characteristics that can change, or vary, in some way.

Several steps are involved in carrying out an experiment, but the process typically begins with the development of one or more hypotheses for the experiment to test (Broota, 1990). Recall, for example, the hypothesis derived by Latané and Darley to test their theory of helping behaviour: The more people who witness an emergency situation, the less likely it is that any of them will help a victim. We can trace the way these researchers designed an experiment to test this hypothesis.

Their first step was to operationalize the hypothesis by conceptualizing it in a way that could be tested. Doing so required that Latané and Darley take into account the fundamental principle of experimental research mentioned earlier. Experimenters must manipulate at least one variable in order to observe the effects of the manipulation on another variable. But the manipulation cannot be viewed by itself, in isolation; if a cause-and-effect relationship is to be established, the effects of the manipulation must be compared with the effects of no manipulation or a different manipulation.

Experimental research requires, then, that the responses of at least two groups be compared with each other. One group will receive some special **treatment**—the manipulation implemented by the experimenter—while another group receives either no treatment or a different treatment. Any group receiving a treatment is called an **experimental group,** while a group that receives no treatment is called the **control group.** (In some experiments there are multiple experimental and control groups, each of which is compared with another.)

experiment: The investigation of the relationship between two (or more) factors by deliberately producing a change in one factor in a situation and observing the effects of that change on other aspects of the situation

experimental manipulation: The change that an experimenter deliberately produces in a situation
variables: Behaviours, events, or other characteristics that can change, or vary, in some way

treatment: The manipulation implemented by the experimenter

experimental group: Any group receiving a treatment
control group: A group that receives no treatment

In this experiment, preschoolers' reactions to the puppet are monitored.

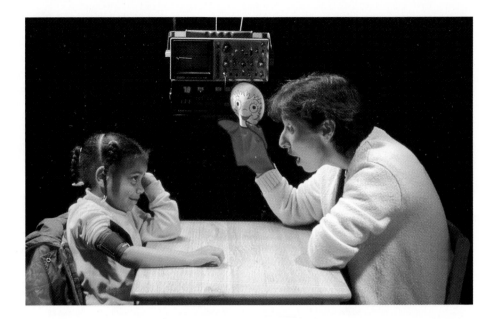

By employing both experimental and control groups in an experiment, researchers are able to rule out the possibility that something other than the experimental manipulation produced the results observed in the experiment. With no control group, we couldn't be sure that some other factor, such as the temperature at the time we were running the experiment, the colour of the experimenter's hair, or even the mere passage of time, wasn't causing the changes observed.

For example, consider a medical researcher who thinks she has invented a medicine that cures the common cold. To test her claim, she gives the medicine one day to a group of 20 people who have colds, and finds that 10 days later all of them are cured. Eureka? Not so fast. An observer viewing this flawed study might reasonably argue that the people would have gotten better even without the medicine. What the researcher obviously needed was a control group consisting of people with colds who *don't* get the medicine, and whose health is also checked 10 days later. Only if there is a difference between the experimental and control groups can the effectiveness of the medicine be assessed. Through the use of control groups, then, researchers can isolate specific causes for their findings—and draw cause-and-effect inferences.

Returning to Latané and Darley's experiment, we note that the researchers needed a means of operationalizing their hypothesis in order to proceed. They decided they would create a bogus emergency situation that would appear to require the aid of a bystander. As their experimental manipulation, they decided to vary the number of bystanders present. They could have had just one experimental group with, say, two people present, and a control group for comparison purposes with just one person present. Instead, they settled on a more complex procedure involving three groups—consisting of two, three, and six people—that could be compared with one another.

Latané and Darley had now identified what is called the experimenter's independent variable. The **independent variable** is the variable that is manipulated by an experimenter. In this experiment, the experimental manipulation was the number of people present.

The next step was to decide how they were going to determine the effect that varying the number of bystanders had on participants' behaviour. Crucial to every experiment is the **dependent variable,** the variable that is measured and is expected to change as a result of changes caused by the experimenter's manipulation.

Latané and Darley had several possible choices for their dependent measure. One might have been a simple Yes/No measure of helping behaviour on the part of the *participants* or *subjects,* the people taking part in the experiment. But the two investigators decided they also wanted a measure that provided a more precise analysis of

independent variable: The variable that is manipulated by an experimenter

dependent variable: The variable that is measured and is expected to change as a result of changes caused by the experimenter's manipulation

helping behaviour. Consequently, they determined that they would also measure the amount of time it took for a participant to provide help.

Latané and Darley now had all the components of an experiment. The independent variable, manipulated by them, was the number of bystanders present in an emergency situation. The dependent variable was whether the bystanders in each of the groups provided help and the amount of time it took them to do so. Like all experiments, then, this one had both an independent and a dependent variable. (To remember the difference, you might recall that a hypothesis predicts how a dependent variable *depends* on the manipulation of the independent variable.) *All* true experiments in psychology fit this straightforward model.

The Final Step: Random Assignment of Participants. To make the experiment a valid test of the hypothesis, the researchers needed to add a final step to the design: properly assigning participants to receive a particular treatment.

The significance of this step becomes clear when we examine various alternative procedures. For example, the experimenters might have assigned just males to the group with two bystanders, just females to the group with three bystanders, and both males and females to the group with six bystanders. Had they done so, however, any differences they found in helping behaviour could not be attributed with any certainty solely to group size, since the differences might just as well be due to the composition of the group. A more reasonable procedure would be to ensure that each group had the same composition in terms of gender; then the researchers would be able to make comparisons across groups with considerably more accuracy.

Participants in each of the experimental groups ought to be comparable, and it is easy enough to create groups that are similar in terms of gender. The problem becomes a bit more tricky, though, when we consider other participant characteristics. How can we ensure that participants in each experimental group will be equally intelligent, extroverted, cooperative, and so forth, when the list of characteristics—any one of which may be important—is potentially endless?

The solution is a simple but elegant procedure called random assignment to condition. In **random assignment to condition,** participants are assigned to different experimental groups or "conditions" on the basis of chance and chance alone. The experimenter might, for instance, put the names of all potential participants into a hat and draw names to make assignments to specific groups. The advantage of this technique is that participant characteristics have an equal chance of being distributed across the various groups. By using random assignment, the experimenter can be confident that each of the groups will have approximately the same proportion of intelligent people, cooperative people, extroverted people, males and females, and so on.

random assignment to condition: A procedure in which participants are assigned to different experimental groups or "conditions" on the basis of chance and chance alone

The following set of key elements is important to keep in mind as you consider whether a research study is truly an experiment:

- An independent variable, the factor that is manipulated by the experimenter

- A dependent variable, the variable that is measured by the experimenter and expected to change

- A procedure that randomly assigns participants to different experimental groups or "conditions" of the independent variable

- A hypothesis that ties the independent and dependent variable together.

Only if each of these elements is present can a research study be considered a true experiment in which cause-and-effect relationships can be determined. (For a summary of the different types of research that we've discussed, see Table 1-1.)

Were Latané and Darley Right? By now, you must be wondering whether Latané and Darley were right when they hypothesized that increasing the number of bystanders in an emergency situation would lower the degree of helping behaviour.

Table 1-1	Research Strategies

Correlational Research		Experimental Research
	General process:	
Researcher observes a previously existing situation but does not intervene		Researcher manipulates a situation in order to observe the outcome of the manipulation
	Intended result:	
Identify associations between factors		Learn how changes in one factor cause changes in another
	Types:	
Archival research (examines records to confirm a hypothesis)		Experiment (investigator produces a change in one factor to observe the effects of that change on other factors)
Naturalistic observation (observation of naturally occurring behaviour, without intervention)		
Survey research (asking questions of people chosen to represent a larger population)		
Case study (intensive investigation of an individual or small group)		

According to the results of the experiment they carried out, their hypothesis was right on target. To test the hypothesis, they used a laboratory setting in which participants were told that the purpose of the experiment was to hold a discussion about personal problems associated with college. The discussion was to be held over an intercom, supposedly to avoid the potential embarrassment of face-to-face contact. Chatting about personal problems was not, of course, the true purpose of the experiment, but participants were told that it was as a way of keeping their expectations about the experiment from biasing their behaviour. (Consider how they would have been affected if they had been told that their helping behaviour in emergencies was being tested. The experimenters could never have gotten an accurate assessment of what the participants would actually do in an emergency. By definition, emergencies are rarely announced in advance.)

The sizes of the discussion groups were two, three, and six people, which constituted the manipulation of the independent variable of group size. Participants were randomly assigned to one of these groups upon their arrival at the laboratory.

As the participants in each group were holding their discussion, they suddenly heard one of the other participants (in reality a trained *confederate,* or employee, of the experimenters) lapse into what sounded like an epileptic seizure:

> I-er-um-I think I-I need-er-if-if- could-er-er-somebody er-er-er-er-er-er-er give me a little-er give me a little help here because-er-I-er-I'm-er-er-h-h- having a-a-a real problem-er-right now and I-er-if somebody could help me out it would-it-would-er-er s-s-sure be-sure be good . . . because-er-there-er- er-a cause I-er-I-uh-I've got a-a one of the-er-sei—er-er-things coming on and-and-and I could really-er-use some help so if somebody would-er-give me a little h-help-uh-er-er-er-er-er c-could somebody-er-er-help-er-us-us-us [choking sounds]. . . . I'm gonna die-er-er-I'm . . . gonna die-er-help-er-er- seizure-er- [choking sounds, then silence] (Latané and Darley, 1970, p. 379).

The participants' behaviour was now what counted. The dependent variable was the time that elapsed from the start of the "seizure" to the time a participant began trying to help the "victim." If six minutes went by without a participant's offering help, the experiment was ended.

As predicted by the hypothesis, the size of the group had a significant effect on whether a participant provided help (Latané & Darley, 1970). In the two-person group (in which participants thought they were alone with the victim), the average elapsed

Pathways Through Psychology

Wendy Josephson

***Associate Professor of Psychology
University of Winnipeg***

Education: *B.A., M.A., Ph.D.
University of Manitoba*

Home: *Winnipeg, Manitoba*

As an undergraduate student in psychology, I took my first course in social psychology from Bob Altemeyer, a wonderful classroom teacher and an inspiring researcher in the area of authoritarianism. I was captivated by social psychology from the very first lecture. Of all the disciplines and sub-disciplines I had encountered, I thought social psychology asked the best questions, and had very interesting answers. I still think that.

As a professor at a small undergraduate university, my work includes teaching courses in social and organizational psychology, research in the areas of violence and aggression, and service to the university and the community. Service to the university includes working on department or university committees and service to the community involves making my research useful to people outside the university world. For example, I have given talks to various educational, community, and industry groups including the Canadian Cable Television Association about the effects of television violence on children. I served as one of the academic advisers to Mediascope and the Children's Action Network. The project was to create a guide to help producers of children's educational television comply with U.S. federal requirements.

There are three accomplishments that I consider most important in my research: The first is a field experiment that I conducted on the effects of television violence on children's play behaviour, which was published in the *Journal of Personality and Social Psychology* in 1987. It demonstrated in a real-life setting that boys' aggressiveness toward each other could be significantly affected by having watched a violent television program, especially if there were other cues in their play setting that were associated with the TV violence.

The second accomplishment is the report that I wrote for the Department of Canadian Heritage in 1995. It reviewed the effects of television violence on children of different ages, and made suggestions for ways in which parents and the television industry could enhance the positive effects of television and reduce its negative effects.

The third is a study that I'm doing now with my colleague Jocelyn Proulx, at the Prairie-based research network called RESOLVE (Research and Education for Solutions to Violence and Abuse). The Social Sciences and Humanities Research Council of Canada (SSHRC) has funded a project in which we provided activities from the Healthy Relationships dating violence prevention curriculum to grade seven, eight and nine students in six Winnipeg schools over a three-year period. We are currently evaluating the effects that the program had on students' knowledge, attitudes and behaviour. This project is important because understanding how to prevent violence early in close relationships could have tremendous impact on individual and family happiness. It was also an opportunity to demonstrate that a lot could be accomplished in a collaboration among academic researchers, school divisions, government (Manitoba Culture, Heritage, and Citizenship) and community organizations (the Halifax group, Men for Change, which developed the Healthy Relationships program).

As a psychologist, I love to do research that answers interesting questions about human behaviour. But the work that is really important to me has to do more than just answer questions. I want the knowledge that is gained from my research to make a difference in people's lives.

Wendy Josephson

Source: Wendy Josephson, Ph.D. University of Winnipeg. <wendy.josephson@uwinnipeg.ca>

time was 52 seconds; in the three-person group (the participant, the victim, and one other person), the average elapsed time was 93 seconds; and in the six-person group (the participant, the victim, and four others), the average time was 166 seconds. Considering a simple Yes/No measure of whether help was given confirms the elapsed-time pattern. Eighty-five percent of the participants in the two-person-group condition helped; 62 percent in the three-person-group condition; and only 31 percent helped in the six-person-group condition.

Because these results are so straightforward, it seems clear that the original hypothesis was confirmed. However, Latané and Darley could not be sure that the results were truly meaningful until they examined their data using formal statistical procedures. As discussed in this book's Appendix, statistical procedures—which entail several kinds of mathematical calculations—allow a researcher to determine precisely the likelihood that results are meaningful and not merely the outcome of chance.

replication: The repetition of findings using other procedures in other settings, with other groups of participants, before full confidence can be placed in the validity of any single experiment

The Latané and Darley study contains all the elements of an experiment: an independent variable, a dependent variable, random assignment to conditions, and multiple experimental groups. Because it does, we can say with some confidence that group size *caused* changes in the degree of helping behaviour.

Of course, one experiment alone does not resolve forever the question of bystander intervention in emergencies. Psychologists require that findings be **replicated,** or repeated, using other procedures in other settings, with other groups of participants, before full confidence can be placed in the validity of any single experiment. [In this case, the experiment has stood the test of time. In a review of some fifty studies carried out in the ten years following the original experiment, the finding that an increase in the number of bystanders leads to decreased helping has been replicated in numerous other studies (Latané & Nida, 1981).

In addition to replicating experimental results, psychologists need to test the limitations of their theories and hypotheses in order to determine under which specific circumstances they do and do not apply. It seems unlikely, for instance, that increasing the number of bystanders *always* results in less helping. Therefore it is critical to understand the conditions in which exceptions to this general rule occur. For example, we might speculate that under conditions of shared outcomes, in which onlookers experience a sense that a victim's difficulties may later affect them in some way, help would be more readily forthcoming (Aronson, 1988). Testing this hypothesis (for which, in fact, there is some support) requires additional experimentation.

Like any science, then, psychology increases our understanding in small, incremental steps, with each step building upon previous work. The work is carried out on many fronts and involves many people—individuals such as Wendy Josephson, whose work is discussed in the Pathways Through Psychology box.

Recap, Review, and Rethink

Recap

- The scientific method is a systematic method of inquiry consisting of identifying questions of interest, formulating an explanation, and carrying out research.

- Theories—broad explanations or predictions about phenomena—and hypotheses—research predictions that can be tested—are two important tools of scientific research.

- Key research methods include archival research, naturalistic observation, survey research, and the case study.

- In correlational research, the relationship between two variables is examined to determine whether they are associated, although cause-and-effect relationships cannot be established.

- In a formal experiment—the only means of determining cause-and-effect associations—the relationship between factors is investigated by deliberately producing a change in one factor and observing changes in the other.

Review

1. An experimenter is interested in studying the relationship between hunger and aggression. He defines aggression as the number of times a participant will hit a punching bag. What is the process of defining this variable called?

2. Match the following forms of research to their definition:
   1. Archival research
   2. Naturalistic observation
   3. Survey research
   4. Case study

   a. Directly asking a sample of people questions about their behaviour
   b. Examining existing records to confirm a hypothesis
   c. Looking at behaviour in its true setting without intervening in the results
   d. In-depth investigation of a person or small group

3. Match each of the following research methods with a problem basic to it:
   1. Archival research
   2. Naturalistic observation
   3. Survey research
   4. Case study

   a. May not be able to generalize to the population at large.
   b. People's behaviour may change if they know they are being watched.
   c. The data may not exist or may be unusable.
   d. People may lie in order to present a good image.

4. A friend tells you that "Anxiety about speaking in public and performance are negatively correlated. Therefore, high anxiety must cause low performance." Is this statement true or false, and why?

5. A psychologist wants to study the effect of attractiveness on willingness to help a person with a math problem. Attractiveness would be the _____ variable, while amount of helping would be the _____ variable.

6. The group in an experiment that receives no treatment is called the _____ group.

Answers to Review Questions are on page 36.

Rethink

1. Can you describe how a researcher might use naturalistic observation, case study methods, and survey research to investigate gender differences in aggressive behaviour at the workplace? First state a hypothesis, then describe your research approaches. What positive and negative features does each method have?

2. Tobacco companies frequently assert that no experiment has ever proved that tobacco use causes cancer. Can you explain this claim in terms of the research procedures and designs discussed in this chapter? What sort of research would establish a cause-and-effect relationship between tobacco use and cancer? Is such a research study possible?

3. In running an experiment, you decide to take the first twenty available participants and assign them to the experimental group and assign the next twenty to the control group. Why might this not be a good idea?

RESEARCH CHALLENGES: EXPLORING THE PROCESS

It is probably apparent by now that there are few simple formulas that psychologists can follow as they carry out research. They must make choices about the type of study to conduct, the measures to take, and the most effective way to analyze the results. Even after they make these essential decisions, they must still consider several critical issues. We turn first to the most fundamental of these issues: ethics.

▶ **What are the major issues that underlie the process of conducting research?**

The Ethics of Research

Put yourself in the place of one of the participants in the Latané and Darley experiment. How would you feel when you learned that the person who you thought was having a seizure was, in reality, a paid accomplice of the experimenter?

Although you might at first experience relief that there had been no real emergency, you might also feel some resentment that you had been deceived by the experimenter. And you might also experience concern that you had been placed in an unusual situation—one that may have dealt a blow to your self-esteem, depending on how you had behaved.

Most psychologists argue that the use of deception is sometimes necessary to prevent participants from being influenced by what they think is the study's true purpose. (If you knew that Latané and Darley were actually studying your helping behaviour, wouldn't you automatically have been tempted to intervene in the emergency?) To avoid such outcomes, researchers must occasionally use deception.

Nonetheless, because research has the potential to violate the rights of participants, psychologists are expected to adhere to a strict set of ethical guidelines aimed at protecting participants (Canadian Psychological Association, 1991). These guidelines are based on the following four principles:

Ethics in Research

*   Respect for the dignity of persons: value the intrinsic worth of the individual.

*   Responsible caring: careful consideration that outcomes will not cause harm.

*   Integrity in relationships: doing what is morally good for the profession.

*   Responsibility to society: promoting the greatest good for society.

In both the United States (APA, 1992) and Canada (CPA, 1991) ethical guidelines do allow the use of deception. All experiments involving deception, in fact, all experiments using human subjects must be reviewed by the responsible agencies. In Canada, this is the Ethics Review Board of the institution to which the researcher belongs. Guidelines for these boards come from the Social Sciences and Humanities Research Council of Canada, which serves as the national funding agency. (Rosnow et. al., 1993; Rosenthal, 1994; Kimmel, 1996; Dunbar, 1998; Stark, 1998).

One of the key ethical principles followed by psychologists is that of **informed consent.** Before participating in an experiment, participants must sign a document affirming that they have been told the basic outlines of the study and are

informed consent: A document signed by participants affirming that they have been told the basic outlines of the study and are aware of what their participation will involve

College students are readily available and widely used research subjects, but they may not be sufficiently representative of the general population.

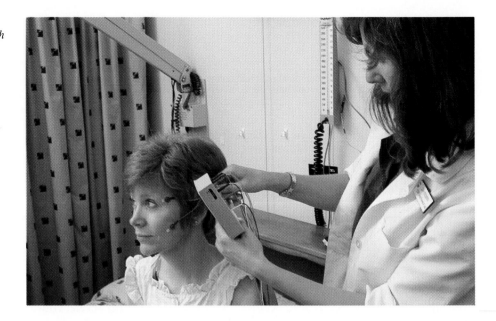

aware of what their participation will involve, what risks the experiment may hold, and the fact that their participation is purely voluntary and may be terminated at any time (Sieber, 1993; Mann, 1994; Stanley & Guido, 1996; Stark, 1998; O'Neill, 1998).

Exploring Diversity

Choosing Participants Who Represent the Scope of Human Behaviour

When Latané and Darley, both college professors, decided who should be used as participants in their experiment, they turned to the people who were most readily accessible to them: college students. In fact, college students are used so frequently in experiments that psychology has been called—somewhat contemptuously—the "science of the behaviour of the college sophomore" (Rubenstein, 1982).

The use of college students as participants has both advantages and drawbacks. The big benefit is their availability. Because most research occurs in university settings, college students are readily available. Typically, they participate for either extra course credit or a relatively small monetary payment, making the cost to the researcher minimal.

The problem with relying on college students for participants is that they may not adequately represent the general population. College students tend to be younger and better educated than a significant percentage of the rest of the population of the United States. Moreover, their attitudes are likely to be less well formed, and they are apt to be more susceptible than older adults to social pressures from authority figures and peers (Sears, 1986).

These concerns apply to Canada as well, where many psychology departments in Canadian universities use introductory psychology students as subjects.

When a science that purports to explain human behaviour in general disregards a significant proportion of the population in drawing conclusions, something is amiss. Conse-

---

Answers to Review Questions:

1. Operationalization.   2. 1. b; 2. c; 3. a; 4. d   3. 1. c; 2. b; 3. d; 4. a   4. False; correlation does not imply causation. Just because two variables are related does not mean that one causes the other. It could be the case that poor performance causes people to become more anxious, or that a third factor causes both of these effects.   5. independent; dependent   6. control

quently, psychological researchers have become increasingly sensitive to the importance of using participants who are fully representative of the general population (Gannon et al., 1992; Youngstrom, 1994). ■

Should Animals Be Used in Research?

It is not just psychologists working with humans who operate under strict ethical constraints; researchers who use animals as subjects in experiments have their own set of exacting guidelines to ensure that animals do not suffer (APA, 1993; CPA, 1996). Specifically, researchers must make every effort to minimize discomfort, illness, and pain, and procedures subjecting animals to distress may be used only when an alternative procedure is unavailable and when the research is justified by its prospective value. In Canada animal welfare is governed under the Criminal Code. There are two provincial acts that are specific to lab animals. However, the primary regulatory body for lab animals is the Canadian Council on Animal Care (CCAC), which was founded in 1968. Most of the universities and private institutions, where animals are used, hold a Certificate of Good Animal Practice from the CCAC. Those that do not would find it very difficult to obtain funding for research (CPA, 1996).

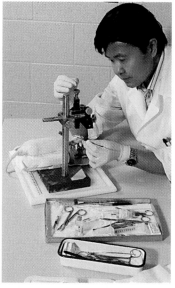

Research involving animals is controversial but, when conducted within ethical guidelines, yields significant benefits for humans.

Why should animals be used for research in the first place? How can we dare to infer human behaviour from the results of research employing rats, gerbils, and pigeons? The answer is that the 7 or 8 percent of psychological research that does employ animals has a different focus and is designed to answer different questions than research that uses humans. For example, the shorter life span of animals (rats live an average of two years) allows researchers to learn about the effects of aging in a much more rapid time frame than if they studied aging using human participants. Moreover, the very complexity of human beings may obscure information about fundamental phenomena that can be more plainly identified in animals. Finally, some studies require large numbers of subjects who share similar backgrounds or who have been exposed to particular environments—conditions that could not practically be met with human beings (Gill et al., 1989; Domjan & Purdy, 1995; Gallagher & Rapp, 1997; Mukerjee, 1997).

Research using animals as subjects has provided psychologists with information that has profoundly benefitted humans. For instance, animal research furnished the keys to detecting eye disorders in children early enough to prevent permanent damage, communicating more effectively with severely retarded children, and reducing chronic pain in people, to name just a few results (APA, 1988; Domjan & Purdy, 1995; Botting & Morrison, 1997).

Animals in Research

Despite the demonstrated value of research that uses animals as subjects, their use in psychological research remains controversial (Orlans, 1993; Plous, 1991, 1996a, 1996b; Birke & Michael, 1995), with some people calling for stringent restrictions or even a complete ban on the practice (Bowd & Shapiro, 1993; Barnard & Kaufman, 1997). However, most psychologists support animal studies that involve observation or confinement, although surveys find that a majority are not supportive of studies that involve pain or death. Furthermore, most believe that existing ethical guidelines are sufficiently stringent to provide protection for animals while still allowing valuable animal research to continue (Plous, 1996a).

Threats to Experiments: Experimenter and Participant Expectations

Even the best-laid experimental plans are susceptible to **experimental bias**—factors that distort an experimenter's understanding of how the independent variable affected the dependent variable. One of the most common forms of experimental bias that experimenters need to exclude is *experimenter expectations,* whereby an experimenter unintentionally transmits cues to participants about the way they are expected to behave in a given experimental condition (Harris, 1991; Blanck, 1993; Rosnow &

experimental bias: Factors that distort an experimenter's understanding of how the independent variable affected the dependent variable

Rosenthal, 1994, 1997). The danger is that these expectations will bring about an "appropriate" behaviour—one that may not have otherwise occurred. For example, if Latané and Darley had unintentionally behaved toward participants in the two-bystander condition as if they expected them to help, but unintentionally let on that they had low expectations for helping in the six-person bystander condition, these variations in experimenter behaviour—no matter how unintended—might have affected the results.

A related problem is *participant expectations* about appropriate behaviour. If you have ever been a participant in an experiment, you know that you quickly develop ideas about what is expected of you, and it is typical for people to develop their own hypotheses about what the experimenter hopes to learn from the study. If these expectations influence a participant's behaviour, it becomes a cause for concern, since in that case it is no longer the experimental manipulation producing an effect, but rather the participant's expectations.

To guard against participant expectations biasing the results of an experiment, the experimenter may try to disguise the true purpose of the experiment. Participants who do not know that helping behaviour is being studied, for example, are more apt to act in a "natural" way than if they are told their helping behaviour is under scrutiny. Latané and Darley decided to misinform their participants, then, telling them that the purpose of the experiment was to hold a discussion among college students about their personal problems. In doing so, they expected that their participants would not suspect the true purpose of the experiment.

In some experiments, it is impossible to hide the actual purpose of the research. In cases such as these, other techniques are available. For example, suppose you were interested in testing the ability of a new drug to alleviate the symptoms of severe depression. If you simply gave the drug to half your participants and not to the other half, participants given the drug might report feeling less depressed merely because they knew they were getting a drug. Similarly, the participants who got nothing might report feeling no better because they knew that they were in a no-treatment control group.

placebo: A bogus treatment, such as a pill, "drug," or other substance without any significant chemical properties or active ingredient

To solve this problem, psychologists typically use a procedure in which all participants receive a treatment, but those in the control group actually receive a placebo treatment. A **placebo** is a bogus treatment, such as a pill, "drug," or other substance without any significant chemical properties or active ingredient. Because members of both groups are kept in the dark as to whether they are getting a real or a bogus treatment, any differences that are found can be attributed to the quality of the drug and not to the possible psychological effects of being administered a pill or other substance (Roberts et al., 1993).

But there is still one more safeguard that a careful researcher must apply in an experiment such as this. To overcome the possibility that experimenter expectations will affect the participant, the person who administers the drug shouldn't know whether it is actually the true drug or the placebo. By keeping both the participant and the experimenter who interacts with the participant "blind" as to the nature of the drug that is being administered, researchers can more accurately assess the effects of the drug. This method is known as the *double-blind procedure*.

The Informed Consumer of Psychology

Thinking Critically about Research

Critical Thinking Skills

If you were about to purchase an automobile, it is unlikely that you would stop at the nearest car dealership and drive off with the first car a salesperson recommended. Instead, you would probably mull over the purchase, read about automobiles, consider the alternatives, talk to others about their experiences, and ultimately put in a fair amount of thought before you made such a major purchase.

In contrast, many of us are considerably less conscientious when we expend our intellectual assets than when we disperse our financial resources. People jump to conclusions on the basis of incomplete and inaccurate information, and only rarely do they take the time to critically evaluate the research and data to which they are exposed.

Because the field of psychology is based on an accumulated body of research, it is crucial for psychologists to scrutinize thoroughly the methods, results, and claims of researchers. Yet it is not just psychologists who need to know how to evaluate research critically; all of us are constantly exposed to the claims of others. Knowing how to approach research and data can be helpful in areas far beyond the realm of psychology.

Several basic questions can help us sort through what is valid and what is not. Among the most important questions to ask are the following:

- What are the foundations of the research? Research studies should evolve from a clearly specified theory. Furthermore, we must take into account the specific hypothesis that is being tested. Unless we know what hypothesis is being examined, it is not possible to judge how successful a study has been. We need to be able to see how the hypothesis has been derived from an underlying theory, and in turn to consider how well the design of the study tests that hypothesis.

- How well was the study conducted? Consider who the participants were, how many were involved, what methods were employed, and what problems in collecting the data the researcher encountered. For instance, there are important differences between a case study that reports the anecdotes of a handful of respondents and a careful survey that collects data from several thousand people.

- What assumptions lie behind the presentation of the results of the study? It is necessary to assess how well the statements being made reflect the actual data, as well as the logic of what is being claimed. For instance, the American Cancer Society announced in 1991 that a woman's odds of getting breast cancer had risen to 1 in 9. It turned out, though, that these were cumulative probabilities, reflecting the likelihood that a woman would develop breast cancer sometime between birth and age 110. For the vast majority of a woman's life, the odds of getting breast cancer are considerably lower. For instance, for women under the age of 50, the risk is closer to 1 in 1,000 (Blakeslee, 1992; Kolata, 1993).

    Similarly, when the manufacturer of Brand X aspirin boasts that "no other aspirin is more effective in fighting pain than Brand X," this does not mean that Brand X is better than every other kind of aspirin. It just means that no other brand of aspirin works better, and that others may actually work just as well as Brand X. Expressed in the latter fashion, the finding doesn't seem worth bragging about.

These basic principles can help you assess the validity of research findings that you come across—both within and outside the field of psychology. The more you know how to evaluate research in general, the better you will be able to assess what the field of psychology has to offer.   ■

Recap, Review, and Rethink

Recap

- Among the major ethical issues faced by psychologists are deception in experiments and the use of animals as subjects.

- Threats to experiments include experimenter expectations and participant expectations.

Review

1. Ethical research begins with the concept of informed consent. Before signing up to participate in an experiment, participants should be informed of

    a. the procedure of the study, stated generally.
    b. the risks that may be involved.
    c. their right to withdraw at any time.
    d. all of the above.

2. List three benefits of using nonhuman animals in psychological research.

3. Deception is one means experimenters can use to try to eliminate participants' expectations. True or false?

4. A procedure in which the experimenter does not know whether participants are receiving an actual treatment or not is known as the _____-_____ procedure.

5. A study is reported which shows that men differ from women in their preference for ice cream flavors. This study was based on a sample of two men and three women. What might be wrong with this study?

Answers to Review Questions are on page 42.

Rethink

1. A pollster studies people's attitudes toward welfare programs by circulating a questionnaire via the Internet. Is this study likely to reflect accurately the views of the general population? Why or why not?

2. A researcher strongly believes that college professors in general show female students less attention and respect in the classroom than they show male students. She sets up an experimental study involving observation of classrooms in different conditions. In explaining the study to the professors and students who will participate, what steps should the researcher take to eliminate experimental bias based on both experimenter expectations and participant expectations?

looking BACK

What is psychology and why is it a science?

1. Although the definition of psychology—the scientific study of behaviour and mental processes—is clear-cut, it is also deceptively simple, since "behaviour" encompasses not just what people do, but their thoughts, feelings, perceptions, reasoning, memory, and biological activities.

What are the different branches of the field of psychology?

2. Psychology includes a number of major specialty areas. Biopsychologists focus on the biological basis of behaviour, while experimental psychologists study the processes of sensing, perceiving, learning, and thinking about the world. Cognitive psychology, an outgrowth of experimental psychology, considers the study of higher mental processes, including thinking, language, memory, problem solving, knowing, reasoning, judging, and decision making.

3. The branches of psychology that study change and individual differences are developmental and personality psychology. Developmental psychologists study how people grow and change throughout the life span. Personality psychologists consider the consistency and change in an individual's behaviour as he or she moves through different situations, as well as the individual differences that distinguish one person's behaviour from another's when each is placed in the same situation.

4. Health, clinical, and counselling psychologists are primarily concerned with promoting physical and mental health. Health psychologists study psychological factors that affect physical disease, while clinical psychologists consider the study, diagnosis, and treatment of abnormal behaviour. Counselling psychologists focus on educational, social, and career adjustment problems.

5. Educational psychologists investigate how the educational process affects students, while school psychologists specialize in assessing and treating children in elementary and secondary schools who have academic and/or emotional problems.

6. Social psychology is the study of how people's thoughts, feelings, and actions are affected by others. The psychology of women concentrates on psychological factors relating to women's behaviour and development. Industrial-organizational psychologists focus on how psychology can be applied to the workplace, while consumer psychologists consider the factors that influence people's buying habits. Cross-cultural psychology examines the similarities and differences in psychological functioning among various cultures. The newest areas of specialization include evolutionary psychology, clinical neuropsychology, environmental psychology, forensic psychology, sport and exercise psychology, and program evaluation.

Where do psychologists work?

7. Psychologists are employed in a variety of settings. Although the primary employment sites are universities and colleges, many psychologists are found in hospitals, clinics, community mental health centres, and counselling centres. Many also have practices in which they treat patients privately.

What are the historical roots of the field of psychology?

8. The foundations of psychology were established by Wilhelm Wundt in Germany in 1879. Early conceptual perspectives that guided the work of psychologists were structuralism, functionalism, and gestalt theory. Structuralism focused on identifying the fundamental elements of the mind, largely by using introspection. Functionalism concentrated on the functions performed by mental activities. Gestalt psychology focused on the study of how perception is organized into meaningful units.

What approaches are used by contemporary psychologists?

9. The biological perspective focuses on the biological functioning of people and animals, reducing behaviour to its most basic components. The psychodynamic perspective takes a very different approach. It suggests that there are powerful, unconscious inner forces and conflicts about which people have little or no awareness and which are primary determinants of behaviour.

10. Cognitive approaches to behaviour consider how people know, understand, and think about the world. Growing out of early work on introspection and later work by the gestaltists and functionalists, cognitive perspectives study how people understand and represent the world within themselves.

11. The behavioural perspective de-emphasizes internal processes and concentrates instead on observable behaviour. It suggests that an understanding and control of a person's environment is sufficient to fully explain and modify behaviour.

12. The humanistic perspective is the newest of the major perspectives of psychology. It emphasizes that people are uniquely inclined toward psychological growth and higher levels of functioning and that they will strive to reach their full potential.

What is the future of psychology likely to hold?

13. Several emerging major trends may influence the future of psychology. Psychology will become increasingly specialized; its explanations will increasingly consider genetic and environmental factors simultaneously; it will take the growing diversity of the countrys population into account more fully; and it will become increasingly concerned with the public interest. In addition, psychological treatment is likely to become more accessible and socially acceptable.

What is the scientific method, and how do psychologists use theory and research to answer questions of interest?

14. The scientific method is an approach psychologists use to understand the unknown. It consists of three steps: identifying questions of interest, formulating an explanation, and carrying out research that is designed to lend support to the explanation.

15. Research in psychology is guided by theories (broad explanations and predictions of phenomena of interest) and hypotheses (derivations of theories that are predictions stated in a way that allows them to be tested).

What are the different research methods employed by psychologists?

16. Archival research uses existing records, such as old newspapers or other documents, to confirm a hypothesis. In naturalistic observation, the investigator acts mainly as an observer, making no change in a naturally occurring situation. In survey research, people are asked a series of questions about their behaviour, thoughts, or attitudes. The case study is an in-depth interview and examination of one person. These methods rely on correlational techniques, which describe associations between various factors but cannot determine cause-and-effect relationships.

How do psychologists establish cause-and-effect relationships in research studies?

17. In a formal experiment, the relationship between factors is investigated by deliberately producing a change—called the experimental manipulation—in one of them and observing changes in the other. The factors that are changed are called variables—behaviours, events, or persons that can change, or vary, in some way. For a hypothesis to be tested, it must be operationalized, a process in which the researcher translates the abstract concepts of the hypothesis into the actual procedures used in the study.

18. In an experiment, at least two groups must be compared with one another to assess cause-and-effect relationships. The group receiving the treatment (the special procedure devised by the experimenter) is the experimental group, while the second group (which receives no treatment) is the control group. There also may be multiple experimental groups, each of which is subjected to a different procedure and then compared with the others. The variable that experimenters manipulate is the independent variable. The variable that they measure and expect to change as a result of manipulation of the independent variable is called the dependent variable.

19. In a formal experiment, participants must be assigned to treatment conditions randomly so that participant characteristics are evenly distributed across the different conditions.

What are the major issues that underlie the process of conducting research?

20. One of the key ethical principals followed by psychologists is that of informed consent. Participants must be informed, prior to participation, about the basic outline of the experiment and the risks and potential benefits of their participation. Researchers working with animals must also follow a rigid set of ethical guidelines for the protection of the animals.

21. Experiments are subject to a number of threats, or biases. Experimenter expectations can produce bias when an experimenter unintentionally transmits cues to participants about his or her expectations regarding their behaviour in a given experimental condition. Participant expectations can also bias an experiment. To help eliminate bias, researchers use placebos and double-blind procedures.

Key Terms and Concepts

psychology (p. 4)
structuralism (p. 14)
introspection (p. 14)
functionalism (p. 15)
gestalt psychology (p. 15)
biological perspective (p. 16)
psychodynamic perspective (p. 16)
cognitive perspective (p. 16)
behavioural perspective (p. 17)
humanistic perspective (p. 17)
free will (p. 17)

scientific method (p. 23)
theories (p. 23)
hypothesis (p. 24)
operationalization (p. 25)
archival research (p. 25)
naturalistic observation (p. 26)
survey research (p. 26)
case study (p. 27)
correlational research (p. 27)
experiment (p. 29)
experimental manipulation (p. 29)

variables (p. 29)
treatment (p. 29)
experimental group (p. 29)
control group (p. 29)
independent variable (p. 30)
dependent variable (p. 30)
random assignment to condition (p. 31)
replication (p. 34)
informed consent (p. 35)
experimental bias (p. 37)
placebo (p. 38)

Epilogue

The field of psychology, as we have seen, is broad and diverse. It encompasses many different branches and specialties practiced in a variety of settings, with new branches arising and coming to prominence all the time. Furthermore, we have seen that even within the various branches of the field, it is possible to adopt several different approaches, including the biological, psychodynamic, cognitive, behavioural, and humanistic perspectives.

We have also seen that, for all its diversity, psychology is united in its use of the scientific method and its reliance on creating productive theories and crafting testable hypotheses. We've considered the basic methods psychologists use to conduct research studies, and we've explored some of the major challenges that psychologists have to deal with when conducting research, including ethical considerations, potential bias, and the question of significance.

Before we turn to the biology of behaviour, return for a moment to the opening prologue of this chapter, which discusses the incidents at the two high schools. In light of what you've learned about the branches, perspectives, and methods of psychology, consider the following questions:

1. How might a psychodynamic perspective explain why the killers decided to go on a shooting spree or why anyone would copy the event? How would the explanation differ from that given by a psychologist using the behavioural perspective?

2. Assume that two developmental psychologists are considering the effects of witnessing the murder of a fellow student on future development. How would the questions and studies of interest to the psychologists differ if one employed the biological perspective and the other the behavioural perspective?

3. How might social psychologists explore the effects of watching news reports of the Columbine incident on viewers' aggression?

4. How might researchers conduct an experiment to test a drug that they believe reduces aggression? What would the independent variable and dependent variable be in such an experiment?

Answers to Review Questions:

1. d   2. (1) We can study some phenomena in animals more easily than we can in people, having greater control over environmental and genetic factors. (2) Large numbers of similar participants can be easily obtained. (3) We can look at generational effects much more easily in animals, because of their shorter life span, than we can with people.   3. true   4. double-blind   5. There are far too few participants. Without a larger sample, no valid conclusions can be drawn about ice cream preferences.

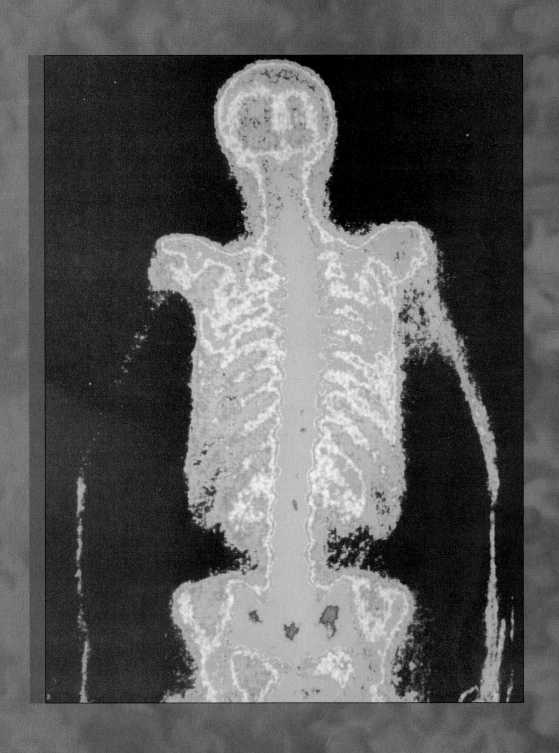

The Biology Underlying Behaviour

Getting stroke victims to the hospital quickly may mean they can benefit from the experimental drug t-PA, which can reverse the damage caused by strokes.

Prologue

Damage Control

Lee Phillips, 62, was shopping at a San Diego mall with her husband Eric when she felt an odd tugging on the right side of her face. Her mouth twisted into a lurid grimace. Suddenly she felt weak. Rushed to the emergency room of a local hospital, she was diagnosed with a stroke.

Peggy Code, 64, was outside a Calgary mall when she lost sensation in the left side of her body. Because she was a nurse, she recognized the symptoms of a stroke.

Every year 500,000 Americans and 50,000 Canadians suffer from strokes. In Canada it costs about $3 billion a year to provide medical care and rehabilitation for stroke victims. The cost in human suffering is immense. Thirty days in hospital and months of rehabilitation are the norm for stroke survivors.

Fortunately for both of these women, a CAT scan and other tests indicated that they were good candidates for an experimental drug called t-PA (tissue plasminogen activator). This drug, if given within 90 minutes of onset, dissolves the blood clot causing the stroke. In the case of these fortunate women the drug worked and both had complete recovery from their paralysis within hours.

Code was particularly fortunate that Canadian stroke expert, Dr. Alastair Buchan was conducting an 18-month trial of this drug at Foothills Hospital in Calgary at the time of her stroke. Because this drug is not effective for every stroke patient it is critical to have appropriate medical evaluation and tests quickly (Gorman, 1996; Bergman, 2000).

looking
AHEAD

The success of t-PA, the drug that surely saved Phillips and Code from a life of severe disability or even death, is little short of miraculous. But the greater miracle is the brain itself. As we shall see in this chapter, the brain, an organ roughly half the size of a loaf of bread, controls our behaviour through every waking and sleeping moment. The brain and the nerves extending throughout the body constitute the human nervous system. Our movements, thoughts, hopes, aspirations, dreams—the very awareness that we are human—are all intimately related to this system.

Because human beings at their most basic level are biological entities, psychologists and researchers from other fields as diverse as computer science, zoology, physiology, and medicine have paid special attention to the biology of the nervous system and its relation to behaviour. These experts are collectively called neuroscientists (Sarter, Berntson, & Cacioppo, 1996; Joseph, 1996; Kolb, 1999). Much knowledge can be gained when researchers in these diverse fields work together. The Program in Neuroscience at the University of Toronto, as an example, includes researchers from 15 departments and faculties, <www.utoronto.ca/neurosci>.

Psychologists who specialize in the relationship between biology and behaviour are known as **biopsychologists**. They seek to answer questions such as these: What are the bases for voluntary and involuntary functioning of the body? How are messages communicated to and from the brain to other parts of the body? What is the physical structure of the brain, and how does this structure affect behaviour? Can the causes of psychological disorders be traced to biological factors, and how can such disorders be treated?

biopsychologists: Psychologists who specialize in considering the ways in which biological structures and functions of the body affect behaviour

This chapter addresses such questions, by focusing on the biological structures that are of interest to biopsychologists. Initially, we discuss nerve cells, called neurons, which allow messages to travel through the brain and body. We learn that through their growing knowledge of neurons and the nervous system, psychologists are increasing their understanding of human behaviour and are uncovering important clues in their efforts to cure certain kinds of diseases. Then we turn to the structure and main divisions of the nervous system, explaining how they work to control voluntary and involuntary behaviours. In the process we also examine how the various parts of the nervous system operate together in emergency situations to produce lifesaving responses to danger.

Next, we consider the brain itself, examining its major structures and the ways in which these affect behaviour. We see how the brain controls movement, our senses, and our thought processes. We also consider the fascinating notion that the two halves of the brain may have different specialties and strengths. Finally, we examine the chemical messenger system of the body, the endocrine system.

Our understanding of human behaviour cannot be complete without knowledge of the fundamentals of the brain and the rest of the nervous system. As we'll see in future chapters, biological factors have an important impact on our sensory experience, states of consciousness, motivation and emotion, sexuality, development throughout the life span, and physical and psychological health. In short, our behaviour—our moods, motivations, goals, and desires—has a good deal to do with our biological makeup.

Neuroscience

NEURONS: THE ELEMENTS OF BEHAVIOUR

If you have ever watched the precision with which a well-trained athlete or dancer executes a performance, you may have marvelled at the complexity—and wondrous abilities—of the human body. But even the most everyday tasks, such as picking up a pencil, writing, and speaking, require a sophisticated sequence of activities that is itself truly impressive. For instance, the difference between saying the words "dime" and "time" rests primarily on whether the vocal cords are relaxed or tense during a period lasting no more than one one-hundredth of a second. Yet it is a distinction that almost everyone can make with ease.

The nervous system provides the pathways that permit us to carry out such precise activities. To understand how it is able to exert such exacting control over our bodies, we must begin by examining neurons, the most basic parts of the nervous system, and considering the way in which nerve impulses are transmitted throughout the brain and body.

The Structure of the Neuron

The ability to play the piano, drive a car, or hit a tennis ball depends, at one level, merely on muscle coordination. But if we consider *how* the muscles involved in such activities are activated, we see that there are more fundamental processes involved. It is necessary for the body to provide messages to the muscles and to coordinate those messages to enable the muscles to produce the complex movements that characterize successful physical activity.

Such messages are passed through specialized cells called **neurons,** the basic elements of the nervous system. Their quantity is staggering; some estimates suggest that there are as many as one *trillion* neurons involved in the control of behaviour (Ferster & Spruston, 1995). Although there are several types of neurons, each has a

▶ **Why do psychologists study the brain and nervous system?**

▶ **What are the basic elements of the nervous system?**

▶ **How does the nervous system communicate electrical and chemical messages from one part to another?**

neurons: Specialized cells that are the basic elements of the nervous system

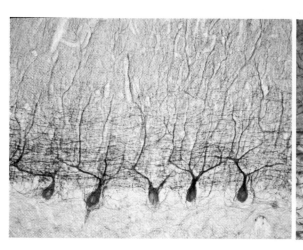
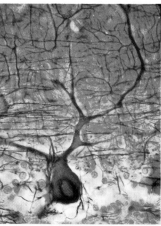

These two photographs, made with an electron microscope, show (left) a group of interconnected neurons in the cerebral cortex and (right) a close-up of a single neuron.

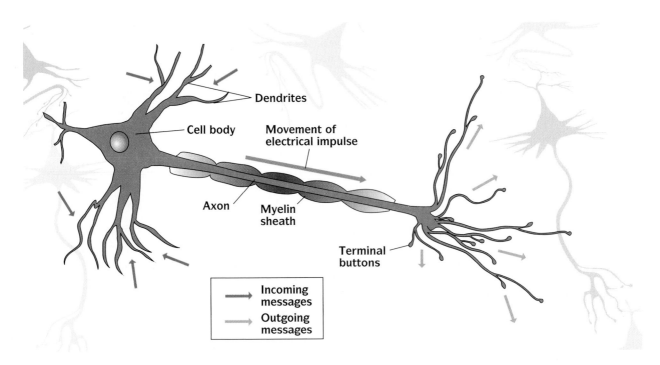

Dendrites

Cell body

Movement of
electrical impulse

Axon

Myelin
sheath

Terminal
buttons

Incoming
messages

Outgoing
messages

FIGURE 2-1 *The primary components of the specialized cell called the neuron, the basic element of the nervous system.*

similar basic structure, as illustrated in Figure 2-1 (Levitan & Kaczmarek, 1991). Like all cells in the body, neurons have a cell body, containing a nucleus. The nucleus incorporates the inherited material that establishes how the cell will function.

In contrast to most other cells, however, neurons have a distinctive feature: the ability to communicate with other cells and transmit information, sometimes across relatively long distances. As you can see in Figure 2-1, neurons have a cluster of fibres called **dendrites** at one end. These fibres, which look like the twisted branches of a tree, receive messages from other neurons. At the opposite end, neurons have a long, slim, tube-like extension called an **axon,** the part of the neuron that carries messages destined for other cells. The axon is considerably longer than the rest of the neuron. Although most axons are several millimetres in length, some may be as long as a metre. Axons end with small bulges called **terminal buttons** from which messages are launched to other cells.

The messages that travel through the neuron are purely electrical in nature. Although there are exceptions, these electrical messages generally move across neurons as if they were travelling on a one-way street. They follow a route that begins with the dendrites, continues into the cell body, and leads ultimately down the tube-like extension, the axon. *D*endrites, then, *d*etect messages from other neurons; *a*xons carry signals *a*way from the cell body.

To prevent messages from short-circuiting one another, it is necessary for the axons to be insulated in some fashion (analogous to the way in which electrical wires must be insulated). In most axons, this is done with a protective coating known as the **myelin sheath,** made up of a series of specialized cells of fat and protein that wrap themselves around the axon.

The myelin sheath also serves to increase the velocity with which the electrical impulses travel through the axons. Those axons that carry the most important and urgently required information have the greatest concentrations of myelin. If your hand touches a hot stove, for example, the information regarding the pain is passed through axons in the hand and arm that contain a relatively large quantity of myelin, speeding the message of pain to the brain. In certain diseases, such as multiple sclerosis, the myelin sheath surrounding the axon deteriorates, exposing parts of the axon that are normally covered. The result is a kind of short circuit that causes a disturbance in mes-

dendrites: A cluster of fibres at one end of a neuron that receive messages from other neurons
axon: The part of the neuron that carries messages destined for other cells

terminal buttons: Small bulges at the end of axons from which messages are launched to other cells

myelin sheath: A series of specialized cells of fat and protein that wrap themselves around the axon providing a protective coating

sages between the brain and muscles and results in symptoms such as the inability to walk, vision difficulties, and general muscle impairment.

Although the electrical impulse moves across the neuron in a dendrite-to-cell body-to-axon sequence, certain substances travel through the neuron in the opposite direction. For instance, axons allow chemical substances needed for nourishment of the cell nucleus to move toward the cell body in a reverse flow. Certain diseases, such as amyotrophic lateral sclerosis (ALS)—also known as Lou Gehrig's disease for its most famous victim—may be caused by the inability of the neuron to transport vital materials in this reverse direction. When this occurs, the neuron eventually dies from starvation. Similarly, rabies is caused by the transmission of the rabies virus by reverse flow along the axon from the terminal buttons.

Firing the Neuron

Like a gun, neurons either fire or don't fire; there is no in-between stage. Pulling harder on a gun trigger is not going to make the bullet travel faster or more surely. Similarly, neurons typically follow an **all-or-none law:** They are either on or off; once triggered beyond a certain point, they will fire. When they are off—that is, in a **resting state**—there is a negative electrical charge of about –70 millivolts within the neuron (a millivolt is one-thousandth of a volt). This charge is caused by the presence of more negatively charged ions (a type of molecule) within the neuron than outside it. You might think of the neuron as one of the poles of a miniature car battery, with the inside of the neuron representing the negative pole and the outside of the neuron the positive pole (Koester, 1991).

However, when a message arrives, the cell walls in the neuron allow positively charged ions to rush in, at rates as high as 100 million ions per second. The sudden arrival of these positive ions causes the charge within that part of the cell to change momentarily from negative to positive. When the charge reaches a critical level, the "trigger" is pulled, and an electrical nerve impulse, known as an **action potential,** travels down the axon of the neuron (Siegelbaum & Koester, 1991; E. Neher, 1992; McCarley, 1994; Siegel et al., 1994; see Figure 2-2).

The action potential moves from one end of the axon to the other like a flame moving across a fuse toward an explosive. As the impulse travels along the axon, the movement of ions causes a sequential change in charge from negative to positive (see Figure 2-3). After the passage of the impulse, positive ions are pumped out of the axon, and the neuron charge returns to negative.

Just after an action potential has passed, the neuron cannot be fired again immediately, no matter how much stimulation it receives. It is as if the gun has to be painstakingly reloaded after each shot. There then follows a period in which though it is possible to fire the neuron, a stronger stimulus is needed than would be needed if sufficient time had passed for the neuron to reach its normal resting state. Eventually, though, the neuron is ready to be fired once again.

These complex events may occur at dizzying speeds, although there is great variation among different neurons. The particular speed at which an action potential travels along an axon is determined by the axon's size and the thickness of the myelin sheath. Axons with small diametres carry impulses at about 3 km per hour; longer and thicker ones can average speeds of more than 360 km per hour.

In addition to varying according to how quickly an impulse moves across the axon, neurons differ in their potential rate of firing. Some neurons have the potential to fire as many as 1,000 times per second; others have a maximum potential rate that is much lower. The intensity of a stimulus that provokes a neuron determines how much of this potential rate is reached. A strong stimulus, such as a bright light or a loud sound, leads to a higher rate of firing than a less intense stimulus does. Thus, while there are no differences in the strength or speed at which an impulse moves across a particular axon—as the all-or-none law suggests—there is variation in the frequency of impulses, providing a mechanism by which we can distinguish the tickle of a feather from the weight of someone standing on our toe.

In 1995 Sue Rodriguez of Vancouver died of ALS. She had fought a brave battle both against her disease and in court where ill and near death she had appealed for the right for physician assisted suicide. Her request was denied.

all-or-none law: The rule that neurons are either on or off
resting state: The state in which there is a negative electrical charge of about –70 millivolts within the neuron
action potential: An electric nerve impulse that travels through a neuron when it is set off by a "trigger," changing the cell's charge from negative to positive

Studying the Neuron

FIGURE 2-2 *Movement of an action potential across an axon. Just prior to time 1, positively charged ions enter the cell walls, changing the charge within that part of the cell from negative to positive. The action potential is thus triggered, travelling down the axon, as illustrated in the changes occurring from Time 1 to Time 3 (from top to bottom in this drawing). Following the passage of the action potential, positive ions are pumped out of the axon, restoring its charge to negative. The change in voltage illustrated at the top of the axon can be seen in greater detail in Figure 2-3.*

FIGURE 2-3 *Changes in the electrical charge of a neuron during the passage of an action potential. In its normal resting state, a neuron has a negative charge of around –70 millivolts. When an action potential is triggered, however, the cell charge becomes positive, increasing to about +40 millivolts. Following the passage of the action potential, the charge becomes even more negative than it is in its typical state. It is not until the charge returns to its resting state that the neuron will be fully ready to be—triggered once again.*

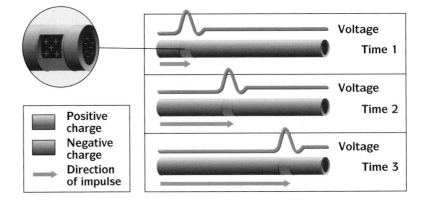

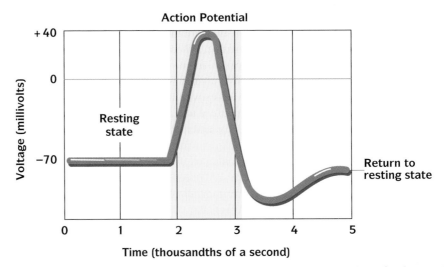

The structure, operation, and functions of the neuron illustrate how fundamental biological aspects of the body underlie several primary psychological processes. Our understanding of the way we sense, perceive, and learn about the world would be greatly restricted without the information about the neuron that biopsychologists and other researchers have acquired.

Where Neuron Meets Neuron: Bridging the Gap

Did you ever put together a child's radio kit? If you have, you may remember that the manufacturer supplied you with wires that had to be painstakingly connected to one another or to some other component of the radio; every piece had to be physically connected to something else.

The brain and body are considerably more sophisticated than a radio—or any other manufactured apparatus, for that matter. Evolution has produced a neural transmission system that at some points has no need for a structural connection between its components. Instead, a chemical connection bridges the gap, known as a **synapse,** between two neurons (see Figure 2-4). When a nerve impulse comes to the end of the axon and reaches a terminal button, the terminal button releases a chemical courier called a neurotransmitter.

Neurotransmitters are chemicals that carry messages across the synapse to the dendrite (and sometimes the cell body) of a receiver neuron. Like a boat that ferries passengers across a river, these chemical messengers move toward the shorelines of other neurons. The chemical mode of message transmission that occurs between neurons is strikingly different from the means by which communication occurs inside neurons. It is important to remember, then, that although messages travel in electrical form *within* a neuron, they move *between* neurons through a chemical transmission system.

synapse: The gap between two neurons, bridged by chemical connections

neurotransmitters: Chemicals that carry messages across the synapse to the dendrite (and sometimes the cell body) of a receiver neuron

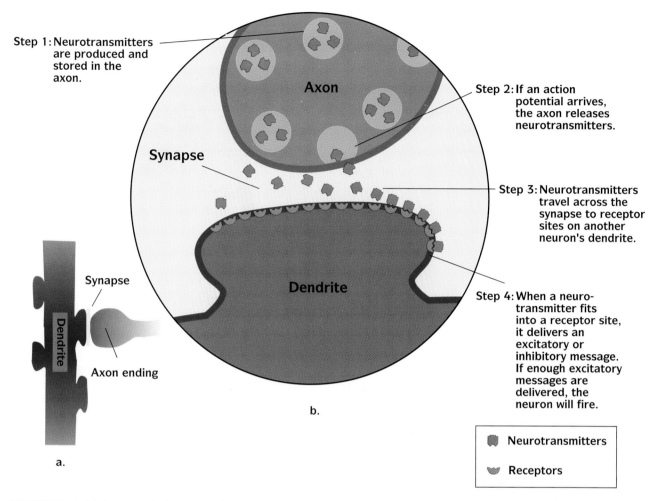

Step 1: Neurotransmitters are produced and stored in the axon.

Axon

Synapse

Step 2: If an action potential arrives, the axon releases neurotransmitters.

Step 3: Neurotransmitters travel across the synapse to receptor sites on another neuron's dendrite.

Dendrite

Step 4: When a neuro-transmitter fits into a receptor site, it delivers an excitatory or inhibitory message. If enough excitatory messages are delivered, the neuron will fire.

Synapse

Dendrite

Axon ending

b.

a.

Neurotransmitters

Receptors

FIGURE 2-4 *(a) A synapse is the junction between an axon and a dendrite. The gap between the axon and the dendrite is bridged by chemicals called neurotransmitters. (b) Just as the pieces of a jigsaw puzzle can fit in only one specific location in a puzzle, each kind of neurotransmitter has a distinctive configuration that allows it to fit into a specific type of receptor site.*

There are several types of neurotransmitters, and not all receiver neurons are capable of making use of the chemical message carried by a particular neurotransmitter. In the same way that a jigsaw puzzle piece can fit in only one specific location in a puzzle, so each kind of neurotransmitter has a distinctive configuration that allows it to fit into a specific type of receptor site on the receiving neuron (see Figure 2-4*b*). It is only when a neurotransmitter fits precisely into a receptor site that successful chemical communication is possible.

If a neurotransmitter does fit into a site on the receiving neuron, the chemical message it delivers is basically one of two types: excitatory or inhibitory. **Excitatory messages** make it more likely that a receiving neuron will fire and an action potential will travel down its axon. **Inhibitory messages,** in contrast, do just the opposite; they provide chemical information that prevents or decreases the likelihood that the receiving neuron will fire.

Because the dendrites of a neuron receive many messages simultaneously, some of which are excitatory and some inhibitory, the neuron must integrate the messages in some fashion (Bariniga, 1995; Brezina, Orekhova, & Weiss, 1996; Abbot et al., 1997; Thomson, 1997). It does this by using a kind of chemical calculator. If the number of excitatory messages outweighs the number of inhibitory ones, the neuron will fire. On the other hand, if the number of inhibitory messages outweighs the excitatory ones, nothing will happen. The neuron will remain in its resting state (see Figure 2-5).

If neurotransmitters remained at the site of the synapse, receptor neurons would be awash in a continual chemical bath, producing constant stimulation of the receptor

excitatory message: A chemical secretion that makes it more likely that a receiving neuron will fire and an action potential will travel down its axon

inhibitory message: A chemical secretion that prevents a receiving neuron from firing

FIGURE 2-5 *Because the dendrites of a neuron receive both excitatory messages (which stimulate it to fire) and inhibitory messages (which tell the neuron not to fire), the neuron must integrate the messages through a summation process. Because in this case the number of excitatory messages is greater than the number of inhibitory messages, it is likely to fire.*

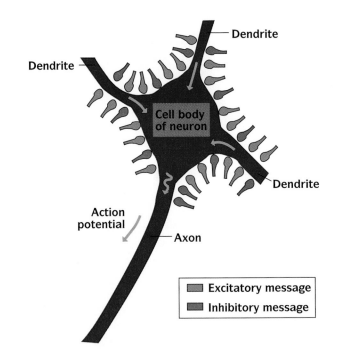

FIGURE 2-5 *Because the dendrites of a neuron receive both excitatory messages (which stimulate it to fire) and inhibitory messages (which tell the neuron not to fire), the neuron must integrate the messages through a summation process. Because in this case the number of excitatory messages is greater than the number of inhibitory messages, it is likely to fire.*

reuptake: The reabsorption of neurotransmitters by a terminal button

Neurotransmitters

neurons. If this were the case, effective communication across the synapse would no longer be possible. To solve this problem, neurotransmitters are either deactivated by enzymes or—more frequently—reabsorbed by the terminal button in an example of chemical recycling called **reuptake.** Like a vacuum cleaner sucking up dust, neurons reabsorb the neurotransmitters that are now clogging the synapse. All this activity occurs at lightning speed, with the process taking just several milliseconds.

Neurotransmitters: Multitalented Chemical Couriers

Neurotransmitters represent a particularly important link between the nervous system and behaviour. Not only are they important for maintaining vital brain and body functions, but having a deficiency or an excess of a neurotransmitter can produce severe behaviour disorders. Over 100 chemicals have been found to act as neurotransmitters, and biopsychologists believe that more may ultimately be identified (Purves et al., 1997).

Neurotransmitters vary significantly in terms of how strong a concentration is required to trigger a neuron to fire. Furthermore, the effects of a given neurotransmitter vary, depending on the portion of the nervous system in which it is produced. The same neurotransmitter, then, can cause a neuron to fire when it is secreted in one part of the brain and can inhibit the firing of neurons when it is produced in another part. (The major neurotransmitters are shown in Table 2-1.)

One of the most common neurotransmitters is *acetylcholine* (or *ACh*, its chemical symbol), which is found throughout the nervous system. ACh is involved in our every move, as—among other things—it transmits messages relating to our skeletal muscles. ACh is also related to the drug curare, used on the tips of poison darts thrown by South American Indians. Curare keeps ACh from reaching receptor cells, thereby paralyzing the skeletal muscles and ultimately producing death by suffocation because the victim cannot breathe.

Some scientists now suggest that Alzheimer's disease, the progressively degenerative disorder that ultimately produces loss of memory, confusion, and personality changes in its victims, is associated with a deficiency in the production of ACh. There is growing evidence that ACh is closely related to memory capabilities. For example, some research now shows that Alzheimer's patients have restricted production of ACh in portions of their brains. The first drug approved in Canada for treatment of this disease is *Aricept*, which acts to increase levels of ACh. (Quirion et al., 1995; Arneric et al., 1995; Selkoe, 1997; Alzheimer's, Manitoba, 1997).

Table 2-1	Some Major Neurotransmitters

Name	Location	Effect	Function
Acetylcholine (ACh)	Brain, spinal cord, peripheral nervous system, especially some organs of the parasympathetic nervous system	Excitatory in brain and autonomic nervous system; inhibitory elsewhere	Muscle movement; cognitive functioning
Glutamate	Brain, spinal cord	Excitatory	Memory
Gamma-amino butyric acid (GABA)	Brain, spinal cord	Main inhibitory neurotransmitter	Eating, aggression, sleeping
Dopamine (DA)	Brain	Inhibitory or excitatory	Muscle disorders, mental disorders, Parkinson's disease
Serotonin	Brain, spinal cord	Inhibitory	Sleeping, eating, mood, pain, depression
Adenosine triphosphate (ATP)	Throughout the nervous system	Excitatory	Memory
Endorphins	Brain, spinal cord	Primarily inhibitory, except in hippocampus	Pain suppression, pleasurable feelings, appetites, placebos

Another common excitatory neurotransmitter, *glutamate,* is related to the chemical basis of memory. As we'll discuss in Chapter 6, memories appear to be produced by specific biochemical changes at particular synapses, and glutamate, along with other neurotransmitters, plays an important role in this process (Kandel, Schwartz, & Jessell, 1995; Kandel & Abel, 1995; Tiunova et al., 1996; M. E. Gibbs et al., 1996).

Gamma-amino butyric acid (GABA), found in both the brain and the spinal cord, appears to be the nervous system's primary inhibitory neurotransmitter. It moderates a variety of behaviours, ranging from eating to aggression. The deadly poison strychnine produces convulsions by disrupting the transmission of GABA across synapses. Strychnine prevents GABA from carrying out its inhibitory role. It permits neurons to fire wildly, thereby producing convulsions. In contrast, some common substances, such as the tranquilizer Valium and alcohol, are effective because they permit GABA to operate more efficiently (F. Petty, 1996; Tabakoff & Hoffman, 1996).

Another major neurotransmitter is *dopamine (DA).* The discovery that certain drugs can have a marked effect on dopamine release has led to the development of effective treatments for a wide variety of physical and mental ailments. For instance, Parkinson's disease, marked by varying degrees of muscular rigidity and shaking, is caused by the destruction of certain neurons, which leads to a deficiency of dopamine in the brain. Techniques for increasing the production of dopamine in Parkinson's patients are proving effective (Hutton et al., 1996; Youdim & Riederer, 1997).

In some cases, *over*production of dopamine seems to produce negative consequences. For instance, researchers have hypothesized that schizophrenia and some other severe mental disturbances are affected or perhaps even caused by the presence of unusually high levels of dopamine. Drugs that block the reception of dopamine have been successful in reducing the abnormal behaviour displayed by some people diagnosed with schizophrenia—as we will examine further when we consider abnormal behaviour and its treatment in Chapter 13 (Siever, 1995; R. S. Kahn, Davidson, & Davis, 1996; McIvor et al., 1996).

Another neurotransmitter, *serotonin,* plays a variety of roles. It is associated with the regulation of sleep, eating, mood, and pain. In fact, a growing body of research points toward an even broader role for serotonin, suggesting its involvement in such diverse behaviours as coping with stress, alcoholism, depression, suicide, impulsivity, and aggression (Higley, Suomi, & Linnoila, 1996).

One of the newest neurotransmitters to be identified is one of the body's most common substances: *adenosine triphosphate,* or *ATP.* Just as gasoline powers an automobile engine, ATP is the fuel used by the body to produce energy within cells, and it

Diagnosed with Parkinson's disease in 1991, Michael J. Fox has recently retired from acting. He has founded a Parkinson's research foundation and plans to work toward finding a cure for this progressive and as yet incurable central nervous system disease. Some symptoms of Parkinson's are rigidity, tremors and gait disorder which are controlled with medication.

now appears that ATP plays an additional role as a neurotransmitter. Although research on ATP is in its infancy, biopsychologists speculate that it may play a major excitatory role. Furthermore, because it works very quickly, ATP may prove to have important therapeutic qualities and may be linked to several basic psychological processes. For example, some investigators hypothesize that ATP is essential in the formation of synapses vital to memory (Ragozzino et al., 1995).

Endorphins, another class of neurotransmitters, are a family of chemicals produced by the brain that are similar in structure to painkilling opiates. The production of endorphins seems to reflect the brain's effort to deal with pain. For instance, people who are afflicted with diseases that produce long-term, severe pain often develop large concentrations of endorphins in their brains—suggesting an effort by the brain to control the pain.

Endorphins may do more than provide mere pain reduction. They may also produce the euphoric feelings that joggers sometimes experience after long runs. It appears that the amount of exercise and perhaps even the pain involved in a long run stimulate the production of endorphins—ultimately resulting in what has been called a "runner's high" (Kremer & Scully, 1994; Dishman, 1997).

Endorphin release may also explain other phenomena that have long puzzled psychologists, such as the reasons that acupuncture and placebos (pills or other substances that contain no actual drugs but that patients *believe* will make them better) may be effective in reducing pain. Some biopsychologists speculate that both acupuncture and placebos induce the release of endorphins. In turn, the endorphins produce a positive bodily state (Mikamo et al., 1994; Murray, 1995; Brown, 1998).

Although it had been thought that all neurotransmitters are produced in the form of chemical liquids, surprising new evidence suggests that at least some chemical communication between neurons also may occur via nitric oxide, a gas. If this speculation is correct, it may mean that chemical gases are a supplementary form of interneuron communication—about whose existence we are just learning (Bach y Rita, 1993; Schuman & Madison, 1994; Purves et al., 1997).

Recap, Review, and Rethink

Recap

- Neurons are the basic elements of the nervous system. They allow the transmission of messages that coordinate the complex activities of the human body.

- All neurons have a similar basic structure. They receive messages through the dendrites and transmit them through the axon to other neurons.

- Neurons fire according to an all-or-none law; they are either firing or resting.

- The specific site of transmission of messages from one neuron to another is called the synapse. Messages moving *across* synapses are chemical in nature, although *within* neurons they travel in electrical form.

- Neurotransmitters are the specific chemicals that make the chemical connection at the synapse. These act either to excite other neurons into firing or to inhibit neurons from firing.

Review

1. The _____ is the fundamental element of the nervous system.

2. Messages are carried through the neuron in what direction?

    a. dendrites —> axon
    b. axon —> dendrites
    c. myelin —> nucleus
    d. terminal button —> brain

3. Just as electrical wires have an outer coating, so axons are insulated by a coating called the _____ _____.

4. The electric nerve impulse that travels down a neuron is called a(n) _____.

5. The _____ law states that a neuron is either firing or resting.

6. The chemical connection between two neurons occurs at a gap known as a(n)

    a. axon.
    b. terminal button.
    c. synapse.
    d. amino acid.

7. _____ are chemical messengers that transmit between neurons.

8. Match the neurotransmitter with its function.

    a. ACh
    b. GABA
    c. Endorphins

    1. Reduce the experience of pain
    2. Moderates eating and aggression
    3. Produces contractions of skeletal muscles

Answers to Review Questions are on page 56.

Rethink

1. What might be the advantage of neurons following the all-or-none law?

2. Can you use your knowledge of psychological research methods to suggest how researchers study the effects of neurotransmitters on human behaviour?

3. In what ways might endorphins help to produce the placebo effect? Is there a difference between *believing* that one's pain is reduced and actually *experiencing* reduced pain? Why or why not?

THE NERVOUS SYSTEM

Given the complexity of individual neurons and the neurotransmission process, it should come as no surprise that the connections and structures formed by the neurons are complicated in their own right. Because just one neuron may be connected to 80,000 other neurons, the total number of possible connections is astonishing. For instance, some estimates of the number of neural connections within the brain fall in the neighborhood of 1 quadrillion—a 1 followed by 15 zeros—while some experts put the number even higher (McGaugh, Weinberger, & Lynch, 1990; Estes, 1991; Eichenbaum, 1993).

Whatever the actual number of neural connections, the human nervous system has both a logic and an elegance. We turn now to its basic structures and its evolutionary foundations.

▶ **In what way are the structures of the nervous system tied together?**

Central and Peripheral Nervous Systems

As you can see from the schematic representation in Figure 2-6, the nervous system is divided into two main parts: the central nervous system and the peripheral

FIGURE 2-6 *A schematic diagram of the relationship of the parts of the nervous system.*

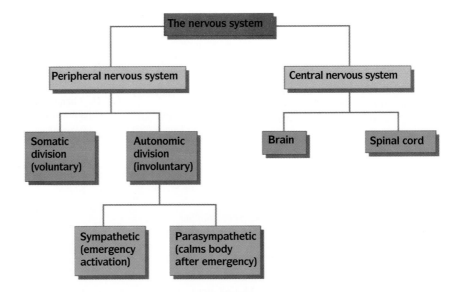

FIGURE 2-6 *A schematic diagram of the relationship of the parts of the nervous system.*

central nervous system (CNS): The system that includes the brain and spinal cord

spinal cord: A bundle of nerves that leaves the brain and runs down the length of the back and is the main means for transmitting messages between the brain and the body

reflexes: Automatic, involuntary response to an incoming stimulus

sensory (afferent) neurons: Neurons that transmit information from the perimeter of the body to the central nervous system

motor (efferent) neurons: Neurons that communicate information from the nervous system to muscles and glands of the body

interneurons: Neurons that connect sensory and motor neurons, carrying messages between the two

peripheral nervous system: The system, made up of long axons and dendrites, that branches out from the spinal cord and brain and reaches the extremities of the body

nervous system. The **central nervous system (CNS)** is composed of the brain and spinal cord. The **spinal cord,** about the thickness of a pencil, contains a bundle of nerves that leaves the brain and runs down the length of the back (see Figure 2-7). It is the main means for transmitting messages between the brain and the body.

However, the spinal cord is not just a communications conduit. It also controls some simple kinds of behaviours on its own, without any involvement of the brain. One example is the way that your knee jerks forward when it is tapped with a rubber hammer. Such behaviours, called **reflexes,** represent an automatic, involuntary response to an incoming stimulus. Similarly, when you touch a hot stove and immediately withdraw your hand, a reflex is at work. Although the brain eventually analyzes and reacts to the situation ("ouch—hot stove—pull away!"), the initial withdrawal is directed only by neurons in the spinal cord.

Three sorts of neurons are involved in reflexes. **Sensory (afferent) neurons** transmit information from the perimeter of the body to the central nervous system. **Motor (efferent) neurons** communicate information from the nervous system to muscles and glands of the body. **Interneurons** connect sensory and motor neurons, carrying messages between the two.

The importance of the spinal cord and reflexes is illustrated by the outcome of accidents in which the cord is injured or severed. Actor Christopher Reeve, who was injured in a horseback-riding accident, suffers from *quadriplegia,* a condition in which voluntary muscle movement below the neck is lost. In a less severe but still debilitating condition, *paraplegia,* people are unable to voluntarily move any muscles in the lower half of their body.

Even though the spinal cord is injured in quadriplegia and paraplegia, undamaged areas of the cord are still able to produce some simple reflex actions, if stimulated appropriately. For instance, if a paraplegic's knee is tapped lightly, the lower leg will jerk forward slightly. Similarly, in some kinds of spinal cord injuries, people will move their legs in an involuntary response to a pinprick, even though they do not experience the sensation of pain.

As suggested by its name, the **peripheral nervous system** branches out from the spinal cord and brain and reaches the extremities of the body. Made up of long axons and dendrites, the peripheral nervous system encompasses all parts of the nervous system other than the brain and spinal cord. There are two major divisions, the

---

Answers to Review Questions:

1. neuron   2. a   3. myelin sheath   4. action potential   5. all-or-none   6. c   7. Neurotransmitters   8. a-3; b-2; c-1

somatic division and the autonomic division, both of which connect the central nervous system with the sense organs, muscles, glands, and other organs. The **somatic division** specializes in the control of voluntary movements—such as the motion of the eyes to read this sentence or of the hand to turn this page—and the communication of information to and from the sense organs. On the other hand, the **autonomic division** is concerned with the parts of the body that keep us alive—the heart, blood vessels, glands, lungs, and other organs that function involuntarily without our awareness. As you read now, the autonomic division of the peripheral nervous system is pumping blood through your body, pushing your lungs in and out, overseeing the digestion of the meal you had a few hours ago, and so on—all without a thought or care on your part.

Activating the Divisions of the Autonomic Nervous System

The autonomic division plays a particularly crucial role during emergency situations. Suppose as you are reading you suddenly sense that a stranger is watching you through the window. As you look up, you see the glint of something that just might be a knife. As confusion races through your mind and fear overcomes your attempts to think rationally, what happens to your body? If you are like most people, you react immediately on a physiological level. Your heart rate increases, you begin to sweat, and you develop goose bumps all over your body.

The physiological changes that occur result from the activation of one of the two parts that make up the autonomic division: the **sympathetic division.** The sympathetic division acts to prepare the body in stressful emergency situations, engaging all the organism's resources to respond to a threat. This response often takes the form of "fight or flight." In contrast, the **parasympathetic division** acts to calm the body after the emergency situation is resolved. When you find, for instance, that the stranger at the window is actually your roommate who has lost his keys and is climbing in the window to avoid waking you, your parasympathetic division begins to predominate, lowering your heart rate, stopping your sweating, and returning your body to the state it was in prior to your fright. The parasympathetic division also provides a means for the body to maintain storage of energy sources such as nutrients and oxygen. The sympathetic and parasympathetic divisions work together to regulate many functions of the body (see Figure 2-8). For instance, sexual arousal is controlled by the parasympathetic division, while sexual orgasm is a function of the sympathetic division.

The Evolutionary Foundations of the Nervous System

The complexities of the nervous system can be understood only by taking the course of evolution into consideration. The forerunner of the human nervous system is found in the earliest, simple organisms to have a spinal cord. Basically, these organisms were simple input-output devices: When the upper side of their spinal cord was stimulated by, for instance, being touched, they reacted with a simple response, such as jerking away. Such responses were completely a consequence of the organism's genetic make-up.

Over millions of years, the front end of the spinal cord became more specialized, and organisms became capable of distinguishing between different kinds of stimuli and responding differently to them. Ultimately, the front end of the spinal cord evolved into what we would consider a primitive brain. At first, it had just three parts, devoted to close stimuli (such as smell), more distant stimuli (such as sights and sounds), and the ability to maintain balance and bodily coordination. In fact, many animals, such as fish, still have a nervous system that is structured in roughly similar fashion today. In contrast, the human brain evolved from this three-part configuration into an organ that is considerably more complex and differentiated (Merlin, 1993).

Furthermore, the nervous system is *hierarchically organized,* meaning that relatively newer (from an evolutionary point of view) and more sophisticated regions of the brain regulate the older, and more primitive, parts of the nervous system. As we move up along the spinal cord and continue upward into the brain, then, the functions controlled by various regions become progressively more advanced.

somatic division: The part of the nervous system that specializes in the control of voluntary movements and the communication of information to and from the sense organs

autonomic division: The part of the nervous system that controls involuntary movement (the actions of the heart, glands, lungs, and other organs)

sympathetic division: The part of the autonomic division of the nervous system that acts to prepare the body in stressful emergency situations, engaging all of the organism's resources to respond to a threat

parasympathetic division: The part of the autonomic division of the nervous system that acts to calm the body after the emergency situation is resolved

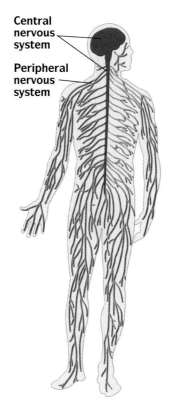

Central nervous system

Peripheral nervous system

FIGURE 2-7 *The central nervous system—consisting of the brain and spinal cord—and the peripheral nervous system.*

FIGURE 2-8 *The major functions of the autonomic nervous system. The sympathetic division acts to prepare certain organs of the body for stressful emergency situations, and the parasympathetic division acts to calm the body after the emergency situation is resolved.*

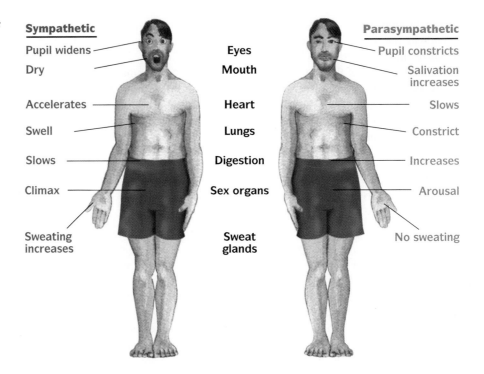

evolutionary psychology: The branch of psychology that seeks to identify behaviour patterns that are a result of our genetic inheritance from our ancestors

Why should we care about the evolutionary background of the human nervous system? The answer comes from researchers working in the area of **evolutionary psychology,** the branch of psychology that seeks to identify how behaviour is influenced and produced by our genetic inheritance from our ancestors. They argue that the course of evolution is reflected in the structure and functioning of the nervous system, and that evolutionary factors consequently have a significant influence on our everyday behaviour. Their work, and that of other scientists, has led to the development of a new field: behavioural genetics.

Behavioural Genetics

behavioural genetics: The study of the effects of heredity on behaviour

Genetics

Our evolutionary heritage manifests itself not only through the structure and functioning of the nervous system, but through our behaviour as well. In the view of a blossoming—as well as controversial—new area of study, people's personality and behavioural habits are affected by evolutionary factors and their genetic heritage. **Behavioural genetics** studies the effects of heredity on behaviour. Behavioural genetics researchers are finding increasing evidence that cognitive abilities, personality traits, sexual orientation, and psychological disorders are affected to some extent by genetic factors (Gilger, 1996; Pillard, 1996; Rieder, Kaufmann, & Knowles, 1996; Funder, 1997).

Behavioural genetics gets to the heart of the nature-nurture issue that we first discussed in Chapter 1. Although no one would argue that our behaviour is *solely* determined by inherited factors, evidence collected by behavioural geneticists does suggest that our genetic inheritance makes us predisposed to respond in particular ways to our environment, and even to seek out particular kinds of environments. For instance, research indicates that genetic factors may be related to such diverse behaviour as level of family conflict, schizophrenia, learning disabilities, and general sociability (Gilger, 1996; Feldman, 1996; Schmitz et al., 1996; Elkins, McGue, & Iacono, 1997).

Furthermore, increasing evidence supports the notion that important human characteristics are related to the presence (or absence) of particular *genes,* the genetic material that controls the transmission of traits. For example, it seems that novelty-seeking behaviour is associated with the presence of a particular gene (Cloninger, Adolfsson & Svrakic, 1996; Benjamin et al., 1996).

Work on genes is just beginning: It is estimated that there are between 50,000 and 100,000 individual genes, and less than 20,000 have been identified and located

(Benjamin et al., 1996; Backlar, 1996; Ebstein et al., 1996; Polymeropoulos et al., 1996; Schuler et al., 1996). Despite its relative infancy, however, the field of behavioural genetics has already made substantial contributions. By understanding the relationship between our genetic heritage and the structures of the nervous system, we are gaining new knowledge about how various behavioural difficulties, such as the psychological disorders we'll discuss in Chapter 12, develop. Perhaps more importantly, behavioural genetics holds the promise of developing new treatment techniques, permitting us to identify how genetic deficiencies that lead to physical and psychological difficulties may be remedied (Bouchard, 1994; Plomin, 1994, 1995; Risch & Merikangas, 1996; Haseltine, 1997). We'll discuss the increasing influence of behavioural genetics further in future chapters.

We turn now to a consideration of the particular structures of the brain and the primary functions to which they are related. However, a caution is in order. Although we'll be discussing the way in which specific brain areas are tied to specific behaviours, this approach is an oversimplification. No simple one-to-one correspondence between a distinct part of the brain and a particular behaviour exists. Instead, behaviour is produced by complex interconnections between sets of neurons located in a variety of parts of the brain. In fact, no portion of the brain is isolated from any other area, and a particular behaviour represents the outcome of the firing of neurons found in multiple areas of the nervous system. In short, our behaviour, emotions, thoughts, hopes, and dreams are produced by a variety of neurons throughout the nervous system, working in concert (Schneider & Tarshis, 1995; Grillner, 1996; Joseph, 1996).

Recap, Review, and Rethink

Recap

- The central nervous system (CNS) is made up of the brain and spinal cord, a thick bundle of nerves running from the brain down the length of the back.

- The peripheral nervous system includes all parts of the nervous system other than the brain and spinal cord. The peripheral nervous system has two major parts: the somatic division (for voluntary movements) and the autonomic division (for involuntary movements).

- The autonomic division, which itself has two parts (sympathetic and parasympathetic divisions), plays a major role during emergency situations.

- Evolutionary psychology relates the evolution of the nervous system to human evolution in general, and seeks to understand how our behaviour patterns result from our genetic inheritance.

- Behavioural genetics, an outgrowth of evolutionary psychology, studies the relationship between evolutionary and genetic factors and human personality and behaviours.

3. The peripheral nervous system includes nerves located in the arms, legs, and spinal cord. True or false?

4. Maria saw a young boy run into the street and get hit by a car. When she got to the fallen child, she was in a state of panic. She was sweating and her heart was racing. Her biological state resulted from the activation of what division of the autonomic nervous system?
   a. parasympathetic
   b. somatic
   c. peripheral
   d. sympathetic

5. The increasing complexity and hierarchy of the nervous system over millions of years is the subject of study for researchers working in the field of _____ _____.

6. The emerging field of _____ _____ studies ways in which our genetic inheritance predisposes us to behave in certain ways.

Answers to Review Questions are on page 60.

Review

1. If you should put your hand on a red-hot piece of metal, the immediate response of pulling it away would be an example of a _____ .

2. The portion of your nervous system that controls functions such as breathing and digestion is known as the _____ nervous system.

Rethink

1. How might communication within the nervous system result in human consciousness?

2. In what ways is the "fight or flight" response helpful to organisms in emergency situations?

3. How might a seemingly personal and individual habit, such as the tendency to seek novelty, be genetically determined? How would researchers study this question?

THE BRAIN

▶ How do researchers identify the major parts and functioning of the brain?

▶ What are the major parts of the brain, and what are the behaviours for which each part is responsible?

Functions of the Brain

It is not much to look at. Soft, spongy, mottled, and pinkish-grey in colour, it can hardly be said to possess much in the way of physical beauty. Despite its physical appearance, however, it ranks as the greatest natural marvel that we know and possesses a beauty and sophistication all its own.

The object to which this description applies: the brain. The brain is responsible for our loftiest thoughts—and our most primitive urges. It is the overseer of the intricate workings of the human body. If one were to attempt to design a computer to mimic the range of capabilities of the brain, the task would be nearly impossible; in fact, it has proved difficult even to come close. The sheer quantity of nerve cells in the brain is enough to daunt even the most ambitious computer engineer. Many billions of nerve cells make up a structure weighing just 1.3 kilograms in the average adult. However, it is not the number of cells that is the most astounding thing about the brain, but its ability to allow human intellect to flourish as it guides our behaviour and thoughts.

Studying the Brain's Structure and Functions: Spying on the Brain

The brain has posed a continual challenge to those wishing to study it. For most of history, its examination was possible only after an individual was dead. Only then could the skull be opened and the brain cut into without the risk of causing serious injury. While informative, such a limited procedure could hardly tell us much about the functioning of the healthy brain.

Today, however, important advances have been made in the study of the brain involving the use of brain scanning techniques, which allow for the investigation of the functioning brain. (Rauch & Renshaw, 1995; Bigler, 1996; Toga & Mazziotta, 1996; Barinaga, 1997). One of the largest scientific communities in North America dedicated to imaging research is The McConnell Brain Imaging Centre of the Montreal Neurological Institute, McGill University which brings together researchers from many disciplines, as a visit to their web site shows, <www.bic.mni.mcgill.ca>. In use there, are all of the major scanning techniques described below, and illustrated in Figure 2-9.

- The *electroencephalogram (EEG)* records the electrical signals being transmitted inside the brain through electrodes placed on the outside of the skull. Although traditionally the EEG could produce only a graph of electrical wave patterns, new techniques are now able to transform the brain's electrical activity into a pictorial representation of the brain that allows the diagnosis of such problems as epilepsy and learning disabilities.

- The *computerized axial tomography (CAT) scan* uses a computer to construct an image of the structures of the brain by combining thousands of separate X rays taken at slightly different angles. It is very useful for showing abnormalities in the structure of the brain, such as swelling and enlargement of certain parts, but does not provide information about brain activity.

- The *functional magnetic resonance imaging (fMRI) scan* produces a powerful magnetic field to provide a detailed, computer-generated image of brain structures and activity. It is also capable of producing vivid images of individual bundles of nerves in other parts of the body, opening the way for improved diagnosis of such ailments as chronic back pain and brain damage (Thatcher et al., 1994; Gonzalez, 1996). Research at the University of Western Ontario uses fMRI to study vision perception (Culham, et al., 1999).

Answers to Review Questions:

1. reflex   2. autonomic   3. False; the spinal cord belongs to the CNS.   4. d   5. evolutionary psychology   6. behavioural genetics

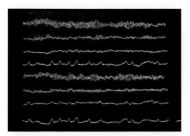

a. EEG

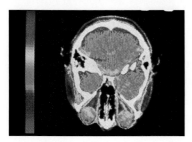

b. CAT scan

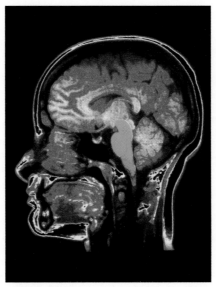

c. fMRI scan

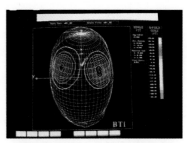

d. SQUID scan

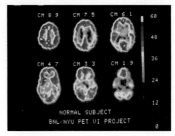

e. PET scan

FIGURE 2-9 *Brain scans produced by different techniques. (a) A computer-produced EEG image. (b) This CAT scan shows the structures of the brain. (c) The fMRI scan uses a magnetic field to detail the parts of the brain. (d) The SQUID scan shows the neural activity of the brain. (e) The PET scan displays the functioning of the brain at a given moment and is sensitive to the person's activities.*

- The *superconducting quantum interference device (SQUID)* is sensitive to tiny changes in magnetic fields that occur when neurons fire. Using SQUID, researchers can pinpoint the location of neural activity (Kuriki, Takeuchi, & Kobayashi, 1994; Sasaki et al., 1995; Forss, Jousmaki, & Hari, 1995).

- The *positron emission tomography (PET) scan* shows biochemical activity within the brain at a given moment in time. PET scans begin with the injection of radioactive (but safe) water into the bloodstream, which wends its way to the brain. By measuring the location of radiation within the brain, a computer can determine which are the more active regions, providing a striking picture of the brain at work. PET scans are used in many kinds of research. For example, to study the neural correlates of memory (Cabeza, et al., 1997), motor-skill learning (Doyon et al., 1996), and cognitive ability (Goel, 1998).

Each of these techniques offers exciting possibilities not only for the diagnosis and treatment of brain disease and injuries, but also for an increased understanding of the normal functioning of the brain. In addition, researchers are developing ways to combine separate scanning techniques (such as integrated, simultaneous PET and fMRI scans) to produce even more effective portraits of the brain (Sarter, Berntson, & Cacioppo, 1996; Service, 1996).

Motor-Skill Learning

Advances in brain scanning are also paving the way for the development of new methods for harnessing the neural signals that emanate from the brain. We consider some of these intriguing findings in the Applying Psychology in the 21st Century box.

The Central Core: Our "Old Brain"

While the capabilities of the human brain far exceed those of the brain of any other species, it is not surprising that the basic functions that we share with more primitive animals, such as breathing, eating, and sleeping, are directed by a relatively primitive part of the brain. A portion of the brain known as the **central core** (see Figure 2-10) is quite similar to that found in all vertebrates (species with backbones). The central core is sometimes referred to as the "old brain" because its evolutionary underpinnings can be traced back some 500 million years to primitive structures found in nonhuman species.

central core: The "old brain" which controls such basic functions as eating and sleeping and is common to all vertebrates

Applying Psychology in the 21st Century

Your Wish Is Its Command

Throw away your computer keyboard. Exterminate your mouse. And of course, get rid of your pens and pencils. Instead, just think a command that you want your computer to follow, and it will do your bidding.

At least that is the scenario that several research teams hope to see in the not-too-distant future. In their view, computers of the future will be able to respond to people's thoughts (Knapp & Lusted, 1992; McFarland et al., 1993; Wolpaw & McFarland, 1994; Lusted & Knapp, 1996).

Researchers expect to accomplish such mind-over-cursor feats by harnessing the brain's electrical impulses. Using electroencephalography, or EEG, techniques, researchers can attach electrodes to an individual's skull and trace the electrical impulses and brain wave patterns that are produced as a person thinks particular kinds of thoughts.

At this point, the process by which brain waves may be harnessed is specula-tive and largely theoretical. For instance, it is difficult enough to recognize from brain waves if people mean "yes" or "no," and nearly impossible to recognize more complicated thinking. Furthermore, so many brain activities occur simultaneously that it is hard to pick out the relevant electrical impulses (Shine, 1994).

Still, there are some current successes. Dr. Emanuel Donchin, a professor of psychology at the University of Illinois, has discovered a technique that lets people type by spelling out words in their minds—although at a rate of only 2.3 characters a minute (Farwell & Donchin, 1988; Pollack, 1993). The system works in a roundabout way. Letters of the alphabet are arranged in rows and columns on a computer screen and are randomly flashed. When the row or column containing the letter that the person is thinking of flashes, the brain emits a telltale signal that typically occurs when people see something that they have been anticipating. By analyzing these signals, another computer is able to identify the relevant letter.

Although the process is slow and tedious, it does work. Moreover, other laboratories are also progressing in their efforts to make computers respond to thought. For instance, researchers at the New York State Department of Health are developing a system that permits people to move a cursor slowly up and down or side-to-side on a computer screen through thinking. The researchers plan to use the system with people who have neurological disorders or physical injuries that prevent them from moving or speaking (Pollack, 1993; Lusted & Knapp, 1996).

Although all the current systems are in the early stages of development, they do seem promising. As our understanding of the brain increases, the potential of mind-over-cursor may well come true (Osman et al., 1992).

With the aid of advanced computer equipment, Heather Black, who has severe cerebral palsy, is able to communicate effectively. When she directs her gaze at one of the flashing squares on the computer screen, electrodes attached to the back of her head detect her reactions to the timing of the flashes, permitting her to make her choice known.

If we were to move up the spinal cord from the base of the skull to locate the structures of the central core of the brain, the first part we would come to would be the *medulla* (see Figure 2-11). The medulla controls a number of critical body functions, the most important of which are breathing and maintenance of heartbeat. The *pons* comes next, joining the two halves of the cerebellum, which lies adjacent to it. Containing large bundles of nerves, the pons acts as a transmitter of motor information, coordinating muscles and integrating movement between the right and left halves of the body. It is also involved in the control of sleep.

The **reticular formation** extends from the medulla through the pons. Like an ever-vigilant guard, the reticular formation is made up of groups of nerve cells that can

reticular formation: The part of the brain from the medulla through the pons made up of groups of nerve cells that can immediately activate other parts of the brain to produce general bodily arousal

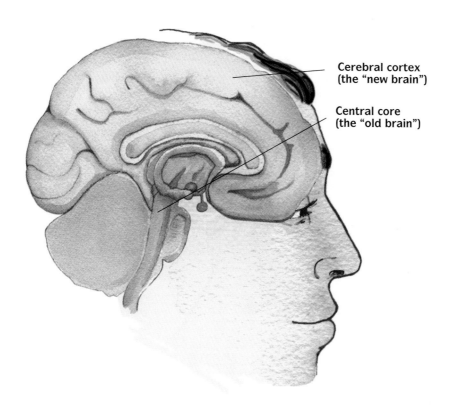

Cerebral cortex (the "new brain")

Central core (the "old brain")

FIGURE 2-10 *The major divisions of the brain: the cerebral cortex and the central core.*

immediately activate other parts of the brain to produce general bodily arousal. If, for example, we are startled by a loud noise, our reticular formation can prompt a heightened state of awareness to determine whether a response is necessary. In addition, the reticular formation serves a different function when we are sleeping, seeming to filter out background stimuli to allow us to sleep undisturbed.

The **cerebellum** is found just above the medulla and behind the pons. Without the help of the cerebellum we would be unable to walk a straight line without staggering and lurching forward, for it is the job of the cerebellum to control bodily balance. It constantly monitors feedback from the muscles to coordinate their placement, movement, and tension. In fact, drinking too much alcohol seems to depress the activity of the cerebellum, leading to the unsteady gait and movement characteristic of drunkenness. Recent research suggests that the cerebellum is also involved in several intellectual functions, ranging from the analysis of sensory information to solving problems (Raymond, Lisberger, & Mauk, 1996; Barinaga, 1996; Gao et al., 1996).

Hidden within the middle of the central core, the **thalamus** acts primarily as a busy relay station, mostly for information concerning the senses. Messages from the eyes, ears, and skin travel to the thalamus to be communicated upward to higher parts of the brain. The thalamus also integrates information from higher parts of the brain, sorting it out so that it can be sent to the cerebellum and medulla.

The **hypothalamus** is located just below the thalamus. Although tiny—about the size of a fingertip—the hypothalamus plays an inordinately important role. One of its major functions is to maintain *homeostasis,* a steady internal environment for the body. As we'll discuss further in Chapter 9, the hypothalamus helps provide a constant body temperature and monitors the amount of nutrients stored in the cells. A second major function is equally important: It produces and regulates behaviour that is critical to the basic survival of the species, known to several generations of anatomy students as the four Fs—fight, flight, feeding, and fornication (Kupfermann, 1991a).

The Limbic System: Beyond the Central Core

In an eerie view of the future, some science fiction writers have suggested that people will someday routinely have electrodes implanted in their brains. These electrodes will

cerebellum (ser uh BELL um): The part of the brain that controls bodily balance

The Cerebellum

thalamus: The part of the brain located in the middle of the central core that acts primarily as a busy relay station, mostly for information concerning the senses

hypothalamus: A tiny part of the brain, located below the thalamus of the brain, that maintains homeostasis and produces and regulates vital, basic behaviour such as eating, drinking, and sexual behaviour

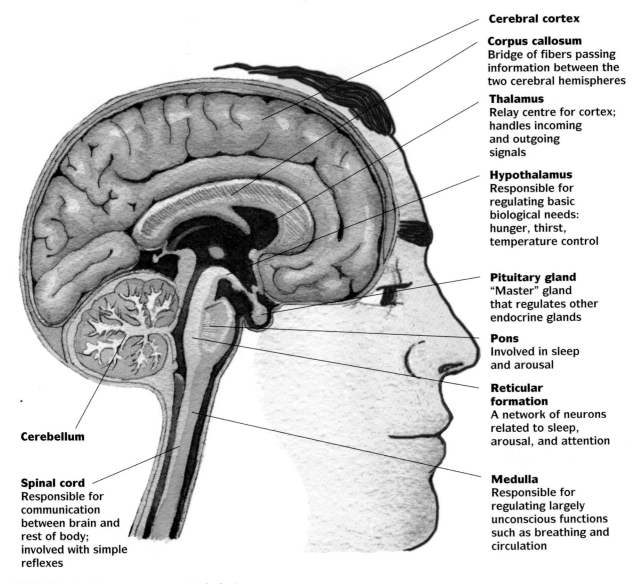

FIGURE 2-11 *The major structures in the brain.*

permit them to receive tiny shocks that produce the sensation of pleasure by stimulating certain centres of the brain. When they feel upset, people will simply activate their electrodes to achieve an immediate high.

Although far-fetched and improbable, such a futuristic fantasy is based on fact. Classic studies by McGill researchers James Olds and Peter Milner identified a pleasure centre in the hypothalamus (1954). In fact, pleasure centres exist in several areas of the brain, including some in the **limbic system** which consists of a series of doughnut-shaped structures including the amygdala, hippocampus, and fornix. The limbic system borders the top of the central core and has connections with the cerebral cortex (see Figure 2-12).

The structures of the limbic system jointly control a variety of basic functions relating to emotions and self-preservation, such as eating, aggression, and reproduction. Injury to the limbic system can produce striking changes in behaviour. It can turn animals that are usually docile and tame into belligerent savages. Conversely, those that are usually wild and uncontrollable may become meek and obedient (Fanelli, Burright, & Donovick, 1983; Bedard & Parsinger, 1995).

Research examining the effects of mild electric shocks to parts of the limbic system and other parts of the brain have produced some thought-provoking findings (Olds & Milner, 1954; Olds & Fobes, 1981). In one experiment, rats who pressed a bar received a mild electric jolt, which produced pleasurable feelings, through an electrode

limbic system: The part of the brain located outside the "new brain" that controls eating, aggression, and reproduction

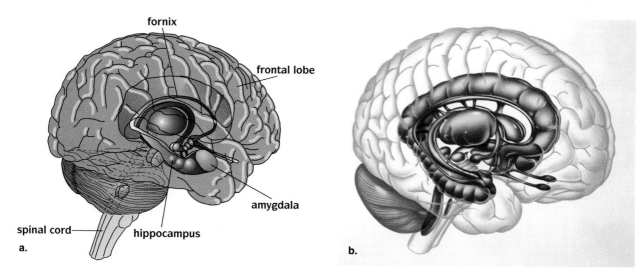

FIGURE 2-12 *(a) The limbic system consists of a series of doughnut-shaped structures that are involved in self-preservation, learning, memory, and the experience of pleasure. (b) This computer-generated image provides another view of the limbic system. Source: Courtesy of Dr. Robert B. Livingston, University of California–San Diego, and Philip J. Mercurio, Neurosciences Institute.*

implanted in their brain. Even starving rats on their way to food would stop to press the bar as many times as they could. Some rats would actually stimulate themselves literally thousands of times an hour—until they collapsed with fatigue (Routtenberg & Lindy, 1965).

The extraordinarily pleasurable quality of certain kinds of stimulation has also been experienced by humans, who, as part of treatment for certain kinds of brain disorders, have received electrical stimulation to certain areas of the limbic system. Although at a loss to describe just what it feels like, these people report the experience to be intensely pleasurable, similar in some respects to sexual orgasm.

The limbic system also plays an important role in learning and memory, a finding demonstrated in patients with epilepsy. In an attempt to stop their seizures, such patients have had portions of their limbic system removed. One unintended consequence of the surgery is that individuals sometimes have difficulty learning and remembering new information. In one case (discussed again when we focus on memory in Chapter 6), a patient who had undergone surgery was unable to remember where he lived, although he had resided at the same address for eight years. Further, even though the patient was able to carry on animated conversations, he was unable, a few minutes later, to recall what had been discussed (Milner, 1966).

The limbic system, then, is involved in several important functions, including self-preservation, learning, memory, and the experience of pleasure. These functions are hardly unique to humans; in fact, the limbic system is sometimes referred to as the "animal brain" because its structures and functions are so similar to those of other mammals. To identify the part of the brain that provides the complex and subtle capabilities that are uniquely human, we need to turn to another structure—the cerebral cortex.

Recap, Review, and Rethink

Recap

- Major brain scanning techniques include the electroencephalogram (EEG), computerized axial tomography (CAT), functional magnetic resonance imaging (fMRI), the superconducting quantum interference device (SQUID), and the positron emission tomography (PET) scan.

- The central core of the human brain is similar to that found in all vertebrates.

- Starting from the top of the spinal cord and moving up into the brain, we first find the medulla, which controls such functions as breathing and heartbeat. Next is the pons, which acts to transmit motor information.

- The reticular formation, extending from the medulla through the pons, arouses and activates the body but also censors outside stimulation during sleep. The cerebellum is involved in the control of motion.

- The thalamus acts primarily as a sensory-information relay centre, whereas the hypothalamus maintains homeostasis, a steady internal environment for the body.

- The limbic system controls a variety of basic functions relating to emotions and self-preservation, such as eating, aggression, and reproduction.

Review

1. The _____ _____ is a procedure whereby a picture of the brain can be taken without opening the skull.

2. Match the name of each brain scan with the appropriate description:

   a. EEG
   b. CAT
   c. fMRI
   d. PET
   e. SQUID

   1. Powerful magnets produce magnetic fields in the brain that provide a computer-generated snapshot.
   2. Location of radioactive isotopes within the brain determines its active regions.
   3. Electrodes record the electrical signals transmitted through the brain.
   4. This scan measures tiny changes in magnetic fields that occur when neurons fire, pinpointing neural activity.
   5. Computer image combines thousands of X-ray pictures into one.

3. Control of such functions as breathing and sleep is located in the recently developed "new brain." True or false?

4. Match the portion of the brain with its function:

   a. medulla
   b. pons
   c. cerebellum
   d. reticular formation

   1. maintains breathing and heartbeat
   2. controls bodily balance
   3. coordinates and integrates muscle movements
   4. activates the brain to produce arousal

5. You receive flowers from a friend. The colour, smell, and feeling of the flowers are relayed through what part of the brain?

6. The _____, a fingertip-sized portion of the brain, is responsible for the maintenance of_____ , the regulation of the body's internal environment.

7. The hypothalamus is responsible for the production and regulation of behaviour that is critical to the basic survival of the species, such as eating, drinking, sexual behaviour, and aggression. True or false?

Answers to Review Questions are on page 68.

Rethink

1. How would you answer the argument that "psychologists should leave the study of neurons and synapses and the nervous system to biologists?"

2. What limitations were imposed on psychologists' understanding of brain-related phenomena by the fact that they could study the brain only after death? In what areas would you expect the most significant advances once brain scanning techniques were possible?

3. What are some implications of the fact that humans and other vertebrates have highly similar limbic systems?

The Cerebral Cortex: Our "New Brain"

As we have proceeded up the spinal cord and into the brain, our discussion has centred on areas of the brain that control functions similar to those found in less sophisticated organisms. But where, you may be asking, are the portions of the brain that enable humans to do what they do best, and that distinguish humans from all other animals? Those unique features of the human brain—indeed, the very capabilities that allow you to come up with such a question in the first place—are embodied in the ability to think, evaluate, and make complex judgments. The principal location of these abilities, along with many others, is the **cerebral cortex.**

cerebral cortex: The "new brain," responsible for the most sophisticated information processing in the brain; contains the lobes

The cerebral cortex, which is sometimes referred to as the "new brain" because of its relatively recent evolution, is a mass of deeply folded, rippled, convoluted tissue. Although only about 2 millimetres thick, it would, if flattened out, cover an area more than .18 square metres. This configuration allows the surface area of the cortex to be considerably greater than if it were smoother and more uniformly packed into the skull. The mottled configuration also permits a high level of neuronal integration, allowing sophisticated processing of information.

lobes: The four major sections of the cerebral cortex—frontal, parietal, temporal, and occipital

The cortex has four major sections, called **lobes.** If we take a side view of the brain, the *frontal lobes* lie at the front center of the cortex, and the *parietal lobes* lie behind them. The *temporal lobes* are found in the lower centre of the cortex, with the *occipital lobes* lying behind them. These four sets of lobes are physically separated by deep grooves called sulci. Figure 2-13*a* shows the four areas.

Another way of describing the brain is by considering the functions associated with a given area. Figure 2-13*b* shows the specialized regions within the lobes related to specific functions and areas of the body. Three major areas have been discovered:

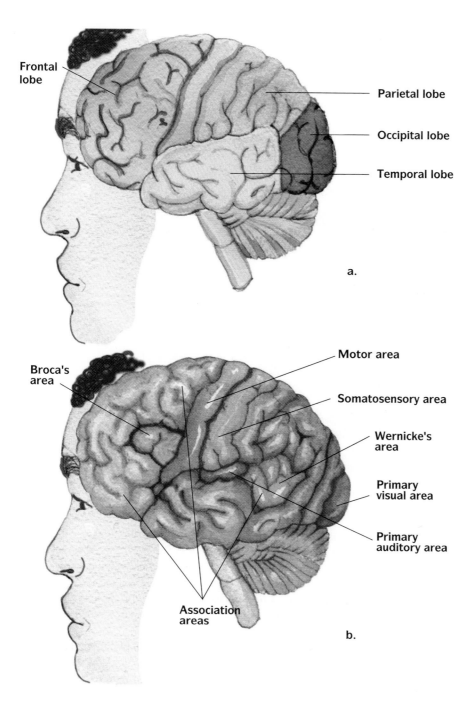

Frontal lobe

Parietal lobe

Occipital lobe

Temporal lobe

a.

Broca's area

Motor area

Somatosensory area

Wernicke's area

Primary visual area

Primary auditory area

Association areas

b.

FIGURE 2-13 *The cerebral cortex of the brain. (a) The major physical structures of the cerebral cortex are called lobes. (b) This figure illustrates the functions associated with particular areas of the cerebral cortex.*

The Brain Structure

the motor areas, the sensory areas, and the association areas. Although we will discuss these areas as though they were separate and independent entities, keep in mind that this is an oversimplification. In most instances, behaviour is influenced simultaneously by several structures and areas within the brain, operating interdependently. Furthermore, even within a given area, additional subdivisions exist (Gibbons, 1990).

The Motor Area of the Cortex

If you look at the frontal lobe in Figure 2-13b, you will see a shaded portion labelled the **motor area**. This part of the cortex is largely responsible for the voluntary movement of particular parts of the body. Every portion of the motor area corresponds to a specific locale within the body. If we were to insert an electrode into a particular part of the motor area of the cortex and apply mild electrical stimulation, there would be involuntary movement in the corresponding part of the body (Kertesz, 1983). If we moved to another part of the motor area and stimulated it, a different part of the body would move.

motor area: The part of the cortex that is largely responsible for the voluntary movement of particular parts of the body

FIGURE 2-14 *The correspondence between the amount and location of tissue in the brain's motor area and the specific body parts where movement is controlled by that tissue. Source: Penfield & Rasmussen, 1950.*

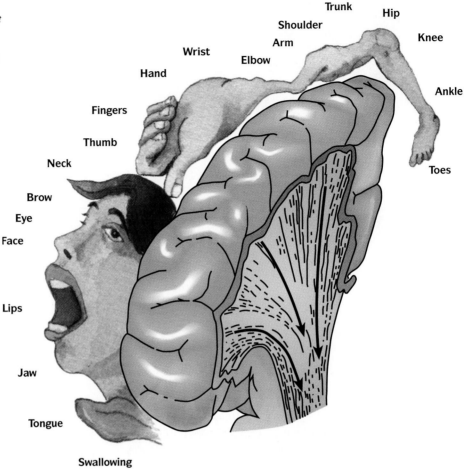

The motor area has been so well mapped that it is possible to devise the kind of schematic representation shown in Figure 2-14. Wilder Penfield, a neurosurgeon at the Montreal Neurological Institute and his colleagues provided us with this knowledge. A map of motor function was important to Penfield's work. He wanted to be sure not to interfere with critical functions, in the process of doing brain surgery. During the course of surgery he stimulated various areas of the cortex and recorded the parts of the patient's body that moved in response to the stimulation.

The model above shows the amount and relative location of cortical tissue that is used to produce movement in specific parts of the human body. As you can see, the control of body movements that are relatively large scale and require little precision, such as movement of a knee or a hip, is centred in a very small space in the motor area. In contrast, movements that must be precise and delicate, such as facial expressions and finger movements are controlled by a considerably larger portion of the motor area (Penfield and Rasmussen, 1950).

In sum, the motor area of the cortex provides a guide to the degree of complexity and the importance of the motor capabilities of specific parts of the body. Keep in mind, however, that such maps are an oversimplification: As we've noted before, behaviour is produced by multiple sets of neurons in the nervous system, linked in elaborate ways. Like other behaviour, movement is produced through the coordinated firing of a complex variety of neurons, working together but not necessarily lined up neatly in the motor area of the cortex (Donoghue & Sanes, 1994; Sanes et al., 1995).

Answers to Review Questions:

1. brain scan   2. a-3; b-5; c-1; d-2; e-4   3. False; it is located in the central core or "old brain."   4. a-1; b-3; c-2; d-4   5. thalamus   6. hypothalamus; homeostasis   7. true

FIGURE 2-15 *The greater the amount of tissue in the somatosensory area of the brain that is related to a specific body part, the more sensitive is that body part. If the size of our body parts reflected the corresponding amount of brain tissue, we would look like this strange creature.*

The Sensory Area of the Cortex

Given the one-to-one correspondence between the motor area and location of body movement, it is not surprising to find a similar relationship between specific portions of the sensory area and the senses. Penfield (1947) also mapped this relationship. Because patients were only under local anesthetic, they were able to report sensation to him as he probed the various areas of the cortex.

The **sensory area** of the cortex includes three regions: one that corresponds primarily to body sensations (including touch and pressure), one relating to sight, and a third relating to sound. For instance, the somatosensory area encompasses specific locations associated with the ability to perceive touch and pressure in a particular area of the body. As with the motor area, the amount of brain tissue related to a particular location on the body determines the degree of sensitivity of that location. The greater the space within the cortex, the more sensitive that area of the body (Penfield and Rasmussen, 1950). As you can see from the weird-looking individual in Figure 2-15, parts such as the fingers are related to proportionally more space in the somatosensory area and are the most sensitive.

The senses of sound and sight are also represented in specific areas of the cerebral cortex. An auditory area located in the temporal lobe is responsible for the sense of hearing. If the auditory area is stimulated electrically, a person will hear sounds such as clicks or hums. It also appears that particular locations within the auditory area respond to specific pitches.

The visual area in the cortex, located in the occipital lobe, operates analogously to the other sensory areas. Stimulation by electrodes produces the experience of flashes of light or colours, suggesting that the raw sensory input of images from the eyes is received in this area of the brain and transformed into meaningful stimuli. The visual area also provides another example of how areas of the brain are intimately related to specific areas of the body. Particular areas of the eye's retina are related to a particular part of the cortex—with, as you might guess, more space in the brain given to the most sensitive portions of the retina (Martin et al., 1995; Miyashita, 1995).

sensory area: The site in the brain containing tissue that corresponds to each of the senses, with the degree of sensitivity relating to the amount of tissue

The Association Areas of the Cortex

Consider the following case:

> Twenty-five-year-old Phineas Gage, a railroad employee, was blasting rock one day in 1848 when an accidental explosion punched a metre-long spike, about 2.5 centimetre in diameter, completely through his skull. The spike entered just under his left cheek, came out the top of his head, and flew into

the air. Gage immediately suffered a series of convulsions, yet a few minutes later was talking with rescuers. In fact, he was able to walk up a long flight of stairs before receiving any medical attention. Amazingly, after a few weeks his wound healed, and he was physically close to his old self again. Mentally, however, there was a difference: Once a careful and hard-working person, Phineas now became enamored with wild schemes and was flighty and often irresponsible. As one of his physicians put it, "Previous to his injury, though untrained in the schools, he possessed a well-balanced mind, and was looked upon by those who knew him as a shrewd, smart businessman, very energetic and persistent in executing all his plans of operation. In this regard his mind was radically changed, so decidedly that his friends and acquaintances said he was 'no longer Gage'" (Harlow, 1869, p. 14).

What had happened to the old Gage? Although there is no way of knowing for sure—science being what it was in the 1800s—we can speculate that the accident may have injured the association areas of the frontal lobes of Gage's cerebral cortex.

If you return one last time to our diagram of the cerebral cortex (Figure 2-13*b*), you will find that the motor and sensory areas take up a relatively small portion of the cortex; the remainder contains the association areas. The **association areas** of the four lobes are generally considered to be the site of higher mental processes such as thinking, language, memory, and speech.

Most of our understanding of the association areas comes from patients who have suffered some type of brain injury. In some cases the injury stemmed from natural causes such as a tumor, disease, or a stroke, any of which would block certain blood vessels within the cerebral cortex. In other cases, accidental causes were the culprits, as was true with Phineas Gage. In any event, damage to these areas can result in unusual behavioural changes, indicating the importance of the association area to normal functioning (Milner & Kolb, 1985; Kupfermann, 1991b; Hoogenraad, Ramos, & van Gijn, 1994).

Gage's case provides evidence that there are specialized areas for making rational decisions. When this area is damaged, people undergo personality changes that affect their ability to make moral judgments and to process emotions. Memory may also be affected (McAndrews & Milner, 1991).

Injuries to other parts of the association areas can produce a condition known as apraxia. *Apraxia* occurs when an individual is unable to integrate activities in a rational or logical manner. For example, a patient asked to get a soda from the refrigerator might go to the refrigerator and open and close the door repeatedly, or might take bottle after bottle of soda out of the refrigerator, dropping each to the floor. Similarly, a person with apraxia who is asked to open a lock with a key may be unable to do so in response to the request—but, if simply left alone in a locked room, will unlock the door if he or she wishes to leave (Lechtenberg, 1982).

Apraxia is clearly not a muscular problem, since the person is capable of carrying out the individual components of the overall behaviour. Moreover, if asked to perform the individual components of a larger behavioural pattern one at a time, a patient is often successful. It is only when asked to carry out a sequence of behaviours requiring a degree of planning and foresight that the patient shows deficits. It appears, then, that the association areas may act as "master planners," that is, organizers of actions.

Other difficulties that arise because of injury to the association area of the brain relate to the use of language. Problems with verbal expression, known as *aphasia,* can take many forms. In *Broca's aphasia* (caused by damage to the part of the brain first identified by a French physician, Paul Broca, in 1861), speech becomes halting, laborious, and often ungrammatical. The speaker is unable to find the right words, in a kind of tip-of-the-tongue phenomenon that we all experience from time to time. In the case of people with aphasia, though, they grope for words almost constantly, eventually blurting out a kind of "verbal telegram." A phrase like "I put the book on the

association areas: One of the major areas of the brain, the site of the higher mental processes such as thought, language, memory, and speech

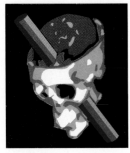

A model of the injury sustained by Phineas Gage. Source: Reprinted with permission of the author and publisher from Science, *Volume 254, May 20, 1994, p. 1104, Copyright 1994 American Association for the Advancement of Science.*

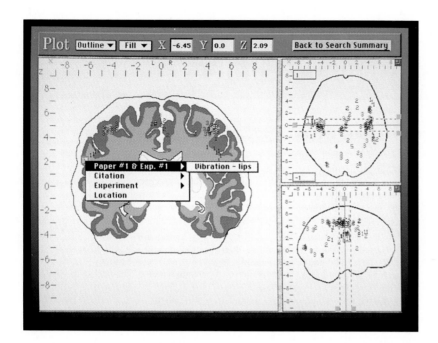

FIGURE 2-16 *A sample computer screen from BrainMap, a computerized data base designed to make every aspect of the brain accessible.*

table" comes out as "I . . . put . . . book . . . table" (Cornell, Fromkin, & Mauner, 1993; Goodglass, 1993; Kirshner, 1995).

Wernicke's aphasia is a disorder named for Carl Wernicke, who identified it in the 1870s. Wernicke's aphasia produces difficulties both in understanding others' speech and in the production of language. Found in patients with damage to an area of the brain first identified by Wernicke, the disorder is characterized by speech that sounds fluent, but makes no sense. For instance, one of Wernicke's patients, Philip Gorgan, was asked what brought him to the hospital. His rambling reply: "Boy, I'm sweating, I'm awful nervous, you know, once in a while I get caught up, I can't mention the tarripoi, a month ago, quite a little" (Gardner, 1975, p. 68).

Brain injuries, such as those that result in aphasia, and brain disorders due to disease and illness have given new impetus to scientists who are seeking to "map" the neural circuitry of the brain. Using sophisticated computer technology, researchers are seeking to create a database encompassing every facet of the brain (see Figure 2-16).

Language and the Brain

Mending the Brain

Shortly after he was born, Jacob Stark's arms and legs started jerking every 20 minutes. Weeks later he could not focus his eyes on his mother's face. The diagnosis: uncontrollable epileptic seizures involving his entire brain.

His mother, Sally Stark, recalled: "When Jacob was two and a half months old, they said he would never learn to sit up, would never be able to feed himself. Nothing could be done to prevent profound retardation. They told us to take him home, love him and find an institution" (Blakeslee, 1992a, p. C3).

Instead, the Starks brought Jacob to the University of California at Los Angeles for brain surgery when he was five months old. Surgeons removed 20 percent of his brain. The operation was a complete success. Three years later, Jacob seems normal in every way, with no sign of seizures.

The surgery that helped Jacob was based on the premise that the diseased part of his brain was producing seizures throughout the entire brain. Surgeons reasoned that if they removed the misfiring portion, the remaining parts of the brain, which appeared intact in PET scans, would take over, and that Jacob could still lead a normal life.

Pathways Through Psychology

Julien Doyon, Professor in Cognitive Neuroscience

Université de Montréal

Adjunct professor in the Department of Neuropsychology, Montreal Neurological Institute, McGill University

Education: *B.A., M.A., Université Laval; Ph.D. McGill University*

Home: *Montréal, Québec*

My interest in cognitive neuroscience began when I was doing my Ph.D at McGill University and taking a course in adult assessment from Laughlin B. Taylor. This interest continued to develop while doing an Internship Practicum, learning how to do clinical assessments of patients with epilepsy who needed surgery of either the frontal or the tempo-

Julien Doyon

ral lobes. I really liked the clinical work and the research questions that can be pursued and asked Brenda Milner to supervise my thesis.

In my clinical practice, I conduct cognitive assessments of patients with a variety of neurological disorders. I also do work in the area of rehabilitation of motor skills. The main focus of my research is understanding and identifying the neural networks involved in learning a motor skill (e.g., playing the piano or playing golf). I am also interested in the plasticity of these networks and in better understanding the brain structures involved at different phases of the learning process.

I believe that, in neuroscience, one must apply different techniques in order to find an answer. I thus use a multifaceted approach in my work. In the case of motor-skill learning, I have carried out experiments looking at the effects of lesions to the brain (striatum and cerebellum for example). A second line of inquiry consists of performing a series of brain imaging studies (PET and fMRI) in normal control subjects and patients with Parkinson's disease. A third line of inquiry involves the rat animal model, in which the effects of lesions to the cerebellum, striatum or frontal cortex are assessed during both the learning of and retention of a motor sequence.

Basic research provides knowledge, which can then be applied to a clinical population. I have recently been using motor imagery as a means of keeping the neural circuits of stroke patients alive in order to improve their chances of re-

covery. If people produce a mental image of a motor activity, the brain circuits for that movement are activated even if the actual performance is not possible at the time because of the stroke.

As a member and past president of both the Canadian Society for Brain, Behaviour and Cognitive Sciences and the International Society for Behavioural Neuroscience I have had the opportunity to extend my network of collaborators and friends.

What has sustained my interest and has provided me with a sense of accomplishment? I would say it would be my work towards understanding the brain structures mediating the learning of motor skills, and work on the neuropathophysiology underlying the cognitive and motor impairment in Parkinson's disease. I have also collaborated with Dr. Jeremy D. Schmahmann of the Massachusetts General Hospital of Harvard University to create a three-dimensional atlas of the human cerebellum. Researchers in the field of brain imaging can use this atlas to locate, with better precision, areas of the cerebellum active during a variety of cognitive and motor tasks.

I believe that brain research is both a fascinating and a necessary endeavour, especially when it allows us to increase our knowledge base and find better treatments for people with neurological disorders.

Source: Julien Doyon, Ph.D, Université of Montréal. <Julien.doyon@umontreal.ca>

The success of such surgery is in part related to new findings about the regenerative powers of the brain and nervous system.

However, new evidence is beginning to suggest otherwise. For instance, researchers have found that the cells from the brains of adult mice can produce new neurons, at least in a test tube environment. Similarly, researchers Henrich Cheng, Yihai Cao, and Lars Olson have reported partial restoration of movement in rats who had a complete gap in their spinal cords and, as a result, were unable to move their hind limbs. Using nerves from the peripheral nervous system, the researchers transplanted neurons and attached them across a gap of about 1 millimetre. The rats were able to flex their legs after the transplantation. One year after the operation, they were able to support themselves and move their legs. Examination of the neurons in the spinal cord showed significant regeneration around the area of the transplantation (Reynolds & Weiss, 1992; Young, 1996; Cheng, Cao, & Olson, 1996).

The future also holds promise for people who suffer from the tremors and loss of motor control produced by Parkinson's disease. Because Parkinson's is caused by a gradual loss of cells that stimulate the production of dopamine in the brain, investigators reasoned that a procedure which would increase the supply of dopamine might be effective. They seem to be on the right track. When certain cells from human fetuses are injected directly into the brains of Parkinson's sufferers, they seem to take root, stimulating dopamine production. For most of those who have undergone this procedure, the preliminary results are promising, with some patients showing great improvement. On the other hand, the technique remains experimental, and it also raises some thorny ethical issues, given that the source of the implanted fetal tissue is aborted fetuses (Thompson, 1992; Widner et al., 1992; Watson, 1994; Kolata, 1995).

The Specialization of the Hemispheres: Two Brains or One?

The most recent development, at least in evolutionary terms, in the organization and operation of our brain probably occurred in the last million years: a specialization of the functions controlled by the two sides of the brain, which has symmetrical left and right halves.

Specifically, the brain can be divided into two roughly similar mirror-image halves or **hemispheres**. The nerves are connected from the brain to the rest of the body in such a way that the left hemisphere of the brain, controls the right side of the body, and the right hemisphere controls the left side of the body. Thus damage to the right side of the brain is typically indicated by functional difficulties in the left side of the body.

Yet the structural similarity between the two hemispheres of the brain is not reflected in all aspects of its functioning. It appears that certain activities are more likely to occur in one hemisphere than in the other. Early evidence for the functional differences between halves of the brain came from studies of people with aphasia. Researchers found that people with the speech difficulties characteristic of aphasia tended to have physical damage to the left hemisphere of the brain. In contrast, physical abnormalities in the right hemisphere of the brain tended to produce far fewer problems with language. This finding led researchers to conclude that for most people, language is **lateralized,** or located more in one hemisphere than the other—in this case, in the left side of the brain (Bradshaw & Rogers, 1993; Zaidel et al., 1995; Grossi et al., 1996).

It now seems clear that the two hemispheres of the brain are somewhat specialized in terms of the functions they carry out. The left hemisphere concentrates more on tasks that require verbal competence, such as speaking, reading, thinking, and reasoning. The right hemisphere has its own strengths, particularly in nonverbal areas such as the understanding of spatial relationships, recognition of patterns and drawings, music, and emotional expression (Zaidel, 1994; Davidson & Hugdahl, 1995; Siegal, Carrington, & Radel, 1996; Mandal et al., 1996; LaMendola & Bever, 1997 see Figure 2-17).

In addition, the way in which information is processed is somewhat different in each hemisphere. The left hemisphere tends to consider information sequentially, one bit at a time, as well as controls the way we search a visual field, while the right hemisphere tends to process information globally, considering it as a whole (Gazzaniga, 1983; Springer & Deutsch, 1989; Turkewitz, 1993; Kingstone, Enns, Mangun and Gazzaniga, 1995).

These differences in specialization of the hemispheres have led researchers to speculate on the relationship of handedness to behaviour and ability. Since the left hand is controlled by the right brain can we assume that a left-handed person is more gifted artistically than a right-handed person? Stanley Coren (1992) of the University of British Columbia has done extensive research in this area and suggests caution. His studies have led him to believe that although some differences do exist they are not significant enough to predict thinking style or specific ability based on handedness.

Other research is amassing evidence that there may be subtle differences in brain lateralization patterns between males and females. In fact, some scientists have sug-

> ► How do the two halves of the brain operate interdependently?

> ► How can an understanding of the nervous system help us to find ways to alleviate disease and pain?

hemispheres: Two symmetrical left and right halves of the brain that control the side of the body opposite to their location

lateralization: The dominance of one hemisphere of the brain in specific functions

FIGURE 2-17 *The series of PET scans shows the activity of the left and right hemispheres while the person is resting, listening to language and music together, language alone, and music alone.*

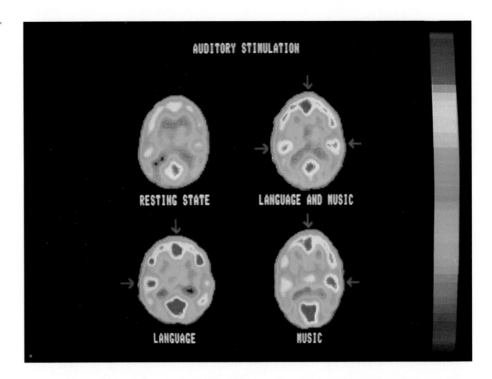

gested that there are slight differences in the structure of the brain that may differ according to gender. Brain lateralization may also be a function of cultural experience. As we see next, such findings have led to a lively and fascinating debate in the scientific community (Geschwind & Galaburda, 1987; Coren, 1992a; Springer & Deutsch, 1993). Two Canadian neuroscientists, Doreen Kimura, and Sandra Witelson have figured prominently in this debate.

Exploring Diversity

Human Diversity and the Brain

The interplay of biology and behaviour is particularly evident when we consider growing evidence suggesting that there are sex differences in brain structure and function. Males and females show some intriguing differences in brain lateralization, although the nature of those differences—and even their very existence—is the source of considerable controversy (Wood, Flowers, & Naylor, 1991; Kimura, 1992; Iaccino, 1993; Kaplan & Rogers, 1994).

Some statements can be made with reasonable confidence. For instance, most males tend to show greater lateralization of language in the left hemisphere. In contrast, women display less lateralization, with language abilities apt to be more evenly divided between the two hemispheres (Gur et al., 1982; Shaywitz et al., 1995; Kulynych et al., 1994). Such differences in brain lateralization may account, in part, for the superiority often displayed by females on certain measures of verbal skills, such as the onset and fluency of speech, and the fact that far more boys than girls have reading problems in elementary school (Kitterle, 1991).

Recent evidence also finds that men and women may process information differently. For example, MRI brain scans of men sounding out words show activation of a small area of the left side of the brain, while women use areas on both sides of the brain (Shaywitz et al., 1995; see Figure 2-18). Similarly, PET brain scans of men and women while they are not engaged in mental activity show differences in the use of glucose (Gur et al., 1995; Gur, 1996). Neuropsychologist Doreen Kimura (1999) has

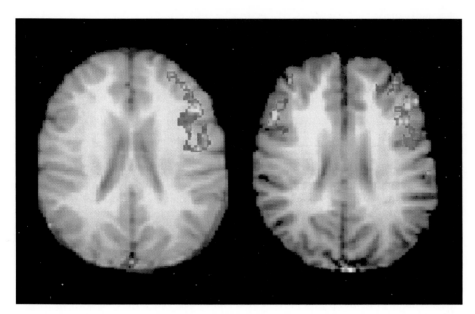

FIGURE 2-18 *These composite MRI brain scans show the distribution of active areas in the brains of males* (left) *and females* (right) *during a verbal task involving rhyming. In males, activation is more lateralized, or confined, to the left hemisphere, while in females, activation is bilateralized, that is, occurring in both hemispheres of the brain. Source: B. A. Shaywitz et al., 1995. NMR/Yale Medical School.*

also investigated the possibility that there are sex differences in problem solving due to hormone differences that affect the brain's early development.

Other research, not without its controversy, points to differences in brain structures between males and females. For example, part of the corpus callosum, a bundle of fibres that connects the hemispheres of the brain, is proportionally larger in women than in men (Witelson, 1995; Driesen & Raz, 1995; Steinmetz et al., 1995; Johnson et al., 1996). Sandra Witelson (1995) has also found evidence of a greater density of neurons in a portion of the temporal cortex of women. Studies conducted on rats, hamsters, and monkeys have also found size and structure differences in male and female brains (Gorski, 1990, 1996; Jacobs & Spencer, 1994).

The meaning of such sex differences is far from clear. Consider one possibility related to the differences that have been found in the proportional size of the corpus callosum. Its increased proportion in women may permit stronger connections to develop between those parts of the brain that control speech. In turn, this would explain why speech tends to emerge slightly earlier in girls than in boys.

Before we rush to such a conclusion, though, it is important to consider an alternative hypothesis: It is plausible that the earlier emergence of verbal abilities in girls is due to the fact that infant girls receive encouragement to verbalize in a more interactive (less direct) and more emotional way than infant boys (Gleason et al., 1994; Perlmann and Gleason, 1990). In turn, this greater early experience may foster growth of certain parts of the brain. Hence, physical brain differences may be a reflection of social and environmental influences, rather than a cause of the differences in men's and women's behaviour. At this point, it is impossible to confirm which of these two alternative hypotheses is correct.

Cultural experience also may give rise to differences in brain lateralization. For example, native speakers of Japanese seem to process information regarding vowel sounds primarily in the brain's left hemisphere. In contrast, North and South Americans, Europeans, and individuals of Japanese ancestry who learn Japanese later in life handle vowel sounds principally in the right hemisphere.

The reason for this cultural difference in lateralization? One explanation may be that certain characteristics of the Japanese language, such as the ability to express complex ideas using only vowel sounds, result in the development of a specific type of brain lateralization in native speakers (Tsunoda, 1985).

In general, scientists are just beginning to understand the extent, nature, and meaning of sex and cultural differences in lateralization and brain structure. At the same time, it is important to keep in mind that the two hemispheres of the brain function in tandem. It is a mistake to think of particular kinds of information as being processed solely in the right or the left hemisphere. The hemispheres work interdependently in deciphering, interpreting, and reacting to the world.

In addition, people who suffer injury to the left side of the brain and lose linguistic capabilities often recover the ability to speak. In such cases, the right side of the brain often pitches in and takes over some of the functioning of the left side. This shift is especially true in young children; the extent of recovery increases the earlier the injury occurs. Overall, then, the brain is remarkably adaptable. It can modify its functioning to a significant extent in response to adverse circumstances (Hellige, 1994; Hoptman & Davidson, 1994; Singer, 1995; Freund, 1996).   ■

Split-Brain Research

The Split Brain: Exploring the Two Hemispheres

When the seizures first started, Cindy Gluccles hoped her physician would give her a drug that would prevent their recurrence. Her physician and her neurologist were both optimistic, maintaining that in most cases seizures could be controlled with the proper drugs. But the seizures got worse and more frequent, and no drug treatment seemed to help. Further examination revealed that the seizures were caused by remarkably large bursts of electrical activity that were starting in one hemisphere and moving to the other. Finally, her doctors prescribed a last-ditch measure: surgically cutting the corpus collusum, the bundle of nerves that connect the two hemispheres. Almost magically, the seizures stopped. The operation was clearly a success—but was Cindy the same person she had been before the operation?

That issue has evoked a great deal of interest on the part of brain researchers and has earned a Nobel Prize for Roger Sperry. Sperry, with a group of colleagues, explored the behaviour of patients whose corpus callosum had been surgically cut. The research team found that in most ways there were no major changes in either personality or intelligence.

split-brain patient: A person who suffers from independent functioning of the two halves of the brain, as a result of which the sides of the body work in disharmony

On the other hand, patients like Cindy Gluccles, called **split-brain patients,** did occasionally display some unusual behaviour. For instance, one patient reported pulling his pants down with one hand and simultaneously pulling them up with the other. In addition, he mentioned grabbing his wife with his left hand and shaking her violently, while his right hand tried to help his wife by bringing his left hand under control (Gazzaniga, 1970).

Interest in this occasional curious behaviour, however, was peripheral to the rare opportunity that split-brain patients provided for researchers investigating the independent functioning of the two hemispheres of the brain, and Sperry developed a number of ingenious techniques for studying how each hemisphere operated (Sperry, 1982). In one experimental procedure, blindfolded subjects were allowed to touch an object with their right hand and were asked to name it. Because the right side of the body is connected to the left side of the brain—the hemisphere that is most responsible for language—the split-brain patient was able to name it. But if the blindfolded subject touched the object with his or her left hand, naming it aloud was not possible. However, the information had registered: When the blindfold was taken off, the subject could choose the object that he or she had touched. Information can be learned and remembered, then, using only the right side of the brain. (By the way, this experiment won't work with you—unless you have had a split-brain operation—since the bundle of fibres connecting the two hemispheres of a normal brain immediately transfers the information from one hemisphere to the other.)

It is clear from experiments like this one that the right and left hemispheres of the brain specialize in handling different sorts of information. At the same time, it is important to realize that they are both capable of understanding, knowing, and being aware of the world, albeit in somewhat different ways. The two hemispheres, then, should be regarded as different in terms of the efficiency with which they process certain kinds of information, rather than as two entirely separate brains. Moreover, in people with normal, nonsplit brains, the hemispheres work interdependently to allow the full range and richness of thought of which humans are capable.

THE ENDOCRINE SYSTEM: OF CHEMICALS AND GLANDS

One aspect of the biopsychology of behaviour that we have not yet considered is the **endocrine system,** a chemical communication network that sends messages throughout the nervous system via the bloodstream. Although not a structure of the brain itself, the endocrine system is intimately tied to the hypothalamus. The job of the endocrine system is to secrete **hormones,** chemicals that circulate through the blood and affect the functioning or growth of other parts of the body (Crapo, 1985; Kravitz, 1988).

Like neurotransmitters, hormones communicate chemical messages throughout the body, although the speed and mode of transmission are quite different. Whereas neural messages are measured in thousandths of a second, hormonal communications may take minutes to reach their destination. Furthermore, neural messages move across neurons in specific lines (as with wires strung along telephone poles), whereas hormones travel throughout the entire body, similar to the way radio waves transmit across the entire landscape. Just as radio waves evoke a response only when a radio is tuned to the correct station, so hormones flowing through the bloodstream activate only those cells that are receptive and "tuned" to the appropriate hormonal message.

A major component of the endocrine system is the **pituitary gland,** found near—and regulated by—the hypothalamus. The pituitary gland has sometimes been called the "master gland," because it controls the functioning of the rest of the endocrine system. But the pituitary gland is more than just the taskmaster of other glands; it has important functions in its own right. For instance, hormones secreted by the pituitary gland control growth. Extremely short people and unusually tall people usually have pituitary gland abnormalities. Other endocrine glands, shown in Figure 2-19, affect emotional reactions, sexual urges, and energy levels.

Despite its designation as the "master gland," the pituitary is actually a servant of the brain, because the brain is ultimately responsible for the endocrine system's functioning. The brain regulates the internal balance of the body, ensuring that homeostasis is maintained through the hypothalamus. Yet the road from brain to endocrine system is not strictly a one-way street. Hormones may permanently modify the way in which brain cells are organized. For example, adult sexual behaviour is thought to be affected by the production of hormones that modify cells in the hypothalamus.

Similarly, particular episodes in our lives can influence the production of hormones. For instance, one experiment in which college students played a computer game against a competitor found that individuals who were winning the game showed a rise in the production of testosterone—a hormone linked to aggressive behaviour (Gladue, Boechler, & McCaul, 1989).

Individual hormones can wear many hats, depending on circumstances. For example, the hormone oxytocin is at the root of many of life's satisfactions and pleasures. In new mothers, oxytocin produces an urge to nurse newborn offspring. The same hormone also seems to stimulate cuddling between species members. And—at least in rats—it encourages sexually active males to seek out females more passionately, and females to be more receptive to males' sexual advances. One study showed that female mice administered oxytocin become 60 to 80 percent more energetic in seeking out males to mount them than a control group of mice who didn't receive oxytocin (Angier, 1991).

endocrine system: A chemical communication network that sends messages throughout the nervous system via the bloodstream

hormones: Chemicals that circulate through the blood and affect the functioning or growth of other parts of the body

pituitary gland: The "master gland," the major component of the endocrine system, which secretes hormones that control growth

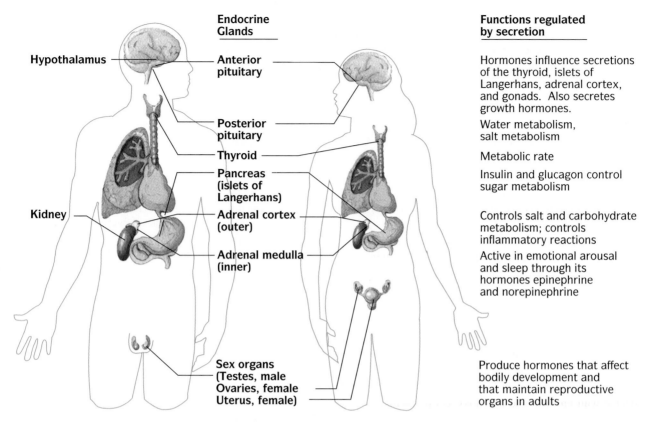

FIGURE 2-19 *Location and function of the major endocrine glands.*

Using biofeedback, people learn to control responses that were once thought involuntary, such as heart rate and blood pressure.

biofeedback: A procedure in which a person learns to control, through conscious thought, internal physiological processes such as blood pressure, heart and respiration rate, skin temperature, sweating, and constriction of particular muscles

The Informed Consumer of Psychology

Learning to Control Your Heart—and Mind—Through Biofeedback

On a June evening in 1985, Tammy DeMichael was cruising along the New York State Thruway with her fiancé when he fell asleep at the wheel. The car slammed into the guardrail and flipped, leaving DeMichael with what the doctors called a "splattered C-6, 7"—a broken neck and crushed spinal cord.

After a year of exhaustive medical treatment, she still had no function or feeling in her arms and legs. "The experts said I'd be a quadriplegic for the rest of my life, able to move only from the neck up," she recalls. "I wouldn't have wanted to keep living."

But DeMichael proved the experts wrong. Today, feeling has returned to her limbs, her arm strength is normal or better, and she no longer uses a wheelchair. "I can walk about 60 feet with just a cane, and I can go almost anywhere with crutches," she says. "I can bench-press 100 pounds, and I ride four miles daily on a stationary bike." (Morrow & Wolff, 1991, p. 64).

The key to DeMichael's astounding recovery: biofeedback. **Biofeedback** is a procedure in which a person learns to control, through conscious thought, internal physiological processes such as blood pressure, heart and respiration rate, skin temperature, sweating, and constriction of particular muscles. It had traditionally been thought that the heart, respiration rate, blood pressure, and other bodily functions were under the control of parts of the brain over which we have no influence. Yet psychologists are finding that these supposedly involuntary biological responses are actually susceptible to voluntary control (Schwartz & Schwartz, 1993; Olson, Schwartz, & Schwartz, 1995; Rau et al., 1996; Grimsley & Karriker, 1996).

In biofeedback, a person is hooked up to electronic devices that provide continuous feedback relating to the physiological response in question. For instance, a person interested in controlling her blood pressure might be hooked up to an apparatus that constantly monitors and displays blood pressure. As she consciously thinks about altering the pressure, she receives immediate feedback on the measure of her success. In this way she can eventually learn to bring her pressure under control. Similarly, if an individual wanted to control headaches through biofeedback, he might have electronic sensors placed on certain muscles in his head and thereby learn to control the constriction and relaxation of those muscles. Then, when he felt a headache coming on, he could relax the relevant muscles and abort the pain.

In DeMichael's case, biofeedback was effective because not all of the nervous system's connections between the brain and her legs were severed. Through biofeedback, she learned how to send messages to specific muscles, "ordering" them to move. Although it took more than a year, DeMichael was successful in restoring a large degree of her mobility.

While the control of physiological processes through the use of biofeedback is not easy to learn, it has been employed with success in a variety of ailments, including emotional problems (such as anxiety, depression, phobias, tension headaches, insomnia, and hyperactivity); medical problems with a psychological component (such as asthma, high blood pressure, ulcers, muscle spasms, and migraine headaches); and physical problems (such as DeMichael's injuries, strokes, cerebral palsy, and—as we see in Figure 2-20—curvature of the spine).

Although biofeedback treatment cannot be successful in every case, it is clear that learning through biofeedback has opened up a number of exciting possibilities for treating people with physical and psychological problems (e.g., Schwartz, 1995; Arena & Blanchard, 1996; Sedlacek & Taub, 1996; Ham & Packard, 1996). Moreover, some psychologists speculate that the use of biofeedback may one day become a part of everyday life.

For instance, one researcher has suggested that students whose minds wander during studying might be hooked up to an apparatus that gives them feedback on whether or not they are paying attention to the information they are studying (Ornstein, 1977). If they stop paying attention, the computer will alert them—putting them back on the right track. ∎

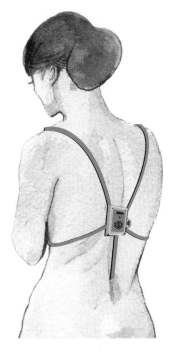

FIGURE 2-20 *The traditional treatment for curvature of the spine employs an unsightly, cumbersome brace. In contrast, biofeedback treatment employs an unobtrusive set of straps attached to a small electronic device that produces tonal feedback when the patient is not standing straight. The person learns to maintain a position that gradually decreases the curvature of the spine until the device is no longer needed. Source: Miller, 1985a.*

Recap, Review, and Rethink

Recap

- The cerebral cortex contains three major areas: the motor, sensory, and association areas. These areas control voluntary movement, the senses, and higher mental processes (including thought, language, memory, and speech), respectively.

- The two halves, or hemispheres, of the brain are structurally similar, but they seem to specialize in different functions. The left side of the brain is most closely related to language and verbal skills; the right side, to nonverbal skills such as musical ability, emotional expression, pattern recognition, and the processing of visual information.

- The endocrine system secretes hormones, chemicals that affect the growth and functioning of the body.

- Biofeedback is a procedure by which a person learns to control certain internal physiological processes, thereby bringing relief from a variety of specific ailments.

Review

1. The _____ lobes lie behind the frontal lobes, and the _____ lobes lie behind the temporal lobes.

2. A surgeon places an electrode on a portion of your brain and stimulates it. Immediately, your right wrist involuntarily twitches. The doctor has most likely stimulated a portion of the _____ area of your brain.

3. The motor area of the brain is divided up into segments that control different body parts. The more precise the movements of these parts need to be, the larger the portion of the motor area devoted to that part. True or false?

4. The sensory areas of the brain are divided up according to the size of the sensory organ. Thus, since there is more skin on a person's back than on his fingertips, the portion of the sensory area that deals with sensations on the back will be larger than the fingertip section. True or false?

5. You see a man who has been asked to sharpen a pencil turn the sharpener for five minutes without putting the pencil into it. The condition that might be responsible for this type of behaviour is called _____ .

6. Brain hemispheres control the side of the body they are located on. The left hemisphere controls the left side of the body, and the right hemisphere controls the right. True or false?

7. Nonverbal realms, such as emotions and music, are controlled primarily by the _____ hemisphere of the brain, while the _____ hemisphere is more responsible for speaking and reading.

Answers to Review Questions are on page 81.

Rethink

1. Suppose that abnormalities in an area of the brain associated with moral judgment were linked through research to serious criminal behaviour. Would you be in favour of mandatory testing of individuals for those abnormalities and surgery to repair or remove them? Why or why not?

2. Could personal differences in people's specialization of right and left hemispheres be related to occupational success? Might an architect who relies on spatial skills have a different pattern of hemispheric specialization from a writer?

3. How might researchers examine whether differences in brain structures between males and females are genetically determined or caused by social and environmental influences? Is it possible to design an *ethical* research study to decide this issue? Might a cross-cultural study provide enlightenment?

looking
BACK

Why do psychologists study the brain and nervous system?

1. A full understanding of human behaviour requires knowledge of the biological influences underlying that behaviour. This chapter reviews what biopsychologists (psychologists who specialize in studying the effects of biological structures and functions on behaviour) have learned about the human nervous system.

What are the basic elements of the nervous system?

2. Neurons, the most basic elements of the nervous system, allow nerve impulses to pass from one part of the body to another. Information generally follows a route that begins with the dendrites, continues into the cell body, and leads ultimately down the tube-like extension, the axon.

How does the nervous system communicate electrical and chemical messages from one part to another?

3. Most axons are protected by a coating called the myelin sheath. When an axon receives a message to fire, it releases an action potential, an electric charge that travels through the neuron. Neurons operate according to an all-or-none law: They are either at rest or an action potential is moving through them. There is no in-between state.

4. Once a neuron fires, nerve impulses are carried to other neurons through the production of chemical substances, neurotransmitters, which actually bridge the gaps—known as synapses—between neurons. Neurotransmitters may be either excitatory, telling other neurons to fire, or inhibitory, preventing or decreasing the likelihood of other neurons firing. Among the major neurotransmitters are acetylcholine (ACh), which produces contractions of skeletal muscles, and dopamine, which has been linked to Parkinson's disease and certain mental disorders such as schizophrenia.

5. Endorphins, another type of neurotransmitter, are related to the reduction of pain. Endorphins aid in the production of natural pain-killers and are probably responsible for creating the kind of euphoria that joggers sometimes experience after running.

In what way are the structures of the nervous system tied together?

6. The nervous system is made up of the central nervous system (the brain and spinal cord) and the peripheral nervous system (the remainder of the nervous system). The peripheral nervous system is made up of the somatic division, which controls voluntary movements and the communication of information to and from the sense organs, and the autonomic division, which controls involuntary functions such as those of the heart, blood vessels, and lungs.

7. The autonomic division of the peripheral nervous system is further subdivided into the sympathetic and parasympathetic divisions. The sympathetic division prepares the body in emergency situations, and the parasympathetic division helps the body return to its typical resting state.

8. Evolutionary psychology—the branch of psychology that seeks to identify behaviour patterns that are a result of our genetic inheritance—has led to increased understanding of the evolutionary basis of the structure and organization of the human nervous system. Behavioural genetics extends this study to include the evolutionary and hereditary basis of human personality traits and behaviour.

How do researchers identify the major parts and functioning of the brain?

9. Brain scans take a "snapshot" of the internal workings of the brain without having to cut surgically into a person's skull. Major brain scanning techniques include the electroencephalogram (EEG), computerized axial tomography (CAT), the functional magnetic resonance imaging (fMRI) scan, the superconducting quantum interference device (SQUID), and the positron emission tomography (PET) scan.

What are the major parts of the brain, and what are the behaviours for which each part is responsible?

10. The central core of the brain is made up of the medulla (which controls such functions as breathing and the heartbeat), the pons (which coordinates the muscles and the two sides of the body), the cerebellum (which controls balance), the reticular formation (which acts to heighten awareness in emergencies), the thalamus (which communicates sensory messages to and from the brain), and the hypothalamus (which maintains homeostasis, or body equilibrium, and regulates basic survival behaviours). The functions of the central core structures are similar to those found in other vertebrates. This part of the brain is sometimes referred to as the "old brain." Increasing evidence also suggests that male and female brains may differ in structure in minor ways.

11. The cerebral cortex—the "new brain"—has areas that control voluntary movement (the motor area); the senses (the sensory area); and thinking, reasoning, speech, and memory (the association area). The limbic system, found on the border of the "old" and "new" brains, is associated with eating, reproduction, and the experiences of pleasure and pain.

How do the two halves of the brain operate interdependently?

12. The brain is divided into left and right halves, or hemispheres, each of which generally controls the opposite side of the body. Each hemisphere can be thought of as specialized in the functions it carries out: The left is best at verbal tasks, such as logical reasoning, speaking, and reading; the right is best at nonverbal tasks, such as spatial perception, pattern recognition, and emotional expression.

13. The endocrine system secretes hormones, allowing the brain to send messages throughout the nervous system via the bloodstream. A major component is the pituitary gland, which affects growth.

How can an understanding of the nervous system help us to find ways to relieve disease and pain?

14. Biofeedback is a procedure by which a person learns to control internal physiological processes. By controlling what were previously considered involuntary responses, people are able to relieve anxiety, tension, migraine headaches, and a wide range of other psychological and physical problems.

Key Terms and Concepts

biopsychologists (p. 46)
neurons (p. 47)
dendrites (p. 48)
axon (p. 48)
terminal buttons (p. 48)
myelin sheath (p. 48)
all-or-none law (p. 49)
resting state (p. 49)
action potential (p. 49)
synapse (p. 50)
neurotransmitters (p. 50)
excitatory message (p. 51)
inhibitory message (p. 51)
reuptake (p. 52)
central nervous system (CNS) (p. 56)

spinal cord (p. 56)
reflexes (p. 56)
sensory (afferent) neurons (p. 56)
motor (efferent) neurons (p. 56)
interneurons (p. 56)
peripheral nervous system (p. 56)
somatic division (p. 57)
autonomic division (p. 57)
sympathetic division (p. 57)
parasympathetic division (p. 57)
evolutionary psychology (p. 58)
behavioural genetics (p. 58)
central core (p. 61)
reticular formation (p. 62)
cerebellum (p. 63)

thalamus (p. 63)
hypothalamus (p. 63)
limbic system (p. 64)
cerebral cortex (p. 66)
lobes (p. 66)
motor area (p. 67)
sensory area (p. 69)
association areas (p. 70)
hemispheres (p. 73)
lateralization (p. 73)
split-brain patient (p. 76)
endocrine system (p. 77)
hormones (p. 77)
pituitary gland (p. 77)
biofeedback (p. 78)

Epilogue

This chapter has traced the ways in which biological structures and functions of the body affect behaviour. Starting with neurons, we considered each of the components of the nervous system, culminating in examining how our brain is able to permit us to think, reason, speak, recall, and experience emotions—the hallmarks of being human.

Before we proceed to the next chapter, where we put our knowledge of the biology of behaviour to use as we turn to sensation and perception, turn back for a moment to the prologue of this chapter, involving the strokes that had the potential to permanently disable or kill Lee Phillips and Peggy Code. Consider the following questions.

1. Using what you now know about brain structures and functioning, can you explain what might have produced these women's strokes in the first place?

2. Strokes often cause paralysis to only one side of the body, leaving the other side unaffected. Why do you think this might be?

3. The drug that treated Phillips's and Code's strokes, t-PA, dissolved the blood clot that had interrupted the blood flow within the brain. Speculate about other treatments that might be used to have a similar effect.

4. Some victims of stroke are able to regain the use of paralyzed limbs or regain lost speech through therapy. Considering what you know about the brain and nervous system, why might such therapy be successful? Would you expect that a younger or older stroke victim would experience greater treatment success?

Answers to Review Questions:

1. parietal, occipital   2. motor   3. true   4. False; it is divided according to the degree of sensitivity needed.   5. apraxia   6. False; they control opposite sides.   7. right; left

The inability to discern colours correctly—a failure of the visual sensory system—is likely to have contributed to this deadly train accident.

Prologue

Deadly Misperceptions

It was an accident that should never have happened. The equipment on the railroad train system was operating properly, and a lighted signal, indicating that the engineer should stop, glowed a bright red. If the engineer, John J. DeCurtis, had perceived it properly, the accident might well have been prevented.

Unfortunately, though, DeCurtis suffered from a colour deficiency, revealed by a routine physical some months earlier. Although he was able to distinguish pure reds, yellows, and greens, he was unable to recognize subtler tests of colour vision during the physical. For instance, he failed almost half the time to distinguish the number of coloured dots inside a circle.

Train systems use red, yellow, and green lights to signal when to stop, when to slow down, and when to speed up, and sometimes two or three lights are used simultaneously. A yellow light over a red light over another red light tells an engineer one thing; a change in configuration means something very different. Furthermore, unlike automotive traffic lights, train signal lights vary only slightly when they change, meaning that the location of the light is of little help in determining what is being signalled. Colour is of primary importance.

Although we can't know for sure, DeCurtis's colour deficiency, coupled with the fatigue he was likely to have experienced as a result of working a shift that already had lasted 14½ hours, may have proved a recipe for disaster. DeCurtis's train barrelled first past a yellow light, and then past a red light, and then into the path of another commuter train in Jersey City, New Jersey. DeCurtis was killed, along with a passenger and the engineer of the other train, and train traffic was disrupted on the busy commuter lines for days (Belluck & Alvarez, 1996; Pérez-Peña, 1996; Wald, 1997).

Fortunately, there are few instances where the inability to sense and perceive the world accurately has such deadly consequences. In fact, our ability to sense the stimuli in our environment typically is remarkable, enabling us to feel the gentlest of breezes, see flickering lights miles away, and hear the soft murmuring of distant songbirds.

In this chapter we focus on the field of psychology that is concerned with the nature of the information our body takes in through its senses and with the way we interpret such information. We will explore both **sensation,** the stimulation of the sense organs, and **perception,** the sorting out, interpretation, analysis, and integration of stimuli involving our sense organs and brain.

To a psychologist interested in understanding the causes of behaviour, sensation and perception are fundamental topics, since our behaviour is so much a reflection of how we react to and interpret stimuli from the world around us. Indeed, questions ranging from what processes enable us to see and hear, to how we know whether sugar or lemon is sweeter, to how we distinguish one person from another all fall into the realm of sensation and perception (Basic Behavioural Science Task Force, 1996).

Although perception clearly represents a step beyond sensation, in practice it is sometimes difficult to distinguish the precise boundary between the two. Indeed, psychologists—and philosophers, as well—have argued for years over the distinction. The primary difference is that sensation can be thought of as an organism's first encounter with a raw sensory stimulus, while perception is the process by which the stimulus is interpreted, analyzed, and integrated with other sensory information. If, for example, we were considering sensation, we might ask about the loudness of a ringing fire alarm. On the other hand, if we were considering perception, we might ask whether someone recognizes the ringing sound as an alarm and identifies its meaning.

The chapter begins with a discussion of the relationship between the characteristics of a physical stimulus and the kinds of sensory responses that it produces. We then examine several of the major senses, including vision, hearing, balance, smell, taste, and the skin senses, which include touch and the experience of pain.

Next, the chapter explains how we organize the stimuli to which our sense organs are exposed. For instance, we consider a number of issues relating to perception, such as how we are able to perceive the world in three dimensions when our eyes are capable only of sensing two-dimensional images. Finally, we examine visual illusions, which provide us with important clues for understanding general perceptual mechanisms. As we explore these issues, we'll see how the senses work together to provide us with an integrated view and understanding of the world.

sensation: The stimulation of the sense organs

perception: The sorting out, interpretation, analysis, and integration of stimuli involving our sense organs and brain

SENSING THE WORLD AROUND US

As she sat down to Thanksgiving dinner, Isabel reflected on how happy she was to be at her parents' home for the holiday. Exhausted from commuting between campus, her apartment, and her job, she was delighted to have someone else doing the cooking. She was especially sick of the tasteless lunches she bolted down at the campus cafeteria.

But these thoughts were soon interrupted when she saw her father carry the turkey in on a tray and place it squarely in the centre of the table. The noise level, already high from the talking and laughter of family members, grew louder still. As Isabel picked up her fork, the smell of the turkey reached her and she felt her stomach growl hungrily. The sight and sound of her family around the table, along with the smells and tastes of the holiday meal, made Isabel feel more relaxed than she had since starting school in the fall.

▶ **What is sensation and how do psychologists study it?**

▶ **What is the relationship between the nature of a physical stimulus and the kinds of sensory responses that result from it?**

Put yourself in this setting and consider how different it might be if any one of your senses was not functioning. What if you were blind and unable to see the faces of your family or the welcome shape of the succulent turkey? What if you had no sense of hearing and could not listen to the conversations of family members, or were unable to feel your stomach growl, or smell the dinner, or taste the food? Clearly, you would experience the dinner very differently from someone whose sensory apparatus was intact.

Moreover, the sensations mentioned above barely scratch the surface of sensory experience. Although most of us have been taught at one time or another that there are just five senses—sight, sound, taste, smell, and touch—this enumeration is too modest, since human sensory capabilities go well beyond the basic five senses. It is well established, for example, that we are sensitive not merely to touch, but to a considerably wider set of stimuli—pain, pressure, temperature, and vibration, to name a few. In addition, the ear is responsive to information that allows us not only to hear but to keep our balance as well. Psychologists now believe that there are at least a dozen distinct senses, all of which are interrelated.

To consider how psychologists understand the senses, and, more broadly, sensation and perception, we first need a basic working vocabulary. In formal terms, if any passing source of physical energy activates a sense organ, the energy is known as a stimulus. A **stimulus,** then, is energy that produces a response in a sense organ.

Stimuli vary in both type and intensity. Different types of stimuli activate different sense organs. For instance, we can differentiate light stimuli, which activate our sense of sight and allow us to see the colours of a tree in autumn, from sound stimuli, which, through our sense of hearing, permit us to hear the sounds of an orchestra.

Each sort of stimulus that is capable of activating a sense organ can also be considered in terms of its strength, or *intensity.* Questions such as how intense a light stimulus needs to be before it is capable of being detected or how much perfume a person must wear before it is noticed by others relate to stimulus intensity.

The issue of how the intensity of a stimulus influences our sensory responses is considered a branch of psychology known as psychophysics. **Psychophysics** is the study of the relationship between the physical nature of stimuli and the sensory responses that they evoke. Psychophysics played a central role in the development of the field of psychology. Many of the first psychologists studied issues related to psychophysics. It is easy to see why: Psychophysics bridges the physical world outside and the psychological world within (Geissler, Link, & Townsend, 1992; Baird, 1997; Gescheider, 1997).

Absolute Thresholds

Just when does a stimulus become strong enough to be detected by our sense organs? The answer to this question requires an understanding of the concept of absolute thresholds. An **absolute threshold** is the smallest intensity of a stimulus that must be present for it to be detected. Consider the following examples of absolute thresholds for the various senses (Galanter, 1962):

- Sight: A candle flame can be seen 48 kilometres away on a dark, clear night.

- Hearing: The ticking of a watch can be heard 6 metres away under quiet conditions.

- Taste: Sugar can be discerned when 1 teaspoon is dissolved in 9 litres of water.

- Smell: Perfume can be detected when one drop is present in a three-room apartment.

- Touch: A bee's wing falling from a distance of 1 centimetre can be felt on the cheek.

Such thresholds permit our sensory apparatus to detect a wide range of sensory stimulation. In fact, the capabilities of our senses are so fine-tuned that we might have problems if they were any more sensitive. For instance, if our ears were just slightly more acute, we would be able to hear the sound of air molecules in our ears knocking into our eardrum—a phenomenon that would surely prove distracting and might even prevent us from hearing sounds outside our bodies.

Of course, the absolute thresholds we have been discussing are measured under ideal conditions. Normally our senses cannot detect stimulation quite as well because of the presence of noise. *Noise,* as defined by psychophysicists, is background stimula-

---

stimulus: Energy that produces a response in a sense organ

psychophysics: The study of the relationship between the physical nature of stimuli and the sensory responses that they evoke

Psychophysics

absolute threshold: The smallest intensity of a stimulus that must be present for it to be detected

The sights, sounds, temperature, and crowded conditions all can be considered as noise *that interferes with sensation.*

tion that interferes with the perception of other stimuli. Hence, noise refers not just to auditory stimuli, the most obvious example, but also to stimuli that affect the other senses. Picture a talkative group of people crammed into a small, crowded, smoke-filled room at a party. The din of the crowd makes it hard to hear individual voices, and the smoke makes it difficult to see, or even taste, the food. In this case, the smoke and crowded conditions would be considered "noise," since they are preventing sensation at more discriminating levels.

Signal Detection Theory

Signal Detection

Will an impending storm strike? Is this aircraft unfit to fly? Is that plane intending to attack this ship? Is this nuclear power plant malfunctioning? Is this assembly-line item flawed? Does this patient have the acquired immunodeficiency syndrome (AIDS) virus? Is this person lying? Is this football player using drugs? Will this school (or job) applicant succeed? (Swets, 1992, p. 522.)

Questions such as these illustrate the range of decisions that people make. Yet for many of these questions, there is no black-and-white answer. Instead, the evidence in favour of or against a particular response is a matter of degree, making the response a question of judgment.

Several factors influence how we answer such questions. For instance, physicians who seek to identify the presence of a tumor in an X ray are influenced by their expectations, knowledge, and experience with patients. Clearly, then, the ability to detect and identify a stimulus is not just a function of the properties of the particular stimulus; it is also affected by psychological factors relating to the person making the judgment.

Signal detection theory explains the role of psychological factors in the judgement of whether a stimulus is present or absent (Green & Swets, 1989; Greig, 1990; Swets, 1992). An outgrowth of psychophysics, the theory acknowledges that observers attempting to detect a stimulus may err in one of two ways: in reporting that a stimulus is present when it is not, or in reporting that a stimulus is not present when it actually is. By applying statistical procedures, psychologists using signal detection theory are able to obtain an understanding of how different kinds of decisions—which may involve such factors as observer expectations and motivation—relate to judgments about sensory stimuli in various situations. Statistical methods also allow psychologists to increase the reliability of predictions about what conditions will cause observers to be most accurate in their judgments (Commons, Nevin, & Davison, 1991; Swets, 1996).

Such findings have immense practical importance, such as in the case of radar operators who are charged with identifying and distinguishing incoming enemy

signal detection theory: The theory that seeks to explain the role of psychological factors in the judgment of whether a stimulus is present or absent

missiles from the radar images of passing birds (Getty et al., 1988; Wickens, 1991). Another arena in which signal detection theory has practical implications is the judicial system (Buckhout, 1976). Witnesses who are asked to view a lineup find themselves in a classic signal detection situation, in which misidentification can have grave consequences for an individual (if an innocent person is incorrectly identified as a perpetrator) and for society (if an actual perpetrator is not detected). However, many witnesses have biases stemming from prior expectations about the socioeconomic status and race of criminals, attitudes toward the police and criminal justice system, and other viewpoints that impede accurate judgment. By using signal detection theory, psychologists have developed procedures that enhance people's chances of accurately identifying witnesses. For example, it is helpful to tell witnesses viewing a lineup that the prime suspect just might not be in the lineup at all. Moreover, justice is better served when the people in the lineup appear equally dissimilar from one another, which seems to reduce the likelihood that witnesses will guess.

Just Noticeable Differences

Suppose you wanted to choose the six best apples from a supermarket display—the biggest, reddest, and sweetest apples. One approach would be to systematically compare one apple with another until you were left with a few so similar that you could not tell the difference between them. At that point, it wouldn't matter which ones you chose.

difference threshold or **just noticeable difference:** The smallest detectable difference between two stimuli

Psychologists have discussed this comparison problem in terms of the **difference threshold,** the smallest detectable difference between two stimuli, also known as a **just noticeable difference.** They have found that the stimulus value that constitutes a just noticeable difference depends on the initial intensity of the stimulus. For instance, you may have noticed that the light change when you switch a three-way bulb from 75 to 100 watts appears greater than when you switch from 100 to 125 watts, even though the wattage increase is the same in both cases. Similarly, when the moon is visible during the late afternoon, it appears relatively dim—yet against a dark night sky, it seems quite bright.

Weber's law: One of the basic laws of psychophysics stating that a just noticeable difference is a constant proportion of the intensity of an initial stimulus

The relationship between changes in the original value of a stimulus and the degree to which the change will be noticed forms one of the basic laws of psychophysics: Weber's law. **Weber's law** (with "Weber" pronounced "vay-ber") states that a just noticeable difference is a constant proportion of the intensity of an initial stimulus. Therefore, if a 1-kilogram increase in a 10-kilogram weight produces a just noticeable difference, it would take a 10-kilogram increase to produce a noticeable difference if the initial weight were 100 kilograms. In both cases, the same proportional increase is necessary to produce a just noticeable difference—1:10 = 10:100. (Actually, Weber found the true proportional increase in weight that produces a just noticeable difference to be between 2 and 3 percent.) Similarly, the just noticeable difference distinguishing changes in loudness between sounds is larger for sounds that are initially loud than for sounds that are initially soft. This principle explains why a person in a quiet room is more apt to be startled by the ringing of a telephone than a person in a room that is already noisy. In order to produce the same amount of reaction in a noisy room, a telephone ring might have to approximate the loudness of cathedral bells.

Visual Illusions

Weber's law seems to hold up for all sensory stimuli, although its predictions are less accurate at extremely high or extremely low levels of stimulation (Sharpe et al., 1989; MacLeod & Willen, 1995). Moreover, the law helps explain psychological phenomena that lie beyond the realm of the senses. For example, imagine that you own a house you would like to sell for $150,000. You might be satisfied if you received an offer of $145,000 from a potential buyer, even though the offer is $5,000 less than the asking price. On the other hand, if you were selling your car and asking $10,000 for it, an offer of $5,000 less than your asking price would probably not make you happy. Although the absolute amount of money is the same in both cases, the psychological value of the $5,000 is very different.

Sensory Adaptation

As the circus strongman carries a group of five acrobats across the circus floor, some-one asks him if they aren't awfully heavy. He replies, "Not if you've just been carry-ing an elephant."

This story illustrates the phenomenon of **adaptation,** an adjustment in sensory capacity following prolonged exposure to stimuli. Adaptation occurs as people get used to a stimulus and change their frame of reference. Consequently, they do not re-spond to the stimulus in the way they did earlier.

One example of adaptation is the decrease in sensitivity that occurs after fre-quent exposure to a stimulus. If, for example, you were to repeatedly hear a loud tone, it would begin to sound softer after a while. This apparent decline in sensitivity to sen-sory stimuli is due to the inability of the sensory nerve receptors to constantly fire off messages to the brain. Because these receptor cells are most responsive to *changes* in stimulation, constant stimulation is not effective in producing a reaction.

Adaptation occurs with all the senses. For example, try to stare unblinkingly at the period at the end of this sentence. (You actually won't be able to do it very well be-cause of involuntary tiny movements of your eye.) But if you could stare long enough, the spot would eventually disappear as the visual neurons lost their ability to fire.

Judgments of sensory stimuli are also affected by the context in which the judg-ments are made. Carrying five acrobats seems insignificant to the strongman who has just carted an elephant around the circus floor. The reason is that judgments are made, not in isolation from other stimuli, but in terms of preceding sensory experience.

You can demonstrate this for yourself by trying a simple experiment. Take two envelopes, one large and one small, and put fifteen nickels in each. Now lift the large envelope, put it down, and lift the small one. Which seems to weigh more? Most peo-ple report that the small one is heavier, although, as you know, the weights are nearly identical. The reason for this misconception is that the physical context of the enve-lope interferes with the sensory experience of weight. Adaptation to the context of one stimulus (the size of the envelope) alters responses to another stimulus (the weight of the envelope) (Coren & Ward, 1989).

adaptation: An adjustment in sensory capacity following prolonged exposure to stimuli

---

Recap, Review, and Rethink

Recap

- Although people have traditionally thought in terms of five senses, psychologists studying sensation have found that there are considerably more.

- Sensation is the stimulation of the sense organs by a form of energy, known as a stimulus. Perception is the sorting out, interpretation, analysis, and integration of stimuli by our sense organs.

- Psychophysics studies the relationship between the physical nature of stimuli and the sensory responses that they evoke.

- An absolute threshold is the smallest amount of physical intensity that will permit a stimulus to be detected.

- Signal detection theory is used to predict the accuracy of sensory judgments.

- The difference threshold, or just noticeable difference, refers to the smallest detectable difference between two stimuli. According to Weber's law, a just noticeable difference is a constant proportion of the intensity of an initial stimulus.

- Sensory adaptation occurs when people are exposed to a stimulus for so long that they become used to it and therefore no longer respond to it.

Review

1. _____ is the stimulation of the sense organs; _____ is the sorting out, interpretation, analysis, and integration of stimuli by our sense organs.

2. The term absolute threshold refers to the largest amount of physical intensity of a stimulus that is detectable without being painful. True or false?

3. According to signal detection theory, in what two ways can people err in making judgments?

4. The proposition that a just noticeable difference is a constant proportion of the intensity of an initial stimulus is known as _____ law.

5. After completing a very difficult rock climb in the morning, Carmella found the afternoon climb unexpectedly easy. This case illustrates the phenomenon of _____.

Answers to Review Questions are on page 92.

Rethink

1. How are both sensation and perception involved in the "fight-or-flight" response to a startling but actually harmless stimulus, such as a loud noise or sudden movement in the dark?

2. Can you think of examples from medicine or another domain in which there is a debate regarding which type of signal detection error is most acceptable (i.e., believing a stimulus to be present when it is not, versus believing a stimulus to be absent when it is present)?

3. Why is sensory adaptation essential for everyday psychological functioning?

VISION: SHEDDING LIGHT ON THE EYE

▶ **What are the basic processes that underlie the sense of vision?**

▶ **How do we see colours?**

When shown a drawing of an asparagus spear and asked what it is, the young man replies, "A rose twig with thorns." Yet when asked to, he can dash off an easily recognizable drawing of asparagus.

When shown a hand-drawn map of his native England with his birthplace marked, he can't identify it—even though he himself drew the map from memory.

Stranger still, the young man can write a letter—but he can't read it. (Bishop, 1993, p. 1.)

Although the visual difficulties of C.K., as he is known in scientific literature, completely disrupted his life, the peculiar nature of his problem presented psychologists with an unusual opportunity to learn more about the operation of vision. C.K., a 33-year-old English immigrant to the United States, experienced brain damage as a result of an auto accident. In studying his condition, scientists discovered an unknown link between the eye and a particular area of the brain where images are stored (Behrmann, Winocur, & Moscovitch, 1992).

C.K.'s case exemplifies the enormous intricacies of vision. These complexities begin with the very stimulus that produces vision: light. Although we are all familiar with light, its underlying physical qualities are more complex than is apparent.

The stimuli that register as light in our eyes are actually electromagnetic radiation waves to which our bodies' visual apparatus happens to be sensitive and capable of responding. As you can see in Figure 3-1, electromagnetic radiation is measured in wavelengths. The size of each wavelength corresponds to different types of energy. The range of wavelengths that humans are sensitive to—called the *visual spectrum*—is actually relatively small. Many nonhuman species have different capabilities. For instance, some reptiles and fish see longer wavelengths than humans, while certain insects see shorter wavelengths than humans.

Light waves coming from some object outside the body (imagine the light reflected off the flower in Figure 3-2) first encounter the only organ that is capable of responding to the visual spectrum: the eye. Strangely enough, most of the eye is not involved with responding directly to light. Instead, its function is to shape the entering image into a form that can be used by the neurons that will serve as messengers to the brain. The neurons themselves take up a relatively small percentage of the total eye. In other words, most of the eye is a mechanical device, analogous in many respects to a camera without film, as you can see in Figure 3-2. At the same time, it is important to realize the limitations of this analogy. Vision involves processes that are far more

Visual Sensation and Perception

FIGURE 3-1 *The visual spectrum—the range of wavelengths to which people are sensitive— represents only a small part of the kinds of wavelengths present in our environment.*

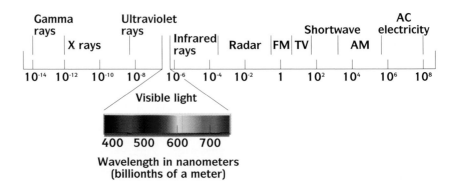

Wavelength in nanometers (billionths of a meter)

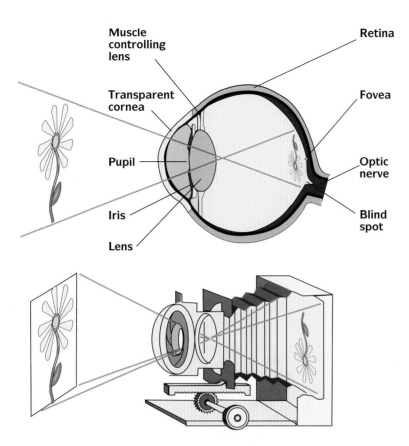

Muscle controlling lens

Transparent cornea

Pupil

Iris

Lens

Retina

Fovea

Optic nerve

Blind spot

FIGURE 3-2 *Although human vision is far more complicated than the most sophisticated camera, in some ways basic visual processes are analogous to those used in photography.*

complex and sophisticated than any camera is capable of mimicking. Once the image reaches the neuronal receptors of the eye, the analogy ends, for the processing of the visual image in the brain is more reflective of a computer than a camera.

Illuminating the Structure of the Eye

The ray of light we are tracing as it is reflected off the flower first travels through the *cornea,* a transparent, protective window that allows light to pass through. After moving through the cornea, the light traverses the pupil. The *pupil* is a dark hole in the centre of the *iris,* the coloured part of the eye, which ranges in humans from a light blue to a dark brown. The size of the pupil opening depends on the amount of light in the environment. The dimmer the surroundings, the more the pupil opens in order to allow more light to enter.

Why shouldn't the pupil be opened all the way all the time, thereby allowing the greatest amount of light into the eye? The answer has to do with the basic physics of light. A small pupil greatly increases the range of distances at which objects are in focus. With a wide-open pupil, the range is relatively small, and details are harder to discern. (Camera buffs experience a similar phenomenon in the aperture or f-stop setting that they must adjust on their cameras.) The eye takes advantage of bright light by decreasing the size of the pupil and thereby becoming more discerning. In dim light the pupil expands to enable us to view the situation better—but at the expense of visual detail. Perhaps one reason that candlelight dinners are often thought of as romantic is that the dimness of the light prevents one from seeing the details of a lover's flaws.

Once light passes through the pupil, it enters the *lens,* which is located directly behind the pupil. The lens acts to bend the rays of light so that they are properly focused on the rear of the eye. The lens focuses light by changing its own thickness, a process called *accommodation.* The kind of accommodation that occurs depends on the location of the object in relation to the viewer's body. Distant objects require a relatively flat lens. In this case, the muscles controlling the lens relax, allowing the lens

FIGURE 3-3 *The basic cells of the eye. Light entering the eye travels through the ganglion and bipolar cells and strikes the light-sensitive rods and cones located at the back of the eye. The rods and cones then transmit nerve impulses to the brain via the bipolar and ganglion cells.*

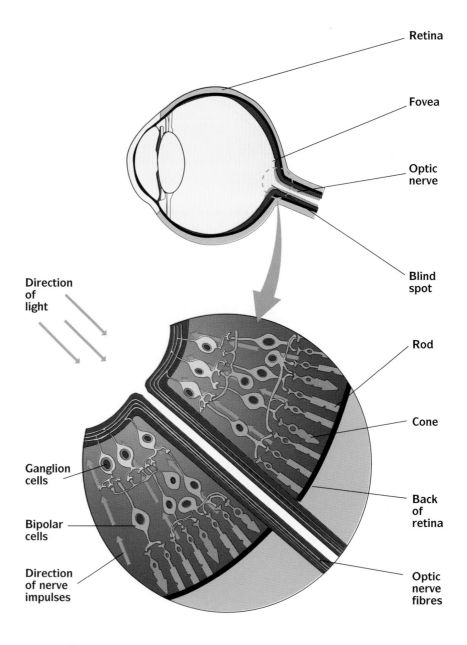

retina: The part of the eye that converts the electromagnetic energy of light into useful information for the brain

to flatten. In contrast, close objects are viewed best through a rounded lens. Here, then, the muscles contract, relieving tension and permitting the lens to become rounder.

Having travelled through the pupil and lens, our image of the flower finally reaches its ultimate destination in the eye—the **retina.** Here the electromagnetic energy of light is converted into messages that the brain can use. It is important to note that because of the physical properties of light, the image has reversed itself in travelling through the lens, and it reaches the retina upside down (relative to its original position). Although it might seem that this reversal would cause difficulties in understanding and moving about the world, this is not the case. The brain interprets the image in terms of its proper orientation.

The retina is actually a thin layer of nerve cells at the back of the eyeball (see Figure 3-3). There are two kinds of light-sensitive receptor cells found in the retina.

Answers to Review Questions:

1. Psychophysics   2. False; it is the smallest amount that is detectable.   3. A stimulus could be reported as present when it isn't, or it could be reported as absent when it is present.   4. Weber's   5. adaptation

The names they have been given describe their shapes: **rods,** which are long and cylindrical, and **cones,** which are short, thick, and tapered. The rods and cones are distributed unevenly throughout the retina. The greatest concentration of cones is on the part of the retina called the *fovea* (refer back to Figure 3-2). The fovea is a particularly sensitive region of the retina. If you want to focus in on something of particular interest, you will probably center the image from the lens onto the area of the fovea.

The density of cones declines just outside the fovea, although cones are found throughout the retina in lower concentrations. On the other hand, there are no rods in the very centre of the fovea, but the density is greatest outside the fovea and then gradually declines toward the edges of the retina. Because the fovea covers only a small portion of the eye, there are fewer cones (about 7 million) than there are rods (about 125 million).

The rods and cones are not only structurally dissimilar, but they play distinctly different roles in vision (Cohen & Lasley, 1986; Buser, Imbert, & Kay, 1992). Cones are primarily responsible for the sharply focused perception of colour, particularly in brightly lit situations, while rods are related to vision in dimly lit situations and are largely insensitive to colour and to details as sharp as those the cones are capable of recognizing. The rods play a key role in *peripheral vision*—seeing objects that are outside the main centre of focus—and in night vision. In both cases, the level of detail that can be discerned is far lower when the rods come into play than when the cones are activated, as you know from groping your way across a dark room at night. Although you may just dimly see the outlines of furniture, it is almost impossible to distinguish colour and the other details of obstacles in your path. You may also have noticed that you can improve your view of a dim star at night by looking slightly away from it. The reason? If you shift your gaze off-centre, the image from the lens falls not on the relatively night-blind cones of the fovea but on the more light-sensitive rods.

The distinctive abilities of rods and cones make the eye analogous to a camera that is loaded with two kinds of film. One type is a highly sensitive black-and-white film (the rods). The other type is a somewhat less sensitive colour film (the cones). Remember, too, that these two types of film are distributed in the eye in different arrangements.

Adaptation: From Light to Dark

Have you ever walked into a movie theatre on a bright, sunny day and stumbled into your seat, barely able to see at all? Do you also recall later getting up to buy popcorn and having no trouble navigating your way up the aisle?

Your ability to see relatively well after you've been in the theatre for a while is due to **dark adaptation,** a heightened sensitivity to light that results from being in relative dimness. The speed at which dark adaptation occurs is a result of the rate of change in the chemical composition of the rods and cones. The changes occur at different speeds for the two kinds of cells, with the cones reaching their greatest level of adaptation in just a few minutes, but the rods taking close to thirty minutes to reach the maximum level. On the other hand, the cones never reach the level of sensitivity to light that the rods attain. When rods and cones are considered jointly, though, dark adaptation is complete in a darkened room in about half an hour (Tamura, Nakatani, & Yau, 1989; Peachey et al., 1992).

Sending the Message from the Eye to the Brain

When light energy strikes the rods and cones, it starts the first in a chain of events that transforms light into neural impulses that can be communicated to the brain. Before the neural message reaches the brain, however, some initial alteration of the visual information takes place.

What happens when light energy strikes the retina depends in part on whether it encounters a rod or a cone. Rods contain *rhodopsin,* a complex, reddish-purple substance whose composition changes chemically when energized by light and thereby

rods: Long, cylindrical, light-sensitive receptors in the retina that perform well in poor light but are largely insensitive to colour and small details

cones: Cone-shaped, light-sensitive receptor cells in the retina that are responsible for sharp focus and colour perception, particularly in bright light

dark adaptation: A heightened sensitivity to light that results from being in relative dimness

FIGURE 3-4 *To find your blind spot, close your right eye and look at the haunted house with your left eye. You will see the ghost on the periphery of your vision. Now, while staring at the house, move the page toward you. When the book is about 30 centimetres from your eye, the ghost will disappear. At this moment, the image of the ghost is falling on your blind spot.*

But also notice how, when the page is at that distance, not only does the ghost seem to disappear, but the line seems to run continuously through the area where the ghost used to be. This shows how we automatically compensate for missing information by using nearby material to complete what is unseen. That's the reason you never notice the blind spot. What is missing is replaced by what is seen next to the blind spot.

optic nerve: A bundle of ganglion axons that carry visual information

Vision

sets off a reaction. The substance found in cone receptors is different, but the principles are similar. Stimulation of the nerve cells in the eye triggers a neural response that is transmitted to other nerve cells, called *bipolar cells* and *ganglion cells,* leading to the brain.

Bipolar cells receive information directly from the rods and cones. This information is then communicated to the ganglion cells. Ganglion cells collect and summarize visual information, which is gathered and moved out of the back of the eyeball through a bundle of ganglion axons called the **optic nerve** (Tessier-Lavigne, 1991; Yang & Masland, 1992).

Because the opening for the optic nerve pushes through the retina, there are no rods or cones in the area, which creates a blind spot. Normally, however, this absence of nerve cells does not interfere with vision, because you automatically compensate for the missing part of your field of vision (O'Regan, 1992; Ramachandran, 1992, 1995; Durgin, Tripathy, & Levi, 1995; Churchland & Ramachandran, 1995). (To find your blind spot, see Figure 3-4.)

Once beyond the eye itself, the neural signals relating to the image move through the optic nerve. As the optic nerve leaves the eyeball, its path does not take the most direct route to the part of the brain right behind the eye. Instead, the optic nerves from each eye meet at a point roughly between the two eyes—called the *optic chiasm*—where each optic nerve then splits.

When the optic nerves split, the nerve impulses coming from the right half of each retina are sent to the right side of the brain, and the impulses arriving from the left half of each retina are sent to the left side of the brain. Because the image on the retinas is reversed and upside down, however, those images coming from the right half of each retina actually originated in the field of vision to the person's left, and images coming from the left half of each retina originated in the field of vision to the person's right (see Figure 3-5). In this way, our nervous system ultimately produces the phenomenon introduced in Chapter 2, in which each half of the brain is associated with the functioning of the opposite side of the body.

One of the most frequent causes of blindness is a restriction of the impulses across the optic nerve. *Glaucoma,* which strikes between 1 and 2 percent of those over age 40, occurs when pressure in the fluid of the eye begins to build up, either because it cannot be properly drained or because too much of it is produced. When this first begins to happen, the nerve cells that communicate information about peripheral vision are constricted, leading to a decline in the ability to see anything outside a narrow circle directly ahead. This is called *tunnel vision.* Eventually, the pressure can become so great that all the nerve cells are contracted, leading to total blindness. Fortunately, if detected early enough, glaucoma is highly treatable, either through medication that reduces the pressure in the eye or through surgery.

Processing the Visual Message

By the time a visual message reaches the brain, it has passed through several stages of processing. One of the initial sites is the ganglion cells (Yang & Masland, 1992). Each

Left visual field | Right visual field

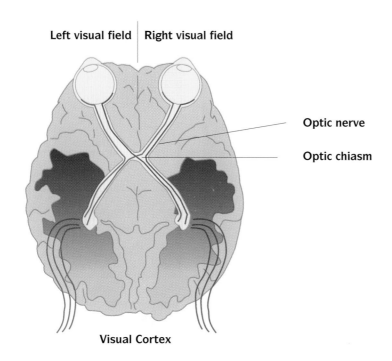

Optic nerve

Optic chiasm

Visual Cortex

FIGURE 3-5 *Because the optic nerve coming from each eye splits at the optic chiasm, the image to a person's right is sent to the left side of the brain, and the image to the person's left is transmitted to the right side of the brain.*

ganglion cell gathers information from a group of rods and cones in a particular area of the eye, and compares the amount of light entering the centre of that area with the amount of light in the area around it. In some cases, ganglion cells are activated by light in the centre (and darkness in the surrounding area). In other cases, the opposite is true, with some ganglion cells activated when there is darkness in the centre and light in the surrounding areas. The ultimate effect of this process is to maximize the detection of variations in light and darkness. The neural image that is passed on to the brain, then, is an enhanced version of the actual visual stimulus outside the body.

The ultimate processing of visual images takes place in the visual cortex of the brain, of course, and it is here that the most complex kinds of processing occur (Hurlbert & Poggio, 1988; DeAngelis, Ohzawa, & Freeman, 1995; Sajda & Finkel, 1995). Canadian psychologist David Hubel and Swedish psychologist Torsten Wiesel won the Nobel Prize for their discovery that many neurons in the cortex are extraordinarily specialized, being activated only by visual stimuli of a particular shape or pattern—a process known as **feature detection.** They found that some cells are activated only by lines of a particular width, shape, or orientation. Other cells are activated only by moving, as opposed to stationary, stimuli (Hubel & Wiesel, 1979; Gallant, Braun, & VanEssen, 1993; Patzwahl, Zanker, & Altenmuller, 1994).

feature detection: The activation of neurons in the cortex by visual stimuli of specific shapes or patterns

More recent work has added to our knowledge of the complex ways in which visual information coming from individual neurons is combined and processed (Milner and Goodale, 1995). Different parts of the brain seem to process nerve impulses in several individual systems simultaneously. For instance, one system relates to shapes, one to colours, and others to movement, location, and depth (Moutoussis & Zeki, 1997).

If separate neural systems exist for the processing of information about specific aspects of the visual world, how are all these data integrated by the brain? Although the exact process is not yet well understood, it seems likely that the brain makes use of information regarding the frequency, rhythm, and timing of the firing of particular sets of neural cells (Ferster & Spurston, 1995). Furthermore, it appears that the brain's integration does not occur in any single step or location in the brain. Instead, integration of visual information is a process that seems to occur on several levels simultaneously (Zeki, 1992; Maunsell, 1995; Schechter, 1996; Moutoussis & Zeki, 1997). The ultimate outcome, though, is indisputable: a vision of the world around us.

FIGURE 3-6 *This is how these hot-air balloons appear, as shown in (a), to someone with normal vision. (b) A person with red-green colour blindness would see the scene like this, in hues of blue and yellow. (c) A person who is blue-yellow blind, conversely, would see it in hues of red and green. (d) To a monochromate, or person with total colour blindness, it would look like this. Source: Joe Epstein/Design Conceptions.*

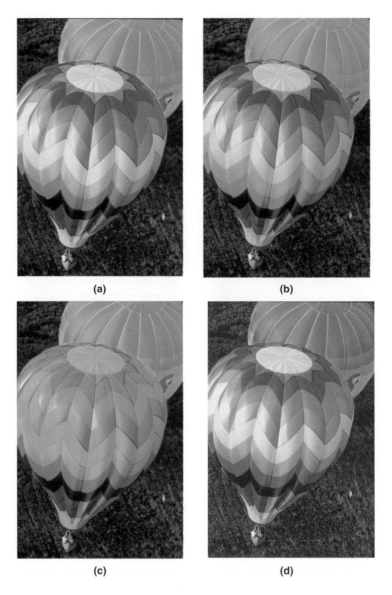

(a)   (b)

(c)   (d)

Colour Blindness

Colour Vision and Colour Blindness: The 7-Million-Colour Spectrum

Although the range of wavelengths to which humans are sensitive is relatively narrow, at least in comparison with the entire electromagnetic spectrum, the portion to which we are capable of responding still allows us great flexibility in sensing the world. Nowhere is this clearer than in terms of the number of colours we can discern. A person with normal colour vision is capable of distinguishing no less than 7 million different colours (Bruce, Green, & Georgeson, 1997).

Although the variety of colours that people are generally able to distinguish is vast, there are certain individuals whose ability to perceive colour is quite limited—the colour-blind. Interestingly, the condition of these individuals has provided some of the most important clues for understanding how colour vision operates (Nathans et al., 1986; Nathans et al., 1989; Shepard & Cooper, 1992; Cowey & Heywood, 1995; Neitz, Neitz, & Kainz, 1996).

Before continuing, though, look at the photos shown in Figure 3-6. If you cannot see any difference in the series of photos, you probably are one of the few people, 1 in 300,000, (Coren, Ward and Enns, 1999) who are completely colour blind.

For most people who are colour blind, the world looks quite dull. Red fire engines appear yellow, green grass seems yellow, and the three colours of a traffic light all look yellow. In fact, in the most common form of colour blindness, all red and green objects

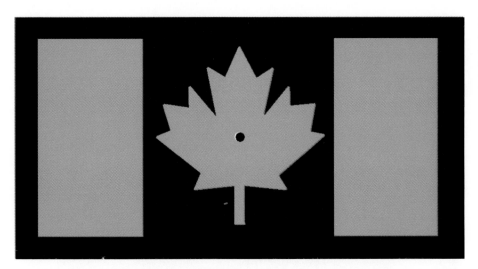

FIGURE 3-7 *If you stare at the dot in this flag for about a minute and then look at the white space below, the afterimage phenomenon will make a traditional red and white flag appear.*

are seen as yellow. There are other forms of colour blindness as well, but they are quite rare. In yellow-blue blindness, people are unable to tell the difference between yellow and blue, and in the most extreme case an individual perceives no colour at all. To such a person the world looks something like the picture on a black-and-white television set.

To understand why some of us are colour blind, it is necessary to consider the basics of colour vision. There appear to be two processes involved. The first process is explained by the **trichromatic theory of colour vision.** The theory suggests that there are three kinds of cones in the retina, each of which responds primarily to a specific range of wavelengths. One is most responsive to blue-violet colours, one to green, and the third to yellow-red (Brown & Wald, 1964). According to trichromatic theory, perception of colour is influenced by the relative strength with which each of the three kinds of cones is activated. If, for instance, we see a blue sky, the blue-violet cones are primarily triggered, while the others show less activity. The trichromatic theory provides a straightforward explanation of colour blindness. It suggests that one of the three cone systems malfunctions, and colours covered by that range are perceived improperly (Nathans et al., 1989).

However, there are phenomena that the trichromatic theory is less successful at explaining. For instance, it cannot account for why pairs of colours can combine to form gray. The theory also does not explain what happens after you stare at something like the flag shown in Figure 3-7 for about a minute. Try this yourself, and then move

trichromatic theory of colour vision: The theory suggesting that there are three kinds of cones in the retina, each of which responds primarily to a specific range of wavelengths

pplying Psychology in the 21st Century

Bringing Sight—Through Sound—to Blind People

Guided by satellites hundreds of miles above, a blind person listens to a synthesized voice produced in a set of stereo earphones. By listening to the directions transmitted through the earphones, the person navigates through a crowded college campus, avoiding obstacles and following an intricate route.

Although it almost sounds like science fiction, the equipment that permitted this blind individual to manoeuvre through his environment exists today, and it may even become commonplace in the not-too-distant future. Sensory perception psychologists Roberta Klatzky and Jack Loomis at the University of California–Santa Barbara are developing what they call a "personal guidance system" to help people with vision limitations to move through their environment (McIntosh, 1994).

The system uses a positioning device that is linked to navigation satellites overhead that are able to map the ground with an accuracy of several feet. Geographic information from the satellites is transmitted to an on-ground receiver and computer weighing 13 kilograms, which is strapped to a person's back. The computer translates the geographic information into acoustic stimulation that is sent to one earphone or the other. The stimulation, which for now is just a code word, becomes softer or louder, depending on the direction the person is supposed to turn. The blind person turns in the direction of the sound, or continues forward if no sound is heard.

Although for the present the computer generates only a single code word, Klatzky and Loomis predict that future versions will provide complete verbal directions, such as "go forward ten feet, and then turn to the right." In addition, the computer will identify landmarks that a person is passing by ("I'm the post office, and I'm 20 feet to your left"). Furthermore, the size of the backpack should shrink significantly, perhaps fitting into a pack around the waist.

The new navigation system is based on basic research on *dead reckoning,* the ability to identify one's position in space accurately. For instance, researchers examined the ways in which both sighted and blind people could use their sense of motion and direction to carry out simple tasks such as returning to a starting point after following

A personal guidance system permits people with blindness to locate where they are at a given moment.

a triangular path while blindfolded. They found that people were reasonably good at the task, although there was a fair amount of error for some individuals. More significantly, the research found that even people who had been blind from an early age were able to do the task about as well as blindfolded, sighted people—suggesting that a system that provided cues about where a person was at a given moment might in fact be effective (Klatzky et al., 1995).

This earlier work led to the idea that a "virtual acoustic display" could be developed. The blind person would experience the virtual display as a mental image of objects and buildings in the current surroundings. The task is difficult, involving such intricacies as the production of simulated echoes to produce a more accurate virtual image of the environment.

Kaltzky and her colleagues expect that it will be another five to ten years before personal guidance systems become available for use by the general public. In fact, she says, "We don't really foresee the personal guidance system being ready to buy off the shelf at K-Mart for a long time."

Other teams of researchers are investigating additional techniques for bringing sight to blind people. For example, some psychologists are considering ways that implants into the optic nerve or the visual cortex of the brain could deliver electrical signals from cameras, potentially permitting blind persons to achieve some degree of vision. Researchers suggest that such systems could be tested within the next few years, and that they may become available to the public in the twenty-first century (McIntosh, 1994; Leutwyler, 1994).

your eyes to the white space below. You will see an image of the traditional red and white Canadian flag. Where there was green, you'll see red, and where there was black, you'll see white.

The phenomenon you have just experienced is called an *afterimage*. It occurs because activity in the retina continues even when you are no longer staring at the original picture. However, it also demonstrates that the trichromatic theory does not explain colour vision completely. Why should the colours in the afterimage be different from those in the original?

Because trichromatic processes do not provide a full explanation of colour vision, vision researchers have developed an alternative explanation. According to the **opponent-process theory of colour vision,** receptor cells are linked in pairs, working in opposition to each other. Specifically, there is a blue-yellow pairing, a red-green pairing, and a black-white pairing. If an object reflects light that contains more blue than yellow, it will stimulate the firing of the cells sensitive to blue, simultaneously discouraging or inhibiting the firing of receptor cells sensitive to yellow—and the object will appear blue. If, on the other hand, a light contains more yellow than blue, the cells that respond to yellow will be stimulated to fire while the blue ones are inhibited, and the object will appear yellow.

The opponent-process theory allows us to explain afterimages very directly. When we stare at the green in the figure, for instance, our receptor cells for the green component of the green-red pairing become fatigued and are less able to respond to green stimuli. On the other hand, the receptor cells for the red part of the pair are not tired, since they are not being stimulated. When we look at a white surface, the light reflected off it would normally stimulate both the green and the red receptors equally. But the fatigue of the green receptors prevents this from happening. They temporarily do not respond to the green, which makes the white light appear to be red. Because the black in the figure does the same thing relative to its specific opponents, while, the afterimage produces the opponent colours—for a while. The afterimage lasts only a short time, since the fatigue of the green receptors is soon overcome, and the white light begins to be perceived more accurately.

It is now clear then that both opponent processes and trichromatic mechanisms are at work in allowing us to see colour. However, they operate in different parts of the visual sensing system. Trichromatic processes work within the retina itself, while opponent mechanisms operate both in the retina and at later stages of neuronal processing (Leibovic, 1990; Gouras, 1991; de Valois & de Valois, 1993).

As our understanding of the processes that permit us to see has increased, some psychologists have begun to develop new techniques to help those with serious vision problems—visually impaired and completely blind people—to overcome their deficiencies. One of the most promising devices is discussed in the Applying Psychology in the 21st Century box.

opponent-process theory of colour vision: The theory that suggests receptor cells are linked in pairs, working in opposition to each other

Recap, Review, and Rethink

Recap

- The eyes are sensitive to electromagnetic radiation waves of certain wavelengths. These waves register as the sensation of light.

- As light enters the eye, it passes through the cornea, pupil, and lens and ultimately reaches the retina, where the electromagnetic energy of light is converted into nerve impulses usable by the brain. These impulses leave the eye via the optic nerve.

- The retina is composed of nerve cells called rods and cones, which play different roles in vision and are responsible for dark adaptation.

- Humans are able to distinguish about 7 million colours. Colour vision involves two processes: trichromatic mechanisms and an opponent-processing system.

Review

1. Light entering the eye first passes through the _____, a protective window.

2. The structure that converts light into usable neural messages is called the _____.

3. Light is focused on the rear of the eye by the iris. True or false?

4. A woman with blue eyes could be described as having blue pigment in her _____.

5. What is the process by which the thickness of the lens is changed in order to focus light properly?

6. The proper sequence of structures that light passes through in the eye is the _____, _____, _____, and _____.

7. Match each type of visual receptor with its function.

   a. rods
   b. cones
   1. used for dim light, largely insensitive to colour
   2. detect colour, good in bright light

8. Paco was to meet his girlfriend in the movie theatre. As was typical, he was late and the movie had begun. He stumbled down the aisle, barely able to see. Unfortunately, the woman he sat down beside and attempted to put his arm around was not his girlfriend. He sorely wished he had given his eyes a chance and waited for _____ adaptation to occur.

9. _____ theory states that there are three types of cones in the retina, each of which responds primarily to a different colour.

Answers to Review Questions are on page 102.

Rethink

1. Why might C.K., the brain-damaged man described at the beginning of this section, be able to write and draw, but be unable to read what he wrote or identify what he drew? Is this a problem with sensation or perception? What part of the overall visual system is probably damaged?

2. Why do you think the eye uses two distinct types of receptor cells called rods and cones? Why would the eye evolve so that the rods, which we rely on in low light, do not provide sharp images? Are there any advantages to this system?

3. If the eye were constructed with a second lens that "unreversed" the image hitting the retina, what changes would you expect to observe in the perception and processing of visual information? Would the hemispheres of the brain function differently?

HEARING AND THE OTHER SENSES

▶ **What role does the ear play in the senses of sound, motion, and balance?**

▶ **How do smell and taste function?**

▶ **What are the skin senses, and how do they relate to the experience of pain?**

The blast-off was easy compared with what the astronaut was experiencing now: space sickness. The constant nausea and vomiting were enough to make him wonder why he had worked so hard to become an astronaut. Even though he had been warned that there was a two-thirds chance that his first experience in space would cause these symptoms, he wasn't prepared for how terribly sick he really felt.

Whether or not our fictional astronaut turns his rocket around and heads back to earth, his experience, a major problem for space travellers, is related to a basic sensory process centred in the ear: the sense of motion and balance. This sense allows people to navigate their bodies through the world and maintain an upright position without falling. Along with hearing, the process by which sound waves are translated into understandable and meaningful forms, the senses of motion and balance represent the major functions of the ear.

Sensing Sound

Although many of us think primarily of the *outer ear* when we consider hearing, this part functions simply as a reverse megaphone, designed to collect and bring sounds into the internal portions of the ear, (see Figure 3-8). However, the location of the outer ears on different sides of the head helps with *sound localization,* the process by which we identify the origin of a sound. Wave patterns in the air enter each ear at a slightly different time, permitting the brain to use the discrepancy to locate the place from which the sound is originating. In addition, the two outer ears delay or amplify sounds of particular frequencies to different degrees (Middlebrooks & Green, 1991; Yost, 1992; Konishi, 1993).

sound: The movement of air molecules brought about by the vibration of an object

eardrum: The part of the ear that vibrates when sound waves hit it

Sound is the movement of air molecules brought about by the vibration of an object. Sounds travel through the air in wave patterns similar in shape to those made by a stone thrown into a still pond. Sounds, arriving at the outer ear in the form of wave vibrations, are funnelled into the *auditory canal,* a tubelike passage that leads to the eardrum. The **eardrum** is aptly named because it operates like a miniature drum, vibrating when sound waves hit it. The more intense the sound, the more the eardrum

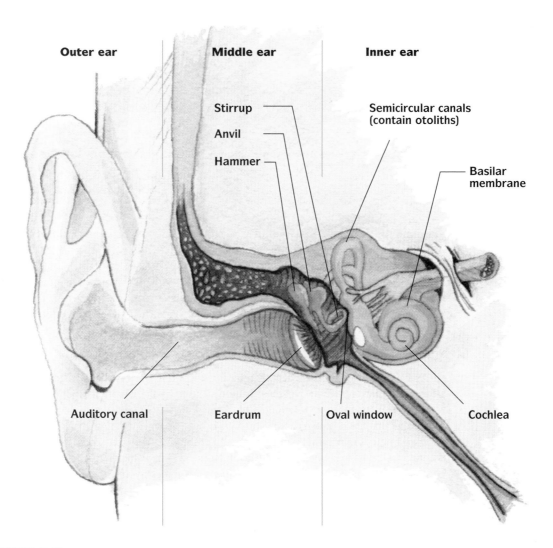

FIGURE 3-8 *The ear.*

vibrates. These vibrations are then transmitted into the *middle ear,* a tiny chamber containing just three bones called, because of their shapes, the *hammer,* the *anvil,* and the *stirrup.* These bones have one function: to transmit vibrations to the *oval window,* a thin membrane leading to the inner ear. Because of their shape, the hammer, anvil, and stirrup do a particularly effective job. Because they act as a set of levers, they not only transmit vibrations but actually increase their strength. Moreover, since the opening into the middle ear (the eardrum) is considerably larger than the opening out of it (the oval window), the force of sound waves on the oval window becomes amplified. The middle ear, then, acts as a tiny mechanical amplifier, making us aware of sounds that would otherwise go unnoticed.

The *inner ear* is the portion of the ear that changes the sound vibrations into a form that allows them to be transmitted to the brain. It also contains the organs that allow us to locate our position and determine how we are moving through space. When sound enters the inner ear through the oval window, it moves into the **cochlea,** a coiled tube filled with fluid that looks something like a snail. Inside the cochlea is the **basilar membrane,** a structure that runs through the centre of the cochlea, dividing it into an upper and a lower chamber (see Figure 3-8). The basilar membrane is covered with **hair cells.** When these hair cells are bent by the vibrations entering the cochlea, a neural message is transmitted to the brain.

Although sound typically enters the cochlea via the oval window, there is an additional method of entry: bone conduction. Because the ear rests on a maze of bones

cochlea (KOKE lee uh): A coiled tube filled with fluid that receives sound via the oval window or through bone conduction

basilar membrane: A structure that runs through the centre of the cochlea, dividing it into an upper and a lower chamber

hair cells: Tiny cells covering the basilar membrane that, when bent by vibrations entering the cochlea, transmit neural messages to the brain

FIGURE 3-9 *The waves produced by different stimuli are transmitted—usually through the air—in different patterns, with lower frequencies indicated by fewer peaks and valleys per second.*

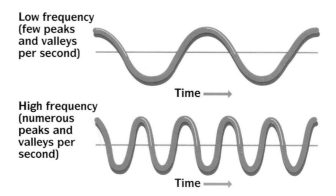

within the skull, the cochlea is able to pick up subtle vibrations that travel across the bones from other parts of the head (Lenhardt et al., 1991; Carlsson, Hakansson, & Ringdahl, 1995). For instance, one of the ways you hear your own voice is through bone conduction. This explains why you sound different to yourself than to other people who hear your voice. (Listen to yourself on a tape recorder sometime to hear what you *really* sound like!) The sound of your voice reaches you both through the air and via bone conduction and therefore sounds richer to you than to everyone else.

The Physical Aspects of Sound

As we mentioned earlier, what we refer to as sound is actually the physical movement of air molecules in regular, wavelike patterns caused by the vibration of an object (see Figure 3-9). Sometimes it is even possible to view these vibrations, as in the case of a stereo speaker that has no enclosure. If you have ever seen one, you know that, at least when the lowest notes are playing, you can see the speaker moving in and out. What is less obvious is what happens next: The speaker pushes air molecules into waves with the same pattern as its movement. These wave patterns soon reach your ear, although their strength has been weakened considerably during their travels. All other stimuli that produce sound work in essentially the same fashion, setting off wave patterns that move through the air to the ear. Air—or some other medium, such as water—is necessary to make the vibrations of objects reach us. This explains why there can be no sound in a vacuum.

Auditory Perception

We are able to see the stereo speaker moving when low notes are played because of a primary characteristic of sound called frequency. *Frequency* is the number of wave crests that occur in a second. With very low frequencies there are relatively few, and therefore slower, up-and-down wave cycles per second. These are visible to the naked eye as vibrations in the speaker. Low frequencies are translated into a sound that is very low in pitch. (*Pitch* is the characteristic that makes sound "high" or "low.") For example, the lowest frequency that humans are capable of hearing is 20 cycles per second. Higher frequencies translate into higher pitch. At the upper end of the sound spectrum, people can detect sounds with frequencies as high as 20,000 cycles per second (Coren, Ward and Enns, 1999).

While sound frequency allows us to enjoy the sounds of the high notes of a piccolo and the bass notes of a tuba, *intensity* is a feature of wave patterns that allows us to distinguish between loud and soft sounds. Intensity refers to the difference between the peaks and valleys of air pressure in a sound wave as it travels through the air. Waves with small peaks and valleys produce soft sounds, while those that are relatively large produce loud sounds.

We are sensitive to a broad range of sound intensity. The loudest sounds we are capable of hearing are about 10 million times as intense as the very weakest sound we can hear. This range is measured in *decibels,* which can be used to place everyday

---

Answers to Review Questions:

1. cornea   2. retina   3. False; it is focused by the lens.   4. iris   5. accommodation   6. cornea, pupil, lens, retina   7. 1-a; 2-b
8. dark   9. Trichromatic

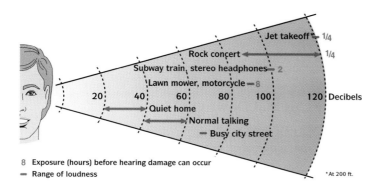

FIGURE 3-10 *Illustrations of decibel levels (sound intensity). The higher the decibel level, the less time it takes for permanent ear damage to occur. Source: Deafness Research Foundation; National Institute on Deafness and Other Communication Disorders.*

sounds along a continuum (see Figure 3-10). When sounds get higher than 120 decibels, they become painful to the human ear. Exposure to such high levels can eventually result in hearing loss, as the hair cells of the basilar membrane lose their elasticity and bend and flatten. Such a loss of hearing is often permanent, although recent findings have shown that hair cells have the potential to repair themselves following damage (Travis, 1992).

Sorting Out Theories of Sound

How are our brains able to sort out wavelengths of different frequencies and intensities? One clue comes from studies of the basilar membrane, the area within the cochlea that translates physical vibrations into neural impulses. It turns out that sounds affect different areas of the basilar membrane, depending on the frequency of the sound wave. The part of the basilar membrane nearest the oval window is most sensitive to high-frequency sounds, while the part nearest the cochlea's inner end is most sensitive to low-frequency sounds. This finding has led to the **place theory of hearing,** which says that different areas of the basilar membrane respond to different frequencies.

On the other hand, place theory does not tell the full story of hearing, since very low frequency sounds trigger neurons across such a wide area of the basilar membrane that no single site is involved. Consequently, an additional explanation for hearing has been proposed: frequency theory. The **frequency theory of hearing** suggests that the entire basilar membrane acts like a microphone, vibrating as a whole in response to a sound. According to this explanation, the nerve receptors send out signals that are tied directly to the frequency (the number of wave crests per second) of the sounds to which we are exposed, with the number of nerve impulses being a direct function of the sound's frequency. Thus, the higher the pitch of a sound (and therefore the greater the frequency of its wave crests), the greater the number of nerve impulses that are transmitted up the auditory nerve to the brain.

According to most contemporary research, both place theory and frequency theory explain at least some of the processes involved in hearing, but neither explanation alone provides the full story (Levine & Shefner, 1991; Hartmann, 1993; Luce, 1993; Hirsh & Watson, 1996). Specifically, place theory provides a better explanation for the sensing of high-frequency sounds, whereas frequency theory explains what happens when low-frequency sounds are encountered. Medium-frequency sounds appear to incorporate both processes.

After an auditory message leaves the ear, it is transmitted to the auditory cortex of the brain through a complex series of neural interconnections. As the message is transmitted, it is communicated through neurons that respond to specific types of sounds. Within the auditory cortex itself, there are neurons that respond selectively to very specific sorts of sound features, such as clicks or whistles. Some neurons respond only to a specific pattern of sounds, such as a steady tone but not an intermittent one. Furthermore, specific neurons transfer information about a sound's location through their particular pattern of firing (Ahissar et al., 1992; Middlebrooks et al., 1994).

place theory of hearing: The theory suggesting that different areas of the basilar membrane respond to different frequencies

frequency theory of hearing: The theory suggesting that the entire basilar membrane acts like a microphone, vibrating as a whole in response to a sound

If we were to analyze the configuration of the cells in the auditory cortex, we would find that neighboring cells are responsive to similar frequencies. The auditory cortex, then, provides us with a "map" of sound frequencies, just as the visual cortex furnishes a representation of the visual field.

Balance: The Ups and Downs of Life

Nick Esasky had just signed a $5.7 million baseball contract with the Atlanta Braves when he began to run into trouble. In his words:

> I felt great about playing in Atlanta, and I was in the best shape of my whole career. But about a week and a half into spring training, things started falling apart. Suddenly I began feeling weak and tired all the time. At first, I thought it was the flu and that it would go away. Then I began to get headaches and nausea, and I felt light-headed and dizzy. Soon it began to affect the way I was playing. At times it was hard for me to follow the ball. It looked hazy, as if it had a glow. I'd catch some off the end of my glove and miss others completely. Other times, a ball would land in my glove and I'd have no idea how it got there (Esasky, 1991, p. 62).

Esasky's problem would not go away, leading to a round of visits to specialists. Finally, after a variety of misdiagnoses, one doctor identified the source of Esasky's difficulty: his ear. Esasky was suffering from *vertigo,* a disorder of the inner ear resulting from a viral infection or head injury. He underwent a gruelling program to bolster his sense of vision and the sense of touch in the soles of his feet, both of which can help compensate for his inner ear problems.

Several structures of the ear are related more to our sense of balance than to our hearing (J. P. Kelly, 1991). The **semicircular canals** of the inner ear consist of three tubes containing fluid that sloshes through them when the head moves, signaling rotational or angular movement to the brain. The pull on our bodies caused by the acceleration of forward, backward, or up-and-down motion, as well as the constant pull of gravity, is sensed by the **otoliths,** tiny, motion-sensitive crystals within the semicircular canals. When we move, these crystals shift like sands on a windy beach. The brain's inexperience in interpreting messages from the weightless otoliths is the cause of the space sickness commonly experienced by two-thirds of all space travelers (Flam, 1991; Weiss, 1992; Clarke, Teiwes, & Scherer, 1993; Mittelstaedt & Glasauer, 1993; Stern & Koch, 1996).

semicircular canals: Structures of the inner ear consisting of three tubes containing fluid that sloshes through them when the head moves, signalling rotational or angular movement to the brain

otoliths: Tiny, motion-sensitive crystals within the semicircular canals that sense body acceleration

Smell and Taste

When Audrey Warner returned home after a day's work, she knew that something was wrong the moment she opened her apartment door. A smell indicative of gas—a strong, sickening odor that immediately made her feel weak—permeated the apartment. She ran to the pay phone across the street and called the gas company. As she was explaining what she smelled, Warner heard a muffled explosion and then saw flames begin to shoot out of her apartment window. Her life had been saved by her ability to smell the gas.

Smell

While there are few instances in which the sense of smell provides such drama, it is clear that our lives would be considerably less interesting if we could not smell freshly mowed hay, sniff a bouquet of flowers, or enjoy the aroma of an apple pie baking. Although many animals have keener abilities to detect odours than we do, since a greater proportion of their brains is devoted to the sense of smell than ours, we are still able to detect more than 10,000 separate smells. We also remember smells, and long-forgotten events and memories can be brought back with the mere whiff of an odour associated with the memory (Schab, 1990, 1991; Herz & Cupchik, 1992; Bartoshuk & Beauchamp, 1994; Gillyatt, 1997).

Results of "sniff tests" have shown that women generally have a better sense of smell than men (Engen, 1987; Ship & Weiffenbach, 1993; Segal et al., 1995). People also seem to have the ability to distinguish males from females on the basis of smell alone. In one experiment, blindfolded students sniffed a sweating hand held one centimetre from their nose. The findings showed that male and female hands could be distinguished from one another with better than 80 percent accuracy (Wallace, 1977). Similarly, experimental participants, asked to sniff the breath of a male or female volunteer who was hidden from view, were able to distinguish the sex of the donor at better than chance levels (Doty et al., 1982).

Our understanding of the mechanisms that underlie the sense of smell is just beginning to emerge. We do know that the sense of smell is sparked when the molecules of a substance enter the nasal passages and meet *olfactory cells*, the receptor cells of the nose, which are spread across the nasal cavity. More than 1,000 separate types of receptor cells have been identified so far. Each of these cells is so specialized that it responds only to a small band of different odours. The responses of the separate olfactory cells are then transmitted to the brain, where they are combined into recognition of a particular smell (Buck & Axel, 1991; Vassar et al., 1994; Fulle et al., 1995).

There's increasing evidence that smell may also act as an involuntary means of communication for humans. It has long been known that animals release *pheromones*, chemicals that produce a reaction in other members of the species, permitting them to send such messages as sexual availability. For instance, certain substances in the vaginal secretions of female monkeys contain pheromones that stimulate sexual interest in male monkeys.

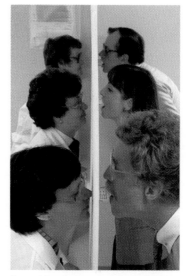

Although it seems reasonable that humans might also communicate through the release of pheromones, the evidence is still scanty. Women's vaginal secretions contain chemicals similar to those found in monkeys, but in humans the smells do not seem to be related to sexual activity. On the other hand, the presence of these substances might explain why women who live together for long periods of time tend to show similarity in the timing of their menstrual cycles. In addition, women are able to identify their babies solely on the basis of smell just a few hours after birth. Finally, studies of women's reactions to androsterone, a component of male sweat, find that most women respond negatively to the smell—except at specific times during their monthly menstrual cycles when they are most likely to become pregnant. At those times the smell doesn't seem to bother them. Apparently, androsterone acts as if it were a pheromone, helping to increase the chances that a female ready to conceive is likely to be receptive to sexual activity (McClintock, 1971; Porter, Cernich, & McLaughlin, 1983; Engen, 1987; Weller & Weller, 1995; Grammer, 1996).

Intrepid volunteers such as those at the left demonstrate that it is possible to differentiate between men and women just by the smell of their breath.

Taste

Unlike smell, which employs more than 1,000 separate types of receptor cells, the sense of taste seems to make do with only a handful of fundamental types of receptors. Most researchers believe that there are just four basic receptor cells, which specialize in either sweet, sour, salty, or bitter flavours. Every other taste is simply a combination of these four basic qualities, in the same way that the primary colours blend into a vast variety of shades and hues (McLaughlin & Margolskee, 1994).

Taste and Smell

The receptor cells for taste are located in *taste buds*, which are distributed across the tongue. However, the distribution is uneven, and certain areas of the tongue are more sensitive to particular fundamental tastes than others (Bartoshuk, 1971). As we can see in Figure 3-11, the tip of the tongue is most sensitive to sweetness. For example, a granule of sugar placed on the rear of the tongue will hardly seem sweet at all. Similarly, only the sides of the tongue are very sensitive to sour tastes, and the rear specializes in bitter tastes.

The different taste areas on the tongue correspond to different locations in the brain. Neurons responding to sour and bitter tastes are located on one end of the area of the cortex corresponding to taste, whereas sweet tastes stimulate neurons on the opposite end of the cortex. In contrast, salty tastes stimulate neurons that are distributed across the entire taste area of the brain (Yamamoto, Yuyama, & Kawamura, 1981).

FIGURE 3-11 *Particular portions of the tongue are sensitive to tastes that are bitter, sour, sweet, or salty.*

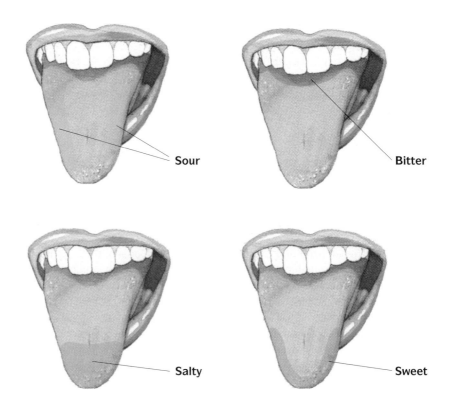

Sour

Bitter

Salty

Sweet

There are significant differences between various individuals' sense of taste, determined largely by genetic factors. Some people, dubbed "supertasters," are highly sensitive to taste; they have twice as many taste receptors as "nontasters," who are relatively insensitive to taste. Supertasters find sweets sweeter, cream creamier, and spicy dishes spicier, and weaker concentrations of flavour are enough to satisfy any cravings they may have. On the other hand, because they aren't so sensitive to taste, nontasters may seek out relatively sweeter and fattier foods in order to maximize the taste. As a consequence, they may be prone to obesity. (To determine your own taste sensitivity, try the test in Figure 3-12; Bartoshuk et al., 1996; Brownlee & Watson, 1997; Bartoshuk & Lucchina, 1997; Bartoshuk & Drewnowski, 1997).

The Skin Senses: Touch, Pressure, Temperature, and Pain

It started innocently, when Jennifer Darling hurt her right wrist during gym class. At first it seemed like a simple sprain. But even though the initial injury healed, the excruciating, burning pain accompanying it did not go away. Instead, it spread to her other arm, and then to her legs. The pain, which Jennifer described as similar to "a hot iron on your arm," was unbearable, and normal painkillers proved ineffective.

The source of the pain turned out to be a rare condition known as "reflex sympathetic dystrophy syndrome," or RSDS for short. For a victim of RSDS, a stimulus as mild as a gentle breeze or the touch of a feather can produce agony. Even bright sunlight or a loud noise can trigger intense pain.

Although a precise explanation for RSDS eludes us, one theory is that messages of pain overwhelm and harm neurons in the nervous system. The body's natural mechanisms that moderate the experience of pain become increasingly less effective, and the brain begins to misinterpret even harmless stimuli such as light or heat as signs of pain.

For Jennifer Darling, knowing the specific causes of RSDS is less important than finding a release from its ravages. Fortunately, she has found a way to gain at least temporary pain relief. Electrodes powered by a battery

TAKE A TASTE TEST

1. Taste Buds count

Punch a hole with a standard hole punch in a square of wax paper. Paint the front of your tongue with a cotton swab dipped in blue food colouring. Put wax paper on the tip of your tongue, just to the right of centre. With a flashlight and magnifying glass, count the number of pink, unstained circles. They contain taste buds.

2. Sweet sensitivity

Rinse your mouth with water before tasting each sample. Put 1/2 cup sugar in a measuring cup, and then add enough water to make 1 cup. Mix. Coat front half of your tongue, including the tip, with a cotton swab dipped in the solution. Wait a few moments. Rate the sweetness according to the scale shown below.

3. Salt sensitivity

Put 2 teaspoons of salt in a measuring cup and add enough water to make 1 cup. Repeat the steps listed above, rating how salty the solution is.

4. Spicy sensitivity

Add 1 teaspoon of Tabasco sauce to 1 cup of water. Apply with a cotton swab to first half inch of the tongue, including the tip. Keep your tongue out of your mouth until the burn reaches a peak, then rate the pain according to the scale.

TASTE SCALE

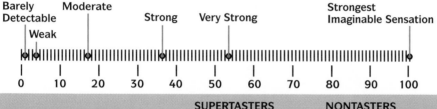

	SUPERTASTERS	NONTASTERS
No. of taste buds	25 on Average	10
Sweet rating	56 on Average	32
Tabasco	64 on Average	31

Average tasters lie in between supertasters and nontasters. Bartoshuk and Lucchina lack the data at this time to rate salt reliably, but you can compare your results with others taking the test.

FIGURE 3-12 *According to Yale University taste researchers Linda Bartoshuk and Laurie Lucchina, all tongues are not created equal. Instead, they suggest that the intensity of a flavour experienced by a given person is determined by their genetic background. This taste test, devised by Bartoshuk and Lucchina, can help determine if you are a Nontaster, Average Taster, or Supertaster. Source: Brownlee, 1997, p. 59.*

have been implanted in her back and right arm. Using a computerized device, she is able to administer mild shocks, which neutralize the pain—at least temporarily. Although not a cure, this treatment at least allows her to have something of a normal life (Bylinsky, 1993).

If pain cannot be relieved, it can devastate a person's life. Yet, a lack of pain may be equally bad. If you never experienced pain, for instance, you might not notice that your arm had brushed against a hot pan, and you would suffer a severe burn. Similarly, without the warning sign of stomach pain that typically accompanies an inflamed appendix, your appendix might eventually rupture, spreading a fatal infection throughout your body.

In fact, all our **skin senses**—touch, pressure, temperature, and pain—play a critical role in survival, making us aware of potential danger to our bodies. Most of these senses operate through nerve receptor cells located at various depths throughout the skin. These cells are not evenly distributed. When we consider receptors sensitive to touch, for example, some areas, such as the fingertips, have many more cells and as a consequence are notably sensitive. In contrast, areas with fewer cells, such as the middle of the back, are considerably less sensitive to touch (see Figure 3-13; Kreuger, 1989).

Probably the most extensively researched skin sense is pain, and with good reason: People consult physicians and take medication for pain more than for any other symptom or condition. Almost 3.9 million Canadians, 17 percent of the population, experience chronic pain, most frequently associated with back problems, arthritis, or rheumatism. Most who suffer severe pain use analgesics, and consult their doctors approximately three times more frequently than those with no pain (Millar, 1996).

skin senses: The senses that include touch, pressure, temperature, and pain

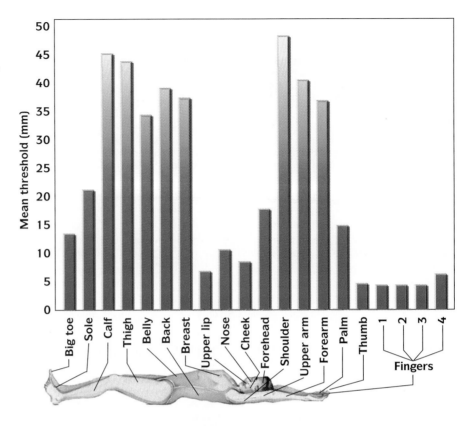

FIGURE 3-13 *Skin sensitivity in various areas of the body. The shorter a line, the more sensitive a body part is. The fingers and thumb, lips, nose, cheeks, and big toe are the most sensitive. Source: After Weinstein, 1968.*

As with our other senses, the perception of pain is not a simple matter of a direct response to certain kinds of stimulation. Some kinds of pain, such as that experienced in childbirth, are moderated by the joyful nature of the situation. At the same time, even a minor stimulus can produce the perception of strong pain, if it occurs in the context of an anxiety-tinged visit to the dentist. Clearly, then, pain is a perceptual response that depends heavily on our emotions and thoughts (Fernandez & Turk, 1992; Cioffi & Holloway, 1993; Schorr, 1993; Turk, 1994; Symbaluk et al., 1997).

Some of the contradictions involved in our responses to stimulation capable of eliciting pain are explained by gate-control theory developed by Canadian psychologist, Ronald Melzack, and his colleague, Patrick Wall. The **gate-control theory of pain** suggests that particular nerve receptors lead to specific areas of the brain related to pain (Melzack & Wall, 1965; Wall & Melzack, 1989; Pancyr & Genest, 1993). When these receptors are activated because of some injury or problem with a part of the body, a "gate" to the brain is opened, allowing us to experience the sensation of pain.

gate-control theory of pain: The theory suggesting that particular nerve receptors lead to specific areas of the brain related to pain

However, another set of neural receptors is able, when stimulated, to close the "gate" to the brain, thereby reducing the experience of pain. The gate may be shut in two different ways. First, other impulses can overwhelm the nerve pathways relating to pain, which are spread throughout the brain (Talbot et al., 1991; Kakigi, Matsuda, & Kuroda, 1993). In this case, nonpainful stimuli compete with and sometimes displace the neuronal message of pain, thereby shutting off the painful stimulus. This explains why rubbing the skin around an injury helps reduce pain. The competing stimuli from the rubbing may overwhelm the painful ones. Similarly, scratching is able to relieve itching (which is technically classified as a kind of pain stimulus).

Psychological factors account for the second way in which a gate may be shut (Turk, 1994). Depending on an individual's current emotions, interpretation of events, and previous experience, the brain may close a gate by sending a message down the spinal cord to an injured area, producing a reduction in or relief from pain. Thus soldiers who are injured in battle may experience no pain. The lack of pain probably occurs because a soldier experiences such relief at still being alive that the brain sends a signal to the injury site to shut down the pain gate (Willis, 1988; Baker & Kirsch, 1991; Azar, 1996a; Rainville et al., 1997).

Pathways Through Psychology

Patrick J. McGrath

Pediatric Pain Researcher
Professor of Psychology, Pediatrics,
Psychiatry and Biomedical
Engineering, Dalhousie University
Psychologist, IWK Grace Health
Centre

Education: *1st year undergraduate*
University of Ottawa; B.A., M.A.
University of Saskatchewan; Ph.D.
(Clinical Psychology) Queen's
University, 1979

Home: *Central Halifax with my*
wife, Anita Unruh, a professor of
Occupational Therapy, our daughter
Mika, our dog, Fergus, and Peaches,
the rabbit.

Dr. Patrick J. McGrath with wife Dr.
Anita Unruh, daughter Mika, and friend

I first became interested in psychology when, at age 9 or 10 years, I met a priest, Canice Connors, who was doing graduate work in psychology. My first year psychology professor, Serge Piccinin at the University of Ottawa, formally introduced me to psychology. I was strongly influenced by Chuck Jillings, a professor at University of Regina, to see psychology as a way of helping people.

Interestingly, I did not like research until John Goodman, my boss at the Children's Hospital of Eastern Ontario in Ottawa, demanded that I do research. I wanted to keep my job and so I began with a small study of recurrent Abdominal Pain because several of my patients had that problem. All of the existing studies—which were not very good—said that this pain was caused by psychological factors. We found that recurrent abdominal pain was not due to psychological problems, although it causes many of them.

Our research was almost always interdisciplinary and I always learned from my colleagues. I kept on doing research because of the challenge in helping to unravel the puzzle of pain, and the fact that research helps more children than I could ever see in clinic.

Today most of my time is spent in research. The Pediatric Pain Research Lab at Dalhousie University and the IWK Grace Health Centre is co-directed by Dr. Allan Finley, an anaesthetist, and myself. Projects include research on Event Related Potentials and pain, measurement of postoperative pain, phantom limb pain, pain in infants and children who have neurological damage, how infants and children learn about pain, and consciousness under anaesthesia. At the Hospital for Sick Children in Toronto we are doing studies on sickle cell pain. We also publish the *Pediatric Pain Letter*, a newsletter of abstracts and commentaries on pediatric pain, and host the International Forum on Pediatric Pain every two years.

What do I find most rewarding about my work? Teaching Introductory Psychology gives me an opportunity to spark students' interest in psychology. The graduate students that I teach help to keep me up-to-date on new developments. Our most important work has been in devising behavioural measures in pain and developing low-cost, distance-education type of treatments for pain. We have also been able to help health professionals realize that children's pain should not be ignored. And seeing patients in the pain service makes me appreciate how much more we have to learn. They are the reason we do the research.

Source: Patrick J. McGrath, Ph.D. Dalhousie University. <www.dal.ca/~pedpain>

Gate-control theory may also explain cultural differences in the experience of pain. Some of these variations are astounding. For example, in India, people who participate in the "hook-swinging" ritual to celebrate the power of the gods, have steel hooks embedded under the skin and muscles of their backs. During the ritual, they swing from a pole, suspended by the hooks. What would seem likely to induce excruciating pain instead produces a state of celebration and near-euphoria. In fact, when the hooks are later removed, the wounds heal quickly, and after two weeks almost no visible marks remain (Kosambi, 1967).

Gate-control theory suggests that the lack of pain is due to a message from the participant's brain, which shuts down the pain pathways. Gate-control theory may also explain the effectiveness of *acupuncture,* an ancient Chinese technique in which sharp needles are inserted into various parts of the body. The sensation from the needles may close the gateway to the brain, reducing the experience of pain. It is also possible that the body's own painkillers, the endorphins (discussed in Chapter 2), as well as positive and negative emotions, may play a role in opening and closing the gate (Wall & Melzack, 1984; Warga, 1987; Murray, 1995; Bromm & Desmedt, 1995). (For a look at someone who deals professionally with pain, see the accompanying Pathways Through Psychology box.)

Recap, Review, and Rethink

Recap

- The senses of hearing, motion, and balance are centred in the ear.

- The major parts of the ear are the outer ear (which includes the auditory canal and eardrum), the middle ear (with the hammer, anvil, and stirrup), and the oval window leading to the inner ear. The inner ear contains the cochlea, basilar membrane, and hair cells.

- The physical aspects of sound include frequency and intensity. Both place and frequency processes are believed to operate in the transformation of sound waves into the experience of sound.

- The sense of balance is located in the ear's semicircular canals and otoliths.

- Less is known about the senses of smell and taste and the skin senses (touch, pressure, temperature, and pain) than about vision and hearing, although each is highly complex.

Review

1. The tubelike passage leading from the outer ear is known as the _____ .

2. The purpose of the eardrum is to protect the sensitive nerves underneath it. It serves no purpose in actual hearing. True or false?

3. To what part of the ear do the three middle ear bones transmit their sound?

4. What theory of hearing states that the entire basilar membrane responds to a sound, vibrating more or less, depending on the nature of the sound?

5. The three fluid-filled tubes in the inner ear that are responsible for our sense of balance are known as the _____.

6. Chemicals that produce a certain reaction in other members of the species are known as _____.

7. _____-_____ theory states that when certain skin receptors are activated as the result of an injury, a "pathway" to the brain is opened, allowing pain to be experienced.

Answers to Review Questions are on page 112.

Rethink

1. Much research is being conducted on repairing faulty sensory organs through such devices as personal guidance systems, eyeglasses, and so forth. Do you think it would be feasible for science to attempt, through similar methods, to augment normal sensory capabilities beyond their "natural" range (such as increasing the capacity of the human visual or audio spectrum)? What benefits might this bring? What problems might it cause?

2. Why might the sensitivity to pheromones have evolved differently in humans than in other species? What cultural factors might have played a role?

3. If the gate-control theory of pain is correct, might it be possible to "train" the brain to shut off painful stimuli at will? Can you think of therapeutic techniques that might be an attempt to accomplish this?

PERCEPTUAL ORGANIZATION: CONSTRUCTING OUR VIEW OF THE WORLD

▶ **What principles underlie our organization of the visual world, allowing us to make sense of our environment?**

▶ **How are we able to perceive the world in three dimensions when our retinas are capable of sensing only two-dimensional images?**

▶ **What clues do visual illusions give us about our understanding of general perceptual mechanisms?**

Consider the vase shown in Figure 3-14a for a moment.

Or is it a vase? Take another look, and instead you may see the profile of two people.

Now that an alternative interpretation has been pointed out, you will probably shift back and forth between the two interpretations. Similarly, if you examine the shapes in Figure 3-14b and 3-14c long enough, you will probably experience a shift in what you're seeing. The reason for these reversals is this: Because each figure is two-dimensional, the usual means we employ for distinguishing the *figure* (the object being perceived) from the *ground* (the background or spaces within the object) do not work.

The fact that we can look at the same figure in more than one way illustrates an important point. We do not just passively respond to visual stimuli that happen to fall on our retinas. Instead, we actively try to organize and make sense of what we see.

We turn now from a focus on the initial response to a stimulus (sensation) to what our minds make of that stimulus—perception. Perception is a constructive process by which we go beyond the stimuli that are presented to us and attempt to construct a meaningful situation (Haber, 1983; Kienker et al., 1986).

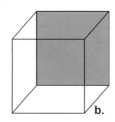

FIGURE 3-14 *When the usual cues we use to distinguish figure from ground are absent, we may shift back and forth between different views of the same figure. If you look at each of these objects long enough you'll probably experience a shift in what you're seeing. In (a), a designer used the profiles of Queen Elizabeth and Prince Philip of England. In (b), the shaded portion of the figure, called a Necker cube, can appear to be either the front or the back of the cube. Finally, in (c), you'll be able to see a face of a woman if you look at the drawing long enough.*

The Gestalt Laws of Organization

Some of the most basic perceptual processes operate according to a series of principles that describe how we organize bits and pieces of information into meaningful wholes. These are known as **gestalt laws of organization,** set forth in the early 1900s by a group of German psychologists who studied patterns, or *gestalts* (Wertheimer, 1923). They discovered a number of important principles that are valid for visual (as well as auditory) stimuli:

gestalt laws of organization: A series of principles that describes how we organize bits and pieces of information into meaningful wholes

- *Closure*. Groupings are usually made in terms of enclosed or complete figures rather than open ones. We tend to ignore the breaks in the figure below and concentrate on the overall form.

- *Proximity*. Elements that are closer together are grouped together. As a result, we tend to see pairs of dots rather than a row of single dots in the following pattern:

. . . .

- *Similarity*. Elements that are similar in appearance are grouped together. We see, then, horizontal rows of circles and squares instead of vertical mixed columns below:

- *Simplicity*. In a general sense, the overriding gestalt principle is simplicity: When we observe a pattern, we perceive it in the most basic, straightforward manner that we can (Hochberg, 1978; Chater, 1996). For example, most of us

FIGURE 3-15 *Although at first it is difficult to distinguish anything in this drawing, keep looking, and eventually you'll probably be able to discern the figure of a dog. Source: Ronald C. James, from Carraher, R. G., and Thurston, J. B. (1966).* Optical Illusions in the Visual Arts. *New York: Van Nostrand Reinhold.*

AND FOR MY NEXT TRICK . . .

© 1996 Ian Falconer originally in The New Yorker. All rights reserved.

feature analysis: An approach to perception that considers how we perceive a shape, pattern, object, or scene by reacting first to the individual elements that make it up

see the figure below as a square with lines on two sides, rather than as the block letter "W" on top of the letter "M." If we have a choice of interpretations, we generally opt for the simpler one.

Although gestalt psychology no longer plays a prominent role in contemporary psychology, its legacy endures (Kubovy & Wagemans, 1995; Sos-Pena, Gabucio, & Tejero, 1995; Kriz, 1995). For instance, one fundamental gestalt principle, which remains influential, is that two objects considered together form a whole that is different than the simple combination of the objects. Gestalt psychologists argued—quite convincingly—that the perception of stimuli in our environment goes well beyond the individual elements that we sense. Instead, it represents an active, constructive process carried out within the brain. There, bits and pieces of sensations are put together to make something greater, and more meaningful, than the separate elements.

Consider, for instance, Figure 3-15. As you examine the black patches, it is likely that you will perceive the form of a dog. The dog represents a gestalt, or perceptual whole. Although you can see the individual parts that make up the figure, putting them together forms something greater than the individual parts. The whole, then, is quite different from the sum of the individual elements.

Feature Analysis: Focusing on the Parts of the Whole

A more recent approach to perception, **feature analysis,** considers how we perceive a shape, pattern, object, or scene by reacting first to the individual elements that make it up. These individual components are then used to understand the overall nature of what we are perceiving. Feature analysis begins with the evidence that individual neurons in the brain are sensitive to specific spatial configurations, such as angles, curves, shapes, and edges, as discussed earlier in the chapter. The presence of these neurons

---

Answers to Review Questions:

1. auditory canal   2. False; it vibrates when sound waves hit it, and transmits the sound.   3. oval window   4. frequency theory
5. semicircular canals   6. pheromones   7. Gate-control

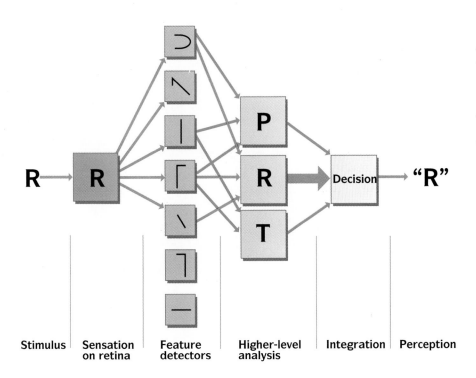

FIGURE 3-16 *According to feature analysis approaches to perception, we break down stimuli into their component parts and then compare these parts to information that is stored in memory. When we find a match, we are able to identify the stimulus. In this example, the process by which we recognize the letter "R" is illustrated.*

suggests that any stimulus can be broken down into a series of component features. For example, the letter "R" is a combination of a vertical line, a diagonal line, and a half circle (see Figure 3-16).

According to feature analysis, when we encounter a stimulus—such as a letter—our brain's perceptual processing system initially responds to its component parts. Each of these parts is compared with information about components that is stored in memory. When the specific components we perceive match up with a particular set of components that we have encountered previously, we are able to identify the stimulus (Spillmann & Werner, 1990; Ullman, 1996).

According to some research, we perceive complex objects in a manner similar to the way in which we perceive simple letters, viewing them in terms of their component elements. For instance, just 36 fundamental components seem to be capable of producing over 150 million objects—more than enough to describe the 30,000 separate objects that the average person can recognize (see Figure 3-17). Ultimately, these component features are combined into a representation of the whole object in the

Pattern Recognition

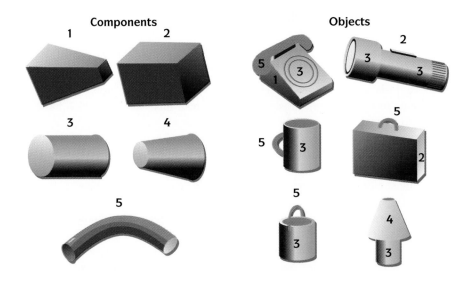

FIGURE 3-17 *Components and simple objects created from them. Source: Adapted from Biederman, 1990.*

FIGURE 3-18 *Double Mona Lisa's? These pictures appear similar at first glance because only our preattentative process is active. When the pictures are seen upright, the true detail in the two faces is revealed. Source: From Julesz, 1986.*

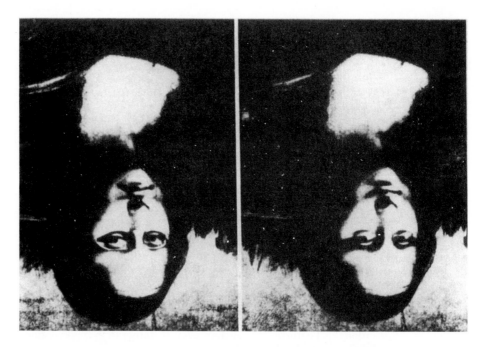

brain. This representation is compared to existing memories, thereby permitting us to identify the object (Biederman, 1987, 1990).

Psychologist Anne Treisman has a different perspective. She suggests that the perception of objects is best understood in terms of a two-stage process. In the *preattentive stage,* we focus on the physical features of a stimulus, such as its size, shape, colour, orientation, or direction of movement. This initial stage takes little or no conscious effort. In the *focused-attention stage,* we pay attention to particular features of an object, choosing and emphasizing features that were initially considered separately (Treisman, 1988, 1993).

For example, take a look at the two upside-down photos in Figure 3-18. Probably, your first impression is that you're viewing two similar photos of the Mona Lisa. But now look at them right side up, and you'll be surprised to note that one of the photos has distorted features. In Treisman's terms, your initial scanning of the photos took place at the preattentive stage. When you turned them over, however, you immediately progressed into the focused-attention stage, where you were able to more carefully consider the actual nature of the stimuli.

Treisman's perspective and other approaches to feature analysis raise a puzzling question about the fundamental nature of perceptual processes: Is perception based mainly on consideration of the component parts of a stimulus, or is it grounded primarily in perception of the stimulus as a whole? This is the issue to which we turn next.

Top-Down and Bottom-Up Processing

Ca- yo- re-d t-is -en-en-e, w-ic- ha- ev-ry -hi-d l-tt-r m-ss-ng? It probably won't take you too long to figure out that it says, "Can you read this sentence, which has every third letter missing?"

If perception were based primarily on breaking down a stimulus into its most basic elements, understanding the sentence, as well as other ambiguous stimuli, would not be possible. The fact that you were probably able to recognize such an imprecise stimulus illustrates that perception proceeds along two different avenues, called top-down processing and bottom-up processing.

In **top-down processing,** perception is guided by higher-level knowledge, experience, expectations, and motivations. You were able to figure out the meaning of the sentence with the missing letters because of your prior reading experience, and because written English contains redundancies. Not every letter of each word is neces-

top-down processing: Perception that is guided by higher-level knowledge, experience, expectations, and motivations

A B C D E F
10 11 12 13 14

sary to decode its meaning. Moreover, your expectations played a role in your being able to read the sentence. You were probably expecting a statement that had *something* to do with psychology, and not the lyrics to a Grateful Dead song.

Top-down processing is illustrated by the importance of context in determining how we perceive objects (Biederman, 1981). Look, for example, at Figure 3-19. Most of us perceive that the first row consists of the letters "A" through "F," while the second contains the numbers 10 through 14. But take a more careful look, and you'll see that the "B" and the "13" are identical. Clearly, our perception is affected by our expectations about the two sequences—even though the two stimuli are exactly the same.

Similarly, when we look at the isolated stimuli shown in Figure 3-20*a* it is almost impossible to tell what they are. But when the same stimuli are placed in the context of a face, they are much easier to identify. Top-down processing, which takes our expectations and understanding of the situation into account, must take place in order for us to understand what we are perceiving.

Yet top-down processing cannot occur on its own. Even though top-down processing allows us to fill in the gaps in ambiguous and out-of-context stimuli, we would be unable to perceive the meaning of such stimuli without bottom-up processing. **Bottom-up processing** consists of recognizing and processing information about the individual components of the stimuli. We would make no headway in our recognition of the sentence without being able to perceive the individual shapes that make up the letters. Some perception, then, occurs at the level of the patterns and features of each of the separate letters.

It should be apparent that top-down and bottom-up processing occur simultaneously, and interact with each other, in our perception of the world around us (Kimchi, 1992; Egeth & Yantis, 1997). It is bottom-up processing that permits us to process the fundamental characteristics of stimuli, whereas top-down processing allows us to bring our experience to bear on perception. And as we learn more about the complex processes involved in perception, we are developing a better understanding of how our brain continually interprets information from our senses and permits us to make responses appropriate to the environment (Rees, Frith, & Lavie, 1997).

bottom-up processing: Perception that consists of recognizing and processing information about the individual components of the stimuli

Perceptual Constancy

Consider what happens as you finish a conversation with a friend and she begins to walk away from you. As you watch her walk down the street, the image on your retina becomes smaller and smaller. Do you wonder why she is shrinking?

Of course not. Despite the very real change in the size of the retinal image, you factor into your thinking the knowledge that your friend is moving further away from you. No matter how far away she progresses, and no matter how small the retinal image becomes as a consequence of her distance, you still perceive her as the same size.

Your friend does not appear to shrink due to perceptual constancy. *Perceptual constancy* is a phenomenon in which physical objects are perceived as unvarying and consistent, despite changes in their appearance or in the physical environment.

One of the most dramatic examples of perceptual constancy involves the rising moon. When the moon first appears at night, close to the horizon, it seems to be huge—considerably larger than when it is high in the sky later in the evening. You may have thought that the apparent size of the moon was caused by the moon's being physically closer to the earth when it first appears. In fact, though, this is not the case at all (Hershenson, 1989).

a. Out of context

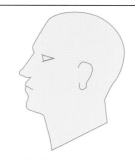

b. In context

FIGURE 3-20 *The odd shapes in (a) become more recognizable when placed on the face of (b). Source: Based on Palmer, 1975.*

Instead, the moon appears to be larger when it is close to the horizon primarily because of a misapplication of perceptual constancy (Coren & Aks, 1990; Coren, 1992b). When the moon is near the horizon, the perceptual cues of intervening terrain and objects such as trees on the horizon produce a misleading sense of distance. Because perceptual constancy leads us to take that distance into account when we view the moon, we perceive the moon as relatively large. On the other hand, when the moon is high in the sky, we see it by itself, and perceptual constancy leads us to perceive it as relatively small. To prove this, try looking at the moon when it is relatively low on the horizon through a paper-towel tube; the moon will suddenly appear to "shrink" back to normal size.

Although other factors help account for the moon illusion, perceptual constancy appears to be a primary ingredient in our susceptibility to the illusion (Coren, 1989; Baird, Wagner, & Fuld, 1990; Coren & Aks, 1990; Suzuki, 1991). Furthermore, perceptual constancy occurs not just in terms of size (as with the moon illusion) but with shape and colour as well (e.g., Brainard, Wandell, & Chichilnisky, 1993). The image on our retina varies as a plane approaches, flies overhead, and disappears, yet we do not perceive the plane as changing shape. Instead, we perceive it as unchanging, despite the physical variations that occur.

Depth Perception: Translating 2-D to 3-D

As sophisticated as the retina is, the images projected onto it are flat and two-dimensional. Yet the world around us is three-dimensional, and we perceive it that way. How do we make the transformation from 2-D to 3-D?

The ability to view the world in three dimensions and to perceive distance—a skill known as *depth perception*—is due largely to the fact that we have two eyes (Regan, 1991). Because there is a certain distance between the eyes, a slightly different image reaches each retina. The brain then integrates these two images into one composite view. But it does not ignore the difference in images, which is known as *binocular disparity* (Howard and Rogers, 1995). The disparity allows the brain to estimate the distance of an object from us.

You can get a sense of binocular disparity for yourself. Hold a pencil at arm's length and look at it first with one eye and then with the other. There is little difference between the two views relative to the background. Now bring the pencil just 15 centimetres away from your face, and try the same thing. This time you will perceive a greater difference between the two views.

The fact that the discrepancy between the images in the two eyes varies according to the distance of objects that we view provides us with a means of determining distance. If we view two objects, and one is considerably closer to us than another, the retinal disparity will be relatively large and we will have a greater sense of depth between the two. On the other hand, if the two objects are a similar distance from us, the retinal disparity will be minor, and we will perceive them as being a similar distance from us.

Filmmakers, whose medium compels them to project images in just two dimensions, have tried to create the illusion of depth perception by using two cameras, spaced slightly apart, to produce slightly different images, each destined for a different eye. In a 3-D movie, the two images are projected simultaneously. This produces a double image, unless special glasses are worn to allow each image to be viewed by the eye for which it is intended. The special glasses—familiar to moviegoers since the first 3-D movie, *Bwana Devil*, appeared in 1952—provide a genuine sense of depth. Similar techniques are being developed to show 3-D movies on television (Rogers, 1988).

monocular cues: Signals that allow us to perceive distance and depth with just one eye

In some cases, certain cues permit us to obtain a sense of depth and distance with just one eye (Burnham, 1983). These cues are known as **monocular cues.** One monocular cue—*motion parallax*—is the change in position of an object on the retina as the head moves from side to side. The brain is able to calculate the distance of the object by the amount of change in the retinal image. Similarly, experience has taught us that if two objects are the same size, the one that makes a smaller image on the retina is farther away than the one that provides a larger image—an example of the monocular cue of *relative size*.

Finally, anyone who has ever seen railroad tracks that seem to join together in the distance knows that distant objects appear to be closer together than nearer ones, a phenomenon called linear perspective. People use *linear perspective* as a monocular cue in estimating distance, allowing the two-dimensional image on the retina to record the three-dimensional world (Bruce, Green, & Georgeson, 1997).

Motion Perception: As the World Turns

When a batter tries to hit a pitched ball, the most important factor is the motion of the ball. How is a batter able to judge the speed and location of a target that is moving at some 145 kilometres per hour?

The answer rests, in part, on several cues that provide us with relevant information about the perception of motion (Movshon & Newsome, 1992). For one thing, the movement of an object across the retina is typically perceived relative to some stable, unmoving background. Moreover, if the stimulus is heading toward us, the image on the retina may expand in size, filling more and more of the visual field. In such cases, we assume that the stimulus is approaching—and not that it is an expanding stimulus viewed at a constant distance.

It is not, however, just the movement of images across the retina that brings about the perception of motion. If it were, we would perceive the world as moving every time we moved our heads. Instead, one of the critical things we learn about perception is to factor information about head and eye movements along with information about changes in the retinal image.

In some cases, movement is so fast that we are unable to follow it. In those instances, we may be able to anticipate where an object will end up on the basis of our prior experience. For example, computer tracking of baseball pitches has shown that most fast balls thrown in major-league games travel too fast for the eye to follow. Indeed, if a batter tried to follow a fast ball from the moment it left a pitcher's hand, the batter would lose sight of it by the time it got about 2 metres from home plate (Bahill & Laritz, 1984). Research suggests that good hitters take their eyes off the ball during the middle of its trip and shift their vision closer to home plate, waiting for the ball's arrival and (hoped-for) impact with the bat. Thus, instead of relying on the raw sensory input from the travelling ball—the phenomenon of sensation—they employ perceptual processes, using what they have learned to expect about how balls travel.

Perceptual Illusions: The Deceptions of Perceptions

> For sight follows gracious contours, and unless we flatter its pleasure by proportionate alternations of these parts (so that by adjustment we offset the amount to which it suffers illusions), an uncouth and ungracious aspect will be presented to the spectators.

Optical Illusions

The phenomenon to which Vitruvius, a Greek architect who lived around 30 B.C., was referring in such elegant language is that people do not always view the world accurately. Consequently, Vitruvius argued, we must consider how people's eyes and brains perceive buildings when designing architectural works.

Consider the Parthenon, one of the most famous buildings of ancient Greece. Although it looks true and straight to the eye, it was actually built with a bulge on one side. This protrusion fools viewers into thinking it is straight. If it didn't have that bulge—and quite a few other "tricks" like it, such as columns that incline inward—it would look as if it were crooked and about to fall down.

The fact that the Parthenon appears to be completely upright, with straight lines and right angles at every corner, is the result of a series of visual illusions. **Visual illusions** are physical stimuli that consistently produce errors in perception. In the case of the Parthenon, the building appears to be completely square, as illustrated in Figure 3-21*a*. However, had it actually been built that way, it would look to us as it does in Figure 3-21*b*. The reason for this is the illusion illustrated in 3-21*c*, which makes angles placed

visual illusions: Physical stimuli that consistently produce errors in perception

FIGURE 3-21 *In building the Parthenon, the Greeks constructed an architectural wonder that looks perfectly straight, with right angles at every corner, as in (a). However, if it had been built with completely true right angles, it would have looked as it does in (b), due to the visual illusion illustrated in (c). To compensate for this illusion, the Parthenon was designed to have a slight upward curvature, as shown in (d). Source: Coren & Ward, 1989, p. 5.*

a.

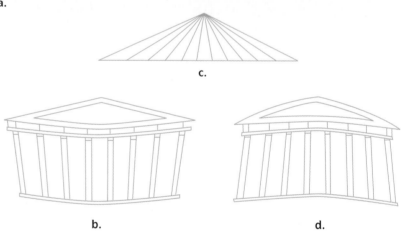

b.   d.

above a line appear as if they were bent. To offset the illusion, the Parthenon was actually constructed as in Figure 3-21*d,* with a slight upward curvature.

Such perceptual insights did not stop with the Greeks. Modern-day architects and designers also take visual distortions into account in their planning. For example, the New Orleans Superdome makes use of several visual tricks. Its seats vary in colour throughout the stadium to give the appearance, from a distance, that there is always a full house. The carpeting in some of the sloping halls has stripes that make people slow their pace by producing the perception that they are moving faster than they actually are. The same illusion is used at toll booths on superhighways. Stripes painted on the pavement in front of the toll booths make drivers feel that they are moving more rapidly than they actually are and cause them to decelerate quickly.

The implications of visual illusions go beyond the attractiveness of buildings. For instance, suppose you were an air traffic controller watching a radar screen like the one shown in Figure 3-22*a.* You might be tempted to sit back and relax as the two planes, whose flight paths are indicated in the figure, drew closer and closer together. If you did, however, the result might be an air disaster. Although it looks as if the two planes will miss each other, they are headed for a collision. Investigation has suggested that some 70 to 80 percent of all airplane accidents are caused by pilot errors of one sort or another (O'Hare & Roscoe, 1990; Baker et al., 1993).

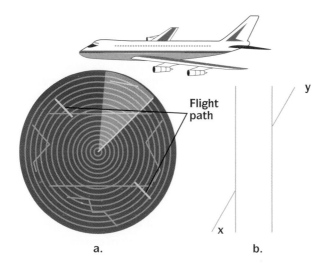

FIGURE 3-22 *(a) Put yourself in the shoes of a flight controller and look at the flight paths of the two planes on this radar screen. A first glance suggests that they are headed on different courses and will not hit each other. But now take a ruler and lay it along the two paths. Your career as a flight controller might well be over if you were guiding the two planes and you allowed them to continue without a change in course (Coren, Porac, & Ward, 1984, p. 7). (b) The Poggendorf illusion, in which the two diagonal lines appear (incorrectly) as if they would not meet if extended toward each other.*

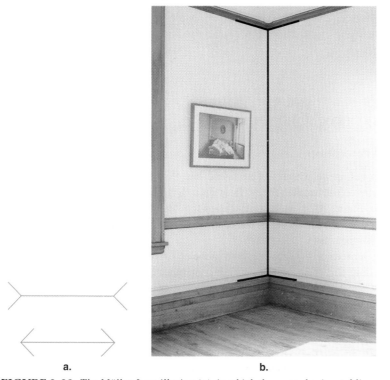

FIGURE 3-23 *The Müller-Lyer illusion (a), in which the upper horizontal line appears longer than the lower one. An explanation for the Müller-Lyer illusion suggests that the line with arrow points directed inward is to be interpreted as the inside corner of a rectangular room extending away from us (b), and the line with arrow points directed outward is viewed as the relatively close corner of a rectangular object, such as the building corner in (c). Our previous experience with distance cues leads us to assume that the outside corner is closer than the inside corner and that the inside corner must therefore be longer.*

The flight-path illustration provides an example of a well-known visual illusion called the *Poggendorf illusion.* As you can see in Figure 3-22*b,* the Poggendorf illusion, when stripped down to its basics, gives the impression that line X would pass *below* line Y if it were extended through the pipe-like figure, instead of heading directly toward line Y as it actually does.

The Poggendorf illusion is just one of many that consistently fool the eye (Perkins, 1983; Greist-Bousquet & Schiffman, 1986). Another, illustrated in Figure 3-23, is called the *Müller-Lyer illusion.* Although the two lines are the same length, the one with the arrow tips pointing inward (Figure 3-23*a,* top) appears to be longer than the one with the arrow tips pointing outward (Figure 3-23*a,* bottom).

Although all kinds of explanations for visual illusions have been suggested, most concentrate either on the eye's visual sensory apparatus itself or on our interpretation of a given figure. Explanations for the Müller-Lyer illusion suggest, for example, that eye movements are greater when the arrow tips point inward, making us perceive the line as longer than when the arrow tips face outward.

Other evidence suggests that the illusion can be attributed to the brain's interpretive errors. For instance, one hypothesis assumes that the Müller-Lyer illusion is a result of the meaning we give to each of the lines (Gregory, 1978; Redding & Hawley, 1993). When we see the top line in Figure 3-23a, we tend to perceive it as if it were the inside corner of a room extending away from us, as illustrated in Figure 3-23b. On the other hand, when we view the bottom line in Figure 3-23a, we perceive it as the relatively close outside corner of a rectangular object such as the building corner in Figure 3-23c. Because previous experience leads us to assume that the outside corner is closer than the inside corner, we make the further assumption that the inside corner must therefore be larger.

Given all the underlying assumptions, it may seem unlikely to you that this explanation is valid. However, there is a good degree of convincing evidence for it. One of the most telling pieces of support comes from cross-cultural studies that show that people raised in areas where there are few right angles—such as the Zulu in Africa—are much less susceptible to the illusion than people who grow up where most structures are built using right angles and rectangles (Segall, Campbell, & Herskovits, 1966).

Exploring Diversity

Culture and Perception

The particular culture in which we are raised has clear consequences for the ways in which we perceive the world (Berry, Poortinga, Segall, and Dasen, 1992). Consider the drawing in Figure 3-24. Sometimes called the "devil's tuning fork," it is likely to produce a mind-boggling effect, as the centre tine of the fork alternates between appearing and disappearing.

Now try to reproduce the drawing on a piece of paper. Chances are that the task is nearly impossible for you—unless you are a member of an African tribe with little exposure to western cultures. For such individuals, the task is simple; they have no trouble reproducing the figure. The reason seems to be that western people automatically interpret the drawing as something that cannot exist in three dimensions, and they are therefore inhibited from reproducing it. The African tribal members, on the other hand, do not make the assumption that the figure is "impossible" and instead view it in two dimensions, which enables them to copy the figure with ease (Deregowski, 1973).

Cultural differences are also reflected in depth perception. A western viewer of Figure 3-25 would interpret the hunter in the drawing as trying to spear the antelope in the foreground, while an elephant stands under the tree in the background. A member of an isolated African tribe, however, interprets the scene very differently by assuming that the hunter is aiming at the elephant. Westerners use the difference in sizes between the two animals as a cue that the elephant is farther away than the antelope (Hudson, 1960).

The misinterpretations created by visual illusions are ultimately due, then, to errors in both fundamental visual processing and the way the brain interprets the information it receives. But visual illusions, by illustrating something fundamental about perception, become more than mere psychological curiosities. There is a basic connection between our prior knowledge, needs, motivations, and expectations about how the world is put together and the way we perceive it. Our view of the world is very much a function, then, of fundamental psychological factors. Furthermore, each person perceives the environment in a way that is unique and special—a fact that allows each of us to make our own special contribution to the world.   ∎

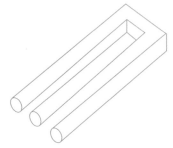

FIGURE 3-24 *The "devil's tuning fork" has three prongs . . . or does it have two?*

Among the most important approaches to fighting chronic pain are the following (Turk & Melzack, 1992; Novy et al., 1995; Langreth, 1996; Gatchel & Turk, 1996):

- *Medication.* Painkilling drugs are the most popular treatment in fighting pain. Drugs range from those that directly treat the source of the pain—such as reducing swelling in painful joints—to those that work on the symptoms of the pain. Medication can be in the form of pills, injections, or liquids. Moreover, in one of the latest innovations, drugs are pumped directly into the spinal cord. Researchers are also working on medications that stimulate the creation of endorphins, the body's own natural painkillers, which we discussed in Chapter 2.

- *Nerve and brain stimulation.* Pain can sometimes be relieved when a low-voltage electric current is passed through the specific part of the body that is in pain. In even more severe cases, electrodes can be surgically implanted directly into the brain, and a handheld battery pack can stimulate nerve cells to provide direct relief (Garrison & Foreman, 1994; Walsh et al., 1995). This process, employed in the case of Jennifer Darling, is known as *transcutaneous electrical nerve stimulation,* or *TENS.*

- *Hypnosis.* For people who can be hypnotized, this method can produce a major degree of pain relief (Erickson, Hershman, & Secter, 1990; Rhue, Lynn, & Kirsch, 1993; Genuis, 1995; Mairs, 1995; Holroyd, 1996; Spiegel, 1996).

- *Biofeedback and relaxation techniques.* As we discussed in the previous chapter, biofeedback is a process through which people learn to control such "involuntary" functions as heartbeat and respiration. If the pain involves muscles, such as in tension headaches or back pain, biofeedback can be helpful. Through biofeedback and the use of other techniques, people can be trained to relax their bodies systematically. Such relaxation is often effective in decreasing the pain caused by tension (Schwartz & Schwartz, 1993; Wauquier et al., 1995; Hermann, Kim, & Blanchard, 1995; NIH, 1996a, b).

- *Surgery.* One of the most extreme methods, surgery can be used to cut certain nerve fibres that carry pain messages to the brain. Still, because of the danger that other bodily functions will be affected, surgery is a treatment of last resort, used most frequently with dying patients.

- *Cognitive restructuring.* People who continually say to themselves, "This pain will never stop," "The pain is ruining my life," or "I can't take it any more" are likely to make their pain even worse. As we'll discuss in Chapter 13, by substituting more positive ways of thinking, people can increase their sense of control—and actually reduce the degree of pain they experience. Teaching people to rewrite the "script" that controls their reaction to pain through therapy can result in significant reductions in the perception of pain (Heyneman et al., 1990; Turk & Nash, 1993; Azar, 1996b).

If you wish to learn more about chronic pain, you can consult the North American Chronic Pain Association of Canada, 150 Central Park Drive, Unit 105, Brampton, Ontario, L6T 2T9. Their web site is <www.chronicpaincanada.org>. In addition, many hospitals have pain clinics that specialize in the treatment of pain. From the web site in the Pathways Box you can locate information about pain in children.   ■

Recap, Review, and Rethink

Recap

- Among the gestalt laws of organization are closure, proximity, similarity, and simplicity.

- People do not respond passively to visual stimuli; rather, they try to separate a given figure from the background.

- Feature analysis considers how people perceive a stimulus, break it down into the individual elements that make it up, and then use those elements to understand what they are seeing.

- Perception occurs through top-down and bottom-up processing.

- Depth perception occurs because of binocular disparity, motion parallax, and the relative size of images on the retina. Motion perception is the result of the movement of images across the retina, combined with information about head and eye movements.

- Visual illusions are physical stimuli that consistently produce errors in perception. Among the most common are the Poggendorf illusion and the Müller-Lyer illusion.

- Subliminal perception and extrasensory perception remain controversial.

Review

1. Match each of the following organizational laws with its meaning:
   a. closure
   b. proximity
   c. similarity
   d. simplicity

   1. Elements close together are grouped together.
   2. Patterns are perceived in the most basic, direct manner possible.
   3. Groupings are made in terms of complete figures.
   4. Elements similar in appearance are grouped together.

2. _____ analysis deals with the way in which we break an object down into its component pieces in order to understand it.

3. Processing that takes into account higher functions such as expectations and motivations is known as _____-_____ processing, while processing that involves recognizing the individual components of a stimulus is known as _____-_____ processing.

4. When a car passes you on the road and appears to shrink as it gets farther away, which perceptual phenomenon permits you to realize that the car is not in fact getting smaller?

5. _____ is the ability to view the world in three dimensions instead of two.

6. The eyes use a technique known as _____, which makes use of the differing images each eye sees to give three dimensions to sight.

7. Match the monocular cues with their definitions.
   1. relative size
   2. linear perspective
   3. motion parallax

   a. Straight lines seem to join together as they become more distant.
   b. An object changes position on the retina as the head moves.
   c. If two objects are the same size, the one producing the smaller retinal image is farther away.

8. Which of the following has *not* been proposed as an explanation of why we perceive visual illusions?

   a. variations in the eye's visual sensory apparatus
   b. small distance between eyeballs
   c. interpretive errors made by the brain
   d. previous learning experience

Answers to Review Questions are on page 126.

Rethink

1. Can you think of examples of the combined use of top-down and bottom-up processing in everyday life? In your examples, which type of processing typically seems to occur first? Why? Is one type of processing superior to the other?

2. In what ways do painters learn to represent 3-D scenes on the 2-D medium of the canvas? Do you think artists in nonwestern cultures use the same or different principles to represent three dimensionality? Why?

3. If the psi experiment described in this chapter is flawed, how can the better-than-chance success of some receivers be explained? How might you improve the design of the experiment?

looking
BACK

What is sensation, and how do psychologists study it?

1. Sensation is the stimulation of the sense organs that comes from our initial encounter with stimuli (forms of energy that activate a sense organ). In contrast, perception is the process by which we sort out, interpret, analyze, and integrate stimuli to which our senses are exposed. Sensation has traditionally been investigated by the branch of psychology called psychophysics, which studies the relationship between the physical nature of stimuli and a person's sensory responses to them.

What is the relationship between the nature of a physical stimulus and the kinds of sensory responses that result from it?

2. One major area of psychophysics is the study of the absolute threshold, the smallest amount of physical intensity

by which a stimulus can be detected. Although under ideal conditions absolute thresholds are extraordinarily sensitive, the presence of noise (background stimuli that interfere with other stimuli) reduces detection capabilities. Moreover, factors such as an individual's expectations and motivations affect success in detecting stimuli. Signal detection theory is now used to predict the accuracy of judgments by systematically taking into account two kinds of errors made by observers—reporting the presence of a stimulus when there is none and reporting the absence of a stimulus when one is actually present.

3. Difference thresholds relate to the smallest detectable difference between two stimuli, known as a just noticeable difference. According to Weber's law, a just noticeable difference is a constant proportion of the intensity of an initial stimulus.

4. Sensory adaptation occurs when we become accustomed to a constant stimulus and change our evaluation of it. Repeated exposure to a stimulus results in an apparent decline in sensitivity to it.

What are the basic processes that underlie the sense of vision?

5. Human sensory experience goes well beyond the traditional five senses, although most is known about just two: vision and hearing. Vision depends on sensitivity to light, electromagnetic waves that are reflected off objects outside the body. The eye shapes the light into an image that is transformed into nerve impulses and interpreted by the brain.

6. When light first enters the eye, it travels through the cornea and then traverses the pupil, a dark hole in the center of the iris. The size of the pupil opening adjusts according to the amount of light entering the eye. Light then enters the lens, which, by a process called accommodation, acts to focus light rays onto the rear of the eye. On the rear of the eye is the retina, which is composed of light-sensitive nerve cells called rods and cones. The rods and cones are unevenly spaced over the retina, with the greatest concentration of cones occurring in an area called the fovea. Because of the phenomenon of adaptation, it takes time to adjust to situations that are darker than the previous environment.

7. The visual information gathered by the rods and cones is transferred via bipolar and ganglion cells through the optic nerve, which leads to the optic chiasm—the point where the optic nerve splits. Because the image on the retina is reversed and upside down, images from the right half of the retina actually originated in the field of vision to the left of the person, and vice versa.

How do we see colours?

8. Colour vision seems to be based on two processes described by the trichromatic theory and the opponent-process theory. The trichromatic theory suggests that there are three kinds of cones in the retina, each of which is responsive to a certain range of colours. The opponent-process theory presumes pairs of different types of cells in the eye. These cells work in opposition to each other.

What role does the ear play in the senses of sound, motion, and balance?

9. Sound, motion, and balance are centred in the ear. Sounds, in the form of vibrating air waves, enter through the outer ear and travel through the auditory canal until they reach the eardrum. The vibrations of the eardrum are transmitted into the middle ear, which consists of three bones: the hammer, the anvil, and the stirrup. These bones transmit vibrations to the oval window, a thin membrane leading to the inner ear. In the inner ear, vibrations move into the cochlea, which encloses the basilar membrane. Hair cells on the basilar membrane change the mechanical energy of sound waves into nerve impulses that are transmitted to the brain. In addition to processing sound, the ear is involved in the sense of balance and motion through the semicircular canals and otoliths.

10. Sound has a number of important characteristics. One is frequency, the number of wave crests that occur in a second. Differences in the frequency of sound waves create different pitches. Another aspect of sound is intensity, the variations in pressure produced by a wave as it travels through the air. Intensity is measured in decibels. The place theory of hearing and the frequency theory of hearing explain the processes by which we distinguish sounds of varying frequency and intensity.

How do smell and taste function?

11. Considerably less is known about smell, taste, and the skin senses than about vision and hearing. Still, it is clear that smell employs olfactory cells (the receptor cells of the nose) and that taste is centred in the tongue's taste buds, which are capable of sensing combinations of sweet, sour, salty, and bitter flavors.

What are the skin senses, and how do they relate to the experience of pain?

12. The skin senses are responsible for the experiences of touch, pressure, temperature, and pain. We know the most about pain, which can be explained by the gate-control theory. The theory suggests that particular nerve receptors lead to specific areas of the brain related to pain. When these receptors are activated, a "gate" to the brain is opened, allowing the sensation of pain to be experienced. In addition, there is another set of receptors which, when stimulated, close the gate, thereby reducing the experience of pain. Endorphins, internal painkillers, may also affect the operation of the gate.

13. Among the techniques used most frequently to alleviate pain are administration of drugs, hypnosis, biofeedback, relaxation techniques, surgery, nerve and brain stimulation, and psychotherapy.

What principles underlie our organization of the visual world, allowing us to make sense of our environment?

14. Work on figure-ground distinctions shows that perception is a constructive process in which people go beyond the stimuli that are physically present and try to construct a meaningful situation. Perception follows the gestalt laws of organization, a series of principles by which we organize bits and pieces of information into meaningful wholes, known as gestalts. Among the most important laws are closure, proximity, similarity, and simplicity. The gestalt psychologists demonstrated convincingly that perception follows the general rule: "The whole is greater than the sum of its parts."

15. Feature analysis pertains to how we consider a shape, pattern, object, or scene in terms of the individual elements that make it up. These component features are then combined into a representation of the whole object in the brain. Finally, this combination of features is compared against existing memories, permitting identification of the object.

16. Processing of perceptual stimuli occurs in both a top-down and a bottom-up fashion. In top-down processing, perception is guided by higher-level knowledge, experience, expectations, and motivations. In bottom-up processing, perception involves recognizing and processing information about the individual components of stimuli.

17. Perceptual constancy permits us to perceive stimuli as unvarying and consistent, despite changes in the environment or the appearance of the objects being perceived. Perceptual constancy occurs in terms of size, shape, and colour constancy.

How are we able to perceive the world in three dimensions when our retinas are capable of sensing only two-dimensional images?

18. Depth perception is the ability to perceive distance and to view the world in three dimensions, even though the images projected on our retinas are two-dimensional. We are able to

judge depth and distance as a result of binocular disparity (the difference in images as seen by each of the eyes) and monocular cues, such as motion parallax (the apparent movement of objects as one's head moves from side to side), the relative size of images on the retina, and linear perspective.

19. Motion perception depends on several cues. They include the perceived movement of an object across our retina and information about how the head and eyes are moving.

What clues do visual illusions give us about our understanding of general perceptual mechanisms?

20. Visual illusions are physical stimuli that consistently produce errors in perception, causing judgments that do not accurately reflect the physical reality of the stimulus. Among the best-known illusions are the Poggendorf illusion and the Müller-Lyer illusion.

21. Visual illusions are usually the result of errors in the brain's interpretation of visual stimuli. Furthermore, the particular culture in which we are raised has clear consequences for the ways in which we perceive the world.

22. Subliminal perception refers to the perception of messages about which we have no awareness, while extrasensory perception does not involve our known senses. The reality of both phenomena is open to question and debate.

Key Terms and Concepts

sensation (p. 85)
perception (p. 85)
stimulus (p. 86)
psychophysics (p.86)
absolute threshold (p. 86)
signal detection theory (p. 87)
difference threshold (p. 88)
just noticeable difference (p. 88)
Weber's law (p. 88)
adaptation (p. 89)
retina (p. 92)
rods (p. 93)
cones (p. 93)

dark adaptation (p. 93)
optic nerve (p. 94)
feature detection (p. 95)
trichromatic theory of colour vision (p. 97)
opponent-process theory of colour vision (p. 99)
sound (p. 100)
eardrum (p. 100)
cochlea (p. 101)
basilar membrane (p. 101)
hair cells (p. 101)
place theory of hearing (p. 103)

frequency theory of hearing (p. 103)
semicircular canals (p. 104)
otoliths (p. 104)
skin senses (p. 107)
gate-control theory of pain (p. 108)
gestalt laws of organization (p. 111)
feature analysis (p. 112)
top-down processing (p. 114)
bottom-up processing (p. 115)
monocular cues (p. 116)
visual illusions (p. 117)
subliminal perception (p. 121)

Epilogue

In this chapter we have noted the important distinction between sensation and perception, and we have examined the processes that underlie both of them. We've seen how external stimuli evoke sensory responses, and how our different senses process the information contained in those responses. We also have focused on the physical structure and internal workings of the individual senses, including vision, hearing, balance, smell, taste, and the skin senses, and we've explored how our brains organize and process sensory information to construct a consistent, integrated picture of the world around us.

Before we proceed to a discussion of consciousness in the next chapter, let's return to the opening prologue of this chapter. Consider the story of the railroad accident and answer the following questions, using your knowledge of sensation and perception.

1. Is the colour deficiency discussed in the prologue primarily a deficiency of sensation or perception? Why?

2. What part of the eye is involved in sensing the colours of train signal lights? Would the eye function differently in daylight versus night?

3. Can the two theories of colour vision discussed in this chapter (the trichromatic theory and the opponent-process theory) help to explain how a train engineer might pass one part of the vision test described in the prologue and fail the other?

4. Can the two theories explain how the engineer might have missed the yellow and the red light signals along his train route just before the accident?

5. How might bottom-up and top-down processing have been involved in the accident? Could the possible fatigue of the engineer have affected either type of processing? How?

Answers to Review Questions:

1. a-3; b-1; c-4; d-2   2. Feature   3. top-down; bottom-up   4. perceptual constancy   5. Depth perception   6. binocular disparity
7. 1-c, 2-a, 3-b   8. b

States of Consciousness

Brett Favre, Green Bay Packer star, fought—and won—his own personal war on drugs.

Prologue

Beating the Blitz

Green Bay Packers quarterback Brett Favre can tell you exactly when he changed his life, even if he doesn't remember it. It was 6 P.M. on February 27, and Favre was in his room at Bellin Hospital in Green Bay, Wisconsin, recovering from ankle surgery. A nurse was about to reinsert his IV, and the oft-injured quarterback was rolling his eyes in resignation at his longtime girlfriend, Deanna Tynes, and their 7-year-old daughter, Brittany. Suddenly he went into convulsions. "His whole body was jerking around, his lip was folded under," says Deanna, 27, who screamed to the nurse to stop him from swallowing his tongue. Asked a terrified Brittany: "Mom, is he going to die?"

In a sense, just the opposite happened. When Favre, 26, regained consciousness minutes later, he awakened to a central fact of his life: He was an addict in need of help. For the previous five months, Favre had been taking the painkiller Vicodin—first to help him deal with a season's worth of injuries and then as a crutch for coping with fame. Doctors could not pinpoint the cause of the seizure, but it seemed clear to Favre that it was related to his dependency on the prescription drug. Three months later he checked into the Menninger Clinic in Topeka, Kansas, for six weeks of rehab (Plummer & Pick, 1996, p. 129).

looking
AHEAD

consciousness: The awareness of the sensations, thoughts, and feelings being experienced at a given moment

Consciousness

Brett Favre was successful in his personal war on drugs: Today, he is free of painkillers, and he was named the National Football League's Most Valuable Player and led his team to two consecutive Super Bowl appearances. Others, though, are not so lucky. Each year, thousands of people die from complications of drug overdoses, and many more are addicted to various kinds of drugs.

What leads people to grow dependent on drugs, or to turn to them as a way to change their normal states of consciousness? More generally, what *is* consciousness, and how does normal waking consciousness relate to states of consciousness such as sleep, hypnotic trances, or drug-induced experiences? In this chapter, we consider these questions.

Consciousness is the awareness of the sensations, thoughts, and feelings being experienced at a given moment. Consciousness is our subjective understanding of both the environment around us and our private internal world, unobservable to outsiders.

Consciousness spans several dimensions, encompassing several levels of awareness. For instance, consciousness ranges from the perceptions we experience while wide awake, concentrating on performing well on a test or seeking to play well in a baseball game, to the minimal level of awareness we experience while sleeping. Consciousness thus varies from an active to a passive state (Hilgard, 1980; Milner & Rugg, 1992). In more active states, we systematically carry out mental activity, focusing our thoughts and absorbing the world around us. In more passive waking states, thoughts and images come to us more spontaneously; we daydream or drift from one thought to another. In the most passive states of consciousness, such as sleeping, we are only minimally aware of the stimuli around us. Still, we remain at least partially aware of events outside our bodies, because we still can be awakened by sufficiently strong stimuli—such as the ringing of a persistent alarm clock.

Because consciousness is so personal a phenomenon, psychologists have sometimes been reluctant to study it (Rychlak, 1997). After all, who can say that your consciousness is similar to or, for that matter, different from anyone else's? In fact, early psychologists suggested that the study of consciousness was out of bounds for the discipline. They argued that because consciousness could be understood only by relying on the "unscientific" introspections of experimental participants about what they were experiencing at a given moment, its study was best left to disciplines such as philosophy. Proponents of this view suggested that philosophers could speculate at their leisure on such knotty issues as whether consciousness is separate from the physical body, how people know they exist, how the body and mind are related to each other, and how we identify what state of consciousness we are in at any given moment in time.

However, most contemporary psychologists reject the view that the study of consciousness is unsuitable for the field of psychology (Block, Flanagan, & Güzeldere, 1997; Shear, 1997). They argue instead that there are several scientific approaches that permit its study. For example, biopsychologists can measure brain wave patterns under conditions of consciousness ranging from sleep to waking to hypnotic trances. Moreover, new understanding of the chemistry of drugs such as marijuana and alcohol has provided insights into the way they produce their pleasurable—as well as adverse—effects.

Another impetus for the study of consciousness is the realization that people in many different cultures routinely seek ways to alter their states of consciousness. Variations in states of consciousness have been found to share some basic characteristics (Ludwig, 1969; Martindale, 1981). One is an alteration in thinking, which may become shallow, illogical, or impaired in some way. In addition, people's sense of time may become disturbed, and their perceptions of the world and of themselves may be changed. They may experience a loss of self-control, doing things that they would never otherwise do. Finally, they may feel a sense of *ineffability*—the inability to understand an experience rationally or describe it in words.

This chapter considers several states of consciousness, beginning with two that we have all experienced: sleeping and dreaming. Next, we turn to states of consciousness found under conditions of hypnosis and meditation. Finally, we examine drug-induced states of consciousness.

SLEEP AND DREAMS

The crowd roared as running back Donald Dorff, age 67, took the pitch from his quarterback and accelerated smoothly across the artificial turf. As Dorff braked and pivoted to cut back over a tackle, a huge defensive lineman loomed in his path. One hundred twenty pounds of pluck, Dorff did not hesitate. But let the retired grocery merchandiser from Golden Valley, Minnesota, tell it:

"There was a 280-pound tackle waiting for me, so I decided to give him my shoulder. When I came to, I was on the floor in my bedroom. I had smashed into the dresser and knocked everything off it and broke the mirror and just made one heck of a mess. It was 1:30 A.M." (Long, 1987, p. 787).

Dorff, it turned out, was suffering from a rare condition afflicting some older men. The problem occurs when the mechanism that usually shuts down bodily movement during dreams does not function properly. People suffering from the malady have been known to hit others, smash windows, punch holes in walls—all while fast asleep.

Donald Dorff's problem had a happy ending. With the help of clonazepam, a drug that suppresses movement during dreams, his malady vanished. He now sleeps through the night undisturbed.

The success of Dorff's treatment illustrates just one of the advances that researchers have made in our understanding of sleep. Yet there are still many unanswered questions, including why we sleep, how much sleep we need, the meaning and function of dreams, and how to avoid insomnia. (Before you read on, you might want to test your knowledge of sleep and dreams by answering the questions in Figure 4-1.)

▶ What are the different states of consciousness?

▶ What happens when we sleep, and what are the meaning and function of dreams?

▶ How much do we daydream?

▶ What are the major sleep disorders and how can they be treated?

The Stages of Sleep

Most of us consider sleep a time of quiet tranquility, as we set aside the tensions of the day and spend the night in uneventful slumber. However, a closer look at sleep shows

FIGURE 4-1 *Testing your knowledge of sleep and dreams. Source: Adapted from Palladino & Carducci, 1984.*

Although sleeping is something we all do for a significant part of our lives, many myths and misconceptions about the topic abound. To test your own knowledge of sleep and dreams, try answering the following questions before reading further.

_____ 1. Some people never dream.
True or false?

_____ 2. Most dreams are caused by bodily sensations such as an upset stomach.
True or false?

_____ 3. It has been proved that eight hours of sleep is needed to maintain mental health.
True or false?

_____ 4. When people do not recall their dreams, it is probably because they are secretly trying to forget them.
True or false?

_____ 5. Depriving someone of sleep will invariably cause the individual to become mentally unbalanced.
True or false?

_____ 6. If we lose some sleep, we will eventually make up all the lost sleep the next night or another night.
True or false?

_____ 7. No one has been able to go for more than forty-eight hours without sleep.
True or false?

_____ 8. Everyone is able to sleep and breathe at the same time.
True or false?

_____ 9. Sleep enables the brain to rest since there is little brain activity taking place during sleep.
True or false?

_____ 10. Drugs have been proved to provide a long-term cure for sleeping difficulties.
True or false?

Scoring: This is an easy set of questions to score, for every item is false. But don't lose any sleep if you missed them; they were chosen to represent the most common myths regarding sleep.

that a good deal of activity occurs throughout the night, and that what at first appears to be a unitary state is, in fact, quite diverse (Broughton and Ogilvie, 1992).

Much of our knowledge of what happens during sleep comes from the *electroencephalogram,* or *EEG,* a measurement of electrical activity within the brain (see Chapter 2). When probes from an EEG machine are attached to the surface of a sleeping person's scalp and face, it becomes readily apparent that instead of being dormant, the brain is active throughout the night. It produces electrical discharges that form systematic, wavelike patterns that change in height (or amplitude) and speed (or frequency) in regular sequences. Instruments that measure muscle and eye movements also reveal a good deal of physical activity.

People progress through four distinct stages of sleep during a night's rest, moving through cycles lasting about 90 minutes. Each of these four sleep stages is associated with a unique pattern of brain waves, as shown in Figure 4-2. Moreover, there are specific biological indicators of dreaming.

When people first go to sleep, they move from a waking state in which they are relaxed with their eyes closed into **stage 1 sleep,** which is characterized by relatively rapid, low-voltage brain waves. This is actually a stage of transition between wakefulness and sleep. During stage 1 images sometimes appear. It's as if we were viewing still photos. However, true dreaming does not occur during the initial entry into this stage.

As sleep becomes deeper, people enter **stage 2 sleep,** which is characterized by a slower, more regular wave pattern. However, there are also momentary interruptions

stage 1 sleep: The state of transition between wakefulness and sleep, characterized by relatively rapid, low-voltage brain waves

stage 2 sleep: A sleep deeper than that of stage 1, characterized by a slower, more regular wave pattern, along with momentary interruptions of "sleep spindles"

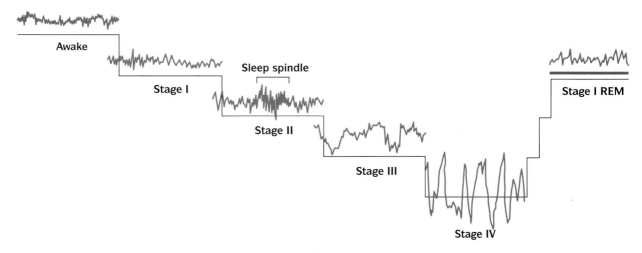

FIGURE 4-2 *Brain-wave patterns (measured by an EEG apparatus) vary significantly during the different stages of sleep. Source: Hobson, 1988.*

of sharply pointed waves called "sleep spindles" because of their configuration. It becomes increasingly difficult to awaken a person from stage 2 sleep, which makes up about half of the total sleep of those in their early twenties.

As people drift into **stage 3 sleep,** the next stage of sleep, the brain waves become slower, with an appearance of higher peaks and lower valleys in the wave pattern. By the time sleepers arrive at **stage 4 sleep,** the pattern is even slower and more regular, and people are least responsive to outside stimulation.

As you can see in Figure 4-3, stage 4 sleep is most likely to occur during the early part of the night. In addition to passing through regular transitions between stages of sleep, then, people tend to sleep less and less deeply over the course of the night. In the first half of the evening, our sleep is dominated by stages 3 and 4. The last half is characterized by lighter stages of sleep—as well as the phase of sleep during which dreams occur, as we discuss next (Dement & Wolpert, 1958).

stage 3 sleep: A sleep characterized by slow brain waves, with greater peaks and valleys in the wave pattern
stage 4 sleep: The deepest stage of sleep, during which we are least responsive to outside stimulation

REM Sleep: The Paradox of Sleep

Several times a night, while sleepers are in stage 1 sleep, something curious happens. Their heart rate increases and becomes irregular, their blood pressure rises, their breathing rate increases, and males—even male infants—have erections. Most characteristic of this period is the back-and-forth movement of their eyes, as if they were

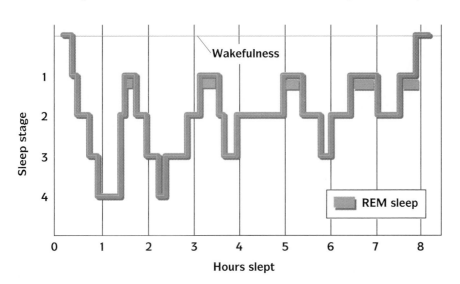

FIGURE 4-3 *During the night, the typical sleeper passes through all four stages of sleep and several REM periods. Source: Hartmann, 1967.*

rapid eye movement (REM)
sleep: Sleep occupying 20 percent of an
adult's sleeping time, characterized by
increased heart rate, blood pressure,
and breathing rate; erections; eye
movements; and the experience of
dreaming

watching an action-filled movie. This period of sleep is called **rapid eye movement,**
or **REM, sleep.** REM sleep occupies a little over 20 percent of adults' total sleeping
time.

Paradoxically, while all this activity is occurring, the major muscles of the body
appear to be paralyzed—except in rare cases such as Donald Dorff's. For this reason,
it is hard to awaken the sleeper. In addition, REM sleep is usually accompanied by
dreams, which—whether or not people remember them—are experienced by *everyone*
during some part of the night.

One possible but still unproven explanation for rapid eye movements is that the
eyes follow the action that is occurring in the dream (Dement, 1979; D. D. Kelly,
1991b). For instance, people who have reported dreaming about watching a tennis
match just before they were awakened showed regular right-left-right eye movements,
as if they were observing the ball flying back and forth across the net.

There is good reason to believe that REM sleep plays an important role in everyday human functioning. People deprived of REM sleep—by being awakened every
time they begin to display the physiological signs of the stage—show a *rebound effect*
when allowed to rest undisturbed. With this rebound effect, REM-deprived sleepers
spend significantly more time in REM sleep than they normally would. It is as if the
body requires a certain amount of REM sleep in order to function properly.

Sleep

How Much Sleep Is Necessary?

Sleep is a requirement for normal human functioning, although, surprisingly, the exact
amount of sleep that people require has not been firmly established. It is reasonable to
expect that our bodies would require a tranquil "rest and relaxation" period in order to
revitalize themselves, and experiments with rats show that total sleep deprivation results in death (Webb, 1992; Porkka-Heiskanen et al., 1997).

Although we know that *some* sleep is necessary, we don't know just how much is
absolutely required. For instance, while most people sleep between seven and eight
hours each night (Farley, 1993), there is wide variability among individuals, with some
people needing as little as three hours (see Figure 4-4). Sleep requirements also vary
over the course of a lifetime: As they age, people generally need less and less sleep.

Furthermore, people who participate in sleep deprivation experiments, in which
they are kept awake for stretches as long as 200 hours, show no lasting effects. It's no
fun—they feel weary and irritable, can't concentrate, and show a loss of creativity,
even after only minor deprivation. They also show a decline in logical reasoning ability, although there are occasional increases at certain times of the day (see Figure 4-5).
However, after being allowed to sleep normally, they bounce back quickly and are
able to perform at pre-deprivation levels after just a few days (Dement, 1976; Webb,
1992; Dinges et al., 1997).

Those of us who worry, then, that long hours of study, work, or perhaps partying
are ruining our health should feel heartened. As far as anyone can tell, most people
suffer no permanent consequences of such temporary sleep deprivation. At the same
time, though, a lack of sleep may make us feel edgy, slow our reaction time, and lower
our performance on academic tasks. We certainly won't feel particularly good. In addition, we put ourselves—and others—at risk when we carry out routine activities,
such as driving, when we're very sleepy. As sleep researcher Stanley Coren suggests,
"Going without sleep is as much of a public and personal safety hazard as going to
work drunk in the morning" (Coren, 1996, p. A10).

Circadian Rhythms: Life Cycles

circadian rhythms: Biological
processes that occur repeatedly on
approximately a 24-hour cycle

The fact that we cycle back and forth between wakefulness and sleep is one example
of our body's circadian rhythms. **Circadian rhythms** (from the Latin *circa dies,* or
"around a day") are biological processes that occur repeatedly in humans and other animals on a daily basis. Sleep and waking, for instance, occur naturally to the beat of an
internal pacemaker that works on a cycle of approximately 24 hours. Several other

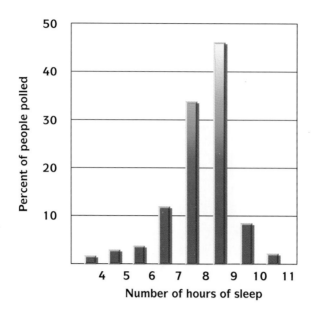

FIGURE 4-4 *Although most people report sleeping between eight and nine hours per night, the amount varies a great deal. Source: From Borbely, A. (1996).* Secrets of sleep. *New York: Basic Books, p. 43. Based on data of Kripke, D. F., et al. (1979).*

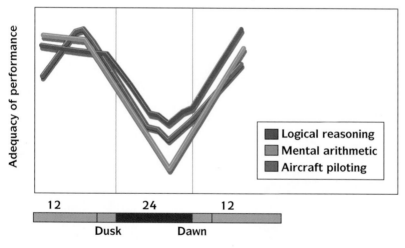

FIGURE 4-5 *Performance on various kinds of tasks improves and declines during certain periods of the day. Source: Moore-Ede, 1993.*

bodily functions, such as temperature, also work on circadian rhythms, regulated by biological mechanisms (Morell, 1996a).

An internal pacemaker or clock mechanism for organizing many circadian rhythms is located in the suprachiasmatic nucleus of the hypothalamus. When Martin Ralph at the University of Toronto transplanted the suprachiasmatic nuclei from a mutant strain of hamsters having a 21-hour cycle into normal hamsters, he found that the normal hamsters changed to a 21-hour cycle (Ralph and Lehman, 1991). Other means of altering circadian rhythms include changing rats' exposure to light (Arvanitogiannis, 1999) and varying hamsters' times for exercise or feeding or both (Mistlberger, 1991).

Circadian cycles are complex. For instance, sleepiness occurs not just in the evening, but throughout the day in regular patterns. As you can see in Figure 4-6, most of us tend to get drowsy in midafternoon—regardless of whether we have eaten a heavy lunch. By making an afternoon siesta part of their everyday habit, people in several cultures take advantage of the body's natural inclination to sleep at this time (Dement, 1989; Stampi, 1992; Ogilvie & Harsh, 1994).

Circadian cycles are powerful—as anyone who has worked a night shift well knows. Not only do night shift workers have trouble staying awake, but they are less productive and more likely to have accidents than day workers. For example, the near-meltdown of the nuclear power plant at Three Mile Island, the Exxon *Valdez* oil spill

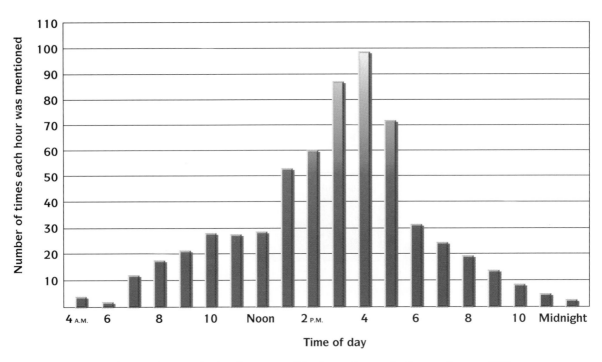

FIGURE 4-6 *The hours that people report having the greatest difficulty staying awake. Source: Dement, 1989.*

Seasonal affective disorder can be relieved by several hours of exposure to special bright lights during the short days of winter.

in Alaska, and the Chernobyl nuclear reactor accident all occurred in the wee hours of the night (Mapes, 1990; Moore-Ede, 1993). Administration of the hormone melatonin may help shift workers deal with night shifts (Folkard et al., 1993).

Although sleep operates on a daily circadian cycle, other bodily rhythms operate on much longer cycles. For instance, some people experience *seasonal affective disorder,* a form of severe depression in which feelings of despair and hopelessness increase during the winter and lift during the rest of the year. The disorder appears to be a result of the brevity and gloom of winter days. Psychologists have found that several hours of daily exposure to bright lights is sometimes sufficient to improve the mood of those with the disorder. Additional experimental treatments, based on variations in hor-

"I've got it again, Larry . . . an eerie feeling like there's something on top of the bed."

mone levels produced by circadian cycles, are being developed to treat other medical problems, including obesity and one form of diabetes (Sack et al., 1990; Roush, 1995; Oren & Terman, 1998).

Another periodic rhythm is the female menstrual cycle. Occurring on a 28-day schedule, the menstrual cycle is regulated by hormone production that ebbs and increases throughout the cycle as women's bodies prepare for the possibility of conception.

Are the physical changes that occur during the phases of the menstrual cycle accompanied by swings in mood? The answer is "probably not," despite the prevalence in the popular press of discussions of "premenstrual syndrome" or "PMS." PMS refers to a grab-bag of symptoms, including irritability, fatigue, anxiety, and volatility, that are assumed to emerge just before menstruation. Although a small proportion of women do suffer relatively intense periodic mood swings related to their menstrual cycles, most do not (McFarlane, Martin, & Williams, 1988; Cotton, 1993; Hunter, Swann, & Ussher, 1995).

The Function and Meaning of Dreaming

I was sitting at my desk when I remembered that this was the day of my chemistry final! I felt awful. I hadn't studied a bit for it. In fact, I couldn't even remember where the class was held, and I had missed every lecture all semester. In a panic, I began running across campus desperately searching for the classroom so that I could beg the professor to give me another chance. But I had to stop at every classroom building, looking in one room after another, hoping to find the professor. It was hopeless; I knew I was going to fail and flunk out of college.

If you have had a similar dream—a surprisingly common dream among people involved in academic pursuits—you know how utterly convincing are the panic and

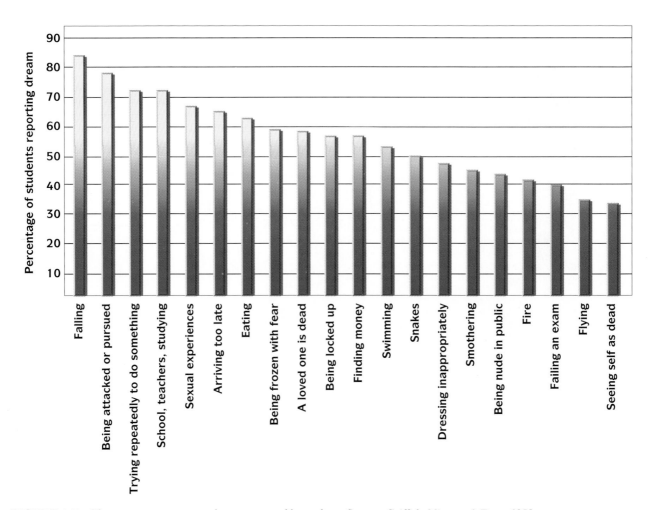

FIGURE 4-7 *The twenty most common dreams reported by students. Source: Griffith, Miyago, & Tago, 1958.*

Dreams

unconscious wish fulfillment theory: Sigmund Freud's theory that dreams represent unconscious wishes that dreamers desire to see fulfilled

latent content of dreams: According to Freud, the "disguised" meanings of dreams, hidden by more obvious subjects

manifest content of dreams: According to Freud, the overt story line of dreams

fear that the events in the dream can bring about. *Nightmares,* unusually frightening dreams, occur fairly often. In one survey, almost half of a group of college students who kept records of their dreams over a two-week period reported having at least one nightmare. This works out to some twenty-four nightmares per person each year, on average (Wood & Bootzin, 1990; Berquier & Ashton, 1992; Tan & Hicks, 1995).

On the other hand, most of the 150,000 dreams the average person experiences by the age of 70 are much less dramatic (Snyder, 1970; Webb, 1992). They typically encompass such everyday events as going to the supermarket, working at the office, or preparing a meal. Students dream about going to class; professors dream about lecturing. Dental patients dream of getting their teeth drilled; dentists dream of drilling the wrong tooth. The English take tea with the Queen in their dreams; in the United States, people go to a bar with the president (K. Wells, 1993; Solomon, 1993; Potheraju & Soper, 1995; Domhoff, 1996; see Figure 4-7 for the most common dreams).

But what, if anything, do all these dreams mean? Whether dreams have a specific significance and function is a question that scientists have considered for many years, and they have developed several alternative theories.

Do Dreams Represent Unconscious Wish Fulfillment?

Sigmund Freud viewed dreams as a guide to the unconscious (Freud, 1900). In his **unconscious wish fulfillment theory,** he proposed that dreams represented unconscious wishes that dreamers desire to see fulfilled. However, because these wishes are threatening to the dreamer's conscious awareness, the actual wishes—called the **latent content of dreams**—are disguised. The true subject and meaning of a dream, then, may have little to do with its overt story line, which Freud called the **manifest content of dreams.**

Table 4-1	Dream Symbolism, According to Freud

Symbol (Manifest Content of Dream)	Interpretation (Latent Content)
Climbing up a stairway, crossing a bridge, riding an elevator, flying in an airplane, walking down a long hallway, entering a room, train travelling through a tunnel	Sexual intercourse
Apples, peaches, grapefruits	Breasts
Bullets, fire, snakes, sticks, umbrellas, guns, hoses, knives	Male sex organs
Ovens, boxes, tunnels, closets, caves, bottles, ships	Female sex organs

To Freud, it was important to pierce the armour of a dream's manifest content to understand its true meaning. To do this, Freud tried to get people to discuss their dreams, associating symbols in the dreams to events in the past. He also suggested that certain common symbols with universal meanings appear in dreams. For example, to Freud, dreams in which the person is flying symbolize a wish for sexual intercourse. (See Table 4-1 for other common symbols.)

Today many psychologists reject Freud's view that dreams typically represent unconscious wishes and that particular objects and events in a dream are symbolic. Instead, the direct, overt action of a dream is considered the focal point in understanding its meaning. For example, a dream in which we are walking down a long hallway to take an exam for which we haven't studied does not relate to unconscious, unacceptable wishes. Instead, it simply may mean we are concerned about an impending test. Even more complex dreams can often be interpreted in terms of everyday concerns and stress (Cook, Caplan, & Wolowitz, 1990; Domhoff, 1996).

Moreover, we now know that some dreams reflect events occurring in the dreamer's environment as he or she is sleeping. For example, sleeping participants in one experiment were sprayed with water while they were dreaming. These unlucky volunteers reported more dreams involving water than a comparison group of participants who were left to sleep undisturbed (Dement & Wolpert, 1958). Similarly, it is not unusual to wake up to find that the doorbell that was being rung in a dream is actually an alarm clock telling us it is time to get up.

Reverse Learning Theory

Although the content of dreams can clearly be affected by environmental stimuli, the question of *why* we dream remains unresolved. Several alternatives to Freud's theory have been proposed. According to the **reverse learning theory,** for instance, dreams have no meaning whatsoever. Instead, they represent a kind of reverse learning, in which we flush away unnecessary information that we have accumulated during the day. In this view, dreaming simply represents the reverse learning of material that ultimately would prove to be confusing to us. Dreams, then, are a kind of mental housecleaning of the brain, but have no meaning in and of themselves (Crick & Mitchison, 1983, 1995).

reverse learning theory: The theory that proposes that dreams have no meaning whatsoever, but instead function to rid us of unnecessary information that we have accumulated during the day

Dreams-for-Survival Theory

The **dreams-for-survival theory** proposes yet another function for dreams. According to this theory, dreams permit information that is critical for our daily survival to be reconsidered and reprocessed during sleep. Dreaming is seen as an inheritance from our animal ancestors, whose small brains were unable to sift sufficient information during waking hours. Consequently, dreaming provided a mechanism that permitted the processing of information twenty-four hours a day.

According to this theory, dreams do have meaning. They represent concerns about our daily lives, illustrating our uncertainties, indecisions, ideas, and desires. Dreams are seen, then, as consistent with everyday living. Rather than being disguised

dreams-for-survival theory: The theory suggesting that dreams permit information that is critical for our daily survival to be reconsidered and reprocessed during sleep

wishes, as Freud suggested, they represent key concerns growing out of our daily experiences (Pavlides & Winson, 1989; Winson, 1990).

Research supports the dreams-for-survival theory, suggesting that certain dreams permit people to focus and consolidate memories, particularly dreams that pertain to "how-to-do-it" memories related to motor skills. For instance, in one experiment, participants learned a visual memory task late in the day. They were then sent to bed, but awakened at certain times during the night. When they were awakened at times that did not interrupt dreaming, their performance on the memory task typically improved the next day. But when they were awakened during Rapid Eye Movement (REM) sleep—the stage of sleep when people dream—their performance declined. The conclusion: Dreaming may play a role in helping us to remember material to which we have been previously exposed (Karni et al., 1992, 1994).

Activation-Synthesis Theory

activation-synthesis theory:
Hobson's theory that the brain produces random electrical energy during REM sleep that stimulates memories lodged in various portions of the brain

The most influential current explanation for dreaming considers dreams as a by-product of fundamental biological activity. According to psychiatrist J. Allan Hobson, who proposed the **activation-synthesis theory,** the brain produces random electrical energy during REM sleep, possibly due to changes in the production of particular neurotransmitters. This electrical energy randomly stimulates memories lodged in various portions of the brain. Because we have a need to make sense of our world, even while asleep, the brain takes these chaotic memories and weaves them into a logical story line, filling in the gaps to produce a rational scenario. In this view, then, dreams are closer to a self-generated game of Madlibs than to significant, meaningful psychological phenomena (J. A. Hobson, 1988, J. A. Hobson, 1996; Porte & Hobson, 1996).

Yet Hobson does not entirely reject the view that dreams reflect unconscious wishes. He suggests that the particular scenario that a dreamer produces is not just random but instead is a clue to the dreamer's fears, emotions, and concerns. Hence, what starts out as a random process culminates in something meaningful.

Evidence that dreaming represents a response to random brain activity comes from work with people who have been injected with drugs similar to the neurotransmitter acetylcholine. Under the influence of the drug, people quickly enter REM sleep and have dreams similar in quality to those that occur during natural sleep. Still, such evidence as this does not confirm that these drug-induced dreams have psychological meaning (Schmeck, 1987; Solms, 1996).

The range of theories about dreaming (summarized in Table 4-2) clearly illustrates that dream researchers have yet to agree on the fundamental meaning of dreams. However, it does seem likely that the specific content of our dreams is unique to us and in some way represents meaningful patterns and concerns. Ultimately, dreams may provide clues about the experiences that on some level of consciousness are most important to us.

| Table 4-2 | Four Views of Dreams |

Theory	Basic Explanation	Meaning of Dreams	Is Meaning of Dream Disguised?
Unconscious wish fulfillment theory (Freud)	Dreams represent unconscious wishes the dreamer wants to fulfill	Latent content reveals unconscious wishes	Yes, by manifest content of dreams
Reverse learning theory	Unnecessary information is "unlearned" and removed from memory	None	No meaning
Dreams-for-survival theory	Information relevant to daily survival is reconsidered and reprocessed	Clues to everyday concerns about survival	Not necessarily
Activation-synthesis theory	Dreams are the result of random activation of various memories, which are tied together in a logical story line	Dream scenario that is constructed is related to dreamer's concerns	Not necessarily

Daydreams: Dreams Without Sleep

It is the stuff of magic: Our past mistakes can be wiped out and the future filled with note-worthy accomplishments. Fame, happiness, and wealth can be ours. In the next moment, though, the most horrible of tragedies can occur, leaving us devastated, alone, and penniless.

The source of these scenarios is **daydreams,** fantasies that people construct while awake. Unlike dreaming that occurs while sleeping, daydreams are more under people's control. Therefore their content is often more closely related to immediate events in the environment than is the content of the dreams that occur during sleep. Although they may include sexual content, daydreams also pertain to other activities or events that are relevant to a person's life.

daydreams: Fantasies that people construct while awake

Daydreams are a typical part of waking consciousness, although our awareness of the environment around us declines. People vary considerably in the amount of day-dreaming they do. For example, around 2 to 4 percent of the population spend at least half their free time fantasizing. Although most people daydream much less frequently, almost everyone fantasizes to some degree. Studies that ask people to identify what they are doing at random times during the day have shown that they are daydreaming about 10 percent of the time. As for the content of fantasies, most concern such mundane, ordinary events as paying the telephone bill, picking up the groceries, or solving a romantic problem (Singer, 1975; Lynn & Rhue, 1988; Lynn et al., 1996).

Although frequent daydreaming might seem to suggest psychological difficul-ties, there actually appears to be little relationship between psychological disturbance and daydreaming. Except in those rare cases in which a daydreamer is unable to distin-guish a fantasy from reality (a mark of serious problems, as we discuss in Chapter 12), daydreaming seems to be a normal part of waking consciousness. Indeed, fantasy may contribute to the psychological well-being of some people by enhancing their creativ-ity and by permitting them to use their imagination to understand what other people are experiencing (Rhue & Lynn, 1987; Lynn & Rhue, 1988; Pihlgren, Gidycz, & Lynn, 1993; Lynn et al., 1996).

Sleep Disturbances: Slumbering Problems

At one time or another, almost all of us have difficulty sleeping—a condition known as *insomnia.* It may be due to a particular situation, such as the breakup of a relationship, or the loss of a job. Some cases of insomnia, however, have no obvious cause. Some people are unable to fall asleep easily, or they go to sleep readily but wake up frequently during the night. Insomnia is a problem that afflicts about a quarter of the population of the United States (Hauri, 1991; Pressman & Orr, 1997). About one million Canadians over the age of 11 used sleeping pills in 1997 (Health Canada, 1999).

Interestingly, many people who *think* they have sleeping problems may be mis-taken. Observers find that patients who enter sleep laboratories for treatment actually sleep much more than they think they do. For example, researchers have found that some people who report being up all night actually fall asleep in thirty minutes and stay asleep all night. Furthermore, some insomniacs can accurately recall sounds that they heard while they were asleep, which gives them the impression that they were ac-tually awake during the night (Engle-Friedman, Baker, & Bootzin, 1985).

The problem for many people, then, is not lack of sleep but faulty perceptions of their sleeping patterns. In many cases, just becoming aware of how long they really do sleep—and understanding the fact that the older they become the less sleep they need—is enough to "cure" people's perception that they have a sleep disorder. In fact, some re-searchers suggest that new drugs for insomnia will function by changing people's *percep-tions* of how much they have slept, rather than actually making them sleep more (Klinkenborg, 1997).

Other sleep problems are less common than insomnia, although they are still widespread (D. D. Kelly 1991a; Bootzin et al., 1993; Buysse, Morin, & Reynolds, 1995). For instance, one million Canadians and over 20 million Americans suffer from *sleep apnea,* a condition in which a person has difficulty breathing and sleeping simul-

Sleep Disorders

Pathways Through Psychology

Robert D. Ogilvie

Sleep Researcher
Brock University, St. Catherines,
Ontario

Education: B.A., Carleton University;
M.A., Hollins College, Virginia; Ph.D.,
Cambridge University

Robert D. Ogilvie

Although I'm officially a psychologist by training, I think of myself as a Sleep Researcher—because that's what I do when I'm not teaching here at Brock University in St. Catherines.

My interest in sleep began almost accidentally in graduate school where I wrote an essay on the effects of sleep and sleep deprivation on early mammalian development. (Try to imagine a world without sleep—it's as essential as air and water.) I soon decided to make sleep the focus of my doctoral work.

Sleep was a relatively new area of study in the late '60s and '70s, when I began to study it, and it was interdisciplinary. Psychologists, psychiatrists, biologists, neurologists, and many others were drawn, like me, to study sleep and dreaming in the years after Aserinsky and Kleitman discovered the link between REM sleep and dreaming. They gave us the first tools with which to link the psychology (dreams and thoughts) and the physiology (Rapid Eye Movements [REM] and brain wave activity) of sleep! This was incredibly exciting and challenging, for it pointed towards a whole new emerging field—one which I've watched and helped to develop.

Now, after 30 years, the knowledge base is solid enough to support a whole new discipline—sleep disorders medicine. Contributing to this creative, dynamic enterprise is amazingly rewarding. I've developed my own expertise within the sleep field: I study the process of falling asleep. As we shift from waking to sleeping mode, our brains and conscious processes undergo a wider array of changes than can be seen at any other time. Studying this transition period can teach us lots about both waking and sleeping.

First, my students and I studied the sequence of changes in brain and behaviour as sleep began in normal sleepers. We found that waking and sleeping systems overlap considerably, and different systems give conflicting signals as to when they themselves have "fallen asleep". For instance, when you are very drowsy and your eyes are closed, slow rolling eye movements begin and last throughout the wake-to-sleep transition.

Next, we began to study sleep onset in people with sleep problems, and soon saw that normal, insomniac, and narcoleptic sleepers entered sleep quite differently. We are presently looking to see whether these different patterns are unique enough to be of diagnostic value.

Why do I do these weird studies, watching others go to sleep? First, as I've mentioned, it is really exciting to place one or two pieces of the Sleep Jig-Saw together in this huge collaborative adventure we call the science of sleep. Second, being a member of this scientific team is rewarding too. I've met fascinating people the world over at sleep conferences. And in the final analysis, being a Sleep Researcher is simply an important part of who I am.

Source: Robert D. Ogilvie, Ph.D. Brock University. <www.psyc.brocku.ca/~rogilvie/ sleep.htm>

---

taneously. The result is disturbed, fitful sleep, as the person is constantly reawakened when the lack of oxygen becomes great enough to trigger a waking response. In some cases, people with apnea wake as many as 500 times during the course of an evening, although they may not even be aware that they have wakened. Not surprisingly, such disturbed sleep results in complaints of fatigue the next day. Sleep apnea may also account for *sudden infant death syndrome,* a mysterious killer of seemingly normal infants who die while sleeping (Ball et al., 1997).

Narcolepsy is an uncontrollable need to sleep for short periods during the day (Dement, 1976; Aldrich, 1992). No matter what the activity—holding a heated conversation, exercising, or driving—the narcoleptic will go directly from wakefulness to REM sleep (Siegel et al., 1991; Tafti et al., 1992; Dantz, Edgar, & Dement, 1994). Narcoleptics experience embarrassment and loss of self-esteem (Broughton and Broughton, 1994). The causes of narcolepsy are not known, although there may be a genetic component.

We know relatively little about sleeptalking and sleepwalking, two sleep disturbances that are usually harmless. Both occur during stage 4 sleep and are more frequent in children than in adults. In most cases, sleeptalkers and sleepwalkers have a vague consciousness of the world around them, and a sleepwalker may be able to walk with agility around obstructions in a crowded room. Unless a sleepwalker wanders into a dangerous environment, sleepwalking typically poses little risk. Moreover, the conventional wisdom that one shouldn't awaken sleepwalkers is wrong: No harm will come from waking them, although they will probably be quite confused (Swanson, 1999).

On the other hand, sleepwalking has a potentially darker side. Consider the following case:

> A 16-year-old Kentucky girl, dreaming that burglars were breaking into her home and murdering her family, got up in her sleep, picked up two revolvers and fired into the dark house, killing her father and 6-year-old brother and injuring her horrified and bewildered mother (J. Brody, 1996, C1).

The defendant argued that because she was sleepwalking, she was not guilty—and a jury concurred. Other defendants have provided similar explanations for violent acts, and sleepwalking is becoming an increasingly popular defense. Still, the number of cases in which sleepwalking is associated with violence remains small (Moldofsky et al., 1995; Nofzinger & Wettstein, 1995; Kryger et al., 1996).

(To read about a psychologist who is a sleep researcher, see the Pathways Through Psychology box opposite.)

The Informed Consumer of Psychology

Sleeping Better

Fortunately, the most severe sleep disorder from which most of us suffer is insomnia. About 35 percent of North American adults suffer from insomnia. Seventeen percent consider their insomnia to be a serious problem because it is so frequent and disruptive (Coren, 1996).

For those of us who spend hours tossing and turning in bed, psychologists studying sleep disturbances have a number of suggestions for overcoming insomnia (Jacobs, Benson, & Friedman, 1993; NIH, 1996; Kupfer & Reynolds, 1997). They include:

- Exercise during the day and avoid naps. Not surprisingly, it helps to be tired before going to sleep! Moreover, learning systematic relaxation techniques and biofeedback (see Chapter 2) can help you unwind from the day's stresses and tensions (Woolfolk & McNulty, 1983; Bootzin, & Perlis, 1992; Rakel, 1993; Lehrer, 1996).

- Choose a regular bedtime and stick to it. Adhering to a habitual schedule helps your internal timing mechanisms regulate your body more effectively.

- Don't use your bed as an all-purpose area; leave studying, reading, eating, watching TV, and other recreational activities to some other part of your living quarters. If you follow this advice, your bed will become a cue for sleeping.

- Avoid drinks with caffeine (such as coffee, tea, and some soft drinks) after lunch. Their effects can linger for as long as eight to twelve hours after they are consumed.

- Drink a glass of warm milk at bedtime. Your grandparents were right, although they probably didn't know why. (Milk contains the chemical tryptophan, which helps people get to sleep.)

- Avoid sleeping pills. Pills can be temporarily effective, but in the long run they may cause more harm than good, since they disrupt the normal sleep cycle. By the way, the advice to avoid sleeping pills unless they are prescribed by a health professional includes such "natural" remedies as melatonin tablets, which are available without prescription in health food stores. On the other hand, sometimes drugs are effective for such short-term sleep disturbances as the disruption in sleeping pattern that often accompanies travel through different time zones (McClusky et al., 1991; Haimov & Lavie, 1996; Zhdanova et al., 1996).

This man's physiological responses during sleep are being studied at the Sleep Disorders Centre in Toronto.

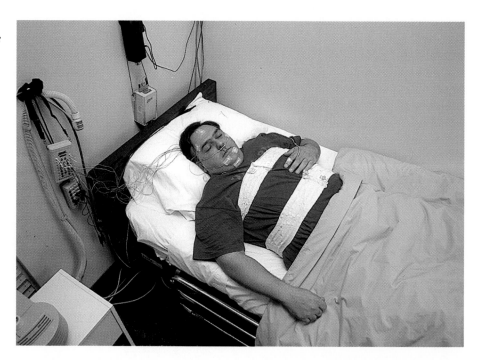

- Try *not* to go to sleep. This advice, which sounds strange at first, actually makes a good deal of sense. Psychologists have found that part of the reason people have difficulty falling asleep is that they are trying so hard. A better strategy is one suggested by Richard P. Bootzin of the University of Arizona, who teaches people to recondition their sleeping habits. He tells them to go to bed only when they feel tired. If they don't get to sleep within ten minutes, they should leave the bedroom and do something else, returning to bed only when they do feel tired. This process should be continued, all night if necessary. But in the morning, the patient must get up at his or her usual hour and must not take a nap during the day. After three to four weeks on this regimen, most people become conditioned to associate their beds with sleep—and fall asleep rapidly at night (Seltzer, 1986; Ubell, 1993; Sloan et al., 1993).

For long-term problems with sleep, you might consider visiting a sleep disorders center. A list of some of the sleep labs and clinics in cities across Canada can be found at the following web site: <www.geocities.com/~sleepawake/can-labs2.html>.   ∎

Recap, Review, and Rethink

Recap

- Consciousness refers to a person's awareness of the sensations, thoughts, and feelings being experienced at a given moment.

- There are four distinct stages of sleep, as well as REM (rapid eye movement) sleep. These stages recur in cycles during the course of a normal night's sleep.

- The four major explanations of dreams are Freud's wish fulfillment theory, reverse learning theory, dreams-for-survival theory, and activation-synthesis theory.

- The major sleep disorders include insomnia, narcolepsy, and sleep apnea.

Review

1. _____ is the term used to describe our understanding of the world external to us, as well as our own internal world.

2. Contrary to popular belief, a great deal of neural activity goes on during sleep. True or false?

3. Dreams occur in what phase of sleep?

4. _____ are internal bodily processes that occur on a daily cycle.

5. Freud's theory of unconscious _____ _____ states that the actual wishes that an individual expresses in dreams are disguised because they are threatening to the person's conscious awareness.

6. Match the theory of dreaming with its definition.
   1. dreams-for-survival theory
   2. reverse learning theory
   3. activation-synthesis theory

   a. Dreams permit necessary information to be reprocessed during sleep.
   b. Random energy produced during sleep stimulates the brain, which then weaves the activated memories into a story line.
   c. Dreams "flush away" excess information gathered during the day.
7. Match the sleep problem with its definition.
   1. insomnia
   2. narcolepsy
   3. sleep apnea

   a. condition that makes breathing while sleeping difficult
   b. difficulty in sleeping
   c. uncontrollable need to sleep during the day

Answers to Review Questions are on page 146.

Rethink

1. How could studying the sleep patterns of nonhuman species potentially enlighten us about the functions of sleep and dreams? Do you think we would find differences between human and nonhuman sleep and eye movement patterns? What sorts of differences might we find?

2. In what ways is the activation-synthesis theory of dreaming similar to Freud's theory? In what ways is it different?

3. Suppose that a new "miracle pill" is developed that will allow a person to function with only one hour of sleep per night. However, because a night's sleep is so short, a person who takes the pill will never dream again. Knowing what you do about the functions of sleep and dreaming, what would be some advantages and drawbacks of such a pill from a personal standpoint? From a societal standpoint? Would you take such a pill?

HYPNOSIS AND MEDITATION

You are feeling relaxed and drowsy. You are getting sleepier and sleepier. Your body is becoming limp. Now you are starting to become warm, at ease, more comfortable. Your eyelids are feeling heavier and heavier. Your eyes are closing; you can't keep them open any more. You are totally relaxed.

Now, as you listen to my voice, do exactly as I say. Place your hands above your head. You will find they are getting heavier and heavier—so heavy you can barely keep them up. In fact, although you are straining as hard as you can, you will be unable to hold them up any longer.

An observer watching the above scene would notice a curious phenomenon occurring. Many of the people listening to the voice would, one by one, drop their arms to their sides, as if they were holding heavy lead weights. The reason for this strange behaviour? The people have been hypnotized.

► Are hypnotized people in a different state of consciousness, and can people be hypnotized against their will?

► What are the consequences of meditation?

Hypnosis: A Trance-Forming Experience?

People under **hypnosis** are in a state of heightened susceptibility to the suggestions of others. In some respects, it appears that they are asleep. Yet other aspects of their behaviour contradict this notion, for people are attentive to the hypnotist's suggestions and may carry out bizarre or silly suggestions.

Despite their compliance when hypnotized, people do not lose all will of their own. They will not perform antisocial behaviours, and they will not carry out self-destructive acts. People will not reveal hidden truths about themselves, and they are capable of lying. Moreover, people cannot be hypnotized against their will—despite popular misconceptions (Pekala, Kumar, & Marcano, 1995; Gwynn & Spanos, 1996).

There are wide variations in people's susceptibility to hypnosis (Lynn et al., 1991; Kirsch & Council, 1992). About 5 to 20 percent of the population cannot be hypnotized at all, while some 15 percent are very easily hypnotized. Most people fall somewhere in between. Moreover, the ease with which a person is hypnotized is related to a number of other characteristics. People who are readily hypnotized are also easily absorbed while reading books or listening to music, becoming unaware of what is happening around them, and they often spend an unusual amount of time daydreaming. In sum, then, they show a high ability to concentrate and to become completely absorbed in what they are doing (Hilgard, 1974; Crawford, 1982; Lynn & Snodgrass, 1987; Rhue, Lynn, & Kirsch, 1993).

hypnosis: A state of heightened susceptibility to the suggestions of others

Hypnosis has been found to be an effective aid in certain cases, including pain relief and smoking cessation.

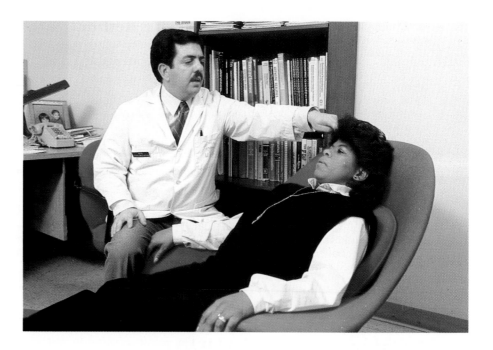

Hypnosis

A Different State of Consciousness?

The issue of whether hypnosis represents a state of consciousness that is qualitatively different from normal waking consciousness has long been a source of controversy among psychologists. Ernest Hilgard (1975) presented one side of the argument when he argued convincingly that hypnosis represents a state of consciousness that differs significantly from other states. He contended that particular behavioural characteristics clearly differentiate hypnosis from other states. These are higher suggestibility; increased ability to recall and construct images, including visual memories from early childhood; a lack of initiative; and the ability to accept suggestions that clearly contradict reality. For example, hypnotized people can be told that they are blind, and subsequently they may report an inability to see objects shown to them (Bryant & McConkey, 1990). Moreover, changes in electrical activity in the brain are associated with hypnosis, supporting the position that hypnosis is a state of consciousness different from normal waking (Spiegel, 1987; Graffin, Ray, & Lundy, 1995).

On the other side of the controversy were theorists who rejected the notion that hypnosis is a significantly different state of consciousness from normal waking consciousness (Spanos, 1986; Spanos & Chaves, 1989). They argued that altered brain wave patterns are not sufficient to demonstrate a qualitative difference, given that no other specific physiological changes occur when a person is in a trance.

Furthermore, people merely pretending to be hypnotized display behaviours that are nearly identical to those of truly hypnotized individuals, and hypnotic susceptibility can be increased through training procedures (Gfeller, Lynn, & Pribble, 1987; Spanos et al., 1987; Spanos et al., 1993). There is also little support for the contention that adults can accurately recall memories of childhood events while hypnotized (Nash, 1987; Frankel, 1993). Such converging evidence suggests that there is nothing qualitatively special about the hypnotic trance (Barber, 1975; Lynn, Rhue, & Weekes, 1990; Spanos et al., 1991; Kirsch & Lynn, 1998).

If hypnosis does not represent a state of consciousness distinct from normal waking consciousness, then why do people *appear* to be in an altered state? To Theodore Sarbin and colleagues, hypnotized people are in a heightened state of sug-

---

Answers to Review Questions:

1. Consciousness   2. true   3. REM   4. Circadian rhythms   5. wish fulfillment   6. 1-a; 2-c; 3-b 7. 1-b; 2-c; 3-a

gestibility, role-playing the state of hypnosis as they understand it. They are not "pretending" to be hypnotized. Instead, they believe they are hypnotized and simply follow the suggestions of the hypnotist in the same way they follow suggestions of employers, bosses, and other persons of authority (Sarbin, 1991, 1993).

Today, there is increasing agreement that the controversy over the nature of hypnosis led to extreme positions on both sides of the issue (Kirsch & Lynn, 1995). More recent approaches suggest that the hypnotic state may best be viewed as lying along a continuum, in which hypnosis is neither a totally different state of consciousness nor totally similar to normal waking consciousness.

As arguments about the true nature of hypnosis continue, though, one thing is clear: Hypnosis has been successfully used to solve practical human problems. In fact, psychologists working in many different areas have found hypnosis to be a reliable, effective tool (Rhue, Lynn, & Kirsch, 1993). Among the range of applications are the following:

- *Controlling pain.* Patients suffering from chronic pain may be given the suggestion, while hypnotized, that their pain is eliminated or reduced. They can be told to feel that a painful area is hot, cold, or numb. They may also be taught to hypnotize themselves to relieve pain or to gain a sense of control over their symptoms. Hypnosis has proved to be particularly useful during childbirth and dental procedures (Erickson, Hershman, & Secter, 1990; Oster, 1994; Enqvist, Von Konow, & Bystedt, 1995; Mairs, 1995; Barber, 1996).

- *Ending tobacco addiction.* Although it hasn't been successful in stopping drug and alcohol abuse, hypnosis is sometimes successful in helping people to stop unwanted behaviour such as smoking. In some approaches, hypnotized smokers are given the suggestion that the taste and smell of cigarettes are unpleasant. Other techniques include teaching self-hypnosis to deal with cravings for cigarettes or suggesting during hypnosis that smokers owe their bodies protection from the ravages of smoking (Erickson, Hershman, & Secter, 1990; Spiegel et al., 1993).

- *Treating psychological disorders.* Hypnosis sometimes is used during treatment for psychological disorders. For example, hypnosis may be employed to heighten relaxation, reduce anxiety, increase expectations of success, or modify thoughts that are self-defeating (Fromm & Nash, 1992).

- *Assisting in law enforcement.* Witnesses and victims are sometimes better able to recall details of a crime when hypnotized. In one well-known case, a witness to the kidnapping of a group of California schoolchildren was placed under hypnosis and was able to recall all but one digit of the license number on the kidnapper's vehicle (Geiselman et al., 1985). On the other hand, the evidence regarding the accuracy of recollections obtained under hypnosis is decidedly mixed. In some cases, accurate recall of specific information increases—but so does the number of errors. Moreover, a person's confidence about the recollections obtained during hypnosis increases, even when the memory is inaccurate. The hypnotic state may simply make people more willing to report whatever they think they remember. Because of these questions about its usefulness, the legal status of hypnosis has yet to be resolved (McConkey & Sheehan, 1995; Gibson, 1995).

- *Improving athletic performance.* Athletes sometimes turn to hypnosis to improve their performance. For example, championship boxer Ken Norton used hypnosis before a bout to prepare himself for the encounter, and baseball star Rod Carew used hypnotism to increase his concentration when batting (Udolf, 1981; Stanton, 1994; Edgette & Edgette, 1995).

Hypnosis, then, has many potential applications. Of course, it is not invariably effective. For the significant number of people who cannot be hypnotized, it offers little help. But for people who make good hypnotic subjects, hypnosis may provide significant benefits.

Drawing by Richter; © 1993 The New Yorker Magazine, Inc.

meditation: A learned technique for refocusing attention that brings about an altered state of consciousness

A design can be used as a mantra to focus one's attention while meditating.

Transcendental Meditation

Meditation: Regulating Our Own State of Consciousness

When traditional practitioners of the ancient eastern religion of Zen Buddhism want to achieve greater spiritual insight, they turn to a technique that has been used for centuries to alter their state of consciousness. This technique is called meditation.

Meditation is a learned technique for refocusing attention that brings about an altered state of consciousness. Although there is an exotic sound to it, some form of meditation is found within every major religion—including Christianity and Judaism. In the United States and Canada today, some of the major proponents of meditation, followers of Maharishi Mahesh Yogi, practice a form of meditation called transcendental meditation, or TM, although many other groups teach various forms of meditation.

The specific meditative technique used in TM involves repeating a *mantra*—a sound, word, or syllable—over and over. In other forms of meditation, the focus is on a picture, flame, or specific part of the body. Regardless of the nature of the particular initial stimulus, in most forms of meditation the key to the procedure is concentrating on it so thoroughly that the meditator becomes unaware of any outside stimulation and reaches a different state of consciousness.

Following meditation, people report feeling thoroughly relaxed. They sometimes relate that they have gained new insights into themselves and the problems they are facing. The long-term practice of meditation may even improve health. One study of a group of elderly nursing-home residents found higher longevity for those who practiced meditation over a three-year period, and another study found that people who meditated regularly had lower medical expenses (Alexander et al., 1989; Goldberg, 1995; Herron et al., 1996).

Meditation brings about several physiological changes. For example, oxygen usage decreases, heart rate and blood pressure decline, and brain wave patterns may change (Sudsuang, Chentanez, & Veluvan, 1991). On the other hand, similar changes occur during relaxation of any sort, so whether these changes qualify as indicators of a true alteration in consciousness remains an open question (Wallace & Benson, 1972; Holmes, 1985; Jevning et al., 1996; Zamarra et al., 1996; see Figure 4-8).

It *is* clear that you too can meditate without exotic trappings by using a few simple procedures developed by Herbert Benson, who has studied meditation extensively. The basics are similar in several respects to those developed as a part of eastern religions but have no spiritual component. They include sitting in a quiet room with your eyes closed, breathing deeply and rhythmically, and repeating a word or sound—such as the word "one"—over and over. Although the procedure is a bit more involved than this, most people find themselves in a deeply relaxed state after just twenty minutes. Practiced twice a day, Benson's meditative techniques seem to be just as effective in bringing about relaxation as more mystical methods (Benson & Friedman, 1985; Benson, 1993; Benson et al., 1994).

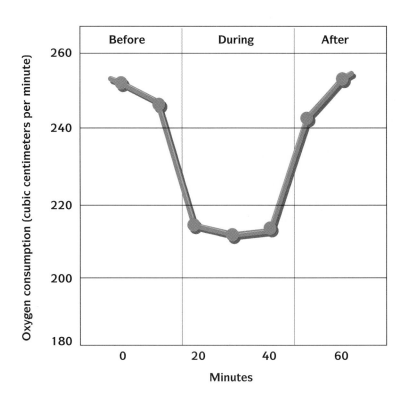

FIGURE 4-8 *The body's use of oxygen declines significantly during meditation. Source: Benson, 1993.*

Exploring Diversity

Cross-cultural Routes to Altered States of Consciousness

- A group of Native American Sioux sit naked in a steaming sweat lodge, as a medicine man throws water on sizzling rocks to send billows of scalding steam into the air.

- Aztec priests smear themselves with a mixture of crushed poisonous herbs, hairy black worms, scorpions, and lizards. Sometimes they drink the potion.

- During the sixteenth century, a devout Hasidic Jew lies across the tombstone of a celebrated scholar. As he murmurs the name of God repeatedly, he seeks to be possessed by the soul of the dead wise man's spirit. If successful, he will attain a mystical state, and the deceased's words will flow out of his mouth.

Each of these rituals has a common goal: suspension from the binds of everyday awareness and access to an altered state of consciousness (Furst, 1977; Fine, 1994). Although they may seem curious and exotic from the vantage point of many western cultures, they represent what seems to be a universal effort to alter consciousness. To members of many nonwestern cultures, the use of meditation, alcohol, and other drugs in western cultures to bring about a change in consciousness may seem equally peculiar. Television, videogames, and virtual reality can also alter consciousness, and these methods may become widespread (Preston, 1998).

Some scholars suggest that the quest to alter consciousness represents a basic human desire. For example, Ronald Siegel (1989) suggests that this need is as basic as requirements for sex, water, and food.

Whether or not one accepts such an extreme view, it is clear that different cultures have developed their own unique forms of consciousness-altering activities. Similarly, as we'll see when we discuss psychological disorders in Chapter 12, what is deemed "abnormal" behaviour varies considerably from one culture to another.

Of course, realizing that efforts to produce altered states of consciousness are widespread throughout the world's societies does not answer a fundamental question: Is the experience of *normal,* unaltered states of consciousness similar across different cultures?

There are two possible responses to this question. Because humans share basic biological commonalities in the ways their brains and bodies are wired, we might assume that the fundamental experience of consciousness is similar across cultures. As a result, we could suppose that consciousness shows some basic similarities across cultures.

On the other hand, the way in which certain aspects of consciousness are interpreted and viewed show substantial difference among different cultures. For example, people in various cultures view the experience of the passage of time in varying ways. One study found, for instance, that Mexicans view time as passing more slowly than other North Americans do (Diaz-Guerrero, 1979).

Whatever the true nature of consciousness and why people seek to alter it, it is clear that people often seek the means to alter their everyday experience of the world. In some cases that need becomes overwhelming, as we see next when we consider the use of drugs.   ∎

Recap, Review, and Rethink

Recap

• Hypnosis places people in a state of heightened susceptibility to the suggestions of others. People cannot be hypnotized against their will, and they vary in their susceptibility to hypnosis.

• One crucial question about hypnosis is whether or not it represents a separate state of consciousness. There is evidence on both sides of the issue.

• Meditation is a learned technique for refocusing attention that is meant to bring about an altered state of consciousness.

• Cultures differ in the routes they choose to bring about altered states of consciousness.

Review

1. _____ is a state of heightened susceptibility to the suggestions of others.

2. A friend tells you "I once heard of a person who was murdered by being hypnotized and then told to jump from the Golden Gate Bridge!" Could such a thing have happened? Why or why not?

3. _____ is a learned technique for refocusing attention to bring about an altered state of consciousness.

4. Leslie repeats a unique sound, known as a _____, when she engages in transcendental meditation.

5. Meditation can be learned only by following procedures that include some spiritual component. True or false?

Answers to Review Questions are on page 152.

Rethink

1. What sorts of mental functioning does hypnosis appear to affect most strongly? Do you think it has more of an effect on the left or right hemisphere of the brain, or does it affect both equally? Why?

2. In what ways is meditation similar to biofeedback? In what ways is it different?

3. If meditation has psychological benefits, does this suggest that we are mentally overburdened in our normal state of consciousness?

DRUG USE: THE HIGHS AND LOWS OF CONSCIOUSNESS

▶ What are the major classifications of drugs, and what are their effects?

As the butane torch flame vaporized the cocaine in the bowl of a glass smoking pipe, Amir Vik-Kiv inhaled deeply, held the smoke in his expanded chest, then exhaled in a breathless rush. Suddenly, his eyes bulged and his hands trembled. Beads of sweat broke out on his forehead, and perspiration stains formed under his arms.

Moments earlier . . . the former television cameraman had "cooked" a gram of refined cocaine in the kitchen of his northeast Washington apartment. Using a simple recipe of water and baking soda, he had reduced the substance to a potent, insidious form known as "crack."

Within an hour he had "burned" about $100 worth of the drug, but what had happened in his brain just seven seconds after taking the first hit was

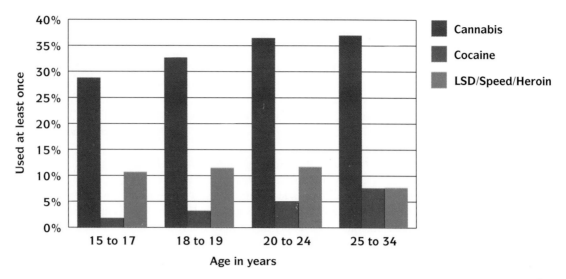

FIGURE 4-9 *How many people have tried illicit drugs? This figure shows the percent of respondents in four age categories who reported using common illicit drugs at least once in a lifetime (Based on CCSA/CAMH, 1999.)*

more like an explosion. Although he had not eaten food in a day or had sex in months, he was no longer hungry for either. . . .

What would happen when the dope ran out was another story. Before long Vik-Kiv would be crawling around the kitchen floor, searching for bits of cocaine that might have spilled. When he found anything white, he would take it—and gag at the taste of what could have been anything from a burning bread crumb to a moldering roach egg (Milloy, 1986, p. 1).

Although few people exhibit such extreme behaviour, drugs are a part of almost all of our lives. From infancy on, most people take vitamins, aspirin, cold-relief medicine, and the like; in fact, in a recent Canadian survey, 70 percent reported using aspirin during the month before the survey (CCSA, 1995a). However, the drugs mentioned have little effect on our consciousness, operating instead primarily on our biological functions (Dortch, 1996).

On the other hand, some substances, known as psychoactive drugs, affect consciousness. **Psychoactive drugs** influence a person's emotions, perceptions, and behaviour. Yet even these drugs are common in most of our lives. If you have ever had a cup of coffee or sipped a beer, you have taken a psychoactive drug.

psychoactive drugs: Drugs that influence a person's emotions, perceptions, and behaviour

A large number of individuals have used more potent—and dangerous—psychoactive drugs than coffee and beer. As Figure 4-9 shows, many young Canadians have tried an illicit drug at least once, especially cannabis. Provincial student drug use surveys show that the drugs used most frequently by Canadian high school students are alcohol, tobacco, and cannabis (CCSA, 1996; AFM, 1997; CAMH, 1999a).

Of course, drugs vary widely in the effects they have on users. The most dangerous drugs are addictive. **Addictive drugs** produce a biological or psychological dependence in the user, and withdrawal from them leads to a craving for the drug that, in some cases, may be nearly irresistible. Addictions may be *biologically based,* in which case the body becomes so accustomed to functioning in the presence of a drug that it cannot function in its absence. Or addictions may be *psychologically based,* in which case people believe that they need the drug in order to respond to the stresses of daily living. Although we generally associate addiction with drugs such as heroin, everyday sorts of drugs like caffeine (found in coffee) and nicotine (found in cigarettes) have addictive aspects as well.

addictive drugs: Drugs that produce a biological or psychological dependence in the user, and withdrawal from them leads to a craving for the drug that, in some cases, may be nearly irresistible

We know surprisingly little about the underlying causes of addiction. One of the problems in identifying the causes is that different drugs (such as alcohol and cocaine) affect the brain in very different ways—and yet may be equally addicting.

Addictions

Furthermore, it takes longer to become addicted to some drugs than to others, even though the ultimate consequences of addiction may be equally grave (Julien, 1995; Hyman, 1996; Leshner, 1997; Lowinson et al., 1997).

Why do people take drugs in the first place? There are many reasons, ranging from the perceived pleasure of the experience itself, to the escape a drug-induced high affords from the everyday pressures of life, to an attempt to achieve a religious or spiritual state. But other factors, ones that have little to do with the nature of the experience itself, also lead people to try drugs (Glantz & Pickens, 1991; Washton, 1995; Mesquita et al., 1995).

For instance, the alleged drug use of well-known role models (such as film star Robert Downey, Jr., or Mayor Marion Barry of Washington, D.C.), the easy availability of some illegal drugs, and the pressures of peers all play a role in the decision to use drugs (Jarvik, 1990; Graham, Marks, & Hansen, 1991; Dupre et al., 1995). In some cases, the motive is simply the thrill of trying something new and perhaps flouting the law (MacCoun, 1993). Finally, the sense of helplessness experienced by poor, unemployed individuals trapped in lives of poverty may lead them to try drugs as a way of escaping the bleakness of their lives. Regardless of the forces that lead a person to begin using drugs, drug addiction is among the most difficult of all behaviours to modify, even with extensive treatment (Hawkins, Catalano, & Miller, 1992; MacCoun, 1993; DiClemente, 1993; Hser, Anglin, & Powers, 1993; Jarvis, Tebbutt, & Mattick, 1995).

Because of the difficulty in treating drug problems, there is little disagreement that the best hope for dealing with the overall societal problem of substance abuse is to prevent people from becoming involved with drugs in the first place. However, there is little accord on how to accomplish this goal. In fact, as we consider in the Applying Psychology in the 21st Century box developing and evaluating effective antidrug programs is challenging.

Stimulants: Drug Highs

stimulants: Drugs that affect the central nervous system by causing a rise in heart rate, blood pressure, and muscular tension

Caffeine and nicotine are two powerful, and widely used, drugs.

It's one o'clock in the morning, and you still haven't finished reading the last chapter of the text on which you will be tested in the morning. Feeling exhausted, you turn to the one thing that may help you stay awake for the next two hours: a cup of strong, black coffee.

If you have ever found yourself in such a position, you have been relying on a major **stimulant,** caffeine, to stay awake. *Caffeine* is one of a number of stimulants that affect the central nervous system by causing a rise in heart rate, blood pressure, and muscular tension. Caffeine is present not only in coffee; it is an important ingredient in tea, soft drinks, and chocolate as well (see Figure 4-10).

Caffeine produces several reactions. The major behavioural effects of caffeine are an increase in attentiveness and a decrease in reaction time. Caffeine can also bring about an improvement in mood, most likely by mimicking the effects of a natural brain chemical, adenosine. Too much caffeine, however, can result in nervousness and insomnia. People can build up a biological dependence on the drug. If they suddenly stop drinking coffee, they may experience headaches or depression. Many people who drink large amounts of coffee on weekdays have headaches on weekends because of a sudden drop in the amount of caffeine they are consuming (Silverman et al., 1992; Silverman et al., 1994; James, 1997).

Nicotine, found in cigarettes, is another common stimulant. The soothing effects of nicotine help explain why cigarette smoking is rewarding for smokers, many of whom continue to smoke despite clear evidence of its long-term health dangers. When we consider health psychology, smoking is addictive. Smokers develop a dependence

Answers to Review Questions:

1. Hypnosis   2. No; people who are hypnotized cannot be made to perform self-destructive acts.   3. Meditation   4. mantra   5. False; some meditative techniques have no spiritual component.

Applying Psychology in the 21st Century

Just Say No? Finding Antidrug Programs that Work

Mark sat in his psychology teacher's office. He explained that he would be missing classes for at least a month, and possibly longer. He wanted to know if he would be able to continue with his college program in the fall. He was going into a residential treatment centre for his drug problem. He didn't want to be dropped from his college program, but he thought the treatment centre was the best way to deal with his substance abuse problems.

The treatment centre Mark had chosen was located in a nearby community. But he would not be able to continue his studies while he was there, or even have contact with anyone outside the centre during the first month. He would go through detailed assessment, detoxification, and begin psychotherapy.

Mark wished his problem had never developed. In fact, he didn't really understand why or how it had. And perhaps it never would have, if Mark had been exposed to effective prevention programs. There are many prevention programs sponsored by local, provincial, and federal agencies. As more programs are evaluated, researchers are discovering which ones are most effective.

Research indicates that substance abuse typically starts early in life. Since Canadians must attend school until age 16, schools provide a captive audience.

The significant issue is how to reach this audience.

An effective strategy is based on the common, but limited notion, that students start to use simply because of peer pressure. Peer influence has been found to be a powerful tool in delivering effective information and skills training programs (CAMH, 1999b). Youth Assisting Peers is a program aimed at grade nine students in which senior students provide information and share opinions with the younger students. Its goals are to dispel myths about substance abuse, to give information (especially harm reduction messages), and to address concerns of ninth graders. Parents Against Drugs is a peer education program in which trained high school students conduct sessions with eighth graders focused on examining and making choices about the use of alcohol and drugs.

Other programs take advantage of the "captive" school audience to deliver programs to at-risk students. For Opening Doors (Addiction Research Foundation, 1995), the target group of students consists of those who are likely to experience problems with low school achievement, violent behaviour, truancy, and drug use. Secondary target groups include parents and members of the school community at large because of their impact on students. Evaluations have demonstrated the effec-

tiveness of this program (CAMH, 1999b). Currently, it is in use in more than fifty Ontario communities, and it will be implemented in other parts of the country as well. The Rural and Northern Youth Intervention Strategy of Manitoba provides counselling to help young people assess the effect of alcohol and drugs on their health, social relations, and other areas of their lives, and promotes general discussion of youth issues.

The Strengthening Families Program targets not only at-risk youth, but also the family. Evaluation of this program in the United States has indicated important criteria for the implementation of family programs (Kumpfer and Alvarado, 1995). The criteria include providing programs of sufficient intensity (e.g., thirty to forty contact hours) that are matched to the developmental stages of children and family needs. The importance of evaluating recruitment procedures, retention, relevance of materials, and overall program effectiveness is also addressed. This program is currently being adapted for use and piloted in Ontario (CAMH, 1999b).

Common themes in program evaluations are that antidrug programs that work involve students actively at all levels (planning, implementation, and as target) and are supported by the larger community.

It has proved difficult to identify antidrug programs that are truly effective.

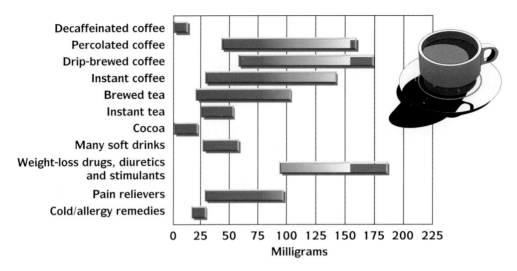

FIGURE 4-10 *How much caffeine are you eating and drinking? This chart shows the range of caffeine found in common foods and drinks. The average American consumes about 200 milligrams of caffeine each day. Source:* The New York Times, *1991, p. c11.*

on nicotine, and those who suddenly stop smoking develop strong cravings for the drug. According to former U.S. Surgeon General C. Everett Koop, who changed the designation of smoking from a "habit" to an "addiction" in 1988, the use of nicotine is "driven by strong, often irresistible urges and can persist despite . . . repeated efforts to quit" (Koop, 1988). This is not surprising: Recent evidence shows that nicotine activates neuronal mechanisms similar to those activated by cocaine, which, as we see next, is also highly addictive (Murray, 1990; Pich et al., 1997).

Cocaine

There is little doubt that the illegal drug that has posed the most serious problems in the last decade has been the stimulant *cocaine* and its derivative, crack. Cocaine is inhaled or "snorted" through the nose, smoked, or injected directly into the bloodstream. It is rapidly absorbed into the body, taking effect almost immediately.

When used in relatively small quantities, cocaine produces feelings of profound psychological well-being, increased confidence, and alertness. (For a summary of the effects of cocaine and other illegal drugs, see Table 4-3.)

Cocaine produces this "high" through the neurotransmitter dopamine. As you'll recall from Chapter 2, dopamine is one of the chemicals that transmits between neurons messages related to ordinary feelings of pleasure. Normally when dopamine is released, excess amounts of the neurotransmitter are reabsorbed by the releasing neuron. However, when cocaine enters the brain, it blocks reabsorption of leftover dopamine. As a result, the brain is flooded with dopamine-produced pleasurable sensations (Self et al., 1996; Balter, 1996; Landry, 1997).

However, there is a steep price to be paid for the pleasurable effects of cocaine. The drug is psychologically and physically addictive, and users may grow obsessed with obtaining it. Cocaine addicts indulge in binge use, administering the drug every ten to thirty minutes if it is available. During these binges, they think of nothing but cocaine; eating, sleeping, family, friends, money, and even survival have no importance. Their lives become tied to the drug. Over time users deteriorate mentally and physically, losing weight and growing suspicious of others. In extreme cases, cocaine can cause hallucinations—a common one is that insects are crawling over one's body. Ultimately, an overdose of cocaine can lead to death (Gawin & Ellinwood, 1988; Mendoza & Miller, 1992; Pottieger et al., 1992).

When cocaine is not available, abusers of the drug go through three distinct phases (see Figure 4-11). In the first stage, users "crash" when the high subsides. They crave cocaine, feel depressed and agitated, and their anxiety intensifies. In the second stage, which begins from nine hours to four days later, heavy users begin the process

Cocaine is an illegal and highly addictive stimulant.

Cocaine

Table 4-3	Drugs and Their Effects

Drug	Street Name	Effects	Withdrawal Symptoms	Adverse/Overdose Reactions
Stimulants				
Cocaine Amphetamines Benzedrine Dexedrine	Coke, blow, toot, snow, lady, crack Speed Speed	Increased confidence, mood elevation, sense of energy and alertness, decreased appetite, anxiety, irritability, insomnia, transient drowsiness, delayed orgasm	Apathy, general fatigue, prolonged sleep, depression, disorientation, suicidal thoughts, agitated motor activity, irritability, bizarre dreams	Elevated blood pressure, increase in body temperature, face-picking, suspiciousness, bizarre and repetitive behaviour, vivid hallucinations, convulsions, possible death
Depressants				
Barbiturates Nembutal Seconal Phenobarbital Alcohol	 Yellowjackets, yellows Reds Booze	Anxiety reduction, impulsiveness, dramatic mood swings, bizarre thoughts, suicidal behaviour, slurred speech, disorientation, slowed mental and physical functioning, limited attention span	Weakness, restlessness, nausea and vomiting, headaches, nightmares, irritability, depression, acute anxiety, hallucinations, seizures, possible death	Confusion, decreased response to pain, shallow respiration, dilated pupils, weak and rapid pulse, coma, possible death
Narcotics				
Heroin Morphine	H, hombre, junk, smack, dope, horse, crap Drugstore dope, cube, first line, mud	Anxiety and pain reduction, apathy, difficulty in concentration, slowed speech, decreased physical activity, drooling, itching, euphoria, nausea	Anxiety, vomiting, sneezing, diarrhea, lower back pain, watery eyes, runny nose, yawning, irritability, tremors, panic, chills and sweating, cramps	Depressed levels of consciousness, low blood pressure, rapid heart rate, shallow breathing, convulsions, coma, possible death
Hallucinogens				
Cannabis Marijuana Hashish Hash oil	Bhang, Kif, ganja, dope, grass, pot, smoke, hemp, joint, weed, bone, Mary Jane, herb, tea	Euphoria, relaxed inhibitions, increased appetite, disoriented behaviour	Hyperactivity, insomnia, decreased appetite, anxiety	Severe reactions are rare but include panic, paranoia, fatigue, bizarre and dangerous behaviour, decreased testosterone over long term; immune-system effects
LSD	Electricity, acid, quasey, blotter acid, microdot, white lightning, purple barrels	Fascination with ordinary objects; heightened aesthetic responses; vision and depth distortion; heightened sensitivity to faces and gestures; magnified feelings; paranoia; panic; euphoria	Not reported	Nausea and chills; increased pulse, temperature, and blood pressure; trembling; slow, deep breathing; loss of appetite; insomnia; longer, more intense "trips"; bizarre, dangerous behaviour
Phencyclidine (PCP)	Angel dust, hog, rocket fuel, superweed, peace pill, elephant tranquilizer, dust, bad pizza	Increased blood pressure and heart rate; sweating; nausea; slowed reflexes; altered body image; altered perception of time and space; impaired memory	Not reported	Highly variable and possibly dose-related: disorientation; loss of recent memory; bizarre, violent behaviour; hallucinations and delusions; coma

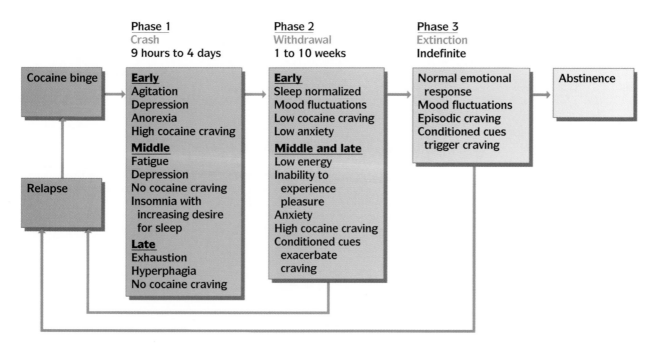

FIGURE 4-11   *Phases of cocaine deprivation. Source: Based on Gawin, 1991.*

of "withdrawal." During this period, they initially crave cocaine less, feel bored and unmotivated, and experience little anxiety.

Later, though, cocaine abusers are highly sensitive to any cues that remind them of their prior cocaine use. These might be a person, event, location, or drug-abuse paraphernalia such as a glass pipe. When this happens, they are susceptible to resuming cocaine use if the drug is available. If addicts are able to pass through the withdrawal stage, they move into the third stage, in which craving for cocaine is further reduced and moods become relatively normal. However, they remain highly sensitive to cues related to cocaine use, and relapses are common. Cocaine abuse, then, has powerful, and lasting, consequences (Waldorf, Reinarman, & Murphy, 1991).

In Canada, the percent of the population who have tried cocaine at least once is highest in 25 to 34 year-olds (8 percent), followed by 20 to 24 year-olds (5 percent) (CCSA/CAMH 1999). In the United States, use is higher (Gawin, 1991; Monitoring the Future Study, 1996).

Amphetamines

Amphetamines are strong stimulants, such as Dexedrine and Benzedrine, popularly known as speed. When their use soared in the 1970s, the phrase "speed kills" became prevalent as the drugs caused an increasing number of deaths. Although amphetamine use has declined from its 1970s peak, many drug experts believe that speed would quickly resurface in large quantities if cocaine supplies were interrupted.

In small quantities, amphetamines bring about a sense of energy and alertness, talkativeness, heightened confidence, and a mood "high." They reduce fatigue and increase concentration. Amphetamines also cause a loss of appetite, increased anxiety, and irritability. When taken over long periods of time, amphetamines can cause feelings of being persecuted by others, as well as a general sense of suspiciousness. People taking amphetamines may lose interest in sex. If taken in too large a quantity, amphetamines overstimulate the central nervous system to such an extent that convulsions and death can occur.

Depressants: Drug Lows

depressants: Drugs that slow down the nervous system

In contrast to the initial effect of stimulants, which is an increase in arousal of the central nervous system, the effect of **depressants** is to impede the nervous system by

Alcohol, a depressant, is the cause of tens of thousands of deaths each year.

causing neurons to fire more slowly. Small doses result in at least temporary feelings of *intoxication*—drunkenness—along with a sense of euphoria and joy. When large amounts are taken, however, speech becomes slurred and muscle control becomes disjointed, making motion difficult. Ultimately, heavy users may lose consciousness entirely.

Alcohol

The most common depressant is *alcohol*, which is used by more people than any other drug. In 1996–97, Canadians drank almost 2 billion litres of beer, 253 million litres of wine, and 130 million litres of spirits. Overall, 42 percent of drinkers reported at least one episode of heavy drinking (consuming 5 or more drinks on a single occasion) during the year, and six percent reported drinking heavily on a weekly basis. The percentages for heavy drinking were highest for young people aged 20 to 24 years. In this age group, 68 percent reported a single occasion of heavy drinking and 13 percent reported heavy drinking on a weekly basis (CCSA/CAMH, 1999; Statistics Canada, 1998). Heavy drinking is also reported by provincial student drug use surveys (CCSA, 1996; AFM, 1997; CAMH, 1999a) and by the Canadian Campus Survey, a nationwide survey of university students (CAMH, 2000). See Figure 4-12.

Students have reported a range of problems related to drinking such as hangovers, vomiting, memory loss, family problems, poor academic performance, and trouble with the law. Of particular concern, is the relation between alcohol consumption and high-risk behaviours such as driving under the influence of alcohol and unplanned sex (MacDonald, Zanna and Fong, 1996).

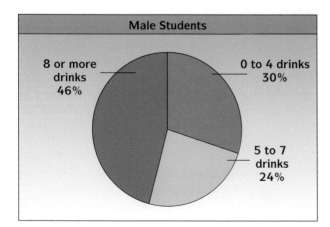
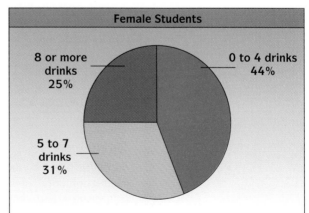

FIGURE 4-12   *Drinking patterns of Canadian university students. The figure shows the percents of male and female students who abstained or drank moderately (0 to 4 drinks), drank heavily (5 to 7 drinks), and drank very heavily (8 or more drinks) on a single occasion during the autumn of 1998. Based on CAMH, 2000.*

Students also experienced problems related to other people's drinking. For example, Ontario university students reported being insulted or humiliated, physically assaulted, and arguing with other students who had been drinking (CCSA, 1995b).

Although alcohol consumption is widespread, significant gender and cultural variations exist in its use. For example, women are typically somewhat lighter drinkers than men are (CCSA/CAMH, 1999), although the gap between the sexes for high school students is small or nonexistent. However, on average, male university students drink more often and have a higher weekly alcohol intake than do female university students (CAMH, 2000). Women are usually more susceptible to the effects of alcohol, because of differences in blood volume and body composition that permit more alcohol to go directly into the bloodstream (Eng, 1990; Hart & Sciutto, 1994; Galanter, 1995; Lex, 1995; National Center on Addiction and Substance Abuse, 1996).

There are also pronounced ethnic differences in alcohol consumption. For example, people of East Asian backgrounds who live in the United States tend to drink significantly less than whites or African Americans, and their incidence of alcohol-related problems is lower. It appears that the physical reactions to drinking, which may include sweating, a quickened heartbeat, and flushing, are more unpleasant for East Asians than for other groups (Akutsu et al., 1989; Mogelonsky, 1996; Smith & Lin, 1996; Garcia-Andrade, Wall, & Ehlers, 1997).

Although alcohol is a depressant, most people claim that it increases their sense of sociability and well-being. The discrepancy between the actual and the perceived effects of alcohol lies in the initial effects it produces in the majority of individuals who use it: release of tension and stress, feelings of happiness, and loss of inhibitions (Steele & Southwick, 1985; Josephs & Steele, 1990; Steele & Josephs, 1990; Sayette, 1993). As the dose of alcohol increases, however, the depressive effects become more pronounced (see Figure 4-13). People may feel emotionally and physically unstable. They also show poor judgment and may act aggressively. Moreover, their memories are impaired, brain processing of spatial information is diminished, and speech becomes slurred and incoherent. Eventually they may fall into a stupor and pass out. If they drink enough alcohol in a short time, they may die of alcohol poisoning (Bushman, 1993; Matthews et al., 1996; Chin & Pisoni, 1997).

Although most people fall into the category of casual users, there are some 18 million alcoholics in the United States. *Alcoholics,* people with alcohol-abuse problems, come to rely on alcohol and continue to drink even though it causes serious difficulties. In addition, they become increasingly immune to the effects of alcohol. Consequently, alcoholics must drink progressively more in order to experience the initial positive feelings that alcohol brings about.

In some cases of alcoholism, people must drink constantly in order to feel well enough to function in their daily lives. In other cases, though, people drink inconsistently, but occasionally go on sporadic binges in which they consume large quantities of alcohol.

It is not clear why certain people become alcoholics and develop a tolerance for alcohol, while others do not. Some evidence suggests a genetic cause. However, not all alcoholics have close relatives who are alcoholics. In these cases, environmental stressors are suspected of playing a larger role (Greenfield et al., 1993; Hester & Miller, 1995; Pennisi, 1997). According to interaction theory, alcoholism develops as a result of interaction between person variables and features of the environment. For example, persons prone to experience anxiety are likely to become alcoholics if alcohol is readily available (Sadava, 1987).

Alcohol Abuse

Barbiturates

Barbiturates, which include such drugs as Nembutal, Seconal, and phenobarbital, are another form of depressant. Frequently prescribed by physicians to induce sleep or to reduce stress, barbiturates produce a sense of relaxation. Yet they too are psychologically and physically addictive and, when combined with alcohol, can be deadly, since such a combination relaxes the muscles of the diaphragm to such an extent that the user suffocates. The street drug known as Quaalude is closely related to the barbiturate family and similar dangers are associated with it.

Number of drinks consumed in 2 hours		Alcohol in blood, percent	Typical effects, average-size adult
	2	0.05	Judgment, thought, and restraint weakened; tension released, giving carefree sensation
	3	0.08	Tensions and inhibitions of everyday life lessened; cheerfulness
	4	0.10	Voluntary motor action affected, making hand and arm movements, walk, and speech clumsy
	7	0.20	Severe impairment—staggering, loud, incoherent, emotionally unstable, 100 times greater traffic risk; exuberance and aggressive inclinations magnified
	9	0.30	Deeper areas of brain affected, with stimulus-response and understanding confused; stuporous; blurred vision
	12	0.40	Incapable of voluntary action, sleepy, difficult to arouse; equivalent of surgical anesthesia
	15	0.50	Comatose; centres controlling breathing and heartbeat anesthetized; death increasingly probable

FIGURE 4-13 *The effects of alcohol.*

Note: A drink refers to a typical 12-ounce bottle of beer, a 1.5-ounce shot of hard liquor, or a 5-ounce glass of wine.

Narcotics: Relieving Pain and Anxiety

Narcotics are drugs that increase relaxation and relieve pain and anxiety. Two of the most powerful narcotics, *morphine* and *heroin*, are derived from the poppy seed pod. Although morphine is used medically to control severe pain, heroin is illegal in Canada and the United States. This has not prevented its widespread use.

Heroin users usually inject the drug directly into their veins with a hypodermic needle. The immediate effect has been described as a "rush" of positive feeling, similar in some respects to a sexual orgasm—and just as difficult to describe. After the rush, a heroin user experiences a sense of well-being and peacefulness that lasts three to five hours. When the effects of the drug wear off, however, the user feels extreme anxiety and a desperate desire to repeat the experience. Moreover, larger amounts of heroin are needed each time to produce the same pleasurable effect. This leads to a cycle of biological and psychological addiction: The user is constantly either shooting

narcotics: Drugs that increase relaxation and relieve pain and anxiety

FIGURE 4-14 *Marijuana use by Ontario students at seven grade levels. (Based on Ontario Student Drug Survey, 1999)*

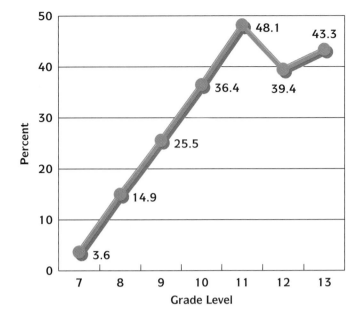

FIGURE 4-14 *Marijuana use by Ontario students at seven grade levels. (Based on Ontario Student Drug Survey, 1999)*

up or attempting to obtain ever-increasing amounts of the drug. Eventually, the life of the addict revolves around heroin.

Because of the powerful positive feelings the drug produces, heroin addiction is particularly difficult to cure. One treatment that has shown some success is the use of methadone. *Methadone* is a synthetic chemical that satisfies a heroin user's physiological cravings for the drug without providing the "high" that accompanies heroin. When heroin users are placed on regular doses of methadone they may be able to function in a relatively normal manner. The use of methadone has one substantial drawback, however. Although it removes the psychological dependence on heroin, it replaces the biological addiction to heroin with a biological addiction to methadone. Researchers, then, are attempting to identify nonaddictive chemical substitutes for heroin, as well as substitutes for other addictive drugs, which do not replace one addiction with another (Waldrop, 1989; Sinclair, 1990; Pulvirenti & Koob, 1994).

Hallucinogens: Psychedelic Drugs

What do mushrooms, jimsonweed, and morning glories have in common? Besides being fairly common plants, each can be a source of a powerful **hallucinogen,** a drug that is capable of producing hallucinations, or changes in the perceptual process.

The most common hallucinogen in widespread use today is *marijuana,* whose active ingredient—tetrahydrocannabinol (THC)—is found in a common weed, cannabis. Marijuana is typically smoked in cigarettes, although it can be cooked and eaten. Between a quarter and a third of high school students, and almost a third of university students use cannabis (CCSA, 1996; CAMH, 1999a; CAMH, 2000). The pattern of use is similar in all provinces: reported use increases from seventh grade through secondary school (see Figure 4-14).

The effects of marijuana vary from person to person, but they typically consist of feelings of euphoria and general well-being. Sensory experiences seem more vivid and intense, and a person's sense of self-importance seems to grow. Memory may be impaired, causing the user to feel pleasantly "spaced out." On the other hand, the effects are not universally positive. Individuals who take marijuana when feeling depressed can end up even more depressed, since the drug tends to magnify both good and bad feelings.

Marijuana has the reputation of being a "safe" drug when used in moderation, and there is little evidence that it produces addiction by itself. There also seems to be little scientific evidence that users "graduate" from marijuana to more dangerous drugs. In fact, in certain cultures, the use of marijuana is routine. For instance, some people in Jamaica habitually drink a marijuana-based tea. In addition, marijuana has several medical

hallucinogen: A drug that is capable of producing hallucinations, or changes in the perceptual process

uses; it can be used to prevent nausea from chemotherapy, treat some AIDS symptoms, and relieve muscle spasms for people with spinal cord injuries. In a controversial move, several states have made the use of the drug legal if it is prescribed by a physician—although it remains illegal under U.S. and Canadian federal law (Brookhiser, 1997).

Still, there are clear risks associated with long-term, heavy marijuana use. For instance, there is some evidence that heavy use at least temporarily decreases the production of the male sex hormone testosterone, potentially affecting sexual activity and sperm count (Jaffe, 1990; Crenshaw & Goldberg, 1996). In addition, marijuana smoked during pregnancy has lasting effects on children who are exposed prenatally. Heavy use also affects the ability of the immune system to fight off germs and increases stress on the heart, although it is unclear how strong these effects are. One negative consequence of smoking marijuana is unquestionable, though: The smoke damages the lungs much the way cigarette smoke does, producing an increased likelihood of developing cancer and other lung diseases (Caplan & Brigham, 1990; Sridhar et al., 1994; Julien, 1995; CR, 1997).

In sum, the *short-term* effects of marijuana use appear to be relatively minor—if users follow obvious cautions, such as avoiding driving or using machinery. However, aside from lung damage, it is less clear whether there are harmful long-term consequences. Additional research is necessary before the question of its safety can be resolved (Zimmer & Morgan, 1997).

Marijuana

LSD and PCP

Two of the strongest hallucinogens are *lysergic acid diethylamide,* or *LSD* (known commonly as acid), and *phencyclidine,* or *PCP* (often referred to as angel dust). Both drugs affect the operation of the neurotransmitter serotonin in the brain, causing an alteration in brain cell activity and perception (Jacobs, 1987; Aghajanian, 1994).

LSD produces vivid hallucinations. Perceptions of colours, sounds, and shapes are altered so much that even the most mundane experience—such as looking at the knots in a wooden table—can seem moving and exciting. Time perception is distorted, and objects and people may be viewed in a new way, with some users reporting that LSD increases their understanding of the world. For others, however, the experience brought on by LSD can be terrifying, particularly if users have had emotional difficulties in the past. Furthermore, people can experience flashbacks, in which they hallucinate long after they initially used the drug.

PCP also causes strong hallucinations. However, the potential side effects associated with its use make the drug even more dangerous than LSD. Large doses may cause paranoid and destructive behavior; in some cases users become violent toward themselves and others.

The Informed Consumer of Psychology

Identifying Drug and Alcohol Problems

In a society bombarded with commercials for drugs that are guaranteed to do everything from curing the common cold to giving new life to "tired blood," it is no wonder that drug-related problems represent a major social issue. Yet many people with drug and alcohol problems deny they have them, and even close friends and family members may fail to realize when occasional social use of drugs or alcohol has turned into abuse.

Certain signs, however, indicate when use becomes abuse (Brody, 1982; Gelman, 1989; NIAAA, 1990; Archambault, 1992). Among them:

- Always getting high to have a good time

- Being high more often than not

- Getting high to get oneself going

- Going to work or class while high

- Missing or being unprepared for class or work because you were high
- Feeling bad later about something you said or did while high
- Driving a car while high
- Coming in conflict with the law because of drugs
- Doing something while high that you wouldn't otherwise do
- Being high in nonsocial, solitary situations
- Being unable to stop getting high
- Feeling a need for a drink or a drug to get through the day
- Becoming physically unhealthy
- Failing at school or on the job
- Thinking about liquor or drugs all the time
- Avoiding family or friends while using liquor or drugs

Any combination of these symptoms should be sufficient to alert you to the potential of a serious drug problem. Because drug and alcohol dependence are almost impossible to cure on one's own, people who suspect that they have a problem should seek immediate attention from a psychologist, physician, or counselor. You can also get help from Alcoholics Anonymous or Narcotics Anonymous. Your local telephone book will have a listing for each of these groups. Finally, you can get information about treatment programs and facilities across Canada from the Canadian Centre on Substance Abuse. You can contact them by phone (613-235-4048), fax (613-235-8101), or mail (75 Albert Street, Suite 300, Ottawa, Ontario, K1P 5E7), or search on their web site <www.ccsa.ca>.   ■

Recap, Review, and Rethink

Recap

- Psychoactive drugs affect a person's emotions, perceptions, and behaviour. The most dangerous drugs are those that are addictive—they produce a biological or psychological dependence.

- Stimulants produce an increase in the arousal of the central nervous system.

- Depressants decrease arousal in the central nervous system; they can produce intoxication.

- Narcotics produce relaxation and relieve pain and anxiety.

- Hallucinogens produce hallucinations and other alterations of perception.

Review

1. What is the technical term for drugs that affect a person's consciousness?

2. Match the type of drug to an example of that type.
   1. barbiturate
   2. amphetamine
   3. hallucinogen

   a. LSD
   b. Phenobarbital
   c. Dexedrine

3. Classify each drug listed as a stimulant (S), depressant (D), hallucinogen (H), or narcotic (N).
   1. PCP _____
   2. nicotine _____
   3. cocaine _____
   4. alcohol _____
   5. heroin _____
   6. marijuana _____

4. The effects of LSD may recur long after the drug has been taken. True or false?

5. _____ is a drug that has been used to cure people of heroin addiction.

6. What is the problem with the use of methadone treatment?

Answers to Review Questions are on page 164.

Rethink

1. People use the word "addiction" loosely, referring to an addiction to candy or a television show. Can you explain the difference between this type of "addiction" and a true physiological addiction? Is there a difference between this type of "addiction" and a psychological addiction?

2. Why do people drink in social situations? How might a life skills training program be helpful in reducing the use of alcohol in such situations?

3. Why is the use of psychoactive drugs and the search for altered states of consciousness found in almost every culture?

What are the different states of consciousness?

1. Consciousness refers to a person's awareness of the sensations, thoughts, and feelings being experienced at a given moment. It can vary from more active states, such as high concentration on a task and focused awareness of the world around us, to more passive states, such as daydreaming and actual sleep.

What happens when we sleep, and what are the meaning and function of dreams?

2. Using the electroencephalogram, or EEG, to study sleep, scientists have found that the brain is active throughout the night, and that sleep proceeds through a series of stages identified by unique patterns of brain waves. Stage 1 is characterized by relatively rapid, low voltage waves, whereas stage 2 shows more regular, spindle patterns. In stage 3, the brain waves become slower, with higher peaks and lower valleys. Finally, stage 4 sleep includes waves that are even slower and more regular.

3. REM (rapid eye movement) sleep is characterized by an increase in heart rate, a rise in blood pressure, an increase in the rate of breathing and, in males, erections. Most striking is the rapid movement of the eyes, which dart back and forth under closed eyelids. Dreams occur during this stage. REM sleep seems to be critical to human functioning, whereas other stages of sleep are less essential.

4. According to Freud, dreams have both a manifest content (their apparent story line) and a latent content (their true meaning). He suggested that the latent content provides a guide to a dreamer's unconscious, revealing unfulfilled wishes or desires. Many psychologists disagree with this view. They suggest that the manifest content represents the true import of the dream.

5. The reverse learning theory suggests that dreams represent a process in which unnecessary information is "unlearned" and removed from memory. In this view, dreams have no meaning. In contrast, the dreams-as-survival theory suggests that information relevant to daily survival is reconsidered and reprocessed in dreams. Finally, the activation-synthesis theory proposes that dreams are a result of random electrical energy. This electrical energy randomly stimulates different memories, which are then woven into a coherent story line.

How much do we daydream?

6. Daydreaming, may occur 10 percent of the time, although wide individual differences exist in the amount of time devoted to it. There is little relationship between psychological disorders and a high incidence of daydreaming.

What are the major sleep disorders and how can they be treated?

7. Insomnia is a sleep disorder characterized by difficulty sleeping. Sleep apnea is a condition in which people experience difficulties in sleeping and breathing at the same time. People with narcolepsy have an uncontrollable urge to sleep. Sleepwalking and sleeptalking are relatively harmless.

8. Psychologists and sleep researchers advise people with insomnia to consider increasing exercise during the day, avoiding caffeine and sleeping pills, drinking a glass of warm milk before bedtime, and avoiding *trying* to go to sleep.

Are hypnotized people in a different state of consciousness, and can people be hypnotized against their will?

9. Hypnosis produces a state of heightened susceptibility to the suggestions of the hypnotist. Although there are no physiological indicators that distinguish hypnosis from normal waking consciousness, significant behavioral changes occur. These include increased concentration and suggestibility, heightened ability to recall and construct images, lack of initiative, and acceptance of suggestions that clearly contradict reality. However, people cannot be hypnotized unwillingly.

What are the consequences of meditation?

10. Meditation is a learned technique for refocusing attention that brings about an altered state of consciousness. In transcendental meditation, the most popular form practiced in Canada and the United States, a person repeats a mantra (a sound, word, or syllable) over and over, concentrating until he or she becomes unaware of any outside stimulation and reaches a different state of consciousness.

11. Different cultures have developed their own unique forms of altering states of consciousness. Some researchers speculate that a universal need exists for altered states of consciousness.

What are the major classifications of drugs, and what are their effects?

12. Drugs can produce an altered state of consciousness. However, they vary in how dangerous they are and in whether or not they are addictive, producing a physical or psychological dependence. People take drugs for several reasons: to perceive the pleasure of the experience itself, to escape from everyday pressures, to attain religious or spiritual states, to follow the model of prestigious users or peers, or to experience the thrill of trying something new and perhaps illegal. Whatever the cause, drug addiction is one of the most difficult behaviors to modify.

13. Stimulants cause arousal in the central nervous system. Two common stimulants are caffeine (found in coffee, tea, and soft drinks) and nicotine (found in cigarettes). More dangerous are cocaine and amphetamines, or "speed." Although in small quantities they bring about increased confidence, a sense of energy and alertness, and a "high," in larger quantities they may overload the central nervous system, leading to convulsions and death.

14. Depressants decrease arousal in the central nervous system, causing the neurons to fire more slowly. They may cause intoxication along with feelings of euphoria. The most common depressants are alcohol and barbiturates.

15. Alcohol is the most frequently used depressant. Although it initially releases tension and produces positive feelings, as the dose of alcohol increases, the depressive effects become

more pronounced. Alcoholics develop a tolerance for alcohol and must drink alcoholic beverages in order to function. Both genetic causes and environmental stressors may lead to alcoholism.

16. Morphine and heroin are narcotics, drugs that produce relaxation and relieve pain and anxiety. Because of their addictive qualities, morphine and heroin are particularly dangerous.

17. Hallucinogens are drugs that produce hallucinations and other changes in perception. The most frequently used hallucinogen is marijuana; its use is common throughout North America. Although occasional, short-term use of marijuana seems to be of little danger, long-term effects are less clear. The lungs can be damaged, there is the possibility that testosterone levels are lowered in males, and the immune system may be affected. Two other hallucinogens, LSD and PCP, affect the operation of neurotransmitters in the brain, causing an alteration in brain-cell activity and perception.

18. A number of signals indicate when drug use becomes drug abuse. These include frequent usage, getting high in order to get to class or work, driving while high, developing legal problems, and getting high alone. A person who suspects that he or she has a drug problem should get professional help. People are almost never capable of solving drug problems on their own.

Key Terms and Concepts

consciousness (p. 130)
stage 1 sleep (p. 132)
stage 2 sleep (p. 132)
stage 3 sleep (p. 133)
stage 4 sleep (p. 133)
rapid eye movement (REM) sleep (p. 134)
circadian rhythms (p. 134)
unconscious wish fulfillment theory (p. 138)

latent content of dreams (p. 138)
manifest content of dreams (p. 138)
reverse learning theory (p. 139)
dreams-for-survival theory (p. 139)
activation-synthesis theory (p. 140)
daydreams (p. 141)
hypnosis (p. 145)

meditation (p. 148)
psychoactive drugs (p. 151)
addictive drugs (p. 151)
stimulants (p. 152)
depressants (p. 156)
narcotics (p. 159)
hallucinogen (p. 160)

Epilogue

In this chapter we discussed consciousness in its full range from active states to passive states. We focused especially on factors that affect consciousness, from natural factors like sleep, dreaming, and daydreaming, to more intentional modes of altering consciousness, including hypnosis, meditation, and drugs. We examined some of the reasons people seek to alter their consciousness, considered both uses and abuses of consciousness-altering strategies, and attempted to address some of the most dangerous ways people affect their consciousness.

Before we turn to the subject of learning in the next chapter, return briefly to the prologue of this chapter, about quarterback Brett Favre's drug dependency. Consider the following questions in light of your understanding of drug use and abuse.

1. What was apparently the cause of Favre's drug dependency? Do you believe he was addicted either physiologically or psychologically to Vicodin?

2. Based on the information in the prologue, to what class of drugs do you think Vicodin apparently belong? What effects would it have had on Favre's state of consciousness? Would the drug have made him a better quarterback? Why or why not?

3. Do you think Favre realized that he was dependent on drugs before his seizure? Why did the seizure change his life?

4. How difficult is it to stop taking a drug like Vicodin? What symptoms would you expect Favre to exhibit during his withdrawal period?

Answers to Review Questions:

1. psychoactive   2. 1-b; 2-c; 3-a   3. 1-H; 2-S; 3-S; 4-D; 5-N; 6-H   4. true   5. Methadone   6. People become addicted to the methadone.

CHAPTER 5

Learning

Jean Little with Ritz, Pippa's predecessor. Seeing Eye dogs can be trained to carry out surprisingly sophisticated tasks using the basic principles of learning.

Prologue

A Friend Named Pippa

Pippa is a wonderful friend and companion, gentle, loyal and giving unselfishly of time and affection. She is ever ready to help, and in return, she asks for little.

Pippa, a three-year-old yellow lab, is a guide dog. She is trained to be a help-mate to her owner Jean Little, a beloved and award winning author who has entertained and inspired Canadian children for over thirty years. Ms. Little does all of the things that you would expect of a well-known author. She travels a lot, often on planes, to schools and conferences. She attends ball games (Pippa is a great Jay's fan). Whether she is in a country lane or on the streets of New York, there is Pippa always a few steps ahead of her.

Trainers, using praise as a reward, have taught Pippa to respond to specific commands. Beyond this, Pippa seems to know that her owner is dependent on her in a way that is different from the sighted person who had trained her. At home and out of harness she is a pet. In harness she is all business, totally in control and responsible for her owner's safety.

Ms. Little who has had two other guide dogs, Zepher and Ritz, since 1982, has spent a number of weeks learning how to work with each one at The Seeing Eye School where the dogs were trained. According to her, a major part of this process is bonding with each other and learning to trust the dog to do what she has learned to do.

Of her dog, Ms. Little says "she guides better than a person and she also provides a bridge to the sighted world". People who might hesitate approaching someone who is blind, find that the dog provides a way of opening communication.

learning: A relatively permanent change in behaviour brought about by experience

Pippa's expertise did not just happen of course. It is the result of painstaking training procedures—the same ones that are at work in each of our lives, illustrated by our ability to write or read a book, drive a car, play scrabble, study for a test, or perform any of the numerous activities that make up our daily routine. Like Pippa, each of us must acquire and refine our skills and abilities through learning.

A fundamental topic for psychologists, learning plays a central role in almost every specialty area of psychology, as we will see throughout this book. For example, a psychologist studying perception might ask, "How do we learn that people who look small from a distance are far away and not simply tiny?" A developmental psychologist might inquire, "How do babies learn to distinguish their mothers from other people?" A clinical psychologist might wonder, "Why do some people learn to be afraid when they see a spider?" A social psychologist might ask, "How do we learn to feel that we are in love?" Each of these questions, although drawn from very different fields of psychology, can be answered only with reference to learning processes.

What do we mean by learning? Although psychologists have identified a number of different types of learning, a general definition encompasses them all: **Learning** is a relatively permanent change in behaviour brought about by experience. What is particularly important about this definition is that it permits us to distinguish between performance changes due to *maturation* (the unfolding of biologically predetermined patterns of behaviour due simply to getting older) and those changes brought about by experience. For instance, children become better tennis players as they grow older partially because their strength increases with their size—a maturational phenomenon. Such maturational changes need to be distinguished from improvements due to learning, which are a consequence of practice.

Similarly, we must distinguish between short-term changes in behaviour that are due to factors other than learning, such as declines in performance resulting from fatigue or lack of effort, and performance changes that are due to actual learning. For example, if Andre Agassi performs poorly in a tennis game because of tension or fatigue, this does not mean that he has not learned to play correctly or has forgotten how to play well.

The distinction between learning and performance is critical, and not always easy to make (Druckman & Bjork, 1994). To some psychologists, we can infer learning only indirectly, by observing changes in performance. Because there is not always a one-to-one correspondence between learning and performance, understanding when true learning has occurred is difficult. (Those of us who have done poorly on an exam because we were tired and made careless mistakes can well understand this distinction.)

We begin this chapter by examining the type of learning that underlies responses ranging from a dog salivating when it sees or hears its owner opening a can of dog food to the emotions we feel when our national anthem is played. We then discuss other theories that consider how learning is a consequence of rewarding circumstances. Finally, we examine approaches that focus on the mental aspects of learning.

CLASSICAL CONDITIONING

Does the mere sight of the golden arches in front of McDonald's make you feel pangs of hunger and think about hamburgers? If it does, then you are displaying a rudimentary form of learning called classical conditioning.

The processes that underlie classical conditioning explain such diverse phenomena as crying at the sight of a bride walking down the aisle at a wedding, fearing the dark, and falling in love with the boy or girl next door. To understand classical conditioning, however, it is necessary to move in time and place to the early part of the twentieth century in Russia.

The Basics of Conditioning

Ivan Pavlov, a Russian physiologist, never intended to do psychological research. In 1904 he won the Nobel Prize for his work on digestion, testimony to his contribution to that field. Yet Pavlov is remembered not for his physiological research, but for his experiments on basic learning processes—work that he began quite accidentally (Windholz, 1997).

Pavlov had been studying the secretion of stomach acids and salivation in dogs in response to the ingestion of varying amounts and kinds of food. While doing so, he observed a curious phenomenon: Sometimes stomach secretions and salivation would begin in the dogs when they had actually eaten no food. The mere sight of a food bowl or of the individual who normally brought the food, or even the sound of that individual's footsteps, was enough to produce a physiological response in the dogs. Pavlov's genius was his ability to recognize the implications of this rather basic discovery. He saw that the dogs were responding not only on the basis of a biological need (hunger), but also as a result of learning—or, as it came to be called, classical conditioning. In **classical conditioning,** an organism learns to respond to a neutral stimulus that normally does not bring about that response.

To demonstrate and analyze classical conditioning, Pavlov conducted a series of experiments (Pavlov, 1927). In one, he attached a tube to the salivary gland of a dog, allowing him to measure precisely the amount of salivation that occurred. He then sounded a tuning fork and, just a few seconds later, presented the dog with meat powder. This pairing, carefully planned so that exactly the same amount of time elapsed between the presentation of the sound and the meat powder, occurred repeatedly. At first the dog would salivate only when the meat powder itself was presented, but soon it began to salivate at the sound of the tuning fork. In fact, even when Pavlov stopped presenting the meat powder, the dog still salivated after hearing the sound. The dog had been classically conditioned to salivate to the tone.

Learning and Instruction

▶ **What is learning?**

▶ **How do we learn to form associations between stimuli and responses?**

classical conditioning: A type of learning in which an organism responds to a neutral stimulus that normally does not bring about that response

Ivan Pavlov (centre, with white beard) is best known for his contributions to the field of classical conditioning.

neutral stimulus: A stimulus that, before conditioning, has no effect on the desired response

unconditioned stimulus (UCS): A stimulus that brings about a response without having been learned

unconditioned response (UCR): A response that is natural and needs no training (e.g., salivation at the smell of food)

As you can see in Figure 5-1, the basic processes of classical conditioning that underlie Pavlov's discovery are straightforward, although the terminology he chose has a technical ring. Consider first the diagram in Figure 5-1a. Before conditioning, there are two unrelated stimuli: the sound of a tuning fork and meat powder. We know that the sound of a tuning fork leads not to salivation but to some irrelevant response, such as perking of the ears or, perhaps, a startle reaction. The sound in this case is therefore called the **neutral stimulus** because it has no effect on the response of interest. We also have meat powder, which, because of the biological makeup of the dog, naturally leads to salivation—the response that we are interested in conditioning. The meat powder is considered an **unconditioned stimulus,** or **UCS,** because food placed in a dog's mouth automatically causes salivation to occur. The response that the meat powder elicits (salivation) is called an **unconditioned response,** or **UCR**—a response that is not associated with previous learning. Unconditioned responses are natural, innate responses that involve no training. They are always brought about by the presence of unconditioned stimuli.

Figure 5-1b illustrates what happens during conditioning. The tuning fork is repeatedly sounded just before presentation of the meat powder. The goal of conditioning is for the tuning fork to become associated with the unconditioned stimulus (meat powder) and therefore to bring about the same sort of response as the unconditioned stimulus. During this period, salivation gradually increases each time the tuning fork is sounded, until the tuning fork alone causes the dog to salivate.

conditioned stimulus (CS): A once-neutral stimulus that has been paired with an unconditioned stimulus to bring about a response formerly caused only by the unconditioned stimulus

conditioned response (CR): A response that, after conditioning, follows a previously neutral stimulus (e.g., salivation at the sound of a tuning fork)

When conditioning is complete, the tuning fork has evolved from a neutral stimulus to what is now called a **conditioned stimulus,** or **CS.** At this time, salivation that occurs as a response to the conditioned stimulus (tuning fork) is considered a **conditioned response,** or **CR.** This situation is depicted in Figure 5-1c. After conditioning, then, the conditioned stimulus evokes the conditioned response.

The sequence and timing of the presentation of the unconditioned stimulus and the conditioned stimulus are particularly important (Rescorla, 1988; Wasserman & Miller, 1997). Like a malfunctioning warning light at a railroad crossing that does not

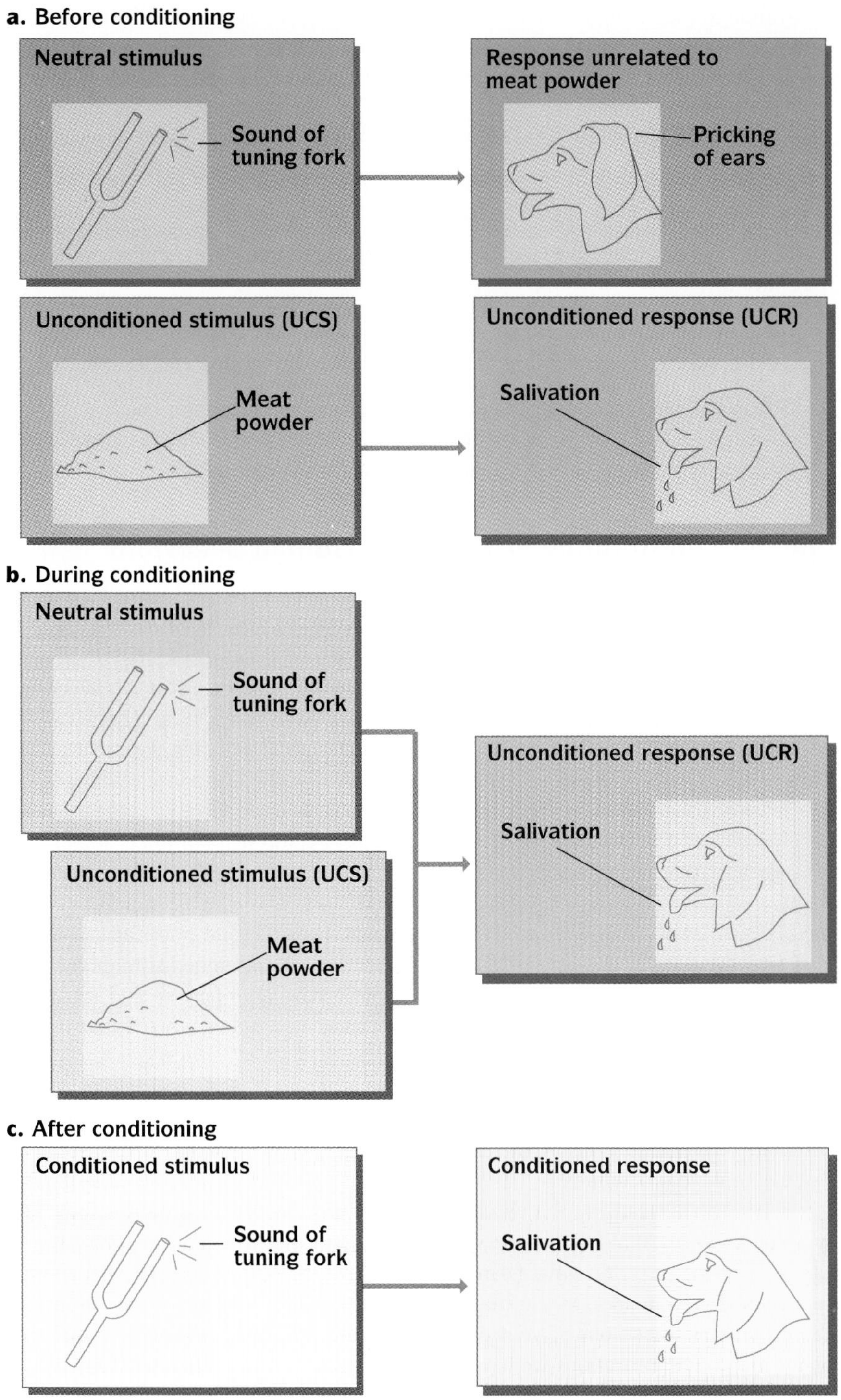

a. Before conditioning

b. During conditioning

c. After conditioning

FIGURE 5-1 *The basic process of classical conditioning. (a) Prior to conditioning, the sound of a tuning fork does not bring about salivation—making the tuning fork a neutral stimulus. On the other hand, meat powder naturally brings about salivation, making the meat powder an unconditioned stimulus and salivation an unconditioned response. (b) During conditioning, the tuning fork is sounded just before the presentation of the meat powder. (c) Eventually, the sound of the tuning fork alone brings about salivation. We can now say that conditioning has been accomplished: The previously neutral stimulus of the tuning fork is now considered a conditioned stimulus that brings about the conditioned response of salivation.*

go on until after a train has passed by, a neutral stimulus that follows an unconditioned stimulus has little chance of becoming a conditioned stimulus. On the other hand, just as a warning light works best if it goes on right before a train passes, a neutral stimulus that is presented just before the unconditioned stimulus is most apt to result in successful conditioning. Research has shown that conditioning is most effective if the neutral stimulus (which will become a conditioned stimulus) precedes the unconditioned stimulus by between a half-second and several seconds, depending on what kind of response is being conditioned.

Although the terminology employed by Pavlov to describe classical conditioning may at first seem confusing, the following rules of thumb can help to make the relationships between stimuli and responses easier to understand and remember:

- *Un*conditioned stimuli lead to *un*conditioned responses.

- *Un*conditioned stimulus-*un*conditioned response pairings are *un*learned and *un*trained.

- During conditioning, previously neutral stimuli are transformed into conditioned stimuli.

- Conditioned stimuli lead to conditioned responses, and conditioned stimulus-conditioned response pairings are a consequence of learning and training.

- Unconditioned responses and conditioned responses are similar (such as salivation in the example described earlier), but the conditioned response is learned, whereas the unconditioned response occurs naturally.

Classical Conditioning

Applying Conditioning Principles to Human Behaviour

Although the initial conditioning experiments were carried out with animals, classical conditioning principles were soon found to explain many aspects of everyday human behaviour. Recall, for instance, the earlier illustration of how people may experience hunger pangs at the sight of McDonald's golden arches. The cause of this reaction is classical conditioning: The previously neutral arches have come to be associated with the food inside the restaurant (the unconditioned stimulus), causing the arches to become a conditioned stimulus that brings about the conditioned response of hunger.

Emotional responses are particularly likely to be learned through classical conditioning processes. For instance, how do some of us develop fears of mice, spiders, and other creatures that are typically harmless? In a now-famous case study designed to show that classical conditioning was at the root of such fears, an 11-month-old infant named Albert, who initially showed no fear of rats, heard a loud noise just as he was shown a rat (Watson & Rayner, 1920). The noise (the unconditioned stimulus) evoked fear (the unconditioned response). After just a few pairings of noise and rat, Albert began to show fear of the rat by itself. The rat, then, had become a CS that brought about the CR, fear. Similarly, the pairing of the appearance of certain species (such as mice or spiders) with the fearful comments of an adult may cause children to develop the same fears their parents have. (By the way, we don't know what happened to the unfortunate Albert, and Watson, the experimenter, has been condemned for using ethically questionable procedures.)

In adulthood, learning via classical conditioning occurs a bit more subtly. You may come to know that a job supervisor is in a bad mood when her tone of voice changes, if in the past you have heard her use that tone only when she was about to criticize someone's work. Or you may have a particular fondness for the colour blue because that was the colour of your childhood bedroom. Classical conditioning, then, explains many of the reactions we have to stimuli in the world around us.

Extinction: Unlearning What We Have Learned

What do you think would happen if a dog who had become classically conditioned to salivate at the sound of a bell never again received food when the bell was sounded? The answer lies in one of the basic phenomena of learning: extinction. **Extinction** occurs when a previously conditioned response decreases in frequency and eventually disappears.

To produce extinction, one needs to end the association between conditioned and unconditioned stimuli. For instance, if we had trained a dog to salivate at the sound of a bell, we could produce extinction by ceasing to provide meat after the bell was sounded. At first the dog would continue to salivate when it heard the bell, but

extinction: One of the basic phenomena of learning that occurs when a previously conditioned response decreases in frequency and eventually disappears

after a few such instances, the amount of salivation would probably decline, and the dog would eventually stop responding to the bell altogether. At that point, we could say that the response had been extinguished. In sum, extinction occurs when the conditioned stimulus is repeatedly presented without the unconditioned stimulus. Extinction does not mean that the original learning is destroyed, only that the organism, over time, pays less attention to the stimulus (Goddard, 1997). We should keep in mind that extinction can be a helpful phenomenon. Consider, for instance, what it would be like if the fear you experienced after watching the famous shower scene in *Psycho* never was extinguished. You might well tremble with fright every time you even thought of showering.

As we will describe more fully in Chapter 13, psychologists have treated people with irrational fears, or phobias, by using a form of therapy called systematic desensitization. The goal of *systematic desensitization* is to bring about the extinction of the phobia. For example, a therapist using systematic desensitization for a client who is afraid of dogs may repeatedly expose the client to dogs, starting with a less frightening aspect (a photo of a cute dog) and moving toward more feared ones (such as an actual encounter with a strange dog). As the negative consequences of exposure to the dog do not materialize, the fear eventually becomes extinguished.

Spontaneous Recovery: The Return of the Conditioned Response

Once a conditioned response has been extinguished, has it vanished forever? Not necessarily. Pavlov discovered this fact when he returned to his previously conditioned dog a week after the conditioned behaviour had been extinguished. If he sounded a tuning fork, the dog once again salivated. Similarly, consider people who have managed to overcome a cocaine addiction. Even though they are "cured," if they are subsequently confronted by a stimulus with strong connections to the drug—such as a white powder or a pipe used for smoking cocaine—they may suddenly experience an irresistible impulse to use the drug again, even after a long absence from drug use (O'Brien et al., 1992; Drummond et al., 1995).

This phenomenon is called **spontaneous recovery**—the reappearance of a previously extinguished response after time has elapsed without exposure to the conditioned stimulus. Usually, however, responses that return through spontaneous recovery are weaker than they were initially and can be extinguished more readily than before.

spontaneous recovery: The reappearance of a previously extinguished response after time has elapsed without exposure to the conditioned stimulus

Generalization and Discrimination

Despite differences in colour and shape, to most of us a rose is a rose is a rose. The pleasure we experience at the beauty, smell, and grace of the flower is similar for different types of roses. Pavlov noticed an analogous phenomenon. His dogs often salivated not only at the sound of the tuning fork that was used during their original conditioning but at the sound of a bell or a buzzer as well.

Such behaviour is the result of stimulus generalization. **Stimulus generalization** takes place when a conditioned response follows a stimulus that is similar to the original conditioned stimulus. The greater the similarity between the two stimuli, the greater the likelihood of stimulus generalization. Baby Albert, who, as we mentioned earlier, was conditioned to be fearful of rats, was later found to be afraid of other furry white things as well. He was fearful of white rabbits, white fur coats, and even a white Santa Claus mask. On the other hand, according to the principle of stimulus generalization, it is unlikely that he would have been afraid of a black dog, since its colour would differentiate it sufficiently from the original fear-evoking stimulus.

stimulus generalization: Response to a stimulus that is similar to but different from a conditioned stimulus; the more similar the two stimuli, the more likely generalization is to occur

The conditioned response elicited by the new stimulus is usually not as intense as the original conditioned response, although the more similar the new stimulus is to the old one, the more similar the new response will be. It is unlikely, then, that Albert's fear of the Santa Claus mask was as great as his learned fear of a rat. Still, stimulus generalization permits us to know, for example, that we ought to brake at all red lights, even if there are minor variations in size, shape, and shade.

If two stimuli are sufficiently distinct from one another so that one evokes a conditioned response but the other does not, we can say that **stimulus discrimination** has occurred. In stimulus discrimination, an organism learns to differentiate among different stimuli and restricts the conditioned response to one stimulus rather than to others. Without the ability to discriminate between a red and a green traffic light, we would be mowed down by oncoming traffic; and if we could not discriminate a cat from a mountain lion, we might find ourselves in uncomfortable straits on a camping trip.

stimulus discrimination: The process by which an organism learns to differentiate among stimuli, restricting its response to one in particular

Higher-Order Conditioning

Suppose a four-year-old boy is knocked over a few times by his neighbor's large and ill-behaved dog, Rags. After a few such incidents, it would not be surprising that merely hearing the dog's name would produce a reaction of fear.

The unpleasant emotional reaction the child experiences on hearing "Rags" represents an example of higher-order conditioning. *Higher-order conditioning* occurs when a conditioned stimulus that has been established during earlier conditioning is then paired repeatedly with a neutral stimulus. If this neutral stimulus, by itself, comes to evoke a conditioned response similar to the original conditioned stimulus, higher-order conditioning has occurred. The original conditioned stimulus acts, in effect, as an unconditioned stimulus.

Our example of Rags can illustrate higher-order conditioning. The child has learned to associate the sight of Rags, who originally was a neutral stimulus, with fear and pain. The mere sight of Rags, then, has become a conditioned stimulus, which evokes the conditioned response of fear.

Later, however, the child makes the association that every time he sees Rags, its owner is calling the dog's name, saying, "Here, Rags." Because of the repeated pairing of the name of Rags (which was originally a neutral stimulus) with the sight of Rags (now a conditioned stimulus), the child becomes conditioned to experience a reaction of fear and loathing whenever he hears the name Rags, even though the child may be safely inside his house. The name "Rags," then, has become a conditioned stimulus because of its earlier pairing with the conditioned stimulus of the sight of Rags. Higher-order conditioning has occurred: The sound of Rags's name has become a conditioned stimulus evoking a conditioned response.

Some psychologists have suggested that higher-order conditioning may provide an explanation for the acquisition and maintenance of prejudice against members of racial and ethnic groups (Staats, 1975). Suppose, for instance, that every time a young girl's parents mentioned a particular racial group, they used such negative words as "stupid" or "filthy." Eventually, the girl might come to associate members of the group with the unpleasant emotional reaction that is evoked by the words "stupid" and "filthy" (reactions learned through prior classical conditioning). Although this is not a complete explanation for prejudice, it is likely that such higher-order conditioning is part of the process.

Beyond Traditional Classical Conditioning: Challenging Basic Assumptions

Theoretically, it ought to be possible to keep producing unlimited higher-order response chains, associating one conditioned stimulus with another. In fact, Pavlov hypothesized that all learning is nothing more than long strings of conditioned responses. However, this notion has not been supported by subsequent research, and it turns out that classical conditioning provides us with only a partial explanation of how people and animals learn (Rizley & Rescorla, 1972; Hollis, 1997).

Some of the other fundamental assumptions of classical conditioning have also been questioned. For example, according to Pavlov, as well as to many contemporary proponents of the traditional view of classical conditioning, the process of linking stimuli and responses occurs in a mechanistic, unthinking way. In contrast to this perspective, learning theorists influenced by cognitive psychology have argued that there is more to classical conditioning than this mechanical view. They contend that learners actively develop an understanding and expectancy about which particular unconditioned stimuli are matched with specific conditioned stimuli. A sounding bell, for instance gives a dog something to think about: the impending arrival of food. In a sense, this view suggests that the learner develops and holds an idea or image about how various stimuli are linked to one another (Rescorla, 1988; Turkkan, 1989; Baker & Mercier, 1989).

Traditional explanations of how classical conditioning operates have also been challenged by John Garcia, a leading researcher in learning processes. He disputes the supposition that optimal learning occurs only when the unconditioned stimulus *immediately* follows the conditioned stimulus (Papini & Bitterman, 1990; Garcia, 1990).

Like Pavlov, Garcia made his major contribution while studying a phenomenon unrelated to learning. He was initially concerned with the effects of exposure to nuclear radiation on laboratory animals. In the course of his experiments, he realized that rats in a radiation chamber drank almost no water, while in their home cage they drank it eagerly. The most obvious explanation—that it had something to do with the radiation—was soon ruled out. Garcia found that even when the radiation was not turned on, the rats still drank little or no water in the radiation chamber.

Initially puzzled by the rats' behaviour, Garcia eventually figured out what was happening. He noticed that the drinking cups in the radiation chamber were made of plastic, thereby giving the water an unusual, plastic-like taste. In contrast, the drinking cups in the home cage were made of glass and left no abnormal taste.

After a series of experiments to rule out several alternative explanations, just one possibility remained: Apparently, the plastic-tasting water had become repeatedly paired with illness brought on by exposure to radiation, and had led the rats to form a classically conditioned association. The process began with the radiation acting as an unconditioned stimulus evoking the unconditioned response of sickness. With repeated pairings, the plastic-tasting water had become a conditioned stimulus that evoked the conditioned response of sickness (Garcia, Hankins, & Rusiniak, 1974).

The problem with this finding was that it violated one of the basic rules of classical conditioning—that an unconditioned stimulus should *immediately* follow the conditioned stimulus for optimal conditioning to occur. Instead, Garcia's findings showed that conditioning could occur even when there was an interval of as long as eight hours between exposure to the conditioned stimulus and the response of sickness. Furthermore, the conditioning persisted over very long periods and sometimes occurred after just one exposure to water that was followed later on by illness.

These findings have had important practical implications. For example, in order to prevent coyotes from killing their sheep, some ranchers now routinely lace a sheep carcass with a drug and leave the carcass in a place where coyotes will find it. The drug temporarily makes the coyotes quite ill, but it does not permanently harm them. After just one exposure to a drug-laden sheep carcass, coyotes tend to avoid sheep, which are normally one of their primary natural victims. The sheep, then, have become a conditioned stimulus to the coyotes. This approach is a far more humane one than shooting the coyotes, the traditional response of ranchers to predators (Gustavson et al., 1974).

Recap, Review, and Rethink

Recap

- Learning is a relatively permanent change in behaviour brought about by experience.

- Classical conditioning is a kind of learning in which an initially neutral stimulus, which does not evoke a relevant response, is paired repeatedly with an unconditioned stimulus. Eventually, the previously neutral stimulus evokes a response similar to that brought about by the unconditioned stimulus.

- Classical conditioning underlies many sorts of everyday learning, such as the acquisition of emotional responses.

- Among the basic phenomena of classical conditioning are extinction, spontaneous recovery, stimulus generalization and discrimination, and higher-order conditioning.

Review

1. _____ involves changes brought about by experience, whereas _____ describes changes due to biological development.

2. _____ is the name of the scientist responsible for discovering the learning phenomenon known as _____ conditioning, in which an organism learns a response to a stimulus to which it would not normally respond.

Refer to the passage below to answer questions 3 through 6:

The last three times Theresa visited Dr. Noble for checkups, he administered a painful preventive immunization shot that left her in tears. Today, when her mother takes her for another checkup, Theresa begins to sob as soon as she comes face-to-face with Dr. Noble, even before he has had a chance to say hello.

3. The painful shot that Theresa received during each visit was a(an) _____ _____, which elicited the _____ _____, her tears.

4. Dr. Noble is upset because his presence has become a _____ _____ for Theresa's crying.

5. When elicited by Dr. Noble's presence alone, Theresa's crying is referred to as a(an) _____ _____.

6. Fortunately, Dr. Noble gave Theresa no more shots for quite some time. Over that time she gradually stopped crying and even came to like him. _____ had occurred.

7. _____ _____ occurs when a stimulus similar to, but not identical to, a conditioned stimulus produces a response. On the other hand, _____ _____ occurs when an organism does not produce a response to a stimulus that is distinct from the CS.

Answers to Review Questions are on page 178.

Rethink

1. Can you think of ways that classical conditioning is used by politicians? Advertisers? Movie makers? Do ethical issues arise from any of these uses?

2. Is it likely that Albert, Watson's experimental subject, went through life afraid of Santa Claus? Describe what probably happened to prevent this.

3. Theoretically, it should be possible to build an infinitely long chain of classically conditioned higher-order responses so that stimuli can be paired together indefinitely. What might prevent this from happening in humans?

OPERANT CONDITIONING

▶ **What is the role of reward and punishment in learning?**

Very good. . . . What a clever idea. . . . Fantastic. . . . I agree. . . . Thank you. . . . Excellent. . . . Super. . . . Right on. . . . This is the best paper you've ever written; you get an A. . . . You are really getting the hang of it. . . . I'm impressed. . . . Let me give you a hug. . . . You're getting a raise. . . . Have a cookie. . . . You look great. . . . I love you. . . .

Few of us mind being the recipient of any of the above comments. But what is especially noteworthy about them is that each of these simple statements can be used, through a process known as operant conditioning, to bring about powerful changes in behaviour and to teach the most complex tasks. Operant conditioning forms the basis for many of the most important kinds of human, and animal, learning.

operant conditioning: Learning in which a voluntary response is strengthened or weakened, depending on its positive or negative consequences

Operant conditioning describes learning in which a voluntary response is strengthened or weakened, depending on its positive or negative consequences. Unlike classical conditioning, in which the original behaviours are the natural, biological responses to the presence of some stimulus such as food, water, or pain, operant conditioning applies to voluntary responses, which an organism performs deliberately, to produce a desirable outcome. The term "operant" emphasizes this point: The organism *operates* on its environment to produce some desirable result. For example, operant conditioning is at work when we learn that toiling industriously can bring about a raise, or that studying hard results in good grades.

As with classical conditioning, the basis for understanding operant conditioning was laid by work with animals. We turn now to some of that early research, which began with a simple inquiry into the behaviour of cats.

Thorndike's Law of Effect

If you placed a hungry cat in a cage and then put a small piece of food outside, chances are the cat would eagerly search for a way out of the cage. The cat might first claw at the sides or push against an opening. Suppose, though, that you had rigged things so that the cat could escape by stepping on a small paddle that released the latch to the door of the cage (see Figure 5-2). Eventually, as it moved around the cage, the cat would happen to step on the paddle, the door would open, and the cat would eat the food.

What would happen if you then returned the cat to the box? The next time, it would probably take a little less time for the cat to step on the paddle and escape. After a few trials, the cat would deliberately step on the paddle as soon as it was placed in the cage. What would have occurred, according to Edward L. Thorndike (1932), who studied this situation extensively, was that the cat would have learned that pressing the paddle was associated with the desirable consequence of getting food. Thorndike summarized that relationship by formulating the *law of effect,* which states that responses that are satisfying are more likely to be repeated, and those that are not satisfying are less likely to be repeated.

Thorndike believed that the law of effect operated as automatically as leaves falling off a tree in autumn. It was not necessary for an organism to understand that there was a link between a response and a reward. Instead, he thought that over time and through experience, the organism would make a direct connection between the stimulus and the response without any awareness that the connection existed.

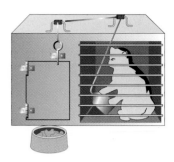

FIGURE 5-2 *Edward L. Thorndike devised this puzzle box to study the process by which a cat learns to press a paddle to escape the box and receive food.*

The Basics of Operant Conditioning

Thorndike's early research served as the foundation for the work of one of the century's most influential psychologists, B. F. Skinner, who died in 1990. You may have heard of the Skinner box (shown in one form in Figure 5-3), a chamber with a highly controlled environment used to study operant conditioning processes with laboratory animals. Whereas Thorndike's goal was to get his cats to learn to obtain food by leaving the box, animals in a Skinner box learn to obtain food by operating on their environment within the box. Skinner became interested in specifying how behaviour varied as a result of alterations in the environment.

Skinner, whose work went far beyond perfecting Thorndike's earlier apparatus, is considered the father of a whole generation of psychologists studying operant conditioning (Delprato & Midgley, 1992; Bjork, 1993; Keehn, 1996). To illustrate Skinner's contribution, let's consider what happens to a pigeon in the typical Skinner box.

Suppose you want to teach a hungry pigeon to peck a key that is located in its box. At first the pigeon will wander around the box, exploring the environment in a relatively random fashion. At some point, however, it will probably peck the key by chance, and when it does, it will receive a food pellet. The first time this happens, the pigeon will not learn the connection between pecking and receiving food and will continue to explore the box. Sooner or later the pigeon will again peck the key and receive

B. F. Skinner, who was the founding father of operant conditioning, developed what came to be called the "Skinner box."

Lever

Food dispenser

FIGURE 5-3 *A Skinner box, used to study operant conditioning. Laboratory animals learn to press the lever in order to obtain food, which is delivered by the dispenser.*

"Oh, not bad. The light comes on, I press the bar, they write me a check. How about you?"

Drawing by Cheney; © 1993 The New Yorker Magazine, Inc.

a pellet, and in time the frequency of the pecking response will increase. Eventually, the pigeon will peck the key continually until it satisfies its hunger, thereby demonstrating that it has learned that the receipt of food is contingent upon the pecking behaviour.

Reinforcing Desired Behaviour

Skinner called the process that leads the pigeon to continue pecking the key "reinforcement." **Reinforcement** is the process by which a stimulus increases the probability that a preceding behaviour will be repeated. In other words, pecking is more likely to occur again due to the stimulus of food.

In a situation such as this one, the food is called a reinforcer. A **reinforcer** is any stimulus that increases the probability that a preceding behaviour will occur again. Hence, food is a reinforcer because it increases the probability that the behaviour of pecking the key (formally referred to as the *response* of pecking) will take place.

What kind of stimuli can act as reinforcers? Bonuses, toys, and good grades can serve as reinforcers—if they strengthen a response that comes before their introduction. In each case, it is critical that the organism learn that the delivery of the reinforcer is contingent on the response occurring in the first place.

Of course, we are not born knowing that a dollar can buy us a chocolate bar. Rather, through experience we learn that money is a valuable commodity because of its association with stimuli, such as food, drink, and shelter, that are naturally reinforcing. This fact suggests a distinction that can be drawn between primary reinforcers and secondary reinforcers. A *primary reinforcer* satisfies some biological need and works naturally, regardless of a person's prior experience. Food for the hungry person, warmth for the cold person, and relief for the person in pain would all be classified as primary reinforcers. A *secondary reinforcer,* in contrast, is a stimulus that becomes reinforcing because of its association with a primary reinforcer. For instance, we know that money is valuable because we have learned that it allows us to obtain other desirable objects, including primary reinforcers such as food and shelter. Money thus becomes a secondary reinforcer.

reinforcement: The process by which a stimulus increases the probability that a preceding behaviour will be repeated
reinforcer: Any stimulus that increases the probability that a preceding behaviour will occur again

---

Answers to Review Questions:

1. Learning; maturation   2. Pavlov; classical   3. unconditioned stimulus; unconditioned response   4. conditioned stimulus
5. conditioned response   6. Extinction   7. Stimulus generalization; stimulus discrimination

What makes something a reinforcer depends on individual preferences. While a Hershey bar may act as a reinforcer for one person, an individual who dislikes chocolate might find a dollar more desirable. The only way we can know if a stimulus is a reinforcer for a given organism is to observe whether the rate of response of a previously occurring behaviour increases after the presentation of the stimulus.

Positive Reinforcers, Negative Reinforcers, and Punishment

In many respects, reinforcers can be thought of in terms of rewards; both a reinforcer and a reward increase the probability that a preceding response will occur again. But the term "reward" is limited to *positive* occurrences, and this is where it differs from a reinforcer—for it turns out that reinforcers can be positive or negative.

A **positive reinforcer** is a stimulus added to the environment that brings about an increase in a preceding response. If food, water, money, or praise is provided following a response, it is more likely that that response will occur again in the future. The paycheck that workers get at the end of the week, for example, increases the likelihood that they will return to their jobs the following week.

In contrast, a **negative reinforcer** refers to an unpleasant stimulus whose *removal* from the environment leads to an increase in the probability that a preceding response will occur again in the future. For example, if you have cold symptoms (an unpleasant stimulus) that are relieved when you take medicine, you are more likely to take the medicine when you experience such symptoms again. Taking medicine, then, is negatively reinforcing, because it removes the unpleasant cold symptoms. Similarly, if the radio volume is so loud that it hurts your ears, you are likely to find that turning it down relieves the problem. Lowering the volume is negatively reinforcing and you are more apt to repeat the action in the future. Negative reinforcement, then, teaches the individual that taking an action removes a negative condition that exists in the environment. Like positive reinforcers, negative reinforcers increase the likelihood that preceding behaviours will be repeated.

Negative reinforcement occurs in two major forms of learning: escape conditioning and avoidance conditioning. In *escape conditioning,* an organism learns to make a response that brings about an end to an aversive situation. Escape conditioning is commonplace, and it often occurs quickly. For example, it doesn't take too long for children to learn to withdraw their hands from a hot radiator—an example of escape conditioning. Similarly, busy college students who take a day off to elude the stress of too heavy a workload are showing escape conditioning.

In contrast to escape conditioning, *avoidance conditioning* occurs when an organism responds to a signal of an impending unpleasant event in a way that permits its evasion. For example, a rat will readily learn to tap a bar to avoid a shock that is signaled by a tone. Similarly, automobile drivers learn to fill up their gas tanks in order to avoid running out of fuel.

It is important to note that whether negative reinforcement consists of escape or avoidance conditioning, it is not the same as punishment. **Punishment** refers to unpleasant or painful stimuli that decrease the probability that a preceding behaviour will occur again. In contrast, negative reinforcement is associated with the removal of an unpleasant or painful stimulus, which produces an *increase* in the behaviour that brought an end to the unpleasant stimulus. If we receive a shock after behaving in a particular fashion, then, we are receiving punishment; but if we are already receiving a shock and do something to stop that shock, the behaviour that stops the shock is considered to be negatively reinforced. In the first case, a specific behaviour is apt to decrease because of the punishment; in the second, it is likely to increase because of the negative reinforcement (Azrin & Holt, 1966).

While punishment is typically considered in terms of applying some aversive stimulus—a spanking for misbehaving or ten years in jail for committing a crime—it may also consist of the removal of something positive. For instance, when a teenager is told she is "grounded" and will no longer be able to use the family car because of her poor grades, or when an employee is informed that he has been demoted with a cut

positive reinforcer: A stimulus added to the environment that brings about an increase in a preceding response

negative reinforcer: An unpleasant stimulus whose removal from the environment leads to an increase in the probability that a preceding response will occur again in the future.

Operant Conditioning

punishment: Unpleasant or painful stimuli that decrease the probability that a preceding behaviour will occur again

Table 5-1	Types of Reinforcement and Punishment	

Kind of Stimulus	When stimulus is *added,* the result is . . .	When stimulus is *removed* or *terminated,* the result is . . .
Positive (pleasant)	*Positive reinforcement* Example: Giving a raise for good performance Result: *Increase* in frequency of response (good performance)	*Punishment by removal* Example: Removal of favourite toy after misbehaviour Result: *Decrease* in frequency of response (misbehaviour)
Negative (unpleasant)	*Punishment by application* Example: Giving a spanking following misbehaviour Result: *Decrease* in frequency of response (misbehaviour)	*Negative reinforcement* Example: Terminating a headache by taking aspirin Result: *Increase* in frequency of response (taking aspirin)

in pay because of poor job evaluations, punishment in the form of the removal of a positive reinforcer is being administered.

The distinctions between the types of punishment, as well as positive and negative reinforcement, may appear confusing initially, but the following rules of thumb (and the summary in Table 5-1) can help you to distinguish these concepts from one another:

- Reinforcement *increases* the behaviour preceding it; punishment *decreases* the behaviour preceding it.

- The *application* of a *positive* stimulus brings about an increase in behaviour and is referred to as positive reinforcement; the *removal* of a *positive* stimulus decreases behaviour because of the omission of reinforcement and is called punishment by removal.

- The *application* of a *negative* stimulus decreases or reduces behaviour and is called punishment by application; the *removal* of a *negative* stimulus that results in an increase in behaviour is termed negative reinforcement.

The Pros and Cons of Punishment: Why Reinforcement Beats Punishment

Punishment

Is punishment an effective means of modifying behaviour? Punishment often appears to present the quickest route to changing behaviour that, if allowed to continue, might be dangerous to an individual. For instance, a parent may not have a second chance to warn a child not to run into a busy street, so punishing the first incidence of this behaviour might prove to be wise.

The subject of punishment is not an insignificant one. Seventy-five percent of Canadian parents use physical discipline in an effort to alter or control the behaviour of their children (Durrant, 1996). This is a topic that raises strong attitudes about its value and effectiveness. As we will see in the discussion that follows, psychologists seriously question the effectiveness of punishment as a means of bringing about behaviour change.

Durrant's study conducted in Toronto and Winnipeg in 1992, provided insight on parents' attitudes about the acceptability and the value of physical punishment. The primary reason cited for using punishment as an acceptable response was if the child was putting themselves in danger or hitting others. The finding that "more than one third of respondents believe that hitting a child is an appropriate way in which to teach a child not to hit others" certainly raises some interesting questions. Another significant finding was that only one fifth of the sample believed that punishment reliably brought about the desired result of behaviour change.

Despite its known disadvantages, punishment is frequently employed in a variety of situations.

Also, several disadvantages make the routine use of punishment questionable. For one thing, it is frequently ineffective, particularly if the punishment is not delivered shortly after the behaviour being suppressed or if the individual is able to withdraw from the setting in which the punishment is being given. An employee who is reprimanded by the boss may quit; a teenager who loses the use of the family car may borrow a friend's instead. In such instances, then, the initial behaviour that is being punished may be replaced by one that is even less desirable.

Even worse, physical punishment may convey to the recipient the idea that physical aggression is permissible and perhaps even desirable. A father who yells at and hits his son for misbehaving teaches the son that aggression is an appropriate, adult response. The son may soon copy his father's behaviour by acting aggressively toward others. In addition, physical punishment is often administered by people who are themselves angry or enraged. It is unlikely that individuals in such an emotional state will be able to think through what they are doing or to carefully control the degree of punishment they are inflicting. Ultimately, those who resort to physical punishment run the risk that they will grow to be feared.

Another disadvantage of punishment is that unless people who are being punished can be made to understand the reasons for it (i.e., that the punishment is meant to change behaviour and that it has nothing to do with the punishers' view of them as individuals) punishment may lead to lowered self-esteem.

Finally, punishment does not convey any information about what an alternative, more appropriate behaviour might be. In order to be useful in bringing about more desirable behaviour in the future, punishment must be accompanied by specific information about the behaviour that is being punished, along with specific suggestions concerning a more desirable behaviour. Punishing a child for staring out the window in school may lead her to stare at the floor instead. Unless we teach her appropriate ways to respond, we have merely managed to substitute one undesirable behaviour for another. If punishment is not followed up with reinforcement for subsequent behaviour that is more appropriate, little will be accomplished.

In sum, reinforcing desired behaviour is a more appropriate technique for modifying behaviour than using punishment. Both in and out of the scientific arena, then, reinforcement usually beats punishment (Sulzer-Azaroff & Mayer, 1991; Seppa, 1996).

Schedules of Reinforcement: Timing Life's Rewards

The world would be a different place if poker players folded for good at their first losing hand, fishermen returned to shore as soon as they missed a catch, or door-to-door

schedules of reinforcement: The
frequency and timing of reinforcement
following desired behaviour
**continuous reinforcement
schedule:** Behaviour that is reinforced
every time it occurs
partial reinforcement schedule:
Behaviour that is reinforced some but
not all of the time

salespeople stopped selling at the first house at which they were turned away. The fact
that such unreinforced behaviours continue, often with great frequency and persistence, illustrates that reinforcement need not be received continually in order for behaviour to be learned and maintained. In fact, behaviour that is reinforced only
occasionally may ultimately be learned better than behaviour that is always reinforced.

When we refer to the frequency and timing of reinforcement following desired
behaviour we are talking about **schedules of reinforcement.** Behaviour that is reinforced every time it occurs is said to be on a **continuous reinforcement schedule;** if it
is reinforced some but not all of the time, it is on a **partial reinforcement schedule.**
Although learning occurs more rapidly under a continuous reinforcement schedule, behaviour lasts longer after reinforcement stops when it is learned under a partial reinforcement schedule.

Why should partial reinforcement schedules result in stronger, longer-lasting
learning than continuous reinforcement schedules? We can answer the question by examining how we might behave when using a soft drink vending machine compared with
a Las Vegas slot machine. When we use a vending machine, prior experience has taught
us that every time we put in the appropriate amount of money, the reinforcement, a soft
drink, ought to be delivered. In other words, the schedule of reinforcement is continuous. In comparison, a slot machine offers a partial reinforcement schedule. We have
learned that after putting in our cash, most of the time we will not receive anything in
return. At the same time, though, we know that we will occasionally win something.

Now suppose that, unbeknownst to us, both the drink vending machine and the
slot machine are broken, so that neither one is able to dispense anything. It would not
be very long before we stopped depositing coins into the broken drink machine. Probably at most we would try only two or three times before leaving the machine in disgust. But the story would be quite different with the broken slot machine. Here, we
would drop in money for a considerably longer time, even though no response would
be forthcoming.

In formal terms, we can see the difference between the two reinforcement schedules: Partial reinforcement schedules (such as those provided by slot machines) maintain performance longer than continuous reinforcement schedules (such as those
established in drink vending machines) before extinction—the disappearance of the
conditioned response—occurs.

Using a *cumulative recorder,* a device that automatically records and graphs the
pattern of responses made in reaction to a particular schedule (see Figure 5-4), learning psychologists have found that certain kinds of partial reinforcement schedules pro-

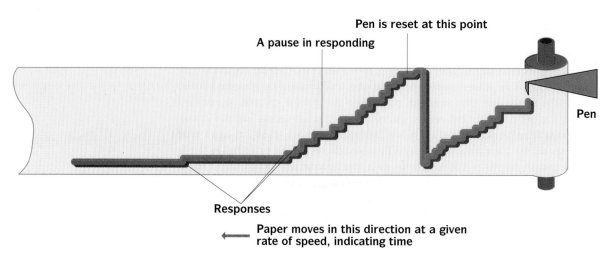

FIGURE 5-4 *A cumulative recorder. As the paper slowly unrolls, the pen indicates when a response has been made by moving a
notch upward. Pauses in responding are indicated by a lack of upward movement of the line. As is the case in this example, it is typical
for the time between initial responses to decrease as the organism learns to make the response.*

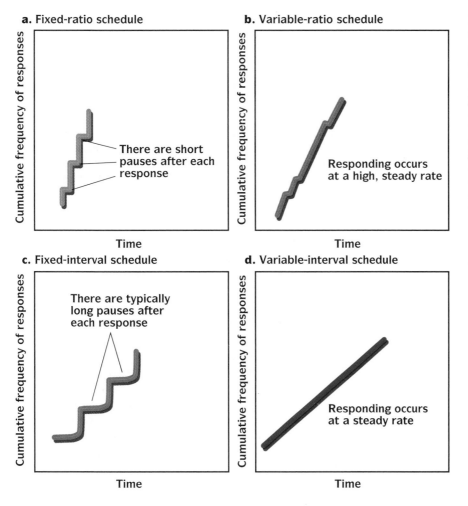

FIGURE 5-5 *Typical outcomes of different reinforcement schedules. (a) In a fixed-ratio schedule, short pauses occur following each response. Because the more responses, the more reinforcement, fixed-ratio schedules produce a high rate of responding. (b) In a variable-ratio schedule, responding also occurs at a high rate. (c) A fixed-interval schedule produces lower rates of responding, especially just after reinforcement has been presented, since the organism learns that a specified time period must elapse between reinforcement. (d) A variable-interval schedule produces a fairly steady stream of responses.*

duce stronger and lengthier responding before extinction than others (King & Logue, 1990). Although many different partial reinforcement schedules have been examined, they can most readily be put into two categories: schedules that consider the *number of responses* made before reinforcement is given, called fixed-ratio and variable-ratio schedules, and those that consider the *amount of time* that elapses before reinforcement is provided, called fixed-interval and variable-interval schedules.

Fixed- and Variable-Ratio Schedules

In a **fixed-ratio schedule,** reinforcement is given only after a certain number of responses are made. For instance, a pigeon might receive a food pellet every tenth time it pecked a key; here, the ratio would be 1:10. Similarly, garment workers are generally paid on fixed-ratio schedules: They receive *x* dollars for every blouse they sew. Because a greater rate of production means more reinforcement, people on fixed-ratio schedules are apt to work as quickly as possible. Even when rewards are no longer offered, responding comes in bursts—although pauses between bursts become longer and longer until the response peters out entirely (see Figure 5-5).

In a **variable-ratio schedule,** reinforcement occurs after a varying number of responses rather than after a fixed number. Although the specific number of responses necessary to receive reinforcement varies, the number of responses usually hovers around a specific average. Probably the best example of a variable-ratio schedule is that encountered by a telephone salesperson. She may make a sale during the third, eighth, ninth, and twentieth calls without being successful during any call in between. Although the number of responses that must be made before making a sale varies, it

fixed-ratio schedule: A schedule whereby reinforcement is given only after a certain number of responses are made

variable-ratio schedule: A schedule whereby reinforcement occurs after a varying number of responses rather than after a fixed number

averages out to a 20 percent success rate. Under these circumstances, you might expect that the salesperson would try to make as many calls as possible in as short a time as possible. Gambling also works on a variable-ratio schedule. The proliferation of casinos in Canada has raised concerns about the pathology of gambling (Ladouceur, 1996). This is the case with all variable-ratio schedules; they promote a high rate of response and a high degree of resistance to extinction.

Fixed- and Variable-Interval Schedules: The Passage of Time

In contrast to fixed- and variable-ratio schedules, in which the crucial factor is the number of responses, fixed-*interval* and variable-*interval* schedules focus on the amount of *time* that has elapsed since a person or animal was rewarded. One example of a fixed-interval schedule is a weekly paycheck. For people who receive regular, weekly paychecks, it typically makes little difference how much they produce in a given week—as long as they show up and do *some* work.

fixed-interval schedule: A schedule that provides reinforcement for a response only if a fixed time period has elapsed, making overall rates of response relatively low

Because a **fixed-interval schedule** provides reinforcement for a response only if a fixed time period has elapsed, overall rates of response are relatively low. This is especially true in the period just after reinforcement when the time before another reinforcement is relatively great. Students' study habits often exemplify this reality. If the periods between exams are relatively long (meaning that the opportunity for reinforcement for good performance is fairly infrequent), students often study minimally or not at all until the day of the exam draws near. Just before the exam, however, students begin to cram for it, signalling a rapid increase in the rate of their studying response (Mawhinney et al., 1971). As you might expect, immediately following the exam there is a rapid decline in the rate of responding, with few people opening a book the day after a test.

variable-interval schedule: A schedule whereby the time between reinforcements varies around some average rather than being fixed

One way to decrease the delay in responding that occurs just after reinforcement, and to maintain the desired behaviour more consistently throughout an interval, is to use a variable-interval schedule. In a **variable-interval schedule,** the time between reinforcements varies around some average rather than being fixed. For example, a professor who gives surprise quizzes that vary from one every three days to one every three weeks, averaging one every two weeks, is using a variable-interval schedule. Compared to the study habits we observed with a fixed-interval schedule, students' study habits under such a variable-interval schedule would most likely be very different. Students would be apt to study more regularly since they would never know when the next surprise quiz would be coming. Variable-interval schedules, in general, are more likely to produce relatively steady rates of responding than fixed-interval schedules, with responses that take longer to extinguish after reinforcement ends.

Discrimination and Generalization in Operant Conditioning

It does not take a child long to learn that a red light at an intersection means stop, while a green light indicates that it is permissible to continue. Just as in classical conditioning, then, operant learning involves the phenomena of discrimination and generalization.

The process by which people learn to discriminate stimuli is known as stimulus control training. In *stimulus control training,* a behaviour is reinforced in the presence of a specific stimulus, but not in its absence. For example, one of the most difficult discriminations many people face is determining when someone's friendliness is not mere friendliness, but a signal of romantic interest. People learn to make the discrimination by observing the presence of certain subtle nonverbal cues—such as increased eye contact and touching—that indicate romantic interest. When such cues are absent, people learn that no romantic interest is indicated. In this case, the nonverbal cue acts as a discriminative stimulus, one to which an organism learns to respond during stimulus control training. A *discriminative stimulus* signals the likelihood that reinforcement will follow a response. For example, if you wait until your roommate is in a good mood before you ask to borrow her favourite compact disc, your behaviour can be said to be under stimulus control since you can discriminate between her moods.

Just as in classical conditioning, the phenomenon of stimulus generalization, in which an organism learns a response to one stimulus and then applies it to other stimuli, is also found in operant conditioning. If you have learned that being polite produces the reinforcement of getting your way in a certain situation, you are likely to generalize your response to other situations. Sometimes, though, generalization can have unfortunate consequences, such as when people behave negatively toward all members of a racial group because they have had an unpleasant experience with one member of that group.

Superstitious Behaviour

- Have you ever knocked on wood after speaking about good fortune?

- After spilling salt, do you quickly throw a pinch over your left shoulder?

- Do you have a lucky pen that you take to all exams?

While it is easy to sneer at such rituals, learning psychologists consider them examples of an interesting class of responses called *superstitious behaviour*. Such behaviour can be explained in terms of the basic principles of reinforcement (Zimmer, 1984; Justice & Looney, 1990; White & Liu, 1995). As we have discussed, behaviour that is followed by a reinforcer tends to be strengthened. Occasionally, however, the behaviour that occurs prior to the reinforcement is entirely coincidental. Imagine, for instance, that a baseball player hits his bat against the ground three times in a row just prior to getting a single. The hit is, of course, coincidental to the batter's hitting the ground, but to the player it may be seen as somehow related. Because the player makes this association he may hit the ground three times every time he is at bat in the future. And because he will be at least partially reinforced for this behaviour—batters usually get a hit 25 percent of the time—his ground-hitting behaviour will probably be maintained.

Do superstitions actually affect subsequent behaviour? In fact, they do. According to some psychologists, superstitious behaviour allows people to cope with anxiety by providing routines or rituals that can give them a sense of control over a situation. In this way, touching a "lucky" pen may help calm a person—which, in fact, may lead to better performance when taking a test or during a stressful interview. Our superstitions, then, may shape our subsequent behaviour (Van Ginkel, 1990; Matute, 1994, 1995).

Shaping: Reinforcing What Doesn't Come Naturally

Consider the difficulty of using operant conditioning to teach people to repair an automobile transmission. If you had to wait until they chanced to fix a transmission perfectly before you provided them with reinforcement, the Model T might be back in style long before they mastered the repair process.

There are many complex behaviours, ranging from auto repair to zither playing, which we would not expect to occur naturally as part of anyone's spontaneous behaviour. In cases such as these, in which there might otherwise be no opportunity to provide reinforcement for the particular behaviour (since it never occurs in the first place), a procedure known as shaping is used. **Shaping** is the process of teaching a complex behaviour by rewarding closer and closer approximations of the desired behaviour. In shaping, any behaviour that is at all similar to the behaviour you want the person to learn is reinforced at first. Later, you reinforce only responses that are closer to the behaviour you ultimately want to teach. Finally, you reinforce only the desired response. Each step in shaping, then, moves only slightly beyond the previously learned behaviour, permitting the person to link the new step to the behaviour learned earlier.

Superstitious behaviour, such as being careful to avoid stepping on cracks in the sidewalk, may be the result of reinforcement that occurs coincidentally.

The Psychology of Superstition

Computer-based instruction relies on the principles of shaping, in which learners are led to provide closer and closer approximations to the desired behaviour.

shaping: The process of teaching a complex behaviour by rewarding closer and closer approximations of the desired behaviour

Pathways Through Psychology

Catharine Rankin

Associate Professor of Psychology, University of British Columbia

Education: B.A., M.A., University of Guelph; B.Ed., University of Western Ontario; Ph.D. (biopsychology) City University of New York

Home: Vancouver, British Columbia

I have always been interested in science, starting with my fossil collection in grade 3. In university, I divided my time between psychology and biology. My Honours project was a study of seal behaviour, my Master's was in cognitive psychology. I then took time out of academics, and did a Bachelor of Education degree and taught grades 4 and 5 in Toronto for two years.

I left there to do a Ph.D. in biopsychology at the City University of New York where I studied the African Electric Catfish in the Animal Behaviour Program at Hunter College and the American Museum of Natural History. As I learned more about behaviour I found myself asking more and more questions about mechanisms. I always wanted to know why and how the animals did what they did.

One summer I took a course at Woods Hole Marine Biological Laboratory called "Neural Systems and Behaviour". It was all about how nervous systems produced behaviour. I was particularly fascinated by the research that used invertebrates to study the biological basis of learning and memory. I decided to pursue that area of research. After finishing my Ph.D. on the electric catfish I went to Yale University to do post-doctoral research on learning in the marine mollusc *Aplysia californica* in the laboratory of Dr. Thomas Carew.

When I came to UBC to set up my own lab, I ended up choosing an even simpler animal to study. My research is on the biological basis of learning and memory in the nematode worm *C. elegans*. This tiny (1mm) worm has only 302 neurons! (Humans have over a trillion neurons—it is impossible to understand what every neuron in a human is doing when it learns—we hope that we can figure out what every neuron in *C. elegans* is doing when it learns.) I am very excited about research—it is like a great mystery to solve. It always feels like the next answer is just around the corner. However, the challenge in research is that every answer leads to more questions! It is very satisfying to understand behaviour enough to be able to predict what an animal is going to do.

Research done by my students and me, has demonstrated that this simple worm can learn (it shows habituation—that is learning not to respond to stimuli that are repeated, but are not important). It also can remember training for at least 24 hours (not bad for a worm that only lives about 12 days). We have used a laser to kill single neurons and then have studied the role of those neurons in habituation. Through this technique we have identified the neurons important for the response we study. We have also studied genetic mutations in *C. elegans* to try to understand what genes are involved in learning and memory. Since *C. elegans* shows habituation in exactly the same way as all other animals, including humans, it is my hope that by understanding the mechanisms of habituation in the worm, I can shed light on mechanisms of human learning. In additon, many human disorders, such as schizophrenia, include deficits in habituation. Understanding the genes that play a role in habituation in the worm may help to understand these human genetic disorders.

Catharine Rankin

Source: Catharine Rankin, Ph.D.
University of British Columbia
<crankin@cortex.psych.ubc.ca>

Biological Constraints on Learning: You Can't Teach an Old Dog Just Any Trick

Keller and Marian Breland were pleased with their idea: As consultants to professional animal trainers, they came up with the notion of having a pig place a wooden disk into a piggy bank. With their experience in training animals through operant conditioning, they thought the task would be easy to teach, given that it was certainly well within the range of the pig's physical capabilities. Yet every time they tried out the procedure, it failed. Upon viewing the disk, the pigs were willing to do nothing but root the wooden disk along the ground. Apparently, the pigs were biologically programmed to push stimuli in the shape of disks along the ground.

Their lack of swine success led the Brelands to substitute a raccoon. Although the procedure worked fine with one disk, when two disks were used, the raccoon refused to deposit either of them and instead rubbed the two together, as if it were washing them. Once again, it appeared that the disks evoked biologically innate behaviours that were impossible to supplant with even the most exhaustive training (Breland & Breland, 1961).

The Brelands' difficulties illustrate an important point: Not all behaviours can be trained in all species equally well. Instead, there are *biological constraints,* built-in limitations, in the ability of animals to learn particular behaviours. In some cases, an organism will have a special bent that will aid in its learning a behaviour (such as behaviours that involve pecking in pigeons); in other cases, biological constraints will act to prevent or inhibit an organism from learning a behaviour. In either instance, it is clear that animals have specialized learning mechanisms that influence how readily both classical and operant conditioning function, and each species is biologically primed to develop particular kinds of associations and to face obstacles in learning others (Hollis, 1984).

Recap, Review, and Rethink

Recap

- Operant conditioning is a form of learning in which a voluntary response is strengthened or weakened, depending on its positive or negative consequences.

- Reinforcement is the process by which a stimulus increases the probability that a preceding behaviour will be repeated.

- A positive reinforcer is a stimulus that is added to the environment to increase the likelihood of a response. A negative reinforcer is a stimulus that removes something unpleasant from the environment, leading to an increase in the probability that a preceding response will occur in the future.

- Punishment involves the administration of an unpleasant stimulus, following a response, which is meant to decrease or suppress behaviour; it may also consist of the removal of a positive reinforcer.

- In punishment, the goal is to decrease or suppress undesired behaviour by administering a stimulus; in negative reinforcement, the goal is to increase a desired behaviour by removing a stimulus.

- Reinforcement need not be constant in order for behaviour to be learned and maintained; partial schedules of reinforcement, in fact, lead to greater resistance to extinction than continuous schedules of reinforcement.

- Generalization, discrimination, and shaping are among the basic phenomena of operant conditioning.

Review

1. _____ conditioning describes learning that occurs as a result of reinforcement.

2. A hungry person would find food to be a _____ reinforcer, while a ten-dollar bill would be a _____ reinforcer.

3. Match the type of operant learning with its definition:
   1. An unpleasant stimulus is presented to decrease behaviour.
   2. An unpleasant stimulus is removed to increase behaviour.
   3. A pleasant stimulus is presented to increase behaviour.

   a. positive reinforcement
   b. negative reinforcement
   c. punishment

4. Sandy had had a rough day, and his son's noisemaking was not helping him relax. Not wanting to resort to scolding, Sandy lowered his tone of voice and told his son in a serious manner that he was very tired and would like the boy to play quietly for an hour. This approach worked. For Sandy, the change in his son's behaviour was

   a. positively reinforcing.
   b. secondarily reinforcing.
   c. punishing.
   d. negatively reinforcing.

5. Sandy was pleased. He had not been happy with himself a week earlier when he had yelled loudly at his son. On that occasion he had halted his son's excessive noise through

   a. removal of a reinforcer.
   b. punishment.
   c. negative reinforcement.
   d. extinction.

6. In a _____ reinforcement schedule, behaviour is reinforced some of the time, while in a _____ reinforcement schedule, behaviour is reinforced all the time.

7. Match the type of reinforcement schedule with its definition.
   1. Reinforcement occurs after a set time period.
   2. Reinforcement occurs after a set number of responses.
   3. Reinforcement occurs after a varying time period.
   4. Reinforcement occurs after a varying number of responses.

   a. fixed-ratio
   b. variable-interval
   c. fixed-interval
   d. variable-ratio

8. Fixed reinforcement schedules produce greater resistance to extinction than variable reinforcement schedules. True or false?

Answers to Review Questions are on page 188.

Rethink

1. B. F. Skinner believed that a person's entire life could be structured according to operant conditioning principles. Do you think this is possible? What benefits and problems would result?

2. Can operant conditioning be used to address serious personal concerns, such as smoking and unhealthy eating? Can it be used to address societal problems, such as environmental pollution and violence? With which type of problem is it likely to be more successful? Why?

3. How might you go about "curing" superstitious behaviour, such as the rituals people undergo before examinations or athletic competitions? Is it important to effect extinction of such behaviours?

COGNITIVE APPROACHES TO LEARNING

▶ **What is the role of cognition and thought in learning?**

▶ **What are some practical methods for bringing about behaviour change, both in ourselves and in others?**

Consider what happens when people learn to drive a car. They don't just get behind the wheel and stumble around until they randomly put the key into the ignition, and later, after many false starts, accidentally manage to get the car to move forward, thereby receiving positive reinforcement. Instead, they may be remembering lessons from driving school.

Clearly, not all learning is due to the unthinking, mechanical, and automatic acquisition of associations between stimuli and responses, as in classical conditioning, or the presentation of reinforcement, as in operant conditioning. In fact, instances such as learning to drive a car imply that some kinds of learning must involve higher-order processes in which people's thoughts and memories and the way they process information account for their responses.

cognitive learning theory: The study of the thought processes that underlie learning

Psychologists who view learning in terms of the thought processes, or cognitions, that underlie it study **cognitive learning theory.** Although psychologists using the cognitive learning perspective do not deny the importance of classical and operant conditioning, they have developed approaches that focus on the unseen mental processes that occur during learning, rather than concentrating solely on external stimuli, responses, and reinforcements.

In its most basic formulation, cognitive learning theory suggests that it is not enough to say that people make responses because there is an assumed link between a stimulus and a response due to a past history of reinforcement for the response. Instead, according to this point of view, people—and even animals—develop an *expectation* that they will receive a reinforcer upon making a response. Studies of animal cognition have examined, among other things, temporal cognition (Wilkie et al., 1997) spatial cognition (Shettleworth and Hampton, 1998), and memory (Broadbeck and Shettleworth, 1995). Marcia Spetch of the University of Alberta conducts extensive research on the cognitive behaviour of both animals and humans. Some studies have presented similar tasks to both pigeons and humans: requiring that they use landmarks to locate a hidden goal. Both similarities and differences in search strategies were examined (Spetch, 1995; Spetch et al., 1996).

Latent Learning

latent learning: Learning in which a new behaviour is acquired but is not demonstrated until reinforcement is provided

Some of the most direct evidence regarding cognitive processes comes from a series of experiments that revealed a type of cognitive learning called latent learning. In **latent learning,** a new behaviour is learned but is not demonstrated until reinforcement is provided for displaying it (Tolman & Honzik, 1930). In the studies, psychologists examined the behaviour of rats in a maze such as the one shown in Figure 5-6a. In one representative experiment, a group of rats was allowed to wander around the maze once a day for seventeen days without ever receiving any reward. Understandably, these rats made many errors and spent a relatively long time reaching the end of the maze. A second group, however, was always given food at the end of the maze. Not surprisingly, these rats learned to run quickly and directly to the food box, making few errors.

A third group of rats started out in the same situation as the unrewarded rats, but only for the first ten days. On the eleventh day, a critical experimental manipulation was introduced: From that point on, the rats in this group were given food for completing the maze. The results of this manipulation were dramatic, as you can see from the graph in Figure 5-6b. The previously unrewarded rats, who had earlier seemed to wander about aimlessly, showed such reductions in running time and declines in error rates that their performance almost immediately matched that of the group that had received rewards from the start.

Answers to Review Questions:

1. Operant   2. primary; secondary   3. 1-c, 2-b, 3-a   4. d   5. b   6. partial, continuous   7. 1-c, 2-a, 3-b, 4-d   8. False; variable ratios are more resistant to extinction.

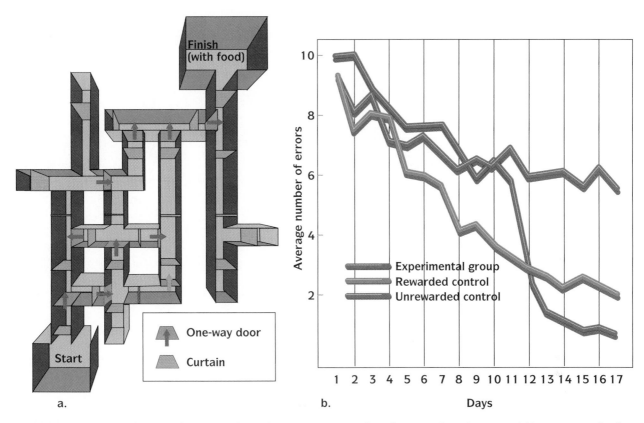

FIGURE 5-6 *(a) In an attempt to demonstrate latent learning, rats were allowed to roam through a maze of this sort once a day for seventeen days. (b) Those rats that were never rewarded (the unrewarded control condition) consistently made the most errors, whereas those that received food at the finish every day (the rewarded control condition) consistently made far fewer errors. But the results also showed latent learning: Rats that were initially unrewarded but began to be rewarded only after the tenth day (the experimental group) showed an immediate reduction in errors and soon became similar to the error rate of the rats that had been consistently rewarded. According to cognitive learning theorists, the reduction in errors indicates that the rats had developed a cognitive map—a mental representation—of the maze.*

To cognitive theorists, it seemed clear that the unrewarded rats had learned the layout of the maze early in their explorations; they just never displayed their latent learning until the reinforcement was offered. Instead, the rats seemed to develop a **cognitive map** of the maze—a mental representation of spatial locations and directions.

cognitive map: A mental representation of spatial locations and directions

People, too, develop cognitive maps of their surroundings, based primarily on particular landmarks. When they first encounter a new environment, their maps tend to rely on specific paths—such as the directions we might give someone unfamiliar with an area: "Turn right at the stop sign, make a left at the bridge, and then go up the hill." However, as people become more familiar with an area, they develop an overall conception of it, which has been called an abstract cognitive map. Using such a map, they are eventually able to take shortcuts as they develop a broad understanding of the area (Garling, 1989; Gale et al., 1990; Plumert et al., 1995).

Unfortunately, though, our cognitive maps are often riddled with errors, representing simplifications of the actual terrain. We tend to develop maps that ignore curving roads and instead conceive of areas in terms of straight grids of intersecting roadways (Tversky, 1981). Our cognitive maps, then, are imperfect versions of actual maps.

Despite their inadequacies, the possibility that we develop our cognitive maps through latent learning presents something of a problem for strict operant conditioning theorists. If we consider the results of Tolman's maze experiment, for instance, it is unclear what the specific reinforcement was that permitted the rats that initially received no reward to learn about the layout of the maze, since there was no obvious reinforcer present. Instead, the results support a cognitive view of learning, in which learning may have resulted in changes in unobservable mental processes.

Observational Learning: Learning Through Imitation

Let's return for a moment to the case of a person learning to drive. How can we account for instances in which an individual with no direct experience in carrying out a particular behaviour learns the behaviour and then performs it? To answer this question, psychologists have proposed social-cognitive learning theory, which is based on observational learning. We observe and copy what other drivers do.

observational learning: Learning through observing the behaviour of another person called a *model*

According to psychologist Albert Bandura and colleagues, a major part of human learning consists of **observational learning,** which they define as learning through observing the behaviour of another person called a *model* (Bandura, 1977). Bandura and his colleagues demonstrated rather dramatically the ability of models to stimulate learning. In what is now considered a classic experiment, young children saw a film of an adult wildly hitting a 5-foot-tall inflatable punching toy called a Bobo doll (Bandura, Ross, & Ross, 1963a, 1963b). Later the children were given the opportunity to play with the Bobo doll themselves and, sure enough, they displayed the same kind of behaviour, in some cases mimicking the aggressive behaviour almost identically.

Not only negative behaviours are acquired through observational learning. In one experiment, for example, children who were afraid of dogs were exposed to a model—dubbed the Fearless Peer—playing with a dog (Bandura, Grusec, & Menlove, 1967). Following exposure, observers were considerably more likely to approach a strange dog than children who had not viewed the Fearless Peer.

Social Learning Theory

According to Bandura, observational learning takes place in four steps: (1) paying attention and perceiving the most critical features of another person's behaviour; (2) remembering the behaviour; (3) reproducing the action; and (4) being motivated to learn and carry out the behaviour. Instead of learning occurring through trial and error, then, with successes being reinforced and failures punished, many important skills are learned through observational processes (Bandura, 1986).

Observational learning is particularly important in acquiring skills in which shaping is inappropriate. Piloting an airplane and performing brain surgery, for example, are behaviours that could hardly be learned using trial-and-error methods without grave cost—literally—to those involved in the learning.

Not all behaviour that we witness is learned or carried out, of course. One crucial factor that determines whether we later imitate a model is the consequences of the model's behaviour. If we observe a friend being rewarded for putting more time into her studies by receiving higher grades, we are more likely to model her behaviour than if her behaviour results in no improvement in her grades but rather greater fatigue and less of a social life. Models who are rewarded for behaving in a particular way are more apt to be mimicked than models who receive punishment. Interestingly, though, observing the punishment of a model does not necessarily stop observers from learning the behaviour. Observers can still recount the model's behaviour—they are just less apt to perform it (Bandura, 1977, 1986, 1994).

Observational learning is central to a number of important issues relating to the extent to which people learn by simply watching the behaviour of others. For instance, the degree to which observation of media aggression produces subsequent aggression on the part of viewers is a crucial—and controversial—question, as we discuss next.

Violence on Television and Film: Does the Media's Message Matter?

Beavis and Butthead, MTV cartoon characters, discuss how much fun it is to set fires. On one occasion, one of them lights a fire in the other's hair by using aerosol spray cans and matches.

Later, five-year-old Austin Messner, who had watched the cartoon, sets his bed on fire with a cigarette lighter. Although he and his mother escape the subsequent blaze, his younger sister dies.

***

The cartoon Beavis and Butthead *depicts a variety of obnoxious and antisocial behaviours, which some viewers may have imitated.*

In a scene from the 1993 film "The Program," a character who wishes to demonstrate his toughness lies down on the centre line of a highway at night as cars and trucks speed by in both directions. In the movie, he walks away unscathed, proving that he's afraid of nothing.

Real life is a little different: Soon after watching the movie, several teenagers were killed in separate incidents in which they lay in the centre of a darkened road and were run over by oncoming traffic (Hinds, 1993).

Does observation of violence and antisocial acts in the media lead viewers to behave in similar ways? Because research on modelling shows that people frequently learn and imitate the aggression that they observe, this question is among the most important being addressed by social psychologists.

Certainly, the amount of violence in the mass media is enormous. Between the ages of 5 and 15, the average Canadian or American child is exposed to no fewer than 13,000 violent deaths on television; the number of fights and aggressive sequences that children view is still higher. Saturday mornings, once filled with relatively peaceful fare, now include cartoon programs with titles such as *X-Men* and *Power Rangers,* which include long sequences of aggressive action (Freedman, 1984; Liebert & Sprafkin, 1988; Signorielli, Gerbner, & Morgan, 1995).

Most research does, in fact, suggest that a significant association exists between watching such violent television programs and displaying aggressive behaviour (Berkowitz, 1993; Boyatzis, Matillo, & Nesbitt, 1995; Hughes & Hasbrouck, 1996). For example, a 1994 study of weapons use in Canadian schools found that sensationalized violence in the media, although not the only factor, was certainly a contributing factor to weapons use in schools (Ministry of the Solicitor General, 1994).

Experts agree that watching media violence can lead to a greater readiness to act aggressively (if not invariably to overt aggression) and to an insensitivity to the suffering of victims of violence (Bushman & Geen, 1990; Comstock & Strasburger, 1990; Huesmann & Moise, 1996). Several factors help explain why the observation of media violence may provoke aggression. For one thing, viewing violence seems to lower inhibitions against the performance of aggression—watching television portrayals of violence makes aggression seem a legitimate response to particular situations.

Both children and adults are exposed to an enormous amount of media aggression.

Media Violence and Children

Furthermore, viewing violence may distort our understanding of the meaning of others' behaviour. We may, for example, be predisposed to view even nonaggressive acts by others as aggressive after watching media aggression, and subsequently may act upon these new interpretations by responding aggressively. Finally, a continual diet of aggression may leave us desensitized to violence, and what previously would have repelled us now produces little emotional response. Our sense of the pain and suffering brought about by aggression may be diminished, and we may find it easier to act aggressively ourselves (Geen & Donnerstein, 1983; Moliter & Hirsch, 1994; Huesmann & Moise, 1996).

Given the probable links between violence and exposure to media aggression, psychologists are working on ways to reduce aggression in frequent viewers. One approach has been to explicitly teach children that televised violence is not representative of the real world, that the viewing of violence is objectionable, and that they should refrain from imitating behaviour seen on television (Eron & Huesmann, 1985; Zillman, 1993; Hughes & Hasbrouck, 1996).

The lessons appear to be effective: As a group, children who are exposed to them act less aggressively than those who have not received lessons. For instance, in one experiment first- and third-grade students who tended to view a lot of television received several training sessions over a nine-month period (Huesmann et al., 1983). During the sessions, the students learned that the aggressive behaviour on television does not approximate what happens in the real world. They were taught about camera techniques and special effects used to produce the illusion of aggression. Moreover, they learned that people generally used alternatives to aggression in seeking solutions to their problems. Finally, they were directly taught the undesirability of watching television violence and how to avoid imitating aggression.

The program was highly successful. Compared to a control group of children who did not receive the training, the students who attended the classes were rated by their classmates as showing significantly lower levels of aggression. Furthermore, the students in the program perceived televised aggression much more negatively than those who did not participate. As a result, the unwanted consequences of viewing media aggression can be reduced through training. Just as people learn through observation to act aggressively, they can learn to become less aggressive.

Other approaches to reducing the link between media violence and viewer aggression have considered whether media portrayals of aggression can be modified, as we discuss in the Applying Psychology in the 21st Century box.

Applying Psychology in the 21st Century

Fight Less, Talk More: Scripts for Reducing Violence

NBC liked television-writer Connie Bottinelli's treatment for a "Movie of the Week" but worried it was too violent. So Ms. Bottinelli called on *Dialogue.*

Dialogue, a newsletter distributed by a small, Washington-based nonprofit group called the Institute for Mental Health Initiatives, illustrates for writers and producers how to avoid violent confrontations on screen. The institute started the four-page newsletter last winter and distributes 20,000 copies quarterly, most to creators of movies and TV shows and often for free.

Ms. Bottinelli's story for NBC was about Vincent, a convicted mobster who is found dead in his prison cell. His wife sues law-enforcement authorities for being responsible for his death.

After looking at the newsletter, Ms. Bottinelli, who lives in Philadelphia, wrote her script to play down Vincent's violent acts and emphasize instead his imprisonment and death. She even added a scene in which Vincent suffers humiliation so that viewers would understand his rage. NBC liked the changes and bought the script (Chang, 1994, p. B1).

Chalk up another success for *Dialogue.* Using the principles derived from the work of psychologists who study the relationship between media violence and viewer aggression, the newsletter offers writers practical ways to deal with portrayals of violence, offensive language, and sex. For instance, one issue provided the following guidelines for presenting violence on TV and in film, which focus on redefining norms about violence and de-glamorizing violence and weapons:

- Minimize violent scenes that do not contribute to the plot or character development or to the story in a true crime piece.
- Depict violence as a last resort for heroes who have used their wits in encountering danger.
- Depict thoughtless violence and use of weapons as weak and shortsighted; depict the verbalization of anger and fear and the struggle to delay action as strong.
- Portray the emotional, social, and economic impact of violence on perpetrators, victims, families, and witnesses (Institute for Mental Health Initiatives, 1993, p. 4).

Such specific advice is useful for screenwriters, who must deal with a variety of pressures from directors, producers, and television and film executives. In fact, with the introduction of a rating system for television shows, the pressures on writers are likely to rise (Institute for Mental Health Initiatives, 1996).

The introduction of the television rating system in early 1997 was a reaction to a growing call for television networks to offer greater guidance to parents. Loosely based on the movie rating system, television ratings use several categories relating to the amount of "adult" content a program contains, ranging from "TV-G" (for general audiences) to "TV-MA" (for mature audiences only). Unfortunately, the guidelines are vague and not well standardized.

Despite the efforts of the media to produce television shows and films that portray violence more appropriately, a more effective approach ultimately may be to teach viewers more discerning viewer skills. In the end, it will probably take a combination of viewer skills and more realistic media presentations to prevent media portrayals of violence from leading to aggression in viewers.

Exploring Diversity

Does Culture Influence How We Learn?

Do the differences in teaching approaches between cultures affect how people learn? According to one school of thought, learners develop *learning styles,* characteristic ways of approaching material, based on their cultural background and unique pattern of abilities (Anderson & Adams, 1992; Milgram, Dunn, & Price, 1993; Chi-Ching & Noi, 1994; Furnham, 1995; Sternberg & Grigorenko, 1997).

Learning styles differ along several dimensions. For example, one central dimension is analytic versus relational approaches to learning (Anderson, 1988; Tharp, 1989). As illustrated in Table 5-2, people with a relational learning style master material best through exposure to a full unit or phenomenon. In contrast, people with an analytical learning style do best when they develop an understanding of the fundamental principles and components, that underlie the full picture.

Although research findings are mixed, some evidence suggests that particular minority groups within western society display characteristic learning styles. For instance, James Anderson and Maurianne Adams (1992) argue that white females and African American, Native American, and Hispanic American males and females are

Table 5-2	Learning Styles

Relational Style	Analytical Style
1. Perceive information as part of total picture	1. Able to dis-embed information from total picture (focus on detail)
2. Exhibit improvisational and intuitive thinking	2. Exhibit sequential and structured thinking
3. More easily learn materials that have a human, social content and are characterized by experiential/cultural relevance	3. More easily learn materials that are inanimate and impersonal
4. Have a good memory for verbally presented ideas and information, especially if relevant	4. Have a good memory for abstract ideas and irrelevant information
5. Are more task-oriented concerning nonacademic areas	5. Are more task-oriented concerning academics
6. Are influenced by authority figures' expression of confidence or doubt in students' ability	6. Are not greatly affected by the opinions of others
7. Prefer to withdraw from unstimulating task performance	7. Show ability to persist at unstimulating tasks
8. Style conflicts with the traditional school environment	8. Style matches most school environments

more apt to use a relational style of learning than Caucasian and Asian American males, who are more likely to employ an analytical style.

The issue of cultural background and learning styles is at the heart of the attempts to transform First Nations education in Canada. Native peoples are struggling to create, for their children, a Native education system to replace years of Eurocentric government mandated (formal) education. This goes far beyond simply reviving Native language and culture although they are important.

Stairs (1995) explains that there are the two different models of education. She uses the Inuit term *isumaqsayuq* to denote a Native educational system that includes knowledge based on real world, practical experience, shared and passed on from those with more experience to the young. Embedded in this knowledge is group identity and values. In contrast she refers to *ilisayuq* as a formal system of education based on abstraction, verbal ability, and preparation for some future endeavour.

Her contention is that the more formal way of transmitting knowledge or educating students runs counter to Native learning styles and in fact disadvantages Native students. Their learning style, especially for those outside of urban centres, is based on repeating practical skills in a variety of settings. These are skills of experience and survival, like hunting and fishing. They are skills that put the group ahead of the individual and will ultimately help to define the person's role in the social community. In a formal classroom where more individualistic behaviour is valued a learning style that is based on cooperation and experience may be misinterpreted as "inattention or even cheating" and may not produce the desired learning outcomes required by a formal education system (Stairs, 1995).

This will naturally have an impact on retention. Aboriginal student retention is a challenging issue. It is impacted by far more than learning styles. It also varies dramatically from one jurisdiction to another. In Ontario for example, retention rates vary from ninety percent in urban centres to as low as nine percent in more remote parts of the province (Mackay and Myles, 1995).

The challenge for Native educators is to find a way to provide the knowledge (content) provided by the formal system using a model of delivery that respects an alternate learning style. This is particularly important for mathematics and science, so that

Native students are not limited in their opportunities in a technologically diverse world.

This is of course not an easy thing to do. One attempt to do this is being tried in northern Alaska, where the *qargi* (a traditional community house where the youth learned from their elders) is being transformed into a "school". In this school Native teachers work with community elders to educate the young. Formal learning, in a subject like mathematics, is applied to real life situations, for example building a boat (Stairs, 1995).

The conclusion that members of particular ethnic and gender groups have similar learning styles is controversial. Because there is so much diversity within each particular racial and ethnic group, critics argue that generalizations about learning styles cannot be used to predict the style of any single individual, regardless of group membership. Instead, they suggest that it is more fruitful to concentrate on determining each individual's particular learning style and pattern of academic and social strengths.

The Informed Consumer of Psychology

Using Behaviour Analysis and Behaviour Modification

A couple who had been living together for three years began to fight more and more frequently. The issues of disagreement ranged from the seemingly petty, such as who was going to do the dishes, to the more profound, such as the quality of their love life and whether they found each other interesting. Disturbed about this increasingly unpleasant pattern of interaction, the couple went to a behaviour analyst, a psychologist who specialized in behaviour-modification techniques. After interviewing each of them alone and then speaking to them together, he asked them to keep a detailed written record of their interactions over the next two weeks—focusing, in particular, on the events that preceded their arguments.

Behaviour Analysis

When they returned two weeks later, he carefully went over the records with them. In doing so, he noticed a pattern that the couple themselves had observed after they had started keeping their records: Each of their arguments had occurred just after one or the other had left some household chore undone. For instance, the woman would go into a fury when she came home from work and found that the man, a student, had left his dirty lunch dishes on the table and had not even started dinner preparations. The man would get angry when he found the woman's clothes draped on the only chair in the bedroom. He insisted it was her responsibility to pick up after herself.

Using the data that the couple had collected, the behaviour analyst devised a system for the couple to try out. He asked them to list all of the chores that could possibly arise and assign each one a point value depending on how long it took to complete. Then he had them divide the chores equally and agree in a written contract to fulfill the ones assigned to them. If either failed to carry out one of the assigned chores, he or she would have to place $1 per point in a fund for the other to spend. They also agreed to a program of verbal praise, promising to verbally reward each other for completing a chore.

Although skeptical about the value of such a program, the couple agreed to try it for a month and to keep careful records of the number of arguments they had during this period. To their surprise, the number declined rapidly, and even the more basic issues in their relationship seemed on the way to being resolved.

The case described above provides an illustration of **behaviour modification,** a formalized technique for promoting the frequency of desirable behaviours and decreasing the incidence of unwanted ones. Using the basic principles of learning theory, behaviour-modification techniques have proved to be helpful in a variety of situations. People with severe mental retardation have learned the rudiments of language and, for

behaviour modification: A formalized technique for promoting the frequency of desirable behaviours and decreasing the incidence of unwanted ones

Behaviour modification for people who want to stop smoking may involve aversive conditioning, in which smoking and cues related to smoking are repeatedly paired with unpleasant stimuli.

Behaviour Analysis

the first time in their lives, have started dressing and feeding themselves. Behaviour modification has also helped people to lose weight, give up smoking, and behave more safely (Bellack, Hersen, & Kazdin, 1990; Sulzer-Azaroff & Mayer, 1991; Malott, Whaley, & Malott, 1993; Walter, Vaughan, & Wynder, 1994).

The techniques used by behaviour analysts are as varied as the list of processes that modify behaviour. These include reinforcement scheduling, shaping, generalization training, discrimination training, and extinction. Participants in a behaviour-change program do, however, typically follow a series of similar basic steps. These steps include:

Identifying goals and target behaviours. The first step is to define "desired behaviour." Is it an increase in time spent studying? A decrease in weight? An increase in the use of language? A reduction in the amount of aggression displayed by a child? The goals must be stated in observable terms and lead to specific targets. For instance, a goal might be "to increase study time," while the target behaviour would be "to study at least two hours per day on weekdays and an hour on Saturdays."

Designing a data-recording system and recording preliminary data. In order to determine whether behaviour has changed, it is necessary to collect data before any changes are made in the situation. This information provides a baseline against which future changes can be measured.

Selecting a behaviour-change strategy. The most crucial step is to select an appropriate strategy. Since all the principles of learning can be employed to bring about behaviour change, a "package" of treatments is normally used. This might include the systematic use of positive reinforcement for desired behaviour (verbal praise or something more tangible, such as food), as well as a program of extinction for undesirable behaviour (ignoring a child who throws a tantrum). Selecting the right reinforcers is critical; it may be necessary to experiment a bit to find out what is important to a given individual. It is best for participants to avoid threats, since they are merely punishing and ultimately not very effective in bringing about long-term changes in behaviour.

Implementing the program. The next step is to institute the program. Probably the most important aspect of program implementation is consistency. It is also important to make sure that one is reinforcing the behaviour he or she wants to reinforce. For example, suppose a mother wants her daughter to spend more time on her homework, but as soon as the child sits down to study, she asks for a snack. If the mother gets one for her, she is likely to be reinforcing her daughter's delaying tactic, not her studying. Instead, the mother might tell her child that she will provide her with a snack after a certain time interval has gone by during which she has studied—thereby using the snack as a reinforcement for studying.

Keeping careful records after the program is implemented. Another crucial task is record keeping. If the target behaviours are not monitored, there is no way of knowing whether the program has actually been successful. Participants are advised not to rely on memory, because memory lapses are all too frequent.

Evaluating and altering the ongoing program. Finally, the results of the program should be compared with preimplementation data to determine its effectiveness. If successful, the procedures employed can gradually be phased out. For instance, if the program called for reinforcing every instance of picking up one's clothes from the bedroom floor, the reinforcement schedule could be modified to a fixed-ratio schedule in which every third instance was reinforced. On the other hand, if the program had not been successful in bringing about the desired behaviour change, consideration of other approaches might be advisable.

Behaviour-change techniques based on these general principles have enjoyed wide success and have proved to be one of the most powerful means of modifying behaviour (Greenwood et al., 1992). Clearly, it is possible to employ the basic notions of learning theory to improve our own lives. ∎

Recap, Review, and Rethink

Recap

- Cognitive learning theory focuses on the unseen, internal mental processes that occur within a person.

- Modelling consists of learning from the observation of others' behaviour. The rewards that a model receives influence the extent to which the model will be imitated.

- Cultural factors are associated with the manner in which people learn.

- Behaviour modification, a technique for promoting desirable behaviours and reducing undesirable ones, has been used successfully in changing both one's own and others' behaviour.

Review

1. A distinguished scientist tells you "Learning can best be understood in terms of underlying thought processes." What theory is being described?

2. In cognitive learning, it is assumed that people develop an _____ about receiving a reinforcer instead of basing behaviour on past reinforcers.

3. _____ learning describes learning that takes place but is not shown until appropriate reinforcement is presented.

4. Bandura's theory of _____ learning states that people learn through watching a _____, which is another person displaying the behaviour of interest.

5. Cognitive learning theorists are concerned only with overt behaviour, not with its internal causes. True or false?

6. A man wishes to quit smoking. Upon the advice of a psychologist, he begins a program in which he sets goals for his withdrawal, carefully records his progress, and rewards himself for not smoking during a certain period of time. What type of program is he following?

Answers to Review Questions are on page 198.

Rethink

1. What is the relationship between a model (in Bandura's sense) and a role model (as the term is used popularly)? Celebrities often complain that their actions should not be scrutinized closely because they do not want to be role models. How would you respond?

2. How could a true experiment be devised that could confirm the long-term consequences of viewing aggression on television?

3. The relational style of learning is said to conflict with the traditional school environment. Could a school environment be created that takes advantage of the characteristics of the relational style? How? Are there types of learning for which the analytical style is decidedly superior?

looking
BACK

What is learning?

1. Learning, a relatively permanent change in behaviour due to experience, is a basic topic of psychology. However, it is a process that must be assessed indirectly—we can only assume that learning has occurred by observing performance, which is susceptible to such factors as fatigue and lack of effort.

How do we learn to form associations between stimuli and responses?

2. One major form of learning is known as classical conditioning. First studied by Ivan Pavlov, classical conditioning occurs when a neutral stimulus—one that brings about no relevant response—is repeatedly paired with a stimulus (called an unconditioned stimulus) that brings about a natural, untrained response. For instance, a neutral stimulus might be a buzzer; an unconditioned stimulus might be a dish of ice cream. The response ice cream might elicit in a hungry person—salivation—is called an unconditioned response; it occurs naturally, owing to the physical makeup of the individual being trained.

3. The actual conditioning occurs when the neutral stimulus is repeatedly presented just before the unconditioned stimulus. After repeated pairings, the neutral stimulus begins to bring about the same response as the unconditioned stimulus. When this occurs, we can say that the neutral stimulus is now a conditioned stimulus, and the response made to it is the conditioned response. For example, after a person has learned to salivate to the sound of the buzzer, we say the buzzer is a conditioned stimulus, and the salivation is a conditioned response.

4. Learning is not always permanent, however. Extinction occurs when a previously learned response decreases in frequency and eventually disappears.

5. Stimulus generalization occurs when a conditioned response follows a stimulus that is similar to the original conditioned stimulus. The greater the similarity between the two stimuli, the greater the likelihood of stimulus generalization; the closer the new stimulus to the old one, the more similar the new response. The converse phenomenon, stimulus discrimination, occurs when an organism learns to respond to one stimulus but not to another.

6. Higher-order conditioning occurs when an established conditioned stimulus is paired with a neutral stimulus, and the new neutral stimulus comes to evoke the same conditioned response as the original conditioned stimulus. The neutral stimulus becomes, then, another conditioned stimulus.

What is the role of reward and punishment in learning?

7. A second major form of learning is operant conditioning. Moving beyond Edward Thorndike's original work on the law of effect, which states that responses that produce satisfying results are more likely to be repeated than those that do not, B. F. Skinner carried out pioneering work on operant learning.

8. According to Skinner, the major mechanism underlying learning is reinforcement, the process by which a stimulus increases the probability that a preceding behaviour will be repeated. We can determine whether a stimulus is reinforcing only by observing its effects upon behaviour. If behaviour increases, the stimulus is, by definition, a reinforcer. Primary reinforcers involve rewards that are naturally effective without prior exposure because they satisfy a biological need. Secondary reinforcers, in contrast, begin to act as if they were primary reinforcers through frequent pairings with a primary reinforcer.

9. Positive reinforcers are stimuli that are added to the environment and lead to an increase in a preceding response. Negative reinforcers are stimuli that remove something unpleasant from the environment, leading to an increase in the preceding response. Negative reinforcement occurs in two major forms. In escape conditioning, an organism learns to make a response that brings about an end to an aversive situation. In avoidance conditioning, an organism responds to a signal of an impending unpleasant event in a way that permits its evasion.

10. Punishment is the administration of an unpleasant stimulus following a response in order to produce a decrease in the incidence of that response. Punishment can also be characterized by the removal of a positive reinforcer. In contrast to reinforcement, in which the goal is to increase the incidence of behaviour, punishment is meant to decrease or suppress behaviour. Although there are some benefits to the use of punishment, its disadvantages usually outweigh its positive effects.

11. Schedules and patterns of reinforcement affect the strength and duration of learning. Generally, partial reinforcement schedules—in which reinforcers are not delivered on every trial—produce stronger and longer-lasting learning than continuous reinforcement schedules.

12. Among the major categories of reinforcement schedules are fixed- and variable-ratio schedules, which are based on the number of responses made, and fixed- and variable-interval schedules, which are based on the time interval that elapses before reinforcement is provided. Fixed-ratio schedules provide reinforcement only after a certain number of

---

Answers to Review Questions:

1. cognitive learning   2. expectation   3. Latent   4. observational; model   5. False; cognitive learning theorists are primarily concerned with mental processes.   6. behaviour modification

responses are made; variable-ratio schedules provide reinforcement after a varying number of responses are made—although the specific number typically settles around some average. In contrast, fixed-interval schedules provide reinforcement after a fixed amount of time has elapsed since the last reinforcement; variable-interval schedules provide reinforcement over varying amounts of time, although the times form a specific average.

13. Generalization and discrimination are phenomena that operate in operant conditioning as well as classical conditioning. Generalization occurs when an organism makes the same or a similar response to a new stimulus that it has learned to make in the past to a similar stimulus. Discrimination occurs when the organism responds to one stimulus, but does not respond to a similar (but different) stimulus.

14. Superstitious behaviour results from the mistaken belief that particular ideas, objects, or behaviour will cause certain events to occur. It occurs as a consequence of learning that is based on the coincidental association between a stimulus and subsequent reinforcement.

15. Shaping is a process for teaching complex behaviours by rewarding closer and closer approximations of the desired final behaviour. Shaping forms the basis for learning many everyday skills and is central to presenting complicated information in textbooks and in computerized programmed instruction.

16. There are biological constraints, or built-in limitations, on the ability of an organism to learn. Because of these constraints, certain behaviours will be relatively easy to learn, whereas other behaviours will be either difficult or impossible to learn.

What is the role of cognition and thought in learning?

17. Cognitive approaches consider learning in terms of thought processes or cognition. Phenomena such as latent learning—in which a new behaviour is learned but not performed until reinforcement is provided for its performance—and the apparent development of cognitive maps support cognitive approaches. Learning also occurs through the observation of behaviour of others, known as models.

18. The major factor that determines whether an observed behaviour will actually be performed is the nature of reinforcement or punishment a model receives.

19. Learning styles are characteristic ways of approaching material, based on a person's cultural background and unique pattern of abilities. One major dimension relates to analytic versus relational approaches to learning. People with relational learning styles master material best through exposure to a full unit or phenomenon. In contrast, people with analytic learning styles make an initial analysis of the underlying principles and components underlying a phenomenon or situation.

What are some practical methods for bringing about behaviour change, both in ourselves and in others?

20. Behaviour modification is a method for formally using the principles of learning theory to promote the frequency of desired behaviours and to decrease or eliminate unwanted ones. The typical steps in a behaviour-change program are identifying goals and target behaviours, designing a data-recording system, recording preliminary data, selecting a behaviour-change strategy, implementing the strategy, keeping careful records, and evaluating and altering the ongoing program.

Key Terms and Concepts

learning (p. 168)
classical conditioning (p. 169)
neutral stimulus (p. 170)
unconditioned stimulus (UCS) (p. 170)
unconditioned response (UCR) (p. 170)
conditioned stimulus (CS) (p. 170)
conditioned response (CR) (p. 170)
extinction (p. 172)
spontaneous recovery (p. 173)
stimulus generalization (p. 173)

stimulus discrimination (p. 174)
operant conditioning (p. 176)
reinforcement (p. 178)
reinforcer (p. 178)
positive reinforcer (p. 179)
negative reinforcer (p. 179)
punishment (p. 179)
schedules of reinforcement (p. 182)
continuous reinforcement schedule (p. 182)
partial reinforcement schedule (p. 182)

fixed-ratio schedule (p. 183)
variable-ratio schedule (p. 183)
fixed-interval schedule (p. 184)
variable-interval schedule (p. 184)
shaping (p. 185)
cognitive learning (p. 188)
latent learning (p. 188)
cognitive map (p. 189)
observational learning (p. 190)
behaviour modification (p. 196)

Epilogue

In this chapter we have discussed several kinds of learning, ranging from classical conditioning, which depends on the existence of natural stimulus-response pairings, to operant conditioning, in which reinforcement is intentionally used to increase desired behaviour. These approaches to learning focus on outward, behavioural learning processes. We have also been introduced to more cognitive and social-cognitive approaches to learning, which focus on mental processes and observational learning to enable learning.

We have also noted that learning, while being both behavioural and cognitive, is also cultural to some extent, and even personal, with individual learning styles potentially affecting the ways in which persons learn most effectively. Finally, we saw some ways in which our learning about learning can be put to practical use, through such means as behaviour modification programs designed to decrease negative behaviours and increase positive ones.

Another complex mental process, memory, is the subject of our next chapter. Before we turn to it, however, return to the prologue of this chapter and consider the following questions in relation to Pippa, the guide dog who helps Jean Little.

1. Is Pippa's learning primarily an example of classical conditioning, operant conditioning, or cognitive learning? Why?

2. Can you describe how the principles of positive reinforcement and negative reinforcement might have been used to teach Pippa her helpful behaviours. Do you think punishment would be an effective learning strategy?

3. How might schedules of reinforcement have been used to train Pippa, including fixed- and variable-ratio schedules and fixed- and variable-interval schedules?

4. In what way would shaping have been used to teach Pippa some of her more complex behaviours, such as navigating the streets of New York?

CHAPTER 6 Memory

Prologue

The Wife Who Forgot She Had a Husband

In the wedding portraits on the walls of their Las Vegas, Nevada, living room, Kim and Krickitt Carpenter look like any young newlyweds—deeply in love and filled with hope for their new life together. But Krickitt admits it causes her some pain now to look at the pictures or to see herself in the wedding video, walking down the aisle in her lacy white gown. "I would almost rather not watch it," she says. "It makes me miss the girl in the picture more and more."

In a sense, that Krickitt is gone, lost forever. Less than ten weeks after the September, 1993 ceremony, the Carpenters were in a nightmarish auto accident that badly injured them both and left Krickitt comatose. Though doctors initially doubted she would survive, she rallied, regaining consciousness and, eventually, most of her physical abilities. But the trauma to her brain caused retrograde amnesia, erasing virtually her entire memory of the previous eighteen months—including any recollection of the man she had fallen in love with and married. "The last 2½ years have been based on a story I'm told," says Krickitt, 26, "because I don't remember any of it" (Fields-Meyer & Haederle, 1996, p. 48).

For Krickitt Carpenter, the road to recovery has been a slow one. Although she retained most of her long-term memories after the accident, she had no recent recollections of her marriage or her husband. Initially, when she returned to living with Kim, it was like being with a stranger toward whom she felt no emotion, and the marriage faltered. However, by retracing the origins of their relationship—they began by having

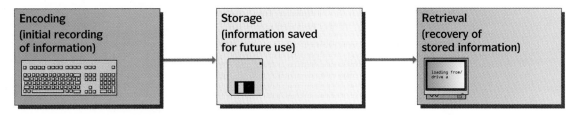

FIGURE 6-1 *Memory is built on these three basic processes.*

"dates"—they were able to reforge the bonds that had been shattered. On Valentine's Day three years after the accident, Kim proposed to Krickitt again, and she accepted. A short time later, the couple exchanged rings and recited new vows.

The Carpenters' story raises several issues regarding the nature of memory loss: What specifically was the nature of the physical trauma that devastated Krickitt's memories? Will the lost memories ever return? Why were only recent memories lost and older ones retained?

But stories like this also illustrate the central role memory plays in our everyday lives. Memory allows us to retrieve a vast amount of information to which we have been exposed. We are able to remember the name of a friend we haven't been in touch with for decades and to recall details of a picture that hung in our bedroom as a child. At the same time, though, memory failures are not uncommon. We may forget where we left the keys to the car or be unable to answer an exam question about material that we studied (and understood) just a few hours earlier.

In this chapter, we address the topic of memory. We examine the ways in which information is stored and retrieved. We discuss approaches that suggest there are actually several separate types of memory, and we explain how each type functions in a somewhat different fashion. We examine the problems of retrieving information from memory, the accuracy of memories, and the reasons information is sometimes forgotten. We also consider the biological foundations of memory. Finally, we discuss some practical means of increasing memory capacity.

ENCODING, STORAGE, AND RETRIEVAL OF MEMORY

You are playing a game of Trivial Pursuit, and winning the game comes down to one question: On what body of water is Bombay located?

As you rack your brain for the answer, several fundamental processes relating to memory come into play. For instance, your difficulty in answering the question may be traced to the initial encoding stage of memory. *Encoding* refers to the process by which information is initially recorded in a form usable to memory. You may never, for instance, have been exposed to information regarding Bombay's location, or if you had been exposed to it, it may simply not have registered in a meaningful way.

On the other hand, even if you had been exposed to the information and originally knew the name of the body of water, you may still be unable to recall it during the game because of a failure in the retention process. Memory specialists speak of *storage,* the maintenance of material saved in the memory system. If the material is not stored adequately, it cannot be recalled later.

Memory also depends on one last process: retrieval. In *retrieval,* material in memory storage is located, brought into awareness, and used. Your failure to recall Bombay's location, then, may rest on your inability to retrieve information that you learned earlier.

In sum, psychologists consider **memory** as the process by which we encode, store, and retrieve information (see Figure 6-1). Each of the three parts of this definition—encoding, storage, and retrieval—represents a different process, which you can think of as analogous to a computer's keyboard (encoding), disk (storage), and screen

▶ What is memory?

▶ Are there different kinds of memory?

Journals

memory: The process by which we encode, store, and retrieve information (retrieval). Only if all three processes have operated will you experience success and be able to recall the body of water on which Bombay is located: the Arabian Sea.

However, before continuing, we should keep in mind the value of memory *failures*. Forgetting is essential to the proper functioning of memory. The ability to forget inconsequential details about experiences, people, and objects allows us to avoid being burdened and distracted by trivial stores of meaningless data. Furthermore, forgetting permits us to combine similar recollections and form general impressions and recollections. For example, it would not be terribly useful to form separate memories of the way friends look every time we see them. Consequently, we tend to forget their clothing, facial blemishes, and other transient features that change from one occasion to the next. Instead, our memories are based on a summary of various critical features—a far more economical use of our memory capabilities. Forgetting unnecessary information, then, is as essential to the proper functioning of memory as is remembering more important material.

The Three Systems of Memory: Memory Storehouses

Although the processes of encoding, storing, and retrieving information are necessary for memory to operate successfully, they do not describe the specific manner in which material is entered into memory. Many psychologists studying memory suggest that there are different systems or stages through which information must travel if it is to be remembered.

According to one of the most influential and enduring theories, there are three kinds of memory storage systems. These storehouses vary in terms of their capacity and the length of time they retain information (Atkinson & Shiffrin, 1968, 1971).

As shown in Figure 6-2, **sensory memory** refers to the initial, momentary storage of information, lasting only an instant. Information is recorded by the person's sensory system as a raw, nonmeaningful stimulus. **Short-term memory** holds information for 15 to 25 seconds. In this system, the information is stored according to its meaning rather than as mere sensory stimulation. The third type of storage system is **long-term memory**. Information is stored in long-term memory on a relatively permanent basis, although it may be difficult to retrieve.

Although we'll be discussing the three types of memory as separate memory stores, keep in mind that these are not mini-warehouses located in particular portions of the brain. Instead, they represent three different types of abstract memory systems with different characteristics. Furthermore, although the three-part model dominated the field of memory research for several decades, recent studies have suggested several different approaches, as we'll discuss later. Still, considering memory in terms of three major kinds of stores has provided us with a useful framework for understanding how information is both recalled and forgotten.

Sensory Memory

A momentary flash of lightning, the sound of a twig snapping, and the sting of a pinprick all represent stimulation of exceedingly brief duration, but they may nonetheless provide important information that can require some response. Such stimuli are initially—and briefly—stored in sensory memory, the first repository of the information that the world presents to us. Actually, the term "sensory memory" encompasses several types of sensory memories, each related to a different source of sensory information. There is **iconic memory**, which reflects information from our visual system; **echoic memory**, which stores information coming from the ears; and corresponding memories for each of the other senses.

Regardless of the individual subtypes, sensory memory in general is able to store information for only a very short time. If information does not pass to short-term memory, it is lost for good. For instance, iconic memory seems to last less than a second, although if the initial stimulus is very bright, the image may last a little longer (Long & Beaton, 1982). Echoic memory fades within three or four seconds (Darwin, Turvey, & Crowder, 1972). However, despite the brief duration of sensory memory,

sensory memory: The initial, momentary storage of information, lasting only an instant
short-term memory: Memory which holds information for fifteen to twenty-five seconds
long-term memory: Memory which stores information on a relatively permanent basis, although it may be difficult to retrieve

Sensory Memory

iconic memory: Memory which reflects information from our visual system
echoic memory: Memory which stores information coming from the ears

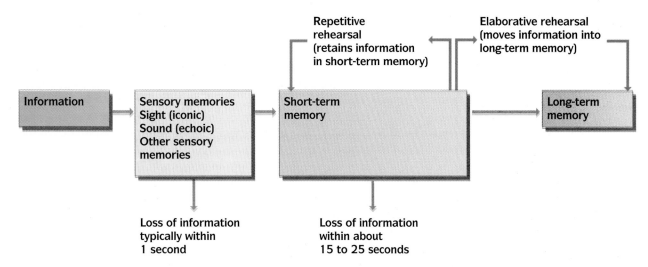

FIGURE 6-2 *In this three-stage model of memory, information initially recorded by the person's sensory system enters sensory memory, which momentarily holds the information. It then moves to short-term memory, which stores the information for 15 to 25 seconds. Finally, the information can move into long-term memory, which is relatively permanent. Whether the information moves from short-term to long-term memory depends on the kind and amount of rehearsal of the material that is carried out. Source: After Atkinson & Shiffrin, 1968.*

its precision is high: Sensory memory can store an almost exact replica of each stimulus to which it is exposed.

If the storage capabilities of sensory memory are so limited and information stored within sensory memory so fleeting, it would seem almost impossible to find evidence for its existence; new information would constantly be replacing older information, even before a person could report its presence. Not until psychologist George Sperling (1960) conducted a series of clever and now-classic studies was sensory memory well understood. Sperling briefly exposed people to a series of twelve letters arranged in the following pattern:

F T Y C

K D N L

Y W B M

When exposed to this array for just one-twentieth of a second, most people could accurately recall only four or five of the letters. Although they knew that they had seen more, the memory of these letters had faded by the time they reported the first few letters. It was possible, then, that the information had initially been accurately stored in sensory memory, but during the time it took to verbalize the first four or five letters the memory of the other letters faded.

To test that possibility, Sperling conducted an experiment in which a high, medium, or low tone sounded just after a person had been exposed to the full pattern of letters. People were told to report the letters in the highest line if a high tone were sounded, the middle line if the medium tone occurred, or the lowest line at the sound of the low tone. Because the tone occurred after the exposure, people had to rely on their memory to report the correct row.

The results of the study clearly showed that people had been storing the complete pattern in memory. They were accurate in their recollection of the letters in the line that had been indicated by the tone, regardless of whether it was the top, middle, or bottom line. Obviously, *all* the lines they had seen had been stored in sensory memory. Despite its rapid loss, then, the information in sensory memory was an accurate representation of what people had seen.

By gradually lengthening the time between the presentation of the visual pattern and the tone, Sperling was able to determine with some accuracy the length of time that information was stored in sensory memory. The ability to recall a particular row of the pattern when a tone was sounded declined progressively as the period between visual exposure and tone increased. This decline continued with recall reaching chance level at about one half of a second. Sperling concluded that the entire visual image was stored in sensory memory for one quarter to one third of a second.

In sum, sensory memory operates as a kind of snapshot that stores information—which may be of a visual, auditory, or other sensory nature—for a brief moment in time. But it is as if each snapshot, immediately after being taken, is destroyed and replaced with a new one. Unless the information in the snapshot is transferred to some other type of memory, it is lost.

Short-Term Memory: Our Working Memory

Short-Term Memory

Because the information that is stored briefly in our sensory memory consists of representations of raw sensory stimuli, it is not meaningful to us. In order for us to make sense of it and to allow for the possibility of long-term retention, the information must be transferred to the next stage of memory, short-term memory.

The specific process by which sensory memories are transformed into short-term memories is not yet clear. Some theorists suggest that the information is first translated into graphical representations or images, and others hypothesize that the transfer occurs when the sensory stimuli are changed to words (Baddeley & Wilson, 1985). Information is held in short-term memory for about 15 to 25 seconds unless it is rehearsed. Craik and Lockhart (1972) refer to the deliberate repetition of information intended to maintain it in short-term memory as rote rehearsal or maintenance rehearsal. For example, if you look up a telephone number in a directory, and then have to walk across a room to get to a phone, you will probably repeat the number in your head (using an "inner voice") to maintain the number in short-term memory until you can make the phone call.

Another feature of short-term memory is that it has a very limited capacity. According to Miller (1956), the limit is 7 ± 2 items or "chunks" of information. A **chunk** is a meaningful grouping of stimuli that can be stored as a unit in short-term memory. Chunks could be individual letters, as in the following list:

chunk: A meaningful grouping of stimuli that can be stored as a unit in short-term memory

C N Q M W N T

Each letter here qualifies as a separate chunk, and—since there are seven of them—they are easily held in short-term memory.

But a chunk might also consist of larger categories, such as words or other meaningful units. For example, consider the following list of twenty-one letters:

C B C N A F T A T V O C N B C T V R C M P

Clearly, because the list exceeds seven chunks, it is difficult to recall the letters after one exposure. But suppose they were presented to you as follows:

CBC NAFTA TVO CN BCTV RCMP

In this case, even though there are still twenty-one letters, it would be possible to store them in memory, since they represent only six chunks.

You can see how chunking works in terms of your own memory process by trying to memorize the shapes in Figure 6-3 after looking at them for just a few moments. Although it may at first seem to be an impossible task, just one hint will guarantee that you can easily memorize all the shapes: Each figure represents some part of a letter in the word "PSYCHOLOGY."

The reason the task suddenly became so simple was that the shapes could be grouped together into one chunk—a word that we all recognize. Rather than being nineteen separate symbols with no meaning, they are recoded as just one chunk.

Chunks can vary in size from single letters or numbers to categories that are far more complicated. The specific nature of what constitutes a chunk varies according to

P S Y C H O L O G Y

one's past experience. You can see this for yourself by trying an experiment that was first carried out as a comparison between expert and inexperienced chess players (deGroot, 1966; Bédard & Chi, 1992; Schneider et al., 1993; Gobet & Simon, 1996).

Examine the first chessboard in Figure 6-4 for about five seconds, and then, after covering up the board, try to reproduce the position of the pieces on the blank chessboard to the right. Unless you are an experienced chess player, you are likely to have great difficulty carrying out such a task. Yet chess masters—the kind who win tournaments—do quite well. They are able to reproduce correctly 90 percent of the pieces on the board. In comparison, inexperienced chess players are typically able to reproduce only 40 percent of the board properly. The chess masters do not have superior memories in other respects; they generally test normally on other measures of memory. What they can do better than others is to see the board in terms of chunks or meaningful units and reproduce the position of the chess pieces by using these units.

Although it is possible to remember seven or so relatively complicated sets of information entering short-term memory, the information, as indicated above, does not remain there for long without rehearsal. Rehearsal also allows us to transfer information from short-term memory to long-term memory. According to memory researchers, Craik and Lockhart (1972), at the University of Toronto, there are two kinds of **rehearsal**: repetition rehearsal and elaborative rehearsal. *Repetition rehearsal* keeps information active in short-term memory. Consider again the earlier example of repeating a phone number while walking from the phone directory to the telephone. This repetition keeps the number current in short-term memory, but it will not necessarily transfer it to long-term memory. As soon as we stop dialing, the number is likely to be replaced by other information and will be completely forgotten.

rehearsal: The repetition or elaboration of information that has entered short-term memory

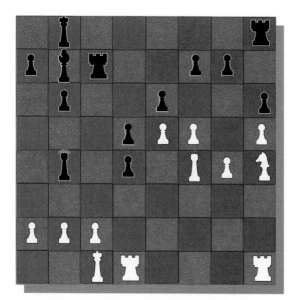 

FIGURE 6-4 *Look at the chessboard on the left for about five seconds, and then cover it with your hand. Now try to recreate the chess pieces on the blank board on the right. Unless you are an experienced chess player, you will probably have a good deal of difficulty recalling the configuration and types of chess pieces. On the other hand, expert chess players have little difficulty recreating the game board. Source: Based on deGroot, 1966.*

Elaborative rehearsal, on the other hand, effectively transfers information to long-term memory. As the name implies, the process of elaborative rehearsal involves elaborating on material by working with or processing its meaning. It occurs when the material is considered and organized. The organization might include expanding the information to make it fit into a logical framework, linking it to another memory, or transforming it in some other way. For example, a list of vegetables to be purchased at a store could be woven together in memory as items being used to prepare a salad; they could be linked to an earlier shopping trip, or they could be thought of in terms of the farm where they are grown. The concept of elaboration will be considered in more detail later in the chapter in the section on levels-of-processing theory.

We can deliberately organize material in a way that increases the likelihood that it will be remembered. By using organizational strategies called *mnemonics* (pronounced "neh MON ix"), we can vastly improve our retention of information. For instance, when a beginning musician learns that the spaces on the musical staff spell the word "FACE," or when we learn the rhyme "Thirty days hath September, April, June, and November …," we are using mnemonics (Mastropieri & Scruggs, 1991; Bellezza, Six, & Phillips, 1992; Schoen, 1996; Goldstein et al., 1996). Strategies for improving memory are discussed in more detail in the Informed Consumer of Psychology section.

Working Memory: The Components of Short-Term Memory. Although short-term memory has traditionally been considered as a single system, more recent evidence suggests that it may actually consist of several components. According to psychologist Alan Baddeley (1992, 1993; Baddeley & Hitch, 1994; Baddeley, 1995a, b), short-term memory is better thought of as a three-part **working memory** (see Figure 6-5). In this view, one component is the *central executive*, which coordinates the material to focus on during reasoning and decision making. The central executive makes use of two subcomponents: the visuospatial sketch pad and the phonological loop. The *visuospatial sketch pad* concentrates on visual and spatial information, while the *phonological loop* is responsible for holding and manipulating material relating to speech, words, and numbers (Gathercole & Baddeley, 1993; Logie, 1995; Della Sala et al., 1995; Baddeley, 1996).

working memory: Baddeley's theory that short-term memory comprises three components, the central executive, the visuospatial sketch pad, and the phonological loop

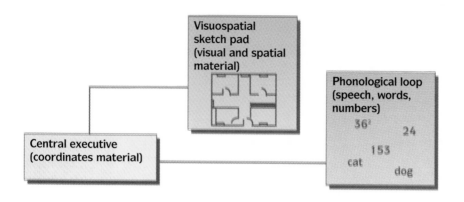

Some researchers suspect that a breakdown in the central executive may result in the memory losses that are characteristic of Alzheimer's disease, the progressively degenerative disorder that produces loss of memory and confusion (Baddeley, 1992; Morris, 1994; Baddeley & Hitch, 1994; Carlesimo et al., 1994; Della Sala et al., 1995; Cherry, Buckwalter, & Henderson, 1996). (We'll discuss Alzheimer's disease and other memory disorders at greater length later in the chapter.)

Long-Term Memory: The Final Storehouse

Material that makes its way from short-term memory to long-term memory enters a storehouse of almost unlimited capacity. Like a new book delivered to a library, the information in long-term memory is filed and catalogued so that it can be retrieved when we need it.

Long-Term Memory

Evidence of the existence of long-term memory, as distinct from short-term memory, comes from a number of sources. For example, people with certain kinds of brain damage have no lasting recall of new information following the damage, although people and events stored in memory prior to the injury remain intact (Milner, 1966). Because short-term memory following the injury appears to be operational—new material can be recalled for a very brief period—and because information that was encoded and stored before the injury can be recalled, we can infer that there are two distinct types of memory—one for short-term and one for long-term storage.

Results from laboratory experiments are also consistent with the notion of separate short- and long-term memories. For example, in one set of studies people were asked to recall a relatively small amount of information (such as a set of three letters). Then, to prevent practice of the initial information, participants were required to recite some extraneous material aloud, such as counting backward by threes (Brown, 1958; Peterson & Peterson, 1959). By varying the amount of time between presentation of the initial material and the need for its recall, investigators found that recall was quite good when the interval was very short but declined rapidly thereafter. After fifteen seconds had gone by, recall hovered at around 10 percent of the material initially presented.

Apparently the distraction of counting backward prevented almost all the initial material from reaching long-term memory. Initial recall was good because it was coming from short-term memory, but these memories were lost at a rapid rate. Eventually, all that could be recalled was the small amount of material that had made its way into long-term storage despite the distraction of counting backward.

The Modules of Memory

Although long-term memory initially was viewed as a unitary entity, most research now suggests that it is composed of several different components, memory modules, or systems. For instance, some researchers have distinguished between declarative and nondeclarative memory (Desmione, 1992; Squire, Knowlton, and Muse, 1993; Eichenbaum, 1997). **Declarative memory** is memory for factual information: names, faces, dates, and the like. Information or knowledge about the world is stored in declarative

declarative memory: Memory for factual information: names, faces, dates, and the like

Although some of these people may not have ridden a bicycle in years, procedural memory enables them to resume riding with little practice.

nondeclarative memory: Memory for skills, habits and the products of conditioning

procedural memory: Memory for skills and habits, such as riding a bike or hitting a baseball

semantic memory: Memory for general knowledge and facts about the world, as well as memory for the rules of logic that are used to deduce other facts

episodic memory: Memory for the biographical details of our individual lives

memory. It includes both general knowledge of the sort acquired through schooling (*semantic memory*), and more personal knowledge such as information about events we have personally experienced (*episodic memory*). In contrast, **nondeclarative memory** is memory for skills, habits, and the products of conditioning. Memory for acquired skills such as how to ride a bike is called *procedural memory*. Information about things is stored in declarative memory; information regarding how to do things is stored in nondeclarative memory.

Endel Tulving, a University of Toronto memory researcher, has conceptualized episodic, semantic, and procedural memories as three distinct memory systems, which have evolved over time (1985, 1993, 2000). In his view, **procedural memory** is the most basic system because it involves "blueprints" for behaviours that allow any organism, that can learn, to adapt to the environment. **Semantic memory** is more specialized knowledge of the world. **Episodic memory** is the most specialized since it involves memories for specific episodes in the past that have personal relevance. Our memories of what we have done and the kinds of experiences we have had constitute episodic memory. Consequently, when we recall our first date, the time we fell off our bicycle, or what we felt like when we graduated from high school, we are recalling episodic memories. (To help your long-term memory keep the distinction between the different types of long-term memory straight, consider Figure 6-6).

Episodic memories can be surprisingly detailed. Consider, for instance, how you'd respond if you were asked to identify what you were doing on a specific day two years ago. Impossible? You might think otherwise as you read the following exchange between a researcher and a subject who was asked, in a memory experiment, what he was doing "on Monday afternoon in the third week of September two years ago."

SUBJECT: Come on. How should I know?
EXPERIMENTER: Just try it anyhow.

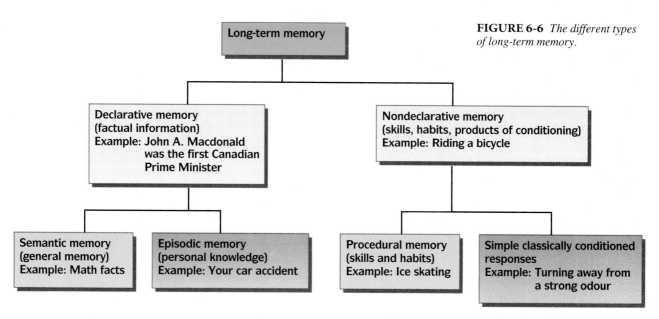

FIGURE 6-6 *The different types of long-term memory.*

SUBJECT: OK. Let's see: Two years ago . . . I would be in high school. . . . That would be my senior year. Third week in September—that's just after summer—that would be the fall term. . . . Let me see. I think I had chemistry lab on Mondays. I don't know. I was probably in chemistry lab. Wait a minute—that would be the second week of school. I remember he started off with the atomic table—a big fancy chart. I thought he was crazy trying to make us memorize that thing. You know, I think I can remember sitting . . . (Lindsay & Norman, 1977).

Episodic memory, then, can provide information from events that happened long in the past (Reynolds & Takooshian, 1988).

But semantic memory is no less impressive, permitting us to dredge up tens of thousands of facts ranging from the date of our birthday to the knowledge that $1 is less than $5. Many psychologists, using **associative models** of memory, argue that semantic memory consists of associations between mental representations of various pieces of information (e.g., Collins & Quillian, 1969; Collins & Loftus, 1975). Consider, for example, Figure 6-7, which shows some of the relationships in memory relating to "animal."

The basic notion behind associative models is that when we think about a particular concept, our semantic memory activates the recall of related concepts, bringing them more readily to mind. For example, thinking about a "robin" activates our recall of related concepts such as "eats worms" and "has a red breast." As a result, if we are trying to remember some specific bit of information (such as where we left our sunglasses), thinking about associated material may help us to recollect it (such as where we were when we last wore the sunglasses).

In such instances, related information helps prime us to recall information that we are otherwise unable to recollect. In **priming,** prior presentation of information subsequently makes it easier to recall related items, even when we have no conscious memory of the original information (Tulving & Schacter, 1990; Toth & Reingold, 1996).

The typical experiment designed to illustrate priming helps clarify the phenomenon. In priming experiments, subjects are first presented with a stimulus such as a word, an object, or perhaps a drawing of a face. The second phase of the experiment is held after an interval ranging from several seconds to several months. At that point, subjects are exposed to incomplete perceptual information that is related to the first

associative models: A technique of recalling information by thinking about related information

priming: A technique of recalling information by having been exposed to related information at an earlier time

FIGURE 6-7 *Associative models suggest that semantic memory consists of relationships between pieces of information, such as those relating to the concept of "animal," shown in this figure. Source: Adapted from Collins & Quillian, 1969.*

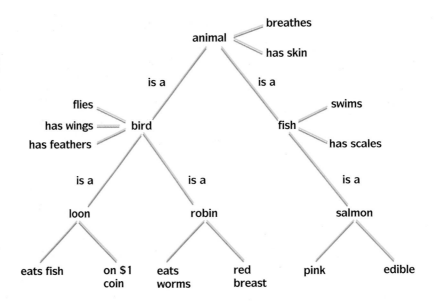

stimulus, and they are asked whether they recognize it. For example, the new material may consist of the first letter of a word that had been presented earlier, or a part of a face that had been shown earlier. If subjects are able to identify the stimulus more readily than they identify stimuli that have not been presented earlier, priming has taken place.

Priming occurs even when subjects report no conscious awareness of having been exposed to a stimulus earlier. For instance, studies have found that people who are anesthetized during surgery can sometimes recall snippets of information that they heard during surgery—even though they have no conscious recollection of the information (Kihlstrom et al., 1990; Sebel, Bonke, & Winogard, 1993; Merikle & Daneman, 1996).

The discovery that people have memories about which they are unaware has been an important one. It has led to speculation that two forms of memory, explicit and implicit, may exist side-by-side. **Explicit memory** refers to intentional or conscious recollection of information. When we try to remember a name or date, we are using explicit memory. In contrast, **implicit memory** refers to memories of which people are not consciously aware, but which can affect subsequent performance and behavior. When an event that we are unable to consciously recall affects our behaviour, implicit memory is at work (Graf & Schacter, 1985; Graf & Masson, 1993; Schacter, Chiu, & Ochsner, 1993; Schacter, 1994b, 1995; Underwood, 1996).

There is considerable disagreement regarding the precise difference between implicit and explicit memory (Lewandowsky, Dunn, & Kirsner, 1989; Roediger, 1990; Schacter, 1993, 1997). Some researchers suggest that two distinct memory systems exist, one for implicit and one for explicit memory (e.g., Weiskrantz, 1989; Schacter, Chiu, Ochsner, 1993; Graf, 1994; Kandel & Hawkins, 1995). In contrast, other researchers have proposed that the two kinds of memory differ simply in the way that information is initially processed and retrieved, and do not constitute independent memory systems (e.g., Roediger, Weldon, & Challis, 1989).

It is still too early to tell which of these views will prevail in the memory research arena. Ongoing studies support both sides of the argument. Larry Jacoby of McMaster University in Hamilton, Ontario, (Jacoby and Kelley, 1992; Jacoby, 1998) has done a number of interesting experiments using the process dissociation procedure. A unique feature of Jacoby's procedure is that he has developed techniques to separate the contribution of different types of processing within a single task. For example, in some experiments, the likelihood of recognition memory was found to differ according to the ways in which the items had been processed earlier (implicitly or explicitly).

explicit memory: Intentional or conscious recollection of information

implicit memory: Memories of which people are not consciously aware, but which can affect subsequent performance and behaviour

Implicit Memory

Rob Rogers reprinted by permission of UFS, Inc.

Levels of Processing

So far, we have relied on a model of memory that suggests that the processing of information in memory proceeds in three sequential stages, starting with sensory memory, advancing to short-term memory, and potentially ending in long-term memory. However, not all memory specialists agree with such a view. Some suggest that a single process accounts for how well information is remembered: the way in which material is first perceived, considered, and understood.

The **levels-of-processing theory** emphasizes the degree to which new material is mentally analyzed (Craik & Lockhart, 1972; Craik, 1990). In contrast to the view that there are sensory, short-term, and long-term memories, levels-of-processing theory suggests that the amount of information processing that occurs when material is initially encountered is central in determining how much of the information is ultimately remembered. According to this approach, the depth of processing during exposure to material—meaning the degree to which it is analyzed and considered—is critical; the greater the intensity of its initial processing, the more likely we are to remember it (Craik & Tulving, 1975).

Because we do not pay close attention to much of the information to which we are exposed, typically only scant mental processing takes place, and we forget new material almost immediately. However, information to which we pay greater attention is processed more thoroughly. Therefore, it enters memory at a deeper level—and is less apt to be forgotten than information processed at shallower levels.

The theory goes on to suggest that there are differences in the ways information is processed. At shallow levels, information is processed in terms of its physical and sensory aspects. For example, we may pay attention only to the shapes that make up the letters in the word "dog." At an intermediate level of processing, the shapes are translated into acoustic units such as names of letters of the alphabet. These letters are considered in the context of words, and specific phonetic sounds may be attached to the letters.

At the deepest level of processing, information is analyzed in terms of its meaning. It may be seen in a wider context, and associations between the meaning of the information and broader networks of knowledge may be drawn. For instance, we may think of dogs not merely as animals with four legs and a tail, but in terms of their relationship to cats and other mammals. We may form an image of our own dog, thereby relating the concept to our own lives. According to the levels-of-processing approach, the deeper the initial level of processing of specific information, the longer the information will be retained. The approach suggests, then, that the best way to remember new information is to consider it thoroughly when you are first exposed to it—reflecting on how it relates to information that you currently know (McDaniel, Riegler, & Waddill, 1990). Even trivial information that is well processed can be remembered (Mitterer and Begg, 1979).

levels-of-processing theory: The theory that emphasizes the degree to which new material is mentally analyzed

The main idea of the levels-of-processing theory is that memory depends on how material has been processed. Deep levels of processing typically produce best memory. However, under some conditions, shallow processing has been found to produce better memory than deep processing (Baddeley, 1978; Cermak and Craik, 1979). Furthermore, no fully adequate means has been found for objectively measuring how deeply material is processed in the first place (Searleman & Herrmann, 1994). In spite of these problems, during the two decades after the publication of the article in which the model was first described (Craik and Lockhart, 1972), this work has been cited 2,000 times in the psychological literature (Payne and Wenger, 1998).

In sum, neither the levels-of-processing model nor the three-stage model of memory is able to account fully for all phenomena relating to memory. As a result, other models of memory have been proposed. For example, one view suggests a model in which short-term storage is considered a part of long-term storage, rather than representing a separate stage. It is probably too early to tell—let alone remember—which of the multiple models of memory gives us the most accurate characterization of memory (Collins et al., 1993; Searleman & Herrmann, 1994; Wolters, 1995; Bjork & Bjork, 1996; Conway, 1997).

Recap, Review, and Rethink

Recap

- Memory is the process by which we encode, store, and retrieve information.

- Sensory memory contains a brief but accurate representation of physical stimuli to which a person is exposed. Each representation is constantly being replaced with a new one.

- Short-term memory has a capacity of seven (plus or minus two) chunks of information. Memories remain in short-term storage for fifteen to twenty-five seconds and are then either transferred to long-term memory or lost.

- Long-term memory consists of declarative and procedural memory. Declarative memory is further subdivided into episodic and semantic memory.

- An alternative to the three-stage model of memory, the levels-of-processing approach, suggests that information is analyzed at different levels rather than through separate stages, with material processed at deeper levels being retained the longest.

Review

1. The process by which information is initially stored in memory is known as _____. _____ is the process by which elements of memory are brought into awareness and used.

2. Match the type of memory with its definition:
   1. long-term memory
   2. short-term memory
   3. sensory memory

   a. holds information fifteen to twenty-five seconds
   b. permanent storage, could be difficult to retrieve
   c. initial storage of information, lasts only a fraction of a second

3. A _____ is a meaningful group of stimuli that can be stored together in short-term memory.

4. _____ are organizational strategies used to organize information.

5. There appear to be two types of long-term memory: _____ memory, which is memory for knowledge and facts, and _____ memory, which is memory for skills, habits, and conditioned responses.

6. _____ models of memory state that long-term memory is stored as associations between pieces of information.

7. You read an article stating that the more a person analyzes a statement, the more likely he or she is to remember it later. What theory is this article describing?

Answers to Review Questions are on page 218.

Rethink

1. What is the difference between sensory memory and the lasting memory that a person has of the sound of a voice, shape of a face, or smell of a perfume? In what part of memory are such lasting sensory experiences stored? How do they get there?

2. It is a truism that "you never forget how to ride a bicycle." Why might this be so? Where is information about bicycle riding stored? What happens when a person has to retrieve that information after not using it for a long time? Is retrieval the same for declarative memory?

3. Priming seems to occur in most cases without conscious awareness. How might this effect be used by advertisers and others to promote their products? What ethical principles are involved?

The tip-of-the-tongue phenomenon is especially frustrating in situations where a person cannot recall the name of someone he or she has just met.

RECALLING LONG-TERM MEMORIES

An hour after his job interview, Ricardo was sitting in a coffee shop, telling his friend Laura how well it had gone, when the woman who had interviewed him walked in. "Well, hello, Ricardo. How are you doing?" Trying to make a good impression, Ricardo began to make introductions, but suddenly realized he could not remember the name of the interviewer. Stammering, he desperately searched his memory, but to no avail. "I *know* her name," he thought to himself, "but here I am, looking like a fool. I can kiss this job goodbye."

▶ **What causes difficulties and failures in remembering?**

Have you ever tried to remember someone's name, convinced that you knew it, but were unable to recall it no matter how hard you tried? This common occurrence—known as the **tip-of-the-tongue phenomenon**—exemplifies the difficulties that can occur in retrieving information stored in long-term memory (Harris & Morris, 1986; A. S. Brown, 1991; Smith, 1994; Riefer, Keveri, & Kramer, 1995).

tip-of-the-tongue phenomenon: The inability to recall information that one realizes one knows—a result of the difficulty of retrieving information from long-term memory

Retrieval Cues

One reason recall is not perfect is the sheer quantity of recollections that are stored in long-term memory. Although the issue is far from settled, many psychologists have suggested that the material that makes its way to long-term memory is relatively permanent (Tulving & Psotka, 1971). If they are correct, this suggests that the capacity of long-term memory is vast, given the broad range of people's experiences and educational backgrounds. For instance, if you are like the average college student, your vocabulary includes some 50,000 words, you know hundreds of mathematical "facts," and you are able to conjure up images—such as the way your childhood home looked—with no trouble at all. In fact, simply cataloging all your memories would probably take years of work.

How do we sort through this vast array of material and retrieve specific information at the appropriate time? One of the major ways is through the use of retrieval cues. A *retrieval cue* is a stimulus that allows us to recall more easily information that is located in long-term memory (Tulving & Thompson, 1973; Ratcliff & McKoon, 1989). It may be a word, an emotion, a sound; whatever the specific cue, a memory will suddenly come to mind when the retrieval cue is present. For example, the smell of roasting turkey may evoke memories of Thanksgiving or family gatherings (Schab & Crowder, 1995).

Retrieval cues guide people through the information stored in long-term memory in much the same way as the cards in an old-fashioned card catalog guided people through a library, or a search engine like "Yahoo" guides people through the World

FIGURE 6-8 *Name the characters in the above figure. Because it is a recall task, it is relatively difficult.* © *Disney Enterprises, Inc.*

> **Answer this recognition question:**
>
> **Which of the following are the names of the seven dwarfs in the Disney movie *Snow White and the Seven Dwarfs*?**
>
> | | |
> |---|---|
> | Goofy | Bashful |
> | Sleepy | Meanie |
> | Smarty | Doc |
> | Scaredy | Happy |
> | Dopey | Angry |
> | Grumpy | Sneezy |
> | Wheezy | Crazy |

FIGURE 6-9 *The recognition problem posed above is considerably easier than the recall task in the previous figure.*

Wide Web. They are particularly important when we are making an effort to *recall* information, as opposed to being asked to *recognize* material stored in memory. In *recall,* a specific piece of information must be retrieved—such as that needed to answer a fill-in-the-blank question or write an essay on a test. In contrast, *recognition* occurs when people are presented with a stimulus and asked whether they have been exposed to it previously, or are asked to identify it from a list of alternatives.

As you might guess, recognition is generally a much easier task than recall (see Figures 6-8 and 6-9). Recall is more difficult because it consists of a series of processes: a search through memory, retrieval of potentially relevant information, and then a decision regarding whether or not the information you have found is accurate. If the information appears correct, the search is over, but if it does not, the search must continue. On the other hand, recognition is simpler since it involves fewer steps (Anderson & Bower, 1972; Miserando, 1991).

Flashbulb Memories

Where were you on the evening of August 31, 1997? You will most likely draw a blank until this piece of information is added: August 31, 1997, was the date that Princess Diana was killed in a car crash.

You probably have little trouble recalling your exact location and a variety of other trivial details that occurred when you heard the news, even though the accident happened years ago. The reason is a phenomenon known as **flashbulb memories**. Flashbulb memories are memories centred around a specific, important, or surprising event that are so vivid it is as if they represented a snapshot of the event.

Several types of flashbulb memories are common among college students. For example, involvement in a car accident, meeting one's roommate for the first time, and the night of high school graduation are all typical flashbulb memories (Rubin, 1985).

Of course, flashbulb memories do not contain every detail of an original scene. For instance, you may remember vividly the huge ball of fire when the space shuttle Challenger exploded on January 28, 1986. But you probably do not recall all the visual details of the space shuttle as it rose into the air just moments before the explosion. And you probably don't remember what you were wearing or what you had for lunch that day. Flashbulb memories, then, are not complete, and just how much their essen-

flashbulb memories: Memories centred around a specific, important, or surprising event that are so vivid it is as if they represented a snapshot of the event

---

Answers to Review Questions:

1. encoding; Retrieval   2. 1-b; 2-a; 3-c   3. chunk   4. Mnemonics   5. declarative; nondeclarative   6. Associative   7. levels-of-processing theory

For many people, the moment that they heard that Princess Diana had been killed in a car crash is a flashbulb memory.

tial nature differs from everyday memories remains an open question (McCloskey et al., 1988; Pillemer, 1990; Winograd & Neisser, 1992; Conway, 1995).

Still, flashbulb memories seem extraordinary because of the details they do include. An analysis of people's recollections of the Kennedy assassination found that their memories tended to have a number of features in common (Brown & Kulik, 1977). Most contained information regarding where the person heard the news, who told him or her about it, what event was interrupted by the news, the emotions of the informant, the person's own emotions, and some personal details of the event (such as seeing a robin fly by while the information was being relayed). (See Figure 6-10.)

On the other hand, we can't be sure that all the details recalled in flashbulb memories are accurate. For example, one day after the *Challenger* accident, psychologists Nicole Harsch and Ulric Neisser asked a group of college students how they had heard the news of the disaster. When they asked the same people the identical question three years later, most responded readily, providing reasonable responses. The trouble was that in about one-third of the cases, their answers were completely wrong (Harsch & Neisser, 1989; Neisser & Harsch, 1992; Winograd & Neisser, 1993).

Flashbulb memories illustrate a more general phenomenon about memory: Memories that are exceptional are more easily retrieved (although not necessarily accurately) than those relating to events that are commonplace. We are more likely, for example, to recall a particular number if it appears in a group of twenty words than if it appears in a group of twenty other numbers. The more distinctive a stimulus, then, the more likely we are to recall it later (von Restorff, 1933; Walker & Jones, 1983; Hunt, 1995).

Flashbulb Memories

Constructive Processes in Memory: Rebuilding the Past

As we have seen, although it is clear that we can have detailed recollections of significant and distinctive events, it is difficult to gauge the accuracy of such memories. In fact, it is apparent that our memories reflect, at least in part, **constructive processes**, processes in which memories are influenced by the meaning that we give to events. When we retrieve information, then, the memory that is produced is affected not just by the direct prior experience we have had with the stimulus, but by our guesses and inferences about its meaning as well.

The notion that memory is based on constructive processes was first put forward by Sir Frederic Bartlett, a British psychologist. He suggested that people tend to remember information in terms of **schemas**, general themes that contain relatively little specific detail (Bartlett, 1932). In a schema, unimportant details are omitted. Instead,

constructive processes: Processes in which memories are influenced by the meaning that we give to events

schemas: General themes that contain relatively little specific detail

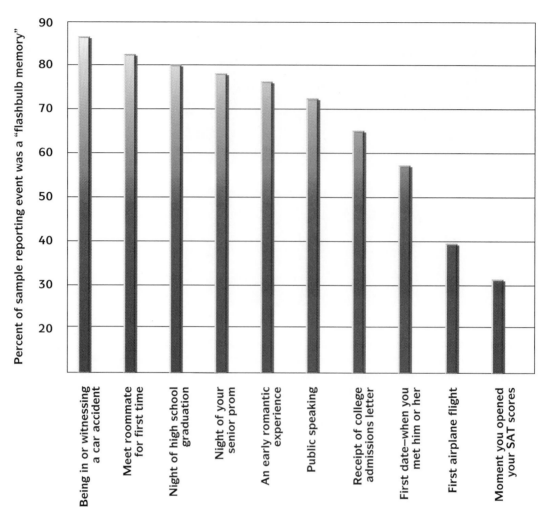

FIGURE 6-10 *The most common "flashbulb memories" of a sample of American college students are shown here. Source: Rubin, 1985.*

memories consist of a general reconstruction of previous experience. Bartlett argued that such schemas were based not only on the specific material to which people are exposed, but also on their understanding of the situation, their expectations about the situation, and their awareness of the motivations underlying the behaviour of others.

In a demonstration of the operation of schemas, researchers have employed a process known as *serial reproduction,* in which information from memory is passed sequentially from one person to another. For an example of serial reproduction, look briefly at the drawing in Figure 6-11, and then try to describe it to someone else without looking back at it. Then ask that person to describe it to another person, and repeat the process with still one more person.

If you listen to the last person's report of the contents of the drawing, you are sure to find that it differs in important respects from the drawing itself. Many people recall the drawing as showing a razor in the hand of the black person—obviously an incorrect recollection, given that the razor is held by the white person (Allport & Postman, 1958).

This example, which is drawn from a classic experiment, illustrates the role of expectations in memory. The migration of the razor in memory from the white person's hand to the black person's hand clearly indicates that expectations about the world—reflecting, in this case, the unwarranted prejudice that blacks may be more violent than whites and thus more apt to be holding a razor—have an impact upon how events are recalled.

Of course, it is not just our expectations that have an impact on what we recall. Our understanding of the motivations of others also contributes to constructive

FIGURE 6-11 *When one person views this picture and then describes it from memory to a second person, who in turn describes it to a third, and so on—in a process known as serial reproduction—the last person to repeat the contents of the cartoon typically gives a description that differs in important respects from the original. Source: Based on Allport & Postman, 1958.*

processes in memory. For example, in what has been called the *soap opera effect,* knowledge about what motivates an individual can lead to elaborations in memory of earlier events involving that person.

The soap opera effect derives its name from soap opera characters who, at least in the eyes of occasional viewers, make seemingly innocent statements. However, to long-term viewers, who are aware of the characters' real motives, the same statements may be fraught with significance. In turn, this information will be remembered differently according to a person's understanding of the motivation behind the statement (Owens, Bower, & Black, 1979).

In short, our understanding of the motivations behind a person's behaviour, as well as our expectations and knowledge, affects the reliability of our memories (Katz, 1989; Ross & Newby, 1996; McDonald & Hirt, 1997). In some cases, the imperfections of people's recollections can have profound implications, as we will see when we now consider memory in the legal realm.

Memory in the Courtroom: The Eyewitness on Trial

The inadequate memories of witnesses cost Thomas Sophonow at least four years of his life. Sophonow was the victim of mistaken identity, when witnesses said they saw him flee from the doughnut shop in Winnipeg where 16-year-old Barbara Stoppel was murdered in 1981. Sophonow has always maintained his innocence, and after three trials and two convictions he was released in 1985. However, it was not until after many more hours were spent going over statements and leads, and after DNA tests were done recently, that the cloud of suspicion around Sophonow disappeared.

Unfortunately Sophonow is not the only victim to whom apologies have had to be made. His case joins other cases of miscarriage of justice (e.g., Donald Marshall, David Milgaard, Guy Paul Morin, Gregory Parsons).

Considerable research has shown that eyewitnesses make errors on identification of suspects and on memory for other details of crime (G.L. Wells, 1993; Ross, Read & Toglia, 1994; Wells, Luus & Windschitl, 1994; Cutler & Penrod, 1995; Egeth, 1995; Sporer, Malpass & Koehnken, 1996). Elizabeth Loftus has argued that eyewitness recall, like other recall, is subject to the effects of reconstruction in memory (Loftus, 1979). John Yuille (University of British Columbia) has also extensively studied eyewitness testimony, and has concluded that real-world witnesses may not be as inaccurate as laboratory studies suggest (Yuille and Tollestrup, 1992; Yuille and Cutshall, 1986). In contrast to Loftus, he has questioned the applicability of laboratory studies to real-world situations. Thus, while it is clear that witnesses make errors in recall, the extent of these errors is not clear.

FIGURE 6-12 *After viewing an accident involving two cars, subjects were asked to estimate the speed of the collision. Estimates varied substantially, depending on the way the question was worded. Source: Loftus & Palmer, 1974.*

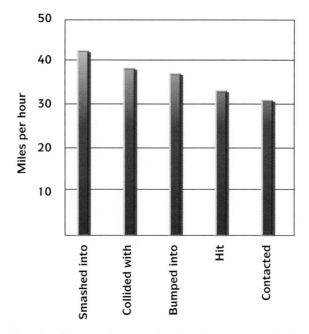

About how fast were the cars going when they _____ each other?

Researchers have found a number of reasons for the inaccuracies in eyewitness testimony. One reason is the impact of weapons used in crimes. When a criminal perpetrator displays a gun or knife, it acts like a perceptual magnet, and the eyes of the witnesses are drawn to the weapon. As a consequence, less attention is paid to other details of crime, and witnesses are less able to recall what actually occurred (Loftus, Loftus and Messo, 1987; Steblay, 1992). Another reason that eyewitnesses are prone to memory-related errors is that specific wording of questions can affect the way in which witnesses recall information. For example, in one experiment participants were shown a film of two cars crashing into each other. Participants who were asked how fast the two cars were going when they *smashed* into each other gave faster estimates (65.7 kph, 40.8 mph) than those asked how fast the cars were going when they *contacted* each other (51.2 kph, 31.8 mph) (Loftus and Palmer, 1974: see Figure 6-12.).

The problem of memory reliability becomes even more acute when children are witnesses, because increasing evidence suggests that children's memories are highly vulnerable to the influence of others (Loftus, 1993; Ceci & Bruck, 1995; Hutcheson et al., 1995; Beal, Schmitt, Dekle, 1995; Cassel, Roebers, & Bjorklund, 1996). For instance, in one experiment, 5- to 7-year-old girls who had just had a routine physical examination were shown an anatomically explicit doll. The girls were shown the doll's genital area and asked, "Did the doctor touch you here?" Three of the girls who did not have a vaginal or anal exam said that the doctor had in fact touched them in the genital area. And one of those three made up the detail, "The doctor did it with a stick" (Saywitz & Goodman, 1990).

Children's memories are especially susceptible to influence when the situation is highly emotional or stressful. For example, in trials in which there is significant pretrial publicity or where alleged victims are repeatedly questioned, often by untrained interviewers, the memories of alleged victims may be influenced by the type of questions they are asked. Yuille has studied the complexities of eliciting and assessing children's statements, and has developed a procedure for interviewing children which has been adopted in most provinces of Canada (Yuille, 1988, 1997; Marxsen, Yuille, and Nisbett, 1995).

In short, the memories of witnesses are far from infallible, and this is especially true when children are involved (Davies, 1993; Ceci & Bruck, 1995; Cassell & Bjorklund, 1995). The question of the accuracy of memories becomes even more complex, however, when we consider the triggering of memories of events that people at first don't even recall happening. As we discuss next, this issue has raised considerable controversy.

Repressed Memories: Truth or Fiction?

Guilty of murder in the first degree.

That was the jury's verdict in the case of George Franklin, Sr., who was charged with murdering his daughter's playmate. But this case was different from most other murder cases: It was based on memories that had been repressed for twenty years. Franklin's daughter claimed that she had forgotten everything she had once known about her father's crime until two years earlier, when she began to have flashbacks of the event. Initially, she had only a memory of her friend's look of betrayal. Over the next year, the memories became richer, and she recalled being together with her father and her friend. Then she remembered her father sexually assaulting her friend. She recalled his lifting a rock over his head, and then seeing her friend lying on the ground, covered with blood. On the basis of these memories, her father was arrested and convicted (although ultimately he gained his freedom following an appeal of the conviction).

But just how accurate were the memories that initially convicted Franklin? Although the prosecutor and jury clearly believed Franklin's daughter, there is good reason to question the validity of *repressed memories,* recollections of events that are initially so shocking that the mind responds by pushing them into the unconscious. Supporters of the notion of repressed memory suggest that such memories may remain hidden, possibly throughout a person's lifetime, unless they are triggered by some current circumstance, such as the probing that occurs during psychological therapy.

However, psychologist Elizabeth Loftus (1997) maintains that so-called repressed memories may well be inaccurate or even wholly false. She notes how easy it is to plant memories that people believe are real. For example, in one experiment, a student named Jack wrote a story for his younger brother Chris, 14, to read. It described an event that never happened:

False Memories

"It was 1981 or 1982. I remember that Chris was 5. We had gone shopping at the University City shopping mall in Spokane. After some panic, we found Chris being led down the mall by a tall, oldish man (I think he was wearing a flannel shirt). Chris was crying and holding the man's hand. The man explained that he had found Chris walking around crying his eyes out just a few moments before and was trying to help him find his parents."

Just a few weeks later, Chris was convinced the event had actually happened. He described the colour of the old man's flannel shirt, his bald head, and how he felt "really scared." Even when informed that the event never happened, Chris clung to his memory, saying "Really? I thought I remembered being lost . . . and looking around for you guys. I do remember that, and then crying, and Mom coming up and saying, 'Where were you? Don't you . . . ever do that again' " (Loftus, 1993, p. 532).

Clearly, people are potentially susceptible to false memories. Why? Some false memories occur when people are unable to recall the source of a memory of a particular event about which they have only vague recollections. When the source of the memory becomes unclear or ambiguous, people may begin to confuse whether they actually experienced the event or whether it was imagined. Ultimately, the memory begins to seem authentic, and people may come to believe that the event actually occurred (Roediger & McDermott, 1995; Zaragoza & Mitchell, 1996; Read, 1996; Payne et al., 1996; Mitchell & Zaragoza, 1996; McDermott, 1996).

In fact, some therapists have been accused of inadvertently encouraging people who come to them with psychological difficulties to recreate false chronicles of childhood sexual experiences (Belicki et al., 1993). For instance, hypnosis, which is sometimes used to help people recall lost memories can actually create false memories. In addition, there have been many well-publicized declarations of repressed memories, such as those of students in residential schools and training centres who remember being abused during their childhood. Such publicity makes the possibility of repressed memories seem more legitimate and may ultimately prime people to recall memories of events that never happened (Lynn, 1997).

On the other hand, many psychologists see repressed memories as a very real phenomenon. Building upon a psychodynamic model of human behaviour that we discussed in Chapter 1, they argue that it is reasonable to assume that some memories will be so painful that they are forced into the unconscious. They suggest that childhood sexual abuse is so traumatic that people are motivated to forget its occurrence. In support of their view, they point to cases in which it is possible to confirm once-repressed memories of childhood abuse (Frederickson, 1992; Whitfield, 1995; Davies, 1996). Kathy Belicki, at Brock University in St. Catherines, has used the analysis of patterns of dreams and sleep experience to identify a history of sexual trauma (Belicki and Cuddy, 1996).

The controversy regarding the legitimacy of repressed memories is unlikely to be resolved soon. Many psychologists, particularly those who provide therapy, give great weight to the reality of repressed memories. On the other side of the issue are many memory researchers, who maintain that there is no scientific support for the existence of such memories (Brown & Pope, 1996; Pezdek & Banks, 1996; Loftus, 1997).

Autobiographical Memory: Where Past Meets Present

autobiographical memories: Our recollections of circumstances and episodes from our own lives

Your memory of experiences in your own past might well be a fiction—or at least a distortion of what actually occurred. The same constructive processes that act to make us inaccurately recall the behaviour of others also reduce the accuracy of autobiographical memories. **Autobiographical memories** are our recollections of circumstances and episodes from our own lives (Mullen & Yi, 1995; Thompson et al., 1996; Rubin, 1996; Stein et al., 1997).

For example, we tend to forget information about our past that is incompatible with the way in which we currently see ourselves. One study found that adults who were well adjusted but who had been treated for emotional problems during the early years of their lives tended to forget important but troubling childhood events. For instance, they forgot such difficult circumstances as their family's receipt of welfare when they were children, being in foster care, and living in a home for delinquents (Robbins, 1988). Similarly, people who are depressed remember sad events from their past more easily than happy people do, and people who report being happy in adulthood remember more happy events than depressing ones (Eich, 1995; Mayer, McCormick, & Strong, 1995; Stein et al., 1996).

It is not just certain kinds of events that are distorted; particular periods of life are remembered more easily than others. For example, when people reach old age, they remember periods of life in which they experienced major transitions, such as attending college or working at their first job, better than their middle-age years (Rubin, 1985; Fitzgerald, 1988; Fromholt & Larsen, 1991).

Exploring Diversity

Are There Cross-cultural Differences in Memory?

Many travellers who have visited areas of the world in which there is no written language have returned with tales of people who have phenomenal memories. Presumably because they have no written records, people in such cultures develop memories that can provide a kind of oral record to keep track of important events in the society's history. For instance, storytellers in some preliterate cultures can recount long chronicles that recall the names and activities of people over many generations (Rubin, 1995).

On the basis of such anecdotes, memory experts initially argued that people in preliterate societies develop a different, and perhaps better, type of memory than those in cultures that employ a written language (Bartlett, 1932; Cole & Gay, 1972). They suggested that in a society that lacks writing, people are motivated to recall information with accuracy, particularly information relating to tribal histories and traditions that would be lost if they were not passed down orally from one generation to another.

However, more recent approaches to cultural differences suggest a different conclusion. For one thing, preliterate peoples don't have an exclusive claim on amazing memory feats. For instance, certain Hebrew scholars know the entire text of the Talmud, a lengthy compilation of biblical commentaries, by heart. Not only have they memorized its thousands of pages, but when given a page number, they can recall the locations of particular words on the page. Similarly, poetry singers in the former Yugoslavia routinely commit to memory a body of at least thirty songs, each several thousand lines long. Even in cultures in which written language exists, astounding feats of memory are possible (Neisser, 1982).

Memory experts suggest that there are both similarities and differences in memory across cultures. According to psychologist Daniel Wagner, basic memory processes, such as short-term memory capacity and the structure of long-term memory, are universal and operate similarly in people of all cultures (Wagner, 1981). In contrast, cultural differences can be seen in the way in which information is acquired, rehearsed, and retrieved from memory. Consequently, culture determines how people consider and frame information initially, how much they practice learning and recalling it, and the strategies they use to try to recall it.

In sum, the association between culture and memory can be compared to the relationship between computer hardware and software. Basic memory processes, analogous to computer "hardware," are universal across cultures. On the other hand, the "software" of memory—the way information is initially acquired, rehearsed, and retrieved—is influenced by the nature of a specific culture.   ■

Recap, Review, and Rethink

Recap

- The tip-of-the-tongue phenomenon refers to the inability to recall something that a person is sure he or she knows.

- Retrieval cues are particularly important when recalling—as opposed to recognizing—information.

- Flashbulb memories are memories centred around a specific, important event that are so clear it is as if they represent a snapshot of the event.

- Memories are affected, at least in part, by constructive processes, which influence the meaning that we give to events. Autobiographical memory, for instance, can be distorted by constructive processes.

- Basic memory processes are universal, although the way in which information is initially acquired, rehearsed, and retrieved differs across cultures.

Review

1. While with a group of friends at a dance, Evita bumps into a man she dated last month. When she tries to introduce him to her friends, she cannot remember his name, though she is positive she knows it. What is the term for this occurrence?

2. _____ is used when a person is asked to retrieve a specific item from memory.

3. A friend of your mother's tells you "I know exactly where I was and what I was doing when I heard that Elvis died." What phenomenon explains this type of recollection?

4. The same person could probably also accurately describe in detail what she was wearing when she heard that Elvis passed on, right down to the colour of the ribbon on her blue suede shoes. True or false?

5. Retrieval of memories is influenced not only by objective reality, but also by our constructions of past events. True or false?

6. _____ are "themes," containing little specific detail, that are used to help us organize information in memory.

Answers to Review Questions are on page 226.

Rethink

1. Are retrieval cues explained by associative models of memory? How do retrieval cues relate to priming?

2. How do schemas help people process information during encoding, storage, and retrieval? In what ways are they helpful? Can they contribute to inaccurate autobiographical memories?

3. How might courtroom procedure be improved, knowing what you now know about memory errors and biases?

FORGETTING: WHEN MEMORY FAILS

▶ **Why do we forget information?**

▶ **What are the biological bases of memory?**

▶ **What are the major memory impairments?**

He could remember, quite literally, nothing—nothing, that is, that had happened since the loss of his brain's temporal lobes and hippocampus during experimental surgery to reduce epileptic seizures. Until that time, his memory had been quite normal. But after the operation he was unable to recall anything for more than a few minutes, and then the memory was seemingly lost forever. He did not remember his address, or the name of the person to whom he was talking. He would read the same magazine over and over again. According to his own description, his life was like waking from a dream and being unable to know where he was or how he got there (Milner, 1966).

The difficulties faced by a person without a normal memory are legion, as the case described above attests. All of us who have experienced even routine instances of forgetting—such as not remembering an acquaintance's name or a fact on a test—understand the serious consequences of memory failure.

The first attempts to study forgetting were made by German psychologist Hermann Ebbinghaus about a hundred years ago. Using himself as his only subject, he memorized lists of three-letter nonsense syllables—meaningless sets of two consonants with a vowel in between, such as FIW and BOZ. By measuring how easy it was to relearn a given list of words after varying periods of time had passed since initial learning, he found that forgetting occurred systematically, as shown in Figure 6-13. As the figure indicates, the most rapid forgetting occurs in the first nine hours, and particularly in the first hour. After nine hours, the rate of forgetting slows and declines little, even after the passage of many days.

Despite his primitive methods, Ebbinghaus's study had an important influence on subsequent research, and his basic conclusions have been upheld (Wixted & Ebbesen, 1991). There is almost always a strong initial decline in memory, followed by a more gradual drop over time. Furthermore, relearning of previously mastered material is almost always faster than starting from scratch, whether the material is academic information or a motor skill such as serving a tennis ball.

Efforts at understanding the problem of *why* we forget have yielded two major solutions. One theory explains forgetting in terms of a process called **decay**, or the loss of information through its nonuse. This explanation assumes that when new material is learned, a **memory trace** or **engram**—an actual physical change in the brain—occurs. In decay, the trace simply fades away with nothing left behind, because of the mere passage of time.

Although there is evidence that decay does occur, it does not seem to be the complete explanation for forgetting. Often there is no relationship between how long ago a person was exposed to information and how well it is recalled. If decay explained all forgetting, we would expect that the longer the time between the initial learning of information and our attempt to recall it, the harder it would be to remember it, since there would be more time for the memory trace to decay. Yet people who take several consecutive tests on the same material often recall more of the initial information when taking later tests than they did on earlier tests. If decay were operating, we would expect the opposite to occur (Payne, 1986).

Because decay does not fully account for forgetting, memory specialists have proposed an additional mechanism: **interference**. In interference, information in memory displaces or blocks out other information, preventing its recall.

To distinguish between decay and interference, think of the two processes in terms of a row of books on a library shelf. In decay, the old books are constantly crumbling and rotting away, leaving room for new arrivals. Interference processes suggest that new books knock the old ones off the shelf, where they become inaccessible.

decay: The loss of information through its nonuse

memory trace or **engram:** An actual physical change in the brain that occurs when new material is learned

interference: The phenomenon by which information in memory displaces or blocks out other information, preventing its recall

---

Answers to Review Questions:

1. tip-of-the-tongue phenomenon   2. Recall   3. flashbulb memory   4. False; small details probably won't be remembered through flashbulb memory.   5. true   6. Schemas

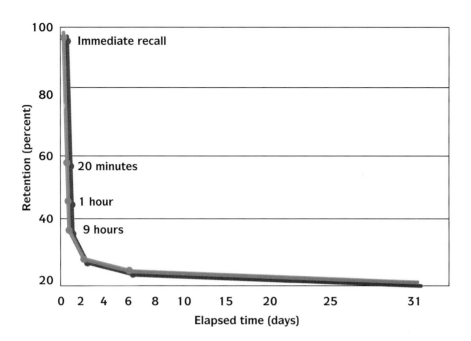

FIGURE 6-13 *In his classic work, Ebbinghaus found that the most rapid forgetting occurs in the first nine hours after exposure to new material. However, the rate of forgetting then slows down and declines very little even after many days have passed. Source: Ebbinghaus, 1885.*

Most research suggests that interference is the key process in forgetting (Potter, 1990; Wang & Arbib, 1993; Mel'nikov, 1993; Bower, Thompson, & Tulving, 1994). We mainly forget things because new memories interfere with the retrieval of old ones, not because the memory trace has decayed.

Although we may view interference negatively, it is important to remember that it may actually enhance our ability to understand and interact with the world around us. Interference assists us in developing general, summary memories of our experiences. For instance, rather than recalling every detail of every encounter with a particular professor, we tend to remember the most important episodes and forget those that are less meaningful. This ability allows us to draw a general, although not necessarily detailed or totally accurate, picture of what our encounters with the professor have been like in the past. Furthermore, it helps us to anticipate the course of future interactions (Potter, 1990).

Proactive and Retroactive Interference: The Before and After of Forgetting

There are actually two sorts of interference that influence forgetting: proactive and retroactive. In *proactive interference,* information learned earlier interferes with recall of newer material. Suppose, as a student of foreign languages, you first learned French in tenth grade, and then in eleventh grade you took Spanish. When in the twelfth grade you take a college achievement test in Spanish, you may find you have difficulty recalling the Spanish translation of a word because all you can think of is its French equivalent.

On the other hand, *retroactive interference* refers to difficulty in recall of information because of later exposure to different material. If, for example, you have difficulty on a French achievement test because of your more recent exposure to Spanish, retroactive interference is the culprit (see Figure 6-14). One way of remembering the difference between proactive and retroactive interference is to keep in mind that *pro*active interference moves forward in time—the past interferes with the present— whereas *retro*active interference retrogresses in time, working backward as the present interferes with the past.

Although the concepts of proactive and retroactive interference suggest why material may be forgotten, they still do not explain whether forgetting due to interference is caused by the actual loss or modification of information, or by problems in the retrieval of information. Most research suggests that material that has apparently been lost because of interference can eventually be recalled if appropriate stimuli are pre-

FIGURE 6-14 *Proactive interference occurs when material learned earlier interferes with recall of newer material. In this example, exposure to psychology prior to learning anthropology interferes with performance on an anthropology test. In contrast, retroactive interference exists when material learned after initial exposure to other material interferes with the recall of the first material. In this case, retroactive interference occurs when recall of psychology is impaired because of later exposure to anthropology.*

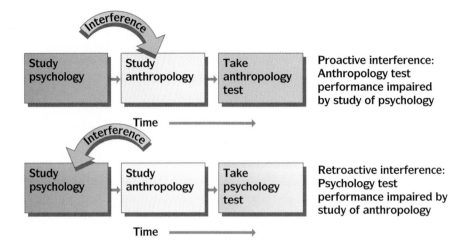

sented (Tulving & Psotka, 1971; Anderson, 1981), but the question has not been fully answered. In an effort to resolve the issue, some psychologists have begun to study the biological bases of memory in order to better understand what is remembered and what is forgotten—an increasingly important avenue of investigation that we turn to now.

The Biological Bases of Memory: The Search for the Engram

Where does memory reside? The search for the engram—the physical change in the brain that corresponds to the memory—has resulted in the development of several imaginative paths of research. This work has extended our knowledge of the biological underpinnings of memory in several directions (Rosenzweig, 1996; Milner, 1996; Galea et al., 1996).

Perhaps the most basic way to answer the question of where memory is "located" is to consider the level of individual neurons and their chemical interconnections. Donald Hebb (1949) first proposed the theory that neural changes occur at synapses that are repeatedly active. Most evidence now suggests that particular memories produce biochemical changes at specific synapses between neurons. Research on the sea snail, a primitive organism that can learn simple responses, has shown that systematic changes occur in its synapses during learning. Specifically, the ability of a particular neuron to release its neurotransmitters increases or declines as a result of learning. If retention of the response is short-term, the neuronal changes will be temporary. On the other hand, if long-term retention occurs, permanent structural changes in the neuronal connections will occur. Obviously, this difference between fleeting and permanent changes in the brain corresponds to the distinction between short- and long-term memory (Kandel & Schwartz, 1982; Mayford et al., 1992; Kandel & Abel, 1995). Research on the nematode worm has also provided interesting information about the biological basis of long-term memory. For example, Rankin and Wicks (2000) found that a mutant strain of worm, unlike the normal strain, did not have long-term memory due to a gene in a neurotransmitter in the sensory neuron.

It is fair to ask just how much we can generalize from the lowly sea snail and worm to humans. However, research using different species has produced results that suggest that the underlying processes are similar. Furthermore, this work is consistent with research on *long-term potentiation*, long-lasting increases in the strength of the responsiveness at various synapses. Certain neural pathways seem to become easily excited as a response is learned, apparently as a memory is formed. The pathways are like a garden hose that expands a bit more each time it was used, thereby allowing more water to be discharged (Martinez & Derrick, 1996; Oliet, Malenka, & Nicoll, 1996; Kilborn, Lynch, & Granger, 1996; Johnston, 1997).

In sum, long-term potentiation increases the excitability of particular neurons and neural pathways. At the same time, changes also occur in the number of synapses, as dendrites branch out. These changes are known as *consolidation,* the process by which memories become fixed and stable in long-term memory. Long-term memories take some time to stabilize, which explains why events and other stimuli are not suddenly fixed in memory. Instead, consolidation may continue for days and even years (Abel et al., 1995; Squire, 1995).

The Site of the Engram

It is clear that memory produces changes on a neuronal level. But just where in the brain does all this activity take place?

This question has proved to be a major puzzle to psychologists interested in memory. The search began in the 1920s, when psychologist Karl Lashley ran a series of experiments in which he removed portions of the cortex of rats. He found that rats who were made to relearn a problem involving running a maze showed learning deficits in proportion to the extent of the damage to their cortex; when more material was removed from the cortex, greater learning difficulties took place.

More intriguing, however, was the finding that the time it took to relearn the problem was unrelated to the specific *location* of the injury. Regardless of the particular portion of the brain that had been removed, the degree of learning deficit was similar, suggesting that memory traces are not strictly localized but somewhat distributed. Results of Lashley's work—summarized in a famous paper titled "In Search of the Engram"—led to the view, which was held for several decades, that stored memories are widely and fairly equally distributed across the brain (Lashley, 1950).

Contemporary research on the biology of learning seems to suggest a different conclusion. Such research shows that separate, distinct areas of the cortex simultaneously process information about particular dimensions of the world, including visual, auditory, and other sensory stimuli. Because different areas of the brain are simultaneously involved in processing information about different aspects of a stimulus, it seems reasonable that information storage might be linked to the sites of processing and therefore located in those particular areas. According to this view then, the location of an engram depends on the nature of the material that is being learned and the specific neural system that processed the information (Alkon, 1987; Matthies, 1989; Desimone, 1992; Squire, 1987, 1993).

How can we reconcile the growing contemporary view that memory is related to specific types of neural processing employed during learning, when we consider Lashley's findings that memory deficits were unrelated to the location of injury to the cortex? One answer is that the contradiction between the two findings is more apparent than real. It is likely, for example, that Lashley's procedure of having rats run through a maze actually involves several kinds of information and learning—including visual information, spatial configuration, smells, and perhaps even sounds. Assuming this to be the case, learning and information processing must have been occurring simultaneously in different locations in the brain. Therefore, removing any particular portion of the cortex would still leave the other memory traces intact—and produce the same apparent deficit in performance regardless of which area of the cortex was removed.

In sum, it appears that memory is localized to specific areas, in the sense that a particular memory trace is related to a particular information processing system in the brain. But in a larger sense, memory traces are distributed throughout the brain, given that several brain processing systems are involved in any learning situation (Squire, 1987; Bear, Cooper, & Ebner, 1987; Cotman & Lynch, 1989; Prado-Alcala, 1995).

Other investigators are following different paths to learn about the biological bases of memory. For instance, recent work suggests that the hippocampus plays a central role in the consolidation of memories, permitting them to be stored in the cerebral cortex of the brain (Zola-Morgan & Squire, 1990, 1993; Gluck & Myers, 1997). Research with food-storing birds such as chickadees has shown a larger hippocampal formation when these birds are allowed to store and search for their food caches (Sherry, Jacobs and Gaulin, 1992; Sherry, 1997; Sherry and Healy, 1998).

Investigators using PET scans, which measure biochemical activity in the brain, have recently found that neuronal memory traces are highly specialized. For instance, subjects in one experiment were given a list of nouns to read aloud. After reading each

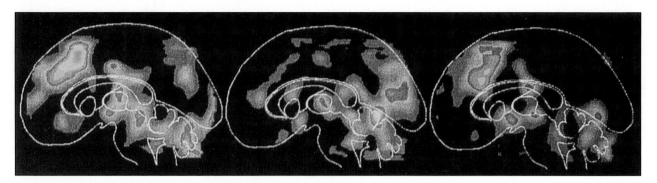

FIGURE 6-15 *PET scans of a subject in an experiment who was first asked to read a list of nouns and produce a related verb (left scan). When asked to repeatedly carry out the task with the same list of nouns, different areas of the brain became active (centre). However, when the subject was given a new list of nouns, the regions of the brain that were initially involved became reactivated (right). Source: Dr. Steven E. Peterson/Washington University.*

noun, they were asked to suggest a related verb. After reading the noun "dog," for example, they might have proposed the verb "bark."

Several distinct areas of the brain showed increased neural activity as subjects first did the task (see Figure 6-15). However, if they repeated the task with the same nouns several times, the activity in the brain shifted to another area. Most interestingly, if they were given a new list of nouns, the activity in the brain returned to the areas that were initially activated.

The results suggest that a particular part of the brain is involved in the production of words, but another part takes over when the process becomes routine—in other words, when memory comes into play. It also suggests that memory is distributed in the brain not just in terms of its content, but in terms of its function (Horgan, 1993; Corbetta et al., 1993; Petersen & Fiez, 1993).

It also appears that certain chemicals and neurotransmitters are linked to the formation, impairment, and improvement of memory. As we discuss in the Applying Psychology in the 21st Century box, such work suggests a futuristic scenario in which people routinely take certain drugs in order to improve their memory.

Memory Dysfunctions: Afflictions of Forgetting

To a casual observer, Harold appears to be a brilliant golfer. He seems to have learned the game perfectly; his shots are almost flawless.

Yet anyone accompanying him on the course is bound to notice some startling incongruities. Although he is immediately able to size up a situation and hit the ball exactly where it should go, he cannot remember where the ball has just landed. At the end of each hole, he forgets the score (Schacter, 1983; Blakeslee, 1984, p. C1).

Alzheimer's Disease

Harold's problem? He suffers from *Alzheimer's disease,* an illness that includes among its symptoms severe memory problems. In Canada, Alzheimer's disease affects one percent of people aged 65 to 74, seven percent of those aged 75 to 84, and 26 percent of those aged 85 and over (Canadian Study of Health and Aging Working Group, 1994).

In its initial stages, Alzheimer's symptoms appear as simple forgetfulness of things like appointments and birthdays. As the disease progresses, memory loss becomes more profound, and even the simplest tasks—such as how to dial a telephone—are forgotten. Ultimately, victims can forget their own names or family members' faces. In addition, physical deterioration sets in, and language abilities may be lost entirely.

Although the causes of Alzheimer's disease are not fully understood, recent evidence suggests that it may be linked to a specific inherited defect. The flaw leads to difficulties in the production of the protein beta amyloid, necessary for the maintenance of nerve cell connections. When the manufacture of beta amyloid goes awry, the result is the deterioration of nerve cells in the brain, which in turn produces the symptoms of Alzheimer's (Kitani,

Applying Psychology in the 21st Century

Are Memory Drugs on the Horizon?

Will our future trips down memory lane begin in the aisles of a drugstore? That strange possibility may become reality one day as researchers find growing evidence that certain drugs may help to improve the memory. This research is leading to the possibility that drugs may be designed to enhance desired memories or even, perhaps, to suppress unwanted ones, such as memories of traumatic events.

According to memory researcher James L. McGaugh, director of the Center for the Neurobiology of Learning and Memory at the University of California at Irvine, "the probability is high that there will be at least a moderately effective memory drug available in the not-too-distant future" (Kotulak, 1995, p. 1).

There are several types of memory-enhancing drugs now being developed. One, a drug called nimodipine, operates by aiding in the initial encoding of material. More specifically, the drug deals with a problem experienced by some older adults in which calcium molecules "leak" from individual neurons in the brain. This leakage interferes with the encoding of new material and subsequently results in less effective recall. Nimodipine reduces neural leakage, thereby boosting the efficiency of neurons in processing electrical charges. In turn, this greater efficiency permits new

material to be learned and later remembered more effectively.

The newest approach to memory enhancement involves increasing the efficiency of long-term potentiation, the process by which particular neural pathways become more readily excited as a memory is formed. Because certain drugs increase long-term potentiation, it seems reasonable that these drugs might be used to enhance memories. According to memory researcher Gary Lynch, "We're talking about a pill that you would take, and two minutes later and for the next several hours, information that you're trying to encode in your brain is going to be encoded better" (Kotulak, 1995, p. 16).

The initial aim of Lynch and colleagues is to provide more effective treatment for people suffering from memory problems brought about by illnesses such as Alzheimer's disease. To accomplish this, Lynch and colleagues have developed a drug called Ampalex, which is currently being studied. Initial results are encouraging. For instance, in one experiment, a group of volunteers in Europe were given doses of the drug. The participants in the study scored four times higher on a battery of memory tests than they did when not taking the drug. In fact, their performance rose to levels achieved by

people some thirty-five years younger (Service, 1994; Beardsley, 1997).

Other researchers are examining drugs that target other molecules in the brain. For instance, researcher Tim Tully and colleagues have found that a protein known as CREB has a marked effect on the ability of fruit flies to remember odors. By genetically altering a particular location in the fruit flies' brains, the researchers were able to affect the production of CREB and change the flies' ability to learn and remember. Tully suggests that drugs that affect the production of CREB may eventually be used not only to enhance memory, but to prevent recurring, intrusive, unpleasant memories that may follow upon a traumatic event. A person might even take such a drug *before* being exposed to a grim situation. For instance, rescue and recovery workers (such as those who searched for victims and debris from the Swissair Flight 111 disaster) might be given a drug before reaching the scene in order to reduce future emotion-laden, grisly memories (Connelly et al., 1996; Schacter, 1996; Beardsley, 1997).

Memory researchers are increasingly optimistic about the possibilities of developing drugs that affect how we remember. In fact, by the start of the twenty-first century, such drugs may be nothing short of memorable.

Some emergency workers continued to be plagued by grisly memories of the Swissair Flight 111 disaster long after the event had occurred. In the future, emergency workers may be able to take drugs before reaching the scene of an accident in order to prevent traumatic memories from developing.

Pathways Through Psychology

Holly Tuokko

Associate Director, Centre on Aging
Associate Professor, Department of
Psychology
University of Victoria, British
Columbia

Education: B.A., M.A., Lakehead
University; Ph.D., University of
Victoria

Home: Victoria

When I began university, I don't think there was such a thing as geriatric neuropsychology and yet somehow I ended up writing a textbook in this field, "An Assessment Guide to Geriatric Neuropsychology," in 1998. This book brings together neuropsychological information of special relevance for those working with older adults. It provides useful summary information on normative data, approaches to assessment, and diagnostic

Holly Tuokko

issues specific to geriatric populations, and fills a gap in the available resources for clinicians.

I first became interested in neuropsychology when I worked as a summer student at an institution for mentally handicapped persons after completing first year university. As part of the Orientation week, the various reasons why people may be mentally handicapped were discussed. This opened my eyes to the connection between the brain and behaviour. Throughout my University training, I continued to be fascinated by brain-behaviour connections and I sought instruction and jobs in settings providing care to persons with mental health problems. After completing my Master's degree in Clinical Psychology at Lakehead University, I worked on research projects with learning disabled children and discovered the growing field of neuropsychology.

After completing my Ph.D., I accepted a position at the Clinic for Alzheimer's Disease and Related Disorders, a research centre affiliated with the University of British Columbia. There I spent 10 years as a scientist/practitioner performing clinical neuropsychological assessment and conducting research on issues related to the identification and care of persons with dementia. This research has included test development and generation of normative data for older adults on a variety of neuropsychological measures. I moved to a mental health outreach team three years before returning to the University of Victoria with the Centre on Aging, an interdisciplinary, applied research centre.

At present, I am the Associate Director of the Centre on Aging at the University of Victoria. I teach courses in the Department of Psychology on adult development and aging, health psychology, and dysfunctional development and aging. My primary research area is mental health and aging. I am conducting rigorous, applied research around issues related to the mental health of older adults. The current focus of my research is the evolution of cognitive disorders in older adults and the impact of these disorders on functional competencies. Specific competencies of interest are driving, financial management, and the types of understanding necessary to consent to health care and consent to receive help or assistance.

I served as a steering committee member on a national epidemiological study examining issues related to the prevalence of cognitive impairment in older Canadians, the Canadian Study of Health and Aging (CSHA). My major contribution was to facilitate the development of a neuropsychological assessment as part of the clinical examination component of this study. This is the first study of its kind to examine neuropsychological functioning of older adults in detail. By being involved in the CSHA, I was able to advocate for and demonstrate the importance of neuropsychology in understanding the cognitive disorders affecting older adults. Neuropsychology has much to contribute to this field.

Source: Holly Tuokko, Ph.D. R.Psych.
University of Victoria <www.coag.uvic.ca/
TuokkoBioframes.htm>

Aoba, & Goto, 1996; Wurtman et al., 1996; Wisniewski & Wegiel, 1996; Selkoe, 1997). (For further discussion of Alzheimer's disease, see the Pathways Through Psychology box.)

Alzheimer's disease is just one of several memory dysfunctions that plague their victims. Another is *amnesia,* memory loss that occurs without other mental difficulties. For example, consider the case of KC who sustained a head injury during a motorcycle accident and suffered loss of memory for events that occurred prior to the accident (Tulving, Hayman and McDonald, 1991). This type of amnesia is known as *retrograde amnesia* and, in reality, is quite rare. There is usually a gradual reappearance of lost memory, although it may take as long as several years for a full restoration to occur. In certain cases, some memories are lost forever (Baddeley, Wilson, & Watts, 1995; Mayes & Downes, 1997; Parkin, 1997).

A second type of amnesia is exemplified by people who remember nothing of their current activities. In *anterograde amnesia,* loss of memory occurs for events following an injury. Information cannot be transferred from short-term to long-term memory, resulting in the inability to remember anything other than what was in long-term storage prior to the accident.

Amnesia is also displayed by people who suffer from *Korsakoff's syndrome,* a disease afflicting long-term alcoholics living under an impaired diet that produces a Vitamin B_1 (thiamine) deficiency. Although many of their intellectual abilities may be intact, Korsakoff's sufferers display a strange array of symptoms, including having hallucinations; repeating questions, even after being told the answer; and repeating the same story over and over again.

Fortunately, most of us have intact memories, and the occasional failures we do suffer may actually be preferable to having a perfect memory. Consider, for instance, the case of a man who had total recall. After reading passages of the *Divine Comedy* in Italian—a language he did not speak—he was able to repeat them from memory even some fifteen years later. He could memorize lists of fifty unrelated words and recall them at will more than a decade later. He could even repeat the same list of words backward, if asked (Luria, 1968).

Such a skill might at first seem to have few drawbacks, but it actually presented quite a problem. The man's memory became a jumble of lists of words, numbers, and names, and when he tried to relax, his mind was filled with images. Even reading was difficult, since every word evoked a flood of thoughts from the past that interfered with his ability to understand the meaning of what he was reading.

The Informed Consumer of Psychology

Improving Your Memory

Memory Aids

Apart from the advantages of forgetting, say, the details of a gruesome science fiction movie, most of us still would like to find ways to improve our memories. Given our understanding of memory, is it possible to find practical ways to increase our recall of information? Most definitely. Research has revealed a number of strategies that can be used to help us develop better memories (Hermann, 1991; Mastropieri & Scruggs, 1992; West, 1995; Herrmann et al., 1996; VanLehn, 1996). Among the best:

- *The keyword technique.* Suppose you are taking a class in a foreign language and need to learn long lists of vocabulary words. One way of easing this process is to use the *keyword technique,* in which a foreign word is paired with a common English word that has a similar *sound.* This English word is known as the keyword. For example, to learn the Spanish word for duck (*pato,* pronounced *pot-o*), you might choose the keyword "pot"; for the Spanish word for horse (*caballo,* pronounced *cob-eye-yo*), the keyword might be "eye."

  Once you have thought of a keyword, you form a mental image of it graphically "interacting" with the English translation of the word. For instance, you might envision a duck taking a bath in a pot to remember the word *pato,* or a horse with a large, bulging eye in the centre of its head to recall *caballo.* This technique has produced considerably superior results in learning foreign language vocabulary than more traditional techniques involving memorization of the words themselves (Pressley & Levin, 1983; Pressley, 1987; Moore & Surber, 1992; Elhelou, 1994; Gruneberg & Pascoe, 1996).

- *Method of loci.* If you have ever had to give a talk in class, you know the difficulty of keeping in mind all the points you want to make. One technique that works quite effectively was developed by the ancient Greeks. When Greek orators sought to memorize long speeches, they used the *method of loci* (*loci* is the Latin word for places) to organize their recollections of what they wanted to say. With this technique, each part of a speech is imagined as "residing" in a different location of a building.

  For instance, you might think of the preface of a talk as being in your house's entryway, the first major point as being in the living room, the next major point residing in the dining room, and so forth, until the end of the speech is reached in the back bedroom of the house.

This technique can easily be adapted to learning lists of words. Each word on the list is imagined as being located in a series of sequential locations. The method works best if you use the most outlandish images possible: If you wanted to use the features of your living room to remember a list of groceries, consisting of bananas, ketchup, and milk, for instance, you might picture a banana entwined in the leaves of your begonia, the ketchup spilled over the end table, and the milk spraying from the top of a table lamp. When you got to the supermarket, you could mentally "walk" through your living room, recalling the items easily.

- *The encoding specificity phenomenon.* Some research suggests that we remember information best in an environment that is the same as or similar to where we initially learned it—a phenomenon known as *encoding specificity* (Tulving & Thompson, 1973). You may do better on a test, then, if you study in the same classroom in which the test is going to be given. On the other hand, if you must take a test in a different room from the one in which you studied, don't despair: The features of the test itself, such as the wording of the test questions, are sometimes so powerful that they overwhelm the subtler cues relating to the original encoding of the material (Bjork & Richardson-Klarehn, 1989).

- *Organization of text material.* Most of life's more important recall tasks involve not lists of words but texts that you have read. How can you facilitate recall of such material? One proven technique for improving recall of written material is to organize the material in memory as it is being read for the first time. To do this, you should first identify any advance information you have about the structure and content of the material—scanning the table of contents, chapter outline, headings, and even the end-of-chapter summary—before reading a given chapter. Understanding the structure of the material will enable you to recall it better.

  Another technique is to ask yourself questions that integrate the material you have read, and then answer them. Asking questions will enable you to make connections and see relationships among the various facts, thereby promoting the processing of the material at a deeper level. As the levels-of-processing approach to memory (discussed earlier) suggests, creating deep connections will aid later recall (Royer & Feldman, 1984). For example, you might at this moment ask yourself, "What are the major techniques for remembering material in textbooks?" and then try to answer the question.

- *Organization of lecture notes.* "Less is more" is perhaps the best advice for taking lecture notes that aid in recall. Rather than trying to jot down every detail of a lecture, it is better to listen and think about the material, taking down the main points after you have considered them in a broader context. In effective note taking, thinking about the material initially is more important than writing it down. This is one reason that borrowing someone else's notes is a bad proposition, since you will have no framework in memory that you can use to understand them (Peper & Mayer, 1978).

- *Practice and rehearsal.* Although practice does not necessarily make perfect, it does help. By studying and rehearsing material past the point of initial mastery—a process called *overlearning*—people are able to show better long-term recall than if they stop practicing after their initial learning of the material.

  Eventually, of course, practice has little or no effect; you probably already know your address so well that no amount of additional practice will make you recall it any better than you already do. But it is safe to say that, given the volume of material covered in most courses, academic material is rarely so securely retained, and you would generally be wise to review material a few times even after you feel you have learned it, in order to reach a true level of overlearning.

  Research on the outcomes of elaborative rehearsal, discussed earlier in the chapter, also suggests the importance of asking and rehearsing the answers to questions in as active a manner as possible. In this way, the connections between the parts of the material are likely to become explicit, aiding in later recall by providing ample retrieval cues.

Finally, people who cram for tests should note that the best retention comes from practice that is distributed over many sessions, rather than left for one long session. Research clearly demonstrates that fatigue and other factors prevent long practice sessions from being as effective as distributed practice. ■

Recap, Review, and Rethink

Recap

- Decay and interference are the primary explanations for forgetting.

- There are two kinds of interference: proactive interference (when information learned earlier interferes with recall of newer information) and retroactive interference (when new information interferes with recall of information learned earlier).

- The major memory dysfunctions include Alzheimer's disease, retrograde amnesia, anterograde amnesia, and Korsakoff's syndrome.

- Specific techniques for increasing the recall of information include the keyword technique, the method of loci, the use of encoding specificity, the organization of information in textbooks, good note taking, and practice and rehearsal.

Review

1. After learning the history of the Roman Empire for a class two years ago, you now find yourself unable to recall what you learned. A friend tells you that nonuse had caused you to lose the information. What is the formal name for this process?

2. An _____ is an actual physical change in the brain brought about by learning.

3. Memory that is difficult to access because of the presence of other information illustrates what phenomenon?

4. _____ interference occurs when previous material is difficult to retrieve because of exposure to later material. _____ interference refers to the difficulty in retrieving later material due to the interference of previous material.

5. Match the following memory disorders with the correct information:
   1. Affects alcoholics; vitamin B_1 (thiamine) deficiency
   2. Memory loss occurring without other mental problems
   3. Beta amyloid defect; progressive forgetting and physical deterioration

   a. Alzheimer's disease
   b. Korsakoff's syndrome
   c. amnesia

Answers to Review Questions are on page 236.

Rethink

1. Does the phenomenon of interference help to explain the unreliability of autobiographical memory? Why or why not?

2. How might biopsychology, especially the knowledge gained by the "search for the engram," aid in the treatment of memory disorders such as amnesia?

3. Can you use memory-related concepts you have learned in this chapter to explain how the method of loci works to improve recall. Why does using outlandish images to link list items with sequential locations help? Can the method of loci be used repeatedly with the same locations, or are the associations between list items and locations permanent? Why?

looking
BACK

What is memory?

1. Memory is the process by which we encode, store, and retrieve information. There are three basic kinds of memory storage: sensory memory, short-term memory, and long-term memory.

Are there different kinds of memory?

2. Sensory memory (made up of memories corresponding to each of the sensory systems) is the first place where information is saved, although the memories are very brief.

For instance, iconic memory (made up of visual sensations) lasts less than a second, and echoic memory (corresponding to auditory sensations) lasts less than four seconds. Despite their brevity, sensory memories are very precise, storing almost an exact replica of each stimulus to which a person is exposed. Unless they are transferred to other types of memory, however, sensory memories appear to be lost.

3. Roughly seven (plus or minus two) chunks of information are capable of being transferred and held in short-term memory. A chunk is a meaningful bit of information,

ranging in size from a letter or a single digit to more complicated categorizations. Information in short-term memory is held from fifteen to twenty-five seconds and, if not transferred to long-term memory, is lost primarily through interference, as well as through decay. Interference is the loss of material through the displacement of older material by newer information, whereas decay is the loss of information through its nonuse.

4. Some theorists suggest that short-term memory is better thought of as a three-part working memory. In this view, there is a central executive, which coordinates the material to focus on during reasoning and decision making, and two subcomponents: the visuospatial sketch pad and the phonological loop.

5. Memories are transferred into long-term storage through rehearsal. The most effective type is elaborative rehearsal, in which the material to be remembered is organized and expanded. Formal techniques for organizing material are called mnemonics.

6. If memories are transferred into long-term memory, they become relatively permanent. Long-term memory is composed of components or modules, each of which is related to separate memory systems in the brain. For instance, we can distinguish between declarative memory (memory for factual information: names, faces, dates, events in our lives, and the like) and procedural memory (memory for skills and habits such as riding a bike or hitting a baseball). Declarative memory is further divided into episodic memory (memories relating to our personal lives) and semantic memory (organized knowledge and facts).

7. Explicit memory refers to intentional or conscious recollection of information. In contrast, implicit memory refers to memories of which people are not consciously aware, but which can improve subsequent performance and behaviour. Some researchers suggest that two distinct memory systems exist, one for implicit and the other for explicit memory. In contrast, other researchers have proposed that the two kinds of memory systems differ simply in the way that information is processed.

8. The levels-of-processing approach to memory suggests that the way in which information is initially perceived and analyzed determines the success with which the information is recalled. The deeper the initial processing, the greater the recall of the material.

What causes difficulties and failures in remembering?

9. The tip-of-the-tongue phenomenon refers to the experience of trying in vain to remember information that one is certain one knows. A major strategy for successfully recalling information is to use retrieval cues, stimuli that permit a search through long-term memory.

10. Flashbulb memories are memories centered around a specific, important event. These memories are so clear that they appear to represent a "snapshot" of the event. Flashbulb memories illustrate the broader point that the more distinctive a memory, the more easily it can be retrieved.

11. Memory is a constructive process in which we relate memories to the meaning, guesses, and expectations that we give to the events the memory represents. Specific information is recalled in terms of schemas, or general themes that contain relatively little detail.

12. Eyewitnesses of crimes are apt to make substantial errors when they try to recall details of criminal activity. The problem of memory reliability becomes even more acute when the witnesses are children. Reliability is also problematic in cases of repressed memories, recollections of events that initially are so shocking that the mind responds by pushing them into the unconscious.

13. Autobiographical memory, which refers to memories of circumstances and episodes from our own lives, is influenced by constructive processes. For example, people forget information about their past that is incompatible with the way they currently see themselves. In addition, although the basic structure of memory is similar across cultures, the way in which memory is acquired, rehearsed, and retrieved may differ from one culture to another.

Why do we forget information?

14. Even with the use of retrieval cues, some information appears irretrievable, owing to decay or interference. Interference seems to be the major cause of forgetting. There are two sorts of interference: proactive interference (when information learned earlier interferes with the recall of material to which one is exposed later) and retroactive interference (when new information interferes with the recall of information to which one was exposed earlier).

What are the biological bases of memory?

15. Current research on the biology underlying memory is concerned with the site of the engram, or memory trace. Certain drugs impair or aid memory in animals, suggesting that drugs may be used in the future to improve the memory of people.

What are the major memory impairments?

16. There are several memory dysfunctions. Among them are Alzheimer's disease, which leads to a progressive loss of memory, and amnesia, a memory loss that occurs without other mental difficulties and that can take two forms. In retrograde amnesia, there is loss of memory for occurrences prior to some event; in anterograde amnesia, there is loss of memory for events following an injury. Korsakoff's syndrome is a disease that afflicts long-term alcoholics, resulting in memory impairment.

17. Psychologists have developed a number of specific techniques to improve memory. These include using the keyword technique to memorize foreign vocabulary; applying the method of loci to learn lists; using the encoding specificity phenomenon; organizing text material and lecture notes; and practicing enough so that overlearning—studying and rehearsing past the point of initial mastery—occurs.

Answers to Review Questions:

1. decay   2. engram (or memory trace)   3. interference   4. Retroactive; Proactive   5. 1-b; 2-c; 3-a

Key Terms and Concepts

memory (p. 205)
sensory memory (p. 206)
short-term memory (p. 206)
long-term memory (p. 206)
iconic memory (p. 206)
echoic memory (p. 206)
chunk (p. 208)
rehearsal (p. 209)
working memory (p. 210)

declarative memory (p. 212)
procedural memory (p. 212)
semantic memory (p. 212)
episodic memory (p. 212)
associative models (p. 213)
priming (p. 213)
explicit memory (p. 214)
implicit memory (p. 214)
levels-of-processing theory (p. 215)

tip-of-the-tongue phenomenon (p. 217)
flashbulb memories (p. 218)
constructive processes (p. 219)
schemas (p. 219)
autobiographical memories (p. 224)
decay (p. 226)
memory trace or engram (p. 226)
interference (p. 226)

Epilogue

In this chapter we have taken a look at memory. We noted that memory comprises the processes of encoding, storage, and retrieval, and we saw that memory can be regarded as having different components. We also encountered several phenomena relating to memory, including the tip-of-the-tongue phenomenon and flashbulb memories. Above all we observed that memory is a constructive process by which interpretations, expectations, and guesses contribute to the nature of our memories.

Before we move on to the next chapter, return briefly to the prologue of this chapter, in which we encountered Krickitt Carpenter and her lost memories of courtship and marriage. Consider the following questions in light of what you know about memory.

1. Krickitt Carpenter's memory loss is called "retrograde amnesia." What does this mean?

2. What would have been the effects on Carpenter's life if her accident had caused anterograde amnesia?

3. What are the chances that Carpenter will recover her lost memories of the 18-month period preceding the accident? How might this happen? Do you think the process can be accelerated by associative techniques?

4. If Krickitt Carpenter suddenly announces that she has recovered her memory, how will doctors know that she is really recalling the past rather than simply accepting as her own memories the stories that others have told her?

5. How might investigators examine Carpenter during her recovery to answer questions about the biological bases of memory? Assuming Carpenter gave her consent to PET scans and other means of looking inside her cerebral cortex, what sorts of questions might be explored?

The ingenuity of inventions such as this bipedal robot (shown with MIT inventor Gil Pratt) illustrates the issues studied by cognitive psychologists.

Prologue

One Man's Mousetraps

His friend was so short that when she was seated at Washington's Kennedy Center her feet barely reached the floor. Could he, she asked, devise some sort of stool on which to rest her feet? One day while driving to work it came to him. You can't walk into a theatre with a stool under your arm. But what about a book? What if an ordinary hard-back book, not much larger than a theatre program, opened up to let two hinged metal flaps swing out and, suitably restrained, form the legs of a stool?

So he took the bound proceedings from a scientific symposium, glued the pages together, hollowed out a section in the middle, cut some sheet aluminum to size, and drilled and screwed the contraption together.

It worked. She was delighted. And so was he.

Years later, before an audience gathered in the elegant reception room of the National Museum of American History in Washington, D.C., Jacob Rabinow showed off the original model, repeatedly metamorphosing it from book to stool and back again, to smiles and nods of appreciation. It was the 150th anniversary of the founding of the modern patent system and this short, stocky, balding inventor, the holder of more than two hundred patents, had been invited to talk about "Inventing for Fun and Occasional Profit. . . ."

Brimming with unapologetic self-confidence, Rabinow told about a method he once cooked up to determine whether frozen foods have remained safely frozen; about his scheme for exploiting natural buoyancy to sculpt monumentally scaled statues underwater; about clutches without clutch plates, mechanical typewriters that justify both margins, and watches that know they're running slow and speed up accordingly. "Invention is an art form," he declared, "and it's no more logical than composing music or writing poetry" (Kanigel, 1987, p. 48).

Is Jacob Rabinow correct in his contention that his inventiveness and creativity amount to an art form, which is not open to scientific analysis? Psychologists would disagree. To them, creativity and inventiveness are topics that not only can be studied scientifically, but involve a number of issues central to understanding behaviour: How do people use and retrieve information to devise innovative solutions to problems? How is such knowledge transformed, elaborated upon, and utilized? More basically, how do people think about, understand, and, through language, describe the world?

In this chapter we consider **cognitive psychology,** the branch of psychology that focuses on the study of cognition. **Cognition** encompasses the higher mental processes of humans, including how people know and understand the world, process information, make judgments and decisions, and describe their knowledge and understanding to others. The realm of cognitive psychology is broad, then, and includes the research on memory examined in the previous chapter and much of the work on intelligence that we discuss in the next chapter (Massaro, 1991; Barsalou, 1992; BBSTF, 1996; Thagard, 1996; Benjafield, 1997).

In this chapter we concentrate on three broad topics that are central to the field of cognitive psychology: thinking and reasoning, problem solving and creativity, and language. We first consider concepts, the building blocks of thinking, and various kinds of reasoning. Then we examine different strategies for approaching problems, means of generating solutions, and ways of making judgments about the usefulness and accuracy of solutions. Finally, in our focus on language, we consider how language is developed and acquired, its basic characteristics, and the relationship between language and thought.

cognitive psychology: The branch of psychology that focuses on the study of cognition

cognition: The higher mental processes of humans, including how people know and understand the world, process information, make judgments and decisions, and describe their knowledge and understanding to others

THINKING AND REASONING

Thinking

What is thinking? The mere ability to pose such a question illustrates the distinctive nature of the human ability to think. No other species can contemplate, analyze, recollect, or plan in the way that humans can. Yet knowing that we think and understanding what thinking is are two different things. Philosophers, for example, have argued for generations about the meaning of thinking, with some placing it at the core of human beings' understanding of their own existence.

To psychologists, **thinking** is the manipulation of mental representations of information. The representation may be a word, a visual image, a sound, or data in any other modality. What thinking does is to transform the representation of information into a new and different form for the purpose of answering a question, solving a problem, or reaching a goal.

Although a clear sense of what specifically occurs when we think remains elusive, the nature of the fundamental elements involved in thinking is becoming increasingly well understood. We begin by considering our use of mental images and concepts, the building blocks of thought.

► **How do we think?**

► **What processes underlie reasoning and decision making?**

thinking: The manipulation of mental representations of information

Mental Images: Examining the Mind's Eye

Think of your best friend. Chances are that you "see" some kind of visual image when asked to think of her or him, or any other person or object, for that matter. To some cognitive psychologists, such mental images represent a major part of thinking.

Mental images are representations in the mind that resemble the object or event being represented. They are not just visual representations; our ability to "hear" a tune in our head also relies on a mental image. In fact, it may be that every sensory modality produces corresponding mental images (Paivio, 1971, 1975; Kosslyn, 1981; Kosslyn et al., 1990; Kosslyn & Shin, 1994).

mental images: Representations in the mind that resemble the object or event being represented

FIGURE 7-1 *Try to mentally rotate one of each pair of patterns to see if it is the same as the other member of the pair. It's likely that the further you have to mentally rotate a pattern, the longer it will take to decide if the patterns match one another. Source: Based on Shepard & Metzler, 1971.*

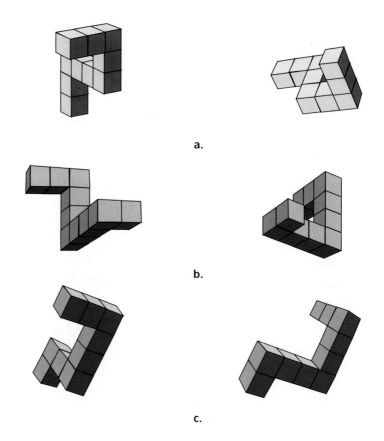

a.

b.

c.

Imagery

Research has found that our representations of mental images have many of the properties of the actual perception of objects being represented. For example, it takes more time to scan the mental visual representations of large objects than small ones, just as it takes more time to scan an actual large object than an actual small one. Similarly, we are able to manipulate and rotate mental visual images of objects, just as we are able to manipulate and rotate them in the real world (Kosslyn, 1981; Cooper & Shepard, 1984; Denis & Greenbaum, 1991; Brandimonte, Hitch, & Bishop, 1992; Sharps, Price, & Williams, 1994; see Figure 7-1).

The production of mental images has been heralded by some as a way to improve performance of various skills. For instance, many athletes use mental imagery in training. Basketball players may try to produce vivid and detailed images of the court, the basket, the ball, and the noisy crowd. They may visualize themselves taking a foul shot, watching the ball, and hearing the swishing sound as it goes through the net (Issac & Marks, 1994). Systematic evaluations of the use of mental imagery by athletes suggest that it is useful in providing a means for improving performance in the sports arena (Druckman & Bjork, 1991).

Mental imagery may produce improvements in other types of skills as well. For example, from the realm of music, researcher Alvaro Pascual-Leone taught a group of people to play a five-finger exercise on the piano. One group practiced every day for five days, while a control group played without any training, just hitting the keys at random. Finally, the members of a third group were taught the exercise but were not allowed to actually try it out on the piano. Instead, they rehearsed it mentally, sitting at the piano and looking at the keys, but not actually touching them.

When brain scans of people in the groups were compared, researchers found a distinct difference between those who manually practiced the exercise and those who just randomly hit keys. However, the most surprising finding came from the group that mentally rehearsed: Their brain scans were virtually identical to those of the people who had actually practiced the exercise manually (see Figure 7-2). Apparently, the same network of brain cells involved in carrying out the task was involved in mentally rehearsing it (Chase, 1993; Pascual-Leone et al., 1995).

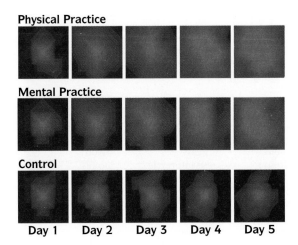

Physical Practice

Mental Practice

Control

Day 1   Day 2   Day 3   Day 4   Day 5

FIGURE 7-2 *Compared with the brain scans of people who actually practiced a piano finger exercise, the brain scans of those who only used mental rehearsal but did not touch the piano were nearly identical. The results of the experiment clearly show the value of mental imagery. Source: Pascual-Leone et al., 1995.*

Such research suggests that children whose parents nag them about practicing an instrument, a dance routine, or some other skill that requires practice can now employ a new excuse: They *are* practicing—mentally.

Concepts: Categorizing the World

If someone asked you what was in your kitchen cabinet, you might answer with a detailed list of every item ("a jar of Skippy peanut butter, three boxes of macaroni and cheese, six unmatched dinner plates," and so forth). More likely, though, you would respond by using some broader categories, such as "food" and "dishes."

The use of such categories reflects the operation of concepts. **Concepts** are categorizations of objects, events, or people that share common properties. By employing concepts, we are able to organize complex phenomena into simpler, and therefore more easily usable, cognitive categories.

Concepts allow us to classify newly encountered objects on the basis of our past experience. For example, we can surmise that a small rectangular box with buttons that is on a chair near a television is probably a remote control—even if we have never encountered that specific brand before. And we may learn to categorize new instances implicitly or explicitly (Brooks, 1978). Ultimately, concepts influence behaviour; we would assume, for instance, that it might be appropriate to pet an animal after determining that it is a dog, while we would behave differently after classifying the animal as a wolf.

When cognitive psychologists first studied concepts, they focused on those that were clearly defined by a unique set of properties or features. For example, an equilateral triangle is a shape that has three sides of equal length. If an object has these characteristics, it is an equilateral triangle; if it does not, then it is not an equilateral triangle.

Other concepts—often those with the most relevance to our everyday lives—are more ambiguous and difficult to define. For instance, concepts such as "table" or "bird" share a set of general, relatively loose characteristic features, rather than unique, clearly defined properties that distinguish an example of the concept from a nonexample. When we consider these more ambiguous concepts, we usually think in terms of examples called prototypes. **Prototypes** are typical, highly representative examples of a concept. For instance, a prototype of the concept "bird" is a robin; a prototype of "table" is a coffee table. Relatively high agreement exists among people as to which examples of a concept are prototypes, as well as which examples are not. For instance, most people consider cars and trucks good examples of vehicles, whereas elevators and wheelbarrows are not viewed as very good examples. Consequently, cars and trucks are prototypes of the concept of vehicle (see Table 7-1).

Concepts enable us to think about and understand more readily the complex world in which we live. For example, the judgments we make about the reasons for

concepts: Categorizations of objects, events, or people that share common properties

prototypes: Typical, highly representative examples of a concept

Table 7-1	Prototypes of Common Concepts			

	Concept Category			
Ranking	Furniture	Vehicle	Weapon	Vegetable
1	Chair	Car	Gun	Peas
2	Sofa	Truck	Knife	Carrots
3	Table	Bus	Sword	String Beans
4	Dresser	Motorcycle	Bomb	Spinach
5	Desk	Train	Hand grenade	Broccoli
6	Bed	Trolley car	Spear	Asparagus
7	Bookcase	Bicycle	Cannon	Corn
8	Footstool	Airplane	Bow and arrow	Cauliflower
9	Lamp	Boat	Club	Brussel sprouts
10	Piano	Tractor	Tank	Lettuce
11	Cushion	Cart	Tear gas	Beets
12	Mirror	Wheelchair	Whip	Tomato
13	Rug	Tank	Ice pick	Lima beans
14	Radio	Raft	Fists	Eggplant
15	Stove	Sled	Rocket	Onion

Prototypes are listed in order of most to least typical. Source: Rosch & Mervis, 1975.

The categorization of objects is an important function of concepts.

other people's behaviour are based on the ways in which we classify their behaviour. Hence, our evaluations of a person who washes her hands twenty times a day could vary, depending on whether we place her behaviour within the conceptual framework of health care worker or mental patient. Similarly, physicians make diagnoses by drawing upon concepts and prototypes of symptoms that they learned about in medical school. Finally, concepts and prototypes facilitate our efforts to draw suitable conclusions through the cognitive process we turn to next: reasoning.

Reasoning: Making Up Your Mind

Professors deciding when students' assignments are due.

An employer determining whom to hire out of a pool of job applicants.

The Prime Minister concluding it is necessary to send troops to a foreign nation.

The common thread among these three circumstances: Each requires reasoning, the process by which information is used to draw conclusions and make decisions.

Although philosophers and logicians have considered the foundations of reasoning for centuries, it is only relatively recently that cognitive psychologists have begun to investigate how people reason and make decisions. Together, their efforts have contributed to our understanding of formal reasoning processes as well as the mental shortcuts we routinely use—shortcuts which may sometimes lead our reasoning capabilities astray (Evans, Newstead, & Byrne, 1994; Johnson-Laird & Shafir, 1994; Corrigan, 1996).

Deductive and Inductive Reasoning

One approach taken by cognitive psychologists in their efforts to understand decision making is to examine how people use formal reasoning procedures. Two major forms exist: deductive reasoning and inductive reasoning (Rips, 1990, 1994a,b 1995). Like other types of complex mental operations, inductive and deductive reasoning are performed by the frontal lobes (Goel et al., 1997).

In **deductive reasoning,** we draw inferences and implications from a set of assumptions and apply them to specific cases (Thompson, 1996). Deductive reasoning

deductive reasoning: A form of reasoning in which a person draws inferences and implications from a set of assumptions and applies them to specific cases

begins with a series of assumptions or premises that are thought to be true, and then derives the implications of these assumptions. If the assumptions are true, then the conclusions must also be true.

A major technique for studying deductive reasoning involves asking people to evaluate syllogisms. A *syllogism* presents a series of two assumptions, or *premises,* that are used to derive a conclusion. By definition, the conclusion must be true if the assumptions or premises are true. For example, consider the following syllogism:

All men are mortal.	[*premise*]
Socrates is a man.	[*premise*]
Therefore, Socrates is mortal.	[*conclusion*]

In this case both premises are true, and so, then, is the conclusion. More abstractly, we can state the syllogism as the following:

All As are B.	[*premise*]
C is an A.	[*premise*]
Therefore, C is a B.	[*conclusion*]

Reasoning

On the other hand, if either or both of the premises in a syllogism are not accurate, then there is insufficient support for the accuracy of the conclusion. Suppose, for example, you saw the following syllogism:

All men are mortal.	[*premise*]
Socrates is a man.	[*premise*]
Therefore, all men are Socrates.	[*conclusion*]

Obviously, such a conclusion makes no sense. We can more easily see why it's unreasonable by restating the syllogism in the abstract, and coming up with an obviously false conclusion:

All As are B.	[*premise*]
C is an A.	[*premise*]
Therefore, all As are C.	[*conclusion*]

The conceptual complement of deductive reasoning is inductive reasoning. In **inductive reasoning,** we infer a general rule from specific cases (Bisanz, Bisanz and Korpan, 1994). Using our observations, knowledge, experiences, and beliefs about the world, we develop a summary conclusion. (You can recall the distinction between deductive and inductive reasoning in this way: In *de*ductive reasoning, the conclusion is *de*rived through the use of general rules, whereas in *in*ductive reasoning, a conclusion is *in*ferred from specific examples.)

Sherlock Holmes used inductive reasoning in his quest to solve mysteries. By amassing clues, he was ultimately able to determine the identity of the criminal. Similarly, we all use inductive reasoning, although typically in more ordinary situations. For instance, if the person in the apartment below you constantly plays Spice Girl's music, you may begin to form an impression of what that individual is like, based on the sample of evidence available to you. Like Sherlock Holmes, you use pieces of evidence to draw a general conclusion.

The limitation of inductive reasoning is that conclusions may be biased if insufficient or invalid evidence is used. Psychologists know this well: The various scientific methods that they may employ in the collection of data to support their hypotheses are prone to several sorts of biases, such as using an inappropriate sample of subjects (see Chapter 1). Similarly, you may fail to draw appropriate conclusions about your neighbor if your impression is based only on the music he or she plays and not on a broader sample of behaviour.

inductive reasoning: A reasoning process whereby a general rule is inferred from specific cases, using observation, knowledge, experience, and beliefs

Applying Psychology in the 21st Century

Can Machines Think?

It may not have ranked as a "defeat for humanity," as one commentator billed it, but ranking world chess champion Gary Kasparov's loss to Deep Blue, an IBM computer, certainly did change the way people viewed the capabilities of computers.

The match was lost when Kasparov blundered in the sixth and final game. Until then, the match had been an even draw. But less than two dozen moves into the last game, Kasparov resigned, realizing his position was hopeless.

However, Kasparov was not ready to turn in his world championship. Although after an early match he had noted, "Suddenly [Deep Blue] played like a god for one moment," he was less conciliatory later. After his loss in the final match, he said, "I think the competition has just started. This is just the beginning." (IBM, 1997; S. Levy, 1997).

Are we facing an age in which machines not only can beat us at chess, but can

claim the ability to think in a manner similar to humans? At the moment, no one can give an accurate response. Part of the difficulty in answering the question is that thinking involves not just the brute force of carrying out a series of mathematical calculations, but a complex web of issues relating to the nature of consciousness, the mind, and the essence of humankind (Chalmers, 1996).

Deep Blue was able to give Kasparov a run for his money because of its ability

Despite Gary Kasporov's chess match loss to IBM's "Deep Blue," no machine has demonstrated the ability to surpass human capabilities of thought.

Algorithms and Heuristics

algorithm: A rule which, if followed, guarantees a solution to a problem

When faced with a decision, we often turn to various kinds of mental shortcuts, known as algorithms and heuristics, to help us. An **algorithm** is a rule which, if followed, guarantees a solution to a problem. We can use an algorithm even if we cannot understand why it works. For example, you may know that the length of the third side of a right triangle can be found using the formula $a^2 + b^2 = c^2$. You may not have the foggiest notion of the mathematical principles behind the formula, but this algorithm is always accurate and therefore provides a solution to a particular problem.

heuristic: A rule of thumb or mental shortcut that may lead to a solution

For many problems and decisions, however, no algorithm is available. In those instances, we may be able to use heuristics to help us. A **heuristic** is a rule of thumb or mental shortcut that may lead to a solution. Heuristics enhance the likelihood of success in coming to a solution but, unlike algorithms, they cannot ensure it. For example, some tic-tac-toe players follow the heuristic of placing an "X" in the center of the squares at the start of the game. This tactic doesn't guarantee that they will win, but it does increase their chances of success. Similarly, some students follow the heuristic of preparing for a test by ignoring the assigned textbook reading and only studying their lecture notes—a strategy that may or may not pay off (Nisbett et al., 1993).

to consider as many as 200 million possible chess positions a second. In and of itself, such sheer calculating speed does not constitute thinking. On the other hand, Herbert Simon, a cognitive psychologist at Carnegie Mellon University and a Nobel Prize winner, argues that the computer did show rudiments of humanlike thinking because of its *selectivity,* its knowledge of where to look—and where not to look—for an answer to a problem. Simon suggests that Deep Blue's capacity to evaluate potential moves and to ignore unimportant possibilities gives it thinking ability (Webber, 1996; Wright, 1996).

Others disagree. For instance, some critics suggest that Deep Blue's ability to consider billions of moves is qualitatively no different from what a simple calculator can do. Perhaps Deep Blue can do more calculations than a pocket calculator, but neither machine is capable of worrying about what comes next, strategizing about how to take account of an opponent's emotions, or dreaming about what one might do with the prize money for winning the tournament. In the view of critics, because such feelings and expectations are not part of the abilities of the computer, it is not engaged in true thinking (Webber, 1996).

Obviously, many of the questions surrounding the ability of computers to think are more philosophical than psychological and are not readily answered. Still, it is clear that computers are becoming increasingly sophisticated, ever more closely approximating human thought processes. For example, psychologists Jack Gelfand and Susan Epstein are developing a computer that can demonstrate expertise in a variety of tasks, rather than being a master at only a single task, such as chess. To do so, they are seeking to design a machine that can learn to play games using experience, memory, and heuristics. The computer also has a visual recognition component, permitting it to perceive patterns in board games. The ability to "see" patterns on the board permits the computer to draw conclusions about whether a specific pattern of game pieces is more or less likely to produce success (Epstein, 1995; Azar, 1997).

One of the computer's programs, called Hoyle, is designed to become an expert game-player. Starting off simply, it plays as a novice would, practicing with "expert" computers designed to play just one game. For instance, it might initially play tic-tac-toe. As it gains experience, it learns strategies, balancing and weighing the different strategies to see which will be most successful. If a strategy is particularly effective, the computer increases its weight, so that strategy counts more in the future; if a strategy is not very useful, its weight decreases. Then, as Hoyle moves on to other games, it can call upon the strategies that applied to earlier games and reuse and adapt them (Epstein, 1995).

Hoyle has so far mastered almost twenty different board games. Because, like humans, it learns some games more quickly than others, it appears to be employing strategies effectively to help it learn. Furthermore, research on the ways in which children learn games suggests that they and Hoyle use similar strategies (Rattermann, 1992).

Is Hoyle thinking like a human? For the moment, the question remains unanswerable. Machines like Hoyle and Deep Blue are clearly making strides toward imitating the moves of expert game players. In fact, it is possible that one day the world chess champion will be a machine. But even if that forecast comes true, the real champions will remain the people who program the computers—the humans behind the machines. Such feats represent, without question, real thinking.

Although heuristics often help people solve problems and make decisions, certain kinds of heuristics may backfire. For example, we sometimes use the *representativeness heuristic,* a rule we apply when we judge people by the degree to which they represent a certain category or group of people. Suppose, for instance, you are the owner of a fast-food store that has been robbed many times by teenagers. The representativeness heuristic would lead you to raise your guard each time someone of this age group enters your store (even though, statistically, it is unlikely that any given teenager will rob the store).

The *availability heuristic* involves judging the probability of an event by how easily the event can be recalled from memory (Tversky & Kahneman, 1974, 1990). According to this heuristic, we assume that events we remember easily are likely to have occurred more frequently in the past than those that are harder to remember. Furthermore, we assume that the same sort of event is more likely to occur in the future. For example, we are more apt to worry about being murdered than dying of diabetes, despite the fact that it is twice as likely that we will die of the disease. We err because of the ease with which we remember dramatic, highly publicized events like murder; this leads us to overestimate the likelihood of their occurrence.

Heuristics

Similarly, many people are more afraid of dying in a plane crash than in an auto accident—despite statistics clearly showing that airplane travel is much safer than auto travel. The reason is that plane crashes receive far more publicity than car crashes, and are therefore more easily remembered. It is the availability heuristic that leads people to conclude that they are in greater jeopardy in an airplane than in a car (Slovic, Fischhoff, & Lichtenstein, 1976; Schwarz et al., 1991).

Are algorithms and heuristics confined to human thinking, or can computers be programmed to use them? As we discussed in the Applying Psychology in the 21st Century box, new research suggests that a future in which machines think is not altogether far-fetched. At the same time, such work raises some fundamental questions about the nature of thought and the mind.

Recap, Review, and Rethink

Recap

- Cognitive psychologists specialize in the study of the higher mental processes of humans, including problem solving, knowing, reasoning, judging, and decision making.

- Thinking is the manipulation of mental representations of information.

- Mental images are representations in the mind that resemble the object or event being represented.

- Concepts are categorizations of objects, events, or people that share common properties.

- In deductive reasoning, we draw inferences and implications from a set of assumptions and apply them to specific cases; in inductive reasoning, we infer a general rule from specific cases.

- When making decisions, people frequently use algorithms (sets of rules that, if followed, guarantee that a solution will be reached) and heuristics (rules of thumb that may lead to a solution).

Review

1. _____ _____ are representations in the mind that resemble the object or event being represented.

2. _____ are categorizations of objects that share common properties.

3. When you think of the term "chair," you immediately think of a comfortable easy chair. A chair of this type could be thought of as a _____ of the category "chair."

4. Match the type of reasoning with its definition:
   1. deductive reasoning
   2. inductive reasoning

   a. deriving the conclusion from a set of premises
   b. inferring a general rule from specific cases

5. When you ask your friend how best to study for your psychology final, he tells you "I've always found it best to skim over the notes once, then read the book, then go over the notes again." What decision-making tool might this example represent?

6. The _____ heuristic is used when one judges the likelihood of an event by the ease with which it is retrieved from memory.

Answers to Review Questions are on page 250.

Rethink

1. In what ways is visualizing hitting a home run different from daydreaming that you are hitting a home run? Which is likely to produce better results? Why?

2. How might the representativeness heuristic and the availability heuristic both contribute to prejudices based on race, age, and gender? Can awareness of these heuristics prevent this from happening?

3. What knowledge of algorithms and heuristics would an expert computer programmer bring to the task of designing a robot that can "learn" (through observation) to play the perfect game of chess and never lose? What problems might the programmer encounter?

PROBLEM SOLVING

▶ **How do people approach and solve problems?**

▶ **What are the major obstacles to problem solving?**

According to an old legend, a group of monks in Vietnam devote much of their time to the effort of solving a problem called the Tower of Hanoi puzzle. The monks believe that, if they succeed, the world as we know it will come to an end (Raphael, 1976). (Should you prefer that the world remain in its present state, there's no need for immediate concern: According to one estimate, the puzzle is so complex that it will take about a trillion years to reach a solution.)

In a simpler version of the puzzle, illustrated in Figure 7-3, three disks are placed on three posts in the order shown. The goal of the puzzle is to move all three disks to the third post, arranged in the same order, using as few moves as possible. But

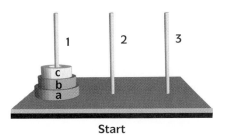 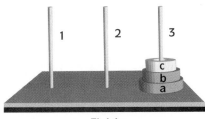

Start   Finish

FIGURE 7-3 *The goal of the Tower of Hanoi puzzle is to move all three disks from the first post to the last and still preserve the orginal order of the disks, using the least number of moves possible while following the rules that only one disk at a time can be moved and no disk can cover a smaller one during a move. Try it yourself before you look at the solution, which is listed according to the sequence of moves. (Solution: Move C to 3, B to 2, C to 2, A to 3, C to 1, B to 3, and C to 3.)*

there are two restrictions: Only one disk can be moved at a time, and no disk can ever cover a smaller one during a move.

Why are cognitive psychologists interested in the Tower of Hanoi problem? The answer is that the way people go about solving this puzzle and simpler ones like it helps illuminate the processes by which people solve complex problems that they encounter in school and at work. For example, psychologists have found that problem solving typically involves three major steps: preparation for the creation of solutions, production of solutions, and evaluation of solutions that have been generated (Sternberg & Frensch, 1991).

Preparation: Understanding and Diagnosing Problems

When approaching a problem like the Tower of Hanoi, most people begin by trying to ensure that they thoroughly understand the problem. If the problem is a novel one, they are likely to pay particular attention to any restrictions placed on coming up with a solution as well as the initial status of the components of the problem. If, on the other hand, the problem is a familiar one, they are apt to spend considerably less time in this stage.

Problems vary from well-defined to ill-defined (Reitman, 1965; Arlin, 1989). In a *well-defined problem*—such as a mathematical equation or the solution to a jigsaw puzzle—both the nature of the problem itself and the information needed to solve it are available and clear. Thus, straightforward judgments can be made about whether a potential solution is appropriate. With an *ill-defined problem*, such as how to increase morale on an assembly line or bring peace to the Middle East, not only may the specific nature of the problem be unclear, but the information required to solve the problem may be even less obvious.

For example, consider the following problem, first devised by Karl Duncker (1945):

> Suppose you are a doctor faced with a patient who has a malignant tumor in his stomach. To operate on the patient is impossible, but unless the tumor is destroyed, the patient will die. A kind of ray, at a sufficiently high intensity, can destroy the tumor. Unfortunately, at this intensity the healthy tissue that the rays pass through on the way to the tumor will also be destroyed. At lower intensities the rays are harmless to healthy tissue but will not affect the tumor, either. How can the rays be used to destroy the tumor without injuring the healthy tissue? (Holyoak, 1990, p. 134.)

Most people have a great deal of difficulty in thinking of even one solution to this problem. The major barrier is that the ill-defined nature of the problem, which involves some vague sort of "rays," doesn't suggest any immediate solutions. However, there is an ingenious solution to the problem: aiming weak rays at the tumor from several different entry points (see Figure 7-4). In this way, no one portion of healthy tissue is damaged, while the tumor receives a full dosage.

Kinds of Problems

Problems typically fall into one of the three categories exemplified in Figure 7-5: arrangement, inducing structure, and transformation (Greeno, 1978; Spitz, 1987). Solving each type requires somewhat different kinds of psychological skills and knowledge.

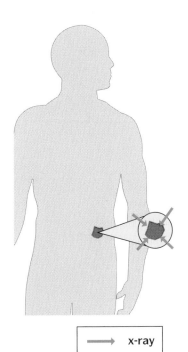

x-ray

FIGURE 7-4 *The solution to the problem of how to direct intense rays at a tumor without the rays damaging healthy tissue: Aiming several lower-intensity rays at the tumor from different positions. In this way, no one portion of healthy tissue is damaged, while the tumor receives a full dosage. Source: Duncker, 1945).*

FIGURE 7-5 *The major categories of problems: (a) arrangement, (b) inducing structure, and (c) transformation. Source: Bourne et al., 1986; hobbit problem: Solso, 1991, p. 448; solutions appear on page 252.*

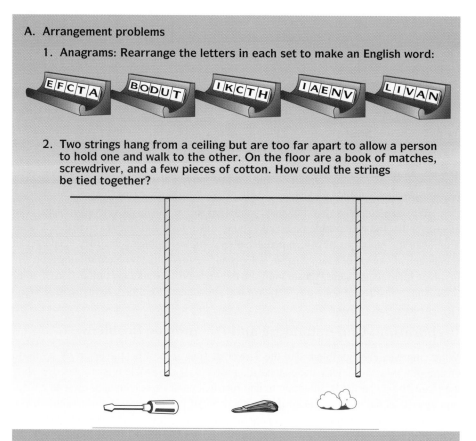

A. Arrangement problems

1. Anagrams: Rearrange the letters in each set to make an English word:

   EFCTA   BODUT   IKCTH   IAENV   LIVAN

2. Two strings hang from a ceiling but are too far apart to allow a person to hold one and walk to the other. On the floor are a book of matches, screwdriver, and a few pieces of cotton. How could the strings be tied together?

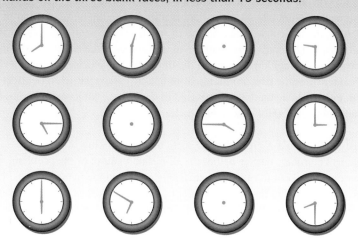

B. Problems of inducing structure

1. What number comes next in the series?

   1 4 2 4 3 4 4 4 5 4 6 4

2. Complete these analogies:

   baseball is to bat as tennis is to _____

   merchant is to sell as customer is to _____

3. The clock faces in each of the three rows are arranged in a logical sequence. Try to find the sequence in each row, and draw the missing hands on the three blank faces, in less than 15 seconds.

Answers to Review Questions:

1. Mental images   2. Concepts   3. prototype   4. 1-a; 2-b   5. heuristic   6. availability

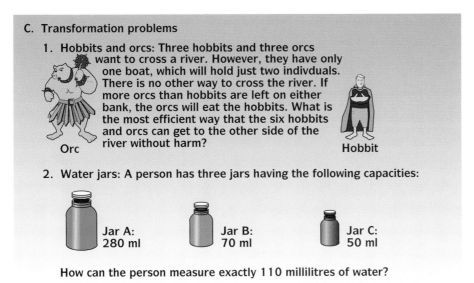

C. Transformation problems

1. Hobbits and orcs: Three hobbits and three orcs want to cross a river. However, they have only one boat, which will hold just two indivduals. There is no other way to cross the river. If more orcs than hobbits are left on either bank, the orcs will eat the hobbits. What is the most efficient way that the six hobbits and orcs can get to the other side of the river without harm?

Orc

Hobbit

2. Water jars: A person has three jars having the following capacities:

Jar A: 280 ml

Jar B: 70 ml

Jar C: 50 ml

How can the person measure exactly 110 millilitres of water?

Arrangement problems require that a group of elements be rearranged or recombined in a way that will satisfy a certain criterion. There are usually several different possible arrangements that can be made, but only one or a few of the arrangements will produce a solution. Anagram problems and jigsaw puzzles represent arrangement problems.

In *problems of inducing structure,* a person must identify the relationships that exist among the elements presented and construct a new relationship among them. In such a problem, it is necessary to determine not only the relationships among the elements, but the structure and size of the elements involved. In the example shown in Figure 7-5, a person must first determine that the solution requires the numbers to be considered in pairs (14-24-34-44-54-64). It is only after that part of the problem is identified that the solution rule (the first number of each pair increases by one, while the second number remains the same) can be determined.

The Tower of Hanoi puzzle represents a third kind of problem. *Transformation problems* consist of an initial state, a goal state, and a series of methods for changing the initial state into the goal state. In the Tower of Hanoi problem, the initial state is the original configuration; the goal state consists of the three disks on the third peg; and the method consists of the rules for moving the disks.

Whether the problem is one of arrangement, inducing structure, or transformation, the initial stage of understanding and diagnosing is critical in problem solving because it allows us to develop our own cognitive representation of the problem and to place it within a personal framework. The problem may be divided into subparts or some information may be ignored as we try to simplify the task. Winnowing out nonessential information (such as the matches and cotton in the hanging strings problem) is often a critical step in problem solving.

Representing and Organizing the Problem

A crucial aspect of the initial encounter with a problem is the way in which we represent it to ourselves and organize the information presented to us (Brown & Walter, 1990, 1993; Davidson, Deuser, & Sternberg, 1994). Consider the following problem:

A man climbs a mountain on Saturday, leaving at daybreak and arriving at the top near sundown. He spends the night at the top. The next day, Sunday, he leaves at daybreak and heads down the mountain, following the same path that he climbed the day before. The question is this: Will there be any time during the second day when he will be at exactly the same point on the mountain as he was at exactly that time on the first day?

SOLUTIONS TO PROBLEMS POSED IN FIGURE 7-5

A. Arrangement problems

1. FACET, DOUBT, THICK, NAIVE, ANVIL

2. The screwdriver is tied to one of the strings. This makes a pendulum that can be swung to reach the other string.

B. Problems of inducing structure

1. 7

2. racket; buy

3. The first blank face should show 5:00 (4½ hours added each time); the second one, 4:30 (45 minutes subtracted each time); the third one, 7:40 (50 minutes added each time).

C. Transformation problems

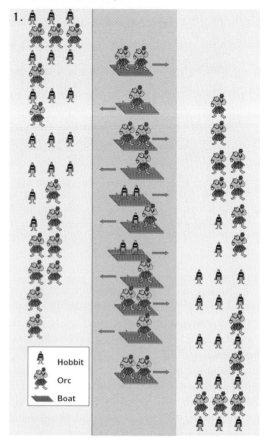

2. Fill jar A; empty into jar B once and into jar C twice. What remains in jar A is 110 millilitres.

If you try to solve this problem by using algebraic or verbal representations, you will have a good deal of trouble. However, if you represent the problem with the kind of simple diagram illustrated in Figure 7-6, the solution becomes apparent.

Successful problem solving, then, requires that a person represent and organize the problem appropriately. However, there is no one optimal way of representing and organizing material, since that depends on the nature of the problem. Sometimes simply restructuring a problem—from a verbal form to a pictorial or mathematical form, for example—can help point out a direct solution (Mayer, 1982).

Production: Generating Solutions

If a problem is relatively simple, a direct solution may already be stored in long-term memory, and all that is necessary is to retrieve the appropriate information. If the solution cannot be retrieved or is not known, we must instigate a process by which possible solutions can be generated and compared with information in long- and short-term memory.

At the most primitive level, solutions to problems can be obtained through trial and error. Thomas Edison was able to invent the light bulb only because he tried thousands of different kinds of materials for a filament before he found one that worked (carbon). The difficulty with trial and error, of course, is that some problems are so complicated it would take a lifetime to try out every possibility. For example, according to one estimate, there are some 10^{120} possible sequences of chess moves.

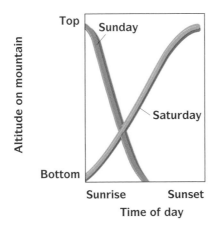

FIGURE 7-6 *It is easy to solve the problem posed in the text by using a graph. Remember, the goal is not to determine the time, but just to indicate whether an exact time exists. Source: Anderson, 1980.*

In place of trial and error, complex problem solving often involves the use of heuristics, which, as we discussed earlier, are rules of thumb that can lead the way to solutions. Probably the most frequently applied heuristic in problem solving is a means-ends analysis. In a **means-ends analysis,** people repeatedly test for differences between the desired outcome and what currently exists. For example, people using a means-ends analysis to search for the correct sequence of roads to get to a city that they can see in the distance would analyze their solutions in terms of how much closer each individual choice of roadway brings them to the ultimate goal of arriving at the city. Such a strategy is only effective, though, if there is a direct solution to the problem. If the problem is such that indirect steps have to be taken that appear to *increase* the discrepancy between the current state and the solution, means-ends analyses can be counterproductive. In our example, if roadways are laid out in such a way that a person must temporarily move *away* from the city in order to reach it eventually, a means-ends analysis will keep the person from reaching the goal.

means-ends analysis: Repeated testing for differences between the desired outcome and what currently exists

For some problems, the converse of a means-ends analysis is the most effective approach: working backward by beginning with the goal and moving toward the starting state. Instead of starting with the current situation and moving closer and closer to the solution, people can work in the opposite direction, starting with the goal and aiming to reach the beginning point (Malin, 1979; Bourne et al., 1986; Hunt, 1994).

Problem-Solving Strategies

Subgoals

Another commonly used heuristic is to divide a problem into intermediate steps, or *subgoals,* and to solve each of those steps. For instance, in our modified Tower of Hanoi problem, there are several obvious subgoals that could be chosen, such as moving the largest disk to the third post.

If solving a subgoal is a step toward the ultimate solution to a problem, then identifying subgoals is an appropriate strategy. There are cases, however, in which the formation of subgoals is not all that helpful and may actually increase the time needed to find a solution (Hayes, 1966; Reed, 1996). For example, some problems cannot be subdivided. Others are so difficult to subdivide that it takes longer to identify the appropriate subdivisions than to solve the problem by other means. Finally, even when a problem is divided into subgoals, it may be unclear what to do after a given subgoal has been reached.

Insight

Some approaches to problem solving focus less on step-by-step processes than on the sudden bursts of comprehension that one may experience during efforts to solve a problem. Just after World War I, German psychologist Wolfgang Köhler examined learning and problem-solving processes in chimps (Köhler, 1927). In his studies, Köhler exposed chimps to challenging situations in which the elements of the solution were all present; all that was needed was for the chimps to put them together.

a.   b.   c.

In an impressive display of insight, Sultan, one of the chimpanzees in Köhler's experiments in problem solving, sees a bunch of bananas that is out of his reach (a). He then carries over several crates (b), stacks them, and stands on them to reach the bananas (c).

insight: A sudden awareness of the relationships among various elements that had previously appeared to be independent of one another

Insight

For example, in one series of studies, chimps were kept in a cage in which boxes and sticks were strewn about, with a bunch of tantalizing bananas hanging out of reach. Initially, the chimps engaged in a variety of trial-and-error attempts at getting to the bananas: They would throw the stick at the bananas, jump from one of the boxes, or leap wildly from the ground. Frequently, they would seem to give up in frustration, leaving the bananas dangling temptingly overhead. But then, in what seemed like a sudden revelation, they would abandon whatever activity they were involved in and stand on a box in order to be able to reach the bananas with a stick. Köhler called the cognitive processes underlying the chimps' behaviour **insight,** a sudden awareness of the relationships among various elements that had previously appeared to be independent of one another.

Although Köhler emphasized the apparent suddenness with which solutions were revealed, subsequent research has shown that prior experience and initial trial-and-error practice in problem solving are prerequisites for "insight" (Metcalfe, 1986). One study demonstrated that only chimps who had experience in playing with sticks could successfully solve the problem; inexperienced chimps never made the connection between standing on the box and reaching the bananas (Birch, 1945). Some researchers have suggested that the behaviour of the chimps represented little more than the chaining together of previously learned responses, no different from the way a pigeon learns, by trial and error, to peck a key (Epstein et al., 1984; Epstein, 1987, 1996). It is clear that insight depends on previous experience with the elements involved in a problem.

Judgment: Evaluating the Solutions

The final step in problem solving is judging the adequacy of a solution. Often, this is a simple matter: If there is a clear solution—as in the Tower of Hanoi problem—we will know immediately whether we have been successful.

On the other hand, if the solution is less concrete, or if there is no single correct solution, evaluating solutions becomes more difficult. In such instances, we must decide which solution alternative is best. Unfortunately, we are often quite inaccurate in estimating the quality of our own ideas (Johnson, Parrott, & Stratton, 1968). For instance, a team of drug researchers working for a particular company may feel that their

THE FAR SIDE   By GARY LARSON

PRIMATE RESEARCH LAB

6-15

© 1981 FarWorks, Inc./Distributed by Universal Press Syndicate

remedy for an illness is superior to all others, overestimating the likelihood of success and belittling the approaches of competing drug companies.

Theoretically, if the heuristics and information we rely on to make decisions are appropriate and valid, we can make accurate choices among problem solutions. However, as we see next, there are several kinds of obstacles to and biases in problem solving that affect the quality of the decisions and judgments we make.

Impediments to Problem Solving

Consider the following problem-solving test (Duncker, 1945):

> You are presented with a set of tacks, candles, and matches in small boxes, and told your goal is to place three candles at eye level on a nearby door, so that wax will not drip on the floor as the candles burn (see Figure 7-7). How would you approach this challenge?

If you have difficulty solving the problem, you are not alone. Most people are unable to solve it when it is presented in the manner illustrated in the figure, in which the objects are located *inside* the boxes. On the other hand, if the objects were presented *beside* the boxes, just resting on the table, chances are you would solve the problem much more readily—which, in case you are wondering, requires tacking the boxes to the door and then placing the candles inside them (see Figure 7-10).

The difficulty you probably encountered in solving the problem stems from its presentation and relates to the fact that you were misled at the initial preparation stage. Actually, significant obstacles to problem solving exist at each of the three major stages. Although cognitive approaches to problem solving suggest that thinking proceeds along fairly rational, logical lines as a person confronts a problem and considers various solutions, a number of factors hinder the development of creative, appropriate, and accurate solutions.

FIGURE 7-7 *The problem here is to place three candles at eye level on a nearby door so that the wax will not drip on the floor as the candles burn—using only the tacks, candles, and matches in the small boxes. The solution is shown in Figure 7-10 on page 258.*

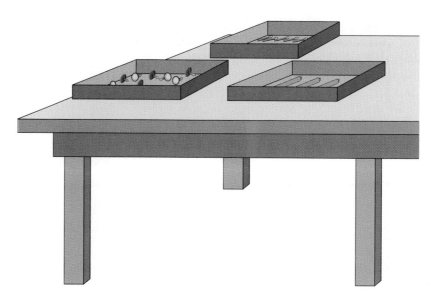

functional fixedness: The tendency to think of an object only in terms of its typical use

mental set: The tendency for old patterns of problem solving to persist

Given jars with these capacities (in litres)

	a	b	c	Obtain
1.	21	127	3	100
2.	14	163	25	99
3.	18	43	10	5
4.	9	42	6	21
5.	20	59	4	31
6.	28	76	3	25

FIGURE 7-8 *Try this classic demonstration, which illustrates the importance of mental set in problem solving. The object is to use the jars in each row to measure out the designated amount of liquid. After you figure out the solution for the first five rows, you'll likely have trouble with the sixth row—even though the solution is actually easier. In fact, if you had tried to solve the problem in the sixth row first, you probably would have had no difficulty at all.*

Functional Fixedness and Mental Set

The reason that most people experience difficulty with the candle problem is a phenomenon known as **functional fixedness,** the tendency to think of an object only in terms of its typical use. For instance, functional fixedness probably leads you to think of the book you are holding in your hands as something to read, as opposed to its value as a doorstop or as kindling for a fire. In the candle problem, functional fixedness occurs because the objects are first presented inside the boxes, which are then seen simply as containers for the objects they hold rather than as a potential part of the solution.

Functional fixedness is an example of a broader phenomenon known as **mental set,** the tendency for old patterns of problem solving to persist. This phenomenon was demonstrated in a classic experiment carried out by Abraham Luchins (1946). As you can see in Figure 7-8, the object of the task is to use the jars in each row to measure out the designated amount of liquid. (Try it yourself to get a sense of the power of mental set before moving on.)

If you have tried to solve the problem, you know that the first five parts are all solved in the same way: Fill the largest jar (B) and from it fill the middle-size jar (A) once and the smallest jar (C) two times. What is left in B is the designated amount. (Stated as a formula, it is B – A – 2C.) The demonstration of mental set comes with the sixth part of the problem, a point at which you probably encountered some difficulty. If you are like most people, you tried the formula and were perplexed when it failed. Chances are, in fact, that you missed the simple (but different) solution to the problem, which merely involves subtracting C from A. Interestingly, those people who were given problem 6 *first* had no difficulty with it at all.

Mental set can also affect perceptions. It can prevent you from seeing your way beyond the apparent constraints of a problem. For example, try to draw four straight lines so that they pass through all nine dots in the grid below—without lifting your pencil from the page.

· · ·
· · ·
· · ·

If you had difficulty with the problem, it was probably because you felt compelled to keep your lines within the grid. If you had gone outside the boundaries, however, you would have succeeded with the solution shown in Figure 7-9.

Inaccurate Evaluation of Solutions

When the nuclear power plant at Three Mile Island in Pennsylvania suffered its initial malfunction in 1979, a disaster that almost led to a nuclear meltdown, the plant operators were faced immediately with solving a problem of the most serious kind. Several monitors indicated contradictory information about the source of the problem: One suggested that the pressure was too high, leading to the danger of an explosion; others indicated that the pressure was too low, which could lead to a meltdown. Although the pressure was in fact too low, the supervisors on duty relied on the one monitor—which was faulty—that suggested the pressure was too high. Once they had made their decision and acted upon it, they ignored the contradictory evidence from the other monitors (Wickens, 1984).

One reason for the operators' mistake is the *confirmation bias,* in which initial hypotheses are favored and contradictory information supporting alternative hypotheses or solutions is ignored. Even when we find evidence that contradicts a solution we have chosen, we are apt to stick with our original hypothesis.

There are several reasons for the confirmation bias. One is that it takes cognitive effort to rethink a problem that appears to be solved already, so we are apt to stick with our first solution. Another is that evidence contradicting an initial solution may present something of a threat to our self-esteem, leading us to hold to the solutions that we have come up with first (Fischoff, 1977; Rasmussen, 1981).

Creativity and Problem Solving

Despite obstacles to problem solving, many people are adept at coming up with creative solutions to problems. One of the enduring questions that cognitive psychologists have sought to answer is what factors underlie **creativity,** the combining of responses or ideas in novel ways (Isaksen & Murdock, 1993; Boden, 1994, 1996; Smith, Ward, & Finke, 1995).

Although identifying the stages of problem solving helps us to understand how people approach and solve problems, it does little to explain why some people—such as Jacob Rabinow, whose inventions were described in the Prologue—come up with better solutions than others. For instance, the possible solutions to even the simplest of problems often show wide discrepancies. Consider, for example, how you might respond to the question, "How many uses can you think of for a newspaper?"

Now compare your own solution with this one proposed by a 10-year-old boy:

> You can read it, write on it, lay it down and paint a picture on it. . . . You could put it in your door for decoration, put it in the garbage can, put it on a chair if the chair is messy. If you have a puppy, you put newspaper in its box or put it in your backyard for the dog to play with. When you build something and you don't want anyone to see it, put newspaper around it. Put newspaper on the floor if you have no mattress, use it to pick up something hot, use it to stop bleeding, or to catch the drips from drying clothes. You can use a newspaper for curtains, put it in your shoe to cover what is hurting your foot, make a kite out of it, shade a light that is too bright. You can wrap fish in it, wipe windows, or wrap money in it. . . . You put washed shoes in newspaper, wipe eyeglasses with it, put it under a dripping sink, put a plant on it, make a paper bowl out of it, use it for a hat if it is raining, tie it on your feet for slippers. You can put it on the sand if you had no towel, use it for bases in baseball, make paper airplanes with it, use it as a dustpan when you sweep, ball it up for the cat to play with, wrap your hands in it if it is cold (Ward, Kogan, & Pankove, 1972).

It is obvious that this list shows extraordinary creativity. Unfortunately, it has proved to be considerably easier to identify *examples* of creativity than to determine its causes. Several factors, however, seem to be associated with creativity (Swede, 1993; Csikszentmihalyi, 1997; Ward, Smith, & Vaid, 1997).

One of these factors is divergent thinking. **Divergent thinking** refers to the ability to generate unusual, yet nonetheless appropriate, responses to problems or questions. This type of thinking contrasts with **convergent thinking,** which produces

FIGURE 7-9 *Solution to the nine-dot problem requires the use of lines drawn beyond the boundaries of the figure—something that our mental set may prevent us from easily seeing.*

creativity: The combining of responses or ideas in novel ways

divergent thinking: The ability to generate unusual, yet nonetheless appropriate, responses to problems or questions
convergent thinking: The ability to produce responses that are based primarily on knowledge and logic

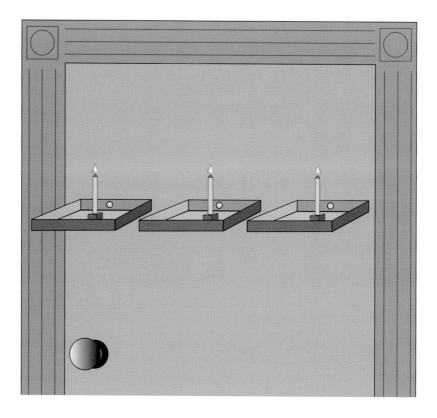

Creativity

responses that are based primarily on knowledge and logic. For instance, someone relying on convergent thinking answers "You read it" to the query "What do you do with a newspaper?" In contrast, "You use it as a dustpan" is a more divergent—and creative—response (Runco, 1991; Baer, 1993; Runco & Sakamoto, 1993; Finke, 1995).

Psychologists Robert Sternberg and Todd Lubart suggest that one important ingredient of creativity is the willingness to take risks that may result in potentially high payoffs (Sternberg & Lubart, 1992, 1995, 1996; Lubart & Sternberg, 1995). In their view, creative people are similar to successful stock market investors, who follow the rule of "buying low and selling high." In an analogous fashion, creative individuals formulate and promote ideas that are, at least for the moment, out-of-synch with prevailing wisdom ("buying low"). Ultimately, though, highly creative people expect that their ideas will rise in value and that others will ultimately find them of value and adopt them ("selling high").

Another ingredient of creativity is *cognitive complexity,* the use of and preference for elaborate, intricate, and complex stimuli and thinking patterns. Similarly, creative people often have a wider range of interests and are more independent and more interested in philosophical or abstract problems than are less creative individuals (Barron, 1990).

One factor that is *not* closely related to creativity is intelligence. Most items on intelligence tests, which are well defined and have only one acceptable answer, focus on convergent thinking skills. Creative people who are divergent thinkers may therefore find themselves at a disadvantage when taking such tests. This may explain why researchers consistently find that creativity is only slightly related to intelligence or school grades, particularly when intelligence is measured using typical intelligence tests (Barron & Harrington, 1981; Sternberg, 1988a; Albert, 1992; Simonton, 1994; Hong, Milgram, & Gorsky, 1995).

Cognitive psychologists have found that creativity and critical thinking skills, such as those involved in the design of this racing wheelchair, can be taught.

The Informed Consumer of Psychology

Thinking Critically and Creatively

Can we learn to be better thinkers? Although we've been considering ways of critically evaluating information in the Informed Consumer of Psychology sections of every chapter so far, our consideration of cognitive psychology presents a good opportunity to review and expand on the techniques for thinking critically and creatively. Cognitive researchers have found that all of us can learn to perform better on decision-making and problem-solving tasks. Abstract rules of logic and reasoning can be taught, and such training can improve the way in which we are able to reason about the underlying causes of everyday life events.

In short, research by cognitive psychologists has suggested that critical and creative thinkers are made, not born. Consider, for instance, some of these suggestions for increasing critical thinking and creativity (Anderson, 1993; Feldman, Coats, & Schwartzberg, 1994; Conti, Amabile, & Pollak, 1995; Halpern, 1995; Schaller et al., 1996; D. A. Levy, 1997; Baer, 1997):

- *Redefine problems.* The boundaries and assumptions we hold can be modified. For example, a problem can be rephrased at either a more abstract or more concrete level.

- *Use fractionation.* In fractionation, an idea or concept is broken down into the parts that make it up. Through fractionation, each part can be examined for new possibilities and approaches, leading to a novel solution for the problem as a whole.

- *Adopt a critical perspective.* Rather than passively accepting assumptions or arguments, we can critically evaluate material by considering its implications and thinking about possible exceptions and contradictions.

- *Consider the opposite.* By considering the opposite of a concept we're seeking to understand, we can sometimes make progress. For example, in order to define "good mental health," it might be useful to consider what is meant by "bad mental health."

- *Use analogies.* Analogies not only help us uncover new understanding, they provide alternative frameworks for interpreting facts. One particularly effective means of coming up with analogies is to look for them in the animal kingdom when the problem concerns people, and in physics or chemistry when the problem concerns inanimate objects. For instance, the idea for the unique packaging of Pringles potato chips reputedly arose when a manufacturer noticed that dry tree leaves, which normally crumble easily, could be packed together tightly if they were moistened slightly (Rice, 1984; Holyoak & Thagard, 1994; Reisberg, 1997; Getner & Holyoak, 1997).

- *Think divergently.* Instead of thinking in terms of the most logical or most common use for an object, we can consider how it might be of help if we were forbidden to use it in its usual way.

- *Take the perspective of another person.* By temporarily adopting the point-of-view of another person, it may be possible to gain a fresh view of the situation.

- *Use heuristics.* As mentioned earlier, heuristics are rules of thumb that can help bring about a solution to a problem. If the nature of the problem is such that it has a single correct answer, and a heuristic is available or can be constructed, using the heuristic frequently helps to develop a solution more rapidly and effectively.

- *Experiment with various solutions.* We shouldn't be afraid to use different routes to find solutions for problems (verbal, mathematical, graphic, even acting out a situation). For instance, we might try to come up with every conceivable idea we can, no matter how wild or bizarre it may seem at first. After we've come up with a list of solutions, we can review each one and try to think of ways of making what at first appeared impractical seem more feasible. ■

Recap, Review, and Rethink

Recap

- In solving problems, people typically pass through a series of three steps: preparation, production, and judgment.

- Insight is a sudden awareness of the relationships among various elements that had earlier seemed independent of one another.

- Among the obstacles to successful problem solving are mental set and functional fixedness, the faulty application of algorithms and heuristics, and the confirmation bias.

- Creativity is related to divergent thinking and cognitive complexity.

- Psychologists have devised several methods for enhancing critical thinking and creative problem solving.

Review

1. Three steps in problem solving studied by psychologists are _____, _____, and _____.

2. Match the type of problem with its definition:
   1. inducing structure
   2. arrangement
   3. transformation

   a. changing the initial state to the goal state
   b. rearranging elements to fit certain criteria
   c. constructing a new relationship between elements

3. Solving a problem by trying to reduce the difference between the current state and the goal state is known as a _____.

4. _____ is the term used to describe the sudden "flash" of revelation that often accompanies the solution to a problem.

5. Thinking of an object only in terms of its typical use is known as _____ _____ . A broader, related tendency for old problem-solving patterns to persist is known as a _____ _____.

6. _____ _____ describes the phenomenon of favouring an initial hypothesis and ignoring subsequent competing hypotheses.

7. Generating unusual but still appropriate responses to a question is known as _____ _____ .

8. Intelligence, as measured on standard intelligence tests, is highly correlated with measures of creativity. True or false?

Answers to Review Questions are on page 262.

Rethink

1. Is the reasoning in the following syllogism correct or incorrect? Why?

   Creative people often have trouble with traditional intelligence tests.

   I have trouble with traditional intelligence tests.

   Therefore, I am a creative person.

2. Are divergent thinking and convergent thinking mutually exclusive or complementary? Why? Are there situations in which one way of thinking is clearly superior? Can the two ways of thinking be combined? How?

3. If certain strategies that enhance creativity can indeed be taught, what potential benefits could this bring in the realms of business? Science? Working with persons who have disabilities?

LANGUAGE

▶ How do people use language?

▶ How does language develop?

'Twas brillig, and the slithy toves
Did gyre and gimble in the wabe:
All mimsy were the borogoves,
And the mome raths outgrabe.

Although few of us have ever come face to face with a tove, we have little diffi-culty in discerning that in Lewis Carroll's (1872) poem "Jabberwocky," the expression "slithy toves" contains an adjective, "slithy," and the noun it modifies, "toves."

Our ability to make sense out of nonsense, if the nonsense follows typical rules of language, illustrates both the sophistication of human language capabilities and the complexity of the cognitive processes that underlie the development and use of language. The use of **language**—the systematic, meaningful arrangement of symbols—clearly represents an important cognitive ability, one that is indispens-able for communicating with others. But language is not only central to communi-cation, it is also closely tied to the very way in which we think about and understand the world, for there is a crucial link between thought and language. It is not surprising, then, that psychologists have devoted considerable attention to studying the topic of language (Harley, 1995; Forrester, 1996; Velichkovsky & Rumbaugh, 1996).

language: The systematic, meaningful arrangement of symbols

Grammar: Language's Language

In order to understand how language develops, and what its relationship to thought is, we first need to review some of the formal elements that constitute language. The basic structure of language rests on grammar. **Grammar** is the system of rules that de-termine how our thoughts can be expressed.

grammar: The system of rules that determines how our thoughts can be expressed

Grammar deals with three major components of language: phonology, syntax, and semantics. **Phonology** is the study of the sound system in language (e.g., rules that determine which sound sequences occur in words). The smallest units of sound that can affect meaning of speech are called **phonemes**. For instance, the "a" in "fat" and the "a" in "fate" represent two different phonemes in English (Halle, 1990; Feldman, 1995; Hirsh-Pasek & Golinkoff, 1996; Vihman, 1996).

phonology: The study of the sound system in language
phonemes: The smallest sound units

Although English speakers use just 42 basic phonemes to produce words, the basic phonemes of other languages range from as few as 15 to as many as 85 (Akmajian, De-mers, & Harnish, 1984). Differences in phonemes are one reason people have difficulty in learning other languages: For example, to the Japanese speaker, whose native language does not have an "r" phoneme, English words such as "roar" present some difficulty.

Syntax refers to the rules that indicate how words and phrases can be combined to form sentences. Every language has intricate rules that guide the order in which words may be strung together to communicate meaning. English speakers have no dif-ficulty recognizing that "Radio down the turn" is not an appropriate sequence, while "Turn down the radio" is. The importance of appropriate syntax is demonstrated in English by the changes in meaning that are caused by the different word orders in the following three utterances: "John kidnapped the boy," "John, the kidnapped boy," and "The boy kidnapped John" (Lasnik, 1990).

syntax: The rules that indicate how words and phrases can be combined to form sentences

The third major component of language is semantics. **Semantics** refers to the rules governing the meaning of words and sentences (Larson, 1990; Hipkiss, 1995; O'Grady & Dobrovolsky, 1996). Semantic rules allow us to use words to convey the subtlest of nuances. For instance, we are able to make the distinction between "The truck hit Laura" (which we would be likely to say if we had just seen the vehicle hit-ting Laura) and "Laura was hit by a truck" (which we would probably say if asked why Laura was missing class while she recuperated).

semantics: The rules governing the meaning of words and sentences

Despite the complexities of language, most of us acquire the basics of grammar without even being aware that we have learned its rules (Pinker, 1994). Moreover, even though we might have difficulty explicitly stating the rules of grammar that we employ, our linguistic abilities are so sophisticated that they enable us to utter an infinite number of different statements. We turn now to a consideration of how such abilities are acquired.

Language Development: Developing a Way with Words

To parents, the sounds of their infant babbling and cooing are music to their ears (except, perhaps, at three o'clock in the morning). These sounds also serve an important function: They mark the first step on the road to the development of language.

Children **babble**—make speechlike but meaningless sounds—from around the ages of 3 months through 1 year. While they babble they may produce, at one time or another, any of the sounds found in all languages, not just the one to which they are exposed. Even deaf children display their own form of babbling: Infants who are unable to hear and who are exposed to sign language from birth "babble," but they do it with their hands (Petitto & Marentette, 1991; Pettito, 1993; Meier & Willerman, 1995).

Babbling increasingly reflects the specific language that is being spoken in the environment, initially in terms of pitch and tone, and eventually in terms of specific sounds (Reich, 1986; Kuhl et al., 1992; Blake and de Boysson-Bardies, 1992; de Boysson-Bardies & Halle, 1994). By the time the child is approximately 1 year old, sounds that are not in the language disappear (Werker, 1989). It is then a short step to the production of actual words. In English, these are typically short words that start with a consonant such as "b," "d," "m," "p," or "t"—which helps to explain why "mama" and "dada" are so often among babies' first words. Of course, even before they produce their first words, children are capable of understanding a fair amount of the language they hear. Language comprehension precedes language production.

After the age of 1 year, children begin to learn more complicated forms of language. They produce two-word combinations, which become the building blocks of sentences, and the number of different words they are capable of using increases sharply. By the age of 2 years, the average child has a vocabulary of more than fifty words. Just six months later, that vocabulary has grown to several hundred words. At that time, children can produce short sentences, although they use **telegraphic speech**—sentences that sound as if they were part of a telegram, in which words not critical to the message are left out. Rather than saying, "I showed you the book," a child using telegraphic speech might say, "I show book"; and "I am drawing a dog" might become "Drawing dog." As the child gets older, of course, the use of telegraphic speech declines and sentences become increasingly complex (Blake, Quartaro and Onorati, 1993).

By age 3, children learn to make plurals by adding "s" to nouns and to form the past tense by adding "ed" to verbs. This ability also leads to errors, since children tend to apply rules too inflexibly. This phenomenon is known as **overgeneralization,** whereby children apply rules even when the application results in an error. Thus, although it is correct to say "he walked" for the past tense of "walk," the "ed" rule doesn't work quite so well when children say "he runned" for the past tense of "run" (Marcus, 1996).

Much of children's acquisition of the basic rules of language is complete by the time they are five. However, a full vocabulary and the ability to comprehend and use subtle grammatical rules are not attained until later. For example, a 5-year-old boy who is shown a blindfolded doll and asked, "Is the doll easy or hard to see?" would have great difficulty responding to the question. In fact, if he were asked to make the doll easier to see, he would probably try to remove the doll's blindfold. On the other hand, 8-year-olds have little difficulty understanding the question, realizing that the doll's blindfold has nothing to do with an observer's ability to see the doll (Chomsky, 1969).

babble: Speechlike but meaningless sounds made by children from the ages of around 3 months through 1 year

A syllable in signed language, similar to this, is found in the manual babbling of deaf infants and in the spoken babbling of hearing infants. The similarities in language structure suggest that language has biological roots.

telegraphic speech: Sentences that sound as if they were part of a telegram, in which words not critical to the message are left out

overgeneralization: The phenomenon whereby children apply rules even when the application results in an error

Answers to Review Questions:

1. preparation, production, judgment   2. 1-c; 2-b; 3-a   3. means-ends analysis   4. Insight   5. functional fixedness; mental set
6. Confirmation bias   7. divergent thinking   8. False; intelligence, as measured on traditional tests, is only slightly related to creativity.

Understanding Language Acquisition: Identifying the Roots of Language

Anyone who spends even a little time with children will notice the enormous strides that they make in language development throughout childhood. However, the reasons for this rapid growth are far from obvious. Two major explanations have been offered: one based on learning theory and the other on innate processes.

The **learning-theory approach** suggests that language acquisition follows the principles of reinforcement and conditioning discussed in Chapter 5. For example, a child who utters the word "mama" is hugged and praised by her mother, which reinforces the behaviour and makes its repetition more likely. This view suggests that children first learn to speak by being rewarded for making sounds that approximate speech. Ultimately, through a process of shaping, language becomes more and more like adult speech (Skinner, 1957).

The learning-theory approach is supported by research that shows that the more parents speak to their young children, the more proficient the children become in language usage (see Figure 7-11). In addition, higher levels of linguistic sophistication in parents' speech to their young children are related to a greater rate of vocabulary growth, vocabulary usage, and even general intellectual achievement by the time the children are 3 years of age (Hart & Risley, 1997).

On the other hand, the learning-theory approach is less successful when it comes to explaining the acquisition of language rules. Children are reinforced not only when they use proper language, but also when they respond incorrectly. For example, parents answer the child's "Why the dog won't eat?" as readily as they do the correctly phrased question "Why won't the dog eat?" Both sentences are understood equally well. Learning theory, then, has difficulty in providing the full explanation for language acquisition.

Pointing to such problems with learning-theory approaches to language acquisition, Noam Chomsky (1968, 1978, 1991), a linguist, provided a ground-breaking alternative. Chomsky argued that humans are born with an innate linguistic capability that emerges primarily as a function of maturation. According to his analysis, all the world's languages share a similar underlying structure called a **universal grammar.** Chomsky suggests that the human brain has a neural system, the **language-acquisition device,** that both permits the understanding of the structure of language and provides strategies and techniques for learning the unique characteristics of a given native language.

learning-theory approach: The theory suggesting that language acquisition follows the principles of reinforcement and conditioning

universal grammar: Noam Chomsky's theory that all the world's languages share a similar underlying structure

language-acquisition device: A neural system of the brain hypothesized to permit understanding of language

FIGURE 7-11 *The greater the number of words that parents say to their children prior to the age of three, the larger their child's vocabulary. Source: Courtesy of Drs. Betty Hart and Todd Risley, 1997.*

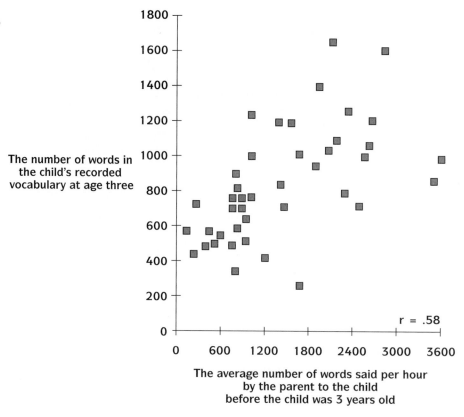

The number of words in the child's recorded vocabulary at age three

The average number of words said per hour by the parent to the child before the child was 3 years old

r = .58

Language Acquisition

In a sense, then, the brain's hard-wired language-acquisition device provides the hardware for our acquisition of language; exposure to language in our environment allows us to develop the appropriate software. Chomsky argues that language is a uniquely human phenomenon made possible by the presence of the language-acquisition device.

Chomsky's view, as you might suspect, is not without its critics. The issue of how humans acquire language remains hotly contested (Rice, 1989; Pinker, 1990, 1994; McDonald, 1997).

Reading: Understanding Written Language

Many psychologists have studied the acquisition of reading skills since proficient reading is important for academic success. In Canadian schools, reading teachers have used the whole language approach, the phonics approach, or a combination of the two. The **whole language approach**, which stresses use of whole and meaningful materials, is supported by research showing that good readers recognize words as visual wholes (Buchanan and Besner, 1993). The **phonics approach**, that emphasizes basic skills such as recognizing and blending constituent sounds in words, is supported by research showing that good readers are superior to poor readers in deciphering unfamiliar words (Barron, 1994; Collins, 1986). Betty Ann Levy (McMaster University) has effectively implemented a sophisticated research-based reading program which involves elements of both approaches in the Hamilton schools (Levy, 1996; Levy et al., 1995).

The Influence of Language on Thinking

Do Inuit living in the frigid Arctic have a more expansive vocabulary for describing snow than people living in more temperate climates? Arguments that the Inuit language has many more words than English for "snow" have been made since the early 1900s. In 1956, the linguist, Benjamin Whorf, put forward the **linguistic-relativity hypothesis**.

whole language approach: Reading instruction that stresses use of whole and meaningful materials

phonics approach: Reading instruction that emphasizes word decoding skills such as analysis and synthesis of constituent sounds in words

linguistic-relativity hypothesis: The theory that language shapes and, in fact, may determine the way people of a particular culture perceive and understand the world

Travelling in countries where a language other than our own is spoken raises the issue of the relationship between language and thought.

According to this hypothesis, language shapes may determine the way people of a particular culture perceive and understand the world (Whorf, 1956; Lucy, 1992, 1996; Smith, 1996). Whorf argued that because snow is so relevant to the daily life of the Inuit they developed a rich vocabulary to describe "snow," and that this vocabulary determined or shaped how they thought about it. Over time, researchers suggested increasingly larger estimates of the number of Inuktitut words for "snow." Indeed, one account estimated 400 such words (Martin and Pullum, 1991; Pinker, 1994). However, research shows that, in fact, Inuktitut does not have more words for "snow" than languages spoken by people living in warmer climates (Martin, 1986).

Was Whorf correct? Does language determine thought? An important study by Eleanor Rosch (1974) demonstrated that language does not determine thought. She compared colour perception and colour names of American English speakers and the Dani tribe of New Guinea. The Dani have only two names for colour: one for cold, dark colours and one for warm, lighter colours. In English, of course, there are hundreds of colour names, but eleven of them represent major colour categories (red, yellow, green, blue, black, gray, white, purple, orange, pink, and brown). Rosch argued that if the linguistic-relativity hypothesis were accurate, English speakers should be more efficient at recognizing and distinguishing colours that represent the major categories than colours that are not members of major categories. In contrast, she reasoned that the Dani tribe members should show no difference in recognition between colours that are members of major or non-major categories, since there are no words in their vocabulary to describe any of them. She found that there was no difference in the way that English speakers and Dani perceived colours; both perceived colours in the major categories more efficiently than colours outside the major categories. Language differences did not lead to perceptual differences. The results did not support the linguistic-relativity hypothesis. Subsequent research has supported Rosch's view, and not the linguistic-relativity hypothesis (Brown, 1986; Pinker, 1990; Laws et al., 1995).

On the other hand, language and culture have been found to influence thinking in some respects. For example, our impressions and memories of others' personalities and behaviours are affected by the linguistic categories we use in comprehending and

Pathways Through Psychology

Fred Genesee

Professor
Department of Psychology
McGill University

Education: B.A., University of Western Ontario; M.A., Ph.D., McGill University

Home: Montreal

My interest in language began when I was an undergraduate; I did an Honours project on lateralization of language functions in the brain. During my first years at McGill I became interested in language acquisition, and in particular, second language acquisition in children. My interest in this topic arose from my belief that studying children acquiring language was a good way to examine biologically factors that influence language learning. Focusing on second language acquisition was a way of examining the limits of the brain to learn language. I was also interested in developmental aspects of language because I wanted to examine how language impacts other aspects of development—social, cognitive, and even educational. For me, language is not only a biological endowment of human beings but a tool that influences diverse aspects of our lives. Language is undoubtedly the most complex accomplishment of human development and I continue to be fascinated by how this miraculous feat of childhood occurs. Bilingual acquisition is even more miraculous since bilingual children acquire two, or more, languages while monolingual children acquire one.

In my early research, I conducted numerous evaluations of second language immersion programs in Canada, and some in the U.S. I was concerned with the impact of immersion on students' first and second language development, their academic achievement, and their sociocultural development (e.g., attitudes towards themselves and others). This research lead me to an interest in the pedagogy of second language instruction and I have written numerous articles and several books that seek to inform second language educators about the implications of research and theory for language teaching and learning in school. Much of what I do in the educational domain now encompasses education for language minority students (ESL) as well as language majority students, who were my original interest. My work has broadened to include consultation and collaboration with educators and policymakers around the world who are concerned with helping school-age children become bilingual—for example in Spain, Estonia, Japan, Germany. Educators and policy-makers worldwide are increasingly adopting educational programs that will promote bilingualism among their students so that they can advance professionally, socio-culturally, and economically. The global village is here and multilingualism is essential.

My research on second language immersion programs has shown that students who come to school speaking society's majority language can be educated effectively through the use of a second language without negative effects on their first language development or their academic achievement. My research has also shown that majority group students with characteristics that normally put them at risk for failure in school can also benefit from immersion in a second language. This research is often consulted by other researchers and professional educators.

My recent research focuses on pre-school children who grow up learning two languages from birth—most of this work has examined French-English bilingual children. We carefully collect language samples from children and analyze transcriptions of their language in order to describe how they become bilingual and to test out various theories or hypotheses. For example, we are examining whether bilingual children go through the same milestones at the same rate in language development as monolingual children, and how they come to know when to use which language with whom.

My research on bilingual acquisition has shown that, from the one-word stage, bilingual children have differentiated linguistic systems and can use their developing languages differentially and appropriately in a variety of contexts. My work has also shown that child bilingual code-mixing (the use of words and structures from two languages in the same sentence) reveals linguistic, cognitive and communicative capacities that are truly unique to bilinguals and speaks to their developing competence.

Many people are skeptical about raising children bilingually. My interest in bilingual acquisition is motivated in part by my academic desire to contribute to theories of language acquisition, but also by my desire to demystify the misperceptions that people often have about bilingual acquisition. I regularly meet with groups who take care of bilingual children and share with them my and other's research so that they can make better decisions in their work with these children. I view myself as a science-broker—someone who translates research and theory into terms that are meaningful and useful to professionals, practitioners, and lay persons.

Fred Genesee

Source: Fred Genesee, Ph.D. McGill University. <www.psych.mcgill.ca/faculty/genesee.html>

remembering (Hoffman et al., 1986; McFadyen, 1996). Culture may also have broad general effects on thinking. Peter Denny, a psychologist at the University of Western Ontario, has suggested that people develop cultural preferences for the habitual use of some cognitive processes rather than others (Denny, 1991).

Do Animals Use Language?

One of the enduring questions that has long puzzled psychologists is whether language is uniquely human or if other animals are able to acquire it as well. It is clear that many animals communicate with one another in some rudimentary forms, such as fiddler crabs that wave their claws to signal, bees whose dance indicates the direction in which food will be found, or certain birds that say "zick, zick" during courtship and "kia" when they are about to fly away. But researchers have yet to demonstrate conclusively that these animals use true language, which is characterized in part by the ability to produce and communicate new and unique meanings following a formal grammar.

Psychologists have, however, been able to teach chimps to communicate at surprisingly high levels. For instance, Kanzi, a 9-year-old pygmy chimpanzee, has linguistic skills that some psychologists claim are close to those of a 2-year-old human being. Psychologist Sue Savage-Rumbaugh and colleagues, who have worked extensively with Kanzi, suggest that he can create sentences that are grammatically sophisticated and can even concoct new rules of syntax (Savage-Rumbaugh et al., 1993).

Despite the skills displayed by primates such as Kanzi, critics contend that the language they use still lacks the grammar and sufficiently complex and novel constructions that characterize the realm of human capabilities (Seidenberg & Petitto, 1987). Instead, they maintain that the chimps are displaying a skill no different from that of a dog that learns to lie down on command in order to get a reward. Furthermore, firm evidence is lacking that animals are able to recognize and respond to the mental states of others of their species, an important aspect of human communication (Cheney & Seyfarth, 1990; Seyfarth & Cheney, 1992, 1996).

Most evidence supports the contention that humans are better equipped than animals to produce and organize language in the form of meaningful sentences. But the issue of whether animals are capable of being taught to communicate in a way that resembles human language remains controversial (Savage-Rumbaugh, 1987; Gibbons, 1991; Cenami-Spada, 1994; Gilbert, 1996; Savage-Rumbaugh & Brakke, 1996).

Exploring Diversity

Linguistic Variety

Linguistic Diversity

In Canada we have two official languages, French and English, which reflect the founding of our country. According to the most recent census (Statistics Canada, 1996, 1999), almost 84 percent of Canadians have English (60 percent) or French (24 percent) as their mother tongue. The remaining portion of the population show great diversity in language having one of about a dozen European or Asian languages or an equal number of aboriginal languages as their mother tongue.

The most common language other than English or French, spoken by Canadians, is Chinese (used by 2.5 percent of the population), followed by Italian (1.8 percent) and German (1.6 percent). Most Chinese speakers live in Ontario and British Columbia. Most Italian and German speakers live in Ontario.

The most frequently spoken aboriginal languages are Cree and Inuktitut. Cree is spoken by almost 10 percent of the aboriginal population, mostly those living in the Prairie Provinces. Inuktitut is spoken by a much smaller percent of aboriginals (3.4 percent) who live mainly in the North West Territories or Quebec.

An increasing number of Canadians (about 17 percent) speak more than one language fluently. Francophones are more often bilingual than anglophones: across

Canada 41 percent of francophones are bilingual compared to nine percent of anglophones. Outside of Quebec most francophones (84 percent) are bilingual, whereas within Quebec most are not (66 percent). In Quebec, 62 percent of anglophones and 34 percent of francophones are bilingual. Bilingualism is more common in Quebec than in any other province. Since 1974, French has been the official language of Quebec. This legislation together with a law that insists on the use of French on all commercial signs has done much to encourage anglophones to become fluent in French, and may, in large measure, account for why almost twice as many anglophones as francophones are bilingual in Quebec.

The language situation is quite different in the United States than it is in Canada. One reason for the differences between the two countries is the prevalence of the concept of multiculturalism in Canada in contrast with the view of society being a "melting pot" in the United States. This view of American society as a "melting pot" underlies the expectation that all citizens will learn to speak English fluently. Some American states have passed laws establishing English as the only official language (Rothstein, 1998). Many Americans consider having one official language important to national unity. A consequence of such laws and attitudes is that American educators find it difficult to provide instruction in any language other than English. Another consequence is that many Americans are not very motivated to learn a language other than English.

In Canada, because we have two official languages, there has been increasing interest in providing second language instruction in an effort to increase bilingualism. Furthermore, research findings show that bilinguals have some distinct advantages compared to monolinguals. For example, speakers of two languages show more cognitive flexibility. They have more linguistic possibilities at hand for contemplating situations they encounter because of their multiple-language abilities. In turn, this permits them to solve problems with greater creativity and flexibility (Bochner, 1996). Bilingual children perform better than monolingual children on both verbal and nonverbal tests of intelligence (Lambert and Anisfeld, 1969; Lambert and Peal, 1972; Hakuta and Garcia, 1989).

Bilingual children also have distinct advantages in learning to read. An important predictor of success in learning to read is metalinguistic awareness (children's awareness and knowledge of the characteristics of language). In her extensive investigation of metalinguistic awareness, Ellen Bialystok (York University) has found that compared to their monolingual peers, young bilingual children have a more fully developed metalinguistic awareness (Bialystok, 1991,1997; Bialystok and Herman, 1999). Norman Segalowitz (Concordia University) has suggested that bilingualism is beneficial for learning to read because the use of more than one set of linguistic signs and categories promotes a more sophisticated understanding of language (Segalowitz, 1997). For example, bilingual and multilingual children learn that more than one word denotes a concept. This experience helps to focus attention and interest on the characteristics of language, thereby enhancing receptivity for language learning.

Canadian psychologists have made important contributions to the study of second-language learning. In 1965, Wallace Lambert of McGill University initiated a French-immersion program for English speaking elementary school children in a Montreal school district (Lambert and Tucker, 1972). Contrary to the fears of some skeptics, Lambert found that the immersion children were as competent in the English language as their peers who had received all their instruction in English. Fred Genesee, also of McGill University, has found that children can be effectively educated in immersion programs, and that children raised as bilinguals have distinct advantages over their monolingual peers (Genesee, 1984; Nicoladis and Genesee, 1997; Cenoz and Genesee, 1998).

Immersion programs developed by psychologists at McGill have served as pedagogical models in other Canadian provinces and in other countries. These psychologists have developed and evaluated programs in second language instruction in Estonia, Germany, Israel, Japan, Spain, Switzerland, and the United States.

For more information about Professor Genesee and his work, see the Pathways Through Psychology box in this chapter. ∎

Recap, Review, and Rethink

Recap

- Language is characterized by grammar, a system of rules that determine how our thoughts can be expressed.

- Language acquisition proceeds rapidly from birth and is largely complete by the age of 5, although there are subsequent increases in vocabulary and sophistication.

- The learning-theory view suggests that language is learned through the principles of reinforcement and conditioning. In contrast, Chomsky's view suggests that language capabilities are innate, a result of the existence of a language-acquisition device in the brain.

- Issues involving the relationship between language and thought, animals' language abilities, and bilingual education are controversial.

Review

1. Match the component of grammar with its definition:
   1. syntax
   2. phonology
   3. semantics

   a. rules showing how words can be combined into sentences
   b. rules governing the meaning of words and sentences
   c. the study of the sound system in language

2. Language production and language comprehension develop in infants at about the same time. True or false?

3. _____ _____ refers to the phenomenon in which young children omit nonessential portions of sentences.

4. A child knows that adding "ed" to certain words puts them in the past tense. As a result, instead of saying "He came," the child says "He comed." This is an example of _____.

5. _____ theory assumes that language acquisition is based on operant learning principles.

6. Chomsky argues that language acquisition is an innate ability tied to the structure of the brain. True or false?

7. Thought has been proved to influence language, but language does not seem to have an influence on thought. True or false?

Answers to Review Questions are on page 271.

Rethink

1. Why is overgeneralization seen as an argument against a strict learning-theory approach to explaining language acquisition?

2. Suppose it is announced that a group of chimpanzees have mastered English (via a computer console) at an eighth-grade level. What effect would this have on current theories of language acquisition? How might this knowledge be applied to humans?

3. Do people with two languages, one at home and one at school, automatically have two cultures? Why might people who speak two languages experience cognitive advantages over those who speak only one?

looking BACK

How do we think?

1. Cognitive psychologists study cognition, which encompasses the higher mental processes. These processes include the way people know and understand the world, process information, make decisions and judgments, and describe their knowledge and understanding to others.

2. Thinking is the manipulation of mental representations of information. Thinking transforms such representations into novel and different forms, permitting people to answer questions, solve problems, or reach goals.

3. Mental images are representations in the mind that resemble the object or event being represented. Mental images have many of the properties of the perceived objects being

represented. For instance, it takes more time to scan the mental visual representations of large objects than small ones. Similarly, people are able to manipulate and rotate mental visual images of objects.

4. Concepts, one of the building blocks of thinking, are categorizations of objects, events, or people that share common properties. Some concepts are thought of in terms of prototypes, representative examples of the concept.

What processes underlie reasoning and decision making?

5. In deductive reasoning, people derive the implications of a set of assumptions that they know to be true. In inductive reasoning, by contrast, people infer a general rule from specific cases. Inductive reasoning allows people to use

their observations, knowledge, experiences, and beliefs about the world to develop summary conclusions.

6. Decisions may be improved through the use of algorithms and heuristics. Algorithms are rules which, if followed, guarantee a solution, while heuristics are rules of thumb that may lead to a solution but are not guaranteed to do so.

7. There are several kinds of heuristics. In the representativeness heuristic, people decide whether a given example is a member of a particular category by evaluating how representative of that category the example is. The availability heuristic consists of judging the probability of an event by how easily other instances of the event can be recalled from memory. Both of these heuristics can lead to error.

How do people approach and solve problems?

8. Problem solving typically involves three major steps: preparation, production of solutions, and evaluation of solutions that have been generated. Preparation begins when people try to understand the problem. Some problems are well defined, with clear solution requirements; other problems are ill defined, with ambiguities in both the information required for a solution and the solution itself.

9. In arrangement problems, a group of elements must be rearranged or recombined in a way that will satisfy a certain criterion. In problems of inducing structure, a person must identify the relationships among the elements presented and construct a new relationship among them. Finally, transformation problems consist of an initial state, a goal state, and a series of methods for changing the initial state into the goal state.

10. A crucial aspect of the preparation stage is the representation and organization of the problem. Sometimes restructuring a problem from a verbal form to a pictorial or mathematical form can help point the way to the solution.

11. In the production stage, people try to generate solutions. The solutions to some problems may already be in long-term memory, available for direct retrieval. Alternatively, some problems may be solved through simple trial and error. More complex problems, however, require the use of algorithms and heuristics.

12. In a means-ends analysis, a person will repeatedly test for differences between the desired outcome and what currently exists, trying each time to come closer to the goal. Another heuristic is to divide a problem into intermediate steps or subgoals and solve each of those steps.

13. One approach to problem solving is exemplified by Köhler's research with chimpanzees, in which the chimps had to manipulate the elements of the situation in a novel fashion in order to solve the problem. Köhler called the cognitive processes underlying the chimps' behaviour "insight"—a sudden awareness of the relationships among elements that had previously seemed independent.

What are the major obstacles to problem solving?

14. Several factors hinder effective problem solving. Functional fixedness (the tendency to think of an object only in terms of its most typical use), is an example of a broader phenomenon known as mental set. Mental set is the tendency for old patterns of problem solving to persist. The inappropriate use of algorithms and heuristics can also act as an obstacle to the production of solutions to problems. Finally, the confirmation bias, in which initial hypotheses

are favoured, can hinder the accurate evaluation of solutions to problems.

15. Creativity is the combining of responses or ideas in novel ways. Divergent thinking, which is associated with creativity, is the ability to respond with unusual, but still appropriate, responses to problems or questions. Cognitive complexity, the use of and preference for elaborate, intricate, and complex stimuli and thinking patterns, is also related to creativity.

16. A growing body of evidence supports the idea that people can learn to perform better in problem-solving situations. By learning abstract rules of logic and reasoning, people are able to think critically about the underlying causes of everyday events.

17. Suggestions for solving problems creatively include redefining the problem, using fractionation, adopting a critical perspective, using analogies, thinking divergently, taking the perspective of another person, using heuristics, and experimenting with different solutions.

How do people use language?

18. Language is the systematic, meaningful arrangement of symbols. All languages have a grammar—a system of rules that determines how thoughts can be expressed. Grammar encompasses the three major components of language: phonology, syntax, and semantics. Phonology refers to the study of the sounds (called phonemes) we make when we speak and the use of those sounds to produce meaning; syntax refers to the rules that indicate how words are joined together to form sentences; and semantics refers to the rules governing the meaning of words and sentences of language.

How does language develop?

19. Language production, preceded by language comprehension, develops out of babbling (speechlike but meaningless sounds), which leads to the production of actual words. After a year, children use two-word combinations and their vocabulary increases. They first use telegraphic speech, in which words not critical to the message are dropped. By the age of 5, acquisition of language rules is relatively complete.

20. There are two major theories of language acquisition. Learning theorists suggest that language is acquired through reinforcement and conditioning. In contrast, Chomsky suggests that there is an innate language acquisition device that guides the development of language.

21. The linguistic-relativity hypothesis suggests that language shapes and may determine the way people think about the world. Most evidence suggests that although language does not determine thought, it does affect the way information is stored in memory and how well it can be retrieved.

22. The degree to which language is a uniquely human skill remains controversial. Although some psychologists contend that certain primates communicate at a high level but nonetheless do not use language, others suggest that they truly understand and produce language in much the same way as humans.

23. People who speak more than one language may have a cognitive advantage over those who speak only one. Research suggests that they have greater cognitive flexibility, are more aware of the rules of language, and may understand concepts more readily.

Key Terms and Concepts

cognitive psychology (p. 241)
cognition (p. 241)
thinking (p. 241)
mental images (p. 241)
concepts (p. 243)
prototypes (p. 243)
deductive reasoning (p. 244)
inductive reasoning (p. 245)
algorithm (p. 246)
heuristic (p. 246)

means-ends analysis (p. 253)
insight (p. 254)
functional fixedness (p. 256)
mental set (p. 256)
creativity (p. 257)
divergent thinking (p. 257)
convergent thinking (p. 257)
language (p. 261)
grammar (p. 261)
phonology (p. 261)

phonemes (p. 261)
syntax (p. 261)
semantics (p. 261)
babble (p. 262)
telegraphic speech (p. 262)
overgeneralization (p. 262)
learning-theory approach (p. 263)
universal grammar (p. 263)
language-acquisition device (p. 263)
linguistic-relativity hypothesis (p. 264)

Epilogue

The topics in this chapter occupy a central place in the field of psychology. We first examined thinking and reasoning, focusing on the importance of mental images and concepts in our understanding of and interactions with the world. We then turned to problem solving, identifying the three steps commonly involved in problem solving: preparation, production of solutions, and evaluation of generated solutions. Finally, we concluded with a discussion of language, describing the components of grammar and tracing language development in children.

We will continue our focus on cognition in the next chapter, as we turn to the subject of intelligence. Before we proceed, however, turn back to the Prologue, where we met the prolific inventor Jacob Rabinow. Consider the following questions in light of what you have learned about reasoning, problem solving, and creativity.

1. What do you think Rabinow means when he says that inventing is as much an art form as composing music or writing poetry? Is he right?

2. Does the notion of prototypes provide clues to the process of invention? Do you think Rabinow's combination book-stool is a prototypical example of a stool?

3. How do the concepts of functional fixedness and mental set relate to Rabinow's inventiveness? Are they related to the notion of prototypes?

4. How do you think insight is involved in Rabinow's inventiveness?

5. In what ways do you think divergent and convergent thinking are involved in the processes of invention? Do they play different roles in the various stages of the act of invention, including identifying the need for an invention, devising possible solutions, and creating a practical invention?

Answers to Review Questions:

1. 1-a; 2-c; 3-b   2. False; language comprehension precedes language production.   3. Telegraphic speech   4. overgeneralization
5. Learning   6. true   7. False; language and thought seem to interact with each other in a variety of ways.

Mindie Crutcher.

Prologue

Mindie Crutcher and Robert Theiss

When Mindie was born, physicians said she would always be hopelessly retarded, that she would never sit up, never walk, never speak. "She will never know you're her mother," they told 25-year-old Diane Crutcher. "Tell relatives your baby is dead."

Today, the child who would never sit up is a lively seventh-grader. The child who would never talk or know her own mother told a symposium of physicians she was "glad Mom and Dad gave me a chance."

Yet the experts were right about one thing: Mindie does have Down syndrome, a genetic disorder, one of the most common birth defects and the leading physical cause of mental retardation (Turkington, 1987, p. 42).

* * *

Imagine—and it takes some doing—being one out of five of the 17,000 grade seven students in Ontario scoring a perfect 100 percent on a math test. Robert Theiss, of Oakville, Ontario is that student. This is no ordinary math test. He wrote The Gauss Mathematics Contest for grade seven and eight students. It is sponsored, in part, by the University of Waterloo and was written by 39,000 students worldwide in 2000. When asked about his ability in math he says that it's probably a blend of genetics and hard work.

The son of two chartered accountants, Robert enjoys spending some of his leisure time solving problems from math books provided by his parents. According to his teachers and his parents he is a well-rounded student who plays soccer and hockey. He reads extensively (100 novels in grade four) and is a gifted artist and creative writer. He hopes one day to have a career that involves mathematics.

looking
AHEAD

Two very different seventh graders—with widely different intellectual capabilities. And yet, one could argue that, Mindie Crutcher and Robert Theiss have much in common. With their personal strengths, motivation and goals moving them forward they may in fact be more similar than different.

In this chapter, we consider intelligence in all its many varieties. Intelligence represents a focal point for psychologists intent on understanding how people are able to adapt their behaviour to the environment in which they live. It also represents a key aspect of how individuals differ from one another in the way in which they learn about and understand the world.

We begin this chapter by considering the challenges involved in defining and measuring intelligence. If you are like most people, you have probably wondered how smart you are. Psychologists, too, have pondered the nature of intelligence. We will examine some of their conceptions of intelligence as well as efforts to develop and use standardized tests as a means of measuring intelligence.

We will also consider the two groups displaying extremes of individual differences in intelligence: people with mental retardation and the gifted. The special challenges of each population will be discussed along with special programs that have been developed to help individuals from both groups reach their full potential.

Finally, we will explore what are probably the two most controversial issues surrounding intelligence. First, we will consider the degree to which intelligence is influenced by heredity and by the environment. Then we will discuss whether traditional tests of intelligence are biased toward the dominant cultural groups in society—a difficult issue that has both psychological and social significance.

▶ **How do psychologists conceptualize and define intelligence?**

▶ **What are the major approaches to measuring intelligence?**

DEFINING INTELLIGENT BEHAVIOUR

It is typical for members of the Trukese, a small tribe in the South Pacific, to sail a hundred miles in open ocean waters. Although their destination may be just a small

dot of land less than a mile wide, the Trukese are able to sail unerringly toward it without the aid of a compass, chronometer, sextant, or any of the other sailing tools that are indispensable to modern western navigation. They are able to sail accurately, even when prevailing winds do not allow a direct approach to the island and they must take a zigzag course (Gladwin, 1964).

How are the Trukese able to navigate so effectively? If you asked them, they could not explain it. They might tell you that they use a process that takes into account the rising and setting of the stars and the appearance, sound, and feel of the waves against the side of the boat. But at any given moment as they are sailing along, they could not identify their position or say why they are doing what they are doing. Nor could they explain the navigational theory underlying their sailing technique.

Some might say the inability of the Trukese to explain in western terms how their sailing technique works is a sign of primitive or even unintelligent behaviour. In fact, if we made Trukese sailors take a standardized western test of navigational knowledge and theory, or, for that matter, a traditional test of intelligence, they might very well do poorly on it. Yet, as a practical matter, it is hard to accuse the Trukese of being unintelligent: Despite their inability to explain how they do it, they are able to navigate successfully through the open ocean waters.

Trukese navigation points out the difficulty in coming to grips with what is meant by intelligence. To a westerner, travelling in a straight line along the most direct and quickest route using a sextant and other navigational tools is likely to represent the most "intelligent" kind of behaviour; on the other hand, a zigzag course, based on the "feel" of the waves, would not seem very reasonable. To the Trukese, who are used to their own system of navigation, however, the use of complicated navigational tools might seem so overly complex and unnecessary that they might think of western navigators as lacking in intelligence.

Intelligence

It is clear that the term "intelligence" can take on many different meanings (Lohman, 1989; Davidson, 1990; Ruzgis & Grigorenko, 1994). If, for instance, you lived in a remote African village, the way you would differentiate between more intelligent and less intelligent people might be very different from the way that someone living in the heart of urban Miami would distinguish individual differences. To the African, high intelligence might be represented by exceptional hunting or other survival skills; to the Miamian, it might be exemplified by dealing effectively with a mass-transit system, by being "street wise," or by avoiding being hustled.

Each of these conceptions of intelligence is reasonable, for each represents an instance in which more intelligent people are better able to use the resources of their environment than less intelligent people, a distinction that we would assume to be basic to any definition of intelligence. Yet it is also clear that these conceptions represent very different views of intelligence.

That two such different sets of behaviour can exemplify the same psychological concept has long posed a challenge to psychologists. For years, they have grappled with the issue of devising a general definition of intelligence that would remain independent of a person's specific culture and other environmental factors. Interestingly, untrained laypersons have fairly clear conceptions of intelligence (Sternberg, 1985b). For example, in one survey that asked a group of people to define what they meant by intelligence, three major components of intelligence emerged (Sternberg et al., 1981). First, there was problem-solving ability: People who reason logically and identify more solutions to problems were seen as intelligent. Second, verbal abilities were thought to exemplify intelligence. Finally, social competence, the ability to show interest in others and interact effectively with them, was viewed as indicating intelligence.

The definition of intelligence that psychologists employ contains some of the same elements found in the layperson's conception. To psychologists, **intelligence** is the capacity to understand the world, think rationally, and use resources effectively when faced with challenges (Wechsler, 1975).

Unfortunately, neither the layperson's nor the psychologist's conception of intelligence is of much help when it comes to distinguishing, with any degree of precision, more intelligent people from less intelligent ones. To overcome this problem, psychologists who study intelligence have focused much of their attention on the development of batteries of tests, known, quite obviously, as **intelligence tests,** and have relied on such tests to identify a person's level of intelligence. These tests have proven to be of great benefit in identifying students in need of special attention in school, in diagnosing cognitive difficulties, and in helping people make optimal educational and vocational choices. At the same time, their use has proved quite controversial.

Measuring Intelligence

The first intelligence tests followed a simple premise: If performance on certain tasks or test items improved with age, then performance could be used to distinguish more intelligent people from less intelligent ones within a particular age group. Using this principle, Alfred Binet, a French psychologist, devised the first formal intelligence test, which was designed to identify the "dullest" students in the Paris school system in order to provide them with remedial aid.

Binet began by presenting tasks to same-age students who had been labelled "bright" or "dull" by their teachers. If a task could be completed by the bright students but not by the dull ones, he retained the task as a proper test item; otherwise it was discarded. In the end he came up with a test that distinguished between the bright and dull groups, and—with further work—one that distinguished among children in different age groups (Binet & Simon, 1916).

On the basis of the Binet test, children were assigned a score that corresponded to their **mental age,** the average age of children taking the test who achieved the same score. For example, if a 9-year-old boy received a score of 45 on the test and this was the average score received by 8-year-olds, his mental age would be considered to be 8 years. Similarly, a 14-year-old girl who scored an 88 on the test—matching the mean score for 16-year-olds—would be assigned a mental age of 16 years.

Assigning a mental age to students provided an indication of whether or not they were performing at the same level as their peers. However, it did not allow for adequate comparisons among people of different *chronological,* or physical, ages. By using mental age alone, for instance, we might assume that an 18-year-old responding at a 16-year-old's level would be as bright as a 5-year-old answering at a 3-year-old's level, when actually the 5-year-old would be displaying a much greater *relative* degree of slowness.

intelligence: The capacity to understand the world, think rationally, and use resources effectively when faced with challenges

intelligence tests: Tests devised to identify a person's level of intelligence

Intelligence: The Controversy

mental age: The average age of children taking the Binet test who achieved the same score

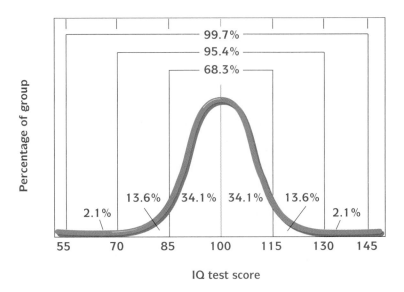

FIGURE 8-1 *The average and most frequent IQ score is 100, and 68.3 percent of all people are within a 30 point range centred on 100. Some 95 percent of the population have scores that are within 30 points above or below 100, and 99.7 percent have scores that are between 55 and 145.*

A solution to the problem came in the form of the **intelligence quotient, or IQ,** a score that takes into account an individual's mental *and* chronological ages. To calculate an IQ score, the following formula is used, in which MA stands for mental age and CA for chronological age:

intelligence quotient (IQ): A score that takes into account an individual's mental *and* chronological ages

$$IQ\ score = \frac{MA}{CA} \times 100$$

Using this formula, we can return to the earlier example of an 18-year-old performing at a mental age of 16 and calculate an IQ score of ($^{16}\!/_8$) × 100 = 88.9. In contrast, the 5-year-old performing at a mental age of 3 comes out with a considerably lower IQ score: ($^3\!/_5$) × 100 = 60.

As a bit of trial and error with the formula will show you, anyone who has a mental age equal to his or her chronological age will have an IQ equal to 100. Moreover, people with a mental age that is greater than their chronological age will have IQs that exceed 100.

Although the basic principles behind the calculation of an IQ score still hold, IQ scores are figured in a somewhat different manner today and are known as *deviation IQ scores*. First, the average test score for everyone of the same age who takes the test is determined, and this average score is assigned an IQ of 100. Then, with the aid of sophisticated mathematical techniques that calculate the differences (or "deviations") between each score and the average, IQ values are assigned to all the other test scores for this age group.

As you can see in Figure 8-1, approximately two-thirds of all individuals fall within fifteen IQ points above and below the average score of 100. As scores increase or fall beyond that range, the percentage of people in a category falls considerably.

Tests of IQ

Just what is an IQ test like? It is probable that sometime during your academic career you have taken one; almost all of us are given IQ tests at one time or another.

Remnants of the original test are still with us, although it has been revised many times and in its modern incarnation bears little resemblance to the original version. Now called the *Stanford-Binet Test,* Fourth Edition, the test consists of a series of items that vary in nature according to the age of the person being tested (Hagen, Sattler, & Thorndike, 1985; Thorndike, Hagan, & Sattler, 1986). For example, young children are asked to copy figures or answer questions about everyday activities. Older people are asked to solve analogies, explain proverbs, and describe similarities that underlie sets of words.

Some intelligence tests include nonverbal items that assess the ability to copy a given pattern using blocks.

The test is administered orally. An examiner begins by finding a mental age level at which the person is able to answer all questions correctly, and then moves on to successively difficult problems. When a mental age level is reached at which no items can be answered, the test is over. By examining the pattern of correct and incorrect responses, the examiner is able to compute an IQ score for the person being tested.

The other IQ test frequently used in North America was devised by psychologist David Wechsler and is known as the *Wechsler Adult Intelligence Scale—III,* or, more commonly, the *WAIS-III.* There is also a children's version, the *Wechsler Intelligence Scale for Children—III,* or *WISC-III.* Both the WAIS-III and the WISC-III have two major parts: a verbal scale and a performance—or nonverbal—scale. As you can see from the sample questions in Figure 8-2, the two scales include questions of very different types. Whereas verbal tasks consist of more traditional kinds of problems, including vocabulary definition and comprehension of various concepts, the nonverbal part involves assembling small objects and arranging pictures in a logical order. Although an individual's scores on the verbal and performance sections of the test are generally within close range of each other, the scores of a person with a language deficiency or a background of severe environmental deprivation may show a relatively large discrepancy between the two scores. By providing separate scores, the WAIS-III and WISC-III give a more precise picture of a person's specific abilities.

Because the Stanford-Binet, WAIS-III, and WISC-III all require individualized administration, it is relatively difficult and time-consuming to administer and score them on a wide-scale basis. Consequently, there are now a number of IQ tests that allow for group administration. Rather than having one examiner ask one person at a time to respond to individual items, group IQ tests are strictly paper-and-pencil measures, in which those taking the tests read the questions and provide their answers in writing. The primary advantage of group tests is their ease of administration (Anastasi & Urbina, 1997).

There are, however, sacrifices made in group testing which, in some cases, may outweigh the benefits. For instance, group tests generally offer a more restricted range of questions than tests administered individually. Furthermore, people may be more motivated to perform at their highest ability level when working on a one-to-one basis with a test administrator than they are in a group. Finally, in some cases, it is simply impossible to employ group tests, particularly with young children or people with unusually low IQs (Aiken, 1996).

Achievement and Aptitude Tests

IQ tests are not the only kind of tests that you may have taken during the course of your schooling. Two other kinds of tests, related to intelligence but designed to measure somewhat different phenomena, are achievement tests and aptitude tests. An **achievement test** is a test meant to ascertain a person's level of knowledge in a given subject area. In Canadian schools these tests are routinely given at least three times, for example in grades three, five and eight. The exact grades differ by province. Rather than measuring general ability, as an intelligence test does, an achievement test concentrates on the specific material that a person has learned.

An **aptitude test** is designed to predict a person's ability in a particular area or line of work. In the process of pursuing admission to university, American students, and Canadian students applying to universities in the United States, take one of the best-known aptitude tests: the Scholastic Assessment Test (SAT). The SAT is meant to predict how well people will do at university, and the scores have proven over the years to correlate moderately well with university grades. For students going on to graduate school, the Graduate Record Exam (GRE) if often required. Aptitude tests are not restricted to application to academic institutions. Air traffic control is one of many training programs for which you would be expected to take the appropriate aptitude test to evaluate your potential for success.

Although in theory the distinction between intelligence, aptitude, and achievement tests can be precisely drawn, as a practical matter there is a good deal of overlap among them. It is difficult to devise tests that predict future performance but do not rely on past achievement.

achievement test: A test meant to ascertain a person's level of knowledge in a given subject area

aptitude test: A test designed to predict a person's ability in a particular area or line of work

Types of Items found on the Wechsler Intelligence Scales for Children—III (WISC-III)

Name	Goal of Item	Example
Verbal scale		
Information	To assess general information	Where does milk come from?
Comprehension	To test understanding and evaluation of social norms and past experience	Why do we put food in the refrigerator?
Arithmetic	To assess math reasoning through verbal problems	Stacy had two crayons and the teacher gave her two more. How many did she have altogether?
Similarities	To test understanding of how objects or concepts are alike, tapping abstract reasoning	In what way are cows and horses alike?
Performance Scale		
Digit symbol	To assess speed of learning	Match symbols to numbers using the key
Picture completion	To identify missing parts, testing visual memory and attention	Identify what is missing 
Object assembly	To test understanding of relationship of parts to wholes	Put pieces together to form a whole 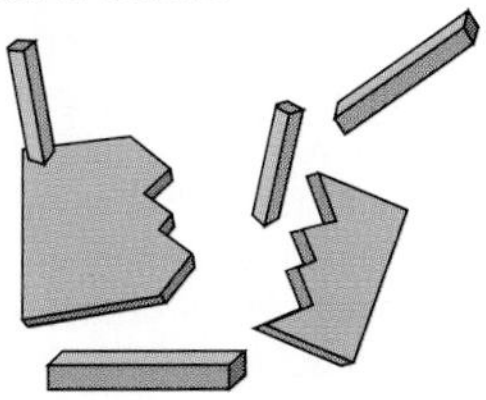

FIGURE 8-2 *Typical kinds of items found on the verbal and performance scales of the Wechsler Intelligence Scales for Children—III (WISC-III).*

The SAT and GRE, as well as other tests, are undergoing a modification in the way that they are administered. In a break from traditional paper-and-pencil tests, the makers of the SAT and GRE will use computers to present a personalized version of the exam to each test-taker. This innovation is only one of several that are changing the way in which people take tests, as we discuss in the Applying Psychology in the 21st Century box.

Reliability and Validity

When we use a ruler, we expect to find that it measures a centimetre in the same way as the last time we used it. When we weigh ourselves on the bathroom scale, we hope that the variations we see on the scale are due to changes in our weight and not to errors on the part of the scale (unless the change in weight is in an unwanted direction!).

Reliability and Validity

Take-at-Home IQ Tests and Take-at-Computer SATs and GREs: Personalized Test Taking

In an age in which home pregnancy testing is routine, it should not be surprising that take-at-home IQ tests might become equally popular. At least that's the hope of a Massachusetts company that has begun to offer a computerized CD-ROM intelligence test for children. The "Children's IQ and Achievement Test" is designed to provide an IQ score for kindergarten through sixth-grade children in the comfort of their homes. According to its developers, the home IQ test is meant to meet the needs of parents who wish to become more involved in their children's education. Bryan Bryant, president of the company that produced the test, says, "Nobody knows more about a child than the parent does. And yet so often at school the parent is a recipient rather than a contributor of information about their child. This can provide another perspective" (Kelly, 1997, p. B7).

Many psychologists and educators disagree, however. Some fear that children will be incorrectly labelled because of potential inaccuracies in the test. Others feel that placing a label on a child at an early age—even an accurate one—may have unfortunate consequences, as children's future treatment is based on the results of the test. Furthermore, even if the test is accurate, it is unclear for what purposes the information will be used (Kelly, 1997).

Take-at-home IQ tests are only one of several innovations that are changing the nature of testing. Another is the use of computers to administer standardized tests. The Educational Testing Service (ETS)—the company that devises the

SAT and the Graduate Record Examination (GRE), used for college and graduate school admission, respectively—is moving to computer administration of all GRE tests by the turn of the century, with SAT administration following suit shortly after.

In the new computerized version, not only will the test questions be viewed and answered on a computer screen, but the test itself will be individualized. In what is known as *adaptive testing,* no two students will receive an identical set of test questions. Instead, the computer will first present a randomly selected question of moderate difficulty. If the test-taker answers it correctly, the computer will then present a randomly chosen item of slightly greater difficulty. If the answer is wrong then the computer will present a slightly easier item. Each question becomes slightly harder or easier than the question preceding it, depending on whether the previous response is correct. Ultimately, the greater the number of difficult questions answered correctly, the higher the score (see Figure 8-3).

Because the test is able to pinpoint a test-taker's level of proficiency fairly quickly, the total time spent taking the exam is shorter than it is when taking a traditional exam. Test-takers are not forced to spend a great deal of time answering questions that are either much easier or much harder than they can handle.

Computerized administration has another feature that may, or may not, be welcomed: presentation of an immediate test score. After completing the test, test-takers are given the option of nullifying

the test if they think they did not do well. If they choose to proceed, however, the computer provides them with their score, which then becomes part of a permanent record.

Computerized adaptive testing has its critics. Some observers suggest that the test discriminates against minorities, who may have limited access to computers and thus may have less practice with them or may be more intimidated by the testing medium (Winerip, 1993). However, ETS disputes the claim, although some of its own research shows that women and older test-takers show greater anxiety at the beginning of the test. Despite this anxiety, however, their performance ultimately is not affected.

Research also suggests that computerized adaptive testing provides scores equivalent to traditional paper-and-pencil measures for most types of testing. (The exception is for "speeded" tests, which involve many relatively easy items that must be completed in a relatively short time.) For tests such as the GRE, however, there appears to be no difference in scores that can be attributed to whether the test is administered traditionally or with a computer.

Whether future tests are administered via computer or more traditional means, what is clear is that testing will be an increasing part of our lives. Ministries of Education in all provinces and territories are requiring standardized testing in the foundation skills of reading comprehension and mathematics at various grade levels.

---

reliability: The concept that tests measure consistently what they are trying to measure

In the same way, we hope that psychological tests have **reliability**—that they measure consistently what they are trying to measure. We need to be sure that each time we administer the test, a test-taker will achieve the same results—assuming that nothing about the person has changed relevant to what is being measured.

Suppose, for instance, that when you first took the SAT exams you scored a 400 on the verbal section of the test. Then, after taking the test again a few months later, you scored a 700. Upon receiving your new score, you might well stop celebrating for a moment to question whether the test is reliable, for it is unlikely that your abilities could have changed enough to raise your score by 300 points.

With the pencil-and-paper version of the Graduate Record Examination all test-takers answer the same questions, which range in difficulty from easy to hard. But the computerized version allows the computer to zero in on the level of difficulty the student can handle. The computer randomly selects a first question of medium difficulty. If the test-taker answers the question correctly, the computer poses a more difficult question. Once the test-taker gives an incorrect answer, he or she is given a question at the next easiest level. Test-takers are graded based on the level of difficulty they master. Below are some sample questions and answers of various difficulty levels.

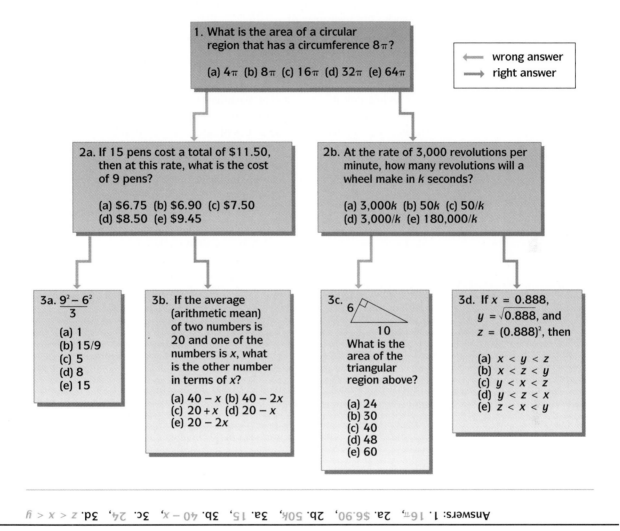

FIGURE 8-3 *In an example of adaptive testing, a computer randomly chooses the initial question, which will be of moderate difficulty. If the test-taker answers correctly, the computer presents a more difficult item; if the answer is wrong, the computer poses an easier item. Ultimately, the greater the number of difficult questions answered correctly, the higher the score. Source: Adapted from the* New York Times, *1993, p. B9.*

But suppose your score changed hardly at all, and both times you received a score of about 400. You couldn't complain about a lack of reliability. However, if you knew your verbal skills were above average, you might be concerned that the test did not adequately measure what it was supposed to measure. In sum, the question has now become one of validity rather than reliability. A test has **validity** when it actually measures what it is supposed to measure.

validity: The concept that tests actually measure what they are supposed to measure

Knowing that a test is reliable is no guarantee that it is also valid. For instance, we could devise a very reliable means for measuring trustworthiness, if we decided that trustworthiness is related to skull size. But there is certainly no guarantee that the test is valid, since one can reasonably assume that skull size has nothing to do with trustworthiness. In this case, then, we have reliability without validity.

On the other hand, if a test is unreliable, it cannot be valid. Assuming that all other factors—motivation to score well, knowledge of the material, health, and so forth—are similar, if a person scores high the first time he or she takes a specific test and low the second time, the test cannot be measuring what it is supposed to measure. Therefore, the test is neither reliable nor valid.

Test validity and reliability are prerequisites for accurate assessment of intelligence—as well as for any other measurement task carried out by psychologists. Consequently, the measures of personality that we'll consider in Chapter 11, clinical psychologists' assessment of psychological disorders discussed in Chapters 12 and 13, and social psychologists' measures of attitudes must meet the tests of validity and reliability in order for the results to be meaningful.

Assuming that a test is both valid and reliable, one further step is necessary in order to interpret the meaning of a particular test-taker's score: the establishment of norms. **Norms** are standards of test performance that permit the comparison of one person's score on the test to the scores of others who have taken the same test. For example, a norm permits test-takers to know that they have scored in the top 15 percent of those who have taken the test.

The basic scheme for developing norms is for test designers to calculate the average score achieved by a particular group of people for whom the test is designed. The test designers can then determine the extent to which each person's score differs from the scores of the others who have taken the test in the past. Test-takers are then able to consider the meaning of their raw scores relative to the scores of others who have taken the test, giving them a qualitative sense of their performance.

Obviously, the samples of test-takers who are employed in the establishment of norms are critical to the norming process. Those people used to determine norms must be representative of the individuals to whom the test is directed.

Alternative Formulations of Intelligence

Although Binet's procedure for measuring intelligence, exemplified by the modern Stanford-Binet and WAIS-III intelligence tests, remains one of the most frequently employed, some theorists argue that it lacks an underlying conception of what intelligence is. To Binet and his followers, intelligence was generally conceived of as a direct reflection of a person's score on his or her test. That was an eminently practical approach, but it depended not on an understanding of the nature of intelligence but primarily on comparing one person's performance with that of others. For this reason, the intelligence tests of Binet and his successors do little to increase our understanding of what intelligence is; they merely measure behaviour assumed to exemplify intelligence.

This is not to say that researchers and theoreticians have ignored the issue of what intelligence really is (Carroll, 1992, 1993, 1994, 1996). One important question they have raised is whether intelligence is a single, unitary factor, or whether it is made up of multiple components (Sternberg, 1990, 1994; Dennis & Tapsfield, 1996; Gottfredson, 1997). The earliest psychologists interested in intelligence assumed that there was a general factor for mental ability, called **g,** or **g-factor** (Spearman, 1927). This factor was thought to underlie performance on every aspect of intelligence, and it was the g-factor that was presumably being measured on tests of intelligence.

More contemporary theoreticians have suggested that there are really two different kinds of intelligence: fluid intelligence and crystallized intelligence (Cattell, 1967, 1987). **Fluid intelligence** reflects reasoning, memory, and information-processing capabilities. If we were asked to solve an analogy, group a series of letters according to some criterion, or to remember a set of numbers, we would be using fluid intelligence.

In contrast, **crystallized intelligence** is the information, skills, and strategies that people have learned through experience and that they can apply in problem-solving situations. We would be likely to rely on crystallized intelligence, for instance, if we were asked to participate in a discussion about the causes of homelessness or to deduce the solution to a mystery. Such tasks allow us to draw upon our own past experiences. The differences between fluid and crystallized intelligence become

norms: Standards of test performance that permit the comparison of one person's score on the test to the scores of others who have taken the same test

g or g-factor: An early theory that assumed there was a general factor for mental ability

fluid intelligence: Intelligence that reflects reasoning, memory, and information processing capabilities

crystallized intelligence: The information, skills, and strategies that people have learned through experience and that they can apply in problem-solving situations

Playing a game like Trivial Pursuit (left) calls mainly for fluid intelligence, which consists of reasoning, memory, and information-processing capabilities. Piloting an airplane (above) requires both fluid intelligence and crystallized intelligence, which is the product of experience and is used in problem-solving situations.

particularly evident in the elderly, who—as we will discuss further in Chapter 10—show declines in fluid, but not crystallized, intelligence (Wang & Kaufman, 1993; Schaie, 1993, 1994; Heidrich & Denney, 1994; Boone, 1995).

Other theoreticians conceive of intelligence as encompassing even more components. For instance, by examining the talents of people who display unusual abilities in certain areas, psychologist Howard Gardner has suggested that we have multiple intelligences, each relatively independent of the others (Gardner, 1983, 1997; Krechevsky & Gardner, 1990; Gardner, Kornhaber, & Wake, 1996). Specifically, he considers intelligence to include the seven spheres illustrated in Figure 8-4.

Although Gardner illustrates his conception of the specific types of intelligence with descriptions of well-known people, it is important to remember that each of us theoretically harbors the same kinds of intelligence. Moreover, although the seven are presented individually, Gardner suggests that these separate intelligences do not operate in isolation. Normally, any activity encompasses several kinds of intelligence working together.

Gardner's model has led to a number of advances in our understanding of the nature of intelligence. For example, one outgrowth of the model is the development of test items in which more than one answer can be correct, providing the opportunity for test-takers to demonstrate creative thinking. According to these approaches, then, different kinds of intelligence may produce different—but equally valid—responses to the same question.

Multiple Intelligences

Is Information Processing Intelligence? Contemporary Approaches

The most recent contribution to understanding intelligence comes from the work of cognitive psychologists. Drawing on the research and theory that we discussed in Chapter 7, cognitive psychologists use an information-processing approach. They assert that the way people store material in memory and use the material to solve intellectual tasks provides the most accurate measure of intelligence. Consequently, cognitive psychologists do not focus on the structure of intelligence or its underlying content or dimensions. Instead, they examine the *processes* involved in producing intelligent behaviour (Sternberg, 1990; Fagan, 1992; Deary & Stough, 1996; Embretson, 1996).

1. Musical intelligence (skills in tasks involving music). Case example:

When he was 3, Yehudi Menuhin was smuggled into the San Francisco Orchestra concerts by his parents. The sound of Louis Persinger's violin so entranced the youngster that he insisted on a violin for his birthday and Louis Persinger as his teacher. He got them both. By the time he was 10 years old, Menuhin was an international performer.

2. Bodily kinesthetic intelligence (skills in using the whole body or various portions of it in the solution of problems or in the construction of products or displays, exemplified by dancers, athletes, actors, and surgeons). Case example:

Fifteen-year old Babe Ruth played third base. During one game, his team's pitcher was doing very poorly and Babe loudly criticized him from third base. Brother Matthias, the coach, called out, "Ruth, if you know so much about it, *you* pitch!" Babe was surprised and embarrassed because he had never pitched before, but Brother Matthias insisted. Ruth said later that at the very moment he took the pitcher's mound, he *knew* he was supposed to be a pitcher.

3. Logical-mathematical intelligence (skills in problem-solving and scientific thinking). Case example:

Barbara McClintock won the Nobel Prize in medicine for her work in microbiology. She describes one of her breakthroughs, which came after thinking about a problem for half an hour . . .: "Suddenly I jumped and ran back to the (corn) field. At the top of the field (the others were still at the bottom) I shouted, 'Eureka, I have it!' "

4. Linguistic intelligence (skills involved in the production and use of language). Case example:

At the age of 10, T. S. Eliot created a magazine called *Fireside*, to which he was the sole contributor. In a three-day period during his winter vacation, he created eight complete issues.

5. Spatial intelligence (skills involving spatial configurations, such as those used by artists and architects). Case example:

Natives of the Caroline Islands navigate at sea without instruments. During the actual trip, the navigator must envision mentally a reference island as it passes under a particular star and from that he computes the number of segments completed, the proportion of the trip remaining, and any corrections in heading.

6. Interpersonal intelligence (skills in interacting with others, such as sensitivity to the moods, temperaments, motivations, and intentions of others). Case example:

When Anne Sullivan began instructing the deaf and blind Helen Keller, her task was one that had eluded others for years. Yet, just two weeks after beginning her work with Keller, Sullivan achieved a great success. In her words, "My heart is singing with joy this morning. A miracle has happened! The wild little creature of two weeks ago has been transformed into a gentle child."

7. Intrapersonal intelligence (knowledge of the internal aspects of oneself; access to one's own feelings and emotions). Case example:

In her essay "A Sketch of the Past," Virginia Woolf displays deep insight into her own inner life through these lines, describing her reaction to several specific memories from her childhood that still, in adulthood, shock her: "Though I still have the peculiarity that I receive these sudden shocks, they are now always welcome; after the first surprise, I always feel instantly that they are particularly valuable. And so I go on to suppose that the shock-receiving capacity is what makes me a writer."

FIGURE 8-4 *Gardner's seven intelligences. Source: Adapted from Walters & Gardner, 1986.*

By breaking tasks and problems into their component parts and identifying the nature and speed of problem-solving processes, researchers have noted distinct differences between those who score high on traditional IQ tests and those who score lower. Take, for example, a college student who is asked to solve the following analogy problem (Sternberg, 1982):

lawyer is to *client* as *doctor* is to:

(a) *patient* or (b) *medicine*

According to Sternberg's theory, a student presented with this analogy tends to move through a series of stages in attempting to reach a solution (see Figure 8-5). First she will *encode* the initial information, which means providing each item with identifying cues that help retrieve relevant information buried in long-term memory. For instance, she may think of lawyer in terms of law school, the Supreme Court, the television program *Law and Order,* and a courtroom. Each of the other terms will be similarly encoded. Next, she will *infer* any possible relationship between lawyer and client. She may infer that the relevant relationship is that a client employs a lawyer, or, alternatively, that a lawyer gives services to a client.

Once this relationship has been inferred, the student must *map* the higher-order relationship between the first half of the analogy and the second half—both deal with people who provide professional services for a fee. The crucial stage that follows is one of *application,* in which the answer options are tried out with the relationship that has been inferred. She will presumably decide that a doctor provides professional services to a patient, not to medicine. Finally, the last component of solving the problem is responding.

By breaking problems into component parts in this manner, it is possible to identify systematic differences in both quantitative and qualitative aspects of problem solving, and to demonstrate that people with higher intelligence levels differ not only in the number of correct solutions they come up with, but in their method of solving problems. For instance, high scorers are apt to spend more time on the initial encoding stages of a problem, identifying the parts of the problem and retrieving relevant information from long-term memory. This initial emphasis on recalling relevant information pays off in the end; those who spend relatively less time on the initial stages tend to be less able to find a solution. The use of such information-processing strategies, therefore, may underlie differences in intelligence.

Applying this cognitive approach to intelligence, psychologist Robert Sternberg (1985a; 1991, 1994, 1996) developed what he calls a triarchic theory of intelligence. The **triarchic theory of intelligence** suggests that there are three major aspects to intelligence: componential, experiential, and contextual (see Figure 8-6). The *componential* aspect focuses on the mental components involved in analyzing information to solve problems, particularly those processes operating when a person displays rational behavior. In contrast, the *experiential* aspect focuses on how a person's prior experiences affect intelligence, and how those experiences are brought to bear on problems. Finally, the *contextual* aspect of intelligence takes into account how successful people are in facing the demands of their everyday environment.

Recent approaches to intelligence have focused most heavily on Sternberg's contextual aspect of intelligence (Sternberg, 1996). Several new theories emphasize *practical intelligence*—intelligence related to overall success in living, rather than to intellectual and academic performance, as we discuss next.

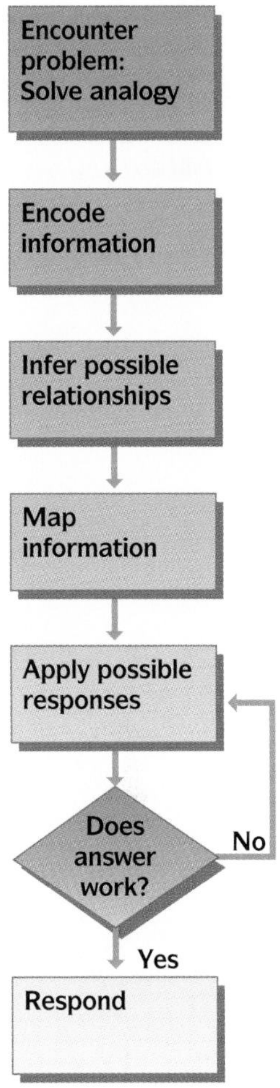

FIGURE 8-5 *Information-processing stages in solving analogies. Source: Sternberg, 1982.*

triarchic theory of intelligence: Robert Sternberg's theory that there are three major aspects to intelligence: componential, experiential, and contextual

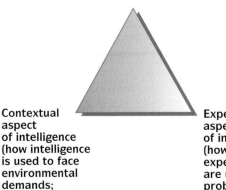

Sternberg's Triarchic Theory of Intelligence

Componential aspect of intelligence (analysis of information to solve problems)

Contextual aspect of intelligence (how intelligence is used to face environmental demands; practical intelligence)

Experiential aspect of intelligence (how prior experiences are used in problem solving)

FIGURE 8-6 *Sternberg's triarchic theory of intelligence. Source: Based on Sternberg, 1985a, 1991.*

Some contemporary approaches to intelligence emphasize practical intelligence, which is intelligence related to success in everyday situations, rather than academic and intellectual performance.

Practical Intelligence: Common Sense

Your year on the job has been generally favourable. Performance ratings for your department are at least as good as they were before you took over, and perhaps even a little better. You have two assistants. One is quite capable. The other just seems to go through the motions and is of little real help. Even though you are well liked, you believe that there is little that would distinguish you in the eyes of your superiors from the nine other managers at a comparable level in the company. Your goal is rapid promotion to an executive position. (Based on Wagner & Sternberg, 1985, p. 447.)

What do you do to meet your goal? The way in which you answer this question may have a lot to do with your future success in a business career, according to its author, psychologist Robert J. Sternberg. The question is one of a series designed to help give an indication of your intelligence. It is not traditional intelligence that the question is designed to tap, but rather intelligence of a particular kind: practical intelligence for business (Wagner & Sternberg, 1991; Sternberg & Wagner, 1986, 1993; Sternberg et al., 1995; Sternberg, 1995, 1996; Wagner, 1997).

The test that Sternberg has devised is one of several recent intelligence measures now taking shape. Each is designed to overcome one of the most glaring limitations of traditional IQ tests: the inability of traditional tests to accurately predict anything other than academic success.

For instance, although not all psychologists agree (e.g., Ree & Earles, 1992), most believe that IQ does not relate particularly well to *career* success (McClelland, 1993). For example, while it is clear that successful business executives usually score at least moderately well on IQ tests, the rate at which they advance and their ultimate business achievements are only minimally associated with their specific IQ scores.

Intelligence Theory

Management

You are responsible for selecting a contractor to reno- vate several large buildings. You have narrowed the choice to two contractors on the basis of their bids, and after further investigation, you are considering awarding the contract to the Wilson & Sons Company. Rate the importance of the following pieces of information in making your decision to award the contract to Wilson & Sons.

_____ The company has provided letters from satisfied former customers.

_____ The Better Business Bureau reports no major complaints about the company.

_____ Wilson & Sons has done good work for your company in the past.

_____ Wilson & Sons' bid was $2,000 less than the other contractor's (approximate total cost of the renovation is $325,000).

_____ Former customers whom you have contacted strongly recommended Wilson & Sons for the job.

Sales

You sell a line of photocopy machines. One of your machines has relatively few features and is inexpen- sive, at $700, although it is not the least expensive model you carry. The $700 photocopy machine is not selling well and it is overstocked. There is a shortage of the more elaborate photocopy machines in your line, so you have been asked to do what you can to improve sales of the $700 machine. Rate the following strategies for maximizing your sales of the slow-moving photocopy machine.

_____ Stress with potential customers that although this model lacks some desirable features, the low price more than makes up for it.

_____ Stress that there are relatively few models left at this price.

_____ Arrange as many demonstrations as possible of the machine.

_____ Stress simplicity of use, since the machine lacks confusing controls that other machines may have.

Academic Psychology

It is your second year as an assistant professor in a prestigious psychology department. This past year you published two unrelated empirical articles in estab- lished journals. You don't, however, believe there is yet a research area that can be identified as your own. You believe yourself to be about as productive as others. The feedback about your first year of teaching has been generally good. You have yet to serve on a university committee. There is one graduate student who has chosen to work with you. You have no ex- ternal source of funding, nor have you applied for any. Your goals are to become one of the top people in your field and to get tenure in your department. The follow- ing is a list of things you are considering doing in the next two months. You obviously cannot do them all. Rate the importance of each by its priority as a means of reaching your goals.

_____ Improve the quality of your teaching.

_____ Write a grant proposal.

_____ Begin a long-term research project that may lead to a major theoretical article.

_____ Concentrate on recruiting more students.

_____ Begin several related short-term research projects, each of which may lead to an empirical article.

_____ Participate in a series of panel discussions to be shown on the local public television station.

College Student Life

You are enrolled in a large introductory lecture course. Requirements consist of 3 exams and a final. Please indicate how characteristic it would be of your behaviour to spend time doing each of the following if your goal were to receive an A in the course.

_____ Attend class regularly.

_____ Attend optional weekly review sections with the teaching fellow.

_____ Read assigned text chapters thoroughly.

_____ Take comprehensive class notes.

_____ Speak with the professor after class and during office hours.

FIGURE 8-7 *Examples of items measuring the type of intelligence useful in several everyday situations, as compared with more traditional types of intelligence. Source: Sternberg & Wagner, 1993, p. 5.*

Sternberg argues that career success requires a type of intelligence that is very different from that involved in academic success. Whereas academic success is based on knowledge of a particular information base obtained from reading and listening, practical intelligence is learned mainly through observation and modelling. People who are high in practical intelligence are able to learn general norms and principles and apply them appropriately (Sternberg et al., 1995; Polk, 1997; see Figure 8-7).

Business is hardly the sole sphere in which this kind of practical intelligence is crucial, and some psychologists have suggested that practical intelligence is essential

"Freeze!. . .Okay, now. . .Whose the brains of
this outfit?"

Table 8-1	Major Approaches to Intelligence

Approach	Characteristics
IQ tests	General measures of intelligence
Fluid and crystallized intelligence	Fluid intelligence relates to reasoning, memory, and information processing capabilities; crystallized intelligence relates to information, skills, and strategies learned through experience
Gardner's multiple intelligences	Seven independent forms of intelligence
Information-processing approaches	Intelligence is reflected in the way people store and use material to solve intellectual tasks
Triarchic theory of intelligence	An information-processing approach suggesting that intelligence has three aspects: componential, experiential, and contextual
Practical intelligence	View intelligence in terms of nonacademic, career, and personal success

Theories of Intelligence

throughout everyday life. For example, psychologist Seymour Epstein has developed a test of what he terms "constructive thinking," which attempts to predict life success (Epstein & Meier, 1989; Epstein, 1994).

　　According to Epstein, constructive thinking underlies success in such domains as happiness with social relationships, job success, and even physical and emotional health. People who think constructively are able to manage their emotions effectively and deal with challenging situations in ways that promote success. Constructive thinkers, for instance, take action in objectionable situations, rather than just complaining about them. Epstein contends that constructive thinking is far more predictive of actual success in life than traditional IQ tests (Epstein, 1994).

In sum, it is clear that there are many ways to demonstrate—and measure—intelligence (summarized in Table 8-1). A high IQ does not guarantee success in life, especially if it is accompanied by low practical intelligence (Goleman, 1995).

The Informed Consumer of Psychology

Can You Do Better on Standardized Tests?

Even though psychologists disagree about the nature of intelligence, intelligence tests—as well as many other kinds of tests—are still widely used in a variety of situations. In school or on the job, almost all of us have had to cope with these formal, standardized tests—tests that have been formulated and verified with large representative samples. And most of us can probably understand the concern of students taking an exam, such as the Graduate Record Exam (GRE), who worry that success in their future lives hangs on one morning's test results.

Although coaching for standardized tests such as the GRE can reliably produce higher scores, much of the gains may come from increased familiarity with test items or with the cognitive growth that occurs over time.

One outcome of the prevalence of tests in our society is the development of numerous coaching services meant to train people to raise their scores by reviewing basic skills and teaching test-taking strategies. But do they work?

The Educational Testing Service (ETS), the creators of the SAT and GRE, at one time suggested that coaching for the SAT was useless. Today, however, ETS acknowledges that the practice may yield benefits. In fact, most research verifies that coaching for the SAT exams produces small, but reliable, effects—usually an increase in verbal and math scores in the range of 15 to 25 points each (Kulik, Bangert-Drowns, & Kulik, 1984; Bond, 1989; Becker, 1990; Powers, 1993; Holmes & Keffer, 1995).

On the other hand, most of the increase in scores following coaching may stem from increased familiarity with the test or from natural growth in cognitive abilities. Some research suggests that the coaching required to bring about average score increases of more than 20 to 30 points is so extensive that it would be the equivalent of going to school full time (Messick & Jungeblut, 1981).

More research is needed before we can ascertain the true value of coaching. At the same time, there are certain steps you can take, without the benefit of coaching, to maximize your opportunity to score well on standardized tests. For example, the following four points provide good advice for anyone taking standardized tests—as well as any other test, for that matter (Crocetti, 1983):

- *Preview each section.* Not only will previewing give you a chance to take a deep breath and prevent you from frantically rushing through a given section, it will also alert you to any unexpected changes in the test format. Previewing will give you a sense of what to expect as you work through each problem.

- *Time yourself carefully.* The computer that scores your test will not care how deeply you have thought out and considered each answer; all it notes is whether or not you have answered a problem correctly. Therefore, it is important not to spend too much time on initial problems at the expense of later ones. If you are unsure of an answer, try to narrow down the options, then guess and go on to the next problem. Perfection is not your goal; maximizing the number of correct responses is.

- *Check the test-scoring policy to determine whether guessing is appropriate.* On the Scholastic Assessment Test, wrong answers are subtracted from your score, making blind guessing a bad strategy. In comparison, the Graduate Record Exam and many other tests do not penalize you for wrong answers. On tests with penalties for wrong answers, guess only if you can narrow the choices down to two or three. On the other hand, for tests in which wrong answers do not lower your score, it pays to guess, even if you have no idea of the correct response.

- *Complete answer sheets accurately.* Obviously, it makes sense to check your answer sheet when you have finished the test. This can be done most efficiently if you have indicated your answers in the test booklet itself, as well as on the separate answer sheet.

These tips won't ensure a high score on the next test you take, but they will help to maximize your opportunity for better performance.   ■

Recap, Review, and Rethink

Recap

- Intelligence is the capacity to understand the world, think rationally, and use resources effectively when faced with challenges.

- The measure of intelligence used in tests is the intelligence quotient, or IQ.

- Tests must be reliable, measuring with consistency what they are trying to measure, and valid, measuring what is supposed to be measured.

- There are a number of alternative formulations of intelligence.

- Coaching has some impact on improving test scores, although there is wide variability in its effectiveness.

Review

1. _____ is a measure of intelligence that takes into account both a person's chronological and mental ages.

2. _____ tests predict a person's ability in a specific area, while _____ tests determine the specific level of knowledge in an area.

3. Some psychologists make the distinction between _____ intelligence, which reflects reasoning, memory, and information-processing capabilities, and _____ intelligence, which is the information, skills, and strategies that people have learned through experience.

4. Cognitive psychologists use an _____-_____ approach to measure intelligence.

Answers to Review Questions are on page 292.

Rethink

1. Job interviews are really a kind of test. In what ways does a job interview resemble an aptitude test? An achievement test? Do you think job interviews can be shown to have validity? Reliability?

2. If such concepts as fluid and crystallized intelligence do exist, how might they be tested? What applications would each of these types of intelligence have?

3. How do the three aspects of intelligence identified in Sternberg's Triarchic Theory of Intelligence (componential, experiential, and contextual) relate to fluid and crystallized intelligence?

VARIATIONS IN INTELLECTUAL ABILITY

► **How can the extremes of intelligence be differentiated?**

► **How can we help people to reach their full potential?**

"Hey, hey, hey, Fact Track!" The 11-year-old speaker chose one of his favourite programs from the table next to the computer in his parents' dining room. He inserted the floppy disc, booted the system, and waited for the program to load.

"What is your name?" appeared on the monitor.

"Daniel Skandera," he typed. A menu scrolled up listing the program's possibilities. Daniel chose multiplication facts, Level 1.

"How many problems do you want to do?" the computer asked.

"20."

"Do you want to set a goal for yourself, Daniel?"

"Yes, 80 sec."

"Get ready!" . . .

Randomly generated multiplication facts flashed on the screen: "4 × 6," "2 × 9," "3 × 3," "7 × 6." Daniel responded, deftly punching in his answers on the computer's numeric key-pad. . . .

The computer tallied the results. "You completed 20 problems in 66 seconds. You beat your goal. Problems correct = 20. Congratulations Daniel!" And with that the 11-year-old retreated hastily to the TV room. The Lakers and 76ers were about to tip off for an NBA championship game, and Daniel wanted to see the first-half before bedtime. (Heward & Orlansky, 1988, p. 100.)

These teenagers are brother and sister. The girl has Down syndrome, a genetic defect that results in mental retardation.

If you view people with mental retardation as inept and dull, it is time to revise your perceptions. As in the case of Daniel, described earlier, individuals with deficits of intellectual abilities can lead full, rounded lives and in some cases even perform competently in certain kinds of academic endeavours.

Both those individuals with low IQs, known as people with mental retardation, and those with unusually high IQs, referred to as the intellectually gifted, require special attention if they are to reach their full potential.

Mental Retardation

Our perception of people's abilities is often affected by the labels we use to identify them. Over the years the people we are referring to as mentally retarded have had other less desirable, yet semi-official, labels used to refer to their level of ability. Today in some jurisdictions, other labels such as developmentally disabled are substituted for mental retardation. Special needs advocates, although constantly searching for more neutral labels face the problem that over time even a new set of labels may take on less than desirable meaning (Weber and Bennett, 1999). With this in mind, we use the term mental retardation simply as a descriptor for a demonstrated level of intellectual ability aware that although this label may be less than perfect it is the most widely accepted frame of reference that we have.

Although sometimes thought of as a rare phenomenon, mental retardation occurs in 1 to 3 percent of the population. There is wide variation among those labelled as mentally retarded, in large part because of the inclusiveness of the definition developed by the American Association on Mental Retardation. The association suggests that **mental retardation** exists when there is "significantly subaverage intellectual functioning," which occurs with related limitations in two or more of the adaptive skill areas of communication, self-care, home living, social skills, community use, self-direction, health and safety, functional academics, leisure and work (AAMR, 1992; Jacobson & Mulick, 1996; Weber and Bennett, 1999).

While "subaverage intellectual functioning" can be measured in a relatively straightforward manner—using standard IQ tests—it is more difficult to determine how to gauge limitations in particular adaptive skill areas. Ultimately, this imprecision leads to a lack of uniformity in how experts apply the label of "mental retardation." And leads to a limited understanding of the variation in the abilities of people who are categorized in this way, ranging from those who can be taught to work and function with little special attention to those who virtually must receive institutional treatment throughout their lives (Matson & Mulick, 1991; Durkin & Stein, 1996; Negrin & Capute, 1996).

mental retardation: A significantly subaverage intellectual functioning that occurs with related limitations in two or more of the adaptive skill areas

Developmental Disability

Down Syndrome

Most people with mental retardation have relatively minor deficits and are classified as having *mild retardation*. These individuals, who have IQ scores ranging from 55 to 69, constitute some 90 percent of all people with mental retardation. Although their development is typically slower than that of their peers, they can function quite independently by adulthood and are able to hold jobs and have families of their own.

At greater levels of retardation—*moderate retardation* (IQs of 40 to 54), *severe retardation* (IQs of 25 to 39), and *profound retardation* (IQs below 25)—the difficulties are more pronounced. This classification system, which is linked to identified ability at each level, is meant to be used in order to provide the support people need to function. Levels of support are intermittent, limited, extensive and pervasive depending on the severity of the disability (Weber and Bennett, 1999).

What are the causes of mental retardation? In nearly one-third of the cases there is an identifiable biological reason. The most common biological cause is Down syndrome, exemplified by Mindie Crutcher in the Prologue of this chapter. Down syndrome is caused by the presence of an extra chromosome (Coyle et al., 1991; Selikowitz, 1997). In other cases, an abnormality occurs in the structure of a chromosome (Oberle et al., 1991; Yu et al., 1991; Rovescalli et al., 1992; Bodensteiner & Schaefer, 1995; Simonoff, Bolton, & Rutter, 1996). Birth complications, such as a temporary lack of oxygen, may also cause retardation.

The majority of cases of mental retardation are classified as familial retardation. In this case individuals have no known biological cause, but do have a history of retardation within their immediate families. Whether this is caused by environmental factors, such as extreme continuous poverty leading to malnutrition, or by some underlying genetic factor is usually impossible to determine for certain (Simonoff, Bolton, & Rutter, 1996).

Regardless of the cause, important advances in the care and treatment of those who are developmentally disabled have been made in the last two decades (Landesman & Ramey, 1989; Gardner, Graeber, & Cole, 1996; Lloyd, Kameenui, & Chard, 1997). Much of this change was instigated by the Education for All Handicapped Children Act of 1975 (Public Law 94-142). In this federal law, the American Congress ruled that people with retardation are entitled to a full education and that they must be educated and trained in the least restrictive environment. Public Law 94-142 had far ranging effects in Canada as well. It gave motivation and support to similar initiatives. Interestingly, two Canadian provinces already had mandatory legislation in place. They were Saskatchewan in 1971 and Nova Scotia in 1973. Mandatory legislation for Ontario came in 1980 with Bill 82. These laws increased educational opportunities, facilitating integration into regular classrooms as much as possible—a process known as mainstreaming (Hocutt, 1996; Weber and Bennett, 1999).

The philosophy behind mainstreaming suggests that this integration into regular classrooms will improve educational opportunities for those students with developmental disabilities, increase their social acceptance, and facilitate their integration into society as a whole. The philosophy at one time was one of segregation into special education classes where students could learn at their own pace along with other handicapped students. Mainstreaming attempts to prevent the isolation inherent in special education classes and to reduce social stigma by allowing interaction with their age peers as much as possible (Mastropieri & Scruggs, 1987; Yell, 1995; Wang, Reynolds, & Walberg, 1996; Phillips-Hershey & Ridley, 1996).

Of course, there are still special education classes; some students function at too low a level to benefit from placement in regular classrooms. Moreover, children mainstreamed into regular classes typically attend special classes for at least part of the day. Still, mainstreaming offers the promise of increasing the integration of developmen-

---

Answers to Review Questions:

1. IQ   2. Aptitude; achievement   3. fluid; crystallized   4. information processing

Pathways Through Psychology

Jo-Anne Trigg

Supervisor of Special Services, Halton District School Board, Burlington, Ontario

Education: *B.A. (psychology), University of Toronto; M.A. (applied child development), University of Guelph; Registered Psychological Associate, College of Psychologists of Ontario*

Home: *Oakville, Ontario*

Jo-Anne Trigg

I work within the Student Services Department of the Halton Board, where my primary responsibility is the education of students with special needs. The role is varied and includes a number of facets. There is case management and problem-solving for children who have serious learning and behaviour problems. There is co-ordination of a Behaviour Action Team; and supervision of a special services team which consists of child and youth counsellors, social workers, psychoeducational consultants, and speech and language pathologists. I also consult two classes of students who have serious behaviour problems and require a specialized setting. I am involved with decisions regarding allocation of resources and staff, policy development, and staff development. Before taking on this role, I worked as a psychoeducational consultant, providing psychological services to a number of schools within the board. That job consisted of direct work and consultation with school staff, students, and their families. I completed psychological assessments including intelligence and achievement tests, among others, was a member of school-based problem-solving teams, completed classroom observations, co-lead groups and did in-class work with students.

When I entered university as an undergraduate student I did not have as a specific goal or plan, to work in the area of psychology. Psychology was not a subject that I was familiar with but I thought that it sounded interesting, so I took a first-year course, and the rest is history. Between my undergraduate and graduate degrees, I worked for a psychologist at the University of Toronto completing experiments in perception, using both human subjects and pigeons. While at university, I came to realize that I wanted to use my psychology to work with people in some capacity. Sometimes pigeons are not very cooperative subjects!

I had not even considered graduate school in my early planning, but the program at Guelph looked both interesting and practical. It included course work, research and field placements so that when I graduated I actually had some direct work experience in the field. This was very helpful when I applied for the position within the psychology department of the school board.

Over the years, there have been many opportunities to develop areas of interest and therefore some expertise. For example, I had the opportunity to work with a committee of staff from the school board and representatives from the broader community to develop a protocol for the assessment of Attention Deficit Hyperactivity Disorder (ADHD), and a manual for schools addressing this condition. Resources were researched and purchased for schools, and inservice on ADHD was conducted.

I have an ongoing interest in the area of autism that developed when increasing numbers of students with this developmental disorder were entering school and there was little known about it. I have been able to learn more about this condition through training opportunities, reading, and working closely with families and the community. This training has taken me to North Carolina, where I have had the opportunity to meet teachers, parents, and other professionals from all over the world. A most fulfilling role was to participate with a group of dedicated parents in the formation of the Halton Chapter of the Autism Society. Recently I chaired a task force made up of board staff, community partners, and parents. The report, which made recommendations about the services and programs required for students with autism, will I hope, direct our planning over the next several years.

I am fortunate to work within an organization and with people who have encouraged me both professionally and personally. In addition, the parents and kids I have met along the way have been instrumental in making my career in psychology a fulfilling one.

Source: Jo-Anne Trigg, M.A., Halton District School Board

tally delayed people into society and allowing them to make their own contributions to the world at large (Fuchs & Fuchs, 1994; Guralnick et al., 1996; Sharpton & West, 1996).

Some educators argue that given the benefits of mainstreaming, an alternative approach, called full inclusion, might also be effective. Full inclusion is the integration of all students, even those with the most severe educational disabilities, into regular classes. Teacher aides are assigned to help the children with special needs progress. Schools having full inclusion have no separate special education classes. However, full inclusion is a controversial practice, and it is not yet widely applied (Kellegrew, 1995; Hocutt, 1996; Siegel, 1996a).

The Intellectually Gifted

Another group of people—the intellectually gifted—differs from those with average intelligence as much as those who are developmentally delayed, although in a different manner. Composing 2 to 4 percent of the population, the **intellectually gifted** have IQ scores greater than 130.

intellectually gifted: Two to four percent of the population who have IQ scores greater than 130

Although the stereotype associated with the gifted suggests that they are awkward, shy, social misfits unable to get along well with peers, most research indicates that just the opposite is true. Like Robert Theiss, described in the Prologue, the intellectually gifted are most often outgoing, well-adjusted, popular people who are able to do most things better than the average person (Subotnik & Arnold, 1993, 1994; Gottfried et al., 1994; Li, 1995; Winner, 1997).

For example, in a long-term study by Lewis Terman that started in the early 1920s and is still going on, 1,500 children who had IQ scores above 140 were followed and examined periodically over the next sixty years (Terman & Oden, 1947; Sears, 1977). From the start, members of this group were physically, academically, and socially more able than their nongifted peers. They were generally healthier, taller, heavier, and stronger than average. Not surprisingly, they did better in school as well. They also showed better social adjustment than average. And all these advantages paid off in terms of career success: As a group, the gifted received more awards and distinctions, earned higher incomes, and made more contributions in art and literature than typical individuals. For example, by the time the members of the group were 40 years old, they had collectively written more than 90 books, 375 plays and short stories, and 2,000 articles, and had registered more than 200 patents. Perhaps most important, they reported greater satisfaction in life than the nongifted.

On the other hand, the picture of these intellectually gifted people was not unvaryingly positive (Shurkin, 1992). Not every member of the group Terman studied was successful, and there were some notable failures. Moreover, other research suggests that high intelligence is not a homogeneous quality; a person with a high overall IQ is not necessarily gifted in every academic subject but may excel in just one or two (Stanley, 1980; Sternberg & Davidson, 1986). A high IQ, then, does not guarantee success in every endeavour.

Although special programs attempting to overcome the deficits of developmentally delayed people abound, only recently have ways of encouraging the talents of the intellectually gifted been developed. This lack of special attention has been due in part to a persistent view that the gifted ought to be able to "make it on their own"; if they can't, then they really weren't gifted in the first place. More enlightened approaches, however, have acknowledged that without some form of special attention, the gifted may become bored and frustrated with the pace of their schooling and may never reach their potential (Gallagher, 1993; Johnson & Ryser, 1996; Plucker & McIntire, 1996; Winner, 1997; Weber and Bennett, 1999; The Association for Bright Children of Ontario).

Giftedness

One particularly successful program for the intellectually gifted is a project called the Study of the Mathematically Precocious Youth (SMPY). In the program, seventh-graders who have shown unusual mathematical ability are enrolled in summer classes in which they are rapidly taught complex mathematical skills, culminating in college-level calculus. In addition, they receive instruction in a variety of other subjects, including the sciences and languages. The ultimate goal of the program, and others like it, is to provide enrichment for gifted students through an accelerated curriculum that will allow their talents to flourish. Such programs increase the likelihood that the gifted will reach their potential (Stanley, 1980; Stanley, 1990; Southern, Jones, & Stanley, 1993).

Recap, Review, and Rethink

Recap

- Mental retardation is defined by significantly subaverage general intellectual functioning along with deficits in adaptive behaviour.

- The levels of retardation include mildly retarded (IQ of 55 to 69), moderately retarded (IQ of 40 to 54), severely retarded (IQ of 25 to 39), and profoundly retarded (IQ below 25).

- The most frequent causes of mental retardation are biological, like Down syndrome and familial influences.

- The intellectually gifted have IQs above 130 and make up 2 to 4 percent of the population.

Review

1. The term mental retardation is applied specifically to people with an IQ below 60. True or false?

2. _____ _____ is a disorder caused by an extra chromosome that is responsible for some cases of mental retardation.

3. _____ is the process by which developmentally disabled students are placed in normal classrooms to facilitate learning and reduce isolation.

4. Some forms of retardation can have a genetic basis, and can be passed through families. True or false?

5. People with high intelligence are generally shy and socially withdrawn. True or false?

Answers to Review Questions are on page 296.

Rethink

1. What advantages and disadvantages do you think full inclusion programs would present for students with developmental disability? For students without mental retardation?

2. Why do you think negative stereotypes persist of gifted individuals and people with developmental disability, even in the face of contrary evidence? How can these stereotypes be changed?

3. Suppose that the federal government set up a $10 billion program to fund special schools exclusively for gifted students. Tuition at these schools would be free to qualified students, with a special tax levied to pay the costs, on the assumption that the future productivity of these students would more than make up for the current expenditure of money. What benefits might come from such a program? What drawbacks might there be?

INDIVIDUAL DIFFERENCES IN INTELLIGENCE: HEREDITARY AND ENVIRONMENTAL DETERMINANTS

Kwang is often washed with a pleck tied to a:
- (*a*) rundel
- (*b*) flink
- (*c*) pove
- (*d*) quirj

If you found this kind of item on an intelligence test, you would probably complain that the test was totally absurd and had nothing to do with your intelligence or anyone else's. How could anyone be expected to respond to items presented in a language that was so unfamiliar?

But suppose you found the following item, which at first glance might look equally strange:

Which word is most out of place here?
- (*a*) splib
- (*b*) blood
- (*c*) gray
- (*d*) spook

Just as absurd? On the contrary, there is considerably more reason to use this second item on an intelligence test than the first example, which was made up of nonsense syllables. Although this second item may appear as meaningless as the first to most of the white population of the United States, to urban African Americans the question might be a reasonable test of their knowledge.

The second item is drawn from a test created by sociologist Adrian Dove, who tried to illustrate a problem that has plagued the developers of IQ tests from the beginning. By using terminology that would be familiar to urban African Americans from

▶ **Are traditional IQ tests culturally biased?**

▶ **Are there racial differences in intelligence?**

▶ **To what degree is intelligence influenced by the environment and to what degree by heredity?**

Differences in some standardized test scores between various racial and ethnic groups have led to a heated controversy concerning the relative contribution of genetic and environmental factors.

inner-city backgrounds, but typically unfamiliar to whites (and to African Americans raised within the dominant white culture), he dramatized the fact that cultural experience could play a critical role in determining intelligence test scores. (The answer to the item presented earlier, by the way, is *c*. To try your hand at other items drawn from Dove's test, see Table 8-2.)

The issue of devising fair intelligence tests that measure knowledge unrelated to cultural and family background and experience would be minor were it not for one important and persistent finding: Members of certain racial and cultural groups consistently score lower on intelligence tests than members of other groups (MacKenzie, 1984; Humphreys, 1992). For example, as a group, African Americans tend to average fifteen IQ points lower than whites. Does this reflect a true difference in intelligence, or are the questions biased in the kinds of knowledge they test? Clearly, if whites perform better because of their greater familiarity with the kind of information that is being tested, their higher IQ scores are not necessarily an indication that they are more intelligent than members of other groups.

There is good reason to believe that some standardized IQ tests contain elements that discriminate against minority group members whose experiences differ from those of the majority. In Canada, this is particularly evident when standardized tests are used with aboriginal youth. In 1972, The National Indian Brotherhood recommended that IQ and other standardized tests not be used to assess Canadian Native students. They believed that since they were not designed for Native students they would not be a fair demonstration of ability. This is complicated by the fact that for many of these students verbal tests are in English, which may not be their first language (Mawhinney, 1983). Even when tests are appropriate, standard English may cause problems for those who may speak nonstandard English (Darou, 1992). Berry emphasizes the role of acculturation in intelligence. Those who do best on standardized intelligence tests are those with more formal schooling. This factor will most certainly disadvantage members of minority groups especially when formal schooling is minimal (Berry, et al., 1992).

However these tests are important as measures of development and useful predictors of success. They allow educators to monitor progress and alter curriculum as needed.

With issues of language in mind and recognizing that studies show that native groups do better on tests of performance rather than on verbal tests. Mawhinney developed a Cree Picture Vocabulary Test (CPVT) for use with the Cree of James Bay. The test was administered in the subject's own language. For speakers of Aboriginal Cana-

---

Answers to Review Questions:

1. False; the term is used to describe a wide range of people with various degrees of mental impairment.   2. Down syndrome
3. Mainstreaming   4. true   5. False; the gifted are generally more socially adept than those of lower IQ.

Table 8-2	A Culture-*Un*fair Intelligence Test

If you have been raised within the dominant white culture, particularly in a suburban or rural environment, you may have difficulty in answering the following questions, which are designed to illustrate the importance of devising culture-fair intelligence tests.

1. Bird, or Yardbird, was the jacket that jazz lovers from coast to coast hung on
   (a) Lester Young
   (b) Peggy Lee
   (c) Benny Goodman
   (d) Charlie Parker
   (e) Birdman of Alcatraz
2. The opposite of square is
   (a) Round
   (b) Up
   (c) Down
   (d) Hip
   (e) Lame
3. If you throw the dice and 7 is showing on the top, what is facing down?
   (a) 7
   (b) Snake eyes
   (c) Boxcars
   (d) Little Joes
   (e) 11
4. Jazz pianist Ahmad Jamal took an Arabic name after becoming really famous. Previously he had what he called his "slave name." What was his previous name?
   (a) Willie Lee Jackson
   (b) LeRoi Jones
   (c) Wilbur McDougal
   (d) Fritz Jones
   (e) Andy Johnson
5. In C. C. Rider, what does "C. C." stand for?
   (a) Civil Service
   (b) Church Council
   (c) County Circuit Preacher
   (d) Country Club
   (e) Cheating Charley (the "Boxcar Gunsel")

Answers: It is obvious how this test illustrates, in an exaggerated reverse fashion, the difficulties that an African American from an inner-city background might have in responding to items on the typical intelligence test, which mirrors the dominant middle- and upper-class white culture. The correct answers are **1.** *d;* **2.** *d;* **3.** *a;* **4.** *d;* **5.** *c.* (Dove, 1968)

---

dian languages, it showed promise as a means to monitor vocabulary development. Another factor mediating in its favour was the fact that its production was a collaborative effort with the Cree people themselves (Mawhinney, 1983).

Exploring Diversity

The Relative Influence of Heredity and of Environment

The efforts of psychologists to produce a **culture-fair IQ test** relate to a lingering controversy over differences in intelligence between members of minority and majority groups. In attempting to identify whether there are differences between such groups, psychologists have had to confront the broader issue of determining the relative contribution to intelligence of genetic factors (heredity) and experience (environment) (Sternberg & Grigorenko, 1996; Scarr, 1996; Petrill et al., 1996; Detterman, 1996; Steen, 1996).

Richard Herrnstein, a psychologist, and Charles Murray, a sociologist, fanned the flames of the debate with the publication of their book, *The Bell Curve,* in 1994 (Herrnstein & Murray, 1994). They argued that an analysis of IQ differences between whites and African Americans demonstrated that, although environmental factors

culture-fair IQ test: A test that does not discriminate against members of any minority group

The Bell Curve Controversy

"I don't know anything about the bell curve, but I say heredity is everything."

played a role, there were also basic genetic differences between the two races. They based their argument on a number of findings. For instance, on average, whites score fifteen points higher than African Americans on traditional IQ tests even when socioeconomic status (SES) is taken into account. According to Herrnstein and Murray, middle- and upper-SES African Americans score lower than middle- and upper-SES whites, just as lower-SES African Americans score lower on average than lower-SES whites. Intelligence differences between African Americans and whites, they concluded, could not be attributed to environmental differences alone.

heritability: A measure of the degree to which a characteristic is related to genetic, inherited factors

Moreover, intelligence in general shows a high degree of **heritability,** a measure of the degree to which a characteristic is related to genetic, inherited factors (e.g., Bouchard et al., 1990; Boomsma, 1993; Li & Watanabe, 1994; Plomin & Petrill, 1997). As can be seen in Figure 8-8, the closer the genetic link between two people, the greater the correspondence of IQ scores. Using data such as these, Herrnstein and Murray argued that differences between races in IQ scores were largely caused by genetically based differences in intelligence.

However, many psychologists reacted strongly to the arguments laid out in *The Bell Curve,* refuting several of the book's contentions (e.g., Nisbett, 1994; Wahlsten, 1995; Fancher, 1995; Block, 1995; Fraser, 1995; Fischer et al., 1996; Neisser et al., 1996). For one thing, even when socioeconomic conditions are supposedly held constant, wide variations remain among individual households, and no one can convincingly assert that living conditions of African Americans and whites are identical even when their socioeconomic status is similar. Second, as we discussed earlier, there is reason to believe that traditional IQ tests may discriminate against lower-SES urban African Americans by asking for information pertaining to experiences they are unlikely to have had.

There is direct evidence that African Americans who are raised in enriched environments do not tend, as a group, to have lower IQ scores than whites in similar environments. For example, a study by Sandra Scarr and Richard Weinberg examined African American children who were adopted at an early age by white middle-class families of above-average intelligence (Scarr & Weinberg, 1976). The IQ scores of the children averaged 106—about fifteen points above the average IQ scores of unadopted African American children reared in their own homes, and above the average scores of the general population. In addition, the younger a child's age at the time of adoption, the higher his or her IQ score tended to be. The evidence that genetic factors play the major role in determining racial differences in IQ, then, is not compelling, although the question still evokes considerable controversy (Neisser et al., 1996).

A similar and very heated controversy exists in Canada. Philippe Rushton has examined the brain size of three racial groups and found differences. According to his research brain size is largest for East-Asians and their descendents followed by Europeans and their descendents and Africans and their descendents. He provides an evolutionary explanation for the difference in size that has to do with races in northern

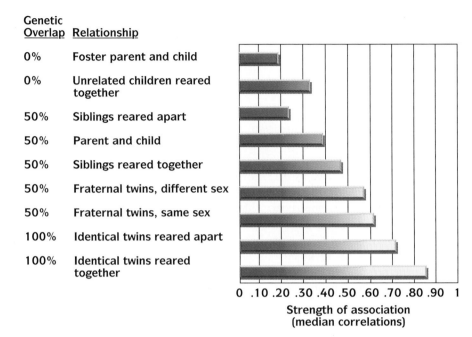

Genetic
Overlap   **Relationship**

0%   Foster parent and child

0%   Unrelated children reared
        together

50%   Siblings reared apart

50%   Parent and child

50%   Siblings reared together

50%   Fraternal twins, different sex

50%   Fraternal twins, same sex

100%   Identical twins reared apart

100%   Identical twins reared
        together

0 .10 .20 .30 .40 .50 .60 .70 .80 .90 1
Strength of association
(median correlations)

FIGURE 8-8 *Summary findings on IQ and closeness of genetic relationship. The bars indicate the median correlations found across many studies, while the percentages indicate the degree of genetic overlap within the relationship. Note, for example, that the median correlation for unrelated people reared apart is quite low, while the correlation for identical twins reared together is substantially higher. In general, the more similar the genetic and environmental background of two people, the greater the correlation. Source: Adapted from Bouchard & McGue, 1981.*

climates having more cognitive demands on them for survival. This required increased problem solving and hence an increased brain size. He then goes on to suggest that the larger the brain the greater the intelligence (Rushton, 1972; Rushton and Ankney, 1995). Michael Peters along with others has criticized Rushton's work. He argues that the research has some major flaws that include questionable measurements, problems inherent in attempts at race classification and disregarding the variation of brain size within racial groups. He finds no evidence to support that any race is genetically more intelligent than another (Peters, 1995). Berry contends that researchers, who take positions like the one Rushton does, show no understanding for cross-cultural research (Berry et al. 1992).

It is also crucial to remember that IQ scores and intelligence have greatest relevance in terms of individuals, not groups. In fact, considering group *racial* differences presents some conceptually troublesome distinctions. *Race* is a biological concept, which is correctly used to refer to classifications based on physical and structural characteristics of a species. Despite its biological origins, however, the term *race* has been used in a variety of ways, to refer to characteristics ranging from skin colour to culture. Furthermore, race is an extraordinarily imprecise concept. Depending on the definition one uses, there are between 3 and 300 races, and no race is pure in a biological sense (Betancourt & Lopez, 1993; Yee et al., 1993; Beutler et al., 1996).

Ultimately, drawing comparisons between different races on any dimension, including IQ scores, is an imprecise, potentially misleading, and often fruitless venture. By far, the greatest discrepancies in IQ scores occur when comparing *individuals,* and not when comparing mean IQ scores of different *groups.* In all racial groups there are people with high intelligence scores and people with low intelligence scores. For the concept of intelligence to aid in the betterment of society, we must examine how *individuals* perform, not the groups to which they belong. We need to focus on the degree to which intelligence can be enhanced in a given person, not in members of a particular group (Angoff, 1988).

Other issues make the heredity-versus-environment debate somewhat irrelevant to practical concerns. For example, as we discussed earlier, there are multiple kinds of intelligence, and traditional IQ scores do not tap many of them. Furthermore, some psychologists argue that IQ scores are only weakly linked to intelligence, and that they are often inadequate predictors of ultimate academic and occupational success.

It also appears that intelligence is not necessarily a fixed characteristic, but may be more flexible and modifiable than originally envisioned. For instance, researchers

FIGURE 8-9 *Although average IQ scores have increased steadily during the 1900s—a phenomenon known as the Flynn effect—the reason for the rise is not at all clear. Source: Horgan, 1995, p. 12.*

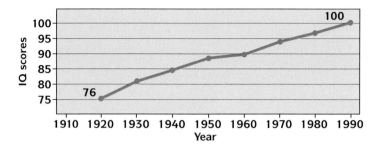

have been increasingly puzzled by data showing a long-term increase in IQ scores that has occurred since the early 1900s. The increase in IQ, called the *Flynn effect* after its discoverer, James Flynn, is not trivial, with the performance of the average 20-year-old today measuring some 15 points higher than the performance of the average 20-year-old in 1940 (Horgan, 1995; Flynn, 1996; see Figure 8-9).

The explanation for the Flynn effect is unclear. It may be that increases in technology have made people better at certain skills that IQ tests measure, or it may be that better nutrition, better parenting, or improvements in the general social environment, including education, may be the cause. Whatever the cause, the change in IQ scores over the century is not due to genetics: This is far too short a time for people to have evolved into a more intelligent species (Neisser, 1996; Shea, 1996b). ■

Placing the Heredity-Environment Question in Perspective

Ultimately, there is no absolute answer to the question of the degree to which intelligence is influenced by heredity and by the environment. We are dealing with an issue for which experiments to determine cause and effect unambiguously cannot be devised for humans (Wahlsten and Gottlieb, 1997). (A moment's thought about how we might experimentally assign infants to enriched or deprived environments will reveal the impossibility of devising ethically reasonable experiments!)

The more critical question to ask, then, is not whether hereditary or environmental factors primarily underlie intelligence, but whether there is anything we can do to maximize the intellectual development of each individual. If we can find ways to do this, we will be able to make changes in the environment—which may take the form of enriched home and school environments—that can lead each person to reach his or her potential (Angoff, 1988; Gardner et al., 1994; Wachs, 1996; Weinberg, 1996).

Recap, Review, and Rethink

Recap

- The issue of whether IQ tests are biased in favour of dominant groups in society arises because of persistent differences in standardized test scores between those groups and some minority groups.

- Attempts have been made to develop culture-fair IQ tests to avoid discriminating against minority groups.

- Probably the most important issue concerning IQ is not the degree to which it is influenced by heredity or the environment, but what we can do to nurture and maximize the development of intelligence in all individuals.

Review

1. Intelligence tests may be biased toward the prevailing culture in such a way that minorities are put at a disadvantage when taking these tests. True or false?

2. A _____-_____ test tries to use only questions appropriate to all people taking the test.

3. IQ tests can accurately determine the intelligence of entire groups of people. True or false?

4. Intelligence can be seen as a combination of _____ and _____ factors.

Answers to Review Questions are on page 302.

Rethink

1. Why might a test that identifies a disproportionate number of minority group members for special educational services and remedial assistance be considered potentially biased? Isn't the purpose of the test to help persons at risk of falling behind academically? How can a test created for a good purpose be biased?

2. What ideas do you have for explaining the Flynn effect, the steady rise in IQ scores over the past half-century? How would you test your ideas?

3. Industrial psychologists use a variety of tests, including intelligence tests, to make hiring and promotion decisions. What recommendations would you suggest for tests of this type?

looking
B A C K

How do psychologists conceptualize and define intelligence?

1. Because intelligence can take many forms, defining it presents a challenge to psychologists. One commonly accepted view is that intelligence is the capacity to understand the world, think rationally, and use resources effectively when faced with challenges.

What are the major approaches to measuring intelligence?

2. Intelligence tests are used to measure intelligence. They provide a mental age which, when divided by a person's chronological age and then multiplied by 100, gives an IQ, or intelligence quotient, score. Specific tests of intelligence include the Stanford-Binet test, the Wechsler Adult Intelligence Scale—III (WAIS-III), and the Wechsler Intelligence Scale for Children—III (WISC-III). In addition to intelligence tests, other standardized tests take the form of achievement tests (which measure level of knowledge in a given area) and aptitude tests (which predict ability in a given area).

3. Although intelligence tests are able to identify individual differences in intelligence, they do not provide us with an understanding of the underlying nature of intelligence. One of the major issues is whether there is a single, unitary factor underlying intelligence or whether intelligence is made up of particular components.

4. Intelligence tests must have reliability and validity. Reliability refers to the consistency with which a test measures what it is trying to measure. A test has validity when it actually measures what it is supposed to measure.

5. The earliest psychologists interested in intelligence made the assumption that there was a general factor for mental ability called *g*. However, later psychologists disputed the view that intelligence was unidimensional.

6. Some researchers suggest that there are two kinds of intelligence: fluid intelligence and crystallized intelligence. Gardner's theory of multiple intelligences proposes that there are seven spheres of intelligence: musical, bodily kinesthetic, logical-mathematical, linguistic, spatial, interpersonal, and intrapersonal.

7. Information-processing approaches suggest that intelligence should be conceptualized as the way in which people represent and use material cognitively. Rather than focusing on the structure of intelligence, this approach examines the processes underlying intelligent behaviour. One example of an information-processing approach is Sternberg's triarchic theory of intelligence, which suggests three major aspects of intelligence: componential, experiential, and contextual.

How can the extremes of intelligence be differentiated?

8. At the two extremes of intelligence are developmentally disabled individuals and the intellectually gifted. The levels of mental retardation include mild retardation (IQ of 55 to 69), moderate retardation (IQ of 40 to 54), severe retardation (IQ of 25 to 39), and profound retardation (IQ below 25). About one-third of the cases of retardation have a known biological cause; Down syndrome being the most common. Most cases, however, are classified as familial retardation, for which there is no known biological cause.

How can we help people to reach their full potential?

9. There have been a number of recent advances in the treatment of both developmentally disabled people and the intellectually gifted, particularly after federal law mandated that mentally retarded people be educated in the least restrictive environment. In mainstreaming, mentally retarded individuals are integrated into regular education classrooms as much as possible. An extension of mainstreaming is full inclusion, the integration of all students, even those with the most severe educational disabilities, into regular classes.

Are traditional IQ tests culturally biased?

10. Traditional intelligence tests have frequently been criticized for being biased in favor of the white middle-class population. This controversy has led to attempts to devise culture-fair tests, IQ measures that avoid questions that depend on a particular cultural background.

Are there racial differences in intelligence?

11. Issues of race and environmental and genetic influences on intelligence represent major controversies.

To what degree is intelligence influenced by the environment and to what degree by heredity?

12. Attempting to distinguish environmental from hereditary factors in intelligence is probably futile and certainly misguided. Because individual IQ scores vary far more than group IQ scores, it is more critical to ask what can be done to maximize the intellectual development of each individual.

Key Terms and Concepts

intelligence (p. 276)
intelligence tests (p. 276)
mental age (p. 276)
intelligence quotient (IQ) (p. 277)
achievement test (p. 278)
aptitude test (p. 278)

reliability (p. 280)
validity (p. 281)
norms (p. 282)
g or g-factor (p. 282)
fluid intelligence (p. 282)
crystallized intelligence (p. 282)

triarchic theory of intelligence (p. 285)
mental retardation (p. 291)
intellectually gifted (p. 294)
culture-fair IQ test (p. 297)
heritability (p. 298)

Epilogue

In this chapter, we looked at one of the most controversial areas of psychology—intelligence. Some of the most heated discussions in all of psychology are focused around this topic, engaging educators, policymakers, politicians, and psychologists alike. The issues include the very meaning of intelligence, its measurement, individual extremes of intelligence, and, finally, the heredity-environment question. We saw that the quest of partitioning intelligence into hereditary factors versus environmental factors is generally pointless. In the area of intelligence, the focus of our efforts should be on making sure that every individual has the opportunity to achieve his or her potential.

Before we leave the topic of intelligence, return to the stories of the two persons of widely different intellectual capabilities discussed in the Prologue, Mindie Crutcher and Robert Theiss. Consider the following questions on the basis of what you have learned about intelligence in this chapter.

1. Mindie Crutcher's physicians concluded in her infancy that she would never be able to sit up, eat, speak, or recognize her mother. Do you think the physicians' conclusions reflect a kind of aptitude testing, achievement testing, or intelligence testing? Why?

2. What can you say about the reliability and validity of the physicians' assessment methods in Mindie Crutcher's case? The reliability and validity of the tests that identified Robert Theiss' talents?

3. In what ways would placing Mindie Crutcher in a separate educational program have helped or hurt her chances of reaching her full potential?

4. Should full inclusion be the model for persons like Mindie? In what realms of human activity—educational, occupational, residential, social, athletic—is full inclusion likely to be most and least successful?

5. In what ways would placing Robert Theiss in a regular (i.e., nonseparate) educational program have helped or hurt his chances of reaching his full potential?

Answers to Review Questions:

1. true   2. culture fair   3. False; IQ tests are used to measure individual intelligence. Within any group there are wide variations in individual intelligence.   4. hereditary; environmental

Emma Robinson (left) and Theresa Luke won gold at the 1999 World Rowing Championships. Both were part of the women's eights team that won bronze at the 2000 Sydney Olympics.

Prologue

Ready to Race

For Canadian Olympic rower, Emma Robinson, the 1999 season was filled with significant victories and serious challenges. At the World Cup Regatta in Lucerne, Emma and her partner, Theresa Luke, broke the record for the pairs event. And in the Pan American Games, they won the Gold Medal. For Emma, this was the third win in as many years, but this time she won with a new partner. Alison Korn, her partner for the previous two wins, had to give up her seat in the boat because of a back injury.

In 1999, Emma overcame a serious challenge to her health. In February of that year, she had surgery to remove her cancerous thyroid. Four days after the surgery she was back in training! Her surgery behind her, Emma found that her biggest problem was overcoming the fatigue associated with the anesthetic. Each day she focused on the training and on the process of getting better rather than on her eventual goal, the Olympics. And finally she was ready for the challenge of the Olympic Games.

In addition to being an accomplished athlete, Emma is a medical student at the University of Toronto. Medical training allows her to combine her interest in science with her interest in people. Becoming a physician offers "huge possibilities." Her current interests are in surgery and pediatrics. She regards medical training and Olympic rowing as similar in at least one respect: both are highly competitive. However, they balance each other, and "moving back and forth between them keeps" her "fresh."

Going to the Olympics is tremendously exciting. Learning to control emotion so that it is not overwhelming is very important. "Mostly what I do," Emma says, "is learn how to use emotion effectively so that I'm ready to race but not overwhelmed."

How do some people like Emma Robinson accomplish so much? Is it the thrill of competing, the anticipation of winning? Or is it the joy of participating? And how can emotions be used to enhance performance?

In this chapter, we consider the issues that can help to answer such questions, as we address the topic of motivation and the related area of emotion. **Motivation** concerns the factors that direct and energize the behaviour of humans and other organisms.

Psychologists who study motivation seek to discover the particular desired goals—the *motives*—that underlie behaviour. Motives are exemplified in behaviour as basic as drinking to satisfy thirst or as inconsequential as taking a stroll to get exercise. To the psychologist specializing in the study of motivation, underlying motives are assumed to steer one's choice of activities.

The study of motivation, then, consists of identifying why people seek to do the things they do. Psychologists studying motivation ask questions such as these: "Why do people choose particular goals for which to strive?" "What specific motives direct behaviour?" "What individual differences in motivation account for the variability in people's behaviour?" "How can we motivate people to behave in particular ways, such as eating certain foods, quitting smoking, or engaging in safer sexual practices?" In this regard, see the Pathways Box later in the chapter.

While motivation is concerned with the forces that direct future behaviour, emotion pertains to the feelings we experience throughout the course of our lives. The study of emotions focuses on our internal experiences at any given moment. Most of us have felt a variety of emotions: happiness at getting a good grade on a difficult exam, sadness brought about by the death of a loved one, anger at being treated unfairly. Emotions are also closely linked to stress, the response to threatening and challenging events. Because emotions not only motivate our behaviour but can also reflect our underlying motivation, they play a broad role in our lives.

In this chapter, we consider motivation, emotion, and stress. We begin by focusing on the major conceptions of motivation, discussing how the different motives and needs people experience jointly affect behaviour. We consider motives that are biologically based and universal in the animal kingdom, such as hunger and sex, as well as motives that are unique to humans, such as needs for achievement, affiliation, and power.

We then turn to the nature of emotional experience. We consider the roles and functions that emotions play in people's lives, discussing a number of theories meant to explain how people understand which emotion they are experiencing at a given moment.

Finally, the chapter ends with a look at stress. We consider the causes of stress and discuss the various ways that people cope with it.

looking
AHEAD

motivation: The factors that direct and energize the behaviour of humans and other organisms

Motivation and Emotion Links

EXPLAINING MOTIVATION

In just an instant, John Thompson's life changed. That's all it took for an auger, an oversized, drill-like piece of farm equipment powered by a tractor, to rip off both of his arms when he slipped, falling against the rotating machinery.

Yet it was in the moments following the accident that Thompson demonstrated incredible bravery. Despite his pain and shock, he ran 120 metres to his house. Using the bone hanging from his left shoulder to open the door, he ran inside and dialed for help with a pen gripped in his teeth. When emergency crews arrived 30 minutes later, he told them where to find ice and plastic bags so that his severed arms could be packed for possible surgical reattachment. Thompson's rescuers came none too soon: By the time surgery could start, he had lost half his blood (Nelson, 1992).

▶ **How does motivation direct and energize behaviour?**

What explains John Thompson's enormous motivation to stay alive? Like many questions involving motivation, this one has no single answer. Clearly, biological aspects of motivation were at work: He obviously experienced a powerful drive to keep himself alive, before he lost so much blood that his life would drain away. But cognitive and social factors, such as his desire to see family and friends, also helped fuel his will to survive.

The complexity of motivation has led to the development of a variety of conceptual approaches to its understanding. Although they vary in the degree to which they focus on biological, cognitive, and social factors, all seek to explain the energy that guides people's behaviour in particular directions.

Instinct Approaches: Born to Be Motivated

instincts: Inborn patterns of behaviour that are biologically determined rather than learned

When psychologists first sought to explain motivation, they turned to **instincts,** inborn patterns of behaviour that are biologically determined rather than learned. According to instinct approaches to motivation, people and animals are born with preprogrammed sets of behaviours essential to their survival. These instincts provide the energy that channels behaviour in appropriate directions. Hence, sex might be explained as a response to an instinct for reproduction, and exploratory behaviour might be viewed as motivated by an instinct to examine one's territory.

There are several difficulties with such a conception, however. For one thing, psychologists have been unable to agree on what the primary instincts are. One early psychologist, William McDougall (1908), suggested that there are eighteen instincts, including pugnacity and gregariousness. Others found even more—with one sociologist claiming that there are exactly 5,759 (Bernard, 1924). Clearly, such an extensive enumeration provides little more than labels for behaviour.

No explanation based on the concept of instincts goes very far in explaining *why* a specific pattern of behaviour, and not some other, has appeared in a given species. Furthermore, the variety and complexity of human behaviour, much of which is clearly learned, are difficult to explain if instincts are the primary motivational force. Therefore, conceptions of motivation based on instincts have been supplanted by newer explanations, although instinct approaches still play a role in certain theories. For example, in later chapters we will discuss Freud's work, which suggests that instinctual drives of sex and aggression motivate behaviour. Moreover, many animal behaviours clearly have an instinctual basis. Finally, evolutionary psychologists, who seek to identify behaviour produced by our genetic makeup suggest that instincts play an important role in directing our behaviour.

Drive-Reduction Approaches: Satisfying Our Needs

drive-reduction approaches to motivation: A theory suggesting that when people lack some basic biological requirement such as water, a drive to obtain that requirement (in this case, the thirst drive) is produced
drive: Motivational tension or arousal that energizes behaviour in order to fulfill some need

In rejecting instinct theory, psychologists first proposed simple drive-reduction theories of motivation in its place (Hull, 1943). **Drive-reduction approaches to motivation** suggest that when people lack some basic biological requirement such as water, a drive to obtain that requirement (in this case, the thirst drive) is produced.

To understand this approach, we need to begin with the concept of drive. A **drive** is motivational tension, or arousal, that energizes behaviour in order to fulfill some need. Many basic kinds of drives, such as hunger, thirst, sleepiness, and sex, are related to biological needs of the body or of the species as a whole. These are called *primary drives.* Primary drives contrast with *secondary drives,* in which no obvious biological need is being fulfilled. In secondary drives, needs are brought about by prior experience and learning. As we will discuss later, some people have strong needs to achieve academically and in their careers. We can say that their achievement need is reflected in a secondary drive that motivates their behaviour.

We usually try to satisfy a primary drive by reducing the need underlying it. For example, we become hungry after not eating for a few hours and may raid the refrigerator, especially if our next scheduled meal is not imminent. If the weather turns cold, we put on extra clothing or raise the setting on the thermostat in order to keep warm. If our body needs liquids in order to function properly, we experience thirst and seek out water.

Homeostasis

The reason for such behaviour is homeostasis, a basic motivational phenomenon underlying primary drives. **Homeostasis** is the process by which an organism strives to maintain some optimal level of internal biological functioning by compensating for deviations from its usual, balanced internal state. Although not all basic biological behaviours related to motivation fit a homeostatic model—sexual behaviour is one example—most of the fundamental needs of life, including the need for food, water, stable body temperature, and sleep, can be explained reasonably well by such an approach.

Unfortunately, although drive-reduction theories provide a good explanation of how primary drives motivate behaviour, they are inadequate when it comes to explaining behaviours in which the goal is not to reduce a drive, but rather to maintain or even to increase a particular level of excitement or arousal. For instance, some behaviours seem to be motivated by nothing more than curiosity. Anyone who has rushed to pick up newly delivered mail, who avidly follows gossip columns in the newspaper, or who yearns to travel to exotic places, knows the importance of curiosity in directing behaviour. And it is not just human beings who display behaviour indicative of curiosity: Monkeys will learn to press a bar just to be able to peer into another room, especially if they can glimpse something interesting (such as a toy train moving along a track). Monkeys will also expend considerable energy solving simple mechanical puzzles, even though their behaviour produces no obvious reward (Harlow, Harlow, & Meyer, 1950; Mineka & Hendersen, 1985; Loewenstein, 1994).

Similarly, many of us go out of our way to seek thrills through such activities as riding a roller coaster and steering a raft down the rapids of a river. Such behaviours certainly don't suggest that people seek to reduce drives, as drive-reduction approaches would indicate.

Both curiosity and thrill-seeking behaviour, then, shed doubt on drive-reduction approaches as a complete explanation for motivation. In both cases, rather than seeking to reduce an underlying drive, people and animals appear to be motivated to *increase* their overall level of stimulation and activity. In order to explain this phenomenon, psychologists have devised an alternative: arousal approaches to motivation.

Arousal Approaches: Beyond Drive Reduction

Arousal approaches seek to explain behaviour in which the goal is to maintain or increase excitement (Berlyne, 1967; Brehm & Self, 1989). According to **arousal approaches to motivation,** each of us tries to maintain a certain level of stimulation and activity. As with the drive-reduction model, if our stimulation and activity levels become too high, we try to reduce them. But in contrast to the drive-reduction model, the arousal model also suggests that if the levels of stimulation and activity are too low, we will try to *increase* them by seeking stimulation.

People vary widely in the optimal level of arousal that they seek out, with some people needing especially high levels of arousal (Babbitt, Rowland, & Franken, 1990; Stacy, Newcomb, & Bentler, 1991; Cocco, Sharpe, & Blaszczynski, 1995). For example, psychologists have hypothesized that individuals such as comic John Belushi, DNA researcher Sir Francis Crick, daredevil Evel Knievel, and bank robbers Bonnie and Clyde exhibited a particularly high need for arousal (Farley, 1986). Such people may attempt to avoid boredom by seeking out challenging situations (Zuckerman, 1991, 1994).

It is not just the celebrated who pursue arousal; many of us characteristically seek out relatively high levels of stimulation. You can get a sense of your own characteristic level of stimulation by completing the questionnaire in Table 9-1.

homeostasis: The process by which an organism strives to maintain some optimal level of internal biological functioning by compensating for deviations from its usual, balanced internal state

arousal approaches to motivation: The belief that we try to maintain a certain level of stimulation and activity, increasing or reducing them as necessary

| Table 9-1 | Do You Seek Out Sensation? |

How much stimulation do you crave in your everyday life? You will have an idea after you complete the following questionnaire, which lists some items from a scale designed to assess your sensation-seeking tendencies. Circle either *A* or *B* in each pair of statements.

1. A I would like a job that requires a lot of travelling.
   B I would prefer a job in one location.
2. A I am invigorated by a brisk, cold day.
   B I can't wait to get indoors on a cold day.
3. A I get bored seeing the same old faces.
   B I like the comfortable familiarity of everyday friends.
4. A I would prefer living in an ideal society in which everyone was safe, secure, and happy.
   B I would have preferred living in the unsettled days of our history.
5. A I sometimes like to do things that are a little frightening.
   B A sensible person avoids activities that are dangerous.
6. A I would not like to be hypnotized.
   B I would like to have the experience of being hypnotized.
7. A The most important goal of life is to live it to the fullest and to experience as much as possible.
   B The most important goal of life is to find peace and happiness.
8. A I would like to try parachute jumping.
   B I would never want to try jumping out of a plane, with or without a parachute.
9. A I enter cold water gradually, giving myself time to get used to it.
   B I like to dive or jump right into the ocean or a cold pool.
10. A When I go on a vacation, I prefer the comfort of a good room and bed.
    B When I go on a vacation, I prefer the change of camping out.
11. A I prefer people who are emotionally expressive, even if they are a bit unstable.
    B I prefer people who are calm and even-tempered.
12. A A good painting should shock or jolt the senses.
    B A good painting should give one a feeling of peace and security.
13. A People who ride motorcycles must have some kind of unconscious need to hurt themselves.
    B I would like to drive or ride a motorcycle.

Scoring Give yourself one point for each of the following responses: 1A, 2A, 3A, 4B, 5A, 6B, 7A, 8A, 9B, 10B, 11A, 12A, 13B. Find your total score by adding up the number of points and then use the following scoring key:

0–3 very low sensation seeking
4–5 low
6–9 average
10–11 high
12–13 very high

Keep in mind, of course, that this short questionnaire, for which the scoring is based on the results of college students who have taken it, provides only a rough estimate of your sensation-seeking tendencies. Moreover, as people get older, their sensation-seeking scores tend to decrease. Still, the questionnaire will at least give you an indication of how your sensation-seeking tendencies compare with those of others.

(Source: Zuckerman, 1978.)

Incentive Approaches: Motivation's Pull

When a luscious dessert is brought to the table after a filling meal, its appeal has little or nothing to do with internal drives or with the maintenance of arousal. Rather, if we choose to eat the dessert, such behaviour is motivated by the external stimulus of the dessert itself, which acts as an anticipated reward. This reward, in motivational terms, is an *incentive*.

incentive approaches to motivation: The theory explaining motivation in terms of external stimuli

Incentive approaches to motivation attempt to explain why behaviour is not always motivated by an internal need, such as the desire to reduce drives or to maintain an optimum level of arousal. Instead of focusing on internal factors, incentive theory explains motivation in terms of the nature of the external stimuli, the incentives that direct and energize behaviour. In this view, properties of external stimuli largely account for a person's motivation.

One explanation of motivation holds that people seek to maintain a certain preferred level of arousal. As the practice of bungee jumping demonstrates, some people seem to need much more excitement than others.

Although the theory explains why we may succumb to an incentive (like a mouth-watering dessert) even though internal cues (like hunger) are lacking, it does not provide a complete explanation of motivation, since organisms seek to fulfill needs even when incentives are not apparent. Consequently, many psychologists believe that the internal drives proposed by drive-reduction theory work in tandem with the external incentives of incentive theory to "push" and "pull" behaviour, respectively. Thus, at the same time that we seek to satisfy our underlying hunger needs (the push of drive-reduction theory), we are drawn to food that appears particularly appetizing (the pull of incentive theory). Rather than contradicting each other, then, drives and incentives may work together in motivating behaviour (Petri, 1996).

Cognitive Approaches: The Thoughts Behind Motivation

Cognitive approaches to motivation focus on the role of our thoughts, expectations, and understanding of the world. For instance, according to one cognitive approach, *expectancy-value theory,* two kinds of cognitions underlie our behaviour. The first is our expectation that a behaviour will cause us to reach a particular goal, and the second is our understanding of the value of that goal to us. For example, the degree to which we are motivated to study for a test will be based jointly on our expectation of how well our studying will pay off (in terms of a good grade) and the value we place on getting a good grade. If both expectation and value are high, we will be motivated to study diligently; but if either one is low, our motivation to study will be relatively lower (Tolman, 1959; McInerney et al., 1997).

Cognitive theories of motivation draw a key distinction between intrinsic and extrinsic motivation. **Intrinsic motivation** causes us to participate in an activity for our own enjoyment, rather than for any tangible reward that it will bring us. In contrast, **extrinsic motivation** causes us to do something for a tangible reward.

cognitive approaches to motivation: Theories that focus on the role of our thoughts, expectations, and understanding of the world in explaining motivation

intrinsic motivation: Motivation by which people participate in an activity for their own enjoyment, not for the reward it will get them

extrinsic motivation: Motivation by which people participate in an activity for a tangible reward

According to research on the two types of motivation, we are more apt to persevere, work harder, and produce work of higher quality when motivation for a task is intrinsic rather than extrinsic (Harackiewicz & Elliot, 1993; Enzle and Anderson, 1993; Ryan & Deci, 1996; Elliot & Harackiewicz, 1996). Some psychologists go farther, suggesting that providing rewards for desirable behaviour may cause intrinsic motivation to decline and extrinsic motivation to increase, although this conclusion is controversial (e.g., Cameron & Pierce, 1994, 1996; Eisenberger & Cameron, 1996; Kohn, 1996; Lepper, Keavney, & Drake, 1996). In one demonstration of this phenomenon, a group of nursery school students were promised a reward for drawing with magic markers (an activity for which they had previously shown high motivation). The reward served to reduce their enthusiasm for the task, for they later showed considerably less zeal for drawing (Lepper & Greene, 1978). It was as if the promise of reward undermined their intrinsic interest in drawing, turning what had been play into work.

Such research suggests the importance of promoting intrinsic motivation and indicates that providing extrinsic rewards (or even just calling attention to them) may actually undermine the effort and quality of performance. Parents might think twice, then, about offering their children monetary rewards for getting good report cards. Instead, the research on intrinsic motivation suggests that better results would come from reminding them of the pleasures that can come from learning and mastering a body of knowledge.

Maslow's Hierarchy: Ordering Motivational Needs

What do Eleanor Roosevelt, Abraham Lincoln, and Albert Einstein have in common? Quite a bit, according to a model of motivation devised by psychologist Abraham Maslow: Each of them reached and fulfilled the highest levels of motivational needs underlying human behaviour.

Maslow's model considers different motivational needs to be ordered in a hierarchy, and it suggests that before more sophisticated, higher-order needs can be met, certain primary needs must be satisfied (Maslow, 1970, 1987). The model can be conceptualized as a pyramid (see Figure 9-1) in which the more basic needs are at the bottom and the higher-level needs are at the top. In order for a particular need to be activated and thereby guide a person's behaviour, the more basic needs in the hierarchy must be met first.

The most basic needs are those described earlier as primary drives: needs for water, food, sleep, sex, and the like. In order to move up the hierarchy, a person must have these basic physiological needs met. Safety needs come next in the hierarchy; Maslow suggests that people need a safe, secure environment in order to function effectively. Physiological and safety needs comprise the lower-order needs.

Only when the basic lower-order needs are met can a person consider fulfilling higher-order needs, such as the need for love and a sense of belonging, esteem, and self-

Needs

FIGURE 9-1 *Maslow's hierarchy shows how our motivation progresses up the pyramid from a basis in the broadest, most fundamental biological needs to higher-order ones. Source: After Maslow, 1970.*

actualization. Love and belongingness needs include the need to obtain and give affection and to be a contributing member of some group or society. After these needs are fulfilled, the person strives for esteem. In Maslow's thinking, esteem relates to the need to develop a sense of self-worth by knowing that others are aware of one's competence and value.

Once these four sets of needs are fulfilled—no easy task—the person is ready to strive for the highest-level need, self-actualization. **Self-actualization** is a state of self-fulfillment in which people realize their highest potential in their own unique way. When Maslow first proposed the concept, he used it to describe just a few well-known individuals such as Eleanor Roosevelt, Lincoln, and Einstein. But self-actualization is not limited to the famous. A parent with excellent nurturing skills who raises a family, a teacher who year after year creates an environment that maximizes students' opportunities for success, and an artist who realizes her creative potential might all be self-actualized. The important thing is that people feel at ease with themselves and satisfied that they are using their talents to the fullest. In a sense, achieving self-actualization produces a decline in the striving and yearning for greater fulfillment that marks most people's lives and instead provides a sense of satisfaction with the current state of affairs (Jones & Crandall, 1991).

Unfortunately, research has not been able to validate the specific ordering of the stages of Maslow's theory, and it has proved difficult to measure self-actualization objectively (Haymes, Green, & Quinto, 1984; Weiss, 1991; Neher, 1991). However, Maslow's model is important for two reasons: It highlights the complexity of human needs, and it emphasizes that until more basic biological needs are met, people will be relatively unconcerned with higher-order needs. If people are hungry, their first interest will be in obtaining food; they will not be concerned with such needs as love and self-esteem. The model helps explain why victims of disasters such as famine and war may suffer the breakdown of normal family ties and be unconcerned with the welfare of anyone other than themselves.

self-actualization: A state of self-fulfillment in which people realize their highest potential in their own unique way

Reconciling the Different Approaches to Motivation

Now that we have examined several different approaches to motivation, it is reasonable to wonder which of them provides the fullest account of motivational phenomena. Actually, many of the conceptual approaches are complementary, rather than contradictory, and it is often useful to employ several theories simultaneously in order to understand a particular motivational system (Deci, 1992). Thus, as we proceed to consider specific motives, such as the needs for food, achievement, affiliation, and power, we will draw upon several of the theories to gain a better understanding of motivation.

Recap, Review, and Rethink

Recap

- The study of motivation looks at the factors that energize and direct people's behaviour.

- A drive is a motivational tension that energizes behaviour to fulfill some need. Primary drives typically operate according to the principle of homeostasis, in which an organism strives to compensate for any deviations from a balanced, preferred internal state.

- Drive-reduction approaches propose that behaviour is motivated by drives to reduce biological needs. Because they do not explain why people sometimes seek stimulation, arousal approaches have been devised.

- To explain why behaviour is not always motivated by the need either to reduce drives or to maintain arousal, incentive approaches have been introduced.

- Cognitive approaches to motivation, exemplified by expectancy-value theory, suggest that people's thoughts, understanding, and interpretation of the world underlie their motivation.

- According to Maslow's motivational model, motivational needs progress in a hierarchy from the most basic to higher-order needs.

Review

1. _____ are forces that guide a person's behaviour in a certain direction.

2. Biologically determined, inborn patterns of behaviour are known as _____.

3. Your psychology professor tells you, "Explaining behaviour is easy! When we lack something we are motivated to get it." Which approach to motivation does your professor subscribe to?

4. By drinking water after running a marathon, a runner tries to keep his or her body at an optimal level of functioning. This process is called _____.

5. Even though I am not thirsty, I am offered and accept a mug of beer. Assuming that I like beer very much, what theory of motivation would predict this behaviour?

6. I help an elderly person across the street because doing a good deed makes me feel good. What type of motivation is at work here? What type of motivation would be at work if I were to help an elderly man across the street because he paid me $20?

7. According to Maslow, a person with no job, no home, and no friends can become self-actualized. True or false?

Answers to Review Questions are on page 316.

Rethink

1. Which approaches to motivation are most commonly used in the workplace? How might each approach be used to design employment policies that can sustain or increase motivation?

2. How does Maslow's hierarchy of needs apply to situations in which workers are paid subsistence wages? How does it apply to situations in which workers receive adequate wages?

3. A writer who works all day composing copy for an advertising firm has a hard time keeping her mind on her work and continually watches the clock. After work she turns to a collection of stories she is creating and writes long into the night, completely forgetful of the clock. What ideas from your reading on motivation help to explain this phenomenon?

HUMAN NEEDS AND MOTIVATION: EAT, DRINK, AND BE DARING

▶ **What are the biological and social factors that underlie hunger?**

▶ **Why, and under what circumstances, do we become sexually aroused?**

▶ **How do most people behave sexually?**

▶ **How are needs relating to achievement, affiliation, and power motivation exhibited?**

To Bob, doing well in university meant that he would get into a good law school, which he saw as a stepping-stone to a successful future. Consequently, he never let up academically and always tried his best to do well in his courses. But his constant academic striving went well beyond the desire to get into law school; he tried not only to get good grades, but to get *better* grades than his classmates.

In fact, Bob was always trying to be the best at everything he did. He could turn the simplest activity into a competition. Bob couldn't even play poker without acting as if his winning the game was essential. There were, however, some areas in which he didn't compete. He was interested only if he thought he had a fighting chance to succeed; he ignored challenges that seemed too difficult as well as those that seemed too easy for him.

What is the motivation behind Bob's consistent striving to achieve? Moreover, why does he welcome some kinds of challenges and avoid others? To answer these questions, we must consider some of the specific kinds of needs that underlie behaviour. In this section, then, we will examine several of the most important human needs. Because human beings are in a fundamental sense biological creatures, we first consider hunger, the primary drive that has received the most attention from researchers. But then we turn to secondary drives—those uniquely human strivings, based on learned needs and past experience, that help explain behaviour such as Bob's.

The Motivation Behind Hunger and Eating

overweight: Having a BMI of 27 or higher

obesity: The state of being more than 20 percent above the average weight for a person of a given height

Thirty percent of Canadians aged 15 or older are **overweight** and 47 percent have some excess weight. Overweight is defined as having a Body Mass Index (BMI) of 27 or higher (where BMI = weight/height^2). Some excess weight is defined as having a BMI of 25 or higher. Canadians are more likely to be overweight if they are male and over 25 years of age (Statistics Canada, 1999).

About one-third of the U.S. population suffers from **obesity,** defined as weighing more than 20 percent above the average weight for a person of a given height. Losing unwanted weight is something of an American obsession, as 60 to 80 *million* women and men struggle to achieve what they perceive to be an ideal weight and body shape—perceptions that are often inaccurate (Thompson, 1992; Brody, 1992; Hall, 1995).

The idea of what constitutes an ideal weight and body shape varies significantly across different cultures and, within western cultures, from one time period to another. For instance, contemporary societal views in many western cultures that stress the importance of slimness in women are relatively recent. In nineteenth-century Hawaii, the most attractive women were those who were the most overweight. Furthermore, for most of the twentieth century—except for a period in the 1920s and the most recent decades—the ideal female figure was relatively full. Even today, weight standards differ among different cultural groups. For instance, African Americans generally judge heavier women more positively than do whites (Silverstein et al., 1986; Heatherton, Kiwan, & Hebl, 1995; Crandall & Martinez, 1996; Greenberg & LaPorte, 1996).

Eating behaviour is clearly complex, involving a variety of mechanisms. In our discussion of what motivates us to eat, we'll start with the biological aspects of eating.

Biological Factors in the Regulation of Hunger

In traditional Hawaiian culture, heavy women are considered the most attractive.

In contrast to human beings, animals are unlikely to become obese. Most nonhuman species, when left in an environment in which food is readily available, do a good job of regulating their intake. You may have observed this with a pet who always has a dish of food available. Cats, for instance, will eat only until their immediate hunger is satisfied; they leave the remaining food untouched, returning to it only when internal cues tell them to eat once again.

Internal mechanisms seem to regulate not only the quantity of food intake in nonhumans, but also the kind of food that animals desired. Hungry rats that have been deprived of particular foods tend to seek out alternatives that contain the specific nutrients their diet is lacking, and laboratory experiments show that animals given the choice of a wide variety of foods choose a fairly well-balanced diet (Rozin, 1977; Bouchard & Bray, 1996).

The mechanisms by which organisms know whether they require food or should stop eating are complex (Keesey & Powley, 1986; Decastro, 1996). It's not just a matter of an empty stomach causing hunger pangs and a full one alleviating hunger. For example, people who have had their stomachs removed still experience the sensation of hunger (Inglefinger, 1944). Consequently, regulation of eating goes beyond the fullness of one's stomach.

Some researchers suggest that changes in the chemical composition of the blood may be an important factor in controlling eating (Logue, 1991). For instance, experiments show that when glucose, a kind of sugar, is injected into the blood, hunger decreases and animals will refuse to eat. On the other hand, when insulin, a hormone involved in the conversion of glucose into stored fat, is introduced into the bloodstream, hunger increases (Rodin, 1985; Campfield et al., 1996).

But what part of the body monitors changes in blood chemistry relating to eating behaviour? The brain's *hypothalamus,* which we discussed in Chapter 2, appears to be primarily responsible for monitoring food intake (Kupfermann, 1991a; Rolls, 1994). Injury to the hypothalamus has been shown to cause radical changes in eating behaviour, depending upon the site of the injury. For example, rats whose *lateral hypothalamus* is damaged may literally starve to death. They refuse food when offered, and unless they are force-fed, eventually die. Rats with an injury to the *ventromedial hypothalamus* display the opposite problem: extreme overeating. Rats with this injury can increase in weight by as much as 400 percent. Similar phenomena occur in humans who have tumours of the hypothalamus.

Although it is clear that the hypothalamus plays an important role in regulating food intake, the exact way in which it operates is still unclear. Some researchers think it affects an organism's sense or perception of hunger; others hypothesize that it directly regulates the neural connections that control the muscles involved in eating behaviour (Stricker & Zigmond, 1976; Kupfermann, 1991a; Capaldi, 1996).

One hypothesis suggests that injury to the hypothalamus affects the weight set point by which food intake is regulated (Nisbett, 1972). According to this hypothesis,

weight set point: The particular level of weight that the body strives to maintain

metabolism: The rate at which food is converted to energy and expended by the body

the **weight set point** is the particular level of weight that the body strives to maintain. Acting as a kind of internal weight thermostat, the hypothalamus calls for either greater or less food intake.

In most cases, the hypothalamus does a good job. People who are not monitoring their weight show only minor weight fluctuations, in spite of substantial day-to-day variations in how much they eat and exercise. However, injury to the hypothalamus drastically raises or lowers the weight set point, and the organism then strives to meet its internal goal by increasing or decreasing its food consumption.

The weight set point may be determined, at least in part, by genetic factors. People seem destined, through heredity, to have a particular **metabolism,** the rate at which food is converted to energy and expended by the body. Some people, with high metabolic rates, are able to eat virtually as much as they want without gaining weight, while others, with low metabolism, may eat literally half as much and yet gain weight readily (Roberts et al., 1988; Friedman, 1995; Leibel, Rosenbaum, & Hirsch, 1995).

Social Factors in Eating

You've just finished a full meal and are completely stuffed. Suddenly, your host announces with great fanfare that he will be serving his "house specialty" dessert, bananas flambé, and that he has spent the better part of the afternoon preparing it. Even though you are full and don't even like bananas, you accept a serving of his dessert and eat it all.

Clearly, internal biological factors do not provide the full explanation for our eating behaviour. External social factors, based on societal rules and conventions and on what we have learned about appropriate eating behaviour, also play an important role. Take, for example, the simple fact that people customarily eat breakfast, lunch, and dinner at approximately the same times every day. Because we are accustomed to eating on schedule every day, we tend to feel hungry as the usual hour approaches, sometimes quite independently of what our internal cues are telling us.

Similarly, we tend to put roughly the same amount of food on our plates every day, even though the amount of exercise we may have had, and consequently our need for energy replenishment, varies from day to day. We also tend to prefer particular foods over others. Rats and dogs may be a delicacy in certain Asian cultures, but few people in western cultures find them appealing, despite their potentially high nutritional value. In sum, cultural influences and our own individual habits play an important role in determining when, what, and how much we eat (Boaks, Popplewell, & Burton, 1987; Rozin, 1990; Booth, 1994; Capaldi, 1996).

Other social factors are related to our eating behaviour as well. Some of us head toward the refrigerator after a difficult day, seeking solace in a pint of Heath Bar Crunch ice cream. Why? Perhaps when we were children, our parents gave us food when we were upset. Eventually, we may have learned, through the basic mechanisms of classical and operant conditioning, to associate food with comfort and consolation. Similarly, we may learn that eating, by focusing our attention on immediate pleasures, provides an escape from unpleasant thoughts. As a consequence, we may eat when we experience distress (Heatherton, Herman, & Polivy, 1992; Greeno & Wing, 1994; McManus & Waller, 1995).

The Roots of Obesity

Given that eating behaviour is influenced by both biological and social factors, determining the causes of obesity has proved to be a challenging task. Researchers have followed several paths.

Some psychologists suggest that an oversensitivity to external eating cues based on social convention, and a parallel insensitivity to internal hunger cues, produce

Obesity

Answers to Review Questions:

1. Motives   2. instincts   3. drive reduction   4. homeostasis   5. incentive   6. intrinsic; extrinsic   7. False; lower-order needs must be fulfilled before self-actualization can occur.

obesity. Research has shown, for example, that obese people who are placed in a room next to an inviting bowl of crackers are apt to eat considerably more than nonobese people—even though they may have just finished a filling sandwich (Schachter, Goldman, & Gordon, 1968). In addition, obese individuals are less apt to eat if doing so involves any sort of work: In one experiment obese participants were less likely to eat nuts that had to be shelled, but ate copious amounts of nuts that already had their shells removed. Nonobese people, in contrast, ate the same amount of nuts, regardless of whether or not they had to be shelled (Nisbett, 1968; Schachter, 1971). Consequently, it appears that many obese people give undue attention to external cues, and are less aware of the internal cues that help nonobese people regulate their eating behaviour.

On the other hand, many individuals who are highly reliant on external cues never become obese, and there are quite a few obese people who are relatively unresponsive to external cues (Rodin, 1981; Herman, 1987). Consequently, some psychologists have turned to weight set point theory as a plausible explanation for the cause of obesity.

Specifically, these researchers suggest that overweight people have higher set points than people of normal weight. Because their set points are unusually high, their attempts to lose weight by eating less may make them especially sensitive to external, food-related cues and therefore more apt to eat, perpetuating their obesity.

But why may some people's weight set points be higher than others? One factor may be the size and number of fat cells in the body, which increase as a function of weight increase. Because the set-point level appears to reflect the number of fat cells a person has, any increase in weight—which produces a rise in fat cells—may raise the set point. Furthermore, any loss of weight after the age of two does not decrease the number of fat cells in the body, although it may cause them to shrink in size. In short, according to the weight set point hypothesis, the presence of too many fat cells may result in the set point becoming "stuck" at a higher level than is desirable. Under such circumstances, losing weight becomes a difficult proposition, because one is constantly at odds with one's own internal set point when dieting (Knittle, 1975; Leibel, Rosenbaum & Hirsch, 1995; Freedman, 1995).

Not everyone agrees with the set point explanation for obesity. Pointing to the rapid rise in obesity that has occurred over the last several decades in the United States, some researchers suggest that there is no fixed set point determining weight that the body attempts to maintain. Instead, they suggest, there is a *settling point,* determined by a combination of our genetic heritage and the nature of the environment in which we live. If high-fat foods are prevalent in our environment, and we are genetically predisposed to obesity, then we settle into an equilibrium that maintains relatively high weight. On the other hand, if our environment is nutritionally healthy, genetic predispositions to obesity will not be triggered, and we will settle into an equilibrium in which our weight is lower (Gibbs, 1996).

Both the set point and settling point explanations for obesity suggest that genetic factors predispose us to obesity—a notion that is receiving increasing support. As we consider in the accompanying Applying Psychology in the 21st Century box, researchers are finding increasing evidence that particular genes control hormones in the body that are linked to weight.

Eating Disorders

A rice cake in the afternoon, an apple for dinner. That was Heather Rhodes's typical diet her freshman year at St. Joseph's College in Rensselaer, Indiana, when she began to nurture a fear (exacerbated, she says, by the sudden death of a friend) that she was gaining weight. But when Rhodes, now 20, returned home to Joliet, Illinois, for summer vacation a year and a half ago, her family thought she was melting away. "I could see the outline of her pelvis in her clothes . . ." says Heather's mother . . . , so she and the rest of the family confronted Heather one evening, placing a bathroom scale in the middle of the family room. "I told them they were attacking me and to go to hell," recalls Heather, who nevertheless reluctantly weighed herself. Her 5'7" frame

Despite looking skeleton-like to others, people with the weight disorder anorexia nervosa see themselves as overweight.

Applying Psychology in the 21st Century

Shedding Obesity's Secrets

The start of a new year is often marked by somber resolutions to lose weight that was put on during the previous year. Yet all too often these good intentions fail, despite the $30 billion that dieters spend each year in the United States to shed excess pounds (Gura, 1997).

Although New Year's resolutions to lose weight at the start of the twenty-first century may be similar to those of the past, the outcomes this time may be more successful, due to a spiraling series of advances in our understanding of the causes of unwanted weight gain.

The initial finding to spark hope that a "cure" for obesity is in the works was the discovery of the fat-dissolving hormone leptin. Researchers found that the fat cells of mice secrete leptin into the blood. The brain, in turn, uses the amount of leptin in the blood as a gauge for maintaining a particular amount of body fat, in the same way that a heater thermostat monitors the temperature of the air to trigger an increase or decrease in heat, as necessary. If there is too much fat, the hormone causes a decrease in appetite and an increase in the use of energy, and higher levels of fat are burned as a result (Campfield et al., 1995; Halaas et al., 1995; Pelleymounter et al., 1995; Rohner-Jeanrenaud, & Jeanrenaud, 1996).

Researchers reasoned that if leptin could be injected into the blood, the brain would assume that smaller numbers of fat cells were needed—and consequently the organism would lose weight. And that is just what happened: Mice who were grossly obese due to a genetic defect shed weight when injected with leptin. Even mice of average weight lost weight when they were inoculated with leptin. Because humans secrete a hormone quite similar to leptin, it is possible

Losing weight is an obsession with many people, some of whom turn to drugs to shed unwanted pounds.

that they, too, may lose weight when leptin levels are increased, although this has yet to be demonstrated (Marco et al., 1996; Gura, 1997).

The discovery of the importance of leptin has been supplemented by additional findings regarding the genetic causes of obesity. At least five separate genes have been identified that produce obesity in mice. The one that has spurred the most interest is the aptly named *obese gene,* or *ob* for short. *Ob* produces leptin, and mutations of the gene produce obesity in mice. Other genes related to weight gain have also been found in mice, including *diabetes, fat, tubby,* and *agouti yellow.* However, it is unlikely that any single gene, or even a combination of a few genes, produces obesity; most researchers believe that multiple genes, interacting with environmental factors, produce weight gain (Zhang et al., 1994; Pelleymounter et al., 1995;

Winters, Boone, & Collins, 1995; Noben-Trauth et al., 1996; Gibbs, 1996).

The new genetic findings do promise fresh approaches to dealing with obesity. Theoretically, at least, it may be possible to "turn off" specific genes that otherwise would produce obesity. Such genetic tinkering, however, remains far in the future.

At the same time that researchers are making advances in our understanding of the causes of obesity, caution is in order over the effectiveness and safety of new treatments. For example, in 1996, the U.S. Federal Drug Administration approved the use of dexfenfluramine ("Redux"), a drug that increases the circulation of serotonin, a neurotransmitter that reduces appetite. Some studies showed that use of the drug in a comprehensive weight-loss program helped people lose weight. However, the drug was withdrawn from the market less than two years later because numerous users developed heart-valve abnormalities (Cowley and Springen, 1997). In 1999, the drug Orlistat, which reduces dietary fat absorption, was approved for use in Canada.

However, it is too early to start filling up on hot fudge sundaes, Big Macs, and fries under the assumption that some miracle cure for obesity will be available soon. For one thing, many drugs found effective with mice, have not been tested with humans. For another, even if drugs without dangerous side effects are found to be effective in reducing obesity in humans, these drugs are unlikely to be totally free of unpleasant side effects. For example, some Orlistat users have experienced gastrointestinal disturbances (Hauptman et al., 2000). Finally, even if people are able to shed pounds because of a new drug, they will remain susceptible to major health risks unless they exercise and reduce fat consumption.

held a mere 85 pounds—down 22 pounds from her senior year in high school. "I told them they rigged the scale," she says. It simply didn't compute with her self-image. "When I looked in the mirror," she says, "I thought my stomach was still huge and my face was fat." (Sandler, 1994, p. 56)

anorexia nervosa: A severe eating disorder in which people may refuse to eat, while denying that their behaviour and appearance—which can become skeletal—are unusual

Heather suffered from the eating disorder anorexia nervosa. **Anorexia nervosa** is a severe eating disorder in which people may refuse to eat, while denying that their behaviour and appearance—which can become skeletonlike—are unusual. Some 15 to 20 percent of anorexics literally starve themselves to death.

Anorexia nervosa afflicts mainly females between the ages of 12 and 40, although both men and women of any age may develop it. People with the disorder typically come from stable homes, and they are often successful, attractive, and relatively affluent. Their lives revolve around food: Although they eat little themselves, they may cook for others, go shopping for food frequently, or collect cookbooks (Hsu, 1990; Button, 1993; Thiel, Broocks, & Schussler, 1995).

A related problem, **bulimia,** is a disorder in which a person binges on incredibly large quantities of food. An entire gallon of ice cream and a whole pie may easily be consumed in a single sitting. Following such a binge, sufferers feel guilt and depression and typically induce vomiting or take laxatives to rid themselves of the food—behaviour known as purging (Hinz & Williamson, 1987). Chronic dieting may lead to bingeing (Polivy and Herman, 1985; Heatherton and Polivy, 1992). Constant bingeing-and-purging cycles and the use of drugs to induce vomiting or diarrhea may create a chemical imbalance that can lead to heart failure. Typically, though, the weight of a person suffering from bulimia remains normal.

> **bulimia:** A disorder in which a person binges on incredibly large quantities of food

Eating disorders represent a growing problem: Between one and four percent of high school and college women are estimated to suffer from either anorexia nervosa or bulimia. What is the cause? Some researchers suspect there is a physiological cause, such as a chemical imbalance in the hypothalamus or pituitary gland (Gold et al., 1986; Brewerton, 1995; Licinio, Wong, & Gold, 1996; Brewerton & Jimerson, 1996). Other psychologists believe that the cause is rooted in societal expectations about the value of slenderness (Crandall & Biernat, 1990; Rothblum, 1990). Anorexics and bulimics take to heart the societal view that one can never be too thin. Consistent with such an explanation is the fact that, as countries become more developed and westernized, and dieting becomes more popular, eating disorders increase. Finally, some psychologists suggest that the disorders occur as a consequence of overdemanding parents or other family problems (Thiel, Broocks, & Schussler, 1995; Schneider, 1996; Wonderlich, Klein, & Council, 1996; Horesh et al., 1996). Anorexics see efforts to control weight as opportunities for success. However, the resulting anxiety may lead to suicide (Buree et al., 1990; Coren & Hewitt, 1998).

Eating Disorders

The complete explanation for anorexia nervosa or bulimia remains elusive. The disorders probably stem from both biological and social causes, and successful treatment is likely to encompass several strategies, including therapy and dietary changes (Brownell & Fairburn, 1995; Crisp & McClelland, 1996; Garner & Garfinkel, 1997).

The Facts of Life: Human Sexual Motivation

Anyone who has seen two dogs mating knows that sexual behaviour has a biological basis. Their sexual behaviour appears to occur spontaneously, without much prompting on the part of others. A number of genetically controlled factors influence the sexual behaviour of animals. For instance, animal behaviour is affected by the presence of certain hormones in the blood. Moreover, females are receptive to sexual advances only at certain relatively limited periods of time during the year (Short & Balaban, 1992; Crews, 1993, 1994).

Human sexual behaviour, by comparison, is more complicated, although the underlying biology is not all that different from that of related species. Consider the functions of the male and female **genitals,** or sex organs. In males, for example, the *testes* begin to secrete **androgens,** male sex hormones, at puberty. Not only do androgens produce secondary sex characteristics, such as the growth of body hair and a deepening of the voice, they also increase the sex drive. Although there are long-term changes in the amount of androgens that the testes produce—with the greatest production occurring just after sexual maturity—the level of production over the short term is fairly constant. Therefore, men are capable of (and interested in) sexual activities without any regard to biological cycles. Given the proper stimuli leading to arousal, male sexual behaviour can occur.

> **genitals:** The male and female sex organs
> **androgens:** Male sex hormones secreted by the testes

Women show a different pattern. When they reach maturity at puberty, the two *ovaries,* the female reproductive organs, begin to produce **estrogen** and **progesterone,**

> **estrogen:** Female sex hormone
> **progesterone:** Female sex hormone

*Beauty standards vary considerably
across different cultures.*

ovulation: The point at which an egg
is released from the ovaries

the female sex hormones. However, these hormones are not produced consistently; instead, their production follows a cyclical pattern. The greatest output occurs during **ovulation,** when an egg is released from the ovaries, making the chances of fertilization by a male sperm cell highest. While in nonhumans the period around ovulation is the only time that the female is receptive to sex, people are different. Although there are variations in reported sex drive, women are receptive to sex throughout their cycles, depending on the external stimuli they encounter in their environment (Hoon, Bruce, & Kinchloe, 1982).

Though biological factors "prime" people for sex, it takes more than hormones to motivate and produce sexual behaviour (McClintock & Herdt, 1996). In animals the presence of a partner who provides arousing stimuli leads to sexual activity. Humans are considerably more versatile; not only other people, but nearly any object, sight, smell, sound, or other stimulus can lead to sexual excitement. Because of prior associations, then, people may be turned on sexually by the smell of Chanel No. 5 or Brut, or the sound of a favourite song. The reaction to a specific, potentially arousing stimulus, is highly individual—what turns one person on may do just the opposite for another.

Sexual fantasies also play an important role in producing sexual arousal. Not only do people have fantasies of a sexual nature during their everyday activities, but about 60 percent of all people have fantasies during sexual intercourse.

Men's and women's fantasies differ little from each other in terms of content or quantity and thoughts of being sexually irresistible and of engaging in oral-genital sex are most common for both sexes (Sue, 1979; McCauley & Swann, 1980; Jones & Barlow, 1990). It is important to note that fantasies are just that; in other words, they do not represent an actual desire to fulfill them in the real world. Thus, we should not assume from data on forced-sex fantasies that females want to be sexually overpowered, nor should we assume that in every male lurks a potential rapist desirous of forcing sexual overtures on a submissive victim.

The Varieties of Sexual Experiences

For most of recorded history, the vast variety of sexual practices remained shrouded in ignorance. However, in the late 1930s, biologist Albert Kinsey undertook the first systematic survey of American sexual behaviour. Kinsey used volunteers, including hospital employees, mental patients, and transients in his study, and therefore did not have a representative sample. The Kinsey Report (1948) shocked people by reports of sexual permissiveness and frequent extramarital affairs. Although it is always difficult to get people to participate in investigations of sexual practices, recently surveys using large random samples of men and women of all ages have been completed in Canada (Barrett et al, 1997) and the United States (Michael et al., 1994). The results portray a more conservative picture than might be anticipated on the basis of publicized findings of less carefully executed research. In both countries adultery is the exception, not the rule. Most married men (Canada, 86 percent; United States, 75 percent) and married women (Canada, 93 percent; United States, 85 percent) have never been unfaithful. By examining the common results gleaned from different samples of subjects, we now have a reasonably complete picture of contemporary sexual practices—to which we turn next.

Masturbation: Solitary Sex

If you were to listen to physicians fifty years ago, you would have been told that **masturbation,** sexual self-stimulation, often using the hand to rub the genitals, would lead to a wide variety of physical and mental disorders, ranging from hairy palms to insanity. Had they been correct, however, most of us would be wearing gloves to hide the sight of our hair-covered palms—for masturbation is one of the most frequently practiced sexual activities. Some 94 percent of all males and 63 percent of all females have masturbated at least once, and among college students, the frequency ranges from "never" to "several times a day" (Hunt, 1974; Houston, 1981; Michael et al., 1994).

Although masturbation is often considered an activity to engage in only if no other sexual outlets are available, this view bears little relationship to reality. Close to three-quarters of married men (age 20 to 40) report masturbating an average of twenty-four times a year, and 68 percent of married women in the same age group masturbate an average of ten times each year (Hunt, 1974; Michael et al., 1994).

Despite the high incidence of masturbation, attitudes toward it still reflect some of the negative views of yesteryear. For instance, one survey found that around 10 percent of the people who masturbated experienced feelings of guilt, and 5 percent of the males and 1 percent of the females considered their behaviour perverted (Arafat & Cotton, 1974). Despite these negative attitudes, however, most experts on sex view masturbation not only as a healthy, legitimate—and harmless—sexual activity, but also as a means of learning about one's own sexuality.

Heterosexuality

People often believe that the first time they have sexual intercourse they have achieved one of life's major milestones. However, **heterosexuality,** sexual attraction and behaviour directed to the opposite sex, consists of far more than male-female intercourse. Kissing, petting, caressing, massaging, and other forms of sex play are all components of heterosexual behaviour. Still, the focus of sex researchers has been on the act of intercourse, particularly in terms of its first occurrence and its frequency.

Premarital Sex

Until fairly recently, premarital sexual intercourse, at least for women, was considered one of the major taboos of our society. Traditionally, women have been warned by society that "nice girls don't do it"; men have been told that although premarital sex is OK for them, they should make sure they marry virgins. This view, that premarital sex is permissible for males but not for females, is called the **double standard.**

Although as recently as the 1960s the majority of adult Americans believed that premarital sex was always wrong, since that time there has been a dramatic change in public opinion. For example, in 1969 the majority of people thought it was wrong for a man and woman to have sexual intercourse before marriage. However, the 1991 figures show a shift; at that point, more people thought it was permissible than thought it wrong.

Changes in attitudes toward premarital sex were matched by changes in actual rates of premarital sexual activity during the same period. For instance, the most recent figures show that just over one-half of women between the ages of 15 and 19 have had premarital sexual intercourse. These figures are close to double the number of women in the same age range who reported having intercourse in 1970 (CDC, 1991b, 1992). Clearly, the trend over the last several decades has been toward more women engaging in premarital sexual activity (Hofferth, Kahn, & Baldwin, 1987; Gerrard, 1988; CDC, 1991b, 1992; Porter et al., 1996).

masturbation: Sexual self-stimulation

Sexuality

heterosexuality: Sexual attraction and behaviour directed to the opposite sex, consisting of far more than male-female intercourse

double standard: The view that premarital sex is permissible for males but not for females

Males, too, have shown an increase in the incidence of premarital sexual intercourse, although the increase has not been as dramatic as it has for females—probably because the rates for males were higher to begin with. For instance, the first surveys of premarital intercourse carried out in the 1940s showed an incidence of 84 percent across males of all ages; recent figures put the figure at closer to 95 percent. Moreover, the average age of males' first sexual experience has also been declining steadily. Some 60 percent of male high school students have had sexual intercourse; and, by the time they reach the age of 20, 80 percent have had intercourse (Arena, 1984; CDC, 1992).

Marital Sex

To judge by the number of articles about sex in marriage, one would think that sexual behaviour was the number one standard by which marital bliss is measured. Married couples are often concerned that they are having too little sex, too much sex, or the wrong kind of sex (Sprecher & McKinney, 1993).

Although there are many different dimensions against which sex in marriage is measured, one is certainly the frequency of sexual intercourse. What is typical? As with most other types of sexual activities, there is no easy answer to the question, since there are such wide variations in patterns between individuals. We do know that 50 percent of Canadians report having sexual intercourse at least once a week, and 14 percent do so two or three times a month (Barrett et al., 1997). In the United States, 36 percent of married couples have intercourse two or three times a week and 43 percent have it a few times a month (Michael et al., 1994). In addition, there are differences according to the number of years a couple has been together: the longer the marriage, the lower the frequency of sex.

The frequency of marital sexual intercourse also appears to be higher at this point in time than in other recent historical periods. A number of factors account for this increase. Increased availability of birth control methods (including birth control pills) and abortion have led couples to be less concerned about unwanted pregnancies. Moreover, several social changes are likely to have had an impact. As women's roles have changed, and the popular media have reinforced the notion that female sexuality is OK, the likelihood that a wife may initiate sex—rather than waiting for her husband's overtures, as in the more traditional scenario—has increased. As sex becomes more openly discussed in magazines, books, and television shows, many married couples have come to believe that the frequency of sex is a critical index of the success of their marriage. Yet the frequency of sexual intercourse does not appear to be associated with happiness in marriage (Goleman, 1985). Sexual satisfaction, on the other hand, has been found to be related to overall satisfaction with a marriage (Blumstein & Schwartz, 1983; Greeley, 1992).

Homosexuality and Bisexuality

Just as there seems to be no genetic or biological reason for heterosexual women to find men's buttocks particularly erotic, humans are not born with an innate attraction to the special characteristics of the opposite sex. We should not find it surprising, then, that some people, **homosexuals,** are sexually attracted to members of their own sex, while others, **bisexuals,** are sexually attracted to people of the same *and* the opposite sex. (Many male homosexuals prefer the term *gay,* and female homosexuals the label *lesbian,* since there are fewer negative stereotypes associated with these words.)

Although people often view homosexuality and heterosexuality as two completely distinct sexual orientations, the issue is not that simple. Pioneering sex researcher Alfred Kinsey acknowledged this when he considered sexual orientation along a scale or continuum, with "exclusively homosexual" at one end and "exclusively heterosexual" at the other. In the middle were people who showed both homosexual and heterosexual behaviour. Updated by sociologist Martin S. Weinberg and colleagues (Weinberg, Williams, & Pryor, 1991), Kinsey's approach suggests that

homosexuals: Persons who are sexually attracted to members of their own sex

bisexuals: Persons who are sexually attracted to people of the same *and* the opposite sex

Athletes face particular pressure to conform, but Canadian swimmer Mark Tewksbury, 1992 Olympic gold medallist in Barcelona, came out as gay in 1999.

sexual orientation is dependent on a person's sexual feelings, sexual behaviours, and romantic feelings.

What determines people's sexual orientation? Although there are a number of theories, none has proved completely satisfactory. Some approaches are biological in nature, suggesting that there may be a genetic or hormonal reason for the development of homosexuality (Berenbaum & Snyder, 1995; Meyer-Bahlburg et al., 1995; Pillard, 1996; Bailey et al., 1997). For example, some evidence suggests a difference in the structure of the anterior hypothalamus, an area of the brain that governs sexual behaviour, between male homosexuals and heterosexuals (LeVay, 1991, 1993; Swaab & Gofman, 1995). Similarly, other research shows that, compared with heterosexual men or women, homosexual men have a larger anterior commissure, which is a bundle of neurons connecting the right and left hemispheres of the brain (Allen & Gorski, 1992; Harrison, Everall, & Catalan, 1994; Byne, 1996). Sandra Witelson (McMaster University) has found different patterns of functional cerebral asymmetry in gay men and lesbian women compared with heterosexuals (McCormick & Witelson. 1994).

Other theories of homosexuality have focused on the childhood and family background of homosexuals (Bailey & Zucker, 1995). For instance, Freud believed that homosexuality occurred as a result of inappropriate identification with the opposite-sex parent during development (Freud, 1922/1959). Similarly, other psychoanalysts suggest that the nature of the parent-child relationship can lead to homosexuality, and that male homosexuals frequently have overprotective, dominant mothers and passive, ineffective fathers (Bieber, 1962).

The problem with such theories is that there are probably as many homosexuals who were not subjected to the influence of such family dynamics as there are homosexuals who were. The evidence does not support explanations that rely on child-rearing practices or on the nature of the family structure (Bell & Weinberg, 1978; Isay, 1990).

Another explanation for homosexuality rests on learning theory (Masters & Johnson, 1979). According to this view, sexual orientation is learned through rewards and punishments in much the same way that we might learn to prefer swimming over tennis. For example, a young adolescent who had an unpleasant heterosexual experience might learn to link unpleasant associations with the opposite sex. If that same person had a rewarding, pleasant homosexual experience, homosexuality might be incorporated into his or her sexual fantasies. If such fantasies are then positively reinforced through association with sexual pleasure, homosexuality may eventually become the preferred form of sexual behaviour.

Sexual Orientation

Although the learning theory explanation is plausible, several difficulties rule it out as a definitive explanation. Because our society tends to hold homosexuality in low esteem, one ought to expect that the punishments involved in homosexual behaviour would outweigh the rewards attached to it. Furthermore, children growing up with a homosexual parent are statistically unlikely to become homosexual, thus contradicting the notion that homosexual behaviour might be learned from others (Victor & Fish, 1995; Tasker & Golombok, 1995; Golombok & Tasker, 1996).

Given the difficulty in finding a consistent explanation, the majority of researchers reject the notion that any single factor orients a person toward homosexuality. Most experts suspect that a combination of biological and environmental factors is at work (Money, 1987; McWhirter, Sanders, & Reinisch, 1990; Greene & Herek, 1994; Bem, 1996).

Although we don't know at this point exactly why people develop a particular sexual orientation, one thing is clear: There is no relationship between psychological adjustment and sexual orientation. Bisexuals and homosexuals enjoy the same overall degree of mental and physical health as heterosexuals do. They hold equivalent ranges and types of attitudes about themselves, independent of sexual orientation. For such reasons, the American Psychological Association and most other mental health organizations have endorsed efforts to reduce discrimination against gay men and lesbians, such as revoking the ban against homosexuals in the military (Gonsiorek, 1991; Herek, 1993; Patterson, 1994; Jones & Koshes, 1995; Shawver, 1995).

Exploring Diversity

Female Circumcision: A Celebration of Culture—or Genital Mutilation?

- On a late-summer night in 1995 in Washington, D.C., one young Ethiopian immigrant confides to another, "Mother says she will do it anyway, herself— when I'm out of the house—if I don't agree to get it done soon….She says she will take a razor blade and do it" (Burstyn, 1995, page 28).

- In Dakar, an office manager at a large European airline returned home at the end of his working day to find his two little daughters lying on the bed terrified. His wife's aunt had come with the excisist and had circumcised the girls against his and his wife's wishes. His wife could do nothing to prevent it; they didn't even have a phone (Armstrong, 1998).

- In Atlanta, Georgia, Hassan and Yasmin Ibrahim are having one of their nightly talks about their three little girls. Both want what is best for their children. Yasmin insists that unless each one of the girls is circumcised, no Somali man will marry them. Hassan says he doesn't want his children to go through the process that most Somali women do (Rosenthal, 1993).

Female circumcision, or female genital mutilation, as the procedure is also called, represents one of the most controversial procedures throughout the world. In one form of the operation, the outer layer of the skin over the clitoris is removed, hence the name female circumcision. Approximately 100 to 135 million women and girls worldwide have undergone some form of this operation (Amnesty International,1998; Burstyn, 1995). Most of these women live in Africa, the Middle East, or Asia. For instance, more than 90 percent of Nigerian women have been circumcised during childhood, and most of them intend to circumcise their daughters. Furthermore, in some cases, more extensive surgery is carried out, in which additional parts of the female genitals are removed and most of the remaining edges sewn together with thorns, catgut, or sewing thread (Ebomoyi, 1987; Rosenthal, 1993; French, 1997; Aikman, n. d.).

Those who practise female circumcision say it upholds an ancient societal tradition, no different from other cultural customs. Its purpose, they say, is to preserve virginity before marriage, to keep women faithful to their husbands after marriage, and to enhance a woman's beauty. Furthermore, proponents believe it differs little from the

Female Genital Cutting

common western practice of male circumcision, in which the foreskin of the penis is surgically removed soon after birth.

Critics, on the other hand, argue that female circumcision is nothing less than female genital mutilation, and that it is a gross violation of human rights. It can lead to constant pain and infection, depending on the nature of the surgery. Because the procedure is traditionally conducted without anesthetic, using a razor blade, sawtooth knife, or glass, it can be physically traumatic (Dugger, 1996).

In the west, this procedure is forbidden by law in Canada, Britain, Denmark, Belgium, the United States, Sweden, and Switzerland (Burstyn,1995; Robinson, 1998). In the United States, the penalty, according to federal law, for performing the surgery on anyone under the age of 18, is five years imprisonment. In Canada, not only is the procedure banned, but the Canadian Criminal Code protects children (who are citizens or landed immigrants) from being taken to another country for the surgery. Medical associations in most Canadian Provinces have strict penalties against female circumcision and reinfibulation (sewing the vagina nearly shut after childbirth) (Burstyn, 1995; Robinson, 1998). In several jurisdictions, women have been granted refugee status on the grounds that they or their daughters would be at risk for female circumcision in their homeland. For example, in Canada in 1993, a Somali woman who fled her country to protect her daughter from the procedure was granted refugee status (Amnesty International, 1998). ■

The Need for Achievement: Striving for Success

While hunger and sex may represent two of the most potent primary drives in our day-to-day lives, we are also motivated by powerful secondary drives that have no clear biological basis (McClelland, 1985; Geen, 1984, 1995). Among the most prominent of these is the need for achievement.

The **need for achievement** is a stable, learned characteristic in which satisfaction is obtained by striving for and attaining a level of excellence (McClelland et al., 1953). People with a high need for achievement seek out situations in which they can compete against some standard—be it grades, money, or winning at a game—and prove themselves successful. But they are not indiscriminate when it comes to picking their challenges: Like Bob, the would-be law student described at the beginning of this section, they tend to avoid situations in which success will come too easily (which would be unchallenging) and situations in which success is unlikely. Instead, people high in achievement motivation are apt to choose tasks that are of intermediate difficulty.

In contrast, people with low achievement motivation tend to be motivated primarily by a desire to avoid failure. As a result, they seek out easy tasks, being sure to avoid failure, or they seek out very difficult tasks for which failure has no negative implications, since almost anyone would fail at them. People with a high fear of failure will stay away from tasks of intermediate difficulty, since they may fail where others have been successful (Atkinson & Feather, 1966; Sorrentino, Hewitt, & Raso-Knott, 1992; Elliot & Church, 1997).

The outcomes of a high need for achievement are generally positive, at least in a success-oriented society such as our own (Heckhausen, Schmalt, & Schneider, 1985; Spence, 1985). For instance, people motivated by a high need for achievement are more likely to attend college than their low-achievement counterparts, and once in college they tend to receive higher grades in classes that are related to their future careers (Atkinson & Raynor, 1974). Furthermore, high achievement motivation is associated with future economic and occupational success (McClelland, 1985).

need for achievement: A stable, learned characteristic in which satisfaction is obtained by striving for and attaining a level of excellence

Theories of Motivation

Measuring Achievement Motivation

How can we measure a person's need for achievement? The technique used most frequently is to administer a *Thematic Apperception Test (TAT)* (Spangler, 1992). In the TAT, people are shown a series of ambiguous pictures, such as the one in Figure 9-2. They are told to write a story that describes what is happening, who the people are, what led to the situation, what the people are thinking or wanting, and what will hap-

FIGURE 9-2 *This ambiguous picture is similar to those used in the Thematic Apperception Test to determine people's underlying motivation. Source: Reprinted by permission of the publisher, from Henry A. Murray,* Thematic Apperception Test, *Cambridge, Mass: Harvard University Press, © 1943 by the President & Fellows of Harvard College, © 1971 by Henry A. Murray.*

pen next. A standard scoring system is then used to determine the amount of achievement imagery in people's stories. For example, someone who writes a story in which the main character is striving to beat an opponent, studying in order to do well at some task, or working hard in order to get a promotion shows clear signs of an achievement orientation. It is assumed that the inclusion of such achievement-related imagery in their stories indicates an unusually high degree of concern with—and therefore a relatively strong need for—achievement.

Other techniques have been developed for assessing achievement motivation on a societal level (Reuman, Alwin, & Veroff, 1984). For example, a good indication of the overall level of achievement motivation in a particular society can be found by assessing achievement imagery in children's stories or folk tales. Researchers who have examined children's reading books for achievement imagery over long periods have found correlations between the amount of such imagery in the books and the economic activity in the society over the next few decades (DeCharms & Moeller, 1962). Whether stories incorporating achievement imagery actually influence children or simply reflect growing economic trends cannot be determined, of course. It is clear, though, that children might be learning more from their books than how to read—they may be acquiring an understanding of the level of achievement motivation that society expects of them.

Race, Culture, Motivation, and Achievement

For almost a century, aboriginal children in Canada were required to attend residential schools in an effort to assimilate Canada's aboriginal population into white culture. Ignoring aboriginal language, tradition, and learning styles, the schools produced educational problems (e.g., 45 percent of those living on reserves were functionally illiterate, Battiste, 1995) and negative attitudes (Barman, 1996). And many students suffered emotional, physical and sexual abuse (O'Hara, 2000).

A common opinion in both Canada and the United States is that blacks achieve less because they are deficient in motivation. Graham (1994) summarized several decades of research and concluded that there is little, if any, reliable evidence to suggest that blacks and whites differ in achievement motivation.

In 1994–1995, the Third International Mathematics and Science Study (TIMSS) was conducted in more than 40 countries. At all five grade levels surveyed, students in Asian countries ranked higher than those in Canada or the United States. Stevenson (1992, 1995, 1997) found that a number of factors contribute to these differences, such as longer school days, a longer school year, and higher parental expectations in Asian countries compared with Canada and the United States.

Taken together, what do these situations and findings tell us about race, culture, motivation, and achievement? Basically, they illustrate a complex interplay among these factors. Motivational differences appear to be largely rooted in different experiences, and motivational differences are one of many factors related to differences in achievement.

The Need for Affiliation: Striving for Friendship

Few of us choose to lead our lives as hermits. Why? One main reason is that most people have a **need for affiliation,** an interest in establishing and maintaining relationships with other people. Individuals with a high need for affiliation write TAT stories that emphasize the desire to maintain or reinstate friendships and show concern over being rejected by friends.

need for affiliation: An interest in establishing and maintaining relationships with other people

People who are higher in affiliation needs are particularly sensitive to relationships with others. They desire to be with their friends more of the time, and alone less often, than people who are lower in the need for affiliation (O'Connor & Rosenblood, 1996). At the same time, affiliation motivation may be less important than gender in determining how much time is actually spent with friends. According to the results of one study, regardless of their affiliative orientation, female students spend significantly more time with their friends and less time alone than male students do (Wong & Csikszentmihalyi, 1991).

The Need for Power: Striving for Impact on Others

If your fantasies include being elected president of the United States or running General Motors, they may be reflecting a high need for power. The **need for power,** a tendency to seek impact, control, or influence over others, and to be seen as a powerful individual, is an additional type of motivation (Winter, 1973, 1987).

need for power: A tendency to seek impact, control, or influence over others, and to be seen as a powerful individual

As you might expect, people with a strong need for power are more apt to belong to organizations and seek office than those low in the need for power. They are also apt to be in professions in which their power needs may be fulfilled, such as business management and—you may or may not be surprised—teaching (Jenkins, 1994). In addition, they seek to display the trappings of power. Even in college, they are more apt to collect prestigious possessions, such as stereos and sports cars.

There are some significant sex differences in the display of the need for power. Men who are high in power needs tend to show unusually high levels of aggression, drink heavily, act in a sexually exploitative manner, and participate more frequently in competitive sports—behaviours that collectively represent somewhat extravagant, flamboyant behaviour (Winter, 1973). In contrast, women display their power needs in a more restrained manner, congruent with traditional societal constraints on women's behaviour. Women high in the need for power are more apt than men to channel their power needs in a socially responsible manner (such as by showing concern for others or displaying highly nurturant behaviour) (Winter, 1988).

In common with other types of motivation, the need for power may express itself in several quite diverse ways (Spangler & House, 1991). How a particular need is manifested reflects a combination of people's skills and values and the specific situation in which they find themselves.

Pathways Through Psychology

Tara K. MacDonald

*Assistant Professor of Psychology
Department of Psychology
Queen's University, Kingston,
Ontario*

*Education: B.A., University of Western
Ontario; Ph.D. University of Waterloo*

Home: Kingston, Ontario

As a first year university student, I had actually intended to pursue an undergraduate degree in English, but found psychology so interesting and exciting that I decided to switch majors. I was especially curious about experimental social psychology—I thought that it was fascinating to learn about clever experiments in the laboratory and the field that were designed to "capture" phenomena that were so interesting and important. I decided to go to graduate school in social psychology. I was interested in the "attitude-behaviour problem," the question of why people do not always engage in behaviours that are consistent with their attitudes and intentions. This is an interesting and potentially important question. For example, most people report very negative attitudes and intentions toward the behaviour of drinking and driving, but unfortunately, statistics show that all too often, people do decide to engage in this risky behaviour.

Dr. Mark Zanna, Dr. Geoffrey Fong and I conducted an initial set of laboratory and field experiments in which we demonstrated that alcohol causes people to be more likely to report intentions to drink and drive. In other experiments, we found that alcohol intoxication also causes people to be more likely to report

Tara K. MacDonald

intentions to engage in unprotected sexual intercourse.

We interpreted our findings as being consistent with Alcohol Myopia, a theory posited by Claude Steele and Robert Josephs in 1990. According to this theory, alcohol intoxication limits people from attending to all of the different cues in the environment, and so intoxicated people are likely to focus on, and act on, the most apparent cues. Interestingly, the alcohol myopia hypothesis suggests that if cues that would deter risky behaviour are highly salient, then alcohol intoxication should be associated with more cautious intentions and behaviour. Indeed, in our most recent research, we have found that when the dangers of unprotected sex-

ual intercourse are made salient, then intoxicated people are less likely than sober people to intend to have unprotected sex.

I enjoy this area of research because it is theoretically interesting, as we are studying how alcohol affects decision-making, and finding that the story is more complicated than most people think. A popular belief is that alcohol simply causes disinhibition; thus, one would expect that alcohol would always lead to risky behaviour. In contrast, we find that alcohol causes people to be highly influenced by the cues in the environment. If cues that emphasize risk are apparent, then alcohol leads to risky intentions; if cues that emphasize caution are apparent, then alcohol leads to more cautious intentions. Also, this research has practical value: it can be applied to efforts to reduce the incidence of risky and costly behaviours associated with alcohol intoxication.

I feel very fortunate to work as a researcher and teacher in a University environment. The job is demanding, to be sure, but it is also very rewarding. I enjoy conducting research and exploring problems that are interesting to me, and then sharing my findings with others through conference presentations and journal publications. I also enjoy teaching psychology—it's a challenge to find ways to present the material so that it is interesting, entertaining, and memorable. Finally, I believe that training future researchers is a very important aspect of my career.

*Source: Tara K. MacDonald, Ph.D. Queen's
University <psyc.queensu.ca/faculty/
macdonald/tara.html>*

Recap, Review, and Rethink

Recap

- Hunger is affected by internal cues that regulate the amount and kind of food eaten. The hypothalamus plays a central role in regulating food intake.

- People's weight set point, their sensitivity to external social cues, the number of fat cells they have, and genetic factors may all affect eating patterns.

- Although biological factors prime people for sex, other stimuli are necessary for sexual excitement to occur.

- Masturbation (sexual self-stimulation) is common among both men and women, although it is still viewed negatively by many people.

- The double standard has declined over the last few decades; tolerance for and actual acts of premarital sex have increased greatly.

- Among the major secondary drives are the needs for achievement, affiliation, and power.

Review

1. Laboratory animals, when deprived of certain nutrients, have been found to instinctively choose foods that contain the nutrients they are lacking. True or false?

2. Match the following terms with their definitions:
   1. hypothalamus
   2. lateral hypothalamic damage
   3. ventromedial hypothalamic damage

   a. leads to refusal of food and starvation
   b. responsible for monitoring food intake
   c. causes extreme overeating

3. The _____ _____ _____ is the particular level of weight the body strives to maintain.

4. _____ is the rate at which energy is produced and expended by the body.

5. _____ is an eating disorder characterized by binge eating, then purging the body by inducing vomiting. A person with the disorder of _____ _____ refuses to eat and denies that his or her behaviour and appearance are unusual.

6. Men's and women's sexual fantasies are essentially similar. True or False?

7. The work carried out by _____ in the 1930s was the first systematic study of sexual behaviour ever undertaken.

8. Although the incidence of masturbation among young adults is high, once men and women become involved in intimate relationships, they typically cease masturbating. True or false?

9. Research comparing homosexuals and heterosexuals clearly demonstrates that there is no difference in the level of adjustment or psychological functioning between the two groups. True or false?

10. Jake is the type of person who constantly strives for excellence. He feels intense satisfaction when he is able to master a new task. Jake most likely has a high need for _____ .

Answers to Review Questions are on page 330.

Rethink

1. In what ways do societal expectations, expressed by television shows and commercials, contribute to both obesity and excessive concern about weight loss? How could television contribute to better eating habits and attitudes toward weight? Should it be required to?

2. What societal factors have led to a reduction in the double standard by which sexuality in men is regarded differently from sexuality in women? Do you think the double standard has completely vanished?

3. Can traits such as need for achievement, need for power, and need for affiliation be used to select workers for jobs? What other criteria, both motivational and personal, would have to be considered when making such a selection?

UNDERSTANDING EMOTIONAL EXPERIENCES

Karl Andrews held in his hands the envelope he had been waiting for. It could be the ticket to his future: an offer of admission to his first-choice university. But what was it going to say? He knew it could go either way: His grades were pretty good, and he had been involved in some extracurricular activities; but his GRE scores had been, to put it bluntly, lousy. He felt so nervous that his hands shook as he opened the thin envelope (not a good sign, he thought). Here it comes. "Dear Mr. Andrews," it read. "The President and Trustees of the University are pleased to admit you. . . ." That was all he needed to see. With a whoop of excitement, Karl found himself jumping up and down gleefully. A rush of emotion overcame him as it sank in that he had, in fact, been accepted. He was on his way.

▶ **What are emotions and how do we experience them?**

▶ **What are the functions of emotions?**

At one time or another, all of us have experienced the strong feelings that accompany both very pleasant and very negative experiences. Perhaps it was the thrill of getting a sought-after job, the joy of being in love, the sorrow over someone's death, or the anguish of inadvertently hurting someone. Moreover, we experience such reactions on a less intense level throughout our daily lives: the pleasure of a friendship, the enjoyment of a movie, or the embarrassment of breaking a borrowed item.

Despite the varied nature of these feelings, they all represent emotions. Although everyone has an idea of what an emotion is, formally defining the concept has proved to be an elusive task. We'll use a general definition: **Emotions** are feelings that generally have both physiological and cognitive elements and that influence behaviour.

Think, for example, about how it feels to be happy. First, we obviously experience a feeling that we can differentiate from other emotions. It is likely that we also experience some identifiable physical changes in our bodies: Perhaps our heart rate increases, or—as in the example of Karl Andrews—we find ourselves "jumping for joy." Finally, the emotion probably encompasses cognitive elements: Our

emotions: Feelings that generally have both physiological and cognitive elements and that influence behaviour

understanding and evaluation of the meaning of what is happening prompt our feelings of happiness.

It is also possible, however, to experience an emotion without the presence of cognitive elements. For instance, we may react with fear to an unusual or novel situation (such as coming into contact with an erratic, unpredictable individual), or we may experience pleasure over sexual excitation, without having cognitive awareness or understanding of just what it is about the situation that is exciting.

Some psychologists argue that there are entirely separate systems governing cognitive responses and emotional responses. One current controversy is whether the emotional response is predominant over the cognitive response or vice versa. Some theorists suggest that we first respond to a situation with an emotional reaction, and later try to understand it (Zajonc, 1985; Zajonc & McIntosh, 1992; Murphy & Zajonc, 1993). For example, we may enjoy a complex modern symphony without at first understanding it or knowing why we like it.

Emotions and Emotional Intelligence

In contrast, other theorists propose that people first develop cognitions about a situation and then react emotionally. This school of thought suggests that it is necessary for us to first think about and understand a stimulus or situation, relating it to what we already know, before we can react on an emotional level (Lazarus, 1991a, 1991b, 1994, 1995).

Both sides of this debate can cite research to support their viewpoints, and so the question is far from resolved. It may be the case that the sequence varies from situation to situation, with emotions predominating in some instances and cognitive processes occurring first in others. What both sides do agree on is that we can experience emotions that involve little or no conscious thought. We may not know why we're afraid of mice, understanding that objectively they represent no danger, but still be frightened out of our wits when we see them.

Regardless of the sequence, it is clear that our emotions play a major role in influencing our behaviour. On the other hand, not everyone seems to experience emotions in an identical way. For instance, there seem to be gender differences in emotional experiences. Results of a variety of studies confirm what popular literature suggests: Compared to men, women consistently report experiencing emotions more intensely and expressing them more readily, a phenomenon that begins as early as the preschool years (Diener, Sandvik, & Larsen, 1985; Larsen & Diener, 1987; Karbon et al., 1992; Brody, 1996).

Although some researchers have suggested that this gender difference is due to innate biological factors (e.g., Pennebaker & Roberts, 1992), a more recent analysis suggests that the variation may be due to different societal expectations for men and women. Psychologists Michele Grossman and Wendy Wood (1993) suggest that women's greater emotional intensity stems from the different social roles played traditionally by women and men in society. Women, for example, are more apt to fill nurturing, caretaker roles in the home, such as those of mother and wife. Furthermore, even when women work outside the home, they are more likely to engage in professions in which nurturance is an important component, such as teaching or nursing.

Because caretaker roles require concern for the needs of others, women may be more apt than men to develop emotional sensitivity. At the same time, men traditionally play roles in which emotional expressivity is downplayed and even discouraged. Traditional societal expectations, then, may lead women to develop more emotionality and men to develop more restrained emotional styles.

The intriguing implication of this analysis is that as society's view of what constitutes appropriate behaviour for men and women changes, the extent of the gender difference in emotionality may decline as well.

Answers to Review Questions:

1. true   2. 1-b; 2-a; 3-c   3. weight set point   4. Metabolism   5. Bulimia; anorexia nervosa   6. true   7. Kinsey   8. False; even people in married relationships show a continued incidence of masturbation.   9. true   10. achievement

The Functions of Emotions

Imagine what it would be like if we didn't experience emotion—no depths of despair, no depression, no remorse, but at the same time no happiness, joy, or love. Obviously life might be considerably less satisfying, and even dull, if we lacked the capacity to sense and express emotion.

But do emotions serve any purpose beyond making life interesting? Indeed they do. Psychologists have identified a number of important functions that emotions play in our daily lives (Scherer, 1984, 1994; Averill, 1994; Oatley & Jenkins, 1996; Greenberg & Paivio, 1997). Among the most important of those functions:

- *Preparing us for action.* Emotions act as a link between events in the external environment and behavioural responses that an individual makes. For example, if we saw an angry dog charging toward us, the emotional reaction (fear) would be associated with physiological arousal of the sympathetic division of the autonomic nervous system (see Chapter 2). The role of the sympathetic division is to prepare us for emergency action, which presumably would get us moving out of the dog's way—quickly. Emotions, then, are stimuli that aid in the development of effective responses to various situations.

- *Shaping our future behaviour.* Emotions serve to promote learning of information that will assist us in making appropriate responses in the future. For example, the emotional response that occurs when a person experiences something unpleasant—such as the threatening dog—teaches that person to avoid similar circumstances in the future. Similarly, pleasant emotions act as reinforcement for prior behaviour and therefore are apt to lead an individual to seek out similar situations in the future. Thus, the feeling of satisfaction that follows giving to a charity is likely to reinforce charitable behaviour and make it more likely to occur in the future.

- *Helping us to regulate social interaction.* As we shall discuss in detail later, the emotions we experience are frequently obvious to observers, as they are communicated through our verbal and nonverbal behaviors. These behaviours can act as a signal to observers, allowing them to better understand what we are experiencing and to predict our future behaviour. In turn, this promotes more effective and appropriate social interaction. For instance, a mother who sees the terror on her 2-year-old son's face when he sees a frightening picture in a book is able to comfort and reassure him, thereby helping him to deal with his environment more effectively in the future.

Determining the Range of Emotions: Labelling Our Feelings

If we were to try to list the words in the English language that have been used to describe emotions, we would end up with at least five hundred different examples (Averill, 1975). The list would range from such obvious emotions as "happiness" and "fear" to less common ones, such as "adventurousness" and "pensiveness."

One challenge for psychologists has been to try to sort through this list in order to identify the most important, fundamental emotions. The issue of cataloguing emotions has been hotly contested, and various emotion theorists have come up with different lists, depending on how they define the concept of emotion. In fact, some reject the question entirely, saying that *no* set of emotions should be singled out as most basic, and that emotions are best understood by breaking them down into their component parts. Other researchers argue that it is best to look at emotions in terms of a hierarchy, dividing them into positive and negative categories, and then organizing them into increasingly narrower subcategories (see Figure 9-3; Fischer, Shaver, & Carnochan, 1990; Carroll & Russell, 1997).

Still, most researchers suggest that a list of basic emotions would include, at the minimum, happiness, anger, fear, sadness, and disgust. Other lists are broader,

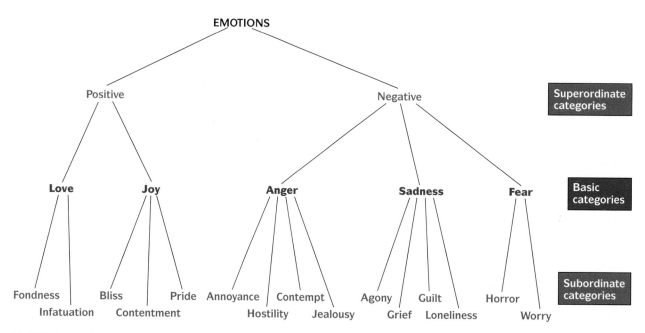

FIGURE 9-3 *One approach to organizing emotions is to use a hierarchy, in which they are divided into increasingly narrow subcategories. Source: Adapted from Fischer, Shaver, & Carnochan, 1990.*

Culture and Emotion

including such emotions as surprise, contempt, guilt, joy (Plutchik, 1980; Ortony & Turner, 1990; Russell, 1991; Ekman, 1994a; Shweder, 1994).

One difficulty in finding a definitive basic set of emotions is that significant differences exist in descriptions of emotions among various cultures. For instance, Germans report experiencing *schadenfreude,* a feeling of pleasure over another person's difficulties, while the Japanese experience *hagaii,* a mood of vulnerable heartache coloured by frustration. In Tahiti, people experience *musu,* a feeling of reluctance to yield to unreasonable demands made by one's parents.

Finding *schadenfreude, hagaii,* and *musu* in a particular culture doesn't mean that inhabitants of other cultures are incapable of experiencing such emotions, of course. It does suggest, though, that the existence of a linguistic category to describe a particular emotion may make it easier to discuss, contemplate, and perhaps experience the emotion (Russell, 1991; Mesquita & Frijda, 1992; Russell & Sato, 1995).

Members of different cultures also experience emotions with differing degrees of intensity. For example, compared with students in Japan, students in the United States report that their emotions last longer and are more intense. In addition, U.S. students say they react more positively to the general experience of emotion than Japanese students (Matsumoto et al., 1988; Lee et al., 1992; Bond, 1993).

Although ultimately it may prove impossible for psychologists to produce a definitive, universal list of the primary emotions, most of us experience a range of emotions throughout the course of our lives. The process by which we come to understand our emotions forms the basis of a number of theories of emotion, which we discuss next.

DECIPHERING OUR EMOTIONS

I've never been so angry before; I feel my heart pounding, and I'm trembling all over. . . . I don't know how I'll get through the performance. I feel like my stomach is filled with butterflies. . . . That was quite a mistake I made! My face must be incredibly red. . . . When I heard the footsteps in the night I was so frightened that I couldn't catch my breath.

If you examine our language, you will find that there are literally dozens of ways to describe how we feel when we experience an emotion, and that the language we use to describe emotions is based, for the most part, on the physical symptoms that are associated with a particular emotional experience (Koveces, 1987).

Consider, for instance, the experience of fear. Pretend that it is late one New Year's Eve. You are walking down a dark road, and you hear a stranger approaching from behind. It is clear that he is not trying to hurry by but is coming directly toward you. You think of what you will do if the stranger attempts to rob you—or worse, hurt you in some way.

While these thoughts are running through your head, it is almost certain that something rather dramatic will be happening to your body. Among the most likely physiological reactions that may occur, which are associated with activation of the autonomic nervous system (see Chapter 2), are those listed here:

- The rate and depth of your breathing will increase.

- Your heart will speed up, pumping more blood through your circulatory system.

- The pupils of your eyes will open wider, allowing more light to enter and thereby increasing your visual sensitivity.

- Your mouth will become dry as the functioning of your salivary glands, and in fact of your entire digestive system, ceases. At the same time, though, your sweat glands may increase their activity, since increased sweating will help you rid yourself of excess heat developed by any emergency activity in which you engage.

- As the muscles just below the surface of your skin contract, your hair may literally stand on end.

Of course, all these physiological changes are likely to occur without your awareness. At the same time, though, the emotional experience accompanying them will be obvious to you: You would most surely report being fearful.

Although it is a relatively straightforward matter to describe the general physical reactions that accompany emotions, defining the specific role that these physiological responses play in the experience of emotions has proved to be a major puzzle for psychologists. As we shall see, some theorists suggest that there are specific bodily reactions that *cause* us to experience a particular emotion—we experience fear, for instance, *because* our hearts are pounding and we are breathing deeply. In contrast, other theorists suggest that the physiological reaction is the *result* of the experience of an emotion. In this view, we experience fear, and this emotional experience causes our hearts to pound and our breathing to deepen.

The James-Lange Theory: Do Gut Reactions Equal Emotions?

To William James and Carl Lange, who were among the first researchers to explore the nature of emotions, emotional experience is, very simply, a reaction to instinctive bodily events that occur as a response to some situation or event in the environment. This view is summarized in James's statement, ". . . we feel sorry because we cry, angry because we strike, afraid because we tremble" (James, 1890).

James and Lange took the view that the instinctive response of crying at a loss leads us to feel sorrow; that striking out at someone who frustrates us results in our feeling anger; that trembling at a menacing threat causes us to feel fear. They suggested that for every major emotion there is an accompanying physiological or "gut" reaction of internal organs—called a *visceral experience*. It is this specific pattern of visceral response that leads us to label the emotional experience.

In sum, James and Lange proposed that we experience emotions as a result of physiological changes that produce specific sensations. In turn, these sensations are interpreted by the brain as particular kinds of emotional experiences (see Figure 9-4). This view has come to be called the **James-Lange theory of emotion** (Laird & Bresler, 1990).

The James-Lange theory has some serious drawbacks, however. In order for the theory to be valid, visceral changes would have to occur at a relatively rapid pace,

James-Lange theory of emotion: The belief that emotional experience is a reaction to bodily events occurring as a result of an external situation ("I feel sad because I am crying")

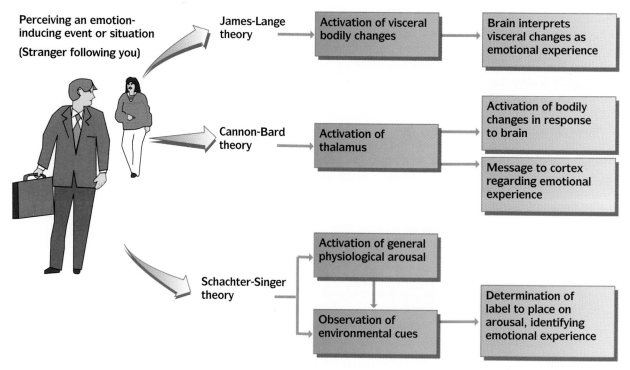

FIGURE 9-4 *A comparison of three models of emotion.*

since we experience some emotions—such as fear upon hearing a stranger rapidly approaching on a dark night—almost instantaneously. Yet emotional experiences frequently occur even before there is time for certain physiological changes to be set into motion. Because of the slowness with which some visceral changes take place, it is hard to see how they could be the source of immediate emotional experience.

The James-Lange theory poses another difficulty: Physiological arousal does not invariably produce emotional experience. For example, a person who is jogging has an increased heartbeat and respiration rate, as well as many of the other physiological changes associated with certain emotions. Yet joggers do not typically think of such changes in terms of emotions. There cannot be a one-to-one correspondence, then, between visceral changes and emotional experience. Visceral changes by themselves may not be sufficient to produce emotion.

Finally, our internal organs produce a relatively limited range of sensations. Although some types of physiological changes are associated with specific emotional experiences (Levenson et al., 1992; Levenson, 1992; Davidson et al., 1994), it is difficult to imagine how the range of emotions that people are capable of experiencing could be the result of unique visceral changes. Many emotions are actually associated with relatively similar sorts of visceral changes, a fact that contradicts the James-Lange theory.

The Cannon-Bard Theory: Physiological Reactions as the Result of Emotions

Cannon-Bard theory of emotion: The belief that both physiological and emotional arousal are produced simultaneously by the same nerve impulse

In response to the difficulties inherent in the James-Lange theory, Walter Cannon, and later Philip Bard, suggested an alternative view. In what has come to be known as the **Cannon-Bard theory of emotion,** they proposed the model illustrated in the second part of Figure 9-4 (Cannon, 1929). The major thrust of the theory is to reject the view that physiological arousal alone leads to the perception of emotion. Instead, the theory assumes that both physiological arousal *and* the emotional experience are produced simultaneously by the same nerve impulse, which Cannon and Bard suggested emanates from the brain's thalamus.

According to the theory, after an emotion-inducing stimulus is perceived, the thalamus is the initial site of the emotional response. In turn, the thalamus sends a signal to the autonomic nervous system, thereby producing a visceral response. At the same time, the thalamus communicates a message to the cerebral cortex regarding the nature of the emotion being experienced. Hence, it is not necessary for different emotions to have unique physiological patterns associated with them—as long as the message sent to the cerebral cortex differs according to the specific emotion.

The Cannon-Bard theory seems to have been accurate in its rejection of the view that physiological arousal alone accounts for emotions. However, more recent research has led to some important modifications of the theory. As you may recall from Chapter 2, we now understand that it is the hypothalamus and the limbic system, and not the thalamus, that play a major role in emotional experience. In addition, the simultaneity of the physiological and emotional responses, which is a fundamental assumption of the theory, has yet to be conclusively demonstrated (Pribram, 1984). This ambiguity has allowed room for yet another theory of emotions: the Schachter-Singer theory.

The Schachter-Singer Theory: Emotions as Labels

Suppose, as you were being followed down a dark street on New Year's Eve, you noticed a man being followed by a shady figure on the other side of the street. Now assume that instead of reacting with fear, the man begins to laugh and act gleeful. Might the reactions of this other individual be sufficient to lay your fears to rest? Might you, in fact, decide there is nothing to fear, and get into the spirit of the evening by beginning to feel happiness and glee yourself?

According to an explanation that focuses on the role of cognition, the **Schachter-Singer theory of emotion,** this might very well happen. This approach to explaining emotions emphasizes that we identify the emotion we are experiencing by observing our environment and comparing ourselves with others (Schachter & Singer, 1962).

A classic experiment found evidence for this hypothesis. In the study, participants were told that they would receive an injection of a vitamin called Suproxin. In reality, they were given epinephrine, a drug that causes an increase in physiological arousal, including higher heart and respiration rates and a reddening of the face, responses that typically occur during strong emotional reactions. Participants in both groups were then individually placed in a situation where a confederate of the experimenter acted in one of two ways. In one condition, he acted angry and hostile, while in the other condition he behaved as if he were exuberantly happy.

The purpose of the experiment was to determine how the participants would react emotionally to the confederate's behaviour. When they were asked to describe their own emotional state at the end of the experiment, those participants exposed to the angry confederate reported that they felt angry, while those exposed to the happy confederate reported feeling happy. In sum, the results suggest that participants turned to the environment and the behaviour of others for an explanation of the physiological arousal they were experiencing.

The results of the Schachter-Singer experiment, then, supported a cognitive view of emotions, in which emotions are determined jointly by a relatively nonspecific kind of physiological arousal *and* the labelling of the arousal based on cues from the environment (refer back to the third part of Figure 9-4).

The Schachter-Singer theory of emotion led to some clever experiments in several areas of psychology, such as the study of how we form attachments to others. In one imaginative experiment, an attractive, college-aged woman stood at the end of a swaying 135-metre suspension bridge that spanned a deep canyon. The woman was ostensibly conducting a survey, and she asked men who made it across the bridge a series of questions. She then gave them her telephone number, telling them that if they were interested in the results of the experiment they could contact her in the upcoming week.

In another condition, an attractive woman asked men who had just strolled across a stable bridge spanning a shallow stream three metres below to complete the same questionnaire. The results showed significant differences in the nature of the

Schachter-Singer theory of emotion: The belief that emotions are determined jointly by a nonspecific kind of physiological arousal and its interpretation, based on environmental cues.

This is Capilano River Bridge (BC), the high, swaying suspension bridge that was used to increase the physiological arousal of male subjects.

men's responses, depending on which bridge they had crossed. For instance, those who crossed the dangerous bridge showed significantly more sexual imagery in their survey responses than those who had crossed the less hazardous span. Furthermore, those crossing the dangerous span were significantly more likely to call the woman in the upcoming week, suggesting that their attraction to her was higher. The men whose arousal was increased by the dangerous bridge seemed to have searched for a reason for their physiological arousal—and ended up attributing the cause to the attractive woman (Dutton & Aron, 1974). Consistent with the Schachter-Singer theory, then, the men's emotional response was based on a labelling of their arousal.

Unfortunately, evidence gathered to confirm the Schachter-Singer theory has not always been so supportive (Reisenzein, 1983; Leventhal & Tomarken, 1986). For instance, some research suggests that physiological arousal is not always essential for emotional experience to occur, and that physiological factors *by themselves* can account for one's emotional state in other instances (Marshall & Zimbardo, 1979; Chwalisz, Diener, & Gallagher, 1988). Thus, certain drugs invariably produce depression as a side effect no matter what the nature of the situation or the environmental cues present.

Still, the Schachter-Singer theory of emotion represented a significant milestone in the study of emotions. The theory paved the way for recent investigations that have focused on the role of appraisal and unexplained physiological arousal. For instance, some work suggests that emotions are produced principally when we evaluate a situation as significant to our personal well-being (Mauro, Sato, & Tucker, 1992; Smith et al., 1993; Sinclair et al., 1994). In short, the Schachter-Singer theory of emotions was important because of its suggestion that, at least under some circumstances, emotional experiences are a joint function of physiological arousal and the labelling of that arousal. When the source of physiological arousal is unclear, we may look to our surroundings to determine just what it is we are experiencing.

Contemporary Perspectives on Emotion

When Schachter and Singer carried out their groundbreaking experiment in the early 1960s, they were relatively limited in the ways that they could evaluate the physiology that accompanies emotion. However, advances in the measurement of the nervous system and other parts of the body have allowed researchers to examine more closely the biological responses that are involved in emotion. As a result, contemporary research on emotion is pointing to a revision of earlier views that physiological responses associated with emotions are undifferentiated. Instead, evidence is growing that specific patterns of biological arousal are associated with individual emotions (Davidson, 1994; Levenson, 1994).

For instance, researchers have found that specific emotions produce activation of very different portions of the brain. In one study using PET brain scans, a group of female participants were asked to recall events that either made them feel sad, such as deaths and funerals, or events that were happy, such as weddings and births. They also looked at photos of faces that were happy or sad. The results were clear: Happiness was related to a decrease in activity in certain areas of the cerebral cortex, while sadness was associated with increases in activity in particular portions of the cortex (see Figure 9-5). Ultimately, it may be possible to map particular emotions to specific sites in the brain (George et al., 1995).

Other approaches to emotion have also evolved. James Russell, at the University of British Columbia, developed a circumplex model as a way of representing the structure of emotional experience and indicating systematic relationships between specific emotions (Russell, 1980). More recently he has developed a prototypical approach to emotion concepts (Russell, 1991; Russell and Fehr, 1994). Keith Oatley, at the University of Toronto, has examined social, cognitive, and experiential aspects of emotions (Oatley, 1992; Oatley and Johnson-Laird, 1987; Oatley and Duncan, 1994).

As new approaches to emotion continue to be developed, it is reasonable to ask why there are so many theories of emotion and, perhaps even more important, which one provides the most complete explanation. There are almost as many theories of

Fear

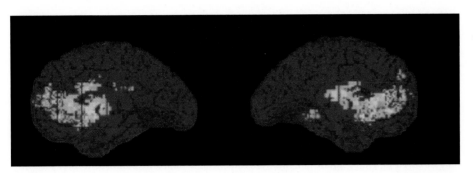

FIGURE 9-5 *The coloured portions of these scans, showing two views of the brain, indicate brain activity that occurs during the experience of sadness, as compared with situations in which no emotion is being experienced. Source: Courtesy of Dr. Mark George.*

emotion as there are individual emotions (e.g., Izard, 1991; Lazarus, 1991b; Ekman and Davidson, 1994; Strongman, 1996; Averill, 1997). Emotions are such complex phenomena, encompassing both biological and cognitive aspects, that no single theory has been able to fully explain all facets of emotional experience. No theory has proved invariably accurate in its predictions. As more evidence is gathered the specific answers to questions about emotions will become clearer.

Recap, Review, and Rethink

Recap

- Emotions are feelings that generally have both a physiological component and a cognitive component.

- Emotions have a number of functions, including preparing us for action, shaping our future behaviour, and regulating social interaction.

- A number of physiological changes accompany strong emotion, including rapid breathing and increased heart rate, opening of the pupils, dryness in the mouth, an increase in sweating, and the sensation of hair "standing on end."

- Major approaches to emotion are the James-Lange, Cannon-Bard, and Schachter-Singer theories. The most recent approaches focus on examining the nature of the biological activation that accompanies emotion.

Review

1. Emotions are always accompanied by a cognitive response. True or false?

2. The _____-_____ theory of emotions states that emotions are a response to instinctive bodily events.

3. Each emotion is accompanied by a unique set of physiological responses, thus proving the James-Lange emotion theory. True or false?

4. According to the _____ - _____ theory of emotion, both an emotional response and physiological arousal are produced simultaneously by nerve impulses.

5. Your friend—a psychology major—tells you, "I was at a party last night. During the course of the evening, my general level of arousal increased. Since I was at a party where people were enjoying themselves, I assumed I must have felt happy." What theory of emotion does your friend subscribe to?

Answers to Review Questions are on page 338.

Rethink

1. Many people enjoy watching movies, sporting events, and music performances in crowded theaters and arenas more than they like watching them at home alone. Which theory of emotions may help explain this? How?

2. If researchers ever learned how to control emotional responses so that targeted emotions and physiological reactions could be induced or decreased at will, what ethical concerns might arise? Would there be ethical uses for such knowledge?

STRESS AND COPING

Tara Knox's day began badly: She slept through her alarm and had to skip breakfast in order to catch the bus to campus. Then, when she went to the library to catch up on the reading she had to do before taking a test the next day, the article she needed was missing. The librarian told her that replacing it would take 24 hours. Feeling exasperated, she walked to the computer lab to print out the paper she had completed the night before. However, she

▶ **What is stress, how does it affect us, and how can we best cope with it?**

couldn't get the computer to read her disk. Although she searched for someone to help her, she was unable to find anyone who seemed to know any more than she did.

It was only 9:42 A.M., and all Tara could think about was how much stress she felt.

Stress: Reacting to Threat and Challenge

stress: The response to events that are threatening or challenging

Stress Links

Most of us need little introduction to the phenomenon of **stress,** the response to events that threaten or challenge a person. Whether it be a paper or exam deadline, a family problem, or even a cumulative series of small events such as those faced by Tara Knox, life is full of circumstances and events, known as *stressors,* that produce threats to our well-being. Even pleasant events—such as planning a party or beginning a sought-after job—can produce stress, although negative events result in greater detrimental consequences than positive ones (Sarason, Johnson, & Siegel, 1978; Brown & McGill, 1989).

All of us face stress in our lives. Some health psychologists believe that daily life actually involves a series of repeated sequences of perceiving a threat, considering ways to cope with it, and ultimately adapting to the threat, with greater or lesser success (Gatchel & Baum, 1983). Although adaptation is often minor and occurs without our being aware of it, in those cases in which the stress is more severe or longer lasting, adaptation requires major effort and may produce physiological and psychological responses that result in health problems.

The High Cost of Stress

Stress can take its toll in many ways, producing both biological and psychological consequences. Often the most immediate reaction to stress is a biological one. Exposure to stressors induces a rise in certain hormones secreted by the adrenal glands, an increase in heart rate and blood pressure, and changes in how well the skin conducts electrical impulses. On a short-term basis, these responses may be adaptive because they produce an "emergency reaction," in which the body prepares to defend itself through activation of the sympathetic nervous system (see Chapter 2). These responses may allow more effective coping with the stressful situation (Selye, 1976; Chrousos et al., 1995; Akil & Morano, 1996).

However, continued exposure to stress results in a decline in the body's overall level of biological functioning due to the constant secretion of stress-related hormones. Over time, stressful reactions can promote deterioration of body tissues such as blood vessels and the heart. Ultimately, we become more susceptible to disease as our ability to fight off infection is lowered (Kiecolt-Glaser & Glaser, 1986; Cohen, Tyrrell, & Smith, 1991; Sapolsky, 1996; Shapiro, 1996).

In addition to major health difficulties, many of the minor aches and pains that we experience may be caused or worsened by stress. These include headaches, backaches, skin rashes, indigestion, fatigue, and constipation. Stress has even been linked to the common cold (Brown, 1984; Cohen, Tyrrell, & Smith, 1994; Cohen, 1996).

psychophysiological disorders: Medical problems caused by an interaction of psychological, emotional, and physical difficulties

Furthermore, an entire class of physical problems, known as **psychophysiological disorders,** often result from stress. These medical problems are caused by an interaction of psychological, emotional, and physical difficulties. Among the common psychophysiological disorders are headaches, skin problems, and high blood pressure (Shorter, 1991; Andreassi, 1995; Lehrer, 1996). In fact, the likelihood of onset of any major illness seems to be related to the number and type of stressful events a person experiences (see Table 9-2).

Answers to Review Questions:

1. False; emotions may occur without a cognitive response.   2. James-Lange   3. False; a large number of emotions are related to similar bodily reactions.   4. Cannon-Bard   5. Schachter-Singer

Table 9-2	Predicting the Illness of the Future from the Stress of the Past

Is there a stress-related illness in your future? Survey research has shown that the nature and number of stressors in a person's life are associated with the experience of a major illness (Rahe & Arthur, 1978).

To find out the degree of stress in your life, take the stressor value given beside each event you have experienced and multiply it by the number of occurrences over the past year (up to a maximum of four), then add up these scores.

87 Experienced the death of a spouse
77 Married
77 Experienced the death of a close family member
76 Were divorced
74 Experienced a marital separation
68 Experienced the death of a close friend
68 Experienced pregnancy or fathered a pregnancy
65 Had a major personal injury or illness
62 Were fired from work
60 Ended a marital engagement or a steady relationship
58 Had sexual difficulties
58 Experienced a marital reconciliation
57 Had a major change in self-concept or self-awareness
56 Experienced a major change in the health or behaviour of a family member
54 Became engaged to be married
53 Had a major change in financial status
52 Took on a mortgage or loan of more than $10,000
52 Had a major change in use of drugs
50 Had a major conflict or change in values
50 Had a major change in the number of arguments with your spouse
50 Gained a new family member
50 Entered college
50 Changed to a new school
50 Changed to a different line of work
49 Had a major change in amount of independence and responsibility
47 Had a major change in responsibilities at work
46 Experienced a major change in use of alcohol
45 Revised personal habits
44 Had trouble with school administration
43 Held a job while attending school
43 Had a major change in social activities
42 Had trouble with in-laws
42 Had a major change in working hours or conditions
42 Changed residence or living conditions
41 Had your spouse begin or cease work outside the home
41 Changed your choice of major field of study
41 Changed dating habits
40 Had an outstanding personal achievement
38 Had trouble with your boss
38 Had a major change in amount of participation in school activities
37 Had a major change in type and/or amount of recreation
36 Had a major change in religious activities
34 Had a major change of sleeping habits
33 Took a trip or vacation
30 Had a major change in eating habits
26 Had a major change in the number of family get-togethers
22 Were found guilty of minor violations of the law

Scoring: If your total score is above 1,435, you are in a high-stress category, which, according to Marx, Garrity, & Bowers (1975), puts you at risk for experiencing a stress-related illness in the future. On the other hand, you should not assume that a high score destines you to a future illness. Because the research on stress and illness is correlational, major stressful events are best viewed as associated with illness—but they may not be its cause. Moreover, some research suggests that future illness is better predicted by the daily, ongoing hassles of life, rather than by the major events depicted in the questionnaire (Lazarus et al., 1985). Still, a high level of stressful events in one's life is a cause for concern, and so it makes sense to take measures to reduce stress (Marx, Garrity, & Bowers, 1975, p. 97; Maddi, Bartone, & Puccetti, 1987; Crandall, 1992).

Stressor

Alarm and mobilization
Meeting and
resisting stressor.

Resistance
Coping with stress and
resistance to stressor.

Exhaustion
Negative consequences
of stress (such as illness)
occur when coping
is inadequate.

FIGURE 9-6 *The general adaptation syndrome suggests that there are three major stages in people's response to stress.*
Source: Selye, 1976.

On a psychological level, high levels of stress prevent people from coping with life adequately. Their view of the environment can become clouded (e.g., a minor criticism made by a friend is blown out of proportion). Moreover, at the greatest levels of stress, emotional responses may be so extreme that people are unable to act at all. People under a lot of stress also become less able to deal with new stressors. The ability to contend with future stress, then, declines as a result of past stress.

In short, stress affects us in multiple ways. It may increase the risk that we will become ill; it may directly produce illness; it may make us less able to recover from a disease; and it may reduce our ability to cope with future stress (Lovallo, 1997).

The General Adaptation Syndrome Model: The Course of Stress

The effects of stress are illustrated in a model devised by the Canadian physician, Hans Selye (pronounced "sell-yea"), a pioneering stress theorist (Selye, 1976, 1993). This model, the **general adaptation syndrome (GAS),** suggests that the same set of physiological reactions to stress occurs regardless of the particular cause of stress.

As shown in Figure 9-6, the model has three phases. The first stage, the *alarm and mobilization stage,* occurs when people become aware of the presence of a stressor. Suppose, for instance, you learned at the end of the first term of college that you were on academic probation because of low grades. You would be likely to respond first with alarm, feeling concerned and upset. Subsequently, though, you would probably begin to mobilize your efforts, making plans and promises to yourself to study harder for the rest of the school year.

On a physiological level, the sympathetic nervous system is energized during the alarm and mobilization phase. Prolonged activation of this system may lead to problems of the blood circulatory system or to stomach ulcers, and the body may become vulnerable to a host of diseases.

If the stressor persists, people move into the next stage of the model. In the *resistance stage,* people prepare themselves to fight the stressor. During resistance, people use various means to cope with the stressor—sometimes successfully—but at a cost of some degree of physical or psychological general well-being. For instance, in the case of your being placed on academic probation, resistance might take the form of devoting long hours to studying. You may ultimately be successful in raising your grades, but this achievement may come at the expense of a loss of sleep and hours of worry.

If resistance is not adequate, the last stage of the model, the *exhaustion stage,* is reached. During the exhaustion stage, a person's ability to adapt to the stressor declines to the point where negative consequences of stress appear: physical illness, psychological symptoms in the form of an inability to concentrate, heightened irritability, or, in severe instances, disorientation and a loss of touch with reality. In a sense, people wear out. For instance, if you become overwhelmed by pressure to perform well in your courses, you may get sick or find it impossible to study altogether.

general adaptation syndrome (GAS): A theory developed by Selye that suggests that a person's response to stress consists of three stages: alarm and mobilization, resistance, and exhaustion

Stress and Stress Management

Of course, not everyone reaches the exhaustion stage. If people can resist a stressor in the second stage, their physical resources are not drained and they can bounce back, thereby avoiding exhaustion.

How do people get beyond the third stage after they have entered it? In some cases, exhaustion allows people to avoid the stressor. For example, people who become ill from overwork may be excused from their duties for a time, thereby giving them a temporary respite from their responsibilities. At least for a time, then, the immediate stress is reduced.

The GAS model has had a substantial impact on our understanding of stress. By suggesting that the exhaustion of resources in the third stage of the model produces physiological damage, it has provided a specific explanation of how stress can lead to illness. Furthermore, the model can be applied to both people and nonhuman species.

On the other hand, some aspects of the GAS model have been questioned. One of the most important criticisms is directed at the theory's supposition about the sympathetic division's emergency reaction, activated during the alarm and mobilization phase. The theory proposes that the reaction is basically the same, regardless of the kind of stressor to which a person is exposed. However, some critics argue that certain stressors produce distinct physiological reactions, such as the secretion of specific hormones. Hence, stress reactions may be less similar to one another than the GAS model implies (Mason, 1974; Hobfoll, 1989).

Furthermore, the model's reliance on physiological factors leaves little room for attention to psychological factors, particularly in terms of the way in which stressors are appraised differently by different people (Mikhail, 1981). Still, the model provides a basis for our understanding of stress.

The Nature of Stressors: My Stress Is Your Pleasure

As noted above, the general adaptation syndrome model is useful in explaining how people respond to stress, but it is not specific about what constitutes a stressor for a given person. Although certain kinds of events, such as the death of a loved one or participation in combat during a war, are universally stressful, other situations may or may not be stressful to a particular person (Fleming, Baum, & Singer, 1984; Pledge, 1992; Affleck et al., 1994; Krohne, 1996).

Consider, for instance, bungee jumping. Some of us would find jumping off a bridge attached to a slender rubber tether to be extremely stressful. However, there are those who see such an activity as challenging and fun-filled. Whether or not bungee jumping is stressful depends in part, then, on individual perceptions of the activity.

For people to consider an event to be stressful, they must perceive it as threatening and must lack the resources to deal with it effectively (Folkman et al., 1986). Consequently, the same event may at times be stressful and at other times provoke no stressful reaction at all. For instance, a young man might experience stress when he is turned down for a date—if he attributes the refusal to his unattractiveness or unworthiness. But if he attributes it to some factor unrelated to his self-esteem, such as a previous commitment of the woman he asked, the experience of being refused might create no stress at all. Hence, cognitive factors relating to our interpretation of events play an important role in the determination of what is stressful.

A number of other variables also influence the severity of stress. For example, stress is greater when the importance and number of goals that are threatened are high, when the threat is immediate, or when the anticipation of the threatening event extends over a long period (Paterson & Neufeld, 1987).

Categorizing Stressors

What kinds of events tend to be seen as stressful? There are three general classes of events: cataclysmic events, personal stressors, and background stressors (Lazarus & Cohen, 1977; Gatchel & Baum, 1983).

Cataclysmic events are strong stressors that occur suddenly and typically affect many people simultaneously. Disasters such as tornadoes and plane crashes are examples of cataclysmic events that can affect hundreds or thousands of people simultaneously.

cataclysmic events: Strong stressors that occur suddenly, affecting many people at once (e.g., natural disasters)

The Quebec ice storm in 1998 caused severe stress in many people.

Although it might seem that cataclysmic events would produce potent, lingering stress, in many cases this is not true. In fact, cataclysmic events may produce less stress in the long run than events that are initially not as devastating. One reason is that cataclysmic events have a clear resolution. Once they are over and done with, people can look to the future knowing that the worst is behind them. Moreover, the stress induced by cataclysmic events is shared by others who have also experienced the disaster. This permits people to offer one another social support and a firsthand understanding of the difficulties the others are going through (Pennebaker & Harber, 1993; Kaniasty & Norris, 1995; Hobfoll et al., 1996).

On the other hand, some victims of major catastrophes can experience **post-traumatic stress disorder** or **PTSD,** in which the original events and the feelings associated with them are reexperienced in vivid flashbacks or dreams. Depending upon what statistics one employs, between 5 and 60 percent of the veterans of the Vietnam War suffer from PTSD. Even the Persian Gulf War, which ended quickly, produced the condition. Furthermore, those who have suffered child abuse or rape, rescue workers facing overwhelming situations, or victims of any sudden natural disaster or accident that produces feelings of helplessness and terror may suffer from the same disorder (Solomon, 1995; LaGreca et al., 1996; Trappler & Friedman, 1996; Saigh, 1996; Friedman & Marsella, 1996; Ward, 1997).

post-traumatic stress disorder (PTSD): A phenomenon in which victims of major catastrophes reexperience the original stress event and associated feelings in vivid flashbacks or dreams

Symptoms of post-traumatic stress disorder include reexperiencing the event, emotional numbing, sleep difficulties, problems in relating to others, alcohol and drug abuse, and—in some cases—suicide. For instance, the suicide rate for Vietnam veterans is as much as 25 percent higher than for the general population (Pollock et al., 1990; Peterson, Prout, & Schwarz, 1991; Wilson & Keane, 1996).

Post-Traumatic Stress Disorder

The second major category of stressor is the personal stressor. **Personal stressors** include major life events such as the death of a parent or spouse, the loss of one's job, a major personal failure, or a diagnosis of a life-threatening illness. Typically, personal stressors produce an immediate major reaction that soon tapers off. For example, stress arising from the death of a loved one tends to be greatest just after the time of death, but people begin to feel less stress and are better able to cope with the loss after the passage of time.

personal stressors: Major life events, such as the death of a family member, that have immediate negative consequences which generally fade with time

In some cases, though, the effects of stress are lingering. Victims of rape sometimes suffer consequences long after the event, facing major difficulties in adjustment. Similarly, the malfunction of the Three Mile Island nuclear plant in Pennsylvania on March 28, 1979, which exposed people to the stressor of a potential nuclear meltdown, produced emotional, behavioural, and physiological consequences that lasted more than a year and a half (Baum, Gatchel, & Schaeffer, 1983; Baum, Cohen, & Hall, 1993; Foa & Riggs, 1995; Valentiner et al., 1996).

Standing in a long line at a bank and getting stuck in a traffic jam are examples of the third major category of stressor: **background stressors** or, more informally, *daily hassles* (Lazarus & Cohen, 1977). These are the minor irritations of life that we all face time and time again: delays, noisy cars and trucks, broken appliances, other people's irritating behaviour, and so on. Another type of background stressor is long-term, chronic problems, such as experiencing dissatisfaction with school or job, being in an unhappy relationship, or living in crowded quarters without privacy.

By themselves, daily hassles do not require much coping or even a response on the part of the individual, although they certainly do produce unpleasant emotions and moods (Clark & Watson, 1988). Yet daily hassles add up—and ultimately they may produce as great a toll as a single, more stressful incident (Kohn and Macdonald, 1992). In fact, there is an association between the number of daily hassles that people face and the number of psychological symptoms they report (Kanner et al., 1981; Zika & Chamberlain, 1987; Chamberlain & Zika, 1990; Roberts, 1995). Even health problems (such as flu, sore throat, headaches, and backaches) have been linked to daily hassles (DeLongis, Folkman, & Lazarus, 1988; Jones, Brantley, & Gilchrist, 1988; Kohn, Lafreniere, & Genrevich, 1991; Fernandez & Sheffield, 1995).

Although the nature of daily hassles differs from day to day and from person to person, background stressors do have certain characteristics in common. One critical factor is related to the degree of control people have over aversive, unpleasant stimuli in the environment (Burger, 1992). When people feel that they can control a situation and determine its outcome, stress reactions are reduced considerably. For instance, although persistent exposure to noise leads to stress, the consequences are less severe if people have some control over its intensity and duration (Sieber et al., 1992; Evans, Hygge, & Bullinger, 1995).

The flip side of hassles are **uplifts,** those minor positive events that make one feel good—even if only temporarily. As indicated in Figure 9-7, uplifts range from relating well to a companion to finding one's surroundings pleasing. What is especially intriguing about uplifts is that they are associated with people's psychological health in just the opposite way that hassles are: The greater the number of uplifts experienced, the fewer the psychological symptoms people later report.

Learned Helplessness

You've probably heard someone complaining about an intolerable situation that he couldn't seem to resolve, saying that he was tired of "hitting his head against the wall" and was giving up and accepting things the way they were. This example illustrates one of the possible consequences of being in an environment in which control over a situation is not possible—a state that produces learned helplessness. According to psychologist Martin Seligman, **learned helplessness** occurs when people conclude that unpleasant or aversive stimuli cannot be controlled—a view of the world that becomes so ingrained that they cease trying to remedy the aversive circumstances, even if they actually can exert some influence (Seligman, 1975; Peterson, Maier, & Seligman, 1993). Victims of the phenomenon of learned helplessness have decided that there is no link between the responses they make and the outcomes that occur.

Take, for example, what often happens to elderly persons when they are placed in nursing homes or hospitals. One of the most striking features of their new environment is that they are no longer independent: They do not have control over the most basic activities in their lives. They are told what and when to eat, and told when they may watch TV or participate in recreational activities. In addition, their sleeping schedules are arranged by someone else. It is not hard to see how this loss of control can have negative effects upon people suddenly placed, often reluctantly, in such a situation.

The results of this loss of control and the ensuing stress are frequently poorer health and even a likelihood of earlier death. These outcomes were confirmed in an experiment conducted in a nursing home where elderly residents in one group were encouraged to make more choices and take greater control of their day-to-day activi-

background stressors ("daily hassles"): Everyday annoyances, such as being stuck in traffic, that cause minor irritations but have no long-term ill effects, unless they continue or are compounded by other stressful events

uplifts: Minor positive events that make one feel good

learned helplessness: A state in which people conclude that unpleasant or aversive stimuli cannot be controlled—a view of the world that becomes so ingrained that they cease trying to remedy the aversive circumstances, even if they actually can exert some influence

FIGURE 9-7 *The most common everyday hassles and uplifts. Source: hassles: Chamberlain & Zika, 1990; uplifts: Kanner et al., 1981.*

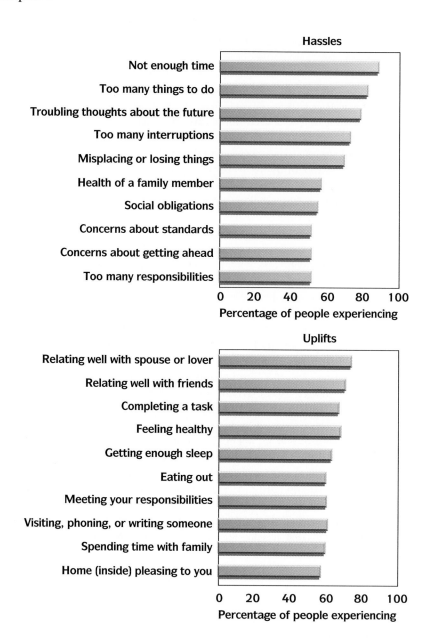

ties (Langer & Janis, 1979). As a result, members of the group were more active and happier than a comparison group of residents who were encouraged to let the nursing home staff take care of them. Moreover, an analysis of the residents' medical records revealed that six months after the experiment, the group encouraged to be self-sufficient showed significantly greater health improvement than the comparison group. Even more startling was an examination of the death rate: Eighteen months after the experiment began, only 15 percent of the "independent" group had died—compared with 30 percent of the comparison group.

Other research confirms that learned helplessness has negative consequences, and not just for elderly people. People of all ages report more physical symptoms and depression when they perceive that they have little or no control than when they feel a sense of control over a situation (Rodin, 1986; Joiner & Wagner, 1995; Shnek et al., 1995).

Coping with Stress

Stress is a normal part of living. As Hans Selye has noted, to avoid stress totally, a person would probably have to cease living. Yet, as we have seen, too much stress can take its toll on both physical and psychological health. How do people deal with stress? Is there a way to reduce its negative effects?

The efforts to control, reduce, or learn to tolerate the threats that lead to stress are known as **coping.** We habitually use certain coping responses to help ourselves deal with stress. Most of the time, we're not aware of these responses—just as we may be unaware of the minor stressors of life until they build up to sufficiently adverse levels.

One means of dealing with stress that occurs on an unconscious level is the use of defense mechanisms. As we will discuss in Chapter 11, **defense mechanisms** are reactions that maintain a person's sense of control and self-worth by distorting or denying the actual nature of the situation. For example, one study examined California students who lived in dormitories close to a geological fault. Those who lived in dorms that were rated as being unlikely to withstand an earthquake were significantly more likely to doubt experts' predictions of an impending earthquake than those who lived in safer structures (Lehman & Taylor, 1988).

Another defense mechanism used to cope with stress is *emotional insulation,* in which a person stops experiencing any emotions at all, thereby remaining unaffected and unmoved by both positive and negative experiences. The problem with defense mechanisms, of course, is that they do not deal with reality but merely hide the problem.

People also use other, more direct and potentially more positive means for coping with stress (Aldwin & Revenson, 1987; Compas, 1987; Miller, Brody, & Summerton, 1988). Specifically, coping strategies fall into two categories: emotion-focused coping and problem-focused coping. *Emotion-focused coping* is characterized by the conscious regulation of emotion in which people seek to change the way they feel or perceive the problem. Examples of emotion-focused strategies include accepting sympathy from others, denial, and avoidance. These strategies may be adaptive or maladaptive (Zeidner & Saklofske, 1996). In contrast, *problem-focused coping* attempts to change the stressful problem or source of the stress. Problem-focused strategies lead to changes in behaviour or to the development of a plan of action to deal with stress. Starting a study group to improve poor classroom performance is an example of problem-focused coping.

In most stressful incidents, people employ *both* emotion-focused and problem-focused strategies. However, they use emotion-focused strategies more frequently when they perceive circumstances as being unchangeable, and problem-focused approaches more often in situations they see as relatively modifiable (Folkman & Lazarus, 1980, 1988; Peacock, Wong, & Reker, 1993; Gottlieb, 1997). Norman Endler (York University) has recently developed a multidimensional interaction model of stress and anxiety (Endler, 1997). According to this model, stressful events, coping strategies, and the consequences of stressful events all interact with each other.

Coping Style: The Hardy Personality

Most of us cope with stress in a characteristic manner, employing a "coping style" that represents our general tendency to deal with stress in a specific way. For example, you may know people who habitually react to even the smallest amount of stress with hysteria, and others who calmly confront even the greatest stress in an unflappable manner. These kinds of people clearly have quite different coping styles (Taylor, 1991; Taylor & Aspinwall, 1996). A recently developed measure of preferred coping styles is the Coping Inventory for Stressful Situations (Endler and Parker, 1993).

Among those who cope with stress most successfully are people with a coping style that has come to be called "hardiness." **Hardiness** is a personality characteristic associated with a lower rate of stress-related illness. It consists of three components: commitment, challenge, and control (Kobasa, 1979; Gentry & Kobasa, 1984).

Commitment is a tendency to throw ourselves into whatever we are doing with a sense that our activities are important and meaningful. Hardy people are also high in a sense of challenge, the second component; they believe that change, rather than stability, is the standard condition of life. To them, the anticipation of change serves as an incentive rather than a threat to their security. Finally, hardiness is marked by a sense of control—the perception that people can influence the events in their lives.

Hardiness seems to act as a buffer against stress-related illness. The hardy individual approaches stress in an optimistic manner, turning stress into a challenge. As a consequence, a person with a hardy personality style is less likely to suffer the negative outcomes of high stress (Wiebe, 1991; Solcova & Tomanek, 1994; Kobasa et al., 1994).

coping: The efforts to control, reduce, or learn to tolerate the threats that lead to stress

defense mechanisms: Unconscious strategies people use to reduce anxiety by concealing its source from themselves and others

Coping with Stress

hardiness: A personality characteristic associated with a lower rate of stress-related illness, consisting of three components: commitment, challenge, and control

The Informed Consumer of Psychology

Effective Coping Strategies

How does one cope most effectively with stress? Researchers have made a number of recommendations for dealing with the problem. There is no universal solution, of course, since effective coping depends on the nature of the stressor and the degree to which control is possible. Still, some general guidelines can be followed (Folkman, 1984; Everly, 1989; Holahan & Moos, 1987, 1990; McCain & Smith, 1994; Zeidner & Endler, 1996):

- *Turning threat into challenge.* When a stressful situation might be controllable, the best coping strategy is to treat the situation as a challenge, focusing on ways to control it. For instance, if you experience stress because your car is always breaking down, you might take an evening course in auto mechanics and learn to deal directly with the car's problems. Even if the repairs prove too difficult to do yourself, at least you'll be in a better position to understand what's wrong.

- *Making a threatening situation less threatening.* When a stressful situation seems to be uncontrollable, a different approach must be taken. It is possible to change one's appraisal of the situation, to view it in a different light, and to modify one's attitudes toward it (Smith & Ellsworth, 1987; Taylor & Aspinwall, 1996). The old truism "Look for the silver lining in every cloud" seems to be supported by research findings that people who discover something good in negative situations show less distress and better coping ability than those who do not (Silver & Wortman, 1980). A sense of humour also helps by acting as a buffer against stress (Martin, 1996). And humour can facilitate changing pessimism to optimism (Lefcourt and Thomas, 1998).

- *Changing one's goals.* When a person is faced with an uncontrollable situation, another reasonable strategy is to adopt new goals that are practical in view of the particular situation. For example, a dancer who has been in an automobile accident and has lost full use of her legs may no longer aspire to a career in dance, but might modify her goals and try to become a dance instructor. Similarly, an executive who has lost his job may change his goal of becoming wealthy to that of obtaining a more modest, but secure, source of income.

- *Taking physical action.* Another approach to coping with stress is to bring about changes in one's physiological reactions to it. For example, biofeedback, discussed in Chapter 2, can alter basic physiological processes, allowing people to reduce blood pressure, heart rate, and other consequences of heightened stress. In addition, exercise can be effective in reducing stress in several ways. For one thing, regular exercise reduces heart rate, respiration rate, and blood pressure (although these responses temporarily increase during exercise periods). Exercise also improves overall health, and it even may reduce the risk of certain diseases, such as breast cancer. Finally, exercise gives people a sense of control over their bodies, as well as a feeling of accomplishment (Mutrie & Biddle, 1995; Dunn et al., 1996; Dishman, 1997; Barinaga, 1997a).

  Finally, sometimes a change in diet is helpful in coping with stress. For instance, people who drink large quantities of caffeine are susceptible to feeling jittery and anxious; simply decreasing the amount they consume may be sufficient to reduce the experience of stress. Similarly, being overweight may itself be a stressor, and losing excess weight may be an effective measure for reducing stress—unless dieting itself becomes stressful.

- *Preparing for stress before it happens.* A final strategy for coping with stress is *inoculation:* preparing for stress before it is encountered. First developed as a means of preventing postsurgical emotional problems among hospital patients, inoculation methods prepare people for stressful experiences—of either a physical or an emotional nature—by explaining, in as much detail as possible, the difficult events they are likely to encounter. As part of the process, people are asked to imagine how they will feel about the circumstances and to consider various ways of dealing with their reactions—all before the experience has actually occurred. Probably the most crucial element, however, is providing individuals with clear, objective strategies for handling the situation, rather than simply telling them what to expect (Janis, 1984).

When carried out properly, inoculation works. People who received inoculation treatments prior to facing a stressful event coped more effectively with their situation than those who did not (Ludwick-Rosenthal & Neufeld, 1988; Register et al., 1991).   ■

Recap, Review, and Rethink

Recap

- Stress is the response to events that threaten an individual's ability to deal adequately with the situation.

- According to Selye's general adaptation model, stress follows three stages: alarm and mobilization, resistance, and exhaustion.

- The specific nature of stressors varies from person to person; what is stressful for one person may be invigorating to another. There are, however, three general categories of stressors: cataclysmic events, personal stressors, and background stressors (or daily hassles).

- Perceptions of control typically reduce stress. In some instances, though, learned helplessness occurs— people perceive that aversive stimuli cannot be controlled.

- Coping devices may take the form of adopting defense mechanisms, turning threat into challenge, reducing the perception of threat, changing goals, or preparing for stress through inoculation.

Review

1. _____ is defined as a response to challenging or threatening events.

2. Match each portion of the GAS with its definition
   1. alarm
   2. exhaustion
   3. resistance

   a. ability to adapt to stress diminishes; symptoms appear
   b. activation of sympathetic nervous system
   c. various strategies used to cope with a stressor

3. _____ _____ _____ _____ occurs when the feelings associated with stressful events are relived after the event is over.

4. Stressors that affect an individual person and produce an immediate major reaction are known as

   a. personal stressors
   b. psychic stressors
   c. cataclysmic stressors
   d. daily stressors

5. Efforts to reduce or eliminate stress are known as _____.

6. People with the personality characteristic of _____ seem to be more able to successfully combat stressors.

Answers to Review Questions are on page 348.

Rethink

1. Why are cataclysmic stressors less stressful in the long run than other types of stressors? Does the reason relate to the coping phenomenon known as social support? How?

2. Which approach to coping with stress do you think is most effective: defense mechanisms, emotion-focused coping, or problem-focused coping? Why?

3. Given what you know about coping strategies, how would you train people to avoid stress in their everyday lives? How would you use this information with a group of Gulf War veterans suffering from post-traumatic stress disorder?

looking
BACK

How does motivation direct and energize behaviour?

1. The topic of motivation includes the factors that direct and energize behaviour. Drive is the motivational tension that energizes behaviour in order to fulfill a need. Primary drives relate to basic biological needs. Secondary drives are those in which no obvious biological need is fulfilled.

2. Motivational drives often operate under the principle of homeostasis, by which an organism tries to maintain an optimal level of internal biological functioning by making up for any deviations from its usual state.

3. A number of broad approaches to motivation move beyond explanations that rely on instincts. Drive-reduction approaches, though useful for primary drives, are inadequate for explaining behaviour in which the goal is not to reduce a drive but to maintain or even increase excitement or arousal. In contrast, arousal approaches suggest that we try to maintain a particular level of stimulation and activity.

4. Incentive approaches, an alternative explanation of motivation, focus on the positive aspects of the environment that direct and energize behaviour. Finally, cognitive approaches to motivation focus on the role of thoughts, expectations, and understanding of the world. One cognitive theory—expectancy-value theory—suggests that expectations that a behaviour will accomplish a particular goal and our understanding of the value of that goal underlie behaviour.

5. Maslow's hierarchy of needs suggests that there are five needs: physiological, safety, love and belongingness, esteem, and self-actualization. Only after the more basic needs are fulfilled is a person able to move toward higher-order needs.

What are the biological and social factors that underlie hunger?

6. Eating behavior is subject to homeostasis, since most people's weight stays within a relatively stable range. Organisms tend to be sensitive to the nutritional value of the food they eat, with the brain's hypothalamus being central to the regulation of food intake.

7. Social factors also play a role in the regulation of eating. For instance, mealtimes, cultural food preferences, and other learned habits determine when and how much one eats. An oversensitivity to social cues and an insensitivity to internal cues may also be related to obesity. In addition, obesity may be caused by an unusually high weight set point—the weight at which the body attempts to maintain homeostasis—and genetic factors.

8. Eating disorders—anorexia nervosa and bulimia are the most prevalent—are a growing problem, especially in the United States. While it is possible that physiological causes may be found, the more likely source of these disorders may be found in societal expectations relating to slenderness, especially for women.

Why, and under what circumstances, do we become sexually aroused?

9. Although biological factors, such as the presence of androgens (male sex hormones) and estrogens and progesterone (female sex hormones) prime people for sex, almost any kind of stimulus can produce sexual arousal, depending on a person's prior experience. Fantasies, thoughts, and images are also important in producing arousal.

How do most people behave sexually?

10. Masturbation is sexual self-stimulation. The frequency of masturbation is high, particularly for males. Although attitudes toward masturbation have become more liberal, they are still somewhat negative—even though no negative consequences have been detected.

11. Heterosexuality, or the sexual attraction to members of the opposite sex, is the most common sexual orientation. The double standard, by which premarital sex is thought to be more permissible for men than for women, has declined, particularly among young people, but it has not disappeared.

12. Homosexuals are sexually attracted to members of their own sex; bisexuals are sexually attracted to people of the same and the opposite sex. About one-quarter of males and 15 percent of females have had at least one homosexual experience, and around 5 to 10 percent of all men and women are exclusively homosexual during extended periods of their lives. No explanation for why people become homosexual has been confirmed; among the possibilities are genetic or biological factors, childhood and family influences, and prior learning experiences and conditioning. What is clear is that there is no relationship between psychological adjustment and sexual orientation.

How are needs relating to achievement, affiliation, and power motivation exhibited?

13. Need for achievement refers to the stable, learned characteristic in which a person strives to attain a level of excellence. People high in the need for achievement tend to seek out tasks that are of moderate difficulty, while those low in the need for achievement seek out only very easy and very difficult tasks. Need for achievement is usually measured through the Thematic Apperception Test (TAT), a series of pictures about which a person writes a story.

14. The need for affiliation is a concern with establishing and maintaining relationships with others, whereas the need for power is a tendency to seek to exert an impact on others.

What are emotions, and how do we experience them?

15. One broad definition of emotions views them as feelings that may affect behaviour and generally have both a physiological and a cognitive component. This definition does not address the issue of whether there are separate systems that govern cognitive and emotional responses, and whether one has primacy over the other.

What are the functions of emotions?

16. Among the functions of emotions are to prepare us for action, to shape future behaviour through learning, and help to regulate social interaction. Although the range of emotions is wide, according to one category system there are only eight primary emotions: joy, acceptance, fear, surprise, sadness, disgust, anger, and anticipation.

17. Among the general physiological responses to strong emotion are opening of the pupils, dryness of the mouth, and increases in sweating, rate of breathing, heart rate, and blood pressure. Because these physiological changes are not the full explanation of emotional experience, a number of distinct theories of emotion have been developed.

18. The James-Lange theory suggests that emotional experience is a reaction to bodily, or visceral, changes that occur as a response to an environmental event. These visceral experiences are interpreted as an emotional response. In

---

Answers to Review Questions:

1. Stress   2. 1-b; 2-a; 3-c   3. Post-traumatic stress disorder   4. a   5. coping   6. hardiness

contrast to the James-Lange theory, the Cannon-Bard theory contends that visceral movements are too slow to explain rapid shifts of emotion and visceral changes do not always produce emotion. Instead, the Cannon-Bard theory suggests that both physiological arousal *and* an emotional experience are produced simultaneously by the same nerve impulse. Therefore, the visceral experience itself does not necessarily differ among differing emotions.

19. A third explanation, the Schachter-Singer theory, rejects the view that the physiological and emotional responses are simultaneous. Instead, it suggests that emotions are determined jointly by a relatively nonspecific physiological arousal and the subsequent labeling of that arousal. This labelling process uses cues from the environment to determine how others are behaving in the same situation.

20. The most recent approaches to emotions focus on their biological aspects. For instance, it now seems that specific patterns of biological arousal are associated with individual emotions. Furthermore, new scanning techniques have identified the specific parts of the brain that are activated during the experience of particular emotions.

What is stress, how does it affect us, and how can we best cope with it?

21. Stress is a response to threatening or challenging environmental conditions. People's lives are filled with stressors—the circumstances that produce stress—of both a positive and negative nature.

22. Stress produces immediate physiological reactions, including a rise in hormonal secretions, heart rate, and blood pressure, and changes in the electrical conductance of the skin. In the short term, these reactions may be adaptive, but in the long term they may have negative consequences, including the development of psychophysiological disorders. The consequences of stress can be explained in part by Selye's general adaptation syndrome (GAS), which suggests there are three stages to stress responses: alarm and mobilization, resistance, and exhaustion.

23. Stress factors are not universal—the way an environmental circumstance is interpreted affects whether it will be considered stressful. Still, there are general classes of events that tend to provoke stress: cataclysmic events, personal stressors, and background stressors or daily hassles. Stress is reduced by the presence of uplifts, minor positive events that make people feel good—even if only temporarily.

24. Stress can be reduced by developing a sense of control over one's circumstances. In some cases, however, people develop a state of learned helplessness—a response to uncontrollable situations that produce the feeling that no behavior will be effective in changing the situation; therefore no response is even attempted. Coping with stress can take a number of forms, including the unconscious use of defense mechanisms and the use of emotion-focused or problem-focused coping strategies.

Key Terms and Concepts

motivation (p. 307)
instincts (p. 308)
drive-reduction approaches to motivation (p. 308)
drive (p. 308)
homeostasis (p. 309)
arousal approaches to motivation (p. 309)
incentive approaches to motivation (p. 310)
cognitive approaches to motivation (p. 311)
intrinsic motivation (p. 311)
extrinsic motivation (p. 311)
self-actualization (p. 313)
obesity (p. 314)
weight set point (p. 316)
metabolism (p. 316)
anorexia nervosa (p. 318)

bulimia (p. 319)
genitals (p. 319)
androgens (p. 319)
estrogen (p. 319)
progesterone (p. 319)
ovulation (p. 320)
masturbation (p. 321)
heterosexuality (p. 321)
double standard (p. 321)
homosexuals (p. 322)
bisexuals (p. 322)
need for achievement (p. 325)
need for affiliation (p. 327)
need for power (p. 327)
emotions (p. 329)
James-Lange theory of emotion (p. 333)

Cannon-Bard theory of emotion (p. 334)
Schachter-Singer theory of emotion (p. 335)
stress (p. 338)
psychophysiological disorder (p. 338)
general adaptation syndrome (GAS) (p. 340)
cataclysmic events (p. 341)
post-traumatic stress disorder (PTSD) (p. 342)
personal stressors (p. 342)
background stressors (p. 343)
uplifts (p. 343)
learned helplessness (p. 343)
coping (p. 345)
defense mechanisms (p. 345)
hardiness (p. 345)

Epilogue

In this chapter, we focused mainly on motivation and emotions, two interrelated aspects of psychology, and on stress. The topic of motivation has spawned a great deal of theory and research in its examination of primary and secondary drives. We then turned to a discussion of emotions, beginning with their functions and proceeding to a review of three major theories that seek to explain what emotions are and how they, and their associated physiological symptoms, emerge in the individual. Finally, we looked at stress and discussed its causes and ways to cope with it.

Return to the opening scenario, which describes Olympic rower Emma Robinson. Using your knowledge of motivation and emotion, consider the following questions:

1. Which approach or approaches to motivation (instinctual, drive reduction, arousal, incentive, or cognitive) most effectively explains why an athlete like Emma Robinson will work exceptionally hard over many years to become an athlete good enough to compete in the Olympic Games?

2. How might the need for achievement and the need for affiliation be related to Emma's efforts as a champion rower and as a medical student?

3. After her surgery, why do you think Emma's strategy of focusing on her training and on getting better each day was effective?

4. How might Emma use emotion to enhance her performance?

5. What are some of the stresses that Emma may have experienced during the 1999 season? Use the information in the scenario to describe interaction among stress, consequences, and coping strategies in accordance with Endler's multidimensional interaction model.

Theodore Kaczynski, the admitted Unabomber.

Prologue

Blood Brothers

A law enforcement official describes them as "anti-Mom diatribes." Beginning in the mid-1980s . . . Ted Kaczynski wrote his mother, Wanda, as many as a dozen letters blaming her for turning him into a recluse. He castigated her for his inability to form relationships, particularly with women. Kaczynski told his brother, David, that he wanted nothing to do with their parents, then dismissed their mother as a "dog."

Blaming one's mother is the oldest and least original excuse in history. In Greek mythology, Oedipus railed against his mother, along with the Fates, after he inadvertently slept with her and killed his father. Teenagers will blame their mothers for almost anything. It may not be fair to hold Wanda Kaczynski, who is described by her neighbors as a sweet old lady, accountable for turning her son into a possible serial killer. Yet . . . *something* must have caused him to go on an 18-year bombing spree that killed three people and wounded twenty-three others.

Why did he do it? Why did the shy, brilliant son of respectable parents become an alleged serial killer? Why did his brother—with the same blood and the same roots—become a gentle social worker? When both dropped out of society, why did only one return? (Thomas, 1996, p. 28)

looking AHEAD

developmental psychology: The branch of psychology that studies the patterns of growth and change occurring throughout life

We may never know the answers to these questions, and it remains a puzzle why the paths of Ted Kaczynski, the Unabomber, and his brother diverged so radically. Their case raises one of the most fundamental issues facing psychologists: How do hereditary and environmental factors interact to produce a unique individual? This question falls within the domain of developmental psychology.

Developmental psychology is the branch of psychology that studies the patterns of growth and change occurring throughout life. In large part, developmental psychologists study the interaction between the unfolding of biologically predetermined patterns of behaviour and a constantly changing, dynamic environment. They ask how our genetic background affects our behaviour throughout our lives, whether our potential is limited by heredity, and how our built-in biological programming affects our day-to-day development. Similarly, they are committed to understanding the way in which the environment works with—or against—our genetic capabilities, how the world we live in affects our development, and how we can be encouraged to develop our full potential.

More than other psychologists, developmental psychologists consider the day-to-day patterns and changes in behaviour that occur across the lifespan. This chapter deals broadly with the entire life cycle, beginning with conception, moving through birth, infancy, and childhood, exploring adolescence and adulthood, and finally proceeding to old age and death.

We begin our discussion of development by examining the approaches that have been used to understand and delineate the environmental and genetic factors that direct a person's development. Then we consider the very start of development, beginning with conception and the nine months of life prior to birth. We describe both genetic and environmental influences on the unborn individual, and how these can affect behavior throughout the remainder of the life cycle.

Next, we examine the physical and perceptual developments that occur after birth, witnessing the enormous and rapid growth that takes place during the early stages of life. We also focus on the developing child's social world, indicating what draws the child into relationships with others and membership in society. Finally, we discuss cognitive growth during infancy and childhood, tracing changes in the ways that children think about the world.

We then examine development from adolescence through young adulthood, middle age, and old age. Our discussion of adolescence focuses on some of the major physical, emotional, and cognitive changes that occur during this transition from childhood to adulthood. Next, we consider early and middle adulthood, stages in which people are at the peak of their physical and intellectual abilities. We discuss the developmental changes people undergo during these periods and their relationship to work, families, and living patterns. Finally, in our discussion of old age, we examine the kinds of physical, intellectual, and social changes that occur as a consequence of the aging process, and we see that aging may bring about both improvements and declines in various kinds of functioning. We end with a discussion of the ways in which people prepare themselves for death.

Child Development

NATURE AND NURTURE: THE ENDURING DEVELOPMENTAL ISSUE

How many bald, six-foot-six, 125-kilogram volunteer fire fighters are there in New Jersey who have droopy mustaches, wear aviator-style eyeglasses, and carry a key ring on the right side of the belt?

The answer is: two. Gerald Levey and Mark Newman are twins, separated at birth. Each twin did not even know the other existed until they were reunited—in a fire station—by a fellow fire fighter who knew Newman and was startled to see Levey at a fire fighters' convention.

The lives of the twins, although separate, took remarkably similar paths. Levey went to college, studying forestry; Newman planned to study forestry in college but instead took a job trimming trees. Both had jobs in supermarkets. One has a job installing sprinkler systems; the other installed fire alarms.

Both men are unmarried and find the same kind of woman attractive: "tall, slender, long hair." They share similar hobbies, enjoying hunting, fishing, going to the beach, and watching old John Wayne movies and professional wrestling. Both like Chinese food and drink the same brand of beer. Their mannerisms are also similar—for example, each one throws his head back when he laughs. And, of course, there is one more thing: They share a passion for fighting fires.

The striking similarities we see in twins Gerald Levey and Mark Newman raise one of the fundamental questions posed by developmental psychologists: How can we

▶ **How do psychologists study the degree to which development is a joint function of hereditary and environmental factors?**

▶ **What is the nature of development prior to birth?**

▶ **What factors affect a child during the mother's pregnancy?**

Gerald Levey and Mark Newman.

nature-nurture issue: The issue of
the degree to which environment and
heredity influence behaviour

distinguish between the causes of behaviour that are *environmental* (the influence of
parents, siblings, family, friends, schooling, nutrition, and all the other experiences to
which a child is exposed) and those causes that are *hereditary* (those based on the genetic makeup of an individual that influence growth and development throughout
life)? This question, which we explored when we considered intelligence in Chapter 8,
is known as the **nature-nurture issue**. In this context, nature refers to heredity factors,
and nurture to environmental influences.

The nature-nurture issue has philosophical roots. English philosopher John
Locke argued in the 1600s that a newborn was, in effect, a blank slate, a *tabula rasa*,
on which the story of his or her individual experience could be written from scratch. In
other words, Locke believed that the environment acted as the sole influence on development. In contrast, the French philosopher Jean Jacques Rousseau suggested in the
1700s a very different notion of development. He believed that people's "natural"
characteristics (namely, genetic factors) were most influential, although subject to
what Rousseau considered to be the corrupting influence of the environment.

Although the question was first posed as the nature-*versus*-nurture question, developmental psychologists today agree that *both* nature and nurture interact to produce
specific developmental patterns and outcomes. The question has changed from *which
one* influences behaviour more to *how and to what degree* environment and heredity
produce their effects. No one grows up free of environmental influences, nor does anyone develop without being affected by his or her inherited *genetic makeup*. However,
the debate over the relative influence of the two factors remains active, with different
approaches and theories of development emphasizing the environment or heredity to a
greater or lesser degree (Scarr, 1996).

For example, some developmental theories stress the role of learning in producing changes in behaviour in the developing child, relying on the basic principles of
learning discussed in Chapter 5. Such theories emphasize the role of environment in
accounting for development. In contrast, other approaches emphasize the influence of
one's physiological makeup and functioning on development. Such theories stress the
role of heredity and *maturation*—the unfolding of biologically predetermined patterns
of behaviour—in producing developmental change. Maturation can be seen, for instance, in the development of sex characteristics (such as breasts or body hair) that occurs at the start of adolescence. Furthermore, developmental psychologists have been
influenced by the work of behavioural geneticists, who study the effects of heredity on
behaviour, and the theories of evolutionary psychologists, whose goal is to identify

Table 10-1	Characteristics with Strong Genetic Components

Physical Characteristics	Intellectual Characteristics	Emotional Characteristics and Disorders
Height	Memory	Shyness
Weight	Ability as measured on intelligence	Extraversion
Obesity	tests	Emotionality
Tone of voice	Age of language acquisition	Neuroticism
Blood pressure	Reading disability	Schizophrenia
Tooth decay	Mental retardation	Anxiety
Athletic ability		Alcoholism
Firmness of handshake		
Age of death		
Activity level		

behaviour patterns that are a result of our genetic inheritance from our ancestors. Both behavioural geneticists and evolutionary psychologists have highlighted the importance of heredity in influencing our behaviour (Bjorklund, 1997; Daly & Wilson, 1983, 1998).

On some points, however, agreement exists among developmental psychologists of different theoretical persuasions. It seems clear that genetic factors not only provide the potential for particular behaviours or traits to emerge, but also place limitations on the emergence of such behaviour or traits. For instance, heredity defines people's general level of intelligence, setting an upper limit which—regardless of the quality of the environment—people cannot exceed. Heredity also provides limits on physical abilities; humans simply cannot run at a speed of 60 kilometres an hour, nor will they grow as tall as 4 metres, no matter what the quality of their environment (Plomin, 1990; Plomin & McClearn, 1993; Steen, 1996).

Table 10-1 lists some of the characteristics that are most affected by heredity. As you consider these items, it is important to keep in mind that these characteristics are not *entirely* determined by heredity. Instead, the best evidence suggests that variations in these factors are largely due to the genetic makeup of an individual.

In most instances, environmental factors play a critical role in enabling people to reach the potential capabilities that their genetic background makes possible. Had Albert Einstein received no intellectual stimulation as a child and not been sent to school, it is unlikely that he would have reached his genetic potential. Similarly, a great athlete like basketball star Michael Jordan would have been unlikely to display much physical skill had he not been raised in an environment that nurtured his innate talent and gave him the opportunity to train and perfect his natural abilities.

Approaches to Studying Development

It is clear that the relationship between heredity and environment is far from simple. As a consequence, developmental psychologists typically take an *interactionist* position on the nature-nurture issue, suggesting that a combination of hereditary and environmental factors influences development (Wahlsten & Gottlieb, 1997). The challenge facing developmental psychologists is to identify the relative strength of each of these influences on the individual, as well as to identify the specific changes that occur over the course of development (Plomin & Neiderhiser, 1992; Wozniak & Fischer, 1993; Saudino & Plomin, 1996).

Determining the Relative Influence of Nature and Nurture

Developmental psychologists use several approaches to determine the relative influence of genetic and environmental factors on behaviour. Researchers can, for example, experimentally control the genetic makeup of laboratory animals by carefully breeding them for specific traits. Just as the people who raise Butterball turkeys have learned to produce a breed that grows especially quickly (so that they can be brought to the marketplace less expensively), psychologists are able to breed strains of laboratory animals that share a similar genetic makeup. Observing animals with similar genetic backgrounds in varied environments allows researchers to ascertain the effects of particular kinds of environmental stimulation. Ultimately, of course, generalizing the findings of animal research to a human population remains problematic. However, findings from animal research provide fundamental information that could not be obtained, for ethical reasons, by using human subjects.

identical twins: Twins who are genetically identical

Human twins also serve as an important source of information about the relative effects of genetic and environmental factors. If **identical twins** (those who are genetically identical) display different patterns of development, such differences have to be attributed to variations in the environment in which the twins were raised. The most useful data come from identical twins (such as Gerald Levey and Mark Newman) who are adopted at birth by different sets of foster parents and raised apart in differing environments. Studies of non-twin siblings who are raised in totally different environments also shed some light on the issue. Because they share relatively similar genetic backgrounds, siblings who show similarities as adults provide strong evidence for the importance of heredity (Lykken et al., 1993; Gottesman, 1997; McClearn et al., 1997).

It is also possible to take the opposite tack. Instead of concentrating on people with similar genetic backgrounds who are raised in different environments, we may consider people raised in similar environments who have totally dissimilar genetic backgrounds. If we find, for example, that two adopted children—who have different genetic backgrounds but have been raised in the same family—develop similarly, we have evidence for the importance of environmental influences on development. Moreover, it is possible to carry out research involving animals with dissimilar genetic backgrounds; by experimentally varying the environment in which they are raised, we can determine the influence of environmental factors (independent of heredity) on development (Segal, 1993; Vernon et al., 1997).

Specific Research Strategies

cross-sectional research: A research method in which people of different ages are compared at the same point in time

Most developmental studies employ one of two major research strategies: cross-sectional research or longitudinal research (Cohen & Reese, 1994; Muir, 1999). In **cross-sectional research**, people of different ages are compared at the same point in time. Cross-sectional studies provide information about differences in development between different age groups.

Suppose, for instance, we were interested in the development of intellectual ability in adulthood. To carry out a cross-sectional study, we might compare a sample of 25-, 45-, and 65-year-olds on an IQ test. We then can determine whether average IQ test scores differ in each age group.

Cross-sectional research has limitations, however. For instance, we cannot be sure that the IQ score differences we might find in our example are due to age differences alone. Instead, they may reflect differences in educational attainment among the three age cohorts. (*Cohort* refers to a group of people who grow up at the same time in the same place.) Specifically, any age differences we find in our cross-sectional study may reflect educational differences among cohorts: People in the older age group may belong to a cohort that was less likely to attend college than those in the younger groups.

longitudinal research: A research method that investigates behaviour as subjects age

One way around the problem is to employ the second major research strategy used by developmental psychologists: a longitudinal study. In **longitudinal research**, the behaviour of one or more subjects is traced as the subjects age. Longitudinal studies assess *change* in intellectual ability over time, unlike cross-sectional studies, which assess *differences* among groups of people.

For instance, consider how we might investigate intellectual development during adulthood using a longitudinal research strategy. First, we might give IQ tests to a group of 25-year-olds. We'd then come back to the same people twenty years later and retest them at age 45. Finally, we'd return to them once more when they were 65 years old and test them again.

By examining changes over several points in time, we can clearly see how individuals develop. Unfortunately, there are also drawbacks to longitudinal research: It requires an enormous expenditure of time (as the researcher waits for the subjects to get older), and subjects who participate at an early stage may drop out, move away, or even die as the research continues. Moreover, subjects who take the same test at several points in time may become "testwise" and perform better each time they take it, having become more familiar with the test.

To make up for the limitations in cross-sectional and longitudinal research, investigators have devised an alternative strategy. Known as **cross-sequential research**, it combines cross-sectional and longitudinal approaches by taking a number of different age groups and examining them over several points in time. For example, investigators might use a group of 3-, 5-, and 7-year-olds, examining them every six months for a period of several years. This technique allows the developmental psychologist to tease out the effects of age changes themselves from other possibly influential factors.

cross-sequential research: A research method that combines cross-sectional and longitudinal research by taking a number of different age groups and examining them over several points in time

The Start of Life: Conception and Beyond

Our understanding of the biology of the start of life—when a male's sperm cell penetrates a female's egg cell, marking the moment of *conception*—makes it no less of a miracle. At that single moment, an individual's genetic endowment is established for the rest of his or her life.

The Basics of Genetics

The one-cell entity that is established at conception contains twenty-three pairs of **chromosomes,** rod-shaped structures that hold the basic hereditary information. One member of each pair is from the mother and the other is from the father.

Each chromosome contains thousands of **genes**—smaller units through which genetic information is transmitted. Either individually or in combination, genes produce the particular characteristics of each person. Composed of sequences of *DNA (deoxyribonucleic acid)* molecules, genes are the biological equivalent of "software" that programs the future development of all parts of the body's hardware. Humans have some 100,000 genes.

chromosomes: Rod-shaped structures that hold the basic hereditary information
genes: The parts of the chromosomes through which genetic information is transmitted

While some genes are responsible for the development of systems common to all members of the human species—the heart, circulatory system, brain, lungs, and so forth—others control the characteristics that make each human unique, such as facial configuration, height, eye colour, and the like. The child's sex is also determined by a particular combination of genes. Specifically, a child inherits an X chromosome from its mother, and either an X or Y chromosome from its father. With an XX combination, the child is a female; with an XY combination, the child will develop as a male. Male development is triggered by a single gene on the Y chromosome, and without the presence of that specific gene, the individual will develop as a female.

As behavioural geneticists are increasingly discovering, genes are also at least partially responsible for a wide variety of personal characteristics, encompassing cognitive abilities, personality traits, sexual orientation, and psychological disorders. Of course, few of these characteristics are determined by a single gene. Instead, most traits are the result of a combination of multiple genes, which operate in tandem with environmental influences (Gilger, 1996; Pillard, 1996; Rieder, Kaufmann, & Knowles, 1996; Funder, 1997).

Behavioural Genetics

In order to better understand how genes influence human characteristics and behaviour an international group of scientists, including researchers from the United States, Britain, Japan, Canada, and Sweden, have been seeking to map the specific location and sequence of *every* gene found in humans. The Human Genome Project is a 15-year-long research investigation, expected to be complete by the year 2005, sponsored by the U.S. government at a cost of $3 billion (Marx, 1995; Beardsley, 1996).

Dr. Lap-Chee Tsui and Dr. Stephen Scherer of the Hospital for Sick Children in Toronto work on a project that focuses on sequencing chromosome 7. Dr. Lap-Chee Tsui, president of the Human Genome Organization, discovered the gene that causes cystic fibrosis.

The idea behind the Human Genome Project is that, once they identify the location of specific genes, researchers will be in a position to help identify people who are likely to suffer from various genetically produced disorders. In fact, the research is further along than was initially expected. In December 1999, researchers announced that they had mapped 700 genes (97 percent) on chromosome 22. This is the second smallest of the 23 pairs and was targeted because mutations of its genes are thought to contribute to heart disease, cancer, retardation, schizophrenia, and diseases of the immune system (Donn, 1999; Nature, 1999). As we consider in the Applying Psychology in the 21st Century box, such identification may very well change the face of health care in the next century.

The Earliest Stages of Development

zygote: The new cell formed by the product of fertilization

When the egg becomes fertilized by the sperm, the result is a one-celled entity called a **zygote** that immediately begins to develop. The zygote starts out as a microscopic speck. Three days after fertilization, though, the zygote consists of around 32 cells, and within a week, it has grown to over 100–150 cells. These first two weeks are known as the *germinal period.*

embryo: A developed zygote that has a heart, brain, and other organs

Two weeks after conception, the developing individual enters the *embryonic period*, which lasts from week two through eight, and he or she is now called an **embryo.** As the embryo develops through an intricate, preprogrammed process of cell division, it grows 10,000 times larger by four weeks of age, attaining a length of about one-fifth of an inch. At this point it has developed a rudimentary heart (that beats), a brain, an intestinal tract, and a number of other organs. Although all these organs are at a primitive stage of development, they are clearly recognizable. Moreover, by the eighth week, the embryo is about an inch long, and has arms, legs, and a face that are discernible.

critical period: One of several stages in development in which specific kinds of growth must occur if the individual is to develop normally

Following the eighth week, the embryo faces what is known as a **critical period**, the first of several stages in prenatal development in which specific kinds of growth must occur if the individual is to develop normally. For example, if the eyes and ears do not develop during this stage, they will never form later on, and if they form abnormally, they will be permanently damaged. During critical periods, organisms are particularly sensitive to environmental influences such as the presence of certain kinds of drugs, which, as we will see later, can have a devastating effect on subsequent development (Bornstein & Bruner, 1989; Eisen, Field, & Larson, 1991; Shatz, 1992).

fetus: A developing child, from eight weeks after conception until birth

From the eighth week and continuing until birth, the developing individual enters the *fetal period* and is now called a **fetus**. At the start of this period, it begins to be responsive to touch; it bends its fingers when touched on the hand. At sixteen to eigh-

Applying Psychology in the 21st Century

Gene Therapy: Tinkering with Our Genetic Underpinnings

As he chats with the young mother, the doctor flicks a cotton swab into the mouth of her infant son, collecting a small sample of mucus from inside his cheek. In the back room of his office, he inserts the sample into a machine, which extracts DNA from the mucus cells and compares it with the genetic material on a dime-size chip. Minutes later, a computer printer begins to spit out a list of the infant's genes. Fortunately, all but a few of the genes are labelled "normal." It is those few that the doctor discusses as he explains the results to the mother. "Your son's genetic inheritance is generally good," he says, "but he is somewhat predisposed to skin lesions. So starting right away, he should be protected against excessive exposure to the sun." And, the doctor warns, "He may well be susceptible to cardiovascular disease later in life. To lessen his risk, after about age two he should begin a lifelong low-fat, high-fiber diet." (Jaroff, 1996, p. 24)

While this scenario is the stuff of fantasy, it is only fantasy for the moment. In the twenty-first century, such a scene, for better or worse, may become quite real. Our increasing understanding of genetics is leading not only to the identification of risk factors in children, but also to the development of new treatments for everything from serious physical illnesses, such as cancer, to psychological disorders like schizophrenia and depression.

Advances are already occurring at a breathtaking rate. For instance, it is already possible to identify whether certain women carry a defect in a gene that has been associated with breast cancer

(*BRCA1* and *BRCA2*). Those with the defect may have as much as an 85 percent chance of developing breast cancer. Women with the predisposition for breast cancer then know that they should be especially vigilant for symptoms of the disease (Runowicz, 1996).

Even more exciting is the possibility of *gene therapy*, in which genes are introduced into existing cells in order to prevent or cure a disorder. For instance, brain tumors are produced by cancer cells that run amok, dividing at a rapid pace due to defects in certain genes located at the site of the tumor. It is possible that other genes, which could destroy the defective tumor cells, could be introduced to the site of the tumor, thereby inactivating the cancer cells. Similarly, it is possible that people who suffer from certain kinds of schizophrenia might one day benefit from an analogous process, in which genes are inserted that deactivate defective areas of the brain, ultimately leading to more normal psychological functioning.

On the other hand, early identification of genetic predispositions may be something of a mixed blessing, raising significant psychological issues. Consider, for instance, people who learn that they have a gene that produces *Huntington's disease*, an inherited muscle disorder that invariably produces death, but whose symptoms do not appear until after the age of 40. Because a genetic test is now available that can unambiguously inform people that they will—or won't—have

the disease, they may know from early in life that they will surely have a lingering and difficult illness and a premature death. According to Nancy Wexler, a clinical psychologist at Columbia University, some 50,000 people now have the knowledge that they carry the gene that produces the illness. Some of them have been hospitalized—not because of the disease, but for depression. In fact, 10 percent of those who find they have the gene that produces Huntington's disease report never fully recovering emotionally (Nowak, 1994c; Jaroff, 1996).

In other cases, the ambiguity of knowing that one is susceptible to a disease and *might* contract it can be as debilitating as the certainty that one is sure to get a disease. For instance, not all women who carry the defective gene that produces some forms of breast cancer will actually get cancer, and in any case knowing in advance that one has the defect cannot prevent the occurrence of cancer. In many instances, then, knowledge that they have a heightened susceptibility to breast cancer simply adds to women's uncertainty (Anderson, 1995; Runowicz, 1996).

We don't know how these psychological issues will play out. What is clear is that our understanding of the genetic basis of an increasing number of disorders is growing at an astounding pace. In fact, some researchers predict that only a few decades from now, virtually every disease will include gene therapy as a treatment (Jaroff, 1996).

teen weeks, the baby's movements become strong enough for the mother to sense. At the same time, hair may begin to grow on the baby's head, and the facial features become similar to those the child will display at birth. The major organs begin to function, although the fetus could not be kept alive outside the mother. In addition, a lifetime's worth of brain neurons are produced—although it is unclear whether the brain is capable of thinking in any real sense at this early stage.

By the twenty-fourth week, a fetus has many of the characteristics it will display as a newborn. In fact, when an infant is born prematurely at this age, it can open and close its eyes; suck; cry; look up, down, and around; and even grasp objects placed in its hands, although it is still unable to survive for long outside the mother.

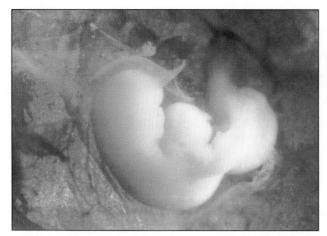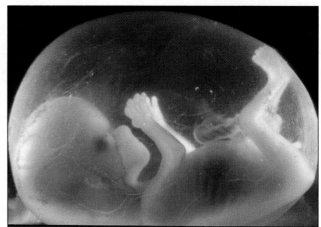

These remarkable photos of live fetuses display the degree of physical development at 4 and 15 weeks.

Darwin Muir of Queens University, a leading expert in the field of infant research, took part in some innovative research designed to investigate development in the womb. Fetal maturational responses in the form of acceleration of the heartbeat and the movement of the fetus in response to vibration were found to develop at different ages; heart rate at 29 weeks gestation and response with body movement at 26 weeks gestation. Understanding this stage of development could shed light on newborn behaviour (Kisilevsky, Muir & Low, 2000).

The fetus continues to develop prior to birth. It begins to grow fatty deposits under the skin and it gains weight. The fetus reaches the **age of viability**, the point at which it can survive if born prematurely, at about twenty-eight weeks, although through advances in medical technology this crucial age is getting earlier. At twenty-eight weeks, the fetus weighs less than 1.5 kilograms and is about 35 centimetres long. It may be capable of learning: One study found that the infants of mothers who had repeatedly read aloud the Dr. Seuss story *The Cat in the Hat* prior to birth preferred the sound of that particular story over other stories after they were born (Spence & De-Casper, 1982).

In the final weeks of pregnancy, the fetus continues to gain weight and grow, becoming increasingly fit. At the end of the normal thirty-eight weeks of pregnancy the fetus typically weighs around 3 kilograms and is about 50 centimetres in length.

age of viability: The point at which the fetus can survive if born prematurely

Prenatal Environmental Influences

Genetic factors are not the only causes of difficulties in fetal development; a number of environmental factors also have an effect on the course of development. The major prenatal environmental influences include:

- *Mother's nutrition and emotional state.* What a mother eats during her pregnancy can have important implications for the health of her baby. Mothers who are seriously undernourished cannot provide adequate nutrition to the growing baby, and they are likely to give birth to underweight babies. Poorly nourished babies are also more susceptible to disease, and a lack of nourishment may have an adverse impact on mental development (Adams & Parker, 1990; Ricciuti, 1993; Sigman, 1995).

  Moreover, there is some evidence that the mother's emotional state affects the baby. Mothers who are anxious and tense during the last months of their pregnancies are more apt to have infants who are irritable and who sleep and eat poorly. The reason? One hypothesis is that the autonomic nervous system of the fetus becomes especially sensitive as a result of the chemical changes produced by the mother's emotional state (Kagan, Kearsley, & Zelazo, 1978).

- *Illness of mother.* Rubella or German measles is a disease that has relatively minor effects on the mother. However it is one of a number of illnesses that can have devastating consequences for the developing fetus when contracted during the early part of a woman's pregnancy especially during the first 16 weeks. Of the 1,150 adult cases a year, 15 percent are women of child-bearing age (Health Canada, 1996). Other maternal diseases that may produce a permanent effect on the fetus include syphilis, diabetes, and high blood pressure.

  Acquired immune deficiency syndrome (AIDS) can be passed from mother to child prior to birth. Sadly, in many cases mothers may not even know they carry the disease and inadvertently transmit it to their children. The AIDS virus can also be passed on through breast-feeding after birth (Heyward & Curran, 1988; Health Canada, 1996); 54,000 Canadians are infected with the Human Immunodeficiency Virus (HIV). This is the virus that causes AIDS and a dozen more Canadians each day are infected. From 1982 to 1990, the median age for HIV dropped from 32 to 23. Many Canadian teens now have HIV (Health Canada, 1998).

- *Mother's use of drugs.* Drugs taken by a pregnant woman can have a tragic effect on the unborn child. Probably the most dramatic example was thalidomide, a tranquilizer that was widely prescribed during the 1960s—until it was discovered that it caused severe birth defects, such as the absence of limbs. Another example is the hormone diethylstilbestrol (DES), prescribed until the 1950s to prevent miscarriages. We now know that daughters whose mothers took DES during pregnancy are at risk for developing abnormalities of the cervix and vagina, and for developing cancer of the uterus. Sons whose mothers took DES have higher rates of infertility and reproductive problems.

  Alcohol and nicotine are also dangerous to fetal development. For example, *fetal alcohol syndrome*, a condition resulting in mental and growth retardation, has been found in the children of mothers who consumed heavy or sometimes even moderate amounts of alcohol during pregnancy. Moreover, mothers who take physically addictive drugs such as cocaine run the risk of giving birth to babies who are similarly addicted. Their newborns suffer painful withdrawal symptoms after birth and sometimes show permanent physical and mental impairment as well (Hunt et al., 1995; Larroque et al., 1995; Short & Hess, 1995; Chandler & Lane, 1996; Karmel & Gardner, 1996).

- *Birth complications.* Although most births are routine, the process sometimes goes awry, resulting in injury to the infant. For example, the umbilical cord connecting the baby to the mother may become compressed, withholding oxygen from the child. If oxygen is withheld too long, the child may suffer permanent brain damage.

A mother's drinking during pregnancy can be dangerous for the unborn child.

A number of other environmental factors have an impact on the child prior to and during birth (see Table 10-2). It is important to keep in mind, however, that development represents the interaction of environmental and genetic influences. Although we have been discussing the influences of genetics and environment separately, neither factor works alone. Moreover, while we have been emphasizing some of the ways in which development can go awry, the vast majority of births occur without difficulty. And in most instances, subsequent development also proceeds routinely, as we discuss next.

Table 10-2	Environmental Factors Affecting Prenatal Development

Factor	Possible Effect
Rubella (German measles)	Blindness, deafness, heart abnormalities, stillbirth
Syphilis	Mental retardation, physical deformities, maternal miscarriage
Addictive drugs	Low birth weight, addiction of infant to drug, with possible death, after birth, from withdrawal
Smoking	Premature birth, low birth weight and length
Alcohol	Mental retardation, lower-than-average birth weight, small head, limb deformities
Radiation from X rays	Physical deformities, mental retardation
Inadequate diet	Reduction in growth of brain, smaller-than-average weight and length at birth
Mother's age—younger than 18 at birth of child	Premature birth, increased incidence of Down syndrome
Mother's age—older than 35 at birth of child	Increased incidence of Down syndrome
DES (diethylstilbestrol)	Reproductive difficulties and increased incidence of genital cancer in children of mothers who were given DES during pregnancy to prevent miscarriage
AIDS	Possible spread of AIDS virus to infant; facial deformities; growth failure

Recap, Review, and Rethink

Recap

- A fundamental issue of developmental psychology is the nature-nurture question, which seeks to determine the relative influence of environmental and genetic factors on development.

- Developmental researchers generally employ cross-sectional, longitudinal, and cross-sequential research strategies to answer questions about development.

- During the course of prenatal development, the one-cell zygote evolves into an embryo and subsequently a fetus. Birth typically occurs thirty-eight weeks after conception.

- Genetic researchers are increasing our knowledge of genetic influences on normal and abnormal development, as well as on a variety of personal characteristics.

Review

1. Developmental psychologists are interested in the effects of both _____ and _____ on development.

2. Environment and heredity both influence development, with genetic potentials generally establishing limits on environmental influences. True or false?

3. By observing genetically similar animals in differing environments, we can increase our understanding of the influences of hereditary and environmental factors in humans. True or false?

4. _____ research studies the same individuals over a period of time, while _____ research studies people of different ages at the same time.

5. Match each of the following terms with its definition.
   1. zygote
   2. gene
   3. chromosome

   a. smallest unit through which genetic information is passed
   b. fertilized egg
   c. rod-shaped structure containing genetic information

6. Specific kinds of growth must take place during a _____ period if the embryo is to develop normally.

Answers to Review Questions are on page 366.

Rethink

1. State a hypothesis relating to the nature-nurture issue that might be studied by the observation of identical twins separated at birth. Do the same for a study involving adopted siblings who are not genetically related. What are the advantages and limitations of both studies?

2. What sort of policy might you create to deal with the notification of persons who have genetically based disorders that can be identified by genetic testing? Would your policy treat potentially fatal disorders differently from less serious ones? Would it make a distinction between treatable and nontreatable disorders?

3. Given the possible effects of the environment on the developing child, do you think expectant mothers should be subject to legal prosecution for their use of alcohol and other drugs that could seriously harm their unborn children? Defend your position.

PHYSICAL AND SOCIAL DEVELOPMENT

His head was molded into a long melon shape and came to a point at the back. . . . He was covered with a thick greasy white material known as "vernix," which made him slippery to hold, and also allowed him to slip easily through the birth canal. In addition to a shock of black hair on his head, his body was covered with dark, fine hair known as "lanugo." His ears, his back, his shoulders, and even his cheeks were furry. . . . His skin was wrinkled and quite loose, ready to scale in creased places such as his feet and hands. . . . His ears were pressed to his head in unusual positions—one ear was matted firmly forward on his cheek. His nose was flattened and pushed to one side by the squeeze as he came through the pelvis (Brazelton, 1969, p. 3).

▶ **What are the major milestones of physical, perceptual, and social development after birth?**

What kind of creature is this? Although the description hardly fits that of the adorable babies seen in advertisements for baby food, we are in fact talking about a normal, completely developed child just after the moment of birth. Called a **neonate**, the newborn presents itself to the world in a form that hardly meets the standards of beauty against which we typically measure babies. Yet ask any parent: No sight is more beautiful or exciting than the first glimpse of their newborn.

neonate: A newborn child

The neonate's flawed appearance is brought about by a number of factors. The trip through its mother's birth canal may have squeezed the incompletely formed bones of the skull together and squashed the nose into the head. It is covered with *vernix*, a white, greasy material that is secreted to protect its skin prior to birth, and it may have *lanugo*, a soft fuzz, over its entire body. Its eyelids may be puffy with an accumulation of fluids because of its upside-down position during birth.

All this changes during the first two weeks of life, as the neonate takes on a more familiar appearance. Even more impressive are the capabilities that the neonate begins to display from the time it is born—capabilities that grow at an astounding rate over the ensuing months and years (Maurer & Maurer, 1988).

The neonate is born with a number of **reflexes**—unlearned, involuntary responses that occur automatically in the presence of certain stimuli. Many of these reflexes are critical for survival and unfold naturally as a part of an infant's ongoing maturation. The *rooting reflex*, for instance, causes neonates to turn their heads toward things that touch their cheeks—such as the nipple of a mother's breast or a bottle. Similarly, a *sucking reflex* prompts the infant to suck at things that touch its lips. Among its other reflexes are a *gag reflex* (to clear its throat); the *startle reflex* (a series of movements in which the infant flings out its arms, fans its fingers, and arches its back in response to a sudden noise); and the *Babinski reflex* (the baby's toes fan out when the outer edge of the sole of its foot is stroked).

reflexes: Automatic, involuntary response to an incoming stimulus

These primitive reflexes are lost after the first few months of life and replaced by more complex and organized behaviours. Although at birth the neonate is capable of only jerky, limited voluntary movements, during the first year of life the ability to move independently grows enormously. The typical baby is able to roll over by the age of 3 months; it can sit without support at 6 months, stand alone at about 11½ months, and walk by the time it is just over a year old. Not only does the ability to make large-scale movements improve during this time, but fine-muscle movements also become increasingly sophisticated (as illustrated in Figure 10-1).

FIGURE 10-1 *Although at birth the neonate is capable of only jerky, limited voluntary movements, during the first year of life the ability to move independently grows enormously.*

0 month: fetal posture	**1 month:** chin up	**2 months:** chest up	**3 months:** reach and miss
4 months: sit with support	**5 months:** sit on lap, grasp object	**6 months:** sit on high chair, grasp dangling object	**7 months:** sit alone
8 months: stand with help	**9 months:** stand holding furniture	**10 months:** creep	**11 months:** walk when led
12 months: pull to stand by furniture	**13 months:** climb stair steps	**14 months:** stand alone	**15 months:** walk alone

Growth After Birth

Perhaps the most obvious sign of development is the physical growth of the child. During the first year of life, children typically triple their birth weight, and their height increases by about half. This rapid growth slows down as the child gets older—think how gigantic adults would be if that rate of growth were constant—and the average rate of growth from age 3 to the beginning of adolescence, around age 13, is a gain of about 2.5 kilos and 7.5 centimetres a year.

The physical changes that occur as children develop are not just a matter of increasing growth; the relationship of the size of the various body parts to one another changes dramatically as children age. As you can see in Figure 10-2, the head of the fetus (and the newborn) is disproportionately large. However, the head soon becomes more proportional in size to the rest of the body as growth occurs mainly in the trunk and legs.

Answers to Review Questions:

1. heredity (or nature); environment (or nurture)   2. true   3. true   4. Longitudinal; cross-sectional   5. 1-b; 2-a; 3-c   6. critical

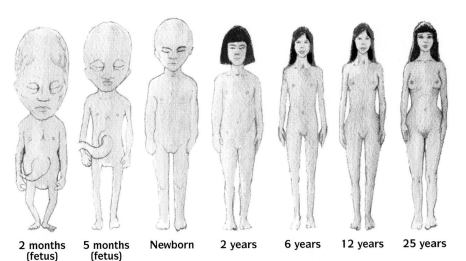

| 2 months (fetus) | 5 months (fetus) | Newborn | 2 years | 6 years | 12 years | 25 years |

FIGURE 10-2 *As development progresses, the relative size of the head—in relation to the rest of the body—decreases until adulthood is reached. Source: Adapted from Robbins, 1929.*

Development of Perception: Taking in the World

When proud parents pick up their neonate and peer into its eyes, is the child able to return their gaze? Although it was thought for some time that newborns could see only a hazy blur, most current findings indicate that the capabilities of neonates are far more impressive (Horowitz & Colombo, 1990; Slater & Morison, 1991). While their eyes have limited capacity to modify the shape of the lens, making it difficult to focus on objects that are not within a 7- to 8-inch distance from the face, neonates are able to follow objects moving within their field of vision. They also show the rudiments of depth perception, as they react by raising their hands when an object appears to be moving rapidly toward the face (Colombo & Mitchell, 1990; Gelman & Au, 1996).

You might think that it would be hard to figure out just how well neonates are able to see, since their lack of both language and reading ability clearly prevents them from saying what direction the "E" on a vision chart is facing. However, a number of ingenious methods, relying on the newborn's biological responses and innate reflexes, have been devised to test perceptual skills (Koop, 1994; Atkinson, 1995).

For instance, infants who are shown a novel stimulus typically pay close attention to it, and, as a consequence, their heart rates increase. But if they are repeatedly shown the same stimulus, their attention to it decreases, as indicated by a return to a slower heart rate. This phenomenon is known as **habituation**, the decrease in the response to a stimulus that occurs after repeated presentations of the same stimulus. By studying habituation, developmental psychologists can tell when a stimulus can be detected and discriminated by a child too young to speak (Bornstein & Lamb, 1992; Peterzell, 1993).

Researchers have developed a number of other methods for measuring neonate and infant perception. One technique, for instance, involves babies sucking on a nipple attached to a computer. A change in the rate and vigor with which they suck is used to infer that they can perceive variations in stimuli. Other approaches include examining babies' eye movements and observing which way babies move their heads when presented with a visual stimulus (Bronson, 1990; Hood & Atkinson, 1993; Teller & Palmer, 1996; Spence & Freeman, 1996; Sansavini, Bertoncini, & Giovanelli, 1997).

Using such research techniques, we now know that infants' visual perception is remarkably sophisticated from the start of life. At birth, babies show preferences for patterns with contours and edges over less distinct patterns, indicating that they are capable of responding to the configuration of stimuli. Furthermore, even newborns are aware of size constancy, apparently sensitive to the phenomenon that objects stay the same size even though the image on the retina may change size as the distance between the object and the retina varies (Slater, Mattock, & Brown, 1990; Slater, 1996).

habituation: The decrease in the response to a stimulus that occurs after repeated presentations of the same stimulus

Infant Hearing

FIGURE 10-3 *This newborn infant is clearly imitating the expressions of the adult model in these amazing photos. Source: From A. N. Meltzoff & M. K. Moore, "Imitations of Facial and Manual Gestures by Human Neonates" in* Science *1997, 198, 75–78.*

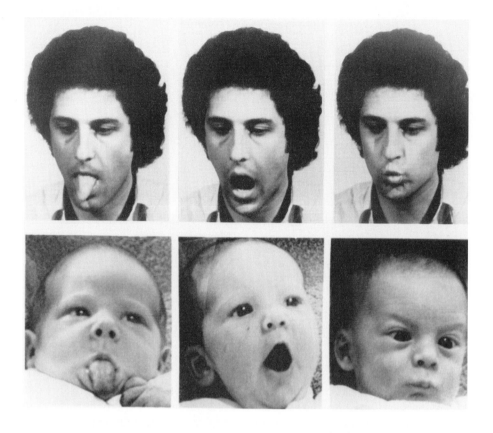

In fact, neonates have the ability to discriminate facial expressions—and even to imitate them (Field, 1982; Meltzoff & Moore, 1993; Meltzoff, 1996). As you can see in Figure 10-3, newborns exposed to an adult with a happy, sad, or surprised facial expression are able to produce a good imitation of the adult's expression. Even very young infants, then, can respond to the emotions and moods that their caregivers' facial expressions reveal. This capability provides the foundation for social interactional skills in children (Phillips et al., 1990; Mumme, Fernald, & Herrera, 1996).

Other visual abilities grow rapidly after birth. By the end of their first month, babies can distinguish some colours from others, and after four months they can readily focus on near or far objects. In fact, from one to three months infants are much more interested in visual pattern than auditory stimuli (Muir, Humphrey, & Humphrey, 1994). By three months infants can discriminate between their mother's face and that of a stranger (Barrera and Maurer, 1981). By 4 or 5 months, they are able to recognize two- and three-dimensional objects, and they can make use of the gestalt patterns that we discussed in relation to adult perception in Chapter 3. Furthermore, there are rapid improvements in perceptual abilities: Sensitivity to visual stimuli, for instance, becomes three to four times greater at 1 year of age than it was at birth (Slater, 1996; Vital-Durand, Atkinson, & Braddick, 1996).

In addition to vision, infants' other sensory capabilities are quite impressive. Newborns can distinguish different sounds to the point of being able to recognize their own mothers' voices at the age of 3 days (DeCasper & Fifer, 1980; Hepper, Scott, & Shahidullah, 1993). They are also capable of making subtle linguistic distinctions that underlie the language abilities described in Chapter 7. At 2 days of age, infants are able to distinguish between their native tongue and foreign languages, and they can discriminate between such closely related sounds as *ba* and *pa* when they are 4 days old (Moon, Cooper, & Fifer, 1993; Jusczyk, 1995). By 6 months of age, they are capable of discriminating virtually any difference in sound that is relevant to the production of language (Aslin, 1987). Moreover, they are capable of discriminating different tastes and smells at a very early age (Steiner, 1979; Mennella & Beauchamp, 1996). There even seems to be something of a built-in sweet tooth: Neonates prefer liquids that have been sweetened with sugar over their unsweetened counterparts.

FIGURE 10-4 *Although the wire "mother" dispensed milk to the hungry infant monkey, the soft, terry cloth "mother" was preferred. Source: Harry Harlow Primate Laboratory/University of Wisconsin.*

Development of Social Behaviour: Taking On the World

As anyone who has seen an infant smiling at the sight of his or her mother can guess, at the same time that infants are growing physically and honing their perceptual abilities, they are also developing socially. Infants as young as three months demonstrate social perception by responding in a reciprocal way to adult eye contact (Muir, Humphrey, & Humphrey, 1994). The nature of a child's early social development provides the foundation for social relationships that will last a lifetime (Schaffer, 1996).

Attachment, the positive emotional bond that develops between a child and a particular individual, is the most important form of social development that occurs during infancy (Greeberg, Cicchetti, & Cummings, 1990). One of the first investigators to demonstrate the importance and nature of attachment was psychologist Harry Harlow. In a classic study, Harlow gave infant monkeys the choice of cuddling a wire "monkey" that provided food, or a soft, terry-cloth "monkey" that was warm but did not provide food. Their choice was clear: They spent most of their time clinging to the warm cloth "monkey," although they made occasional forays to the wire monkey to nurse (Harlow & Zimmerman, 1959). It was obvious that the cloth monkey provided greater comfort to the infants; food alone was insufficient to create attachment (see Figure 10-4).

attachment: The positive emotional bond that develops between a child and a particular individual

Building on this pioneering work, other researchers have suggested that attachment grows through the responsiveness of infants' caregivers to the signals the babies provide, such as cries, smiles, reaching, and clinging. The greater the responsiveness of the caregiver to the child's signals, the more likely it is that the child will become securely attached. Full attachment eventually develops as a result of a complex series of interactions between caregiver and child known as the Attachment Behavioural System (Bell & Ainsworth, 1972; Pederson et al., 1998). It is important to note that the infant plays as critical and active a role in the formation of a bond as the caregiver. Infants who respond positively to a caregiver promote more positive behaviour on the part of the caregiver, which in turn elicits an even stronger degree of attachment from the child.

Measuring Attachment

Developmental psychologists have devised a quick and direct way of measuring attachment. Developed by Mary Ainsworth (See Chapter 1), the *Ainsworth strange situ-*

Attachment Theory

ation consists of a sequence of events involving a child and (typically) his or her mother. Initially, the mother and baby enter an unfamiliar room, and the mother permits the baby to explore while she sits down. An adult stranger then enters the room, after which the mother leaves. The mother then returns, and the stranger leaves. The mother then once again leaves the baby alone, and the stranger returns. Finally, the stranger leaves, and the mother returns (Ainsworth et al., 1978).

Babies' reactions to the strange situation vary drastically, depending, according to Ainsworth, on their degree of attachment to the mother. One-year-old children who are labelled "securely attached" employ the mother as a kind of home base, exploring independently but returning to her occasionally. When she leaves, they exhibit distress, and they go to her when she returns. Children termed "avoidant" do not cry when the mother leaves, but they seem to avoid her when she returns, appearing to be angry with her. Finally, "ambivalent" children display anxiety before they are separated and are upset when the mother leaves, but they may show ambivalent reactions to her return, such as seeking close contact but simultaneously hitting and kicking her. Using this model, Benoit and Parker (2000) studied triads made up of grandmother/mother and infant. Sixty-five percent of the triads had corresponding attachment patterns across generations.

The nature of attachment between children and their mothers has far-reaching consequences for later development. For example, one study found that boys who were securely attached at age 1 showed fewer psychological difficulties when they were older than did avoidant or ambivalent youngsters (Lewis et al., 1984). Moreover, children who are securely attached to their mothers tend to be more socially and emotionally competent than their less securely attached peers, and they are viewed as more cooperative, capable, and playful (Ainsworth & Bowlby, 1991; Kerns & Barth, 1995; Coble, Gantt, & Mallinckrodt, 1996; Rose-Krasnor et al., 1996; Greenberg, 1997).

On the other hand, children who lack secure attachment do not always have difficulties later in life, and being securely attached at an early age does not guarantee good adjustment later. Furthermore, some cultures foster higher levels of secure attachment than others. In short, attachment is related to the social environment that children encounter as they are growing up (Nakagawa, Lamb, & Miyaki, 1992; Fox, 1995).

The Father's Role

For many years, the father stood in the shadows behind the mother—at least as far as developmental research was concerned. Because the traditional view was that the mother-infant bond was the most crucial in a child's life, researchers in earlier decades focused on the mother's relationship with her children. However, the last decade has seen an increase in studies that highlight the father's role in parenting (Phares, 1992; Parke, 1996).

More than 15 percent of single parent households in Canada and the United States are headed by the father (Walker and Henning, 1997).

On the other hand, fathers by and large spend less time caring for and playing with their children than do mothers, and many fathers view child-care activities as a voluntary choice, rather than a necessity or duty. However, the strength of attachment between fathers and their children can be as great as between mothers and their children. Although children can be simultaneously attached to both parents, the nature of attachment is not always identical between children and mothers and children and fathers. For instance, infants tend to prefer to be soothed by their mothers, even though fathers are just as adept at comforting and nurturing babies (Lamb, 1982; Larson, Richards, & Perry-Jenkins, 1994).

The reason for differences in attachment to mothers and fathers may be that mothers spend a greater proportion of their time feeding and directly nurturing their children, whereas fathers spend more time, proportionately, playing with them. Moreover, the quality of fathers' play is often different from that of mothers. Fathers engage in more physical, rough-and-tumble sorts of activities, whereas mothers play more verbally oriented and traditional games such as peekaboo. Such differences in play style are typically very pronounced, and occur even in the minority of families in which the mother works to support the family and the father stays at home with the children (Parke, 1981; Power & Parke, 1982; Labrell, 1996).

At about age 2, children begin to become independent of their parents, preferring to play with friends—even though at that age they are more likely to play side by side than together.

Despite the differences between the behaviour of fathers and mothers, each parent is an important attachment figure and plays a major role in the social development of a child. Furthermore, the sheer amount of time an adult spends with a child is often less important than the quality of that time (Hetherington & Parke, 1993).

Social Relationships with Peers

Anyone who watches a preschooler rush off to play with a neighborhood friend is aware of the enjoyment that children derive from being with their peers. Such friendships are crucial to a child's social development (Lewis & Feinman, 1991; Laursen, Hartup, & Koplas, 1996; Bukowski, Newcomb, & Hartup, 1996). According to developmental psychologist Willard Hartup, experience is necessary in both "vertical" relationships (those with people of greater knowledge and social power, such as parents) and "horizontal" relationships (those with people who have the same amount of knowledge and social power) if children are to develop social competence (Hartup, 1996).

By the time they are 2 years old, children start to become less dependent on their parents and more self-reliant, increasingly preferring to play with friends. During childhood there is a preference for friendships with same sex peers. This will change in adolescence to a more positive attitude towards friendships with other sex peers (Sippola, Bukowski, & Noll, 1997). Initially, play is relatively independent: Even though they may be sitting side-by-side, 2-year-olds pay more attention to toys than to one another when playing. Later, however, children actively interact, modifying one another's behaviour and later exchanging roles during play.

As children reach school age, their social interactions become increasingly formalized, as well as more frequent. They may engage in elaborate games involving complex scenarios. Play also becomes more structured, involving teams and games with rigid rules (Mueller & Lucas, 1975; Stambak & Sinclair, 1993).

It is important to realize that children's play serves purposes other than mere enjoyment (Asher & Parker, 1991; Cohen, 1993). Play allows children to become increasingly competent in their social interactions with others. Through play they learn to take the perspective of other people and to infer others' thoughts and feelings, even when these are not being directly expressed. In sum, social interaction aids children in interpreting the meaning of others' behaviour and developing the capacity to respond appropriately (Crick & Dodge, 1994; Pellegrini, 1995).

Furthermore, children learn physical and emotional self-control: They learn to avoid hitting an adversary who bests them, to be polite, and to control their emotional displays and facial expressions (e.g., smiling even when receiving a disappointing gift). Situations that provide children with opportunities for social interaction, then, may enhance their social development (Selman et al., 1983; Feldman, 1982, 1993; Fox, 1994; Pulkkinen, 1994).

When women began to enter the work force in record numbers in the 1970s, concern arose that paid day care would interfere with children's attachment to their parents. Research has shown that that fear was largely unfounded.

The Benefits of Day Care

Research on the importance of social interaction is corroborated by work that examines the benefits of day care, which is an important part of an increasing number of children's lives. For instance, over 70 percent of Canadian parents with infants and toddlers have used out-of-home care arrangements (Parlow, 1997).

Do out-of-the-home child-care arrangements benefit children's development? Most research suggests that the answer is yes. For example, children who attend high-quality child-care centres may not only do as well as children who stay at home with their parents, but in some respects may actually do better (Clarke-Stewart, Gruber, & Fitzgerald, 1994; Hagekull & Bohlin, 1995; Lamb, 1996; Burchinal et al., 1996). Children in child care are generally more considerate and sociable than other children, and they interact more positively with teachers (e.g., Phillips, McCartney, & Scarr, 1987). They may also be more compliant and regulate their own behaviour more effectively (Volling & Feagans, 1995).

In addition, especially for children from poor or disadvantaged homes, child care in specially enriched environments—those with many toys, books, a variety of children, and high-quality care providers—often proves to be more intellectually stimulating than the home environment. Such child care can lead to increased intellectual achievement, demonstrated in higher IQ scores and better language development (Lee et al., 1990). In fact, some research suggests that children in child-care centres score higher on tests of cognitive abilities than those who are cared for by their mothers or by sitters or home day-care providers (Clark-Stewart, 1991; Feagans, Fendt, & Farran, 1995; Broberg et al., 1997). However, a Canadian study on day care in Montreal (Schliecker, White and Jacobs, 1991) found that there was a relationship between the quality of day care and vocabulary comprehension. Children in lower-quality day care had poorer vocabulary comprehension. This was regardless of socioeconomic levels of the parents.

What about the relationaship between day care and attachment to parents? The research findings on the issue are inconsistent. Some evidence suggests that infants who are involved in outside care more than twenty hours a week in their first year show less attachment to their mothers than those who have not been in day care (Belsky & Rovine, 1988; Morgan, 1996). On the other hand, most other research finds little or no difference in the strength of parental attachment bonds of infants and toddlers who have been in day care compared with those raised solely by their parents, regardless of how long they have been in day care. Furthermore, there is no evidence that children in day-care centres are more attached to their day-care workers than to their parents; in fact, the children almost always appear to be more attached to their parents (Ragozin, 1980; Rutter, 1982). In short, most evidence suggests that children who are

Table 10-3	Child-Rearing Patterns	
Parental Style	**Parenting Behaviour**	**Children's Behaviour**
Authoritarian	Rigid, punitive, strict standards	Unsociable, unfriendly, withdrawn
Permissive	Lax, inconsistent, undemanding	Immature, moody, dependent, low self-control
Authoritative	Firm, set limits and goals, use reasoning, encourage independence	Good social skills; likable, self-reliant, independent

in day care are no less attached to their parents than those who are not in day care (NICHD Early Child Care Research Network, 1997).

Overall, there may be significant benefits from the social interaction and intellectual stimulation afforded by high-quality day-care centres. However, the key here is *high-quality* day care (which may not be easy to find). In contrast, low-quality day-care centres provide few or no advantages. Furthermore, we don't know yet whether the benefits of day care last through adulthood. Still, it is clear that participation in day care provides the opportunity for social interaction and stimulation that may prove to be beneficial (Zaslow, 1991; Zigler & Lang, 1991; Ziegler & Styfco, 1993; Clarke-Stewart, Gruber, & Fitzgerald, 1994).

Parenting Styles and Social Development

Although many advances in social development are prompted by peer interaction, parents' child-rearing patterns also shape their children's social competence. Psychologist Diana Baumrind (1971, 1980) found that parenting styles fall into three main categories. **Authoritarian parents** are rigid and punitive and value unquestioning obedience from their children. They have strict standards and discourage expressions of disagreement. **Permissive parents** give their children lax or inconsistent direction and, although warm, require little of them. Finally, **authoritative parents** are firm, setting limits for their children. As the children get older, these parents try to reason and explain things to them. They also set clear goals and encourage their children's independence (see Table 10-3).

As you might expect, the three kinds of child-rearing styles were associated with very different kinds of behaviour in children (although there were, of course, many exceptions). Children of authoritarian parents tend to be unsociable, unfriendly, and relatively withdrawn. In contrast, permissive parents' children are immature, moody, and dependent and have low self-control. The children of authoritative parents fare best: Their social skills are high—they are likable, self-reliant, independent, and cooperative.

Before we rush to congratulate authoritative parents and condemn authoritarian and permissive parents, it is important to note that in many cases authoritarian and permissive parents produce children who are perfectly well adjusted. Moreover, children are born with a particular **temperament**—a basic, innate disposition. Some children are naturally easy-going and cheerful, whereas others are irritable and fussy. The kind of temperament a baby is born with may in part elicit particular kinds of parental child-rearing styles (Goldsmith et al., 1987; Goldsmith & Harman, 1994; Kendler, 1996). In a study of infant care decisions and attachment security, McKim and others, (1999) gathered information on 189 families in the Ottawa-Carleton area. Among other things, they found that "Difficult temperament children were less secure in their relationships with their mothers generally, but difficult infants in extensive out-of-home care appeared to be buffered against this effect." (p.104) They go on to suggest that both mother and child benefit from this arrangement.

Furthermore, the findings regarding child-rearing styles are chiefly applicable to North American society, in which a dominant value is that children should learn to be in-

authoritarian parents: Parents who are rigid and punitive and value unquestioning obedience from their children

permissive parents: Parents who give their children lax or inconsistent direction and, although warm, require little of them

authoritative parents: Parents who are firm, set clear limits, reason with their children, and explain things to them

temperament: Basic, innate disposition

Characteristics of Temperament

"Please, Jason. Don't you want to grow up to be an autonomous person?"

dependent and not rely too heavily on their parents. In contrast, Japanese parents encourage dependence in order to promote the values of cooperation and community life. These differences in cultural values result in very different philosophies of child rearing. For example, Japanese mothers believe it is a punishment to make a young child sleep alone, so many children sleep next to their mothers throughout infancy and toddlerhood (Kagan, Kearsley, & Zelazo, 1978; Miyake, Chen, & Campos, 1985; Kawasaki et al., 1994).

In sum, a child's upbringing is a consequence of the child-rearing philosophy parents hold, the specific practices they employ, and the nature of their own and their child's personality. As is the case with other aspects of development, then, behaviour is a function of a complex interaction of environmental and genetic factors (Maccoby, 1992; Ge et al., 1996; Gottlieb, 1996; Kagan, 1997).

Erikson's Theory of Psychosocial Development

In trying to trace the course of social development, some theorists have considered how society and culture present challenges that change as the individual matures. Following this path, psychoanalyst Erik Erikson developed one of the most comprehensive theories of social development. According to Erikson (1963), the developmental changes occurring throughout our lives can be viewed as a series of eight stages of psychosocial development. **Psychosocial development** encompasses changes in our interactions and understanding of one another as well as in our knowledge and understanding of ourselves as members of society.

Erikson suggests that passage through each of the stages necessitates resolution of a crisis or conflict. Accordingly, each of Erikson's eight stages is represented as a pairing of the most positive and most negative aspects of the crisis of the period. Although each crisis is never resolved entirely—life becomes increasingly complicated as we grow older—it needs to be resolved sufficiently so that we are equipped to deal with demands made during the following stage of development.

In the first stage of psychosocial development, the **trust-versus-mistrust stage** (birth to 1½ years), infants develop feelings of trust if their physical requirements and psychological needs for attachment are consistently met and their interactions with the world are generally positive. On the other hand, inconsistent care and unpleasant interactions with others can lead to the development of mistrust and leave the infant unable to meet the challenges required in the next stage of development.

In the second stage, the **autonomy-versus-shame-and-doubt stage** (1½ to 3 years), toddlers develop independence and autonomy if exploration and freedom are encouraged, or they experience shame, self-doubt, and unhappiness if they are overly

psychosocial development: Development of individuals' interactions and understanding of each other and of their knowledge and understanding of themselves as members of society

trust-versus-mistrust stage: According to Erikson, the first stage of psychosocial development, occurring from birth to 18 months of age, during which infants develop feelings of trust or lack of trust

autonomy-versus-shame-and-doubt stage: The period during which, according to Erikson, toddlers (ages 18 months to 3 years) develop independence and autonomy if exploration and freedom are encouraged, or shame and self-doubt if they are restricted and overprotected

restricted and protected. According to Erikson, the key to the development of autonomy during this period is for the child's caregivers to provide the appropriate amount of control. If parents provide too much control, children will be unable to assert themselves and develop their own sense of control over their environment; if parents provide too little control, children themselves become overly demanding and controlling.

The next crisis that children face is that of the **initiative-versus-guilt stage** (ages 3 to 6). In this stage, the major conflict is between a child's desire to initiate activities independently and the guilt that comes from the unwanted and unexpected consequences of such activities. If parents react positively to the child's attempts at independence, they help their child to resolve the initiative-versus-guilt crisis positively.

The fourth and last stage of childhood is the **industry-versus-inferiority stage** (ages 6 to 12). During this period, successful psychosocial development is characterized by increasing competency in all areas, be they social interactions or academic skills. In contrast, difficulties in this stage lead to feelings of failure and inadequacy.

Erikson's theory suggests that psychosocial development continues throughout life, and he proposes that there are four more crises to face beyond childhood. Although his theory has been criticized on several grounds—such as the imprecision of the concepts he employs and his greater emphasis on male development than female development—it remains influential and is one of the few theories of social development that encompass the entire lifespan.

initiative-versus-guilt stage: According to Erikson, the period during which children ages 3 to 6 years experience conflict between independence of action and the sometimes negative results of that action

industry-versus-inferiority stage: According to Erikson, the last stage of childhood during which children aged 6 to 12 years may develop positive social interactions with others or may feel inadequate and become less sociable

COGNITIVE DEVELOPMENT

Suppose you had two drinking glasses of different shapes—one short and broad, and one tall and thin. Now imagine that you filled the short, broad one with juice about halfway and then poured the liquid from that glass into the tall one. The juice appears to fill about three-fourths of the second glass. If someone asked you whether there was more juice in the second glass than there had been in the first, what would you say?

You might think that such a simple question hardly deserves an answer; of course there is no difference in the amount of juice in the two glasses. However, most 4-year-olds would be likely to say that there is more juice in the second glass. If you then poured the juice back into the short glass, they would say there is now less juice than there was in the taller glass.

Why are young children confused by this problem? The reason is not immediately obvious. Anyone who has observed preschoolers must be impressed by how far they have progressed from the early stages of development. They speak with ease, know the alphabet, count, play complex games, use tape players, tell stories, and communicate quite effectively.

Yet, despite this outward sophistication, there are profound gaps in children's understanding of the world. Some theorists have suggested that children are incapable of understanding certain ideas and concepts until they reach a particular stage of **cognitive development**—the process by which a child's understanding of the world changes as a function of age and experience. In contrast to the theories of physical and social development discussed earlier (such as those of Erikson), theories of cognitive development seek to explain the quantitative and qualitative intellectual advances that occur during development.

▶ **How can we best describe cognitive development?**

cognitive development: The process by which a child's understanding of the world changes as a function of age and experience

Piaget's Theory of Cognitive Development

No theory of cognitive development has had more impact than that of Swiss psychologist Jean Piaget. Piaget (1970) suggested that children throughout the world proceed through a series of four stages in a fixed order. He maintained that these stages differ not only in the *quantity* of information acquired at each stage, but in the *quality* of knowledge and understanding as well. Taking an interactionist point of view, he suggested that movement from one stage to the next occurred when the child reached an appropriate level of maturation *and* was exposed to relevant types of experiences.

Table 10-4	A Summary of Piaget's Stages of Cognitive Development	

Stage	Approximate Age Range	Major Characteristics
Sensorimotor	Birth–2 years	Development of object permanence, development of motor skills, little or no capacity for symbolic representation
Preoperational	2–7 years	Development of language and symbolic thinking, egocentric thinking
Concrete operational	7–12 years	Development of conservation, mastery of concept of reversibility
Formal operational	12–adulthood	Development of logical and abstract thinking

Without such experiences, children were assumed to be incapable of reaching their highest level of cognitive growth.

Piaget's four stages are known as the sensorimotor, preoperational, concrete operational, and formal operational stages (see Table 10-4). Let's examine each of them and the approximate ages that they span.

Sensorimotor Stage: Birth to Two Years

sensorimotor stage: According to Piaget, the stage from birth to 2 years during which a child has little competence in representing the environment using images, language, or other symbols

object permanence: The awareness that objects—and people—continue to exist even if they are out of sight

During the initial part of the **sensorimotor stage** children have relatively little competence in representing the environment using images, language, or other kinds of symbols. Consequently, infants have no awareness of objects or people that are not immediately present at a given moment, lacking what Piaget calls **object permanence.** Object permanence is the awareness that objects—and people—continue to exist even if they are out of sight.

How can we know that children lack object permanence? Although we cannot ask infants, we can observe their reactions when a toy that they are playing with is hidden under a blanket. Until the age of about 9 months, children will make no attempt to locate the toy. However, soon after this age they will begin to search actively for the object when it is hidden, indicating that they have developed a mental representation of the toy. Object permanence, then, is a critical development during the sensorimotor stage.

Preoperational Stage: Two to Seven Years

preoperational stage: According to Piaget, the period from 2 to 7 years of age that is characterized by language development

The most important development during the **preoperational stage** is the use of language, described in more detail in Chapter 7. Children develop internal representational systems that allow them to describe people, events, and feelings. They even use symbols in play, pretending, for example, that a book pushed across the floor is a car.

egocentric thought: A way of thinking in which the child views the world entirely from his or her own perspective

Although children's thinking is more advanced in this stage than it was in the earlier sensorimotor stage, it is still qualitatively inferior to that of adults. We see this when we observe the preoperational child engrossed in **egocentric thought,** a way of thinking in which the child views the world entirely from his or her own perspective. Preoperational children think that everyone shares their own perspective and knowledge. Thus, children's stories and explanations to adults can be maddeningly uninformative, as they are described without any context. For example, a preoperational child may start a story with "He wouldn't let me go," neglecting to mention who "he" is or where the storyteller wanted to go. Egocentric thinking is also seen when children at the preoperational stage play hiding games. For instance, 3-year-olds frequently hide with their faces against a wall, covering their eyes—although they are still in plain view. It seems to them that if *they* cannot see, no one else will be able to see them, since they assume that others share their view.

principle of conservation: The knowledge that quantity is unrelated to the arrangement and physical appearance of objects

Another deficiency of preoperational children is demonstrated by their inability to understand the **principle of conservation,** which is the knowledge that quantity is unrelated to the arrangement and physical appearance of objects. Children who have not

Type of conservation	Modality	Change in physical appearance	Average age of full mastery
Number	Number of elements in a collection	Rearranging or dislocating elements	6–7
Substance (mass)	Amount of a malleable substance (e.g., clay or liquid)	Altering shape	7–8
Length	Length of a line or object	Altering shape or configuration	7–8
Area	Amount of surface covered by a set of plane figures	Rearranging the figures	8–9
Weight	Weight of an object	Altering shape	9–10
Volume	Volume of an object (in terms of water displacement)	Altering shape	14–15

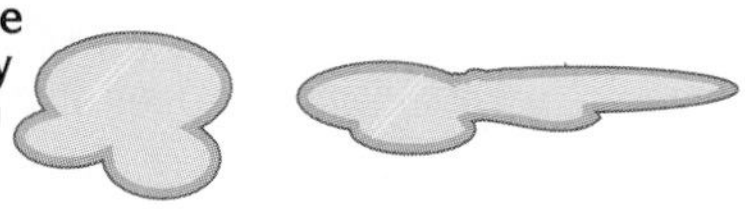

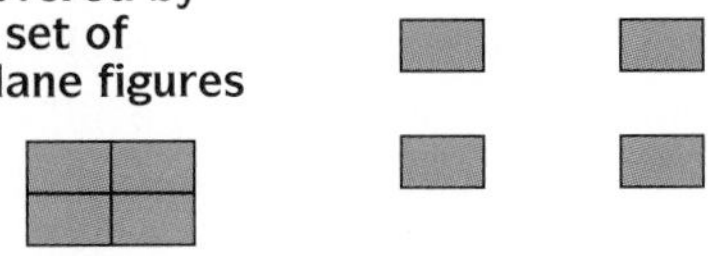

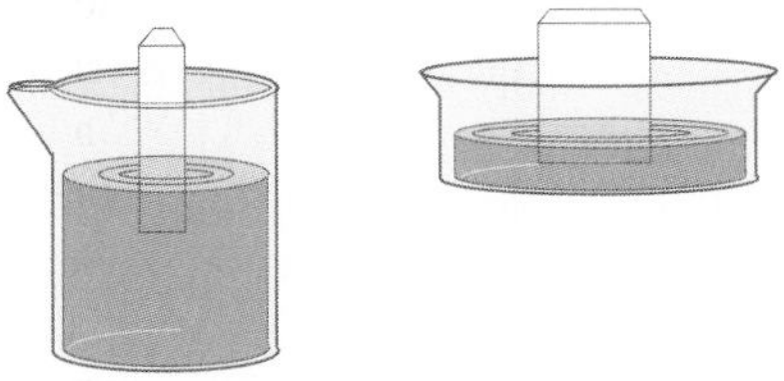

FIGURE 10-5 *These tests are among those used most frequently to assess whether children have learned the principle of conservation across a variety of dimensions.*

mastered this concept do not know that the amount, volume, or length of an object does not change when its shape or configuration is changed. The question about the two glasses—one short and broad, the other tall and thin—with which we began our discussion of cognitive development illustrates this point quite clearly. Children who do not understand the principle of conservation invariably state that the amount of liquid changes as it is poured back and forth. They cannot comprehend that a transformation in appearance does not imply a transformation in amount. Instead, it seems just as reasonable to the child that there is a change in quantity as it does to the adult that there is no change.

Preoperational Cognitive Development

There are a number of other ways, some quite startling, in which their failure to understand the principle of conservation affects children's responses. Research demonstrates that principles that are obvious and unquestioned by adults may be completely misunderstood by children during the preoperational period, and that it is not until the next stage of cognitive development that children grasp the concept of conservation. (Several examples of conservation are illustrated in Figure 10-5.)

Concrete Operational Stage: Seven to Twelve Years

concrete operational stage:
According to Piaget, the period from 7 to 12 years of age that is characterized by logical thought and a loss of egocentrism

The beginning of the **concrete operational stage** is marked by mastery of the principle of conservation. However, there are still some aspects of conservation—such as conservation of weight and volume—that are not fully understood for a number of years.

During the concrete operational stage, children develop the ability to think in a more logical manner, and they begin to overcome some of the egocentrism characteristic of the preoperational period. One of the major principles that children are able to grasp during this stage is reversibility, the idea that some changes can be undone by reversing an earlier action. For example, they can understand that when a ball of clay is rolled into a long sausage shape, it is possible to recreate the original ball by reversing the action. They can even conceptualize this principle in their heads, without having to see the action performed before them.

Although children make important advances in their logical capabilities during the concrete operational stage, there is still one major limitation in their thinking: They are largely bound to the concrete, physical reality of the world. For the most part, they have difficulty understanding questions of an abstract or hypothetical nature.

Formal Operational Stage: Twelve Years to Adulthood

formal operational stage:
According to Piaget, the period from age 12 to adulthood that is characterized by abstract thought

The **formal operational stage** produces a new kind of thinking, which is abstract, formal, and logical. Thinking is no longer tied to events that are observed in the environment but makes use of logical techniques to resolve problems.

The emergence of formal operational thinking is illustrated by the way in which children approach the "pendulum problem," devised by Piaget (Piaget & Inhelder, 1958). The problem solver is asked to figure out what determines how fast a pendulum swings. Is it the length of the string, the weight of the pendulum, or the force with which the pendulum is pushed? (For the record, the answer is the length of the string.)

Children in the concrete operational stage approach the problem haphazardly, without a logical or rational plan of action. For example, they may simultaneously change the length of the string *and* the weight on the string *and* the force with which they push the pendulum. Since they are varying all factors at once, they are unable to tell which factor is the critical one. In contrast, people in the formal operational stage approach the problem systematically. Acting as if they were scientists conducting an experiment, they examine the effects of changes in just one variable at a time. This ability to rule out competing possibilities is characteristic of formal operational thought.

Although formal operational thought emerges during the teenage years, this type of thinking is, in some cases, used only infrequently (Burbules & Linn, 1988). Moreover, it appears that many individuals never reach this stage at all; most studies show that only 40 to 60 percent of college students and adults fully reach it, with some estimates running as low as 25 percent in the general population (Keating & Clark, 1980). In addition, in certain cultures—particularly those that are less technologically sophisticated than most western societies—almost no one reaches the formal operational stage (Chandler, 1976; Super, 1980).

Stages Versus Continuous Development: Is Piaget Right?

No other theorist has given us as comprehensive a theory of cognitive development as Piaget. Still, many contemporary theorists suggest that a better explanation of how children develop cognitively can be provided by theories that do not subscribe to a stage approach. For instance, children are not always consistent in their performance of tasks that—if Piaget's theory were accurate—ought to be performed equally well at a given stage (Siegler, 1994).

Furthermore, some developmental psychologists suggest that cognitive development proceeds in a more continuous fashion than Piaget's stage theory implies. They propose that cognitive development is primarily quantitative in nature, rather than qualitative. They argue that although there are differences in when, how, and to what extent a child is capable of using given cognitive abilities—reflecting quantitative changes—the underlying cognitive processes change relatively little with age (Gelman & Baillargeon, 1983; Case, 1991; Case et al., 1993; Case & Okamoto, 1996).

Another criticism levelled at Piaget is that he underestimated the age at which infants and children are able to understand specific concepts and principles. In fact, they do seem to be more sophisticated in their cognitive abilities than Piaget believed (Tomlinson-Keasey et al., 1979; Bornstein & Sigman, 1986). For instance, recent evidence suggests that infants as young as five months have rudimentary mathematical skills and can calculate the outcome of simple addition and subtraction problems (Wynn, 1992, 1993, 1995).

Despite such criticisms, most developmental psychologists agree that, although the processes that underlie changes in cognitive abilities may not unfold in the manner suggested by his theory, Piaget has generally provided us with an accurate account of age-related changes in cognitive development. Moreover, the influence of his theory has been enormous (Ginsburg & Opper, 1988; Beilin & Pufall, 1992; Demetriou, Shayer, & Efklides, 1993; Siegler & Ellis, 1996). For example, Piaget suggests that increases in cognitive performance cannot be attained unless both cognitive readiness brought about by maturation *and* appropriate environmental stimulation are present. This view has been influential in determining the nature and structure of educational curricula and how children are taught. Piaget's theory and methods have also been used to investigate issues surrounding animal cognition, such as whether primates show object permanence (they seem to); (Gagnon & Dore, 1994; Funk, 1996; Ha, Kimpo, & Sackett, 1997).

Information-Processing Approaches

If cognitive development does not proceed as a series of stages, as Piaget suggested, what *does* underlie the enormous growth in children's cognitive abilities that is apparent to even the most untutored eye? To many developmental psychologists, changes in **information processing**, the way in which people take in, use, and store information, account for cognitive development (Siegler, 1991; Berndt, 1997).

information processing: The way in which people take in, use, and store information

According to this approach, quantitative changes occur in children's ability to organize and manipulate information. From this perspective, children become increasingly adept at information processing, much as a computer program might become more sophisticated as a programmer modifies it on the basis of experience. Information-processing approaches consider the kinds of "mental programs" that children invoke when approaching problems (Siegler, 1989; Mehler & Dupoux, 1994).

Cognitive Development

Several significant changes occur in children's information-processing capabilities. For one thing, speed of processing increases with age, as some abilities become more automatic. The speed at which stimuli can be scanned, recognized, and compared with other stimuli increases with age. With increasing age, children can pay attention to stimuli longer and discriminate between different stimuli more readily, and they are less easily distracted (Jensen & Neff, 1993; Mayr, Kliegl, & Krampe, 1996; Miller & Vernon, 1997).

Memory also improves dramatically with age. You may recall from Chapter 6 that adults are able to keep seven, plus or minus two, chunks of information in short-term memory. In contrast, preschoolers can hold only two or three chunks; 5-year-olds can hold four; and 7-year-olds can hold five. The size of chunks also grows with age, as does the sophistication and organization of knowledge stored in memory (Bjorklund, 1985; Ornstein & Naus, 1988). Still, memory capabilities are impressive at a very early age: Even before they can speak, infants can remember for months events in which they were active participants, according to recent research (Rovee-Collier, 1993; Myers, Perris, & Speaker, 1994; Bauer, 1996).

Finally, improvement in information processing is tied to advances in **metacognition**, an awareness and understanding of one's own cognitive processes. Metacogni-

metacognition: An awareness and understanding of one's own cognitive processes

tion involves the planning, monitoring, and revising of cognitive strategies. Younger children, who lack an awareness of their own cognitive processes, are often ignorant of their incapabilities. Thus, when they misunderstand others, they may fail to recognize their own errors. It is only later, when metacognitive abilities become more sophisticated, that children are able to know when they *don't* understand. Such increasing sophistication reflects a change in children's *theory of mind*, their knowledge and beliefs about the way the mind operates (Flavell, 1993; Bartsch & Estes, 1996; Chandler & Lalonde, 1996; Taylor, 1996).

Vygotsky's View of Cognitive Development: Considering Culture

Vygotsky's Approach to Cognitive Development

According to Russian developmental psychologist Lev Vygotsky, the culture in which we are raised has an important influence on our cognitive development. In an increasingly influential view, Vygotsky suggests that the focus on individual performance (found in both Piagetian and information-processing approaches) is misplaced. Instead, he holds that we cannot understand cognitive development without taking into account the social aspects of learning (Vygotsky, 1979, 1926/1997; Wertsch & Tulviste, 1992; Beilin, 1996; Daniels, 1996).

Vygotsky argues that cognitive development occurs as a consequence of social interactions in which children work with others to jointly solve problems. Through such interactions, children's cognitive skills increase, and they gain the ability to function intellectually on their own. More specifically, Vygotsky suggests that children's cognitive abilities increase when they are exposed to information that falls within their zone of proximal development. The **zone of proximal development,** or **ZPD,** is the level at which a child can almost, but not fully, comprehend or perform a task on his or her own. When children encounter information that falls within the ZPD, they are able to increase their understanding or master a new task. On the other hand, if the information lies outside children's ZPD, they will not be able to master it (Belmont, 1995).

zone of proximal development (ZPD): According to Vygotsky, the level at which a child can almost, but not fully, comprehend or perform a task on his or her own

In short, cognitive development occurs when parents, teachers, or skilled peers assist the child by presenting information that is both new and within the ZPD (Rogoff, 1990; Steward, 1995). This type of assistance is called *scaffolding*, the support for learning and problem solving that encourages independence and growth (Bruner, 1983). Vygotsky claims that scaffolding not only promotes the solution of specific problems, it also aids in the development of overall cognitive abilities.

More than other approaches to cognitive development, Vygotsky's theory considers how the specific cultural and social context of society affects intellectual growth. The way in which children understand the world is seen as an outgrowth of interactions with parents, peers, and other members of a given culture. Furthermore, as we see next, cultural influences on cognitive development also result in significant differences in scholastic success.

Exploring Diversity

Understanding Children's School Achievement: Science, Mathematics, and Spelling

By the time that they complete public school, most students know whether they are good at mathematics or science or spelling. Those who are proficient in these subject areas will likely have more choices in high school, college, university, and employment than students who are not.

A dedicated group of psychologists in the Centre for Research in Child Development, at the University of Alberta, are studying scientific literacy (Gay Bisanz and Jeffrey Bisanz), mathematical thinking (Jeffrey Bisanz), and spelling literacy (Connie Varnhagen). They, along with other colleagues, are interested in understanding

Children's ability to critically evaluate the information that they receive from many media sources is a skill learned both in and out of school.

the cognitive processes and social forces that contribute to proficiency in these subject areas.

In the area of scientific literacy, research focuses on how media reports of scientific research are understood and interpreted by children and adolescents. What skills are employed in order to understand scientific information? The researchers believe that the ability to question information effectively is dependent on the science education that has been received. This ability translates into being an informed consumer at both a personal and societal level (Korpan et al. 1997a). Research also investigates how young children are exposed to science information outside of school, in family, or play related activity. (Korpan et al. 1997b). The hope is to translate this knowledge into improved science education.

Cognitive development in mathematical thinking is examined in children and adults. Strategies used by both good and poor math students have been examined. Research has shown that children as young as five can invent and use "computational shortcuts" which many adults are unable to do (Bisanz, 1999a, Bisanz, 1999b). Studies are also underway to identify the role of culture and types of schooling as they relate to ability in mathematics. Again this understanding of how children do math may help contribute to new ways to teach the subject. It may also provide knowledge about how a curriculum might be altered to accommodate learners with different ability levels.

Examining how children spell by identifying the strategies that they use has led Connie Varnhagen (1997) and colleagues to believe that rather than employing a specific strategy based on age and cognitive development, children employ strategies that are related to whether they are able to spell the word. Like the work on science and mathematics, the work on spelling may well provide more effective ways to teach spelling and therefore improve literacy. ■

Recap, Review, and Rethink

Recap

- The neonate is born with a number of reflexes, including the rooting, sucking, startle, and Babinski reflexes.

- Physical growth is initially rapid: During the first year, children typically triple their birth weight, and height increases by 50 percent. Rate of growth declines after age 3, averaging about 2.5 kilos and 7.5 centimetres a year until adolescence.

- The perceptual abilities of infants grow rapidly, although they are remarkably sophisticated at birth.

- Social development is demonstrated through the growth of attachment, the positive emotional bond that develops between a child and a particular individual. As a child ages, relationships with friends become increasingly important.

- Parents generally use one of three main parenting styles: authoritarian, permissive, and authoritative. In North American culture, the authoritative style seems most effective and appears to produce the best behaviour in children.

- Erikson's theory suggests that there are four stages of psychosocial development within childhood, with four other stages spanning the rest of life.

- The major theory of cognitive development—the way in which children's understanding of the world changes as a function of age and experience—is Piaget's theory. Piaget proposes four major stages: sensorimotor, preoperational, concrete operational, and formal operational.

- Although Piaget's description of what happens within the various stages of cognitive development has largely been upheld, some theorists argue that development is more gradual and continuous and due more to quantitative than to qualitative changes in cognition.

- Information-processing approaches to cognitive development focus on the quantitative changes that occur in the way in which people take in, use, and store information. Major changes occur with age in speed of processing, length of attention span, memory, and metacognitive abilities.

- Vygotsky's approach maintains that cognitive development occurs through social interactions in which children and others jointly pose and solve problems that are within the child's zone of proximal development.

Review

1. Researchers studying newborns use _____, or the decrease in the response to a stimulus that occurs after repeated presentations of the same stimulus, as an indicator of a baby's interest.

2. The emotional bond that develops between a child and its caregiver is known as _____.

3. Children develop an attachment to their mothers only; the father's role is important, but children do not become attached to their fathers. True or false?

4. Match the parenting style with its definition.
   1. permissive
   2. authoritative
   3. authoritarian

   a. rigid; highly punitive; demand obedience
   b. give little direction; lax on obedience
   c. firm but fair; try to explain their decisions

5. Similar child-rearing styles have been documented around the world. True or false?

6. Erikson's theory of _____ development involves a series of eight stages, each of which must be resolved in order for a person to develop optimally.

7. _____ suggested four stages of cognitive development, each of which is dependent on maturational and environmental factors.

8. Match the stage of development with the thinking style characteristic of the stage.
   1. egocentric thought
   2. object permanence
   3. abstract reasoning
   4. conservation; reversibility

   a. sensorimotor
   b. formal operational
   c. peroperational
   d. concrete operational

9. Current research suggests that child development may proceed in a continuous fashion, rather than in stages as suggested by Piaget. True or false?

10. _____ theories of development suggest that the way in which a child handles information is critical to his or her development.

11. According to Vygotsky, information that is within a child's _____ _____ _____ _____ is most likely to result in cognitive development.

Answer to Review Questions are on page 384.

Rethink

1. In what ways might the infant's major reflexes—the rooting, sucking, gagging, and Babinski reflexes—have had survival value, from an evolutionary perspective? Does the infant's ability to mimic the facial expressions of adults have a similar value?

2. Do you think the growing trend toward greater parental involvement by fathers will have effects on the child-rearing styles to which children are exposed? Will it affect attachment? Psychosocial development? Why or why not?

3. According to Piaget's theory, a child must have reached a certain level of maturity before particular kinds of information can be learned. Do you think that there could be any advantages to exposing a child to more complex material at an early age? What might information-processing theory have to say about this?

4. It is stated in this chapter that "even before they can speak, infants can remember for months events in which they were active participants." Knowing what you do about research involving infants, how might researchers have studied this question?

ADOLESCENCE: BECOMING AN ADULT

▶ **What major physical, social, and cognitive transitions characterize adolescence?**

Turning 13 was an important period of my life. It was the time when I started to mature physically. It also was the time when more girls started to notice me. My personality changed a lot from a boring nerd to an energetic, funny, and athletic kid.

As my year went on as a 13-year-old, as if things couldn't get better, they surprisingly did! My life as a child had ended. I was now a teenager. This just goes to show you that turning 13 meant turning into a new person.

Patrick Backer (1993, p. 2)

As you go to school, things get harder. You sort of realize that you're getting older. Adults treat you like an adult and don't give you the breaks you got when you're a child.

To be 13 you have journeyed only half way to the *real* world. Then you notice that you're going to high school and think of the next four years and then college. Next you vote, a house, job and kids. It seems your life passes right before your eyes.

Mieko Ozeki (1993, p. 2)

When I turned 13 it was like starting a new life. It was the year I was finally going to be allowed to do more things. For one thing I was able to hang out later. I wasn't a child anymore. I knew it and my parents knew it, too.

I really can't think of a more important birthday besides your first one.

Dmitri Ponomarev (1993, p. 2)

As these essays indicate, the thirteenth birthday has a significance that extends beyond simply marking the passage of another year. Instead, for many people, it is a moment that signifies the transition into adolescence.

Adolescence, the developmental stage between childhood and adulthood, is a critical period. It is a time of profound changes and, occasionally, turmoil. Considerable biological change occurs as adolescents attain sexual and physical maturity. At the same time, these physiological changes are rivaled by important social, emotional, and cognitive changes that occur as adolescents strive for independence and move toward adulthood.

adolescence: The developmental stage between childhood and adulthood

Because many years of schooling precede most people's entry into the workforce in western society, the stage of adolescence is a fairly lengthy one, beginning just before the teenage years and ending just after them. No longer children, but considered by society to be not quite adults, adolescents face a period of rapid physical, cognitive, and social change that affects them for the rest of their lives.

Adolescents' development is also affected by dramatic transformations in society. Many of Canada's children will spend some of their childhood or adolescence in single-parent families, and by age 16 many adolescents will witness the divorce or remarriage of their parents. Furthermore, adolescents spend considerably less time with their parents, and more with their peers, than they did several decades ago. Finally, the ethnic and cultural diversity of adolescents is increasing dramatically. These societal changes are sure to impact the transition from childhood to adulthood in significant ways (Dreman, 1997).

Adolescent Studies

Physical Development: The Changing Adolescent

If you think back to the start of your own adolescence, it is likely that the most dramatic changes you remember are of a physical nature. A spurt in height, the growth of breasts in girls, deepening voices in boys, the development of body hair, and intense sexual feelings are a source of curiosity, interest, and sometimes embarrassment for individuals entering adolescence.

The physical changes that occur at the start of adolescence are largely a result of the secretion of various hormones (see Chapter 2), and they affect virtually every aspect of the adolescent's life. Not since infancy has development been so dramatic. Weight and height increase rapidly due to a growth spurt that begins at around age 10 for girls and age 12 for boys. Adolescents may grow as much as 12.5 centimetres in one year.

Puberty, the period at which maturation of the sexual organs occurs, begins at about age 11 or 12 for girls and 13 or 14 for boys. However, there are wide variations, and it is not uncommon for a girl to begin to menstruate—the first sign of sexual maturity in females—as early as age 8 or 9 or as late as age 16. In both boys and girls, sexual *attraction* to others begins even before the maturation of the sexual organs, at around the age of 10 (Eveleth & Tanner, 1976; Tanner, 1990; McClintock & Herdt, 1996).

puberty: The period at which maturation of the sexual organs occurs, begins at about age 11 or 12 for girls and 13 or 14 for boys

Significant cultural and situational variations occur in the timing of first menstruation. For example, the average Lumi girl in New Guinea does not begin menstruating until she is 18. In western cultures, the average age at which adolescents reach sexual maturity has been steadily decreasing over the last century, most likely a result of improved nutrition and medical care (Dreyer, 1982). In fact, in all regions of the world, girls living in affluent homes begin to menstruate at an earlier age than those from economically disadvantaged homes. The onset of puberty, then, provides a good illustration of how changes in the environment interact with heredity to affect development.

The age at which puberty begins has important implications for the way adolescents feel about themselves—as well as how others treat them. Early-maturing boys have a distinct advantage over later-maturing boys. They do better in athletics, are generally more popular with peers, and have more positive self-concepts (Peterson, 1985). On the other hand, they are more likely to have difficulties at school, to commit minor acts of delinquency, and to become involved with alcohol abuse. One reason for such behaviour seems to be that early-maturing boys are more likely to become friends with older, and therefore more influential, boys, who may lead them into age-inappropriate activities. On balance, though, the consequences of early maturation for boys are basically positive; early maturers, compared to later maturers, are typically somewhat more responsible and cooperative in later life (Duncan et al., 1985; Anderson & Magnusson, 1990).

The picture is different for girls. Although early-maturing girls are more sought after as dates and have better self-esteem than later-maturing girls, some of the consequences of their early physical maturation may be less positive. For example, the development of such obvious characteristics as breasts may set them apart from their peers and be a source of ridicule (Simmons & Blyth, 1987; Ge, Conger, & Elder, 1996).

Late maturation also produces certain psychological difficulties. Boys who are smaller and less coordinated than their more mature peers tend to be ridiculed and seen as less attractive. In time, they may come to view themselves in the same way. The consequences of late maturation may extend well into a male's thirties (Mussen & Jones, 1957). Similarly, late-maturing girls are at a disadvantage in high school. They hold relatively low social status, and they may be overlooked in dating and other male-female activities (Apter et al., 1981; Clarke-Stewart & Friedman, 1987).

Clearly, the rate at which physical changes occur during adolescence can have significant effects on the ways in which people are viewed by others and the ways in which they view themselves. Just as important as physical changes, however, are the psychological and social changes that unfold during adolescence.

Moral and Cognitive Development: Distinguishing Right from Wrong

In Europe, a woman is near death from a special kind of cancer. The one drug that the doctors think might save her is a form of radium that a druggist in the same town has recently discovered. The drug is expensive to make, and the druggist is charging ten times the cost, or $2,000, for a small dose. The sick woman's husband, Heinz, approaches everyone he knows in hopes of borrowing money, but he can get together only about $1,000. He tells the druggist that his wife is dying and asks him to lower the price of the drug or let him pay later. The druggist says, "No, I discovered the drug and I'm going to make money from it." Heinz is desperate and considers breaking into the man's store to steal the drug for his wife.

What would you tell Heinz to do?

Kohlberg's Theory of Moral Development

In the view of psychologist Lawrence Kohlberg, the advice you give Heinz is a reflection of your level of moral development. According to Kohlberg, people pass through a series of stages in the evolution of their sense of justice and in the kind of reasoning they use to make moral judgments (Kohlberg, 1984). Largely because of the various cognitive deficits that Piaget described, preadolescent children tend to think either in terms of concrete, unvarying rules ("It is always wrong to steal" or "I'll be punished if I steal") or in terms of the rules of society ("Good people don't steal" or "What if everyone stole?").

Although moral development generally advances during adolescence, there are significant differences among adolescents in the stage of moral reasoning and behaviour that they have achieved.

Adolescents, however, are capable of reasoning on a higher plane, having typically reached Piaget's formal operational stage of cognitive development. Because they are able to comprehend broad moral principles, they can understand that morality is not always black and white and that conflict can exist between two sets of socially accepted standards.

Kohlberg (1984) suggests that the changes occurring in moral reasoning can be understood best as a three-level sequence, with each level divided into two stages. These three levels and six stages, along with samples of subjects' reasoning at each stage, are described in Table 10-5. Note that arguments either in favor of or against stealing the drug can be classified as belonging to the same stage of moral reasoning. It is the nature and sophistication of the argument that determine the category into which it falls.

Kohlberg's theory assumes that people move through the six stages in a fixed order, and that they are not capable of reaching the highest stage until about the age of 13—primarily because of deficits in cognitive development that are not overcome until that age. However, many people never reach the highest level of moral reasoning. In fact, Kohlberg suggests that only about 25 percent of all adults rise above stage 4 of his model (Kohlberg & Ryncarz, 1990).

Cultural Universals

Extensive research has shown that the stages identified by Kohlberg generally provide a valid representation of moral development. Yet the research also raises several methodological issues. One major problem is that Kohlberg's procedure measures moral *judgments*, not *behaviour*. Although Kohlberg's theory seems to be a generally accurate account of how moral reasoning develops, some research finds that moral reasoning is not always related to moral behaviour (Snarey, 1985; Malinowski & Smith, 1985; Damon, 1988; Straughan, 1994). At the same time, other investigators suggest that a relationship between moral judgments and behaviour does exist. For example, students who are most likely to commit acts of civil disobedience are those whose moral judgments are at the highest levels (Candee & Kohlberg, 1987). Still, the evidence is mixed on this question; knowing right from wrong does not mean that we will always act in accordance with our judgments (Darley & Shultz, 1990; Thoma, Rest, & Davison, 1991; Killen & Hart, 1995; Coles, 1997).

Moral Development in Women

Psychologist Carol Gilligan (1982, 1987, 1993) has identified an important shortcoming of Kohlberg's original research: It was carried out using only male subjects and is thus more applicable to men than to women. Furthermore, she argues convincingly that because of their distinctive socialization experiences, a fundamental difference exists in the manner in which men and women view moral behaviour. According to Gilligan, men view morality primarily in terms of broad principles, such as justice and fairness. In contrast, women see it in terms of responsibility toward individuals and willingness to make sacrifices to help a specific individual within the context of a par-

Table 10-5	Kohlberg's Levels of Moral Reasoning

		Sample Moral Reasoning of Subjects	
Level	Stage	In Favour of Stealing	Against Stealing
Level 1 Preconventional morality: At this level, the concrete interests of the individual are considered in terms of rewards and punishments.	*Stage 1* Obedience and punishment orientation: At this stage, people stick to rules in order to avoid punishment, and obedience occurs for its own sake.	"If you let your wife die, you will get in trouble. You'll be blamed for not spending the money to save her, and there'll be an investigation of you and the druggist for your wife's death."	"You shouldn't steal the drug because you'll be caught and sent to jail if you do. If you do get away, your conscience will bother you thinking how the police will catch up with you at any minute."
	Stage 2 Reward orientation: At this stage, rules are followed only for a person's own benefit. Obedience occurs because of rewards that are received.	"If you do happen to get caught, you could give the drug back and you wouldn't get much of a sentence. It wouldn't bother you much to serve a little jail term, if you have your wife when you get out."	"You may not get much of a jail term if you steal the drug, but your wife will probably die before you get out, so it won't do much good. If your wife dies, you shouldn't blame yourself; it isn't your fault she has cancer."
Level 2 Conventional morality: At this level, people approach moral problems as members of society. They are interested in pleasing others by acting as good members of society.	*Stage 3* "Good boy" morality: Individuals at this stage show an interest in maintaining the respect of others and doing what is expected of them.	"No one will think you're bad if you steal the drug, but your family will think you're an inhuman husband if you don't. If you let your wife die, you'll never be able to look anybody in the face again."	"It isn't just the druggist who will think you're a criminal; everyone else will too. After you steal the drug, you'll feel bad thinking how you've brought dishonor on your family and yourself; you won't be able to face anyone again."
	Stage 4 Authority and social-order-maintaining morality: People at this stage conform to society's rules and consider that "right" is what society defines as right.	"If you have any sense of honour, you won't let your wife die just because you're afraid to do the only thing that will save her. You'll always feel guilty that you caused her death if you don't do your duty to her."	"You're desperate and you may not know you're doing wrong when you steal the drug. But you'll know you did wrong after you're sent to jail. You'll always feel guilty for your dishonesty and lawbreaking."
Level 3 Postconventional morality: At this level, people use moral principles which are seen as broader than those of any particular society.	*Stage 5* Morality of contract, individuals rights, and democratically accepted law: People at this stage do what is right because of a sense of obligation to laws which are agreed upon within society. They perceive that laws can be modified as part of changes in an implicit social contract.	"You'll lose other people's respect, not gain it, if you don't steal. If you let your wife die, it will be out of fear, not out of reasoning. So you'll just lose self-respect and probably the respect of others too."	"You'll lose your standing and respect in the community and violate the law. You'll lose respect for yourself if you're carried away by emotion and forget the long-range point of view."
	Stage 6 Morality of individual principles and conscience: At this final stage, a person follows laws because they are based on universal ethical principles. Laws that violate the principles are disobeyed.	"If you don't steal the drug, and if you let your wife die, you'll always condemn yourself for it afterward. You won't be blamed and you'll have lived up to the outside rule of the law but you won't have lived up to your own standards of conscience."	"If you steal the drug, you won't be blamed by other people, but you'll condemn yourself because you won't have lived up to your own conscience and standards of honesty."

ticular relationship. Compassion for individuals is a more salient factor in moral behaviour for women than it is for men (Gilligan, Ward, & Taylor, 1988; Gilligan, Lyons, & Hanmer, 1990).

Consequently, because Kohlberg's model conceives of moral behaviour largely in terms of abstract principles such as justice and fairness, it is inadequate in describ-

Table 10-6	Gilligan's Stages of Moral Development	
Stage	**Major Characteristics**	**Samples of Reasoning Used by Women Contemplating Having an Abortion**
Stage 1 Orientation toward individual survival	Focus on what is practical, best for self; concern for survival	Having a baby would prevent her "from doing other things" but would be "the perfect chance to move away from home."
Stage 2 Goodness as self-sacrifice	Sacrifice of own wishes to help others	"I think what confuses me is a choice of either hurting myself or hurting other people around me. What is more important?"
Stage 3 Morality of nonviolence	Hurting anyone, including oneself, is immoral	"The decision has got to be, first of all, something that the woman can live with . . . and it must be based on where she is at and other significant people in her life are."

ing the moral development of females. This factor accounts for the puzzling finding that women typically score at a lower level than men on tests of moral judgment using Kohlberg's stage sequence. In Gilligan's view, women's morality is centred on individual well-being and social relationships rather than on moral abstractions. For this reason, she maintains that the highest levels of morality are represented by compassionate concern for the welfare of others.

According to Gilligan's research, which investigated moral dilemmas such as deciding whether to have an abortion, women's moral development proceeds in three stages (see Table 10-6). In the first stage, termed "orientation toward individual survival," a woman concentrates on what is practical and best for her. During this stage, there is a transition from selfishness to responsibility, in which the woman thinks about what would be best for others.

At the second stage of moral development, termed "goodness as self-sacrifice," a woman begins to think that she must sacrifice her own wishes for the sake of what other people want. Ultimately, though, she makes the transition from "goodness" to "truth," in which she takes into account her own needs plus those of others. In the third stage, "morality of nonviolence," a woman comes to see that hurting anyone is immoral—including hurting herself. This realization establishes a moral equality between herself and others and represents, according to Gilligan, the most sophisticated level of moral reasoning.

As you can see, Gilligan's sequence of stages is very different from that presented by Kohlberg, and some psychologists have suggested that her rejection of Kohlberg's work is too sweeping (Colby & Damon, 1987). Other research has questioned whether there is a difference in the development of men's and women's morality (Hoff-Sommers, 2000). Lawrence Walker of the University of British Columbia (1984) examined over eighty studies, which included 108 samples with over 8,000 subjects. These studies were chosen because they included both males and females and were examining sex differences in moral reasoning. Included are some of Gilligan's studies. In his conclusion Walker states "… contrary to the prevailing stereotype, very few sex differences in moral development have been found" (p. 688). Concerns raised by Hoff-Sommers (2000) have opened a dialogue between her and Carol Gilligan (*The Atlantic Monthly*, August 2000). The controversy will undoubtedly continue.

Moral Development

Social Development: Finding Oneself in a Social World

"Who am I?" "How do I fit into the world?" "What is life all about?"

| Table 10-7 | A Summary of Erikson's Stages |

Stage	Approximate Age	Positive Outcomes	Negative Outcomes
1. Trust-vs.-mistrust	Birth–1½ years	Feelings of trust from environmental support	Fear and concern regarding others
2. Autonomy-vs.-shame-and-doubt	1½–3 years	Self-sufficiency if exploration is encouraged	Doubts about self, lack of independence
3. Initiative-vs.-guilt	3–6 years	Discovery of ways to initiate actions	Guilt from actions and thoughts
4. Industry-vs.-inferiority	6–12 years	Development of sense of competence	Feelings of inferiority, no sense of mastery
5. Identity-vs.-role-confusion	Adolescence	Awareness of uniqueness of self, knowledge of role to be followed	Inability to identify appropriate roles in life
6. Intimacy-vs.-isolation	Early adulthood	Development of loving, sexual relationships and close friendships	Fear of relationships with others
7. Generativity-vs.-stagnation	Middle adulthood	Sense of contribution to continuity of life	Trivialization of one's activities
8. Ego-integrity-vs.-despair	Late adulthood	Sense of unity in life's accomplishments	Regret over lost opportunities of life

Questions such as these assume particular significance during the teenage years, as adolescents seek to find their place in the broader social world. As we will see, this quest takes adolescents along several routes.

Erikson's Theory of Psychosocial Development: The Search for Identity

Erikson's theory of psychosocial development emphasizes the search for identity during the adolescent years. As noted earlier, psychosocial development encompasses how people's understanding of themselves, one another, and the world around them changes during the course of development (Erikson, 1963).

The fifth stage of Erikson's theory (summarized, with the other stages, in Table 10-7) is labelled the **identity-versus-role confusion stage** and encompasses adolescence. This stage is a time of major testing, as people try to determine what is unique and special about themselves. They attempt to discover who they are, what their strengths are, and what kinds of roles they are best suited to play for the rest of their lives—in short, their **identity**. Confusion over the most appropriate role to follow in life can lead to lack of a stable identity, adoption of a socially unacceptable role such as that of a social deviant, or difficulty in maintaining close personal relationships later in life (Kahn et al., 1985; Archer & Waterman, 1994; Kidwell et al., 1995).

During the identity-versus-role-confusion period, pressures to identify what one wants to do with one's life are acutely felt. Because these pressures come at a time of major physical changes as well as important changes in what society expects of them, adolescents can find the period a particularly difficult one. The identity-versus-role-confusion stage has another important characteristic: a decline in reliance on adults for information, with a shift toward using the peer group as a source of social judgments. The peer group becomes increasingly important, enabling adolescents to form close, adultlike relationships and helping them to clarify their personal identities.

According to Erikson, the identity-versus-role-confusion stage during adolescence marks a pivotal point in psychosocial development, paving the way for continued growth and the future development of personal relationships. For instance, during college, people move into the **intimacy-versus-isolation stage** (spanning the period of

identity-versus-role-confusion stage: According to Erikson, a time in adolescence of testing to determine one's unique qualities

identity: The distinguishing character of the individual: who each of us is, what our roles are, and what we are capable of

intimacy-versus-isolation stage: According to Erikson, a period during early adulthood that focuses on developing close relationships

The attitudes of a girl's peer group can influence her reaction to early maturation.

early adulthood, from around age 18 to age 30), in which the focus is on developing close relationships with others. Difficulties during this stage result in feelings of loneliness and a fear of relationships with others, while successful resolution of the crises of the stage results in the possibility of forming relationships that are intimate on a physical, intellectual, and emotional level.

Development continues during middle adulthood as people enter the **generativity-versus-stagnation stage**. Generativity refers to a person's contribution to his or her family, community, work, and society as a whole. Success in this stage results in positive feelings about the continuity of life, while difficulties lead to feelings of triviality regarding one's activities and a sense of stagnation or of having done nothing for upcoming generations. In fact, if a person has not successfully resolved the identity crisis of adolescence, he or she may still be floundering as far as identifying an appropriate career is concerned.

Finally, the last stage of psychosocial development, the period of **ego-integrity-versus-despair**, comprises later adulthood and continues until death. Success in resolving the difficulties presented by this stage of life is signified by a sense of accomplishment; difficulties result in regret over what might have been achieved, but was not.

One of the most noteworthy aspects of Erikson's theory is its suggestion that development does not stop at adolescence but continues throughout adulthood, a view that a substantial amount of research now confirms (Peterson & Stewart, 1993; Hetherington & Weinberger, 1993; Mansfield & McAdams, 1996; McAdams et al., 1997). For instance, a twenty-two-year study by psychologist Susan Whitbourne found considerable support for the fundamentals of Erikson's theory, determining that psychosocial development continues through adolescence and adulthood (Whitbourne et al., 1992). In sum, adolescence is not an endpoint but rather a way station on the path of psychosocial development.

Stormy Adolescence: Myth or Reality?

Does puberty invariably foreshadow a stormy, rebellious period of adolescence? At one time most children entering adolescence were thought to be beginning a period fraught with stress and unhappiness, but psychologists are now finding that this characterization is largely a myth. Most young people, it seems, pass through adolescence

generativity-versus-stagnation stage: According to Erikson, a period in middle adulthood during which we take stock of our contributions to family and society

ego-integrity-versus-despair stage: According to Erikson, a period from late adulthood until death during which we review life's accomplishments and failures

Pathways Through Psychology

Lorrie K Sippola

Assistant Professor, University of Saskatchewan
Academic Coordinator, RESOLVE Saskatchewan (Research and Education for Solutions to Violence) University of Saskatchewan

Education: B.A. M.A. Ph.D. Concordia University, Montreal

Home: Saskatoon, Saskatchewan

My interest in adolescent development stems primarily from earlier intervention work with young offenders and, later, with adult male sexual offenders in the criminal justice system. At that time, clinical literature suggested that early developmental challenges were contributing factors to criminal behaviour and sexual deviance. From my perspective, then, it made sense to work from a preventative model, which focused on understanding the factors contributing to development of a particular outcome. This perspective is in contrast to an intervention model that focuses on treating outcome after onset. From my clinical experiences, adolescence appeared to be a crucial stage of development for various behaviours. In particular, relationships during this period of development seemed to provide a window of opportunity for change. From my own observations, positive relational experiences in adolescence seemed to provide opportunities to repair damage from earlier experiences. Alternatively, challenging relationships during this time seemed to

Lorrie Sippola and Kita

contribute to the onset of particular problems. The road to my current career was not a straight path with clearly defined goals and aspirations. But, eventually, these ideas lead me to study the role of interpersonal relationships in adolescent development.

Currently, we know little about the development of healthy, intimate relationships between romantic partners. Much of the research in the area has focused on factors predicting early onset of intercourse or teenage pregnancy. I'm interested in extending this work by examining platonic but emotionally engaged relationships between boys and girls and how these relationships change over time. To do this, students in my lab and I

pursue the following questions: What are the features of adolescent cross-sex friendships? How are these relationships similar to and different from relationships with same-sex peers? How does gender influence adolescents' experience of cross-sex relationships and how do cross-sex relationships influence adolescents' understanding of the concept of gender?

The question regarding important accomplishments is a difficult one to answer. I guess the obvious ones would be winning awards for my dissertation, receiving a post-doctoral fellowship to continue my training at Radcliffe College at Harvard University, and recently receiving external funding for two longitudinal projects that are currently ongoing in Saskatoon. These awards reflect recognition for my research from my peers. This is always satisfying. However, I have recently become involved in a research project at an inner-city high school. Sharing my research skills to address questions raised by the teachers, guidance counsellors, and social workers at the school has been most rewarding. These educators have taught me a great deal about how basic, developmental science can be used to address real-world problems. This has been an important and meaningful personal and professional experience.

Source: Lorrie K. Sippola, Ph.D., University of Saskatchewan
<www.usask.ca/psychology/faculty/lsippola.htm>

without appreciable turmoil in their lives (Petersen, 1988; Steinberg, 1993; Crockett & Crouter, 1995; Petersen, Silbereisen, & Soreson, 1996).

This is not to say that adolescence is completely tranquil (Laursen & Collins, 1994; Eccles, Lord, & Roeser, 1996). In most families, there is clearly a rise in the amount of arguing and bickering that goes on. Young teenagers, as part of their search for identity, tend to experience a degree of tension between their attempts to become independent from their parents and their actual dependence on them. They may experiment with a range of behaviours, flirting with a variety of activities that their parents, and even society as a whole, find objectionable. Happily, though, for the majority of families such tensions tend to stabilize during middle adolescence—around age 15 or 16—and eventually decline around age 18 (Montemayor, 1983; Galambos, 1992; Montemayor, Adams, & Gullotta, 1994).

One reason for the increase in discord during adolescence appears to be the protracted period in which children stay at home with their parents. In prior historical periods—and in some nonwestern cultures today—children leave home immediately after puberty and are considered adults. Today, however, sexually mature adolescents may spend as many as seven or eight years with their parents (Steinberg, 1989). Current statistics even hint at an extension of the conflicts of adolescence beyond the teenage years for a significant number of people. Some one-third of all unmarried men and one-fifth of unmarried women between the ages of 25 and 34 continue to reside with their parents (Gross, 1991).

Adolescence also introduces a variety of stresses outside the home. Starting with the move from elementary to high school, and the relationships with friends and peers, both are particularly volatile (Berndt, 1992; Berndt & Keefe, 1995; Graber, Brooks-Gunn, & Petersen, 1996; Cotterell, 1996; Keefe & Berndt, 1996). Many adolescents hold part-time jobs, increasing the demands of school, work, and social activities on their time. Such stressors can lead to tensions at home. Adolescents from vulnerable and stressed family environments are more at risk for loss of self-esteem than those with more family support (Steinberg & Dornbusch, 1991; Gauze et al, 1996). (See the Pathways Through Psychology box for someone whose work is directly involved with the period of adolescence.)

EARLY AND MIDDLE ADULTHOOD: THE MIDDLE YEARS OF LIFE

Psychologists generally consider early adulthood to begin around age 20 and last until about age 40 to 45, and middle adulthood to last from about age 40 to 45 to around age 65. Despite the enormous importance of these periods of life in terms of both the accomplishments that occur within them and their overall length (together they span some 45 years)—they have been studied less than any other stage by developmental psychologists. One reason is that the physical changes that occur during these periods are less apparent and more gradual than those at other times during the lifespan. In addition, the social changes that arise during this period are so diverse that they defy simple categorization. Still, there has been a recent upsurge of interest in adulthood among developmental psychologists, with a special focus on the effects of social changes on the family, marriage, divorce, and women's careers.

▶ **What are the principal kinds of physical, social, and intellectual changes that occur in early and middle adulthood, and what are their causes?**

Physical Development: The Peak of Health

For most people, early adulthood marks the peak of physical health. From about 18 to 25 years of age, people's strength is greatest, their reflexes are quickest, and their chances of dying from disease are quite slim. Moreover, reproductive capabilities are at their highest level.

The changes that begin at age 25 are largely of a quantitative rather than a qualitative nature. The body begins to operate slightly less efficiently and becomes somewhat more prone to disease. Overall, however, ill health remains the exception; most people stay remarkably healthy. (Can you think of any machine other than the body that can operate without pause for so long a period?)

The major biological change that does occur pertains to reproductive capabilities during middle adulthood. On average, during their late forties or early fifties, women begin **menopause**, the point at which they stop menstruating and are no longer fertile. Because menopause is accompanied by a significant reduction in the production of estrogen, a female hormone, women sometimes experience symptoms such as hot flashes, or sudden sensations of heat. However, most symptoms of menopause can be successfully treated with artificial estrogen, if the symptoms are severe enough to warrant medical intervention.

Menopause was once blamed for a host of psychological symptoms, including depression and memory loss. However, most research now suggests that such

menopause: The point at which women stop menstruating and are no longer fertile

Women's Health

THE FOUR AGES OF MAN

INFANCY   CHILDHOOD   YOUTH   MATURITY

problems, if they do occur, are caused more by women's perceived reactions to reaching an "old" age in a society that highly values youth, rather than by menopause itself.

In fact, researchers have found that women's reactions to menopause vary significantly across cultures. According to anthropologist Yewoubdar Beyene, the more a society values old age, the less difficulty its women have during menopause. In her study of women in Mayan villages, Beyene found that women looked forward to menopause, because they then stopped having children. In addition, they didn't even experience some of the classic symptoms of menopause; hot flashes, for example, were unheard of. A society's attitudes, then, more than the physiological changes of menopause, may produce psychological difficulties (Ballinger, 1981; Beyene, 1989; Beck, 1992; Figueiras & Marteau, 1995).

For men, the aging process during middle adulthood is somewhat subtler. There are no physiological signals of increasing age equivalent to the end of menstruation in women, so no male menopause exists. In fact, men remain fertile and are capable of fathering children until well into old age. On the other hand, some gradual physical declines occur: Sperm production decreases and the frequency of orgasm tends to decline. Once again, though, any psychological difficulties associated with these changes that men may experience are usually brought about not so much by physical deterioration as by the inability of the aging individual to meet the exaggerated standards of youthfulness held in high regard by our society.

Social Development: Working at Life

Whereas physical changes during adulthood reflect development of a quantitative nature, social developmental transitions are more profound. It is during this period that people typically launch themselves into careers, marriage, and families.

According to psychologist Daniel Levinson (1986, 1990, 1996), people pass through several stages from the entry into early adulthood through the end of middle adulthood. During early adulthood, the stages relate to leaving one's family and entering the adult world. An individual envisions what Levinson calls "The Dream"—an all-encompassing vision about the goals that one desires from life, be it writing the great American novel or becoming a physician. People make, and perhaps discard, career choices during early adulthood, until eventually they reach long-term decisions. This leads to a period of settling down in the late thirties, during which people establish themselves in a particular set of roles and begin to develop and work toward a vision of their own future.

In their early forties, people sometimes begin to question their lives as they enter a period called the **midlife transition**, and the idea that life is finite becomes paramount in their thinking. Rather than maintaining a future-oriented view of life, people begin to ask questions about their past accomplishments, assessing what they have done and how satisfying it has been to them (Gould, 1978). They realize that they will not accomplish everything they had hoped to before their life ends.

midlife transition: Beginning around the age of 40, a period during which we come to the realization that life is finite

In some cases, people's assessments of their lives are negative, and they may enter what has been popularly labelled a **midlife crisis**. At the same time that they face signs of physical aging, they become aware that their careers are not going to progress considerably further. Even if they have attained the heights to which they aspired—be it company president or well-respected community leader—they find that the satisfaction they derive from their accomplishments is not all that they had hoped it would be. As they look at their past, they may also be motivated to try to define what went wrong and how they can remedy previous dissatisfaction.

midlife crisis: The realization that we have not accomplished in life what we had hoped to, leading to negative feelings

In most cases, though, the passage into middle age is relatively placid, and some developmental psychologists even question whether most people experience a midlife crisis (Whitbourne, 1986; Kruger, 1994). Most 40-year-olds view their lives and accomplishments positively enough to have their midlife transition proceed relatively smoothly, and the forties and fifties are a particularly rewarding period of life. Rather than looking to the future, people at this stage concentrate on the present, and their involvement with their families, friends, and other social groups takes on new importance. A major developmental thrust of this period of life is learning to accept that the die has been cast, and that one must come to terms with one's circumstances.

Finally, during the last stages of middle adulthood—the fifties—people generally become more accepting of others and their lives, and less concerned about issues or problems that once bothered them. Rather than being driven to achieve as they were in their thirties, they come to accept the realization that death is inevitable, and they try to understand their accomplishments in terms of the broader meaning of life (Gould, 1978). Although people may begin, for the first time, to label themselves as "old," many also develop a sense of wisdom and feel freer to enjoy life (Karp, 1988, 1991).

Although Levinson's model of adult development has been influential, it does have a serious limitation: the nature of the original participants in his research. He studied only forty men, all of whom were white and middle class. Furthermore, he never conducted any scientifically controlled experiments to validate his findings. Finally, the lack of attention to women's life cycles, as well as those of minorities, limits the generalizability of Levinson's work.

Because most work on the phases of social development in adulthood has been based on the study of men's lives, it is important to consider whether women's lives follow the same patterns. We might expect significant gender differences on several grounds. For one thing, women often play different roles in society than men, either by choice or because of societal expectations. Moreover, women's roles have undergone rapid social change in the last decade, as we shall discuss next, making generalizations about women's development during early and middle adulthood difficult (Gilligan, 1982; Mercer, Nichols, & Doyle, 1989; Gilligan, Lyons, & Hanmer, 1990; Garbarino et al., 1995; Clausen, 1995; Roberts & Helson, 1997).

For these reasons, there is as yet no clear answer to the question of how women's social development differs from men's, since researchers have only begun to accumulate a large enough body of data focusing directly on women. Some recent research suggests, however, that there are both similarities and differences between men and women. Levinson, for example, argues that women generally go through the same stages at the same ages as men, although disparities exist in the specific details of some of the stages. For instance, important differences appear during "The Dream," the stage in which people develop a vision of what their future life will encompass. Women often have greater difficulty than men in forming a clear dream, for they may experience conflict between the goals of working and of raising a family. For men, this conflict tends to be much less important, since a man who wishes to marry and have a family usually views employment as the means of taking care of his family (Levinson & Levinson, 1996).

Marriage, Children, and Divorce: Family Ties

In the typical ending of many a fairy tale, a dashing young man and a beautiful young woman marry, have children, and live happily ever after. Unfortunately, such a

The high divorce rate has meant that growing numbers of children are being raised primarily by one parent—usually the mother, but increasingly often the father.

Parenting

scenario is more common in fairy tales than real life. In most cases it does not match the realities of love and marriage in the 1990s. Today, it is just as likely that the man and woman would first live together, then get married and have children—but ultimately end up getting divorced (Gottfried & Gottfried, 1994).

In 1996, 11.7 percent of all couples in Canada were cohabiting and 47 percent of these unions involved children. Nine out of ten Canadians will marry and 30 to 40 percent will end in divorce. The divorce rate has accelerated over the last several decades in most industrialized countries except for Japan and Italy (Cherlin et al., 1991; Cherlin, 1993; Goode, 1993; Ahrons, 1995; Statistics Canada, 1996).

Because of these matrimonial and divorce trends, the number of single-parent households has more than doubled over the past two decades. In fact, families with only one parent made up 14 percent of all families and of those 83 percent were headed by women, according to Statistics Canada (1996).

Divorce and subsequent life in a single-parent household may lead to several kinds of psychological difficulties, both for parents and for children (Gottman, 1993; Guttman, 1993; Kurtz, 1994; Weiss, 1994; Simons, 1996). Children may initially be exposed to high levels of parental conflict, leading to heightened anxiety and aggressive behaviour. Later separation from one or the other parent is a painful experience and may result in obstacles to establishing close relationships throughout life. Children may blame themselves for the breakup or may feel pressure to take sides. In many cases, good child care is hard to find, producing psychological stress and sometimes guilt over the arrangements working parents must make for economic reasons. Time is always at a premium in single-parent families (Whitehead, 1993).

On the other hand, little consistent evidence suggests that children from single-parent families are less well adjusted than those from two-parent families (Barber & Eccles, 1992). Moreover, it is clear that children are more successful growing up in a relatively tranquil single-parent family than in a two-parent family in which the parents are engaged in continuous conflict with one another. In fact, the emotional and behavioural problems displayed by some children of divorced parents may stem more from family problems that existed prior to the divorce than from the divorce itself (Cherlin, 1993; Gelles, 1994; Gottfried & Gottfried, 1994; Harold et al., 1997).

Do current divorce statistics suggest that marriage is as obsolete as the horse and buggy? At first they may seem to, but a closer look reveals that this is not the case. For one thing, survey data show that most people want to get married at some time in their lives, and close to 95 percent eventually do. Even people who divorce are more likely than not to get remarried, some of them three or more times—a phenomenon known as serial marriage. Finally, individuals who are married report being happier than those who are not (DeWitt, 1992; Hallberg, 1992; Bird & Melville, 1994; Tepperman & Curtis, 1995; Nock, 1995; Rosewicz, 1996).

The Changing Face of Marriage

Marriage remains an important institution in western cultures, and identifying a mate is a critical issue for the majority of people during adulthood. On the other hand, the nature of marriage has changed over the last few decades, as the roles played by men and women have evolved. More women than ever before either want to or are forced by their economic situation to act simultaneously as wives, mothers, and wage earners—in contrast to women in traditional marriages, in which the husband is the sole wage earner and the wife assumes primary responsibility for care of the home and children. In Canada, 63 percent of mothers with children under the age of 16 and 57 percent of mothers with children under the age of 6 work outside the home (Ghalam, 1994).

Although married women are more likely than they once were to be out of the house working, they are not free of household responsibilities. Even in marriages in which the spouses hold jobs of similar status and that require similar hours, the distribution of household tasks between husbands and wives has not changed substantially. Working wives are still more likely to view themselves as responsible for traditional homemaking tasks such as cooking and cleaning. In contrast, husbands of working wives still view themselves as responsible primarily for such household tasks as repairing broken appliances, putting up screens in the summer, and doing yard work (Schellhardt, 1990; Biernat & Wortman, 1991; Perry-Jenkins, 1993).

On the other hand, not all couples divide responsibilities along traditional lines. For instance, husbands who strongly subscribe to feminist ideals are more likely to spend time taking care of their children. Moreover, homosexual couples tend to share domestic chores equitably, splitting tasks so that each partner carries out an equal number of different activities (Deutsch, Lussier, & Servis, 1993; Kurdek, 1993; Gilbert, 1993).

In addition, there is a difference in the way married men and women spend their time during the average week. Although child care represents the biggest time investment for both husbands and wives when they are home, husbands spend significantly less time caring for their children (19 percent) than wives (32 percent) (Robinson & Godbey, 1997).

In general, working women spend more time than working men on combined job and family demands. In fact, the number of hours put in by working mothers can be staggering. For instance, one survey found that employed mothers of children under 3 years of age worked an average of ninety hours per week! Sociologist Arlie Hochschild refers to the additional work experienced by women as the "second shift." According to her analysis of national statistics, women who both work and are mothers spend an extra month of 24-hour days during the course of a year (Hochschild, 1990, 1997; Hochschild, Machung, & Pringle, 1995). Furthermore, similar patterns are seen in many developing societies throughout the world, with women working at full-time jobs and also having primary responsibilities for child care (Googans & Burden, 1987; Mednick, 1993).

In short, many families in which both parents work still tend to view the mother as holding primary responsibility for child rearing. Consequently, rather than careers being a substitute for what women do at home, they often exist in addition to the role of homemaker. It is not surprising that some wives feel resentment toward husbands who spend less time on child care and housework than the wives had expected before the birth of their children (Williams & McCullers, 1983; Ruble et al., 1988; DeMeis & Perkins, 1996).

On the other hand, many wives report feeling relatively accepting of this unequal distribution. One reason is that traditional societal standards still provide relatively strong support for women who play a dominant role in child care and housework (Major, 1993). In addition, for many women the benefits of work may outweigh the disadvantages of having major responsibilities in multiple roles. For instance, women who work, particularly those in high-prestige occupations, report feeling a greater sense of mastery, pride, and competence than women who stay at home. The value of work, then, goes beyond merely earning a salary. Work provides personal satisfaction as well as a sense of contributing to society. In fact, some critics contend that work is valued because it provides an escape from the rigours of home and child care. For some people, then, work acts as an escape from a frenetic, stress-filled home life (Crosby, 1991; Barnett, Marshall, & Singer, 1992; Schwartzberg & Dytell, 1996; Steil & Hay, 1997; Hochschild, 1997).

It is clear that success at work has important psychological consequences for both men and women. People report feeling happier and more in control of their lives, have higher self-esteem, and even feel that they have better marriages when they are successful at their jobs. Conversely, work failures—such as being laid off or fired—can lead to anxiety, depression, and a host of other psychological symptoms. In sum, for men and women in the middle years of life, job-related achievement represents an important aspect of continued growth and development (Price, 1992; Barnett et al., 1993).

THE LATER YEARS OF LIFE: GROWING OLD

▶ **How does the reality of old age differ from the stereotypes about the period?**

▶ **How can we adjust to death?**

I've always enjoyed doing things in the mountains—hiking or, more recently, active cliff-climbing. When climbing a route of any difficulty at all, it's absolutely necessary to become entirely absorbed in what you're doing. You look for a crack that you can put your hand in. You have to think about whether the foothold over there will leave you in balance or not. Otherwise you can get trapped in a difficult situation. And if you don't remember where you put your hands or feet a few minutes before, then it's very difficult to climb down.

The more difficult the climb, the more absorbing it is. The climbs I really remember are the ones I had to work on. Maybe a particular section where it took two or three tries before I found the right combination of moves that got me up easily—and, preferably, elegantly. It's a wonderful exhilaration to get to the top and sit down and perhaps have lunch and look out over the landscape and be so grateful that it's still possible for me to do that sort of thing (Lyman Spitzer, quoted in Kotre & Hall, 1990, pp. 358–359).

Late Adulthood

Lyman Spitzer. Age: 74.

If you can't quite picture a 74-year-old climbing rocks, some rethinking of your view of old age might well be in order. In spite of the societal stereotype of old age as a time of inactivity and physical and mental decline, *gerontologists*, specialists who study aging, are beginning to paint quite a different portrait of late adulthood.

By focusing on the period of life that starts at around age 65, gerontologists are making important contributions to clarifying the capabilities of older adults. Their work is demonstrating that significant developmental processes continue even during old age. And as life expectancy increases, the number of people who reach older adulthood will continue to grow substantially. Consequently, developing an understanding of late adulthood has become a critical priority for psychologists (Cavanaugh & Park, 1993; Birren, 1996; Binstock et al., 1996).

Physical Changes in Late Adulthood: The Old Body

Napping, eating, walking, conversing. It probably doesn't surprise you that these relatively unvigorous activities represent the typical pastimes of late adulthood. But what is striking about this list is that these activities are identical to the most common leisure activities reported in a survey of college students. Although the students cited more active pursuits—such as sailing and playing basketball—as their favourite activities, in actuality they engaged in such sports relatively infrequently, spending most of their free time napping, eating, walking, and conversing (Harper, 1978).

Although the leisure activities in which older adulthood engage may not differ all that much from those that younger people pursue, many physical changes are, of course, brought about by the aging process. The most obvious are in appearance—hair thinning and turning gray, skin wrinkling and folding, and sometimes a slight loss of height as the size of the disks between vertebrae in the spine decreases—but there are also subtler changes in the body's biological functioning (DiGiovanna, 1994).

For example, sensory acuity decreases as a result of aging; vision and hearing are less sharp, and smell and taste are not as sensitive. Reaction time slows. There are changes in physical stamina. Because oxygen intake and heart-pumping ability decline, the body is unable to replenish lost nutrients as quickly—and therefore the rebound from physical activity is slower (Shock, 1962; Perlmutter & Hall, 1992). Of course, none of these changes begins suddenly at age 65. Gradual declines in some kinds of functioning start earlier. It is in old age, however, that these changes become more apparent (Perlmutter, 1994; Schneider & Rowe, 1996).

What are the reasons for these physical declines? There are two major explanations: genetic preprogramming theories and wear-and-tear theories. **Genetic preprogramming theories of aging** suggest that there is a built-in time limit to the reproduction of human cells, and that after a certain time they are no longer able to divide (Hayflick, 1974, 1994). A variant of this idea is that some cells are genetically preprogrammed to become harmful to the body after a certain amount of time has gone by, causing the internal biology of the body to "self-destruct" (Finch, 1990; Ricklefs & Finch, 1995; Finch & Tanzi, 1997).

The second approach to understanding physical declines due to aging is based on the same factors that force people to buy new cars every so often: Mechanical devices wear out. According to **wear-and-tear theories of aging**, the mechanical functions of the body simply stop working efficiently. Moreover, waste by-products of

genetic preprogramming theories of aging: Theories that suggest there is a built-in time limit to the reproduction of human cells, and that after a certain time they are no longer able to divide

wear-and-tear theories of aging: Theories that suggest that the mechanical functions of the body simply stop working efficiently

energy production eventually accumulate, and mistakes are made when cells reproduce. Eventually the body, in effect, wears out.

We do not know which of these theories provides a better explanation of the physical aging process; it may be that both contribute (Rusting, 1992; Austad, 1997; Kitcher,
1997). It is important to realize, however, that physical aging is not a disease, but rather
a natural biological process. Many physical functions do not decline with age. For example, sex remains pleasurable well into old age (although the frequency of sexual activity
decreases), and some people even report that the pleasure they derive from sex increases
during late adulthood (Rowe & Kahn, 1987; Olshansky, Carnes, & Cassel, 1990).

Furthermore, neither genetic preprogramming theories nor wear-and-tear theories successfully explain a fact that is immediately apparent to anyone studying aging:
Women live longer than men. Life expectancy in Canada is 81.4 years for women and
75.7 years for men (Health Canada, 1996). Throughout the industrialized world,
women outlive men by a margin of four to ten years. The female advantage begins just
after conception. Although more males are conceived than females, males have a higher
rate of prenatal, infant, and childhood death, and by age 30 there are equal numbers of
males and females. By age 65, 84 percent of females and 70 percent of males are still
alive. Although some observers have suggested that the gender gap is a result of the
superiority of women's health habits, that is not the full explanation; in fact, a full explanation of why women live longer than men remains to be found (Edmondson, 1997).

Cognitive Changes: Thinking About—and During—Old Age

Three women were talking about the inconveniences of growing old.

"Sometimes," one of them confessed, "when I go to my refrigerator, I
can't remember if I'm putting something in or taking something out."

"Oh, that's nothing," said the second woman. "There are times when I
find myself at the foot of the stairs wondering if I'm going up or if I've just
come down."

"Well, my goodness!" exclaimed the third woman. "I'm certainly glad I
don't have any problems like that"—and she knocked on wood. "Oh," she said,
starting up out of her chair, "there's someone at the door" (Dent, 1984, p. 38).

At one time, many gerontologists would have agreed with the view—suggested by
the story above—that older adults are forgetful and confused. Today, however, most research tells us that this is far from an accurate assessment of older people's capabilities.

One reason for the change in view is the availability of more sophisticated research techniques for studying cognitive changes that occur in late adulthood. For example, if we were to give a group of older adults an IQ test, we might find that the average
score was lower than the score achieved by a group of younger people. We might conclude that this signifies a decline in intelligence. Yet if we looked a little closer at the
specific test, we might find that such a conclusion was unwarranted. For instance, many
IQ tests include portions based on physical performance (such as arranging a group of
blocks) or on speed. In such cases, poorer performance on the IQ test may be due to
decrements in reaction time—a physical decline that accompanies old age and has little
or nothing to do with the intellectual capabilities of older adults (Schaie, 1991).

Other difficulties hamper research into cognitive functioning during late adulthood. For example, older adults are more likely than younger people to suffer from
physical ill health. Some studies of IQ in the past inadvertently compared a group of
physically healthy younger people with a group of older people who were generally
less healthy, with the finding of significantly lower scores for the older group. However, when only *healthy* older adults are observed, intellectual declines are markedly
less evident (Riegel & Riegel, 1972; Avorn, 1983; Kausler, 1994). Furthermore, it is
unfair to compare the test results of an older group with those of a younger group of
subjects when the mean level of education is probably lower in the older group (for
historical reasons) than in the younger one.

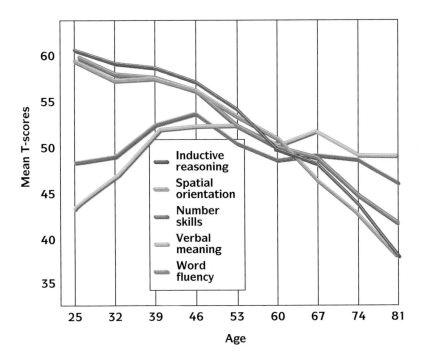

FIGURE 10-6 *Age-related changes in intellectual skills vary according to the specific cognitive ability in question. Source: Schaie, 1994.*

Similarly, declines in the IQ scores of older adults may be caused by their having lower motivation to perform well on intelligence tests than younger people. Finally, traditional IQ tests may not be the most appropriate measures of intelligence in late adulthood. For example, as we discussed in Chapter 8, some researchers contend that several kinds of intelligence exist, and others have found that older adults perform better on tests of everyday problems and social competence than do younger individuals (Cornelius & Caspi, 1987; Willis & Schaie, 1994).

On the other hand, researchers have found some declines in intellectual functioning during late adulthood, even when using more sophisticated research methods. However, as can be seen in Figure 10-6, the pattern of age differences is not uniform for different types of cognitive abilities. Furthermore, the differences are not identical for men and women (Schaie, 1993, 1994; Powell & Whitla, 1994a).

In general, age-related changes in cognitive abilities can be summarized in terms of differences in fluid and crystallized intelligence. You may recall from Chapter 8 that *fluid intelligence* refers to reasoning, memory, and information-processing capabilities, while *crystallized intelligence* is intelligence based on the information, skills, and strategies that people have learned through experience and that can be applied in problem-solving situations.

Although fluid intelligence shows declines in old age, crystallized intelligence remains steady and in some cases actually improves. For example, an older woman asked to solve a geometry problem (which taps fluid intelligence) might have greater difficulty than she once did, but she might be better at solving verbal problems that require reasoned conclusions (Baltes & Schaie, 1974; Schaie, 1993; Salthouse, 1996).

One reason for developmental changes in intellectual functioning is that certain types of abilities may be more sensitive to changes in the nervous system than others. Another factor may be the degree to which the two kinds of intelligence are used during a person's lifetime. Whatever the reason, people compensate for the decline. They can still learn what they want to; it may just take more time. Furthermore, teaching older adults strategies for dealing with new problems can prevent declines in performance (Storandt et al., 1984; Willis & Nesselroade, 1990; Grasel, 1994; Powell & Whitla, 1994b; Raykov, 1995).

Memory Changes in Old Age: Are Older Adults Forgetful?

One of the characteristics most frequently attributed to late adulthood is forgetfulness. How accurate is this assumption?

Most evidence suggests that memory change is *not* an inevitable part of the aging process. For instance, research shows that older people in cultures in which older adults are held in high esteem, such as in mainland China, are less likely to show memory losses than those living in cultures in which the expectation is that memory will decline. Similarly, when older people in western societies are reminded of the advantages of age ("age brings wisdom"), they tend to do better on tests of memory (Levy & Langer, 1994; Levy, 1996).

Even when people do show memory declines during late adulthood, their deficits tend to be limited to particular types of memory. For instance, losses tend to be limited to episodic memories, which relate to specific experiences about our lives. Other types of memories, such as semantic memories (which refer to general knowledge and facts) and implicit memories (which are memories about which we are not consciously aware) are largely unaffected by age (Graf, 1990; Russo & Parkin, 1993).

Declines in episodic memories can often be traced to changes in the lives of older adults. For instance, it is not surprising that a retired person, who may no longer face the same kind of consistent intellectual challenges encountered on the job, might well be less practiced in using memory or even be less motivated to remember things, leading to an apparent decline in memory. Even in cases in which long-term memory declines, older adults can usually profit from compensatory efforts. Training older adults to use the kinds of mnemonic strategies described in Chapter 6 not only may prevent their long-term memory from deteriorating, but may actually improve it (Perlmutter & Mitchell, 1986; Brody, 1987; Ratner et al., 1987; Kotler-Cope & Camp, 1990; Verhaeghen, Marcoen, & Goossens, 1992; West, 1995).

In the past, older adults with severe cases of memory decline, accompanied by other cognitive difficulties, were viewed as suffering from senility. *Senility* is a broad, imprecise term typically applied to older adults who experience progressive deterioration of mental abilities, including memory loss, disorientation to time and place, and general confusion. Once thought to be an inevitable state that accompanies aging, senility is now viewed by most gerontologists as a label that has outlived its usefulness. Rather than senility being the cause of certain symptoms, the symptoms are deemed to be caused by some other factor.

However, some cases of memory loss are produced by actual disease. For instance, *Alzheimer's disease* is the progressive brain disorder discussed in Chapter 6 that leads to a gradual and irreversible decline in cognitive abilities. In other cases, the declines are caused by temporary anxiety and depression, which may be successfully treated, or may even be due to overmedication. The danger is that people suffering such symptoms may be labelled senile and left untreated, thereby continuing their decline—even though treatment would have been beneficial (Selkoe, 1997).

In sum, declines in cognitive functioning in old age are, for the most part, not unavoidable. The key to maintaining cognitive skills may lie in intellectual stimulation. Like the rest of us, older adults need a stimulating environment in order to hone and maintain their skills.

The Social World of Late Adulthood: Old But Not Alone

Aging and Health

Just as the view that mental declines are an inevitable outcome of old age has proved to be wrong, so has the view that old age inevitably brings loneliness. People in late adulthood most often see themselves as functioning members of society, with one representative poll showing that just 12 percent of people 65 and over view loneliness as a serious problem (Harris Poll, 1975; Binstock & George, 1996).

Still, the social patterns and behaviours of older adults are different in some respects from those of younger individuals. Two major approaches have been suggested to explain older adult's social environment: disengagement theory and activity theory.

The **disengagement theory of aging** sees aging as a gradual withdrawal from the world on physical, psychological, and social levels (Cummings & Henry, 1961). Physically, lower energy levels produce less activity; psychologically, the focus shifts from others to the self; and socially, there is less interaction with others and a reduction in the level of participation in society at large. But rather than viewing this disengagement in a negative light, some theorists suggest that it should be seen positively. Such disengagement provides the opportunity for increased reflectiveness and decreased emotional investment in others at a time of life when social relationships will inevitably be ended by death.

Disengagement theory has been criticized because of its suggestion that disengagement is an automatic process, marking a sharp departure from earlier behaviour patterns. Even more important are data showing that the older adults who report being the happiest are those who remain the most active (Havighurst, 1973). Such criticisms and findings have led to the development of an alternative approach to describing social adjustment to aging. The **activity theory of aging** suggests that the people who age most successfully are those who maintain the interests and activities they pursued during middle age and who resist any decrease in the amount and kind of social interaction they have with others (Blau, 1973). According to activity theory, late adulthood should reflect a continuation, as much as possible, of the activities in which people participated during the earlier part of their lives, as well as activities to replace those lost through changes such as retirement.

However, activity alone does not guarantee happiness. Rather, the *nature* of activities in which people engage is probably more critical (Gubrium, 1973; Kozma, Stones, & McNeil, 1991). Albert Kozma of Memorial University in Newfoundland has done extensive research on aging. In terms of physical activity, walking is correlated with reduction of depression and organized exercise programs increased happiness. This may well be related to the social as well as the physical aspects of the activity (Kozma, Stones, & McNeil, 1991). Furthermore, not all people in late adulthood need a life filled with activities and social interaction to be happy; as in every stage of life, there are those who are just as satisfied leading a relatively inactive, solitary existence (Hansson & Carpenter, 1994; Harlow & Cantor, 1996). Active or solitary, the question of how satisfied people are in late adulthood is correlated to their appraisal of their situation. Kozma and others have examined psychological well-being (PWB) in older adults. They found that subjective feelings were a better predictor of satisfaction than were objective realities. For example subjective health had a component of comparison to the state of health of other people and predicted PWB better that the objective health situation of the person. In the same way, subjective feeling about income, housing, marital status, and job satisfaction all were more highly correlated to PWB than the objective state (Kozma, Stones & McNeil, 1991).

We cannot say whether disengagement theory or activity theory presents a more accurate view of those in late adulthood, probably because there are vast individual differences in how people cope with the aging process. Clearly, however, people in late adulthood are not just marking time until death. Rather, old age is a time of continued growth and development, as important as any other period of life (Wong, 1989).

disengagement theory of aging: A theory that suggests that aging is a gradual withdrawal from the world on physical, psychological, and social levels

activity theory of aging: A theory that suggests that the people who age most successfully are those who maintain the interests and activities they had during middle age

The Informed Consumer of Psychology

Adjusting to Death

At some time in our lives, we all face death—certainly our own, as well as the deaths of friends, loved ones, and even strangers. Although there is nothing more inevitable in life, death remains a frightening, emotion-laden topic. Certainly, little is more stressful than the death of a loved one or the contemplation of our own imminent death, and preparing for death is one of our most crucial developmental tasks.

Not too long ago, talk of death was taboo. The topic was never mentioned to dying people, and gerontologists had little to say about it. That changed, however, with the pioneering work of Elisabeth Kübler-Ross (1969), who brought the subject out into the open with her observation that those facing death tend to move through five broad stages.

- *Denial.* In this first stage, people resist the idea that they are dying. Even if told that their chances for survival are small, they refuse to admit that they are facing death.

- *Anger.* After moving beyond the denial stage, dying people become angry—angry at people around them who are in good health, angry at medical professionals for being ineffective, angry at God. They ask the question "Why me?" and are unable to answer it without feeling anger.

- *Bargaining.* Anger leads to bargaining, in which the dying try to think of ways to postpone death. They may decide to dedicate their lives to religion if God saves them; they may say, "If only I can live to see my son married, I will accept death then." Such bargains are rarely kept, most often because the dying person's illness keeps progressing and invalidates any "agreements."

- *Depression.* When dying people come to feel that bargaining is of no use, they move to the next stage: depression. They realize that the die is cast, that they are losing their loved ones, and that their lives really are coming to an end. They are experiencing what Kübler-Ross calls "preparatory grief" for their own death.

- *Acceptance.* In this last stage, people are past mourning for the loss of their own lives, and they accept impending death. Usually they are unemotional and uncommunicative; it is as if they have made peace with themselves and are expecting death without rancor.

It is important to keep in mind that not everyone experiences each of these stages in the same way. In fact, Kübler-Ross's stages pertain only to people who are fully aware that they are dying and have the time to evaluate their impending death. Furthermore, vast differences occur in how specific individuals react to impending death. The specific cause and duration of dying, as well as the person's sex, age, and personality and the type of support received from family and friends, all have an impact on how people respond to death (Zautra, Reich, & Guarnaccia, 1990; Stroebe, Stroebe, & Hansson, 1993).

Few of us enjoy the contemplation of death. Yet awareness of its psychological aspects and consequences can make its inevitable arrival less anxiety-producing and perhaps more understandable.   ■

Recap, Review, and Rethink

Recap

- Several critical physical changes occur during puberty. Early maturing is generally socially beneficial, whereas late maturing is usually disadvantageous.

- According to Kohlberg, moral development passes through a series of stages, each of which represents an increasingly sophisticated level. In Gilligan's contrasting view of moral development, women, more than men, focus on principles involving compassion toward the individual rather than on abstract principles of justice or fairness.

- During adolescence, people enter Erikson's crucial identity-versus-role-confusion stage, which may include an identity crisis. This is followed in later life by the last three of Erikson's stages: intimacy-versus-isolation, generativity-versus-stagnation, and ego-integrity-versus-despair.

- Although adolescence was once thought of as a stormy, rebellious period, psychologists now believe that such a view reflects more myth than reality.

- According to a model developed by Levinson, social development during early and middle adulthood proceeds through a series of stages, notably including a midlife transition, which may produce a midlife crisis.

- Important changes are taking place in marriage and family life because of societal developments such as increased divorce, a higher incidence of single-parent families, and the rise of working mothers and the two-income household.

- The physical declines of the elderly are explained by two classes of theories: genetic preprogramming theories and wear-and-tear theories.

- Fluid intelligence and memory are affected by aging, but crystallized intelligence remains largely intact and overall cognitive declines among older adults have been greatly exaggerated and can often be avoided.

- Kübler-Ross identified five stages through which people pass when facing death: denial, anger, bargaining, depression, and acceptance.

Review

1. Delayed maturation typically provides both males and females with a social advantage. True or false?

2. _____ proposed a set of six stages of moral development ranging from reasoning based on rewards and punishments to abstract thinking involving concepts of justice.

3. Match each of Gilligan's stages of women's moral development with its definition:
   1. Morality of nonviolence
   2. Orientation toward individual survival
   3. Goodness as self-sacrifice

   a. The focus is on what is best for the woman in particular.
   b. A woman must sacrifice her wants to what others want.
   c. Hurting anyone, including oneself, is immoral.

4. Emotional and psychological changes that sometimes accompany menopause are probably not due to menopause itself. True or false?

5. Forty-year-old Rob recently found himself surveying his goals and accomplishments to date. Although he has accomplished a lot, he realizes that many of his goals will not be met in his lifetime. Levinson would term this stage in Rob's life the _____.

6. In households where both partners have similar jobs, the division of labour for household chores is generally the same as in "traditional" households where the husband works and the wife stays home. True or false?

7. Lower IQ test scores during late adulthood do not necessarily mean that intelligence has decreased. True or false?

8. During old age, a person's _____ intelligence continues to increase, while _____ intelligence may decline.

9. Lavinia feels that, in her old age, she has gradually decreased her social contacts and has become more self-oriented. A proponent of _____ theory interprets the situation as a result of Lavinia's not maintaining her past interests. A supporter of _____ theory views her behavior in a more positive light, suggesting that it is a natural process accompanied by enhanced reflectiveness and declining emotional investment.

10. In Kübler-Ross's _____ stage, people resist the idea of death. In the _____ stage, they attempt to make deals to avoid death, while in the _____ stage, they passively await death.

Answers to Review Questions are on page 404.

Rethink

1. In what ways do school cultures help or hurt teenage students who are going through adolescence? What school policies might benefit early-maturing girls and late-maturing boys? Would same-sex schools help, as some have argued?

2. Given the current divorce rate and the number of households in which both parents work, do you think it is reasonable to think in terms of a "traditional" household in which the father is the breadwinner while the wife is a homemaker? What problems might such a definition cause for children whose homes do not match this definition?

3. Many people today suffer from misconceptions about people in late adulthood, thinking of them as senile, slow, lonely, and so forth. How might you go about proving these stereotypes wrong? What advantages might a change in our misconceptions have in terms of the resources that those in late adulthood can provide?

looking
BACK

How do psychologists study the degree to which development is a joint function of hereditary and environmental factors?

1. Developmental psychology is the branch of psychology that studies growth and change throughout life. One fundamental question is how much developmental change is due to nature—hereditary factors—and how much to nurture—environmental factors. Most developmental psychologists believe that heredity defines the upper limits of our growth and change, whereas the environment affects the degree to which the upper limits are reached.

2. Cross-sectional research compares people of different ages with one another at the same point in time. In contrast, longitudinal research traces the behaviour of one or more subjects as the subjects become older. Finally, cross-sequential research combines the two methods by taking several different age groups and examining them over several points in time.

What is the nature of development prior to birth?

3. At the moment of conception, a male's sperm cell and a female's egg cell unite, with each contributing to the new individual's genetic makeup. The union of sperm and egg produces a new cell, called a zygote, which contains twenty-three pairs of chromosomes—with one member of each pair coming from the father and the other from the mother. Each chromosome contains thousands of genes, through which genetic information is transmitted. Genes, which are composed of DNA sequences, are the "software" that programs the future development of the body's hardware.

4. After the zygote is formed, it immediately begins to grow. After two weeks it is an embryo, and after four weeks it is about one-fifth of an inch long. By the eighth week, the embryo is called a fetus and is responsive to touch and other stimulation. At about twenty-four weeks it reaches the age

of viability, which means it may survive if born prematurely. A fetus is normally born after thirty-eight weeks of pregnancy, weighing around 7 pounds and measuring about 20 inches.

5. Researchers, including behavioural geneticists, are beginning to unravel the mysteries of human genes, discovering that genes affect not only physical attributes but also a wide array of personal characteristics, such as cognitive abilities, personality traits, sexual orientation, and psychological disorders. The Human Genome Project is a lengthy study designed to map the location and sequence of every human gene, which will help researchers understand the origin of genetically produced disorders and also support gene therapy, the genetically based treatment of diseases.

What are the major milestones of physical, perceptual, and social development after birth?

6. The newborn, or neonate, has many capabilities. Among them are the rooting reflex, the startle reflex, and the Babinski reflex. After birth, physical development is rapid; children typically triple their birth weights in a year. Perceptual abilities also increase rapidly; infants can distinguish colour and depth after just one month. Other sensory capabilities are also impressive at birth; infants can distinguish sounds and discriminate tastes and smells. However, the development of more sophisticated perceptual abilities depends on increased cognitive abilities.

7. Social development in infancy is marked by the phenomenon of attachment—the positive emotional bond between a child and a particular individual. Attachment is measured in the laboratory using the Ainsworth strange situation and is related to later social and emotional adjustment.

8. As children become older, the nature of their social interactions with peers changes. Initially play occurs relatively independently but it becomes increasingly cooperative. Play enhances social competence and self-control.

9. Different styles of child rearing result in differing outcomes. Authoritarian parents are firm, punitive, and strict. Their children tend to be unsociable and withdrawn. Permissive parents provide lax or inconsistent discipline, although they are warm. Their children tend to be immature, moody, dependent, and low in self-control. Finally, authoritative parents are firm, setting limits, but using reasoning and explanations. Their children tend to be likable, self-reliant, independent, and high in social skills. Of course, there are many exceptions, depending in part on the children's temperament and on the culture in which they are raised.

10. According to Erikson, eight stages of psychosocial development encompass people's changing interactions and understanding of themselves and others. During childhood, there are four stages, each of which relates to a crisis that requires resolution. These stages are labeled trust-versus-mistrust (birth to 18 months), autonomy-versus-shame-and-doubt (18 months to 3 years), initiative-versus-guilt (3 to 6 years), and industry-versus-inferiority (6 to 12 years).

How can we best describe cognitive development?

11. Piaget's theory suggests that cognitive development proceeds through four stages in which qualitative changes occur in thinking. In the sensorimotor stage (birth to 2 years), children develop object permanence, the awareness that objects and people continue to exist even if they are out of sight. In the preoperational stage (2 to 7 years), children display egocentric thought, and by the end of the stage they begin to understand the principle of conservation—the knowledge that quantity is unrelated to the arrangement and physical appearance of an object. The conservation principle is not fully grasped until the concrete operational stage (7 to 12 years), in which children begin to think more logically, and to understand the concept of reversibility. In the final stage, the formal operational period (12 years to adulthood), thinking becomes abstract, formal, and fully logical.

12. Although Piaget's theory has had an enormous influence, some theorists suggest that the notion of developmental stages is inaccurate. They say that development is more continuous and that the changes occurring within and between stages are reflective of quantitative advances in cognitive development rather than qualitative changes in thinking.

13. Information-processing approaches suggest that quantitative changes occur in children's ability to organize and manipulate information about the world, such as significant increases in speed of processing, attention span, and memory. In addition, there are advances in metacognition, the awareness and understanding of one's own cognitive processes.

14. According to the Russian developmental psychologist Lev Vygotsky, learning and development are essentially social in nature. Children's cognitive development occurs as a consequence of social interactions in which children and others work together to solve problems. When the information that children need and use to solve problems with others is within the children's zone of proximal development, cognitive development is most effectively supported.

What major physical, social, and cognitive transitions characterize adolescence?

15. Adolescence, the developmental stage between childhood and adulthood, is marked by the onset of puberty, the point at which sexual maturity occurs. The age at which puberty begins has implications for the way people view themselves and the way they are seen by others.

16. Moral judgments during adolescence increase in sophistication, according to Kohlberg's three-level, six-stage model. Although Kohlberg's stages are an adequate description of males' moral judgments, they do not seem to be as applicable in describing females' judgments. Specifically, Gilligan suggests that women view morality in terms of concern for individuals rather than in terms of broad, general principles of justice or fairness. In her view, moral development in women proceeds in three somewhat different stages from those identified by Kohlberg.

Answers to Review Questions:

1. False; both male and female adolescents suffer if they mature late.   2. Kohlberg   3. 1-c; 2-a; 3-b   4. true   5. midlife transition
6. true   7. true   8. crystallized; fluid   9. activity; disengagement   10. denial; bargaining; acceptance

17. According to Erikson's model of psychosocial development, adolescence may be accompanied by an identity crisis, although this is by no means universal. Adolescence is followed by three stages of psychosocial development that cover the remainder of the lifespan.

What are the principal kinds of physical, social, and intellectual changes that occur in early and middle adulthood, and what are their causes?

18. Early adulthood marks the peak of physical health. Physical changes occur relatively gradually in men and women during adulthood, although one major change occurs at the end of middle adulthood for women: They begin menopause, after which they are no longer fertile. For men, the aging process is subtler, since they remain fertile.

19. Levinson's model of adult development begins with entry into early adulthood at around age 20 and ends at around age 60 or 65. One of the most critical transitions—at least for men—occurs during midlife (around age 40 to 45), when people typically experience a midlife transition in which the notion that life is not unending becomes more important. In some cases this can lead to a midlife crisis; usually, however, the passage into middle age is relatively calm. Although Levinson suggests that women's lives follow basically the same pattern as men's, there are likely to be several gender differences.

20. As aging continues during middle adulthood, people realize in their fifties that their lives and accomplishments are fairly well set, and they try to come to terms with them.

21. Among the most important developmental milestones during adulthood are marriage, family changes, and divorce. Although divorce is more prevalent than ever before, most people still view marriage as important and desirable. Another important determinant of adult development is work. In the last several decades, women have joined the work force in increasingly high numbers.

How does the reality of old age differ from the stereotypes about the period?

22. Old age may bring marked physical declines. Although the activities of people in late adulthood are not all that different from those of younger people, older adults do experience decrements in reaction time, as well as sensory declines and a decrease in physical stamina. These declines might be caused by genetic preprogramming, which sets a time limit on the reproduction of human cells, or they may simply be due to wear and tear on the mechanical parts of the body.

23. Although intellectual declines were once thought to be an inevitable part of aging, most research suggests that this is not necessarily the case. Fluid intelligence does decline with age, and long-term memory abilities are sometimes impaired. In contrast, crystallized intelligence shows slight increases with age, and short-term memory remains at about the same level.

24. Disengagement theory sees successful aging as a process accompanied by gradual withdrawal from the physical, psychological, and social worlds. In contrast, activity theory suggests that the maintenance of interests and activities from earlier years leads to successful aging. Because there are vast individual differences, it is unclear whether either of the two theories is completely accurate.

How can we adjust to death?

25. According to Kübler-Ross, dying people move through five stages as they face death: denial, anger, bargaining, depression, and acceptance. However, people's reactions to death vary significantly.

Key Terms and Concepts

developmental psychology (p. 354)
nature-nurture issue (p. 356)
identical twins (p. 358)
cross-sectional research (p. 358)
longitudinal research (p. 358)
cross-sequential research (p. 359)
chromosomes (p. 359)
genes (p. 359)
zygote (p. 360)
embryo (p. 360)
critical period (p. 360)
fetus (p. 360)
age of viability (p. 361)
neonate (p. 365)
reflexes (p. 365)
habituation (p. 367)
attachment (p. 369)
authoritarian parents (p. 373)

permissive parents (p. 373)
authoritative parents (p. 373)
temperament (p. 373)
psychosocial development (p. 374)
trust-versus-mistrust stage (p. 374)
autonomy-versus-shame-and-doubt stage (p. 374)
initiative-versus-guilt stage (p. 375)
industry-versus-inferiority stage (p. 375)
cognitive development (p. 375)
sensorimotor stage (p. 376)
object permanence (p. 376)
preoperational stage (p. 376)
egocentric thought (p. 376)
principle of conservation (p. 376)
concrete operational stage (p. 378)
formal operational stage (p. 378)
information processing (p. 379)

metacognition (p. 379)
zone of proximal development (ZPD) (p. 380)
adolescence (p. 383)
puberty (p. 383)
identity-versus-role-confusion stage (p. 388)
identity (p. 388)
intimacy-versus-isolation stage (p. 389)
generativity-versus-stagnation stage (p. 389)
ego-integrity-versus-despair stage (p. 389)
menopause (p. 391)
midlife transition (p. 392)
midlife crisis (p. 393)
genetic preprogramming theories of aging (p. 398)
wear-and-tear theories of aging (p. 398)
disengagement theory of aging (p. 401)
activity theory of aging (p. 401)

Epilogue

We have traced major events in human development across the lifespan, including changes in physical, social, and cognitive abilities. We first noted that children advance rapidly after birth in all these areas, developing abilities upon which they build further in adolescence and later life. We observed that development continues throughout the lifespan, even into old age.

As we explored each area of development, we encountered anew the nature-nurture issue, concluding in every significant instance that both nature and nurture contribute to a person's development of skills, personality, and interactions. Specifically, our genetic inheritance—nature—lays down general boundaries within which we can advance and grow, and our environment helps to determine the extent to which we take advantage of our potential.

Our consideration of development included a look at the major theories of development, especially Erik Erikson's theory of psychosocial development, Jean Piaget's theory of cognitive development, Lev Vygotsky's theory of cognitive development, Kohlberg's theory of moral development—and Gilligan's corresponding theory for women.

Before proceeding to the next chapter, turn once again to the prologue that introduced this one, on Unabomber suspect Ted Kaczynski. Using your knowledge of childhood development, consider the following questions.

1. How does Ted Kaczynski's claim that his upbringing caused him to have difficulty forming relationships pertain to the issue of attachment? What sort of attachment style would you expect him to have exhibited as a child? Why?

2. How might a person with difficulty forming attachments and a severe distrust and loathing of his mother have navigated the conflicts described by Erikson's theory of psychosocial development? What sorts of problems might such a person have encountered?

3. What sort of lifestyle would you expect a person with severe attachment difficulties and psychosocial impairments to lead, in terms of living arrangements, occupation, marital status, and relationships with other people? If Ted Kaczynski exhibited such a lifestyle, would it be fair to assert in court that this indicated that he was the Unabomber?

4. How would you unravel the different effects that nature and nurture might have had on a person like Kaczynski? What questions would you ask his brother and his mother?

5. Why might Kaczynski and his brother have taken such different paths, in terms of interpersonal relationships and lifestyle, when both presumably had similar upbringings?

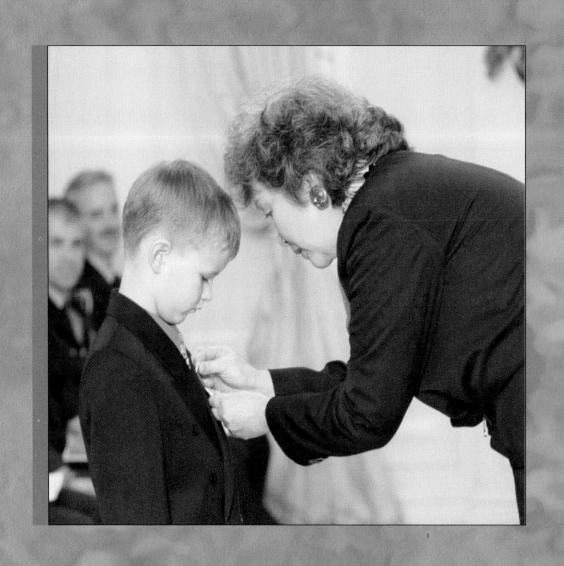

Personality

Canadian astronaut, Julie Payette.

Prologue

A Dream Fulfilled: Becoming an Astronaut

As a child, Julie Payette was fascinated by televised accounts of the Apollo space missions, and she read everything she could about space. Her parents encouraged her curiosity and helped her to set high standards for achievement. The family lived in Montreal where her mom worked in accounting and her dad was an engineer. One of her mother's favourite sayings was "there's always room for improvement" (Branswell, 1999, page 57).

As a young woman, Payette prepared for a career in space by earning a Bachelor of Engineering at McGill University, and a Master of Applied Science (Computer Engineering) at the University of Toronto. She learned to fly jet aircraft at CFB Moose Jaw, and qualified for captaincy in 1996. Her work experience has included research in computer systems as well as speech and language processing in Canada and Switzerland.

In 1992, several months before her twenty-ninth birthday, Payette was accepted as an astronaut, and began training in Canada. Seven years later, she flew on the Space Shuttle Discovery, fulfilling an ambition she had harboured since she was nine years old—operating the robotic manipulator, Canadarm. The crew moved tons of equipment and supplies to the International Space Station so that another group of astronauts would be able to live on the Space Station for a year. On her trip Payette flew a total of four million miles.

Payette has many talents and interests. She speaks six languages, including Russian, and is a gifted musician (pianist, flutist, and singer) and athlete (squash, badminton, raquetball and scuba diving). Her biographical data on the NASA web site tell us that she has received scholarships to support her university education, a post-graduate scholarship and a fellowship, an award for exceptional achievement, and several honorary doctorates. Payette is the eighth Canadian to travel in space.

looking AHEAD

personality: The relatively enduring characteristics that differentiate people—those behaviors that makes each individual unique

▶ How do psychologists define and use the concept of personality?

▶ What do the theories of Freud and his successors tell us about the structure and development of personality?

Julie Payette is a truly exceptional young woman. What combination of personality characteristics, abilities and experiences have determined her interests and contributed to her many accomplishments?

Psychologists who specialize in **personality** seek to understand the characteristic ways in which people behave. Personality encompasses the relatively enduring characteristics that differentiate people—those behaviours that make each of us unique. It is also personality that leads us to act in a consistent and predictable manner both in different situations and over extended periods of time.

In this chapter we consider a number of approaches to personality. We begin with the broadest and most comprehensive theory: Freud's psychoanalytic theory. Next, we turn to more recent theories of personality. We consider approaches that concentrate on identifying the most fundamental personality traits; on theories that view personality as a set of learned behaviours; on biological and evolutionary perspectives on personality; and on approaches, known as humanistic theories, that highlight the uniquely human aspects of personality. We end our discussion by focusing on how personality is measured and how personality tests can be used.

PSYCHOANALYTIC APPROACHES TO PERSONALITY

Oscar Madison: sloppy, dishevelled, unkempt.

Felix Unger: neat, precise, controlled.

As anyone who has seen the play or the old television series *The Odd Couple* can attest, it would seem that Oscar and Felix could hardly possess more dissimilar personalities. Yet to one group of personality theorists—*psychoanalysts*—the two men might actually be quite similar, at least in terms of the underlying part of personality that motivates their behaviour. According to psychoanalysts, our behaviour is triggered largely by powerful forces within our personalities of which we are not aware. These hidden forces, shaped by childhood experiences, play an important role in energizing and directing our everyday behaviour.

The most important theorist to hold such a view, and indeed one of the best-known figures in all psychology, is Sigmund Freud. An Austrian physician, Freud originated **psychoanalytic theory** in the early 1900s.

psychoanalytic theory: Freud's theory that unconscious forces act as determinants of personality

Freud's Psychoanalytic Theory

The college student was intent on sounding smooth and making a good first impression on an attractive woman whom he had spotted across a crowded room at a party. As he walked toward her, he mulled over a line he had heard in an old movie the night before: "I don't believe we've been properly introduced yet." To his horror, what came out was a bit different. After threading his way through the crowded room, he finally reached the woman and blurted out, "I don't believe we've been properly seduced yet."

Although this statement may seem to be merely an embarrassing slip of the tongue, according to psychoanalytic theory such a mistake is not an error at all (Motley, 1987). Rather, it is an indication of deeply felt emotions and thoughts that are harbored in the **unconscious,** a part of the personality of which a person is not aware. The unconscious contains *instinctual drives*: infantile wishes, desires, demands, and needs that are hidden from conscious awareness because of the conflicts and pain they would cause us if they were part of our everyday lives. Many of life's experiences are painful, and the unconscious provides a "safe" haven for our recollections of such events. Uncomfortable memories can remain in our unconscious without continually disturbing us.

unconscious: A part of the personality of which a person is not aware, and which is a potential determinant of behaviour

To Freud, conscious experience is just the tip of the psychological iceberg. Like the unseen mass of a floating iceberg, the material in the unconscious far surpasses in quantity the information about which we are aware. Much of people's everyday behaviour is viewed as being motivated by unconscious forces. For example, a child's concern over being unable to please her strict and demanding parents may lead her to have low self-esteem as an adult, even though she may be highly accomplished. Moreover, on a conscious level she may recall her childhood with great pleasure; it is her unconscious, holding her painful memories, that provokes the low self-evaluation.

According to Freud, to fully understand personality, it is necessary to illuminate and expose what is in the unconscious. But because the unconscious disguises the meaning of the material it holds, it cannot be observed directly. It is therefore necessary to interpret clues to the unconscious—slips of the tongue, fantasies, and dreams—in order to understand the unconscious processes that direct behaviour. A slip of the tongue such as the one quoted earlier (sometimes termed a *Freudian slip*) might be interpreted as revealing the speaker's underlying unconscious sexual desires.

Freud

If the notion of an unconscious does not seem so farfetched to most of us, it is only because Freudian theory has had such a widespread influence in western cultures, with applications in fields ranging from literature to religion. In Freud's day, however, the idea that the unconscious could harbor painful material from which people were protecting themselves was revolutionary. The best minds of the time found the notion laughable and summarily rejected Freud's ideas as being without basis. It is a tribute to the influence of Freud's theory that the concept of the unconscious is readily accepted by people today (Moore & Fine, 1990; Westen, 1990; Mitchell & Black, 1996).

Structuring Personality: Id, Ego, and Superego

To describe the structure of personality, Freud developed a comprehensive theory, which held that personality consisted of three separate but interacting components: the id, the ego, and the superego. Freud suggested that the three structures can be depicted

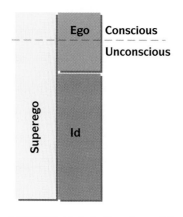

FIGURE 11-1 *In Freud's model of personality, there are three major components: the id, the ego, and the superego. As the schematic shows, only a small portion of personality is conscious. This diagram should not be thought of as an actual, physical structure, but rather as a model of the interrelationships among the parts of personality.*

id: The raw, unorganized, inborn part of personality, whose sole purpose is to reduce tension created by primitive drives related to hunger, sex, aggression, and irrational impulses

libido: According to Freud, the "psychic energy" that fuels the primary drives of hunger, sex, aggression, and irrational impulses.

ego: The part of the personality that provides a buffer between the id and the outside world

superego: According to Freud, the final personality structure to develop that represents the rights and wrongs of society as handed down by a person's parents, teachers, and other important figures

oral stage: According to Freud, a stage from birth to 12–18 months, in which an infant's centre of pleasure is the mouth

diagrammatically to show how they are related to the conscious and the unconscious (see Figure 11-1).

Although Freud described the three components of personality in very concrete terms, it is important to realize that they are not actual physical structures found in a certain part of the brain. Instead, they represent abstract conceptions of a general *model* of personality that describes the interaction of various processes and forces within one's personality that motivate behaviour.

If personality consisted only of primitive, instinctual cravings and longings, it would have just one component: the id. The **id** is the raw, unorganized, inborn part of personality. From the time of birth, the sole purpose of the id is to reduce tension created by primitive drives related to hunger, sex, aggression, and irrational impulses. These drives are fuelled by "psychic energy" or **libido,** as Freud called it. The id operates according to the *pleasure principle,* in which the goal is the immediate reduction of tension and the maximization of satisfaction.

Unfortunately for the id—but luckily for people and society—reality prevents the fulfillment of the demands of the pleasure principle in most cases. Instead, the world produces constraints: We cannot always eat when we are hungry, and we can discharge our sexual drives only when time, place—and partner—are willing. To account for this fact of life, Freud suggested a second component of personality, which he called the ego.

The **ego** provides a buffer between the id and the realities of the objective, outside world. In contrast to the pleasure-seeking nature of the id, the ego operates according to the *reality principle,* in which instinctual energy is restrained in order to maintain the safety of the individual and help integrate the person into society. In a sense, then, the ego is the "executive" of personality: It makes decisions, controls actions, and allows thinking and problem solving of a higher order than the id's capabilites. The ego is also the seat of higher cognitive abilities such as intelligence, thoughtfulness, reasoning, and learning.

The **superego,** the final personality structure to develop, represents the rights and wrongs of society as handed down by a person's parents, teachers, and other important figures. It becomes a part of personality when children learn right from wrong and continues to develop as people begin to incorporate into their own standards the broad moral principles of the society in which they live.

The superego actually has two components, the *conscience* and the *ego-ideal.* The conscience prevents us from doing morally bad things, while the ego-ideal motivates us to do what is morally proper. The superego helps us to control impulses coming from the id, making our behaviour less selfish and more virtuous.

Although on the surface the superego appears to be the opposite of the id, the two share an important feature: Both are unrealistic in that they do not consider the practical realities imposed by society. Thus the superego pushes the person toward greater virtue; if left unchecked, it would create perfectionists, unable to make the compromises that life requires. Similarly, an unrestrained id would create a primitive, pleasure-seeking, thoughtless individual, seeking to fulfill every desire without delay. The ego, then, must compromise between the demands of the superego and the id, thereby enabling a person to resist some of the gratification sought by the id while at the same time keeping the moralistic superego in check so that it does not prevent the person from obtaining any gratification at all.

Developing Personality: A Stage Approach

Freud also provided us with a view of how personality develops throughout a series of stages during childhood. What is especially noteworthy about the sequence he proposed is that it explains how experiences and difficulties during a particular childhood stage may predict specific sorts of idiosyncrasies in adult personality. The theory is also unique in focusing each stage on a major biological function, which Freud assumed to be the focus of pleasure in a given period.

In the first stage of development, called the **oral stage,** the baby's mouth is the focal point of pleasure (see Table 11-1 for a summary of the stages). During the first

Table 11-1	Freud's Stages of Personality Development	

Stage	Age	Major Characteristics
Oral	Birth to 12–18 months	Interest in oral gratification from sucking, eating, mouthing, biting
Anal	12–18 months to 3 years	Gratification from expelling and withholding feces; coming to terms with society's controls relating to toilet training
Phallic	3 to 5–6 years	Interest in the genitals; coming to terms with Oedipal conflict, leading to identification with same-sex parent
Latency	5–6 years to adolescence	Sexual concerns largely unimportant
Genital	Adolescence to adulthood	Reemergence of sexual interests and establishment of mature sexual relationships

12 to 18 months of life, children suck, mouth, and bite anything that will fit into their mouths. To Freud, this behaviour suggested that the mouth was the primary site of a kind of sexual pleasure. If infants were either overly indulged (perhaps by being fed every time they cried) or frustrated in their search for oral gratification, they might become fixated at this stage. Displaying **fixation** means that an adult shows personality traits characteristic of an earlier stage of development due to an unresolved conflict stemming from the earlier period. For example, fixation at the oral stage might produce an adult who was unusually interested in overtly oral activities—eating, talking, smoking—or who showed symbolic sorts of oral interests: being either "bitingly" sarcastic or very gullible ("swallowing" anything).

From around 12 to 18 months until 3 years of age—where the emphasis in western cultures is on toilet training—the child enters the **anal stage.** At this point, the major source of pleasure changes from the mouth to the anal region, and children derive considerable pleasure from both retention and expulsion of feces. If toilet training is particularly demanding, the result may be fixation. If fixation occurs during the anal stage, Freud suggested that adults might show unusual rigidity, orderliness, punctuality—or extreme disorderliness or sloppiness, as in our earlier examples of Felix and Oscar.

At about age 3, the **phallic stage** begins, at which point there is another major shift in the primary source of pleasure for the child. This time, interest focuses on the genitals and the pleasures derived from fondling them. This is also the stage of one of the most important points of personality development, according to Freudian theory: the **Oedipal conflict.** As children focus their attention on their genitals, the differences between male and female anatomy become more salient. Furthermore, at this time Freud believed that the male begins to develop sexual interests in his mother, starts to see his father as a rival, and harbours a wish to kill his father—as Oedipus did in the ancient Greek tragedy. But because he views his father as too powerful, he develops a fear of retaliation in the form of "castration anxiety." Ultimately, this fear becomes so powerful that the child represses his desires for his mother and instead chooses *identification* with his father, trying to be as much like him as possible.

For girls, the process is different. Freud reasoned that girls begin to experience sexual arousal toward their fathers and—in a suggestion that was later to bring serious accusations that he viewed women as inferior to men—that they begin to experience *penis envy.* They wish they had the anatomical part that, at least to Freud, seemed most clearly "missing" in girls. Blaming their mothers for their lack of a penis, girls come to believe that their mothers are responsible for their "castration." As with males, though, they find that in order to resolve such unacceptable feelings, they must identify with the same-sex parent by behaving like her and adopting her attitudes and values. In this way, a girl's identification with her mother is completed.

At this point, the Oedipal conflict is said to be resolved, and Freudian theory assumes that both males and females move on to the next stage of development. If

According to psychoanalytic theory, toilet training is a crucial event in the formation of an individual's personality.

fixation: Personality traits characteristic of an earlier stage of development due to an unresolved conflict stemming from the earlier period

anal stage: According to Freud, a stage from 12–18 months to 3 years of age, in which a child's pleasure is centred on the anus

phallic stage: According to Freud, a period beginning around age 3 during which a child's interest focuses on the genitals

Oedipal conflict: A child's sexual interest in his or her opposite-sex parent, typically resolved through identification with the same-sex parent

Table 11-2	Freud's Defense Mechanisms	
Defense Mechanism	**Explanation**	**Example**
Repression	Unacceptable or unpleasant impulses are pushed back into the unconscious	A woman is unable to recall that she was raped
Regression	People behave as if they were at an earlier stage of development	A boss has a temper tantrum when an employee makes a mistake
Displacement	The expression of an unwanted feeling or thought is redirected from a more threatening, powerful person to a weaker one	A brother yells at his younger sister after a teacher gives him a bad grade
Rationalization	A distortion of reality in which a person justifies what happens	A person who is passed over for an award says she didn't really want it in the first place
Denial	Refusal to accept or acknowledge an anxiety-producing piece of information	A student refuses to believe that he has flunked a course
Projection	Attributing unwanted impulses and feelings to someone else	A man who is angry at his father acts lovingly to his father but complains that his father is angry with him
Sublimation	Diversion of unwanted impulses into socially approved thoughts, feelings, or behaviours	A person with strong feelings of aggression becomes a soldier

difficulties arise during this period, however, all sorts of problems are thought to occur, which include improper sex-role behaviour and the failure to develop a conscience.

Following the resolution of the Oedipal conflict, typically at around age 5 or 6, children move into the **latency period,** which lasts until puberty. During this period, little of interest is occurring, according to Freud. Sexual concerns are more or less put to rest, even in the unconscious. Then, during adolescence, sexual feelings reemerge, marking the start of the final period, the **genital stage,** which extends until death. The focus during the genital stage is on mature, adult sexuality, which Freud defined as sexual intercourse.

Defense Mechanisms

Freud's efforts to describe and theorize about the underlying dynamics of personality and its development were motivated by very practical problems that his patients faced in dealing with *anxiety,* an intense, negative emotional experience. According to Freud, anxiety is a danger signal to the ego. Although anxiety may arise from realistic fears—such as seeing a poisonous snake about to strike—it may also occur in the form of *neurotic anxiety,* in which irrational impulses emanating from the id threaten to burst through and become uncontrollable.

Because anxiety, obviously, is unpleasant, Freud believed that people develop a range of defense mechanisms to deal with it. **Defense mechanisms** are unconscious strategies that people use to reduce anxiety by concealing the source from themselves and others. Freud, and later his daughter Anna Freud (who became a well-known psychoanalyst in her own right), formulated an extensive list of potential defense mechanisms; the major ones are summarized in Table 11-2 (Cooper, 1989; Conte & Plutchik, 1995; Basch, 1996).

The primary defense mechanism is *repression,* in which unacceptable or unpleasant id impulses are pushed back into the unconscious. Repression is the most

latency period: According to Freud, the period between the phallic stage and puberty during which children's sexual concerns are temporarily put aside
genital stage: According to Freud, the period from puberty until death, marked by mature sexual behaviour (i.e., sexual intercourse)

defense mechanisms: Unconscious strategies that people use to reduce anxiety by concealing the source from themselves and others

direct method of dealing with anxiety; instead of handling an anxiety-producing impulse on a conscious level, one simply ignores it. For example, a college student who feels hatred for her mother might repress these personally and socially unacceptable feelings. They remain lodged within the id, since acknowledging them would provoke anxiety. This does not mean, however, that they have no effect: True feelings might be revealed through dreams, slips of the tongue, or symbolically in some other fashion. The student might, for instance, have difficulty with authority figures such as teachers and do poorly in school. Alternatively, she might join the military, where she could ultimately give harsh orders to others without having them questioned.

If repression is ineffective in keeping anxiety at bay, other defense mechanisms may be called upon. For example, *regression* might be used, whereby people behave as if they were at an earlier stage of development. By retreating to a younger age—for instance by complaining and throwing tantrums—they might succeed in having fewer demands put upon them. For example, a student who is overwhelmed by exams might act in a childish, immature manner to escape his responsibilities.

Anyone who has ever been angered by the unfairness of a professor and then returned to the dorm and yelled at his or her roommate knows what displacement is all about. In *displacement,* the expression of an unwanted feeling or thought is redirected from a more threatening, powerful person to a weaker one. A classic case is yelling at one's secretary after being criticized by the boss.

Rationalization, another defense mechanism, occurs when we distort reality by justifying what happens to us. We develop explanations that allow us to protect our self-esteem. If you've ever heard someone say that he didn't mind being stood up for a date because he really had a lot of studying to do that evening, you have probably seen rationalization at work.

In *denial,* a person simply refuses to accept or acknowledge an anxiety-producing piece of information. For example, when told that his wife has died in an automobile crash, a husband may at first deny the tragedy, claiming that there must be some mistake, and only gradually come to conscious acceptance that she has actually been killed. In extreme cases, denial may linger; the husband may continue to expect that his wife will return home.

Projection is a means of protecting oneself by attributing unwanted impulses and feelings to someone else. For example, a man who feels sexually inadequate may complain to his wife that *she* is sexually inept.

Finally, one defense mechanism that Freud considered to be healthy and socially acceptable is sublimation. In *sublimation,* people divert unwanted impulses into socially approved thoughts, feelings, or behaviors. For example, a person with strong feelings of aggression may become a football player or karate instructor. Sublimation affords the opportunity not only to release psychic tension but to do so in a way that is socially acceptable.

All of us employ defense mechanisms to some degree, according to Freudian theory, and they can serve a useful purpose by protecting us from unpleasant information. Yet some people use them to such an extent that a large amount of psychic energy must constantly be directed toward hiding and rechanneling unacceptable impulses. When this occurs, everyday living becomes difficult. In such cases, the result is what Freud called "neurosis," a mental disorder produced by anxiety.

Evaluating Freudian Theory

More than almost any other psychological theory we have discussed, Freud's personality theory presents an elaborate and complicated set of propositions—some of which are so removed from everyday explanations of behaviour that they may appear difficult to accept (Crews, 1993; Webster, 1995). But lay people are not the only ones concerned about the validity of Freud's theory; personality psychologists, too, have criticized its inadequacies.

Among the most compelling criticisms is the lack of scientific data to support the theory. Although a wealth of individual assessments of particular people *seem* to support the theory, we lack definitive evidence showing that the personality is structured and operates along the lines Freud laid out. This is due, in part, to the fact that Freud's conception of personality is built on unobservable abstract conceptions. Moreover, while we can readily employ Freudian theory in after-the-fact explanations, it is extremely difficult to predict how certain developmental difficulties will be displayed in the adult. For instance, if a person is fixated at the anal stage, he might, according to Freud, be unusually messy—or he might be unusually neat. Freud's theory offers us no way to predict which manifestations of the difficulty will occur. It produces good history, then, but not such good science (Macmillan, 1991; Crews, 1996).

Finally, Freud made his observations—admittedly insightful ones—and derived his theory from a limited population. His theory was based almost entirely on upper-class Austrian women living in the strict, puritanical era of the early 1900s. How far one can generalize beyond this population is a matter of considerable debate. For instance, in some Pacific Island societies, the role of disciplinarian is played by a mother's oldest brother, not the father. In such a culture, it wouldn't make sense to argue that the Oedipal conflict would progress in the same way that it did in Austrian society, where the father typically was the major disciplinarian—a view supported by studies in such societies. In sum, cross-cultural research raises questions about the universality of Freud's view of personality development (Doi, 1990; Brislin, 1993; Altman, 1996).

Despite these criticisms, which cannot be ignored, Freud's theory has had an enormous impact on the field of psychology—and indeed on all of western thinking. The ideas of the unconscious, anxiety, defense mechanisms, and the childhood causes of adult psychological difficulties have permeated people's views of human behaviour, including their understanding of the causes of their own behaviour (Baumeister, 1997).

Furthermore, Freud's emphasis on the unconscious has been partially supported by some of the current research findings of cognitive psychologists. This work has revealed that mental processes about which people are unaware have an important impact on thinking and actions. In addition, experimental techniques derived from procedures used to study implicit memory (Chapter 6) allow the unconscious to be studied in a more scientifically sophisticated manner. The techniques help overcome the reliance of traditional Freudian approaches on single-participant case studies and unconfirmable theoretical interpretations of dreams and slips of the tongue for support (Kihlstrom, 1987; Westen, 1990; Jacoby & Kelley, 1992).

The importance of psychoanalytic theory is underscored by the fact that it spawned a significant—and enduring—method of treating psychological disturbances, as we will discuss further in Chapter 13. For a variety of reasons, then, Freud's psychoanalytic theory remains a significant contribution to our understanding of personality.

The Neo-Freudian Psychoanalysts

One particularly important outgrowth of Freud's theorizing was the work done by a series of successors who were trained in traditional Freudian theory but who later rejected some of its major points. These theorists are known as **neo-Freudian psychoanalysts.**

neo-Freudian psychoanalysts: Psychoanalysts who were trained in traditional Freudian theory but who later rejected some of its major points

The neo-Freudians placed greater emphasis than Freud did on the functions of the ego, suggesting that it had more control than the id over day-to-day activities. They also paid greater attention to social factors and the effects of society and culture on personality development. Carl Jung (pronounced "yoong"), for example, who initially adhered closely to Freud's thinking, later rejected the notion of the primary importance of unconscious sexual urges—a key notion of Freudian theory. Instead he looked at the primitive urges of the unconscious more positively, suggesting that people had a **collective unconscious,** a set of influences we inherit from our own particular ancestors, the whole human race, and even animal ancestors from the distant past. This collective unconscious is shared by everyone and is displayed by behaviour that is common across diverse cultures—such as love of mother, belief in a supreme being, and even behaviour as specific as fear of snakes.

collective unconscious: A set of influences we inherit from our own particular ancestors, the whole human race, and even animal ancestors from the distant past

In Jungian terms, Batman and the Joker are archetypes, or universally recognizable symbols, of good and evil.

Jung went on to propose that the collective unconscious contained *archetypes,* universal symbolic representations of a particular person, object, or experience. For instance, a mother archetype, which contains reflections of our ancestors' relationships with mother figures, is suggested by the prevalence of mothers in art, religion, literature, and mythology. (Think of the Virgin Mary, Earth Mother, wicked stepmothers of fairy tales, Mother's Day, and so forth!)

Jung

To Jung, archetypes play an important role in determining our day-to-day reactions, attitudes, and values. For instance, Jung might explain the popularity of a movie such as the original *Batman* as being due to its use of broad archetypes of good (Batman), evil (the Joker), and innocence (Vicki Vail).

Alfred Adler, another important neo-Freudian psychoanalyst, also considered Freudian theory's emphasis on sexual needs to be misplaced. Instead, Adler proposed that the primary human motivation was a striving for superiority, not in terms of superiority over others, but as a quest to achieve self-improvement and perfection. Adler used the term **inferiority complex** to describe situations in which adults have not been able to overcome the feelings of inferiority that they developed as children, when they were small and limited in their knowledge about the world. Early social relationships with parents have an important effect on how well children are able to outgrow feelings of personal inferiority and instead orient themselves toward attaining more socially useful goals, such as improving society.

Other neo-Freudians, such as Erik Erikson (whose theory we discussed in Chapter 10) and Karen Horney (1937), also focused less than Freud on inborn sexual and aggressive drives and more on the social and cultural factors behind personality. Horney (pronounced "HORN-eye") was one of the first psychologists who championed women's issues. She suggested that personality develops in terms of social relationships and depends particularly on the relationship between parents and child and how well the child's needs were met. She rejected Freud's suggestion that women had penis envy, asserting that what women envied most in men was not their anatomy but the independence, success, and freedom that women were often denied.

inferiority complex: According to Adler, a situation in which adults have not been able to overcome the feelings of inferiority that they developed as children, when they were small and limited in their knowledge about the world

Recap, Review, and Rethink

Recap

- Freud's psychoanalytic theory proposes that personality consists of three components: the id, the ego, and the superego.

- According to psychoanalytic theory, personality develops during a series of stages in which the focus of pleasure is on a particular part of the body.

- Defense mechanisms are unconscious strategies that people use to reduce anxiety by concealing its source. Among the most important are repression, regression, displacement, rationalization, denial, projection, and sublimation.

- Among the neo-Freudian psychoanalysts who built and modified psychoanalytic theory are Jung, Adler, and Horney.

Review

1. _____ theory states that behaviour is motivated primarily by unconscious forces.

2. Match each component of the personality (according to Freud) with its description.
   1. ego
   2. id
   3. superego

   a. determines right from wrong on the basis of cultural standards
   b. operates according to the "reality principle"; energy is redirected to integrate the person into society
   c. seeks to reduce tension brought on by primitive drives

3. Within the superego, the _____-_____ motivates us to do what is right, while the _____ prevents us from doing what is unacceptable.

4. Which of the following represents the proper order of personality development according to Freud?

   a. oral, phallic, latency, anal, genital
   b. anal, oral, phallic, genital, latency
   c. oral, anal, phallic, latency, genital
   d. latency, phallic, anal, genital, oral

5. In the resolution of the _____ complex, Freud believed that boys learn to repress their desire for their mother and identify with their father.

6. _____ _____ is the term Freud used to describe unconscious strategies used to reduce anxiety.

Answers to Review Questions are on page 420.

Rethink

1. List some ways in which Freud's theories of unconscious motivations are commonly used in popular culture. How accurately do you think such popular uses of Freudian theories reflect Freud's ideas?

2. A friend tells you that whenever he gets really angry, he goes to the gym and works out vigorously until he feels better. Which of Freud's defense mechanisms might this behaviour represent?

3. Give some examples of archetypes in addition to those mentioned in this chapter. In what ways are archetypes similar to and different from stereotypes?

OTHER MAJOR APPROACHES TO PERSONALITY: IN SEARCH OF HUMAN UNIQUENESS

▶ **What are the major aspects of trait, learning, biological and evolutionary, and humanistic approaches to personality?**

"Tell me about Nelson," said Johnetta.

"Oh, he's just terrific. He's the friendliest guy I know—goes out of his way to be nice to everyone. He hardly ever gets mad. He's just so even-tempered, no matter what's happening. And he's really smart, too. About the only thing I don't like is that he's always in such a hurry to get things done. He seems to have boundless energy, much more than I have."

"He sounds great to me, especially in comparison to Rico," replied Johnetta. "He is so self-centred and arrogant it drives me crazy. I sometimes wonder why I ever started going out with him."

Friendly. Even-tempered. Smart. Energetic. Self-centred. Arrogant.

The interchange above is made up of a series of trait characterizations of the boyfriends being discussed. In fact, most of our understanding of the reasons behind others' behaviour is based on the premise that people possess certain traits that are assumed to be consistent across different situations. A number of formal theories of personality employ variants of this approach. We turn now to a discussion of these and other personality approaches, all of which provide alternatives to the psychoanalytic emphasis on unconscious processes in determining behaviour.

Mother Teresa exemplified the humanistic approach to personality, which emphasizes people's basic goodness.

Trait Approaches: Placing Labels on Personality

If someone were to ask you to characterize another person, it is probable that—like the two people in the conversation just presented—you would come up with a list of that individual's personal qualities, as you see them. But how would you know which of these qualities were most important to an understanding of that person's behaviour?

Personality psychologists have asked similar questions themselves. In order to answer them, they have developed a model of personality known as **trait theory.** **Traits** are enduring dimensions of personality characteristics along which people differ.

Trait theorists do not assume that some people have a trait and others do not; rather, they propose that all people possess certain traits, but that the degree to which a given trait applies to a specific person varies and can be quantified. For instance, you might be relatively friendly, whereas I might be relatively unfriendly. But we both have a "friendliness" trait, although your degree of "friendliness" would be higher than mine. The major challenge for trait theorists taking this approach has been to identify the specific primary traits necessary to describe personality. As we shall see, different theorists have come up with surprisingly different sets of traits (Wiggins, 1997).

Allport's Trait Theory: Identifying the Basics

When personality psychologist Gordon Allport systematically leafed through an unabridged dictionary, he came up with some 18,000 separate terms that could be used to describe personality. Although he was able to pare down the list to a mere 4,500 descriptors after eliminating synonyms, he was obviously still left with a problem crucial to all trait approaches: Which of these were the most basic?

Allport answered this question by suggesting that there are three basic categories of traits: cardinal, central, and secondary (Allport, 1961, 1966). A *cardinal trait* is a single characteristic that directs most of a person's activities. For example, a totally selfless woman might direct all her energy toward humanitarian activities; an intensely power-hungry person might be driven by an all-consuming need for control.

Most people, however, do not develop all-encompassing cardinal traits. Instead, they possess a handful of central traits that make up the core of personality. *Central traits,* such as honesty and sociability, are the major characteristics of an individual; they usually number from five to ten in any one person. Finally, *secondary traits* are characteristics that affect behaviour in fewer situations and are less influential than central or cardinal traits. For instance, a preference for ice cream or a dislike of modern art would be considered secondary traits.

trait theory: A model of personality that seeks to identify the basic traits necessary to describe personality

traits: Enduring dimensions of personality characteristics along which people differ

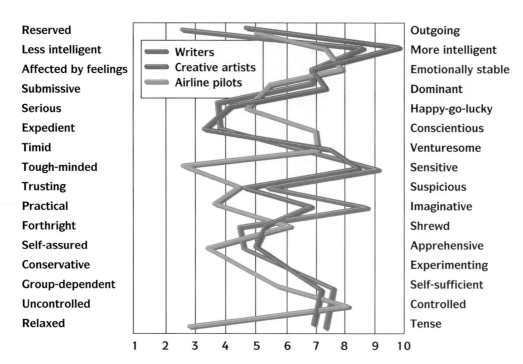

FIGURE 11-2 *Personality profiles for source traits developed by Cattell for three groups of subjects: writers, creative artists, and airline pilots. The average score for the general population is between 4.5 and 6.5 on each scale.*

The Theories of Cattell and Eysenck: Factoring Out Personality

More recent attempts to identify primary traits have centred on a statistical technique known as factor analysis. *Factor analysis* is a method of summarizing the relationships among a large number of variables into fewer, more general patterns. For example, a personality researcher might administer a questionnaire to many participants, asking them to describe themselves by referring to an extensive list of traits. By statistically combining responses and computing which traits are associated with one another in the same person, a researcher can identify the most fundamental patterns or combinations of traits—called factors—that underlie participants' responses.

Using factor analysis, personality psychologist Raymond Cattell (1965) suggested that the characteristics that can be observed in a given situation represent forty-six *surface traits,* or clusters of related behaviours. For example, you might encounter a friendly, gregarious librarian who goes out of his way to be helpful to you, and from your interactions with him decide that he possesses the trait of sociability—in Cattell's terms, a surface trait.

However, such surface traits are based on people's perceptions and representations of personality; they do not necessarily provide the best description of the underlying personality dimensions that are at the root of all behaviour. Carrying out further factor analysis, Cattell found that sixteen *source traits* represented the basic dimensions of personality. Using these source traits, he developed the Sixteen Personality Factor Questionnaire, or 16 PF, a measure that provides scores for each of the source traits. Figure 11-2 shows the pattern of average scores on each of the source traits for three different groups of participants—writers, creative artists, and airplane pilots (Cattell, Cattell, & Cattell, 1993).

Another trait theorist, psychologist Hans Eysenck (1975a, 1994a; Eysenck & Eysenck, 1985; Eysenck et al., 1992), also used factor analysis to identify patterns of

---

Answers to Review Questions:

1. Psychoanalytic   2. 1-b; 2-c; 3-a   3. ego ideal; conscience   4. c   5. Oedipal   6. Defense mechanisms

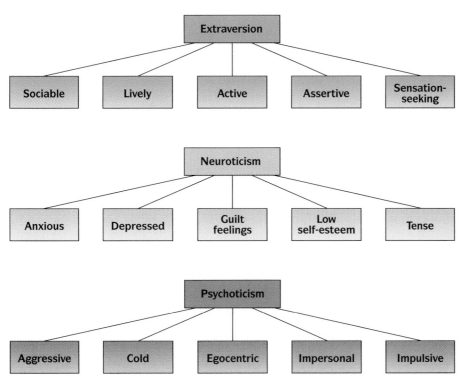

FIGURE 11-3 *According to Eysenck, personality could best be described in terms of just three major dimensions: extraversion, neuroticism, and psychoticism. Eysenck has been able to predict behaviour accurately in a variety of types of situations by evaluating people along these three dimensions.*

traits, but he came to a very different conclusion about the nature of personality. He found that personality could best be described in terms of just three major dimensions: *extraversion, neuroticism,* and *psychoticism.* The extraversion dimension relates to the degree of sociability, while the neurotic dimension encompasses emotional stability. Finally, psychoticism refers to the degree to which reality is distorted. By evaluating people along these three dimensions, Eysenck has been able to predict behaviour accurately in a variety of types of situations. Figure 11-3 illustrates specific traits associated with each of the dimensions.

Most contemporary trait theorists argue that five broad trait factors lie at the core of personality. The five factors, which have come to be called the "Big Five," are *extraversion, agreeableness, conscientiousness, neuroticism* (emotional stability), and *openness to experience* (Digman, 1990; Funder, 1991; Costa & McCrae, 1995; Paunonen et al., 1996; Wiggins, 1996; see Table 11-3). There is a growing consensus that these five factors represent the best description of personality. Still, the evidence is not conclusive, and the specific number and kinds of traits that are considered fundamental remain a source of debate (and investigation) among trait theorists (Block, 1995; Jackson, Ashton, & Tomes, 1996; Jackson et al., 1996; McCrae & Costa, 1997; Wiggins & Trapnell, 1997). There is more research published on traits than on any other topic in personality psychology (Endler & Speer, 1998).

Five-Factor Model of Personality

Evaluating Trait Approaches to Personality

Trait approaches have several virtues. They provide a clear, straightforward explanation of people's behavioural consistencies. Traits are useful in studying people's lives (Wiggins & Pincus, 1992). Furthermore, they allow us to readily compare one person with another. Because of these advantages, trait conceptions of personality have influenced the development of several personality measures discussed later in the chapter (Buss, 1989; Funder, 1991; Wiggins, 1997).

On the other hand, trait approaches have some drawbacks. For example, as we have seen, there is some disagreement among trait theorists regarding how many and which traits are fundamental. Another issue concerns the hierarchical structure of trait models (see Figure 11-3 and Table 11-3). For example, would it be better to assess the factor, Conscientiousness, or its related sample traits, in order to predict or account for

Table 11-3	The Big Five Personality Factors and Sample Traits

Extraversion

quiet	talkative
reserved	assertive
shy	active
silent	energetic

Agreeableness

fault-finding	sympathetic
cold	kind
unfriendly	appreciative
quarrelsome	affectionate

Conscientiousness

careless	organized
disorderly	thorough
frivolous	planful
irresponsible	efficient

Neuroticism

tense	stable
anxious	calm
nervous	contented
moody	unemotional

Openness to experience

commonplace	wide interests
narrow interests	imaginative
simple	intelligent
shallow	original

Source: Adapted from Pervin, Chapter 3.

behaviour? Tests at the level of specific traits appear to be sensitive to the common variance attributable to the higher level factors as well as to the variance associated with the specific lower level traits (Paunonen, 1998).

And there is an even more fundamental difficulty with trait approaches. Traits label or describe personality, but they do not explain it. Describing someone as generous does not tell us why that person donates money to charity or the reasons for generosity in a particular situation.

Learning Approaches: We Are What We've Learned

The psychoanalytic and trait approaches we've discussed concentrate on the "inner" person—the stormy fury of an unobservable but powerful id or a hypothetical but critical set of traits. In contrast, learning approaches to personality focus on the "outer" person. To a strict learning theorist, personality is simply the sum of learned responses to the external environment. Internal events such as thoughts, feelings, and motivations are ignored. Although their existence is not denied, learning theorists say that personality is best understood by looking at features of a person's environment.

According to the most influential of the learning theorists, B. F. Skinner (whom we discussed first in terms of operant conditioning in Chapter 5), personality is a collection of learned behaviour patterns (Skinner, 1975). Similarities in responses across different situations are caused by similar patterns of reinforcement that have been received in such situations in the past. If I am sociable both at parties and at meetings, it is because I have been reinforced previously for displaying social behaviours—not because I am fulfilling some unconscious wish based on experiences during my child-hood or because I have an internal trait of sociability.

Strict learning theorists such as Skinner are less interested in the consistencies in behaviour across situations, however, than in ways of modifying behaviour. Their view is that humans are infinitely changeable. If one is able to control and modify the patterns of reinforcers in a situation, behaviour that other theorists would view as stable and unyielding can be changed and ultimately improved. Learning theorists are optimistic in their attitudes about the potential for resolving personal and societal problems through treatment strategies based on learning theory—methods we will discuss in Chapter 13.

Social-Cognitive Approaches to Personality

Not all learning theories of personality take such a strict view in rejecting the importance of what is "inside" the person by focusing solely on the "outside." Unlike other learning approaches to personality, **social-cognitive approaches** emphasize the influence of a person's cognitions—thoughts, feelings, expectations, and values—in determining personality. According to Albert Bandura, one of the main proponents of this point of view, people are able to foresee the possible outcomes of certain behaviours in a given setting without actually having to carry them out. This takes place mainly through the mechanism of *observational learning*—viewing the actions of others and observing the consequences (Bandura, 1977, 1986).

For instance, as we first discussed in Chapter 5, children who view a model behaving in an aggressive manner tend to copy the behaviour if the consequences of the model's behaviour are seen to be positive. If, on the other hand, the model's aggressive behaviour has resulted in no consequences or negative consequences, children are considerably less likely to act aggressively. According to social-cognitive approaches, personality thus develops by repeated observation of the behaviour of others.

Bandura places particular emphasis on the role played by *self-efficacy*, learned expectations that one is capable of carrying out a behaviour or producing a desired outcome. Self-efficacy underlies people's faith in their ability to carry out a particular behaviour. The greater a person's sense of self-efficacy, the more persistent he or she will be, and the more likely it is that the individual will be successful. For instance, students high in self-efficacy regarding scholastic accomplishments will be more likely to achieve academic success (Scheier & Carver, 1992; Pajares, 1996; Zimmerman, 1995, 1996).

Self-efficacy also determines the kinds of goals that people set for themselves and how hard they will try to reach those goals. High self-efficacy leads to higher aspirations and to foreseeing future success (Bandura, 1997).

Compared to other learning theories of personality, social-cognitive approaches are distinctive in their emphasis on the reciprocity between individuals and their environment. Not only is the environment assumed to affect personality, but people's behaviour and personalities are assumed to "feed back" and modify the environment—which in turn affects behaviour in a web of reciprocity.

In fact, Bandura has suggested that reciprocal determinism is the key to understanding behaviour. *Reciprocal determinism* refers to the way in which the interaction of environment, behaviour, and individual ultimately causes people to behave as they do (Bandura, 1981, 1986). For instance, suppose a man with aggressive needs gets into a fight at a hockey game. He may later seek out hockey games in part to fulfill his enjoyment of fighting. At the same time, his drive to be aggressive may increase because of his fighting. In sum, the environment of the hockey game, the behaviour of fighting, and the individual's characteristics interact with one another in a reciprocal fashion.

Evaluating Learning Approaches of Personality

By ignoring the internal processes that are uniquely human, traditional learning theorists such as Skinner have been accused of oversimplifying personality to such an extent that the concept becomes meaningless. Reducing behavior to a series of stimuli and responses, and excluding thoughts and feelings from the realm of personality, leaves behaviourists practicing an unrealistic and inadequate form of science, in the eyes of their critics.

social-cognitive approaches to personality: The theory that emphasizes the influence of a person's cognitions—thoughts, feelings, expectations, and values—in determining personality

Self-Efficacy

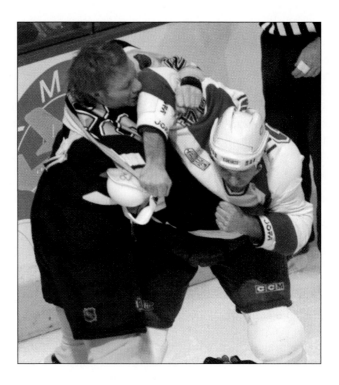

Learning theory approaches to personality suggest that reinforcement we receive from behaving in a certain manner—such as behaving aggressively—may lead to that behaviour becoming a consistent aspect of our personality.

Of course, some of these criticisms are blunted by social-cognitive approaches, which explicitly consider the role of cognitive processes in personality. Still, learning approaches tend to share a highly *deterministic* view of human behaviour, a view maintaining that behaviour is shaped primarily by forces beyond the control of the individual. According to some critics, determinism disregards the ability of people to pilot their own course through life.

On the other hand, learning approaches have had a major impact in a variety of ways. For one thing, they have helped make the study of personality an objective, scientific venture by focusing on observable behaviour and environment. In addition, learning approaches have produced important, successful means of treating personality disorders. The degree of success these treatments have enjoyed is testimony to the merits of learning theory approaches to personality.

Biological and Evolutionary Approaches: Are We Born with Personality?

biological and evolutionary approaches to personality: The theory that suggests that important components of personality are inherited

Do we inherit our personality? That's the question raised by **biological and evolutionary approaches** to personality, which suggest that important components of personality are inherited. Building on the work of behavioural geneticists (first discussed in Chapter 2), researchers using biological and evolutionary approaches argue that personality is determined at least in part by particular combinations of genes, in much the same way that our height is largely a result of genetic contributions from our ancestors (Kupfermann, 1991d; Plomin & McClearn, 1993; Jang, Livesley, & Vernon, 1996a, 1996b; Cipriani, 1996; Buss, 1997).

The importance of genetic factors in personality has been illustrated by studies of twins. Auke Tellegen and his colleagues at the University of Minnesota gave pairs of twins, who were genetically identical but raised apart from each other, a battery of personality tests, including one that measured eleven key personality traits (Tellegen et al., 1988). Results indicated that in major respects the twins were quite similar in personality. However, some traits were more influenced by heredity than others. For example, social potency had particularly strong genetic components, whereas social closeness had relatively weak genetic components. See Figure 11-4.

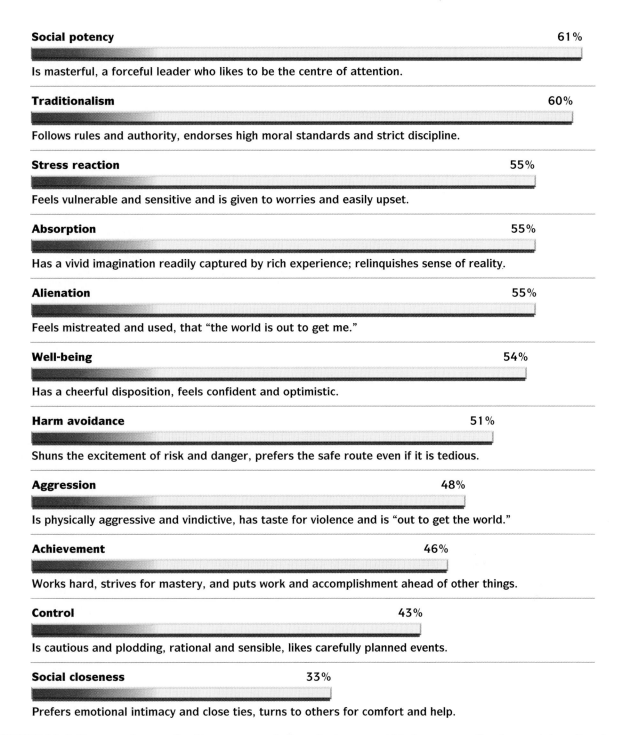

Social potency 61%

Is masterful, a forceful leader who likes to be the centre of attention.

Traditionalism 60%

Follows rules and authority, endorses high moral standards and strict discipline.

Stress reaction 55%

Feels vulnerable and sensitive and is given to worries and easily upset.

Absorption 55%

Has a vivid imagination readily captured by rich experience; relinquishes sense of reality.

Alienation 55%

Feels mistreated and used, that "the world is out to get me."

Well-being 54%

Has a cheerful disposition, feels confident and optimistic.

Harm avoidance 51%

Shuns the excitement of risk and danger, prefers the safe route even if it is tedious.

Aggression 48%

Is physically aggressive and vindictive, has taste for violence and is "out to get the world."

Achievement 46%

Works hard, strives for mastery, and puts work and accomplishment ahead of other things.

Control 43%

Is cautious and plodding, rational and sensible, likes carefully planned events.

Social closeness 33%

Prefers emotional intimacy and close ties, turns to others for comfort and help.

FIGURE 11-4 *The roots of personality. The percentages indicate the degree to which eleven personality characteristics reflect the influence of heredity. Source: Tellegen et al., 1988.*

In a study of the sources of personality differences in identical twins and siblings, Canadian psychologist, Philip Vernon and his colleagues found that Extraversion and Openness were highly heritable personality traits. Autonomy was the least heritable of the traits, and both Neuroticism and Conscientiousness were also influenced by environmental factors (Vernon et al., 1997).

Furthermore, it is increasingly clear that the roots of adult personality emerge at the earliest periods of life. Infants are born with a particular **temperament,** a basic, innate disposition. Temperament encompasses several dimensions, including general activity level and mood. For instance, some individuals are quite active, while others are relatively placid. Similarly, some are relatively easygoing, while others are irritable, easily upset,

temperament: A basic, innate disposition

Applying Psychology in the 21st Century

Born To Be Mild? Determining the Roots of Shyness—and Finding Ways to Change It

If any child seemed destined to grow up afraid of her shadow and just about anything else that moved, it was 2-year-old Marjorie. She was so painfully shy that she wouldn't talk to or look at a stranger. She was even afraid of friendly cats and dogs. When Jerome Kagan, a Harvard professor who discovered that shyness has a strong genetic component, sent a clown to play with Marjorie, she ran to her mother. "It was as if a cobra entered that room," Kagan says. His diagnosis: Marjorie showed every sign of inherited shyness, a condition in which the brain somehow sends out messages to avoid new experiences. But as Kagan continued to examine her over the years, Marjorie's temperament changed. When she started school, she gained confidence from ballet classes and her good grades, and she began to make friends. Her parents even coaxed her into taking horseback-riding lessons. Marjorie may have been born shy, but she has grown into a bubbly second-grader (Peyser & Underwood, 1997, p. 60).

For Marjorie, biology was not destiny. Shy from birth, she was able, like some other children who display similar early shyness, to become more outgoing. On the other hand, some individuals never outgrow their initial shyness, and shyness remains a dominant part of their personality throughout their lives.

Determining why some children remain shy—and what makes them shy in the first place—is the question being asked by psychologist Jerome Kagan, who has studied the trait extensively. Kagan and other researchers have found

that even some unborn fetuses will show signs that indicate later shyness. For instance, their hearts beat around 140 beats per minute, significantly faster than typical. Furthermore, they are more reactive to physical stimulation, even in the womb (DiPietro et al., 1996).

These same children begin to show overt signs of shyness as early as two months after birth. They spontaneously frown, even while resting quietly—a rarity in young infants. Later, they are unusually fearful of the sight of an unfamiliar adult, and they fret when confronted with unfamiliar objects or new settings. By the time they are 3 or 4 years old, their parents and teachers label them as "shy."

To Kagan, such behaviour is characteristic of inhibited children. *Inhibited children*, possibly representing as many as 10 percent of all children, are consistently shy and emotionally restrained in unfamiliar situations. When placed in a novel environment or when meeting people for the first time, they become noticeably quiet. When asked, in experiments, questions of just moderate difficulty by an unfamiliar adult, they become anxious, which has the effect of hindering their performance. They are more likely than other children to show unusual fears, such as a fear of going into their bedrooms by themselves at night or speaking aloud in class. In contrast, uninhibited children show little fear of strangers or of new situations, and act in a sociable and relaxed manner when encountering novel situations (Kagan, 1989a, 1997).

Inhibited children differ from uninhibited ones on a biological level. Inhibited children show higher muscle tension at age 5, particularly in the vocal cords and larynx. They tend to have more rapid resting heartbeats, and their heartbeats increase more when confronted with a new situation. Inhibited and uninhibited children also show hormonal differences and variations in the excitability of the limbic system of the brain (Kagan & Snidman, 1991; Kagan, 1994; Arcus, 1994).

Based on this evidence, Kagan has suggested that the differences between inhibited and uninhibited children can be explained by the inhibited children's greater physiological reactivity—an inborn characteristic. According to this hypothesis, some infants, due to their genetic endowment, are more reactive to novel stimuli than others. Even the mildest stress raises their heartbeat, increases muscle tension, and causes changes in hormonal levels. It is this characteristic reactivity that ultimately leads most of the infants who show this pattern to display shyness later in social situations (Kagan, 1997; Newman et al., 1997). Psychophysiological correlates of shyness have also been observed in older children and adults. In one study, shy 7-year-olds showed a greater increase in right frontal EEG activity and a greater increase in heart rate than their nonshy peers as a task became more demanding (Schmidt et al., 1999). Shy adults have shown an increase in autonomic activity in situations involving social stress (Schmidt & Fox, 1994) and risk-taking (Addison & Schmidt, 1999).

and difficult to soothe. Temperament is quite consistent, with significant stability from infancy well into adolescence (Riese, 1990; Pedlow et al, 1993; Guerin & Gottfried, 1994; Sanson et al., 1994; Caspi et al., 1995; Gunnar et al., 1995; Hart et al., 1997). Research on the genetic basis of personality at different ages suggests that the genetic contribution to personality traits increases with age (Jang et al., 1996a).

Current research is seeking to identify whether specific genes are related to personality, and significant progress is being made along these lines. For example, recent studies have found that people with a longer variety of a dopamine-4 receptor gene are more likely to be thrill seekers than those without such a gene. These thrill seekers

Shyness may stem from genetic factors. However, this genetic predisposition can be overcome if children are exposed to situations that encourage them to behave in a more outgoing fashion.

On the other hand, not all infants born with easily aroused nervous systems later become shy: About one-quarter overcome their biological predisposition and do not exhibit shyness in later years. The outcome is determined by the environment that is provided by parents and other adults. Individuals whose parents encourage them to be outgoing by arranging opportunities for them to interact with others and to become involved in new activities often overcome their shyness. In contrast, children raised in stressful environments, such as households in which marital strife or chronic illness is present, are more apt to remain shy throughout childhood and potentially beyond (Kagan, Arcus, & Snidman, 1993; Pedlow et al., 1993; Rothbart, Ahodi & Hershey, 1994; Rubin, Stewart, & Coplan, 1995).

Individuals who remain shy as adults experience significant disadvantages. For example, in small leaderless discussion groups involving third-year university students who were strangers, the shy students were initially judged to be lower in intelligence (Paulhus & Morgan, 1997). The implications of these findings for social and academic situations as well as for job interviews are obviously undesirable.

Because research on overcoming genetic predispositions toward shyness is relatively recent, we don't know if strategies to make children less shy are effective in modifying personality throughout adulthood. However, work with nonhumans suggests that these efforts may indeed last a lifetime. For instance, psychologist Stephen Suomi of the National Institute of Child Health and Human Development has found that certain rhesus monkeys possess a genetic predisposition to behave shyly. But their shyness can be overcome if they are adopted by "expert" mothers, who somehow convey the abilities needed to be socially skilled in the monkey world. Such adopted monkeys can go on to be leaders and later to be effective parents. In fact, even though they pass on genes to their own children that predispose the children to behave shyly, they are able to convey to their offspring the behaviours that prevent shyness from appearing (Higley, Suomi, & Linnoila, 1990; Boyce et al., 1995).

In short, it is important to keep in mind that genes alone do not represent our destiny. Even if inherited factors predispose us to act in certain ways, these predispositions can be overcome. As Jerome Kagan puts it, "Sometimes human behaviour is the result of deliberation and will imposed on the invisible forces of biology and personal history" (Kagan, 1990, p. 5).

tend to be extroverted, impulsive, quick-tempered, and always on the prowl for excitement and novel situations (Benjamin et al., 1996).

Does the identification of specific genes linked to personality, coupled with the existence of temperaments from the time of birth, mean that we are destined to have certain types of personalities? Hardly. First, it is unlikely that any single gene is linked to a specific trait. For instance, the dopamine-4 receptor only accounts for around 10 percent of the variations in novelty seeking between different individuals. The rest of the variation is accounted for by other genes and environmental factors, according to Dean Hamer, one of the researchers who identified the dopamine-4 receptor gene (Angier, 1996).

More importantly, genes and the environment never work in isolation. As we saw in our discussions of the heritability of intelligence (Chapter 8) and the nature-nurture issue (Chapter 10), it is impossible to completely divorce genetic factors from environmental factors. Although studies of identical twins raised in different environments are helpful, they are not definitive, because it is impossible to fully assess and control environmental factors. Furthermore, estimates of the influence of genetics are just that—estimates—and they apply to groups, not individuals. Consequently, findings such as those shown in Figure 11-4 must be regarded as approximations.

Finally, even if more genes are found to be linked to specific personality characteristics, they still cannot be viewed as the sole cause of personality. For one thing, genetically determined behaviours may not occur if they are not "turned on" by particular environmental experiences. Furthermore, the appearance of behaviours produced by genes in some ways may produce a particular environment. For instance, a cheerful, smiley baby may lead her parents to smile more and act more responsive, thereby creating an environment that is supportive and pleasant. On the other hand, the parents of a cranky, fussy baby may be less inclined to smile at the child; in turn, the environment in which that child is raised will be a less supportive and pleasant one. In a sense, then, genes not only influence a person's behaviour—they also help produce the environment in which the person is raised (Scarr, 1992, 1993; Saudino et al., 1997).

Although an increasing number of personality theorists are taking biological and evolutionary factors into account (e.g., DeKay & Buss, 1992; Cipriani, 1996; Buss, 1997), at the present time no comprehensive, unified theory that considers biological and evolutionary factors is widely accepted. Still, it is clear that certain personality traits have substantial genetic components, and heredity and environment interact to determine personality. (For more on how heredity and environment are related to personality, see the accompanying Applying Psychology in the 21st Century box.)

Evolutionary Psychology

Humanistic Approaches: The Uniqueness of You

Where, in all these approaches to personality, is there an explanation for the saintliness of a Mother Teresa, the creativity of a Michelangelo, the brilliance and perseverance of an Einstein? An understanding of such unique individuals—as well as more ordinary sorts of people who share some of the same attributes—comes from humanistic theory.

According to humanistic theorists, all of the approaches to personality that we have previously discussed share a fundamental misperception in their views of human nature. Instead of seeing people as controlled by unconscious, unseen forces (as do psychoanalytic approaches), a set of stable traits (trait approaches), situational reinforcements and punishments (learning theory), or inherited factors (biological and evolutionary approaches), **humanistic approaches** emphasize people's basic goodness and their tendency to grow to higher levels of functioning. It is this conscious, self-motivated ability to change and improve, along with people's unique creative impulses, that make up the core of personality.

The major proponent of the humanistic point of view is Carl Rogers (1971). Rogers suggests that people have a need for positive regard that reflects a universal requirement to be loved and respected. Because others provide this positive regard, we grow dependent on them. We begin to see and judge ourselves through the eyes of other people, relying on their values.

According to Rogers, one outgrowth of placing importance on the opinions of others is that there may be a conflict between people's actual experiences and their *self-concepts,* or self-impressions. If the discrepancies are minor, so are the consequences. But if they are great, they will lead to psychological disturbances in daily functioning, such as the experience of frequent anxiety.

Rogers suggests that one way of overcoming the discrepancy between experience and self-concept is through the receipt of unconditional positive regard from another person—a friend, a spouse, or a therapist. As we will discuss further in

humanistic approaches to personality: The theory that emphasizes people's basic goodness and their tendency to grow to higher levels of functioning

"So, while extortion, racketeering, and murder may be bad acts, they don't make you a bad person."

Chapter 13, *unconditional positive regard* refers to an attitude of acceptance and respect on the part of an observer, no matter what a person says or does. This acceptance, says Rogers, allows people the opportunity to evolve and grow both cognitively and emotionally and to develop more realistic self-concepts.

To Rogers and other humanistic personality theorists such as Abraham Maslow (whose theory of motivation we discussed in Chapter 9), an ultimate goal of personality growth is self-actualization. **Self-actualization** is a state of self-fulfillment in which people realize their highest potential. This, Rogers would argue, occurs when their everyday experience and their self-concept are closely matched. People who are self-actualized accept themselves as they are in reality, which enables them to achieve happiness and fulfillment (Ford, 1991).

self-actualization: A state of self-fulfillment in which people realize their highest potential in their own unique way

Evaluating Humanistic Approaches

An important contribution of humanistic approaches has been to highlight the uniqueness of human beings. Another significant contribution has been to help focus attention and research on the self. At present, research on the self-concept and self-esteem accounts for a large proportion of the research published in personality journals (Endler & Speer, 1998). See the Pathways Through Psychology box to read about Romin Tafarodi, a Canadian psychologist whose research concerns the self-concept (Tafarodi & Vu, 1997; Tafarodi, 1998).

One criticism of humanistic approaches concerns the difficulty of verifying basic assumptions of the perspective. For example, humanistic theorists make the assumption that people are basically "good," which is unverifiable. Many people find this assumption difficult to accept. Another criticism concerns the relative importance of unconditional positive regard for adjustment.

Comparing Approaches to Personality

Given the multiple approaches to personality that we have discussed, you may be wondering which of the theories provides the most accurate approach to personality. It is a question that cannot be answered with precision. Each theory holds distinct premises and looks at somewhat different aspects of personality. Furthermore, in many cases personality is most reasonably viewed from a number of perspectives simultaneously. Of course, at some point a unified theory of personality may be developed, but the field has not yet reached that juncture and appears unlikely to do so in the near future.

In the meantime, the various theories highlight different aspects of personality. Table 11-4 compares them along several fundamental dimensions.

Table 11-4	Comparing Approaches to Personality			
Theoretical Approach	Conscious Versus Unconscious Determinants of Personality	Nature (Genetic Factors) Versus Nurture (Environmental Factors)	Freedom Versus Determinism	Stability Versus Modifiability
Psychoanalytic	Emphasizes the unconscious	Stresses the innate, inherited structure of personality	Stresses determinism, the view that behaviour is directed and caused by factors outside one's control	Emphasizes the stability of characteristics throughout a person's life
Trait	Disregards both conscious and unconscious	Approaches vary	Stresses determinism, the view that behaviour is directed and caused by factors outside one's control	Emphasizes the stability of characteristics throughout a person's life
Learning	Disregards both conscious and unconscious	Focuses on the environment	Stresses determinism, the view that behaviour is directed and caused by factors outside one's control	Stresses that personality remains flexible and resilient throughout one's life
Biological and Evolutionary	Disregards both conscious and unconscious	Stresses the innate, inherited structure of personality	Stresses determinism, the view that behaviour is directed and caused by factors outside one's control	Emphasizes the stability of characteristics throughout a person's life
Humanistic	Stresses the conscious	Stresses the interaction between both nature and nurture	Stresses the freedom of individuals to make their own choices	Stresses that personality remains flexible and resilient throughout one's life

Recap, Review, and Rethink

Recap

- Traits are relatively enduring dimensions along which people's personalities differ. Trait theorists have tried to identify the major traits that characterize personality.

- Learning theories of personality concentrate on how environmental factors shape personality. Among the most important approaches are Skinner's reinforcement theory and cognitive social approaches.

- Biological and evolutionary approaches focus on the degree to which personality characteristics are inherited.

- Humanistic theories view the core of personality as the ability to change, improve, and be creative in a uniquely human fashion.

- The major dimensions along which personality theories differ include the role of the unconscious versus the conscious, nature (genetic factors) versus nurture (environmental factors), freedom versus determinism, and stability versus modifiability of personality characteristics.

Review

1. Carl's determination to succeed is the dominant force in all his activities and relationships. According to Gordon Allport's theory, this is an example of a _____ trait. In contrast, Cindy's fondness for old Western movies is an example of a _____ trait.

2. Which trait theorist used surface traits and source traits to explain behavior on the basis of sixteen personality dimensions?
   a. Hans Eysenck
   b. Walter Mischel
   c. Gordon Allport
   d. Raymond Cattell

3. A person who enjoys such activities as parties and hang gliding might be described by Eysenck as high on what trait?

4. Proponents of which approach to personality would be most likely to agree with the statement "Personality can be thought of as learned responses to a person's environment"?
   a. humanistic approaches
   b. biological and evolutionary approaches
   c. learning approaches
   d. trait approaches

5. A person who would make the statement "I know I can't do it" would be rated by Bandura as low on _____-_____.

6. Which approach to personality emphasizes the innate goodness of people and their desire to grow?
   a. humanistic
   b. psychoanalytic
   c. learning
   d. biological and evolutionary

Answers to Review Questions are on page 432.

Rethink

1. If personality traits are merely descriptive and not explanatory, of what use are they? Can assigning a trait to a person be harmful? Would the world be a better place without convenient labels for personality traits? Why or why not?

2. In what ways are Cattell's sixteen source traits, Eysenck's three dimensions, and the "Big Five" factors similar, and in what ways are they different? Which traits seem to appear in all three schemes (under one name or another) and which are unique to one scheme? Is this significant?

3. Which of these theories of personality is most appealing to you? Which seems to make the most sense? If you were asked to write an essay providing "the definitive definition of personality," how would you use the information on personality in this chapter to do it?

ASSESSING PERSONALITY: DETERMINING WHAT MAKES US SPECIAL

You have a need for other people to like and admire you.

You have a tendency to be critical of yourself.

You have a great deal of unused potential that you have not turned to your advantage.

Although you have some personality weaknesses, you are generally able to compensate for them.

Relating to members of the opposite sex has presented problems to you.

While you appear to be disciplined and self-controlled to others, you tend to be anxious and insecure inside.

At times you have serious doubts as to whether you have made the right decision or done the right thing.

You prefer a certain amount of change and variety and become dissatisfied when hemmed in by restrictions and limitations.

You do not accept others' statements without satisfactory proof.

You have found it unwise to be too frank in revealing yourself to others.

▶ **How can we most accurately assess personality?**

▶ **What are the major types of personality measures?**

If you think these statements provide a surprisingly accurate account of your personality, you are not alone: Most college students think that the descriptions are tailored just to them. In fact, the statements are intentionally designed to be so vague as to be applicable to just about anyone (Forer, 1949; Russo, 1981).

The ease with which we can agree with such imprecise statements underscores the difficulty in coming up with accurate and meaningful assessments of people's personalities (Johnson et al., 1985; Prince & Guastello, 1990). Just as trait theorists were faced with the problem of determining the most critical and important traits, psychologists interested in assessing personality must be able to define the most meaningful ways of discriminating between one person's personality and another's. To do this, they use **psychological tests,** standard measures devised to assess behaviour objectively. Such tests are used by psychologists to help people make decisions about their lives and understand more about themselves. They are also employed by researchers interested in the causes and consequences of personality (Groth-Marnat, 1990, 1996; Matarazzo, 1992; Kaplan & Saccuzzo, 1997; Aiken, 1997).

Like the intelligence assessments that we discussed in Chapter 8, all psychological tests must have reliability and validity. *Reliability,* you may recall, refers to the measurement consistency of a test. If a test is reliable, it yields the same result each time it is administered to a given person or group. In contrast, unreliable tests give different results each time they are administered.

Tests also must be valid in order to draw meaningful conclusions. Tests have *validity* when they actually measure what they are designed to measure. If a test is constructed to measure sociability, for instance, we need to know that it actually measures sociability and not some other trait.

Personality Tests

psychological tests: Standard measures devised to assess behaviour objectively and used by psychologists to help people make decisions about their lives and understand more about themselves

Finally, psychological tests are based on *norms,* standards of test performance that permit the comparison of one person's score on the test to the scores of others who have taken the same test. For example, a norm permits test-takers to know that they have scored in the top 10 percent of those who have taken the test.

Basically, norms are established by administering a particular test to a large number of people and determining the typical scores. It is then possible to compare a single person's score to the scores of the group, providing a comparative measure of test performance against the performance of others who have taken the test.

The establishment of appropriate norms is not a simple endeavor. For instance, the specific group that is employed to determine norms for a test has a profound effect on how an individual's performance is evaluated.

Exploring Diversity

Personality and Culture

Is personality structure the same across cultures or does it vary? During the first half of the twentieth century a popular view held that each culture had a "national character" composed of a specific combination of traits. The results of more recent research suggest that the main dimensions of personality are similar in different cultures.

Psychologists at the University of Western Ontario together with their colleagues in other countries have used both a verbal self-report measure and a nonverbal measure in cross-cultural research. The verbal measure, the Personality Research Form (PRF), was developed by Douglas Jackson. This test is the fourth most cited personality test used by personality researchers (Mitchell, 1983). In order to investigate personality across cultures, the PRF was translated into other languages.

An issue in personality research has been whether the observed organization of personality traits, such as indicated by the Five-Factor Model of personality (see Table 11-3), is the result of shared meanings of words used to label and measure traits. Therefore, it is important to have a personality test that is not dependent on language.

Sampo Paunonen and Douglas Jackson (University of Western Ontario) and Mirja Keinonen (University of Helsinki) developed the Nonverbal Personality Questionnaire (NPQ). This test has 136 line drawings of a person engaging in various trait-related behaviours. Respondents indicate the likelihood that they would engage in behaviours similar to those pictured (Paunonen et al., 1990).

The use of both a verbal and a nonverbal measure is advantageous because each measure alone has some problems. On the one hand, translating tests is difficult because of a lack of correspondence between words, idioms and grammar across languages. Subtle differences in content of test items may occur. On the other hand, in constructing a nonverbal test, it is difficult to represent all traits in pictorial format. Also, some aspects of a trait can be better represented in pictures than other aspects. An important advantage of using both the PRF and the NPQ is that together they have been found to measure many of the dimensions of personality of the Five Factor Model (Ashton et al., 1998).

Paunonen and his colleagues used these tests to assess personality in six cultures, including Canada, Finland, Poland, Germany, Russia, and Hong Kong (Paunonen at al. 1992, 1996). They discovered that the factors identified in each culture's data resembled the personality dimensions of the Five-Factor Model.

Michelle Yik, Paul Trapnell, and Delroy Lucas at the University of British Columbia, together with colleagues elsewhere, have used a translation of the Revised NEO Personality Inventory (a test based on the Five-Factor Model) to investigate personal-

---

Answers to Review Questions:

1. cardinal; secondary   2. d   3. extraversion   4. c   5. self efficacy   6. a

Canada's population is increasingly diverse, but research studies here and in other countries support the hypothesis that basic personality dimensions are the same across cultures.

ity structure in Chinese undergraduates in Hong Kong and Canada. They found that the basic dimensions of personality were the same in the two groups of Chinese speaking students. However, the profiles developed from the subscale data had some differences, which they interpreted as largely cultural in origin (McCrae et al., 1998).

Together, these studies provide support for the hypothesis that the basic dimensions of personality are the same across cultures. And they also support the view that how these dimensions manifest themselves is subject to both hereditary and environmental influences. ■

Self-Report Measures of Personality

If someone wanted to assess your personality, one possible approach would be to carry out an extensive interview with you in order to determine the most important events of your childhood, your social relationships, and your successes and failures. Obviously, though, such a technique would be extraordinarily costly in time and effort.

It is also unnecessary. Just as physicians draw only a small sample of your blood to test it, psychologists can utilize **self-report measures** that ask people about a relatively small sample of their behaviour. This sampling of self-report data is then used to infer the presence of particular personality characteristics (Conoley & Impara, 1997).

One of the best examples of a self-report measure, and the most frequently used personality test, is the **Minnesota Multiphasic Personality Inventory-2 (MMPI-2).** Although the original purpose of the measure was to differentiate people with specific sorts of psychological difficulties from those without disturbances, it has been found to predict a variety of other behaviours. For instance, MMPI scores have been shown to be good predictors of whether college students will marry within ten years and whether they will get an advanced degree. Police departments use the test to measure whether police officers are prone to use their weapons. Psychologists in the former Soviet Union even administered a modified form of the MMPI to their cosmonauts and Olympic athletes (Dworkin & Widom, 1977; Holden, 1986; Hathaway & McKinley, 1989; Greene, 1991; Butcher, 1995; Duckworth & Anderson, 1995).

The test itself consists of a series of 567 items to which a person responds "true," "false," or "cannot say." The questions cover a variety of issues, ranging from mood ("I feel useless at times") to opinions ("people should try to understand their dreams") to physical and psychological health ("I am bothered by an upset stomach several times a week" and "I have strange and peculiar thoughts"). There are no right or wrong answers. The test yields scores on separate subscales. The interpretation of results depends on the pattern of these subscale scores.

How did the authors of the MMPI determine what specific patterns of responses indicate? The procedure they used is typical of personality test construction—a process known as **test standardization.** To devise the test, groups of psychiatric patients with a specific diagnosis, such as depression or schizophrenia, were asked to

self-report measures: A method of gathering data about people by asking them questions about a sample of their behaviour

Minnesota Multiphasic Personality Inventory-2 (MMPI-2): A test used to identify people with psychological difficulties as well as predicting a variety of other behaviours

MMPI-2

test standardization: A technique used to validate questions in personality tests by studying the response of people with known diagnoses

Pathways Through Psychology

Romin Tafarodi

Assistant Professor of Psychology University of Toronto, Toronto, Ontario

Education: B.A., University of Waterloo; Ph.D., University of Texas at Austin

Home: Toronto.

My interest in psychology stems from a childhood tendency to think too much about why I am who I am and do what I do. By the time I reached adulthood, I realized that the answers to those questions might also apply to understanding others. I've always been fascinated by our ability to conceive of ourselves as persons and why this ability becomes a blessing for some but a curse for others.

I came from a small family and was a bit of a loner growing up. When in the company of others, I tended to be acutely aware of their presence and its influence on my behaviour. My interest in social dynamics as causes and consequences of personality is an outgrowth of this early awareness. As a child, I was uncomfortable with the idea that we are self-made, autonomous agents. Rather, I felt that genetics and social experience were the building blocks of personality. Moreover, because personality itself is really nothing more than consistency in behaviour, I concluded that the real causes of what we do cannot be found in our experience of choice. I've maintained that position ever since, although at times I've wished that I believed otherwise. I suppose I was at-

Romin Tafarodi

tracted to science in part because it is a haven for unrepentant determinists. As I've always been much more interested in people than in plants, animals, or inanimate objects, psychology was the natural choice. Psychology is a relatively young science and I'm often struck by how little we really know about the mind. This realization is more exciting than discouraging, as it presents the possibility of major theoretical advances in the near future. It is this promise that inspires me.

My parents were Iranian immigrants who struggled to build a new life for themselves in Canada. The challenges of their cultural transition became a major

theme in my life and led to interests that are reflected in my work on cross-cultural differences in self-identity. Much of my research to date has focused on the attitude that people hold toward themselves—their self-esteem. I have proposed that self-esteem, even in its most generalized form, consists of two distinct aspects, one involving the perception of power, or efficacy, and the other the perception of goodness, or social worth. Conceiving of self-esteem as two-dimensional helps us better understand those who see themselves as competent yet worthless, or incompetent yet worthy. Given that the two dimensions have distinct origins and sensitivities, it also helps us predict how different types of life events, and changing cultural conditions, impact self-esteem. Such knowledge may prove useful in treating those who suffer from self-esteem problems and for promoting the development of healthy self-esteem in children and adolescents. Though researchers continue to disagree on what self-esteem is, where it comes from, and what it affects, nearly all see it as a central feature of personality and perhaps our most important attitude. The consensus assures me that I'm at least working in the right area. I'm currently looking at how choice, distinctiveness, family dynamics, and cultural conditions affect self-esteem and other aspects of self-identity.

Source: Romin Tafarodi, Ph.D., University of Toronto.
<psych.utoronto.ca/~tafarodi>

---

complete a large number of items. The test authors then determined which items best differentiated members of these groups from a comparison group of normal participants, and these specific items were included in the final version of the test. By systematically carrying out this procedure on groups with different diagnoses, the test authors were able to devise a number of subscales that identified different forms of abnormal behaviour (see Figure 11-5).

The MMPI is the most widely used personality test; it has been translated into more than one hundred languages (Graham, 1990; Helmes & Reddon, 1993; Greene & Clopton, 1994). However, like other personality tests, it does present opportunities for abuse. For example, employers who use it as a job-screening tool may lack the skill required for interpretation of results.

A problem common to self-report measures is that people may fake answers intentionally or otherwise. The MMPI has a "lie scale" that indicates when people are falsifying their answers (Butcher et al., 1990; Graham, 1990; Bagby, Buis, & Nichol-

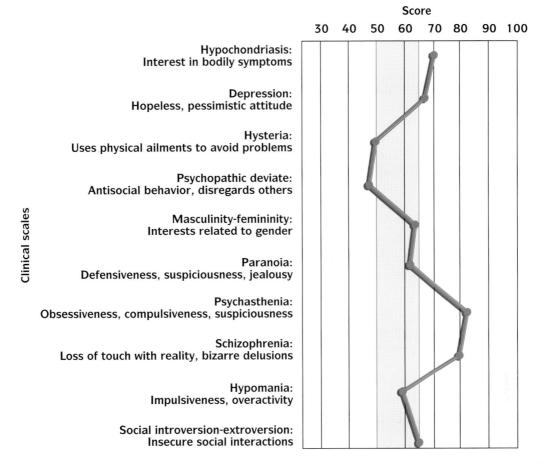

Score

FIGURE 11-5 *A sample profile on the MMPI-2 of a person who suffers from obsessional anxiety, social withdrawal, and delusional thinking. Source: Based on data from Halgin & Whitbourne, 1994, p. 72; and Minnesota Multiphasic Personality Inventory-2. Copyright © by the Regents of the University of Minnesota, 1942, 1943 (renewed 1970, 1989).*

son, 1995). For self-report measures that do not include a "lie scale," an effective strategy for detecting faking is to measure response times (Holden & Hibbs, 1995).

Projective Methods

If you were shown the shape presented in Figure 11-6 and asked what it represented to you, you might not think that your impressions would mean very much. But to a psychoanalytic theoretician, your responses to such an ambiguous figure would provide valuable clues to the state of your unconscious, and ultimately to your general personality characteristics.

The shape in the figure is representative of inkblots used in **projective personality tests,** in which a person is shown an ambiguous stimulus and asked to describe it or tell a story about it. The responses are then considered to be "projections" of what the person is like.

The best-known projective test is the **Rorschach test.** Devised by Swiss psychiatrist Hermann Rorschach (1924), the test consists of showing a series of symmetrical stimuli, similar to the one in Figure 11-6, to people who are then asked what the figures represent to them. Their responses are recorded, and through a complex set of clinical judgments on the part of the examiner, people are classified into different personality types. For instance, respondents who see a bear in one inkblot are thought to have a strong degree of emotional control, according to the rules developed by Rorschach (Weiner, 1994; Hurt, Reznikoff, & Clarkin, 1995; Meloy et al., 1997; Misra et al., 1997).

The **Thematic Apperception Test (TAT)** is another well-known projective test. As noted when we discussed achievement motivation in Chapter 9, the TAT consists

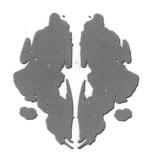

FIGURE 11-6 *This inkblot is similar to the type used in the Rorschach personality test. What do you see in it?*

projective personality test: A test in which a person is shown an ambiguous stimulus and asked to describe it or tell a story about it

Rorschach test: A test developed by Swiss psychiatrist Hermann Rorschach that consists of showing a series of symmetrical stimuli to people who are then asked what the figures represent to them

Thematic Apperception Test (TAT): A test consisting of a series of pictures about which a person is asked to write a story

of a series of pictures about which a person is asked to write a story. The stories are then used to draw inferences about the writer's personality characteristics (Bellak, 1993; Cramer, 1996).

Tests with stimuli as ambiguous as the Rorschach and TAT require unusual skill and care in their interpretation—too much, in many critics' estimation. The Rorschach, in particular, has been criticized for requiring too much inference on the part of the examiner, and attempts to standardize scoring have frequently failed. Furthermore, many critics complain that the Rorschach does not provide much valid information about underlying personality traits. In fact, some researchers suggest that the test is more useful for permitting a clinical psychologist to get to know a test-taker in the context of therapy than for gathering much reliable information about the test-taker's personality. Despite such problems, both the Rorschach and TAT are widely used, particularly in clinical settings, and their proponents suggest that their reliability and validity are high enough to provide useful inferences about personality (Piotrowski & Keller, 1989; Dawes, 1994; Wood, Nezworski, & Stejskal, 1996; Weiner, 1996; Bornstein, 1996).

Behavioural Assessment

behavioural assessment: Direct measures of an individual's behaviour used to describe characteristics indicative of personality

If you were a psychologist subscribing to a learning approach to personality, you would be likely to object to the indirect nature of projective tests. Instead, you would be more apt to use **behavioural assessment**—direct measures of an individual's behaviour used to describe characteristics indicative of personality. As with observational research (discussed in Chapter 1), behavioural assessment may be carried out naturalistically by observing people in their own settings: in the workplace, at home, or in school, for instance. In other cases, behavioural assessment occurs in the laboratory, under controlled conditions in which a psychologist sets up a situation and observes an individual's behaviour.

Regardless of the setting in which behaviour is observed, an effort is made to ensure that behavioural assessment is carried out objectively, quantifying behaviour as much as possible. For example, an observer might record the number of social contacts a person initiates, the number of questions asked, or the number of aggressive acts. Another method is to measure duration of events: the duration of a temper tantrum in a child, the length of a conversation, the amount of time spent working, or the time spent in cooperative behaviour.

Behavioural assessment is particularly appropriate for observing—and eventually remedying—specific behavioural difficulties, such as increasing socialization in shy children. It provides a means of assessing the specific nature and incidence of a problem and subsequently allows psychologists to determine whether intervention techniques have been successful.

Behavioural Assessment

Behavioural assessment techniques based on learning theories of personality have also made important contributions to the treatment of certain kinds of psychological difficulties. Indeed, the knowledge of normal personality provided by the theories we have discussed throughout this chapter has led to significant advances in our understanding and treatment of both physical and psychological disorders.

The Informed Consumer of Psychology

Assessing Personality Assessments

Wanted: People with "kinetic energy," "emotional maturity," and the ability to "deal with large numbers of people in a fairly chaotic situation."

Although this job description may seem most appropriate for the job of co-host of *Wheel of Fortune,* in actuality it is part of an advertisement for managers for American MultiCinema's theaters (Dentzer, 1986). To find people with such qualities, AMC has developed a battery of personality measures for job applicants to complete. In developing its own tests, AMC joined scores of companies, ranging from General Motors to J.C. Penney, that employ personality tests to help determine who gets hired (Hogan, Hogan, & Roberts, 1996).

Individuals, too, have come to depend on personality testing. Many organizations will—for a hefty fee—administer a battery of personality tests that purport to steer people toward a career for which their personality is particularly suited. Before relying too heavily on the results of such personality testing, either in the role of potential employee, employer, or consumer of testing services, you should keep several points in mind:

- Understand what the test purports to measure. Standard personality measures are accompanied by information that discusses how the test was developed, to whom it is most applicable, and how the results should be interpreted. If possible, you should read the accompanying literature; it will help you understand the meaning of any results.

- No decision should be based solely on the results of any one test. Test results should be interpreted in the context of other information—academic records, social interests, and home and community activities. Without these data, individual scores are relatively uninformative at best and may even be harmful.

- Tests are not infallible. The results may be in error; the test may be unreliable or invalid. You may, for example, have had a "bad day" when you took the test, or the person scoring and interpreting the test may have made a mistake. You should not place undue stock in the results of the single administration of any test.

In sum, it is important to keep in mind the complexity of human behaviour—particularly your own. No one test can provide an understanding of the intricacies of someone's personality without considering a good deal more information than can be provided in a single testing session. ■

Recap, Review, and Rethink

Recap

- Psychological tests are standard measures used to assess behaviour objectively. They must be reliable, measuring with consistency what they are trying to measure, and valid, measuring what they are supposed to measure.

- Self-report measures of personality ask people about a sample range of their behaviours. The results are then used to infer personality characteristics.

- Projective personality tests present ambiguous stimuli which the person is asked to describe or tell a story about. Responses are used as an indication of aspects of the individual's personality.

- Behavioral assessment employs direct measures of an individual's behaviour to describe characteristics indicative of personality.

Review

1. _____ is the consistency of a personality test, while _____ is the ability of a test to actually measure what it is designed to measure.

2. _____ are standards used to compare scores of different people taking the same test.

3. Tests such as the MMPI-2, in which a small sample of behaviour is assessed to determine larger trends, are examples of
   a. cross-sectional tests.
   b. projective tests.
   c. achievement tests.
   d. self-report tests.

4. A person shown a picture and asked to make up a story about it would be taking a _____ personality test.

Answers to Review Questions are on page 438.

Rethink

1. What do you think are some of the problems that developers and interpreters of self-report personality tests must deal with in their effort to provide valid and reliable information about test-takers? Why is a "lie scale" included on such measures?

2. How would you assess the reliability of a projective test, such as the Rorschach test or the Thematic Apperception Test? What would be an acceptable standard of reliability?

3. Should personality tests be used for personnel decisions? Should they be used for other social purposes, such as identifying individuals at risk for certain types of personality disorders? What sorts of policies would you devise to ensure that such tests were used ethically?

looking
BACK

How do psychologists define and use the concept of personality?

1. In this chapter, we have examined characteristics and behaviours that make people different from one another—those behaviours that psychologists consider to be at the root of personality. Personality refers to the relatively enduring characteristics that differentiate one person from another and that lead them to act in a consistent and predictable manner, both in different situations and over extended periods of time.

What do the theories of Freud and his successors tell us about the structure and development of personality?

2. According to psychoanalysts, much of behaviour is caused by parts of personality that are found in the unconscious and of which we are unaware. Freud's theory suggests that personality is composed of the id, the ego, and the superego. The id is the unorganized, inborn part of personality whose purpose is to immediately reduce tensions relating to hunger, sex, aggression, and other primitive impulses. The ego restrains instinctual energy in order to maintain the safety of the individual and to help the person to be a member of society. The superego represents the rights and wrongs of society and consists of the conscience and the ego-ideal.

3. Freud's psychoanalytic theory suggests that personality develops through a series of stages, each of which is associated with a major biological function. The oral stage is the first period, occurring during the first year of life. Next comes the anal stage, lasting from approximately age 1 to age 3. The phallic stage follows, with interest focusing on the genitals. At age 5 or 6, near the end of the phallic stage, children experience the Oedipal conflict, a process through which they learn to identify with the same-sex parent by acting as much like that parent as possible. Then follows a latency period lasting until puberty, after which people move into the genital stage, a period of mature sexuality.

4. Defense mechanisms, used for dealing with anxiety relating to impulses from the id, provide people with unconscious strategies to reduce anxiety. The most common defense mechanisms are repression, regression, displacement, rationalization, denial, projection, and sublimation.

5. Freud's psychoanalytic theory has provoked a number of criticisms. These include a lack of supportive scientific data, the theory's inadequacy in making predictions, and its reliance on a highly restricted population. Still, the theory remains a pivotal one. For instance, the neo-Freudian psychoanalytic theorists built on Freud's work, although they placed greater emphasis on the role of the ego and paid greater attention to social factors in determining behaviour.

What are the major aspects of trait, learning, biological and evolutionary, and humanistic approaches to personality?

6. Trait approaches have tried to identify the most basic and relatively enduring dimensions along which people differ from one another—dimensions known as traits. For example, Allport suggested that there are three kinds of traits—cardinal, central, and secondary. Later theorists employed a statistical technique called factor analysis to identify the most crucial traits. Using this method, Cattell identified sixteen basic traits, while Eysenck found three major dimensions: extraversion, neuroticism, and psychoticism.

7. Learning approaches to personality concentrate on observable behaviour. To the strict learning theorist, personality is the sum of learned responses to the external environment. In contrast, social-cognitive approaches concentrate on the role of cognitions in determining personality. Social-cognitive approaches pay particular attention to self-efficacy and reciprocal determinism in determining behaviour.

8. Biological and evolutionary approaches to personality focus on how personality characteristics are inherited. For example, studies of children's temperament suggest that there is a distinction between inhibited and uninhibited children, which is reflected in differences both in biological reactivity and in shyness.

9. Humanistic approaches emphasize the basic goodness of people. They consider the core of personality in terms of a person's ability to change and improve. Roger's concept of the need for positive regard suggests that a universal requirement to be loved and respected underlies personality.

10. The major personality approaches differ along a number of important dimensions, including the role of the unconscious versus the conscious, nature versus nurture, freedom versus determinism, and stability versus modifiability of personality characteristics.

How can we most accurately assess personality?

11. Psychological tests are standard assessment tools that objectively measure behaviour. They must be reliable, measuring what they are trying to measure consistently, and valid, measuring what they are supposed to measure.

What are the major types of personality measures?

12. Self-report measures ask people about a sample range of their behaviours. These reports are used to infer the presence of particular personality characteristics. The most commonly used self-report measure is the Minnesota Multiphasic Personality Inventory-2 (MMPI-2), designed to differentiate people with specific sorts of psychological difficulties from normal individuals.

Answers to Review Questions:

1. Reliability, validity   2. Norms   3. d   4. projective

13. Projective personality tests present an ambiguous stimulus; the observer's responses are then used to infer information about the observer. The two most frequently used projective tests are the Rorschach, in which reactions to inkblots are employed to classify personality types, and the Thematic Apperception Test (TAT), in which stories about ambiguous pictures are used to draw inferences about the storyteller's personality.

14. Behavioural assessment is based on the principles of learning theory. It employs direct measurement of an individual's behaviour to determine characteristics related to personality.

Key Terms and Concepts

personality (p. 410)
psychoanalytic theory (p. 411)
unconscious (p. 411)
id (p. 412)
libido (p. 412)
ego (p. 412)
superego (p. 412)
oral stage (p. 412)
fixation (p. 413)
anal stage (p. 413)
phallic stage (p. 413)
Oedipal conflict (p. 413)
latency period (p. 414)

genital stage (p. 414)
defense mechanisms (p. 414)
neo-Freudian psychoanalysts (p. 416)
collective unconscious (p. 416)
inferiority complex (p. 417)
trait theory (p. 419)
traits (p. 419)
social-cognitive approaches to personality (p. 423)
biological and evolutionary approaches to personality (p. 424)
temperament (p. 425)

humanistic approaches to personality (p. 428)
self-actualization (p. 429)
psychological tests (p. 431)
self-report measures (p. 433)
Minnesota Multiphasic Personality Inventory-2 (MMPI-2) (p. 433)
test standardization (p. 434)
projective personality test (p. 435)
Rorschach test (p. 435)
Thematic Apperception Test (TAT) (p. 435)
behavioral assessment (p. 436)

Epilogue

In this chapter, we have discussed the different ways in which psychologists have interpreted the development and structure of personality. The perspectives we've examined range from Freud's analysis of personality based primarily on internal, unconscious factors, to the externally based view of personality as a learned set of traits and actions that is championed by the learning theorists. We have also noted that there are many ways to interpret personality, and by no means does a consensus exist on what the key traits are that are central to personality.

Before proceeding to the next chapter, return to the Prologue and consider the personality of Julie Payette. Use your understanding of personality to consider the following questions.

1. What part of the description of Julie Payette would a psychodynamic theorist use to explain the source of some of her behaviour? What sort of interpretation might be made?

2. Using Cattell's sixteen source traits, what sort of profile do you think Julie Payette would display if she were tested? Where would she fall on Eysenck's major personality dimensions?

3. Do you think a personality profile of Julie Payette taken when she was a child would have changed or remained the same when she reached adulthood? Why?

4. What details would a behaviourist select as reinforcers? Suggest some possible effects of these reinforcers.

12 Psychological Disorders

Prologue

Lori Schiller

Lori Schiller thinks it all began one night at summer camp when she was 15.

Suddenly, she was hearing voices, "You must die! Die! Die!" they screamed. The voices drove her from her bunk, out into the dark, where she thought she could escape. Camp officials found her jumping frantically on a trampoline, screaming. "I thought I was possessed," says Ms. Schiller, now 33. Terrified, she told no one about the voices when she first heard them. The camp sent her home sick. Says Nancy Schiller, her mother: "We thought she had the flu."

After Lori came home "sick" from summer camp, it was easy enough for everyone to shrug off the subtle changes in her personality. When she refused to make phone calls, her family wrote it off to adolescence. When she would lie on the sofa facing the wall as the rest of the family watched television, they figured she just wasn't interested in the show that was on. They didn't see it as a serious sign of withdrawal. . . .

In reality, she now says, she was frightened. Voices had begun sliding down the telephone wire; they were assaulting her from the TV screen. "The people on TV were telling me it was my responsibility to save the world, and if I didn't I would be killed," she says. . . .

Keeping her secret wasn't difficult at first. She could dodge the still-infrequent voices by taking a walk, or by retreating into sleep. But the voices were very real. "I was sure everyone else could hear them, and I was embarrassed because they were saying such bad things about me," she recalls.

Her behaviour became erratic, wilder. On a whim one day, she hopped into her car, drove four hours home to Scarsdale, changed her mind and drove back. She went sky diving. She got stopped by police for speeding. She had fits of hysterical laughter. . . .

As time went on, Lori had more and more trouble concentrating, and more difficulty in controlling her impulses, one of which was to commit suicide. "I used to sit in the library, up all these stairs, and think about jumping," she recalls. Finally, in her senior year, she told her parents she "had problems" and asked to see a counsellor (Bennett, 1992, pp. A1, A10).

Although she initially managed to hide her disorder from everyone, Lori Schiller was losing her hold on reality. Less than a year after graduating from college, her parents convinced her to go to a private mental hospital. She would spend the next decade in and out of institutions, suffering from schizophrenia, one of the most severe psychological disorders.

Schiller's case raises several questions. What caused her disorder? Were genetic factors involved, or were stresses primarily responsible for her disorder? Were there signs that others should have noticed earlier? Could her schizophrenia have been prevented? What were the specific symptoms of her abnormal behaviour? And, more generally, how do we distinguish normal from abnormal behaviour, and how can Lori's behaviour be categorized and classified in such a way as to pinpoint the specific nature of her problem?

We address some of the issues raised by Lori Schiller's case in this and the following chapter. We begin by discussing the subtle distinctions that exist between normal and abnormal behaviour. We examine the various approaches that have been used to explain psychological disorders, ranging from explanations based on superstition to those based on more scientific approaches.

The heart of the chapter consists of a description of the various types of psychological disorders. Using a classification system employed by mental health practitioners, we examine the most significant kinds of disorders. The chapter also includes a discussion of how to evaluate one's own behaviour to determine whether it is advisable to seek help from a mental health professional.

NORMAL VERSUS ABNORMAL: MAKING THE DISTINCTION

Universally that person's acumen is esteemed very little perceptive concerning whatsoever matters are being held as most profitable by mortals with sapience endowed to be studied who is ignorant of that which the most in doctrine erudite and certainly by reason of that in them high mind's ornament deserving of veneration constantly maintain when by general consent they affirm that other circumstances being equal by no exterior splendour is the prosperity of a nation more efficaciously asserted than by the measure of how far forward may have progressed the tribute of its solicitude for that proliferent continuance which of evils the original if it be absent when fortunately present constitutes the certain sign of omnipollent nature's incorrupted benefaction.

It would be easy to conclude that these words were the musings of a madman. The passage does not seem to make any sense at all. But literary scholars would disagree. In actuality this passage is from James Joyce's classic *Ulysses,* which has been hailed as one of the major works of twentieth-century literature (Joyce, 1934, p. 377).

As this example illustrates, a cursory examination of a person's writing is insufficient to determine the degree to which he or she is "normal." But even when we consider more extensive samples of a person's behaviour, we find that there may be only a fine line between behaviour that is considered normal and that which is considered abnormal.

▶ **How can we distinguish normal from abnormal behaviour?**

▶ **What are the major models of abnormal behaviour used by mental health professionals?**

▶ **What classification system is used to categorize abnormal behaviour?**

Mental Health Issues

Defining Abnormality

The difficulty in distinguishing normal from abnormal behaviour has inspired a diversity of approaches for devising a precise, scientific definition of "abnormal behaviour." Over the years, such approaches have varied considerably. For instance, consider the following definitions:

- *Abnormality as deviation from the average.* This statistically based approach views abnormality as deviation from average behaviour. To determine abnormality, we simply observe what behaviours are rare or infrequent in a given society or culture and label these deviations from the norm "abnormal."

  Although such a definition may be appropriate in some instances, its drawback is that some behaviours that are statistically rare clearly do not lend themselves to classification as abnormal. If most people prefer to have Corn Flakes for breakfast, but you prefer Raisin Bran, this hardly makes your behaviour abnormal. Similarly, such a conception of abnormality would unreasonably label a person who has an unusually high IQ as abnormal, simply because a high IQ is statistically rare. A definition of abnormality that rests on deviation from the average, then, is insufficient by itself.

- *Abnormality as deviation from the ideal.* An alternative approach considers abnormality in relation to the standard toward which most people are striving— the ideal. This sort of definition considers behaviour abnormal if it deviates enough from some kind of ideal or cultural standard. Unfortunately, the definition suffers from even more difficulties than the deviation-from-the-average definition, since society has so few standards about which people agree. Moreover, the standards that do arise tend to change over time, making the deviation-from-the-ideal approach inadequate.

Defining abnormality is difficult, and psychological and legal definitions sometimes clash. A person who is unable to function effectively in day-to-day life may be regarded as psychologically abnormal; yet Paul Bernardo, convicted of rape and two gruesome murders, was considered sane and therefore deserving of legal punishment by the court.

Forensic Psychology

- *Abnormality as a sense of subjective discomfort.* Given the drawbacks of both the deviation-from-the-average and deviation-from-the-ideal definitions of abnormality, we must turn to more subjective approaches. One of the most useful definitions of abnormal behaviour concentrates on the psychological consequences of the behaviour for the individual. In this approach, behaviour is considered abnormal if it produces a sense of distress, anxiety, or guilt in an individual—or if it is harmful to others in some way.

  Even a definition that relies on subjective discomfort has its drawbacks, for in some particularly severe forms of mental disturbance, people report feeling euphoric and on top of the world, even though their behaviour seems bizarre to others. In this case, then, there is a subjective state of well-being, yet the behaviour is within the realm of what most people would consider abnormal. This discrepancy suggests that a definition of abnormality that does not consider people's ability to function effectively is inadequate. Thus psychologists have developed one final approach to distinguishing between normal and abnormal behaviour.

- *Abnormality as the inability to function effectively.* Most people are able to feed themselves, hold a job, get along with others, and in general live as productive members of society. Yet there are those who are unable to adjust to the demands of society or function effectively.

  According to this view of abnormality, people who are unable to function effectively and adapt to the demands of society are considered abnormal. For example, an unemployed, homeless woman living on the street might be considered unable to function effectively. Therefore her behaviour would be viewed as abnormal, even if she had made the choice to live in this particular fashion. Her inability to adapt to the requirements of society is what makes her "abnormal," according to this approach.

- *Abnormality as a legal concept.* In one of Canada's most high profile trials, Paul Bernardo was found guilty of rape and murder and sentenced as a dangerous offender to an indeterminate jail term. To most people, the horrendous crimes committed by Bernardo are abnormal. However by law he was mentally fit to stand trial. In Canada, fitness to stand trial has two components. A person can be found, upon psychiatric examination, to be unfit to stand trial if he, because of mental illness, is unable to understand the court proceedings. If he is found fit to stand trial he may be found "not criminally responsible due to mental disorder". In each province there is a provincial review board that appoints a multi-disciplinary team made up of both legal and health care professionals to decide these matters. In either case, if the person is found to be "not fit" or "not

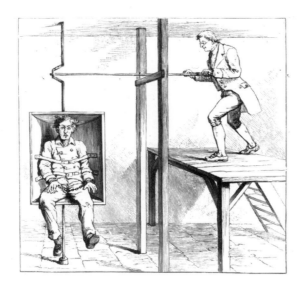

responsible" he is usually placed in the care of a psychiatric facility. Bernardo was legally both fit to stand trial and to take responsibility for his crimes.

Gradations of Abnormal and Normal Behaviour: Drawing the Line on Abnormality

Clearly, none of the previous definitions is broad enough to cover all instances of abnormal behaviour. Consequently, the distinction between normal and abnormal behaviour often remains ambiguous even to trained professionals. Furthermore, the label "abnormal behaviour" is influenced to a large extent by cultural expectations for "normal" behaviour in a particular society.

Probably the best way to deal with this imprecision is to view abnormal and normal behaviour as marking two ends of a continuum rather than as absolute states. Behaviour should then be evaluated in terms of gradations, ranging from completely normal functioning to extremely abnormal behaviour. Obviously, behaviour typically falls somewhere between these two extremes.

Models of Abnormality: From Superstition to Science

For much of the past, abnormal behaviour was linked to superstition and witchcraft. People displaying abnormal behaviour were accused of being possessed by the devil or some sort of demonic god. Authorities felt justified in "treating" abnormal behaviour by attempting to drive out the source of the problem. This typically involved whipping, immersion in hot water, starvation, or other forms of torture in which the cure was often worse than the affliction (Howells & Osborn, 1984; Berrios, 1996).

Contemporary approaches take a more enlightened view, and six major perspectives on abnormal behaviour predominate: the medical model, the psychoanalytic model, the behavioural model, the cognitive model, the humanistic model, and the sociocultural model. These models suggest not only different causes of abnormal behaviour but—as we shall see in the next chapter—different treatment approaches as well. (Table 12-1 summarizes the models and the way in which they can be applied to the case of Lori Schiller described in the Prologue.)

The Medical Model

When people display the symptoms of tuberculosis, we generally find the tuberculin germ in their body tissue. In the same way, the **medical model of abnormality** suggests that when an individual displays symptoms of abnormal behaviour, the root cause will be found in a physical examination of the individual, which may reveal a hormonal imbalance, a chemical deficiency, or a brain injury. Indeed, when we speak

medical model of abnormality: The model that suggests that when an individual displays symptoms of abnormal behaviour, the root cause will be found in a physical examination of the individual, which may reveal a hormonal imbalance, a chemical deficiency, or a brain injury

Table 12-1	Models of Psychological Disorder

In considering the case of Lori Schiller, discussed at the start of the chapter, we can employ each of the different models of abnormal behaviour. Note, however, that given the nature of her psychological disorder, some of the models are considerably more applicable than others.

Model	Description	Possible Application of Model to Schiller's Case
Medical model	Suggests that physiological causes are at the root of abnormal behaviour	Examine Schiller for medical problems, such as a brain tumor, chemical imbalance in the brain, or disease
Psychoanalytic model	Abnormal behaviour stems from childhood conflicts	Seek out information about Schiller's past, considering possible childhood conflicts
Behavioural model	Abnormal behaviour is a learned response	Concentrate on rewards and punishments for Schiller's behaviour, and identify environmental stimuli that reinforce her behaviour
Cognitive model	Assumes cognitions (people's thoughts and beliefs) are central to abnormal behaviour	Focus on Schiller's perceptions of herself and her environment
Humanistic model	Emphasizes people's control and responsibility for their own behaviour	Consider Schiller's behaviour in terms of the choices she has freely made
Sociocultural model	Assumes behaviour is shaped by family, society, and culture	Focus on how societal demands contributed to Schiller's disorder

of mental "illness," the "symptoms" of abnormal behaviour, and mental "hospitals," we are using terminology associated with the medical model.

Because many sorts of abnormal behaviours have been linked to biological causes, the medical model is a reasonable approach. Yet serious criticisms have been levelled against it. For one thing, there are many forms of abnormal behaviour for which no biological cause has been identified. In addition, some critics have argued that the use of the term "illness" implies that people displaying abnormal behaviour hold no responsibility for their actions (Szasz, 1982, 1994).

Still, recent advances in our understanding of the biological bases of behaviour have supported the importance of considering physiological factors in abnormal behaviour. For instance, we'll see later in the chapter that some of the most severe forms of psychological disturbance are the result of genetic factors, or malfunctions in neurotransmitter transmission (Resnick, 1992; Brunner et al., 1993; Crow, 1995; Petronis & Kennedy, 1995).

The Psychoanalytic Model

psychoanalytic model of abnormality: The model that suggests that abnormal behaviour stems from childhood conflicts over opposing wishes regarding sex and aggression

Whereas the medical model suggests that biological causes are at the root of abnormal behaviour, the **psychoanalytic model of abnormality** holds that abnormal behaviour stems from childhood conflicts over opposing wishes regarding sex and aggression. As we discussed in Chapter 11, Freud believed that children pass through a series of stages in which sexual and aggressive impulses take different forms and stimulate conflicts that require resolution. If these childhood conflicts are not dealt with successfully, they remain unresolved in the unconscious and eventually bring about abnormal behaviour during adulthood.

To understand the roots of people's disordered behaviour, the psychoanalytic model scrutinizes their early life history. However, because there is no conclusive way of linking people's childhood experiences with the abnormal behaviours they display as adults, we can never be sure that the mechanisms suggested by psychoanalytic theory are accurate. Moreover, psychoanalytic theory paints a picture of people as having little control over their behaviour, since it is guided by unconscious impulses.

On the other hand, the contributions of psychoanalytic theory have been significant. More than any other approach to abnormal behaviour, this model highlights the fact that people can have a rich, involved inner life and that prior experiences can have a profound effect on current psychological functioning (Horgan, 1996).

The Behavioural Model

Both the medical and psychoanalytic models look at abnormal behaviours as *symptoms* of some underlying problem. In contrast, the **behavioural model of abnormality** looks at the behaviour itself as the problem. Using the principles of learning discussed in Chapter 5, behavioural theorists see both normal and abnormal behaviours as responses to a set of stimuli, responses that have been learned through past experience and that are guided in the present by stimuli in the individual's environment. To explain why abnormal behaviour occurs, one must analyze how an abnormal behaviour has been learned and observe the circumstances in which it is displayed.

behavioural model of abnormality: The model that looks at the behaviour itself as the problem

The emphasis on observable behaviour represents both the greatest strength and the greatest weakness of the behavioural approach to abnormal behaviour. Because of its emphasis on the present immediate behaviour, this model is the most precise and objective approach for examining manifestations of abnormal behaviour. At the same time, though, critics charge that the model ignores the rich inner world of thoughts, attitudes, and emotions that may contribute to abnormal behaviour.

The Cognitive Model

The medical, psychoanalytic, and behavioural models view people's behaviour as being caused by factors largely beyond their control. To many critics, however, people's thoughts cannot be ignored.

In response to such concerns, some psychologists employ a **cognitive model of abnormality.** Rather than considering only external behaviour, as in traditional behavioural approaches, the cognitive approach assumes that *cognitions* (people's thoughts and beliefs) are central to a person's abnormal behaviour. A primary goal of treatment using the cognitive model is to explicitly teach new, more adaptive ways of thinking.

cognitive model of abnormality: The model that suggests that people's thoughts and beliefs are a central component of abnormal behaviour

For instance, a student who has the erroneous cognition, "This exam is crucial to my future," whenever taking an exam might be led, through therapy, to hold the more realistic thought: "My entire future is not dependent on this one exam." By changing cognitions in this way, psychologists working within a cognitive framework seek to allow people to free themselves from maladaptive thoughts and behaviours.

The Humanistic Model

Psychologists who subscribe to the **humanistic model of abnormality** emphasize the control and responsibility that people have for their own behaviour, even when such behaviour is abnormal. The humanistic model of abnormality concentrates on what is uniquely human, viewing people as basically rational, oriented toward a social world, and motivated to get along with others (Rogers, 1980).

humanistic model of abnormality: The model that emphasizes the control and responsibility that people have for their own behaviour, even when such behaviour is abnormal

Humanistic approaches focus on the relationship of the individual to society, considering the ways in which people view themselves in relation to others and see their place in the world. People are viewed as having an awareness of life and of themselves that leads them to search for meaning and self-worth. Rather than assuming that a "cure" is required, the humanistic model suggests that individuals can, by and large, set their own limits of what is acceptable behaviour. As long as they are not hurting others and do not feel personal distress, people should be free to choose the behaviours they engage in.

Although the humanistic model has been criticized for its reliance on unscientific, unverifiable information and its vague, almost philosophical, formulations, it offers a distinctive view of abnormal behaviour. The model stresses the unique aspects of being human and provides a number of important suggestions for helping those with psychological problems.

sociocultural model of abnormality: The model that makes the assumption that people's behaviour —both normal and abnormal—is shaped by the kind of family group, society, and culture in which they live

The Sociocultural Model

The **sociocultural model of abnormality** makes the assumption that people's behaviour—both normal and abnormal—is shaped by the kind of family group, society, and culture in which they live. According to this view, the nature of one's relationships with others may support abnormal behaviours and even cause them to occur. Consequently, the kinds of stresses and conflicts people experience as part of their daily interactions with others in their environment can promote and maintain abnormal behaviour.

Statistical support for the position that sociocultural factors shape abnormal behaviour can be found in the fact that some kinds of abnormal behaviour are far more prevalent among certain social groups than others. For instance women are twice as likely as men to suffer from depression. Some other high-risk groups for depression are people who are seriously ill or recently bereaved. Increasing numbers of Canadian children, estimates up to 26 percent, suffer from mental health problems. (Feightner, 1994; Nelson et al., 1996)).

Furthermore, poor economic times tend to be linked to general declines in psychological functioning, and social problems such as homelessness are associated with psychological disorders (Pines, 1981; Schweitzer & Hier, 1993; Bhugra, 1996; Nelson et al., 1996).

As with the other theories, the sociocultural model does not have unequivocal support. Alternative explanations abound for the association between abnormal behaviour and social factors. For example men may be less likely than women to seek help. Furthermore, sociocultural explanations provide relatively little in the way of direct guidance for the treatment of individuals showing mental disturbance, since the focus is on broader societal factors. Their identification does however highlight the need for prevention programs. This is important because it is unrealistic to think that there are adequate resources to provide individual interventions to all in need (Nelson et al., 1996).

Classifying Abnormal Behaviour: The ABCs of *DSM*

Crazy. Nutty as a fruitcake. Loony. Insane. Neurotic. Psycho. Strange. Demented. Odd. Possessed.

Society has long placed labels on people who display abnormal behaviour. Unfortunately, most of the time these labels have reflected intolerance and have been used with little thought to what the label signifies.

Providing appropriate and specific names and classifications for abnormal behaviour has presented a major challenge to psychologists. It is not too hard to understand why, given the difficulties discussed earlier in simply distinguishing normal from abnormal behaviour. Yet classification systems are necessary in order to be able to describe and ultimately to diagnose abnormal behaviour.

DSM-IV: Determining Diagnostic Distinctions

Over the years many different classification systems have been used, varying in terms of their utility and how universally they have been accepted by mental health workers. Today, however, one standard system, devised by the American Psychiatric Association, has emerged; it is employed by most professionals in Canada and the United States to diagnose and classify abnormal behaviour. The classification system is known as the ***Diagnostic and Statistical Manual of Mental Disorders, Fourth Edition (DSM-IV).***

Diagnostic and Statistical Manual of Mental Disorders, Fourth Edition (DSM-IV): A system devised by the American Psychiatric Association used by most professionals to diagnose and classify abnormal behaviour

Published in 1994, *DSM-IV* presents comprehensive and relatively precise definitions for more than 200 separate diagnostic categories. By following the criteria presented in the system, diagnosticians can clearly describe the specific problem an individual is experiencing. (Table 12-2 provides a brief outline of the major diagnostic categories.)

DSM-IV evaluates behaviour according to five separate dimensions, or *axes*. The first three axes assess the primary disorder; the nature of any longstanding personality

Pathways Through Psychology

Sylvia Geist

Community and Clinical Psychologist, Geist Family Centre, Toronto, Ontario

Education: B.A. York University; M. Ed.; Ed.D. University of Toronto Registered Psychologist (C. Psych.), Province of Ontario

Home: Toronto, Ontario

My interest in psychological disorders or mental illnesses was sparked in 1980 when I began to listen to families attending the family support group at the

Sylvia Geist

Centre for Addiction and Mental Health (formerly the Clarke Institute of Psychiatry). It was there that I first learned about the devastating consequences of these brain disorders on individuals and their families. Their voices became the focus of my doctoral dissertation entitled: "Impact of Schizophrenia on the Family: A Voyage Through Turbulence." My research highlighted the families as reactors to mental illness and not as causes of the illness. This shift in thinking contrasted with the literature at the time that discussed mental illness as the result of family dynamics or faulty parenting. My thesis was published as a video that is being used as an educational and training tool for professionals and families.

I have held various employment positions at the Centre for Addiction and Mental Health (formerly Queen Street Mental Health Centre). As a psychometrist, I provided case management and clinical services to persons with serious mental illnesses and as an administrator of a community clinic of the Centre I developed and implemented (within a multi-disciplinary team) community rehabilitation programs. I created a family psychoeducational program and facilitated a support group for families whose loved ones were patients of the hospital. As a volunteer, I actively participated for many years in Schizophrenia Society of Ontario. Later, as President of the Schiz-

ophrenia Society of Canada, I was able to advocate for the improvement of services and to work towards the elimination of the stigma that keeps mental illnesses "in the closet." I am continually involved in advocacy activities as founding and past Chairperson of the Canadian Alliance of Mental Illnesses and Mental Health (CAMIMH), an Alliance of five national organizations whose mandate is to place mental illnesses and mental health as a priority on the Canadian political and social agendas.

My understanding of mental illnesses was formed from a number of perspectives gleaned from these positions. Over my twenty years of working in the field I have had the privilege of receiving several awards for my work and have had the opportunity to work with many dedicated individuals (researchers, professionals, families, politicians, media, etc.). The recent opening of the Geist Family Centre (Toronto) that focuses on services for mental illnesses and mental health is a continuation of work as a community and clinical psychologist. My belief that I could make a difference in the quality of life of "marginalized" Canadian citizens has made my career as a psychologist both meaningful and sustaining.

Source: Sylvia Geist, Ed.D., C. Psych., Geist Family Centre
<sgeiste@netcom.ca>

problems in adults or any specific developmental problems in children and adolescents that may be relevant to treatment; and any physical disorders or illnesses that may also be present. The fourth and fifth axes take broader considerations into account. They focus on the severity of stressors present and on the person's general level of functioning over the past year in social relationships, work, and the use of leisure time.

One noteworthy feature of *DSM-IV* is that it is designed to be primarily descriptive and devoid of suggestions as to the underlying causes of an individual's behaviour and problems (Millon, 1991). Why should this be important? For one thing, it allows communication between mental health professionals of diverse backgrounds and approaches. In addition, precise classification enables researchers to make progress on exploring the causes of a problem. If the manifestations of an abnormal behaviour cannot be reliably described, researchers will be hard-pressed to find ways of investigating the disorder. Finally, *DSM-IV* provides a kind of conceptual shorthand through which professionals can describe the behaviours that tend to occur together in an individual (Widiger et al., 1990; DeAngelis, 1991; Frances, First, & Pincus, 1995; Halling & Goldfarb, 1996).

DSM-IV Link

| Table 12-2 | Major *DSM-IV* Diagnostic Categories |

The following list of disorders represents the major categories from *DSM-IV*. This is only a partial list of the over 200 disorders found in *DSM-IV*.

Anxiety disorders (problems in which anxiety impedes daily functioning)
    Subcategories: generalized anxiety disorder, panic disorder, phobic disorder, obsessive-compulsive disorder, post-traumatic stress disorder

Somatoform disorders (psychological difficulties displayed through physical problems)
    Subcategories: hypochondriasis, conversion disorder

Dissociative disorders (the splitting apart of crucial parts of personality that are usually integrated)
    Subcategories: dissociative identity disorder (multiple personality), dissociative amnesia, dissociative fugue

Mood disorders (emotions of depression or euphoria that are so strong they intrude on everyday living)
    Subcategories: major depression, bipolar disorder

Schizophrenia (declines in functioning, thought and language disturbances, perception disorders, emotional disturbances, and withdrawal from others)
    Subcategories: disorganized, paranoid, catatonic, undifferentiated, residual

Personality disorders (problems that create little personal distress but that lead to an inability to function as a normal member of society)
    Subcategories: antisocial (sociopathic) personality disorder, narcissistic personality disorder

Sexual disorders (problems related to sexual arousal from unusual objects or problems related to sexual functioning)
    Subcategories: paraphilia, sexual dysfunction

Substance-related disorders (problems related to drug dependence and abuse)
    Subcategories: alcohol, cocaine, hallucinogens, marijuana

Delirium, dementia, amnesia, and other cognitive disorders

Classification Concerns

Like any classification system, *DSM-IV* has its drawbacks. For instance, critics charge that it relies too much on the medical model of psychological disorder. Because it was drawn up by psychiatrists—who are physicians—some condemn it for viewing abnormal behaviours primarily in terms of symptoms of some underlying physiological disorder. Moreover, other critics suggest that *DSM-IV* pigeonholes people into inflexible categories, and that it would be more reasonable to use systems that classify people in terms of gradations.

Other concerns with *DSM-IV* are more subtle, but equally important to consider. For instance, some critics argue that labelling an individual as abnormal provides a lifetime stigma that is dehumanizing. Furthermore, after an initial diagnosis is made, other diagnostic possibilities may be overlooked by mental health professionals, who concentrate on the initial diagnostic category (Szasz, 1961, 1994; Kirk, 1992).

The notion that diagnostic categories provide rigid labels was illustrated in a now-classic experiment conducted in the early 1970s (Rosenhan, 1973). In the study, Rosenhan and seven of his colleagues presented themselves at the doors of separate mental hospitals across the United States and sought admission. The reason, they each stated, was that they were hearing voices—"unclear voices" which said "empty," "hollow," and "thud." Aside from changing their names and occupations, *everything* else they did and said was representative of their true behaviour, including the responses they gave during extensive admission interviews and answers to the battery of tests they were asked to complete. In fact, as soon as they were admitted, they said they no longer heard any voices. In sum, each of the pseudo-patients acted in a "normal" way.

One would assume that Rosenhan and his colleagues would have been quickly discovered as the impostors they were, but this was not the case. Instead, each of them was diagnosed as severely abnormal on the basis of observed behaviour. Most were labeled as suffering from schizophrenia, and they were kept in the hospital from three to fifty-two days, with the average stay being nineteen days. In most cases, they were not allowed to leave without the assistance of people outside the hospital. Even when they were discharged, most of the patients left with the label "schizophrenia—in remission," implying that the abnormal behaviour had only temporarily subsided and could recur at any time. Most disturbing of all, none of the pseudo-patients was identified by the staff of the hospitals as impostors. In sum, placing labels on people powerfully influences how their actions are perceived and interpreted.

Still, despite the drawbacks inherent in any labeling system, *DSM-IV* has had an important influence on the way in which mental health professionals consider psychological disorders. It has increased both the reliability and validity of diagnostic categorization. In addition, it provides us with a logical way to organize our examination of the major types of mental disturbance, to which we turn next.

Recap, Review, and Rethink

Recap

- Definitions of abnormality include those based on deviation from the average, deviation from the ideal, the psychological consequences of the behaviour for the individual, the individual's ability to function effectively and adapt as a member of society, and legal definitions.

- Abnormal and normal behaviour may best be viewed in terms of gradations, ranging from completely normal functioning to extreme abnormal behaviour.

- Current theories view abnormality in terms of six major models: the medical, psychoanalytic, behavioural, cognitive, humanistic, and sociocultural models.

- The *Diagnostic and Statistical Manual of Mental Disorders, Fourth Edition (DSM-IV)* provides a description of over 200 separate diagnostic categories of psychological disorders.

Review

1. One problem in defining abnormal behaviour is that
   a. statistically rare behaviour may not be abnormal.
   b. not all abnormalities are accompanied by feelings of discomfort.
   c. cultural standards are too general to use as a measuring tool.
   d. all of the above are correct.

2. If abnormality is defined as experiencing subjective discomfort or causing harm to others, which of the following people is most likely to need treatment?
   a. An executive is afraid to accept a promotion because it would require moving from his ground-floor office to the top floor of a tall office building.
   b. A woman quits her job and chooses to live on the street.
   c. A man believes that friendly spacemen visit his house every Thursday.
   d. A photographer lives with nineteen cats in a small apartment.

3. Virginia's mother thinks that Virginia's behaviour is clearly abnormal because, despite being offered admission to medical school, she decides to become a waitress. What approach is Virginia's mother using to define abnormal behaviour?

4. Which of the following is a strong argument against the medical model?
   a. Physiological abnormalities are almost always impossible to identify.
   b. There is no conclusive way to link past experience and behaviour.
   c. The medical model rests too heavily on the effects of nutrition.
   d. Assigning behaviour to a physical problem takes responsibility away from the individual for changing his or her behaviour.

5. Cheryl is painfully shy. According to the behavioural model, the best way to deal with her "abnormal" behaviour is to
   a. treat the underlying physical problem.
   b. use the principles of learning theory to modify her shy behaviour.
   c. express a great deal of caring.
   d. uncover her negative past experiences through hypnosis.

6. *DSM-IV* is intended both to describe psychological disorders and to suggest their underlying causes. True or false?

Answers to Review Questions are on page 452.

Rethink

1. Imagine that an acquaintance of yours was recently arrested for shoplifting a $15 necktie. What sort of explanation for this behaviour would be provided by proponents of *each* model of abnormality, including the medical model, the psychoanalytic model, the behavioural model, the cognitive model, the humanistic model, and the sociocultural model?

2. In what ways do you think the *DSM-IV* has increased both the reliability and validity of diagnostic categorization? Do you think the advantages of the system outweigh the concern that diagnostic categories can become overly rigid?

3. Do you agree or disagree that *DSM* should be updated every few years? What makes abnormal behaviour so variable? Why can't there be one definition of abnormal behaviour that is unchanging?

MAJOR DISORDERS

► What are the major psychological disorders?

Sally experienced her first panic attack out of the blue 3 weeks after completing her final year in college. She had just finished a job interview and was meeting some friends for dinner. In the restaurant, she began to feel dizzy. Within a few seconds, her heart was pounding and she was feeling breathless, as though she might pass out. Her friends noticed that she did not look well and offered to drive her home. Sally suggested they stop at the hospital emergency room instead. Although she felt better by the time they arrived at the hospital, and tests indicated nothing wrong, Sally experienced a similar episode a week later while at a movie. . . .

Her attacks became more and more frequent. Before long, she was having several attacks per week. In addition, she constantly worried about having attacks. She began to avoid exercise and other activities that produced physical sensations. She also noticed the attacks were worse when she was alone. She began to avoid driving, shopping in large stores, and eating in all restaurants. Some weeks she avoided leaving the house completely. Sally stopped looking for work, fearing that she would be unable to stay at her job in the event of a panic attack (Antony, Brown, & Barlow, 1992, p. 79).

The diagnosis: Sally suffered from one of the major forms of psychological disturbance, known as an anxiety disorder.

Anxiety disorders are one of a number of major forms of abnormal behaviour that we will consider. Keep in mind that we are focusing on those disorders that are most common, serious, or harmful to everyday functioning, and that many other types of disorders have been identified. It is also important to note that although we'll be discussing these disturbances in a dispassionate manner, each represents a very human set of difficulties that influence, and in some cases wreak considerable havoc on, people's lives.

Anxiety Disorders

A study on psychiatric disorders done in Edmonton found an 11.2 percent lifetime prevalence for anxiety disorders, with the highest number (7.2 percent) suffering from specific phobias (Bland, Newman, and Orn, 1988). There also appears to be a gender factor. A study done by the Ontario Ministry of Health (1994) found that 9 percent of men and 16 percent women had suffered anxiety disorders in the previous twelve months (Antony and Swinson, 1996).

All of us, at one time or another, experience *anxiety,* a feeling of apprehension or tension, in reaction to stressful situations. There is nothing "wrong" with such anxiety; everyone feels it to some degree, and usually it is a reaction to stress that helps, rather than hinders, our daily functioning. Without anxiety, for instance, most of us would not be terribly motivated to study hard, to undergo physical exams, or to spend long hours at our jobs.

But some people experience anxiety in situations in which there is no external reason or cause. When anxiety occurs without external justification and begins to impede people's daily functioning, it is considered a psychological problem known as an **anxiety disorder.** There are four main types of anxiety disorders: phobic disorder, panic disorder, generalized anxiety disorder, and obsessive-compulsive disorder.

anxiety disorder: The occurrence of anxiety without obvious external cause, intruding on daily functioning

Phobic Disorder

Claustrophobia. Acrophobia. Xenophobia. Although these sound like characters in a Greek tragedy, they are actually members of a class of psychological disorders known as phobias. **Phobias** are intense, irrational fears of specific objects or situations. For example, claustrophobia is a fear of enclosed places, acrophobia a fear of high places,

phobias: Intense, irrational fears of specific objects or situations

---

Answers to Review Questions:

1. d   2. a   3. deviation from the ideal   4. d   5. b   6. False; *DSM-IV* is intended to be descriptive only.

Table 12-3	Giving Fear A Proper Name		
Phobia	**Trigger**	**Phobia**	**Trigger**
Aerophobia	Flying	Hydrophobia	Water
Anthrophobia	People	Mikrophobia	Germs
Arachnophobia	Spiders	Murophobia	Mice
Astraphobia	Lightning	Mysophobia	Dirt or germs
Brontophobia	Thunder	Nyctophobia	Darkness
Cynophobia	Dogs	Ochlophobia	Crowds
Gephyrophobia	Bridges	Ophidiophobia	Snakes
Herpetophobia	Reptiles	Trichophobia	Hair

and xenophobia a fear of strangers. Although the objective danger posed by an anxiety-producing stimulus (which can be just about anything, as you can see from the list in Table 12-3) is typically small or nonexistent, to the individual suffering from the phobia the danger is great, and a full-blown panic attack may follow exposure to the stimulus. Phobic disorders differ from generalized anxiety disorders and panic disorders in that there is a specific, identifiable stimulus that sets off the anxiety reaction.

Phobias may have only a minor impact on people's lives if those who suffer from them can avoid the things they fear. Unless one is a professional firefighter or tightrope walker, for example, a fear of heights may have little impact on one's daily life. On the other hand, a fear of strangers presents a more serious problem. In one extreme case, a Washington woman left her home just three times in thirty years—once to visit her family, once for a medical operation, and once to purchase ice cream for a dying companion (Adler, 1984).

Panic Disorder

In another type of anxiety disorder, **panic disorder,** *panic attacks* occur that last from a few seconds to as long as several hours. Unlike phobias, which are brought about by specific objects or situations, panic disorders are not triggered by any identifiable stimulus. Instead, during an attack, such as the ones experienced by Sally in the case described earlier, anxiety suddenly—and without warning—rises to a peak, and an individual feels a sense of impending, unavoidable doom. Panic disorder may sometimes be accompanied by agorophobia (PDA), which is the fear of open spaces or crowded places (Cox, Endler, & Swinson, 1995; Cox et al., 1994). Although symptoms differ from person to person, they may include heart palpitations, shortness of breath, unusual amounts of sweating, faintness and dizziness, an urge to urinate, gastric sensations and—in extreme cases—a sense of imminent death. After such an attack, it is no wonder that people tend to feel exhausted (Antony, Brown, & Barlow, 1992; McNally, 1994; Asnis & van Praag, 1995; Rachman & deSilva, 1996).

panic disorder: Anxiety that manifests itself in the form of panic attacks that last from a few seconds to as long as several hours

Generalized Anxiety Disorder

As the name implies, people with **generalized anxiety disorder** experience long-term, consistent anxiety without knowing why. They feel worried or afraid of *something* but are unable to articulate what it is. Because of their anxiety, they are unable to function normally. They cannot concentrate, cannot set their worry and fears aside, and their lives become centred around their anxiety. Their anxiety may eventually result in physiological problems. Because of heightened muscle tension and arousal, individuals with generalized anxiety disorder may begin to experience headaches, dizziness, heart palpitations, or insomnia. The most frequent symptoms are given in Figure 12-1.

generalized anxiety disorder: The experience of long-term anxiety with no explanation

Obsessive-Compulsive Disorder

In **obsessive-compulsive disorder,** people are plagued by unwanted thoughts, called obsessions, or feel that they must carry out some actions, termed compulsions, against their will.

obsessive-compulsive disorder: A disorder characterized by obsessions or compulsions

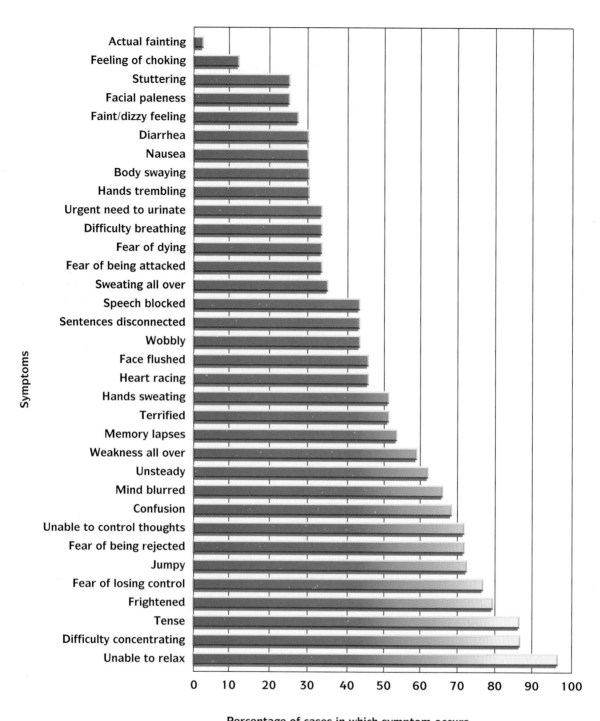

FIGURE 12-1 *Frequency of symptoms in cases of generalized anxiety disorder. Source: Adapted from Beck & Emery, 1985, pp. 87–88.*

obsession: A thought or idea that keeps recurring in one's mind

An **obsession** is a thought or idea that keeps recurring in one's mind. For example, a student may not be able to stop feeling that he has neglected to put his name on a test and may think about it constantly for the two weeks it takes to get the paper back. A man may go on vacation and wonder the whole time whether he locked his house. A woman may hear the same tune running through her head over and over again. In each case, the thought or idea is unwanted and difficult to put out of mind. Of course, many of us suffer from mild obsessions from time to time, but usually such thoughts persist only for a short period. For people with serious obsessions, however, the thoughts persist for days or months and may consist of bizarre, troubling images. In one classic case of an obsession, the patient complained of experiencing "terrible" thoughts:

> When she thought of her boyfriend she wished he were dead; when her mother went down the stairs, she "wished she'd fall and break her neck"; when her sister spoke of going to the beach with her infant daughter, the patient "hoped that they would both drown." These thoughts "make me hysterical. I love them; why should I wish such terrible things to happen? It drives me wild, makes me feel I'm crazy and don't belong to society" (Kraines, 1948, p. 199).

As part of an obsessive-compulsive disorder, people may also experience **compulsions,** urges to repeatedly carry out some act that seems strange and unreasonable, even to them. Whatever the compulsive behaviour, people experience extreme anxiety if they cannot carry it out, even if it is something they want to stop. The acts involved may be relatively trivial, such as repeatedly checking the stove to make sure all the burners are turned off, or more unusual, such as continuously washing oneself (Rachman & Hodgson, 1980; Carter, Pauls, & Leckman, 1995). For example, consider this case report of a 27-year-old woman with a cleaning ritual:

compulsion: An urge to repeatedly carry out some act that seems strange and unreasonable, even if the sufferer realizes it is unreasonable

> Bess would first remove all of her clothing in a preestablished sequence. She would lay out each article of clothing at specific spots on her bed, and examine each one for any indications of "contamination." She would then thoroughly scrub her body, starting at her feet and working meticulously up to the top of her head, using certain washcloths for certain areas of her body. Any articles of clothing that appeared to have been "contaminated" were thrown into the laundry. Clean clothing was put in the spots that were vacant. She would then dress herself in the opposite order from which she took the clothes off. If there were any deviations from this order, or if Bess began to wonder if she had missed some contamination, she would go through the entire sequence again. It was not rare for her to do this four or five times in a row on certain evenings (Meyer & Osborne, 1987, p. 156).

Unfortunately for those experiencing an obsessive-compulsive disorder, little or no reduction in anxiety results from carrying out a compulsive ritual. They tend to lead lives filled with unrelenting tension (Bouchard, Rhéaume, & Ladouceur, 1999).

The Causes of Anxiety Disorders

No one mechanism fully explains all cases of anxiety disorders, and each of the models of abnormal behaviour that we discussed earlier has something to say about their causes. However, the medical, behavioural, and cognitive models have been particularly influential in psychologists' thinking.

Anxiety Disorders

Biological approaches, stemming from the medical model, have shown that genetic factors play a role in anxiety disorders. For example, if one member of a pair of identical twins has panic disorder, there is a 30 percent chance that the other twin will have it also. Furthermore, recent research shows that a person's characteristic level of anxiety is related to a specific gene that is involved in the production of the neurotransmitter serotonin. This work is consistent with findings indicating that certain chemical deficiencies in the brain appear to produce some kinds of anxiety disorder (Hoehn-Saric, 1993; Lesch et al., 1996; Rieder, Kaufmann, & Knowles, 1996).

Psychologists employing the behavioural model have taken a different approach, emphasizing environmental factors. They consider anxiety to be a learned response to stress. For instance, suppose a young girl is bitten by a dog. When she next sees a dog, she is frightened and runs away—a behaviour that relieves her anxiety and thereby reinforces her avoidance behaviour. After repeated encounters with dogs in which she is reinforced for her avoidance behaviour, she may develop a full-fledged phobia regarding dogs.

Finally, the cognitive model suggests that anxiety disorders are an outgrowth of inappropriate and inaccurate cognitions about circumstances in a person's world. For example, people with anxiety disorders may view a friendly puppy as a ferocious and savage pit bull, or they may see an air disaster looming every moment they are in the vicinity of an airplane. According to the cognitive perspective, it is people's faulty thinking about the world that is at the root of an anxiety disorder.

Somatoform Disorders

Most of us know people who cannot wait to regale us with their latest physical problems; even an innocent "How are you?" brings a long list of complaints in response. People who consistently report physical problems, have a preoccupation with their health, and have unrealistic fears of disease may be experiencing a problem known as hypochondriasis. In *hypochondriasis* there is a constant fear of illness, and physical sensations are misinterpreted as signs of disease. It is not that the "symptoms" are faked; hypochondriacs actually experience the aches and pains that most of us feel as we go through an active existence. It is the misinterpretation of these sensations as symptoms of some dread disease—often in the face of inarguable medical evidence to the contrary—that characterizes hypochondriasis (Barsky et al., 1992; Noyes et al., 1993; Cantor & Fallon, 1996; Lautenbacher, & Rollman, 1999).

somatoform disorder:
Psychological difficulties that take on a physical (somatic) form of one sort or another

Hypochondriasis is just one example of a class of disorders known as **somatoform disorders,** psychological difficulties that take on a physical (somatic) form of one sort or another. Even though an individual with a somatoform disorder reports physical symptoms, there is no underlying physical problem, or, if a physical problem does exist, the person's reaction greatly exaggerates what would be expected from the medical problem alone. Only when a physical examination rules out actual physiological difficulties can a diagnosis of somatoform disorder be made.

conversion disorder: A major somatoform disorder that involves an actual physical disturbance, such as the inability to use a sensory organ or the complete or partial inability to move an arm or leg

In addition to hypochondriasis, the other major somatoform disorder is **conversion disorder.** Unlike hypochondriasis, in which there is no actual physical problem, conversion disorders involve an actual physical disturbance, such as the inability to use a sensory organ or the complete or partial inability to move an arm or leg. The *cause* of such a physical disturbance is purely psychological. There is no biological reason for the problem. Some of Freud's classic cases involved conversion disorders. For instance, one patient of Freud's was suddenly unable to use her arm, without any apparent physiological cause. Later, just as abruptly, she regained its use.

Conversion disorders are often characterized by rapid onset. People wake up one morning blind or deaf, or they experience numbness that is restricted to a certain part of the body. A person's hand, for example, might become entirely numb, while an area above the wrist—controlled by the same nerves—remains inexplicably sensitive to touch. Such a condition is referred to as "glove anesthesia," because the area that is numb is the part of the hand covered by a glove, and not a region related to pathways of the nervous system (see Figure 12-2).

One of the most surprising characteristics frequently found in people experiencing conversion disorders is a lack of concern over symptoms that most of us would expect to be highly anxiety-producing (Ford & Folks, 1985). For instance, a person in good health who wakes up blind might react in a bland, matter-of-fact way. Considering how most of us would feel if we woke up blind, this unemotional reaction (called *"la belle indifference,"* a French phrase meaning "a great indifference") hardly seems appropriate.

Conversion disorders generally occur when an individual is under some kind of emotional stress that could be reduced by a physical symptom. The physical condition creates an unconscious defense or means to escape or reduce the source of stress. An emotional problem is turned, then, into a physical ailment that acts to relieve the source of the original emotional problem.

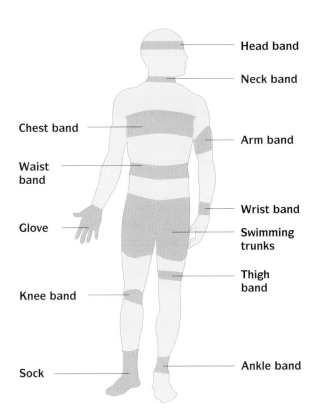

Head band

Neck band

Chest band

Arm band

Waist band

Glove

Wrist band

Swimming trunks

Knee band

Thigh band

Sock

Ankle band

FIGURE 12-2 *The shaded areas of the body indicate places where numbness might occur as a result of a psychological disorder rather than actual nerve damage.*

Dissociative Disorders

The most dramatic and celebrated cases of psychological dysfunction (although they are actually rare) have been **dissociative disorders.** The movie *The Three Faces of Eve,* the book *Sybil* (about a girl who allegedly had sixteen personalities), and cases of people found wandering the streets with no notion of who they are or where they came from exemplify dissociative disorders. The key factor in such problems is the splitting apart (or dissociation) of critical parts of personality that are normally integrated and work together. This lack of integration acts to allow certain parts of a personality to avoid stress—since another part can be made to face it. By dissociating themselves from key parts of their personality, individuals with the disorder can eliminate anxiety (Ross et al., 1990; Putnam, 1995a; Spiegel, 1996).

Three major types of dissociative disorders have been distinguished: dissociative identity disorder, dissociative amnesia, and dissociative fugue. A person with a **dissociative identity disorder** (or multiple personality) displays characteristics of two or more distinct personalities. Each personality has a unique set of likes and dislikes and its own reactions to situations. Some people with multiple personalities even carry several pairs of glasses because their vision changes with each personality. Moreover, each individual personality can be well adjusted when considered on its own (Ross, 1996; Kluft, 1996). This disorder is most often found in women and there is a very high correlation with sexual and physical abuse in childhood (Ross, 1994).

Reports of multiple personality have risen dramatically over the last few decades, with more cases being reported during a 5-year period in the 1980s than in the preceding 200 years (Putnam et al., 1986). Although one explanation for this increase is that diagnostic techniques have become more precise, some psychologists argue that it is the result of a self-fulfilling prophecy. In this view, the publicity accompanying well-known cases has led people to increasingly interpret their own psychological symptoms as signs of multiple personality. Subsequently, they may describe their symptoms to therapists in a manner that predisposes the therapists to view them as signs of multiple personality disorder. In short, according to this explanation, it is people's expectations about what they are experiencing that has led to the

dissociative disorder:
Psychological dysfunctions characterized by the splitting apart of critical personality facets that are normally integrated, allowing stress avoidance by escape

dissociative identity disorder:
A disorder in which a person displays characteristics of two or more distinct personalities

apparently higher incidence of the disorder. Ultimately, however, the recent rise in incidence of multiple personalities remains unexplained (McHugh, 1993; Spanos, 1994, 1996; Cote, 1994).

dissociative amnesia: A failure or inability to remember past experiences

Dissociative amnesia, another dissociative disorder, is a failure or inability to remember past experiences. Dissociative amnesia is unlike simple amnesia, which, as we discussed in Chapter 6, involves an actual loss of information from memory, typically due to a physiological cause. In contrast, in cases of dissociative amnesia, the "forgotten" material is still present in memory—it simply cannot be recalled.

In the most severe forms, individuals cannot recall their names, are unable to recognize parents and other relatives, and do not know their addresses. In other respects, though, they may appear quite normal. Apart from an inability to remember certain facts about themselves, they may be able to recall skills and abilities that they developed earlier. For instance, even though a chef may not remember where he grew up and received training, he may still be able to prepare gourmet meals.

In some cases of dissociative amnesia, the memory loss is quite profound. For example, a woman—dubbed Jane Doe by her rescuers—was found by a Florida park ranger in the early 1980s. Incoherent, thin, and only partially clothed, Doe was unable to recall her name, her past, and even how to read and write. On the basis of her accent, authorities thought the woman was from Illinois, and interviews conducted while she was given tranquilizing drugs revealed that she had had a Catholic education. However, the childhood memories she revealed were so universal that her background could not be further pinpointed. In a desperate attempt to rediscover her identity, she appeared on the television show *Good Morning America,* and ultimately a couple from Roselle, Illinois, whose daughter had moved to Florida, stepped forward, saying that they were her parents. However, Jane Doe never regained her memory (Carson, Butcher & Coleman, 1992).

dissociative fugue: An amnesiac condition in which people take sudden, impulsive trips, sometimes assuming a new identity

A more unusual form of amnesia is a condition known as **dissociative fugue.** In this state, people take an impulsive, sudden trip, often assuming a new identity. After a period of time—days, months, or sometimes even years—they suddenly realize that they are in a strange place and completely forget the time that they have spent wandering. Their last memories are those from the time just before they entered the fugue state. It is very rare and in some cases may be undiagnosed multiple personality disorder (Ross, 1994).

What the dissociative disorders have in common is that they allow people to escape from some anxiety-producing situation. Either the person produces a new personality to deal with stress, or the situation that caused the stress is forgotten or left behind as the individual journeys to some new—and perhaps less anxiety-ridden—environment (Spiegel & Cardena, 1991; Putnam, 1995b).

Recap, Review, and Rethink

Recap

- Anxiety disorders occur when anxiety is so great that it impedes people's everyday functioning.

- Somatoform disorders are psychological problems that take on a physical form.

- Dissociative disorders occur when normally integrated parts of personality split apart.

Review

1. Kathy is terrified of elevators. She is likely to be suffering from a(n)
   a. obsessive-compulsive disorder.
   b. phobic disorder.
   c. panic disorder.
   d. generalized anxiety disorder.

2. Carmen described an incident in which her anxiety suddenly rose to a peak and she felt a sense of impending doom. Carmen had experienced a(n) _____.

3. Troubling thoughts that persist for days or months are known as
   a. obsessions.
   b. compulsions.
   c. rituals.
   d. panic attacks.

4. An overpowering urge to carry out a strange ritual is called a(n) _____ .

5. In what major way does conversion disorder differ from hypochondriasis?

6. The splitting apart of the personality, providing escape from stressful situations, is the key factor in _____ disorders.

Answers to Review Questions are on page 460.

Rethink

1. Genetic factors have been found to play an important role in anxiety disorders. What other factors may contribute, and how can both the behavioural and cognitive models be used as a basis for treatment of anxiety disorders?

2. Which model do you think would provide the most effective means of dealing with somatoform disorders? Why?

3. Do you think the behavioural model would be effective in dealing with dissociative disorders? Why or why not? Which model do you think would be most promising for this type of disorder?

Mood Disorders

I felt very withdrawn. I felt very much to myself. The sleeping problem was back from the previous week, and there was a lot of anxiety. . . . I wasn't eating anything. I had a lot of things going together (Harnisch, 1997).

▶ **What are the most severe forms of psychological disorders?**

Did you ever apply for a job you really wanted, and for which you had a terrific interview, only to learn later that you didn't get it? Although your emotional reaction was probably not as strong as the one described above by New York Mets baseball pitcher Pete Harnisch, you probably experienced a feeling of depression, an emotional reaction of sadness and melancholy. Unlike Harnisch, though, who suffered from feelings of depression for extended periods, more than likely you returned to a more positive frame of mind relatively quickly.

We all experience mood swings. Sometimes we are happy, perhaps even euphoric; at other times we feel upset, saddened, or depressed. Such changes in mood are a normal part of everyday life. In some people, however, moods are so pronounced and so long-lasting that they interfere with the ability to function effectively. In extreme cases a mood may become life-threatening, and in others it may cause the person to lose touch with reality. Situations such as these represent **mood disorders,** disturbances in emotional feelings strong enough to intrude on everyday living.

mood disorder: Affective disturbances severe enough to interfere with normal living

Major Depression

Moses. Rousseau. Dostoevsky. Queen Victoria. Lincoln. Tchaikovsky. Freud.

The common link among these people? Each is believed to have suffered from periodic attacks of **major depression,** one of the most common forms of mood disorders. A major study for 1996–97 released by Health Canada in 1999 reported that 4 percent of Canadians twelve years of age and older had reported a major episode of depression. This is equivalent to 1 million people. Of this number 45 percent were in a depressed state for between 5 and 26 weeks.

major depression: A severe form of depression that interferes with concentration, decision making, and sociability

Women are twice as likely to experience major depression as men. The group with the highest rate of depression (8 to 9 percent), in Canada, is young women ages 15 to 19. For both sexes depression is more likely at younger ages. However as people get older their depression tends to last longer, from an average of 5 weeks for 12- to 19-year-olds to an average of 10.3 weeks for age 75 and older (Health Canada, 1999).

Depressive Disorders

When psychologists speak of major depression they do not mean the sadness that comes from experiencing one of life's disappointments. Some depression is normal following the breakup of a long-term relationship, the death of a loved one, or the loss of a job. It is even normal for less serious problems: doing badly in school or not getting into the college of one's choice.

People who suffer from major depression experience similar sorts of feelings, but the severity tends to be considerably greater. They may feel useless, worthless, and lonely and may despair over the future. These feelings may continue for months or even years. Of people who suffer from major depression, 50 percent will recover within a year. However, the other 50 percent will suffer from chronic depression (Feightner, 1994). They may have uncontrollable crying jags and disrupted sleep. The

In a tangle of chronic stomach pain, drug abuse, and persistent depression, Kurt Cobain of the rock group Nirvana committed suicide at the age of 27.

depth of such behaviour and the length of time it lasts are the hallmarks of major depression. (Table 12-4 provides a quick assessment of the severity of depression.)

Mania and Bipolar Disorders

mania: An extended state of intense euphoria and elation

While those with severe depression descend into depths of despair, another type of psychological disorder causes people to soar high emotionally, experiencing what is called mania. **Mania** refers to an extended state of intense euphoria and elation. People experiencing mania feel intense happiness, power, invulnerability, and energy:

> … During my depression I was quite introspective. As a hypomanic, however, I didn't stop to analyze my thoughts feelings or behaviour. I was much too busy and didn't always stop to think about what I was doing… At times I seemed to have lost my sense of judgement. This was quite different from my usual pattern of behavior, but I was not aware of the discrepancy (Endler, 1982, p. 86).

The above exerpt was written by Norman Endler, a clinical psychologist and professor of psychology at York University. His book, *Holiday of Darkness*, is the story of his battle with bipolar disorder. It is a book that is both a text on depressive illness and the story of a personal journey. He addresses with great honesty his feelings, the issue of the stigma of mental illness and the powerful healing force of his therapy and his family.

bipolar disorder: A disorder in which a person alternates between euphoric feelings of mania and bouts of depression

The alternation of mania and depression is called **bipolar disorder** (or, as it used to be known, manic-depressive disorder). The swings between highs and lows may occur as frequently as a few days apart or they may alternate over a period of years. In addition, the periods of depression tend to be longer in most individuals than the periods of mania, although this pattern is reversed in some.

Ironically, some of society's most creative individuals may suffer from forms of bipolar disorder. The imagination, drive, excitement, and energy that they display dur-

---

Answers to Review Questions:

1. b   2. panic attack   3. a   4. compulsion   5. In conversion disorder, an actual physical disturbance is present   6. dissociative

Table 12-4	A Test for Depression

This test was distributed by mental-health organizations during National Depression Screening Day in the early 1990s, a nationwide event that sought to identify people who suffered from depression severe enough to warrant psychological intervention. On the day of the screening, the organizations received some 30,000 inquiries (Hill, 1992).

To complete the questionnaire, count the number of statements with which you agree:

1. I feel downhearted, blue, and sad.
2. I don't enjoy the things that I used to.
3. I feel that others would be better off if I were dead.
4. I feel that I am not useful or needed.
5. I notice that I am losing weight.
6. I have trouble sleeping through the night.
7. I am restless and can't keep still.
8. My mind isn't as clear as it used to be.
9. I get tired for no reason.
10. I feel hopeless about the future.

Scoring If you agree with at least five of the statements, including either item 1 or 2, and if you have had these symptoms for at least two weeks, help from a professional is strongly recommended. If you answer yes to number 3, you should get help immediately.

ing manic stages allow them to make unusually creative contributions. For instance, historical analysis of the composer Robert Schumann's music shows that he was most prolific during the periods of mania he suffered periodically. In contrast, his output dropped off drastically during periods of depression (see Figure 12-3). On the other hand, the high output associated with mania does not necessarily lead to higher quality: Some of Schumann's greatest works were created outside his periods of mania (Jamison, 1993, 1995; Weisberg, 1994; Week & James, 1995; Ludwig, 1996).

Bipolar Disorder

Despite the creative fires that may be lit by mania, persons who experience this disorder often show a recklessness that produces self-injury—emotionally and sometimes physically. They may alienate others with their talkativeness, inflated self-esteem, and indifference to the needs of others.

Causes of Mood Disorders

Because they represent a major mental health problem, mood disorders—and, in particular, depression—have received a good deal of study. Several approaches have been used to explain the disorder. Psychoanalytic approaches, for example, see depression as the result of feelings of loss (real or potential) or of anger directed at oneself. In one psychoanalytic approach, for instance, depression is thought to be produced by the loss or threatened loss of a parent early in life. In another psychoanalytic view, people are thought to feel responsible for the bad things that happen to them and to direct their anger inward.

On the other hand, convincing evidence has been found that both bipolar disorder and major depression may have genetic and biochemical roots. For example, heredity plays a role in bipolar disorder: The affliction clearly runs in some families (Gershon et al., 1990; Morell, 1996b; Berrettini & Pekkarinen, 1996; De-bruyn et al., 1996). Furthermore, several neurotransmitters appear to play a role in depression. For instance, alterations in the functioning of serotonin and norepinephrine in the brain are related to the disorder (Cooper, Bloom, & Roth, 1991; Horton & Katona, 1991; Jacobs, 1994).

Some explanations for mood disorders are based on cognitive factors (Gotlib, 1992; Costello, 1993). Psychologist Martin Seligman suggests that depression is

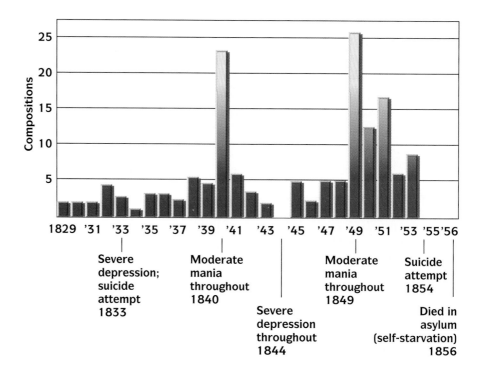

learned helplessness: A state in which people conclude that unpleasant or aversive stimuli cannot be controlled—a view of the world that becomes so ingrained that they cease trying to remedy the aversive circumstances, even if they actually can exert some influence

largely a response to learned helplessness. **Learned helplessness** is a state in which people perceive and eventually learn that there is no way to escape from or cope with stress. As a consequence, they simply give up fighting stress and submit to it, thereby spawning depression (Seligman, 1975, 1988; Peterson, Maier, & Seligman, 1993). Building on Seligman's notions, other psychologists suggest that depression may be a result of hopelessness, a combination of learned helplessness and an expectation that negative outcomes in one's life are inevitable (Abramson, Metalsky, & Alloy, 1989; Nunn, 1996).

Clinical psychologist Aaron Beck has proposed that faulty cognitions underlie people's depressed feelings. Specifically, his cognitive theory of depression suggests that depressed individuals typically view themselves as life's losers, blaming themselves whenever anything goes wrong. By focusing on the negative side of situations, they feel inept and unable to act constructively to change their environment. In sum, their negative cognitions lead to feelings of depression (Sacco & Beck, 1995; Wright & Beck, 1996).

Building on the work of Beck, Canadian researchers have made significant contributions to the cognitive model of depression, with a focus on negative self schemas. Research suggests that knowledge, stored in stable units called schemas, influences the selection and interpretation of future information. Depressed people appear to have more negative self-schemas and access them more readily than do non-depressed people. Although it is not possible to say that these schemas cause depression, they might help to maintain it (Segal & Vella, 1990; Segal et al., 1995; Rector et al., 1998).

In a study that used a narrative report, a group of psychiatric patients at a Calgary hospital, were found to employ one of four distinct strategies to deflect the responsibility for their condition away from themselves. Unlike the traditional findings of cognitive research with an emphasis on negative self schemes, this study found the participants blamed others or circumstance for their situation (Drew, Dobson & Stam, 1999).

The various theories of depression have still not provided a complete answer to an elusive question that has dogged researchers: Why is the incidence of depression twice as high for women as for men? One explanation is that the stress experienced by women may be greater than that experienced by men at certain points in their lives—

such as when a woman must simultaneously earn a living and be the primary caregiver for her children. In addition, women have a higher risk for physical and sexual abuse, typically earn lower wages than men, and report greater unhappiness with their marriages (McGrath et al., 1990; Strickland, 1992; Nolen-Hoeksema & Girgus, 1994; Brems, 1995; Nolen-Hoeksema, 1995).

But biological factors may also explain some women's depression. For example, 25 to 50 percent of women who take oral contraceptives report symptoms of depression, and depression that occurs following the birth of a child is linked to hormonal changes (Strickland, 1992).

It is clear, ultimately, that researchers have discovered no definitive solutions to the puzzle of depression, and there are many alternative explanations. Most likely, mood disorders are caused by a complex interaction of several factors (Ingram, 1990; Wolman & Stricker, 1990; Jarrett, 1991).

Schizophrenia

MYTH: Schizophrenia is split personality or multiple personality disorder.

FACT: Schizophrenia is often confused with split personality. They are NOT the same thing. The confusion arose because the word schizophrenia comes form two Greek roots meaning "split mind." The splitting or fragmentation referred to is the breakdown of an individual's thinking and feeling processes, not a division of the person into two separate personalities. The popular use of the word "schizophrenic" to describe a mixture of contradictory qualities is completely different from the correct psychiatric use of the term (The World Psychiatric Association Program to Fight Stigma Due to Schizophrenia. www.openthedoors.com).

Mental Health

Schizophrenia is one of the most severe forms of mental disturbance. People with schizophrenia make up by far the largest percentage of those hospitalized for mental disorders. In Canada 1 percent of the population suffers from schizophrenia. Schizophrenic patients occupy 1 in 12 hospital beds in Canada (Schizophrenic Society of Canada). They are also in many respects the least likely to recover from their psychological difficulties.

Schizophrenia refers to a class of disorders in which severe distortion of reality occurs. Thinking, perception, and emotion may deteriorate; there may be a withdrawal from social interaction; and there may be displays of bizarre behaviour. Although several types of schizophrenia (see Table 12-5) have been observed, the distinctions between them are not always clear-cut (Fenton & McGlashan, 1991a; Bentall, 1992). Moreover, the symptoms displayed by persons with schizophrenia may vary considerably over time, and people with schizophrenia show significant differences in the pattern of their symptoms even when they are labeled with the same diagnostic category. Nonetheless, a number of characteristics reliably distinguish schizophrenia from other disorders. They include:

schizophrenia: A class of disorders in which severe distortion of reality occurs

- *Decline from a previous level of functioning.* An individual can no longer carry out activities he or she was once able to do.

- *Disturbances of thought and language.* People with schizophrenia have a number of neurocognitive deficits. They use logic and language in a peculiar way. Their thinking often does not make sense, and their information processing is frequently faulty (Heinrichs and Zakzanis, 1998). They also do not follow conventional linguistic rules (Penn et al., 1997). Consider, for example, the following response to the question "Why do you think people believe in God?"

    Uh, let's, I don't know why, let's see, balloon travel. He holds it up for you, the balloon. He don't let you fall out, your little legs sticking down

Table 12-5	The Major Types of Schizophrenia

Type	Symptoms
Disorganized (hebephrenic) schizophrenia	Inappropriate laughter and giggling, silliness, incoherent speech, infantile behaviour, strange and sometimes obscene behaviour
Paranoid schizophrenia	Delusions and hallucinations of persecution or of greatness, loss of judgment, erratic and unpredictable behaviour
Catatonic schizophrenia	Major disturbances in movement; in some phases, loss of all motion, with patient frozen into a single position, remaining that way for hours and sometimes even days; in other phases, hyperactivity and wild, sometimes violent, movement
Undifferentiated schizophrenia	Variable mixture of major symptoms of schizophrenia; classification used for patients who cannot be typed into any of the more specific categories
Residual schizophrenia	Minor signs of schizophrenia following a more serious episode

through the clouds. He's down to the smokestack, looking through the smoke trying to get the balloon gassed up you know. Way they're flying on top that way, legs sticking out (Chapman & Chapman, 1973, p. 3).

As this selection illustrates, although the basic grammatical structure may be intact, the substance of thinking that is characteristic of schizophrenia may be illogical, garbled, and lacking in meaningful content.

- *Delusions.* People with schizophrenia often have *delusions,* firmly held, unshakable beliefs with no basis in reality. Among the most common delusions experienced by people with schizophrenia are the beliefs that they are being controlled by someone else, that they are being persecuted by others, and that their thoughts are being broadcast so that others are able to know what they are thinking.

- *Perceptual disorders.* People with schizophrenia do not perceive the world as most other people do. They may see, hear, or smell things differently from others (see Figure 12-4) and do not even have a sense of their bodies in the way that others do. Some reports suggest that individuals with schizophrenia have difficulty determining where their own bodies stop and the rest of the world begins (Ritzler & Rosenbaum, 1974). They may also have *hallucinations,* the experience of perceiving things that do not actually exist (McGuire, Shah, & Murray, 1993; Ruppin, Reggia, & Horn, 1996; Reichman & Rabins, 1996).

- *Emotional disturbances.* People with schizophrenia sometimes show a bland lack of emotion in which even the most dramatic events produce little or no emotional response. Conversely, they may display emotion that is inappropriate to a situation. For example, a person with schizophrenia might laugh uproariously at a funeral or may react with anger when being helped by someone.

- *Withdrawal.* People with schizophrenia may have little interest in others. They may not socialize or hold real conversations with others, although they may talk *at* another person. In the most extreme cases they do not even acknowledge the presence of other people, appearing to be in their own isolated world.

The symptoms of schizophrenia follow two primary courses. In *process schizophrenia,* the symptoms develop relatively early in life, slowly and subtly. There may be a gradual withdrawal from the world, excessive daydreaming, and a blunting of emotion, until eventually the disorder reaches the point where others cannot overlook it. In other cases, known as *reactive schizophrenia,* the onset of symptoms is sudden and conspicuous. The treatment outlook for reactive schizophrenia is relatively favorable; process schizophrenia has proved to be much more difficult to treat.

A relatively recent addition to the classifications used in schizophrenia distinguishes *positive-symptom schizophrenia* from *negative-symptom schizophrenia* (Fenton & McGlashan, 1994; Tandon, 1995; Hafner & Maurer, 1995). Positive-symptom schizophrenia is indicated by the presence of disordered behaviour such as hallucinations, delusions, and extremes of emotionality. In contrast, negative-symptom schizophrenia means an absence or loss of normal functioning, such as social withdrawal or blunted emotions. The distinction is becoming increasingly important because it suggests that two different underlying processes may explain the roots of schizophrenia—which remains one of the greatest mysteries facing psychologists who deal with disordered behaviour (Fenton & McGlashan, 1991b; Heinrichs, 1993).

FIGURE 12-4 *This haunting art was created by an individual suffering from schizophrenia.*

Solving the Puzzle of Schizophrenia: Biological Causes

Although it is clear that schizophrenic behaviour departs radically from normal behaviour, its causes are less apparent. It does appear, however, that schizophrenia has both biological and environmental components at its roots.

Let's first consider the evidence pointing to a biological cause of schizophrenia. Because schizophrenia is more common in some families than in others, genetic factors seem to be involved in producing at least a susceptibility to or readiness for developing schizophrenia (Gottesman, 1991; Verdoux et al., 1996; Tsuang & Faraone, 1996). For example, research has shown that the closer the genetic link between a person with schizophrenia and another individual, the higher the likelihood that the other person will experience the disorder (see Figure 12-5).

Because if genetics alone were responsible, the chance of the identical twin of a twin with schizophrenia having schizophrenia would be 100 percent instead of just under 50 percent, since identical twins share the same genetic makeup. Moreover, research that has sought to find a link between schizophrenia and a particular gene has been only partly successful (e.g., Crowe et al., 1991; Wang et al., 1993; Chen et al., 1996). However researchers feel that they are getting closer. In early 2000, Dr. Anne Bassett, of the University of Toronto, announced that she and her colleagues had identified the chromosome on which they believe they will find the gene for schizophrenia. The research was conducted by a Canadian-American team. The subjects were 304 Canadians from families who appeared to have an inherited predisposition for the disorder. Although this research is promising, Dr. Basset believes that more than one gene is probably involved as well as environmental factors (Mary Vallis). Apparently schizophrenia is produced by more than genetic factors alone (Iacono & Grove, 1993; Kendler et al., 1996; Ingraham & Chan, 1996; Franzek & Beckmann, 1996).

One of the most intriguing biological hypotheses to explain schizophrenia is that the brains of victims harbour either a biochemical imbalance or a structural abnormality. For example, the *dopamine hypothesis* suggests that schizophrenia occurs when there is excess activity in those areas of the brain that use dopamine as a neurotransmitter (Wong et al., 1988; Seeman, 1993). This hypothesis came to light after the discovery that drugs that block dopamine action in brain pathways can be highly effective in reducing the symptoms of schizophrenia.

Unfortunately, the dopamine hypothesis does not provide the whole story. Drugs that block dopamine action produce a biological reaction just a few hours after they're taken—yet the symptoms of schizophrenia do not subside for weeks. If the hypothesis were entirely correct, we would expect an immediate improvement in schizophrenic symptoms. Moreover, these drugs are effective in reducing symptoms not only in people with schizophrenia but also in those suffering from very different sorts of psychological problems, such as mania and depression. Such evidence has led some researchers to hypothesize that dopamine is not the full explanation, but that it oper-

FIGURE 12-5 *The closer the genetic links between two people, the greater the likelihood that if one experiences schizophrenia, so will the other. Source: Gottesman, 1991.*

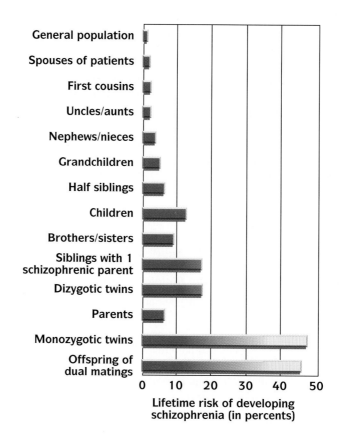

ates in conjunction with other neurotransmitters such as serotonin (Lieberman & Koreen, 1993; Kahn et al., 1993; Hsiao et al., 1993; Kapur & Remington, 1996; Abi-Dargham et al., 1997).

Other biological explanations for schizophrenia propose that structural abnormalities exist in the brains of people with the disorder, perhaps due to abnormal prenatal development (Wyatt, Apud, & Potkin, 1996; Brown et al., 1996). For example, some research suggests that the hippocampus and ventricles of the brains of those with schizophrenia differ in size from those of people who do not have the disorder (Lim et al., 1996; Fukuzako et al., 1996). Furthermore, increasing evidence shows that the neural circuits of the cortex and limbic system of individuals with schizophrenia are abnormal (Benes, 1996). Consistent with such research, people with schizophrenia and those without the disorder show different brain functioning (Andreasen et al., 1992; Bogerts, 1993; Andreasen et al., 1994; Frazier et al., 1996; Pearlson et al., 1996; O'Leary et al., 1996). The brain scans shown in Figures 12-6 and 12-7 illustrate some of these differences.

Environmental Perspectives on Schizophrenia

Although biological factors provide some pieces of the puzzle of schizophrenia, we still need to consider past and current experiences in the environments of people who develop the disturbance.

For instance, theories that look toward the emotional and communication patterns of families of people with schizophrenia suggest that schizophrenia is affected by high levels of expressed emotion. *Expressed emotion* is an interaction style characterized by criticism, hostility, and emotional intrusiveness by family members. Some researchers suggest that faulty communication patterns lie at the heart of schizophrenia (Weisman et al., 1993; Mueser et al., 1993; Bayer, 1996; Linszen et al., 1997).

Psychologists who take a cognitive perspective on schizophrenia suggest that the problems in thinking experienced by people with the disorder point to a cognitive cause for the disorder. Some suggest that schizophrenia is the result of *overattention* to stimuli in the environment. Rather than being able to screen out unimportant or inconsequential stimuli and focus on the most important things in the environment, people with schizophrenia are excessively receptive to data. As a consequence, their information processing capabilities become overloaded and eventually break down. On the other hand, other cognitive experts argue that schizophrenia is the result of *underattention* to certain stimuli. According to this explanation, people with schizophrenia fail to focus on important stimuli sufficiently, and pay attention to other, less important information in their surroundings (Braff, 1993).

Although it is plausible that overattention and underattention are related to different forms of schizophrenia, these phenomena do not explain the origins of such information processing disorders. Consequently, cognitive approaches—like other environmental explanations—are not the full explanation of the disorder.

The Multiple Causes of Schizophrenia

We have seen that several different biological and environmental factors are related to schizophrenia. It is likely, then, that not just one but several causes jointly explain the onset of the disorder. The predominant approach used today, the *predisposition model of schizophrenia,* considers a number of factors simultaneously (Cornblatt & Erlenmeyer-Kimling, 1985; Fowles, 1992; Breier, 1995). This model suggests that individuals may inherit a predisposition or an inborn sensitivity to schizophrenia that makes them particularly vulnerable to stressful factors in the environment. The stressors may vary—social rejection or dysfunctional family communication patterns—but if they are strong enough and are coupled with a genetic predisposition, the result will be the onset of schizophrenia. Similarly, if the genetic predisposition is strong enough, schizophrenia may occur even when the environmental stressors are relatively weak.

In short, schizophrenia is associated with several kinds of biological and environmental factors. It is increasingly clear, then, that schizophrenia is produced not by any single factor but by a combination of interrelated variables (Fowles, 1992; Hirsch, Cramer, & Bowen, 1992; Straube & Oades, 1992; Kety, 1996).

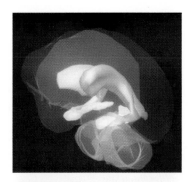

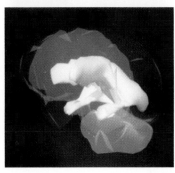

FIGURE 12-6 *Structural changes in the brain have been found in people with schizophrenia. In the top MRI reconstruction of the brain of a patient with schizophrenia, the hippocampus is shrunken, and the ventricles are enlarged and fluid-filled. In contrast, the brain (below) of a person without the disorder appears structurally different. Source: N. C. Andreasen, University of Iowa.*

Personality Disorders

> Canada's most notorious and reviled criminal is Clifford Olson, a serial murderer sentenced in January 1982 to life imprisonment for the torture and killing of eleven boys and girls. These crimes were the latest and most despicable in a string of antisocial and criminal acts extending back to his early childhood. Although some psychopaths are not violent and few are as brutal as he is, Olson is the prototypical psychopath.
>
> … In the years since his imprisonment Olson has continued to bring grief to the families of his victims by sending them letters with comments about the murders of their children. He has never shown any guilt or remorse for his depredations… (Hare, 1993, p. 132).

Olson's behaviour is a clear example of a person with a personality disorder. **Personality disorders** are different from the other problems that we have discussed in this chapter, because there is often little sense of personal distress associated with the psychological maladjustment of those affected. In fact, people with personality disorders frequently lead seemingly normal lives. However, just below the surface lies a set of inflexible, maladaptive personality traits that do not permit such individuals to function appropriately as members of society (Derksen, 1995; Clarkin & Lenzenweger, 1996; Millon & Davis, 1995, 1996; Millon, 1997).

The best-known type of personality disorder is the **antisocial or sociopathic** (often known as psychopathic) **personality disorder.** As the Olson example shows, individuals with this disturbance tend to display no regard for the moral and ethical rules of society or the rights of others. Although they appear intelligent and are usually likable at first, upon closer examination they can be seen as manipulative and deceptive. Moreover, they lack a conscience; they feel no guilt or anxiety over their wrong-

personality disorder: A mental disorder characterized by a set of inflexible, maladaptive personality traits that keep a person from functioning properly in society

antisocial or sociopathic personality disorder: A disorder in which individuals tend to display no regard for the moral and ethical rules of society or the rights of others

FIGURE 12-7 *Compare these PET scans, which show differences in functioning between two people, one of whom has been diagnosed with schizophrenia. Both are performing a task involving vision. In the person without schizophrenia, the task increases prefrontal cortex metabolism (right). For the person with schizophrenia, however, this does not occur (left). Source: M. S. Buchsbaum, University of California–Irvine.*

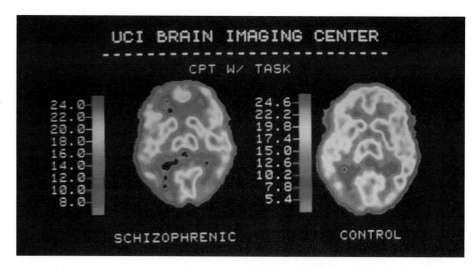

Antisocial Personality Disorder

doing. When those with an antisocial personality behave in a way that injures someone else, they understand intellectually that they have caused the harm but feel no remorse (Lykken, 1995).

People with antisocial personalities are often impulsive, and they lack the ability to withstand frustration. Finally, they can be extremely manipulative. They may have excellent social skills, be charming, engaging, and able to convince others to do what they want. Some of the best con men have antisocial personalities. Although many psychopaths end up in prison for criminal activity, many live out their lives in the community bringing personal and economic pain to those with whom they interact (Hare, 1993).

What causes such an unusual constellation of problems? A variety of factors have been suggested, ranging from a biologically induced inability to experience emotions appropriately to problems in family relationships (e.g., Gillstrom & Hare, 1988; Nigg & Goldsmith, 1994; Rosenstein & Horowitz, 1996). For example, in many cases of antisocial behavior, the individual has come from a home in which a parent has died or left, or one in which there is a lack of affection, a lack of consistency in discipline, or outright rejection. Other explanations concentrate on sociocultural factors, since an unusually high proportion of antisocial personalities come from lower socioeconomic groups. Some researchers have suggested that the breakdown of societal rules, norms, and regulations that may be found in severely deprived economic environments may encourage the development of antisocial personalities (Melges & Bowlby, 1969). Still, no one has been able to pinpoint the specific causes of antisocial personalities, and it is likely that some combination of factors is responsible (Hare, Hart, & Harpur, 1991).

There is very little evidence that treatment has any effect on psychopathic behaviour (Hare, 1993). Recognized as a world authority on psychopaths, Robert Hare, of the University of British Columbia, was approached by the Canadian government to design a treatment and management program for psychopaths. He brought together a group of international experts and has devised an experimental treatment plan. Believing that attempts to develop empathy or conscience are wasted, the program will focus on intensive and tightly controlled efforts to foster a sense of responsibility. Clients will be encouraged to meet their needs in a more socially acceptable way, on the premise that their self-interest is not being well served in jail. Hare (1993) does caution that even this program may not help non-custodial psychopaths whose behaviour cannot be controlled

borderline personality disorder:
A disorder in which individuals have difficulty in developing a secure sense of who they are

People with **borderline personality disorder,** another personality disorder, have difficulty in developing a secure sense of who they are. As a consequence, they tend to rely on relationships with others to define their identity. The problem with this strategy is that rejections are devastating. Furthermore, people with this disorder are distrustful of others and have difficulty controlling their anger. Their emotional volatility leads to impulsive and self-destructive behaviour. Glenn Close's character in the film *Fatal Attraction* typifies the behaviour characteristic of borderline personality disorder (Horwitz et al., 1996).

Individuals with borderline personality disorder often feel empty and alone. They may form intense, sudden, one-sided relationships, demanding the attention of another person and then feeling angered when they don't receive it. In fact, they often appear intensely angry to others.

Another example of a personality disturbance is the **narcissistic personality disorder,** characterized by an exaggerated sense of self-importance. Those with the disorder expect special treatment from others, while at the same time disregarding others' feelings. In some ways, in fact, the main attribute of the narcissistic personality is an inability to experience empathy for other people.

There are several other categories of personality disorder, ranging in severity from individuals who may simply be regarded by others as eccentric, obnoxious, or difficult, to people who act in a manner that is criminal and dangerous to others. Although they are not out of touch with reality in the way that people with schizophrenia are, people with personality disorders lead lives that are on the fringes of society.

narcissistic personality disorder: A personality disturbance that is characterized by an exaggerated sense of self-importance

Recap, Review, and Rethink

Recap

- Mood disorders are characterized by disturbances in affect that are so great they impede daily living.

- Schizophrenia is the most common diagnosis for those hospitalized for mental disturbance.

- People with personality disorders do not feel the personal distress associated with other disorders, but they do have maladaptive traits that prevent them from functioning as typical members of society.

Review

1. Henry's feelings of deep despair, worthlessness, and loneliness have persisted for months. His symptoms are indicative of
   a. an adjustment reaction.
   b. normal depression.
   c. major depression.
   d. affective depression.

2. States of extreme euphoria and energy paired with severe depression characterize _____ disorder.

3. Arthur's belief that his thoughts are being controlled by beings from outer space is an example of a

   _____ .

4. _____ schizophrenia is characterized by symptoms that are sudden and of easily identifiable onset, while _____ schizophrenia develops gradually over a person's lifespan.

5. The _____ _____ states that schizophrenia may be caused by an excess of certain neurotransmitters in the brain.

6. Which of the following theories states that schizophrenia is caused by the combination of a genetic predisposition and environmental stressors?
   a. learned-inattention
   b. predisposition model
   c. dopamine hypothesis
   d. learned-helplessness theory

7. The _____ personality disorder is characterized by a disregard for societal rules or others' rights.

Answers to Review Questions are on page 470.

Rethink

1. Given the association between talent and bipolar disorder, do you think some talented people may be encouraged to tolerate or even nurture mood swings?

2. Do any of the explanations of schizophrenia offer the promise of a treatment or cure of the disorder? Do any of the explanations permit us to predict who will be affected by the disorder? How is explanation different from treatment and prediction?

3. Personality disorders are often not apparent to others, and many people with these problems seem to live basically normal lives and are not a threat to others. Since these people can function well in society, why should they be considered "ill"?

BEYOND THE MAJOR DISORDERS: ABNORMAL BEHAVIOUR IN PERSPECTIVE

The various forms of abnormal behaviour described in *DSM-IV* cover much wider ground than we have been able to discuss in this chapter. Some we have considered in earlier chapters, such as *psychoactive substance-use disorder,* in which problems arise from the

▶ **What indicators signal a need for the help of a mental health practitioner?**

abuse of drugs (Chapter 4), *eating disorders* (Chapter 9), and *sexual disorders,* in which one's sexual activity is unsatisfactory. Another important class of disorders that we have previously touched upon is *organic mental disorders.* These are problems that have a purely biological basis. There are other disorders we have not mentioned at all, and each of the classes we have discussed can be divided into several subcategories.

Keep in mind that the specific nature of the disorders included in *DSM-IV* is a reflection of late-twentieth-century western cultures. The classification system is a snapshot of how its authors viewed mental disorder when it was published in 1994. In fact, the development of the latest version of *DSM* was a source of great controversy, in part reflecting issues that divide society.

For example, two disorders were particularly controversial during the revision process. One, known as the "self-defeating personality disorder," was a category that ultimately was removed from the appendix, where it had appeared in the previous revision. The term "self-defeating personality disorder" was meant to apply to cases in which people in relationships in which they receive unpleasant and demeaning treatment neither leave nor take other action. It was typically used to describe people who remained in abusive relationships.

Although some clinicians argued that it was a valid category, one that they observed in their clinical practice, there ultimately seemed to be a lack of research evidence supporting its existence. Furthermore, some critics complained that use of the label had the effect of condemning targets of abuse for their plight—a blame-the-victim phenomenon—and as a result, the category was removed from the manual.

A second and even more controversial category was "premenstrual dysphoric disorder." The disorder was characterized by severe, incapacitating mood changes or depression related to a woman's menstrual cycle. Some critics argued that the classification simply labelled normal female behaviour as a disorder. The former U.S. Surgeon General, Antonia Novello, suggested that what "in women is called PMS [premenstrual syndrome, a similar classification] in men is called healthy aggression and initiative" (Cotton, 1993, p. 270). Advocates for including the disorder prevailed, however, and "premenstrual dysphoric disorder" appears in the appendix of *DSM-IV.*

In many cultures, the ability to hear the voices of departed spirits is considered a divine gift. In modern, industrialized societies, however, hearing voices is viewed as a sign of psychological disturbance.

Answers to Review Questions:

1. c   2. bipolar   3. delusion   4. Reactive; process   5. dopamine hypothesis   6. b   7. antisocial or sociopathic

Such controversies underline the fact that our understanding of abnormal behaviour is a reflection of the society and culture in which we live. Future revisions of *DSM* may include a different catalogue of disorders. Even now, other cultures might well include a list of disorders that look very different from the list that appears in the current *DSM,* as we discuss next.

Exploring Diversity

DSM and Culture—and the Culture of *DSM*

In most people's estimation, a person who hears voices of the recently deceased is probably a victim of some psychological disturbance. Yet members of the Plains Indian tribe routinely hear the voices of the dead calling to them from the afterlife.

This is but one example of the role that culture plays in the labelling of behaviour as "abnormal." In fact, of all the major adult disorders found within the *DSM* categorization, just four are found across all cultures of the world: schizophrenia, bipolar disorder, major depression, and anxiety disorders (Kleinman, 1991; Lewis-Fernandez & Kleinman, 1995; Kleinman, 1996). *All* the rest are particular to North America and western Europe.

Take, for instance, anorexia nervosa, first discussed in Chapter 9. Anorexia nervosa is a disorder in which people, particularly young women, develop inaccurate views of their body appearance, become obsessed with their weight, and refuse to eat, sometimes starving in the process. This disorder occurs only in cultures holding the societal standard that slender female bodies are most desirable. Because for most of the world such a standard does not exist, anorexia nervosa does not occur. Interestingly, there is no anorexia nervosa in all of Asia, with two exceptions: the upper and upper-middle classes of Japan and Hong Kong, where western influence tends to be great. It is also noteworthy that anorexia nervosa is a fairly recent disorder even in western cultures. In the 1600s and 1700s it did not occur because the ideal female body in western cultures at that time was a plump one.

Dissociative Identity Disorder

Similarly, dissociative identity disorder (multiple personality) makes sense as a problem only in societies in which a sense of self is fairly concrete. In India, the self is based more on external factors that are relatively independent of the person. There, when an individual displays symptoms of what people in a western society would call dissociative identity disorder, it is assumed that that person is possessed either by demons (which is viewed as a malady) or by gods (which is not a cause for treatment).

Furthermore, even though such disorders as schizophrenia are found throughout the world, the particular symptoms of the disorder are influenced by cultural factors. Hence, catatonic schizophrenia, in which unmoving patients appear to be frozen, sometimes for days, in the same position is rare in North America and western Europe. In contrast, in India, 80 percent of those with schizophrenia are catatonic.

Other cultures have disorders that do not appear in the west. For example, in Malaysia, a behavior called "amok" is characterized by a wild outburst in which a person, usually quiet and withdrawn, kills or severely injures another. Another example is "koro," found in southeast Asian males who develop an intense panic that their penis is about to withdraw into their abdomen. Finally, a disorder sometimes found among children in the Andean mountains is "susto," in which those afflicted suffer are apathetic, unable to sleep, depressed, and anxious. This condition is brought on by fear that the soul will be lost because of contact with the supernatural (witches or the evil eye) (Durst & Rosca-Rebaudengo, 1991; Stix, 1996; Berry et al., 1992).

In sum, we should not assume that *DSM* provides the final word on psychological disorders. The disorders it includes are very much a creation and function of western cultures at a particular moment in time, and its categories should not be seen as universally applicable. ∎

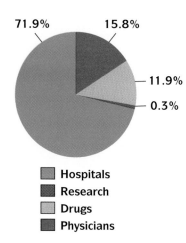

71.9%   15.8%

— 11.9%

— 0.3%

■ Hospitals
■ Research
□ Drugs
■ Physicians

FIGURE 12-8 *Distribution of direct costs for mental health care in Canada. Source: Health Canada, Economic Burden of Illness in Canada, 1993.*

The Prevalence of Psychological Disorders

Health Canada predicts that there will be 18 million hospital patient days for mental disorders by 2002–3. This is an increase of two thirds since 1982–3 (Stephens, 1998). In Canada, education and occupational status are highly correlated with mental health. Unemployment and disability are related to negative mental health. Social support is another significant factor. Canadians with the lowest levels of support are six times more likely to have mental health problems. Age is also a factor, with positive mental health increasing with age.

Poor mental health is very costly. First on a personal level in terms of suffering, and then on a national or provincial level in terms of dollars spent. Mental health care in Canada costs $7.8 billion a year. Of this amount, approximately five billion goes to direct costs (drugs, physicians, hospitals, and research). Figure 12-8 shows the breakdown of these expenditures. The rest of the money goes to pay indirect costs such as premature death, and long and short-term disability (Stephens, 1998).

Mental health is a matter for global concern. According to the World Health Organization, 1.5 billion people world wide are suffering, at any given time, from some kind of neuropsychiatric disorder such as depression, anxiety, schizophrenia, dementia, and epilepsy. Three quarters of them live in developing countries (World Health Organization, 1999).

In a massive study, in the United States, researchers conducted face-to-face interviews with more than 8,000 men and women between the ages of 15 and 54 years. The sample was designed to be representative of the population of the United States. According to results of the study, 48 percent of those interviewed experienced a disorder at some point in their lives. In addition, 30 percent experience a disorder in any given year (Kessler et al., 1994).

Despite the relatively high prevalence of psychological disorders in Canada and the United States, the findings do not suggest that either country is on the verge of a collective breakdown. Although the results indicate that more people than expected experience the symptoms of psychological disorder, they do not indicate what effect the disorders have had on people's family, schooling, or working situations.

Finally, it is important to keep in mind that the findings are representative only of people living in North America. For instance, cross-cultural surveys show that the incidence of major depression varies significantly from one culture to another. The probability of suffering at least one episode of depression is only 1.5 percent in Taiwan and 2.9 percent in Korea, compared to 11.6 percent in New Zealand and 16.4 percent in France. Such notable differences underscore the importance of considering the cultural context of psychological disorders (Weissman et al., 1996).

The prevalence figures for the United States and Canada suggest that psychological disorders are far from rare, and yet significant prejudice and discrimination are directed toward people with psychological disorders. The stigma (a label that leads people to be seen as different and therefore defective) against people who experience a psychological disorder remains real. However, as discussed in the accompanying Applying Psychology in the 21st Century box, this stigma is gradually being reduced.

The Informed Consumer of Psychology

Deciding When You Need Help

After you consider the range and variety of psychological disturbances that can afflict people, it would not be surprising if you began to feel that you were suffering from one (or more) of the problems we have discussed. In fact, there is a name for this perception: *medical student's disease*. Although in the present case it might more aptly be labeled "psychology student's disease," the basic symptoms are the same: feeling that you suffer from the same sorts of problems you are studying.

Applying Psychology in the 21st Century

Erasing the Stigma of Psychological Disorders

"A great soldier, a great patriot, a great humanitarian" who bears a great burden.

These remarks by Art Eggleton, Canada's Defence Minister, were delivered in recognition of the career of Lt. General Roméo Dallaire who resigned recently after a 35-year career in the Canadian Forces. Dallaire who retired early for medical reasons refers to himself as "a casualty of Rwanda, an injured officer of the Rwandan war." As the commanding officer of a United Nations' peace keeping mission to Rwanda in 1994, Dallaire and his troops were helpless in the face of the massive genocide which occurred. It is estimated that up to one million people died including thousands of women, children, as well as a number of peacekeepers.

The injury suffered by Dallaire was not caused by a bullet; but by the terrible things he saw and was unable to do anything about. He, like as many as 10 percent of Canadian soldiers, suffers from an anxiety disorder known as post-traumatic stress disorder (PTSD) (Thompson, 2000).

Research done on peacekeeping stress at the University of Guelph (Lamerson and Kelloway, 1996) cite the work of Everly (1989) and Everly and Mitchell (1992) as identifying PTSD as "the most severe and disabling variation of occupational stress known". Lamerson and Kelloway (1996) believe that Canadian peacekeepers may be particularly vulnerable because of the frequency with which they are sent on these missions. Also peacekeepers operate under very stringent guidelines that add to already heightened stress. Being in a war zone, often shot at, and not able to take action creates what the authors term a multiplicative effect for stress.

Lt. General Roméo Dallaire is fighting to overcome post-traumatic stress disorder.

PTSD has many symptoms. They include inability to sleep, memory problems, survivor guilt, emotional numbness, reliving the trauma, headaches, digestive problems, and substance abuse. Depression may develop. Work and family situations may become a casualty. The cost on a personal and organizational level is extremely high (Lamerson and Kelloway, 1996).

For a number of years Dallaire was in denial, believing that hard work would erase the terrible memories. This effort accompanied by an inability to eat or sleep properly led to total collapse. Dail-

laire talks about anger and depression so severe that he could not function. He finds the dark and silence difficult. Unexpected flashbacks occur when even something as simple as bushes at the side of the road appear to become piles of corpses. In a moment of great dispair, General Dallaire attempted suicide. He survived and with the support of his family and professional help he is attempting to put his life back together. Of professional help he says, "you literally cannot get out of this without professional help. There is absolutely no way." (Thompson, 2000).

By being so open about his condition Dallaire joins other well known individuals who are beginning to admit publicly that they suffer from a serious psychological disorder—and who, in the process, are helping to erase the stigma regarding abnormal behaviour. For instance Academy Award-winner Rod Steiger has lectured about his eight years of depression, which he describes as producing pain so searing that it "skins you alive." Singer Naomi Judd, suffered from panic attacks that made it difficult to leave home. Ted Turner, who founded CNN and Turner Broadcasting, has discussed suffering from bipolar disorder. American General Colin Powell when asked at a news conference about his wife's rumored depression, replied "My wife has depression. It's not a family secret. It is very easily controlled with proper medication, just as my blood pressure is."

Such public admissions, as well as raising awareness, often are a force for social change. For example General Dallaire continues to encourage the Canadian military to imporve support for personnel suffering from PTSD (Thompson, 2000).

Most often, of course, your concerns will be unwarranted. As we have discussed, the differences between normal and abnormal behaviour are often so fuzzy that it is easy to jump to the conclusion that one has the same symptoms that are involved in serious forms of mental disturbance.

Before coming to such a conclusion, though, it is important to keep in mind that from time to time we all experience a wide range of emotions and subjective experiences, and it is not unusual to feel deeply unhappy, to fantasize about bizarre situations, or to feel anxiety about life's circumstances. It is the persistence, depth, and consistency of such behaviour that set normal reactions apart from abnormal ones. If you have not previously had serious doubts about the normality of your behaviour, it is unlikely that reading about others' psychological disorders should prompt you to reevaluate your earlier conclusion.

On the other hand, many people do have problems that warrant concern, and in such cases it is important to consider the possibility that professional help is warranted. The following list of symptoms can serve as a guideline to help you determine if outside intervention might be useful (Engler & Goleman, 1992):

- Long-term feelings of distress that interfere with your sense of well-being, competence, and ability to function effectively in daily activities
- Occasions in which you experience overwhelmingly high stress, accompanied by feelings of inability to cope with the situation
- Prolonged depression or feelings of hopelessness, particularly when they do not have any clear cause (such as the death of someone close)
- Withdrawal from other people
- A chronic physical problem for which no physical cause can be determined
- A fear or phobia that prevents you from engaging in everyday activities
- Feelings that other people are out to get you or are talking about and plotting against you
- The inability to interact effectively with others, preventing the development of friendships and loving relationships

This list offers a rough set of guidelines for determining when the normal problems of everyday living escalate beyond your ability to deal with them yourself. In such situations, the least reasonable approach would be to pore over the psychological disorders we have discussed in an attempt to pigeonhole yourself into a specific category. A more reasonable strategy is to consider seeking professional help—a possibility that we discuss in the next chapter. ■

Recap, Review, and Rethink

Recap

- Sexual disorders, psychoactive substance-use disorders, and organic mental disorders are other prevalent forms of abnormal behaviour.

- What is considered abnormal behaviour varies from one culture to another.

- A global concern, 1.5 billion people worldwide suffer from a neuropsychiatric disorder.

- Several guidelines can be used to determine when professional help is warranted for a psychological disorder.

Review

1. The latest version of *DSM* is considered to be the definitive guideline on defining mental disorders. True or False?

2. _____ _____ _____, characterized by severe, incapacitating mood changes or depression related to a woman's menstrual cycle, was eventually added to the appendix of *DSM-IV* despite controversy surrounding its inclusion.

3. Match the disorder with the culture in which it is most common.
   1. amok
   2. anorexia nervosa
   3. susto
   4. catatonic schizophrenia

   a. India
   b. Malaysia
   c. United States
   d. Andean mountains

4. Recent research on the prevalence of psychological disorders has found that _____ is the most common disorder, with 17 percent of those surveyed reporting a major episode at least once in their lifetime.

Answers to Review Questions are on page 476.

Rethink

1. Why is inclusion in the *DSM-IV* of "borderline" disorders such as self-defeating personality disorder and premenstrual dysphoric disorder so controversial and political? What disadvantages does inclusion bring? Does inclusion bring any benefits?

2. Society and culture can have a strong impact on determining what passes for normal and abnormal behaviour. How would you "revise" *DSM-IV* to more accurately reflect cultural differences in determining psychological disorders?

3. What societal changes would have to occur for psychological disorders to be regarded as the equivalent of appendicitis or another treatable physical disorder? Do you think a person who has been treated for a psychological disorder could become president of the United States? Should such a person become president?

looking
BACK

How can we distinguish normal from abnormal behaviour?

1. The most satisfactory definition of abnormal behaviour is one based on the psychological consequences of the behaviour, which are thought of as abnormal if they produce a sense of distress, anxiety, or guilt, or if they are harmful to others. Another useful definition considers people who cannot adapt to society and who are unable to function effectively to be abnormal. There are also legal definitions that focus on whether a person is "insane," which is a legal, not psychological, term.

2. No single definition is totally adequate. Therefore, it is reasonable to consider abnormal and normal behaviour in terms of gradations, ranging from completely normal functioning to extremely abnormal behaviour. Obviously, behaviour typically falls somewhere between these two extremes.

What are the major models of abnormal behaviour used by mental health professionals?

3. The medical model of abnormal behaviour views abnormality as a symptom of an underlying disease that requires a cure. Psychoanalytic models suggest that abnormal behaviour is caused by conflicts in the unconscious stemming from past experience. In order to resolve psychological problems, people need to resolve the unconscious conflicts.

4. In contrast to the medical and psychoanalytic models, behavioural approaches view abnormal behaviour not as a symptom of some underlying problem, but as the problem itself. To resolve the problem, one must change the behaviour.

5. The cognitive approach, often referred to as the cognitive behavioural perspective, suggests that abnormal behaviour is the result of faulty cognitions. In this view, abnormal behaviour can be remedied through a change in cognitions (thoughts and beliefs).

6. Humanistic approaches view people as rational and motivated to get along with others; abnormal behaviour is seen as a difficulty in fulfilling one's needs. People are considered to be in control of their lives and able to resolve their own problems.

7. Sociocultural approaches view abnormal behaviour in terms of difficulties arising from family and other social relationships. The sociocultural model concentrates on such factors as socioeconomic status and the social rules society creates to define normal and abnormal behaviour.

What classification system is used to categorize abnormal behaviour?

8. The system for classifying abnormal behaviours that is used most widely today is *DSM-IV—Diagnostic and Statistical Manual of Mental Disorders, Fourth Edition.*

What are the major psychological disorders?

9. Anxiety disorders are present when a person experiences so much anxiety that it impedes daily functioning. Specific types of anxiety disorders include phobic disorder, panic disorder, generalized anxiety disorder, and obsessive-compulsive disorder. Phobic disorders are characterized by intense, irrational fears of specific objects or situations, while panic disorders are marked by panic attacks, which are sudden, intense feelings of anxiety. Generalized anxiety disorder occurs when a person experiences long-term anxiety with no apparent cause. People with obsessive-compulsive disorders display obsessions (recurring thoughts or ideas) or compulsions (repetitious, unwanted behaviours).

10. Somatoform disorders are psychological difficulties that are displayed through physical problems. An example is hypochondriasis, in which there is a constant fear of illness and a preoccupation with disease. Another somatoform disorder is conversion disorder, in which there is an actual physical difficulty that occurs without a physiological cause.

11. Dissociative disorders are marked by the splitting apart, or dissociation, of crucial parts of personality that are usually integrated. The three major kinds of dissociative disorders are dissociative identity disorder (multiple personality), dissociative amnesia, and dissociative fugue.

What are the most severe forms of psychological disorders?

12. Mood disorders are characterized by emotional states of depression or euphoria so strong that they intrude on everyday living. In major depression, people experience sorrow so deep that they may become suicidal. In bipolar disorder, stages of mania, in which there is an extended sense of elation and powerfulness, alternate with depression.

13. Schizophrenia is one of the severest forms of mental illness. The manifestations of schizophrenia include declines in functioning, thought and language disturbances, perceptual disorders, emotional disturbance, and withdrawal from others. There is strong evidence linking schizophrenia to genetic, biochemical, and environmental factors. According to the predisposition model, an interaction among various factors produces the disorder.

14. People with personality disorders experience little or no personal distress, but they do suffer from an inability to function as normal members of society. The best-known type of personality disorder is the antisocial or sociopathic personality disorder, in which the moral and ethical rules of society are ignored. People with borderline personality disorder have difficulty with identity, are distrustful and often angry, and form intense, sudden relationships. The narcissistic personality is characterized by an exaggerated sense of importance.

15. There are many other categories of disorders, including sexual disorders, psychoactive substance-use disorders, and organic mental disorders.

16. Students of psychology are susceptible to the same sort of "disease" that afflicts medical students: the perception that they suffer from the problems they are studying. Unless their psychological difficulties are persistent, deep, and consistent, however, it is unlikely that their concerns are valid.

What indicators signal a need for the help of a mental health practitioner?

17. A number of signals indicate a need for professional help. These include long-term feelings of psychological distress, feelings of inability to cope with stress, withdrawal from other people, prolonged feelings of hopelessness, chronic physical problems with no apparent causes, phobias and compulsions, paranoia, and an inability to interact with others.

Key Terms and Concepts

medical model of abnormality (p. 445)
psychoanalytic model of abnormality (p. 446)
behavioural model of abnormality (p. 447)
cognitive model of abnormality (p. 447)
humanistic model of abnormality (p. 447)
sociocultural model of abnormality (p. 448)
Diagnostic and Statistical Manual of Mental Disorders, Fourth Edition (DSM-IV) (p. 448)
anxiety disorder (p. 452)
phobias (p. 452)

panic disorder (p. 453)
generalized anxiety disorder (p. 453)
obsessive-compulsive disorder (p. 453)
obsession (p. 454)
compulsion (p. 455)
somatoform disorder (p. 456)
conversion disorder (p. 456)
dissociative disorder (p. 457)
dissociative identity disorder (p. 457)
dissociative amnesia (p. 458)
dissociative fugue (p. 458)

mood disorder (p. 459)
major depression (p. 459)
mania (p. 460)
bipolar disorder (p. 460)
learned helplessness (p. 462)
schizophrenia (p. 463)
personality disorder (p. 467)
antisocial or sociopathic personality disorder (p. 467)
borderline personality disorder (p. 468)
narcissistic personality disorder (p. 469)

Answers to Review Questions:

1. False; the development of the latest version of *DSM* was a source of great controversy, in part reflecting issues that divide society.
2. Premenstrual dysphoric disorder   3. 1-b, 2-c, 3-d, 4-a   4. depression

Epilogue

In this chapter, we discussed a few of the many types of psychological disorders to which people are prone, noting the difficulty that psychologists and physicians have in clearly differentiating normal from abnormal behaviour, and looking at some of the approaches that have been taken to explain and treat psychological disorders. We took note of what is currently the most commonly used classification scheme, categorized in *DSM-IV*, and we examined some of the most prevalent forms of psychological disorders. In order to gain a perspective on the topic of psychological disorders, we discussed the surprisingly broad incidence of psychological disorders in U.S. society and the cultural nature of such disorders.

Before we proceed to focus on treatment of such disorders, turn back to the Prologue, in which the case of Lori Schiller was described. Using the knowledge you gained from this chapter, consider the following questions.

1. Which definitions of abnormality (i.e., deviation from the average, deviation from the ideal, subjective discomfort, inability to function effectively, and legal definitions) appear to fit the case of Lori Schiller? If a person in Schiller's condition commits a serious crime in response to internal voices, would a plea of "not criminally responsible due to mental disorder" be appropriate?

2. Which model of abnormality (i.e., medical, psychoanalytic, behavioural, cognitive, humanistic, or sociocultural) do you think would be most likely to produce positive results in Schiller's case? Would it be advisable to try different approaches in succession? Could two or more approaches be used together?

3. Schiller was diagnosed as suffering from schizophrenia. What elements of her behaviour seem to fit the description of schizophrenia provided by *DSM-IV* (and summarized in Table 12-2)?

4. From which type of schizophrenia (i.e., disorganized, paranoid, catatonic, undifferentiated, or residual; see Table 12-5) do you think Schiller was probably suffering? Why?

5. Were there signs of psychological disorder in Schiller's actions during adolescence? Why do you think Schiller's family failed to notice that she needed help? Why do you think it took so long for Schiller to tell her parents she had problems?

13 Treatment of Psychological Disorders

Brandon Fitch, a person diagnosed with schizophrenia being successfully treated with clozapine, is finally able to enjoy the prom that his illness caused him to miss some fifteen years before.

Prologue

Conquering Schizophrenia

For weeks they had practiced dance steps, shopped for formals, fretted about hairstyles and what on earth to say to their partners. Now the Big City Band was pumping up the volume, and the whole ballroom was beginning to shake. Brandon Fitch, wearing a pinstripe suit and an ear-to-ear grin, shimmied with a high-stepping blonde. Daphne Moss, sporting a floral dress and white corsage, delighted her dad by letting him cut in. The usually quiet Kevin Buchberger leaped onto the dance floor and flat-out boogied for the first time in his life, while Kevin Namkoong grabbed an electric guitar and jammed with the band. The prom at Case Western Reserve University had hit full tilt.

But this was a prom that almost never was. Most of the 175 participants were in their 30s; they had missed the proms of their youth—along with other adolescent rites of passage. Don't ask where they were at 18 or 21. The memories are too bleak, too fragmented to convey. They had organized this "better-late-than-never" prom to celebrate their remarkable "awakening" to reality after many years of being lost in the darkness of schizophrenia. The revellers were, in a sense, the laughing, dancing embodiments of a new wave of drug therapy that is revolutionizing the way doctors are dealing with this most devilish of mental illnesses. . . .

Moss, Buchberger, Fitch, and their fellow promgoers were awakened from their long nightmare of insanity by a remarkable drug called clozapine (brand name: Clozaril). The dinner dance, organized with help from psychiatrists and counsellors at Case Western Reserve's affiliated University Hospitals, in Cleveland, served as a bittersweet celebration of shared loss and regained hope. "Those of us who are ill travel on a different road," said prom chairman Fitch in a welcoming address to his fellow refugees from madness. "We would have liked to have gone to our senior proms, but fate didn't give us that chance" (Wallis & Willwerth, 1992, p. 53).

The drug that has brought new life to people like Daphne Moss, Kevin Buchberger, and Brandon Fitch is just one of many that, along with other new treatment approaches, have revolutionized the treatment of psychological disorders in the last several decades. Although there are literally hundreds of different treatment approaches, ranging from one-meeting informal counseling sessions to long-term drug therapy, all have a common objective: the relief of psychological disorder, with the ultimate aim of enabling individuals to achieve richer, more meaningful, and more fulfilling lives.

In this chapter, we explore a number of basic issues related to the treatment of abnormal behaviour: How do we treat people with psychological disorders? Who is

Table 13-1	Getting Help from the Right Person

Clinical Psychologists

Ph.D.s who have also completed a postgraduate internship. They specialize in assessment and treatment of psychological difficulties.

Counselling Psychologists

Psychologists with Ph.D. or Ed.D. who typically treat day-to-day adjustment problems, often in a university mental health clinic.

Psychiatrists

M.D.s with postgraduate training in abnormal behaviour. Because they can prescribe medication, they often treat the most severe disorders.

Psychoanalysts

Either M.D.s or psychologists who specialize in psychoanalysis, the treatment technique first developed by Freud.

Clinical or Psychiatric Social Workers

Professionals with a master's degree and specialized training who may provide therapy, usually regarding common family and personal problems.

Each of these trained professionals could be expected to give helpful advice and direction. However, the nature of the problem a person is experiencing may make one or another more appropriate. For example, a person who is suffering from severe disturbance and who has lost touch with reality will typically require some sort of biologically based drug therapy. In that case, a psychiatrist—who is a physician—would be the professional of choice. On the other hand, those suffering from milder disorders, such as difficulty in adjusting to the death of a family member, have a broader choice that might include any of the professionals listed above. The decision can be made easier by initial consultations with professionals in mental health facilities in communities, colleges, and health organizations, who can provide guidance in selecting an appropriate therapist.

the most appropriate person to provide treatment? What is the future like for people with severe disturbances? What is the most reasonable therapeutic approach to use? Is one form of therapy better than the others? Does any therapy *really* work? How does a person choose the "right" kind of therapy and therapist?

Most of the chapter focuses on the various approaches used by providers of treatment for psychological disturbances. Despite their diversity, these approaches fall into two main categories: psychologically based and biologically based therapy. Psychologically based therapy, or **psychotherapy,** is the process in which a patient (often referred to as the client) and a professional attempt to remedy psychological difficulties. In psychotherapy, the emphasis is on change as a result of discussions and interactions between therapist and client. In contrast, **biomedical therapy** relies on drugs and other medical procedures to improve psychological functioning.

As we describe the various approaches to therapy, it is important to keep in mind that although the distinctions may seem clear-cut, there is a good deal of overlap in the classifications and procedures employed, and even in the training and titles of various kinds of therapists (see Table 13-1). In fact, many therapists today use a variety of methods with a given person, in what is referred to as an *eclectic approach to therapy.* Assuming that abnormal behaviour is often the product of both psychological and biological processes, eclectic therapists may draw from several perspectives simultaneously, in an effort to address both the psychological and the biological aspects of a person's problems (Stricker & Gold, 1993; Beutler, Consoli, & Williams, 1995; Goldfried & Norcross, 1995; Racey, 1996; Wachtel & Messer, 1997).

psychotherapy: The process in which a patient (often referred to as the client) and a professional attempt to remedy psychological difficulties

biomedical therapy: Therapy that relies on drugs and other medical procedures to improve psychological functioning

PSYCHOTHERAPY: PSYCHOLOGICAL APPROACHES TO TREATMENT

▶ **What are the goals of psychologically and biologically based treatment approaches?**

▶ **What are the basic kinds of psychotherapies?**

Psychotherapy

Alice: I was thinking about this business of standards. I somehow developed a sort of a knack, I guess, of—well—habit—of trying to make people feel at ease around me, or to make things go along smoothly. . . .

Therapist: In other words, what you did was always in the direction of trying to keep things smooth and to make other people feel better and to smooth the situation.

Alice: Yes. I think that's what it was. Now the reason why I did it probably was—I mean, not that I was a good little Samaritan going around making other people happy, but that was probably the role that felt easiest for me to play. I'd been doing it around home so much. I just didn't stand up for my own convictions, until I don't know whether I have any convictions to stand up for.

Therapist: You feel that for a long time you've been playing the role of kind of smoothing out the frictions or differences or what not. . . .

Alice: M-hm.

Therapist: Rather than having any opinion or reaction of your own in the situation. Is that it? (Rogers, 1951, pp. 152–153).

***

Martha: The basic problem is that I'm worried about my family. I'm worried about money. And I never seem to be able to relax.

Therapist: Why are you worried about your family? Let's go into that, first of all. What's to be concerned about? They have certain demands which you don't want to adhere to.

Martha: I was brought up to think that I mustn't be selfish.

Therapist: Oh, we'll have to knock that out of your head! . . .

Martha: My mother feels that I shouldn't have left home—that my place is with them. There are nagging doubts about what I should—

Therapist: Why are there doubts? Why *should* you?

Martha: I think it's a feeling I was brought up with that you always have to give of yourself. If you think of yourself, you're wrong.

Therapist: That's a *belief.* Why do you have to keep believing that—at *your* age? You believed a lot of superstitions when you were younger. Why do you have to retain them? Your parents indoctrinated you with this nonsense, because that's *their* belief. But why do you still have to believe that one should not be self-interested; that one should be self-sacrificial? Who needs that philosophy? All it's gotten you, so far, is guilt. And that's all it ever *will* get you. (Ellis, 1974, pp. 223–286).

***

Sandy: My father . . . never took any interest in any of us. (Begins to weep.) It was my mother—rest her soul—who loved us, not our father. He worked her to death. Lord, I miss her. (Weeps uncontrollably.)—I must sound angry at my father. Don't you think I have a right to be angry?

Therapist: Do you think you have a right to be angry?

Sandy: Of course, I do! Why are you questioning me? You don't believe me, do you?

Therapist: You want me to believe you.

Sandy: I don't care whether you believe me or not. As far as I'm concerned, you're just a wall that I'm talking to—I don't know why I pay for this rotten therapy.—Don't you have any thought

or feelings at all? I know what you're thinking—you think I'm
crazy—you must be laughing at me—I'll probably be a case in
your next book! You're just sitting there—smirking—making me
feel like a bad person—thinking I'm wrong for being mad, that I
have no right to be mad.

Therapist: Just like your father.

Sandy: Yes, you're just like my father.—Oh my God! Just now—I—I—
thought I was talking to him (Sue, Sue, & Sue, 1990,
pp. 514–515).

As these excerpts from actual therapy sessions illustrate, therapy for psychological disorders is far from a uniform process. In the first case, the therapist painstakingly
mirrors what Alice has said, reflecting back her observations. In contrast, the therapist
in the second excerpt is considerably more active, prodding and inflaming the patient.
Finally, the third case shows a therapist who says very little at all; the responses to
Sandy's declarations are fundamentally noncommittal.

Although diverse in many respects, all psychological approaches see treatment
as a way of solving psychological problems by modifying people's behaviour and
helping them gain a better understanding of themselves and their pasts, presents, and
futures. We will consider four major kinds of psychotherapies: psychodynamic, behavioural, cognitive, and humanistic, all of which are based on the different models of
abnormal behaviour discussed in Chapter 12.

Psychodynamic Treatment: Piercing the Unconscious

Psychodynamic therapy is based on the premise, first suggested by Freud in his psychoanalytic approach to personality, that the primary sources of abnormal behaviour
are unresolved past conflicts and the possibility that unacceptable unconscious impulses will enter consciousness. To guard against this anxiety-provoking possibility,
individuals employ *defense mechanisms,* psychological strategies to protect themselves from these unconscious impulses (see Chapter 11).

psychodynamic therapy: First
suggested by Freud, therapy that is based
on the premise that the primary sources
of abnormal behaviour are unresolved
past conflicts and the possibility that
unacceptable unconscious impulses will
enter consciousness

The most common defense mechanism is repression, in which threatening conflicts and impulses are pushed back into the unconscious. However, since unacceptable conflicts and impulses can never be completely buried, some of the anxiety
associated with them can produce abnormal behaviour in the form of what Freud
called *neurotic symptoms.*

How does one rid oneself of the anxiety produced by unconscious, unwanted
impulses and drives? To Freud, the answer was to confront the conflicts and impulses
by bringing them out of the unconscious part of the mind and into the conscious part.
Freud assumed that this technique would reduce anxiety stemming from past conflicts
and that the patient could then participate in his or her daily life more effectively.

The challenge facing a psychodynamic therapist, then, is to find a way to facilitate patients' attempts to explore and understand their unconscious. Freud's development of "talking cures" is likely to be acknowledged as his greatest contribution to
medical science (Murray et al., 2000). Basically, the technique consists of leading patients to consider and discuss in detail their past experiences from the time of their first
memories. The process assumes that the person will eventually stumble upon the anxiety producing conflicts. They will then be able to "work through" these difficulties.

Psychoanalysis: Freud's Therapy

Classic Freudian psychodynamic therapy, called **psychoanalysis,** tends to be a lengthy
and expensive affair. Patients typically meet with their therapists an hour a day, four to
six days a week, for several years. In their sessions, they often use a technique developed by Freud called *free association.* Patients are told to say aloud whatever comes to
mind, regardless of its apparent irrelevance or senselessness. In fact, they are urged
not to try to make sense of things or impose logic upon what they are saying, since it is

psychoanalysis: Psychodynamic
therapy that involves frequent sessions
and often lasts for many years

assumed that the ramblings evoked during free association actually represent important clues to the unconscious, which has its own logic. It is the analyst's job to recognize and label the connections between what is being said and the patient's unconscious (Auld & Hyman, 1991; Weinshel & Renik, 1996; Galatzer-Levy & Cohler, 1997).

Another important tool of the therapist is *dream interpretation*. As we discussed in Chapter 4, this is an examination of patients' dreams to find clues to the unconscious conflicts and problems they are experiencing. According to Freud, dreams provide a close look at the unconscious because people's defenses tend to be lowered when they are asleep. But even in dreaming there is a censoring of thoughts; events and people in dreams are usually represented by symbols. Because of this phenomenon, one must move beyond the surface description of the dream (called the *manifest content* of dreams), and consider its underlying meaning (the *latent content* of dreams), which reveals the true message of the dream.

The processes of free association and dream interpretation do not always move forward easily. The same unconscious forces that initially produced repression may work to keep past difficulties out of the conscious, producing resistance. *Resistance* is an inability or unwillingness to discuss or reveal particular memories, thoughts, or motivations. Resistance can be expressed in a number of ways. For instance, patients may be discussing a childhood memory and suddenly forget what they were saying, or they may completely change the subject. It is the therapist's job to pick up instances of resistance and to interpret their meaning, as well as to ensure that patients return to the subject—which is likely to hold difficult or painful memories for them.

Because of the close, almost intimate interaction between patient and psychoanalyst, the relationship between the two often becomes emotionally charged and takes on a complexity unlike most others. Patients may come to see the analyst as symbolic of significant others in their past, perhaps a parent or a lover, and apply some of their feelings for that person to the analyst—a phenomenon known as *transference* (Mann, 1997).

Transference can be used by a therapist to help the patient recreate past relationships that were psychologically difficult. For instance, if a patient undergoing transference views his therapist as symbolic of his father—with whom he had a difficult relationship—the patient and therapist may "redo" an earlier interaction, this time including more positive aspects. Through this process, conflicts regarding the real father may be resolved. (Practitioners of psychoanalysis would see transference at work in the therapy excerpt at the beginning of the chapter, when Sandy says to the therapist "you're just like my father.")

Contemporary Alternatives to Psychoanalysis

Time and money are commodities of which patients in psychoanalysis need a lot. As you can imagine, few people have the time, money, or patience that participating in years of traditional psychoanalysis requires. Moreover, there is no conclusive evidence that psychoanalysis, as originally conceived by Freud, works better than other, more contemporary versions of psychodynamic therapy. Today, for instance, psychodynamic therapy tends to be shorter, usually lasting no longer than three months or twenty sessions (DeLuca, Grayston & Romano, 1999). The therapist takes a more active role than Freud would have liked, controlling the course of therapy and prodding and advising the patient with considerable directness. Finally, there is less emphasis on a patient's past history and childhood. Instead, a more here-and-now approach is used, in which the therapist concentrates on an individual's current relationships, emotions, and specific complaints (MacKenzie, 1990; Ursano, Sonnenberg, & Lazar, 1991; HMHL, 1994b; Greenberg & Paivio, 1997).

Even with its current modifications, psychodynamic therapy has its critics. It is still relatively time-consuming and expensive, especially in comparison with other forms of psychotherapy that we will discuss later. Moreover, certain kinds of patients tend to be well suited for this method, especially those who suffer from anxiety disorders and those who are highly articulate. These characteristics have been designated as a stereotype of the perfect patient known as YAVIS: a patient who is young, attractive, verbal, intelligent, and successful (Schofield, 1964).

Ultimately, the most important concern about psychodynamic treatment is whether it actually works, and here we find no pat answer. Psychodynamic treatment techniques have been controversial since Freud introduced them. Part of the problem is the difficulty in establishing whether or not patients have improved following psychodynamic therapy. One must depend on reports from the therapist or the patients themselves, reports that are obviously open to bias and subjective interpretation.

Critics have questioned the entire theoretical basis of psychodynamic theory, maintaining that there is no proof that such constructs as the unconscious exist. Despite the considerable criticism, though, the psychodynamic treatment approach has remained viable. To proponents, it not only provides effective treatment in many cases of psychological disturbance, but it also permits the potential development of an unusual degree of insight into one's life (Fonagy & Moran, 1990; Crits-Cristoph, 1992; Shapiro & Emde, 1994; Barber & Lane, 1995).

Psychotherapy: Evaluation

Behavioural Approaches to Treatment

Perhaps, as a child, you were rewarded by your parents with an ice cream cone when you were especially good . . . or sent to your room if you misbehaved. As we saw in Chapter 5, the principles behind such a child-rearing strategy are valid: Good behaviour is maintained by reinforcement, and unwanted behaviour can be eliminated by punishment.

These principles represent the basic underpinnings of **behavioural treatment approaches.** Building upon the basic processes of learning embodied in classical and operant conditioning, behavioural treatment approaches make a fundamental assumption: both abnormal behaviour and normal behaviour are *learned*. People who display abnormal behaviour either have failed to learn the skills needed to cope with the problems of everyday living or have acquired faulty skills and patterns that are being maintained through some form of reinforcement. To modify abnormal behaviour, then, behavioural approaches propose that people must learn new behaviour to replace the faulty skills they have developed and unlearn their maladaptive behaviour patterns (Bellack, Hersen, & Kazdin, 1990; Bergin & Garfield, 1994; Hayes, Folette & Follette, 1995; Agras & Berkowitz, 1996).

To behavioural psychologists, it is not necessary to delve into people's pasts or their psyches. Rather than viewing abnormal behaviour as a symptom of some underlying problem, they consider the abnormal behaviour itself as the problem in need of modification. Changing people's behaviour to allow them to function more effectively

behavioural treatment approaches: Approaches that build upon the basic processes of learning embodied in classical and operant conditioning

Behavioural approaches to treatment would seek to modify the behaviour of this couple, rather than focusing on the underlying causes of the behaviour.

Chapter 13

These participants in a systematic desensitization program have worked to overcome their fear of flying and are about to "graduate" by taking a brief flight.

solves the problem—with no need for concern about the underlying cause. In this view, then, if you can change abnormal behaviour, you've cured the problem.

Classical Conditioning Approaches

Suppose you bite into your favourite chocolate bar and find that it is not only infested with ants, but that you've swallowed a bunch of them. You immediately become sick to your stomach and throw up. Your long-term reaction? You never eat that kind of chocolate bar again, and it may actually be months before you eat any type of chocolate.

This simple example hints at how classical conditioning might be used to modify behaviour. Recall from our discussion in Chapter 5 that when a stimulus that naturally evokes a negative response (such as an unpleasant taste or a puff of air in the face) is paired with a previously neutral stimulus (such as the sound of a tone), the neutral stimulus can come to elicit a similar negative reaction by itself. Using this procedure, first developed by Ivan Pavlov, we may create unpleasant reactions to stimuli that an individual previously enjoyed—possibly to excess. The technique, known as *aversive conditioning,* has been used in cases of alcoholism, drug abuse, and smoking.

The basic procedure in aversive conditioning is relatively straightforward. For example, a person with a drinking problem might be given an alcoholic drink along with a drug that causes severe nausea and vomiting. After these two are paired a few times, the alcohol alone becomes associated with the vomiting and loses its appeal. In fact, what typically happens is that just the sight or smell of alcohol triggers the aversive reaction.

Although aversion therapy works reasonably well to inhibit substance abuse problems such as alcoholism and certain kinds of sexual disorders, its long-term effectiveness is questionable. Moreover, there are important ethical concerns about aversion techniques that employ such potent stimuli as electric shock—used only in the most extreme cases, such as self-mutilation—instead of drugs that merely induce gastric discomfort (Yuskauskas, 1992). It is clear, though, that aversion therapy is an important procedure for eliminating maladaptive responses for some period of time—a respite that provides, even if only temporarily, the opportunity to encourage more adaptive behaviour patterns (Harris & Handleman, 1990).

The most successful treatment based on classical conditioning is known as systematic desensitization. In **systematic desensitization,** a person is taught to relax and then is gradually exposed to an anxiety-producing stimulus in order to extinguish the response of anxiety (Wolpe, 1990; Smith, 1990; Morris, 1991; St. Onge, 1995b).

Suppose, for instance, you were extremely afraid of flying. The very thought of being in an airplane made you begin to sweat and shake, and you'd never even been able to get yourself near enough to an airport to know how you'd react if you actually

systematic desensitization: A form of treatment in which a person is taught to relax and then is gradually exposed to an anxiety-producing stimulus in order to extinguish the response of anxiety

Table 13-2 | How to Elicit the Relaxation Response

Step 1. Pick a focus word or short phrase that's firmly rooted in your personal belief system. For example, a nonreligious individual might choose a neutral word like *one* or *peace* or *love*. A Christian person desiring to use a prayer could pick the opening words of Psalm 23. *The Lord is my shepherd;* a Jewish person could choose *Shalom.*

Step 2. Sit quietly in a comfortable position.

Step 3. Close your eyes.

Step 4. Relax your muscles.

Step 5. Breathe slowly and naturally, repeating your focus word or phrase silently as you exhale.

Step 6. Throughout, assume a passive attitude. Don't worry about how well you're doing. When other thoughts come to mind, simply say to yourself, "Oh, well," and gently return to the repetition.

Step 7. Continue for 10 to 20 minutes. You may open your eyes to check the time, but do not use an alarm. When you finish, sit quietly for a minute or so, at first with your eyes closed and later with your eyes open. Then do not stand for one or two minutes.

Step 8. Practice the technique once or twice a day.

had to fly somewhere. Using systematic desensitization to treat your problem, you would first be trained in relaxation techniques by a behaviour therapist (see Table 13-2), learning to relax your body fully—a highly pleasant state, as you might imagine.

The next step would involve the construction of a *hierarchy of fears*—a list, in order of increasing severity, of the things that are associated with your fears. For instance, your hierarchy might resemble this one:

1. Watching a plane fly overhead

2. Going to an airport

3. Buying a ticket

4. Stepping into the plane

5. Seeing the plane door close

6. Having the plane taxi down the runway

7. Taking off

8. Being in the air

Once this hierarchy had been developed and you had learned relaxation techniques, the two sets of responses would be associated with each other. To do this, your therapist might ask you to put yourself into a relaxed state and then to imagine yourself in the first situation identified in your hierarchy. After you were able to consider that first step while remaining relaxed, you would move on to the next situation, eventually moving up the hierarchy in gradual stages until you could imagine yourself being in the air without experiencing anxiety. In some cases, all this would take place in a psychologist's office, while in others, people would actually be placed in the fear-evoking situation. Thus, it would not be surprising if you were brought, finally, to an airplane to use your relaxation techniques.

Systematic desensitization has proved to be an effective treatment for a number of problems, including phobias, anxiety disorders, and even impotence and fear of sexual contact (Bellack, Hersen, & Kazdin, 1990; Mendez & Garcia, 1996; Rachman, 1990, 1991, 1997). Furthermore, therapists are harnessing new technologies, such as virtual reality displays, to broaden the effectiveness of the procedure.

Psychotherapy: Links

Observational Learning and Modelling

If we had to be hit by a car in order to learn the importance of looking both ways before crossing the street, the world would probably suffer from a serious underpopulation problem. Fortunately, this is not necessary, for we learn a significant amount through **observational learning,** by modelling the behaviour of other people.

observational learning: Learning by watching others' behaviour and the consequences of that behaviour

Applying Psychology in the 21st Century

Gambling: A Personal and Social Problem

With the legalization of gambling in Canada, and the opening of more than 50 casinos across the country, concern has rapidly grown about the increased number of problem or pathological gamblers (Nicol & Nolen, 1998). Pathological gambling was added to the Diagnostic and Statistical Manual of Mental Disorders in 1980. It has been classified as an impulse control disorder characterized by 11 criteria, including loss of control over gambling, deception about the extent of one's gambling, chasing losses, and disruption at home and work (APA, 1994). One to two percent of Canadians are pathological gamblers (Ladouceur, 1996).

Gambling is a complex behaviour, which has been conceptualized using many perspectives (Inter-Provincial Task Force on Problem Gambling, 1999), including most of those in the current chapter and Chapter 11. Information in the report by the Task Force, that pertains to the perspectives in this textbook is summarized here. According to psychodynamic models, gamblers use gambling activities to cope with conflict or heal a deep emotional wound. Numerous psychodynamic concepts have been used to account for gambling: an unconscious desire to hurt one's father, female masochism, aggressive impulses, lack of power in childhood, and sexual excitement.

Trait and biological approaches have focused on individual characteristics. For example, gambling has been linked to a high desire for control, and the needs for dominance and achievement. Biological models have emphasized variables such as EEG waves, arousal, plasma endorphin levels, and chemical imbalances in the brain.

Learning approaches include both behavioural and cognitive perspectives. Behavioural models have focused on the reinforcing aspects of gambling such as the arousal of winning and the powerful control of the partial reinforcement schedule (see Chapter 5). Cognitive models, on the other hand, have stressed irrational thought processes that support gambling behaviour (e.g., illusion of control).

Treatment for gambling is as varied as the models that describe it. For a number of years, Robert Ladouceur (University of Laval) and his colleagues have researched gambling behaviours and their treatment (Ladouceur et al., 1994; Ladouceur & Mireault, 1988; Bujold et al., 1994). Treatment has emphasized cognitive and behavioural strategies, such as the correction of misperceptions about gambling, problem-solving training, social-skills training, and relapse prevention (Sylvain et al., 1997; Ladouceur et al., 1998). They have demonstrated that these strategies are effective, and that therapeutic gains last for as long as 12 months following therapy (Sylvain et al., 1997).

The Inter-Provincial Task Force on Problem Gambling (1999) has developed a community health model of gambling. The model specifies the dimensions of the problem and difficulties associated with gambling. They have also developed a measure of problem gambling indicators. So far, they have not reported on implications for therapy.

The Canadian Centre for Substance Abuse has a listing of government-funded help lines located in cities across Canada. This list is available on the Internet at <www.ccsa.ca/gambdir/dirhelp.htm>.

Having fun in the casino may lead to problems requiring therapeutic intervention for gambling.

Behaviour therapists have used *modelling* to systematically teach people new skills and ways of handling their fears and anxieties. For example, some people have never learned fundamental social skills such as maintaining eye contact with those to whom they are speaking. A therapist can model the appropriate behaviour and thereby teach it to someone deficient in such skills. Children with dog phobias have also been able to overcome their fears by watching another child—called the "Fearless Peer"—repeatedly walk up to a dog, touch it, pet it, and finally play with it. Modelling, then, can play an effective role in resolving some kinds of behaviour difficulties, especially if the model is rewarded for his or her behaviour (Bandura, Grusec, & Menlove, 1967; Rosenthal & Steffek, 1991; St. Onge, 1995a).

Operant Conditioning Approaches

Consider the A we get for a good paper . . . the raise for fine on-the-job performance . . . the gratitude for helping an elderly person cross the street. Such rewards for our behaviour produce a greater likelihood that we will repeat that behaviour in the future. Similarly, behavioural approaches using operant conditioning techniques (which demonstrate the effects of rewards and punishments on future behaviour) are based on the notion that we should reward people for carrying out desirable behaviour, and extinguish behaviour that we wish to eliminate by either ignoring or punishing it (Kazdin, 1989, 1994).

Probably the best example of the systematic application of operant conditioning principles is the *token system,* whereby a person is rewarded for desired behaviour with a token such as a poker chip or some kind of play money. The behaviour may range from such simple things as keeping one's room neat to personal grooming or interacting with other people. The tokens earned can be exchanged for some desired object or activity, such as snacks, new clothes, or viewing a movie.

Although it is most frequently employed in institutional settings for individuals with relatively serious problems, the system is not unlike what parents do when they give children money for being well behaved—money that they can later exchange for something they want. In fact, contingency contracting, a variant of the more extensive token system, has proved quite effective in producing behaviour modification. In *contingency contracting,* a written agreement is drawn up between therapist and client (or teacher and student or parent and child). The contract states a series of behavioural goals that the client hopes to attain. It also specifies the positive consequences for the client if the goals are reached—usually some explicit reward such as money or additional privileges. Contracts frequently state negative consequences if the goals are not met.

For instance, suppose a person is having difficulty quitting smoking. He and his therapist might devise a contract in which he would pledge that for every day he went without a cigarette he would receive a reward. On the other hand, the contract could include punishments for failure. If the patient smoked on a given day, the therapist might send a check—written out in advance by the patient and given to the therapist to hold—to a cause the patient had no interest in supporting (for instance, to the Maple Leaf Gun Club if the patient is a staunch advocate of gun control).

How Does Behaviour Therapy Stack Up?

Behaviour therapy is most helpful for certain kinds of problems. For instance, behaviour therapy works well for phobias and compulsions, for establishing control over impulses, and for learning complex social skills to replace maladaptive behaviour. More than any of the other therapeutic techniques, it has produced methods that can be employed by nonprofessionals to change their own behaviour. Moreover, it tends to be economical in terms of time, since it is directed toward the solution of carefully defined problems (Wilson et al., 1987; Wilson & Agras, 1992).

On the other hand, behaviour therapy is not always effective. For instance, it is not particularly successful in treating deep depression or personality disorders (Brody, 1990). In addition, it has been criticized for its emphasis on external behaviour, and its consequent devaluation of internal thoughts and expectations. Finally, the long-term success of behaviour therapy is sometimes less impressive than its effectiveness in

In family therapy, the family system as a whole—not just one family member identified as the "problem"—is treated.

the short run. Because of such concerns, some psychologists have turned to cognitive approaches.

Cognitive Approaches to Therapy

If you assumed that faulty, maladaptive cognitions lie at the heart of abnormal behaviour, wouldn't the most direct treatment route be to teach people new, more adaptive modes of thinking? The answer is yes, according to psychologists who take a cognitive approach to treatment.

The goal of cognitive approaches is to change people's faulty cognitions about themselves and the world. Because of their reliance on basic principles of learning, these strategies have often been called the **cognitive-behavioural approach** (Beck, 1991, Basco & Rush, 1996; Dobson & Craig, 1996; Jacobson et al., 1996). In his cognitive behavioural modification, Meichenbaum emphasized the importance of changes in self-instruction (the messages people give themselves) for changes in behaviour (Meichenbaum, 1977, 1991).

One of the best examples of cognitive behavioural treatment is rational-emotive therapy. **Rational-emotive therapy** attempts to restructure a person's belief system into a more realistic, rational, and logical set of views. According to psychologist Albert Ellis (1987, 1995, 1996a), many people lead unhappy and sometimes even psychologically disordered lives because they harbour such irrational, unrealistic ideas as these:

- It is necessary to have the love or approval of virtually every significant other person for everything we do.

- We should be thoroughly competent, adequate, and successful in all possible respects if we are to consider ourselves worthwhile.

In order to lead their clients to eliminate such maladaptive cognitions and adopt more effective thinking, rational-emotive therapists take an active, directive role during therapy, openly challenging patterns of thought that appear to be dysfunctional. (Martha's case excerpt at the beginning of the chapter is a good example of the approach.) For instance, a therapist might bluntly dispute the logic employed by a person in treatment by saying, "Why does the fact that your girlfriend left you mean that *you* are a bad person?" By pointing out the problems in clients' logic, therapists believe they can help people to adopt a more realistic view of themselves and their circumstances (Dryden & DiGiuseppe, 1990; Bernard & DiGiuseppe, 1993; Dryden, 1995; Ellis, 1996b; Ellis & Dryden, 1997).

cognitive-behavioural approach: A process by which people's faulty cognitions about themselves and the world are changed to more accurate ones

rational-emotive therapy: A form of therapy that attempts to restructure a person's belief system into a more realistic, rational, and logical set of views

Rational Emotive Therapy

"To this day, I can hear my mother's voice—harsh, accusing. 'Lost your mittens? You naughty kittens! Then you shall have no pie!' "

Another form of therapy that builds on a cognitive perspective is that of Aaron Beck (Beck, 1991, 1995). Like the goal of rational-emotive therapy, the basic goal of Beck's **cognitive therapy** is to change people's illogical thoughts about themselves and the world. However, cognitive therapy is considerably less confrontational and challenging than rational-emotive therapy. Clients are urged to obtain information on their own that will lead them to discard their inaccurate thinking. They are helped to discover ways of thinking more appropriately about themselves and others (Castonguay et al., 1996; Wright & Beck, 1996; Alford & Beck, 1997).

Cognitive approaches to therapy have proved successful in dealing with a broad range of disorders. For example, they have been applied to pathological gambling (Sylvain et al., 1997; Ladouceur et al., 1998), depression (Hurst & Genest, 1995), panic disorder (Néron, Lacroix & Chaput, 1995) and phobias (Rachman, 1990). The ability of cognitive therapy to incorporate additional treatment approaches has made it particularly effective (Whisman, 1993; Shapiro et al., 1995; Dobson & Craig, 1996; Hayes et al., 1996). As a result of reviewing treatment outcome studies for Generalized Anxiety Disorder, Dugas and his colleagues (1996) concluded that the most effective treatment combined awareness training, problem solving strategies, and exposure to mental images associated with worry.

cognitive therapy: Psychotherapy based on Beck's goal to change people's illogical thoughts about themselves and the world

Recap, Review, and Rethink

Recap

- Psychotherapy is psychologically based therapy in which the emphasis is on producing change through discussion and interaction between client and therapist. Biomedical therapy uses drugs and other medical procedures.

- Psychodynamic therapy is based on Freud's notion that psychological disorders are produced by unconscious conflicts and anxiety.

- Behavioural approaches to therapy assume that people who display abnormal behaviour have either failed to acquire appropriate skills or have learned faulty or maladaptive skills.

- Cognitive approaches to therapy seek to change faulty cognitions that people hold about the world and themselves.

Review

1. A remedy for a psychological disorder that is based on discussion and interaction between therapist and client is known as _____.

2. Match the following mental health practitioners with the appropriate description.
   1. psychiatrist
   2. clinical psychologist
   3. counselling psychologist
   4. psychoanalyst

   a. Ph.D. specializing in treatment of psychological disorders
   b. professional specializing in Freudian therapy techniques
   c. M.D. trained in abnormal behaviour
   d. Ph.D. specializing in adjustment of day-to-day problems

3. According to Freud, people use _____ _____ as a means to ensure that unwanted impulses will not intrude on conscious thought.

4. In dream interpretation, a psychoanalyst must learn to distinguish between the _____ content of a dream, which is what appears on the surface, and the _____ content, its underlying meaning.

5. Which of the following treatments deals with phobias by gradual exposure to the item producing the fear?
   a. systematic desensitization
   b. partial reinforcement
   c. behavioral self-management
   d. aversion therapy

Answers to Review Questions are on page 494.

Rethink

1. Compare and contrast psychoanalysis and cognitive therapy.

2. In what situations might behavioural therapy be most useful? In what situations might a therapeutic technique that deals with thoughts rather than actions be more suitable?

3. How would you construct an experiment to demonstrate the effectiveness of psychoanalytic techniques? Behavioural and cognitive approaches? How might you examine the reliability of dream interpretation?

Humanistic Approaches to Therapy

▶ **What are humanistic approaches to treatment?**

▶ **How does group therapy differ from individual types of therapy?**

▶ **How effective is therapy, and which kind of therapy works best in a given situation?**

humanistic therapy: Therapy in which the underlying assumption is that people have control of their behaviour, can make choices about their lives, and are essentially responsible for solving their own problems

As you know from your own experience, it is impossible to master the material covered in a course without some hard work, no matter how good the teacher and the textbook are. *You* must take the time to study, to memorize the vocabulary, to learn the concepts. Nobody else can do it for you. If you choose to put in the effort, you'll succeed; if you don't, you'll fail. The responsibility is primarily yours.

Humanistic therapy draws upon this philosophical perspective of self-responsibility in developing treatment techniques. Although many different types of therapy fit into this category, the ideas that underlie them are the same: We have control of our own behaviour; we can make choices about the kinds of lives we want to live; and it is up to us to solve the difficulties that we encounter in our daily lives.

Instead of being the directive figures they are in some psychodynamic and behavioural approaches, humanistic therapists view themselves as guides or facilitators. Therapists using humanistic techniques seek to lead people to realizations about themselves and to help them find ways to come closer to the ideal they hold for themselves. In this view, psychological disorders are the result of people's inability to find meaning in life and of feeling lonely and unconnected to others.

Humanistic approaches have spawned a number of therapeutic techniques. Among the most important are client-centred therapy, existential therapy, and gestalt therapy.

Client-Centred Therapy

If you refer back to the case of Alice described earlier in the chapter on page 482, you'll see that the therapist's comments are not interpretations or answers to questions that the client has raised. Instead, they tend to clarify or reflect back what the client has said (e.g., "In other words, what you did . . ."; "You feel that . . ."; "Is that it?"). This therapeutic technique is known as *nondirective counselling*, and it is at the heart of client-centred therapy. First practiced by Carl Rogers, client-centred therapy is the best-known and most frequently used type of humanistic therapy (Rogers, 1951, 1980; Raskin & Rogers, 1989).

client-centred therapy: Therapy in which the goal is to reach one's potential for self-actualization

The goal of **client-centred therapy** is to enable people to reach their potential for *self-actualization*. By providing a warm and accepting environment, therapists hope to motivate clients to air their problems and feelings, which, in turn, will enable the clients to make realistic and constructive choices and decisions about the things that bother them in their current lives. Instead of directing the choices clients make, then, the therapist provides what Rogers calls *unconditional positive regard*—expressing acceptance and understanding, regardless of the feelings and attitudes the client expresses. In doing so, the therapist hopes to create an atmosphere in which clients are able to come to decisions that can improve their lives (Farber, Brink, & Raskin, 1996).

Furnishing unconditional positive regard does not mean that the therapist must approve of everything the client says or does. Rather, it means that the therapist must convey that the client's thoughts and behaviours are seen as genuine reflections of what the client is experiencing (Lietaer, 1984; Mearns, 1994).

It is relatively rare for client-centred therapy to be used today in its purest form. Contemporary approaches are apt to be somewhat more directive, with therapists nudging clients toward insights rather than merely reflecting back their statements. However, clients' insights are still seen as central to the therapeutic process.

Existential Therapy

What is the meaning of life? Although we have probably all pondered this question, for some people it is a central issue in their daily lives. For people who experience psychological problems as a result of difficulty in finding a satisfactory answer, existential therapy is particularly appropriate.

In contrast to other humanistic approaches that view humans' unique freedom and potential as a positive force, **existential therapy** is based on the premise that the inability to deal with such freedom can produce anguish, fear, and concern (May, 1969, 1990). In existential therapy, the goal is to allow individuals to come to grips with the freedom they have and to begin to understand how they fit in with the rest of the world. Existential therapists try to make their patients aware of the importance of free choice and the fact that they have the ultimate responsibility for making their own choices about their lives.

Therapists providing existential therapy are exceedingly directive, probing and challenging their client's views of the world. In addition, therapists try to establish a deep and binding relationship with their clients. Their objective is to allow clients to see that they share in the difficulties and experiences that arise in trying to deal with the freedom that is part of being human (Bugental & Bracke, 1992; Schneider & May, 1995).

existential therapy: A humanistic approach that addresses the meaning of life and human freedom

Gestalt Therapy

Have you ever thought back to some childhood incident in which you were treated unfairly and again felt the rage that you had experienced at that time? To therapists working in a gestalt perspective, the healthiest thing for you to do psychologically might be to act out that rage—by hitting a pillow, kicking a chair, or yelling in frustration. This sort of activity represents an important part of what goes on in gestalt therapy sessions, in which the client is encouraged to act out past conflicts and difficulties.

Gestalt Therapy

The rationale for this approach to treatment is that it is necessary for people to integrate their thoughts, feelings, and behaviours into a *gestalt,* the German term for "whole" (as we discussed in reference to perception in Chapter 3). According to Fritz Perls (1967, 1970), who developed **gestalt therapy,** the way for people to do this is to examine their earlier experience and complete any "unfinished business" from their past that still affects and colours present-day relationships. Specifically, Perls assumed that people should reenact during therapy the specific conflicts that they experienced earlier. For instance, a client might first play the part of his angry father and then play himself when his father yelled at him. Gestalt therapists claim that by increasing their perspective on a situation, clients are better able to understand the source of their psychological disorders. Ultimately, the goal is to experience life in a more unified and complete way (Perls, Hefferline, & Goodman, 1994; Yontef, 1995).

gestalt therapy: An approach to therapy that attempts to integrate a client's thoughts, feelings, and behaviour into a whole

Humanistic Approaches in Perspective

The notion that psychological disorders are the consequence of restricted growth potential is philosophically appealing to many people. Furthermore, the acknowledgment of humanistic therapists that the freedom we possess can lead to psychological difficulties provides an unusually supportive environment for therapy. In turn, this atmosphere can aid clients in finding solutions to difficult psychological problems.

On the other hand, the lack of specificity of the humanistic treatments is a problem that has troubled critics. Humanistic approaches are not very precise and are probably the least scientifically and theoretically developed type of treatment. Moreover, this form of treatment is best suited for the same type of highly verbal client who

In group therapy, people with psychological difficulties meet with a therapist to discuss their problems.

profits most from psychoanalytic treatment. Still, humanistic treatment approaches have been influential.

Group Therapy

group therapy: Therapy in which people discuss problems with a group

Although most treatment takes place between a single individual and a therapist, some forms of therapy involve groups of people seeking treatment. In **group therapy,** several unrelated people meet with a therapist to discuss some aspect of their psychological functioning.

People typically discuss their problems with the group, which is often centred around a common difficulty, such as a lack of social skills. The other members of the group provide emotional support and dispense advice on ways in which they have coped effectively with similar problems (Kaplan & Sadock, 1993; Yalom, 1995, 1997; Vinogradov & Yalom, 1996). For example, young offenders convicted of physical and sexual assaults participated in a group therapy program to gain self-knowledge regarding their maladaptive behaviours and develop empathy for their victims (Mamabolo, 1996).

Groups vary greatly in terms of the particular model they employ; there are psychoanalytic groups, humanistic groups, and groups corresponding to the other therapeutic approaches. Furthermore, groups also differ in the degree of guidance the therapist provides (Flowers & Booraem, 1990; Spira, 1997).

Because several people are treated simultaneously in group therapy, it is a much more economical means of treatment than individual psychotherapy. On the other hand, critics argue that group settings do not afford the individual attention inherent in one-to-one therapy, and especially shy and withdrawn individuals may not receive the attention they need in a group setting.

Family Therapy

family therapy: An approach that focuses on the family as a whole unit to which each member contributes

One specialized form of group therapy is family therapy. As the name implies, **family therapy** involves two or more members of the same family, one (or more) of whose problems led to treatment. But rather than focusing simply on members of the family who present the initial problem, family therapists consider the family as a whole unit,

---

Answers to Review Questions:

1. psychotherapy   2. 1-c; 2-a; 3-d; 4-b   3. defense mechanisms   4. manifest; latent   5. a

to which each member contributes. By meeting with the entire family simultaneously, family therapists attempt to obtain a sense of how the family members interact with one another (Nichols & Schwartz, 1995; Piercy et al., 1996; Rolland & Walsh, 1996).

Family therapists view the family as a "system," and they assume that the separate individuals in the family cannot improve without understanding the conflicts that are to be found in the interactions of the family members. Thus each member is expected to contribute to the resolution of the problem being addressed.

Many family therapists assume that family members fall into rigid roles or set patterns of behaviour, with one person acting as the scapegoat, another as a bully, and so forth. In their view, family disturbances are perpetuated by this system of roles. One goal of this type of therapy, then, is to get the family members to adopt new, more constructive roles and patterns of behaviour (Minuchin, 1974; Kaslow, 1991; Minuchin & Nichols, 1992; Sprenkle & Moon, 1996).

Evaluating Psychotherapy: Does Therapy Work?

Your best friend at school, Ben, comes to you because he just hasn't been feeling right about things lately. He's upset because he and his girlfriend aren't getting along, but his difficulties go beyond that. He can't concentrate on his studies, has a lot of trouble getting to sleep, and—this is what really bothers him—he's begun to think that people are ganging up on him, talking about him behind his back. It just seems that no one really cares about or understands him or makes any effort to see why he's become so miserable.

Ben is aware that he ought to get *some* kind of help, but he is not sure where to turn. He is fairly skeptical of psychologists, thinking that a lot of what they say is just mumbo-jumbo, but he's willing to put his doubts aside and try anything to feel better. He also knows there are many different types of therapy, and he doesn't have a clue as to which would be best for him. He turns to you for advice, because he knows you are taking a psychology course. He asks, "Which kind of therapy works best?"

Is Therapy Effective?

Such a question requires a complex response, for there is no easy answer. In fact, identifying which form of treatment is most appropriate is a controversial, and still unresolved, task for psychologists specializing in abnormal behaviour. For example, even before considering whether any one form of therapy works better than another, we need to determine whether therapy in *any* form is effective in alleviating psychological disturbances.

Psychotherapy: Effectiveness

Until the 1950s most people simply assumed that therapy, on the face of it, was an effective strategy for resolving psychological difficulties. But in 1952, psychologist Hans Eysenck published an influential article reviewing the published literature on the subject, which challenged this widely held assumption. He claimed that people who received psychodynamic treatment and related therapies were no better off at the end of treatment than those people who were placed on a waiting list for treatment—but never received it. According to his analysis, about two-thirds of the people who reported suffering from "neurotic" symptoms believed that those symptoms had disappeared after two years, regardless of whether or not they had been in therapy. Eysenck concluded that people suffering from neurotic symptoms would go into **spontaneous remission,** recovery without treatment, if they were simply left alone—certainly a cheaper and simpler process.

spontaneous remission: Recovery without treatment

As you can imagine, Eysenck's review was controversial from the start, and its conclusions were quickly challenged. Critics pointed to the inadequacy of the data he reviewed, suggesting that he was basing his conclusions on studies that contained a number of flaws.

Nevertheless, Eysenck's early review served to stimulate a continuing stream of better controlled, more carefully crafted studies on the effectiveness of psychotherapy, and today most psychologists agree: Therapy does work. Several comprehensive reviews indicate that therapy brings about greater improvement than no treatment at all, with the rate of spontaneous remission (recovery without treatment) being fairly low.

FIGURE 13-1 *Estimates of the effectiveness of different types of treatment, in comparison to control groups of untreated people. The percentile score shows how much more effective a particular type of treatment is for the average patient than is no treatment. For example, people given psychodynamic treatment score, on average, more positively on outcome measures than about three-quarters of untreated people. Source: Adapted from Smith, Glass, & Miller, 1980.*

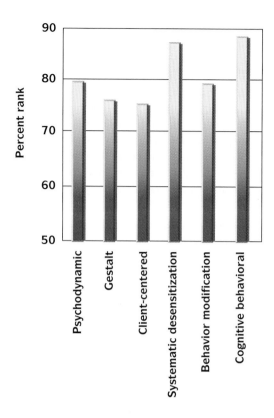

In most cases, then, the symptoms of abnormal behaviour do not go away by themselves if left untreated—although the issue continues to be hotly debated (Kazdin, 1993; Bergin & Garfield, 1994; M. E. P. Seligman, 1995, 1996; Scott, 1996; Sohn, 1996).

Which Kind of Therapy Works Best?

Although most psychologists feel confident that psychotherapeutic treatment *in general* is more effective than no treatment at all, the question of whether any specific form of treatment is superior to any other has yet to be answered definitively (Garfield, 1990; Jacobson & Truax, 1991; Barber & Lane, 1995; Pratt & Moreland, 1996).

For instance, one classic study comparing the effectiveness of various approaches found that while there is some variation among the success rates of the various treatment forms, most treatments show success rates that are fairly close to one another. As Figure 13-1 indicates, the success rates ranged from about 70 to 85 percent greater success for treated than for untreated individuals (Smith, Glass, & Miller, 1980). There was a slight tendency for behavioural approaches and cognitive approaches to be more successful, but this result may have been due to differences in the severity of cases treated (Orwin & Condray, 1984).

Other research, relying on *meta-analytic* procedures, in which data from a large number of studies are statistically combined, yields similar general conclusions. Furthermore, a large-scale survey of 186,000 individuals found that although survey respondents felt they had benefitted substantially from psychotherapy (see Figure 13-2), there was little difference in "consumer satisfaction" based on the specific type of treatment they had received (Strupp & Binder, 1992; Giles, 1993; Weisz et al., 1995; CR, 1995; Seligman, 1995; Kotkin, Daviet, & Gurin, 1996; Strupp, 1996).

In short, converging evidence allows us to draw several conclusions about the effectiveness of psychotherapy (Strupp & Binder, 1992; Seligman, 1996):

- For most people, psychotherapy is effective. This conclusion holds over different lengths of treatment, specific kinds of psychological disorders, and types of treatment. Thus, the question "Does psychotherapy work?" appears to be convincingly answered: It does (Lipsey & Wilson, 1993; Seligman, 1996).

How much can therapy help?

Almost everyone got some relief from the problems that brought them to a therapist, no matter how poorly they felt at the start.

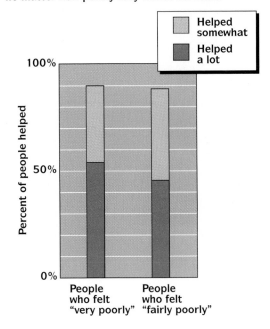

FIGURE 13-2 *A large-scale survey of 186,000 individuals found that while the respondents had benefitted substantially from psychotherapy there was little difference in "consumer satisfaction" based on the specific type of treatment they had received.*

- On the other hand, psychotherapy doesn't work for everyone. As many as 10 percent of people show no improvement or actually deteriorate (Lambert, Shapiro, & Bergin, 1986; Luborsky, 1988).

- Certain specific types of treatments are somewhat, although not invariably, better for specific types of problems. For example, systematic desensitization relieves specific phobias quite effectively (Seligman, 1995). However, there are many exceptions, and often the differences in success rates for different types of treatment are not substantial.

- No single form of therapy works best on every problem. Consequently, there is no definitive answer to the question "Which therapy works best?"

Because no one type of psychotherapy is invariably effective, eclectic approaches to therapy are becoming increasingly popular. In an **eclectic approach to therapy,** a therapist uses a variety of techniques, integrating several perspectives, to treat a person's problems. By using eclectic procedures, the therapist is able to choose the appropriate mix in accordance with the specific needs of the individual (Prochaska, 1995; Goldfried, 1995; Beutler, Consoli, & Williams, 1995; Racey, 1996; Leger, 1998). For example, some clients may lack the patience and ability required for introspection, and consequently behavioural therapy is probably more suitable than psychodynamic therapy for these individuals. Also, not every sort of therapy is equally suited for treatment of every psychological disorder.

In selecting and using specific therapeutic techniques, it is important to acknowledge influences of the broader social context of everyday life. For example, in the treatment of women suffering from depression, it is important to understand how social and cultural factors shape and regulate their lives. This knowledge will help the therapist and client avoid the problem of disempowerment associated with drug therapy. It may also help them deal with inappropriate beliefs about the self and the experience of depression that may arise in cognitive therapy (Stoppard, 1999; Gammell and Stoppard, 1999; Hurst, 1999; Hurst and Genest, 1995). See the Pathways Through Psychology box to read about Janet Stoppard and her work on women and depression.

eclectic approach to therapy: An approach to therapy that uses techniques taken from a variety of treatment methods, rather than just one

Because cultural and environmental factors can be related to a person's psychological difficulties, many psychotherapists believe it is important to take the race and ethnicity of people they treat into consideration.

Suicide

Exploring Diversity

Youth Suicide in the General Population and Aboriginal Communities

Between 3,500 and 4,000 Canadians commit suicide annually (Statistics Canada, 1998). Not only is Canada's suicide rate higher than that of the United States, but it is above average in comparison with other countries (National Task Force, 1994). Lester and Leenaars (1998) have described suicide as a major health problem in Canada.

The comparatively high number of Canadian youths who take their own lives is particularly distressing. Although the conditions of each individual victim's circumstances are unique in many ways, there are also factors that distinguish youth suicide in the aboriginal population from youth suicide in the general population.

Consider the situation of youth in the general population. From the 1960s to the 1990s, teen suicides quadrupled, giving Canada the third highest rate among industrialized nations (Nemeth, 1994). For young males aged 20 to 24 years, the incidence of suicide is as high (24.9 per 100,000 of population) as it is for the traditional high-risk group: males aged 50 and older (Statistics Canada, 1998). Predisposing factors for this group of young people include family problems, problems in peer relationships, previous attempts, and diagnosis of mental illness. Trigger events are interpersonal conflicts, legal problems, loss of a valued relationship and school problems (White, 1998; Heikkinen et al., 1993).

There are a number of distinctive features of aboriginal life in Canada that have been linked to the high suicide rates in aboriginal communities: rates that are two to four times as high as rates for the general population. Suicide is particularly high among aboriginal youths aged 15 to 30 (Sakinofsky, 1998; National Task Force, 1994). In both First Nations and Innuit communities, the erosion of traditional cultural values is a significant factor. In First Nations communities, Federal Government policies aimed at assimilation have contributed to chaotic conditions that have produced serious conflict concerning a sense of identity. First Nations youth grow up thinking that the history of their people is either irrelevant or nonexistent (Sinclair, 1998). In Innuit communities, the rate of cultural change is related to the suicide rate. The encroachment of the majority culture into Innuit communities is linked to family instability, feelings of alienation, and substance abuse problems. These conditions contribute to the high suicide rate among Innuit youth (Kirmayer et al., 1998).

Common characteristics of youths at risk for suicide in the general population and in the aboriginal population are withdrawal, feelings of alienation, and personal problems. However, there are significant differences between aboriginal and other youth concerning the sources and types of personal problems.

The National Task Force (1994) has suggested the following prevention strategies: improvement of social conditions, educational programs to promote awareness and improved social skills, and reduction in access to lethal means. The Royal Commission on Aboriginal People (1995) has outlined prevention strategies at three levels: crisis services, community development, and Federal commitment to self-determination of aboriginal peoples. ■

Recap, Review, and Rethink

Recap

- Humanistic approaches view therapy as a way to help people solve their own problems.

- In group therapy, several unrelated people meet with a therapist to discuss some aspect of their psychological functioning.

- A long-standing issue is whether psychotherapy is effective, and, if it is, whether one kind is superior to others.

- Racial, ethnic, and cultural factors must be taken into account during treatment for psychological disorders.

Review

1. Match each of the following treatment strategies with the statement you might expect to hear from a therapist using that strategy.
   1. gestalt therapy
   2. group therapy
   3. unconditional positive regard
   4. behavioural therapy
   5. nondirective counselling

   a. "In other words, you don't get along with your mother because she hates your girlfriend, is that right?"
   b. "I want you all to take turns talking about why you decided to come, and what you hope to gain from therapy."
   c. "I can understand why you wanted to wreck your friend's car after she hurt your feelings. Now, tell me more about the accident."
   d. "That's not appropriate behaviour. Let's work on replacing it with something else."
   e. "Remember the anger you felt and scream until you feel better."

2. _____ therapies assume people are responsible for their own lives and the decisions they make.

3. _____ therapy emphasizes the integration of thoughts, feelings, and behaviours.

4. One of the major criticisms of humanistic therapies is that
   a. they are too imprecise and unstructured.
   b. they treat only the symptom of the problem.
   c. the therapist dominates the patient-therapist interaction.
   d. it works well only on lower-class clients.

5. In a controversial study, Eysenck found that some people go into _____ _____ , or recovery without treatment, if they are simply left alone instead of treated.

6. Treatments that combine techniques from all the theoretical approaches are called _____ procedures.

Answers to Review Questions are on page 500.

Rethink

1. Computer programs have been created to simulate the responses of a therapist. Which of the therapeutic approaches that you have studied lend themselves most readily to computer simulation? Why?

2. How can people be successfully treated in group therapy when individuals with the "same" problem are so different? What advantages might group therapy offer over individual therapy?

3. List some examples of behaviour that might be considered abnormal among members of one cultural or economic group and normal by members of a different cultural or economic group. Suppose that most therapies had been developed by psychologists from minority culture groups and lower socioeconomic status; how might they differ from current therapies?

BIOMEDICAL THERAPY: BIOLOGICAL APPROACHES TO TREATMENT

If you get a kidney infection, you're given an antibiotic and, with luck, about a week later your kidney is as good as new. If your appendix becomes inflamed, a surgeon removes it and your body functions normally once more. Could an analogous approach, focusing on the body's physiology, be taken with psychological disturbances?

▶ How are drug, electroconvulsive, and psychosurgical techniques used today in the treatment of psychological disorders?

According to biological approaches to treatment, the answer is yes. Biomedical therapies are used routinely for certain kinds of problems. The basic model suggests that rather than focusing on a patient's psychological conflicts or past traumas, or on environmental variables that may support abnormal behaviour, it is more appropriate in certain cases to treat brain chemistry and other neurological factors directly. This can be done through the use of drugs, electric shock, or surgery.

Drug Therapy

drug therapy: Control of psychological problems through drugs

Are we close to the day when we will take a pill each morning to maintain good psychological health, in the same way that we now take a vitamin pill to help us stay physically healthy? Although that day has not yet arrived, there are quite a few forms of **drug therapy** that successfully alleviate symptoms of a number of psychological disturbances.

Drug therapies work by altering the operation of neurotransmitters and neurons in the brain. Some drugs operate by inhibiting neurotransmitters or receptor neurons, thus reducing activity at particular synapses, the sites where nerve impulses travel from one neuron to another in the brain. Other drugs do just the opposite: They increase the activity of certain neurotransmitters or neurons, allowing particular neurons to fire more frequently.

Antipsychotic Drugs

antipsychotic drugs: Drugs that temporarily alleviate psychotic symptoms such as agitation and overactivity

Probably no greater change has occurred in mental hospitals than the successful introduction in the mid-1950s of **antipsychotic drugs**—drugs used to alleviate severe symptoms of disturbance, such as loss of touch with reality, agitation, and overactivity. Previously, the typical mental hospital fulfilled all the stereotypes of the insane asylum, with screaming, moaning, clawing patients displaying the most bizarre behaviours. Suddenly, in just a matter of days, the hospital wards became considerably calmer environments in which professionals could do more than just try to get the patients through the day without causing serious harm to themselves or others.

This dramatic change was brought about by the introduction of a drug called *chlorpromazine*. This drug, and others of a similar nature, rapidly became the most popular and successful treatment for schizophrenia. Today drug therapy is the preferred treatment for most cases of severely abnormal behaviour, and as such, is used for most hospitalized patients with psychological disorders. For instance, the antipsychotic drugs *clozapine* and *haloperidol* represent the current generation of antipsychotics. Clozapine was the drug used so successfully to treat those attending the prom described in the Prologue (Wallis & Willwerth, 1992; Meltzer, 1993; Rosenheck et al., 1997).

How do antipsychotic drugs work? Most operate by blocking the dopamine receptors at the brain's synapses. On the other hand, some newer drugs, like clozapine, amplify the release of dopamine in certain parts of the brain, such as those related to planning and goal-directed activity (Barreira, 1996; Green & Patel, 1996; Mrzljak et al., 1996).

Despite the effectiveness of antipsychotic drugs, they do not produce a "cure" in the same way that, say, penicillin cures an infection. As soon as the drug is withdrawn, the original symptoms tend to reappear. Furthermore, such drugs can have long-term side effects, such as dryness of the mouth and throat, dizziness, and sometimes tremors and loss of muscle control that may continue even after drug treatments are stopped—a permanent condition called *tardive dyskinesia* (Kane, 1992; Shriqui & Annable, 1995).

Perhaps even more devastating than these physical side effects are the numbing effects of antipsychotic drugs on the emotional responses of some patients. For exam-

Drug Therapy

ple, Mark Vonnegut (son of author Kurt Vonnegut) describes his reactions to the use of the antipsychotic drug *thorazine* while he was institutionalized for schizophrenia:

> What the drug is supposed to do is keep away hallucinations. What I think it does is just fog up your mind so badly you don't notice the hallucinations or much else. . . . On thorazine everything's a bore. Not a bore, exactly. Boredom implies impatience. You can read comic books . . . you can tolerate talking to jerks forever. . . . The weather is dull, the flowers are dull, nothing's very impressive (Vonnegut, 1975, pp. 196–197).

Antidepressant Drugs

As you might guess from the name, **antidepressant drugs** are a class of medications used in cases of severe depression to improve the moods of patients. They were discovered quite by accident: It was found that patients suffering from tuberculosis who were given the drug *iproniazid* suddenly became happier and more optimistic. When the same drug was tested on people suffering from depression, a similar result occurred, and drugs became an accepted form of treatment for depression (Glick, 1995; Shuchter, Downs, & Zisook, 1996).

antidepressant drugs: Medication that improves a depressed patient's mood and feeling of well-being

Most antidepressant drugs work by allowing an increase in the concentration of particular neurotransmitters in the brain. For example, tricyclic drugs modify the amount of norepinephrine and serotonin at the synapses of neurons in the brain. Others, such as bupropion, operate by affecting the neurotransmitter dopamine (Zito, 1993; Berman, Krystal, & Charney, 1996).

Although antidepressant drugs may produce side effects such as drowsiness and faintness, their overall success rate is quite good. Unlike antipsychotic drugs, antidepressants can produce lasting, long-term recoveries from depression. In many cases, even after patients stop taking the drugs, their depression does not return (Spiegel, 1989; Zito, 1993; Julien, 1995).

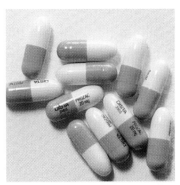

Prozac is a widely prescribed—and controversial—antidepressant.

Antidepressant drugs have become among the most heavily prescribed of all drugs. In 1996, some $6 billion was spent worldwide on antidepressants, and sales are increasing at a rate of more than 20 percent a year. In particular, the antidepressant *fluoxetine,* sold under the trade name *Prozac,* has graced the cover of magazines such as *Newsweek* and has been the topic of bestsellers (Kramer, 1993).

Is Prozac as revolutionary as its proponents claim? In some respects, the drug does merit accolades. Despite its high expense—each daily dose costs about $2—it has significantly improved the lives of thousands of depressed individuals.

Prozac (and its cousins Zoloft and Paxil) work by blocking reabsorption of the neurotransmitter serotonin. Compared to other antidepressants, Prozac has relatively few side effects. Furthermore, many people who do not respond to other types of antidepressants do well on Prozac.

On the other hand, the drug has not been used long enough for us to know all of its potential side effects, and some reports suggest that Prozac may have a darker side. For example, between 20 and 30 percent of users report the side effects of nausea and diarrhea, and a smaller number report sexual dysfunctions (Barondes, 1994).

Furthermore, the reputation of Prozac as an all-purpose mood booster raises troublesome issues. The wave of publicity about the drug increases the likelihood that patients with mild forms of depression or even other disorders will forgo alternative, more suitable types of treatment such as psychotherapy. Instead, they may aggressively seek prescriptions for Prozac.

Many health providers are more than willing to oblige requests for the drug. Over 20,000 Canadians take Prozac (Nichols, 1994). In the United States, Prozac is prescribed more than one million times a month, most often by practitioners who do not specialize in psychological disorders (Cowley, 1994).

The widespread use of Prozac and other antidepressants, and the accolades they have attained, raise a more difficult, and ultimately philosophical, question: Are the positive changes in mood, attitudes, and outlook on life supposedly produced by Prozac completely desirable? Although proponents of the drug argue that it allows the "real person" to emerge, some observers argue that the personality that shows itself under the influence of Prozac is less than genuine. They contend that people may not be better off, after all, in escaping from unpleasant feelings. To critics, people who take drugs such as Prozac may be unmotivated to seek the insights and experiences that can make life truly meaningful and worthwhile.

In short, although Prozac and other antidepressants have important benefits, they are not wonder drugs. Until the long-term biological and psychological effects are fully known, their use requires caution.

Ironically, despite the widespread use of antidepressants, a recent assessment by depression experts found that depression is actually undertreated. According to their statistics, half of the people suffering from serious depression for twenty years or more have never taken an antidepressant. Even most of those who do take medicine often fail to take a sufficient dosage for a long enough time to alleviate their symptoms (Gilbert, 1997).

Lithium

lithium: A form of simple mineral salts that has been used very successfully in cases of bipolar disorders

Lithium, a form of simple mineral salts, is a drug that has been used very successfully in cases of bipolar disorders. Although no one knows definitely why it works, it is effective in reducing manic episodes some 70 percent of the time. On the other hand, its effectiveness in resolving depression is not as impressive. It works only in certain cases, and, like other antidepressants, it can produce a number of side effects (Coppen, Metcalfe, & Wood, 1982).

Lithium has a quality that sets it apart from other drug treatments: More than any other drug, it represents a *preventive* treatment, forestalling episodes of manic depression. Often, people who have been subject to bipolar disorder episodes in the past can take a daily dose of lithium that prevents a recurrence of their symptoms. In contrast, most other drugs are useful only after symptoms of psychological disturbance occur.

Antianxiety Drugs

If the names Valium and Xanax sound familiar to you, you are not alone: They are among the drugs most frequently prescribed by physicians. Both are members of a class of drugs known as antianxiety drugs, which are prescribed—often by family physicians—to alleviate the stress and anxiety experienced by patients during particularly difficult periods. In fact, more than half of all Americans have a family member who has taken such a drug at one time or another.

antianxiety drugs: Drugs that reduce the level of anxiety a person experiences, essentially by reducing excitability and in part by increasing drowsiness

As the name implies, **antianxiety drugs** reduce the level of anxiety a person experiences, essentially by reducing excitability and in part by increasing drowsiness. They are used not only to reduce general tension in people who are experiencing temporary difficulties but also to aid in the treatment of more serious anxiety disorders (Zito, 1993).

Although the popularity of antianxiety drugs suggests that they hold few risks, they can produce a number of potentially serious side effects. For instance, they can cause fatigue, and long-term use can lead to dependence. Moreover, taken in combination with alcohol, some antianxiety drugs can become lethal. But a more important issue concerns their use to suppress anxiety. Almost every approach to psychological disturbance views continuing anxiety as a signal of some sort of problem. Thus, drugs that mask anxiety may simply be hiding difficulties. Consequently, rather than confronting their underlying problems, people may simply be hiding from them through the use of antianxiety drugs. In general, anxiety disorders are dealt with more effectively by a combination of antianxiety drugs and behavioural or cognitive therapy than by drugs alone (Gauthier, 1999; Bouchard et al., 1996). Cognitive therapy provides opportunities to confront the catastrophic thoughts in panic disorder (Cox, 1996).

Electroconvulsive Therapy (ECT)

ECT

Martha Manning had contemplated all kinds of suicide—by pills, hanging, even guns. Her depression was so deep that she lived each minute "afraid I [wouldn't] make it to the next hour." But she balked when her therapist recommended electroconvulsive therapy, commonly known as "shock treatment." Despite her training and practice as a clinical psychologist, Manning immediately flashed to scenes from *One Flew Over the Cuckoo's Nest,* "with McMurphy and the Chief jolted with electroshock, their bodies flailing with each jolt" (Guttman, 1995, p. 16).

The reality, it turned out, was quite different. Although it did produce some memory loss and temporary headaches, the procedure also brought Manning back from the brink of suicide.

First introduced in the 1930s, **electroconvulsive therapy (ECT)** is a procedure in which an electric current of 70 to 150 volts is briefly administered to a patient's head, causing a loss of consciousness and often seizures. Usually the patient is sedated and receives muscle relaxants prior to administration of the current, which helps to prevent violent muscle contractions. The typical patient receives about ten such treatments in the course of a month, but some patients continue with maintenance treatments for months afterward (Fink, 1994, 1997; Calev, Shapira, & Pass, 1995; Nierenberg, 1998).

ECT is a controversial technique. Apart from the obvious distastefulness of a treatment that evokes images of capital punishment by electrocution, there are frequently side effects. For instance, following treatment patients often experience disorientation, confusion, and sometimes memory loss that may remain for months. Furthermore, many patients fear ECT, even though they are anesthetized during the actual treatment and thus experience no pain. Finally, we still do not know how or why ECT works, and critics suggest that the treatment may produce permanent damage to the brain (Fisher, 1985; Valente, 1991). However, the Canadian Psychiatric Association has concluded that ECT is safe and effective if it is properly used (Enns & Reiss, 1992).

Given the drawbacks to ECT, why is it used at all? The basic reason is that in many cases it seems to be an effective treatment for severe cases of depression. For instance, it may prevent depressed, suicidal individuals from committing suicide, and it can act more quickly than antidepressive medications, which may take longer to become effective. Still, ECT tends to be used only when other treatments have proved ineffective (Thienhaus, Margletta, & Bennett, 1990; APA Task Force, 1990; Coffey, 1993; Foderaro, 1993; Sackeim et al., 1996).

electroconvulsive therapy (ECT): A procedure in which an electric current of 70 to 150 volts is briefly administered to a patient's head, causing a loss of consciousness and often seizures

Psychosurgery

If ECT strikes you as a questionable procedure, the use of **psychosurgery**—brain surgery in which the object is to alleviate symptoms of mental disorder—is likely to appear even more so. A technique that is used only rarely today, psychosurgery was first introduced as a "treatment of last resort" in the 1930s.

The initial form of psychosurgery, a *prefrontal lobotomy,* consisted of surgically destroying or removing parts of a patient's frontal lobes that were thought to control emotionality. In the 1930s and 1940s, the procedure was performed on thousands of patients, often with little precision (Miller, 1994).

Such psychosurgery often did improve a patient's behaviour—but not without drastic side effects. For along with remission of symptoms of mental disorder, patients sometimes suffered personality changes, becoming bland, colourless, and unemotional. In other cases, patients became aggressive and unable to control their impulses. In the worst cases, treatment resulted in the death of the patient.

With the advent of effective drug treatments—and the obvious ethical questions regarding the appropriateness of forever altering someone's personality—psychosurgery became nearly obsolete. However, it is still used in very rare cases when all other procedures have failed and the patient's behaviour presents a high risk to self and others. Today, a more precise form of psychosurgery called a *cingulotomy* is sometimes employed in rare cases of obsessive-compulsive disorder (Chiocca & Martuza, 1990; Baer et al., 1995). Psychosurgery is also occasionally used in dying patients with severe, uncontrollable pain. Still, even these cases raise

psychosurgery: Brain surgery once used to alleviate symptoms of mental disorders but rarely used today

important ethical issues, and psychosurgery remains a highly controversial treatment (Rappaport, 1992; Miller, 1994).

Biomedical Therapies in Perspective: Can Abnormal Behaviour Be Cured?

In some respects, there has been no greater revolution in the field of mental health than that represented by the biological approaches to treatment. As previously violent, uncontrollable patients have been calmed by the use of drugs, mental hospitals have been able to concentrate more on actually helping patients and less on custodial functions. Similarly, patients whose lives have been disrupted by depression or bipolar episodes have been able to function normally, and other forms of drug therapy have also shown remarkable results.

On the other hand, biomedical therapies are not without their detractors. For one thing, critics charge that they merely provide relief of the *symptoms* of mental disorder; as soon as the drugs are withdrawn, the symptoms return. Biomedical treatment may not solve the underlying problems that led a patient to therapy in the first place. Moreover, biomedical therapies can produce side effects, ranging from physical reactions to the development of *new* symptoms of abnormal behaviour (Elkin, 1986). For these reasons, then, biologically based treatment approaches do not represent a cure-all for psychological disorders.

Community Psychology: Focus on Prevention

Each of the treatments that we have reviewed in this chapter has a common element: It is a "restorative" treatment, aimed at alleviating psychological difficulties that already exist. However, a relatively new movement, dubbed **community psychology,** is geared toward a different aim: to prevent or minimize the incidence of psychological disorders.

community psychology: A movement aimed toward preventing or minimizing psychological disorders in the community

Community psychology came of age in the 1960s, when plans were developed for a nationwide network of community mental health centres in the United States. These centres were meant to provide low-cost mental health services, including short-term therapy and community educational programs. With the development of effective drug therapy, the population of mental hospitals and psychiatric wards has decreased substantially in Canada and the United States during the last thirty years. In Canada, 78 percent of the in-patient beds were closed (Freeman, 1994). This change has been accompanied by a shift from institutional-based care to private practice on the part of clinical psychologists (Goodman, 2000). The influx of former mental patients into the community, known as **deinstitutionalization**, further spurred the community psychology movement. Currently, this movement is concerned with providing treatment and protecting the rights of deinstitutionalized patients (Melton & Garrison, 1987).

deinstitutionalization: The transfer of former mental patients from institutions into the community

In Canada, the recent need to control rising costs in health care has led to government restructuring of health care systems. This restructuring has been a factor in deinstitutionalization. To address the needs of those with mental health problems, the Canadian Mental Health Association has developed a national framework for mental health policy (Trainor, Pomeroy & Pape, 1999). This framework is based on the use of mental health services, and the development of a resource base in the community. The conceptual model for the resource base places the person with a mental health problem at the centre. Surrounding the person are four fundamental elements of life (housing, income, work, and education) and four sources of support (family and friends, community and service groups, consumer groups and organizations, and mental health services). The goal is sufficient development of the sources of support to ensure that the person has access to the four fundamental elements of life.

On a more immediate level, community psychology has led to the development of telephone "hot lines" and crisis centres. In many North American cities, people experiencing acute stress can dial a telephone number at any time of the day or night and talk to a trained, sympathetic listener who can provide immediate—although obviously limited—treatment or support (Tolan et al., 1990; Boehm et al., 1995; Twine &

Pathways Through Psychology

Janet Stoppard

Professor, Psychology Department, University of New Brunswick

Education: *Ph.D. (Queen's University, Kingston); M.Sc. (Queen's University, Belfast, Northern Ireland); B.Sc. (Exeter University, UK)*

Home: *Fredericton, New Brunswick*

Janet Stoppard

I became interested in Psychology as a teenager after reading a book about "altered states of consciousness". I decided then to study psychology at university. After completing my undergraduate degree, I moved to Belfast in Northern Ireland to do a master's degree in clinical psychology. This was followed by several years working in child psychological services. Around this time (early 1970s), Belfast was becoming a difficult place to live because of the "troubles", and I made the decision to emigrate to Canada. I applied for a position as a clinical psychologist in Halifax, Nova Scotia and once there, soon realised that having a Ph.D. would increase my career options. Less than two years after coming to Canada, I was a doctoral student in clinical psychology at another Queen's University, this time in Kingston, Ontario.

The early 1970s in Canada was an exciting time to be a graduate student in psychology. The "Women's Movement" was raising issues about the social and economic conditions of women's lives and feminist concerns were receiving increased attention with the 1970 report of the Royal Commission on the Status of Women. As a student, I was involved in the Kingston Women's Centre and debates about the status of women were a regular feature of campus life. The study of gender issues in psychology was a new and burgeoning research area. The appearance in 1972 of Phyllis Chesler's

book "Women and Madness" inspired feminist critiques of mainstream clinical psychology. Gender bias in clinical practice became an important topic for research; feminist approaches to therapy began to be developed; and psychology of women emerged as a legitimate field of study. It was in this climate that I carried out my thesis research on the social psychology of gender stereotypes. By this time, my career goals had shifted toward academia. With an academic job in mind, I spent 1976–77 as a post-doctoral clinical fellow at UBC, based at the Health Sciences Centre Hospital, where my work focused on treatment of depression. I was struck by the preponderance of women among the depressed patients I saw. This observation stayed with me and when I moved back to the Maritimes, and my current position at UNB, I pursued my interests in women's mental health and began to explore issues surrounding women's vulnerability to depression.

Since 1979, I have been a psychology professor at UNB, where I'm involved with the graduate program in Clinical Psychology and the undergraduate Women's

Studies program. I helped to establish the Women's Studies program and was the program's first coordinator. I also teach a course on women and mental health that is part of the Women's Studies program. During the 1980s, I was involved with the Canadian Mental Health Association (CMHA) and in 1985–86, while on sabbatical in Toronto, co-ordinated a group that prepared a report for CMHA entitled "Women and Mental Health in Canada: Strategies for Change" (1987). This report, which documented ways in which women's mental health is disadvantaged, attracted considerable media attention and stimulated a number of national conferences on women's mental health. At the same time, I was researching explanations for gender-related differences in depression and this lead to an evaluation of cognitive-behavioural theories of depression. My paper on this work, "An Evaluation of the Adequacy of Cognitive/Behavioural Theories for Understanding Depression in Women", was published in 1989 in *Canadian Psychology*. Most recently, my research has been focused on the contributions of qualitative research for understanding women's depression. In 1999, I was guest editor (with Linda McMullen, University of Saskatchewan) for a special theme issue of *Canadian Psychology* which contained papers describing qualitative studies of women's experiences with depression. As well, my book *Understanding Depression: Feminist Social Constructionist Approaches* was published recently (Routledge, 2000). Writing this book gave me an opportunity to bring together ideas about women's depression that I've been developing over the last few years.

Source: Janet Stoppard, Ph.D., University of New Brunswick.
<www.unb.ca/psychology/faculty/stoppard.htm>

Barraclough, 1998). Even in remote areas of the Canadian North, people can contact a crisis line. The Baffin Crisis Line, Kamatsiaqtut, provides a telephone counselling and contact service (Levy & Fletcher, 1998). The service is provided by northerners who understand the culture, setting, and problems of the North and it is provided in three languages: Inuktitut, French and English. Many cities have crisis centres and drop-in centres. Colleges and universities frequently offer crisis counselling as part of their student counselling services, using both fully credentialled and peer counsellors.

Unfortunately, the original goals of community psychology have not been met. For instance, the incidence of mental disorders has not declined. And many people do not get the care they need (Kiesler & Simpkins, 1991, 1993; Torrey, 1996, 1997; Hwang, 2000). In comparison to the United States, Ontario and Quebec invest proportionately more in prevention. However, when overall health care spending is taken into account, prevention typically receives low funding in Canada (Nelson, Prilleltensky, Laurendeau & Powell, 1996).

The Informed Consumer of Psychology

Choosing the Right Therapist

If you make the decision to seek therapy, you're faced with a daunting task. There are, however, a number of guidelines that can help you determine if you've chosen the right therapist (Engler & Goleman, 1992):

Choosing a Therapist

- The relationship between client and therapist should be comfortable. You should not be intimidated by, or in awe of, a therapist. Instead, you should trust the therapist and feel free to discuss even the most personal issues without fearing a negative reaction. In sum, the "personal chemistry" should feel right.

- Therapists and clients should agree on the goals for treatment. They should be clear, specific, and attainable.

- The therapist should have appropriate training and credentials for the type of therapy he or she is conducting and should be registered. The Canadian Psychological Association recently reaffirmed the doctorate as the minimum requirement for registration (Goodman, 2000). However, they advocate the availability of additional training for those at mid-career. Currently, in some Canadian jurisdictions there is some master's-level registration, usually with the designation "Psychological Associate." Check the therapist's membership in professional associations, and at the initial consultation query her or him about cost and billing practices.

- Clients should feel that they are making progress toward resolving their psychological difficulties after therapy has begun, despite occasional setbacks. Although there is no set timetable, the most obvious changes resulting from therapy tend to occur relatively early in the course of treatment. For instance, half of patients in psychotherapy improve by the eighth session and three-fourths by the twenty-sixth session (see Figure 13-3; Howard et al., 1986; Howard & Zola, 1988; HMHL, 1994b).

If a client has no sense of improvement after repeated visits, this issue should be frankly discussed, with an eye toward the possibility of making a change. Today, most

Drawing by Gahan Wilson © 1994 The New Yorker Magazine, Inc.

"Looking good!"

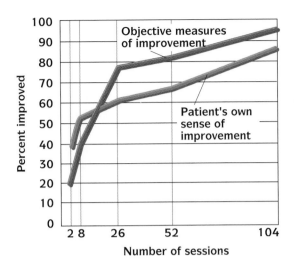

FIGURE 13-3 *For most patients, improvements in psychological functioning occur relatively soon after therapy has begun. Source: Howard et al., 1986.*

therapy is of fairly brief duration, especially that involving college students—who average just five sessions (Crits-Cristoph, 1992; Messer & Warren, 1995; Quick, 1996; Bloom, 1997; Lazarus, 1997).

Clients should be aware that they will have to put in a great deal of effort in therapy. Although ours is a culture that promises quick cures for any problem—as anyone who has perused the self-help shelves of bookstores knows—in reality, solving difficult problems is not easy. People must be committed to making therapy work and should know that it is they, and not the therapist, who must do most of the work to resolve their problems. The potential is there for the effort to pay off handsomely—as people experience more positive, fulfilling, and meaningful lives. ■

Recap, Review, and Rethink

Recap

- Biomedical treatment approaches encompass drug therapy, electroconvulsive therapy, and psychosurgery.

- Drug therapy has produced dramatic reductions in psychotic behaviour. Among the medications used are antipsychotic drugs, antidepressant drugs, and antianxiety drugs.

- Electroconvulsive therapy (ECT) consists of passing an electric current through the brain of patients suffering from severe psychological disturbances, particularly schizophrenia and depression.

- The most extreme form of biomedical therapy is psychosurgery, in which patients undergo brain surgery. Although rarely used today, prefrontal lobotomies were once a common form of treatment.

- Community psychology aims to prevent or minimize psychological disorders.

Review

1. Antipsychotic drugs have provided effective, long-term, and complete cures for schizophrenia. True or false?

2. One of the most effective biomedical treatments for psychological disorders, used mainly to arrest and prevent manic-depressive episodes, is
   a. chlorpromazine.   c. Librium.
   b. lithium.   d. Valium.

3. Originally a treatment for schizophrenia, _____ involves administering electric current to a patient's head.

4. Psychosurgery has grown in popularity as a method of treatment as surgical techniques have become more precise. True or false?

5. The trend toward releasing more patients from mental hospitals into the community is known as

   _____.

Answers to Review Questions are on page 508.

Rethink

1. One of the main criticisms of biological therapies is that they treat the symptoms of mental disorder without uncovering and treating the underlying problems from which people are suffering. Do you agree with this criticism or not? Why?

2. Does the fact that no one understands why ECT is effective mean that its use should be avoided? In general, should treatments that are seemingly effective, but for unknown reasons, be employed?

3. If a dangerously violent person could be "cured" of violence through a new psychosurgical technique, would you approve the use of this technique? Suppose the person agreed to—or requested—the technique? What sort of policy would you develop for the use of psychosurgery?

What are the goals of psychologically and biologically based treatment approaches?

1. Although the specific treatment types are diverse, psychotherapy (psychologically based therapy) and biomedical therapy (biologically based therapy) share the goal of resolving psychological problems by modifying people's thoughts, feelings, expectations, evaluations, and ultimately their behaviour.

What are the basic kinds of psychotherapies?

2. Psychoanalytic treatment is based on Freud's psychodynamic theory. It seeks to bring unresolved past conflicts and unacceptable impulses from the unconscious into the conscious, where the problems may be dealt with more effectively. To do this, patients meet frequently with their therapists and use techniques such as free association and dream interpretation. The process can be a difficult one because of patient resistance and transference, and there is no conclusive evidence that the process works.

3. Behavioural approaches to treatment view abnormal behaviour itself as the problem, rather than viewing the behaviour as a symptom of some underlying cause. To bring about a "cure," this view suggests that the outward behaviour must be changed. In aversive conditioning, unpleasant stimuli are linked to a behaviour that the patient enjoys but wants to stop. Systematic desensitization uses the opposite procedure. A stimulus that evokes pleasant feelings is repeatedly paired with a stimulus that evokes anxiety in order to reduce that anxiety. Observational learning is another behavioural treatment used to teach new, more appropriate behaviour, as are techniques such as token systems.

4. Cognitive approaches to treatment, which are often referred to as cognitive-behavioural therapy, suggest that the goal of therapy should be a restructuring of a person's belief system into a more realistic, rational, and logical view of the world. Two examples of cognitive treatments are the rational-emotive therapy of Ellis and Beck's cognitive therapy.

What are humanistic approaches to treatment?

5. Humanistic therapy is based on the premise that people have control of their behaviour, that they can make choices about their lives, and that it is up to them to solve their own problems. Humanistic therapists take a nondirective approach, acting more as guides who facilitate a client's search for answers. One example of humanistic therapy is Carl Rogers's client-centred therapy, in which the goal is to allow people to reach the potential good assumed to be characteristic of every human being. Existential therapy helps people cope with the unique freedom and potential that human existence offers, whereas gestalt therapy is directed toward aiding people in the integration of their thoughts, feelings, and behaviour.

How does group therapy differ from individual types of therapy?

6. In group therapy, several unrelated people meet with a therapist to discuss some aspect of their psychological functioning, often centring on a common problem such as alcoholism or problems in relating to others. Groups vary greatly in the therapeutic approach that is used.

How effective is therapy, and which kind of therapy works best in a given situation?

7. Most research suggests that, in general, therapy is more effective than no therapy, although how much more effective is not known. The answer to the more difficult question of which therapy works best is even less clear, in part because the therapies are so qualitatively different, and in part because the definition of "cure" is so vague. It is indisputable, though, that particular kinds of therapy are more appropriate for some problems than for others.

How are drug, electroconvulsive, and psychosurgical techniques used today in the treatment of psychological disorders?

8. Biological treatment approaches suggest that therapy ought to focus on the physiological causes of abnormal behaviour, rather than considering psychological factors. Drug therapy, the best example of biomedical treatments, has been effective in bringing about dramatic reductions in the appearance of severe signs of mental disturbance.

9. Antipsychotic drugs such as chlorpromazine are very effective in reducing psychotic symptoms, although they can produce serious side effects. Antidepressant drugs, such as Prozac, reduce depression so successfully that they are very widely used. The antianxiety drugs, or minor tranquilizers, are among the most frequently prescribed medications of any sort; they act to reduce the experience of anxiety.

10. Electroconvulsive therapy (ECT) consists of passing an electric current of 70 to 150 volts through the head of a patient, who loses consciousness and has a strong seizure. This procedure is an effective treatment for severe cases of schizophrenia and depression. Another biomedical treatment is psychosurgery. The typical procedure consists of surgically destroying certain parts of a patient's brain in an operation known as a prefrontal lobotomy. Given the grave ethical problems and possible adverse side effects, the procedure is rarely used today.

11. Community psychology aims to prevent or minimize psychological disorders. The movement was spurred in part by deinstitutionalization, in which previously hospitalized mental patients were released into the community. A notable by-product of the movement has been the installation of telephone hot lines and campus crisis centres throughout the country.

Answers to Review Questions:

1. False; schizophrenia can be controlled, but not cured, by medication.   2. b   3. electroconvulsive therapy (ECT)   4. False; psychosurgery is now used only as a treatment of last resort.   5. deinstitutionalization

Key Terms and Concepts

psychotherapy (p. 481)
biomedical therapy (p. 481)
psychodynamic therapy (p. 483)
psychoanalysis (p. 483)
behavioural treatment approaches (p. 485)
systematic desensitization (p. 486)
observational learning (p. 487)
cognitive-behavioural approach (p. 490)
rational-emotive therapy (p. 490)

cognitive therapy (p. 491)
humanistic therapy (p. 492)
client-centred therapy (p. 492)
existential therapy (p. 493)
gestalt therapy (p. 493)
group therapy (p. 494)
family therapy (p. 494)
spontaneous remission (p. 495)
eclectic approach to therapy (p. 497)

drug therapy (p. 500)
antipsychotic drugs (p. 500)
antidepressant drugs (p. 501)
lithium (p. 502)
antianxiety drugs (p. 502)
electroconvulsive therapy (ECT) (p. 503)
psychosurgery (p. 503)
community psychology (p. 504)
deinstitutionalization (p. 504)

Epilogue

In this chapter we have examined how psychological professionals treat people with psychological disorders. We considered a range of approaches, including both psychologically based and biologically based therapies. It is clear that substantial progress has been made in recent years, both in terms of treating the symptoms of mental disorders and in understanding their underlying causes.

Before we leave the topic of psychological disorders, turn back to the Prologue, in which several former sufferers of schizophrenia held a belated prom to celebrate their liberation from that disorder. Based on your understanding of the treatment of psychological disorders, consider the following questions.

1. The promgoers in the story were treated using drug therapy. How would their treatment have proceeded if they had undergone Freudian psychoanalysis? What sorts of issues might a psychoanalyst have examined?

2. Do you think any behavioural therapies would have been helpful in treating the promgoers' schizophrenia? Could behavioural therapies have helped them control the outward exhibition of symptoms?

3. Would cognitive or humanistic approaches have had any effect on schizophrenia? In what ways might such approaches have fallen short?

4. Do you think that people who recover from schizophrenia can quickly and calmly reenter the world and take up their lives as if nothing had happened to them? What sorts of adjustments might lifelong sufferers now in their thirties have to make?

5. Antipsychotic drugs sometimes have the side effect of numbing emotional responses. If it could be known ahead of time that the promgoers would eventually experience this side effect, do you think the drug therapy would still have been advisable? Why or why not?

A family and a country united in grief at the death of Pierre Elliott Trudeau (1919–2000), former Prime Minister of Canada.

Prologue

… And They Brought Roses

In Ottawa, some 60,000 mourners stood patiently in line for many hours to pay their final respects to Pierre Elliott Trudeau; many brought with them Trudeau's trademark red rose. Thousands more would gather on station platforms as the train bearing his body went by; others stood outside Notre-Dame Basilica in Montreal for the funeral service.

It was an outpouring of grief unprecedented in Canada for a political figure. Paralleled only, some thought, to the grief at the death of Princess Diana in 1997.

The diversity of the mourners in terms of age, ethnicity, language, and culture mirrored the population of the most culturally diverse country in the world. This was a fitting tribute for the man who became Canada's Prime Minister in 1968 and held that position for most of the next sixteen years. Trudeau was a charismatic and intellectual man with a vision of a just society and under whose leadership Canada's constitution was repatriated from Britain, bilingualism and multiculturalism were protected, and programs for youth were given prominence.

looking AHEAD

social psychology: The study of how people's thoughts, feelings, and actions are affected by others

The extraordinary response to Trudeau's death raises many interesting questions. Why the outpouring of grief from people too young to remember the man? What made him such a powerful communicator? What drew international politicians like Jimmy Carter (United States) and Fidel Castro (Cuba) to consider him a friend? Will Trudeau's red rose become a symbol for renewed commitment to a just society or will it only be a flower left at his grave?

Each of these questions can be answered only by studying the field of social psychology, the branch of psychology that focuses on those aspects of human behaviour that unite—and separate—us from one another. **Social psychology** is the study of how people's thoughts, feelings, and actions are affected by others. Social psychologists consider the nature and causes of individual behaviour in social situations.

The broad scope of social psychology is conveyed by the kinds of questions social psychologists ask, such as: How can we convince people to change their attitudes or to adopt new ideas and values? In what ways do we come to understand what others are like? How are we influenced by what others do and think? Why do some people display such violence, aggression, and cruelty toward others that people throughout the world live in fear of annihilation at their hands? And why, on the other hand, do some people place their own lives at risk to help others?

In this chapter, we explore social psychological approaches to these and other issues. Not only do we examine those processes that underlie social behaviour, we also discuss strategies for confronting and solving a variety of problems and issues that all of us face—ranging from achieving a better understanding of persuasive tactics to forming more accurate impressions of others.

We begin with a look at attitudes, our evaluations of people and other stimuli. We examine how people form judgments about others and the causes of their behaviour. Next, we discuss social influence, the process by which the actions of an individual (or a group) affect the behaviour of others.

We then consider stereotypes, prejudice, and discrimination, focusing on their roots and the ways in which they can be reduced. Finally, we consider examples of positive and negative social behaviour. After examining what social psychologists have learned about the ways in which people become attracted to one another, form relationships, and fall in love, the chapter concludes with a look at the factors that underlie aggression and helping.

ATTITUDES AND SOCIAL COGNITION

What do Wayne Gretzky, Rosie O'Donnell, and Tiger Woods have in common? Each has appeared in a television commercial, exhorting us to purchase some particular brand-name product.

These commercials were just a few of the thousands that appear on our screens, all designed to persuade us to purchase specific products. These attempts illustrate basic principles that have been articulated by social psychologists who study **attitudes,** learned predispositions to respond in a favourable or unfavourable manner to a particular person, behaviour, belief, or thing (Eagly & Chaiken, 1993, 1995; Petty et al., 1997).

Our attitudes, of course, are not restricted to consumer products. We also develop attitudes toward specific individuals, and to more abstract issues. For example, when you think of the various people in your life, you no doubt hold vastly differing attitudes toward them, depending on the nature of your interactions with them. These attitudes may range from highly positive, as in the case of a lover, to extremely negative, as with a despised rival. Attitudes are also likely to vary in importance. Whereas our attitudes toward friends, family, and peers are generally central to our interactions in the social world, our attitudes toward, say, television newscasters may be relatively insignificant.

Social psychologists generally consider attitudes to follow the **ABC model,** which suggests that an attitude has three components: affect, behaviour, and cognition (Zanna & Remple, 1988; Rajecki, 1989). The *affect component* encompasses our positive or negative emotions about something—how we feel about it. The *behaviour component* consists of a predisposition or intention to act in a particular manner that is relevant to our attitude. Finally, the *cognition component* refers to the beliefs and thoughts we hold about the object of our attitude. For example, someone's attitude toward Celine Dion may consist of a positive emotion (the affect component), an intention to buy her latest recording (the behaviour component), and the belief that she is a good singer (the cognition component). (See Figure 14-1.)

Every attitude has these three interrelated components, although they vary in terms of which element predominates and in the nature of their relationship. All

▶ **What are attitudes and how are they formed, maintained, and changed?**

▶ **How do we form impressions of what others are like and of the causes of their behaviour?**

▶ **What are the biases that influence the ways in which we view others' behaviour?**

attitudes: Learned predispositions to respond in a favourable or unfavourable manner to a particular person, behaviour, belief, or thing

ABC model of attitudes: The model suggesting that an attitude has three components: affect, behaviour, and cognition

FIGURE 14-1 *Like all attitudes, this attitude on abortion is composed of an affect component, behaviour component, and cognition component.*

Affect
"I like to make my own decisions."
"It angers me when others restrict my rights."

Attitude
"I am in favor of legalized abortion."

Behaviour
"I intend to support legislative means to permit abortions."
"I would consider getting an abortion if necessary."

Cognition
"I believe poor women suffer if they cannot obtain an abortion."
"I believe it is a woman's right to deal with her own body."

Attitudes

attitudes, however, form, are maintained, and change according to general principles that social psychologists have discovered—principles that we discuss next.

Forming and Maintaining Attitudes

Although people do not enter the world holding well-defined attitudes toward any particular person or object, anyone who has seen an infant smile at her parents knows that at least certain attitudes develop quickly. Interestingly, some of the same principles that govern how attitudes are acquired and develop in the youngest of children continue to operate throughout life.

Classical Conditioning and Attitudes

One of the basic processes underlying attitude formation and development can be explained by learning principles (McGuire, 1985; Cacioppo et al., 1992). The same classical conditioning processes that made Pavlov's dogs salivate at the sound of a bell can explain how attitudes are acquired. As we discussed in Chapter 5, people develop associations between various objects and the emotional reactions that accompany them. For example, many soldiers who were stationed in the sandy Persian Gulf during the war with Iraq reported afterwards that they never again wanted to sit on a sandy beach. Put another way, they developed an association between their war experiences and sand, and consequently their attitude about sand turned negative. Similarly, positive associations can develop through classical conditioning. We may come to hold a positive attitude toward a particular perfume because a favourite aunt wears it.

Advertisers make use of the principles of classical conditioning of attitudes by attempting to link a product they want consumers to buy with a positive feeling or event (Alsop, 1988; Kim, Allen, & Kardes, 1996). For instance, many advertisements feature young, attractive, healthy men and women using a product—even if it is one as uninteresting as toothpaste. The idea behind such advertisements is to create a classically conditioned response to the product, so that just glimpsing a tube of Crest toothpaste evokes a positive feeling.

Operant Conditioning Approaches to Attitude Acquisition

Another basic learning process, operant conditioning, also underlies attitude acquisition. Attitudes that are reinforced, either verbally or nonverbally, tend to be maintained. Conversely, a person who states an attitude that elicits ridicule from others

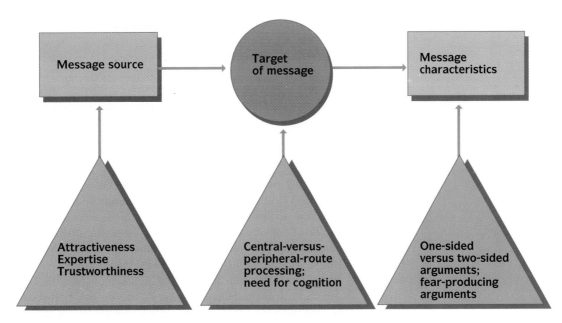

FIGURE 14-2 *In this model of the critical factors affecting persuasion, the message source and message characteristics are shown to influence the recipient or target of a persuasive message.*

may modify or abandon the attitude. But it is not only direct reinforcement or punishment that can influence attitudes. *Vicarious learning,* in which a person learns something through the observation of others, can also account for attitude development—particularly when the person has no direct experience with the object about which the attitude is held. It is through vicarious learning processes that children pick up the prejudices of their parents. For example, even if they have never met a blind person, children whose parents remark that "blind people are incompetent" may adopt such an attitude themselves (Guerin, 1994).

We also learn attitudes vicariously through television, films, and other media. For instance, movies that glorify violence reinforce positive attitudes regarding aggression (as we discuss later in the chapter), and portrayals of women as subservient to men shape and bolster sexist attitudes.

Persuasion: Changing Attitudes

Why did the makers of Reeboks conclude that an endorsement by Shaquille O'Neal would lead people to use more of their product?

According to professionals working in the field of advertising, each of these celebrity endorsements is a carefully selected match between the product and the individual chosen to represent it. It's not just a matter of finding a well-known celebrity; the person must also be believable and trustworthy and reflect the qualities that advertisers want their particular product to project (Misra & Beatty, 1990; Kamins & Gupta, 1994).

The work of advertisers draws heavily upon findings from social psychology regarding persuasion. This research has identified a number of factors (see Figure 14-2) that promote effective persuasion—many of which you will recognize if you consider for a moment some of the advertisements with which you are most familiar (Tesser & Shaffer, 1990; Johnson, 1991).

Message Source

The individual who delivers a persuasive message, known as the attitude communicator, has a major impact on the effectiveness of that message. Communicators who are both physically and socially attractive seem to produce greater attitude change (Chaiken, 1979). Moreover, the expertise and trustworthiness of a communicator are

Sports stars such as Shaquille O'Neal, as well as other celebrities, are used by advertisers to persuade consumers to buy certain brands.

related to the impact of a message—except in situations in which the communicator is believed to have an ulterior motive. If a prestigious communicator seems to be benefitting from persuading others, the message may be discounted (Hovland, Janis, & Kelly, 1953; Eagly, Wood, & Chaiken, 1978). For example, a prestigious scientist who argues that a drug is safe would generally be a particularly influential source, unless it is revealed that the scientist has a financial interest in the drug's manufacturer and stands to benefit financially from its widespread use (Wu & Shaffer, 1987; Roskos & Fazio, 1992; DeBono & Klein, 1993; Priester & Petty, 1995).

Characteristics of the Message

As you might expect, it is not just *who* delivers a message but *what* the message is like that affects attitude and behaviour change. One-sided arguments—in which only the communicator's side is presented—are probably best if the communicator's message is initially viewed favourably by the target of the message. But if the target receives a message presenting an unpopular viewpoint, two-sided messages—which include both the communicator's position and the one he or she is arguing against—are more effective, probably because they are seen as more precise and thoughtful (Karlins & Abelson, 1979). In addition, fear-producing messages ("If you don't practice safer sex, you'll get AIDS") are generally effective, although not always. For instance, if the fear aroused is too strong, messages may evoke people's defense mechanisms and may be ignored. In such cases, fear appeals work best if they include precise recommendations for actions to avoid danger (Leventhal, 1970; Boster & Mongeau, 1985; Sutton, 1992; Perloff, 1993; Rosenthal, 1997).

Characteristics of the Target

Once a message has been communicated, the characteristics of the *target* of the message determine whether the message will be accepted. For example, it seems reasonable to assume that recipients' intelligence would be related to their persuasibility—and it is, although the relationship is complex. Specifically, high intelligence both aids and hinders persuasion. Because higher intelligence enables people to understand a message better and later recall it more easily, persuasion may be more likely. On the other hand, higher intelligence is associated with greater knowledge about a subject and more confidence in one's own opinions, and so messages of opposing viewpoints may be more likely to be rejected.

How do social psychologists reconcile these conflicting predictions? Although the question has yet to be definitively resolved, most research suggests that highly intelligent people are more resistant to persuasion than those who are less intelligent (Rhodes & Wood, 1992; Wood & Stagner, 1994).

Some gender differences in persuasibility also seem to exist. For instance, social psychologist Alice Eagly (1989) has found that women are somewhat more easily persuaded than men, particularly when they have less knowledge of the message topic. However, the magnitude of the differences between men and women is not large.

One factor that clearly underlies whether recipients will be receptive to persuasive messages relates to the type of information processing in which they engage. Social psychologists have discovered two primary information-processing routes to persuasion: central-route and peripheral-route processing (Eagly, 1983; Cialdini, 1984; Petty & Cacioppo, 1986; Petty, 1994). **Central-route processing** occurs when the recipient thoughtfully considers the issues and arguments involved in persuasion. **Peripheral-route processing,** in contrast, occurs when people are persuaded on the basis of factors unrelated to the nature or quality of the content of a persuasive message. Instead, they are influenced by factors that are irrelevant or extraneous to the attitude topic or issue, such as who is providing the message or how long the arguments are (Petty & Cacioppo, 1986; Mackie, 1987; Petty et al., 1994).

In general, central-route processing results in the most lasting attitude change. However, if central-route processing cannot be employed (for instance, if the target is inattentive, bored, or distracted), then the nature of the message becomes less important, and peripheral factors more critical (Petty & Cacioppo, 1984; Heppner et al., 1995).

central-route processing: Message interpretation characterized by thoughtful consideration of the issues and arguments used to persuade
peripheral-route processing: Message interpretation characterized by consideration of the source and related general information rather than of the message itself

Table 14-1	The Need for Cognition

Which of the following statements apply to you?

1. I really enjoy a task that involves coming up with new solutions to problems.
2. I would prefer a task that is intellectual, difficult, and important to one that is somewhat important but does not require much thought.
3. Learning new ways to think doesn't excite me very much.
4. The idea to rely on thought to make my way to the top does not appeal to me.
5. I think only as hard as I have to.
6. I like tasks that require little thought once I've learned them.
7. I prefer to think about small, daily projects rather than long-term ones.
8. I would rather do something that requires little thought than something that is sure to challenge my thinking abilities.
9. I find little satisfaction in deliberating hard and for long hours.
10. I don't like to be responsible for a situation that requires a lot of thinking.

Scoring: The more you agree with statements 1 and 2, and disagree with the rest, the greater the likelihood that you have a high need for cognition. (Source: Adapted from Cacioppo et al., 1996).

The Process of Persuasion

Advertising that uses celebrities to sell a product, then, seeks to produce change through the peripheral route. In fact, it is possible that well-reasoned, carefully crafted messages will be *less* effective when delivered by a celebrity than by an anonymous source—if the target pays greater attention to the celebrity (leading to peripheral-route processing) than to the message (which would have led to central-route processing). On the other hand, since recipients of advertising messages are often in a fairly inattentive state, the use of celebrities is probably an excellent strategy.

Are some people more likely than others to use central-route processing rather than peripheral-route processing? The answer is yes. People who are high in the *need for cognition*, a person's habitual level of thoughtfulness and cognitive activity, are more likely to employ central-route processing. Consider the statements shown in Table 14-1. People who agree with the first two statements, and disagree with the rest, have a relatively high need for cognition (Cacioppo, Berntson, & Crites, 1996).

People who are high in the need for cognition enjoy thinking, philosophizing, and pondering about the world. As a consequence, they tend to reflect more on persuasive messages using central-route processing, and they are likely to be persuaded by complex, logical, and detailed messages. In contrast, those who are low in the need for cognition become impatient when forced to spend too much time thinking about an issue. Consequently, they are more apt to use peripheral-route processing and to be more persuaded by factors other than the quality and detail of messages (Haugtvedt, Petty, & Cacioppo, 1992).

Advertisers also take such basic characteristics as target age, race, ethnicity, religion, income, and marital status into account in their advertisements by using psychographic data. *Psychographics* is a technique for dividing people into lifestyle profiles that are related to purchasing patterns. For instance, Health Canada, in an attempt to reduce tobacco use among young people, needed to know what advertising appeals might be the most successful. A study of 11- to 17-year-olds identified seven different character-type profiles. Interestingly, smoking behaviour was different for each group. Using knowledge from these profiles, advertising was targeted at the highest using group using the image of an adolescent girl morphing into a distorted cigarette (Gilbert & Warren, 1995; Heath, 1996; Mintz et al., 1997).

The Link Between Attitudes and Behaviour

Not surprisingly, attitudes influence behaviour. If you like hamburgers (the affect component), are predisposed to eat at McDonald's or Burger King (the behaviour component), and believe hamburgers are a good source of protein (the cognitive com-

Pathways Through Psychology

James Alcock

Professor of Psychology and Director of the Graduate Program in Psychology at York University, Toronto, Ontario

Education: B.Sc., McGill University; Ph.D., McMaster University

Home: Toronto, Ontario

Most of my research and writing activity has had to do with the psychology of belief. I first became interested in this as a graduate student, when I became puzzled by the explosion of interest in putative psychic phenomena such as extrasensory perception. As I began to study both the extent of such belief and the factors that give rise to it, I became more and more aware that belief in paranormal and supernatural phenomena is often held with great tenacity, even though it may be at odds with other important beliefs of the individual.

My work has consisted of such things as presenting to subjects "impossible" demonstrations, assessing the extent to which their beliefs are affected by experiences that seem to defy common sense, and trying to understand how it is that "irrational" beliefs become part of their larger belief system. For example, in one study, subjects were asked if one could increase the area of a piece of paper by cutting it up and rearranging the order of the pieces. Subjects who were certain that this was impossible were then shown a demonstration in which such an event actually seemed to occur. Half of the subjects switched their belief from being certain that this could not happen to being certain that it could. The other half maintained their earlier belief despite the evidence of their eyes. I became interested in

James Alcock

how and why some individuals stick with "theory" and ignore the "data," while others go with the data, and forget the theory.

In later years, I became more involved internationally. I was part of a group that was invited to China to give lectures, and to examine possible instances of psychic phenomena. Under test conditions these claims were not substantiated. I was asked by the National Research Council in the United States to prepare a comprehensive review of all research involving so-called human operator influence over the output of random number generators, in light of claims made by some scientists that they had demonstrated that thought could influence such devices. I found that there was no evidence for such a phenomenon and that the various research studies backing such claims suffered from serious methodological flaws.

Over the years, my interest in psychology has been sustained through work with both students and colleagues and by my research and writing. Bill Carment, Stan Sadava and I continue with our collaboration on *A Textbook of Social Psychology*. In 1981, *Parapsychology: Science or Magic?* was published. In it, I set out to show how ordinary psychological processes can't account for the many weird and seemingly paranormal experiences that people report. This marked a highlight of my continued interest in the paranormal research. As did the invitation to publish a target article, outlining my criticisms of parapsychological research, in *Behavioural and Brain Sciences*. The article was accompanied by the responses to my arguments by a large group of scholars from around the world.

These things are important to me, both professionally and personally, because I believe that as psychologists, we need to study the experiences that are important to people, and supposed psychic experiences typically are seen as very important. It is not enough simply to reject the psychic interpretation out of hand. We need to understand the nature of the experience, even if, as I personally believe, these experiences do not actually involve anything paranormal or supernatural, because they are so important to people. By understanding them we widen our knowledge of the human psyche, and the propensity in some circumstances to believe things that run quite counter to our logic.

Source: James Alcock, Ph.D., York University
<jalcock@glendon.yorku.ca>

ponent), it is very likely that you will eat hamburgers frequently. The strength of the link between particular attitudes and behaviour varies, of course, but generally people strive for consistency between their attitudes and their behaviour (Kraus, 1995). Furthermore, our beliefs can be very powerful (See Pathways Through Psychology).

Interestingly, the consistency that leads attitudes to influence behaviour sometimes works the other way around, for in some cases it is our behaviour that shapes our attitudes. Consider, for instance, the following incident:

You've just spent what you feel is the most boring hour of your life, turning pegs for a psychology experiment. Just as you're finally finished and about to leave, the experimenter asks you to do him a favour. He tells you that he needs a helper for future experimental sessions to introduce subsequent participants to the peg-turning task. Your specific job would be to tell them that turning the pegs is an interesting, fascinating experience. Each time you tell this tale to another participant, you'll be paid $1.

If you agree to help out the experimenter, you may be setting yourself up for a state of psychological tension that is known as cognitive dissonance. According to a major social psychologist, Leon Festinger (1957), **cognitive dissonance** occurs when a person holds two attitudes or thoughts (referred to as *cognitions*) that contradict each other.

cognitive dissonance: The conflict that occurs when a person holds two attitudes or thoughts (referred to as *cognitions*) that contradict each other

A participant in the situation just described is left with two contradictory thoughts: (1) I believe the task is boring; but (2) I said it was interesting with little justification ($1). According to the theory, dissonance should be aroused. But how can such dissonance be reduced? One can't very well deny having said that the task was interesting without making a fairly strong break with reality. But, relatively speaking, it is easy to change one's attitude toward the task—and thus the theory predicts that participants will reduce dissonance by adopting more positive attitudes toward the task (Johnson, Kelly, & LeBlanc, 1995).

This prediction was confirmed in a classic experiment (Festinger & Carlsmith, 1959). The experiment followed essentially the same procedure outlined earlier, in which a participant was offered $1 to describe a boring task as interesting. In addition, as a control, a condition was included in which participants were offered $20 to say that the task was interesting. The reasoning behind this condition was that $20 was so much money that participants in this condition had a good reason to be conveying incorrect information; dissonance would *not* be aroused, and *less* attitude change would be expected. The results supported this notion. Participants who were paid $1 changed their attitudes more (becoming more positive toward the peg-turning task) than participants who were paid $20.

We now know that dissonance explains a number of everyday occurrences involving attitudes and behaviour. For example, a smoker who knows that smoking leads to lung cancer holds contradictory cognitions: (1) I smoke; and (2) smoking leads to lung cancer. The theory predicts that these two thoughts will lead to a state of cognitive dissonance. More important, it predicts that the individual will be motivated to reduce such dissonance by one of the following methods: (1) modifying one or both of the cognitions; (2) changing the perceived importance of one cognition; (3) adding cognitions; or (4) denying that the two cognitions are related to each other. Hence the smoker might decide that he really doesn't smoke all that much (modifying the cognition), that the evidence linking smoking to cancer is weak (changing the importance of a cognition), that the amount of exercise he gets compensates for the smoking (adding cognitions), or that there is no evidence linking smoking and cancer (denial). Whatever technique is used, the result is a reduction in dissonance (see Figure 14-3).

Social Cognition: Understanding Others

We all know people, whether they are public figures or personal friends, with whom we disagree. People who do things we may disapprove of. However, rather than feel negatively towards this person we may genuinely like them, ignoring the behaviour.

Situations such as this illustrate the power of our impressions and attest to the importance of determining how people develop an understanding of others. One of the dominant areas of study in social psychology during the last few years has focused on learning how we come to understand what others are like and how we explain the reasons underlying others' behaviour (Fiske & Taylor, 1991; Devine, Hamilton, & Ostrom, 1994; Augoustinos & Walker, 1995).

FIGURE 14-3 *The presence of two contradictory cognitions ("I smoke" and "Smoking leads to cancer") produces dissonance, which may be reduced through several methods.*

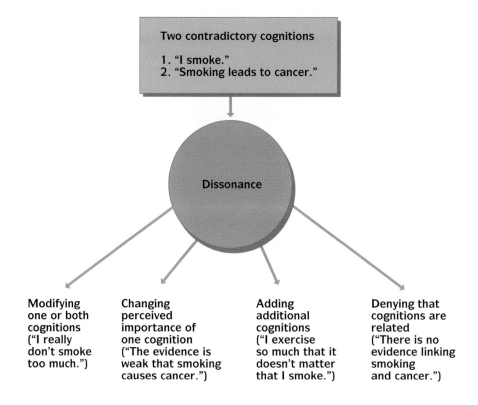

Two contradictory cognitions

1. "I smoke."
2. "Smoking leads to cancer."

Dissonance

Modifying one or both cognitions ("I really don't smoke too much.")

Changing perceived importance of one cognition ("The evidence is weak that smoking causes cancer.")

Adding additional cognitions ("I exercise so much that it doesn't matter that I smoke.")

Denying that cognitions are related ("There is no evidence linking smoking and cancer.")

social cognition: The processes that underlie our understanding of the social world

schemas: Sets of cognitions about people and social experiences

Understanding What Others Are Like

Consider for a moment the enormous amount of information about other people to which we are exposed. How are we able to decide what is important and what is not, and to make judgments about the characteristics of others? Social psychologists interested in this question study **social cognition**—the processes that underlie our understanding of the social world. They have learned that individuals have highly developed **schemas,** sets of cognitions about people and social experiences. These schemas organize information stored in memory, represent in our minds the way the social world operates, and give us a framework to categorize, store, remember, and interpret information relating to social stimuli (Fiske & Taylor, 1991; Cowan, 1992; Fiske, 1992).

We typically hold schemas for particular types of people in our environments. Our schema for "teacher," for instance, generally consists of a number of characteristics: knowledge of the subject matter he or she is teaching, a desire to impart that knowledge, and an awareness of the student's need to understand what is being said. Or we may hold a schema for "mother" that includes the characteristics of warmth, nurturance, and caring. Regardless of their accuracy—and, as we shall see, very often their inaccuracy—schemas are important because they organize the way in which we recall, recognize, and categorize information about others. Moreover, they allow us to make predictions of what others are like on the basis of relatively little information, since we tend to fit people into schemas even when there is not much concrete evidence to go on (Snyder & Cantor, 1979; Smith, 1984; Baldwin, 1995; Bargh et al., 1995).

Impression Formation

How do we decide that Gail is a flirt, or Andy is a jerk, or Jon is a really nice guy? The earliest work on social cognition was designed to examine *impression formation,* the process by which an individual organizes information about another person to form an overall impression of that person. In one classic study, for instance, students were told that they were about to hear a guest lecturer (Kelley, 1950). One group of students was told that the lecturer was "a rather warm person, industrious, critical, practical, and determined," while a second group was told that he was "a rather cold person, industrious, critical, practical, and determined."

The simple substitution of "cold" for "warm" was responsible for drastic differences in the way the students in each group perceived the lecturer, even though he gave the same talk in the same style in each condition. Students who had been told he was "warm" rated him considerably more positively than students who had been told he was "cold."

The findings from this experiment led to additional research on impression formation that focused on the way in which people pay particular attention to certain unusually important traits—known as **central traits**—to help them form an overall impression of others. According to this work, the presence of a central trait alters the meaning of other traits (Asch, 1946; Widmeyer & Loy, 1988). Hence the description of the lecturer as "industrious" presumably meant something different according to whether it was associated with the central trait "warm" or "cold."

central traits: The major traits considered in forming impressions of others

Other work on impression formation has used information-processing approaches (see Chapter 6) to develop mathematically oriented models of how individual personality traits are combined to create an overall impression (Anderson, 1974, 1996). Generally, the results of this research suggest that in forming an overall judgment of a person, we use a psychological "average" of the individual traits we see, in a manner that is analogous to finding the mathematical average of several numbers (Kaplan, 1975; Anderson, 1991).

Of course, as we gain more experience with people and see them exhibiting behaviour in a variety of situations, our impressions of them become more complex (Anderson & Klatzky, 1987; Casselden & Hampson, 1990; Sherman & Klein, 1994) they may also become more accurate (Paulhus & Bruce, 1992). However, because there usually are gaps in our knowledge of others, we still tend to fit them into personality schemas that represent particular "types" of people. For instance, we might hold a "gregarious person" schema, made up of the traits of friendliness, aggressiveness, and openness. The presence of just one or two of these traits might be sufficient to make us assign a person to a particular schema.

Unfortunately, the schemas that we employ are susceptible to a variety of factors that affect the accuracy of our judgments. For example, our mood affects how we perceive others. People who are happy form more favourable impressions and make more positive judgments than people who are in a bad mood (Erber, 1991; Kenny, 1991, 1994; Abele & Petzold, 1994; Bernieri et al., 1994).

Even when schemas are not entirely accurate, they serve an important function. They allow us to develop expectations about how others will behave, permitting us to plan our interactions with others more easily, and serving to simplify a complex social world.

Attribution Processes: Understanding the Causes of Behaviour

When Barbara Washington, a new employee at the Ablex Computer Company, completed a major staffing project two weeks early, her boss, Yolanda, was delighted. At the next staff meeting, she announced how pleased she was with Barbara and explained that *this* was an example of the kind of performance she was looking for in her staff. The other staff members looked on resentfully, trying to figure out why Barbara had worked night and day to finish the project not just on time, but two weeks early. She must be an awfully compulsive person, they decided.

Most of us have, at one time or another, puzzled over the reasons behind someone's behaviour. Perhaps it was in a situation similar to the one above, or it may have been under more formal circumstances, such as serving as a judge on a student judiciary board in a cheating case. In contrast to work on social cognition, which describes how people develop an overall impression about others' personality traits, **attribution theory** seeks to explain how we decide, on the basis of samples of an individual's behaviour, what the specific causes of that person's behaviour are (Weiner, 1985a, 1985b; Jones, 1990; White, 1992).

attribution theory: The theory of personality that seeks to explain how we decide, on the basis of samples of an individual's behaviour, what the specific causes of that person's behaviour are

FIGURE 14-4 *The general process we use to determine the causes of behaviour and other social occurrences proceeds in several steps. Source: Adapted from Krull & Anderson, 1997.*

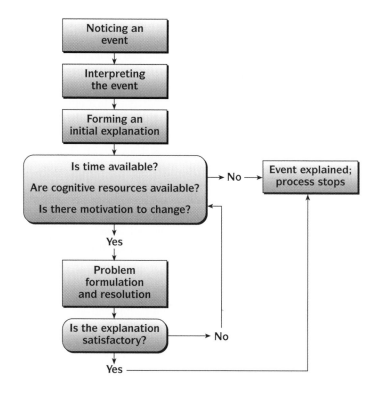

The general process we use to determine the causes of behaviour and other social occurrences proceeds in several steps, as illustrated in Figure 14-4. After first noticing that a behavioural event has occurred, we must interpret the meaning of the event. This leads to the formulation of an initial explanation. Depending on the time available, the cognitive resources on hand (such as the attention that can be given to the matter), and the motivation of the perceiver (determined in part by how important the event is), we may then choose to accept our initial explanation or seek to modify it. If we have the time, cognitive resources, and motivation, then the event becomes the trigger for deliberate problem solving as we seek a fuller explanation. During the problem formulation and resolution stage, we may try out several possibilities before determining that a solution has been reached (Krull & Anderson, 1997).

In seeking an explanation for behaviour, one central question we must answer is whether the cause is situational or dispositional (Heider, 1958). **Situational causes** are those brought about by something in the environment. For instance, someone who knocks over a quart of milk and then cleans it up is probably doing so not because he or she is necessarily a terribly neat person, but because the *situation* is one that requires it. In contrast, a person who spends hours shining the kitchen floor is probably doing so because he or she *is* a neat person—hence, the behaviour has a **dispositional cause,** prompted by the person's disposition (his or her internal traits or personality characteristics).

In our example involving Barbara, her fellow employees attributed her behaviour to her disposition rather than to the situation. But from a logical standpoint, it is equally plausible that there was something about the situation that caused the behaviour. If asked, Barbara might attribute her accomplishment to situational factors, explaining that she had so much other work to do that she just had to get the project out of the way, or that the project was not all that difficult and so it was easy to complete ahead of schedule. To her, then, the reason for her behaviour might not be dispositional at all; it could be situational.

situational causes (of behaviour): A cause of behaviour that is based on environmental factors

dispositional causes (of behaviour): A cause of behaviour that is based on internal traits or personality factors

Biases in Attribution: To Err Is Human

If we always processed information in the rational manner that attribution theory suggests, the world might run a lot more smoothly. Unfortunately, although attribution theory generally makes accurate predictions, people do not always process information about others in as logical a fashion as the theory seems to suggest (Gilbert, Jones, & Pelham, 1987; Piattelli-Palmarini, 1994; Heath et al., 1994). In fact, research reveals consistent biases in the ways people make attributions. Among the most typical:

- *The fundamental attribution error.* One of the most common biases in people's attributions is the tendency to over-attribute others' behaviour to dispositional causes, and the corresponding failure to recognize the importance of situational causes. Known as the **fundamental attribution error,** this tendency is quite prevalent (Ross, 1977; Ross & Nisbett, 1991). We tend to exaggerate the importance of personality characteristics (dispositional causes) in producing others' behaviour, minimizing the influence of the environment (situational factors).

  fundamental attribution error: A tendency to attribute others' behaviour to dispositional causes and the tendency to minimize the importance of situational causes

  Why should the fundamental attribution error be so common? One reason pertains to the nature of information that is available to the people making an attribution. When we view the behaviour of another person in a particular setting, the information that is most conspicuous is the person's behaviour itself. Because the individual's immediate surroundings are relatively unchanging, the person whose behaviour we're considering is the centre of our attention. In contrast, the person's environment is less attention-grabbing. Consequently, we are more likely to make attributions based on personal, dispositional factors and less likely to make attributions relating to the situation (Gilbert & Malone, 1995).

- *The halo effect.* Harry is intelligent, kind, and loving. Is he also conscientious? If you were to hazard a guess, your most likely response would be "yes." Your guess reflects the **halo effect,** a phenomenon in which an initial understanding that a person has positive traits is used to infer other uniformly positive characteristics (Petzold, 1992). The opposite would also hold true. Learning that Harry was unsociable and argumentative would probably lead you to assume he was lazy as well.

  halo effect: A phenomenon in which an initial understanding that a person has positive traits is used to infer other uniformly positive characteristics

  The reason for the halo effect is that we hold *implicit personality theories,* theories reflecting our notions of a combination of traits found in particular individuals. These theories are based on both experience and logic. Our perception of the world may be flawed, however, because application of our theory can be singularly inappropriate for a given individual, or it may simply be wrong. Most people have neither uniformly positive nor uniformly negative traits, but instead possess a combination of the two.

- *Assumed-similarity bias.* How similar to you—in terms of attitudes, opinions, and likes and dislikes—are your friends and acquaintances? Most people believe that their friends and acquaintances are fairly similar to themselves. But this feeling goes beyond just people we know; there is a general tendency—known as the **assumed-similarity bias**—to think of people as being similar to oneself, even when meeting them for the first time (Ross, Greene, & House, 1977; Hoch, 1987; Marks & Miller, 1987).

  assumed-similarity bias: The tendency to think of people as being similar to oneself, even when meeting them for the first time

  If other people are, in fact, different from oneself, the assumed-similarity bias reduces the accuracy of the judgments being made. Moreover, it suggests an interesting possibility: It may be that a judgment about another individual better defines the judge's characteristics than those of the person being rated. In some cases, then, the portrait we draw of another person—particularly one about whom we have little information—may in reality be a sketch of the way we view ourselves.

Exploring Diversity

Ethnicity in the Twenty-First Century

"Ethnicity is likely to be to the twenty-first century what class was to the twentieth—a major source of social tensions and political conflicts; hence it will be a major focus of attention for an academia that will be asked to provide facts, explanations, and theories" (Berry and Laponce, 1994, p. 3). Berry and Laponce also point out that it will be a source of creative energy.

This is very evident in Canada. Since 1971, Canada has had an official multicultural policy. In 1982 multiculturalism and equality rights became a part of the Canadian constitution under the Charter of Rights and Freedoms.

Multiculturalism is a strategy to manage cultural diversity. The multicultural hypothesis suggests that when individuals maintain their unique ethnic identity they feel more secure. This security then translates into positive feelings about other ethnic groups, allowing for peaceful and productive co-existence and fair treatment for all.

Canadian social psychologists have become world leaders in research into bilingualism, multiculturalism, immigrant acculturation, ethnic identity, prejudice, stereotypes and discrimination (Alcock, Carment, and Sadava, 2000). To social psychologists falls the role of analysis and research, often commissioned and funded by the government which may translate into public policy (Tepper,1994). Applied social psychology therefore extends knowledge in order "...to understand and, perhaps solve contemporary social problems." (Sadava,1997, p. 8).

One area where social-psychological research is influential is in the study of attitudes. According to Kalin and Berry (1994), for multicultural policies to be successful they must have the support of individuals in the society. Personal attitudes are a key element to understanding others and potentially avoiding conflict. Although a match between policy and public views will contribute to success of that policy, official policy may also be designed to encourage attitude change. Research projects are often designed to monitor such change (Berry, 1999).

In a test of the multicultural hypothesis, Kalin and Berry, (1994) found that those who scored as insecure on measures of cultural and economic security were less favourable in their attitudes towards other ethnic groups. Those who scored higher on security were more tolerant of others.   ■

Recap, Review, and Rethink

Recap

- Attitudes are learned predispositions to respond in a favorable or unfavorable manner to a particular object. They have three components: affect, behaviour, and cognition.

- The major factors promoting persuasion relate to the message source, characteristics of the message, and characteristics of the recipient or target.

- People strive to fit their attitudes and behaviour together in a logical framework, and they attempt to overcome any inconsistencies that they perceive.

- Social cognition is concerned with the processes that underlie our understanding of the social world.

- Attribution theory explains the processes that underlie how we attribute the causes of others' behaviour, particularly in terms of situational versus dispositional causes.

Review

1. A learned predisposition to respond in a favourable or an unfavourable manner to a particular object is called a(n) _____.

2. Match each component of the ABC model of attitudes with its definition.
   1. affect
   2. behaviour
   3. cognition

   a. thoughts and beliefs
   b. positive or negative emotions
   c. predisposition to act in a particular way

3. One brand of peanut butter advertises its product by describing its taste and nutritional value. It is hoping to persuade customers through _____-route processing. In ads for a competing brand, a popular actor happily eats the product—but does not describe it. This approach hopes to persuade customers through _____-route processing.

4. Cognitive dissonance theory suggests that we commonly change our behaviour to keep it consistent with our attitudes. True or false?

5. A _____ provides a mental framework for us to organize and interpret information about the social world.

6. Monica was happy to lend her textbook to a fellow student who seemed bright and friendly. She was surprised when her classmate did not return it. Her assumption that the bright and friendly student would also be responsible reflects the _____ effect.

Answers to Review Questions are on page 526.

Rethink

1. Suppose you were assigned to develop a full advertising campaign for a product, including television, radio, and print ads. How might the theories in this chapter guide your strategy to suit the different media?

2. How do the props used in television commercials contribute to peripheral- or central-route processing?

3. Joan sees Annette, a new coworker, act in a way that seems abrupt and curt. Joan concludes that Annette is unkind and unsociable. The next day Joan sees Annette acting kindly to another worker. Is Joan likely to change her impression of Annette? Why or why not? Finally, Joan sees several friends of hers laughing and joking with Annette, treating her in a very friendly fashion. Is Joan likely to change her impression of Annette? Why or why not?

SOCIAL INFLUENCE

You have just transferred to a new college and are attending your first class. When the professor enters, your fellow classmates instantly rise, bow to the professor, and then stand quietly, with their hands behind their backs. You've never encountered such behaviour, and it makes no sense to you. Is it more likely that you will (1) jump up to join the rest of the class or (2) remain seated?

Based on what research has told us about **social influence,** the process by which the actions of an individual or group affect the behaviour of others, the answer to the question would almost always be the first option. As you undoubtedly know from your own experience, pressures to conform can be painfully strong, and they can bring about changes in behavior that, when considered in perspective, otherwise never would have occurred.

Conformity: Following What Others Do

Conformity is a change in behaviour or attitudes brought about by a desire to follow the beliefs or standards of other people. The classic demonstration of pressure to conform comes from a series of studies carried out in the 1950s by Solomon Asch (Asch, 1951). In the experiments, participants thought they were participating in a test of perceptual skills with a group of six other participants. The participants were shown one card with three lines of varying length and a second card that had a fourth line that matched one of the first three (see Figure 14-5). The task was seemingly straightforward: The participants had to announce aloud which of the first three lines was identical in length to a "standard" line. Because the correct answer was always obvious, the task seemed easy to the participants.

Indeed, since the participants all agreed on the first few trials, the procedure appeared to be quite simple. But then something odd began to happen. From the perspective of the participant in the group who got to answer last, all of the first six participants' answers seemed to be wrong—in fact, unanimously wrong. And this pattern persisted. Over and over again, the first six participants provided answers that contradicted what the last participant believed to be correct. The dilemma that this situation posed for the last participant was whether to follow his or her own perceptions or to follow the group and repeat the answer that everyone else was giving.

As you might have guessed, the situation in the experiment was more contrived than it first appeared. The first six participants were actually confederates of the experimenter and had been instructed to give unanimously erroneous answers in many of the trials. And the study had nothing to do with perceptual skills. Instead, the issue under investigation was conformity.

▶ **What are the major sources and tactics of social influence?**

social influence: The process by which the actions of an individual or group affect the behaviour of others

conformity: A change in behaviour or attitudes brought about by a desire to follow the beliefs or standards of other people

Standard line

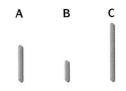

Comparison lines

FIGURE 14-5 *Subjects in Asch's conformity experiment were first shown a "standard" line and then asked to identify which of the three comparison lines was identical in length. As this example illustrates, there was always a correct answer.*

What Asch found was that in about one-third of the trials, participants conformed to the unanimous but erroneous group answer, with about 75 percent of all participants conforming at least once. However, there were strong individual differences. Some participants conformed nearly all the time, whereas others never did so.

Since Asch's pioneering work, literally hundreds of studies have examined the factors affecting conformity, and we now know a great deal about the phenomenon (Tanford & Penrod, 1984; Moscovici, 1985; Wood et al., 1994). Among the most important variables producing conformity are the following:

- *The characteristics of the group.* The more attractive a group is to its members, the greater its ability to produce conformity (Hogg & Hardie, 1992). Furthermore, a person's relative **status,** the social rank held within a group, is critical: The lower a person's status in the group, the greater the power of the group over that person's behaviour.

status: The social rank held within a group

- *The nature of the individual's response.* Conformity is considerably higher when people must make a response publicly than when they can respond privately, as our founding fathers noted when they authorized secret ballots in voting.

- *The kind of task.* People working on tasks and questions that are ambiguous (having no clear answer) are more susceptible to social pressure. Asked to give an opinion, such as on what type of clothing is fashionable, a person is more likely to yield to conformist pressures than if asked a question of fact. Moreover, tasks at which an individual is less competent relative to the group create conditions in which conformity is more likely.

- *Unanimity of the group.* Conformity pressures are most pronounced in groups that are unanimous in their support of a position. But what of the case in which people with dissenting views have an ally in the group, known as a **social supporter,** who agrees with them? Having just one person present who shares the unpopular point of view is sufficient to reduce conformity pressures (Allen, 1975; Levine, 1989).

social supporter: A person who shares an unpopular opinion or attitude of another group member, thereby encouraging nonconformity

Groupthink: Caving in to Conformity

Although we usually think of conformity in terms of interpersonal effects, in some instances conformity pressures can lead to disastrous effects with long-term consequences. For instance, consider NASA's decision to launch the space shuttle *Challenger* on the morning after a night of subfreezing temperatures. Despite a recommendation from engineers involved in the manufacture of the shuttle that extreme temperatures could make a set of rubber seals so brittle that they could deteriorate, leading to potential disaster, a consensus formed to proceed with the launch. In fact, NASA officials were so eager to get the shuttle off the ground that they ordered the engineers to rethink their recommendation. Ultimately, the individual who made the final decision was not even informed of the engineers' concerns; subordinate members of the launch team sought to "protect" him from dissenting information. We now know that the engineers were correct: The rubber seals did fail, leading to the disastrous rocket explosion that killed all seven astronauts on board.

With the clarity of hindsight, it is clear that NASA's decision was wrong. How could such a poor decision have been made?

A phenomenon known as groupthink provides an explanation. *Groupthink* is a type of thinking in which group members share such a strong motivation to achieve consensus that they lose the ability to critically evaluate alternative points of view. Groupthink is most likely to occur when there is a popular or powerful leader who is

---

Answers to Review Questions:

1. attitude   2. 1-b; 2-c; 3-a   3. central; peripheral   4. False; we typically change our attitudes, not our behaviour, to reduce cognitive dissonance.   5. schema   6. halo

surrounded by people of lower status—obviously the case with any U.S. president and his advisors, but also true in a variety of other organizations (Janis, 1972, 1989; t'Hart, 1990; Manz & Sims, 1992; Neck & Moorhead, 1995).

The phenomenon of groupthink is apt to occur in several types of situations (McCauley, 1989):

- There is an illusion that the group is invulnerable and cannot make major errors in judgment.

- Information that is contradictory to the dominant group view tends to be ignored, discounted, or minimized.

- Pressures are placed on group members to conform to the majority view— although the pressures may be relatively subtle.

- The pressure to conform discourages minority viewpoints from being brought before the group. Consequently, there *appears* to be unanimity in the group, even if this is not really the case.

- There is an illusion of morality. Because the group views itself as representing something just and moral, members assume that any judgment that the group reaches will be just and moral as well.

The consequences of groupthink are numerous, and nearly always negative. Groups tend to limit their list of possible solutions to just a few, and they spend relatively little time considering any alternatives once the leader seems to be leaning toward a particular solution. In fact, they may completely ignore information that challenges a developing consensus. Because research shows that more than a few historical episodes reflect the workings of groupthink, it is important for members of any group to be on guard (Tetlock et al., 1992, 1993; Cline, 1994; Schafer & Crichlow, 1996).

Groupthink is not the only impediment to successfully solving problems. Other situations involving groups may also lead to poor decision making—with sometimes deadly results, as we discuss in the Applying Psychology in the 21st Century box.

Compliance: Submitting to Direct Social Pressure

When we discuss conformity, we are usually talking about a phenomenon in which the social pressure is subtle or indirect. But in some situations social pressure is much more obvious, and there is direct, explicit pressure to endorse a particular point of view or to behave in a certain way. Social psychologists call the type of behaviour that occurs in response to direct social pressure **compliance.**

Several specific sales tactics represent attempts to gain compliance. Among the most frequently employed are the following:

- *The foot-in-the-door technique.* A salesperson comes to your door and asks you to accept a small sample. You agree, thinking you have nothing to lose. A little later comes a larger request, which, because you have already agreed to the first one, you have a harder time turning down.

  The salesperson in this case is employing a tried-and-true strategy that social psychologists call the foot-in-the-door technique. According to the *foot-in-the-door technique,* you first ask a person to agree to a small request and later to comply with a more important one. It turns out that compliance with the ultimate request increases significantly when the person first agrees to the smaller favour.

  The foot-in-the-door phenomenon was first demonstrated in a study in which a number of experimenters went door-to-door asking residents to sign a petition in favour of safe driving (Freedman & Fraser, 1966). Almost everyone complied with this small, benign request. However, a few weeks later, different experimenters contacted the residents again and made a much larger request: that the residents erect a huge sign reading "Drive Carefully" on their front

Social Influence

compliance: Behaviour that occurs in response to direct social pressure

Applying Psychology in the 21st Century

Producing Good Decisions in the Air: Helping People to Work Together More Effectively

As the DC-8, carrying 189 people, began its initial descent into the Portland, Oregon, airport, the pilot noticed that a signal light had failed to go on. The absence of the light suggested that some of the wheels of the plane might collapse when the plane landed, leading to a fire or damage to the body of the plane.

Rather than continuing with the approach, the pilot began to circle the airport, while seeking to determine the nature of the problem. However, as time went by, the fuel began to dwindle. Even though the flight engineer repeatedly warned about the decreasing

fuel problem, the pilot focused on the landing gear problem. Eventually, the plane ran so low on fuel that the pilot could not reach the runway, and the plane plunged into a wooded area near the airport. Ten people were killed (Helmreich, 1997).

The disaster could have been avoided—if the members of the crew had worked together more effectively. Instead, the pilot virtually ignored the flight engineer, and the engineer, outranked by the pilot, raised the problem so tentatively that he was unable to capture the pilot's attention.

This is hardly the only incident in which pilot miscalculations have led to fatal accidents. In fact, more than two-thirds of accidents involve at least a certain degree of human error. Furthermore, most of these errors are the result of poor cockpit decisions stemming from a lack of teamwork, communication errors, and failures of human interaction. In short, aviation accidents are often the result of the failure of cockpit personnel to work effectively in groups.

In an effort to raise the level of cockpit group performance, social psychologist

Social psychologists studying group processes among aircraft crew members have sought to increase air safety.

lawns. The results were clear: 55 percent of those who had signed the petition agreed to the request, whereas only 17 percent of people in a control group who had not been asked to sign the petition agreed.

Subsequent research has confirmed the effectiveness of the foot-in-the-door technique (Beaman et al., 1983; Dillard, 1991; Bell et al., 1994; Dolin & Booth-Butterfield, 1995; Gorassini & Olson, 1995). Why does it work? One reason is that involvement with the small request leads to an interest in an issue, and taking an action—any action—makes the individual more committed to the issue, thereby increasing the likelihood of future compliance. Another explanation revolves around people's self-perceptions. By complying with the initial request, individuals may come to see themselves as the kind of person who provides help when asked. Then, when confronted with the larger request, they agree in order to maintain the kind of consistency in attitudes and behaviour that we described earlier. Although we don't know which of these

Robert Helmreich and colleagues at the University of Texas in Austin are developing a new instructional approach known as crew resource management, or CRM (Helmreich & Foushee, 1993; Helmreich, Wiener, & Kanki, 1993). A major goal is to reduce cockpit errors by teaching flight crews to collaborate more closely. During training seminars, crews are presented with actual case studies that illustrate important principles. For example, the case of an Air Florida jetliner that crashed into the Potomac River in Washington, D.C., in January 1982 is used to illustrate the effects of faulty communications. Consider, for instance, the following excerpt from that flight's voice recorder, in which the first officer seems to understand that there is a problem with the plane's speed, but is unable to articulate his worries effectively to the captain:

First officer:	Ah, that's not right.
Captain:	Yes, it is, there's 80 [referring to ground speed].
First officer:	Nah, I don't think it's right. Ah, maybe it is.
Captain:	Hundred and twenty.
First officer:	I don't know.

If the first officer had been more forceful, the crash might well have been avoided.

Other techniques for strengthening flight crew communications involve the use of flight simulators, which replicate the cockpit of a jet. An instructor who has received special training in group behaviour accompanies a crew on a simulated flight, starting with pre-takeoff preparations and ending with the landing. Various problems and full-scale catastrophes are programmed into the computer, and the crew's mission is to practice communicating as effectively as possible. During "post-flight" debriefings, the crew reviews video tapes of its performance, and the instructor suggests ways that communication can be improved.

CRM is also helpful in improving the interface between crew members and in-flight computers. Despite, or perhaps because of, their sophistication, computers used in modern aircraft bring about their own set of safety issues. For example, when crew members alter flight coordinates and other pieces of information by entering data directly into the computer, other crew members may not observe what they have done and may be unaware of the change. In contrast, changes made by a crew member in older airplanes were usually very obvious, and instrument displays reflected the changes in a way that was evident to the entire flight crew. Unless pilots state their computer entries out loud, an important means of verification is lost. Similarly, the need to make computer entries can be distracting in and of itself, because pilots must turn their eyes from the outside of the plane or the instrument panel and instead look at the computer entry pad.

Finally, the norms that pilots follow also affect safety. For instance, traditional pilot norms emphasize a kind of rugged individualism in which the pilot has enormous authority and power. Such norms may make pilots unwilling to admit they are fatigued or susceptible to stress. Furthermore, there are cultural factors that have an impact on safety issues. For example, surveys show that only one-third of pilots from one Asian country thought that other (subordinate) crew members should voice their safety concerns on a flight, while almost all pilots in the United States felt that concerns should be expressed (Johnston, 1993; Merritt & Helmreich, 1996).

Ultimately, Helmreich argues that the ideal cockpit crew would have several characteristics:

- Adopt a strong orientation to teamwork.
- Use a leadership style that encourages divergent points of view.
- Support norms that encourage subordinate crew members to suggest alternate courses of action.
- Adher to standard safety practices, but not so rigidly that they do not make exceptions to the rules.

These techniques are not only effective for airplane cockpits, but for any situation in which highly trained people of different status work together using complex technologies. For instance, the same general principles suggested by CRM are effective in reducing error in hospital operating rooms (Helmreich & Schaefer, 1994; Belkin, 1997).

two explanations is more accurate, it is clear that the foot-in-the-door strategy is effective (Dillard, 1991; Gorassini & Olson, 1995).

- *The door-in-the-face technique.* A fund-raiser comes to your door and asks for a $500 contribution. You laughingly refuse, telling her that the amount is way out of your league. She then asks for a $10 contribution. What do you do? If you are like most people, you'll probably be a lot more compliant than if she hadn't asked for the huge contribution first. The reason lies in the *door-in-the-face technique,* in which a large request, refusal of which is expected, is followed by a smaller one. This strategy, which is the opposite of the foot-in-the-door approach, has also proved to be effective (Dillard, 1991; Reeves et al., 1991; Abrahams & Bell, 1994).

One example of its success was shown in a field experiment in which college students were stopped on the street and asked to agree to a substantial favour—acting as unpaid counsellors for juvenile offenders two hours a week for two years (Cialdini et al., 1975). Not surprisingly, no one agreed to make such an enormous commitment. But when they were later asked the considerably smaller favour of taking a group of the juveniles on a two-hour trip to the zoo, half the people complied. In comparison, only 17 percent of a control group of participants who had not first received the larger request agreed.

The use of this technique is widespread in everyday life. You may have used it at some point yourself, perhaps by asking your parents for a very large increase in your allowance and later settling for less. Similarly, television writers sometimes sprinkle their scripts with obscenities that they know will be cut out by network censors, hoping to keep other key phrases intact (Cialdini, 1988).

• *The that's-not-all technique.* In the *that's-not-all technique,* you're offered a deal at an inflated price. But immediately following the initial offer, the salesperson offers an incentive, discount, or bonus to clinch the deal.

Although it sounds transparent, such a practice can be quite effective. In one study, the experimenters set up a booth and sold cupcakes for 75 cents each. In one condition, customers were told directly that the price was 75 cents. But in another condition, they were told the price was $1, but had been reduced to 75 cents. As the that's-not-all technique would predict, more cupcakes were sold at the "reduced" price—even though it was identical to the price in the other experimental condition (Burger, 1986).

• *The not-so-free sample.* If you're ever given a free sample, keep in mind that it comes with a psychological cost. Although they may not couch it in these terms, salespeople who provide samples to potential customers do so in order to instigate the norm of reciprocity. The *norm of reciprocity* is the well-accepted societal standard dictating that we should treat other people as they treat us. Receipt of a *not-so-free sample,* then, suggests the need for reciprocation—in the form of a purchase, of course (Cialdini, 1988).

Obedience: Obeying Direct Orders

obedience: A change in behaviour due to the commands of others

Compliance techniques provide a means by which people are gently led toward agreement with another person's request. In some cases, however, requests are geared toward producing **obedience,** a change in behaviour due to the commands of others. Although obedience is considerably less common than conformity and compliance, it does occur in several specific kinds of relationships. For example, we may show obedience to our boss, teacher, or parent, merely because of the power they hold to reward or punish us.

To acquire an understanding of obedience, consider, for a moment, how you might respond if a stranger said to you:

I've devised a new way of improving memory. All I need is for you to teach people a list of words and then give them a test. The test procedure requires only that you give learners a shock each time they make a mistake on the test. To administer the shocks you will use a "shock generator" that gives shocks ranging from 30 to 450 volts. You can see that the switches are labeled from "slight shock" through "danger: severe shock" at the top level, where there are three red X's. But don't worry; although the shocks may be painful, they will cause no permanent damage.

Presented with this situation, you would be likely to think that neither you nor anyone else would go along with the stranger's unusual request. Clearly, it lies outside the bounds of what we consider good sense.

Or does it? Suppose the stranger asking for your help were a psychologist conducting an experiment. Or suppose it were your teacher, your employer, or your

FIGURE 14-6 *This impressive looking "shock generator" was used to lead participants to believe they were administering electric shocks to another person, who was connected to the generator by electrodes that were attached to the skin. Source: Copyright 1965 by Stanley Milgram. From the film* Obedience, *distributed by the New York University Film Library and Pennsylvania State University, PCR.*

military commander—all people in authority with some seemingly legitimate reason for their request.

If you still believe it unlikely that you would comply—think again. For the situation presented above describes a now-classic experiment conducted by social psychologist Stanley Milgram in the 1960s (Milgram, 1974). In the study, participants were placed in a situation in which they were told by an experimenter to give increasingly strong shocks to another person as part of a study on learning (see Figure 14-6). In reality, the experiment had nothing to do with learning; the real issue under consideration was the degree to which participants would comply with the experimenter's requests. In fact, the "learner" supposedly receiving the shocks was actually a confederate who never really received any punishment.

Most people who hear a description of the experiment feel that it is unlikely that *any* participant would give the maximum level of shock—or, for that matter, any shock at all. Even a group of psychiatrists to whom the situation was described predicted that fewer than 2 percent of the participants would fully comply and administer the strongest shocks.

However, the actual results contradicted both experts' and nonexperts' predictions. Some 65 percent of the participants eventually used the highest setting on the shock generator, 450 volts, to shock the learner. This obedience occurred even though the learner, who had mentioned at the start of the experiment that he had a heart condition, demanded to be released, screaming "Let me out of here! Let me out of here! My heart's bothering me. Let me out of here!" Still, despite the learner's pleas, most participants continued to administer the shocks.

Why did so many individuals comply with the experimenter's demands? Extensive interviews were carried out with participants following the experiment. They showed that participants were obedient primarily because they believed that the experimenter would be responsible for any potential ill effects that befell the learner. The experimenter's orders were accepted, then, because the participants thought that they personally could not be held accountable for their actions—they could always blame the experimenter (Darley, 1995; Blass, 1996).

Although the Milgram experiment has been criticized for creating an extremely trying set of circumstances for the participants—thereby raising serious ethical questions—and on methodological grounds (Orne & Holland, 1968; A. G. Miller, 1986; Miller, Collins, & Brief, 1995), it remains one of the strongest laboratory demonstrations of obedience (Blass, 1991; Blass & Krackow, 1991). We need only consider actual instances of obedience to authority to witness some frightening real-life parallels. For instance, a major defense offered after World War II by Nazi

Obedience to Authority

officers to excuse their participation in atrocities during the war was that they were "only following orders." Milgram's experiment, which was motivated in part by his desire to explain the behaviour of everyday Germans during World War II, forces each of us to ask ourselves this question: Would we be able to withstand the intense power of authority?

Recap, Review, and Rethink

Recap

- Social influence encompasses situations in which the actions of one individual or group affect the behaviour of another.

- Conformity is a change in attitude or behaviour brought about by a desire to follow the beliefs or standards of others.

- Groupthink is a type of conformity in which group members' desire to reach consensus outweighs their ability to evaluate alternative points of view critically.

- Compliance is a change in behaviour made in response to more explicit social pressure. Obedience, in contrast, is a change in behaviour resulting from a direct command.

Review

1. A _____ _____, or person who agrees with the dissenting viewpoint, is likely to reduce conformity.

2. Who pioneered the study of conformity?
   a. Skinner
   b. Asch
   c. Milgram
   d. Fiala

3. Which of the following techniques asks a person to comply with a small initial request to enhance the likelihood that the person will later comply with a larger request?
   a. door-in-the-face
   b. foot-in-the-door
   c. that's-not-all
   d. not-so-free sample

4. The _____-_____-_____-_____ technique begins with an outrageous request which then makes a smaller request seem reasonable.

5. _____ is a change in behaviour that is due to another person's orders.

Answers to Review Questions are on page 534.

Rethink

1. Do you think conformity is more of an issue at certain periods during life, or is it a force to be faced throughout the life span?

2. Given that persuasive techniques like those described in this section are so powerful, should there be laws against the use of such techniques? Should people be taught defenses against such techniques? Is the use of such techniques ethically and morally defensible?

3. Why do you think the Milgram experiment is so controversial? What sorts of effects might the experiment have had on participants? Do you think the experiment would have had similar results if it had been conducted not in a laboratory setting, but among members of a social group (such as a fraternity or sorority) with strong pressures to conform?

PREJUDICE AND DISCRIMINATION

► **What is the distinction among stereotypes, prejudice, and discrimination?**

► **How can we reduce prejudice and discrimination?**

stereotypes: Generalized beliefs and expectations about social groups and their members

What do you think of when someone says, "He's an immigrant," or "She's homeless," or "woman driver"? If you're like most people, you'll probably automatically form some sort of impression of what that individual is like.

Labels do affect our perception. Victoria Esses of the University of Western Ontario whose research interests include **stereotypes**, prejudice and discrimination has found that our attitudes about groups are affected by the labels we use to identify them. In a study using the labels Aboriginal Peoples, Native Indians, First Nations people, Native Canadians, and Native Peoples. Findings indicated that people reacted with less favourable attitudes to some labels than to others (Donakowski and Esses, 1996). Suggesting that we have certain beliefs or stereotypes attached to these and other labels. Stereotypes, which may be negative or positive, are the outgrowth of our tendency to categorize and organize the vast amount of information we encounter in our everyday lives. All stereotypes share the common feature of oversimplifying the world: We view individuals not in terms of their individual characteristics, but in terms of their membership in a particular group (Mackie & Hamilton, 1993; Jussim et al., 1996; Macrae, Stangor, & Hewstone, 1996; Sherman, 1996).

Stereotypes can lead to **prejudice,** the negative (or positive) evaluations of groups and their members. For instance, racial prejudice occurs when a member of a racial group is evaluated in terms of race and not because of his or her own characteristics or abilities.

prejudice: The negative (or positive) evaluations of groups and their members

The most common stereotypes and forms of prejudice have to do with racial, religious, gender, and ethnic categorizations. Over the years, various groups have been called "lazy" or "shrewd," or "cruel," or aggressive with varying degrees of regularity by nongroup members (Katz & Braly, 1933; Devine & Elliot, 1995; Johnston, 1996; Dion, 1975; Kalin & Berry, 1996).

Although usually backed by little or no evidence, stereotypes often have harmful consequences. When people act on negative stereotypes, the result is **discrimination**—negative behaviour toward members of a particular group. Discrimination can lead to exclusion from jobs, neighbourhoods, or educational opportunities, and may result in members of particular groups receiving lower salaries and benefits.

discrimination: Negative behaviour toward members of a particular group

High-profile cases of restitution for discrimination against, as an example, Native Canadians, Japanese Canadians, or those labelled mentally defective" and sterilized by eugenics boards, might suggest that prejudice and discrimination are a thing of the past. In Canada the law prohibits overt discrimination, but the reality may be somewhat different. Although in the minority, white supremacist groups, which have chapters in Canada, continue to draw members, and promote racial hatred and harm (Alcock, et al., 1997). At the societal level, black and Aboriginal people continue to be over represented in the criminal justice system (Report of the Commission on Systemic Racism in the Ontario Criminal Justice System, 1995).

Stereotyping leads not only to overt discrimination; it can actually *cause* members of stereotyped groups to behave in ways that reflect the stereotype through a phenomenon known as the *self-fulfilling prophecy.* Self-fulfilling prophecies are expectations about the occurrence of a future event or behaviour that act to increase the likelihood that the event or behaviour *will* occur. For example, if people think that members of a particular group lack ambition, they may treat them in a way that actually brings about a lack of ambition. Similarly, people holding a stereotype may be "primed" to interpret the behaviour of the stereotyped group as representative of the stereotype, even when the behaviour depicts something entirely different (Slusher & Anderson, 1987; Harris-Kern, & Perkins, 1995; Jussim & Eccles, 1995; Madon, Jussim, & Eccles, 1997).

Antidiscrimination

The Foundations of Prejudice

No one has ever been born disliking a particular racial, religious, or ethnic group. People learn to hate, in much the same way that they learn the alphabet.

According to *social learning approaches* to stereotyping and prejudice, people's feelings about members of various groups are shaped by the behaviour of parents, other adults, and peers (Kryzanowski & Stewin, 1985; Fagot, Leinbach, & O'Boyle, 1992; Yenerall, 1995). Right-wing authoritarianism (RWA) is a term used to describe a highly prejudiced personality type. Research by Bob Altemeyer of the University of Manitoba (1981, 1994) suggests that three traits underlie this personality type: submission (to authority figures), aggression (against those they believe threaten the system) and conventionalism (adherence to perceived established norms). People who measure as high on the RWA are highly bigoted and may commend ... their children for expressing attitudes in favour of prejudice. Likewise, young children learn prejudice by imitating the behaviour of adult models. Such learning starts at an early age, since children as young as three years of age begin to show preferences for members of their own race (Katz, 1976).

The mass media also provide a major source of information about stereotypes, not just for children, but for adults as well. Even today, some television shows and movies portray Italians as Mafia-like mobsters who invariably inhabit the "mean streets" of U.S. cities. Or Aboriginal people as dependent, uneducated, deviant, and alcoholic. A study done by Claxton-Oldfield and Keefe (1999) did a content analysis of

Tiger Woods, who calls himself "Cablinasian"—a phrase he made up to refer to his racial heritage of Caucasian, Black, Indian, and Asian—broke through the colour barrier in professional golf.

a daily newspaper to examine potential stereotypes of the Innu of Labrador and found most stories depicted the Innu as dependent, in conflict with authority, or deviant. The authors found these stereotypes reflected in research on student's impressions of the Innu people. When such portrayals are the primary source of information about minority groups, they can lead to the development and maintenance of unfavorable stereotypes (Hammer, 1992; Evans, 1993; Bryant & Zillman, 1994; Campbell, 1995; Herrett-Skjellum, & Allen, 1996).

Social learning theory does not provide the full story of stereotyping and prejudice. For instance, some psychologists argue that prejudice results when there is competition for scarce societal resources. This type of prejudice has more to do with belief about the impact of a group on your life rather that a negative stereotype that is held. Mark Zanna, of the University of Waterloo (1994) has proposed that there may be prejudice based on affect and symbolic belief as well as on stereotypes. Affect prejudice is based on emotions or feelings towards another group. Symbolic belief prejudice is based on beliefs about how a group helps or hinders the attainment of goals.

Further Zanna's research showed that we may be prejudiced against different groups for different reasons and that these reasons may change with circumstance. So if a group is believed to be taking jobs away or using other scarce resources, prejudice towards that group may have a high symbolic belief component.

Other explanations of prejudice focus on mood states and their relationship to prejudice. When individuals are dissatisfied with their life circumstances they may look to blame someone or something. This behaviour is known as scapegoating. A series of five studies on the relationship between mood and prejudice were carried out by Esses, Haddock and Zanna (1994). Using both males and females and members of a number of ethnic groups they found that when people were in a negative (bad) mood they were extremely likely to evaluate other ethnic groups in a highly unfavourable way. In addition, other explanations for prejudice emphasize human cognitive limitations that lead us to categorize people on the basis of visually conspicuous physical features such as race, sex, and ethnic group. Such categorization can lead to the development of stereotypes and, ultimately, to discriminatory behaviour (Mackie & Hamilton, 1993; Brewer & Harasty, 1996; Fiske & Morling, 1996; Fiske et al., 1998).

Working to End Prejudice and Discrimination

How can we diminish the effects of prejudice and discrimination? Psychologists have developed several strategies that have proven effective. Among them:

- *Increasing contact between the target of stereotyping and the holder of the stereotype*. Research has shown that increasing the amount of interaction between people can reduce negative stereotyping. But only certain kinds of contact are likely to foster a reduction in prejudice and discrimination. Situations where there is relatively intimate contact, where the individuals are of equal status, or where participants must cooperate with one another or are dependent on one another are most likely to bring about a reduction of stereotyping. Contact seems to be effective in part because people's understanding of stereotyped groups becomes more detailed, individualized, and accurate as the amount of interaction increases. This finding provides part of the basis for such social practices as school integration and fair housing laws (Desforges et al., 1991; Hawley & Jackson, 1995; Gaertner et al., 1996; Pettigrew, 1997).

Answers to Review Questions:

1. social supporter   2. b   3. b   4. door-in-the-face   5. Obedience

- *Making positive values and norms against prejudice more conspicuous.* It is not always necessary to rely on contact to reduce prejudice and discrimination. An additional approach is to demonstrate to people the inconsistencies between values they hold regarding equality and fair treatment of others, and negative stereotyping. For instance, people who are made to understand that their values regarding equality and fairness are inconsistent with their negative perceptions of minority group members are more likely to work actively against prejudice in the future (Rokeach, 1971). Similarly, people who hear others making strong, vehement antiracist statements are subsequently more likely to strongly condemn racism. The reason? Public denunciations of racism make public standards, or norms, against racism more prominent. A few outspoken individuals, then, may create an atmosphere in which prejudice is viewed considerably more negatively than in a situation in which others take no stand or take only weak stands (Blanchard, Lilly, & Vaughn, 1991).

- *Educating for tolerance.* Probably the most direct means of changing stereotypical and discriminatory attitudes is through education Even five-year-olds can display high levels of prejudice (Aboud,1988; Doyle and Aboud,1995). Efforts that could make use of the formal education system to reduce prejudice would be valuable. For example, studies done in Toronto in 1975 (Reich and Purbhoo) and 1981 (Ziegler) showed that students in more ethnically heterogeneous settings were more tolerant of diversity.

Support Networks

Two Quebec researchers studied white third and fourth grade students to see if conversations between dyads of high prejudice and low prejudice students would affect the levels of tolerance. High prejudice children did become more tolerant after listening to their partners express a balanced and more tolerant attitude (Aboud,1996).

Another strategy is teaching people to be more aware of the positive characteristics of targets of stereotyping. For instance, when the meaning of puzzling behaviour is explained to people holding stereotypes, they may come to appreciate its true significance—even though it may still appear foreign and perhaps even threatening. Furthermore, training in statistical reasoning, which illustrates various logical fallacies, can inhibit the formation of certain stereotypes (Landis et al., 1976; Langer, Bashner, & Chanowitz, 1985; Schaller et al., 1996).

An area of education that has been found to reduce prejudice is bilingual education. Extensive research on second language learning has been carried out by researchers at McGill University in Montreal (see chapter 7). In general findings from Canada and other parts of the world show that people who acquire a second language are less prejudiced. This is particularly true if the language is acquired out of interest in the other culture rather that simply to seek employment. (Noels and Clément, 1998; Alcock, Carment & Sadava, 2000)

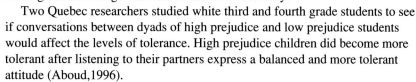

Recap, Review, and Rethink

Recap

- Stereotypes are generalized beliefs and expectations about members of a group formed simply on the basis of their membership in that group.

- Prejudice is the negative (or positive) evaluation of members of a group based primarily on membership in the group rather than on individual behaviour.

- Discrimination is negative behaviour toward members of a particular group.

- Among the ways of reducing stereotyping and prejudice are increasing contact, making positive values and norms against prejudice conspicuous, education.

Review

1. Any expectation—positive or negative—about an individual based solely on that person's membership in a group can be a stereotype. True or false?

2. The negative (or positive) evaluations of groups and their members is called

   a. stereotyping.
   b. prejudice.
   c. self-fulfilling prophecy.
   d. discrimination.

3. Paul is a store manager who does not expect women to succeed in business. He therefore offers important, high-profile responsibilities only to men. If the female employees fail to move up in the company, this could be an example of a _____-_____ prophecy.

Answers to Review Questions are on page 538.

Rethink

1. How are stereotypes, prejudice, and discrimination related? In a society committed to equality, which of the three should be changed first? Why?

2. A growing number of popular sports and entertainment figures are members of minority groups. Is this trend likely to change stereotypes about minority group members? Why or why not? What sorts of public roles played by minority group members are likely to have the greatest positive effect on stereotypical attitudes?

3. Do you think women can be victims of stereotype vulnerability? Can you explain how this would happen? Can men be victims of stereotype vulnerability?

POSITIVE AND NEGATIVE SOCIAL BEHAVIOUR

▶ **Why are we attracted to certain people, and what progression do social relationships follow?**

▶ **What factors underlie aggression and prosocial behaviour?**

Are people basically good or bad? Like philosophers and theologians, social psychologists have pondered the basic nature of humanity. Is it represented by the violence and cruelty we see throughout the world, or is there something special about human nature that permits loving, considerate, unselfish, and even noble behaviour?

We turn to two routes that social psychologists have followed in seeking answers to these questions. We first consider what they have learned about the sources of our attraction to others, and we end the chapter with a look at two sides of the coin of human behaviour: aggression and helping.

Liking and Loving: Interpersonal Attraction and the Development of Relationships

When nineteenth-century poet Elizabeth Barrett Browning wrote "How do I love thee? Let me count the ways," she was expressing feelings about a topic that is central to most people's lives—and one that has developed into a major subject of investigation by social psychologists: loving and liking. Known more formally as the study of **interpersonal attraction** or close relationships, this topic encompasses the factors that lead to positive feelings for others.

interpersonal attraction: Positive feelings for others; liking and loving

How Do I Like Thee? Let Me Count the Ways

By far the greatest amount of research has focused on liking, probably because it has always proved easier for investigators conducting short-term experiments to produce states of liking in strangers whom one has just met than to promote and observe loving relationships over long periods of time. Hence traditional studies have given us a good deal of knowledge about the factors that initially attract two people to each other (Berscheid, 1985; Simpson & Harris, 1994). Among the most important factors considered by social psychologists are the following:

- *Proximity.* If you live in a dormitory or an apartment, consider the friends you made when you first moved in. Chances are you became friendliest with those who lived geographically closest to you. In fact, this is one of the most firmly established findings in the interpersonal attraction literature: *Proximity* leads to liking (Festinger, Schachter & Back, 1950; Nahome & Lawton, 1976).

- *Mere exposure.* Repeated exposure to a person is often sufficient to produce attraction. Interestingly, repeated exposure to *any* stimulus—a person, picture, compact disc, or what have you—usually makes us like the stimulus more.

Becoming familiar with a stimulus can evoke positive feelings; the positive feelings stemming from familiarity are then transferred to the stimulus itself. There are exceptions, though. In cases in which the initial interactions are strongly negative, repeated exposure is unlikely to cause us to like another person more; instead, the more we are exposed to him or her, the more we may dislike such an individual (Zajonc, 1968; Bornstein & D'Agostino, 1992, 1994; Moreland & Beach, 1992; Kruglanski, Freund, & Bar Tal, 1996).

- *Similarity.* Folk wisdom tells us that birds of a feather flock together. Unfortunately, it also maintains that opposites attract. Social psychologists have come up with a clear verdict regarding which of the two statements is correct: We tend to like those who are similar to us. Discovering that others are similar in terms of attitudes, values, or traits promotes liking for them. Furthermore, the more similar others are, the more we like them (Byrne, 1969; Lancaster, Royal, & Whiteside, 1995; McCaul et al., 1995; Glaman, Jones, & Rozelle, 1996).

  One reason similarity increases the likelihood of interpersonal attraction is that we assume that people with similar attitudes will evaluate us positively (Condon & Crano, 1988). Because there is a strong **reciprocity-of-liking effect** (a tendency to like those who like us), knowing that someone evaluates us positively will promote attraction to that person. In addition, we assume that when we like someone else, that person likes us in return (Tagiuri, 1958; Metee & Aronson, 1974).

- *Need complementarity.* We all know exceptions to the general rule that similarity is related to attraction. Some couples seem totally mismatched in terms of personality, interests, and attitudes, yet are clearly quite captivated with one another. Social psychologists have explained instances in which people are attracted to dissimilar others by considering the needs that their partners fulfill. According to this reasoning, we may be attracted to people who fulfill the greatest number of needs for us. Thus a dominant person may seek out someone who is submissive; at the same time, the submissive individual may be seeking someone who is dominant. Although their dissimilarity often makes others expect them to be incompatible, by forming a relationship they are able to fulfill each other's complementary needs.

  The hypothesis that people are attracted to others who fulfill their needs—dubbed the **need-complementarity hypothesis**—was first proposed in the late 1950s in a classic study that found that a sample of married couples appeared to have complementary needs (Winch, 1958). Although research attempting to support the concept since that time has been wildly inconsistent, it does seem that in some realms the hypothesis holds. For example, people with complementary abilities may be attracted to one another. In one study, schoolchildren developed friendships with others whose academic skills were in areas distinct from those in which they felt particularly competent, thereby allowing them to stand out in different subjects from their friends. A good mathematics student, then, might form a friendship with someone particularly good in English (Tesser, 1988).

  In general, though, most evidence suggests that attraction is related more to similarity than to complementarity (e.g., Meyer & Pepper, 1977). Whether in the area of attitudes, values, or personality traits, then, similarity remains one of the best predictors of whether two people will be attracted to each other.

- *Physical attractiveness.* For most people, the equation *beautiful = good* is quite true. As a result, people who are physically attractive are more popular than those who are physically unattractive, if all other factors are equal. This finding, which contradicts the values that most people would profess, is apparent even in childhood—with nursery-school-age children rating popularity on the basis of attractiveness (Dion & Berscheid, 1974)—and continues into adulthood. Indeed, physical attractiveness may be the single most important element promoting

reciprocity-of-liking effect: A tendency to like those who like us

Relationship Research

need-complementarity hypothesis: The hypothesis that people are attracted to others who fulfill their needs

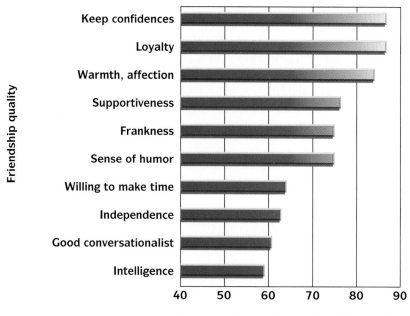

FIGURE 14-7 *These are the key qualities looked for in a friend, according to some 40,000 respondents to a questionnaire.*

Relationships

initial liking in college dating situations, although its influence eventually decreases when people get to know each other better (Hatfield & Sprecher, 1986; Agnew & Thompson, 1994; Kowner & Ogawa, 1995; Zuckerman, Miyake, & Elkin, 1995; Keller & Young, 1996; Hadjistavropoulos and Genest, 1994).

The factors that we have discussed are not, of course, the only constituents of liking. For example, surveys have sought to identify the factors critical in friendships. In a questionnaire answered by some 40,000 respondents, the qualities that were most valued in a friend were identified as the ability to keep confidences, loyalty, and warmth and affection, followed closely by supportiveness, frankness, and a sense of humor (Parlee, 1979). The results are summarized in Figure 14-7.

How Do I Love Thee? Let Me Count the Ways

Whereas our knowledge of what makes people like one another is extensive, our understanding of love is more limited in scope and recently acquired. For some time, many social psychologists believed that love was a phenomenon too difficult to observe and study in a controlled, scientific way. However, love is such a central issue in most people's lives that, in time, social psychologists could not resist its allure and became infatuated with the topic (Aron et al., 1997).

As a first step, researchers tried to identify the characteristics that distinguished between mere liking and full-blown love (Sternberg, 1987). Using this approach, they discovered that love is not simply liking of a greater quantity, but a qualitatively different psychological state (Walster & Walster, 1978). For instance, at least in its early stages, love includes relatively intense physiological arousal, an all-encompassing interest in another individual, fantasizing about the other, and relatively rapid swings of emotion. Similarly, love, unlike liking, includes elements of passion, closeness, fascination, exclusiveness, sexual desire, and intense caring. Partners are idealized; we exaggerate their good qualities and minimize their imperfections (Davis, 1985; Hendrick & Hendrick, 1989; Murray, Holmes, & Griffin, 1996; Murray & Holmes, 1997). Karen and Ken Dion of the University of Toronto (1991,1993,1996) study romantic love. They are particularly interested in the role of personality and culture in love relationships.

Answers to Review Questions:

1. true   2. b   3. self-fulfilling

Several social psychologists have tried to capture the elusive nature of love using paper-and-pencil measures. For example, Zick Rubin (1970, 1973) tried to differentiate between love and liking using a paper-and-pencil scale. Keep a particular individual in mind as you answer these questions from his scale:

I feel I can confide in _____ about virtually everything.
I would do almost anything for _____.
I feel responsible for _____'s well-being.

A positive response to each question provides an indication of love for the individual you have in mind. Now answer these questions, also drawn from Rubin's scale:

I think that _____ is unusually well adjusted.
I think that _____ is one of those people who quickly wins respect.
_____ is one of the most likable people I know.

These three questions are designed to measure liking, as opposed to loving. Researchers have found that couples scoring high on the love scale differ considerably from those with low scores. They gaze at each other more, and their relationships are more likely to be intact six months later than are the relationships of those who score low on the scale.

Other experiments have found evidence suggesting that the heightened physiological arousal hypothesized to be characteristic of loving is indeed present when a person reports being in love. Interestingly, though, it may not be just arousal of a sexual nature. Berscheid & Walster (1974) have theorized that when we are exposed to *any* stimulus that increases physiological arousal—such as danger, fear, or anger—we may label our feelings as love for another person present at the time of the arousal. This is most likely to occur if there are situational cues that suggest that "love" is an appropriate label for the feelings being experienced. In sum, we perceive we are in love when instances of general physiological arousal are coupled with the thought that the cause of the arousal is most likely love.

This theory explains why a person who keeps being rejected or hurt by another can still feel "in love" with that person. If the rejection leads to physiological arousal, but the arousal still happens to be attributed to love—and not to rejection—then a person will still feel "in love."

Other researchers have theorized that there are actually several kinds of love (Soble, 1990; Fehr & Russell, 1991; Hendrick & Hendrick, 1992). Some distinguish between two main types of love: passionate love and companionate love. **Passionate (or romantic) love** represents a state of intense absorption in someone. It includes intense physiological arousal, psychological interest, and caring for the needs of another. In contrast, **companionate love** is the strong affection that we have for those with whom our lives are deeply involved. The love we feel for our parents, other family members, and even some close friends falls into the category of companionate love (Hendrick & Hendrick, 1992; Hatfield & Rapson, 1993; Singelis, Choo, & Hatfield, 1995).

According to psychologist Robert Sternberg (1986, 1988b), an even finer differentiation between types of love is in order. He proposes that love is made up of three components: an *intimacy component,* encompassing feelings of closeness and connectedness; a *passion component,* made up of the motivational drives relating to sex, physical closeness, and romance; and a *decision/commitment component,* encompassing the initial cognition that one loves someone, and the longer-term feelings of commitment to maintain love.

Tracing the Course of Relationships: The Rise and Fall of Liking and Loving

With more than one out of two marriages ending in divorce, and broken love affairs a common phenomenon, it is not surprising that social psychologists have begun to turn their attention increasingly toward understanding how relationships develop, are maintained—and, in some cases, dissolve (Tzeng, 1992; Duck, 1994b; Adelmann, Chadwick, & Baerger, 1996; Bui, Peplau, & Hill, 1996).

passionate (or romantic) love: A state of intense absorption in someone that includes intense physiological arousal, psychological interest, and caring for the needs of another
companionate love: The strong affection that we have for those with whom our lives are deeply involved

The disruption of communication patterns may be both a cause and an effect of the decline of a relationship.

The behaviour of couples in developing relationships changes in fairly predictable patterns (Huston & Vangelisti, 1991; Carstensen, Gottman, & Levenson, 1995). The most frequent pattern follows this course:

- People interact more often, for longer periods of time, and in a widening array of settings.

- They seek each other's company.

- They increasingly "open up" to each other, disclosing secrets and sharing physical intimacies. They are more willing to share both positive and negative feelings and are increasingly willing to provide praise and criticism.

- They begin to understand each other's point of view and way of looking at the world.

- Their goals and behaviour become more in tune, and they begin to share greater similarity in attitudes and values.

- Their investment in the relationship—in terms of time, energy, and commitment—increases.

- They begin to feel that their psychological well-being is tied to the well-being of the relationship. They come to see the relationship as unique and irreplaceable.

- They start behaving like a couple, rather than like two separate individuals.

Although this sequence of transitions is typical, it is difficult to predict the exact point in a relationship when each will occur. One important reason is that at the same time the relationship is evolving, the two individuals may be going through personal growth and change themselves. In addition, the people in the relationship may have differing goals for its outcome; one partner may be interested in marriage, while the other may only be looking for a relatively short-term relationship.

Finally, even if both partners have an underlying concern about finding a marriage partner, the kind of mate for whom one partner is looking may be very different from that sought by the other (Sprecher, Sullivan, & Hatfield, 1994; Hatfield & Sprecher, 1995; Goode, 1996). For instance, a survey of close to 10,000 individuals across the world found that people had considerably different preferences regarding qualities in a mate, depending both on their culture and their sex. For example, people in Canada rated mutual attraction and love as the first and second most important characteristics. In contrast, men in China rated good health as most important, and women rated emotional stability and maturity as most important. In Zulu South Africa, men rated emotional stability first and women rated dependable character first (Buss et al., 1990; see Table 14-2).

Once relationships have evolved, how can we distinguish successful ones from those that will ultimately fail? One approach is to examine the rate at which the various components of love develop. According to Sternberg's theory of love, the three individual components of love—intimacy, passion, and decision/commitment—vary in their influence over time and follow distinct courses. In strong loving relationships, for instance, the level of commitment peaks and then remains stable, while intimacy continues to grow over the course of a relationship (see Figure 14-8). Passion, on the other hand, shows a marked decline over time, reaching a plateau fairly early in a relationship. Still, it remains an important component of loving relationships.

The Decline of a Relationship

What is it that causes some relationships to founder? Social psychologist George Levinger (1983) has speculated on the reasons behind the deterioration of relationships. One important factor appears to be a change in judgments about the meaning of a partner's behaviour. Behaviour that was once viewed as "charming forgetfulness" comes to be seen as "boorish indifference," and the partner becomes less valued. In addition, communications may be disrupted. Rather than listening to what the other

| Table 14-2 | Rank Ordering of Desired Characteristics in a Mate |

	China		South Africa Zulu		Canada English		Canada French	
	Males	Females	Males	Females	Males	Females	Males	Females
Mutual attraction—love	4	8	10	5	1	1	2	2
Emotional stability and maturity	5	1	1	2	3	3	1	1
Dependable character	6	7	3	1	2	2	6	4
Pleasing disposition	13	16	4	3	4	4	3	5
Education and intelligence	8	4	6	6	6	8	7	7
Good health	1	3	5	4	5	5	8	9
Good looks	11	15	14	16	7	6	5	6
Sociability	12	9	11	8	8	9	9	11
Desire for home and children	2	2	9	9	11	12	4	3
Refinement, neatness	7	10	7	10	10	7	10	8
Ambition and industriousness	10	5	8	7	9	13	11	15
Similar education	15	12	12	12	13	11	14	14
Good cook and housekeeper	9	11	2	15	15	10	13	10
Favourable social status or rating	14	13	17	14	12	15	12	12
Similar religious background	18	18	16	11	14	14	15	13
Good financial prospect	16	14	18	13	16	16	16	16
Chastity (no prior sexual intercourse)	3	6	13	18	17	18	17	18
Similar political background	17	17	15	17	18	17	18	17

Source: Buss et al., 1990. (1 indicates most desirable characteristic)

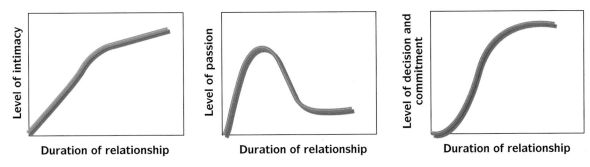

FIGURE 14-8 *The changing ingredients of love. The three components of love vary in strength over the course of a relationship.*
Source: Sternberg, 1986.

person is saying, each partner becomes bent on justifying himself or herself, and communication deteriorates. Eventually, a partner may begin to invite and agree with criticism of the other partner from people outside the relationship, and look to others for the fulfillment of basic needs that were previously met by the partner.

Just as developing relationships tend to follow a common pattern, relationships that are on the decline conform to a pattern of stages (Duck, 1988; see Figure 14-9). The first phase occurs when a person decides that he or she can no longer tolerate being in a relationship. During this stage, the focus is on the other person's behaviour and an evaluation of the extent to which this behaviour provides a basis for terminating the relationship.

In the next phase, a person decides to confront the partner and determines whether to attempt to repair, redefine, or terminate the relationship. For example, a redefinition might encompass a qualitative change in the level of the relationship. ("We can still be friends" might replace "I'll love you forever.")

If the decision is made to terminate the relationship, the person then enters a period in which there is public acknowledgment that the relationship is being dissolved and an accounting is made to others regarding the events that led to the termination of

FIGURE 14-9 *Endings: The*
stages of relationship dissolution.
Source: Based on Duck, 1984, p. 16.

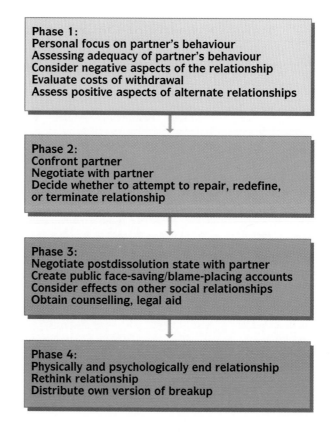

the relationship. The last stage is a "grave-dressing" phase, in which the major activity is to physically and psychologically end the relationship. One of the major concerns of this period is to rethink the entire relationship, making what happened seem reasonable and in keeping with one's self-perceptions.

Just how much distress do people experience when a relationship ends? The degree of anguish depends on what the relationship was like before its end. In the case of undergraduate dating couples who break up, partners who report the most distress are those who had been especially close to one another over a long period and had spent a considerable amount of time exclusively together. They had participated in many activities with their partners and report having been influenced strongly by them. Finally, the degree of distress is related to holding the expectation that it will be difficult to find a new, replacement partner. If no alternatives are on the horizon, people are apt to look more longingly at what they once had (Simpson, 1987).

Aggression and Prosocial Behaviour: Hurting and Helping Others

School shootings, carjackings, and road rage are just some of the examples of violence that seem all too common today. Yet we also find examples of generous, unselfish, thoughtful behaviour that suggest a more optimistic view of humankind. Consider, for instance, people who minister to the homeless, or individuals like Oscar Schindler, who helped Jews escape from Nazi death camps during World War II. Or contemplate the simple kindnesses of life: lending a valued compact disc, stopping to help a child who has fallen off her bicycle, or merely sharing a chocolate bar with a friend. Such instances of helping are no less characteristic of human behaviour than the distasteful examples of aggression. In this last part of the chapter, we explore how social psychologists have sought to explain instances of both aggressive and helping behaviour.

Hurting Others: Aggression

We need look no further than our daily paper or the nightly news to be bombarded with examples of aggression, both on a societal level (war, invasion, assassination)

Table 14-3	Is This Aggression?

To see for yourself the difficulties involved in defining aggression, consider each of the following acts and determine whether it represents aggressive behaviour—according to your own definition of aggression.

1. A spider eats a fly.
2. Two wolves fight for the leadership of the pack.
3. A soldier shoots an enemy at the front line.
4. The warden of a prison executes a convicted criminal.
5. A man viciously kicks a cat.
6. A man, while cleaning a window, knocks over a flower pot, which, in falling, injures a pedestrian.
7. Mr. X, a notorious gossip, speaks disparagingly of many people of his acquaintance.
8. A man mentally rehearses a murder he is about to commit.
9. An angry son purposely fails to write to his mother, who is expecting a letter and will be hurt if none arrives.
10. An enraged boy tries with all his might to inflict injury on his antagonist, a bigger boy, but is not successful in doing so. His efforts simply amuse the bigger boy.
11. A senator does not protest the escalation of bombing to which she is morally opposed.
12. A farmer beheads a chicken and prepares it for supper.
13. A hunter kills an animal and mounts it as a trophy.
14. A physician gives a flu shot to a screaming child.
15. A boxer gives his opponent a bloody nose.
16. A Girl Scout tries to assist an elderly woman but trips her by accident.
17. A bank robber is shot in the back while trying to escape.
18. A tennis player smashes her racket after missing a volley.
19. A person commits suicide.
20. A cat kills a mouse, parades around with it, and then discards it.

(Source: Adapted from Benjamin, 1985, p. 41.)

and on an individual level (crime, child abuse, and the many petty cruelties that humans are capable of inflicting on one another). Is such aggression an inevitable part of the human condition? Or is aggression primarily a product of particular circumstances that, if changed, could lead to its reduction?

The difficulty of answering such knotty questions becomes quickly apparent as soon as we consider how best to define the term "aggression." Depending on the way we define the word, many examples of inflicted pain or injury may or may not qualify as aggression (see Table 14-3). It is clear, for instance, that a rapist is acting with aggression toward his victim. On the other hand, it is less certain that a physician carrying out an emergency medical procedure without an anesthetic, thereby causing incredible pain to the patient, should be considered aggressive.

Most social psychologists define aggression in terms of the intent and purpose behind the behaviour. **Aggression** is intentional injury or harm to another person (Berkowitz, 1993). Under this definition, it is clear that the rapist in our example is acting aggressively, whereas the physician causing pain during a medical procedure is not.

We turn now to several approaches to aggressive behaviour developed by social psychologists (Berkowitz, 1993; Huesmann, 1994).

Driver Aggression

aggression: Intentional injury or harm to another person

Instinct Approaches: Aggression as a Release

If you have ever punched an adversary in the nose, you may have experienced a certain satisfaction, despite your better judgment. Instinct theorists, noting the prevalence of aggression not only in humans but in animals as well, propose that aggression is primarily the outcome of innate—or inborn—urges.

The major proponent of the instinct approach is Konrad Lorenz, an ethologist (a scientist who studies animal behaviour) who suggested that humans, along with members of other species, have a fighting instinct, which in earlier times ensured protection of food supplies and weeded out the weaker of the species (Lorenz, 1966, 1974). The controversial notion arising from Lorenz's instinct approach is that aggressive energy is constantly being built up within an individual until it is finally discharged in a

catharsis: The process of discharging built-up aggressive energy

process called **catharsis.** The longer the energy is built up, says Lorenz, the greater will be the magnitude of the aggression displayed when it is discharged.

Probably the most controversial idea to come out of instinct theories of aggression is Lorenz's proposal that society ought to provide acceptable means of catharsis through, for instance, participation in sports and games, in order to prevent its discharge in less socially desirable ways. Although the notion makes logical sense, there is no possible way to devise an adequate experiment to test it. Relatively little support exists for instinct theories in general, because of the difficulty in finding evidence for any kind of pent-up reservoir of aggression (Geen & Donnerstein, 1983; Berkowitz, 1993). Most social psychologists suggest that we should look to other approaches to explain aggression.

Frustration-Aggression Approaches: Aggression as a Reaction to Frustration

Suppose you've been working on a paper that is due for a class early the next morning, and your word processor printer runs out of ink just before you can print out the paper. You rush to the store to buy more ink, only to find the salesclerk locking the door for the day. Even though the clerk can see you gesturing and literally begging him to open the door, he refuses, shrugging his shoulders and pointing to a sign that indicates when the store will open the next day. At that moment, the feelings you experience toward the salesclerk probably place you on the verge of real aggression, and you are undoubtedly seething inside.

frustration: The thwarting or blocking of some ongoing, goal-directed behaviour

Frustration-aggression theory tries to explain aggression in terms of events like this one. When first put forward, the theory said flatly that frustration *always* led to aggression of some sort, and that aggression was *always* the result of some frustration, where **frustration** is defined as the thwarting or blocking of some ongoing, goal-directed behaviour (Dollard et al., 1939). More recent formulations, however, have modified the original one, suggesting instead that frustration produces anger, leading to a *readiness* to act aggressively. Whether or not actual aggression occurs depends on the presence of *aggressive cues,* stimuli that have been associated in the past with actual aggression or violence and that will trigger aggression again (Berkowitz, 1984). In addition, frustration is assumed to produce aggression only to the extent that the frustration produces negative feelings (Berkowitz, 1989, 1990).

What kinds of stimuli act as aggressive cues? They can range from the most overt, such as the presence of weapons, to the subtlest, such as the mere mention of the name of an individual who has behaved violently in the past. For example, in one experiment, angered participants behaved significantly more aggressively when in the presence of a rifle and revolver than in a comparable situation in which no guns were present (Berkowitz & LePage, 1967). Similarly, frustrated participants in an experiment who had viewed a violent movie were more physically aggressive toward a confederate with the same name as the star of the movie than toward a confederate with a different name (Berkowitz & Geen, 1966). It appears, then, that frustration does lead to aggression, at least when aggressive cues are present (Carlson, Marcus-Newhall, & Miller, 1990).

Observational Learning Approaches: Learning to Hurt Others

Violence on Television

Do we learn to be aggressive? The observational learning (sometimes called social learning) approach to aggression says we do. Taking an almost opposite view from instinct theories, which focus on innate explanations of aggression, observational learning theory (see Chapter 5) emphasizes that social and environmental conditions can teach individuals to be aggressive. Aggression is seen not as inevitable, but rather as a learned response that can be understood in terms of rewards and punishments (Bandura, 1973, 1983; Fry, 1992; MacEwen, 1993).

Suppose, for instance, that a girl hits her younger brother when he damages one of her new toys. Whereas instinct theory would suggest that the aggression had been pent up and was now being discharged, and frustration-aggression theory would examine the girl's frustration at no longer being able to use her new toy, observational learning theory would look to previous reinforcement that the girl had received for being aggressive. Perhaps she had learned that aggression resulted in her getting attention from her parents, or perhaps in the past her brother had apologized after being hit. In either case, observational learning theory views the aggression as a result of past rewards the girl had obtained for such behaviour.

Observational learning theory pays particular attention not only to direct rewards and punishments that individuals themselves receive, but to the rewards and punishments that models—individuals who provide a guide to appropriate behaviour—receive for their aggressive behaviour. According to observational learning theory, people observe the behaviour of models and the subsequent consequences of the behaviour. If the consequences are positive, the behaviour is likely to be imitated when observers find themselves in a similar situation.

This basic formulation of observational learning theory has received wide research support. For example, nursery-school-age children who have watched an adult behave aggressively display the same behaviour themselves if they have been previously angered (Bandura, Ross, & Ross, 1963a, 1963b). It turns out, though, that exposure to models typically leads to spontaneous aggression only if the observer has been angered, insulted, or frustrated after exposure (Bandura, 1973, 1983).

Helping Others: The Brighter Side of Human Nature

Turning away from aggression, we move now to the opposite—and brighter—side of the coin of human nature: helping behaviour. Helping behaviour, or **prosocial behaviour** as it is more formally known, has been considered under many different conditions (McGuire, 1994). However, the question that psychologists have looked at most closely relates to bystander intervention in emergency situations. What are the factors that lead someone to help a person in need?

As we noted in Chapter 1, one critical factor is the number of others present. When more than one person bears witness to an emergency situation, a sense of diffusion of responsibility can arise among bystanders. **Diffusion of responsibility** is the tendency for people to feel that responsibility for acting is shared, or diffused, among those present. The more people that are present in an emergency, then, the less personally responsible each individual feels—and therefore the less help that is provided (Latané & Nida, 1981; Kalafat, Elias, & Gara, 1993; Bickman, 1994).

Although the majority of research on helping behaviour supports the diffusion-of-responsibility formulation, other factors are clearly involved in helping behaviour. According to a model developed by Latané and Darley (1970), the process of helping involves four basic steps:

- *Noticing a person, event, or situation that may require help.*

- *Interpreting the event as one that requires help.* Even if an event is noticed, it may be sufficiently ambiguous to be interpreted as a nonemergency situation (Shotland, 1985; Harrison & Wells, 1991). It is here that the presence of others first affects helping behaviour. The presence of inactive others may indicate to the observer that a situation does not require help—a judgment not necessarily made if the observer is alone.

- *Assuming responsibility for taking action.* It is at this point that diffusion of responsibility is likely to occur if others are present. Moreover, a bystander's particular expertise is apt to play a role in determining whether helping occurs. For instance, if people with training in medical aid or lifesaving techniques are present, untrained bystanders are less apt to intervene because they feel they have less expertise. This point was well illustrated in a study by Jane and Irving Piliavin (1972), who conducted a field experiment in which an individual seemed to collapse in a subway car with blood trickling out of the corner of his mouth. The results of the experiment showed that bystanders were less likely to help when a person (actually a confederate) appearing to be an intern was present than when the "intern" was not present.

prosocial behaviour: Helping behaviour

diffusion of responsibility: The tendency for people to feel that responsibility for acting is shared, or diffused, among those present

Altruism is often the only bright side of a natural disaster. A volunteer helps Pine Lake, Alberta, victims of a July 2000 tornado that killed 11.

- *Deciding on and implementing the form of assistance.* After an individual assumes responsibility for helping, the decision must be made as to how assistance will be provided. Helping can range from very indirect forms of intervention, such as calling the police, to more direct forms, such as giving first aid or taking the victim to a hospital. Most social psychologists use a *rewards-costs approach* for helping to predict the nature of assistance that a bystander will choose to provide. The general notion is that the rewards of helping, as perceived by the bystander, must outweigh the costs if helping is to occur, and most research tends to support this notion (Bell et al., 1995).

After the nature of assistance is determined, one step remains: the actual implementation of the assistance. A rewards-costs analysis suggests that the least costly form of implementation is the most likely to be used. However, this is not always the case: In some situations, people behave altruistically. **Altruism** is helping behaviour that is beneficial to others but clearly requires self-sacrifice. For example, an instance in which a person runs into a burning house to rescue a stranger's child might be considered altruistic, particularly when compared with the alternative of simply calling the fire department (Batson, 1990, 1991; Dovidio, Allen, & Schroeder, 1990; Shapiro & Gabbard, 1994). (Figure 14-10 summarizes the basic steps of helping.)

Some research suggests that people who intervene in emergency situations tend to possess certain personality characteristics that differentiate them from nonhelpers. For example, helpers tend to be more self-assured. Other research has found that individuals who are characteristically high in sympathy, *empathy* (a personality trait in which someone observing another person experiences the emotions of that person), and emotional understanding are more likely to respond to others' needs (Cialdini et al., 1987; Eisenberg & Fabes, 1991; Knight et al., 1994; Shaw, Batson, & Todd, 1994; Batson et al., 1995; Sibicky, Schroeder, & Dovidio, 1995).

Still, most social psychologists agree that no single set of attributes differentiates helpers from nonhelpers. Temporary, situational factors play the predominant role in determining whether an individual intervenes in a situation requiring aid (Carlson, Charlin, & Miller, 1988; Carlo et al., 1991; Knight et al., 1994).

For instance, our mood helps determine how helpful we are. Not surprisingly, being in a good mood encourages helping. What doesn't make as much sense, at least at first, is the finding that bad moods, too, seem to encourage helping behaviour. There are some reasonable explanations, however, for this finding. For one thing, we may think that helping will enable us to view ourselves more positively, thereby raising our spirits and getting us out of our bad mood. Similarly, if a bad mood leads us to focus on ourselves, the values we hold about helping may become more conspicuous—leading us to help more (Cialdini & Fultz, 1990; Eisenberg, 1991; Salovey, Charlin, & Miller, 1991; Wegener & Petty, 1994; Carlson, Charlin, & Miller, 1994).

altruism: Helping behaviour that is beneficial to others but clearly requires self-sacrifice

FIGURE 14-10 *The basic steps of helping. Source: Based on Latané & Darley, 1970.*

The Informed Consumer of Psychology

Dealing with Anger Effectively

At one time or another, almost everyone feels angry. The anger may have come as a result of a frustrating situation, or it may be due to the behaviour of another individual. How we deal with such anger may determine the difference between a promotion and a lost job or a broken relationship and one that mends itself.

Social psychologists who have studied the topic suggest that there are several good ways to deal with anger, strategies that maximize the potential for positive consequences (Deffenbacher, 1988, 1996; Pennebaker, 1990; Redmond & Redmond, 1994; Nay, 1995; Bass, 1996). Among the most useful strategies are the following:

- Look at the situation that is producing anger from the perspective of others. By taking others' point of view, you may be able to understand the situation better, and with increased understanding may become more tolerant of the apparent shortcomings of others.

- Reduce the importance of the situation. Does it really matter that someone is driving too slowly and that you'll be late to an appointment as a result? Reinterpret the situation in a way that is less bothersome.

- Fantasize about getting even—but don't act on it. Fantasy provides a safety valve. In your fantasies, you can yell at that unfair professor all you want and suffer no consequences at all. However, don't spend too much time brooding: Fantasize, but then move on.

- Relax. By teaching yourself the kind of relaxation techniques used in systematic desensitization (see Table 13-2 in the previous chapter), you can help reduce your reactions to anger. In turn, your anger may dissipate.

No matter which of these strategies you try, above all don't ignore anger. People who always strive to suppress their anger may experience a variety of consequences, such as self-condemnation and even physical illness (Pennebaker, 1990; Eysenck, 1994b; Engebretson & Stoney, 1995; Sharma, Ghosh, & Spielberger, 1995). ■

Recap, Review, and Rethink

Recap

- Studies of interpersonal attraction and close relationships consider liking and loving.

- Among the most important elements that affect liking are proximity, mere exposure, similarity, and physical attractiveness.

- Love is assumed to be distinct from liking in qualitative, as well as quantitative, respects. In addition, several different kinds of love can be distinguished.

- Aggression refers to intentional injury of or harm to another person.

- Helping in emergencies involves four steps.

Review

1. We tend to like those people who are similar to us. True or false?

2. _____ _____ predicts that we will be attracted to those people with needs different from our own.

3. According to Berscheid, a person can still feel in love with another even when constantly rejected if _____ is present and is misinterpreted as "love."

4. Which of the following sets are the three components of love proposed by Sternberg?
   a. passion, closeness, sexuality
   b. attraction, desire, complementarity
   c. passion, intimacy, commitment
   d. commitment, caring, sexuality

5. According to survey research, people have similar preferences for a mate, relatively independent of their sex and cultural background. True or false?

6. Which hypothesis states that frustration produces anger, which in turn produces a readiness to act aggressively?
   a. frustration-aggression
   b. observational learning
   c. catharsis
   d. instinctual aggression

7. Based on the research evidence, which of the following might be the best way to reduce the amount of fighting a young boy does?
   a. Take him to the gym and let him work out on the boxing equipment.
   b. Take him to see *Terminator 2* several times in the hopes that it will provide catharsis.
   c. Reward him if he doesn't fight during a certain period.
   d. Ignore it and let it die out naturally.

8. If a person in a crowd does not help in an apparent emergency situation because many other people are present, that person is falling victim to the phenomenon of _____ ___ _____.

Answers to Review Questions are on page 548.

Rethink

1. Can love be adequately studied? Is there an "intangible" quality to love that renders it at least partially unknowable? How would you define "falling in love"? How would you study it?

2. Why do people feel the need to create a public face-saving or blame-placing account of the dissolution of a relationship, and why do they have to rethink the relationship in order to make the breakup seem reasonable? Does this have anything to do with the phenomenon of cognitive dissonance?

3. How would the aggression of a Timothy McVeigh, convicted of blowing up a federal building in Oklahoma City, be interpreted by the three main approaches to the study of aggression: instinct approaches, frustration-aggression approaches, and observational learning approaches? Do you think any of these approaches fits the McVeigh case more closely than the others?

looking
BACK

What are attitudes and how are they formed, maintained, and changed?

1. In this chapter, we discussed social psychology, the study of the ways in which people's thoughts, feelings, and actions are affected by others, and the nature and causes of individual behaviour in social situations.

2. Attitudes, a central topic of study in social psychology, are learned predispositions to respond in a favourable or unfavourable manner to a particular object. The ABC model of attitudes suggests that they have three components: the affect component, the behaviour component, and the cognition component. Attitudes can be acquired through several processes. These include classical conditioning, in which a previously neutral object begins to evoke the attitudes associated with another object due to repeated pairings, and operant conditioning, in which reinforcement acts to maintain an attitude.

3. A number of theories suggest that people try to maintain consistency between attitudes. Cognitive dissonance occurs when two cognitions—attitudes or thoughts—contradict each other and are held simultaneously by an individual. To resolve the contradiction, the person may modify the cognition, change its importance, or deny it, thereby bringing about a reduction in dissonance. However, alternative explanations based on self-perception theory have been proposed to explain dissonance phenomena.

How do we form impressions of what others are like and of the causes of their behaviour?

4. Impressions of others are formed through social cognitions—the processes that underlie our understanding of the social world. People develop schemas, which organize information about people and social experiences in memory. Such schemas represent our social life and allow us to interpret and categorize information about others.

5. One of the ways in which people form impressions of others is through the use of central traits, personality characteristics that are given unusually heavy weight when an impression is formed. Information-processing approaches have found that we tend to average sets of traits to form an overall impression.

6. Attribution theory tries to explain how we understand the causes of behaviour, particularly with respect to situational or dispositional factors.

What are the biases that influence the ways in which we view others' behaviour?

7. Even though logical processes are involved, attribution is still prone to error. For instance, the fundamental attribution error is the tendency to over-attribute others' behaviour to dispositional causes, and the corresponding failure to recognize the importance of situational causes. Other biases include the halo effect, in which the initial understanding that a person has positive traits is used to infer other positive characteristics, and the assumed-similarity bias, the tendency to think of people as being similar to oneself.

What are the major sources and tactics of social influence?

8. Social influence is the area of social psychology concerned with situations in which the actions of an individual or group affect the behaviour of others.

9. Conformity refers to changes in behaviour or attitudes that occur as the result of a desire to follow the beliefs or standards of others. Among the factors affecting conformity are the nature of the group, the nature of the response required, the kind of task, and the unanimity of the group. One manifestation of conformity is groupthink, the desire to achieve consensus even at the expense of critical analysis of other perspectives.

10. Compliance is behaviour that occurs as a result of direct social pressure. Two important means of eliciting compliance are the foot-in-the-door technique, in which people are initially asked to agree to a small request but later asked to respond to a larger one, and the door-in-the-face procedure, in which a large request, designed to be refused, is followed by a smaller one. Other tactics include the that's-not-all technique and the not-so-free sample. In contrast to compliance, obedience is a change in behaviour in response to the commands of others.

What is the distinction among stereotypes, prejudice, and discrimination?

11. Stereotypes are the negative (or positive) evaluations of groups and their members. Although they are most frequently applied to racial and ethnic groups, stereotypes are also found in categorizations of gender and age groups. Prejudice is the negative (or positive) evaluation of groups and their members.

12. Stereotyping and prejudice can lead to discrimination, negative behaviour toward members of a particular group. It also leads to self-fulfilling prophecies, expectations about the occurrence of future events or behaviours that act to increase the likelihood that the events or behaviours will actually occur.

13. According to social learning approaches, people learn stereotyping and prejudice by observing the behaviour of parents, other adults, and peers. In addition, social identity theory suggests that group membership is used as a source of pride and self-worth, which may lead people to think of their own group as better than others.

How can we reduce prejudice and discrimination?

14. Among the ways of reducing prejudice and discrimination are increasing contact, making positive values against prejudice apparent, and educating for tolerance.

Answers to Review Questions:

1. true   2. Need complementarity   3. arousal   4. c   5. False; they have distinct patterns of preferences.   6. a   7. c   8. diffusion of responsibility

15. Stereotype vulnerability, obstacles to performance that stem from awareness of society's stereotypes regarding minority group members, can be combated by specific training programs that address the vulnerability of minority group members to stereotypes and illustrate that the stereotypes are inaccurate.

Why are we attracted to certain people, and what progression do social relationships follow?

16. The study of interpersonal attraction, or close relationships, considers liking and loving. Among the primary determinants of liking are proximity, mere exposure, similarity, and physical attractiveness.

17. Loving is distinguished from liking by the presence of intense physiological arousal, an all-encompassing interest in another, fantasies about the other, rapid swings of emotion, fascination, sexual desire, exclusiveness, and strong feelings of caring. According to one approach, love can be categorized into two types: passionate and companionate.

18. Recent work has examined the development, maintenance, and deterioration of relationships. Relationships tend to move through stages, and the various components of love—intimacy, passion, and decision/commitment—vary in their influence over time.

What factors underlie aggression and prosocial behavior?

19. Aggression is intentional injury of or harm to another person. Instinct approaches suggest that humans have an innate drive to behave aggressively and that if aggression is not released in socially desirable ways, it will be discharged in some other form—an idea for which there is relatively little research support. Frustration-aggression theory suggests that frustration produces a readiness to be aggressive—if aggressive cues are present. Finally, observational learning theory hypothesizes that aggression is learned through reinforcement—particularly reinforcement that is given to models.

20. Helping behaviour in emergencies is determined in part by the phenomenon of diffusion of responsibility, which results in a lower likelihood of helping when more people are present. Deciding to help is the outcome of a four-stage process consisting of noticing a possible need for help, interpreting the situation as requiring aid, assuming responsibility for taking action, and deciding on and implementing a form of assistance.

Key Terms and Concepts

social psychology (p. 512)
attitudes (p. 513)
ABC model of attitudes (p. 513)
central-route processing (p. 516)
peripheral-route processing (p. 516)
cognitive dissonance (p. 519)
social cognition (p. 520)
schemas (p. 520)
central traits (p. 521)
attribution theory (p. 521)
situational causes (of behaviour) (p. 522)
dispositional causes (of behaviour) (p. 522)

fundamental attribution error (p. 523)
halo effect (p. 523)
assumed-similarity bias (p. 523)
social influence (p. 525)
conformity (p. 525)
status (p. 526)
social supporter (p. 526)
compliance (p. 527)
obedience (p. 530)
stereotypes (p. 532)
prejudice (p. 533)
discrimination (p. 533)

interpersonal attraction (p. 536)
reciprocity-of-liking effect (p. 537)
need-complementarity hypothesis (p. 537)
passionate (or romantic) love (p. 539)
companionate love (p. 539)
aggression (p. 543)
catharsis (p. 544)
frustration (p. 544)
prosocial behaviour (p. 545)
diffusion of responsibility (p. 545)
altruism (p. 546)

Epilogue

In this chapter we have touched on some of the major ideas, research topics, and experimental findings of social psychology. We have examined how people form, maintain, and change attitudes; and how they form impressions of others and assign attributions to them. We have also seen how groups, through conformity and tactics of compliance, can influence individuals' actions and attitudes. We also discussed interpersonal relationships, including both liking and loving, and we looked at the two sides of a coin that represent the extremes of social behavior: aggression and prosocial behaviour.

Turn back to the Prologue, which described reactions to the death of Pierre Trudeau. Use your understanding of social psychology to consider the following questions.

1. How does the ABC model of attitudes—encompassing affect, behaviour, and cognition—apply to the attitudes of many people toward Pierre Trudeau? Which component do you think was strongest in most people's attitudes toward him?

2. Trudeau was a vocal advocate for bilingualism and multiculturalism. Can you discuss, in terms of findings regarding persuasion, the renewed attention that these issues received following his death?

3. What sort of impression did most people mourning Trudeau have of him? How might they have formed that impression? Did people have the same impression of other Canadian politicians?

4. To which biases, if any, do you think people's attitudes toward Pierre Trudeau might have been subject?

5. What similarities do you see between the death of Princess Diana and the death of Pierre Elliot Trudeau?

Glossary

A

ABC model of attitudes: The model suggesting that an attitude has three components: affect, behaviour, and cognition (Ch. 14)

absolute threshold: The smallest intensity of a stimulus that must be present for it to be detected (Ch. 3)

achievement test: A test meant to ascertain a person's level of knowledge in a given subject area (Ch. 8)

action potential: An electric nerve impulse that travels through a neuron when it is set off by a "trigger," changing the cell's charge from negative to positive (Ch. 2)

activation-synthesis theory: Hobson's theory that the brain produces random electrical energy during REM sleep that stimulates memories lodged in various portions of the brain (Ch. 4)

activity theory of aging: A theory that suggests that the people who age most successfully are those who maintain the interests and activities they had during middle age (Ch. 10)

adaptation: An adjustment in sensory capacity following prolonged exposure to stimuli (Ch. 3)

addictive drugs: Drugs that produce a biological or psychological dependence in the user, and withdrawal from them leads to a craving for the drug that, in some cases, may be nearly irresistible (Ch. 4)

adolescence: The developmental stage between childhood and adulthood (Ch. 10)

age of viability: The point at which the fetus can survive if born prematurely (Ch. 10)

aggression: Intentional injury or harm to another person (Ch. 14)

algorithm: A rule which, if followed, guarantees a solution to a problem (Ch. 7)

all-or-none law: The rule that neurons are either on or off (Ch. 2)

altruism: Helping behaviour that is beneficial to others but clearly requires self-sacrifice (Ch. 14)

anal stage: According to Freud, a stage from 12–18 months to 3 years of age, in which a child's pleasure is centred on the anus (Ch. 11)

androgens: Male sex hormones secreted by the testes (Ch. 9)

anorexia nervosa: A severe eating disorder in which people may refuse to eat, while denying that their behaviour and appearance—which can become skeletal—are unusual (Ch. 9)

antianxiety drugs: Drugs that reduce the level of anxiety a person experiences, essentially by reducing excitability and in part by increasing drowsiness (Ch. 13)

antidepressant drugs: Medication that improves a depressed patient's mood and feeling of well-being (Ch. 13)

antipsychotic drugs: Drugs that temporarily alleviate psychotic symptoms such as agitation and overactivity (Ch. 13)

antisocial or sociopathic personality disorder: A disorder in which individuals tend to display no regard for the moral and ethical rules of society or the rights of others (Ch. 12)

anxiety disorder: The occurrence of anxiety without obvious external cause, intruding on daily functioning (Ch. 12)

aptitude test: A test designed to predict a person's ability in a particular area or line of work (Ch. 8)

archival research: Research in which existing records, such as census data, birth certificates, or newspaper clippings, are examined to confirm a hypothesis (Ch. 1)

arousal approaches to motivation: The belief that we try to maintain a certain level of stimulation and activity, increasing or reducing them as necessary (Ch. 9)

association areas: One of the major areas of the brain, the site of the higher mental processes such as thought, language, memory, and speech (Ch. 2)

associative models: A technique of recalling information by thinking about related information (Ch. 6)

assumed-similarity bias: The tendency to think of people as being similar to oneself, even when meeting them for the first time (Ch. 14)

attachment: The positive emotional bond that develops between a child and a particular individual (Ch. 10)

attitudes: Learned predispositions to respond in a favourable or unfavourable manner to a particular person, behaviour, belief, or thing (Ch. 14)

attribution theory: The theory of personality that seeks to explain how we decide, on the basis of samples of an individual's behaviour, what the specific causes of that person's behaviour are (Ch. 14)

authoritarian parents: Parents who are rigid and punitive and value unquestioning obedience from their children (Ch. 10)

authoritative parents: Parents who are firm, set clear limits, reason with their children, and explain things to them (Ch. 10)

autobiographical memories: Our recollections of circumstances and episodes from our own lives (Ch. 6)

autonomic division: The part of the nervous system that controls involuntary movement (the actions of the heart, glands, lungs, and other organs) (Ch. 2)

autonomy-versus-shame-and-doubt stage: The period during which, according to Erikson, toddlers (ages 18 months to 3 years) develop independence and autonomy if exploration and freedom are encouraged, or shame and self-doubt if they are restricted and overprotected (Ch. 10)

axon: The part of the neuron that carries messages destined for other cells (Ch. 2)

B

babble: Speechlike but meaningless sounds made by children from the ages of around 3 months through 1 year (Ch. 7)

background stressors ("daily hassles"): Everyday annoyances, such as being stuck in traffic, that cause minor irritations but have no long-term ill effects, unless they continue or are compounded by other stressful events (Ch. 9)

basilar membrane: A structure that runs through the centre of the cochlea, dividing it into an upper and a lower chamber (Ch. 3)

behaviour modification: A formalized technique for promoting the frequency of desirable behaviours and decreasing the incidence of unwanted ones (Ch. 5)

behavioural assessment: Direct measures of an individual's behaviour used to describe characteristics indicative of personality (Ch. 11)

behavioural genetics: The study of the effects of heredity on behaviour (Ch. 2)

behavioural model of abnormality: The model that looks at the behaviour itself as the problem (Ch. 12)

behavioural perspective: The psychological model that suggests that observable behaviour should be the focus of study (Ch. 1)

behavioural treatment approaches: Approaches that build upon the basic processes of learning embodied in classical and operant conditioning (Ch. 13)

biofeedback: A procedure in which a person learns to control, through conscious thought, internal physiological processes such as blood pressure, heart and respiration rate, skin temperature, sweating, and constriction of particular muscles (Ch. 2)

biological and evolutionary approaches to personality: The theory that suggests that important components of personality are inherited (Ch. 11)

biological perspective: The psychological model that views behaviour from the perspective of biological functioning (Ch. 1)

biomedical therapy: Therapy that relies on drugs and other medical procedures to improve psychological functioning (Ch. 13)

biopsychologists: Psychologists who specialize in considering the ways in which biological structures and functions of the body affect behaviour (Ch. 2)

bipolar disorder: A disorder in which a person alternates between euphoric feelings of mania and bouts of depression (Ch. 12)

bisexuals: Persons who are sexually attracted to people of the same *and* the opposite sex (Ch. 9)

borderline personality disorder: A disorder in which individuals have difficulty in developing a secure sense of who they are (Ch. 12)

bottom-up processing: Perception that consists of recognizing and processing information about the individual components of the stimuli (Ch. 3)

bulimia: A disorder in which a person binges on incredibly large quantities of food (Ch. 9)

C

Cannon-Bard theory of emotion: The belief that both physiological and emotional arousal are produced simultaneously by the same nerve impulse (Ch. 9)

case study: An in-depth, intensive investigation of an individual or small group of people (Ch. 1)

cataclysmic events: Strong stressors that occur suddenly, affecting many people at once (e.g., natural disasters) (Ch. 9)

catharsis: The process of discharging built-up aggressive energy (Ch. 14)

central core: The "old brain" which controls such basic functions as eating and sleeping and is common to all vertebrates (Ch. 2)

central nervous system (CNS): The system that includes the brain and spinal cord (Ch. 2)

central-route processing: Message interpretation characterized by thoughtful consideration of the issues and arguments used to persuade (Ch. 14)

central traits: The major traits considered in forming impressions of others (Ch. 14)

cerebellum (ser uh BELL um): The part of the brain that controls bodily balance (Ch. 2)

cerebral cortex: The "new brain," responsible for the most sophisticated information processing in the brain; contains the lobes (Ch. 2)

chromosomes: Rod-shaped structures that hold the basic hereditary information (Ch. 10)

chunk: A meaningful grouping of stimuli that can be stored as a unit in short-term memory (Ch. 6)

circadian rhythms: Biological processes that occur repeatedly on approximately a 24-hour cycle (Ch. 4)

classical conditioning: A type of learning in which an organism responds to a neutral stimulus that normally does not bring about that response (Ch. 5)

client-centred therapy: Therapy in which the goal is to reach one's potential for self-actualization (Ch. 13)

cochlea (KOKE lee uh): A coiled tube filled with fluid that receives sound via the oval window or through bone conduction (Ch. 3)

cognition: The higher mental processes of humans, including how people know and understand the world, process information, make judgments and decisions, and describe their knowledge and understanding to others (Ch. 7)

cognitive approaches to motivation: Theories that focus on the role of our thoughts, expectations, and understanding of the world in explaining motivation (Ch. 9)

cognitive-behavioural approach: A process by which people's faulty cognitions about themselves and the world are changed to more accurate ones (Ch. 13)

cognitive development: The process by which a child's understanding of the world changes as a function of age and experience (Ch. 10)

cognitive dissonance: The conflict that occurs when a person holds two attitudes or thoughts (referred to as *cognitions*) that contradict each other (Ch. 14)

cognitive learning theory: The study of the thought processes that underlie learning (Ch. 5)

cognitive map: A mental representation of spatial locations and directions (Ch. 5)

cognitive model of abnormality: The model that suggests that people's thoughts and beliefs are a central component of abnormal behaviour (Ch. 12)

cognitive perspective: The psychological model that focuses on how people know, understand, and think about the world (Ch. 1)

cognitive psychology: The branch of psychology that focuses on the study of cognition (Ch. 7)

cognitive therapy: Psychotherapy based on Beck's goal to change people's illogical thoughts about themselves and the world (Ch. 13)

collective unconscious: A set of influences we inherit from our own particular ancestors, the whole human race, and even animal ancestors from the distant past (Ch. 11)

community psychology: A movement aimed toward preventing or minimizing psychological disorders in the community (Ch. 13)

companionate love: The strong affection that we have for those with whom our lives are deeply involved (Ch. 14)

compliance: Behaviour that occurs in response to direct social pressure (Ch. 14)

compulsion: An urge to repeatedly carry out some act that seems strange and unreasonable, even if the sufferer realizes it is unreasonable (Ch. 12)

concepts: Categorizations of objects, events, or people that share common properties (Ch. 7)

concrete operational stage: According to Piaget, the period from 7 to 12 years of age that is characterized by logical thought and a loss of egocentrism (Ch. 10)

conditioned response (CR): A response that, after conditioning, follows a previously neutral stimulus (e.g., salivation at the sound of a tuning fork) (Ch. 5)

conditioned stimulus (CS): A once-neutral stimulus that has been paired with an unconditioned stimulus to bring about a response formerly caused only by the unconditioned stimulus (Ch. 5)

cones: Cone-shaped, light-sensitive receptor cells in the retina that are responsible for sharp focus and colour perception, particularly in bright light (Ch. 3)

conformity: A change in behaviour or attitudes brought about by a desire to follow the beliefs or standards of other people (Ch. 14)

consciousness: The awareness of the sensations, thoughts, and feelings being experienced at a given moment (Ch. 4)

constructive processes: Processes in which memories are influenced by the meaning that we give to events (Ch. 6)

continuous reinforcement schedule: Behaviour that is reinforced every time it occurs (Ch. 5)

control group: A group that receives no treatment (Ch. 1)

convergent thinking: The ability to produce responses that are based primarily on knowledge and logic (Ch. 7)

conversion disorder: A major somatoform disorder that involves an actual physical disturbance, such as the inability to use a sensory organ or the complete or partial inability to move an arm or leg (Ch. 12)

coping: The efforts to control, reduce, or learn to tolerate the threats that lead to stress (Ch. 9)

correlational research: The relationship between two sets of factors is examined to determine whether they are associated, or "correlated" (Ch. 1)

creativity: The combining of responses or ideas in novel ways (Ch. 7)

critical period: One of several stages in development in which specific kinds of growth must occur if the individual is to develop normally (Ch. 10)

cross-sectional research: A research method in which people of different ages are compared at the same point in time (Ch. 10)

cross-sequential research: A research method that combines cross-sectional and longitudinal research by taking a number of different age groups and examining them over several points in time (Ch. 10)

crystallized intelligence: The information, skills, and strategies that people have learned through experience and that they can apply in problem-solving situations (Ch. 8)

culture-fair IQ test: A test that does not discriminate against members of any minority group (Ch. 8)

D

dark adaptation: A heightened sensitivity to light that results from being in relative dimness (Ch. 3)

daydreams: Fantasies that people construct while awake (Ch. 4)

decay: The loss of information through its nonuse (Ch. 6)

declarative memory: Memory for factual information: names, faces, dates, and the like (Ch. 6)

deductive reasoning: A form of reasoning in which a person draws inferences and implications from a set of assumptions and applies them to specific cases (Ch. 7)

defense mechanisms: Unconscious strategies people use to reduce anxiety by concealing its source from themselves and others (Ch. 9, 11)

deinstitutionalization: The transfer of former mental patients from institutions into the community (Ch. 13)

dendrites: A cluster of fibres at one end of a neuron that receive messages from other neurons (Ch. 2)

dependent variable: The variable that is measured and is expected to change as a result of changes caused by the experimenter's manipulation (Ch. 1)

depressants: Drugs that slow down the nervous system (Ch. 4)

developmental psychology: The branch of psychology that studies the patterns of growth and change occurring throughout life (Ch. 10)

Diagnostic and Statistical Manual of Mental Disorders, Fourth Edition (DSM-IV): A system devised by the American Psychiatric Association used by most professionals to diagnose and classify abnormal behaviour (Ch. 12)

difference threshold: The smallest detectable difference between two stimuli,

also known as a **just noticeable difference** (Ch. 3)

diffusion of responsibility: The tendency for people to feel that responsibility for acting is shared, or diffused, among those present (Ch. 14)

discrimination: Negative behaviour toward members of a particular group (Ch. 14)

disengagement theory of aging: A theory that suggests that aging is a gradual withdrawal from the world on physical, psychological, and social levels (Ch. 10)

dispositional causes (of behaviour): A cause of behaviour that is based on internal traits or personality factors (Ch. 14)

dissociative amnesia: A failure or inability to remember past experiences (Ch. 12)

dissociative disorder: Psychological dysfunctions characterized by the splitting apart of critical personality facets that are normally integrated, allowing stress avoidance by escape (Ch. 12)

dissociative fugue: An amnesiac condition in which people take sudden, impulsive trips, sometimes assuming a new identity (Ch. 12)

dissociative identity disorder: A disorder in which a person displays characteristics of two or more distinct personalities (Ch. 12)

divergent thinking: The ability to generate unusual, yet nonetheless appropriate, responses to problems or questions (Ch. 7)

double standard: The view that premarital sex is permissible for males but not for females (Ch. 9)

dreams-for-survival theory: The theory suggesting that dreams permit information that is critical for our daily survival to be reconsidered and reprocessed during sleep (Ch. 4)

drive: Motivational tension or arousal that energizes behaviour in order to fulfill some need (Ch. 9)

drive-reduction approaches to motivation: A theory suggesting that when people lack some basic biological requirement such as water, a drive to obtain that requirement (in this case, the thirst drive) is produced (Ch. 9)

drug therapy: Control of psychological problems through drugs (Ch. 13)

E

eardrum: The part of the ear that vibrates when sound waves hit it (Ch. 3)

echoic memory: Memory which stores information coming from the ears (Ch. 6)

eclectic approach to therapy: An approach to therapy that uses techniques taken from a variety of treatment methods, rather than just one (Ch. 13)

ego: The part of the personality that provides a buffer between the id and the outside world (Ch. 11)

egocentric thought: A way of thinking in which the child views the world entirely from his or her own perspective (Ch. 10)

ego-integrity-versus-despair stage: According to Erikson, a period from late adulthood until death during which we review life's accomplishments and failures (Ch. 10)

electroconvulsive therapy (ECT): A procedure in which an electric current of 70 to 150 volts is briefly administered to a patient's head, causing a loss of consciousness and often seizures (Ch. 13)

embryo: A developed zygote that has a heart, brain, and other organs (Ch. 10)

emotions: Feelings that generally have both physiological and cognitive elements and that influence behaviour (Ch. 9)

endocrine system: A chemical communication network that sends messages throughout the nervous system via the bloodstream (Ch. 2)

episodic memory: Memory for the biographical details of our individual lives (Ch. 6)

estrogen: Female sex hormone (Ch. 9)

evolutionary psychology: The branch of psychology that seeks to identify behaviour patterns that are a result of our genetic inheritance from our ancestors (Ch. 2)

excitatory message: A chemical secretion that makes it more likely that a receiving neuron will fire and an action potential will travel down its axon (Ch. 2)

existential therapy: A humanistic approach that addresses the meaning of life and human freedom (Ch. 13)

experiment: The investigation of the relationship between two (or more) factors by deliberately producing a change in one factor in a situation and observing the effects of that change on other aspects of the situation (Ch. 1)

experimental bias: Factors that distort an experimenter's understanding of how the independent variable affected the dependent variable (Ch. 1)

experimental group: Any group receiving a treatment (Ch. 1)

experimental manipulation: The change that an experimenter deliberately produces in a situation (Ch. 1)

explicit memory: Intentional or conscious recollection of information (Ch. 6)

extinction: One of the basic phenomena of learning that occurs when a previously conditioned response decreases in frequency and eventually disappears (Ch. 5)

extrinsic motivation: Motivation by which people participate in an activity for a tangible reward (Ch. 9)

F

family therapy: An approach that focuses on the family as a whole unit to which each member contributes (Ch. 13)

feature analysis: An approach to perception that considers how we perceive a shape, pattern, object, or scene by reacting first to the individual elements that make it up (Ch. 3)

feature detection: The activation of neurons in the cortex by visual stimuli of specific shapes or patterns (Ch. 3)

fetus: A developing child, from eight weeks after conception until birth (Ch. 10)

fixation: Personality traits characteristic of an earlier stage of development due to an unresolved conflict stemming from the earlier period (Ch. 11)

fixed-interval schedule: A schedule that provides reinforcement for a response only if a fixed time period has elapsed, making overall rates of response relatively low (Ch. 5)

fixed-ratio schedule: A schedule whereby reinforcement is given only after a certain number of responses are made (Ch. 5)

flashbulb memories: Memories centred around a specific, important, or surprising event that are so vivid it is as if they represented a snapshot of the event (Ch. 6)

fluid intelligence: Intelligence that reflects reasoning, memory, and information-processing capabilities (Ch. 8)

formal operational stage: According to Piaget, the period from age 12 to adulthood that is characterized by abstract thought (Ch. 10)

free will: The human ability to make decisions about one's life (Ch. 1)

frequency theory of hearing: The theory suggesting that the entire basilar membrane acts like a microphone, vibrating as a whole in response to a sound (Ch. 3)

frustration: The thwarting or blocking of some ongoing, goal-directed behaviour (Ch. 14)

functional fixedness: The tendency to think of an object only in terms of its typical use (Ch. 7)

functionalism: An early approach to psychology that concentrated on what the mind does—the functions of mental activity—and the role of behaviour in allowing people to adapt to their environments (Ch. 1)

fundamental attribution error: A tendency to attribute others' behaviour to dispositional causes and the tendency to minimize the importance of situational causes (Ch. 14)

G

g or g-factor: An early theory that assumed there was a general factor for mental ability (Ch. 8)

gate-control theory of pain: The theory suggesting that particular nerve receptors lead to specific areas of the brain related to pain (Ch. 3)

general adaptation syndrome (GAS): A theory developed by Selye that suggests that a person's response to stress consists of three stages: alarm and mobilization, resistance, and exhaustion (Ch. 9)

generalized anxiety disorder: The experience of long-term anxiety with no explanation (Ch. 12)

generativity-versus-stagnation stage: According to Erikson, a period in middle adulthood during which we take stock of our contributions to family and society (Ch. 10)

genes: The parts of the chromosomes through which genetic information is transmitted (Ch. 10)

genetic preprogramming theories of aging: Theories that suggest there is a built-in time limit to the reproduction of human cells, and that after a certain time they are no longer able to divide (Ch. 10)

genital stage: According to Freud, the period from puberty until death, marked by mature sexual behaviour (i.e., sexual intercourse) (Ch. 11)

genitals: The male and female sex organs (Ch. 9)

gestalt (geh SHTALLT) psychology: An approach to psychology that focuses on the organization of perception and thinking in a "whole" sense, rather than on the individual elements of perception (Ch. 1)

gestalt laws of organization: A series of principles that describes how we organize bits and pieces of information into meaningful wholes (Ch. 3)

gestalt therapy: An approach to therapy that attempts to integrate a client's thoughts, feelings, and behaviour into a whole (Ch. 13)

grammar: The system of rules that determines how our thoughts can be expressed (Ch. 7)

group therapy: Therapy in which people discuss problems with a group (Ch. 13)

H

habituation: The decrease in the response to a stimulus that occurs after repeated presentations of the same stimulus (Ch. 10)

hair cells: Tiny cells covering the basilar membrane that, when bent by vibrations entering the cochlea, transmit neural messages to the brain (Ch. 3)

hallucinogen: A drug that is capable of producing hallucinations, or changes in the perceptual process (Ch. 4)

halo effect: A phenomenon in which an initial understanding that a person has positive traits is used to infer other uniformly positive characteristics (Ch. 14)

hardiness: A personality characteristic associated with a lower rate of stress-related illness, consisting of three components: commitment, challenge, and control (Ch. 9)

hemispheres: Two symmetrical left and right halves of the brain that control the side of the body opposite to their location (Ch. 2)

heritability: A measure of the degree to which a characteristic is related to genetic, inherited factors (Ch. 8)

heterosexuality: Sexual attraction and behaviour directed to the opposite sex, consists of far more than male-female intercourse (Ch. 9)

heuristic: A rule of thumb or mental shortcut that may lead to a solution (Ch. 7)

homeostasis: The process by which an organism strives to maintain some optimal level of internal biological functioning by compensating for deviations from its usual, balanced internal state (Ch. 9)

homosexuals: Persons who are sexually attracted to members of their own sex (Ch. 9)

hormones: Chemicals that circulate through the blood and affect the functioning or growth of other parts of the body (Ch. 2)

humanistic approaches to personality: The theory that emphasizes people's basic goodness and their tendency to grow to higher levels of functioning (Ch. 11)

humanistic model of abnormality: The model that emphasizes the control and responsibility that people have for their own behaviour, even when such behaviour is abnormal (Ch. 12)

humanistic perspective: The psychological model that suggests that people are in control of their lives (Ch. 1)

humanistic therapy: Therapy in which the underlying assumption is that people have control of their behaviour, can make choices about their lives, and are essentially responsible for solving their own problems (Ch. 13)

hypnosis: A state of heightened susceptibility to the suggestions of others (Ch. 4)

hypothalamus: A tiny part of the brain, located below the thalamus of the brain, that maintains homeostasis and produces and regulates vital, basic behaviour such as eating, drinking, and sexual behaviour (Ch. 2)

hypothesis: A prediction, stemming from a theory, stated in a way that allows it to be tested (Ch. 1)

I

iconic memory: Memory which reflects information from our visual system (Ch. 6)

id: The raw, unorganized, inborn part of personality, whose sole purpose is to reduce tension created by primitive drives related to hunger, sex, aggression, and irrational impulses (Ch. 11)

identical twins: Twins who are genetically identical (Ch. 10)

identity: The distinguishing character of the individual: who each of us is, what our roles are, and what we are capable of (Ch. 10)

identity-versus-role-confusion stage: According to Erikson, a time in adolescence of testing to determine one's unique qualities (Ch. 10)

implicit memory: Memories of which people are not consciously aware, but which can affect subsequent performance and behaviour (Ch. 6)

incentive approaches to motivation: The theory explaining motivation in terms of external stimuli (Ch. 9)

independent variable: The variable that is manipulated by an experimenter (Ch. 1)

inductive reasoning: A reasoning process whereby a general rule is inferred from specific cases, using observation, knowledge, experience, and beliefs (Ch. 7)

industry-versus-inferiority stage: According to Erikson, the last stage of childhood during which children aged 6 to 12 years may develop positive social interactions with others or may feel inadequate and become less sociable (Ch. 10)

inferiority complex: According to Adler, a situation in which adults have not been able to overcome the feelings of inferiority that they developed as children, when they were small and limited in their knowledge about the world (Ch. 11)

information processing: The way in which people take in, use, and store information (Ch. 10)

informed consent: A document signed by participants affirming that they have been told the basic outlines of the study and are aware of what their participation will involve (Ch. 1)

inhibitory message: A chemical secretion that prevents a receiving neuron from firing (Ch. 2)

initiative-versus-guilt stage: According to Erikson, the period during which children ages 3 to 6 years experience conflict between independence of action and the sometimes negative results of that action (Ch. 10)

insight: A sudden awareness of the relationships among various elements that had previously appeared to be independent of one another (Ch. 7)

instincts: Inborn patterns of behaviour that are biologically determined rather than learned (Ch. 9)

intellectually gifted: Two to four percent of the population who have IQ scores greater than 130 (Ch. 8)

intelligence: The capacity to understand the world, think rationally, and use resources effectively when faced with challenges (Ch. 8)

intelligence quotient (IQ): A score that takes into account an individual's mental *and* chronological age (Ch. 8)

intelligence tests: Tests devised to identify a person's level of intelligence (Ch. 8)

interference: The phenomenon by which information in memory displaces or blocks out other information, preventing its recall (Ch. 6)

interneurons: Neurons that connect sensory and motor neurons, carrying messages between the two (Ch. 2)

interpersonal attraction: Positive feelings for others; liking and loving (Ch. 14)

intimacy-versus-isolation stage: According to Erikson, a period during early adulthood that focuses on developing close relationships (Ch. 10)

intrinsic motivation: Motivation by which people participate in an activity for their own enjoyment, not for the reward it will get them (Ch. 9)

introspection: A procedure used to study the structure of the mind, in which subjects are asked to describe in detail what they are experiencing when they are exposed to a stimulus (Ch. 1)

J

James-Lange theory of emotion: The belief that emotional experience is a reaction to bodily events occurring as a result of an external situation ("I feel sad because I am crying") (Ch. 9)

just noticeable difference: See **difference threshold** (Ch. 3)

L

language: The systematic, meaningful arrangement of symbols (Ch. 7)

language-acquisition device: A neural system of the brain hypothesized to permit understanding of language (Ch. 7)

latency period: According to Freud, the period between the phallic stage and puberty during which children's sexual concerns are temporarily put aside (Ch. 11)

latent content of dreams: According to Freud, the "disguised" meanings of dreams, hidden by more obvious subjects (Ch. 4)

latent learning: Learning in which a new behaviour is acquired but is not demonstrated until reinforcement is provided (Ch. 5)

lateralization: The dominance of one hemisphere of the brain in specific functions (Ch. 2)

learned helplessness: A state in which people conclude that unpleasant or aversive stimuli cannot be controlled—a view of the world that becomes so ingrained that they cease trying to remedy the aversive circumstances, even if they actually can exert some influence (Ch. 9, 12)

learning: A relatively permanent change in behaviour brought about by experience (Ch. 5)

learning-theory approach: The theory suggesting that language acquisition follows the principles of reinforcement and conditioning (Ch. 7)

levels-of-processing theory: The theory that emphasizes the degree to which new material is mentally analyzed (Ch. 6)

libido: According to Freud, the "psychic energy" that fuels the primary drives of hunger, sex, aggression, and irrational impulses (Ch. 11)

limbic system: The part of the brain located outside the "new brain" that controls eating, aggression, and reproduction (Ch. 2)

linguistic-relativity hypothesis: The theory that language shapes and, in fact, may determine the way people of a particular culture perceive and understand the world (Ch. 7)

lithium: A form of simple mineral salts that has been used very successfully in cases of bipolar disorders (Ch. 13)

lobes: The four major sections of the cerebral cortex—frontal, parietal, temporal, and occipital (Ch. 2)

longitudinal research: A research method that investigates behaviour as subjects age (Ch. 10)

long-term memory: Memory which stores information on a relatively permanent basis, although it may be difficult to retrieve (Ch. 6)

M

major depression: A severe form of depression that interferes with concentration, decision making, and sociability (Ch. 12)

mania: An extended state of intense euphoria and elation (Ch. 12)

manifest content of dreams: According to Freud, the overt story line of dreams (Ch. 4)

masturbation: Sexual self-stimulation (Ch. 9)

means-ends analysis: Repeated testing for differences between the desired outcome and what currently exists (Ch. 7)

medical model of abnormality: The model that suggests that when an individual displays symptoms of abnormal behaviour, the root cause will be found in a physical examination of the individual, which may reveal a hormonal imbalance, a chemical deficiency, or a brain injury (Ch. 12)

meditation: A learned technique for refocusing attention that brings about an altered state of consciousness (Ch. 4)

memory: The process by which we encode, store, and retrieve information (Ch. 6)

memory trace or **engram:** An actual physical change in the brain that occurs when new material is learned (Ch. 6)

menopause: The point at which women stop menstruating and are no longer fertile (Ch. 10)

mental age: The average age of children taking the Binet test who achieved the same score (Ch. 8)

mental images: Representations in the mind that resemble the object or event being represented (Ch. 7)

mental retardation: A significantly subaverage intellectual functioning that occurs with related limitations in two or more of the adaptive skill areas (Ch. 8)

mental set: The tendency for old patterns of problem solving to persist (Ch. 7)

metabolism: The rate at which food is converted to energy and expended by the body (Ch. 9)

metacognition: An awareness and understanding of one's own cognitive processes (Ch. 10)

midlife crisis: The realization that we have not accomplished in life what we had hoped to, leading to negative feelings (Ch. 10)

midlife transition: Beginning around the age of 40, a period during which we come to the realization that life is finite (Ch. 10)

Minnesota Multiphasic Personality Inventory-2 (MMPI-2): A test used to identify people with psychological difficulties as well as predicting a variety of other behaviours (Ch. 11)

monocular cues: Signals that allow us to perceive distance and depth with just one eye (Ch. 3)

mood disorder: Affective disturbances severe enough to interfere with normal living (Ch. 12)

motivation: The factors that direct and energize the behaviour of humans and other organisms (Ch. 9)

motor area: The part of the cortex that is largely responsible for the voluntary movement of particular parts of the body (Ch. 2)

motor (efferent) neurons: Neurons that communicate information from the nervous system to muscles and glands of the body (Ch. 2)

myelin sheath: A series of specialized cells of fat and protein that wrap themselves around the axon providing a protective coating (Ch. 2)

N

narcissistic personality disorder: A personality disturbance which is characterized by an exaggerated sense of self-importance (Ch. 12)

narcotics: Drugs that increase relaxation and relieve pain and anxiety (Ch. 4)

naturalistic observation: Research in which an investigator simply observes some naturally occurring behaviour and does not intervene in the situation (Ch. 1)

nature-nurture issue: The issue of the degree to which environment and heredity influence behaviour (Ch. 10)

need for achievement: A stable, learned characteristic in which satisfaction is obtained by striving for and attaining a level of excellence (Ch. 9)

need for affiliation: An interest in establishing and maintaining relationships with other people (Ch. 9)

need for power: A tendency to seek impact, control, or influence over others, and to be seen as a powerful individual (Ch. 9)

need-complementarity hypothesis: The hypothesis that people are attracted to others who fulfill their needs (Ch. 14)

negative reinforcer: An unpleasant stimulus whose removal from the environment leads to an increase in the probability that a preceding response will occur again in the future (Ch. 5)

neo-Freudian psychoanalysts: Psychoanalysts who were trained in traditional Freudian theory but who later rejected some of its major points (Ch. 11)

neonate: A newborn child (Ch. 10)

neurons: Specialized cells that are the basic elements of the nervous system (Ch. 2)

neurotransmitters: Chemicals that carry messages across the synapse to the dendrite (and sometimes the cell body) of a receiver neuron (Ch. 2)

neutral stimulus: A stimulus that, before conditioning, has no effect on the desired response (Ch. 5)

nondeclarative memory: Memory for skills, habits, and the products of conditioning (Ch. 6)

norms: Standards of test performance that permit the comparison of one person's score on the test to the scores of others who have taken the same test (Ch. 8)

O

obedience: A change in behaviour due to the commands of others (Ch. 14)

obesity: The state of being more than 20 percent above the average weight for a person of a given height (Ch. 9)

object permanence: The awareness that objects—and people—continue to exist even if they are out of sight (Ch. 10)

observational learning: Learning by watching others' behaviour and the consequences of that behaviour (Ch. 13)

observational learning: Learning through observing the behaviour of another person called a *model* (Ch. 5)

obsession: A thought or idea that keeps recurring in one's mind (Ch. 12)

obsessive-compulsive disorder: A disorder characterized by obsessions or compulsions (Ch. 12)

Oedipal conflict: A child's sexual interest in his or her opposite-sex parent, typically resolved through identification with the same-sex parent (Ch. 11)

operant conditioning: Learning in which a voluntary response is strengthened or weakened, depending on its positive or negative consequences (Ch. 5)

operationalization: The process of translating a hypothesis into specific, testable procedures that can be measured and observed (Ch. 1)

opponent-process theory of colour vision: The theory that suggests receptor cells are linked in pairs, working in opposition to each other (Ch. 3)

optic nerve: A bundle of ganglion axons that carry visual information (Ch. 3)

oral stage: According to Freud, a stage from birth to 12–18 months, in which an infant's centre of pleasure is the mouth (Ch. 11)

otoliths: Tiny, motion-sensitive crystals within the semicircular canals that sense body acceleration (Ch. 3)

overgeneralization: The phenomenon whereby children apply rules even when the application results in an error (Ch. 7)

overweight: Having a BMI of 27 or higher (Ch. 9)

ovulation: The point at which an egg is released from the ovaries (Ch. 9)

P

panic disorder: Anxiety that manifests itself in the form of panic attacks that last from a few seconds to as long as several hours (Ch. 12)

parasympathetic division: The part of the autonomic division of the nervous system that acts to calm the body after the emergency situation is resolved (Ch. 2)

partial reinforcement schedule: Behaviour that is reinforced some but not all of the time (Ch. 5)

passionate (or romantic) love: A state of intense absorption in someone that includes intense physiological arousal, psychological interest, and caring for the needs of another (Ch. 14)

perception: The sorting out, interpretation, analysis, and integration of stimuli involving our sense organs and brain (Ch. 3)

peripheral nervous system: The system, made up of long axons and dendrites, that branches out from the spinal cord and brain and reaches the extremities of the body (Ch. 2)

peripheral-route processing: Message interpretation characterized by consideration of the source and related general information rather than of the message itself (Ch. 14)

permissive parents: Parents who give their children lax or inconsistent direction and, although warm, require little of them (Ch. 10)

personal stressors: Major life events, such as the death of a family member, that have immediate negative consequences which generally fade with time (Ch. 9)

personality: The relatively enduring characteristics that differentiate people—those behaviours that makes each individual unique (Ch. 11)

personality disorder: A mental disorder characterized by a set of inflexible, maladaptive personality traits that keep a person from functioning properly in society (Ch. 12)

phallic stage: According to Freud, a period beginning around age 3 during which a child's interest focuses on the genitals (Ch. 11)

phobias: Intense, irrational fears of specific objects or situations (Ch. 12)

phonemes: The smallest sound units (Ch. 7)

phonics approach: Reading instruction that emphasizes word decoding skills such as analysis and synthesis of constituent sounds in words (Ch. 7)

phonology: The study of the sound system in language (Ch. 7)

pituitary gland: The "master gland," the major component of the endocrine system, which secretes hormones that control growth (Ch. 2)

place theory of hearing: The theory suggesting that different areas of the basilar membrane respond to different frequencies (Ch. 3)

placebo: A bogus treatment, such as a pill, "drug," or other substance without any significant chemical properties or active ingredient (Ch. 1)

positive reinforcer: A stimulus added to the environment that brings about an increase in a preceding response (Ch. 5)

post-traumatic stress disorder (PTSD): A phenomenon in which victims of major catastrophes reexperience the original stress event and associated feelings in vivid flashbacks or dreams (Ch. 9)

prejudice: The negative (or positive) evaluations of groups and their members (Ch. 14)

preoperational stage: According to Piaget, the period from 2 to 7 years of age that is characterized by language development (Ch. 10)

priming: A technique of recalling information by having been exposed to related information at an earlier time (Ch. 6)

principle of conservation: The knowledge that quantity is unrelated to the arrangement and physical appearance of objects (Ch. 10)

procedural memory: Memory for skills and habits, such as riding a bike or hitting a baseball, sometimes referred to as "nondeclarative memory" (Ch. 6)

progesterone: Female sex hormone (Ch. 9)

projective personality test: A test in which a person is shown an ambiguous stimulus and asked to describe it or tell a story about it (Ch. 11)

prosocial behaviour: Helping behaviour (Ch. 14)

prototypes: Typical, highly representative examples of a concept (Ch. 7)

psychoactive drugs: Drugs that influence a person's emotions, perceptions, and behaviour (Ch. 4)

psychoanalysis: Psychodynamic therapy that involves frequent sessions and often lasts for many years (Ch. 13)

psychoanalytic model of abnormality: The model that suggests that abnormal behaviour stems from childhood conflicts over opposing wishes regarding sex and aggression (Ch. 12)

psychoanalytic theory: Freud's theory that unconscious forces act as determinants of personality (Ch. 11)

psychodynamic perspective: The psychological model based on the belief that behaviour is motivated by inner forces over which the individual has little control (Ch. 1)

psychodynamic therapy: First suggested by Freud, therapy that is based on the premise that the primary sources of abnormal behaviour are unresolved past conflicts and the possibility that unacceptable unconscious impulses will enter consciousness (Ch. 13)

psychological tests: Standard measures devised to assess behaviour objectively and used by psychologists to help people make decisions about their lives and understand more about themselves (Ch. 11)

psychology: The scientific study of behaviour and mental processes (Ch. 1)

psychophysics: The study of the relationship between the physical nature of stimuli and the sensory responses that they evoke (Ch. 3)

psychophysiological disorders: Medical problems caused by an interaction of psychological, emotional, and physical difficulties (Ch. 9)

psychosocial development: Development of individuals' interactions and understanding of each other and of their knowledge and understanding of themselves as members of society (Ch. 10)

psychosurgery: Brain surgery once used to alleviate symptoms of mental disorders but rarely used today (Ch. 13)

psychotherapy: The process in which a patient (often referred to as the client) and a professional attempt to remedy psychological difficulties (Ch. 13)

puberty: The period at which maturation of the sexual organs occurs, begins at about age 11 or 12 for girls and 13 or 14 for boys (Ch. 10)

punishment: Unpleasant or painful stimuli that decrease the probability that a preceding behaviour will occur again (Ch. 5)

R

random assignment to condition: A procedure in which participants are assigned to different experimental groups or "conditions" on the basis of chance and chance alone (Ch. 1)

rapid eye movement (REM) sleep: Sleep occupying 20 percent of an adult's sleeping time, characterized by increased heart rate, blood pressure, and breathing rate; erections; eye movements; and the experience of dreaming (Ch. 4)

rational-emotive therapy: A form of therapy that attempts to restructure a person's belief system into a more realistic, rational, and logical set of views (Ch. 13)

reciprocity-of-liking effect: A tendency to like those who like us (Ch. 14)

reflexes: Automatic, involuntary response to an incoming stimulus (Ch. 2, 10)

rehearsal: The repetition of information that has entered short-term memory (Ch. 6)

reinforcement: The process by which a stimulus increases the probability that a preceding behaviour will be repeated (Ch. 5)

reinforcer: Any stimulus that increases the probability that a preceding behaviour will occur again (Ch. 5)

reliability: The concept that tests measure consistently what they are trying to measure (Ch. 8)

replication: The repetition of findings using other procedures in other settings, with other settings, with other groups of participants, before full confidence can be placed in the validity of any single experiment (Ch. 1)

resting state: The state in which there is a negative electrical charge of about −70 millivolts within the neuron (Ch. 2)

reticular formation: The part of the brain from the medulla through the pons made up of groups of nerve cells that can immediately activate other parts of the brain to produce general bodily arousal (Ch. 2)

retina: The part of the eye that converts the electromagnetic energy of light into useful information for the brain (Ch. 3)

reuptake: The reabsorption of neurotransmitters by a terminal button (Ch. 2)

reverse learning theory: The theory that proposes that dreams have no meaning whatsoever, but instead function to rid us of unnecessary information that we have accumulated during the day (Ch. 4)

rods: Long, cylindrical, light-sensitive receptors in the retina that perform well in poor light but are largely insensitive to colour and small details (Ch. 3)

Rorschach test: A test developed by Swiss psychiatrist Hermann Rorschach that consists of showing a series of symmetrical stimuli to people who are then asked what the figures represent to them (Ch. 11)

S

Schachter-Singer theory of emotion: The belief that emotions are determined jointly by a nonspecific kind of physiological arousal and its interpretation, based on environmental cues (Ch. 9)

schedules of reinforcement: The frequency and timing of reinforcement following desired behaviour (Ch. 5)

schemas: General themes that contain relatively little specific detail (Ch. 6)

schemas: Sets of cognitions about people and social experiences (Ch. 14)

schizophrenia: A class of disorders in which severe distortion of reality occurs (Ch. 12)

scientific method: The approach used by psychologists to systematically acquire knowledge and understanding about behaviour and other phenomena of interest (Ch. 1)

self-actualization: A state of self-fulfillment in which people realize their highest potential in their own unique way (Ch. 9, Ch. 11)

self-report measures: A method of gathering data about people by asking them questions about a sample of their behaviour (Ch. 11)

semantic memory: Memory for general knowledge and facts about the world, as well as memory for the rules of logic that are used to deduce other facts (Ch. 6)

semantics: The rules governing the meaning of words and sentences (Ch. 7)

semicircular canals: Structures of the inner ear consisting of three tubes containing fluid that sloshes through them when the head moves, signalling rotational or angular movement to the brain (Ch. 3)

sensation: The stimulation of the sense organs (Ch. 3)

sensorimotor stage: According to Piaget, the stage from birth to 2 years during which a child has little competence in representing the environment using images, language, or other symbols (Ch. 10)

sensory (afferent) neurons: Neurons that transmit information from the perimeter of the body to the central nervous system (Ch. 2)

sensory area: The site in the brain of the tissue that corresponds to each of the senses, with the degree of sensitivity relating to the amount of tissue (Ch. 2)

sensory memory: The initial, momentary storage of information, lasting only an instant (Ch. 6)

shaping: The process of teaching a complex behaviour by rewarding closer and closer approximations of the desired behaviour (Ch. 5)

short-term memory: Memory which holds information for fifteen to twenty-five seconds (Ch. 6)

signal detection theory: The theory that seeks to explain the role of psychological factors in the judgment of whether a stimulus is present or absent (Ch. 3)

situational causes (of behaviour): A cause of behaviour that is based on environmental factors (Ch. 14)

skin senses: The senses that include touch, pressure, temperature, and pain (Ch. 3)

social cognition: The processes that underlie our understanding of the social world (Ch. 14)

social-cognitive approaches to personality: The theory that emphasizes the influence of a person's cognitions—thoughts, feelings, expectations, and values—in determining personality (Ch. 11)

social influence: The process by which the actions of an individual or group affect the behaviour of others (Ch. 14)

social psychology: The study of how people's thoughts, feelings, and actions are affected by others (Ch. 14)

social supporter: A person who shares an unpopular opinion or attitude of another group member, thereby encouraging nonconformity (Ch. 14)

sociocultural model of abnormality: The model that makes the assumption that people's behaviour—both normal and abnormal—is shaped by the kind of family group, society, and culture in which they live (Ch. 12)

somatic division: The part of the nervous system that specializes in the control of voluntary movements and the communication of information to and from the sense organs (Ch. 2)

somatoform disorder: Psychological difficulties that take on a physical (somatic) form of one sort or another (Ch. 12)

sound: The movement of air molecules brought about by the vibration of an object (Ch. 3)

spinal cord: A bundle of nerves that leaves the brain and runs down the length of the back and is the main means for transmitting messages between the brain and the body (Ch. 2)

split-brain patient: A person who suffers from independent functioning of the two halves of the brain, as a result of which the sides of the body work in disharmony (Ch. 2)

spontaneous recovery: The reappearance of a previously extinguished response after time has elapsed without exposure to the conditioned stimulus (Ch. 5)

spontaneous remission: Recovery without treatment (Ch. 13)

stage 1 sleep: The state of transition between wakefulness and sleep, characterized by relatively rapid, low-voltage brain waves (Ch. 4)

stage 2 sleep: A sleep deeper than that of stage 1, characterized by a slower, more

regular wave pattern, along with momentary interruptions of "sleep spindles" (Ch. 4)

stage 3 sleep: A sleep characterized by slow brain waves, with greater peaks and valleys in the wave pattern (Ch. 4)

stage 4 sleep: The deepest stage of sleep, during which we are least responsive to outside stimulation (Ch. 4)

status: The social rank held within a group (Ch. 14)

stereotypes: Generalized beliefs and expectations about social groups and their members (Ch. 14)

stimulants: Drugs that affect the central nervous system by causing a rise in heart rate, blood pressure, and muscular tension (Ch. 4)

stimulus: Energy that produces a response in a sense organ (Ch. 3)

stimulus discrimination: The process by which an organism learns to differentiate among stimuli, restricting its response to one in particular (Ch. 5)

stimulus generalization: Response to a stimulus that is similar to but different from a conditioned stimulus; the more similar the two stimuli, the more likely generalization is to occur (Ch. 5)

stress: The response to events that are threatening or challenging (Ch. 9)

structuralism: Wundt's model that focuses on the fundamental elements that form the foundation of thinking, consciousness, emotions, and other kinds of mental states and activities (Ch. 1)

subliminal perception: The perception of messages about which we have no awareness (Ch. 3)

superego: According to Freud, the final personality structure to develop that represents the rights and wrongs of society as handed down by a person's parents, teachers, and other important figures (Ch. 11)

survey research: Research in which people chosen to represent some larger population are asked a series of questions about their behaviour, thoughts, or attitudes (Ch. 1)

sympathetic division: The part of the autonomic division of the nervous system that acts to prepare the body in stressful emergency situations, engaging all the organism's resources to respond to a threat (Ch. 2)

synapse: The gap between two neurons, bridged by chemical connections (Ch. 2)

syntax: The rules that indicate how words and phrases can be combined to form sentences (Ch. 7)

systematic desensitization: A form of treatment in which a person is taught to relax and then is gradually exposed to an anxiety-producing stimulus in order to extinguish the response of anxiety (Ch. 13)

T

telegraphic speech: Sentences that sound as if they were part of a telegram, in which words not critical to the message are left out (Ch. 7)

temperament: A basic, innate disposition (Ch. 10, 11)

terminal buttons: Small bulges at the end of axons from which messages are launched to other cells (Ch. 2)

test standardization: A technique used to validate questions in personality tests by studying the response of people with known diagnoses (Ch. 11)

thalamus: The part of the brain located in the middle of the central core that acts primarily as a busy relay station, mostly for information concerning the senses (Ch. 2)

Thematic Apperception Test (TAT): A test consisting of a series of pictures about which a person is asked to write a story (Ch. 11)

theories: Broad explanations and predictions concerning phenomena of interest (Ch. 1)

thinking: The manipulation of mental representations of information (Ch. 7)

tip-of-the-tongue phenomenon: The inability to recall information that one realizes one knows—a result of the difficulty of retrieving information from long-term memory (Ch. 6)

top-down processing: Perception that is guided by higher-level knowledge, experience, expectations, and motivations (Ch. 3)

trait theory: A model of personality that seeks to identify the basic traits necessary to describe personality (Ch. 11)

traits: Enduring dimensions of personality characteristics along which people differ (Ch. 11)

treatment: The manipulation implemented by the experimenter (Ch. 1)

triarchic theory of intelligence: Robert Sternberg's theory that there are three major aspects to intelligence: componential, experiential, and contextual (Ch. 8)

trichromatic theory of colour vision: The theory suggesting that there are three kinds of cones in the retina, each of which responds primarily to a specific range of wavelengths (Ch. 3)

trust-versus-mistrust stage: According to Erikson, the first stage of psychosocial development, occurring from birth to 18 months of age, during which time infants develop feelings of trust or lack of trust (Ch. 10)

U

unconditioned response (UCR): A response that is natural and needs no training (e.g., salivation at the smell of food) (Ch. 5)

unconditioned stimulus (UCS): A stimulus that brings about a response without having been learned (Ch. 5)

unconscious: A part of the personality of which a person is not aware, and which is a potential determinant of behaviour (Ch. 11)

unconscious wish fulfillment theory: Sigmund Freud's theory that dreams represent unconscious wishes that dreamers desire to see fulfilled (Ch. 4)

universal grammar: Noah Chomsky's theory that all the world's languages share a similar underlying structure (Ch. 7)

uplifts: Minor positive events that make one feel good (Ch. 9)

V

validity: The concept that tests actually measure what they are supposed to measure (Ch. 8)

variable-interval schedule: A schedule whereby the time between reinforcements varies around some average rather than being fixed (Ch. 5)

variable-ratio schedule: A schedule whereby reinforcement occurs after a varying number of responses rather than after a fixed number (Ch. 5)

variables: Behaviours, events, or other characteristics that can change, or vary, in some way (Ch. 1)

visual illusions: Physical stimuli that consistently produce errors in perception (Ch. 3)

W

wear-and-tear theories of aging: Theories that suggest that the mechanical functions of the body simply stop working efficiently (Ch. 10)

Weber's law: One of the basic laws of psychophysics stating that a just noticeable difference is a constant proportion of the intensity of an initial stimulus (Ch. 3)

weight set point: The particular level of weight that the body strives to maintain (Ch. 9)

whole language approach: reading instruction that stresses use of whole and meaningful materials (Ch.7)

working memory: Baddeley's theory that short-term memory comprises three components, the central executive, the visuospatial sketch pad, and the phonological loop (Ch. 6)

Z

zone of proximal development (ZPD): According to Vygotsky, the level at which a child can almost, but not fully, comprehend or perform a task on his or her own (Ch. 10)

zygote: The new cell formed by the product of fertilization (Ch. 10)

References

*denotes Canadian research

Aamodt, M. G. (1996). *Applied industrial/organizational psychology* (2nd ed.). Pacific Grove, CA: Brooks/Cole.

AAMR (American Association on Mental Retardation). (1992). Mental retardation: Definition, classification, and systems of support. Washington, DC: American Association on Mental Retardation.

AAUW (American Association of University Women). (1992). How schools shortchange women: The A.A.U.W. Report. Washington, DC: American Association of University Women Educational Foundation.

AAUW (American Association of University Women). (1993). *Hostile hallways.* Washington, DC: American Association of University Women Educational Foundation.

Abbot, L. F., Varela, J. A., Sen, K., & Nelson, S. B. (1997, January 10). Synaptic depression and cortical gain control. *Science, 275,* 220–224.

Abel, T., Alberini, C., Ghiradi, M., Huang, Y. Y., Nguyen, P., & Kandel, E. R. (1995). Steps toward a molecular definition of memory consolidation. In D. L. Schacter (Ed.), *Memory distortions: How minds, brains, and societies reconstruct the past.* Cambridge, MA: Harvard University Press.

Abele, A., & Petzold, P. (1994). How does mood operate in an impression formation task? An information integration approach. Special Issue: Affect in social judgments and cognition. *European Journal of Social Psychology, 24,* 173–187.

Abi-Dargham, A., Laruelle, M., Aghajanian, G. K., Charney, D., et al. (1997). The role of serotonin in the pathophysiology and treatment of schizophrenia. *Journal of Neuropsychiatry and Clinical Neurosciences, 9,* 1–17.

Aboud, F. E. (1988). *Children and prejudice.* New York: Blackwell.*

Aboud, F. E. & Doyle, A. B. (1996). Does talk of race foster prejudice or tolerance in children? *Canadian Journal of Behavioural Science, 28,* 161–170.*

Abrahams, M. F., & Bell, R. A. (1994). Encouraging charitable contributions: An examination of three models of door-in-the-face compliance. *Communication Research, 21,* 131–153.

Abramson, L. Y., Metalsky, G. I., & Alloy, L. B. (1989). Hopelessness depression: A theory-based subtype. *Psychological Review, 96,* 358–372.

Adams, B., & Parker, J. D. (1990). Maternal weight gain in women with good pregnancy outcome. *Obstetrics and Gynecology, 76,* 1–7.

Addictions Foundation of Manitoba. (1997). *Student survey on alcohol and other drugs.* Winnipeg: AFM.*

Addiction Research Foundation. (1995). *Opening Doors: A personal and social skills program.* Toronto: ARF.*

Addison, T. L., & Schmidt, L. A. (1999). Are women who are shy reluctant to take risks? Behavioural and psychophysiological correlates. *Journal of Research in Personality, 33,* 352–357.

Adelmann, P. K., Chadwick, K., & Baerger, D. R. (1996). Marital quality of Black and White adults over the life course. *Journal of Social and Personal Relationships, 13,* 361–384.

Adler, J. (1984, April 23). The fight to conquer fear. *Newsweek,* pp. 66–72.

Adler, P. A., & Adler, P. (1994). Observational techniques. In N. K. Denzin, & Y. S. Lincoln (Eds.), *Handbook of qualitative research.* Thousand Oaks, CA: Sage.

Adler, T. (1991, June). Primate rules focus on mental well-being. *APA Monitor, 6.*

Affleck, G., Tennen, H., Urrows, S., & Higgins, P. (1994). Person and contextual features of daily stress reactivity: Individual differences in relations of undesirable daily events with mood disturbance and chronic pain intensity. *Journal of Personality and Social Psychology, 66,* 329–340.

Aggleton, P., O'Reilly, K., Slutkin, G., & Davies, P. (July 15, 1994). Risking everything? Risk behavior, behavior change, and AIDS. *Science, 265,* 341–345.

Aghajanian, G. K. (1994). Serotonin and the action of LSD in the brain. *Psychiatric Annals, 24,* 137–141.

Agnew, C. R., & Thompson, V. D. (1994). Causal inferences and responsibility attributions concerning an HIV-positive target: The double-edged sword of physical attractiveness. *Journal of Social Behavior & Personality, 9,* 181–190.

Agras, W. S., & Berkowitz, R. I. (1996). Behavior therapy. In R. E. Hales, & S. C. Yudofsky (Eds.), *The American Psychiatric Press synopsis of psychiatry.* Washington, DC: American Psychiatric Press.

Ahissar, M., Ahissar, E., Bergman, H., & Vaadia, E. (1992). Encoding of sound-source location and movement: Activity of single neurons and interactions between adjacent neurons in the monkey auditory cortex. *Journal of Neurophysiology, 67,* 203–215.

Ahrons, C. (1995). *The good divorce: Keeping your family together when your marriage comes apart.* New York: HarperPerennial.

Aiken, L. R. (1996). *Assessment of intellectual functioning* (2nd ed.). New York: Plenum.

Aiken, L. R. (1997). *Psychological testing and assessment* (9th ed.). Boston: Allyn & Bacon.

Aikman, P. (n.d.) Female genital mutilation: Human rights abuse or protected cultural practice. Available: <http://meds.queensu.ca/hsj/vol1-1/fgm.html>.

Ainsworth, M. D. S. (1989). Attachments beyond infancy. *American Psychologist, 44,* 709–716.

Ainsworth, M. D. S., Blehar, M. C., Waters, E., & Wall, S. (1978). *Patterns of attachment: A psychological study of the strange situation.* Mahwah, NJ: Erlbaum.

Ainsworth, M. D. S., & Bowlby, J. (1991). An ethological approach to personality development. *American Psychologist, 46,* 333–341.

Akbarian, S., Kim, J. J., Potkin, S. G., Hetrick, & W. P., et al. (1996). Maldistribution of interstitial neurons in prefrontal white matter of the brains of schizophrenic patients. *Archives of General Psychiatry, 53,* 425–436.

Akil, H., & Morano, M. I. (1996). The biology of stress: From periphery to brain. In S. J. Watson (Ed.), *Biology of schizophrenia and affective disease.* Washington, DC: American Psychiatric Press.

Akmajian, A., Demers, R. A., & Harnish, R. M. (1984). *Linguistics.* Cambridge, MA: MIT Press.

Akutsu, P. D., Sue, S., Zane, N. W. S., & Nakamura, C. Y. (1989). Ethnic differences in alcohol consumption among Asians and Caucasians in the United States: An investigation of cultural and physiological factors. *Journal of Studies on Alcohol, 50,* 261–267.

Alan Guttmacher Institute. (1993a). Report on viral sexual diseases. Chicago: Alan Guttmacher Institute.

Alan Guttmacher Institute. (1993b). Survey of male sexuality. Chicago: Alan Guttmacher Institute.

Albee, G. W. (1978, February 12). I.Q. tests on trial. *New York Times,* p. E-13.

Albert, R. S. (Ed.). (1992). *The social psychology of creativity and exceptional achievement* (2nd ed.). New York: Pergamon.

Alcock, J. E. (1981). *Parapsychology: Science or magic?* London: Pergamon.*

Alcock, J. E. (1987). The status of parapsychology in the world of science. *Behaviour and Brain Sciences, 10,* 553–564.*

Alcock, J. E. (1998). Science, pseudoscience and anomaly. *Behaviour and Brain Sciences, 21,* 303.*

Alcock, J. E., Carment, D. W., & Sadava, S. W. (2000). *A textbook of social psychology.* Scarborough, Ontario: Pearson Education Canada.*

Alcock, J. E., Carment, D. W., Sadava, S. W., Collins, J. E., & Green, J. M. (1997). *A textbook of social psychology: Brief edition.* Scarborough, Ontario, Prentice Hall Allyn and Bacon.*

Aldrich, M. S. (1992). Narcolepsy. *Neurology, 42,* 34–43.

Aldwin, C. M., & Revenson, T. A. (1987). Does coping help? A reexamination of the relation between coping and mental health. *Journal of Personality and Social Psychology, 53,* 337–348.

Alexander, C. N., Langer, E. J., Newman, R. I., Chandler, H. M., & Davies, J. L. (1989). Transcendental meditation, mindfulness, and longevity: An experimental study with the elderly. *Journal of Personality and Social Psychology, 57,* 950–964.

Alford, B. A., & Beck, A. T. (1997). *The integrative power of cognitive therapy.* New York: Guilford Press.

Alkon, D. L. (1987). *Memory traces in the brain.* New York: Cambridge University Press.

Allen, L. S., & Gorski, R. A. (1992). Sexual orientation and the size of the anterior commissure in the human brain. *Proceedings of the National Academy of Sciences, 89,* 7199.

Allen, L. S., Hines, M., Shryne, J. E., & Gorski, R. A. (1989). Two sexually dimorphic cell groups in the human brain. *Journal of Neuroscience, 9,* 497–506.

Allen, V. L. (1965). Situational factors in conformity. In L. Berkowitz (Ed.), *Advances in experimental social psychology* (Vol. 1). New York: Academic Press.

Allen, V. L. (1975). Social support for nonconformity. In L. Berkowitz (Ed.), *Advances in experimental and social psychology* (Vol. 8). New York: Academic Press.

Alliger, G. M., Lilienfeld, S. O., & Mitchell, K. E. (1996). The susceptibility of overt and covert integrity tests to coaching and faking. *Psychological Science, 7,* 32–39.

Allison, J. A., & Wrightsman, L. S. (1993). *Rape: The misunderstood crime.* Newbury Park, CA: Sage.

Allison, K. W., Crawford, I., Echemendia, R., Robinson, L., & Knepp, D. (1994). Human diversity and professional competence: Training in clinical and counseling psychology revisited. *American Psychologist, 49,* 792–796.

Allport, G. W. (1961). *Pattern and growth in personality.* New York: Holt, Rinehart and Winston.

Allport, G. W. (1966). Traits revisited. *American Psychologist, 21,* 1–10.

Allport, G. W., & Postman, L. J. (1958). The basic psychology of rumor. In E. D. Maccoby, T. M. Newcomb, & E. L. Hartley (Eds.), *Readings in social psychology* (3rd ed.). New York: Holt, Rinehart and Winston.

Alonso, A., & Swiller, H. I. (Eds.). (1993). *Group therapy in clinical practice.* Washington, DC: American Psychiatric Press.

Alper, J. (1993, April 16). The pipeline is leaking women all the way along. *Science, 260,* 409–411.

Alsop, R. (1988, May 13). Advertisers put consumers on the couch. *Wall Street Journal,* p. 21.

Altman, N. (1996). The accommodation of diversity in psychoanalysis. In R. P. Foster, M. Moskowitz, & R. A. Javier (Eds.), *Reaching across boundaries of culture and class: Widening the scope of psychotherapy.* Northvale, NJ: Jason Aronson, Inc.

Altemeyer, B. (1981). *Right-wing authoritarianism.* Winnipeg: University of Manitoba Press.*

Altemeyer, B. (1994). Reducing prejudice in right-wing authoritarians. In M. P. Zanna & J. M. Olson (Eds.), *The psychology of prejudice: The Ontario Symposium,* (Vol. 7).*

Alwitt, L., & Mitchell, A. A. (1985). *Psychological processes and advertising effects: Theory, research, and applications.* Mahwah, NJ: Erlbaum.

Alzheimer's Manitoba. Available: <http://www.alzheimer.mb.ca/media/#aricept>.

American College Health Association. (1989). *Guidelines on acquaintance rape.* Washington, DC: American College Health Association.

American Psychiatric Association. (1994). *Diagnostic and statistical manual* (4th ed.). Washington, DC.

American Psychological Association. (1992). Ethical principles of psychologists and code of conduct. *American Psychological Association.* Washington, DC: American Psychological Association.

American Psychological Association. (1993, January/February). Subgroup norming and the Civil Rights Act. *Psychological Science Agenda, 5,* 6.

American Psychologist: A Public Interest Directorate. (1993, August 10). *Violence and youth: Psychology's response.* Washington, DC: American Psychological Association.

Amir, Y. (1976). The role of intergroup contact in change of prejudice and ethnic relations. In P. Katz (Ed.), *Towards the elimination of racism.* New York: Pergamon.

Amnesty International. (1998). Female genital mutilation—A human rights information package. Available: <http://www.amnesty.org/ailib/intcam/femgen/fgm3.htm>.

Amsel, A. (1988). *Behaviorism, neobehaviorism, and cognitivism in learning theory.* Mahwah, NJ: Erlbaum.

Anastasi, A. (1988). *Psychological testing* (6th ed.). New York: Macmillan.

Anastasi, A. (1996). *Psychological testing* (7th ed.). New York: Macmillan.

Anastasi, A., & Urbina, S. (1997). *Psychological testing* (7th ed.). Englewood Cliffs, NJ: Prentice Hall.

Andersen, B. L., Kiecolt-Glaser, J. K., & Glaser, R. (1994). A biobehavioral model of cancer stress and disease course. *American Psychologist, 49,* 389–404.

Anderson, B. F. (1980). *The complete thinker: A handbook of techniques for creative and critical problem solving.* Englewood Cliffs, NJ: Prentice-Hall.

Anderson, C. A., & Anderson, K. B. (1996). Violent crime rate studies in philosophical context: A destructive testing approach to heat and southern culture of violence effects. *Journal of Personality and Social Psychology, 70,* 740–756.

Anderson, J. (1988). Cognitive styles and multicultural populations. *Journal of Teacher Education, 39,* 2–9.

Anderson, J. A., & Adams, M. (1992). Acknowledging the learning styles of diverse student populations: Implications for instructional design. *New Directions for Teaching and Learning, 49,* 19–33.

Anderson, J. R. (1981). Interference: The relationship between response latency and response accuracy. *Journal of Experimental Psychology: Human Learning and Memory, 7,* 311–325.

Anderson, J. R. (1993). Problem solving and learning. *American Psychologist, 48,* 35–44.

Anderson, J. R., & Bower, G. H. (1972). Recognition and retrieval processes in free recall. *Psychological Review, 79,* 97–123.

Anderson, K. B., Cooper, H., & Okamura, L. (1997). Individual differences and attitudes toward rape: A meta-analytic review. *Personality and Social Psychology Bulletin, 23,* 295–315.

Anderson, N. H. (1974). Cognitive algebra integration theory applied to social attribution. In L. Berkowitz (Ed.), *Advances in experimental social psychology* (Vol. 7, pp. 1–101). New York: Academic Press.

Anderson, N. H. (1996). *A functional theory of cognition.* Mahwah, NJ: Erlbaum.

Anderson, N. H. (Ed.). (1991). *Contributions to information integration theory: Vol. 2. Social.* Mahwah, NJ: Erlbaum.

Anderson, S. M., & Klatzky, R. L. (1987). Traits and social stereotypes: Levels of categorization in person perception. *Journal of Personality and Social Psychology, 53,* 235–246.

Anderson, T., & Magnusson, D. (1990). Biological maturation in adolescence and the development of drinking habits and alcohol abuse among young males: A prospective longitudinal study. *Journal of Youth and Adolescence, 19,* 33–42.

Anderson, W. F. (1995, September). Gene therapy. *Scientific American,* 123–128.

Andreasen, N. C. (1985). Positive vs. negative schizophrenia: A critical evaluation. *Schizophrenia, 11,* 380–389.

Andreasen, N. C. (1997, March 14). Linking mind and brain in the study of mental illnesses: A project for a scientific psychopathology. *Science, 275,* 1586–1593.

Andreasen, N. C., Arndt, S., Swayze, V. W., II, Cizadlo, T., Flaum, M., O'Leary, D., Ehrhardt, J. C., & Yuh, W. T. C. (1994, October 14). Thalamic abnormalities in schizophrenia visualized through magnetic resonance image averaging. *Science, 266,* 294–298.

Andreasen, N. C., Rezai, K., Alliger, R., Swayze, V. W., II, Flaum, M., Kirchner, P., Cohen, G., & O'Leary, D. S. (1992). Hypofrontality in neuroleptic-naïve patients and in patients with chronic schizophrenia: Assessment with Xenon 133 single-photon emission computed tomography and the Tower of London. *Archives of General Psychiatry, 49,* 943–958.

Andreasen, N. C. (1989). Neural mechanisms of negative symptoms. *British Journal of Psychiatry, 155,* 93–98.

Andreassi, J. L. (1995). *Psychophysiology: Human behavior and physiological response* (3rd ed.). Mahwah, NJ: Erlbaum.

Angier, N. (1990, May 15). Cheating on sleep: Modern life turns America into the land of the drowsy. *New York Times,* pp. C1, C8.

Angier, N. (1991, January 22). A potent peptide prompts an urge to cuddle. *New York Times,* p. C1.

Angier, N. (1996, Nov. 1). Maybe gene isn't to blame for thrill-seeking manner. *The New York Times,* p. A12.

Angoff, W. H. (1988). The nature-nurture debate, aptitudes, and group differences. *American Psychologist, 43,* 713–720.

Anstey, K., Stankov, L., & Lord, S. (1993). Primary aging, secondary aging, and intelligence. *Psychology and Aging, 8,* 562–570.

Antony, M. M., Brown, T. A., & Barlow, D. H. (1992). Current perspectives on panic and panic disorder. *Current Directions in Psychological Science, 1,* 79–82.

Antony, M. M., & Swinson, R. P. (1996). Anxiety disorders: Future directions for research and treatment. Health Canada.*

APA (American Psychiatric Association) Task Force on Electroconvulsive Therapy. (1990). *The practice of electroconvulsive therapy: Recommendations for treatment, training, and privileging.* Washington, DC: American Psychiatric Association.

APA (American Psychological Association). (1986, March). Council resolution on polygraph tests. *APA Monitor.*

APA (American Psychological Association). (1988). *Behavioral research with animals.* Washington, DC: American Psychological Association.

APA (American Psychological Association). (1993). *Employment survey.* Washington, DC: American Psychological Association.

APA (American Psychological Association). (1994). *Careers in psychology.* Washington, DC: American Psychological Association.

APA (American Psychological Associaton). (1996). *Psychology careers for the twenty-first century.* Washington, DC: American Psychological Association.

APA Public Interest Directorate. (1993, August 10). *Violence and youth: Psychology's response.* Washington, DC: American Psychological Association.

Aponte, J. F., Rivers, R. Y., & Wohl, J. (Eds.). (1995). *Psychological interventions and cultural diversity.* New York: Longwood.

Apter, A., Galatzer, A., Beth-Halachmi, N., & Laron, Z. (1981). Self-image in adolescents with delayed puberty and growth retardation. *Journal of Youth and Adolescence, 10,* 501–505.

Apter, A., & Tyano, S. (1996). *Adolescent suicide and attempted suicide.* In F. L. Mak, & C. C. Nadelson (Eds.), *International*

review of psychiatry (Vol. 2). Washington, DC: American Psychiatric Press.

Arafat, I., & Cotton, W. L. (1974). Masturbation practices of males and females. *Journal of Sex Research, 10,* 293–307.

Archambault, D. L. (1992). Adolescence: A physiological, cultural, and psychological no man's land. In G. W. Lawson, & A. W. Lawson (Eds.), *Adolescent substance abuse: Etiology, treatment, and prevention.* Gaithersburg, MD: Aspen.

Archer, D., & McDaniel, P. (1995). Violence and gender: Differences and similarities across societies. In R. B. Ruback, & N. A. Weiner (Eds.), *Interpersonal violent behaviors: Social and cultural aspects.* New York: Springer.

Archer, D., Pettigrew, T. F., & Aronson, E. (1992). Making research apply. *American Psychologist, 47,* 1233–1236.

Archer, J. (1996). Sex differences in social behavior: Are the social role and evolutionary explanations compatible? *American Psychologist, 51,* 909–917.

Archer, S. L., & Waterman, A. S. (1994). Adolescent identity development: Contextual perspectives. In C. B. Fisher, & R. M. Lerner (Eds.), *Applied developmental psychology.* New York: McGraw-Hill.

Archibald, W. P. (1974). Alternative explanations for the self-fulfilling prophecy. *Psychological Bulletin, 81,* 74–84.

Arcus, D. (1994). Biological mechanisms and personality: Evidence from shy children. *Advances, 10,* 40–50.

Arena, J. G., & Blanchard, E. B. (1996). Biofeedback and relaxation therapy for chronic pain disorders. In R. J. Gatchel, & D. C. Turk (Eds.), *Psychological approaches to pain management: A practitioner's handbook.* New York: Guilford Press.

Arena, J. M. (1984, April). A look at the opposite sex. *Newsweek on Campus,* p. 21.

Arlin, P. K. (1989). The problem of the problem. In J. D. Sinnott (Ed.), *Everyday problem solving: Theory and applications.* New York: Praeger.

Armstrong, R. A., Slaven, A., & Harding, G. F. (1991). Visual evoked magnetic fields to flash and pattern in 100 normal subjects. *Vision Research, 31,* 1859–1864.

Armstrong, Sally. (1998, Nov/Dec). Not my daughter. Homemaker's, 66–83.

Arneric, S. P., Sullivan, J. P., Decker, M. W., Brioni, J. D., et al. (1995). Potential treatment of Alzheimer disease using cholinergic channel activators (ChCAs) with cognitive enhancement, anxiolytic-like, and cytoprotective properties. Special Issue: Cholinergic signaling in Alzheimer disease: Therapeutic strategies. *Alzheimer Disease and Associated Disorders, 9,* (Suppl. 2), 50–61.

Aron, A., Melinat, E., Aronon, E. N., Vallone, R. D., & Bator, R. J. (1997). The experimental generation of interpersonal closeness: A procedure and some preliminary findings. *Personality and Social Psychology Bulletin, 23,* 363–377.

Aronow, E., Reznikoff, M., & Moreland, K. (1994). *The Rorschach technique: Perceptual basics, content interpretation, and applications.* Boston: Longwood.

Aronson, E. (1988). *The social animal* (3rd ed.). San Francisco: Freeman.

Aronson, E., Ellsworth, P. C., Carlsmith, J. M., & Gonzales, M. H. (1990). *Methods of research in social psychology* (2nd ed.). New York: McGraw-Hill.

Arvanitogiannis, A. (1999). Resetting the rat circadian clock by ultra-short light flashes. *Neuroscience Letters, 261,* 159–162.*

Asch, S. E. (1946). Forming impressions of personality. *Journal of Abnormal and Social Psychology, 41,* 258–290.

Asch, S. E. (1951). Effects of group pressure upon the modification and distortion of judgments. In H. Guetzkow (Ed.), *Groups, leadership, and men.* Pittsburgh: Carnegie Press.

Asher, S. R., & Parker, J. G. (1991). Significance of peer relationship problems in childhood. In B. H. Schneider, G. Attili, J. Nadel, & R. P. Weissberg (Eds.), *Social competence in developmental perspective.* Amsterdam: Kluwer Academic.

Ashton, M. C., Jackson, D. N., Helmes, E., & Paunonen, S. V. (1998). Joint factor analysis of the Personality Research Form and the Jackson Personality Inventory: Comparisons with the Big Five. *Journal of Research in Personality, 32,* 243–250.*

Aslin, R. N. (1987). Visual and auditory development in infancy. In J. Osofsky (Ed.), *Handbook of infant development* (2nd ed.). New York: Wiley.

Aslin, R. N., & Smith, L. B. (1988). Perceptual development. *Annual Review of Psychology, 39,* 435–473.

Asnis, G. M., & van Praag, H. M. (Eds.). (1995). *Panic disorder: Clinical, biological, and treatment aspects.* New York: Wiley.

Association for Bright Children of Ontario. Available <http://www.kanservu.ca/~abc/>.

Atkinson, H. (Ed.). (1997, January 21). Understanding your diagnosis. *HealthNews,* p. 3.

Atkinson, J. (1995). Through the eyes of an infant. In R. L. Gregory, J. Harris, P. Heard, & D. Rose (Eds.), *The artful eye.* Oxford, England: Oxford University Press.

Atkinson, J., & Braddick, O. (1989). Development of basic visual functions. In A. M. Slater, & J. G. Bremner (Eds.), *Infant development.* Mahwah, NJ: Erlbaum.

Atkinson, J. W., & Feather, N. T. (1966). *Theory of achievement motivation.* New York: Krieger.

Atkinson, J. W., & Raynor, J. O. (Eds.). (1974). *Motivation and achievement.* Washington, DC: Winston.

Atkinson, J. W., & Shiffrin, R. M. (1971, August). The control of short-term memory. *Scientific American,* pp. 82–90.

Atkinson, R. C., & Shiffrin, R. M. (1968). Human memory: A proposed system and its control processes. In K. W. Spence, and J. T. Spence (Eds.), *The psychology of learning and motivation: Advances in research and theory* (Vol. 2, pp. 80–195). New York: Academic Press.

Augoustinos, M., & Walker, I. (1995). *Social cognition: An integrated introduction.* London: Sage.

Auld, F., & Hyman, M. (1991). *Resolution of inner conflict: An introduction to psychoanalytic therapy.* Washington, DC: American Psychological Association.

Austad, S. N. (1997). *Why we age. What science is discovering about the body's journey through life.* New York: Wiley.

Averill, J. R. (1975). A semantic atlas of emotional concepts. *Catalog of Selected Documents in Psychology, 5,* 330.

Averill, J. R. (1994). Emotions are many splendored things. In P. Ekman, & R. J. Davidson (Eds.), *The nature of emotion: Fundamental questions.* New York: Oxford, University Press.

Averill, J. R. (1997). The emotions: An integrative approach. In R. Hogan, J. Johnson, & S. Briggs (Eds.), *Handbook of personality psychology.* Orlando, FL: Academic Press.

Avison, W. R., & Gotlib, I. H. (Eds.). (1994). *Stress and mental health.* New York: Plenum.

Avorn, J. (1983). Biomedical and social determinants of cognitive impairment in the elderly. *Journal of the American Geriatric Society, 31,* 137–143.

Ayoub, D. M., Greenough, W. T., & Juraska, J. M. (1983). Sex differences in dendritic structure in the preoptic area of the juvenile macaque monkey brain. *Science, 219,* 197–198.

Azar, B. (1996a, December). Behavioral interventions are proven to reduce pain. *APA Monitor,* Washington, DC: American Psychological Association.

Azar, B. (1996b, December). Psychosocial factors provide clues to pain. *APA Monitor,* p. 20.

Azar, B. (1997, April). Psychologists are watching debate over 2000 census. *APA Monitor,* p. 28.

Azrin, N. H., & Holt, N. C. (1966). Punishment. In W. A. Honig (Ed.), *Operant behavior: Areas of research and application* (pp. 380–447). New York: Appleton.

B.B.S.T.F. (Basic Behavioral Science Task Force). (1996). Basic behavioral science research for mental health: Thought and communication. *American Psychologist, 51,* 181–189.

Baba, T. W., Trichel, A. M., An, L., Liska, V., Martin, L. N., Murphey-Corb, M., & Ruprecht, R. M. (June 7, 1996). Infection and AIDS in adult macaques after nontraumatic oral exposure to cell-free HIV. *Science, 272,* 1486–1489.

Babbitt, T., Rowland, G., & Franken, R. (1990). Sensation seeking and participation in aerobic exercise classes. *Personality and Individual Differences, 11,* 181–184.

Bach y Rita, P. (1993). Nonsynaptic diffusion neurotransmission (NDN) in the brain. *Neurochemistry International, 23,* 297–318.

Backer, P. (1993, February 28). On turning 13: Reports from the front lines. *New York Times,* sec 4, p. 2.

Backlar, P. (1996). Genes and behavior: Will genetic information change the way we see ourselves? *Community Mental Health Journal, 32,* 205–209.

Baddeley, A. (1982). *Your memory: A user's guide.* New York: Macmillan.

Baddeley, A. (1992, January 31). Working memory. *Science, 255,* 556–559.

Baddeley, A. (1993). Working memory and conscious awareness. In A. F. Collins, S. E. Gathercole, M. A. Conway, & P. E. Morris (Eds.), *Theories of memory.* Mahwah, NJ: Erlbaum.

Baddeley, A. D. (1978). The trouble with levels: A reexamination of Craik and Lockhart's framework for memory research. *Psychological Review, 85,* 139–152.

Baddeley, A. D. (1995a). The psychology of memory. In A. D. Baddeley, B. A. Wilson, & F. N. Watts (Eds.), *Handbook of memory disorders.* Chichester, England: Wiley.

Baddeley, A. D. (1995b). Working memory. In M. S. Gazzaniga (Ed.), *The cognitive neurosciences.* Cambridge, MA: MIT Press.

Baddeley, A. D. (1996). Exploring the central executive. *Quarterly Journal of Experimental Psychology, Human Experimental Psychology, 49A,* 5–28.

Baddeley, A. D., & Hitch, G. J. (1994). Developments in the concept of working memory. Special Section: Working memory. *Neuropsychology, 8,* 485–493.

Baddeley, A., & Wilson, B. (1985). Phonological coding and short-term memory in patients without speech. *Journal of Memory and Language, 24,* 490–502.

Baddeley, A., Wilson, B., & Watts, F. (Eds.). (1995). *Handbook of memory disorders.* New York: Wiley.

Baer, J. (1993). *Creativity and divergent thinking: A task-specific approach.* Mahwah, NJ: Erlbaum.

Baer, J. (1997). *Creative teachers, creative students.* Boston, MA: Allyn & Bacon.

Baer, L., Rauch, S. L., Ballantine, H. T., Jr., Martuza, R., Cosgrove, R., Cassem, E., Giriunas, I., Manzo, P. A., Dimino, C., & Jenike, M. A. (1995). Cingulotomy for intractable obsessive-compulsive disorder. Prospective long-term follow-up of 18 patients. *Archives of General Psychiatry, 52,* 384–392.

Bagby, R. M., Buis, T., & Nicholson, R. A. (1995). Relative effectiveness of the standard validity scales in detecting fake-bad and fake-good responding: Replication and extension. *Psychological Assessment, 7,* 84–92.

Bahill, T. A., & Laritz, T. (1984). Why can't batters keep their eyes on the ball? *American Scientist, 72,* 249–253.

Bahrick, H. P., Hall, L. K., & Berger, S. A. (1996). Accuracy and distortion in memory for high school grades. *Psychological Science, 7,* 265–269.

Bailey, J. M. (1995). Biological perspectives on sexual orientation. In A. R. D'Augelli, & C. J. Patteson (Eds.), *Lesbian, gay, and bisexual identities over the lifespan: Psychological perspectives.* New York: Oxford University Press.

Bailey, J. M., & Pillard, R. C. (1991). A genetic study of male sexual orientation. *Archives of General Psychiatry, 48,* 1089–1096.

Bailey, J. M., Pillard, R. C., Kitzinger, C., & Wilkinson, S. (1997). Sexual orientation: Is it determined by biology? In M. R. Walsh (Ed.), *Women, men, & gender: Ongoing debates.* New Haven, CT: Yale University Press.

Bailey, J. M., Pillard, R. C., Neale, M. C., & Agyei, Y. (1993). Heritable factors influence sexual orientation in women. *Archives of General Psychiatry, 50,* 217–223.

Bailey, J. M., & Zucker, K. J. (1995). Childhood sex-typed behavior and sexual orientation: A conceptual analysis and quantitative review. *Developmental Psychology, 31,* 43–55.

Bailey, J. M., & Pillard, R. C. (1994, January). The innateness of homosexuality. *Harvard Mental Health Letter, 10,* 4–6.

Baird, J. C. (1997). *Sensation and judgment: Complementarity theory of psychophysics.* Mahwah, NJ: Erlbaum.

Baird, J. C., Wagner, M., & Fuld, K. (1990). A simple but powerful theory of the moon illusion. *Journal of Experimental Psychology Human Perception and Performance, 16,* 675–677.

Baker, A. G., & Mercier, P. (1989). Attention, retrospective processing and evolution of a structured connectionist model of Pavlovian conditioning (AESOP). In S. B. Klein, & R. R. Mowrer (Eds.), *Contemporary learning theories: Vol. I. Pavlovian conditioning and the status of traditional learning theory.* Mahwah, NJ: Erlbaum.

Baker, J. N. (1987, July 27). Battling the IQ-test ban. *Newsweek,* p. 53.

Baker, R. (Ed.). (1989). *Panic disorder: Theory, research and therapy.* New York: Wiley.

Baker, S. L., & Kirsch, I. (1991). Cognitive mediators of pain perception and tolerance. *Journal of Personality and Social Psychology, 61,* 504–510.

Baker, S. P., Lamb, M. W., Li, G., & Dodd, R. S. (1993). Human factors in crashes of commuter airplanes. *Aviation, Space, and Environmental Medicine, 64,* 63–68.

Baldwin, M. W. (1995). Relational schemas and cognition in close relationships. Special Section: Study of relationships. *Journal of Social and Personal Relationships, 12,* 547–552.

Bales, J. (1988, April). Polygraph screening banned in Senate bill. *APA Monitor, 10.*

Ball, E. M., Simon, R. D., Tall, A. A., Banks, M. B., Nino-Murcia, G., & Dement, W. C. (1997, February 24). Diagnosis and treatment of sleep apnea within the community. *Archive of Internal Medicine, 157,* 419–424.

Ballinger, B., & Yalom, I. (1994). Group therapy in practice. In B. Bongar, & L. E. Beutler (Eds.), *Comprehensive textbook of psychotherapy: Theory and practice.* New York: Oxford University Press.

Ballinger, C. B. (1981). The menopause and its syndromes. In J. G. Howells (Ed.), *Modern perspectives in the psychiatry of middle age* (pp. 279–303). New York: Brunner/Mazel.

Balter, M. (1996, February 16). New clues to brain dopamine control, cocaine addiction. *Science, 271,* 909.

Baltes, P. B., & Schaie, K. W. (1974, March). The myth of the twilight years. *Psychology Today,* pp. 35–38ff.

Bandura, A. (1973). *Aggression: A social learning analysis.* Englewood Cliffs, NJ: Prentice-Hall.

Bandura, A. (1977). *Social learning theory.* Englewood Cliffs, NJ: Prentice-Hall.

Bandura, A. (1981). In search of pure unidirectional determinants. *Behavior Therapy, 12,* 30–40.

Bandura, A. (1983). Psychological mechanisms of aggression. In R. G. Geen, & E. I. Donnerstein (Eds.), *Aggression: Theoretical and empirical reviews, Vol. 1: Theoretical and methodological issues.* New York: Academic Press.

Bandura, A. (1986). *Social foundations of thought and action: A social cognitive theory.* Englewood, Cliffs, NJ: Prentice-Hall.

Bandura, A. (1994). Social cognitive theory of mass communication. In J. Bryant, & D. Zillmann (Eds.), *Media effects: Advances in theory and research. LEA's communication series.* Mahwah, NJ: Erlbaum.

Bandura, A. (Ed.). (1995). *Self-efficacy in changing societies.* New York: Cambridge University Press.

Bandura, A. (1997). *Self-efficacy: The exercise of control.* New York: Freeman.

Bandura, A., Grusec, J. E., & Menlove, F. L. (1967). Vicarious extinction of avoidance behavior. *Journal of Personality and Social Psychology, 5,* 16–23.

Bandura, A., O'Leary, A., Taylor, C. B., Gauthier, J., & Gossard, D. (1987). Perceived self-efficacy and pain control: Opioid and non-opioid mechanism. *Journal of Personality and Social Psychology, 53,* 563–571.

Bandura, A., Ross, D., & Ross, S. (1963a). Imitation of film-mediated aggressive models. *Journal of Abnormal and Social Psychology, 66,* 3–11.

Bandura, A., Ross, D., & Ross, S. (1963b). Vicarious reinforcement and imitative learning. *Journal of Abnormal and Social Psychology, 67,* 601–607.

Banks, T., & Dabbs, J. M., Jr. (1996). Salivary testosterone and cortisol in delinquent and violent urban subculture. *Journal of Social Psychology, 136,* 49–56.

Barbaro, N. M. (1988). Studies of PAG/PVG stimulation for pain relief in humans. *Progress in Brain Research, 77,* 165–173.

Barber, B. L., & Eccles, J. S. (1992). Long-term influence of divorce and single parenting on adolescent family- and work-related values, behaviors, and aspirations. *Psychological Bulletin, 111,* 108–126.

Barber, J. (Ed.). (1996). *Hypnosis and suggestion in the treatment of pain: A clinical guide.* New York: Norton.

Barber, S., & Lane, R. C. (1995). Efficacy research in psychodynamic therapy: A critical review of the literature. *Psychotherapy in Private Practice, 14,* 43–69.

Barber, T. X. (1975). Responding to "hypnotic" suggestions: An introspective report. *American Journal of Clinical Hypnosis, 18,* 6–22.

Barefoot, J. C., & Schroll, M. (1996). Symptoms of depression, acute myocardial infarction, and total mortality in a community sample. *Circulation, 93,* 1976–1980.

Bargh, J., & Pietromonaco, P. (1982). Automatic information processing and social perception: The influence of trait information presented outside of conscious awareness on impression formation. *Journal of Personality and Social Psychology, 43,* 437–449.

Bargh, J. A., & Raymond, P. (1995). The naive misuse of power: Nonconscious sources of sexual harassment. Special Issue: Gender stereotyping, sexual harassment, and the law. *Journal of Social Issues, 51,* 85–96.

Bargh, J. A., Raymond, P., Pryor, J. B., & Strack, F. (1995). Attractiveness of the underling: An automatic power sex association and its consequences for sexual harassment and aggression. *Journal of Personality and Social Psychology, 68,* 768–781.

Barinaga, M. (1991, June 14). Sexism charged by Stanford physician. *Science, 252,* 1484.

Barinaga, M. (1994, December 2). Watching the brain remake itself. *Science, 266,* 1475–1476.

Barinaga, M. (1995, April 14). Dendrites shed their dull image. *Science, 268,* 200–201.

Barinaga, M. (1996, April 26). The cerebellum: Movement coordinator or much more? *Science, 272,* 482–483.

Barinaga, M. (1997a, May 30). How much pain for cardiac gain? *Science, 276,* 1324–1327.

Barinaga, M. (1997b, June 27). New imaging methods provide a better view into the brain. *Science, 276,* 1974–1976.

Barland, G. H., & Raskin, D. C. (1975). An evaluation of field techniques in detection of deception. *Psychophysiology, 12,* 321–330.

Barman, J. (1996). Aboriginal education at the crossroads: The legacy of residential schools and the way ahead. In D. A. Long & O. P. Dickason (Eds.), *Visions of the heart: Canadian aboriginal issues.* Toronto: Harcourt Brace.*

Barnard, N. D., & Kaufman, S. R. (1997, February). Animal research is wasteful and misleading. *Scientific American, 276,* 80–82.

Barnett, R. C., Marshall, N. L., Raudenbush, S. W., & Brennan, R. T. (1993). Gender and the relationship between job experiences and psychological distress: A study of dual-earner couples. *Journal of Personality and Social Psychology, 64,* 794–806.

Barnett, R. C., Marshall, N. L., & Singer, J. D. (1992). Job experiences over time, multiple roles, and women's mental health: A longitudinal study. *Journal of Personality and Social Psychology, 67,* 634–644.

Barnett, W. S. (1993). Benefit-cost analysis of preschool education: Findings from a 25-year follow-up. *Journal of Orthopsychiatry, 63,* 500–508.

Baron, J. (1993). Why teach thinking?—An essay. *Applied Psychology: An International Review, 42,* 191–237.

Baron, J. B., & Sternberg, R. J. (1986). *Teaching thinking skills.* New York: Freeman.

Baron, R. A., & Bronfen, M. I. (1994). A whiff of reality: Empirical evidence concerning the effects of pleasant fragrances on work-related behavior. *Journal of Applied Social Psychology, 24,* 1179–1203.

Baron, R. A., & Byrne, D. (1988). *Social psychology: Understanding human interaction* (5th ed.). Boston: Allyn & Bacon.

Barondes, S. H. (1994, February 25). Thinking about Prozac. *Science, 263,* 1102–1103.

Barreira, P. T. (1996). New medications: Major antipsychotic psychopharmacologic advances. In S. M. Soreff (Ed.), *Handbook for the treatment of the seriously mentally ill.* Seattle, WA: Hogrefe & Huber.

Barrera, M. E. & Maurer, D. (1981) Discrimination of strangers by the three month old. *Child Development, 52(2),* 558–563.*

Barrett, M. C., King, A., Lévy, J., Maticka-Tyndale, E., & McKay, A. (1997). Canada. In R. T. Francoeur (Ed.), *The international encyclopedia of sexuality (Vol. 1): Argentina to Greece.* New York: Continuum.*

Barringer, F. (1989, June 9). Doubt on "trial marriage" raised by divorce rates. *New York Times,* pp. 1, 28.

Barringer, F. (1993a, April 1). Viral sexual diseases are found in 1 of 5 in U.S. *New York Times,* pp. A1, B9.

Barringer, F. (1993b, May 16). Pride in a soundless world: Deaf oppose a hearing aid. *New York Times,* pp. 1, 22.

Barron, F. (1990). *Creativity and psychological health: Origins of personal vitality and creative freedom.* Buffalo, NY: Creative Education Foundation.

Barron, F., & Harrington, D. M. (1981). Creativity, intelligence, and personality. *Annual Review of Psychology, 32,* 439–476.

Barron, R. W. (1994). The sound-to-spelling connection: Orthographic activation in auditory word recognition and its implications for the acquisition of phonological awareness and literacy skills. In V. W. Berninger (Ed.), *The varieties of orthographic knowledge I: Theoretical and developmental issues.* Dordrecht, the Netherlands: Kluwer.*

Barry, H., III, Josephson, L., Lauer, E., & Marshall, C. (1976). Traits inculcated in childhood: V. Cross-cultural codes. *Ethnology, 15,* 83–114.

Barsalou, L. W. (1992). *Cognitive psychology: An overview for cognitive scientists.* Mahwah, NJ: Erlbaum.

Barsky, A. J., Cleary, P. D., Wyshak, G., Spitzer, R. L., Williams, J. B. W., & Klerman, G. L. (1992). A structure diagnostic interview for hypochondriasis: A proposed criterion standard. *Journal of Nervous and Mental Disease, 180,* 20–27.

Bartecchi, C. E., MacKenzie, T. D., & Schrier, R. W. (1995, May). The global tobacco epidemic. *Scientific American,* pp. 44–51.

Bartlett, F. (1932). *Remembering: A study in experimental and social psychology.* Cambridge, England: Cambridge University Press.

Bartlett, J. A., Demetrikopoulos, M. K., Schleifer, S. J., & Keller, S. J. (1996). Stress, depression, mood, and immunity. In C. R. Pfeffer (Ed.), *Severe stress and mental disturbance in children.* Washington, DC: American Psychiatric Press.

Bartoshuk, L., & Drewnowski, A. (1997, February). Symposium presented at the annual meeting of the American Association for the Advancement of Science, Seattle.

Bartoshuk, L., & Lucchina, L. (1997, January 13). Are you a supertaster? *U.S. News & World Report*, pp. 58, 59.

Bartoshuk, L. M. (1971). The chemical senses: I. Taste. In J. N. Kling, & L. A. Riggs (Eds.), *Experimental psychology* (3rd ed.). New York: Holt, Rinehart and Winston.

Bartoshuk, L. M., & Beauchamp, G. K. (1994). Chemical senses. *Annual Review of Psychology, 45,* 419–449.

Bartoshuk, L. M., Duffy, V. B., Reed, D., & Williams, A. (1996). Supertasting, earaches and head injury: Genetics and pathology alter our taste worlds. *Neuroscience and Biobehavioral Review, 20,* 79–87.

Bartsch, K., & Estes, D. (1996). Individual differences in children's developing theory of mind and implications for metacognition. *Learning and Individual Differences, 8,* 281–304.

Basch, M. F. (1996). Affect and defense. In D. L. Nathanson (Ed.), *Knowing feeling: Affect, script, and psychotherapy.* New York: Norton.

Basco, M. R., & Rush, A. J. (1996). *Cognitive-behavioral therapy for bipolar disorder.* New York: Guilford Press.

Bashore, T. R., & Rapp, P. E. (1993). Are there alternatives to traditional polygraph procedures? *Psychological Bulletin, 113,* 3–22.

Basic Behavioral Science Task Force. (1996). Basic behavioral science research for mental health: Perception, attention, learning, and memory. *American Psychologist, 51,* 133–142.

Bass, A. (1996, April 21). Is anger good for you? *Boston Globe Magazine,* pp. 20–41.

Bass, B. M. (1990). *Bass & Stogdill's handbook of leadership: Theory, research, & managerial applications* (3rd ed.). New York: Free Press.

Batson, C. D. (1990). How social an animal? The human capacity for caring. *American Psychologist, 45,* 336–346.

Batson, C. D. (1991). *The altruism question: Toward a social-psychological answer.* Mahwah, NJ: Erlbaum.

Batson, C. D., Batson, J. G., Slingsby, J. K., Harrell, K. L., Peekna, H. M., & Todd, R. M. (1991). Empathic joy and the empathy-altruism hypothesis. *Journal of Personality and Social Psychology, 61,* 413–426.

Batson, C. D., Batson, J. G., Todd, R. M., & Brummett, B. H. (1995). Empathy and the collective good: Caring for one of the others in a social dilemma. *Journal of Personality & Social Psychology, 68,* 619–631.

Battiste, M. (1995). Introduction. In M. Battiste & J. Barman (Eds.), *First Nations education in Canada: The circle unfolds* (pp. vii–xx). Vancouver: University of British Columbia Press.*

Bauer, P. J. (1996). What do infants recall of their lives? Memory for specific events by one- to two-year-olds. 102nd Annual Convention of the American Psychological Association. (1994, Los Angeles, California, US) *American Psychologist, 51,* 29–41.

Baum, A., Cohen, L., & Hall, M. (1993). Control and instrusive memories as possible determinants of chronic stress. *Psychosomatic Medicine, 55,* 274–286.

Baum, A., Gatchel, R. J., & Schaeffer, M. A. (1983). Emotional, behavioral, and physiological effects of chronic stress at Three Mile Island. *Journal of Consulting and Clinical Psychology, 51,* 565–572.

Baumeister, R. (1997). Was Freud right? Psychoanalytic theories in modern social-personality research. Paper presented at APA Annual Convention Symposium, Washington, DC.

Baumrind, D. (1971). Current patterns of parental authority. *Developmental Psychology Monographs, 4* (1, pt. 2).

Baumrind, D. (1980). New directions in socialization research. *Psychological Bulletin, 35,* 639–652.

Bayer, D. L. (1996). Interaction in families with young adults with a psychiatric diagnosis. *American Journal of Family Therapy, 24,* 21–30.

Beal, C. R., Schmitt, K. L., & Dekle, D. J. (1995). Eyewitness identification of children: Effects of absolute judgments, nonverbal response options, and event encoding. *Law and Human Behavior, 19,* 197–216.

Beall, A. E., & Sternberg, R. J. (Eds.). (1993). *The psychology of gender.* New York: Guilford.

Beaman, A. L., Cole, C. M., Preston, M., Klentz, B., & Steblay, N. M. (1983). Fifteen years of foot-in-the-door research: A meta-analysis. *Personality and Social Psychology Bulletin, 9,* 181–196.

Bear, M. F., Cooper, L. N., & Ebner, F. F. (1987). A physiological basis for a theory of synapse modification. *Science, 237,* 42–48.

Beardsley, T. (1996, March). Vital data. *Scientific American,* pp. 100–105.

Beardsley, T. (1997, March). Memories are made of . . . *Scientific American,* pp. 32–33.

Beck, A. T. (1976). *Cognitive therapy and emotional disorders.* New York: International Universities Press.

Beck, A. T. (1982). Cognitive therapy of depression: New perspectives. In P. Clayton, & J. Barrett (Eds.), *Treatment of depression: Old controversies and new approaches.* New York: Raven.

Beck, A. T. (1991). Cognitive therapy: A 30-year perspective. *American Psychologist, 46,* 368–375.

Beck, A. T. (1995). Cognitive therapy: Past, present, and future. In M. J. Mahoney (Ed.), *Cognitive and constructive psychotherapies: Theory, research, and practice.* New York: Springer.

Beck, A. T., & Emery, G., with Greenberg, R. L. (1985). *Anxiety disorders and phobias: A cognitive perspective.* New York: Basic Books.

Beck, A. T., & Haaga, D. A. F. (1992). The future of cognitive therapy. *Psychotherapy, 29,* 34–38.

Beck, M. (1992, May 25). Menopause. *Newsweek,* pp. 71–79.

Beck, M., & Wingert, P. (1993, June 23). The young and the gifted. *Newsweek,* pp. 52–53.

Becker, B. J. (1990). Coaching for the Scholastic Aptitude Test: Further synthesis and appraisal. *Review of Educational Research, 60,* 373–417.

Beckham, E. E., & Leber, W. R. (Eds.). (1997). *Handbook of Depression* (2nd ed.). New York: Guilford Press.

Beckman, H. B., & Frankel, R. M. (1984). The effect of physician behavior on the collection of data. *Annals of Internal Medicine, 101,* 692–696.

Beckman, J. C., Keefe, F. J., Caldwell, D. S., & Brown, C. J. (1991). Biofeedback as a means to alter electromyographic activity in a total knee replacement patient. *Biofeedback and Self Regulation, 16,* 23–35.

Bedard, J., & Chi, M. T. H. (1992). Expertise. *Current Directions in Psychological Science, 1,* 135–139.

Bedard, W. W., & Parsinger, M. A. (1995). Prednisolone blocks extreme intermale social aggression in seizure-induced, brain-damaged rats: Implications for the amygdaloid central nucleus, corticotrophin-releasing factor, and electrical seizures. *Psychological Reports, 77,* 3–9.

Begley, S. (1993, December 20). "We slam-dunked it": NASA's shuttle mission fixes Hubble Telescope. *Newsweek,* pp. 100–102.

Begley, S. (1996, July 1). To stand and raise a glass. *Newsweek,* pp. 52–55.

Behrmann, M., Winocur, G., & Moscovitch, M. (1992). Dissociation between mental imagery and object recognition in a brain-damaged patient. *Nature, 359,* 636–637.

Beilin, H. (1996). Mind and meaning: Piaget and Vygotsky on causal explanation. *Human Development, 39,* 277–286.

Beilin, H., & Pufall, P. (Eds.). (1992). *Piaget's theory: Prospects and possibilities.* Mahwah, NJ: Erlbaum.

Belicki, K., & Cuddy, M. (1996). Identifying a history of sexual trauma from patterns of dream and sleep experience. In D. Barrett (Ed.), *Trauma and dreams* (pp. 46–55). Boston: Harvard University Press.*

Belkin, L. (1997, June 15). How can we save the next victim? *New York Times Magazine,* pp. 28–33, 44, 50, 63, 66, 70.

Bell, A., & Weinberg, M. S. (1978). *Homosexuality: A study of diversities among men and women.* New York: Simon & Schuster.

Bell, J., Grekul, J., Lamba, N., & Minas, C. (1995). The impact of cost on student helping behavior. *Journal of Social Psychology, 135,* 49–56.

Bell, R. A., Cholerton, M., Fraczek, K. E., & Rohlfs, G. S. (1994). Encouraging donations to charity: A field study of competing and complementary factors in tactic sequencing. *Western Journal of Communication, 58,* 98–115.

Bell, S. M., & Ainsworth, M. D. S. (1972). Infant crying and maternal responsiveness. *Child Development, 43,* 1171–1190.

Bellack, A. S., Hersen, M., & Kazdin, A. E. (1990). *International handbook of behavior modification and therapy.* New York: Plenum.

Bellak, L. (1993). *The T.A.T., C.A.T., and S.A.T. in clinical use* (5th ed.). Boston: Longwood.

Beller, M., & Gafni, N. (1996). 1991 International assessment of educational progress in mathematics and sciences: The gender differences perspective. *Journal of Educational Psychology, 88*, 365–377.

Bellezza, F. S., Six, L. S., & Phillips, D. S. (1992). A mnemonic for remembering long strings of digits. *Bulletin of the Psychonomic Society, 30*, 271–274.

Belluck, P., & Alvarez, L. (1996, February 18). Danger rode on New Jersey transit engineer's coveted shift. *New York Times*, pp. 37, 40.

Belmont, J. M. (1995). Discussion: A view from the empiricist's window. Special Issue: Lev S. Vygotsky and contemporary educational psychology. *Educational Psychologist, 30*, 99–102.

Belsky, J., & Rovine, M. (1988). Nonmaternal care in the first year of life and infant-parent attachment security. *Child Development, 59*, 157–167.

Bem, D. J. (1996). Exotic becomes erotic: A developmental theory of sexual orientation. *Psychological Review, 103*, 320–335.

Bem, D. J., & Honorton, C. (1994). Does psi exist? Replicable evidence for an anomalous process of information transfer. *Psychological Bulletin, 115*, 4–18.

Bem, S. (1987). Gender schema theory and its implications for child development: Raising gender-aschematic children in a gender-schematic society. In M. R. Walsh (Ed.), *The psychology of women: Ongoing debates*. New Haven, CT: Yale University Press.

Bem, S. L. (1993). *Lenses of gender*. New Haven, CT: Yale University Press.

Benbow, C. P., Lubinski, D., & Hyde, J. S. (1997). Mathematics: Is biology the cause of gender differences in performance? In M. R. Walsh (Ed.), *Women, men, & gender: Ongoing debates*. New Haven, CT: Yale University Press.

Benes, F. M. (1996, November). Altered neural circuits in schizophrenia. *The Harvard Mental Health Letter*, pp. 5–7.

Benjafield, J. G. (1996). *A history of psychology*. Boston: Allyn & Bacon.*

Benjafield, J. G. (1997). *Cognition* (2nd ed.). Upper Saddle, NJ: Prentice Hall.*

Benjamin, J., et al. (1996). Population and familial association between the D4 dopamine receptor gene and measures of novelty seeking. *Nature and Genetics, 12*, 81–84.

Benjamin, L. T., Jr. (1985, February). Defining aggression: An exercise for classroom discussion. *Teaching of Psychology, 12* (1), 40–42.

Benjamin, L. T., Jr. (1997). The psychology of history and the history of psychology: A historiographical introduction. In L. T. Benjamin (Ed.), *A history of psychology: Original sources and contemporary research* (2nd ed.). New York: McGraw-Hill.

Benjamin, L. T., Jr., & Shields, S. A. (1990). Foreword. In H. Hollingworth, *Leta Stetter Hollingworth: A biography*. Boston, MA: Anker Publishing.

Bennett, A. (1992, October 14). Lori Schiller emerges from the torments of schizophrenia. *Wall Street Journal*, pp. A1, A10.

Bennett, P. (1994). Type A behaviour: A suitable case for treatment? Special Issue: Heart disease: The psychological challenge. *Irish Journal of Psychology, 15*, 43–53.

Bennett, W., & Gurin, J. (1982). *The dieter's dilemma: Eating less and weighing more*. New York: Basic Books.

Benoit, D., & Parker, K. (2000). Stability and transmission of attachment across three generations. In D. Muir & A. Slater (Eds.), *Infant development: The essential readings*. Oxford: Blackwell Publishers.*

Ben-Sira, Z. (1976). The function of the professional's affective behavior in client satisfaction: A revised approach to social interaction theory. *Journal of Health and Social Behavior, 17*, 3–11.

Benson, D. J., & Thomson, G. E. (1982). Sexual harassment on a university campus: The confluence of authority relations, sexual interest and gender stratification. *Social Problems, 29*, 236–251.

Benson, H. (1993). The relaxation response. In D. Goleman, & J. Guerin (Eds.), *Mind-body medicine: How to use your mind for better health*. Yonkers, NY: Consumer Reports Publications.

Benson, H., & Friedman, R. (1985). A rebuttal to the conclusions of Davis S. Holmes's article, "Meditation and somatic arousal reduction." *American Psychologist, 40*, 725–726.

Benson, H., Kornhaber, A., Kornhaber, C., LeChanu, M. N., et al. (1994). Increases in positive psychological characteristics with a new relaxation-response curriculum in high school students. *Journal of Research and Development in Education, 27*, 226–231.

Bentall, R. P. (1992). The classification of schizophrenia. In D. J. Kavanagh (Ed.), *Schizophrenia: An overview and practical handbook*. London: Chapman & Hall.

Boehm, K. E., Schondel, C. K., Marlowe, A. L., & Rose, J. S. (1995). Adolescents calling a peer-listening phone service: Variations in calls by gender, age, and season of year. *Adolescence, 30*, 863–871.

Berenbaum, S. A., & Hines, M. (1992). Early androgens are related to childhood sex-typed toy preferences. *Psychological Science, 3*, 203–206.

Berenbaum, S. A., & Snyder, E. (1995). Early hormonal influences on childhood sex-typed activity and playmate preferences: Implications for the development of sexual orientation. *Developmental Psychology, 31*, 31–42.

Berg, L., Danzinger, W. L., Storandt, M., Coben, L. A., Gado, M., Hughes, C. P., Knesevich, J. W., & Botwinick, J. (1984). Predictive features in mild senile dementia of the Alzheimer type. *Neurology, 34*, 563–569.

Bergen, D. J., & Williams, J. E. (1991). Sex stereotypes in the United States revisited: 1972–1988. *Sex Roles, 24*, 413–423.

Bergener, M., Ermini, M., & Stahelin, H. B. (Eds.). (1985, February). *Thresholds in aging*. The 1984 Sandoz Lectures in Gerontology, Basel, Switzerland.

Berger, J. (1993, May 30). The long days and short life of a medical student. *New York Times*, p. B4.

Bergin, A. E., & Garfield, S. L. (Eds.). (1994). *Handbook of psychotherapy and behavior change*. New York: Wiley.

Bergman, B. (2000, March 20) Taming the stroke. *Maclean's.*

Berkowitz, L. (1974). Some determinants of impulsive aggression: The role of mediated associations with reinforcements for aggression. *Psychological Review, 81*, 165–176.

Berkowitz, L. (1984). Aversive conditioning as stimuli to aggression. In R. J. Blanchard, & C. Blanchard (Eds.), *Advances in the study of aggression* (Vol. 1). New York: Academic Press.

Berkowitz, L. (1987). Mood, self-awareness, and willingness to help. *Journal of Personality and Social Psychology, 52*, 721–729.

Berkowitz, L. (1989). Frustration-aggression hypothesis. *Psychological Bulletin, 106*, 59–73.

Berkowitz, L. (1990). On the formation and regulation of anger and aggression: A cognitive-neoassociationistic analysis. *American Psychologist, 45*, 494–503.

Berkowitz, L. (1993). *Aggression: Its causes, consequences, and control*. New York: McGraw-Hill.

Berkowitz, L., & Geen, R. G. (1966). Film violence and the cue properties of available targets. *Journal of Personality and Social Psychology, 3*, 525–530.

Berkowitz, L., & LePage, A. (1967). Weapons as aggression-eliciting stimuli. *Journal of Personality and Social Psychology, 7*, 202–207.

Berlyne, D. (1967). Arousal and reinforcement. In D. Levine (Ed.), *Nebraska symposium on motivation*. Lincoln: University of Nebraska Press.

Berman, A. L., & Jobes, D. A. (1991). *Adolescent suicide: Assessment and intervention*. Washington, DC: American Psychological Association.

Berman, A. L., & Jobes, D. A. (1995). Suicide prevention in adolescents (age 12–18). In M. M. Silverman, & R. W. Maris (Eds.), *Suicide prevention: Toward the year 2000*. New York: Guilford Press.

Berman, R. M., Krystal, J. H., & Charney, D. S. (1996). Mechanism of action of antidepressants: Monoamine hypotheses and beyond. In S. J. Watson (Ed.), *Biology of schizophrenia and affective disease*. Washington, DC: American Psychiatric Press.

Berman, S. L., Kurtines, W. M., Silverman, W. K., & Serafini, L. T. (1996). The impact of exposure to crime and violence on urban youth. *American Journal of Orthopsychiatry, 66*, 329–336.

Bernard, J. (1982). *The future of marriage* (2nd ed.). New York: Bantam.

Bernard, L. L. (1924). *Instinct: a study in social psychology*. New York: Holt.

Bernard, M. E., & DiGiuseppe, R. (Eds.). (1993). *Rational-emotive consultation in applied settings*. Mahwah, NJ: Erlbaum.

Berndt, T. J. (1992). Friendship and friends' influence in adolescence. *Current Directions in Psychological Science, 1*, 156–159.

Berndt, T. J. (1997). *Child development* (2nd ed.). Madison, WI: Brown & Benchmark.

Berndt, T. J., & Keefe, K. (1995). Friends' influence on adolescents' adjustment to school. *Child Development, 66,* 1312–1329.

Bernieri, F. J., Zuckerman, M., Koestner, R., & Rosenthal, R. (1994). Measuring person perception accuracy: Another look at self-other agreement. *Personality and Social Psychology Bulletin, 20,* 367–378.

Berquier, A., & Ashton, R. (1992). Characteristics of the frequent nightmare sufferer. *Journal of Abnormal Psychology, 101,* 246–250.

Berrettini, W. H., & Pekkarinen, P. H. (1996). Molecular genetics of bipolar disorder. *Annals of Medicine, 28,* 191–194.

Berrios, G. E. (1996). *The history of mental symptoms: Descriptive psychopathology since the nineteenth century.* Cambridge, England: Cambridge University Press.

Berry, J. W. (1999). Intercultural relations in plural societies. *Canadian Psychology, 40,* 12–21.*

Berry, J. W., Poortinga, Y. H., Segall, M. H., & Dasen, P. R. (1992). *Cross-cultural psychology: Research and applications.* New York: Cambridge University Press.*

Berry, J. W., & Laponce, J. A. (Eds.). (1994). *Ethnicity and culture in Canada: The research landscape.* Toronto: University of Toronto Press.*

Berscheid, E. (1985). Interpersonal attraction. In G. Lindzey, & E. Aronson (Eds.), *Handbook of social psychology* (3rd ed.). New York: Random House.

Berscheid, E., & Walster, E. (1974). Physical attractiveness. In L. Berkowitz (Ed.), *Advances in experimental social psychology* (Vol. 7, pp. 157–215). New York: Academic Press.

Bersoff, D. N. (1995). *Ethical conflicts in psychology.* Washington, DC: American Psychological Association.

Bersoff, D. N., & Ogden, D. W. (1991). APA Amicus Curiae briefs: Furthering lesbian and gay male civil rights. *American Psychologist, 46,* 950–956.

Betancourt, H., & Lopez, S. R. (1993). The study of culture, ethnicity, and race in American psychology. *American Psychologist, 48,* 1586–1596.

Beutler, L. E., Brown, M. T., Crothers, L., Booker, K., et al. (1996). The dilemma of factitious demographic distinctions in psychological research. *Journal of Consulting and Clinical Psychology, 64,* 892–902.

Beutler, L. E., Consoli, A. J., & Williams, R. E. (1995). Integrative and eclectic therapies in practice. In B. M. Bongar, & L. E. Beutler (Eds.), *Comprehensive textbook of psychotherapy: Theory and practice.* Oxford textbooks in clinical psychology, Vol. 1. New York: Oxford University Press.

Beyene, Y. (1989). *From menarche to menopause: Reproductive lives of peasant women in two cultures.* Albany: State University of New York Press.

Beyer, S. (1990). Gender differences in the accuracy of self-evaluations of performance. *Journal of Personality and Social Psychology, 59,* 960–970.

Bhugra, D. (Ed.). (1996). *Homelessness and mental health.* Cambridge, England: Cambridge University Press.

Bialystok, E. (1991). *Language processing in bilingual children.* London: Cambridge University Press.*

Bialystok, E. (1997). Effects of bilingualism and biliteracy on children's emerging concepts of print. *Developmental Psychology, 33,* 429–440.*

Bialystok, E., & Herman, J. (1999). Does bilingualism matter for early literacy? *Bilingualism: Language and Cognition, 2,* 35–44.*

Bickman, L. (1994). Social influence and diffusion of responsibility in an emergency. In B. Puka (Ed.), *Reaching out: Caring, altruism, and prosocial behavior. Moral development: A compendium,* Vol. 7. New York: Garland.

Bieber, I. (1962). *Homosexuality: A psychoanalytic study.* New York: Basic Books.

Biederman, I. (1981). On the semantics of a glance at a scene. In M. Kubovy, and J. R. Pomerantz (Eds.), *Perceptual organization.* Mahwah, NJ: Erlbaum.

Biederman, I. (1987). Recognition-by-components: A theory of human image understanding. *Psychological Review, 94,* 115–147.

Biederman, I. (1990). Higher-level vision. In D. N. Osherson, S. Kosslyn, & J. Hollerbach (Eds.), *An invitation to cognitive science: Visual cognition and action.* Cambridge, MA: MIT Press.

Biernat, M., & Wortman, C. B. (1991). Sharing of home responsibilities between professionally employed women and their husbands. *Journal of Personality and Social Psychology, 60,* 844–860.

Bigler, E. D. (Ed.). (1996). *Neuroimaging.* New York: Plenum.

Binet, A., & Simon, T. (1916). *The development of intelligence in children (The Binet-Simon Scale).* Baltimore: Williams & Wilkins.

Bini, L. (1938). Experimental research on epileptic attacks induced by the electric current. *American Journal of Psychiatry (Suppl. 94),* 172–183.

Binstock, R. H., George, L. K., Marshall, V. W., Myers, G. C., & Schulz, J. H. (Eds.). (1996). *Handbook of aging and the social sciences* (4th ed.). San Diego, CA: Academic Press.

Birch, H. G. (1945). The role of motivation factors in insightful problem solving. *Journal of Comparative Psychology, 38,* 295–317.

Birchwood, M., Hallett, L., & Preston, R. (1989). In M. Birchwood et al., *Schizophrenia: An integrated approach to research and treatment.* New York: New York University Press.

Bird, G., & Melville, K. (1994). *Families and intimate relationships.* New York: McGraw-Hill.

Birke, L., & Michael, M. (1995). Raising the profile of welfare: Scientists and their use of animals. *Anthrozoos, 8,* 90–99.

Birren, J. E. (Ed.). (1996). *Encyclopedia of gerontology: Age, aging and the aged.* San Diego, CA: Academic Press.

Bisanz, J. (1999a). The development of mathematical cognition: Arithmetic. *Journal of Experimental Child Psychology, 74,* 153–156.*

Bisanz, J. (1999b). The development of mathematical cognition: Numerical processes and concepts. *Journal of Experimental Child Psychology, 74,* 283–285.*

Bisanz, J., Bisanz, G. L., & Korpan, C. A. (1994). Inductive reasoning. In R. J. Sternberg (Ed.), *Thinking and problem-solving.* San Diego, CA: Academic Press.

Bishop, J. E. (1993, September 30). The knowing eye: One man's accident is shedding new light on human perception. *Wall Street Journal,* pp. A1, A8.

Bjork, D. W. (1993). *B. F. Skinner: A life.* New York: Basic Books.

Bjork, D. W. (1997). *William James: The center of his vision.* Washington, DC: American Psychological Association.

Bjork, E. L., & Bjork, R. A. (Eds.). (1996). *Memory.* New York: Academic Press.

Bjork, R. A., & Richardson-Klarehn, A. (1989). On the puzzling relationship between environmental context and human memory. In C. Izawa (Ed.), *Current issues in cognitive processes: The Tulane-Floweree symposium on cognition.* Mahwah, NJ: Erlbaum.

Bjorklund, D. F. (1985). The role of conceptual knowledge in the development of organization in children's memory. In C. J. Brainerd & M. Pressley (Eds.), *Basic process in memory development.* New York: Springer-Verlag.

Bjorklund, D. F. (1997). In search of a metatheory for cognitive development (or, Piaget is dead and I don't feel so good myself). *Child Development, 68,* 144–148.

Blake, J., & de Boysson-Bardies, B. (1992). Patterns in babbling: A cross-linguistic study. *Journal of Child Language, 19,* 51–74.*

Blake, J., Quartaro, G., & Onorati, S. (1993). Evaluating quantitative measures of grammatical complexity in spontaneous speech samples. *Journal of Child Language, 20,* 139–152.

Blakeslee, S. (1984, August, 14). Scientists find key biological causes of alcoholism. *The New York Times,* p. C-1.

Blakeslee, S. (1992a, August 11). Finding a new messenger for the brain's signals to the body. *New York Times,* p. C3.

Blakeslee, S. (1992b, November 10). Missing limbs, still atingle, are clues to changes in the brain. *New York Times,* pp. C1, C12.

Blanchard, F. A., Lilly, R., & Vaughn, L. A. (1991). Reducing the expression of racial prejudice. *Psychological Science, 2,* 101–105.

Blanck, P. D. (Ed.). (1993). *Interpersonal expectations: Theory, research and applications.* Cambridge, England: Cambridge University Press.

Bland, R. C., Newman, S. C., & Orn, H. (1998). Period prevalence of psychiatric disorders in Edmonton. *Acta Psychiatrica Scandanvica, 77,* 33–42.*

Blascovich, J., Wyer, N. A., Swart, L. A., & Kibler, J. L. (1997). Racism and racial categorization. *Journal of Personality and Social Psychology, 72,* 1364–1372.

Blascovich, J. J., & Katkin, E. S. (Eds.). (1993). *Cardiovascular reactivity to psychological stress and disease.* Washington, DC: American Psychological Association.

Blass, T. (1991). Understanding behavior in the Milgram obedience experiment: The role of personality, situations, and their interactions. *Journal of Personality and Social Psychology, 60,* 398–413.

Blass, T. (1996). Attribution of responsibility and trust in the Milgram obedience experiment. *Journal of Applied Social Psychology, 26,* 1529–1535.

Blass, T., & Krackow, A. (1991, June). *The Milgram obedience experiments: Students' views vs. scholarly perspectives and actual findings.* Paper presented at the annual meeting of the American Psychological Society, Washington, DC.

Blau, Z. S. (1973). *Old age in a changing society.* New York: New Viewpoints.

Block, J. (1995). A contrarian view of the five-factor approach to personality description. *Psychological Bulletin, 117,* 187–215.

Block, N. (1995). How heritability misleads about race. *Cognition, 56,* 99–128.

Block, N., Flanagan, O., & Güzeldere, G. (Eds.). (1997). *The nature of consciousness: Philosophical debates.* Cambridge, MA: MIT Press.

Bloom, B. L. (1997). *Planned short-term psychotherapy: A clinical handbook* (2nd ed.). Boston: Allyn & Bacon.

Blum, K., Noble, E. P., Sheridan, P. J., Montgomery, A., Ritchie, T., Jagadeeswaran, P., Nogami, H., Briggs, A. H., & Cohn, J. B. (1990, April 18). Allelic association of human dopamine D2 receptor gene in alcoholism. *Journal of the American Medical Association, 263,* 2055–2059.

Blumenfield, M., Levy, N. B., & Kaplan, D. (1979). The wish to be informed of a fatal illness. *Omega, 9,* 323–326.

Blumstein, P. W., & Schwartz, P. (1983). *American couples.* New York: Morrow.

Boakes, R. A., Popplewell, D. A., & Burton, M. J. (Eds.). (1987). *Eating habits: Food, physiology, and learned behaviour.* New York: Wiley.

Bochner, S. (1996). The learning strategies of bilingual versus monolingual students. *British Journal of Educational Psychology, 66,* 263–268.

Boden, M. A. (Ed.). (1994). *Dimensions of creativity.* Cambridge, MA: MIT Press.

Boden, M. A. (1996). Creativity. In M. A. Boden (Ed.), *Artificial intelligence. Handbook of perception and cognition* (2nd ed.). San Diego, CA: Academic Press.

Bodensteiner, J. B., & Schaefer, G. B. (1995). Evaluation of the patient with idiopathic mental retardation. *Journal of Neuropsychiatry and Clinical Neurosciences, 7,* 361–370.

Boehm, K. E., & Campbell, N. B. (1995). Suicide: A review of calls to an adolescent peer listening phone service. *Child Psychiatry and Human Development, 26,* 61–66.

Bogerts, B. (1993). Recent advances in the neuropathology of schizophrenia. *Schizophrenia Bulletin, 19,* 431–445.

Bohan, J. S. (1992). *Re-placing women in psychology: Readings toward a more inclusive history.* Dubuque, IA: Kendall/Hunt.

Bolger, N., & Eckenrode, J. (1991). Social relationships, personality, and anxiety during a major stressful event. *Journal of Personality and Social Psychology, 61,* 440–449.

Bolles, R. C., & Fanselow, M. S. (1982). Endorphins and behavior. *Annual Review of Psychology, 33,* 87–101.

Bolos, A. M., Dean, M., & Rausburg, M. (1990, December 26). Population and pedigree studies reveal a lack of association between the dopamine D2 receptor gene and alcoholism. *Journal of the American Medical Association, 264,* 3156.

Bond, L. (1989). The effects of special preparation on measures of scholastic ability. In R. L. Linn (Ed.), *Educational measurement* (3rd ed.). The American Council on Education/Macmillan series on higher education. New York: Macmillan.

Bond, M. H. (1993). Emotions and their expression in Chinese culture. *Journal of Nonverbal Behavior, 17,* 245–263.

Boneau, C. A. (1992). Observations of psychology's past and future. *American Psychologist, 47,* 1586–1596.

Bonta, B. D. (1997). Cooperation and competition in peaceful societies. *Psychological Bulletin, 121,* 299–320.

Boone, D. E. (1995). A cross-sectional analysis of WAIS-R aging patterns with psychiatric inpatients: Support for Horn's hypothesis that fluid cognitive abilities decline. *Perceptual and Motor Skills, 81,* 371–379.

Boosma, D. I. (1993). Current status and future prospects in twin studies of the development of cognitive abilities: Infancy to old age. In T. J. Bouchard, Jr., & P. Propping (Eds.), *Twins as a tool of behavioral genetics. Life sciences research report, 53.* Chichester, England: Wiley.

Boosma, D. I., & Koopmans, J. R. (1994). Genetic and social influences on starting to smoke: A study of Dutch adolescent twins and their parents. *Addiction, 89,* 219–226.

Booth, A. (Ed.). (1992). *Child care in the 1990s: Trends and consequences.* Mahwah, NJ: Erlbaum.

Booth, D. A. (1994). *Psychology of nutrition.* London: Taylor & Francis.

Bootzin, R. R., Manber, R., Perlis, M. L., Salvio, M. A., & Wyatt, J. K. (1993). Sleep disorders. In P. B. Sutker, & H. E. Adams (Eds.), *Comprehensive handbook of psychopathology* (2nd ed.). New York: Plenum Press.

Bootzin, R. R., & Perlis, M. L. (1992). Nonpharmacologic treatments of insomnia. Roundtable conference: Low-dose benzodiazepine therapy in the treatment of insomnia (1991, Chicago, Illinois). *Journal of Clinical Psychiatry, 53* (Suppl), 37–41.

Borland, J. H. (1989). *Planning and implementing programs for the gifted.* New York: Teachers College Press.

Bornstein, M. H. (1989). Sensitive periods in development: Structural characteristics and causal interpretations. *Psychological Bulletin, 105,* 179–197.

Bornstein, M. H. (Ed.). (1995). *Handbook of parenting, Vol. 4: Applied and practical parenting.* Mahwah, NJ: Erlbaum.

Bornstein, M. H., & Bruner, J. S. (Eds.). (1989). *Interaction on human development: Crosscurrents in contemporary psychology services.* Mahwah, NJ: Erlbaum.

Bornstein, M. H., & Krasnegor, N. A. (Eds.). (1989). *Stability and continuity in mental development: Behavioral and biological perspectives.* Mahwah, NJ: Erlbaum.

Bornstein, M. H., & Lamb, M. E. (1992). *Development in infancy* (3rd ed.). New York: McGraw-Hill.

Bornstein, M. H., & Sigman, M. D. (1986). Continuity in mental development from infancy. *Child Development, 57,* 251–274.

Bornstein, R. F. (1996). Construct validity of the Rorschach Oral Dependency Scale: 1967–1995. *Psychological Assessment, 8,* 200–205.

Bornstein, R. F., & D'Agostino, P. R. (1992). Stimulus recognition and the mere exposure effect. *Journal of Personality and Social Psychology, 63,* 545–552.

Bornstein, R. F., & D'Agostino, P. R. (1994). The attribution and discounting of perceptual fluency: Preliminary tests of a perceptual fluency/attributional model of the mere exposure effect. *Social Cognition, 12,* 103–128.

Boster, F. J., & Mongeau, P. (1985). Fear-arousing persuasive messages. In R. N. Bostrom (Ed.), *Communication yearbook* (Vol. 8). Beverly Hills, CA: Sage.

Botting, J. H., & Morrison, A. R. (1997, February). Animal research is vital to medicine. *Scientific American, 276,* 83–86.

Botvin, G. J., & Botvin, E. M. (1992). Adolescent tobacco, alcohol, and drug abuse: Prevention strategies, empirical findings, and assessment issues. *Journal of Developmental and Behavioral Pediatrics, 13,* 290–301.

Botvin, G. J., Schinke, S. P., Epstein, J. A., & Diaz, T. (1994). Effectivenenss of culturally focused and generic skills training approaches to alcohol and drug abuse prevention among minority youths. *Psychology of Addictive Behaviors, 8,* 116–127.

Botvin, G. J., Schinke, S. P., Epstein, J. A., & Diaz, T., et al. (1995). Effectiveness of culturally focused and generic skills training approaches to alcohol and drug abuse prevention among minority adolescents: Two-year follow-up results. *Psychology of Addictive Behaviors, 9,* 183–194.

Bouchard, C., & Bray, G. A. (Eds.). (1996). *Regulation of body weight: Biological and behavioral mechanisms.* New York: Wiley.

Bouchard, C., Rhéaume, J., & Ladouceur, R. (1999). Responsibility and perfectionism in OCD: An experimantal study. *Behaviour Research and Therapy, 37,* 239–248.*

Bouchard, C., Tremblay, A., Despres, J. P., Nadeau, A., et al. (1990, May 24). The response to long-term overfeeding in identical twins. *New England Journal of Medicine, 322,* 1477–1482.

Bouchard, S., Gauthier, J., LaBerge, B., Plamondon, J., French, D., Pelletier, M. H., & Godbout, C. (1996). Exposure versus cognitive restructuring in the treatment of panic disorder with agoraphobia. *Behaviour Research and Therapy, 34,* 213–224.*

Bouchard, T. J., Jr. (1994, June 17). Genes, environment, and personality. *Science, 264,* 1700–1701.

Bouchard, T. J., & McGue, M. (1981). Familial studies of intelligence: A review. *Science, 212,* 1055–1059.

Bourne, L. E., Dominowski, R. L., Loftus, E. F., & Healy, A. F. (1986). *Cognitive processes* (2nd ed.). Englewood Cliffs, NJ: Prentice-Hall.

Bowd, A. D., & Shapiro, K. J. (1993). The case against laboratory animal research in psychology. *Journal of Social Issues, 49,* 133–142.

Bowen, D. J., Kahl, K., Mann, S. L., & Peterson, A. V. (1991). Descriptions of early triers. *Addictive Behaviors, 16,* 95–101.

Bower, G., & Cohen, P. R. (1982). Emotional influences in memory and thinking: Data and theory. In M. S. Clark, & S. T. Fiske (Eds.), *Affect and cognition.* Mahwah, NJ: Erlbaum.

Bower, G. H. (1993). The fragmentation of psychology? *American Psychologist, 48,* 905–907.

Bower, G. H., Thompson, S., & Tulving, E. (1994). Reducing retroactive interference: An interference analysis. *Journal of Experimental Psychology Learning, Memory, and Cognition, 20,* 51–66.

Bower, T. (1989). The perceptual world of the newborn child. In A. M. Slater, & J. G. Bremner (Eds.), *Infant development.* Mahwah, NJ: Erlbaum.

Boyatzis, C. J., Matillo, G. M., & Nesbitt, K. M. (1995). Effects of the "Mighty Morphin Power Rangers" on children's aggression with peers. *Child Study Journal, 25,* 45–55.

Boyce, W. T., Champoux, M., Suomi, S. J., & Gunnar, M. R. (1995). Salivary cortisol in nursery-reared rhesus monkeys: Reactivity to peer interactions and altered circadian activity. *Developmental Psychobiology, 28,* 257–267.

Bradshaw, J. L., & Rogers, L. J. (1993). *The evolution of lateral asymmetries, language, tool use, and intellect.* San Diego, CA: Academic Press.

Braff, D. L. (1993). Information processing and attention dysfunctions in schizophrenia. *Schizophrenia Bulletin, 19,* 233–259.

Brainard, D. H., Wandell, B. A., & Chichilnisky, E. (1993). Color constancy: From physics to appearance. *Current Directions in Psychological Science, 2,* 165–170.

Brainerd, C. J., Reyna, V. F., & Brandse, E. (1995). Are children's false memories more persistent than their true memories? *Psychological Science, 6,* 359–364.

Brand, D. (1987, August 31). The new whiz kids. *Time,* pp. 42–51.

Brandimonte, M. A., Hitch, G. J., & Bishop, D. V. (1992). Manipulation of visual mental images in children and adults. *Journal of Experimental Child Psychology, 53,* 300–312.

Brandon, R., & Davies, C. (1973). *Wrongful imprisonment: Mistaken convictions and their consequences.* Hamden, CT: Archon Books.

Brandon, T. H. (1994). Negative affect as motivation to smoke. *Current Directions in Psychological Science, 3,* 33–37.

Bransford, J. D., & Johnson, M. K. (1972). Contextual prerequisites for understanding: Some investigations of comprehension and recall. *Journal of Verbal Learning and Verbal Behavior, 11,* 717–721.

Branswell, B. (1999, May 17). Ambition accomplished. *Maclean's, 112,* 57–58.*

Braun, B. (1985, May 21). Interview by D. Goleman: New focus on multiple personality. *New York Times,* p. C-1.

Brazelton, T. B. (1969). *Infants and mothers: Differences in development.* New York: Dell.

Breakwell, G. M., Hammond, S., & Fife-Schaw, C. (Eds.). (1995). *Research methods in psychology.* Newbury Park, CA: Sage.

Brehm, J. W., & Self, E. A. (1989). The intensity of motivation. *Annual Review of Psychology, 40,* 109–131.

Brehm, S. S., & Brehm, J. W. (1981). *Psychological reactance.* New York: Academic Press.

Breier, A. (1995). Stress, dopamine, and schizophrenia: Evidence for a stress-diathesis model. In C. M. Mazure (Ed.), *Does stress cause psychiatric illness? Progress in psychiatry, No. 46.* Washington, DC: American Psychiatric Press.

Breland, K., & Breland, M. (1961). Misbehavior of organisms. *American Psychologist, 16,* 681–684.

Brems, C. (1995). Women and depression: A comprehensive analysis. In E. E. Beckham, & W. R. Leber (Eds.), *Handbook of depression* (2nd ed.). New York: Guilford Press.

Breu, G. (1992, November 23). A heart stopper. *People Weekly,* pp. 87–88.

Brewer, M. B. (1988). A dual process model of impression formation. In T. K. Srull, & R. S. Wyer, Jr. (Eds.), *Advances in social cognition* (Vol. 1, pp. 1–36). Mahwah, NJ: Erlbaum.

Brewer, M. B., & Harasty, A. S. (1996). Seeing groups as entities: The role of perceiver motivation. In R. M. Sorrentino, & E. T. Higgins (Eds.), *Handbook of motivation and cognition, Vol. 3: The interpersonal context. Handbook of motivation and cognition.* New York: Guilford Press.

Brewer, M. B., & Lui, L. L. (1989). The primacy of age and sex in the structure of person categories. *Social Cognition, 7,* 262–274.

Brewerton, T. D. (1995). Toward a unified theory of serotonin dysregulation in eating and related disorders. *Psychoneuroendocrinology, 20,* 561–590.

Brewerton, T. D., & Jimerson, D. C. (1996). Studies of serotonin function in anorexia nervosa. *Psychiatry Research, 62,* 31–42.

Brewin, C. R., MacCarthy, B., Duda, K., & Vaughn, C. E. (1991). Attribution and expressed emotion in the relatives of patients with schizophrenia. *Journal of Abnormal Psychology, 100,* 546–554.

Brezina, V., Orekhova, I. V., & Weiss, K. R. (1996, August 9). Functional uncoupling of linked neurotransmitter effects by combinatorial convergence. *Science, 272,* 806–810.

Bridges, J. S. (1988). Sex differences in occupational performance expectations. *Psychology of Women Quarterly, 12,* 75–90.

Brislin, R. (1993). *Understanding culture's influence on behavior.* Fort Worth, TX: Harcourt Brace Jovanovich.

Broberg, A. G., Wessels, H., Lamb, M. E., & Hwang, C. P. (1997). Effects of day care on the development of cognitive abilities in 8-year-olds: A longitudinal study. *Developmental Psychology, 33,* 62–69.

Brody, G. H., Neubaum, E., & Forehand, R. (1988). Serial marriage: A heuristic analysis of an emerging family form. *Journal of Personality and Social Psychology, 103,* 211–222.

Brody, J. (1982). *New York Times guide to personal health.* New York: Times Books.

Brody, J. (1996, January 16). When can killers claim sleepwalking as a legal defense? *New York Times,* pp. C1, C5.

Brody, J. E. (1987, November 19). Encouraging news for the absent-minded: Memory can be improved, with practice. *New York Times,* p. C1.

Brody, J. E. (1992, November 23). For most trying to lose weight, dieting only makes things worse. *New York Times,* pp. A1, A8.

Brody, L. R. (1996). Gender, emotional expression, and parent-child boundaries. In R. D. Kavanaugh, B. Zimmerberg, & S. Fein (Eds.), *Emotion: Interdisciplinary perspectives.* Mahwah, NJ: Erlbaum.

Brody, N. (1990). Behavior therapy versus placebo: Comment on Bowers and Clum's meta-analysis. *Psychological Bulletin, 107,* 106–109.

Bromm, B., & Desmedt, J. E. (Eds.). (1995). *Pain and the brain: From nociception to cognition.* New York: Raven Press.

Bronson, G. W. (1990). The accurate calibration in infants' scanning records. *Journal of Experimental Child Psychology, 49,* 79–100.

Brookhiser, R. (1997, January 13). Lost in the weed. *U.S. News & World Report,* p. 9.

Brooks, L. R. (1978). Nonanalytic concept formation and memory for instances. In E. Rosch & B. B. Lloyd (Eds.), *Cognition and categorization.* Mahwah, NJ: Erlbaum.*

Broota, K. D. (1990). *Experimental design in behavioral research.* New York: Wiley.

Brossard, M. A., & Morin, R. (1996, Sept. 15). American voters focus on worries close to home. (Washington Post public opinion poll.) *The Washington Post,* p. A1.

Broughton, R. J., & Ogilvie, R. D. (Eds.). (1992). *Sleep, arousal and performance: Problems and promises.* Boston: Birkhauser.*

Broughton, W. A., & Broughton, R. J. (1994). Psychosocial impact of narcolepsy. *Sleep, 17 (8 Suppl),* 45–49.

Brown, A. S. (1991). A review of the tip-of-the-tongue experience. *Psychological Bulletin, 109,* 204–223.

Brown, A. S., Susser, E. S., Butler, P. D., Andrews, R. R., et al. (1996). Neurobiological plausibility of prenatal nutritional deprivation as a risk factor for schizophrenia. *Journal of Nervous and Mental Disease, 184,* 71–85.

Brown, B. (1984). *Between health and illness.* Boston: Houghton Mifflin.

Brown, J. D. (1991). Staying fit and staying well: Physical fitness as a moderator of life stress. *Journal of Personality and Social Psychology, 60,* 555–561.

Brown, J. D., & McGill, K. L. (1989). The cost of good fortune: When positive life events produce negative health consequences. *Journal of Personality and Social Psychology, 57,* 1103–1110.

Brown, L. S., & Pope, K. S. (1996). *Recovered memories of abuse: Assessment, therapy, forensics.* Washington, DC: American Psychological Association.

Brown, P. (1986). Simbu aggression and the drive to win. *Anthropolitical Quarterly, 59,* 165–170.

Brown, P. K., & Wald, G. (1964). Visual pigments in single rod and cones of the human retina. *Science, 144,* 45–52.

Brown, R. (1958). How shall a thing be called? *Psychological Review, 65,* 14–21.

Brown, R. (1986). *Social psychology* (2nd ed.). New York: Macmillan.

Brown, R., & Kulik, J. (1977). Flashbulb memories. *Cognition, 5,* 73–99.

Brown, R. J., Williams, J. (1984). Group identification: The same thing to all people? *Human Relations, 37,* 547–564.

Brown, S. I., & Walter, M. I. (Eds.). (1990). *The art of problem posing* (2nd ed.). Mahwah, NJ: Erlbaum.

Brown, S. I., & Walter, M. I. (Eds.). (1993). *Problem posing: Reflections and applications.* Mahwah, NJ: Erlbaum.

Brown, W. A. (January, 1998). The placebo effect. *Scientific American,* pp. 90–95.

Browne, A., & Finkelhor, D. (1986). Impact of child sexual abuse: A review of the research. *Psychological Bulletin, 99,* 66–77.

Brownell, K. D. (1989, June). When and how to diet. *Psychology Today,* pp. 40–89.

Brownell, K. D., & Fairburn, C. G. (Eds.). (1995). *Eating disorders and obesity: A comprehensive handbook.* New York: Guilford Press.

Brownell, K. D., & Rodin, J. (1994). The dieting maelstrom: Is it possible and advisable to lose weight? *American Psychologist, 49,* 781–791.

Brownlee, S., & Watson, T. (1997, January 13). The senses. *U.S. News & World Report,* pp. 51–59.

Bruce, B., & Wilfley, D. (1996, January). Binge eating among the overweight population: A serious and prevalent problem. *Journal of the American Dietetic Association, 96,* 58–61.

Bruce, V., & Green, P. R. (1990). *Visual perception: Physiology, psychology, and ecology* (2nd ed.). Mahwah, NJ: Erlbaum.

Bruce, V., Green, P. R., & Georgeson, M. (1997). *Visual perception: Physiology, psychology, and ecology* (3rd ed.). Mahwah, NJ: Erlbaum.

Bruner, J. (1983). *Child's talk: Learning to use language.* Oxford: Oxford University Press.

Brunner, H. G., Nelen, M., Breakefield, X. O., Ropers, H. H., & van Oost, B. A. (1993, October 22). Abnormal behavior associated with a point mutation in the structural gene for monoamine oxidase A. *Science, 262,* 578–580.

Bryant, F. B., & Yarnold, P. R. (1990). The impact of Type A behavior on subjective life quality: Bad for the heart, good for the soul? *Journal of Social Behavior and Personality, 5,* 369–404.

Bryant, J., & Zillman, D. (Eds.). (1994). *Media effects: Advances in theory and research.* Mahwah, NJ: Erlbaum.

Bryant, R. A., & McConkey, K. M. (1990). Hypnotic blindness and the relevance of cognitive style. *Journal of Personality and Social Psychology, 59,* 756–761.

Buchanan, L., & Besner, D. (1993). Reading aloud: Evidence for the use of a whole word nonsemantic pathway. *Canadian Journal of Experimental Psychology, 47,* 133–152.*

Buck, L., & Axel, R. (1991, April 5). A novel multigene family may encode odorant receptors: A molecular basis for odor recognition. *Cell, 65,* 167–175.

Buckhout, R. (1975). Eyewitness testimony. *Scientific American,* pp. 23–31.

Buckhout, R. (1976). Eyewitness testimony. In R. Held, & W. Richards (Eds.), *Recent progress in perception.* San Francisco: Freeman.

Bugental, J. F. T., & Bracke, P. E. (1992). The future of existential-humanistic psychotherapy. *Psychotherapy, 29,* 28–33.

Bugental, J. F. T., & McBeath, B. (1994). Depth existential therapy: Evolution since World War II. In B. Bongar, & L. E. Beutler (Eds.), *Comprehensive textbook of psychotherapy: Theory and practice.* New York: Oxford University Press.

Bui, K.-V. T., Peplau, L. A., & Hill, C. T. (1996, December). Testing the Rusbult Model of Relationship Commitment and Stability in a 15-year study of heterosexual couples. *Personality and Social Psychology Bulletin, 22,* 1244–1257.

Bujold, A., Ladouceur, R., Sylvain, C., & Boisvert, J. (1994). Treatment of pathological gamblers: An experimental study. *Journal of Behaviour Therapy and Experimental Psychiatry, 25,* 275–282.*

Bukowski, W. M., Newcomb, A. F., & Hartup, W. W. (Eds.). (1996). *The company they keep: Friendship in childhood and adolescence.* New York: Cambridge University Press.

Bully B'ware Productions. Coquitlam, B.C.* <www.bullybeware.com>.

Burbules, N. C., & Linn, M. C. (1988). Response to contradiction: Scientific reasoning during adolescence. *Journal of Educational Psychology, 80,* 67–75.

Burchinal, M. R., Roberts, J. E., Nabors, L. A., & Bryant, D. M. (1996). Quality of center child care and infant cognitive and language development. *Child Development, 67,* 606–620.

Bureau of Justice Statistics (1995). National crime victimization survey. Washington, DC: Department of Justice.

Bureau of Labor Statistics (1997). Household demographics. Washington, DC: Bureau of Labor Statistics.

Buree, B. U., Papageoris, D., & Hare, R. D. (1990). Eating in anorexia-nervosa and bulimia nervosa: An application of the tripartite model of anxiety. *Canadian Journal of Behavioural Science, 22,* 207–218.*

Burger, J. M. (1986). Increasing compliance by improving the deal: The that's-not-all technique. *Journal of Personality and Social Psychology, 51,* 277–283.

Burger, J. M. (1992). *Desire for control: Personality, social and clinical perspectives.* New York: Plenum Press.

Burgess, D., & Borgida, E. (1997). Sexual harassment: An experimental test of sex-role spillover theory. *Personality and Social Psychology Bulletin, 23,* 63–75.

Burgess, R. L., & Huston, T. L. (Eds.). (1979). *Social exchanges in developing relationships.* New York: Academic Press.

Burgoon, J. K., & Dillman, L. (1995). Gender, immediacy, and nonverbal communication. In P. J. Kalbfleisch, & M. J. Cody (Eds.), *Gender, power, and communication in human relationships. LEA's communication series.* Mahwah, NJ: Erlbaum.

Burman, S., & Allen-Meares, P. (1994). Neglected victims of murder: Children's witness to parental homicide. *Social Work, 39,* 28–34.

Burnham, D. K. (1983). Apparent relative size in the judgment of apparent distance. *Perception, 12,* 683–700.

Burns, A., & Scott, C. (1994). *Mother-headed families and why they have increased.* Mahwah, NJ: Erlbaum.

Burstyn, L. (1995, October). Female circumcision comes to America. *Atlantic Monthly, 276,* 28–35.

Buser, P., Imbert, M., & Kay, R. H. (Trans.). (1992). *Vision.* Cambridge, MA: MIT Press.

Bush, P. J., & Osterweis, M. (1978). Pathways to medicine use. *Journal of Health and Social Behavior, 19,* 179–189.

Bushman, B. J. (1993). Human aggression while under the influence of alcohol and other drugs: An integrative research review. *Current Directions in Psychological Science, 2,* 148–152.

Bushman, B. J. (1995). Moderating role of trait aggressiveness in the effects of violent media on aggression. *Journal of Personality and Social Psychology, 69,* 950–960.

Bushman, B. J., & Geen, R. G. (1990). Role of cognitive-emotional mediators and individual differences in the effects of media violence on aggression. *Journal of Personality and Social Psychology, 58,* 156–163.

Buss, A. H. (1989). Personality as traits. *American Psychologist, 44,* 1378–1388.

Buss, D. M. (1997). Evolutionary foundations of personality. In R. Hogan, J. Johnson, & S. Briggs (Eds.), *Handbook of personality psychology.* Orlando, FL: Academic Press.

Buss, D. M., et al. (1990). International preferences in selecting mates: A study of

37 cultures. *Journal of Cross-Cultural Psychology, 21,* 5–47.

Buss, D. M., Larsen, R. J., Westen, D., & Semmelroth, J. (1992). Sex differences in jealousy: Evolution, physiology, and psychology. *Psychological Science, 3,* 251–255.

Butcher, J. N. (1990). *The MMPI-2 in psychological treatment.* New York: Oxford University Press.

Butcher, J. N. (1995). Interpretation of the MMPI-2. In L. E. Beutler, & M. R. Berren (Eds.), *Integrative assessment of adult personality.* New York: Guilford Press.

Butcher, J. N., Graham, J. R., Dahlstrom, W. G., & Bowman, E. (1990). The MMPI-2 with college students. *Journal of Personality Assessment, 54,* 1–15.

Butler, R. A. (1954). Incentive conditions which influence visual exploration. *Journal of Experimental Psychology, 48,* 19–23.

Butler, R. A. (1987). An analysis of the monaural displacement of sound in space. *Perception & Psychophysics, 41,* 1–7.

Button, E. (1993). *Eating disorders: Personal construct theory and change.* New York: Wiley.

Buunk, B. P., Angleitner, A., Oubaid, V., & Buss, D. M. (1996). Sex differences in jealousy in evolutionary and cultural perspective: Tests from the Netherlands, Germany, and the United States. *Psychological Science, 7,* 359–363.

Buysse, D. J., Morin, C. M., & Reynolds, C. F., III. (1995). Sleep disorders. In G. O. Gabbard (Ed.), *Treatments of psychiatric disorders* (2nd ed.), Vols. 1 & 2. Washington, DC: American Psychiatric Press, Inc.

Bylinsky, G. (1993, March 22). New gains in the fight against pain. *Fortune,* pp. 107–118.

Byne, W. (1996). Biology and homosexuality: Implications of neuroendocrinological and neuroanatomical studies. In R. P. Cabaj, & T. S. Stein (Eds.), *Textbook of homosexuality and mental health.* Washington, DC: American Psychiatric Press, Inc.

Byne, W., & Parsons, B. (1994, February). Biology and human sexual orientation. *Harvard Mental Health Letter, 10,* 5–7.

Byrne, D. (1969). Attitudes and attraction. In L. Berkowitz (Ed.), *Advances in experimental social psychology* (Vol. 4, pp. 35–89). New York: Academic Press.

Cabeza, R., Mangels, J., Nyberg, L., Habib, R., Houle, S., McIntosh, A. R., & Tulving, E. (1997). Brain regions differentially involved in remembering what and when. *Neuron, 19,* 863–870.*

Cacioppo, J. T., Berntson, G. G., & Crites, S. L., Jr. (1996). Social neuroscience: Principles of psychophysiological arousal and response. In E. T. Higgins, & A. W. Kruglanski (Eds.), *Social psychology: Handbook of basic principles.* New York: Guilford Press.

Cacioppo, J. T., Marshall-Goodell, B. S., Tassinary, L. G., & Petty, R. E. (1992). Rudimentary determinants of attitudes: Classical conditioning is more effective when prior knowledge about the attitude stimulus is low than high. *Journal of Experimental Social Psychology, 28,* 207–233.

Cacioppo, J. T., & Tassinary, L. G. (1990). Inferring psychological significance from physiological signals. *American Psychologist, 45,* 16–28.

Cairns, H. S., & Cairns, C. E. (1976). *Psycholinguistics: A cognitive view of language.* New York: Holt, Rinehart & Winston.

Calev, A., Shapira, B., & Pass, H. L. (1995). Recent advances in the treatment of depression with electroconvulsive therapy (ECT). In G. Ben-Shakhar, & A. Lieblich (Eds.), *Studies in psychology in honor of Solomon Kugelmass.* Publications of the Hebrew University of Jerusalem, Vol. 36. Jerusalem: Magnes Press.

Calkins, B. J. (1993). *Advancing the science: A psychologist's guide to advocacy.* Washington, DC: American Psychological Association.

Camara, W. J., & Schneider, D. L. (1994). Integrity tests: Facts and unresolved issues. *American Psychologist, 49,* 112–119.

Cameron, J., & Pierce, W. D. (1994). Reinforcement, reward, and intrinsic motivation: A meta-analysis. *Review of Educational Research, 64,* 363–423.

Cameron, J., & Pierce, W. D. (1996). The debate about rewards and intrinsic motivation: Protests and accusations do not alter the results. *Review of Educational Research, 66,* 39–51.

CAMH. (1999a). *Ontario student drug survey.* Toronto: CAMH.*

CAMH. (1999b). Alcohol and drug prevention programs for youth: What really works.* Available: <http://www.camh.net/prevention/best_prevention_youth.html>.

CAMH. (2000). Canadian Campus Survey Executive Summary.* Available: <http://www.camh.net/press-releases>.

Campbell, C. P. (1995). *Race, myth, and the news.* Thousand Oaks, CA: Sage.

Campfield, L. A., Smith, F. J., Guisez, Y., Devos, R., & Burn, P. (1995, July 28). Recombinant mouse OB protein: Evidence for a peripheral signal linking adiposity and central neural networks. *Science, 269,* 546–550.

Campfield, L. A., Smith, F. J., Rosenbaum, M., & Hirsch, J. (1996). Human eating: Evidence for a physiological basis using a modified paradigm. Special Issue: Society for the Study of Ingestive Behavior, Second Independent Meeting. *Neuroscience and Biobehavioral Reviews, 20,* 133–137.

Camras, L. A., Holland, E. A., & Patterson, M. J. (1993). Facial expression. In M. Lewis, & J. M. Haviland (Eds.), *Handbook of emotions.* New York: Guilford Press.

Canadian Centre for Substance Abuse. (1995a). *Alcohol and drug use: Results from the 1993 General Social Survey.* Ottawa: CCSA.*

Canadian Council on Animal Care (1989). *Ethics of animal investigation.* Ottawa: Author.*

Canadian Psychological Association (1991). *Canadian code of Ethics for psychologists.* Revised. Ottawa: Author.*

Canadian Psychological Association (1996). *Guidelines for the use of animals in research and instruction in psychology: Commentary and elaboration.* Ottawa: Author.

Canadian Study of Health and Aging Working Group. (1994). Canadian study of health and aging: Study methods and prevalence of dimentia. *Canadian Medical Association Journal, 150,* 899–913.*

Candee, D., & Kohlberg, L. (1987). Moral judgment and moral action: A reanalysis of Haan, Smith, and Block's (1968) free-speech data. *Journal of Personality and Social Psychology, 52,* 554–564.

Cannon, W. B. (1929). Organization for physiological homeostatics. *Physiological Review, 9,* 280–289.

Canter, M. B., Bennett, B. E., Jones, S. E., & Nagy, T. F. (1994). *Ethics for psychologists: A commentary on the APA ethics code.* Washington, DC: American Psychological Association.

Cantor, C., & Fallon, B. A. (1996). *Phantom illness: Shattering the myth of hypochondria.* Boston: Houghton Mifflin.

Capaldi, E. D. (Ed.). (1996). *Why we eat what we eat: The psychology of eating.* Washington, DC: American Psychological Association.

Caplan, G. A., & Brigham, B. A. (1990). Marijuana smoking and carcinoma of the tongue: Is there an association? *Cancer, 66,* 1005–1006.

Cappella, J. N. (1993). The facial feedback hypothesis in human interaction: Review and speculation. Special Issue: Emotional communication, culture, and power. *Journal of Language and Social Psychology, 12,* 13–29.

Caramazza, A., & Hillis, A. E. (1991, February 28). Lexical organization of nouns and verbs in the brain. *Nature, 349,* 788–790.

Carlesimo, G. A., Fadda, L., Lorussa, S., Caltagirone, C. (1994). Verbal and spatial memory spans in Alzheimer's and multi-infarct dementia. *Acta Neurologica Scandinavica, 89,* 132–138.

Carli, L. L. (1990). Gender, language, and influence. *Journal of Personality and Social Psychology, 59,* 941–951.

Carli, L. L., Ganley, R., & Pierce-Otay, A. (1991). Similarity and satisfaction in roommate relationships. *Personality and Social Psychology Bulletin, 17,* 419–426.

Carlo, G., Eisenberg, N., Troyer, D., Switzer, G., & Speer, A. L. (1991). The altruistic personality: In what contexts is it apparent? *Journal of Personality and Social Psychology, 61,* 450–458.

Carlson, M., Charlin, V., & Miller, N. (1988). Positive mood and helping behavior: A test of six hypotheses. *Psychological Bulletin, 55,* 211–229.

Carlson, M., Charlin, V., & Miller, N. (1994). Positive mood and helping behavior: A test of six hypotheses. In B. Puka (Ed.), *Reaching out: Caring, altruism, and prosocial behavior. Moral development: A compendium, Vol. 7.* New York: Garland.

Carlson, M., Marcus-Newhall, A., & Miller, N. (1989). Evidence for a general construct of aggression. *Personality and Social Psychology Bulletin, 15*, 377–389.

Carlson, M., Marcus-Newhall, A., & Miller, N. (1990). Effects of situational aggression cues: A quantitative review. *Journal of Personality and Social Psychology, 58*, 622–633.

Carlsson, P., Hakansson, B., & Ringdahl, A. (1995). Force threshold for hearing by direct bone conduction. *Journal of the Acoustical Society of America, 97*, 1124–1129.

Carmelli, D., Swan, G. E., Robinette, D., & Fabsitz, R. (1992, September 17). Genetic influences on smoking—a study of male twins. *New England Journal of Medicine, 327*, 829–933.

Carnegie Council on Adolescent Development. (1995). *Great transitions: Preparing adolescents for a new century.* New York: Carnegie Corporation of New York.

Carnegie Task Force on Meeting the Needs of Young Children. (1994). *Starting points: Meeting the needs of our youngest children.* New York: Carnegie Corporation.

Carney, P. (1999). School violence: The school setting is only part of the picture. *Psynopsis,* Summer, 1999.*

Carroll, J. B. (1992). Cognitive abilities: The state of the art. *Psychological Science, 3*, 266–270.

Carroll, J. B. (1993). *Human cognitive abilities: A survey of factor-analytic studies.* Cambridge, England: Cambridge University Press.

Carroll, J. B. (1994). An alternative, Thurstonian view of intelligence. *Psychological Inquiry, 5*, 195–197.

Carroll, J. B. (1996). A three-stratum theory of intelligence: Spearman's contribution. In I. Dennis, & P. Tapsfield (Eds.), *Human abilities: Their nature and measurement.* Mahwah, NJ: Erlbaum.

Carroll, J. M., & Russell, J. A. (1997). Facial expressions in Hollywood's portrayal of emotion. *Journal of Personality and Social Psychology, 72*, 164–176.

Carson, R. C., Butcher, J. N., & Coleman, J. C. (1992). *Abnormal psychology and modern life* (9th ed.). New York: HarperCollins.

Carstensen, L. L., Gottman, J. M., & Levenson, R. W. (1995). Emotional behavior in long-term marriage. *Psychology & Aging, 10*, 140–149.

Carter, A. S., Pauls, D. L., & Leckman, J. F. (1995). The development of obsessionality: Continuities and discontinuities. In D. Cicchetti, & D. J. Cohen (Eds.), *Developmental psychopathology, Vol. 2: Risk, disorder, and adaptation.* Wiley series on personality processes. New York: Wiley.

Carter, B. (1991, May 1). Children's TV, where boys are king. *New York Times,* pp. A1, C18.

Caruso, D. A., Horm-Wingerd, D. M., & Dickinson, L. (1996). Head Start teaching center: Describing the initiation of a new approach to Head Start staff development. *Child and Youth Care Forum, 25*, 89–99.

Carver, C. (1990). *Optimism and coping with cancer.* Paper presented at the conference on "Hostility, coping and health," Lake Arrowhead, CA.

Carver, C. S., Pozo, C., Harris, S. D., Noriega, V., Scheier, M. F., Robinson, D. S., Ketchan, A. S., Moffat, F. L., Jr., & Clark, K. C. (1993). How coping mediates the effect of optimism on distress: A study of women with early stage breast cancer. *Journal of Personality and Social Psychology, 65*, 372–390.

Casas, J. M. (1994). Counseling and psychotherapy with racial/ethnic minority groups in theory and practice. In B. Bongar, & L. E. Beutler (Eds.), *Comprehensive textbook of psychotherapy: Theory and practice.* New York: Oxford University Press.

Cascio, W. F. (1995). Whiter industrial and organization psychology in a changing world of work? *American Psychologist, 50*, 928–939.

Case, R. (Ed.). (1991). *The mind's staircase: Exploring the conceptual underpinnings of children's thought and knowledge.* Mahwah, NJ: Erlbaum.

Case, R., & Okamoto, Y. (1996). The role of central conceptual structures in the development of children's thought. *Monographs of the Society for Research in Child Development, 61*, v–265.

Case, R., Okamoto, Y., Henderson, B., & McKeough, A. (1993). Individual variability and consistency in cognitive development: New evidence for the existence of central conceptual structures. In R. Case, & W. Edelstein (Eds.), *The new structuralism in cognitive development: Theory and research on individual pathways. Contributions to human development, Vol. 23.* Basel, Switzerland: S. Karger, AG.

Caspi, A., Henry, B., McGee, R. O., Moffitt, T. E., & Silva, P. A. (1995). Temperamental origins of child and adolescent behavior problems: from age three to age fifteen. *Child Development, 66*, 55–68.

Cassel, W. S., & Bjorklund, D. F. (1995). Developmental patterns of eyewitness memory and suggestibility: An ecologically based short-term longitudinal study. *Law and Human Behavior, 19*, 507–532.

Cassel, W. S., Roebers, C. E. M., & Bjorklund, D. F. (1996). Developmental patterns of eyewitness responses to repeated and increasingly suggestive questions. *Journal of Experimental Child Psychology, 61*, 116–133.

Casselden, P. A., & Hampson, S. E. (1990). Forming impressions from incongruent traits. *Journal of Personality and Social Psychology, 59*, 353–362.

Castonguay, L. G., Goldfried, M. R., Wiser, S., et al. (1996) Predicting the effect of cognitive therapy for depression: A study of unique and common factors. *Journal of Consulting and Clinical Psychology, 64*, 497–504.

Catalano, E. M., & Johnson, K. (Eds.). (1987). *A patient's guide to the management of chronic pain.* Oakland, CA: New Harbinger.

Catania, J. A., Coates, T. J., Stall, R., Turner, H., Peterson, J., Hearst, N., Dolcini, M. M., Hudes, E., Gagnon, J., Wiley, J., & Groves, R. (1992). Prevalence of AIDS-related risk factors and condom use in the United States. *Science, 258*, 1101–1106.

Cattell, R. B. (1965). *The scientific analysis of personality.* Chicago: Aldine.

Cattell, R. B. (1967). *The scientific analysis of personality.* Baltimore: Penguin.

Cattell, R. B. (1987). *Intelligence: Its structure, growth, and action.* Amsterdam: North-Holland.

Cattell, R. B., Cattell, A. K., & Cattell, H. E. P. (1993). *Sixteen personality factor questionnaire* (5th ed.). San Antonio, TX: Harcourt Brace.

Caudill, M. A. (1995). *Managing pain before it manages you.* New York: Guilford Press.

Cavanaugh, J. C., & Park, D. C. (1993, December). The graying of America: An aging revolution in need of a national research agenda. *American Psychologist Observer,* p. 3.

CBS News. (1997, January 30–February 1). Public survey. New York: CBS News.

CCSA. (1995b). University student drug use and lifestyle behaviours. Ottawa: CCSA.* Available: <http://www.ccsa.ca/clip11.htm>.

CCSA. (1996). Atlantic student drug use surveys.* Highlights available: <http://www.ccsa.ca/student.htm>.

CCSA/CAMH. (1999). *Canadian profile 1999: Alcohol, tobacco and other drugs.* Ottawa: CCSA/CAMH.*

CDC (Centers for Disease Control). (1991a). *1988 smoking survey.* Atlanta, GA: Centers for Disease Control.

CDC (Centers for Disease Control). (1991b). *Incidence of sexually transmitted disease.* Atlanta, GA: Centers for Disease Control.

CDC (Centers for Disease Control). (1992). *Most students sexually active: Survey of sexual activity.* Atlanta, GA: Centers for Disease Control.

CDC (Centers for Disease Control and Prevention). (1994). Cigarette smoking among adults—United States, 1993. *Morbidity and Mortality Weekly Report, 43*, 925–930.

Ceci, S. J., & Bruck, M. (1995). *Jeopardy in the courtroom: A scientific analysis of children's testimony.* Washington, DC: American Psychological Association.

Cemini-Spada, E. (1994). Animal mind—human mind: The continuity of mental experience with or without language. *International Journal of Comparative Psychology, 7*, 159–193.

Cenoz, J., & Genesee, F. (1998). *Beyond bilingualism: Multilingualism and multilingual education.* Clevedon, England: Multilingual Matters.*

Center on Addiction and Substance Abuse. (1994). *Report on college drinking.* New York: Columbia University.

Center on Addiction and Substance Abuse. (1996). Gender and drug and alcohol abuse. New York: Center on Addiction and Substance Abuse.

Centre for Addiction and Mental Health. (2000). *Canadian Campus Survey.* Ottawa: CAMH.*

Cermak, L. S., & Craik, F. I. M. (Eds.). (1979). *Levels of processing in human memory.* Mahwah, NJ: Erlbaum.

Chaiken, S. (1979). Communicator physical attractiveness and persuasion. *Journal of Personality and Social Psychology, 37,* 1387–1397.

Chalmers, D. (1996). *The conscious mind.* New York: Oxford University Press.

Chamberlain, K., & Zika, S. (1990). The minor events approach to stress: Support for the use of daily hassles. *British Journal of Psychology, 81,* 469–481.

Chandler, L. S., & Lane, S. J. (Eds.). (1996). *Children with prenatal drug exposure.* New York: Haworth Press.

Chandler, M., & Lalonde, C. (1996). Shifting to an interpretive theory of mind: 5- to 7-year-olds' changing conceptions of mental life. In A. J. Sameroff, & M. M. Haith (Eds.), *The five to seven year shift: The age of reason and responsibility. The John D. and Catherine T. MacArthur Foundation Series on Mental Heath and Development.* Chicago: University of Chicago Press.

Chandler, M. J. (1976). Social cognition and life-span approaches to the study of child development. In H. W. Reese, & L. P. Lipsitt (Eds.), *Advances in child development and behavior* (Vol. 11), New York: Academic Press.

Chang, Y. (1994, July 27). Tip sheet for scriptwriters: Fight less, talk more. *Wall Street Journal,* pp. B1, B8.

Chapman, L. J., & Chapman, J. P. (1973). *Disordered thought in schizophrenia.* New York: Appleton-Century-Crofts.

Chase, M. (1993, October 13). Inner music: Imagination may play role in how the brain learns muscle control. *Wall Street Journal,* pp. A1, A6.

Chater, N. (1996). Reconciling simplicity and likelihood principles in perceptual organization. *Psychological Review, 103,* 566–581.

Chen, A. C. H., Kalsi, G., Brynjolfsson, J., & Sigmundsson, T. (1996). Lack of evidence for close linkage of the glutamate GluR6 receptor gene with schizophrenia. *American Journal of Psychiatry, 153,* 1634–1636.

Chen, C., & Stevenson, H. W. (1995). Motivation and mathematics achievement: A comparative study of Asian-American, Caucasian-American, and East Asian high school students. *Child Development, 66,* 1215–1234.

Cheney, C. D. (1996). Medical nonadherence: A behavior analysis. In J. R. Cautela, & W. Ishaq (Eds.), *Contemporary issues in behavior therapy: Improving the human condition. Applied clinical psychology.* New York: Plenum Press.

Cheney, D. L., & Seyfarth, R. M. (1990). *How monkeys see the world: Inside the mind of another species.* Chicago: University of Chicago Press.

Cheng, H., Cao, Y., & Olson, L. (1996, July 26). Spinal cord repair in adult paraplegic rats: Partial restoration of hind limb function. *Science, 273,* 510–513.

Cherlin, A. (1993). *Marriage, divorce, remarriage.* Cambridge, MA: Harvard University Press.

Cherlin, A. J., Furstenberg, F. F., Jr., Chase-Lansdale, P. L., Kiernan, K. E., Robins, P. K., Morrison, D. R., & Teitler, J. O. (1991, June 7). Longitudinal studies of effects of divorce on children in Great Britain and the United States. *Science, 252,* 1386–1389.

Cherry, B. J., Buckwalter, J. G., & Henderson, V. W. (1996). Memory span procedures in Alzheimer's disease. *Neuropsychology, 10,* 286–293.

Chi-Ching, Y., & Noi, L. S. (1994). Learning styles and their implications for cross-cultural management in Singapore. *Journal of Social Psychology, 134,* 593–600.

Chin, J. L., De La Cancela, V., & Jenkins, Y. M. (1993). *Diversity in psychotherapy: The politics of race, ethnicity, and gender.* New York: Praeger.

Chin, J. L., Liem, J. H., Ham, M. D., & Hong, G. K. (1993). *Transference and empathy in Asian American psychotherapy.* New York: Praeger.

Chin, S. B., & Pisoni, D. B. (1997). *Alcohol and speech.* New York: Academic Press.

Chiocca, E. A., & Martuza, R. L. (1990). Neurosurgical therapy of the patient with obsessive-compulsive disorder. In M. A. Jenike, L. Baer, & W. E. Minichiello (Eds.), *Obsessive compulsive disorders: Theory and management* (2nd ed.). Chicago: Yearbook Medical Publishers.

Chodorow, N. (1978). *The reproduction of mothering.* Berkeley: University of California Press.

Chomsky, N. (1968). *Language and mind.* New York: Harcourt Brace Jovanovich.

Chomsky, N. (1969). *The acquisition of syntax in children from five to ten.* Cambridge, MA: MIT Press.

Chomsky, N. (1978). On the biological basis of language capacities. In G. A. Miller, & E. Lennenberg (Eds.), *Psychology and biology of language and thought* (pp. 199–220). New York: Academic Press.

Chomsky, N. (1991). Linguistics and cognitive science: Problems and mysteries. In A. Kasher (Ed.), *The Chomskyan turn.* Cambridge, MA: Blackwell.

Chrisler, J. C., Golden, C., & Rozee, P. D. (Eds.). (1996). *Lectures on the psychology of women.* New York: McGraw-Hill.

Chrousos, G. P., McCarty, R., Pacak, K., Cizza, G., & Sternberg, E. (Eds.). (1995). *Stress: Basic mechanisms and clinical implications.* New York: New York Academy of Sciences.

Church, A. T., & Burke, P. J. (1994). Exploratory and confirmatory tests of the big five and Tellegen's three- and four-dimensional models. *Journal of Personality and Social Psychology, 66,* 93–114.

Churchland, P. S., & Ramachandran, V. S. (1995). Filling in: Why Dennett is wrong. In B. Dahlbom (Ed.), *Dennett and his critics: Demystifying mind. Philosophers and their critics.* Oxford, England: Blackwell.

Churchland, P. S., & Sejnowski, T. J. (1992). *The computational brain.* Cambridge, MA: Bradford.

Chwalisz, K., Diener, E., & Gallagher, D. (1988). Autonomic arousal feedback and emotional experience: Evidence from the spinal-cord injured. *Journal of Personality and Social Psychology, 54,* 820–828.

Cialdini, R. (1993). *Influence: Science and practice* (3rd ed.). New York: HarperCollins.

Cialdini, R., & Fultz, J. (1990). Interpreting the negative mood-helping literature via "Mega"-analysis: A contrary view. *Psychological Bulletin, 107,* 210.

Cialdini, R. B. (1984). *Social influence.* New York: William Morrow.

Cialdini, R. B. (1988). *Influence: Science and practice* (2nd ed.). Glenview, IL: Scott, Foresman.

Cialdini, R. B. (1997). Professionally responsible communication with the public: Giving psychology a way. *Personality and Social Psychology Bulletin, 23,* 675–683.

Cialdini, R. B., Schaller, M., Houlihan, D., Arps, K., Fultz, J., & Beaman, A. L. (1975). Reciprocal concessions procedure for inducing compliance: The door-in-the-face technique. *Journal of Personality and Social Psychology, 31,* 206–215.

Cialdini, R. B., Schaller, M., Houlihan, D., Arps, K., Fultz, J., & Beaman, A. L. (1987). Empathy-based helping: Is it selflessly or selfishly motivated? *Journal of Personality and Social Psychology, 52,* 749–758.

Cicchetti, D., & Beeghly, M. (Eds.). (1990). *Children with down syndrome.* Cambridge, England: Cambridge University Press.

Cicchetti, D., & Cohen, D. J. (Eds.), (1995). *Developmental psychopathology, Vol. 2: Risk, disorder, and adaptation.* Wiley series on personality processes. New York: Wiley & Sons.

Cimbolic, P., & Jobes, D. A. (Eds.). (1990). *Youth suicide: Issues, assessment, and intervention.* Springfield, IL: Thomas.

Cioffi, D., & Holloway, J. (1993). Delayed costs of suppressed pain. *Journal of Personality and Social Psychology, 64,* 274–282.

Cipriani, D. C. (1996). Stability and change in personality across the life span: Behavioral-genetic versus evolutionary approaches. *Genetic, Social, and General Psychology Monographs, 122,* 55–74.

CIRE (Cooperative Institutional Research Program of the American Council on Education). (1990). *The American freshman: National norms for fall 1990.* Los Angeles: American Council on Education.

Clare, A. (1993). Communication in medicine. Jansson Memorial Lecture (1992, Dublin, Ireland). *European Journal of Disorders of Communication, 28,* 1–12.

Clark, L. A., & Watson, D. (1988). Mood and the mundane: Relations between daily life events and self-reported mood. *Journal of Personality and Social Psychology, 54,* 296–308.

Clark, M. (1987, November 9). Sweet music for the deaf. *Newsweek,* p. 73.

Clark, M. S., & Reis, H. T. (1988). Interpersonal processes in close relationships. *Annual Review of Psychology, 39,* 609–672.

Clarke, A. H., Teiwes, W., & Scherer, H. (1993). Evaluation of the torsional VOR in weightlessness. Special Issue: Space and the Vestibular System. *Journal of Vestibular*

Research Equilibrium and Orientation, 3, 207–218.

Clarke-Stewart, K. A. (1991). A home is not a school: The effects of child care on children's development. *Journal of Social Issues, 47,* 105–123.

Clarke-Stewart, K. A., & Friedman, S. (1987). *Child development: Infancy through adolescence.* New York: Wiley.

Clarke-Stewart, K. A., Gruber, C. P., & Fitzgerald, L. M. (1994). *Children at home and in day care.* Mahwah, NJ: Erlbaum.

Clarkin, J. F., & Lenzenweger, M. F. (Ed.). (1996). *Major theories of personality disorder.* New York: Guilford Press.

Clausen, J. A. (1995). Gender, contexts, and turning points in adults' lives. In P. Moen, G. H. Elder, Jr., & K. Luscher (Eds.), *Examining lives in context: Perspectives on the ecology of human development.* Washington, DC: American Psychological Association.

Claxton-Oldfield, S., & Keefe, S. M. (1999). Assessing Stereotypes about the Innu of Davis Inlet, Labrador. *Canadian Journal of Behavioural Science, 31,* 86–91.*

Clayton, R. R., Cattarello, A. M., & Johnstone, B. M. (1996). The effectiveness of Drug Abuse Resistance Education (project DARE): 5-year follow-up results. *Preventative Medicine, 25,* 307–318.

Clayton, R. R., Leukefeld, C. G., Harrington, N. G., & Cattarello, A. (1996). DARE (Drug Abuse Resistance Education): Very popular but not very effective. In C. B. McCoy, L. R. Metsch, & J. A. Inciardi (Eds.), *Intervening with drug-involved youth.* Thousand Oaks, CA: Sage.

Cline, R. J. W. (1994). Groupthink and the Watergate cover-up: The illusion of unanimity. In L. R. Frey (Ed.), *Group communication in context: Studies of natural groups.* LEA's communication series. Mahwah, NJ: Erlbaum.

Cloninger, C. R., Adolfsson, R., & Svrakic, N. M. (1996). Mapping genes for human personality. *Nature Genetics, 12,* 3–4.

Coats, E. J., & Feldman, R. S. (1996). Gender differences in nonverbal correlates of social status. *Personality and Social Psychology Bulletin, 22,* 1014–1022.

Coble, H. M., Gantt, D. L., & Mallinckrodt, B. (1996). Attachment, social competency, and the capacity to use social support. In G. R. Pierce, B. R. Sarason, & I. G. Sarason (Eds.), *Handbook of social support and the family. Plenum series on stress and coping.* New York: Plenum Press.

Cocco, N., Sharpe, L., & Blaszczynski, A. P. (1995). Differences in preferred level of arousal in two sub-groups of problem gamblers: A preliminary report. *Journal of Gambling Studies, 11,* 221–229.

Coffey, C. E. (1993). *The clinical science of electroconvulsive therapy.* Washington, DC: American Psychiatric Press.

Cohen, D. (1993). *The development of play* (2nd ed.). London: Routledge.

Cohen, D. (1996). Law, social policy, and violence: The impact of regional cultures. *Journal of Personality and Social Psychology, 70,* 961–978.

Cohen, D., & Nisbett, R. E. (1994). Self-protection and the culture of honor: Explaining Southern violence. Special Issue: The self and the collective. *Personality & Social Psychology Bulletin, 20,* 551–567.

Cohen, D. B. (1979). *Sleep and dreaming: Origins, nature, and functioning.* New York: Pergamon.

Cohen, G. (1989). *Memory in the real world.* Mahwah, NJ: Erlbaum.

Cohen, S. (1996, June). Psychological stress, immunity, and upper respiratory infections. *Current Directions in Psychological Science, 5,* 86–90.

Cohen, S., Tyrrell, D. A., & Smith, A. P. (1993). Negative life events, perceived stress, negative affect, and susceptibility of the common cold. *Journal of Personality and Social Psychology, 64,* 131–140.

Cohen, S., Tyrrell, D. A. J., & Smith, A. P. (1991). Psychological stress and susceptibility to the common cold. *New England Journal of Medicine, 325,* 606–612.

Cohen, S., Tyrrell, D. A. J., & Smith, A. P. (1994). Psychological stress and susceptibility to the common cold. In A. Steptoe, & J. Wardle, (Eds.), *Psychosocial processes and health: A reader.* Cambridge, England: Cambridge University Press.

Cohen, S., & Williamson, G. M. (1991). Stress and infectious disease in humans. *Psychological Bulletin, 109,* 5–24.

Cohen, S. H., & Reese, H. W. (Eds.). (1991). *Life-span developmental psychology: Methodological innovations.* Mahwah, NJ: Erlbaum.

Cohen, S. H., & Reese, H. W. (Eds.). (1994). *Life-span developmental psychology: Methodological contributions.* Mahwah, NJ: Erlbaum.

Cohen, T. E., & Lasley, D. J. (1986). Visual sensitivity. In M. R. Rosenzweig, & L. Porter (Eds.), *Annual Review of Psychology, 37.*

Cohen, Y., Spirito, A., & Brown, L. K. (1996). Suicide and suicidal behavior. In R. J. DiClemente, W. B. Hansen, & L. E. Ponton (Eds.), *Handbook of adolescent health risk behavior. Issues in clinical child psychology.* New York: Plenum Press.

Coie, J. D., Watt, N. F., West, S. G., Hawkins, J. D., Asarnow, J. R., Markman, H. J., Ramey, S. L., Shure, M. B., & Long, B. (1993). The science of prevention: A conceptual framework and some directions for a national research program. *American Psychologist, 48,* 1013–1022.

Colby, A., & Damon, W. (1987). Listening to a different voice: A review of Gilligan's *In a different voice.* In M. R. Walsh (Ed.), *The psychology of women.* New Haven, CT: Yale University Press.

Cole, M., & Gay, J. (1972). Culture and memory. *American-Anthropologist, 74,* 1066–1084.

Coles, R., (1997). *The moral intelligence of children.* New York: Random House.

Coles, R., & Stokes, G. (1985). *Sex and the American teenager.* New York: Harper & Row.

Collaer, M. L., & Hines, M. (1995). Human behavioral sex differences: A role for gonadal hormones during early

development? *Psychological Bulletin, 118,* 55–107.

Collin, C. A., DiSano, F., & Malik, R. (1994). Effects of confederate and subject gender on conformity in a color classification task. *Social Behavior & Personality, 22,* 355–364.

Collins, A. F., Gathercole, S. E., Conway, M. A., & Morris, P. E. (Eds.). (1993). *Theories of memory.* Mahwah, NJ: Erlbaum.

Collins, A. F., Gathercole, S. E., Conway, M. A., & Nirrusm, P. E. (Eds.). (1993). *Theories of memory.* Hove, England: Erlbaum.

Collins, A. M., & Loftus, E. F. (1975). A spreading-activation theory of semantic processing. *Psychological Review, 82,* 407–428.

Collins, A. M., & Quillian, M. R. (1969). Retrieval times from semantic memory. *Journal of Verbal Learning and Verbal Behavior, 8,* 240–247.

Collins, J. D. (1986). *Encoding speed in children who differ in reading ability.* Unpublished doctoral dissertation, University of Toronto: Toronto.*

Colombo, J., & Mitchell, D. W. (1990). Individual differences in early visual attention. In J. Colombo, & J. W. Fagen (Eds.), *Individual differences in infancy: Reliability, stability, and prediction.* Mahwah, NJ: Erlbaum.

Commons, M. L., Nevin, J. A., & Davison, M. C. (Eds.). (1991). *Signal detection: Mechanism, models, and applications.* Mahwah, NJ: Erlbaum.

Compas, B. E. (1987). Coping with stress during childhood and adolescence. *Psychological Bulletin, 101,* 393–403.

Compas, B. E., Ey, S., & Grant, K. E. (1993). Taxonomy, assessment, and diagnosis of depression during adolescence. *Psychological Bulletin, 114,* 323–344.

Comstock, G., & Strasburger, V. C. (1990). Deceptive appearances: Television violence and aggressive behavior. Conference: Teens and television (1988, Los Angeles, California). *Journal of Adolescent Health Care, 11,* 31–44.

Condon, J. W., & Crano, W. D. (1988). Inferred evaluation and the relation between attitude similarity and interpersonal attraction. *Journal of Personality and Social Psychology, 54,* 789–797.

Connolly, J. B., Roberts, I. J. H., Armstrong, J. D., Kaiser, K., Forte, M., Tully, T., & O'Kane, C. J. (1996, December 20). Associative learning disrupted by impaired Gs signaling in drosophila mushroom bodies. *Science, 274,* 2104.

Conoley, J. C., & Impara, J. C. (Eds.). (1997). *The 12th mental measurements yearbook.* Lincoln, NE: Buros Institute.

Conte, H. R., & Plutchik, R. (Eds.). (1995). *Ego defenses: Theory and measurement.* New York: Wiley.

Conti, R., Amabile, T. M., & Pollak, S. (1995). The positive impact of creative activity: Effects of creative task engagement and motivational focus on college students' learning. *Personality and Social Psychology Bulletin, 21,* 1107–1116.

Conway, M., & Rubin, D. (1993). The structure of autobiographical memory. In A. F. Collins, S. E. Gathercole, M. A. Conway, & P. E. Morris (Eds.), *Theories of memory.* Mahwah, NJ: Erlbaum.

Conway, M. A. (1995). *Flashbulb memories.* Mahwah, NJ: Erlbaum.

Conway, M. A. (Ed.). (1997). *Cognitive models of memory.* Cambridge, MA: MIT Press.

Cook, C. A. L., Caplan, R. D., & Wolowitz, H. (1990). Nonwaking responses to waking stressors: Dreams and nightmares. *Journal of Applied Social Psychology, 20,* 199–226.

Cook, T. D., & Shadish, W. R. (1994). Social experiments: Some developments over the past fifteen years. *Annual Review of Psychology, 45,* 545–580.

Cooper, H., & Hedges, L. F. (Eds.). (1994). *The handbook of research synthesis.* New York: Russell Sage Foundation.

Cooper, I. S. (1981). *Living with chronic neurological disease.* New York: Norton.

Cooper, J. R., Bloom, F. E., & Roth, R. H. (1991). *The biochemical basis of neuropharmacology.* New York: Oxford University Press.

Cooper, L. A., & Shepard, R. N. (1984, December). Turning something over in the mind. *Scientific American,* pp. 106–114.

Cooper, S. H. (1989). Recent contributions to the theory of defense mechanism: A comparative view. *Journal of the American Psychoanalytic Association, 37,* 865–892.

Coppen, A., Metcalfe, M., & Wood, K. (1982). Lithium. In E. S. Paykel (Ed.), *Handbook of affective disorders.* New York: Guilford Press.

Corbetta, M., Miezin, F. M., Shulman, G. L., & Petersen, S. E. (1993, March). A PET study of visuospatial attention. *Journal of Neuroscience, 13,* 1202–1226.

Coren, S. (1989). The many moon illusions: An integration through analysis. In M. Hershenson (Ed.), *The moon illusion.* Mahwah, NJ: Erlbaum.*

Coren, S. (1992a). *The left-handed syndrome.* New York: The Free Press.*

Coren, S. (1992b). The moon illusion: A different view through the legs. *Perceptual and Motor Skills, 75,* 827–831.*

Coren, S. (1996). *Sleep thieves: An eye-opening exploration into the science and mysteries of sleep.* New York: Free Press.*

Coren, S., & Aks, D. J. (1990). Moon illusion in pictures: A multimechanism approach. *Journal of Experimental Psychology: Human Perception and Performance, 16,* 365–380.*

Coren, S., & Hewitt, P. L. (1998). Is anorexia nervosa associated with elevated rates of suicide? *American Journal of Public Health, 88,* 1206–1207.*

Coren, S., Porac, C., & Ward, L. M. (1979). *Sensation and perception.* New York: Academic Press.*

Coren, S., Porac, C., & Ward, L. M. (1984). *Sensation and perception* (2nd ed.). New York: Academic Press.*

Coren, S., & Ward, L. M. (1989). *Sensation and perception* (3rd ed.). San Diego, CA: Harcourt Brace Jovanovich.*

Coren, S., Ward, L. M., & Enns, J. T. (1999). *Sensation and perception* (5th ed.). Fort Worth: Harcourt Brace.*

Corina, D. P., Vaid, J., & Bellugi, U. (1992). The linguistic basis of left hemisphere specialization. *Science, 255,* 1258.

Cornblatt, B., & Erlenmeyer-Kimling, L. E. (1985). Global attentional deviance in children at risk for schizophrenia: Specificity and predictive validity. *Journal of Abnormal Psychology, 94,* 470–486.

Cornelius, S. W., & Caspi, A. (1987). Everyday problem solving in adulthood and old age. *Psychology and Aging, 2,* 144–153.

Cornell, T. L., Fromkin, V. A., & Mauner, G. (1993). A linguistic approach to language processing in Broca's aphasia: A paradox resolved. *Current Directions in Psychological Science, 2,* 47–52.

Corrigan, P. W. (1996). Models of "normal" cognitive functioning. In P. W. Corrigan, & S. C. Yudofsky (Eds.), *Cognitive rehabilitation for neuropsychiatric disorders.* Washington, DC: American Psychiatric Press.

Costa, P. T., Jr., & McCrae, R. R. (1985). Hypochondriasis, neuroticism, and aging. *American Psychologist, 40,* 19–28.

Costa, P. T., Jr., & McCrae, R. R. (1997). Longitudinal stability of adult personality. In R. Hogan, J. Johnson, & S. Briggs (Eds.), *Handbook of personality psychology.* Orlando, FL: Academic Press.

Costa, P. T., Jr., & McCrae, R. R. (1995). Solid ground in the wetlands of personality: A reply to Block. *Psychological Bulletin, 117,* 216–220.

Costello, C. G. (1993). Cognitive causes of psychopathology. In C. G. Costello (Ed.), *Basic issues in psychopathology.* New York: Guilford Press.

Cote, I. (1994). Current perspectives on multiple personality disorder. *Hospital and Community Psychiatry, 45,* 827–829.

Cotman, C. W., & Lynch, G. S. (1989). The neurobiology of learning and memory. *Cognition, 33,* 201–241.

Cotterell, J. (1996). *Social networks and social influences in adolescence.* London: Routledge.

Cotton, P. (1993, July 7). Psychiatrists set to approve DSM-IV. *Journal of the American Medical Association, 270,* 13–15.

Council of Scientific Affairs (1985, April 5). Scientific status of refreshing recollection by the use of hypnosis. *Journal of the American Medical Association, 253,* 1130–1134.

Cowan, N. (1988). Evolving conceptions of memory storage, selective attention, and their mutual constraints within the human information-processing system. *Psychological Bulletin, 104,* 163–191.

Cowey, A., & Heywood, C. A. (1995). There's more to colour than meets the eye. 25th Annual Meeting of the European Brain and Behaviour Society. *Behavioural Brain Research, 71,* 89–100.

Cowley, G. (1994, February 7). The culture of Prozac. *Newsweek,* pp. 41–42.

Cowley, G., & Springen K. (1997, September 29). After Fen-Phen. *Newsweek,* 46–48.

Cox, B. J. (1996). The nature and assessment of catastrophic thoughts in panic disorder. *Behaviour Research and Therapy, 34,* 363–374.*

Cox, B. J., Endler, N. S., & Swinson, R. P. (1995). An examination of levels of agoraphobic severity in panic disorder. *Behaviour Research and Therapy, 33,* 57–62.*

Cox, B. J., Swinson, R. P., Endler, N. S. & Norton, G. R. (1994). The sympton structure of panic attacks. *Comprehensive Psychiatry, 35,* 349–353.

Coyle, J. T., Oster-Granite, M. L., Reeves, R., Hohmann, C., Corsi, P., & Gearhart, J. (1991). Down syndrome and trisomy 16 mouse: Impact of gene imbalance on brain development and aging. In P. R. McHuagh, & V. A. McKusick (Eds.), *Genes, brain, and behavior. Research publications: Association for Research in Nervous and Mental Disease,* Vol. 69. New York: Raven.

CR (Consumer Reports). (1993, June). Dieting and weight loss. *Consumer Reports,* p. 347.

CR (Consumer Reports). (1995, November). Mental health: Does therapy help? *Consumer Reports,* pp. 734–739.

CR (Consumer Reports). (1997, May). Marijuana as medicine: How strong is the science? *Consumer Reports,* pp. 62–63.

Crabb, P. B., & Pristash, D. (1992, June). Gender-typing of material culture in children's books, 1937–1989. Paper presented at the annual meeting of the American Psychological Society, San Diego, CA.

Craig, W. M. & Pepler, D. J. (1996). Bullying and victimization at school: What can we do about it? In S. Miller, J. Brodine & T. Miller (Eds.), *Safe by design: Planning for peaceful school communities.* Seattle: Committee for Children.*

Craik, F. I.M., & Lockhart, R. S. (1972). Levels of processing: A framework for memory research. *Journal of Verbal Behavior, 11,* 671–684.*

Craik, F. I. M. (1990). Levels of processing. In M. E. Eysenck (Ed.), *The Blackwell dictionary of cognitive psychology.* London: Blackwell.*

Craik, F. I. M., & Tulving, E. (1975). Depth of processing and the retention of words in episodic memory. *Journal of Experimental Psychology, 104,* 268–294.*

Cramer, J. A. (1995). Optimizing long-term patient compliance. *Neurology, 45,* s25–s28.

Cramer, P. (1987). The development of defense mechanisms. *Journal of Personality, 55,* 597–614.

Cramer, P. (1996). *Storytelling, narrative, and the Thematic Apperception Test.* New York: Guilford Press.

Crandall, C., & Biernat, M. (1990). The ideology of anti-fat attitudes. *Journal of Applied Social Psychology, 20,* 227–243.

Crandall, C. S. (1988). Social contagion of binge eating. *Journal of Personality and Social Psychology, 55,* 588–598.

Crandall, C. S. (1992). Psychophysical scaling of stressful life events. *Psychological Science, 3,* 256–258.

Crandall, C. S., & Martinez, R. (1996). Culture, ideology, and antifat attitudes.

Personality and Social Psychology Bulletin, 22, 1165–1176.

Crapo, L. (1985). *Hormones, the messengers of life.* New York: Freeman.

Crawford, C., & Krebs, D. (Eds.). (1997). *Handbook of evolutionary psychology: Ideas, issues and applications.* Mahwah, NJ: Erlbaum.

Crawford, H. J. (1982). Hypnotizability, daydreaming styles, imagery vividness, and absorption: A multidimensional study. *Journal of Personality and Social Psychology, 42,* 915–926.

Crawford, M. (1995). *Talking difference: On gender and language.* Thousand Oaks, CA: Sage.

Crease, R. P. (1993, July 30). Biomedicine in the age of imaging. *Science, 261,* 554–561.

Crenshaw, T. L., & Goldberg, J. P. (1996). *Sexual pharmacology: Drugs that affect sexual functioning.* New York: Norton.

Creswell, J. W. (1994). *Research design.* Newbury Park, CA: Sage.

Crews, D. (1993). The organizational concept and vertebrates without sex chromosomes. *Brain, Behavior, and Evolution, 42,* 202–214.

Crews, D. (1994, January). Animal sexuality. *Science, 263,* 108–114.

Crews, F. (1993, November 18). The unknown Freud. *New York Review,* pp. 55–66.

Crews, F. (1996). The verdict on Freud. *Psychological Science, 7,* 63–68.

CRHL. (1990, February). How to lose weight and keep it off. *Consumer Reports Health Letter, 2,* 9–11.

Crick, F., & Mitchison, G. (1983). The function of dream sleep. *Nature, 304,* 111–114.

Crick, F., & Mitchison, G. (1995). REM sleep and neural nets. Special Issue: The function of sleep. *Behavioural Brain, 69,* 147–155.

Crick, N. R., & Dodge, K. A. (1994). A review and reformulation of social information-processing mechanisms in children's social adjustment. *Psychological Bulletin, 115,* 74–101.

Crisp, A. H., & McClelland, L. (1996). *Anorexia nervosa: Guidelines for assessment and treatment in primary and secondary care* (2nd ed.). Mahwah, NJ: Erlbaum.

Crits-Christoph, P. (1992). The efficacy of brief dynamic psychotherapy: A meta-analysis. *American Journal of Psychiatry, 149,* 151–158.

Crits-Christoph, P., & Mintz, J. (1991). Implications of therapist effects for the design and analysis of comparative studies of psychotherapies. *Journal of Consulting and Clinical Psychology, 59,* 20–26.

Crittendon, K. S. (1996). Causal attribution processes among the Chinese. In M. H. Bond (Ed.), *The handbook of Chinese psychology.* Hong Kong: Oxford University Press.

Crocetti, G. (1983). *GRE: Graduate record examination general aptitude test.* New York: Arco.

Crockett, L. J., & Crouter, A. C. (Eds.). (1995). *Pathways through adolescence: Individual development in relation to social contexts.* Mahwah, NJ: Erlbaum.

Cromwell, R. L., & Snyder, C. R. (1993). *Schizophrenia: Origins, processes, treatment, and outcome.* New York: Oxford University Press.

Cronkite, K. (1994). *On the edge of darkness: Conversations about depression.* New York: Doubleday.

Crosby, F. J. (1991). *Juggling: The unexpected advantages of balancing career and home for women, their families, and society.* New York: Free Press.

Cross, S. E., & Markus, H. R. (1993). Gender in thought, belief, and action. In A. E. Beall, & R. J. Sternberg (Eds.), *The psychology of gender.* New York: Guilford.

Crow, T. J. (1990). The continuum of psychosis and its genetic origins: The sixty-fifth Maudsley lecture. *British Journal of Psychiatry, 156,* 788–797.

Crow, T. J. (1995). A theory of the evolutionary origins of psychosis. *European Neuropsychopharmacology, 5,* 59–63.

Crowe, R. R., Black, D. W., Wesner, R., Andreasen, N. C., Cookman, A., & Roby, J. (1991). Lack of linkage to chromosome 5q11–q13 in six schizophrenia pedigrees. *Archives of General Psychiatry, 48,* 357–361.

Croyle, R. T., & Hunt, J. R. (1991). Coping with health threat: Social influence processes in reactions to medical test results. *Journal of Personality and Social Psychology, 60,* 382–389.

Csikszentmihalyi, M. (1997). *Creativity: Flow and the psychology of discovery and invention.* New York: BasicBooks/ Mastermind Series.

Culbertson, F. M. (1997, January). Depression and gender: An international review. *American Psychologist, 52,* 25–31.

Culham, J. C., Dukelow, S. P., Vilis, T., Hassard, F. A., Gati, J. S., Menon, R. S. & Goodale, M. A. Recovery of fMRI activation in motion area MT following storage of the motion after effect. *Journal of Neurophysiology, 81,* 388–393.

Culotta, E., & Koshland, D. E., Jr. (1992, December 18). No news is good news. *Science, 258,* 1862–1865.

Cummings, E., & Henry, W. E. (1961). *Growing old.* New York: Basic Books.

Cummings, J. (1987, October 6). An earthquake aftershock: Calls to mental health triple. *New York Times,* p. A1.

Cushner, K., & Brislin, R. W. (1996). *Intercultural interactions: A practical guide* (2nd ed.). Thousand Oaks, CA: Sage.

Cutler, B. L., & Penrod, S. D. (1995). *Mistaken identification: The eyewitness, psychology, and the law.* New York: Cambridge University Press.

Czeisler, C. A., Johnson, M. P., & Duffy, J. F. (1990, May 3). Exposure to bright light and darkness to treat physiological maladaption to night work. *New England Journal of Medicine, 322,* 1253.

Czeisler, C. A., Kronauer, R. E., Allan, J. S., Duffy, J. F., Jewett, M. E., Brown, E. N., & Ronda, J. M. (1989, June 16). Bright light induction of strong (Type O) resetting of the human circadian pacemaker. *Science, 244,* 1328–1333.

Dabbs, J. M., Jr. (1993). Salivary testosterone measurements in behavioral studies. In D. Malamud, & L. A. Tabak (Eds.), *Saliva as a diagnostic fluid. Annals of the New York Academy of Sciences, Vol. 694.* New York: New York Academy of Sciences.

Dabbs, J. M., Carr, T. S., Frady, R. L., & Riad, J. K. (1995). Testosterone, crime, and misbehavior among 692 male prison inmates. *Personality and Individual Differences, 18,* 627–633.

Dabbs, J. M., Jr., Hargrove, M. F., & Heusel, C. (1996). Testosterone differences among college fraternities: Well-behaved vs. rambunctious. *Personality and Individual Differences, 20,* 157–161.

Dabbs, J. M., Jr., & Morris, R. (1990). Testosterone, social class, and antisocial behavior in a sample of 4,462 men. *Psychological Science, 1,* 209–211.

Dabiri, L., Pasta, D., Darby, J. K., & Mosbacher, D. (1994). Vitamin E in tardive dyskinesia. *American Journal of Psychiatry, 151,* 925–926.

Daly, M., & Wilson, M. (1983). Sex, evolution, and behavior. Boston: Willard Grant Press.*

Daly, M., & Wilson, M. (1998). *The truth about Cinderella: A Darwinian view of parental love.* London: Weidenfeld & Nicolson.*

Damasio, H., Grabowski, T., Frank, R., Galaburda, A. M., & Damasio, A. R. (1994, May 20). The return of Phineas Gage: Clues about the brain from the skull of a famous patient. *Science, 264,* 1102–1105.

Damon, W. (1988). *The Moral Child.* New York: Free Press.

Dana, R. H. (1993). *Multicultural assessment perspectives for professional psychology.* Boston: Allyn & Bacon.

Daniels, H. (Ed.). (1996). *An introduction to Vygotsky.* London: Routledge.

Dantz, B., Edgar, D. M., & Dement, W. C. (1994). Circadian rhythms in narcolepsy: Studies on a 90 minute day. *Electroencephalography and Clinical Neurophysiology, 90,* 24–35.

Darley, J. M. (1995). Constructive and destructive obedience: A taxonomy of principal-agent relationships. *Journal of Social Issues, 51,* 125–154.

Darley, J. M., & Latané, B. (1968). Bystanders intervention in emergencies: Diffusion of responsibility. *Journal of Personality and Social Psychology, 8,* 377–383.

Darley, J. M., & Shultz, T. R. (1990). Moral rules: Their content and acquisition. *Annual Review of Psychology, 41,* 525–556.

Darling, N., & Steinberg, L. (1993). Parenting style as context: An integrative model. *Psychological Bulletin, 113,* 487–496.

Darnton, N. (1990, June 4). Mommy vs. Mommy. *Newsweek,* pp. 64–67.

Darnton, N. (1991, October 7). The pain of the last taboo. *Newsweek,* pp. 70–72.

Darwin, C. (1859). *On the origin of species.* New York: New York University Press, 1988.

Darwin, C. J., Turvey, M. T., & Crowder, R. G. (1972). An auditory analogue of the Sperling partial-report procedure: Evidence for brief auditory storage. *Cognitive Psychology, 3,* 255–267.

Davidson, J. E. (1990). Intelligence recreated. *Educational Psychologist, 25,* 337–354.

Davidson, J. E., Deuser, R., & Sternberg, R. J. (1994). The role of metacognition in problem solving. In J. Metcalfe, & A. P. Shimamura (Eds.), *Metacognition: Knowing about knowing.* Cambridge, MA: MIT Press.

Davidson, R. J. (1994). Complexities in the search for emotion-specific physiology. In P. Ekman, & R. J. Davidson (Eds.), *The nature of emotion: Fundamental questions.* New York: Oxford University Press.

Davidson, R. J., Gray, J. A., LeDoux, J. E., Levenson, R. W., Pankseep, J., & Ekman, P. (1994). Is there emotion-specific physiology? In P. Ekman, & R. J. Davidson (Eds.), *The nature of emotions: Fundamental questions.* New York: Oxford University Press.

Davidson, R. J., & Hugdahl, K. (Eds.). (1995). *Brain asymmetry.* Cambridge, MA: MIT Press.

Davies, G., Lloyd-Bostock, S., McMurran, M., & Wilson, C. (Eds.). (1995). *Psychology, law, and criminal justice: International developments in research and practice.* Berlin, Germany: Walter de Gruyter.

Davies, G. M. (1993). Children's memory for other people: An integrative review. In C. A. Nelson (Ed.), *Memory and affect in development. The Minnesota Symposia on Child Psychology, Vol. 26.* Mahwah, NJ: Erlbaum.

Davies, J. M. (1996). Dissociation, repression and reality testing in the countertransference: The controversy over memory and false memory in the psychoanalytic treatment of adult survivors of childhood sexual abuse. *Psychoanalytic Dialogues, 6,* 189–218.

Davies, J. M., & Frawley, M. G. (1994). *Treating the adult survivor of childhood sexual abuse: A psychoanalytic perspective.* New York: Basic Books.

Davis, J. A., & Smith, T. (1991). *General social surveys, 1972–1991.* Storrs, CT: University of Connecticut, Roper Center for Public Opinion Research.

Davis, J. M., & Sandoval, J. (1991). *Suicidal youth.* San Francisco: Jossey-Bass.

Davis, R. (1986). Assessing the eating disorders. *The Clinical Psychologist, 39,* 33–36.

Dawes, R. M. (1994). *House of cards: Psychology and psychotherapy built on myth.* New York: Free Press.

DeAngelis, G. C., Ohzawa, I., & Freeman, R. D. (1995). Neuronal mechanisms underlying stereopsis: How do simple cells in the visual cortex encode binocular disparity? *Perception, 24,* 3–31.

DeAngelis, T. (1991, June). DSM being revised, but problems remain. *APA Monitor,* p. 7.

DeAngelis, T. (1994, June). New test allows takers to tackle real-life problems. *APA Monitor,* p. 14.

Deary, I. J. (1996). Intelligence and inspection time: Achievements, prospects, and problems. *American Psychologist, 51,* 599–608.

Deary, I. J., & Stough, C. (1996). Intelligence and inspection time: Achievements, prospects, and problems. *American Psychologist, 51,* 599–608.

Deaux, K. (1995). How basic can you be? The evolution of research on gender stereotypes. *Journal of Social Issues, 51,* 11–20.

deBono, E. (1967). *The five day course in thinking.* New York: Basic Books.

DeBono, K. G., & Klein, C. (1993). Source expertise and persuasion: The moderating role of recipient dogmatism. *Personality & Social Psychology Bulletin, 19,* 167–173.

de Boysson-Bardies, B., & Halle, P. A. (1994). Speech development: Contributions of cross-linguistic studies. In A. Vyt, H. Bloch, & M. H. Bornstein (Eds.), *Early child development in the French tradition: Contributions from current research.* Mahwah, NJ: Erlbaum.

De bruyn, A., Souery, D., Mendelbaum, K., Mendlewicz, J., et al. (1996). Linkage analysis of families with bipolar illness and chromosome 18 markers. *Biological Psychiatry, 39,* 679–688.

Debul, A. J., & Russo, N. F. (1996). Rethinking psychological theory to encompass issues of gender and ethnicity: Focus on achievement. In K. F. Wyche, & F. J. Crosby (Eds.), *Women's ethnicities: Journeys through psychology.* Boulder, CO: Westview Press.

DeCasper, A. J., & Fifer, W. D. (1980). Of human bonding: Newborns prefer their mothers' voices. *Science, 208,* 1174–1176.

DeCastrim J. M. (1996). How can eating behavior be regulated in the complex environments of free-living humans? Society for the Study of Ingestive Behavior (1994, Hamilton, Canada). *Neuroscience and Biobehavioral Reviews, 20,* 119–131.

DeCastro, J. M. (1996). How can eating behavior be regulated in the complex environments of free-living humans? Society for the Study of Ingestive Behavior (1994, Hamilton, Canada). *Neuroscience and Biobehavioral Reviews, 20,* 119–131.

DeCharms, R., & Moeller, G. H. (1962). Values expressed in American children's readers, 1800–1950. *Journal of Abnormal and Social Psychology, 64,* 136–142.

Deci, E. L. (1992). On the nature and functions of motivation theories. *Psychological Science, 3,* 167–176.

Deci, E. L., & Ryan, R. M. (1985). *Intrinsic motivation and self-determination in human behavior.* New York: Plenum Press.

Deffenbacher, J. L. (1988). Cognitive relaxation and social skills treatments of anger: A year later. *Journal of Consulting Psychology, 35,* 309–315.

Deffenbacher, J. L. (1996). Cognitive-behavioral approaches to anger reduction. In K. S. Dobson, & K. D. Craig (Eds.), *Advances in cognitive-behavioral therapy, Vol. 2.* Banff international behavioral science series. Thousand Oaks, CA: Sage.

DeGaston, J. F., Week, S., & Jensen, L. (1996). Understanding gender differences in adolescent sexuality. *Adolescence, 31,* 217–231.

deGroot, A. D. (1966). Perception and memory versus thought: Some old ideas and recent findings. In B. Kleinmuntz (Ed.), *Problem solving: Research, method, and theory.* New York: Wiley.

DeKay, W. T., & Buss, D. M. (1992). Human nature, individual differences, and the importance of context: Perspectives from evolutionary psychology. *Current Directions in Psychological Science, 1,* 184–189.

de la Cancela, V., & Sotomayer, G. M. (1993). Rainbow warriors: Reducing institutional racism in mental health. *Journal of Mental Health Counseling, 15,* 55–71.

Delaney, C. H. (1995). Rites of passage in adolescence. *Adolescence, 30,* 891–897.

Delaney, S. L., & Hearth, A. H. (1997). *On my own at 107: Reflections on life without Bessie.* New York: HarperSanFrancisco.

Della Sala, S., Baddeley, A. D., Papagno, C., & Spinnler, H. (1995). Dual-task paradigm: A means to examine the central executive. In J. Grafman, K. J. Holyoak, & F. Boller (Eds.), *Structure and functions of the human prefrontal cortex.* Annals of the New York Academy of Sciences, Vol. 769. New York: New York Academy of Sciences.

DeLongis, A., Folkman, S., & Lazarus, R. S. (1988). The impact of daily stress on health and mood: Psychological social resources as mediators. *Journal of Personality and Social Psychology, 54,* 486–495.

Delprato, D. J., & Midgley, B. D. (1992). Some fundamentals of B. F. Skinner's behaviorism. *American Psychologist, 47,* 1507–1520.

DeLuca, R. V., Grayston, A. G., & Romano, E. (1999). Time-limited group therapy for sexually abused boys. In C. Schaefer (Ed.), *Short-term psychotherapy groups for children.* New York: Aronson.*

DeMeis, D. K., & Perkins, H. W. (1996). "Supermoms" of the nineties: Homemaker and employed mothers; performance and perceptions of the motherhood role. *Journal of Family Issues, 17,* 777–792.

Dement, W. C. (1989). *Sleep and alertness: Chrono-biological, behavioral, and medical aspects of napping.* New York: Raven Press.

Dement, W. C. (1976). *Some must watch while some must sleep.* New York: Norton.

Dement, W. C. (1979). Two kinds of sleep. In D. Goleman, & R. J. Davidson (Eds.), *Consciousness: Brain, states of awareness, and mysticism* (pp. 72–75). New York: Harper & Row.

Dement, W. C., & Wolpert, E. A. (1958). The relation of eye movements, body mobility, and external stimuli to dream content. *Journal of Experimental Psychology, 55,* 543–553.

Demetriou, A., Shayer, M., & Efklides, A. (1993). *Neo-Piagetian theories of cognitive development.* London: Routledge.

Denis, M., & Greenbaum, C. (Trans.). (1991). *Image and cognition.* London, England: Harverster Wheatsheaf.

Denmark, F. L. (1994). Engendering psychology. *American Psychologist, 49,* 329–334.

Denmark, F. L., & Fernandez, L. C. (1993). Historical development of the psychology of women. In F. L. Denmark, & M. A. Paludi

(Eds.), *A handbook of issues and theories.* Westport, CT: Greenwood Press.

Dennett, D. C. (1991). *Consciousness explained.* Boston: Little, Brown.

Dennis, D. L., Buckner, J. C., Lipton, F. R., & Levine, I. S. (1991). A decade of research and services for homeless mentally ill persons: Where do we stand? *American Psychologist, 46,* 1129–1138.

Dennis, I., & Tapsfield, P. (Eds.). (1996). *Human abilities: Their nature and measurement.* Mahwah, NJ: Erlbaum.

Denny, J. P. (1991). Rational thought in oral culture and literate decontextualization. In D. R. Olson & N. Torrance (Eds.), *Literacy and orality* (pp. 66–89). London: Cambridge University Press.*

Dent, J. (1984, March). *Reader's Digest, 124,* 38.

Denton, K., & Krebs, D. (1990). From the scene of the crime: The effect of alcohol and social context on moral judgment. *Journal of Personality and Social Psychology, 59,* 242–248.

Dentzer, S. (1986, May 5). Can you pass the job test? *Newsweek,* pp. 46–53.

Deregowski, J. B. (1973). Illusion and culture. In R. L. Gregory, & G. H. Combrich (Eds.), *Illusion in nature and art* (pp. 161–192). New York: Scribner.

Derksen, J. J. L. (1995). *Personality disorders: Clinical and social perspectives.* Somerset, NJ: Wiley.

Desforges, D. M., Lord, C. G., Ramsey, S. L., Mason, J. A., VanLeeuwen, M. D., West, S. C., & Lepper, M. R. (1991). Effects of structured cooperative contact on changing negative attitudes toward stigmatized social groups. *Journal of Personality and Social Psychology, 60,* 531–544.

Desimone, R. (1992, October 9). The physiology of memory: Recordings of things past. *Science, 258,* 245–255.

DeSteno, D. A., & Salovey, P. (1996). Evolutionary orgins of sex differences in jealousy? Questioning the "fitness" of the model. *Psychological Science, 7,* 367–372.

Detterman, D. K. (Ed.). (1996). *The environment.* Norwood, NJ: Ablex.

Deutsch, F. M., Lussier, J. B., & Servis, L. J. (1993). Husbands at home: Predictors of paternal participation in childcare and housework. *Journal of Personality and Social Psychology, 65,* 1154–1166.

Deutsch, M. (1993). Educating for a peaceful world. *American Psychologist, 48,* 510–517.

Deutsch, M. (1994). Constructive conflict resolution: Principles, training, and research. *Journal of Social Issues, 50,* 13–32.

de Valois, R. L., & de Valois, K. K. (1993). A multi-stage color model. *Vision Research, 33,* 1053–1065.

Devenport, L. D., & Devenport, J. A. (1990). The laboratory animal dilemma: A solution in our backyards. *Psychological Science, 1,* 215–216.

Devine, P. G., & Baker, S. M. (1991). Measurement of racial stereotype subtyping. *Personality and Social Psychology Bulletin, 17,* 44–50.

Devine, P. G., & Elliot, A. J. (1995, November). Are racial stereotypes *really*

fading? The Princeton trilogy revisited. *Personality and Social Psychology Bulletin, 21,* 1139–1150.

Devine, P. G., Hamilton, D. L., & Ostrom, T. M. (Eds.). (1994). *Social cognition: Impact on social psychology.* San Diego, CA: Academic Press.

DeWitt, P. M. (1992). The second time around. *American Demographics, 14,* 60–63.

Diaz-Guerrero, R. (1979). Culture and personality revisited. *Annals of the New York Academy of Sciences, 285,* 119–130.

Dickinson, A. (1991). Helpless to save her sister from Alzheimer's, an anguished actress provides what comfort she can. *People Weekly,* 75–78.

DiClemente, C. C. (1993). Changing addictive behaviors: A process perspective. *Current Directions in Psychological Science, 2* (4), 101–106.

Diefenbach, M. A., & Leventhal, H. (1996). The common sense model of illness representation: Theoretical and practical considerations. *Journal of Social Distress & the Homeless, 5,* 11–38.

Diener, E., Sandvik, E., & Larsen, R. J. (1985). Age and sex effects for emotional intensity. *Developmental Psychology, 21,* 542–546.

DiGiovanna, A. G. (1994). *Human aging: Biological perspectives.* New York: McGraw-Hill.

Digman, J. M. (1990). Personality structure: Emergence of the five-factor model. *Annual Review of Psychology, 41,* 417–440.

Dillard, J. P. (1991). The current status of research on sequential-request compliance techniques. Special issue: Meta-analysis in personality and social psychology. *Personality and Social Psychology Bulletin, 17,* 283–288.

DiMatteo, M. R. (1997). Health behaviors and care decisions: An overview of professional-patient communications. In D. S. Gochman (Ed.), *Handbook of health behavior research.* New York: Plenum Press.

DiMatteo, M. R., & DiNicola, D. D. (1982). *Achieving patient compliance: The psychology of the medical practitioner's role.* New York: Pergamon.

Dinges, D. F., Pack, F., Williams, K., Gillen, K. A., Powell, J. W., Ott, G. E., Aptowicz, C., & Pack, A. I. (1997). Cumulative sleepiness, mood disturbance, and psychomotor vigilance performance decrements during a week of sleep restricted to 4–5 hours per night. *Sleep, 20,* 267–273.

Dion, K. K., & Berscheid, E. (1974). Physical attractiveness and peer perception among children. *Sociometry, 37,* 1–12.

Dion, K. K., & Dion, K. L. (1991). Psychological individualism and love. *Journal of Social Behaviour and Personality, 6,* 17–33.*

Dion, K. K., & Dion, K. L. (1993). Individualistic and collectivistic perspectives on gender and the cultural context of love and intimacy. *The Journal of Social Issues, 49,* 53–69.*

Dion, K. K., & Dion, K. L. (1996). Cultural perspectives on romantic love. *Personal Relationships, 3,* 5–17.*

Dion, K. L. (1975). Women's reactions to discrimination from members of the same or opposite sex. *Journal of Research in Personality, 9,* 294–306.*

DiPietro, J. A., Hodgson, D. M., Costigan, K. A., & Johnson, T. R. B. (1996). Fetal antecedents of infant temperament. *Child Development, 67,* 2568–2583.

Dishman, R. K. (1997, January). Brain monoamines, exercise, and behavioral stress: Animal models. *Medical Science Exercise, 29,* 63–74.

Dobson, K. S. (1995). Psychology in Canada: The future is not the past. *Canadian Psychology, 36(1),* 1–11.*

Dobson, K. S., & Breault, L. (1998). The Canadian code of ethics and the regulation of psychology. *Canadian Psychology, 39 (3),* 212–220.*

Dobson, K. S., & Craig, K. D. (Eds.). (1996). *Advances in cognitive-behavioral therapy, Vol. 2.* Thousand Oaks, CA: Sage.

Dobson, K. S., & Shaw, B. F. (1994). Cognitive therapies in practice. In B. Bongar, & L. E. Beutler (Eds.), *Comprehensive textbook of psychotherapy: Theory and practice.* New York: Oxford University Press.

Dodge, K. A., Bates, J. E., & Petit, G. S. (1990, December 20). Mechanisms in the cycle of violence. *Science, 250,* 1678–1683.

Doi, T. (1990). The cultural assumptions of psychoanalysis. In J. W. Stigler, R. A. Shweder, & G. Herdt (Eds.), *Cultural psychology: Essays on comparative human development.* New York: Cambridge University Press.

Dolce, J. J., & Raczynski, J. M. (1985). Neuromuscular activity and electromyography in painful backs: Psychological and bio-mechanical models in assessment and treatment. *Psychological Bulletin, 97,* 502–520.

Dolin, D. J., & Booth-Butterfield, S. (1995). Foot-in-the-door and cancer prevention. *Health Communication, 7,* 55–66.

Dollard, J., Doob, L., Miller, N., Mower, O. H., & Sears, R. R. (1939). *Frustration and aggression.* New Haven, CT: Yale University Press.

Domhoff, G. W. (1996). *Finding meaning in dreams: A quantitative approach.* New York: Plenum Press.

Dominowski, R. L., & Bourne, L. E., Jr. (1994). History of research on thinking and problem-solving. In R. J. Sternberg (Ed.), *Thinking and problem-solving.* San Diego, CA: Academic Press.

Domjan, M., & Purdy, J. E. (1995). Animal research in psychology: More than meets the eye of the general psychology student. *American Psychologist, 50,* 496–503.

Donakowski, D. W., & Esses, V. M. (1996). Native Canadians, First Nations, or Aboriginals: The effect of labels on attitudes toward Native Peoples. *Canadian Journal of Behavioural Science, 28,* 86–91.*

Donn, J. (1999). Genome scientists triumph: Map of 22nd chromosome virtually completed. Associated Press <http://polydb.union.rpi.edu/article/40143/genome.html>.

Donoghue, J. P., & Sanes, J. N. (1994). Motor areas of the cerebral cortex. *Journal of Clinical Neurophysiology, 11,* 382–396.

Dore, F. Y., & Dumas, C. (1987). Psychology of animal cognition: Piagetian studies. *Psychological Bulletin, 102,* 219–233.

Dorris, J. (Ed.). (1991). *The suggestibility of children's recollections: Implications for eyewitness testimony.* Hyattsville, MD: American Psychological Association.

Dortch, S. (1996, October.) Our aching heads. *American Demographics,* pp. 4–8.

Doty, R. L., Green, P. A., Ram, C., & Yankell, S. L. (1982). Communication of gender from human breath odors: Relationship to perceived intensity and pleasantness. *Hormones and Behavior, 16,* 13–22.

Dove, A. (1968, July 15). Taking the chitling test. *Newsweek,* p. 32.

Dovidio, J. F., Allen, J. L., & Schroeder, D. A. (1990). Specificity of empathy-induced helping: Evidence for altruistic motivation. *Journal of Personality and Social Psychology, 59,* 249–260.

Dovidio, J. F., Ellyson, S. L., Keating, C. F., Heltman, K., & Brown, C. E. (1988). The relationship of social power to visual displays of dominance between men and women. *Journal of Personality and Social Psychology, 54,* 233–242.

Doyle, A. B., & Aboud, F. E. (1995). A longitudinal study of white children's racial prejudice as a social cognitive development. Merrill-Palmer.*

Doyon, J., & Milner, B. (1991). Right temporal-lobe contribution to global visual processing. *Neuropsychologia, 29(5),* 343–360.*

Doyon, J., Owen, A. M., Sziklas, V., Petrides, M., & Evans, A. C. (1996). Functional anatomy of visuomotor skill learning in human subjects examined with positron emission tomography. *European Journal of Neuroscience, 8,* 637–648.*

Dreman, S. (1997). *The family on the threshold of the 21st century.* Mahwah, NJ: Erlbaum.

Dressler, W. W., & Oths, K. S. (1997). Cultural determinants of health behavior. In D. S. Gochman (Ed.), *Handbook of Health Behavior Research.* New York: Plenum Press.

Drew, M. L., Dobson, K. S., & Stam, H. J. (1999). The negative self-concept in clinical depression: A discourse analysis. *Canadian Psychology, 40,* 192–204.*

Dreyer, P. H. (1982). Sexuality during adolescence. In B. B. Wolman (Ed.), *Handbook of developmental psychology.* Englewood Cliffs, NJ: Prentice-Hall.

Driesen, N. R., & Raz, N. (1995). The influence of sex, age, and handedness on corpus callosum morphology: A meta-analysis. *Psychobiology, 23,* 240–247.

Druckman, D., & Bjork, R. A. (1991). *In the mind's eye: Enhancing human performance.* Washington, DC: National Academy Press.

Druckman, D., & Bjork, R. A. (Eds.). (1994). *Learning, remembering, believing: Enhancing human performance.* Washington, DC: National Academy Press.

Drum, D. J. (1990). Group therapy review. *Counseling Psychologist, 18,* 131–138.

Drummond, D. C., Tiffany, S. T., Glautier, S., & Remington, B. (Eds.). (1995). *Addictive behaviour: Cue exposure theory and practice.* Chichester, England: Wiley.

Dryden, W. (Ed.). (1995). *Rational emotive behavior therapy.* Newbury Park, CA: Sage.

Dryden, W., & DiGiuseppe, R. (1990). *A primer on rational-emotive therapy.* Champaign, IL: Research Press.

Duck, S. (Ed.). (1984). *Personal relationships.* New York: Academic Press.

Duck, S. (1988). *Relating to others.* Chicago: Dorsey.

Duck, S. (1994a). Attaching meaning to attachment. *Psychological Inquiry, 5,* 34–38.

Duck, S. (1994b). *Dynamics of relationships.* Newbury Park, CA: Sage.

Duck, S. W. (1982). A topography of relationship disengagement and dissolution. In S. W. Duck (Ed.), *Personal relationships: Vol. 4. Dissolving personal relationships.* New York: Academic Press.

Duckitt, J. (1992). Psychology and prejudice: A historical analysis and integrative framework. *American Psychologist, 47,* 1182–1193.

Duckworth, J. C., & Anderson, W. P. (1995). *MMPI & MMPI-2: Interpretation manual for counselors and clinicians* (4th ed.). Bristol, PA: Accelerated Development, Inc.

Dugas, M. J., Ladouceur, R., Boisvert, J. M., & Freeston, M. H. (1996). Le trouble d'anxiété généralisée: Éléments fondamentaux et interventions psychologiques. *Canadian Psychology, 37,* 40–53.*

Dugger, C. W. (1996, December 28). Tug of taboos: African genital rite vs. U.S. law. *New York Times,* pp. 1, 9.

Duke, M., & Nowicki, S., Jr. (1979). *Abnormal psychology: Perspectives on being different.* Monterey, CA: Brooks/Cole.

Dulac, C. & Axel, R. (1995, Oct 20). A novel family of genes encoding putative pheromone receptors in mammals. *Cell, 83,* 195–206.

Duncan, P. D., et al. (1985). The effects of pubertal timing on body image, school behavior, and deviance. Special Issue: Time of maturation and psychosocial functioning in adolescence: I. *Journal of Youth and Adolescence, 14,* 227–235.

Duncker, K. (1945). On problem solving. *Psychological Monographs, 58* (5, whole no. 270).

Dunham, R. M., Kidwell, J. S., & Wilson, S. M. (1986). Rites of passage at adolescence: A ritual process paradigm. *Journal of Adolescent Research, 1,* 139–153.

Dunn, A. L., Reigle, T. G., Youngstedt, S. D., Armstrong, R. B., & Dishman, R. K. (1996, February). Brain norepinephrine and metabolites after treadmill training and wheel running in rats. *Medical Science Exercise, 28,* 204–209.

Dunne, E. J., McIntosh, J. L., & Dunne-Maxim, K. (Eds.). (1987). *Suicide and its aftermath: Understanding and counseling the survivors.* New York: Norton.

Dupre, D., Miller, N., Gold, M., & Rospenda, K. (1995). Initiation and progression of alcohol, marijuana, and cocaine use among adolescent abusers. *American Journal on Addictions, 4,* 43–48.

Durgin, F. H., Tripathy, S. P., & Levi, D. M. (1995). On the filling in of the visual blind spot: Some rules of thumb. *Perception, 24,* 827–840.

Durkin, M. S., & Stein, Z. A. (1996). Classification of mental retardation. In J. W. Jacobson, & J. A. Mulick (Eds.), *Manual of diagnosis and professional practice in mental retardation.* Washington, DC: American Psychological Association.

Durrant, J.E. (1996). Public attitudes toward corporal punishment in Canada. In D. Frehsee, W. Horn, & K. D. Bussman (Eds.), *Family violence against children: A challenge for society.* Berlin: de Gruyter.

Durst, R., & Rosca-Rebandengo, P. (1991). The disorder named Koro. *Behavioral Neurology, 4,* 1–13.

Dusenbury, L., & Botvin, G. J. (1992). Substance abuse prevention: Competence enhancement and the development of positive life options. *Journal of Addictive Diseases, 11,* 29–45.

Dutton, D. G., & Aron, A. P. (1974). Some evidence for heightened sexual attraction under conditions of high anxiety. *Journal of Personality and Social Psychology, 30,* 510–517.

Dworkin, R. H., & Widom, C. S. (1977). Undergraduate MMPI profiles and the longitudinal prediction of adult social outcome. *Journal of Consulting and Clinical Psychology, 45,* 620–625.

Dywan, J., & Bowers, K. (1983). The use of hypnosis to enhance recall. *Science, 222,* 184–185.

Eagly, A. (1978). Sex differences in influenceability. *Psychological Bulletin, 85,* 86–116.

Eagly, A. (1989, May). Meta-analysis of sex differences. Annual conference on adversity, University of Massachusetts, Amherst.

Eagly, A., & Chaiken, S. (1993). *The psychology of attitudes.* Fort Worth, TX: Harcourt Brace Jovanovich.

Eagly, A. H. (1983). Gender and social influence: A social psychological analysis. *American Psychologist, 38,* 971–981.

Eagly, A. H., & Carle, L. L. (1981). Sex of researchers and sex-typed communications as determinants of sex differences in influenceability: A meta-analysis of social influence studies. *Psychological Bulletin, 90,* 1–20.

Eagly, A. H., & Chaiken, S. (1995). Attitude strength, attitude structure, and resistance to change. In R. E. Petty, & J. A. Krosnick (Eds.), *Attitude strength: Antecedents and consequences.* Ohio State University series on attitudes and persuasion, Vol. 4. Mahwah, NJ: Erlbaum.

Eagly, A. H., & Steffen, V. J. (1986). Gender and aggressive behavior: A meta-analytic review of the social psychological literature. *Psychological Bulletin, 100,* 309–330.

Eagly, A. H., Wood, W., & Chaiken, S. (1978). Causal inferences about communicators and their effect on opinion change. *Journal of Personality and Social Psychology, 36,* 424–435.

Ebbinghaus, H. (1885/1913). *Memory: A contribution to experimental psychology.* (H. A. Roger, & C. E. Bussenius, Trans.). New York: Columbia University Press.

Ebomoyi, E. (1987). Prevalence of female circumcision in two Nigerian communities. *Sex Roles, 17,* 13–152.

Ebstein, R. P., Novick, O., Umansky, R., Priel, B., Osher, Y., Blaine, D., Bennett,

E. R., Nemanov, L., Katz, M., & Belmaker, R. H. (1996). Dopamine D4 receptor (DSDR) exon III polymorphism associated with the human personality trait of novelty seeking. *Nature and Genetics, 12,* 78–80.

Eccles, J. S. (1987). Gender roles and women's achievement-related decisions. *Psychology of Women Quarterly, 11,* 135–171.

Eccles, J. S., Jacobs, J. E., & Harold, R. D. (1990). Gender role stereotypes, expectancy effects, and parents' socialization of gender differences. *Journal of Social Issues, 46,* 183–201.

Eccles, J. S., Lord, S. E., & Roeser, R. W. (1996). In D. Cicchetti, & S. L. Toth (Eds.), *Adolescence: Opportunities and challenges. Rochester symposium on developmental psychopathology,* Vol. 7. Rochester, NY: University of Rochester Press.

Ecenbarger, W. (1993, April 1). America's new merchants of death. *The Reader's Digest,* p. 50.

Eckenrode, J. (1984). Impact of chronic and acute stressors on daily reports of mood. *Journal of Personality and Social Psychology, 46,* 907–918.

Eckes, T. (1994). Features of men, features of women: Assessing stereotypic beliefs about gender subtypes. *British Journal of Social Psychology, 33,* 107–123.

Eckholm, E. (1988, April 17). Exploring the forces of sleep. *New York Times Magazine,* pp. 26–34.

Edgette, J. H., & Edgette, J. S. (1995). *The handbook of hypnotic phenomena in psychotherapy.* New York: Brunner/Mazel.

Edmondson, B. (1996, October). The minority majority in 2001. *American Demographics,* 16–17, 39–41.

Edmondson, B. (1997, February). Two words and a number. *American Demographics,* pp. 10–15.

Edmondson, B. (1997, April). The facts of death. *American Demographics,* 47–53.

Edwards, F. A., Gibb, A. J., & Colquhoun, D. (1992, September 10). ATP receptor-mediated synaptic currents in the central nervous system. *Nature, 359,* 144–147.

Egan, T. (1994, January 30). A Washington city full of Prozac. *New York Times,* p. A16.

Egeland, J. A., Gerhard, D. S., Pauls, D. L., Sussex, J. N., Kidd, K. K., Allen, C. R., Hostetter, A. M., & Housman, D. E. (1987). Bipolar effective disorders linked to DNA markers on chromosome 11. *Nature, 325,* 783–787.

Egeth, H. (1995). Expert psychological testimony about eyewitnesses: An update. In F. Kessel (Ed.), *Psychology, science, and human affairs: Essays in honor of William Bevan.* Boulder, CO: Westview Press.

Egeth, H. E., & Yantis, S. (1997). Visual attention: Control, representation, and time course. *Annual Review of Psychology, 48,* 269–297.

Ehrenreich, B. (1997). *Blood rites: Origins and history of the passion of war.* New York: Henry Holt.

Ehrman, R. N., Robbins, S. J., Childress, A. R., & O'Brien, C. P. (1992). Conditioned responses to cocaine-related stimuli in cocaine abuse patients. *Psychopharmacology, 107,* 523–529.

Eich, E. (1995). Searching for mood dependent memory. *Psychological Science, 6,* 67–75.

Eichenbaum, H. (1993, August 20). Thinking about brain cell assemblies. *Science, 261,* 993–994.

Eichenbaum, H. (1997). Declarative memory: Insights from cognitive neurobiology. *Annual Review of Psychology, 48,* 547–572.

Eimas, P. D. (1996). The perception and representation of speech by infants. In J. L. Morgan, & K. Demuth (Eds.), *Signal to syntax: Bootstrapping from speech to grammar in early acquisition.* Mahwah, NJ: Erlbaum.

Eisen, L., Field, T. M., & Larson, S. K. (1991). Environmental effects on the fetus: The examples of alcohol, cocaine, and exercise. In L. Diamant (Ed.), *Mind-body maturity: Psychological approaches to sports, exercise, and fitness.* New York: Hemisphere.

Eisenberg, N. (1991). Meta-analytic contributions to the literature on prosocial behavior. *Personality and Social Psychology Bulletin, 17,* 273–282.

Eisenberg, N. (1994). *Social development.* Newbury Park, CA: Sage.

Eisenberg, N., & Fabes, R. A. (1991). Prosocial behavior and empathy: A multimethod developmental perspective. In M. S. Clark (Ed.), *Prosocial behavior.* Newbury Park, CA: Sage.

Eisenberger, R., & Cameron, J. (1996). Detrimental effects of reward. *American Psychologist, 51,* 1153–1166.

Ekman, P. (1972). Universals and cultural differences in facial expressions of emotion. In J. Cole (Ed.), *Darwin and facial expression: A century of research in review* (pp. 169–222). New York: Academic Press.

Ekman, P. (1993). Facial expression and emotion. *American Psychologist, 48,* 384–392.

Ekman, P. (1994). All emotions are basic. In P. Ekman, & R. J. Davidson (Eds.), *The nature of emotion: Fundamental questions.* New York: Oxford University Press.

Ekman, P. (1994b). Strong evidence for universals in facial expressions: A reply to Russell's mistaken critique. *Psychological Bulletin, 115,* 268–287.

Ekman, P., & Davidson, R. J. (1994). *The nature of emotion: Fundamental questions.* New York: Oxford University Press.

Ekman, P., Davidson, R. J., & Friesen, W. V. (1990). Emotional expression and brain physiology II: The Duchenne smile. *Journal of Personality and Social Psychology, 58,* 342–353.

Ekman, P., Levenson, R. W., & Friesen, W. V. (1983, September 16). Autonomic nervous system activity distinguishes among emotions. *Science, 223,* 1208–1210.

Ekman, P., & O'Sullivan, M. (1991). Facial expression: Methods, means, and moues. In R. S. Feldman, & B. Rimé (Eds.), *Fundamentals of nonverbal behavior.* Cambridge, England: Cambridge University Press.

Elhelou, M-W. A. (1994). Arab children's use of the keyword method to learn English vocabulary words. *Educational Research, 36,* 295–302.

Elkin, I. (1986, May). *NIMH treatment of depression: Collaborative research program.* Paper presented at the annual meeting of the American Psychiatric Association, Washington, DC.

Elkind, D. (1981). *The hurried child.* Reading, MA: Addison-Wesley.

Elkind, D. (1988). *Miseducation.* New York: Knopf.

Elkins, I. J., McGue, M., & Iacono, W. G. (1997). Genetic and environmental influences on parent–son relationships: Evidence for increasing genetic influence during adolescence. *Developmental Psychology, 33,* 351–363.

Elliot, A. J., & Church, M. A. (1997). A hierarchical model of approach and avoidance achievement motivation. *Journal of Personality and Social Psychology, 72,* 218–232.

Elliot, A. J., & Harackiewicz, J. M. (1996). Approach and avoidance achievement goals and intrinsic motivation: A mediational analysis. *Journal of Personality and Social Psychology, 70,* 461–475.

Elliott, S. (1997, June 21). Industry still has many weapons available. *New York Times,* p. 10.

Ellis, A. (1974). *Growth through reason.* Hollywood, CA: Wilshire Books.

Ellis, A. (1987). The impossibility of achieving consistently good mental health. *American Psychologist, 42,* 364–375.

Ellis, A. (1995). Thinking processes involved in irrational beliefs and their disturbed consequences. *Journal of Cognitive Psychotherapy, 9,* 105–116.

Ellis, A. (1996a). *Better, deeper, and more enduring brief therapy: The rational emotive behavior therapy approach.* New York: Brunner/Mazel.

Ellis, A. (1996b). How I learned to help clients feel better and get better. *Psychotherapy, 33,* 149–151.

Ellis, A., & Dryden, W. (1987). *The practice of rational-emotive therapy (RET).* New York: Springer.

Ellis, A., & Dryden, W. (1997). *The practice of rational emotive behavior therapy* (2nd ed.). New York: Springer.

Ellis, H. C. (1992). Graduate education in psychology: Past, present, and future. *American Psychologist, 47,* 570–576.

Ellyson, S. L., & Dovidio, J. F. (Eds.). (1985). *Power, dominance, and nonverbal behavior.* New York: Springer-Verlag.

Ellyson, S. L., Dovidio, J. F., & Brown, C. E. (1992, April). Visual dominance of behavior in mixed-sex interaction: A meta-analysis. Paper presented at the annual meeting of the Eastern Psychological Association, Boston.

Embretson, S. E. (1996). Multidimensional latent trait models in measuring fundamental aspects of intelligence. In I. Dennis, & P. Tapsfield (Eds.), *Human abilities: Their nature and measurement.* Mahwah, NJ: Erlbaum.

Endler, N. S. (1997). Stress, anxiety and coping: The multidimensional interaction model. *Canadian Psychology, 38,* 136–153.*

Endler, N. S., & Parker, J. D. (1993). The multidimensional assessment of coping: Concepts, issues, and measurement. In G. L. Van Heck, & P. Bonaiuto (Eds.),

Personality psychology in Europe (Vol. 4). Tilburg, Netherlands: Tilburg University Press.*

Endler, N. S., & Speer, R. L. (1998). Personality psychology: Research trends for 1993–1995. *Journal of Personality, 66,* 621–669.*

Eng, R. C. (Ed.). (1990). *Women: Alcohol and other drugs.* Dubuque, IA: Kendall/Hunt.

Engebretson, T. O., & Stoney, C. M. (1995). Anger expression and lipid concentrations. *International Journal of Behavioral Medicine, 2,* 281–298.

Engen, T. (1982). *Perception of odors.* New York: Academic Press.

Engen, T. (1987, September–October). Remembering odors and their names. *American Scientist, 75,* 497–503.

Engle-Friedman, M., Baker, A., & Bootzin, R. R. (1985). Reports of wakefulness during EEG identified stages of sleep. *Sleep Research, 14,* 152.

Engler, J., & Goleman, D. (1992). *The consumer's guide to psychotherapy.* New York: Simon & Schuster.

Ennett, S. T., & Bauman, K. E. (1994). The contribution of influence and selection to adolescent peer group homogeneity: The case of adolescent cigarette smoking. *Journal of Personality and Social Psychology, 67,* 653–663.

Enns, M. W., & Reiss, J. P. R. (1992). Electroconvulsive therapy. *Canadian Journal of Psychiatry, 37,* 671–678.*

Enqvist, B., Von Konow, L., & Bystedt, H. (1995). Stress reduction, preoperative hypnosis, and perioperative suggestion in maxillofacial surgery: Somatic responses and recovery. *Stress Medicine, 11,* 229–233.

Enzle, M. E., & Anderson, S. C. (1993). Surveillant intentions and intrinsic motivation. *Journal of Personality and Social Psychology, 64,* 257–266.*

Epperson, S. E. (1988, September 16). Studies link subtle sex bias in schools with women's behavior in the workplace. *Wall Street Journal,* p. 19.

Epstein, L. H., Grunberg, N. E., Lichtenstein, E., & Evans, R. I. (1989). Smoking research: Basic research, intervention, prevention, and new trends. *Health Psychology, 8,* 705–721.

Epstein, R. (1987). The spontaneous interconnection of four repertoires of behavior in a pigeon. *Journal of Comparative Psychology, 101,* 197–201.

Epstein, R. (1996). *Cognition, creativity, and behavior: Selected essays.* Westport, CT: Praeger Publishers/Greenwood Publishing Group.

Epstein, R., Kirshnit, C. E., Lanza, R. P., & Rubin, L. C. (1984). Insight in the pigeon: Antecedents and determinants of intelligent performance. *Nature, 308,* 61–62.

Epstein, S. (1994). An integration of the cognitive and the psychodynamic unconscious. *American Psychologist, 49,* 709–724.

Epstein, S., & Meier, P. (1989). Constructive thinking: A broad coping variable with specific components. *Journal of Personality and Social Psychology, 57,* 332–350.

Epstein, S., & O'Brien, E. J. (1985). The person-situation debate in historical and current perspective. *Psychological Bulletin, 98,* 513–537.

Epstein, S. L. (1992). The role of memory and concepts in learning. *Minds and Machines, 2,* 239–265.

Epstein, S. L. (1995). Learning in the right places. *Journal of the Learning Sciences, 4,* 281–319.

Erber, R. (1991). Affective and semantic priming: Effects of mood on category accessibility and inference. *Journal of Experimental Social Psychology, 27,* 480.

Erickson, M. H., Hershman, S., & Secter, I. I. (1990). *The practical application of medical and dental hypnosis.* New York: Brunner/Mazel.

Erikson, E. H. (1963). *Childhood and society* (2nd ed.). New York: Norton.

Erlandson, D. A., Harris, E. L., Skipper, B. L., & Allen, S. D. (1993). *Doing naturalistic inquiry: A guide to methods.* Newbury Park, CA: Sage.

Eron, L. D. (1982). Parent-child interaction, television violence, and aggression of children. *American Psychologist, 37,* 197–211.

Eron, L. D. (1992). Gender differences in violence: Biology and/or socialization? In K. Bjorkqvist, & P. Niemela (Eds.), *Of mice and women: Aspects of female aggression.* San Diego, CA: Academic Press.

Eron, L. D., & Huesmann, L. R. (1985). The control of aggressive behavior by changes in attitude, values, and the conditions of learning. In R. J. Blanchard, & C. Blanchard (Eds.), *Advances in the study of aggression.* New York: Academic Press.

Eron, L. D., Huesmann, L. R., Lefkowitz, M. M., & Walden, L. O. (1972). Does television cause aggression? *American Psychologist, 27,* 253–263.

Esasky, N. (1991, March). His career threatened by dizzying attacks of vertigo: A ballplayer struggles to regain his field of dreams. *People Weekly,* pp. 61–64.

Esser, J. K., & Lindoerfer, J. S. (1989). Groupthink and the space shuttle Challenger accident: Toward a quantitative case analysis. *Journal of Behavioral Decision Making, 2,* 167–177.

Esses, V. M., Haddock, G., & Zanna, M. (1994). The role of mood in the expression of intergroup stereotypes. In M. P. Zanna & J. M. Olson (Eds.), *The psychology of prejudice: The Ontario Symposium,* (Vol. 7).*

Estes, W. K. (1991). Cognitive architectures from the standpoint of an experimental psychologist. *Annual Review of Psychology, 42,* 1–28.

Estes, W. K. (1997). Significance testing in psychological research: Some persisting issues. *Psychological Science, 8,* 18–19.

Evans, D. L. (1993, March 1). The wrong examples. *Newsweek,* p. 10.

Evans, G. W., Hygge, S., & Bullinger, M. (1995). Chronic noise and psychological stress. *Psychological Science, 6,* 333–338.

Evans, J. S. B. T., Newstead, S. E., & Byrne, R. M. E. (1994). *Human reasoning: The psychology of deduction.* Mahwah, NJ: Erlbaum.

Evans, P. D. (1990). Type A behavior and coronary heart disease: When will the jury return? *British Journal of Psychology, 81,* 147–157.

Evans, R. J., Derkach, V., & Surprenant, A. (1992, June 11). ATP (adenosine triphosphate) mediates fast synaptic transmission in mammalian neurons. *Nature, 357,* 503–505.

Eveleth, P., & Tanner, J. (1976). *World-wide variation in human growth.* New York: Cambridge University Press.

Everly, G. S., Jr. (1989). *A clinical guide to the treatment of the human stress response.* New York: Plenum.*

Everly, G. S., & Mitchell, J. T. (1992). The prevention of work-related post traumatic stress: The critical incident stress debriefing process (CSID). Paper presented at the second APA-NIOSH conference on occupational stress, Washington, DC.*

Evinger, S. (1996, May). How to record race. *American Demographics,* 36–41.

Ewbank, J. J., Barnes, T. M., Lakowski, B., Lussier, M., Bussey, H., & Hekimi, S. (1997, February 14). Structural and functional conservation of the caenorhabditis elegans timing gene clk-1. *Science, 275,* 980.

Exner, J. E., Jr. (1993). *The Rorschach: A comprehensive system.* New York: Wiley.

Eysenck, H. J. (1975). *Eysenck on extroversion.* New York: Wiley.

Eysenck, H. J. (1975). The structure of social attitudes. *British Journal of Social and Clinical Psychology, 14,* 323–331.

Eysenck, H. J. (1985). Race, social class, and individual differences in IQ. *Personality and Individual Differences, 6,* 287.

Eysenck, H. J. (1994a). The big five or giant three: Criteria for a paradigm. In C. F. Halverson, Jr., G. A. Kohnstamm, & R. P. Martin (Eds.), *The developing structure of temperament and personality from infancy to adulthood.* Mahwah, NJ: Erlbaum.

Eysenck, H. J. (1994b). Cancer, personality, and stress: Prediction and prevention. *Advances in Behaviour Research and Therapy, 16,* 167–215.

Eysenck, H. J., Barrett, P., Wilson, G., & Jackson, C. (1992). Primary trait measurement of the 21 components of the P-E-N system. *European Journal of Psychological Assessment, 8,* 109–117.

Eysenck, H. J., & Eysenck, M. W. (1985). *Personality and individual differences: A natural science approach.* New York: Plenum.

Fagan, J. F., III. (1992). Intelligence: A theoretical viewpoint. *Current Directions in Psychological Science, 1,* 82–86.

Fagot, B. I., Leinbach, M. D., & O'Boyle, C. (1992). Gender labeling, gender stereotyping, and parenting behaviors. *Developmental Psychology, 28,* 225–230.

Fairburn, C. C., Jones, R., Peveler, R. C., et al. (1993). Psychotherapy and bulimia nervosa. *Archives of General Psychiatry, 50,* 419–428.

Fajardo, D. M. (1985). Author race, essay quality, and reverse discrimination. *Journal of Applied Social Psychology, 15*, 255–268.

Fancher, R. E. (1995). The Bell Curve on separated twins. Special Issue: Canadian perspectives on *The Bell Curve*. *Alberta Journal of Educational Research, 41*, 265–270.

Fanelli, R. J., Burright, R. G., & Donovick, P. J. (1983). A multivariate approach to the analysis of genetic and septal lesion effects on maze performance in mice. *Behavioral Neuroscience, 97*, 354–369.

Farber, B. A., Brink, D. C., & Raskin, P. M. (Eds.). (1996). *The psychotherapy of Carl Rogers: Cases and commentary.* New York: Guilford Press.

Farley, C. F. (1993, April 19). CNN/Time national poll. *Time*, p. 15.

Farley, F. (1986, May). The big T in personality. *Psychology Today*, pp. 44–52.

Farwell, L. A., & Donchin, E. (1988). Talking off the top of your head: Toward a mental prosthesis utilizing event-related brain potentials. *Electroencephalography and Clinical Neurophysiology, 70*, 510–523.

Farwell, L. A., & Donchin, E. (1991). The truth will out: Interrogative polygraphy ("lie detection") with event-related brain potentials. *Psychophysiology, 28*, 531–547.

Fawzy, F. I. (1994). The benefits of a short-term group intervention for cancer patients. *Advances, 10*, 17–19.

Fay, R. E., Turner, C. F., Klassen, A. D., & Gagnon, J. H. (1989). Prevalence and patterns of same-gender sexual contact among men. *Science, 243*, 338–348.

Feagans, L. V., Fendt, K., & Farran, D. C. (1995). The effects of day care intervention on teacher's ratings of the elementary school discourse skills in disadvantaged children. *International Journal of Behavioral Development, 18*, 243–261.

Fehr, B., & Russell, J. A. (1991). The concept of love viewed from a prototype perspective. *Journal of Personality and Social Psychology, 60*, 425–438.

Feifel, H. (1963). In N. L. Farberow (Ed.), *Taboo topics* (pp. 8–12). New York: Atherton.

Feightner, J. W. (1994). Early detection of depression. In Canadian Task Force on the Periodic Health Examination. *Canadian Guide to Clinical Preventive Health Care.* Ottawa: Health Canada, 450–454.*

Feingold, A. (1992). Good-looking people are not what we think. *Psychological Bulletin, 111*, 304–341.

Feingold, A. (1994). Gender differences in personality: A meta-analysis. *Psychological Bulletin, 116*, 429–456.

Feldman, E. J. (1996). The recognition and investigation of X-linked learning disability syndromes. *Journal of Intellectual Disability Research, 40*, 400–411.

Feldman, L. B. (Ed.). (1995). *Morphological aspects of language processing.* Mahwah, NJ: Erlbaum.

Feldman, R. S. (Ed.). (1982). *Development of nonverbal behavior in children.* New York: Springer-Verlag.

Feldman, R. S. (Ed.). (1993). *Applications of nonverbal behavioral theories and research.* Mahwah, New Jersey: Erlbaum.

Feldman, R. S., Coats, E. J., & Schwartzberg, S. (1994). *Case studies and critical thinking about psychology.* New York: McGraw-Hill.

Feldman, R. S., Philippot, P., & Custrini, R. J. (1991). Social competence and nonverbal behavior. In R. S. Feldman, & B. Rimé (Eds.), *Fundamentals of nonverbal behavior.* Cambridge, England: Cambridge University Press.

Felson, R. B., & Tedeschi, J. T. (Eds.). (1993). *Aggression and violence: Social interactionist perspectives.* Washington, DC: American Psychological Association.

Fenton, W. S., & McGlashan, T. H. (1991a). Natural history of schizophrenia subtypes: I. Longitudinal study of paranoid, hebephrenic, and undifferentiated schizophrenia. *Archives of General Psychiatry, 48*, 969–977.

Fenton, W. S., & McGlashan, T. H. (1991b). Natural history of schizophrenia subtypes: II. Positive and negative symptoms and long-term course. *Archives of General Psychiatry, 48*, 978–986.

Fenton, W. S., & McGlashan, T. H. (1994). Antecedents, symptom progression, and long-term outcome of the deficit syndrome in schizophrenia. *American Journal of Psychiatry, 151*, 351–356.

Ferguson, G. A. (1993). Psychology in Canada 1939–1945. *Canadian Psychology, 33(4)*, 697–705.*

Ferguson, T. (1993). Working with your doctor. In D. Goleman, & J. Gurin (Eds.), *Mind-body medicine.* Yonkers, NY: Consumer Reports Books.

Fernandez, E., & Sheffield, J. (1995). Psychosocial stressors predicting headache occurrence: The major role of minor hassles. *Headache Quarterly, 6*, 215–220.

Fernandez, E., & Turk, D. C. (1992). Sensory and affective components of pain: Separation and synthesis. *Psychological Bulletin, 112*, 205–217.

Ferster, D., & Spruston, N. (1995, November 3). Cracking the neuronal code. *Science, 270*, 756–757.

Feshbach, S. (1990). Psychology, human violence, and the search for peace: Issues in science and social values. *Journal of Social Issues, 46*, 183–198.

Festinger, L. (1957). *A theory of cognitive dissonance.* Stanford, CA: Stanford University Press.

Festinger, L., & Carlsmith, J. M. (1959). Cognitive consequences of forced compliance. *Journal of Abnormal and Social Psychology, 58*, 203–210.

Festinger, L., Schachter, S., & Back, K. W. (1950). *Social pressure in informal groups.* New York: Harper.

Fichter, M. M. (Ed.). (1990). *Bulimia nervosa: Basic research, diagnosis and therapy.* New York: Wiley.

Fiedler, F. E., Mitchell, R., & Triandis, H. C. (1971). The culture assimilator: An approach to cross-cultural training. *Journal of Applied Psychology, 55*, 95–102.

Field, T. (1982). Individual differences in the expressivity of neonates and young infants. In R. S. Feldman (Ed.), *Development of nonverbal behavior in children.* New York: Springer-Verlag.

Field, T. M. (1978). Interaction of primary versus secondary caretaker fathers. *Developmental Psychology, 14*, 183–184.

Fields-Meyer, T., & Haederle, M. (1996, June 24). Married to a stranger. *People*, pp. 48–51.

Figueiras, M. J., & Marteau, T. M. (1995). Experiences of the menopause: A comparison between Portugal and the United Kingdom. *Analise Psicologica, 13*, 163–171.

Filler, A. G., Howe, F. A., Hayes, C. E., Kliot, M., Winn, H. R., Bell, B. A., Griffiths, J. R., & Tsuruda, J. S. (1993, March 13). Magnetic resonance neurography. *The Lancet, 341*, 659–661.

Finch, C. E. (1990). *Longevity, senescence, and the genome.* Chicago: University of Chicago Press.

Finch, C. E. & Tanzi, R. E. (1997, October). Genetics of aging. *Science, 278*, 407–410.

Fine, L. (1994). Personal communication.

Fingerhut, L., Ingram, D., & Feldman, J. (1992). Firearm and nonfirearm homicide among persons 15 through 19 years of age. *Journal of the American Medical Association, 267*, 3048–3053.

Fingerhut, L. A., & Kleinman, J. C. (1990). International and interstate comparisons of homicide among young males. *Journal of the American Medical Association, 263*, 3292–3295.

Fink, A. (1993). *Evaluation fundamentals.* Newbury Park, CA: Sage.

Fink, M. (1990, April). Continuation of ECT. *Harvard Medical School Mental Health Letter, 6*, 8.

Fink, M. (1994, May). Can ECT be an effective treatment for adolescents? *Harvard Mental Health Letter, 10*, 8.

Fink, M. (1997, June). What is the role of ECT in the treatment of mania? *The Harvard Mental Health Letter*, 8.

Finke, R. A. (1995). Creative insight and preinventive forms. In R. J. Sternberg, & J. E. Davidson (Eds.), *The nature of insight.* Cambridge, MA: MIT Press.

Finkelhor, D. (1984). *Child sexual abuse: New theory and research.* New York: Free Press.

Fiore, M. C. (1992). Trends in cigarette smoking in the United States: The epidemiology of tobacco use. *Medical Clinics of North America 76*, 289–303.

Firestein, B. A. (Ed.). (1996). *Bisexuality: The psychology and politics of an invisible minority.* Thousand Oaks, CA: Sage.

Fischer, C. S., Hout, M., Jankowski, M. S., Lucas, S. R., Swidler, A., & Voss, K. (1996). *Inequality by design: Cracking The Bell Curve Myth.* Princeton, NJ: Princeton University Press.

Fischer, K. W., Shaver, P. R., & Carnochan, P. (1990). How emotions develop and how they organize development. *Cognition and Emotion, 4*, 81–127.

Fischman, J. (1987). Type A on trial. *Psychology Today*, pp. 42–50.

Fischoff, B. (1977). Perceived informativeness of facts. *Journal of Experimental*

Psychology: Human Perception and Performance, 3, 349–358.

Fisher, C. B., & Fyrberg, D. (1994). Participant partners: College students weigh the costs and benefits of deceptive research. *American Psychologist, 49,* 417–427.

Fisher, J. D., & Fisher, W. A. (1992). Changing AIDS-risk behavior. *Psychological Bulletin, 111,* 455–474.

Fisher, K. (1985, March). ECT: New studies on how, why, who. *APA Monitor,* pp. 18–19.

Fiske, A. (1991). *Structures of social life.* New York: Free Press.

Fiske, A. P., Kitayama, S., Markus, H. R., & Nisbett, R. E. (1998). The cultural matrix of social psychology. In D. Gilbert, S. Fiske, & G. Lindzey (Eds.), *Handbook of Social Psychology.* New York: McGraw-Hill.

Fiske, S. T. (1987). People's reaction to nuclear war: Implications for psychologists. *American Psychologist, 42,* 207–217.

Fiske, S. T. (1992). Thinking is for doing: Portraits of social cognition from daguerreotype to laserphoto. *Journal of Personality and Social Psychology, 63,* 877–889.

Fiske, S. T. (1997). Stereotyping, prejudice, and discrimination. In D. T. Gilbert, S. T. Fiske, & G. Lindzey (Eds.), *The handbook of social psychology* (4th ed.). New York: McGraw-Hill.

Fiske, S. T., & Glick, P. (1995). Ambivalence and stereotypes cause sexual harassment: A theory with implications for organizational change. *Journal of Social Issues, 51,* 97–115.

Fiske, S. T., & Morling, B. (1996). Stereotyping as a function of personal control motives and capacity constraints: The odd couple of power and anxiety. In R. M. Sorrentino, & E. T. Higgins (Eds.), *Handbook of motivation and cognition, Vol. 3: The interpersonal context. Handbook of motivation and cognition.* New York: Guilford Press.

Fiske, S. T., Pratto, F., & Pavelchak, M. A. (1983). Social science and the politics of the arms race. *Journal of Social Issues, 39,* 161–180.

Fiske, S. T., & Taylor, S. E. (1991). *Social cognition* (2nd ed.). New York: McGraw-Hill.

Fitzgerald, J. M. (1988). Vivid memories and the reminiscence phenomenon: The role of a self narrative. *Human Development, 31,* 261–273.

Fitzgerald, L. F. (1993). Sexual harassment: Violence against women in the workplace. *American Psychologist, 48,* 1070–1076.

Flam, F. (1991, June 14). Queasy riders. *Science, 252,* 1488.

Flavell, J. H. (1993). Young children's understanding of thinking and consciousness. *Current Directions in Psychological Science, 2,* 40–43.

Flavell, J. H., Green, F. L., & Flavell, E. R. (1990). Developmental changes in young children's knowledge about the mind. *Cognitive Development, 5,* 1–27.

Fleming, R., Baum, A., & Singer, J. E. (1984). Toward an integrative approach to the study

of stress. *Journal of Personality and Social Psychology, 46,* 939–949.

Flippen, A. R., Hornstein, H. A., Siegal, W. E., & Weitzman, E. A. (1996). A comparison of similarity and interdependence as triggers for in-group formation. *Personality and Social Psychology Bulletin, 22,* 882–893.

Flowers, J. V., & Booraem, C. D. (1990). The effects of different types of interventions on outcome in group therapy. *Group, 14,* 81–88.

Flynn, J. R. (1987). Massive IQ gains in 14 nations: What IQ tests really measure. *Psychological Bulletin, 101,* 171–191.

Flynn, J. R. (1996). What environmental factors affect intelligence: The relevance of IQ gains over time. In D. K. Detterman (Ed.), *Current topics in human intelligence, Volume 5, The Environment.* Norwood, NJ: Ablex.

Foa, E. B. & Riggs, D. S. (1995). Posttraumatic stress disorder following assault: Theoretical considerations and empirical findings. *Current Directions in Psychological Science, 4,* 61–65.

Foderaro, L. W. (1993, July 19). With reforms in treatment, shock therapy loses shock. *New York Times,* pp. A1, B2.

Folkard, S., Arendt, J., & Clark, M. (1993). Can melatonin improve shift-workers' tolerance of the night shift? Some preliminary findings. *Chronobiology International, 10,* 315–320.

Folkman, S. (1984). Personal control and stress and coping processes: A theoretical analysis. *Journal of Personality and Social Psychology, 46,* 839–852.

Folkman, S. (1995, Fall). Coping with caregiving and bereavement. *Psychology & Aids Exchange.* Washington, DC: American Psychological Association.

Folkman, S., & Lazarus, R. S. (1980). An analysis of coping in a middle-aged community sample. *Journal of Health and Social Behavior, 21,* 219–239.

Folkman, S., & Lazarus, R. S. (1988). Coping as a mediator of emotion. *Journal of Personality and Social Psychology, 54,* 466–475.

Folkman, S., Lazarus, R. S., Dunkel-Schetter, C., DeLongis, A., & Green, R. J. (1986). Dynamics of a stressful encounter: Cognitive appraisal, coping, and encounter outcome. *Journal of Personality and Social Psychology, 50,* 992–1003.

Fonagy, P., & Moran, G. S. (1990). Studies of the efficacy of child psychoanalysis. *Journal of Consulting and Clinical Psychology, 58,* 684–695.

Ford, C. S., & Beach, F. A. (1951). *Patterns of sexual behavior.* New York: Harper.

Ford, C. V., & Folks, D. G. (1985). Conversion disorders: An overview. *Psychosomatics, 26,* 371–383.

Ford, J. G. (1991). Rogers's theory of personality: Review and perspectives. In A. Jones, & R. Crandall (Eds.), Handbook of self-actualization [Special issue]. *Journal of Social Behavior and Personality, 6,* 19–44.

Forer, B. (1949). The fallacy of personal validation: A classroom demonstration of

gullibility. *Journal of Abnormal and Social Psychology, 44,* 118–123.

Foreyt, J. P., & Goodrick, G. K. (1994). *Living without dieting.* New York: Warner.

Forgas, J. P., & Bower, G. H. (1987). Mood effects on person-perception judgments. *Journal of Personality and Social Psychology, 53,* 53–60.

Forrester, M. A. (1996). *Psychology of language: A critical introduction.* Thousand Oaks, CA: Sage.

Forss, N., Jousmaki, V., & Hari, R. (1995). Interaction between afferent input from fingers in human somatosensory cortex. *Brain Research, 685,* 68–76.

Forss, N., Makela, J. P., McEvoy, L., & Hari, R. (1993). Temporal integration and oscillatory responses of the human auditory cortex revealed by evoked magnetic fields to click trains. *Hearing Research, 68,* 89–96.

Fowers, B. J., & Richardson, F. C. (1996). Why is multiculturalism good? *American Psychologist, 51,* 609–621.

Fowler, F. J., Jr. (1995). *Improving survey questions: Design and evaluation.* Newbury Park, CA: Sage.

Fowler, R. D. (1993). New stats add weight to member director. *APA Monitor,* p. 2.

Fowles, D. C. (1992). Schizophrenia: Diathesis-stress revisited. *Annual Review of Psychology, 43,* 303–336.

Fox, N. (Ed.). (1994). The development of emotion regulation: Biological and behavioral consideration. *Monographs of the SRCD, 12,* 88–95.

Fox, N. A. (1995). Of the way we were: Adult memories about attachment experiences and their role in determining infant-parent relationships: A commentary on van IJzendoorn (1995). *Psychological Bulletin, 117,* 404–410.

Fox, R. E. (1994). Training professional psychologists for the twenty-first century. *American Psychologist, 49,* 200–206.

Frances, A., First, M. B., & Pincus, H. A. (1995). *DSM-IV guidebook.* Washington, DC: American Psychiatric Press.

Frank, S. J., Jacobson, S., & Tuer, M. (1990). Psychological predictors of young adults' drinking behaviors. *Journal of Personality and Social Psychology, 59,* 770–780.

Frankel, F. H. (1993). Adult reconstruction of childhood events in the multiple personality literature. *American Journal of Psychiatry, 150,* 954–958.

Frankel, R. M. (1995). Emotion and the physician-patient relationship. *Motivation and Emotion, 19,* 163–173.

Frankenburg, W. K., & Dodds, J. B. (1967). The Denver developmental screening test. *Journal of Pediatrics, 71,* 181–191.

Franzek, E., & Beckmann, H. (1996). Gene-environment interaction in schizophrenia: Season-of-birth effect reveals etiologically different subgroups. *Psychopathology, 29,* 14–26.

Fraser, S. (Ed.). (1995). *The bell curve wars: Race, intelligence, and the future of America.* New York: Basic Books, Inc.

Frazier, J. A., Guide, J. M., Hamburger, S. D., et al. (1996, July). Brain anatomic magnetic resonance imaging in childhood-onset schizophrenia. *Archives of General Psychiatry, 53,* 617–624.

Frederick, C. J. (1993). Terrorism and hostage taking. In A. A. Leenaars, A. L. Berman, P. Cantor, R. E. Litman, & R. W. Maris (Eds.), *Suicidology: Essays in honor of Edwin S. Shneidman.* Northvale, NJ: Jason Aronson.

Frederickson, R. (1992). *Repressed memories: A journey to recovery from sexual abuse.* Fireside Books.

Freedheim, D. K. (Ed.). (1992). *History of psychotherapy: A century of change.* Washington, DC: American Psychological Association.

Freedman, D., Pisani, R., Purves, R., & Adhikari, A. (1991). *Statistics* (2nd ed.). New York: Norton.

Freedman, D. S. (1995). The importance of body fat distribution in early life. *American Journal of the Medical Sciences, 310,* S72–S76.

Freedman, J. (1996, May). Violence in the mass media and violence in society: The link is unproven. *Harvard Mental Health Letter,* pp. 4–6.

Freedman, J. L. (1984). Effects of television violence on aggressiveness. *Psychological Bulletin, 96,* 227–246.

Freedman, J. L., & Fraser, S. C. (1966). Compliance without pressure: The foot-in-the-door technique. *Journal of Personality and Social Psychology, 4,* 195–202.

Freeman, P. (1990, December 17). Silent no more. *People Weekly,* pp. 94–104.

Freeman, S. J. (1994). An overview of Canada's mental health system. In L. L. Bachrach, P. Goering, & D. Wasylenki (Eds.), *Mental health care in Canada. New directions for mental health services.* San Fransisco: Jossey-Bass.*

Freeman, W. (1959). Psychosurgery. In *American handbook of psychiatry* (Vol. 2, pp. 1521–1540). New York: Basic Books.

Freiberg, P. (1995, March). Psychologists wary of AIDS home test. *APA Monitor,* p. 34.

French, H. W. (1997, February 2). Africa's culture war: Old customs, new values. *New York Times,* pp. 1E, 4E.

Freud, S. (1900). *The interpretation of dreams.* New York: Basic Books.

Freud, S. (1922/1959). *Group psychology and the analysis of the ego.* London: Hogarth.

Freund, H. (1996, June 21). Remapping the brain. *Science, 272,* 1754.

Friedman, H. S., Hawley, P. H., & Tucker, J. S. (1994). Personality, health, and longevity. *Current Directions in Psychological Science, 3,* 37–41.

Friedman, H. S., Tucker, J. S., Tomlinson-Keasey, C., Schwartz, J., et al. (1993). Does childhood personality predict longevity? *Journal of Personality and Social Psychology, 65,* 176–185.

Friedman, L. (1989). Mathematics and the gender gap: A meta-analysis of recent studies on sex differences in mathematical tasks. *Review of Educational Research, 59,* 185–213.

Friedman, M., Thoresen, C. E., Gill, J. J., Powell, L. H., Ulmer, D., Thompson, L., Price, V. A., Rabin, D. D., Breall, W. S., Dixon, T., Levy, R., & Bourg, E. (1984). Alteration of Type A behavior and reduction in cardiac recurrences in postmyocardial infarction patients. *American Heart Journal, 108* (2), 237–248.

Friedman, M. I. (1995). Control of energy intake by energy metabolism. *American Journal of Clinical Nutrition, 62,* 1096S–1100S.

Friedman, M. J., & Marsella, A. J. (1996). Post-traumatic stress disorder: An overview of the concept. In A. J. Marsella, M. J. Friedman, E. T. Gerrity, & R. M. Scurfield (Eds.), *Ethnocultural aspects of post-traumatic stress disorder: Issues, research, and clinical applications.* Washington, DC: American Psychological Association.

Friedman, W. J. (1993). Memory for the time of past events. *Psychological Bulletin, 113,* 44–66.

Friend, T. (1994, March). River, with love and anger. *Esquire,* pp. 108–117.

Frijda, N. H. (1988). The laws of emotion. *American Psychologist, 43,* 349–358.

Frijda, N. H., Kuipers, P., & terSchure, E. (1989). Relations among emotion, appraisal, and emotional action readiness. *Journal of Personality and Social Psychology, 57,* 212–228.

Frishman, R. (1996). Don't be a wimp in the doctor's office. *The Harvard Health Letter, 21,* 1–2.

Fromholt, P., & Larsen, S. F. (1991). Autobiographical memory in normal, aging, and primary degenerative dementia (dementia of Alzheimer type). *Journal of Gerontology, 46,* 85–91.

Fromm, E., & Nash, M. (Eds.). (1992). *Contemporary hypnosis research.* New York: Guilford Press.

Fry, D. P. (1992). "Respect for the rights of others is peace": Learning aggression versus nonaggression among the Zapotec. *American Anthropologist, 94,* 621–639.

Fuchs, D., & Fuchs, L. S. (1994). Inclusive schools movement and the radicalization of special education reform. *Exceptional Children, 60,* 294–309.

Fukuzako, H., Fukuzako, T., Hashiguchi, T., Hokazono, Y., et al. (1996). Reduction in hippocampal formation volume is caused mainly by its shortening in chronic schizophrenia: Assessment by MRI. *Biological Psychiatry, 39,* 938–945.

Fulle, H. J., Vassar, R., Foster, D. C., Yang, R. B., Axel, R., & Garbers, D. L. (1995, April 11). A receptor guanylyl cyclase expressed specifically in olfactory sensory neurons. *Proceedings of the National Academy of Sciences, 92,* 3571–3575.

Funder, D. C. (1991). Global traits: A neo-Allportian approach to personality. *Psychological Science, 2,* 31–39.

Funder, D. C. (1997). *The personality puzzle.* New York: Norton.

Funder, D. C. F. (1987). Errors and mistakes: Evaluating the accuracy of social judgment. *Psychological Bulletin, 101,* 75–90.

Funk, M. S. (1996). Development of object permanence in the New Zealand parakeet (*Cyanoramphus auriceps*). *Animal Learning and Behavior, 24,* 375–383.

Furnham, A. (1994). The psychology of common sense. In J. Siegfried (Ed.), *The status of common sense in psychology.* Norwood, NJ: Ablex.

Furnham, A. (1995). The relationship of personality and intelligence to cognitive learning style and achievement. In D. H. Saklofske, & M. Zeidner (Eds.), *International handbook of personality and intelligence. Perspectives on individual differences.* New York: Plenum Press.

Furst, P. T. (1977). "High states" in culture-historical perspective. In N. E. Zinberg (Ed.), *Alternate states of consciousness.* New York: Free Press.

Gabriel, M. T., Critelli, J. W., & Ee, J. S. (1994). Narcissistic illusions in self-evaluations of intelligence and attractiveness. *Journal of Personality, 62,* 143–155.

Gaertner, S. L., Mann, J. A., Dovidio, J. F., Murrell, A. J., & Pomare, M. (1990). How does cooperation reduce intergroup bias? *Journal of Personality and Social Psychology, 59,* 692–704.

Gaertner, S. L., Rust, M. C., Dovidio, J. F., Bachman, B. A., et al. (1996). The contact hypothesis: The role of a common ingroup identity on reducing intergroup bias among majority and minority group members. In J. L. Nye, & A. M. Brower (Eds.), *What's social about social cognition? Research on socially shared cognition in small groups.* Thousand Oaks, CA: Sage.

Gage, N. L. (1991, January–February). The obviousness of social and educational research results. *Educational Researcher,* pp. 10–16.

Gagnon, G. H. (1977). *Human sexualities.* Glenview, IL: Scott, Foresman.

Gagnon, S., & Dore, F. X. (1994). Cross-sectional study of object permanence in domestic puppies (*Canis familiaris*). *Journal of Comparative Psychology, 108,* 220–232.

Gakkagher, D. J. (1996). Personality, coping, and objective outcomes: Extraversion, neuroticism, coping styles, and academic performance. *Personality and Individual Differences, 21,* 421–429.

Galambos, N. L. (1992). Parent-adolescent relations. *Current Directions in Psychological Science, 1,* 146–149.

Galanter, E. (1962). Contemporary psychophysics. In R. Brown, E. Galanter, E. Hess, & G. Maroler (Eds.), *New directions in psychology* (pp. 87–157). New York: Holt.

Galanter, M. (Ed.). (1995). *Recent developments in alcoholism, Vol. 12: Alcoholism and women.* New York: Plenum Press.

Galatzer-Levy, R. M., & Cohler, B. J. (1997). *Essential psychoanalysis: A contemporary introduction.* New York: Basic Books.

Galavotti, C., Saltzman, L. E., Sauter, S. L., & Sumartojo, E. (1997, February). Behavioral science activities at the Centers for Disease Control and Prevention: A selected overview of exemplary programs. *American Psychologist, 52,* 154–166.

Gale, N., Golledge, R. G., Pellegrino, J. W., & Doherty, S. (1990). The acquisition and integration of route knowledge in an unfamiliar neighborhood. *Journal of Environmental Psychology, 10,* 3–25.

Galea, L. A. M., Kavaliers, M., & Ossenkopp, K. P. (1996). Sexually-dimorphic spatial learning in meadow voles, microbus pennsylvanicus, and deer mice, peromyscus maniculatus. *Journal of Experimental Biology, 199*, 195–200.*

Gallagher, J. J. (1993). Current status of gifted education in the United States. In K. A. Heller, F. J. Monks, & A. H. Passow (Eds.), *International handbook of research and development of giftedness and talent.* Oxford, England: Pergamon.

Gallagher, J. J. (1994). Teaching and learning: New models. *Annual Review of Psychology, 45*, 171–195.

Gallagher, M., & Rapp, R. R. (1997). The use of animal models to study the effects of aging on cognition. *Annual Review of Psychology, 48*, 339–370.

Gallant, J. L, Braun, J., & VanEssen, D. C. (1993, January 1). Selectivity for polar, hyperbolic, and cartesian gratings in macaque visual cortex. *Science, 259*, 100–103.

Gammell, D. J., & Stoppard, J. M. (1999). Women's experiences of treatment of depression: Medicalization or empowerment? *Canadian Psychology, 40*, 112–128.*

Gannon, L., Luchetta, T., Rhodes, K., Pardie, L., & Segrist, D. (1992). Sex bias in psychological research. *American Psychologist, 47*, 389–396.

Ganrud, C. (Ed.). (1993). *Visual perception and cognition in infancy.* Mahwah, NJ: Erlbaum.

Gao, J., Parsons, L. M., Bower, J. M., Xiong, J., Li, J., & Fox, P. T. (1996, April 26). Cerebellum implicated in sensory acquisition and discrimination rather than motor control. *Science, 272*, 545–547.

Garbarino, J., Gaa, J. P., Swank, P., McPherson, R., et al. (1995). The relation of individuation and psychosocial development. *Journal of Family Psychology, 9*, 311–318.

Garber, H. L. (1988). *The Milwaukee Project: Preventing mental retardation in children at risk.* Washington, DC: American Association on Mental Retardation.

Garcia, J. (1990). Learning without memory. *Journal of Cognitive Neuroscience, 2*, 287–305.

Garcia, J., Brett, L., & Rusiniak, K. (1989). Limits of Darwinian conditioning. In S. B. Klein, & R. R. Mowrer (Eds.), *Contemporary learning theories* (Vol. 2). Mahwah, NJ: Erlbaum.

Garcia, J., Hankins, W. G., & Rusiniak, K. W. (1974). Behavioral regulation of the milieu intern in man and rat. *Science, 185*, 824–831.

Garcia-Andrade, C., Wall, T. L., & Ehlers, C. L. (1997). The firewater myth and response to alcohol in Mission Indians. *Journal of Psychiatry, 154*, 983–988.

Gardner, H. (1975). *The shattered mind: The person after brain damage.* New York: Knopf.

Gardner, H. (1983). *Frames of mind: The theory of multiple intelligences.* New York: Basic Books.

Gardner, H. (1993). *Multiple intelligences.* New York: Basic Books.

Gardner, H. (1997). *Extraordinary minds.* New York: Basic Books.

Gardner, H., Kornhaber, M. L., & Wake, W. K. (1996). *Intelligence: Multiple perspectives.* Fort Worth, TX: Harcourt.

Gardner, H., Krechevsky, M., Sternberg, R. J., & Okagaki, L. (1994). Intelligence in context: Enhancing students' practical intelligence for school. In K. McGilly (Ed.), *Classroom lessons: Integrating cognitive theory and classroom practice.* Cambridge, MA: MIT Press.

Gardner, W. I., Graeber, J. L., & Cole, C. L. (1996). Behavior therapies: A multimodal diagnostic and intervention model. In J. W. Jacobson, & J. A. Mulick (Eds.), *Manual of diagnosis and professional practice in mental retardation.* Washington, DC: American Psychological Association.

Garfield, S. L. (1990). Issues and methods in psychotherapy process research. *Journal of Consulting and Clinical Psychology, 58*, 273–280.

Garland, A. F., & Zigler, E. (1993). Adolescent suicide prevention: Current research and social policy implications. *American Psychologist, 48*, 169–182.

Garling, T. (1989). The role of cognitive maps in spatial decisions. *Journal of Environmental Psychology, 9*, 269–278.

Garner, D. M., & Garfinkel, P. E. (1997). *Handbook of treatment for eating disorders.* New York: Guilford Press.

Garnett, L. R. (1996). Taking emotions to heart. *Harvard Health Letter, 21*, 1–3.

Garrison, D. W., & Foreman, R. D. (1994). Decreased activity of spontaneous and noxiously evoked dorsal horn cells during transcutaneous electrical nerve stimulation (TENS). *Pain, 58*, 309–315.

Gartell, N. N. (1982). Hormones and homosexuality. In W. Paul et al. (Eds.), *Homosexuality: Social, psychological, and biological issues.* Beverly Hills, CA: Sage.

Gatchel, R. J., & Baum, A. (1983). *An introduction to health psychology.* Reading, MA: Addison-Wesley.

Gatchel, R. J., & Turk, D. C. (Eds.). (1996). *Psychological approaches to pain management: A practitioner's handbook.* New York: Guilford Press.

Gathercole, S. E., & Baddeley, A. D. (1993). *Working memory and language processing.* Mahwah, NJ: Erlbaum.

Gauthier, J. G. (1999). Bridging the gap between biological and psychological perspectives in the treatment of anxiety disorders. *Canadian Psychology, 40*, 1–11.*

Gauthier, J. G., & Phillips, A. G. (Eds.). (1997) *National conference on psychology as a science, May 8–11, 1997: Final report.* Canadian Psychological Association.*

Gauze, C., Bukowski, W. M., Aquan-Assee, J., & Sippola, L. K. (1996). Interactions between family environment and friendship and associations with self-perceived well-being during early adolescence. *Child Development, 67*, 2201–2216.*

Gawin, F. H. (1991, March 29). Cocaine addiction: Psychology and neurophysiology. *Science, 251*, 1580–1586.

Gawin, F. H., & Ellinwood, E. H. (1988). *New England Journal of Medicine, 318*, 1173.

Gazzaniga, M. S. (1970). *The bisected brain.* New York: Plenum Press.

Gazzaniga, M. S. (1983). Right-hemisphere language following brain bisection: A twenty-year perspective. *American Psychologist, 38*, 525–537.

Gazzaniga, M. S. (1989, September 1). Organization of the human brain. *Science, 245*, 947–952.

Gazzaniga, M. S. (1992). Brain modules and belief formation. In F. S. Kessel, P. M. Cole, & D. L. Johnson (Eds.), *Self and consciousness: Multiple perspectives.* Mahwah, NJ: Erlbaum.

Gazzaniga, M. S. (Ed.). (1994). *The cognitive neurosciences.* Cambridge, MA: MIT Press.

Ge, X., Conger, R. D., Cadoret, R. J., Neiderhiser, J. M., et al. (1996). The developmental interface between nature and nurture: A mutual influence model of child antisocial behavior and parent behaviors. *Developmental Psychology, 32*, 574–589.

Ge, X., Conger, R. D., & Elder, G. H., Jr., (1996). Coming of age too early: Pubertal influences on girls' vulnerability to psychological distress. *Child Development, 67*, 3386–3400.

Geary, D. C., Bow-Thomas, C. C., Fan, L., & Siegler, R. S. (1993). Even before formal instruction, Chinese children outperform American children in mental addition. *Cognitive Development, 8*, 517–529.

Geary, D. C., Fan, L., & Bow-Thomas, C. C. (1992). Numerical cognition: Loci of ability differences comparing children from China and the United States. *Psychological Science, 3*, 180–185.

Geen, R. G. (1984). Human motivation: New perspectives on old problems. In A. M. Rogers, & C. J. Scheirer (Eds.), *The G. Stanley Hall Lecture Series* (Vol. 4). Washington, DC: American Psychological Association.

Geen, R. G. (1995). *Human motivation: A social psychological approach.* Pacific Grove, CA: Brooks/Cole.

Geen, R. G., & Donnerstein, E. (1983). *Aggression: Theoretical and empirical reviews.* New York: Academic Press.

Geis, F. L. (1993). Self-fulfilling prophecies. In A. E. Beall, & R. J. Sternberg (Eds.), *The psychology of gender.* New York: Guilford Press.

Geiselman, R. E., Fisher, R. P., MacKinnon, D. P., & Holland, H. L. (1985). Eyewitness memory enhancement in the police interview: Cognitive retrieval mnemonics versus hypnosis. *Journal of Applied Psychology, 70*, 401–412.

Geisinger, K. F. (Ed.). (1992). *Psychological testing of Hispanics.* Washington, DC: American Psychological Association.

Geissler, H., Link, S. W., & Townsend, J. T. (1992). *Cognition, information processing, and psychophysics.* Mahwah, NJ: Erlbaum.

Gelles, R. J. (1994). *Contemporary families.* Newbury Park, CA: Sage.

Gelman, D. (1989, February 20). Roots of addiction. *Newsweek*, pp. 52–57.

Gelman, D. (1994, April 18). The mystery of suicide. *Newsweek*, pp. 44–49.

Gelman, R., & Baillargeon, R. (1983). A review of some Piagetian concepts. In J. H. Flavell, & E. M. Markman (Eds.), *Handbook of child psychology: Vol. 3. Cognitive development* (4th ed.). New York: Wiley.

Gelman, R., & Kit-Fong Au, T. (Eds.). (1996). *Perceptual and cognitive development.* New York: Academic Press.

Genesee, F. (1984). Beyond bilingualism: Social psychological studies of French immersion programs in Canada. *Canadian Journal of Behavioural Science, 16,* 338–352.*

Gentry, W. D., & Kobasa, S. C. O. (1984). Social and psychological resources mediating stress-illness relationships in humans. In W. D. Gentry (Ed.), *Handbook of behavioral medicine.* New York: Guilford Press.

Genuis, M. L. (1995). The use of hypnosis in helping cancer patients control anxiety, pain, and emesis: A review of recent empirical studies. *American Journal of Clinical Hypnosis, 37,* 316–325.

George, M. S., Wassermann, E. M., Williams, W. A., Callahan, A., et al. (1995). Daily repetitive transcranial magnetic stimulation (rTMS) improves mood in depression. *Neuroreport: An International Journal for the Rapid Communication of Research in Neuroscience, 6,* 1853–1856.

Gerbner, G., Gross, L., Jackson-Beeck, M., Jeffries-Fox, S., & Signorielli, N. (1978). Cultural indicators: Violence profile No. 9. *Journal of Communication, 28,* 176–207.

Gerbner, G., Morgan, M., & Signorielli, N. (1993). Television violence. Unpublished study, University of Pennsylvania, Philadelphia.

Gergen, K. J., Gulerce, A., Lock, A., & Misra, G. (1996). Psychological science in cultural context. *American Psychologist, 51,* 496–503.

Gerrard, M. (1988). Sex, sex guilt, and contraceptive use revisited: The 1980s. *Journal of Personality and Social Psychology, 57,* 973–980.

Gerrard, M., Gibbons, F. X., & Bushman, B. J. (1996). Relation between perceived vulnerability to HIV and precautionary sexual behavior. *Psychological Bulletin, 119,* 390–409.

Gerrig, R. J., & Banaji, M. R. (1994). Language and thought. In R. J. Sternberg (Ed.), *Thinking and problem-solving.* San Diego, CA: Academic Press.

Gerritsen, W., Heijnen, C. J., Weigant, V. M., Bermond, B., et al. (1996). Experimental social fear: Immunological, hormonal, and autonomic concomitants. *Psychosomatic Medicine, 58,* 273–296.

Gershon, E. S., Martinez, M., Goldin, L. R., & Gejman, P. V. (1990). Genetic mapping of common disease: The challenges of manic-depressive illness and schizophrenia. *Trends in Genetics, 6,* 282–287.

Gescheider, G. A. (1997). *Psychophysics: The fundamentals* (3rd ed.). Mahwah, NJ: Erlbaum.

Geschwind, N., & Galaburda, A. M. (1987). *Cerebral lateralization: Biological mechanism, associations, and pathology.* Cambridge, MA: MIT Press.

Getchell, T. V., Chen, Y., Strotmann, J., Breer, H., & Getchell, M. L. (1993). Expression of a mucociliary-specific epitome in human olfactory epithelium. *Neuroreport, 4,* 623–626.

Getner, D., & Holyoak, K. J. (1997, January) Reasoning and learning by analogy. *American Psychologist, 52,* 32–34.

Getty, D. J., Pickett, R. M., D'Orsi, C. J., & Swets, J. A. (1988). Enhanced interpretation of diagnostic images. *Investigative Radiology, 23,* 240–252.

Gfeller, J. D., Lynn, S. J., & Pribble, W. E. (1987). Enhancing hypnotic susceptibility: Interpersonal and rapport factors. *Journal of Personality and Social Psychology, 52,* 586–595.

Ghalum, N. Z. (1994). Women in the workplace. In C. McKie & K. Thompson (Eds.), Canadian Social Trends, 12. Toronto: Thompson Educational Publishing.

Ghez, C. (1991). The cerebellum. In E. R. Kandel, J. H. Schwartz, & T. M. Jessell (Eds.), *Principles of neural science* (3rd ed.). New York: Elsevier.

Gibb, C. A. (1969). Leadership. In G. Lindzey & E. Aronson (Eds.), *Handbook of social psychology* (2nd ed.). Reading, MA: Addison-Wesley.

Gibbons, A. (1990, July 13). New maps of the human brain. *Science, 249,* 122–123.

Gibbons, A. (1991, March 29). Deja vu all over again: Chimp-language wars. *Science, 251,* 1561–1562.

Gibbs, M. E., & Ng, K. T. (1977). Psychobiology of memory: Towards a model of memory formation. *Behavioral Reviews, 1,* 113–136.

Gibbs, M. E., O'Dowd, B. S., Hertz, L., Robinson, S. R., et al. (1996). Inhibition of glutamine synthetase activity prevents memory consolidation. *Cognitive Brain Research, 4,* 57–64.

Gibbs, N. (1989, January 9). For goodness' sake. *Time,* pp. 20–24.

Gibbs, W. W. (1996, August). Gaining on fat. *Scientific American,* pp. 88–94.

Gibson, B. (1997). Smoker-nonsmoker conflict: Using a social psychological framework to understand a current social controversy. *Journal of Social Issues, 53,* 97–112.

Gibson, E. J. (1994). Has psychology a future? *Psychological Science, 5,* 69–76.

Gibson, H. B. (1995). A further case of the misuse of hypnosis in a police investigation. *Contemporary Hypnosis, 12,* 81–86.

Gidron, Y., & Davidson, K. (1996). Development and preliminary testing of a brief intervention for modifying CHD-predictive hostility components. *Journal of Behavioral Medicine, 19,* 203–220.

Gilbert, B. (1996). New ideas in the air at the National Zoo. *Smithsonian,* pp. 32–43.

Gilbert, D. G. (1995). *Smoking: Individual differences, psychopathology, and emotion.* Philadelphia: Taylor & Francis.

Gilbert, D. T., Jones, E. E., & Pelham, B. W. (1987). Influence and inference: What the active perceiver overlooks. *Journal of Personality and Social Psychology, 52,* 861–870.

Gilbert, D. T., & Malone, P. S. (1995). The correspondence bias. *Psychological Bulletin, 117,* 21–38.

Gilbert, F. W., & Warren, W. E. (1995). Psychographic constructs and demographic segments. *Psychology & Marketing, 12,* 223–237.

Gilbert, L. A. (1993). *Two careers/one family: The promise of gender equality.* Newbury Park, CA: Sage.

Gilbert, S. (1997, January 22). Lag seen in aid for depression; antidepressants are safe, effective and underused, a panel concludes. *The New York Times,* p. B11.

Giles, T. R. (Ed.). (1993). *Handbook of effective psychotherapy.* New York: Plenum Press.

Gilger, J. W. (1996). How can behavioral genetic research help us understand language development and disorders? In M. L. Rice (Ed.), *Toward a genetics of language.* Mahwah, NJ: Erlbaum.

Gill, T. J., Jr., Smith, G. J., Wissler, R. W., & Kunz, H. W. (1989, July 29). The rat as an experimental animal. *Science, 245,* 269–276.

Gilligan, C. (1982). *In a different voice: Psychological theory and women's development.* Cambridge, MA: Harvard University Press.

Gilligan, C. (1987). Adolescent development reconsidered. *New Directions for Child Development, 37,* 63–92.

Gilligan, C. (1993). Woman's place in man's life cycle. In A. Dobrin (Ed.), *Being good and doing right: Readings in moral development.* Lanham, MD: University Press of America.

Gilligan, C., Lyons, N. P., & Hanmer, T. J. (Eds.). (1990). *Making connections.* Cambridge, MA: Harvard University Press.

Gilligan, C., Ward, J. V., & Taylor, J. M. (Eds.). (1988). *Mapping the moral domain: A contribution of women's thinking to psychological theory and education.* Cambridge, MA: Harvard University Press.

Gillstrom, B. J., & Hare, R. D. (1988). Language-related hand gestures in psychopaths. *Journal of Personality Disorders, 1,* 21–27.

Gillyatt, P. (1997, February). When the nose doesn't know. *Harvard Health Letter,* pp. 6–7.

Ginsburg, H. P., & Opper, S. (1988). *Piaget's theory of intellectual development* (3rd ed.). Englewood Cliffs, NJ: Prentice-Hall.

Gladue, B. (1984). Hormone markers for homosexuality. *Science, 225,* 198.

Gladue, B. A. (1995). The biopsychology of sexual orientation. *Current Directions in Psychological Science, 3,* 150–154.

Gladue, B. A., Boechler, M., & McCaul, K. D. (1989). Hormonal response to competition in human males. *Aggressive Behavior, 15,* 409–422.

Gladwin, T. (1964). Culture and logical process. In N. Goodenough (Ed.), *Explorations in cultural anthropology: Essays in honor of George Peter Murdoch.* New York: McGraw-Hill.

Glaman, J. M., Jones, A. P., & Rozelle, R. M. (1996). The effects of co-worker similarity on the emergence of affect in work teams.

Group and Organization Management, 21, 192–215.

Glantz, M., & Pickens, R. (Eds.). (1991). *Vulnerability to drug abuse.* Washington, DC: American Psychological Association.

Glaser, R. (1990). The reemergence of learning theory within instructional research. *American Psychologist, 45,* 29–39.

Glaser, R., & Kiecolt-Glaser, J. (Eds.). (1994). *Handbook of human stress and immunity.* San Diego, CA: Academic Press.

Glaser, R., Rice, J., Speicher, C. E., Stout, J. C., & Kiecolt-Glaser, J. K. (1986). Stress depresses interferon production by leukocytes concomitant with a decrease in natural killer cell activity. *Behavioral Neuroscience, 100,* 675–678.

Glass, D. C., & Singer, J. E. (1972). *Urban stress.* New York: Academic Press.

Glass, S. (1997, March 3). Don't you D.A.R.E. *New Republic,* pp. 18–28.

Glassman, A. H., & Koob, G. F. (1996, February 22). Neuropharmacology. Psychoactive smoke. *Nature, 379,* 677–678.

Glautier, S. (1994). Classical conditioning, drug cues, and drug addiction. In C. R. Legg, & D. A. Booth (Eds.). *Appetite: Neural and behavioural bases. European Brain & Behaviour Society Publications Series, 1.* Oxford, England: Oxford University Press.

Glenn, N. D. (1987, October). Marriage on the rocks. *Psychology Today,* pp. 20–21.

Glick, I. (Ed.). (1995). *Treating depression.* New York: Jossey-Bass.

Glick, P., & Fiske, S. T. (1996). The ambivalent sexism inventory: Differentiating hostile and benevolent sexism. *Journal of Personality and Social Psychology, 70,* 491–512.

Glick, P., Zion, C., & Nelson, C. (1988). What mediates sex discrimination in hiring decisions? *Journal of Personality and Social Psychology, 55,* 178–186.

Glover, J. A., Ronning, R. R., & Reynolds, C. R. (Eds.). (1989). *Handbook of creativity.* New York: Plenum Press.

Gluck, M., & Rosenthal, E. (1996). *OTA report: The effectiveness of AIDS prevention efforts.* Washington, DC: American Psychological Association Office on AIDS.

Gluck, M. A., & Myers, C. E. (1997). Psychobiological models of hippocampal function in learning and memory. *Annual Review of Psychology, 48,* 481–514.

Gobet, F., & Simon, H. A. (1996). Recall of random and distorted chess positions: Implications for the theory of expertise. *Memory and Cognition, 24,* 493–503.

Gochman, D. S. (Ed.). (1997). *Handbook of health behavior research.* New York: Plenum Press.

Goddard, M. J. (1997). Spontaneous recovery in U.S. extinction. *Learning and Motivation, 28,* 118–128.*

Goel, V., Gold, B., Kapur, S., & Houle, S. (1997). The seats of reason: A localization study of deductive and inductive reasoning using PET (015) blood flow technique. *NeuroReport, 8,* 1305–1310.*

Goel, V., Gold, B., Kapur, S., & Houle, S. (1998). Neuroanatomical correlates of

human reasoning. *Journal of Cognitive Neuroscience, 10(3),* 293–302.*

Goelman, D. (1995). *Emotional intelligence: Why it can matter more than IQ.* New York: Bantam.

Gold, P. W., Gwirtsman, H., Avgerinos, P. C., Nieman, L. K., Gallucci, W. T., Kaye, W., Jimerson, D., Ebert, M., Rittmaster, R., Loriaux, L., & Chrousos, G. P. (1986). Abnormal hypothalamic-pituitary-adrenal function in anorexia nervosa. *New England Journal of Medicine, 314,* 1335–1342.

Goldberg, B. (1995). Slowing down the aging process through the use of altered states of consciousness: A review of the medical literature. *Psychology: A Journal of Human Behavior, 32,* 19–21.

Goldberg, L. R. (1990). An alternative "Description of Personality": The big-five factor structure. *Journal of Personality and Social Psychology, 59,* 1216–1229.

Goldberger, N. R., & Veroff, J. B. (Eds.). (1995). *The culture and psychology reader.* New York: New York University Press.

Golden, W. L., Gersh, W. D., & Robbins, D. M. (1992). *Psychological treatment of cancer patients: A cognitive behavioral approach.* Boston: Allyn & Bacon.

Goldfried, M., & Davison, G. (1976). *Clinical behavior therapy.* New York: Holt, Rinehart and Winston.

Goldfried, M. R. (1995). *From cognitive-behavior therapy to psychotherapy integration: An evolving view.* New York: Springer.

Goldfried, M. R., & Castonguay, L. G. (1992). The future of psychotherapy integration. *Psychotherapy, 29,* 4–10.

Goldfried, M. R., & Norcross, J. C. (1995). Integrative and eclectic therapies in historical perspective. In B. M. Bongar, & L. E. Beutler (Eds.), *Comprehensive textbook of psychotherapy: Theory and practice.* Oxford textbooks in clinical psychology, Vol. 1. New York: Oxford University Press.

Goldman-Rakic, P. S. (1988). *Neurobiology of neocortex.* New York: Wiley.

Goldsmith, H. H., Buss, A. H., Plomin, R., Rothbart, M. K., Thomas, A., Chess, S., Hinde, R. A., & McCall, R. B. (1987). Roundtable: What is temperament? Four approaches. *Child Development, 58,* 505–529.

Goldsmith, H. H., & Harman, C. (1994). Temperament and attachment; individuals and relationships. *Current Directions in Psychological Science, 3,* 53–56.

Goldstein, A. P. (1994). *The ecology of aggression.* New York: Plenum Press.

Goldstein, G., Beers, S. R., Longmore, S., & McCue, M. (1996). Efficacy of memory training: A technological extension and replication. *Clinical Neuropsychologist, 10,* 66–72.

Goleman, D. (1985, February 5). Mourning: New studies affirm its benefits. *New York Times,* pp. C1–C2.

Goleman, D. (1988, January 21). Physicians may bungle key part of treatment: The medical interview. *New York Times,* p. B16.

Goleman, D. (1989, August 29). When the rapist is not a stranger: Studies seek new understanding. *New York Times,* pp. C1, C6.

Goleman, D. (1991, October 22). Sexual harassment: It's about power, not sex. *New York Times,* pp. C1, C12.

Goleman, D. (1993a, July 21). "Expert" babies found to teach others. *New York Times,* p. C10.

Goleman, D. (1993b, September 7). Pollsters enlist psychologists in quest for unbiased results. *New York Times,* pp. C1, C11.

Goleman, D. (1995, October 4). Eating disorder rates surprise experts. *The New York Times,* p. C11.

Golombok, S., & Tasker, F. (1996). Do parents influence the sexual orientation of their children? Findings from a longitudinal study of lesbian families. *Developmental Psychology, 32,* 3–11.

Gonsiorek, J. C. (1991). The empirical basis for the demise of the illness model of homosexuality. In J. Gonsiorek, & J. Weinrich (Eds.), *Homosexuality: Research implications for public policy.* Newbury Park, CA: Sage.

Gonzalez, R. G. (1996). Molecular and functional magnetic resonance neuroimaging for the study of dementia. In R. J. Wurtman, S. Corkin, J. H. Growdon, & R. M. Nitsch (Eds.), *The neurobiology of Alzheimer's disease. Annals of the New York Academy of Sciences, Vol. 777.* New York: New York Academy of Sciences.

Goodchilds, J. D. (Ed.). (1991). *Psychological perspectives on human diversity in America.* Washington, DC: American Psychological Association.

Good, E. (1996). Gender and courtship entitlement: Responses to personal ads. *Sex Roles, 34,* 141–169.

Goode, W. J. (1993). *World changes in divorce patterns.* New Haven, CT: Yale University Press.

Goodglass, H. (1993). *Understanding aphasia.* San Diego: Academic Press.

Goodman, J. T. (2000). Three decades of professional psychology: Reflections and future challenges. *Canadian Psychology, 41,* 25–33.*

Goodwin, F. K., & Jamison, K. R. (1990). *Manic-depressive illness.* New York: Oxford University Press.

Googans, B., & Burden, D. (1987). Vulnerability of working parents: Balancing work and home roles. *Social Work, 32,* 295–300.

Gorassini, D. R., & Olson, J. M. (1995). Does self-perception change explain the foot-in-the-door effect? *Journal of Personality and Social Psychology, 69,* 91–105.

Gorman, C. (1996, Fall). *Time Special Issue,* p. 31–35.

Gorman, J. M., Liebowitz, M. R., Fyer, A. J., & Stein, J. (1989). A neuroanatomical hypothesis for panic disorder. *American Journal of Psychiatry, 146,* 148–161.

Gorski, R. A. (1990). Structural sexual dimorphisms in the brain. In N. A. Krasnegor, & R. S. Bridges (Eds.), *Mammalian parenting: Biochemical, neurobiological, and behavioral determinants.* New York: Oxford University Press.

Gorski, R. A. (1996, March). Paper presented at the annual meeting of the American

Association for the Advancement of Science, Baltimore, Maryland.

Gotlib, I. H. (1992). Interpersonal and cognitive aspects of depression. *Current Directions in Psychological Science, 1,* 149–154.

Gottesman, I. I. (1991). *Schizophrenia genesis: The origins of madness.* New York: Freeman.

Gottesman, I. I. (1997, June 6). Twin: En route to QTLs for cognition. *Science, 276,* 1522–1523.

Gottfredson, L. S. (1994). The science of politics and race-norming. *American Psychology, 49,* 955–963.

Gottfredson, L. S. (1997). Why *g* matters: The complexity of everyday life. *Intelligence, 24,* 79–132.

Gottfried, A. E., & Gottfried, A. W. (Eds.). (1988). *Maternal employment and children's development.* New York: Plenum Press.

Gottfried, A. E., & Gottfried, A. W. (Eds.). (1994). *Redefining families.* New York: Plenum Press.

Gottfried, A. W., Gottfried, A. E., Bathurst, K., & Guerin, D. W. (1994). *Gifted IQ: Early developmental aspects—The Fullerton Longitudinal Study.* New York: Plenum Press.

Gottlieb, B. H. (Ed.). (1997). *Coping with chronic stress.* New York: Plenum.

Gottlieb, G. (1996). Developmental psychobiological theory. In R. B. Cairns, G. H. Elder, Jr., & E. J. Costello (Eds.), *Developmental science. Cambridge studies in social and emotional development.* New York: Cambridge University Press.

Gottman, J. M. (1993). *What predicts divorce? The relationship between marital processes and marital outcomes.* Mahwah, NJ: Erlbaum.

Gould, A. (1992). *A history of hypnotism.* Cambridge, England: Cambridge University Press.

Gould, R. L. (1978). *Transformations.* New York: Simon and Schuster.

Gouras, P. (1991). Color vision. In E. R. Kandel, J. H. Schwartz, & T. M. Jessell (Eds.), *Principles of neural science* (3rd ed.). New York: Elsevier.

Gove, W. R. (1982). Labeling theory's explanation of mental illness: An update of recent evidence. *Deviant Behavior, 3,* 307–327.

Graber, J. A., Brooks-Gunn, J., & Petersen, A. C. (Eds.). (1996). *Transitions through adolescence: Interpersonal domains and context.* Mahwah, NJ: Erlbaum.

Graf, P. (1990, Spring). Paper on episodic memory in *Psychonomic Science.*

Graf, P. (1994). Explicit and implicit memory: A decade of research. In C. Umilta, & M. Moscovitch (Eds.), *Attention and performance 15: Conscious and nonconscious information processing. Attention and performance series.* Cambridge, MA: MIT Press.

Graf, P., & Masson, M. E. J. (Eds.). (1993). *Implicit memory: New directions in cognition, development, and neuropsychology.* Mahwah, NJ: Erlbaum.

Graf, P., & Schacter, D. L. (1985). Implicit and explicit memory for new associations in normal and amnesic subjects. *Journal of Experimental Psychology: Learning, Memory, and Cognition, 11,* 501–518.*

Graff, M. R. (1997). AADE legislative advocacy: Perspectives on prevention. *Diabetes Education, 23,* 241.

Graffin, N. F., Ray, W. J., & Lundy, R. (1995). EEG concomitants of hypnosis and hypnotic susceptibility. *Journal of Abnormal Psychology, 104,* 123–131.

Graham, J. R. (1990). *MMPI-2: Assessing personality and psychopathology.* New York: Oxford University Press.

Graham, J. W., Marks, G., & Hansen, W. B. (1991). Social influence processes affecting adolescent substance use. *Journal of Applied Psychology, 76,* 291–298.

Graham, S. (1992). "Most of the subjects were white and middle class": Trends in published research on African Americans in selected APA journals, 1970–1989. *American Psychologist, 47,* 629–639.

Graham, S. (1994). Motivation in African Americans. *Review of Educational Research, 64,* 55–117.

Graham, S. (1997). Using attribution theory to understand social and academic motivation in African American youth. *Educational Psychologist, 32,* 21–34.

Graham, S., & Hudley, C. (1992). An attributional approach to aggression in African-American children. In D. Schunk, & J. Meece (Eds.), *Student perceptions in the classroom.* Mahwah, NJ: Erlbaum.

Grammar, K. (1996, June). Sex and olfaction. Paper presented at the annual meeting of the Human Behavior and Evolution Society. Evanston, Illinois.

Grasel, E. (1994). Non-pharmacological intervention strategies on aging processes: Empirical data on mental training in "normal" older people and patients with mental impairment. Vth Congress of the International Association of Biomedical Gerontology (1993, Budapest, Hungary). *Archives of Gerontology and Geriatrics, Suppl 4,* 91–98.

Graziano, A. M., & Raulin, M. L. (1997). *Research methods: A process of inquiry* (3rd ed.). Reading, MA: Addison-Wesley.

Greeberg, M. T., Cicchetti, D., & Cummings, E. M. (Eds.). (1990). *Attachment in the preschool years: Theory, research, and intervention.* Chicago: University of Chicago Press.

Greeley, A. M. (1992, Oct. 4). Happiest couples in study have sex after 60. *New York Times,* p. 13.

Green, A. I., & Patel, J. K. (1996, December). The new pharmacology of schizophrenia. *The Harvard Mental Health Letter,* pp. 5–7.

Green, D. M., & Swets, J. A. (1966). *Signal detection theory and psychophysics.* Los Altos, CA: Peninsula Publishing.

Green, D. M., & Swets, J. A. (1989). *A signal detection theory and psychophysics.* Los Altos, CA: Peninsula.

Green, R. (1978). Sexual identity of 37 children raised by homosexual or transsexual parents. *American Journal of Psychiatry, 135,* 687–692.

Greenberg, D. R., & LaPorte, D. J. (1996). Racial differences in body type preferences of men for women. *International Journal of Eating Disorders, 19,* 275–278.

Greenberg, L. S., & Paivio, S. C. (1997). *Working with emotions in psychotherapy.* New York: Guilford.*

Greenberg, P., Stiglin, L. E., Finkelstein, S. N., & Berndt, E. R. (1993a). The economic burden of depression in 1990. *Journal of Clinical Psychiatry, 54,* 405–418.

Greenberg, P., Stiglin, L. E., Finkelstein, S. N., & Berndt, E. R. (1993b). Depression: A neglected major illness. *Journal of Clinical Psychiatry, 54,* 419–424.

Greenberg, S. H. (1997, Spring/Summer). The loving ties that bond. *Newsweek,* pp. 68–72.

Greene, B., & Herek, G. (1993). *Lesbian and gay psychology: Theory, research, and clinical applications.* Newbury Park, CA: Sage.

Greene, R. L. (1991). *The MMPI-2/MMPI: An interpretive manual.* Boston: Longwood.

Greene, R. L., & Clopton, J. R. (1994). Minnesota Multiphasic Personality Inventory-2. In M. E. Maruish (Ed.), *The use of psychological tests for treatment planning and outcome assessment.* Mahwah, NJ: Erlbaum.

Greenfield, P. M. (1997). You can't take it with you. Why ability assessments don't cross cultures. *American Psychologist, 52,* 1115–1124.

Greenfield, S. F., Swartz, M. S., Landerman, L. R., & George, L. K. (1993). Long-term psychosocial effects of childhood exposure to parental problem drinking. *American Journal of Psychiatry, 150,* 608–613.

Greenglass, E. R. (1991). Burnout and gender: Theoretical and organizational implications. *Canadian Psychology, 32(4),* 562–574.*

Greenhouse, L. (1997, April 11). Justices grapple with merits of polygraphs at trials. *The New York Times,* p. A19.

Greeno, C. G., & Wing, R. R. (1994). Stress-induced eating. *Psychological Bulletin, 115,* 444–464.

Greeno, J. G. (1978). Natures of problem-solving abilities. In W. K. Estes (Ed.), *Handbook of learning and cognitive processes.* Mahwah, NJ: Erlbaum.

Greenwald, A. G., Draine, S. C., & Abrams, R. L. (1996, September 20). Three cognitive markers of unconscious semantic activation. *Science, 272,* 1699–1702.

Greenwald, A. G., Spangenberg, E. R., Pratkanis, A. R., & Eskenzai, J. (1991). Double-blind tests of subliminal self-help audiotapes. *Psychological Science, 2,* 119–122.

Greenwood, C. R., Carta, J. J., Hart, B., Kamps, D., Terry, B., Arreaga-Mayer, C., Atwater, J., Walker, D., Risley, T., & Delquadri, J. C. (1992). Out of the laboratory and into the community: 26 years of applied behavior analysis at the Juniper Gardens children's project. *American Psychologist, 47,* 1464–1474.

Gregory, R. L. (1978). *The psychology of seeing* (3rd ed.). New York: McGraw-Hill.

Gregory, S. (1856). *Facts for young women.* Boston.

Greig, G. L. (1990). On the shape of energy-detection ROC curves. *Perception & Psychophysics, 48,* 77–81.

Greist-Bousquet, S., & Schiffman, H. R. (1986). The basis of the Poggendorff effect: An additional clue for Day and Kasperczyk. *Perception and Psychophysics, 39,* 447–448.

Griffith, R. M., Miyago, O., & Tago, A. (1958). The universality of typical dreams: Japanese vs. Americans. *American Anthropologist, 60,* 1173–1179.

Grillner, S. (1996, January). Neural networks for vertebrate locomotion. *Scientific American,* 64–69.

Grimsley, D. L., & Karriker, M. W. (1996). Bilateral skin temperature, handedness, and the biofeedback control of skin temperature. *Journal of Behavioral Medicine, 19,* 87–94.

Grohol, J. M. (1997). *The insider's guide to health resources online.* New York: Guilford Press.

Gross, J. (1991, June 16). More young single men hang onto apron strings. *New York Times,* pp. 1, 18.

Grossberg, S. (1995). The attentive brain. *American Scientist, 83,* 438–449.

Grossi, G., Semenza, C., Corazza, S., & Volterra, V. (1996). Hemispheric specialization for sign language. *Neuropsychologia, 34,* 737–740.

Grossman, M., & Wood, W. (1993). Sex differences in intensity of emotional experience: A social role interpretation. *Journal of Personality and Social Psychology, 65,* 1010–1022.

Groth-Marnat, G. (1990). *Handbook of psychological assessment* (2nd ed.). New York: Wiley.

Groth-Marnat, G. (1996). *Handbook of psychological assessment* (3rd ed.). Somerset, NJ: Wiley.

Grube, J. W., Rokeach, M., & Getzlaf, S. B. (1990). Adolescents' value images of smokers, ex-smokers, and nonsmokers. *Addictive Behaviors, 15,* 81–88.

Gruneberg, M. M., & Pascoe, K. (1996). The effectiveness of the keyword method for receptive and productive foreign vocabulary learning in the elderly. *Contemporary Educational Psychology, 21,* 102–109.

Guarino, M., Fridrich, P., & Sitton, S. (1994). Male and female conformity in eating behavior. *Psychological Reports, 75,* 603–609.

Gubrium, J. G. (1973). *The myth of the golden years: A socioenvironmental theory of aging.* Springfield, IL: Thomas.

Gudjonsson, G. H. (1996). Psychology and the law. In C. R. Hollin (Ed.), *Working with offenders: Psychological practice in offender rehabilitation.* Chichester, England: Wiley.

Guerin, B. (1994). Attitudes and beliefs as verbal behavior. Special Section: Attitudes and behavior in social psychology. *Behavior Analyst, 17,* 155–163.

Guerin, D. W., & Gottfried, A. W. (1994). Developmental stability and change in parent reports of temperament: A ten-year longitudinal investigation from infancy through preadolescence. *Merrill Palmer Quarterly, 40,* 334–355.

Guetzkow, H. (1968). Differentiation of roles in task-oriented groups. In D. Cartwright, & A. Zander (Eds.), *Group dynamics: Research and theory* (3rd ed.). New York: Harper & Row.

Gunnar, M. R., Porter, F. L., Wolf, C. M., Rigatuso, J., et al. (1995). Neonatal stress reactivity: Predictions to later emotional temperament. *Child Development, 66,* 1–13.

Gur, R. C. (1996, March). Paper presented at the annual meeting of the American Association for the Advancement of Science, Baltimore, Maryland.

Gur, R. C., Gur, R. E., Obrist, W. D., Hungerbuhler, J. P., Younkin, D., Rosen, A. D., Skilnick, B. E., & Reivich, M. (1982). Sex and handedness differences in cerebral blood flow during rest and cognitive activity. *Science, 217,* 659–661.

Gur, R. C., Mozley, L. H., Mozley, P. D., Resnick, S. M., Karp, J. S., Alavi, A., Arnold, S. E., & Gur, R. E. (1995, January 27). Sex differences in regional cerebral glucose metabolism during a resting state. *Science, 267,* 528–531.

Gura, T. (1997, February 7). Obesity sheds its secrets. *Science, 275,* 751–753.

Guralnick, M. J., Connor, R. T., Hammond, M., Gottman, J. M. et al. (1996). Immediate effects of mainstreamed settings on the social interactions and social integration of preschool children. *American Journal on Mental Retardation, 100,* 359–377.

Gurin, J. (1989, July). Leaner, not lighter. *Psychology Today,* pp. 32–36.

Gurman, E. B. (1994). Debriefing for all concerned: Ethical treatment of human subjects. *Psychological Science, 5,* 139.

Gustavson, C. R., Garcia, J., Hankins, W. G., & Rusniak, K. W. (1974). Coyote predation control by aversive conditioning. *Science, 184,* 581–583.

Gutek, B. (1985). *Sex and the workplace.* San Francisco: Jossey-Bass.

Gutek, B. (1993). Responses to sexual harassment. In S. Oskamp, & M. Costanzo (Eds.), *Advances in applied social psychology.* Newbury Park, CA: Sage.

Gutek, B. A., Cohen, A. G., & Tsui, A. (1996). Reactions to perceived sex discrimination. *Human Relations, 49,* 791–813.

Gutek, B. A., & O'Connor, M. O. (1995). The empirical basis for the reasonable woman standard. *Journal of Social Issues, 51,* 151–166.

Guthrie, G., & Lonner, W. (1986). Assessment of personality and psychopathology. In W. Lonner, & J. Berry (Eds.), *Field methods in cross-cultural research.* Newbury Park, CA: Sage.

Guttman, J. (1993). *Divorce in psychosocial perspective: Theory and research.* Mahwah, NJ: Guttmann.

Guttman, M. (1995, March 3–5). She had electroshock therapy. *USA Weekend,* p. 16.

Gwynn, M. I., & Spanos, N. P. (1996). Hypnotic responsiveness, nonhypnotic suggestibility, and responsiveness to social influence. In R. G. Kunzendorf, N. P. Spahos, & B. Wallace (Eds.), *Hypnosis and imagination. Imagery and human*

development series. Amityville, NY: Baywood.

Ha, J. C., Kimpo, C. L., & Sackett, G. P. (1997). Multiple-spell, discrete-time survival analysis of developmental data: Object concept in pigtailed macaques. *Developmental Psychology, 33,* 1054–1059.

Haber, R. N. (1983). Stimulus information processing mechanisms in visual space perception. In J. Beck, B. Hope, & A. Rosenfeld (Eds.), *Human and machine vision.* New York: Academic Press.

Hadjistavropoulos, T., & Genest, M. (1994). The underestimation of the role of physical attractiveness in dating preferences: Ignorance or taboo? *Canadian Journal of Behavioural Science, 26,* 298–318.*

Hafen, B. Q., Karren, K. J., Frandsen, K. J., & Smith, N. L. (1996). *Mind/body health: The effects of attitudes, emotions, and relationships.* Boston: Allyn & Bacon.

Hafner, H., & Maurer, K. (1995). Epidemiology of positive and negative symptoms in schizophrenia. In C. L. Shriqui, & H. A. Nasrallah (Eds.), *Contemporary issues in the treatment of schizophrenia.* Washington, DC: American Psychiatric Press.

Hagekull, B., & Bohlin, G. (1995). Day care quality, family and child characteristics, and socioemotional development. *Early Childhood Research Quarterly, 10,* 505–526.

Hagen, E., Sattler, J. M., & Thorndike, R. L. (1985). *Stanford-Binet test.* Chicago: Riverside.

Haimov, I., & Lavie, P. (1996). Melatonin: A soporific hormone. *Current Directions in Psychological Science, 5,* 106–111.

Hakuta, K. U., & Garcia, E. E. (1989). Bilingualism and education. *American Psychologist, 44,* 374–379.

Halaas, J. L, Gajiwala, K. S., Maffei, M., Cohen, S. L., Chait, B. T., Rabinowitz, D., Lallone, R. L., Burley, S. K., & Friedman, J. M. (1995, July 28). Weight-reducing effects of the plasma protein encoded by the obese gene. *Science, 269,* 543–546.

Halberstadt, A. G. (1991). Toward an ecology of expressiveness: Family socialization in particular and a model in general. In R. S. Feldman, & B. Rimé (Eds.), *Fundamentals of nonverbal behavior.* Cambridge, England: Cambridge University Press.

Haley, W. E., Clair, J. M., & Saulsberry, K. (1992). Family caregiver satisfaction with medical care of their demented relatives. *Gerontologist, 32,* 219–226.

Halgin, R. P., & Vivona, J. M. (1996). Adult survivors of childhood sexual abuse: Diagnostic and treatment challenges. In R. S. Feldman (Ed.), *The psychology of adversity.* Amherst, MA: University of Massachusetts Press.

Halgin, R. P., & Whitbourne, S. K. (1994). *Abnormal psychology.* Fort Worth, TX: Harcourt Brace.

Hall, C. C. I. (1995). Asian eyes: Body image and eating disorders of Asian and Asian American women. *Eating Disorders. The Journal of Treatment and Prevention, 3,* 8–19.

Hall, G. C. N. (1996). *Theory-based assessment, treatment, and prevention of sexual aggression.* New York: Oxford University Press.

Hall, G. C. N., & Barongan, C. (1997). Prevention of sexual aggression: Sociocultural risk and protective factors. *American Psychologist, 52,* 5–14.

Hall, J. A. (1978). Gender effects in decoding nonverbal cues. *Psychological Bulletin, 85,* 845–857.

Hall, J. A., Roter, D. L., & Katz, N. R. (1988). Task versus socioemotional behaviors in physicians. *Medical Care, 25,* 399–412.

Hall, P. (Ed.). (1997). *Race, ethnicity, and multiculturalism.* Hamden, CT: Garland.

Hall, S. S. (1992). *Mapping the next millennium.* New York: Random House.

Hall, S. S. (1998, February 15). Or memories, our selves. *New York Times Magazine,* pp. 26–57.

Hallberg, H. (1992). Life after divorce: A five-year follow-up study of divorced middle-aged men in Sweden. *Family Practice, 9,* 49–56.

Halle, M. (1990). Phonology. In D. N. Osherson, & H. Lasnik (Eds.), *Language.* Cambridge, MA: MIT Press.

Halling, S., & Goldfarb, M. (1996). The new generation of diagnostic manuals (DSM-III, DSM-III-R, and DSM-IV): An overview and a phenomenologically based critique. *Journal of Phenomenological Psychology, 27,* 49–71.

Halpern, D. F. (1991). *Sex differences in cognitive abilities* (2nd ed.). Mahwah, NJ: Erlbaum.

Halpern, D. F. (1995). *Thought & knowledge: An introduction to critical thinking,* (3rd ed.). Mahwah, NJ: Erlbaum.

Ham, L. P., & Packard, R. C. (1996). A retrospective, follow-up study of biofeedback-assisted relaxation therapy in patients with post-traumatic headache. *Biofeedback and Self Regulation, 21,* 93–104.

Hamer, D. H., Hu, S., Magnuson, V. L., Hu, N., & Pattatucci, A. M. L. (1993, July 16). A linkage between DNA markers on the X chromosome and male sexual orientation. *Science, 261,* 321–327.

Hamilton, D. L., Stroessner, S. J., & Mackie, D. M. (1993). The influence of affect on stereotyping: The case of illusory correlations. In D. M. Mackie, & D. L. Hamilton (Eds.), *Affect, cognition, and stereotyping: Interactive processes in group perception.* San Diego, CA: Academic Press.

Hamilton, M., & Yee, J. (1990). Rape knowledge and propensity to rape. *Journal of Research in Personality, 24,* 111–122.

Hammer, J. (1992, October 26). Must Blacks be buffoons? *Newsweek,* pp. 70–71.

Hammond, R., & Yung, B. (1991). Preventing violence in at-risk African American youth. *Journal of Health Care for the Poor and Underserved, 2,* 359–373.

Hammond, S. L., & Lambert, B. L. (1994a). Communicating about medications: Directions for research. Special Issue: Communicating with patients about their medications. *Health Communication, 6,* 247–251.

Hammond, S. L., & Lambert, B. L. (Eds.). (1994b). *Communicating with patients about their medications.* Mahwah, NJ: Erlbaum.

Hammond, W. R., & Yung, B. (1993). Psychology's role in the public health response to assaultive violence among young African American men. *American Psychologist, 48,* 142–154.

Handler, A., Franz, C. E., & Guerra, M. (1992, April). Sex differences in moral orientation in midlife adults: A longitudinal study. Paper presented at the meetings of the Eastern Psychological Association, Boston.

Hanisch, K. A. (1996). An integrated framework for studying the outcomes of sexual harassment: Consequences for individuals and organizations. In M. S. Stockdale (Ed.), *Sexual harassment in the workplace: Perspectives, frontiers, and response strategies. Women and work: A research and policy series, Vol. 5.* Thousand Oaks, CA: Sage.

Hanna, E., & Meltzoff, A. N. (1993). Peer imitation by toddlers in laboratory, home, and day-care contexts: Implications for social learning and memory. *Developmental Psychology, 29,* 701–710.

Hanna, J. L. (1984). Black/white nonverbal differences, dance, and dissonance: Implications for desegregation. In A. Wolfgang (Ed.), *Nonverbal behavior: Perspectives, applications, intercultural insights.* Lewiston, NY: Hogrefe.

Hansen, B., & Knopes, C. (1993, July 6). Prime time tuning out varied culture. *USA Today,* pp. 1A, 3D.

Hanson, S. J., & Olson, C. R. (Eds.). (1990). *Connectionist modeling and brain function.* Cambridge, MA: MIT Press.

Hansson, R. O., & Carpenter, B. N. (1994). *Relationships in old age: Coping with the challenge of transition.* New York: Guilford Press.

Harackiewicz, J. M., & Elliot, A. J. (1993). Achievement goals and intrinsic motivation. *Journal of Personality and Social Psychology, 65,* 904–915.

Hare, R. D. (1993). *Without conscience.* New York: The Guildford Press.*

Hare, R. D., Hart, S. D., & Harpur, T. J. (1991). Psychopathy and the DSM-IV criteria for antisocial personality disorder. *Journal of Abnormal Psychology, 100,* 391–398.*

Harley, T. A. (1995). *The psychology of language: From data to theory.* Mahwah, NJ: Erlbaum.

Harlow, H. F., Harlow, M. K., & Meyer, D. R. (1950). Learning motivated by a manipulation drive. *Journal of Experimental Psychology, 40,* 228–234.

Harlow, H. F., & Zimmerman, R. R. (1959). Affectional responses in the infant monkey. *Science, 130,* 421–432.

Harlow, J. M. (1869). Recovery from the passage of an iron bar through the head. *Massachusetts Medical Society Publication, 2,* 329–347.

Harlow, R. E., & Cantor, N. (1996). Still participating after all these years: A study of life task participation in later life. *Journal of Personality and Social Psychology, 71,* 1235–1249.

Harnisch, P. (1997, April). Press conference. New York, NY.

Harold, G. T., Fincham, F. D., Osborne, L. N., & Conger, R. D. (1997). Mom and dad are at it again: Adolescent perceptions of marital conflict and adolescent psychological distress. *Developmental Psychology, 33,* 333–350.

Harper, T. (1978, November 15). It's not true about people 65 or over. *Green Bay (Wis.) Press-Gazette,* p. D-1.

Harrington, L., Hull, C., Crittenden, J., & Greider, C. (1995). Gel shift and UV cross-linking analysis of Tetrahymena telomerase. *Journal of Biological Chemistry, 270,* 8893–8901.

Harris Poll: National Council on the Aging. (1975). *The myth and reality of aging in America.* Washington, DC: National Council on the Aging.

Harris, C. R., & Christenfeld, N. (1996). Gender, jealousy, and reason. *Psychological Science, 7,* 364–366.

Harris, D. (1996, February). How does your pay stack up? *Working Woman,* pp. 27–28.

Harris, J. E., & Morris, P. E. (1986). *Everyday memory and action and absent mindedness.* New York: Academic Press.

Harris, L. E., Luft, F. C., Rudy, D. W., & Tierney, W. M. (1995). Correlates of health care satisfaction in inner-city patients with hypertension and chronic renal insufficiency. *Social Science and Medicine, 41,* 1639–1645.

Harris, M. J. (1991). Controversy and cumulation: Meta-analysis and research on interpersonal expectancy effects. *Personality and Social Psychology Bulletin, 17,* 316–322.

Harris, S. L., & Handleman, J. S. (1990). *Aversive and nonaversive interventions.* New York: Springer.

Harris vs. Forklift Systems. 510 U.S. 17. (1993).

Harris-Kern, M. J., & Perkins, R. (1995). Effects of distraction on interpersonal expectancy effects: A social interaction test of the cognitive busyness hypothesis. *Social Cognition, 13,* 163–182.

Harrison, J. A., & Wells, R. B. (1991). Bystander effects on male helping behavior: Social comparison and diffusion of responsibility. *Representative Research in Social Psychology, 19,* 53–63.

Harrison, P. J., Everall, I. P., & Catalan, J. (1994). Is homosexual behaviour hard-wired? Sexual orientation and brain structure. *Psychological Medicine, 24,* 811–816.

Harsch, N., & Neisser, U. (1989). Substantial and irreversible errors in flashbulb memories of the Challenger explosion. Poster presented at the meeting of the Psychonomic Society, Atlanta.

Hart, B., & Risley, T. (1997). Use of language by three-year-old children. Courtesy of Drs. Betty Hart & Todd Risley.

Hart, B., & Risley, T. R. (1997). *Meaningful differences.* Baltimore, MD: Brookes.

Hart, D., Hofmann, V., Edelstein, W., & Keller, M. (1997). The relation of childhood personality types to adolescent behavior and development: A longitudinal study of Icelandic children. *Developmental Psychology, 33,* 195–205.

Hart, J., Jr., & Gordon, B. (1992, September 3). Neural subsystems for object knowledge. *Nature, 359,* 60–64.

Hart, K. E., & Sciutto, M. J. (1994, April). Gender differences in alcohol-related problems. Paper presented at the annual meeting of the Eastern Psychological Association, Providence, RI.

Hartman, W., & Fithian, M. (1984). *Any man can.* New York: St. Martin's.

Hartmann, E. (1967). *The biology of dreaming.* Springfield, IL: Charles C Thomas.

Hartmann, W. M. (1993). On the origin of the enlarged melodic octave. *Journal of the Acoustical Society of America, 93,* 3400–3409.

Hartup, W. W. (1989). Social relationships and their developmental significance. *American Psychologist, 44,* 120–126.

Hartup, W. W. (1996). The company they keep: Friendships and their developmental significance. Society for Research in Child Development Biennial Meetings: Presidential address (1995, Indianapolis, Indiana, US) *Child Development, 67,* 1–13.

Hartup, W. W., & Moore, S. G. (1993). Early peer relations: Developmental significance and prognostic implications. *Early Childhood Research Quarterly, 5,* 1–17.

Haseltine, W. A. (1997, March). Discovering genes for new medicines. *Scientific American,* pp. 92–97.

Haslam, N. (1997). Evidence that male sexual orientation is a matter of degree. *Journal of Personality and Social Psychology, 73,* 862–870.

Haslam, S. A., McGarty, C., & Brown, P. M. (1996). The search for differentiated meaning is a precursor to illusory correlation. *Personality and Social Psychology Bulletin, 22,* 611–619.

Hass, N. (1994, March 21). Fighting and switching. *Newsweek,* pp. 52–53.

Hatchett, L., Friend, R., Symister, P., & Wadhwa, N. (1997). Interpersonal expectations, social support, and adjustment to chronic illness. *Journal of Personality and Social Psychology, 73,* 560–573.

Hatfield, E., & Rapson, R. L. (1993). *Love, sex, and intimacy: Their psychology, biology, and history.* New York: HarperCollins.

Hatfield, E., & Sprecher, S. (1986). *Mirror, mirror: The importance of looks in everyday life.* Albany: State University of New York Press.

Hatfield, E., & Sprecher, S. (1995). Men's and women's preferences in marital partners in the United States, Russia, and Japan. *Journal of Cross Cultural Psychology, 26,* 728–750.

Hathaway, B. (1984, July). Running to ruin. *Psychology Today,* pp. 14–15.

Hathaway, S. R., & McKinley, J. C. (1989). *MMPI-2: Minnesota Multiphasic Personality Inventory-2.* Minneapolis: University of Minnesota Press.

Haugtvedt, C. P., Petty, R. E., & Cacioppo, J. T. (1992). Need for cognition and advertising: Understanding the role of personality variables in consumer behavior. *Journal of Consumer Psychology, 1,* 239–260.

Hauptman, J., Lucas, C., Boldrin, M. N., Collins, H., & Segal, K. R. (2000). Orlistat in the long-term treatment of obesity in primary care settings. *Archives of Family Medicine, 9,* 160–167.*

Hauri, P. J. (Ed.). (1990). *Case studies in insomnia.* New York: Plenum.

Havighurst, R. J. (1973). Social roles, work, leisure, and education. In C. Eisdorfer, & M. P. Lawton (Eds.), *The psychology of adult development and aging.* Washington, DC: American Psychological Association.

Hawkins, D. J., Catalano, R. F., & Miller, J. Y. (1992). Risk and protective factors for alcohol and other drug problems in adolescence and early adulthood: Implications for substance abuse prevention. *Psychological Bulletin, 112,* 64–105.

Hawley, W. D., & Jackson, A. W. (Eds.). (1995). *Toward a common destiny: Improving race and ethnic relations in America.* San Francisco, CA: Jossey-Bass.

Hawton, K. (1986). *Suicide and attempted suicide among children and adolescents.* Newbury Park, CA: Sage.

Hayes, A. M., Castonguay, L. G., & Goldfried, M. R. (1996). Effectiveness of targeting the vulnerability factors of depression in cognitive therapy. *Journal of Consulting and Clinical Psychology, 64,* 623–627.

Hayes, J. R. (1966). Memory, goals, and problem solving. In B. Kleinmuntz (Ed.), *Problem solving: Research, method, and theory.* New York: Wiley.

Hayes, J. R. (1989). *The complete problem solver* (2nd ed.). Mahwah, NJ: Erlbaum.

Hayes, S. C., Folette, W. C., & Follette, V. M. (1995). Behavior therapy: A contextual approach. In A. S. Gurman, & Stanley B. Messer (Eds.), *Essential psychotherapies: Theory and practice.* New York: Guilford Press.

Hayflick, L. (1974). The strategy of senescence. *Journal of Gerontology, 14,* 37–45.

Hayflick, L. (1994). *How and why we age.* New York: Ballatine Books.

Haymes, M., Green, L., & Quinto, R. (1984). Maslow's hierarchy, moral development, and prosocial behavioral skills within a child psychiatric population. *Motivation and Emotion, 8,* 23–31.

Haynes, J. D. (1995). A critique of the possibility of genetic inheritance of homosexual orientation. Special Issue: Sex, cells, and same-sex desire: The biology of sexual preference: I. *Journal of Homosexuality, 28,* 91–113.

Haynes, R. B., Wang, E., & Gomes, M. D. M. (1987). A critical review of interventions to improve compliance with prescribed medications. *Patient Education and Counseling, 10,* 155–166.

Hazen, R. M., & Trefil, J. (1991). *Science matters: Achieving scientific literacy.* New York: Doubleday.

Health Canada (1993). Economic burden of illness in Canada. Minister of Public Works and Government Services Canada, Catalogue No. H21–136/1993E.*

Health Canada (1996). Surveillance of congenital rubella syndrome and other rubella-associated adverse pregnancy outcomes. *Canada communicable disease report, Volume 22–5.**

Health Canada (1996). Life expectancy has increased in the 20th century. Canada's seniors at a glance.* Available: <http://www.hc-sc.gc.ca/seniors-aines/ pubs/poster/seniors/page3e.htm>.

Health Canada (1998). The AIDS/HIV files.* Available: <http://www.hc-sc.gc.ca/real/ aids/screens.html>.

Health Canada. (1999). Statistical report on the health of Canadians.* Available: <http://www.hc-sc.gc.ca/hppb/phdd/ report/stat/eng/index.html>.

Heath, A. C., & Madden, P. A. F. (1995). Genetic influences on smoking behavior. In J. R. Turner, L. R. Cardon, & J. K. Hewitt (Eds.), *Behavior genetic approaches in behavioral medicine. Perspectives on individual differences.* New York: Plenum.

Heath, L., Tindale, R. S., Edwards, J., Posavac, E. J., Bryant, F. B., Henderson-King, E., Suarez-Balcazar, Y., & Myers, J. (Eds.). (1994). *Applications of heuristics and biases to social issues.* New York: Plenum.

Heath, R. P. (1996, July). The frontiers of psychographics. *American Demographics,* pp. 38–43.

Heatherton, T. F., Herman, C. P., & Polivy, J. (1992). Effects of distress on eating: The importance of ego-involvement. *Journal of Personality and Social Psychology, 62,* 801–803.

Heatherton, T. F., & Polivy, J. (1992). Chronic dieting and eating disorders: A spiral model. In J. H. Crowther, S. E. Hobfall, M. A. P. Stephens, & D. L. Tennenbaum (Eds.), *The etiology of bulimia: The individual and familial context.* Washington, DC: Hemisphere.*

Heatherton, T. F., Kiwan, D., & Hebl, M. R. (1995, August). *The stigma of obesity in women: The difference is black and white.* Paper presented at the annual meeting of the American Psychological Association, New York.

Hebb, D. O. (1949). *The organization of behaviour.* New York: Wiley.*

Heckhausen, H., Schmalt, H. D., & Schneider, K. (1985). *Achievement motivation in perspective* (M. Woodruff, & R. Wicklund, Trans.). Orlando, FL: Academic Press.

Hedges, L. V., & Nowell, A. (1995, July). Sex differences in mental test scores, variability, and numbers of high-scoring individuals. *Science, 269,* 41–45.

Heider, F. (1958). *The psychology of interpersonal relations.* New York: Wiley.

Heidrich, S. M., & Denney, N. W. (1994). Does social problem solving differ from other types of problem solving during the adult years? *Experimental Aging Research, 20,* 105–126.

Heikkinen, M., Aro, H., & Lönnqvist, J. (1993). Life events and social support in suicide. *Suicide and Life-Threatening Behaviour, 23,* 343–358.*

Heilman, M. E., & Stopeck, M. H. (1985). Attractiveness and corporate success: Different causal attributions for men and women. *Journal of Applied Psychology, 70,* 379–388.

Heinrichs, R. W. (1993). Schizophrenia and the brain: Conditions for neuropsychology of madness. *American Psychologist, 48,* 221–233.*

Heinrichs, R. W., & Zakzanis, K. K. (1998). Neurocognitive deficit in schizophrenia: A quantitative review of the evidence. *Neuropsychology, 12,* 426–445.*

Heishman, S. J., Kozlowski, L. T., & Henningfield, J. E. (1997). Nicotine addiction: Implications of public health policy. *Journal of Social Issues, 53,* 13–33.

Hellige, J. B. (1990). Hemispheric asymmetry. *Annual Review of Psychology, 41,* 55–80.

Hellige, J. B. (1993). Unity of thought and action: Varieties of interaction between the left and right cerebral hemispheres. *Current Directions in Psychological Science, 2,* 21–25.

Hellige, J. B. (1994). *Hemispheric asymmetry: What's right and what's left.* Cambridge, MA: Harvard University Press.

Helmes, E., & Reddon, J. R. (1993). A perspective on developments in assessing psychopathology: A critical review of the MMPI and MMPI-2. *Psychological Bulletin, 113,* 453–471.

Helmreich, R. L. (1997, May). Managing human error in aviation. *Scientific American,* pp. 62–67.

Helmreich, R. L., & Foushee, H. C. (1993). Why crew resource management? Empirical and theoretical bases of human factors training in aviation. In E. L. Wiener, B. Kanki, & R. Helmreich, *Team performance in the operating room.* San Diego: Academic Press.

Helmreich, R. L., & Schaefer, H. G. (1994). Team performance in the operating room. In M. S. Bogner (Ed.), *Human error in medicine.* Mahwah, NJ: Erlbaum.

Helmreich, R. L., Wiener, E. L., & Kanki, B. G. (1993). The future of crew resource management in the cockpit and elsewhere. In E. L. Wiener, B. Kanki, & R. Helmreich (Eds.), *Team performance in the operating room.* San Diego: Academic Press.

Helms, J. E. (1992). Why is there no study of cultural equivalence in standardized cognitive ability testing? *American Psychologist, 47,* 1083–1101.

Henderson-King, E. I., & Nisbett, R. E. (1996). Anti-black prejudice as a function of exposure to the negative behavior of a single black person. *Journal of Personality and Social Psychology, 71,* 654–664.

Hendrick, S. S., & Hendrick, C. (1992). *Romantic love.* Newbury Park, CA: Sage.

Hendrick, S. S., Hendrick, C., & Adler, N. L. (1988). Romantic relationships: Love, satisfaction, and staying together. *Journal of Personality and Social Psychology, 54,* 980–988.

Henneberger, M. (1993). Secrets of long life from two who ought to know. *New York Times,* pp. B1, B10.

Hepper, P. G., Scott, D., & Shahidullah, S. (1993). Newborn and fetal response to maternal voice. Special Issue: Prenatal and perinatal behaviour. *Journal of Reproductive and Infant Psychology, 11,* 147–153.

Heppner, M. J., Good, G. E., Hillenbrand-Gunn, T. L., & Hawkins, A. K. (1995). Examining sex differences in altering attitudes about rape: A test of the Elaboration Likelihood Model. *Journal of Counseling & Development, 73,* 640–647.

Herbert, T. B., & Cohen, S. (1993). Depression and immunity: A meta-analytic review. *Psychological Bulletin, 113,* 472–486.

Herek, G. M. (1993). Sexual orientation and military service: A social science perspective. *American Psychologist, 48,* 538–549.

Herholz, K. (1995). FDG PET and differential diagnosis of dementia. *Alzheimer Disease and Associated Disorders, 9,* 6–16.

Herman, C. P. (1987). Social and psychological factors in obesity: What we don't know. In H. Weiner, & A. Baum (Eds.), *Perspectives in behavioral medicine: Eating regulation and discontrol.* Mahwah, NJ: Erlbaum.

Hermann, C., Kim, M., & Blanchard, E. B. (1995). Behavioral and prophylactic pharmacological intervention studies of pediatric migraine: An exploratory meta-analysis. *Pain, 60,* 239–255.

Hermann, D. J. (1991). *Super memory.* Emmaus, PA: Rodale Press.

Herrett-Skjellum, J., & Allen, M. (1996). Television programming and sex stereotyping: A meta-analysis. In B. R. Burleson (Ed.), *Communication Yearbook 19.* Thousand Oaks, CA: Sage.

Herrmann, D., McEvoy, C., Hertzog, C., Hertel, P., & Johnson, M. (Eds.). (1996). *Basic and applied research. Volume 1: Theory and context. Volume 2: Practical applications.* Mahwah, NJ: Erlbaum.

Herrnstein, R. J., & Murray, D. (1994). *The bell curve.* New York: Free Press.

Herron, R. E., Hillis, S. L., Mandarino, J. V., et al. (1996). The impact of the Transcendental Meditation program on government payments to physicians in Quebec. *American Journal of Health Promotion, 10,* 208–216.

Hersh, S. M. (1994, June). The wild east. *Atlantic Monthly,* pp. 61–86.

Hershenson, M. (Ed.). (1989). *The moon illusion.* Mahwah, NJ: Erlbaum.

Herz, R. S., & Cupchik, G. C. (1992). An experimental characterization of odor-evoked memories in humans. *Chemical Senses, 17,* 519–528.

Hester, R. K., & Miller, W. R. (Eds.). (1995). *Handbook of alcoholism treatment approaches: Effective alternatives* (2nd ed.). Needham Heights, MA: Allyn & Bacon.

Hetherington, E. M., & Parke, R. D. (1993). *Child psychology: A contemporary viewpoint* (4th ed.). New York: McGraw-Hill.

Hetherington, T. F., & Weinberger, J. (Eds.). (1993). *Can personality change?* Washington, DC: American Psychological Association.

Heubusch, K. (1997, March). More teens lighting up. *American Demographics,* p. 36.

Heward, W. L., & Orlansky, M. D. (1988). *Exceptional children* (3rd ed.). Columbus, OH: Merrill.

Heyneman, N. E., Fremouw, W. J., Gano, D., Kirkland, F., & Heiden, L. (1990). Individual differences and the effectiveness of different coping strategies for pain. *Cognitive Therapy and Research, 14,* 63–77.

Heyward, W. L., & Curran, J. W. (1988, October). The epidemiology of AIDS in the U.S. *Scientific American,* pp. 72–81.

Higbee, K. L. (1988). *Your memory: How it works and how to improve it.* New York: Paragon House.

Higbee, K. L., & Kunihira, S. (1985). Cross-cultural applications of Yodni mnemonics in education. *Educational Psychologist, 20,* 57–64.

Higley, J. D., Suomi, S. J., & Linnoila, M. (1990). Developmental influences on the serotonergic system and timidity in the nonhuman primate. In E. F. Cocaro, & D. L. Murphy (Eds.), *Serotonin in major psychiatric disorders.* Washington, DC: American Psychiatric Press.

Higley, J. D., Suomi, S. J., & Linnoila, M. (1996). A nonhuman primate model of Type II alcoholism? Part 2. Diminished social competence and excessive aggressive correlates with low cerebrospinal fluid 5-hydroxyindoleacetic acid concentrations. *Alcoholism Clinical and Experimental Research, 20,* 643–650.

Hilgard, E. R. (1974). Imaginative involvement: Some characteristics of the highly hypnotizable and the nonhypnotizable. *International Journal of Clinical and Experimental Hypnosis, 22,* 138–156.

Hilgard, E. R. (1975). Hypnosis. *Annual Review of Psychology, 26,* 19–44.

Hilgard, E. R. (1980). Consciousness in contemporary psychology. *Annual Review of Psychology, 31,* 1–26.

Hilgard, E. R., Leary, D. E., & McGuire, G. R. (1991). The history of psychology: A survey and critical assessment. *Annual Review of Psychology, 42,* 79–107.

Hill, C. T., & Stull, D. E. (1981). Sex differences in effects of social and value similarity in same-sex friendship. *Journal of Personality and Social Psychology, 41,* 488–502.

Hill, H., Soriano, F. I., Chen, A., & LaFromboise, T. D. (1994). Socio-cultural factors in the etiology and prevention of violence among ethnic minority youth. In L. D. Eron, J. H. Genry, & P. Schlegel (Eds.), *Reason to hope: A psychosocial perspective on violence & youth* (pp. 59–97). Washington, DC: American Psychological Association.

Hill, W. (1992). Personal communication. Public Affairs Network Coordinator for the American Psychiatric Association.

Hilton, A., Patuin, L., & Sachder, I. (1989). Ethnic relations in rental housing: A social psychological approach. *Canadian Journal of Behavioural Science, 21,* 121–131.

Hinds, M. C. (1993, October 19). Not like the movie: A dare leads to death. *New York Times,* p. A11.

Hine, D. W., Summers, C., Tilleczek, K., & Lewko, J. (1997). Expectancies and mental models as determinants of adolescents' smoking decision. *Journal of Social Issues, 53,* 35–52.

Hinz, L. D., & Williamson, D. A. (1987). Bulimia and depression: A review of the affective-variant hypothesis. *Psychological Bulletin, 102,* 150–158.

Hipkiss, R. A. (1995). *Semantics: Defining the discipline.* Mahwah, NJ: Erlbaum.

Hirsch, S., Cramer, P., & Bowen, J. (1992). The triggering hypothesis of the role of life events in schizophrenia. *British Journal of Psychiatry, 161,* 84–87.

Hirschman, R. S., Leventhal, H., & Glynn, K. (1984). The development of smoking behavior: Conceptualization and supportive cross-sectional survey data. *Journal of Applied Social Psychology, 14,* 184–206.

Hirsh, I. J., & Watson, C. S. (1996). Auditory psychophysics and perception. *Annual Review of Psychology, 47,* 461–484.

Hirsh-Pasek, K., & Golinkoff, R. M. (1996). *The origins of grammar: Evidence from early language comprehension.* Cambridge, MA: MIT Press.

HMHL. (Harvard Mental Health Letter). (1994a, January). AIDS and mental health—Part I. *Harvard Mental Health Letter, 10,* 1–4.

HMHL. (Harvard Mental Health Letter). (1994b, March). Brief psychodynamic therapy—Part I. *Harvard Mental Health Letter,* p. 10.

HMHL. (Harvard Mental Health Letter). (1994c, February). AIDS and mental health—Part II. *Harvard Mental Health Letter, 10,* 1–4.

HMHL. (Harvard Mental Health Letter). (1996, November). Suicide. *Harvard Mental Health Letter, 13,* 1–5,

HMHL. (Harvard Mental Health Letter). (1997, June). Nicotine dependence—Part II. *Harvard Mental Health Letter,* pp. 1–4.

Hobfoll, S. E. (1989). Conservation of resources: A new attempt at conceptualizing stress. *American Psychologist, 44,* 513–524.

Hobfoll, S. E. (1996). *Social support: Will you be there when I need you?* Pacific Grove, CA: Brooks/Cole.

Hobfoll, S. E., Freedy, J. R., Green B. L., & Solomon, S. D. (1996). Coping in reaction to extreme stress: The roles of resource loss and resource availability. In M. Zeidner, & N. S. Endler (Eds.), *Handbook of coping: Theory, research, applications.* New York: Wiley.

Hobfoll, S. E., Spielberger, C. D., Breznitz, S., Figley, C., Folkman, S., Lepper-Green, B., Meichenbaum, D., Milgram, N. A., Sandler, I., Sarason, I., & van der Kolk, B. (1991). War-related stress: Addressing the stress of war and other traumatic events. *American Psychologist, 46,* 848–855.

Hobson, J. A. (1988). *The dreaming brain.* New York: Basic Books.

Hobson, J. A. (1996, February). How the brain goes out of its mind. *Harvard Mental Health Letter,* pp. 3–5.

Hobson, J. A., & McCarley, R. W. (1977). The brain as a dream state generator: An activation-synthesis hypothesis of the dream

process. *American Journal of Psychiatry, 134,* 1335–1348.

Hoch, S. J. (1987). Perceived consensus and predictive accuracy: The pros and cons of projection. *Journal of Personality and Social Psychology, 53,* 221–234.

Hochberg, J. E. (1978). *Perception.* Englewood Cliffs, NJ: Prentice-Hall.

Hochschild, A. (1997). *The time bind. When work becomes home and home becomes work.* New York: Henry Holt.

Hochschild, A. R. (1990). The second shift: Employed women and putting in another day of work at home. *Utne Reader, 38,* 66–73.

Hochschild, A. R. (1997, April 20). There's no place like work. *New York Times Magazine,* 51–84.

Hochschild, A. R., & Machung, A. (1990). *The second shift: Working parents and the revolution at home.* New York: Viking.

Hochschild, A. R., Machung, A., & Pringle, R. (1995). The architecture of gender: Women, men, and inequality. In D. M. Newman (Ed.), *Sociology: Exploring the architecture of everyday life: Readings.* Thousand Oaks, CA: Sage.

Hocutt, A. M. (1996). Effectiveness of special education: Is placement the critical factor? *The Future of Children, 6,* 77–102.

Hoehn-Saric, R. (Ed.). (1993). *Biology of anxiety disorders.* Washington, DC: American Psychiatric Association.

Hoeller, K. (Ed.). (1990). *Readings in existential psychology & psychiatry.* Seattle, WA: Review of Existential Psychology & Psychiatry.

Hoff-Sommers, C. (2000) The war against boys. *The Atlantic Monthly, Vol. 285(5),* 59–74.

Hofferth, S. L., Kahn, J. R., & Baldwin, W. (1987). Premarital sexual activity among U.S. teenage women over the past three decades. *Family Planning Perspectives, 19,* 46–53.

Hoffman, C., Lau, I., & Johnson, D. R. (1986). The linguistic relativity of person cognition: An English-Chinese comparison. *Journal of Personality and Social Psychology, 51,* 1097–1105.

Hoffman, L. W. (1989). Effects of maternal employment in the two-parent family. *American Psychologist, 44,* 283–292.

Hoffman, M. (1991, June 28). A new role for gases: Neurotransmission. *Science, 252,* 1788.

Hofstede, G. (1980). *Culture's consequences.* Beverly Hills, CA: Sage.

Hofstee, W. K. B., de Raad, B., & Goldberg, L. R. (1992). Integration of the big five and circumflex approaches to trait structure. *Journal of Personality and Social Psychology, 63,* 146–163.

Hogan, R., Curphy, G. J., & Hogan, J. (1994). What we know about leadership: Effectiveness and personality. *American Psychologist, 49,* 493–504.

Hogan, R., Hogan, J., & Roberts, B. W. (1996). Personality measurement and employment decisions: Questions and answers. *American Psychologist, 51,* 469–477.

Hogan, R., Johnson, J., & Briggs, S. (Eds.). (1997). *Handbook of personality psychology.* Orlando, FL: Academic Press.

Hogg, M. A., & Hardie, E. A. (1992). Prototypicality, conformity, and depersonalized attraction: A self-categorization analysis of group cohesiveness. *British Journal of Social Psychology, 31,* 41–56.

Holahan, C. J., & Moos, R. H. (1987). Personal and contextual determinants of coping strategies. *Journal of Personality and Social Psychology, 52,* 946–955.

Holahan, C. J., & Moos, R. H. (1990). Life stressors, resistance factors, and improved psychological functioning: An extension of the stress resistance paradigm. *Journal of Personality and Social Psychology, 58,* 909–917.

Holden, C. (1986, September 19). Researchers grapple with problems of updating classic psychological test. *Science, 233,* 1249–1251.

Holden, C. (1987, October 9). Why do women live longer than men? *Science, 238,* 158–160.

Holden, C. (1991, January 11). Probing the complex genetics of alcoholism. *Science, 251,* 163–164.

Holden, C. (1993, January 15). Wake-up call for sleep research. *Science, 259,* 305.

Holden, R. R., & Hibbs, N. (1995). Incremental validity of response latencies for detecting fakers on a personality test. *Journal of Research in Personality, 29,* 362–372.*

Holland, J. C. (1996, September). Cancer's psychological challenges. *Scientific American,* pp. 158–161.

Holland, J. C., & Lewis, S. (1993). Emotions and cancer: What do we really know? In D. Goleman, & J. Gurin (Eds.), *Mind-body medicine.* Yonkers, NY: Consumer Reports Books.

Hollander, E. P. (1985). Leadership and power. In G. Lindzey, & E. Aronson (Eds.), *Handbook of social psychology* (3rd ed.). New York: Random House.

Hollingshead, A. B., & Redich, F. C. (1958). *Social class and mental illness.* New York: Wiley.

Hollingworth, H. L. (1943/1990). *Leta Stetter Hollingworth: A biography.* Boston, MA: Anker.

Hollingworth, L. S. (1928). *The psychology of the adolescent.* New York: Appleton.

Hollis, K. L. (1984). The biological function of Pavlovian conditioning: The best defense is a good offense. *Journal of Experimental Psychology: Animal Behavior Processes, 10,* 413–425.

Hollis, K. L. (1997, September). Contemporary research on Pavlovian conditioning: A "new" functional analysis. *American Psychologist, 52,* 956–965.

Hollister, L. E. (1988). Cannabis—1988. *Acta Psychiatry Scandinavia, 78,* Suppl. 345, 108–118.

Holmes, C. T., & Keffer, R. L. (1995). A computerized method to teach Latin and Greek root words: Effect on verbal SAT scores. *Journal of Educational Research, 89,* 47–50.

Holmes, D. S. (1985). To meditate or rest? The answer is rest. *American Psychologist, 40,* 728–731.

Holmes, J. (1994). *John Bowlby and attachment theory.* New York: Routledge.

Holroyd, J. (1996). Hypnosis treatment of clinical pain: Understanding why hypnosis is useful. *International Journal of Clinical and Experimental Hypnosis, 44,* 33–51.

Holyoak, K. J. (1990). Problem solving. In D. N. Osherson, & E. E. Smith (Eds.), *Thinking.* Cambridge, MA: MIT Press.

Holyoak, K. J., & Thagard, P. (1994). *Mental leaps: Analogy in creative thought.* Cambridge, MA: MIT Press.

Holzman, P. S., & Matthysse, S. (1990). The genetics of schizophrenia: A review. *Psychological Science, 1,* 279–286.

Hong, E., Milgram, R. M., & Gorsky, H. (1995). Original thinking as a predictor of creative performance in young children. *Roeper Review, 18,* 147–149.

Honts, C. R., Hodes, R. L., & Raskin, D. C. (1985). Effects of physical countermeasures on the physiological detection of deception. *Journal of Applied Psychology, 70,* 177–187.

Honts, C. R., & Kircher, J. C. (1994). Mental and physical countermeasures reduce the accuracy of polygraph tests. *Journal of Applied Psychology, 79,* 252–259.

Honts, C. R., Raskin, D. C., & Kircher, J. C. (1987). Effects of physical countermeasure and their electromyographic detection during polygraphy tests for deception. *Journal of Psychophysiology, 1,* 241–247.

Hood, B. M., & Atkinson, J. (1993). Disengaging visual attention in the infant and adult. *Infant Behavior and Development, 16,* 405–422.

Hoogenraad, T. U., Ramos, L. M. P., & van Gijn, J. (1994). Visually induced central pain and arm withdrawal after right parietal lobe infarction. *Journal of Neurology, Neurosurgery, and Psychiatry, 57,* 850–852.

Hoon, P. W., Bruce, K., & Kinchloe, B. (1982). Does the menstrual cycle play a role in sexual arousal? *Psychophysiology, 19,* 21–26.

Hoptman, M. J., & Davidson, R. J. (1994). How and why do the two cerebral hemispheres interact? *Psychological Bulletin, 116,* 195–219.

Horesh, N., Apter, A., Ishai, J., Danziger, Y., et al. (1996). Abnormal psychosocial situations and eating disorders in adolescence. *Journal of the American Academy of Child and Adolescent Psychiatry, 35,* 921–927.

Horgan, J. (1993, December). Fractured functions: Does the brain have a supreme integrator? *Scientific American,* pp. 36–37.

Horgan, J. (1995, November). Get smart, take a test. *Scientific American,* pp. 12–14.

Horgan, J. (1996, December). Why Freud isn't dead. *Scientific American,* pp. 106–111.

Horn, J. L. (1985). Remodeling old models of intelligence. In B. B. Wolman (Ed.), *Handbook of intelligence.* New York: Wiley.

Horney, K. (1937). *Neurotic personality of our times.* New York: Norton.

Horowitz, F. D., & Colombo, J. (Eds.). (1990). *Infancy research: A summative evaluation and a look to the future.* Detroit: Wayne State University.

Horowitz, F. D., & O'Brien, M. (Eds.). (1987). *The gifted and talented: Developmental perspectives.* Washington, DC: American Psychological Association.

Horton, R., & Katona, C. (Eds.). (1991). *Biological aspects of affective disorders.* San Diego, CA: Academic Press.

Horwitz, L., Gabbard, G. O., Allen, J. G., Frieswyk, S. H., Colson, D. B., Newsom, G. E., & Coyne, L. (1996). *Borderline personality disorder: Tailoring the psychotherapy to the patient.* Washington, DC: American Psychiatric Press.

Hosoi, J., Murphy, G. F., Egan, C. L., Lerner, E. A., Grabbe, S., Asahina, A., & Granstein, R. D. (1993, May 13). Regulation of Langerhans cell function by nerves containing calcitonin gene-related peptide. *Nature, 363,* 159–163.

House, J. S., Landis, K. R., & Umberson, D. (1989, July 29). Social relationships and health. *Science, 241,* 540–545.

Houston, L. N. (1981). Romanticism and eroticism among black and white college students. *Adolescence, 16,* 263–272.

Hovland, C., Janis, I., & Kelly, H. H. (1953). *Communication and persuasion.* New Haven, CT: Yale University Press.

Howard, A., Pion, G. M., Gottfredson, G. D., Flattau, P. E., Oskamp, S., Pfafflin, S. M., Bray, D. W., & Burstein, A. D. (1986). The changing face of American psychology: A report from the committee on employment and human resources. *American Psychologist, 41,* 1311–1327.

Howard, I. P., & Rogers, B. J. (1995). *Binocular vision and stereopsis.* New York: Oxford University Press.*

Howard, K. I., & Zola, M. A. (1988). Paper presented at the annual meeting of the Society for Psychotherapy Research. Chicago.

Howells, J. G., & Osborn, M. L. (1984). *A reference companion to the history of abnormal psychology.* Westport, CT: Greenwood Press.

Howes, C. (1990). Can the age of entry into child care and the quality of child care predict adjustment in kindergarten? *Developmental Psychology, 26,* 292–303.

Hser, Y., Anglin, M. D., & Powers, K. (1993). A 24-year follow-up of California narcotics addicts. *Archives of General Psychiatry, 50,* 577–584.

Hsiao, J. K., Colison, J., Bartko, J. J., Doran, A. R., Konicki, P. E., Potter, W. Z., & Pickar, D. (1993). Monoamine neurotransmitter interactions in drug-free and neuroleptic-treated schizophrenics. *Archives of General Psychiatry, 50,* 606–614.

Hsu, L. K. G. (1990). *Eating disorders.* New York: Guilford Press.

Hubel, D. H., & Wiesel, T. N. (1979). Brain mechanisms of vision. *Scientific American,* pp. 150–162.

Hudson, W. (1960). Pictorial depth perception in subcultural groups in Africa. *Journal of Social Psychology, 52,* 183–208.

Huesmann, L. R. (1994). *Aggressive behavior: Current perspectives.* New York: Plenum Press.

Huesmann, L. R., & Eron, L. D. (Eds.). (1986). *Television and the aggressive child: A cross-national comparison.* Mahwah, NJ: Erlbaum.

Huesmann, L. R., Eron, L. D., Klein, R., Brice, P., & Fischer, P. (1983). Mitigating the imitation of aggressive behaviors by changing children's attitudes about media violence. *Journal of Personality and Social Psychology, 5,* 899–910.

Huesmann, L. R., & Moise, J. (1996, June). Media violence: A demonstrated public health threat to children. *Harvard Mental Health Letter,* pp. 5–7.

Hughes, J. N., & Hasbrouck, J. E. (1996). Television violence: Implications for violence prevention. *School Psychology Review, 25,* 134–151.

Hull, C. L. (1943). *Principles of behavior.* New York: Appleton-Century-Crofts.

Human Capital Initiative. (1997). *Reducing violence: A research agenda.* Washington, DC: American Psychological Association.

Humphreys, L. G. (1992). Commentary: What both critics and users of ability tests need to know. *Psychological Science, 3,* 271–274.

Hunsley, J., & Lefebvre, M. (1990). A survey of the practices and activities of Canadian clinical psychologists. *Canadian Psychology, 350–358.*

Hunt, E. (1994). Problem solving. In R. J. Sternberg (Ed.), *Thinking and problem solving. Handbook of perception and cognition* (2nd ed.). San Diego, CA: Academic Press.

Hunt, E., Streissguth, A. P., Kerr, B., & Olson, H. C. (1995). Mothers' alcohol consumption during pregnancy: Effects on spatial-visual reasoning in 14-year-old children. *Psychological Science, 6,* 339–342.

Hunt, M. (1974). *Sexual behaviors in the 1970s.* New York: Dell.

Hunt, M. (1993). *The story of psychology.* New York: Doubleday.

Hunt, M. (1997). *How science takes stock: The story of meta-analysis.* New York: Russell Sage Foundation.

Hunt, R. R. (1995). The subtlety of distinctiveness: What von Restorff really did. *Psychonomic Bulletin and Review, 2,* 105–112.

Hunter, J. A., Platow, M. J., Howard, M. L., & Stringer, M. (1996). Social identity and intergroup evaluative bias: Realistic categories and domain specific self-esteem in a conflict setting. *European Journal of Social Psychology, 26,* 631–647.

Hunter, J. A., Stringer, M., & Watson, R. P. (1991). Intergroup violence and intergroup attributions. *British Journal of Social Psychology, 30,* 261–266.

Hunter, M. S., Swann, C., & Ossher, J. M. (1995). Seeking help for premenstrual syndrome: Women's self-reports and treatment preferences. *Sexual and Marital Therapy, 10,* 253–262.

Hurlburt, A. C., & Poggio, T. A. (1988, January 29). Synthesizing a color algorithm from examples. *Science, 239,* 482–485.

Hurst, S. A. (1999). Legacy of betrayal: A grounded theory of becoming demoralized from the perspective of women who have been depressed. *Canadian Psychology, 40,* 179–191.*

Hurst, S. A., & Genest, M. (1995). Cognitive-behavioural therapy with a feminist orientation: A perspective for therapy with depressed women. *Canadian Psychology, 36,* 236–257.*

Hurt, S. W., Reznikoff, M., & Clarkin, J. F. (1995). The Rorschach. In L. E. Beutler, & M. R. Berren (Eds.), *Integrative assessment of adult personality.* New York: Guilford Press.

Huston, T. L., & Vangelisti, A. L. (1991). Socioemotional behavior and satisfaction in marital relationships: A longitudinal study. *Journal of Personality and Social Psychology, 61,* 721–733.

Hutcheson, G. D., Baxter, J. S., Telfer, K., & Warden, D. (1995). Child witness statement quality: Question type and errors of omission. *Law and Human Behavior, 19,* 631–648.

Hutchison, J. B. (Ed.). (1978). *Biological determinants of sexual behavior.* New York: Wiley.

Hutton, J. T., Koller, W. C., Ahlskog, J. E., Pahwa, R., et al. (1996). Multicenter, placebo-controlled trial of cabergoline taken once daily in the treatment of Parkinson's disease. *Neurology, 46,* 1062–1065.

Hwang, S. W. (2000). Mortality among men using homeless shelters in Toronto, Ontario. *Journal of the American Medical Association, 283,* 2152–2157.*

Hyde, J. S., Fennema, E., & Lamon, S. J. (1990). Gender differences in mathematics performance: A meta-analysis. *Psychological Bulletin, 107,* 139–155.

Hyde, J. S., & Linn, M. C. (1988). Gender differences in verbal ability: A meta-analysis. *Psychological Bulletin, 104,* 53–69.

Hyler, S. E., Gabbard, G. O., & Schneider, I. (1991). Homicidal maniacs and narcissistic parasites: Stigmatization of mentally ill persons in the movies. Annual Meeting of the American Psychiatric Association (1989, San Francisco, California). *Hospital and Community Psychiatry, 42,* 1044–1048.

Hyman, R. (1994). Anomaly or artifact? Comments on Bem and Honorton. *Psychological Bulletin, 115,* 19–24.

Hyman, S. E. (1996, August 2). Shaking out the cause of addiction. *Science, 273,* 611–612.

Iaccino, J. F. (1993). *Left brain-right brain differences: Inquiries, evidence, and new approaches.* Mahwah, NJ: Erlbaum.

Iacono, W. G. (1991). Can we determine the accuracy of polygraph tests? In P. K. Ackles, J. R. Jennings, & M. G. H. Coles (Eds.), *Advances in psychophysiology* (Vol. 4). Greenwich, CT: JAI Press.

Iacono, W. G., & Grove, W. M. (1993). Schizophrenia reviewed: Toward an integrative genetic model. *Psychological Science, 4,* 273–276.

IBM (1997, May 15.) "Deep Blue vs. Gary Kasparov." WWW site.

Ingelfinger, F. J. (1944). The late effects of total and subtotal gastrectomy. *New England Journal of Medicine, 231,* 321–377.

Ingraham, L. J., & Chan, T. F. (1996). Is there psychopathology in the coparents of schizophrenic adoptees' half-siblings. *Psychological Reports, 79,* 1296–1298.

Ingram, R. E. (Ed.). (1990). *Contemporary psychological approaches to depression: Theory, research, and treatment.* New York: Plenum.

Institute for Mental Health Initiatives. (1993). Violence. *Dialogue, 1,* 1–4.

Institute for Mental Health Initiatives. (1996). Language, sex, violence, children. *Dialogue, 4,* 1–4.

Inter-Provincial Task Force on Problem Gambling. (1999). Measuring problem gambling in Canada: Final report — Phase 1. Ottawa: CCSA.* Available: <http://www.ccsa.ca/Final.htm>.

Irani, K., Xia, Y., Zweier, J. L., Sollott, S. J., Der, C. J., Fearon, E. R., Sundaresan, M., Finkel, T., Goldschmidt-Clermont, P. J. (1997). Mitogenic signaling mediated by oxidants in ras-transformed fibroblasts. *Science, 275,* 1649.

Isaksen, S. G., & Murdock, M. C. (1993). The emergence of a discipline: Issues and approaches to the study of creativity. In S. G. Isaksen, M. C. Murdock, R. L. Firestein, & D. J. Treffinger (Eds.), *The emergence of a discipline* (Vol. 1). Norwood, NJ: Ablex.

Isay, R. A. (1990). *Being homosexual: Gay men and their development.* New York: Avon.

Issac, A. R., & Marks, D. F. (1994). Individual differences in mental imagery experience: Developmental changes and specialization. *British Journal of Psychology, 85,* 479–500.

Izard, C. E. (1990). Facial expressions and the regulation of emotions. *Journal of Personality and Social Psychology, 58,* 487–498.

Izard, C. E. (1991). *The psychology of emotions.* New York: Plenum.

Izard, C. E. (1994). Innate and universal facial expressions: Evidence from developmental and cross-cultural research. *Psychological Bulletin, 115,* 288–299.

Jacklin, C. N., & Reynolds, C. (1993). Gender and childhood socialization. In A. E. Beall, & R. J. Sternberg (Eds.), *The psychology of gender.* New York: Guilford Press.

Jackson, D. N., Ashton, M. C., & Tomes, J. L. (1996). The six-factor model of personality: Facets from the big five. *Personality and Individual Differences, 21,* 391–402.

Jackson, D. N., Paunonen, S. V., Fraboni, M., & Goffin, R. D. (1996). A five-factor versus six-factor model of personality structure. *Personality and Individual Differences, 20,* 33–45.

Jackson, T. L. (Ed.). (1996). *Acquaintance rape: Assessment, treatment, and prevention.* Sarasota, FL: Professional Resource Press/Professional Resource Exchange, Inc.

Jacobs, B. L. (1987, July–August). How hallucinogenic drugs work. *American Scientist, 75,* 386–392.

Jacobs, B. L. (1994, September–October). Serotonin, motor activity, and depression-related disorders. *American Scientist, 82,* 456–463.

Jacobs, G. D., Benson, H., & Friedman, R. (1993). Home-based central nervous system assessment of a multifactor behavioral intervention for chronic sleep-onset insomnia. *Behavior Therapy, 24,* 159–174.

Jacobs, L. F., & Spencer, W. D. (1994). Natural space-use patterns and hippocampal size in kangaroo rats. *Brain, Behavior and Evolution, 44,* 125–132.

Jacobs, M. K., & Goodman, G. (1989). Psychology and self-helping groups: Predictions on a partnership. *American Psychologist, 44,* 536–545.

Jacobson, J. W., & Mulick, J. A. (Eds.). (1996). *Manual of diagnosis and professional practice in mental retardation.* Washington, DC: American Psychological Association.

Jacobson, N. S., Dobson, K. S., Truax, P. A., et al. (1996). A component analysis of cognitive-behavioral treatment for depression. *Journal of Consulting and Clinical Psychology, 64,* 295–304.

Jacobson, N. S., & Truax, P. (1991). Clinical significance: A statistical approach to defining meaningful change in psychotherapy research. *Journal of Consulting and Clinical Psychology, 59,* 12–19.

Jacobson, P. B., Perry, S. W., & Hirsch, D. (1990). Behavioral and psychological responses to HIV antibody testing. *Journal of Consulting and Clinical Psychology, 58,* 31–37.

Jacobson, P. D., Wasserman, J., & Anderson, J. R. (1997). Historical overview of tobacco legislation and regulation. *Journal of Social Issues, 53,* 75–95.

Jacoby, L. L. (1998). Invariance in automatic influences of memory: Toward a user's guide for the process-dissociation procedure. *Journal of Experimental Psychology: Learning, Memory, and Cognition, 24,* 3–26.*

Jacoby, L. L., & Kelley, C. (1992). Unconscious influences of memory: Dissociations and automaticity. In A. D. Milner, & M. D. Rugg (Eds.), *The neuropsychology of consciousness* (pp. 201–233) San Diego: Academic Press.*

Jacoby, L. L., & Kelley, C. M. (1992). A process-dissociation framework for investigating unconscious influences: Freudian slips, projective tests, subliminal perception, and signal detection theory. *Current Directions in Psychological Science, 1,* 174–179.*

Jaffe, J. W. (1990). Drug addiction and drug abuse. In A. G. Gilman, T. W. Rall, A. S. Nies, & P. Taylor (Eds.), *Goodman and Gilman's The pharmacological basis of therapeutics* (8th ed.). New York: Pergamon.

Jaffe, P. G., & Baker, L. L. (1999). Why changing the YOA does not impact youth crime: Developing effective prevention programs for children and adolescents. *Canadian Psychology, 40(1),* 22–29.*

James, J. E. (1997). *Understanding caffeine: A biobehavioral analysis.* Newbury Park, CA: Sage.

James, W. (1890). *The principles of psychology.* New York: Holt.

Jamison, K. R. (1993). *Touched with fire: Manic depressive illness and the artistic temperament.* New York: Free Press.

Jamison, K. R. (1995, February). Manic-depressive illness and creativity. *Scientific American,* pp. 62–67.

Janda, L. H., & Klenke-Hamel, K. E. (1980). *Human sexuality.* New York: Van Nostrand.

Jang, K. L., Livesley, W. J., & Vernon, P. A. (1996a). The genetic basis of personality at different ages: A cross-sectional twin study. *Personality and Individual Difference, 21,* 299–301.

Jang, K. L., Livesley, W. J., & Vernon, P. A. (1996b). Heritability of the big five personality dimensions and their facets: A twin study. *Journal of Personality, 64,* 577–591.

Janis, I. (1972). *Victims of groupthink: A psychological study of foreign policy decisions and fiascoes.* Boston: Houghton Mifflin.

Janis, I. (1984). Improving adherence to medical recommendations: Descriptive hypothesis derived from recent research in social psychology. In A. Baum, J. E. Singer, & S. E. Taylor (Eds.), *Handbook of medical psychology* (Vol. 4). Mahwah, NJ: Erlbaum.

Janis, I. L. (1989). *Crucial decisions: Leadership in policy-making management.* New York: Free Press.

Janis, I. L., & Frick, F. (1943). The relationship between attitudes toward conclusions and errors in judging logical validity of syllogisms. *Journal of Experimental Psychology, 33,* 73–77.

Janssen, E. (1995). Understanding the rapist's mind. *Perspectives in Psychiatric Care, 31,* 9–13.

Jaret, P. (1992, November/December). Mind over malady. *Health,* pp. 87–94.

Jaroff, L. (1996, Fall). Keys to the kingdom. *Time,* pp. 24–29.

Jarrett, R. B. (1991). University of Texas Southwestern Medical Center at Dallas: Psychosocial Research Program in Mood Disorders. In L. E. Beutler, & M. Crago (Eds.), *Psychotherapy research: An international review of programmatic studies.* Washington, DC: American Psychiatric Press, Inc.

Jarvik, M. E. (1990, October 19). The drug dilemma: Manipulating the demand. *Science, 250,* 387–392.

Jarvis, T. J., Tebbutt, J., & Mattick, R. P. (1995). *Treatment approaches for alcohol and drug dependence.* New York: Wiley.

Jenkins, B. M. (1983). *Some reflections on recent trends in terrorism.* Santa Monica, CA: Rand Corporation.

Jenkins, C. D., Zyzanski, S. J., & Rosenman, R. H. (1978). Coronary-prone behavior: One pattern or several? *Psychosomatic Medicine, 40,* 25–43.

Jenkins, S. R. (1994). Need for power and women's careers over 14 years: Structural power, job satisfaction, and motive change. *Journal of Personality and Social Psychology, 66,* 155–165.

Jensen, J. K., & Neff, D. L. (1993). Development of basic auditory discrimination in preschool children. *Psychological Science, 4,* 104–107.

Jervis, R., Lebow, R. N., & Stein, J. G., with Moragan, P. M., & Snyder, J. L. (1985). *Psychology and deterrence.* Baltimore: Johns Hopkins University Press.

Jessell, T. M., & Kelly, D. D. (1991). Pain and analgesia. In E. R. Kandel, J. H. Schwartz, & T. M. Jessell (Eds.), *Principles of neural science* (3rd ed.). New York: Elsevier.

Jevning, R., Anand, R., Biedebach, M., & Fernando, G. (1996). Effects on regional cerebral blood flow of transcendental meditation. *Physiological Behavior, 59,* 399–402.

Jhally, S., Goldman, R., Cassidy, M., Katula, R., Seiter, E., Pollay, R. W., Lee, J. S., Carter-Whitney, D., Steinem, G., et al. (1995). Advertising. In G. Dines, & J. M. Humez (Eds.), *Gender, race, and class in media: A text-reader.* Thousand Oaks, CA: Sage.

Jiang, W., Babyak, M., Krantz, D. S., Waugh, R. A., Coleman, R. E., Hanson, M. M., Frid, D. J., McNulty, S., Morris, J. J., O'Connor, C. M., & Blumenthal, J. A. (1996, June 5). Mental stress-induced myocardial ischemia and cardiac events. *Journal of the American Medical Association, 275,* 1651–1656.

Johnsen, S. K. & Ryser, G. R. (1996). An overview of effective practices with gifted students in general-education settings. *Journal for the Education of the Gifted, 19,* 379–404.

Johnson, A. M., Wadsworth, J., Wellings, K., & Bradshaw, S. (1992). Sexual lifestyles and HIV risk. *Nature, 360,* 410–412.

Johnson, B. T. (1991). Insights about attitudes: Meta-analytic perspectives. *Personality and Social Psychology Bulletin, 17,* 289–299.

Johnson, D. M., Parrott, G. R., & Stratton, R. P. (1968). Production and judgment of solutions to five problems. *Journal of Educational Psychology Monograph Supplement, 59* (6, pt. 2).

Johnson, J. T., Cain, L. M., Falke, T. L., Hayman, J., & Perillo, E. (1985). The "Barnum Effect" revisited: Cognitive and motivational factors in the acceptance of personality descriptions. *Journal of Personality and Social Psychology, 49,* 1378–1391.

Johnson, M. G., & Henley, T. (1990). *Reflections on the principles of psychology.* Mahwah, NJ: Erlbaum.

Johnson, R. W., Kelly, R. J., & LeBlanc, B. A. (1995). Motivational basis of dissonance: Aversive consequences of inconsistency. *Personality & Social Psychology Bulletin, 21,* 850–855.

Johnson, S. C., Pinkston, J. B., Bigler, E. D., & Blatter, D. D. (1996). Corpus callosum morphology in normal controls and traumatic brain injury: Sex differences, mechanisms of injury, and neuropsychological correlates. *Neuropsychology, 10,* 408–415.

Johnson-Laird, P. N. (1983). *Mental models: Towards a cognitive science of language, inference, and consciousness.* Cambridge, MA: Harvard University Press.

Johnson-Laird, P. N., Byrne, R. M., & Schaeken, W. (1992). Propositional reasoning by model. *Psychological Review, 99,* 418–439.

Johnson-Laird, P. N., & Shafir, E. (Eds.). (1994). *Reasoning and decision making.* New York: Blackwell.

Johnston, D. (1997, October 17). A missing link? LTP and learning. *Science, 278,* 401–402.

Johnston, L. (1996). Resisting change: Information-seeking and stereotype change. *European Journal of Social Psychology, 26,* 799–825.

Johnston, L., Bachman, J., & O'Malley, P. (1996). *Monitoring the future: A continuing study of the lifestyles and values of youth.* Ann Arbor: University of Michigan Institute of Social Research.

Johnston, N. (1993). CRM: Cross-cultural perspectives. In E. L. Wiener, B. Kanki, & R. Helmreich (Eds.), *Team performance in the operating room.* San Diego: Academic Press.

Joiner, T. E., & Wagner, K. D. (1995). Attribution style and depression in children and adolescents: A meta-analytic review. *Clinical Psychology Review, 15,* 777–798.

Jones, A., & Crandall, R. (Eds.). (1991). Handbook of self-actualization. *Journal of Social Behavior and Personality, 6,* 1–362.

Jones, E. E. (1990). *Interpersonal perception.* New York: Freeman.

Jones, F. D., & Koshes, R. J. (1995). Homosexuality and the military. *American Journal of Psychiatry, 152,* 16–21.

Jones, G. N., Brantley, P. J., & Gilchrist, J. C. (1988, August). The relation between daily stress and health. Paper presented at the annual meeting of the American Psychological Association, Atlanta.

Jones, J. C., & Barlow, D. H. (1990). Self-reported frequency of sexual urges, fantasies, and masturbatory fantasies in heterosexual males and females. *Archives of Sexual Behavior, 19,* 269–279.

Jones, J. M. (1994). Our similarities are different: Toward a psychology of affirmative diversity. In E. J. Trickett, R. J. Watts, & D. Birman (Eds.), *Human diversity: Perspectives on people in context.* The Jossey-Bass social and behavioral science series. San Francisco: Jossey-Bass.

Jones, L. V. (1984). White-black achievement differences: The narrowing gap. *American Psychologist, 39,* 1207–1213.

Joseph, R. (1996). *Neuropsychiatry, neuropsychology, and clinical neuroscience: Emotion, evolution, cognition, language, memory, brain damage, and abnormal behavior* (2nd ed.). Baltimore, MD: Williams & Wilkins.

Josephs, R. A., Markus, H. R., & Tafarodi, R. W. (1992). Gender and self esteem. *Journal of Personality and Social Psychology, 63,* 391–402.

Josephs, R. A., & Steele, C. M. (1990). The two faces of alcohol myopia: Attentional mediation of psychological stress. *Journal of Abnormal Psychology, 99,* 115–126.

Josephson, W. L. (1995). *Television violence: A review of the effects on children of different ages.* Ottawa: Department of Canadian Heritage and Health Canada.*

Josephson, W. L., Proulx, J., Safer, A., & Davison, P. (1999). Dating violence prevention in schools: A community-academic partnership. *Canadian Psychology, 40(2a),* 73.*

Joyce, J. (1934). *Ulysses.* New York: Random House.

Julesz, B. (1986). Stereoscopic vision. *Vision Research, 26,* 1601–1612.

Julien, R. M. (1991). *A primer of drug action* (7th ed.). New York: Freeman.

Julien, R. M. (1995). *Primer of drug action* (8th ed.). New York: Freeman.

Julius, M. (1990). Paper presented at the Gerontological Society of America on women who suppress their anger.

Juristat (1999). Youth violent crime (Vol. 19, no. 13).*

Jusczyk, P. W. (1986). Toward a model of the development of speech perception. In J. S. Perkell, & D. H. Klatt (Eds.), *Invariance and variability in speech processes.* Mahwah, NJ: Erlbaum.

Jusczyk, P. W. (1995). Language acquisition: Speech sounds and the beginning of phonology. In J. L. Miller, & P. D. Eimas (Eds.), *Speech, language, and communication. Handbook of perception and cognition* (2nd ed.). San Diego, CA: Academic Press, Inc.

Jusczyk, P. W. (1997). *The discovery of spoken language.* Cambridge, MA: MIT Press.

Jusczyk, P. W., & Derrah, C. (1987). Representation of speech sounds by young infants. *Developmental Psychology, 23,* 648–654.

Jussim, L., & Eccles, J. (1995). Naturally occurring interpersonal expectancies. In N. Eisenberg, (Ed.), *Social development. Review of personality and social psychology* (p. 15). Thousand Oaks, CA: Sage.

Jussim, L., Fleming, C. J., Coleman, L., & Kohberger, C. (1996). The nature of stereotypes: II. A multiple-process model of evaluations. *Journal of Applied Social Psychology, 26,* 283–312.

Jussim, L., Milburn, M., & Nelson, W. (1991). Emotional openness: Sex-role stereotypes and self-perceptions. *Representative Research in Social Psychology, 19,* 35–52.

Justice, T. C., & Looney, T. A. (1990). Another look at "superstitions" in pigeons. *Bulletin of the Psychonomic Society, 28,* 64–66.

Kagan, J. (1989a). Temperamental contributions to social behavior. *American Psychologist, 44,* 668–674.

Kagan, J. (1989b). *Unstable ideas: Temperament, cognition, and self.* Cambridge, MA: Harvard University Press.

Kagan, J. (1990). Temperament and social behavior. *Harvard Medical School Mental Health Letter, 6,* 4–5.

Kagan, J. (1994). Inhibited and uninhibited temperaments. In W. B. Carey, & S. C. McDevitt (Eds.), *Prevention and early intervention: Individual differences as risk factors for the mental health of children: A festschrift for Stella Chess and Alexander Thomas.* New York: Brunner/Mazel.

Kagan, J. (1997). Temperament and the reactions to unfamiliarity. *Child Development, 68,* 139–143.

Kagan, J., Arcus, D., & Snidman, N. (1993). The idea of temperament: Where do we go from here? In R. Plomin, & G. E. McClearn (Eds.), *Nature, nurture, & psychology.* Washington, DC: American Psychological Association.

Kagan, J., Kearsley, R., & Zelazo, P. R. (1978). *Infancy: Its place in human development.* Cambridge, MA: Harvard University Press.

Kagan, J., & Snidman, N. (1991). Infant predictors of inhibited and uninhibited profiles. *Psychological Science, 2,* 40–44.

Kahn, M. W., Hannah, M., Hinkin, C., Montgomery, C., & Pitz, D. (1987). Psychopathology on the streets: Psychological measurements of the homeless. *Professional Psychology, 22,* 103–109.

Kahn, R. S., Davidson, M., & Davis, K. L. (1996). Dopamine and schizophrenia revisited. In S. J. Watson (Ed.), *Biology of schizophrenia and affective disease.* Washington, DC: American Psychiatric Press.

Kahn, R. S., Davidson, M., Knott, P., Stern, R. G., Apter, S., & Davis, K. L. (1993). Effect of neuroleptic medication on cerebrospinal fluid monoamine metabolite concentrations in schizophrenia. Serotonin-dopamine interactions as a target for treatment [see comments]. *Archives of General Psychiatry, 50,* 599–605.

Kahn, S., Zimmerman, G., Csikszentmihalyi, M., & Getzels, J. W. (1985). Relations between identity in young adulthood and intimacy at midlife. *Journal of Personality and Social Psychology, 49,* 1316–1322.

Kail, R. (1991). Processing time declines exponentially during childhood and adolescence. *Developmental Psychology, 27,* 259–266.

Kakigi, R., Matsuda, Y., & Kuroda, Y. (1993). Effects of movement-related cortical activities on pain-related somatosensory evoked potentials following CO_2 laser stimulation in normal subjects. *Acta Neurologica Scandinavica, 88,* 376–380.

Kalafat, J., Elias, M., & Gara, M. A. (1993). The relationship of bystander intervention variables to adolescents' responses to suicidal peers. *Journal of Primary Prevention, 13,* 231–244.

Kalichman, S. C. (1998). *Preventing AIDS: A sourcebook for behavioral interventions.* Mahwah, NJ: Erlbaum.

Kalin, R., & Berry, J. W. (1994). Ethnic and multicultural attitudes. In J. W. Berry & J. Laponce (Eds.), *Ethnicity and culture in Canada: The research landscape.* Toronto: University of Toronto Press.*

Kalin, R., & Berry, J. W. (1996). Interethnic attitudes in Canada: Ethnocentrism, consensual hierarchy and reciprocity. *Canadian Journal of Behavioural Science, 28,* (253–261).*

Kamins, M. A., & Gupta, K. (1994). Congruence between spokesperson and product type: A matchup hypothesis perspective. *Psychology and Marketing, 11,* 569–586.

Kandel, E., & Abel, T. (1995, May 12). Neuropeptides, adenylyl cyclase, and memory storage. *Science, 268,* 825–826.

Kandel, E., Schwartz, R., & Jessell, T. M. (1995). *Essentials of neural science and behavior.* New York: Appleton & Lange.

Kandel, E. R., & Hawkins, R. D. (1995). Neuronal plasticity and learning. In R. D. Broadwell (Ed.), *Neuroscience, memory, and language. Decade of the brain, Vol. 1.* Washington, DC: U.S. Government Printing Office.

Kandel, E. R., & Schwartz, J. H. (1982). Molecular biology of learning: Modulation or transmitter release. *Science, 218,* 433–442.

Kandel, E. R., Siegelbaum, S. A., & Schwartz, J. H. (1991). Synaptic transmission. In E. R. Kandel, J. H. Schwartz, & T. M. Jessell (Eds.), *Principles of neural science* (3rd ed.). New York: Elsevier.

Kane, J. M. (1992). *Tardive dyskinesia.* Washington, DC: American Psychiatric Association Press.

Kaniasty, K., & Norris, F. H. (1995, June). Mobilization and deterioration of social support following natural disasters. *Current Directions in Psychological Science, 4,* 94–98.

Kanigel, R. (1987, May 17). One man's mousetraps. *New York Times Magazine,* 48–54.

Kanner, A. D., Coyne, J. C., Schaefer, C., & Lazarus, R. (1981). Comparison of two modes of stress measurement: Daily hassles and uplifts versus major life events. *Journal of Behavioral Medicine, 4,* 14.

Kanner, B. (1989, May 8). Mind games. *New York Magazine,* pp. 34–40.

Kantrowitz, B. (1991, October 21). Striking a nerve. *Newsweek,* pp. 34–40.

Kantrowitz, B. (1992, August 3). Teenagers and AIDS. *Newsweek,* pp. 44–49.

Kaplan, G., & Rogers, L. J. (1994). Race and gender fallacies: The paucity of biological determinist explanations of difference. In E. Tobach, & B. Rossoff (Eds.), *Challenging racism and sexism: Alternatives to genetic explanations. Genes and gender, 7.* New York: Feminist Press at The City University of New York.

Kaplan, H. I., & Sadock, B. J. (Eds.). (1993). *Comprehensive group psychotherapy* (4th ed.). Baltimore: Williams and Wilkins.

Kaplan, H. S. (1974). *The new sex therapy.* New York: Brunner-Mazel.

Kaplan, M. F. (1975). Information integration in social judgment: Interaction of judge and informational components. In M. Kaplan, & S. Schwartz (Eds.), *Human development and decision processes.* New York: Academic Press.

Kaplan, R. M., & Saccuzzo, D. P. (1997). *Psychological testing: Principles, applications, and issues* (4th ed.). Pacific Grove, CA: Brooks/Cole.

Kaplan, R. M., Sallis, J. F., Jr., & Patterson, T. L. (1993). *Health and human behavior.* New York: McGraw-Hill.

Kapur, S., & Remington, G. (1996). Serotonin-dopamine interaction and its relevance to schizophrenia. *American Journal of Psychiatry, 153*, 466–476.

Karbon, M., Fabes, R. A., Carlo, G., & Martin, C. L. (1992). Preschoolers' beliefs about sex and age differences in emotionality. *Sex Roles, 27*, 377–390.

Karlins, M., & Abelson, H. I. (1979). *How opinions and attitudes are changed.* New York: Springer-Verlag.

Karmel, B. Z., & Gardner, J. M. (1996). Prenatal cocaine exposure effects on arousal-modulated attention during the neonatal period. *Developmental Psychology, 29*, 463–480.

Karni, A., Tanne, D., Rubenstein, B. S., Askenazy, J. J. M., & Sagi, D. (1992, October). No dreams—no memory: The effect of REM sleep deprivation on learning a new perceptual skill. *Society for Neuroscience Abstracts, 18*, 387.

Karni, A., Tanne, D., Rubenstein, B. S., Askenazy, J. J. M., & Sagi, D. (1994, July 29). Dependence on REM sleep of overnight improvement of a perceptual skill. *Science, 265*, 679–682.

Karoly, P., & Kanfer, F. H. (1982). *Self-management and behavior change.* New York: Pergamon.

Karp, D. A. (1988). A decade of remembrances: Changing age consciousness between fifty and sixty years old. *The Gerontologist, 28*, 727–738.

Karp, D. A. (1991). A decade of reminders: Changing age consciousness between fifty and sixty years old. In B. B. Hess, & E. W. Markson (Eds.), *Growing old in America* (4th ed.). New Brunswick, NJ: Transaction Publishers.

Kaslow, F. W. (1991). The art and science of family psychology: Retrospective and perspective. *American Psychologist, 46*, 621–626.

Kasparov, G. (1996, March 25). The day that I sense a new kind of intelligence. *Time*, p. 55.

Kassin, S. M. (1983). Deposition testimony and the surrogate witness: Evidence for a "messenger effect" in persuasion. *Personality and Social Psychology Bulletin, 9*, 281–288.

Katigbak, M. S., & Akamine, T. X. (1994, August). Relating indigenous Philippine dimension to the big five model. Paper presented at the 102nd Annual Convention of the American Psychological Association, Los Angeles, CA.

Katz, A. N. (1989). Autobiographical memory as a reconstructive process: An extension of Ross's hypothesis. *Canadian Journal of Psychology, 43*, 512–517.

Katz, D., & Braly, K. W. (1933). Racial stereotypes of 100 college students. *Journal of Abnormal and Social Psychology, 4*, 280–290.

Katz, P. A. (Ed.). (1976). *Towards the elimination of racism.* New York: Pergamon.

Kaufman, J., & Zigler, E. (1987). Do abused children become abusive parents? *American Journal of Orthopsychiatry, 57*, 186–192.

Kaufman, M. T. (1992, November 28). Teaching compassion in theater of death. *New York Times.*

Kausler, D. H. (1994). *Learning and memory in normal aging.* San Diego, CA: Academic.

Kavanaugh, R. D., Zimmerberg, B., & Fein, S. (Eds.). (1995). *Emotion: Interdisciplinary perspectives.* Mahwah, NJ: Erlbaum.

Kawachi, I., Colditz, G. A., Speizer, F. E., Manson, J. E., Stampfer, M. J., Willett, W. C., & Hennekens, C. H. (1997). A prospective study of passive smoking and coronary heart disease. *Circulation, 95*, 2374–2379.

Kawasaki, C., Nugent, J. K., Miyashita, H., Miyahara, H., et al. (1994). The cultural organization of infants' sleep. Special Issue: Environments of birth and infancy. *Children's Environment, 11*, 135–141.

Kay, F. M., & Hagan, J. (1995). The persistent glass ceiling: Gendered inequalities in the earnings of lawyers. *British Journal of Sociology, 46*, 279–310.

Kazdin, A. E. (1989). *Behavior modification in applied settings* (4th ed.). Pacific Grove, CA: Brooks/Cole.

Kazdin, A. E. (1993). Psychotherapy for children and adolescents: Current progress and future research directions. *American Psychologist, 48*, 644–657.

Kazdin, A. E. (1994). *Behavior modification in applied settings* (5th ed.). Pacific Grove, CA: Brooks/Cole.

Keating, D. P., & Clark, L. V. (1980). Development of physical and social reasoning in adolescence. *Developmental Psychology, 16*, 23–30.

Keefe, K., & Berndt, T. J. (1996). Relations of friendship quality to self-esteem in early adolescence. *Journal of Early Adolescence, 16*, 110–129.

Keehn, J. D. (1996). *Master builders of modern psychology: From Freud to Skinner.* New York: New York University Press.

Keesey, R. E., & Powley, T. L. (1986). The regulation of body weight. *Annual Review of Psychology, 37*, 109–133.

Keith, S., Regier, D., Rae, D., & Matthews, S. (1992). The prevalence of schizophrenia: Analysis of demographic features, symptom patterns, and course. In A. Z. Schwartzberg, A. H. Essman, S. C. Feinstein, & S. Lebovici (Eds.), *International annals of adolescent psychiatry*, Vol. 2. Chicago: University of Chicago Press.

Keith, S. J., Regier, D. A., & Rae, D. S. (1991). Schizophrenic disorders. In L. N. Robins, & D. A. Regier (Eds.), *Psychiatric disorders in America.* New York: Free Press.

Kellegrew, D. H. (1995). Integrated school placements for children with disabilities. In R. L. Koegel, & L. K. Koegel (Eds.), *Teaching children with autism: Strategies for initiating positive interactions and improving learning opportunities.* Baltimore, MD: Brookes.

Keller, M. C., & Young, R. K. (1996). Mate assortment in dating and married couples. *Personality and Individual Differences, 21*, 217–221.

Kelley, H. (1950). The warm-cold variable in first impressions of persons. *Journal of Personality and Social Psychology, 18*, 431–439.

Kelley, H. H. (1992). Common-sense psychology and scientific psychology. *Annual Review of Psychology, 43*, 1–23.

Kelley, J., & Evans, M. D. (1993). The legitimation of inequality: Occupational earnings in nine nations. *American Journal of Sociology, 99*, 75–125.

Kelly, D. D. (1991a). Disorders of sleep and consciousness. In E. R. Kandel, J. H. Schwartz, & T. M. Jessell (Eds.), *Principles of neural science* (3rd ed.). New York: Elsevier.

Kelly, D. D. (1991b). Sexual differentiation of the nervous system. In E. R. Kandel, J. H. Schwartz, & T. M. Jessell (Eds.), *Principles of neural science* (3rd ed.). New York: Elsevier.

Kelly, D. D. (1991c). Sleep and dreaming. In E. R. Kandel, J. H. Schwartz, & T. M. Jessell (Eds.), *Principles of neural science* (3rd ed.). New York: Elsevier.

Kelly, E. S. (1997, January 22). The latest in take-at-home tests: I.Q. *New York Times*, p. B7.

Kelly, J. A. (1995). *Changing HIV risk behavior: Practical strategies.* New York: Guilford Press.

Kelly, J. A., & Kalichman, S. C. (1995). Increased attention to human sexuality can improve HIV-AIDS prevention efforts: Key research issues and directions. *Journal of Consulting and Clinical Psychology, 63*, 907–918.

Kelly, J. A., Murphy, D. A., Sikkema, K. J., & Kalichman, S. C. (1993). Psychological interventions to prevent HIV infection are urgently needed. *American Psychologist, 48*, 1023–1034.

Kelly, J. P. (1991). The sense of balance. In E. R. Kandel, J. H. Schwartz, & T. M. Jessell (Eds.), *Principles of neural science* (3rd ed.). New York: Elsevier.

Kempton, W., Darley, J. M., & Stern, P. C. (1992). Psychological research for the new energy problems: Strategies and opportunities. *American Psychologist, 47*, 1213–1223.

Kendall, P. C. (Ed.). (1991). *Child and adolescent therapy: Cognitive-behavioral procedures.* New York: Guilford Press.

Kendler, K. S. (1996). Parenting: A genetic-epidemiologic perspective. *American Journal of Psychiatry, 153*, 11–20.

Kendler, K. S., MacLean, C. J., O'Neill, A., & Burke, J. (1996). Evidence for a schizophrenia vulnerability locus on chromosome 8p in the Irish study of high-density schizophrenia families. *American Journal of Psychiatry, 153*, 1534–1540.

Kenny, D. A. (1991). A general model of consensus and accuracy in interpersonal perception. *Psychological Review, 98*, 155–163.

Kenny, D. A. (1994). *Interpersonal perception.* New York: Guilford Press.

Kerns, K. A., & Barth, J. M. (1995). Attachment and play: Convergence across components of parent-child relationships and their relations to peer competence. *Journal of Social and Personal Relationships, 12,* 243–260.

Kershner, R. (1996). Adolescent attitudes about rape. *Adolescence, 31,* 29–33.

Kertesz, A. E. (1983). Cyclofusion and stereopsis. *Perception and Psychophysics, 33,* 99–101.

Kessler, R. C., McGonagle, K. A., Zhao, S., Nelson, C. B., Hughes, M., Eshleman, S., Wittchen, H., & Kendler, K. S. (1994). Lifetime and 12-month prevalence of DSM-III-R psychiatric disorders in the United States. *Archives of General Psychiatry, 51,* 8–19.

Kety, S. S. (1996). Genetic and environmental factors in the etiology of schizophrenia. In S. Matthysse, D. L. Levy, J. Kagan, & F. M. Benes (Eds.), *Psychopathology: The evolving science of mental disorder.* New York: Cambridge University Press.

Keyes, R. (1980). *The height of your life.* Boston: Little, Brown.

Kidwell, J. S., Dunham, R. M., Bacho, R. A., Pastorino, E., et al. (1995). Adolescent identity exploration: A test of Erikson's theory of transitional crisis. *Adolescence, 30,* 785–793.

Kiecolt-Glaser, J. K., & Glaser, R. (1986). Behavioral influences on immune function: Evidence for the interplay between stress and health. In T. Field, P. McCabe, & N. Schneiderman (Eds.), *Stress and coping* (Vol. 2). Mahwah, NJ: Erlbaum.

Kienker, P. K., Sejnowski, T. J., Hinton, G. E., & Schumacher, L. E. (1986). Separating figure from ground with a parallel network. *Perception, 15,* 197–216.

Kiesler, C. A., & Simpkins, C. (1991, June). The de facto national system of psychiatric inpatient care. *American Psychologist, 46,* 579–584.

Kiesler, C. A., & Simpkins, C. G. (1993). *The unnoticed majority in psychiatric inpatient care.* New York: Plenum.

Kiesler, S. (Ed.). (1996). *Culture of the Internet.* Mahwah, NJ: Erlbaum.

Kihlstrom, J. F. (1987, September 18). The cognitive unconscious. *Science, 237,* 1445–1452.

Kihlstrom, J. F., Schacter, D. L., Cork, R. C., Hurt, C. A., & Behr, S. E. (1990). Implicit and explicit memory following surgical anesthesia. *Psychological Science, 1,* 303–306.

Kilborn, K., Lynch, G., & Granger, R. (1996). Effects of LTP on response selectivity of simulated cortical neurons. *Journal of Cognitive Neuroscience, 8,* 328–343.

Killen, M., & Hart, D. (Eds.). (1995). *Morality in everyday life: Developmental perspectives.* Cambridge, England: Cambridge University Press.

Kilpatrick, D. G., Edmunds, C. S., & Seymour, A. K. (1992, November 13). *Rape in America: A report to the nation.* Arlington, VA: National Victims Center and Medical University of South Carolina.

Kim, J., Allen, C. T., & Kardes, F. R. (1996). An investigation of the mediational mechanisms underlying attitudinal conditioning. *Journal of Marketing Research, 33,* 318–328.

Kim, U., Triandis, H. C., Kagitcibasi, C., & Yoon, G. (1994). *Individualism and collectivism: Theory, method, and applications.* Newbury Park, CA: Sage.

Kimble, G. A. (1989). Psychology from the standpoint of a generalist. *American Psychologist, 44,* 491–499.

Kimble, G. A. (1994). A frame of reference for psychology. *American Psychologist, 49,* 510–519.

Kimchi, R. (1992). Primacy of wholistic processing and global/local paradigm: A critical review. *Psychological Bulletin, 112,* 24–38.

Kimmel, A. J. (1996). *Ethical issues in behavioral research: A survey.* Oxford, England: Blackwell.

Kimura, D. (1992, September). Sex differences in the brain. *Scientific American,* pp. 119–125.

Kimura, D. (1999). *Sex and Cognition.* Cambridge, Mass: Bradford.

Kimura, D., & Hampson, E. (1988). Reciprocal effects of hormonal fluctuations on human motor and perceptual-spatial skills. *Behavioral Neuroscience, 102,* 456–459.

Kimura, D., & Hampson, E. (1994). Cognitive pattern in men and women is influenced by fluctuations in sex hormones. *Current Directions in Psychological Science, 3,* 57–61.*

King, G. R., & Logue, A. W. (1990). Humans' sensitivity to variation in reinforcer amount: Effects of the method of reinforcer delivery. *Journal of the Experimental Analysis of Behavior, 53,* 33–46.

King, S. H. (1993). The limited presence of African American teachers. *Review of Educational Research, 63,* 114–149.

Kingstone, A., Enns, J. T., Mangun, G. R., Gazzaniga, M. S. (1995). Guided visual search is a left-hemisphere process in split-brain patients. *Psychological Science, 6(2),* 118–121.*

Kinsey, A. C., Pomeroy, W. B., & Martin, C. E. (1948). *Sexual behavior in the human male.* Philadelphia: Saunders.

Kinsey, A. C., Pomeroy, W. B., Martin, C. E., & Gebhard, P. H. (1953). *Sexual behavior in the human female.* Philadelphia: Saunders.

Kirby, D. (1977). The methods and methodological problems of sex research. In J. S. DeLora, & C. A. B. Warren (Eds.), *Understanding sexual interaction.* Boston: Houghton Mifflin.

Kirk, S. A. (1992). *The selling of DSM: The rhetoric of science in psychiatry.* Hawthorne, NY: Aldine de Gruyter.

Kirmayer, L. J., Fletcher, C., & Boothroyd, L. J. (1998). Suicide among the Inuit of Canada. In A. A. Leenaars, S. Wenckstern, I. Sakinofsky, R. J. Dyck, M. J. Kral, & R. C. Bland (Eds.), *Suicide in Canada* (pp. 189–211). Toronto: University of Toronto Press.*

Kirsch, B. (1989, October 8). Breaking the sound barrier. *New York Times Magazine,* pp. 64–66, 68–70.

Kirsch, I., & Council, J. R. (1992). Situational and personality correlates of suggestibility. In E. Fromm, & M. Nash (Eds.), *Contemporary perspectives in hypnosis research.* New York: Guilford Press.

Kirsch, I., & Lynn, S. J. (1995). The altered state of hypnosis: Changes in the theoretical landscape. *American Psychologist, 50,* 846–858.

Kirsch, I., & Lynn, S. J. (1998). Dissociation theories of hypnosis. *Psychological Bulletin, 123,* 100–115.

Kirshner, H. S. (1995). Alexias. In H. S. Kirshner (Ed.), *Handbook of neurological speech and language disorders. Neurological disease and therapy, Vol. 33.* New York: Dekker.

Kislevsky, B. S., Muir, D. W., & Low, J. A. (2000). Maturation of human fetal responses to vibroacoustic stimulation. In D. Muir & A. Slater (Eds.), *Infant development: The essential readings.* Oxford: Blackwell Publishers.*

Kitani, K., Aoba, A., & Goto, S. (Eds.). (1996). *Pharmacological intervention in aging and age-associated disorders. Annals of the New York Academy of Sciences, 786.* New York: New York Academy of Sciences.

Kitayama, S., & Markus, H. R. (Eds.). (1994). *Emotion and culture: Empirical studies of mutual influence.* Washington, DC: American Psychological Association.

Kitcher, P. (1997). *The lives to come.* New York: Touchstone Books.

Kitterle, F. L. (Ed.). (1991). *Cerebral laterality: Theory and research.* Mahwah, NJ: Erlbaum.

Klatzky, R. L., Colledge, R. G., Loomis, J. M., Cicinelli, J. G., et al. (1995). Performance of blind and sighted persons on spatial tasks. *Journal of Visual Impairment and Blindness, 89,* 70–82.

Klein, S. B., & Mowrer, R. R. (1989). *Contemporary learning theories, instrumental conditioning theory and the impact of biological constraints on learning.* Mahwah, NJ: Erlbaum.

Kleinke, C. L., Peterson, T. R., & Rutledge, T. R. (1998). Effects of self-generated facial expressions on mood. *Journal of Personality and Social Psychology, 74,* 272–279.

Kleinman, A. (1991, July). The psychiatry of culture and culture of psychiatry. *Harvard Mental Health Letter.*

Kleinman, A. (1996). How is culture important for DSM-IV? In J. E. Mezzich, A. Kleinman, H. Fabrega, Jr., & D. L. Parron (Eds.), *Culture and psychiatric diagnosis: A DSM-IV perspective.* Washington, DC: American Psychiatric Press, Inc.

Klineberg, O. (1990). A personal perspective on the development of social psychology. *Annals of the New York Academy of Sciences, 602,* 35–50.

Klinkenborg, V. (1997, January 5). Awakening to sleep. *New York Times Magazine,* pp. 26–31, 41, 51, 55.

Kluft, R. P. (1996). Dissociative identity disorder. In L. K. Michelson, & W. J. Ray (Eds.), *Handbook of dissociation: Theoretical, empirical, and clinical perspectives.* New York: Plenum.

Kluger, J. (1996, November 25). Can we stay young? *Time*, pp. 89–98.

Knapp, R. B., & Lusted, H. S. (1992). Biocontrollers for the physically disabled: A direct link from nervous system to computer. In H. J. Murphy (Ed.), *Virtual reality and persons with disabilities: Proceedings*. California State University.

Knight, G. P., Johnson, L. G., Carlo, G., & Eisenberg, N. (1994). A multiplicative model of the dispositional antecedents of prosocial behavior: Predicting more of the people more of the time. *Journal of Personality and Social Psychology, 66*, 178–183.

Knittle, J. L. (1975). Early influences on development of adipose tissue. In G. A. Bray (Ed.), *Obesity in perspective*. Washington, DC: U.S. Government Printing Office.

Kobasa, S. C. (1979). Stressful life events, personality, and health: An inquiry into hardiness. *Journal of Personality and Social Psychology, 37*, 1–11.

Kobasa, S. C. O., Maddi, S. R., Puccetti, M. C., & Zola, M. A. (1994). Effectiveness of hardiness, exercise, and social support as resources against illness. In A. Steptoe, & J. Wardle (Eds.), *Psychosocial processes and health: A reader*. Cambridge, England: Cambridge University Press.

Koch, S. (1993). "Psychology" or "The psychological studies"? *American Psychologist, 48*, 902–904.

Koester, J. (1991). Membrane potential. In E. R. Kandel, J. H. Schwartz, & T. M. Jessell (Eds.), *Principles of neural science* (3rd ed.). New York: Elsevier.

Kohlberg, L. (1969). Stage and sequence: The cognitive-developmental approach to socialization. In D. Goslin (Ed.), *Handbook of socialization theory and research*. Chicago: Rand McNally.

Kohlberg, L. (1984). *The psychology of moral development: Essays on moral development* (Vol. 2). San Francisco: Harper & Row.

Kohlberg, L., & Ryncarz, R. A. (1990). Beyond justice reasoning: Moral development and consideration of a seventh stage. In C. N. Alexander, & E. J. Langer (Eds.), *Higher stages of human development: Perspectives on adult growth*. New York: Oxford University Press.

Köhler, W. (1927). *The mentality of apes*. London: Routledge & Kegan Paul.

Kohn, A. (1990). *You know what they say*. New York: HarperCollins.

Kohn, A. (1996). By all available means: Cameron and Pierce's defense of extrinsic motivators. *Review of Educational Research, 66*, 1–4.

Kohn, P. M., Lafreniere, K., & Genrevich, M. (1991). Hassles, health, and personality. *Journal of Personality and Social Psychology, 61*, 478–482.*

Kohn, P. M., & Macdonald, J. E. (1992). Hassles, anxiety, and negative well-being. *Anxiety, stress and coping, 5*, 151–163.*

Kolata, G. (1987, May 15). Early signs of school-age IQ. *Science, 236*, 774–775.

Kolata, G. (1988, February 25). New obesity studies indicate metabolism is often to blame. *New York Times*, pp. A1, B5.

Kolata, G. (1991, May 15). Drop in casual sex tied to AIDS peril. *New York Times*.

Kolata, G. (1993, February 28). Rethinking the statistics of "epidemic" breast cancer. *New York Times*.

Kolata, G. (1995, March 16). Parkinson's sufferers gamble on surgery with great risks. *New York Times*, p. A1.

Kolb, B. (1999). The twentieth century belongs to neuropsychology. *Brain Research Bulletin, 50*, 409–410.*

Kolb, B., & Whishaw, I. Q. (1990). *Fundamentals of human neuropsychology* (3rd ed.). New York: Freeman.*

Konishi, M. (1993, April). Listening with two ears. *Scientific American*, pp. 66–73.

Konner, M. (1988, January 17). Caffeine high. *New York Times Magazine*, pp. 47–48.

Konrad, W. (1994, April). Ten things your doctor won't tell you. (Report of study in *Annals of Internal Medicine*). *Smart Money*, p. 76.

Koop, C. B. (1994). Infant assessment. In C. B. Fisher, & R. M. Lerner (Eds.), *Applied developmental psychology*. New York: McGraw-Hill.

Koop, C. E. (1988). *The health consequences of smoking*. Washington, DC: Government Printing Office.

Korb, M. P., Gorrell, J., & VanDeRiet, V. (1989). *Gestalt therapy: Practice and theory* (2nd ed.). New York: Pergamon.

Korpan, C. A., Bisanz, G. L., Bisanz, J., & Henderson, J. (1997). Assessing literacy in science: Evaluation of scientific news briefs. *Science Education, 81*, 515–532.*

Korpan, C., Bisanz, G. L., Bisanz, J., Boehme, C. & Lynch, M. N. (1997). What did you learn outside of school today? Using unstructured interviews to document home and community activities related to science and technology. *Science Education 81*, 651–662.*

Korsch, B. M., & Negrete, V. F. (1972). Doctor-patient communication. *Scientific American*, pp. 66–74.

Kosambi, D. D. (1967). Living prehistory in India. *Scientific American*, p. 105.

Kosik, K. S. (1992, May 8). Alzheimer's disease: A cell biological perspective. *Science, 256*, 780–783.

Koss, M. P. (1993). Rape: Scope, impact, interventions, and public policy responses. *American Psychologist, 48*, 1062–1069.

Koss, M. P., & Burkhart, B. R. (1989). A conceptual analysis of rape victimization. *Psychology of Women Quarterly, 13*, 27–40.

Koss, M. P., & Butcher, J. N. (1986). Research on brief psychotherapy. In S. L. Garfield, & A. E. Bergin (Eds.), *Handbook of psychotherapy and behavior change* (3rd ed.). New York: Wiley.

Koss, M. P., Dinero, T. E., Seibel, C. A., & Cox, S. L. (1988). Stranger and acquaintance rape: Are there differences in the victim's experience? *Psychology of Women Quarterly, 12*, 1–24.

Kosslyn, S. M. (1981). The medium and the message in mental imagery. *Psychological Review, 88*, 46–66.

Kosslyn, S. M., Seger, C., Pani, J. R., & Hillger, L. A. (1990). When is imagery used in everyday life? A diary study. *Journal of Mental Imagery, 14*, 131–152.

Kosslyn, S. M., & Shin, L. M. (1994). Visual mental images in the brain: Current issues. In M. J. Farah, & G. Ratcliff (Eds.), *The neuropsychology of high-level vision: Collected tutorial essays. Carnegie Mellon symposia on cognition*. Mahwah, NJ: Erlbaum.

Kostses, H., et al. (1991). Long-term effects of biofeedback-induced facial relaxation on measures of asthma severity in children. *Biofeedback and Self-Regulation, 16*, 1–22.

Kotkin, M., Daviet, C., & Gurin, J. (1996, October). Comment. *American Psychologist, 51*, 1080–1088.

Kotler, P. (1986). *Principles of marketing* (3rd ed.). Englewood Cliffs, NJ: Prentice-Hall.

Kotler-Cope, S., & Camp, C. J. (1990). Memory interventions in aging populations. In E. A. Lovelace (Ed.), *Aging and cognition: Mental processes, self-awareness, and interventions. Advances in psychology*. Amsterdam, Netherlands: North-Holland.

Kotre, J., & Hall, E. (1990). *Seasons of life*. Boston: Little, Brown.

Kotulak, R. (1995, January 7). Memory drug is probable in near future. *The Arizona Daily Star*, pp. 1, 16A.

Koveces, Z. (1987). *The container metaphor of emotion*. Paper presented at the University of Massachusetts, Amherst.

Kowner, R., & Ogawa, T. (1995). The role of raters' sex, personality, and appearance in judgments of facial beauty. *Perceptual & Motor Skills, 81*, 339–349.

Kozma, A., Stones, M. J., & McNeil, J. K. (1991). *Psychological well-being in later life*. Toronto: Butterworths Canada.*

Kraines, S. H. (1948). *The therapy of the neuroses and psychoses* (3rd ed.). Philadelphia: Lea & Febiger.

Kramer, P. (1993). *Listening to Prozac*. New York: Viking.

Krantz, D. S., Glass, D. C., Schaeffer, M. A., & Davia, J. E. (1982). Behavior patterns and coronary disease: A critical evaluation. In J. T. Cacioppo, & R. E. Petty (Eds.), *Focus on cardiovascular psychophysiology* (pp. 315–346). New York: Guilford Press.

Kraus, S. J. (1995, January). Attitudes and the prediction of behavior: A meta-analysis of the empirical literature. *Personality and Social Psychology Bulletin, 21*, 58–75.

Kravitz, E. A. (1988). Hormonal control of behavior: Amines and the biasing of behavioral output in lobsters. *Science, 241*, 1775–1782.

Krechevsky, M., & Gardner, H. (1990). The emergence and nurturance of multiple intelligences: The Project Spectrum approach. In M. J. A. Howe (Ed.), *Encouraging the development of exceptional skills and talents*. Leicester, England: British Psychological Society.

Kremer, J. M. D., & Scully, D. M. (1994). *Psychology in sport*. London, England: Taylor & Francis.

Kreuger, L. E. (1989). *The world of touch*. Mahwah, NJ: Erlbaum.

Kriz, J. (1995). Naturwissenschaftliche Konzepte in der gegenwartigen Diskussion zum Problem der Ordnung. (The contribution of natural science concepts to the current discussion of order.) *Gestalt Theory, 17,* 153–163.

Krohne, H. W. (1996). Individual differences in coping. In M. Zeidner, & N. S. Endler (Eds.), *Handbook of coping: Theory, research, applications.* New York: Wiley.

Kruger, A. (1994). The midlife transition: Crisis or chimera? *Psychological Reports, 75,* 1299–1305.

Kruger, L. (Ed.). (1996). *Pain and touch.* New York: Academic Press.

Kruglanski, A. W., Freund, T., & Bar Tal, D. (1996). Motivational effects in the mere-exposure paradigm. *European Journal of Social Psychology, 26,* 479–499.

Krull, D. S., & Anderson, C. A. (1997). The process of explanation. *Current Directions in Psychological Science, 6,* 1–5.

Kryger, M. H., Roos, L., Delaive, K., Walld, R., & Horrocks, J. (1996). Utilization of health-care services in patients with severe obstructive sleep apnea. *Sleep, 19 (Suppl.),* S111–S116.

Kryzanowski, E., & Stewin, L. (1985). Developmental implications in youth counseling: Gender socialization. *International Journal for the Advancement of Counseling, 8,* 265–278.

Kübler-Ross, E. (1969). *On death and dying.* New York: Macmillan.

Kubovy, M., & Wagemans, J. (1995). Grouping by proximity and multistability in dot lattices: A quantitative gestalt theory. *Psychological Science, 6,* 225–233.

Kubzansky, L. D., Kawachi, I, Spria, A., III, Weiss, S. T., Vokonas, P. S., & Sparrow, D. (1997). Is worrying bad for your heart? A prospective study of worry and coronary heart disease in the Normative Aging Study. *Circulation, 95,* 818–824.

Kucharski, D., & Hall, W. G. (1987). New routes to early memories. *Science, 238,* 786–788.

Kuczmarski, R. J., Flegal, K. M., Campbell, S. M., & Johnson, C. L. (1994, July 20). Increasing prevalence of overweight among U.S. adults. *Journal of the American Medical Association, 272,* 205–211.

Kuhl, P. K., Williams, K. A., Lacerda, F., Stevens, K. N., & Lindblom, B. (1992, January 31). Linguistic experience alters phonetic perception in infants by 6 months of age. *Science, 255,* 606–608.

Kulik, J. A., Bangert-Drowns, R. L., & Kulik, C. C. (1984). Effectiveness of coaching for aptitude tests. *Psychological Bulletin, 95,* 179–188.

Kulynych, J. J., Vladar, K., Jones, D. W., & Weinberger, D. R. (1994). Gender differences in the normal lateralization of the supratemporal cortex: MRI surface-rendering morphometry of Heschl's gyrus and the planum temporale. *Cerebral Cortex, 4,* 107–118.

Kumpfer, K. L., & Alvarado, R. (1995). Strengthening families to prevent drug use in multiethnic youth. In G. J. Botvin, S. Schinke, and M. A. Orlandi (Eds.), *Drug abuse prevention with multiethnic youth* (pp. 255–294). Thousand Oakes, CA: Sage.*

Kupfer, D. J., Reynolds, C. F., III. (1997, January 30). Management of insomnia. *New England Journal of Medicine, 336,* 341–346.

Kupfermann, I. (1991a). Hypothalamus and limbic system: Motivation. In E. R. Kandel, J. H. Schwartz, & T. M. Jessell (Eds.), *Principles of neural science* (3rd ed.). New York: Elsevier.

Kupfermann, I. (1991b). Hypothalamus and limbic system: Peptidergic neurons, homeostasis, and emotional behavior. In E. R. Kandel, J. H. Schwartz, & T. M. Jessell (Eds.), *Principles of neural science* (3rd ed.). New York: Elsevier.

Kupfermann, I. (1991c). Localization of higher cognitive and affective functions: The association cornices. In E. R. Kandel, J. H. Schwartz, & T. M. Jessell (Eds.), *Principles of neural science* (3rd ed.). New York: Elsevier.

Kupfermann, I. (1991d). Genetic determinants of behavior. In E. R. Kandel, J. H. Schwartz, & T. M. Jessell (Eds.), *Principles of neural science* (3rd ed.). New York: Elsevier.

Kurdek, L. A. (1993). The allocation of household labor in gay, lesbian, and heterosexual married couples. *Journal of Social Issues, 49,* 127–139.

Kuriki, S., Takeuchi, F., & Kobayashki, T. (1994). Characteristics of the background fields in multichannel-recorded magnetic field responses. *Electroencephalography and Clinical Neurophysiology Evoked Potentials, 92,* 56–63.

Kurtz, L. (1994). Psychosocial coping resources in elementary school-age children of divorce. *American Journal of Orthopsychiatry, 64,* 554–563.

Kvale, S. (1996). *Interviews: An introduction to qualitative research interviewing.* Newbury Park, CA: Sage.

Labrell, F. (1996). Paternal play with toddlers: Recreation and creation. *European Journal of Psychology of Education, 11,* 43–54.

Lacayo, R. (1997, January 6). *Time,* pp. 82–85.

Ladd, G. W. (1990). Having friends, keeping friends, making friends, and being liked by peers in the classroom: Predictors of children's early school adjustment? *Child Development, 61,* 1081–1100.

Ladouceur, R. (1996). The prevalence of pathological gambling in Canada. *Journal of Gambling Studies, 12,* 129–142.*

Ladouceur, R., Boisvert, J., & Dumont, J. (1994). Cognitive-behavioural treatment for adolescent gamblers. *Behaviour Modification, 18,* 230–242.*

Ladouceur, R., & Mireault, C. (1988). Gambling behaviours among high school students in the Quebec area. *Journal of Gambling Behaviour, 4,* 3–12.*

Ladouceur, R., Sylvain, C., Letarte, H., Giroux, I., & Jacques, C. (1998). Cognitive treatment of pathological gamblers. *Behaviour Research and Therapy, 36,* 1111–1119.*

LaFromboise, T., Coleman, H. L., & Gerton, J. (1993). Psychological impact of biculturalism: Evidence and theory. *Psychological Bulletin, 114,* 395–412.

LaGreca, A. M., Silverman, W. K., Vernberg, E. M., & Prinstein, M. J. (1996). Symptoms of post-traumatic stress in children after Hurricane Andrew: A prospective study. *Journal of Consulting and Clinical Psychology, 64,* 712–723.

Laird, J. D., & Bresler, C. (1990). William James and the mechanisms of emotional experience. *Personality and Social Psychology Bulletin, 16,* 636–651.

Laird, J. D., & Bresler, C. (1992). The process of emotional experience: A self-perception theory. In M. S. Clark (Ed.), *Review of personality and social psychology.* Newbury Park, CA: Sage.

Lakowski, B., & Hekimi, S. (1996, May 17). Determination of life-span in caenorhabditis elegans by four clock genes. *Science, 272,* 1010.

Lamal, P. A. (1979). College students' common beliefs about psychology. *Teaching of Psychology, 6,* 155–158.

Lamb, M. (1982). The bonding phenomenon: Misinterpretations and their implications. *Journal of Pediatrics, 101,* 555–557.

Lamb, M. E. (Ed.). (1987). *The father's role.* Mahwah, NJ: Erlbaum.

Lamb, M. E. (1996). Effects of nonparental child care on child development: An update. *Canadian Journal of Psychiatry, 41,* 330–342.

Lambert, M. J., Shapiro, D. A., & Bergin, A. E. (1986). The effectiveness of psychotherapy. In S. L. Garfield, & A. E. Bergin (Eds.), *Handbook of psychotherapy and behavior change* (3rd ed.). New York: Wiley.

Lambert, W. E., & Anisfeld, E. (1969). A note on the relationship of bilingualism and intelligence. *Canadian Journal of Behavioural Science, 1,* 123–128.*

Lambert, W. E., & Peal, E. (1972). The relation of bilingualism to intelligence. In A. S. Dil (Ed.), *Language, psychology, and culture.* Stanford, CA: Stanford University Press.

Lambert, W. E., & Tucker, G. R. (1972). *Bilingual education in children: The St. Lambert experiment.* Rowley, MA: Newbury House.*

Lambert, W. W. (1971). *Comparative perspectives on social psychology.* Boston: Little, Brown.

LaMendola, N. P., & Bever, T. G. (1997, October 17). Peripheral and cerebral asymmetries in the rat. *Science, 278,* 483–486.

Lamerson, C. D., & Kelloway, E. K. (1996). Towards a model of peacekeeping stress: Traumatic and Contextual Influences. *Canadian Psychology, 37,* 195–204.*

Lancaster, L., Royal, K. E., & Whiteside, H. D. (1995). Attitude similarity and evaluation of a women's athletic team. *Journal of Social Behavior and Personality, 10,* 885–890.

Landesman, S., & Ramey, C. (1989). Developmental psychology and mental retardation: Integrating scientific principles with treatment practices. *American Psychologist, 44,* 409–415.

Landis, D., Day, H. R., McGrew, P. L., Thomas, J. A., & Miller, A. B. (1976). Can a black "culture assimilator" increase racial understanding? *Journal of Social Issues, 32,* 169–183.

Landry, D. W. (1997, February). Immunotherapy for cocaine addiction. *Scientific American*, 41–45.

Lang, J. S. (1987, April 13). Happiness is a reunited set of twins. *U.S. News & World Report*, pp. 63–66.

Lang, S. S., & Patt, R. B. (1994). *You don't have to suffer*. New York: Oxford University Press.

Langer, E., Bashner, R. S., & Chanowitz, B. (1985). Decreasing prejudice by increasing discrimination. *Journal of Personality and Social Psychology, 49,* 113–120.

Langer, E., & Janis, I. (1979). *The psychology of control*. Beverly Hills, CA: Sage.

Langer, E., Janis, I. L., & Wolfer, J. A. (1975). Reduction of psychological stress in surgical patients. *Journal of Experimental Social Psychology, 11,* 155–165.

Langer, E. J. (1983). *The psychology of control*. Beverly Hills, CA: Sage.

Langreth, R. (1996, August 20). Science yields powerful new therapies for pain. *Wall Street Journal*, pp. B1, B4.

Larroque, B., Kaminski, M., Dehaene, P., Subtil, D., et al. (1995). Moderate prenatal alcohol exposure and psychomotor development at preschool age. *American Journal of Public Health, 85,* 1654–1661.

Larsen, R. J., & Diener, E. (1987). Affect intensity as an individual characteristic: A review. *Journal of Research in Personality, 21,* 1–39.

Larsen, R. J., Kasimatis, M., & Frey, K. (1992). Facilitating the furrowed brow: An unobtrusive test of the facial feedback hypothesis applied to unpleasant affect. *Cognition and Emotion, 6,* 321–338.

Larson, R. K. (1990). Semantics. In D. N. Osherson, & H. Lasnik (Eds.), *Language*. Cambridge, MA: MIT Press.

Larson, R. W., Richards, M. H., & Perry-Jenkins, M. (1994). Divergent worlds: The daily emotional experience of mothers and fathers in the domestic and public spheres. *Journal of Personality and Social Psychology, 67,* 1034–1046.

Lashley, K. S. (1950). In search of the engram. *Symposia of the Society for Experimental Biology, 4,* 454–482.

Lask, B., & Bryant-Waugh, R. (Eds.). (1993). *Childhood onset of anorexia nervosa and related eating disorders*. Mahwah, NJ: Erlbaum.

Lasnik, H. (1990). Syntax. In D. N. Osherson, & H. Lasnik (Eds.), *Language*. Cambridge, MA: MIT Press.

Lassner, J. B., Matthews, K. A., & Stoney, C. M. (1994). Are cardiovascular reactors to asocial stress also reactors to social stress? *Journal of Personality and Social Psychology, 66,* 69–77.

Latané, B., & Darley, J. M. (1970). *The unresponsive bystander: Why doesn't he help?* New York: Appleton-Century-Crofts.

Latané, B., & Nida, S. (1981). Ten years of research on group size and helping. *Psychological Bulletin, 89,* 308–324.

Lau, R. R. (1997). Cognitive representation of health and illness. In D. S. Gochman (Ed.), *Handbook of health behavior research*. New York: Plenum Press.

Laumann, E., Gagnon, J. H., Michael, R. T., & Michaels, S. (1994). *The social organization of sexuality*. Chicago: University of Chicago Press.

Laursen, B., & Collins, W. A. (1994). Interpersonal conflict during adolescence. *Psychological Bulletin, 115,* 197–209.

Laursen, B., Hartup, W. W., & Koplas, A. L. (1996). Towards understanding peer conflict. *Merrill-Palmer Quarterly, 42,* 76–102.

Lautenbacher, S. & Rollman, G. B. (1999). Somatization, hypochondriasis, and related conditions. In A. R. Block, E. F. Kremer, & E. Fernandez (Eds.), *Handbook of Pain syndromes: Biopsychosocial perspectives*. Mahwah, NJ: Erlbaum.*

Laws, G., Davies, I., & Andrews, C. (1995). Linguistic structure and non-linguistic cognition: English and Russian blues compared. *Language and Cognitive Processes, 10,* 59–94.

Lazarus, A. A. (1997). *Brief but comprehensive psychotherapy: The multimodal way*. New York: Springer.

Lazarus, A. A., Beutler, L. E., & Norcross, J. C. (1992). The future of technical eclecticism. *Psychotherapy, 29,* 11–20.

Lazarus, R. (1994). Appraisal: The long and short of it. In P. Ekman, & R. J. Davidson (Eds.), *The nature of emotion: Fundamental questions*. New York: Oxford University Press.

Lazarus, R. S. (1984). On the primacy of cognition. *American Psychologist, 39,* 124–129.

Lazarus, R. S. (1991a). Cognition and motivation in emotion. *American Psychologist, 46,* 352–367.

Lazarus, R. S. (1991b). *Emotion and adaptation*. New York: Oxford University Press.

Lazarus, R. S. (1995). Emotions express a social relationship, but it is an individual mind that creates them. *Psychological Inquiry, 6,* 253–265.

Lazarus, R. S., & Cohen, J. B. (1977). Environmental stress. In I. Altman, & J. F. Wohlwill (Eds.), *Human behavior and the environment: Current theory and research* (Vol. 2). New York: Plenum Press.

Lazarus, R. S., DeLongis, A., Folkman, S., & Gruen, R. (1985). Stress and adaptational outcomes: The problem of confounded measures. *American Psychologist, 40,* 770–779.

Lazarus, R. S., & Lazarus, B. N. (1994). *Passion and reason: Making sense of our emotions*. New York: Oxford University Press.

Leahey, T. H. (1994). Is this a dagger I see before me? Four theorists in search of consciousness. *Contemporary Psychology, 39,* 575–581.

Leary, W. E. (1996, November 20). U.S. rate of sexual diseases highest in developed world. *New York Times*, p. C21.

Lebow, R. N., & Stein, J. G. (1987). Beyond deterrence. *Journal of Social Issues, 43,* 5–71.

Lechtenberg, R. (1982). *The psychiatrist's guide to diseases of the nervous system*. New York: Wiley.

Lee, F., Hallahan, M., & Herzog, T. (1996). Explaining real-life events: How culture and domain shape attributions. *Personality and Social Psychology Bulletin, 22,* 732–741.

Lee, F. R. (1993, October 4). On the campus, testing for AIDS grows common. *New York Times*, pp. A1, B2.

Lee, M. E., Matsumoto, D., Kobayashi, M., Krupp, D., Maniatis, E. F., & Roberts, W. (1992). Cultural influences on nonverbal behavior in applied settings. In R. S. Feldman (Ed.), *Applications of nonverbal behavioral theory and research*. Mahwah, NJ: Erlbaum.

Lee, V. E., Brooks-Gunn, J., Schnur, E., & Liaw, F. (1990). Are Head Start effects sustained? A longitudinal follow-up comparison of disadvantaged children attending Head Start, no preschool, and other preschool programs. *Child Development, 61,* 495–507.

Lee, Y. (1994). Why does American psychology have cultural limitations? *American Psychologist, 49,* 524.

Leenaars, A. A. (1991). Suicide notes and their implications for intervention. *Crisis, 12,* 1–20.

Lefcourt, H. M., & Thomas, S. (1998). Humor and stress revisited. In W. Ruch (Ed.), *The sense of humor*. Berlin: Mouton de Gruyter.*

Leger, F. T. (1998). *Beyond the therapeutic relationship: Behavioural, biological, and cognitive foundations of psychotherapy*. New York: Haworth.*

Lehman, D. R., Lempert, R. O., & Nisbett, R. E. (1988). The effects of graduate training on reasoning: Formal discipline and thinking about everyday-life events. *American Psychologist, 43,* 431–442.

Lehman, D. R., & Taylor, S. E. (1988). Date with an earthquake: Coping with a probable, unpredictable disaster. *Personality and Social Psychology Bulletin, 13,* 546–555.

Lehrer, P. M. (1996). Recent research findings on stress management techniques. In Editorial Board of Hatherleigh Press, *The Hatherleigh guide to issues in modern therapy. The Hatherleigh guides series, Vol. 4*. New York: Hatherleigh Press.

Leibel, R. L., Rosenbaum, M., & Hirsch, J. (1995). Changes in energy expenditure resulting from altered body weight [see comments] [published erratum appears in New England Journal of Medicine 1995 Aug 10;333(6):399] *New England Journal of Medicine, 332,* 621–628.

Leibovic, K. N. (Ed.). 1990. *Science of vision*. New York: Springer-Verlag.

Leigh, H., & Reiser, M. F. (1980). *The patient*. New York: Plenum Press.

Lemoine, P., & Lemoine, P. (1992). Outcome of children of alcoholic mothers (study of 105 cases followed to adult age) and various prophylactic findings. *Annals of Pediatrics—Paris, 39,* 226–235.

Lenhardt, M. L., Skellett, R., Wang, P., & Clarke, A. M. (1991, July 5). Human ultrasonic speech perception. *Science, 253,* 82–85.

Leong, F. T., & Austin, J. T. (Eds.). (1996). *The psychology research handbook: A guide for graduate students and research assistants*. Thousand Oaks, CA: Sage.

Lepore, S. J., Evans, G. W., & Schneider, M. L. (1991). Dynamic role of social support in the link between chronic stress and psychological distress. *Journal of Personality and Social Psychology, 61,* 899–909.

Lepowsky, M. (1994). *Fruit of the motherland: Gender in an egalitarian society.* New York: Columbia University Press.

Lepper, H. S., Martin, L. R., & DiMatteo, M. R. (1995). A model of nonverbal exchange in physician-patient expectations for patient involvement. *Journal of Nonverbal Behavior, 19,* 207–222.

Lepper, M. R., & Greene, D. (1975). Turning play into work: Effects of adult surveillance and extrinsic rewards on children's intrinsic motivation. *Journal of Personality and Social Psychology, 31,* 479–486.

Lepper, M. R., & Greene, D. (Eds.). (1978). *The hidden costs of reward.* Mahwah, NJ: Erlbaum.

Lepper, M. R., Keavney, M., & Drake, M. (1996). Intrinsic motivation and extrinsic rewards: A commentary on Cameron and Pierce's meta-analysis. *Review of Educational Research, 66,* 5–32.

Lesch, K. P., Bengel, D., Heils, A., Sabol, S. Z., Greenberg, B. D., Petri, S., Benjamin, J., Muller, C. R., Hamer, D. H., & Murphy, D. L. (1996, November 29). Association of anxiety-related traits with a polymorphism in the serotonin transporter gene regulatory region. *Science, 274,* 1527–1531.

Leshner, A. I. (1997, October 3). Addiction is a brain disease, and it matters. *Science, 278,* 45–47.

Leshowitz, B., Jenkens, K., Heaton, S., & Bough, T. L. (1993). Fostering critical thinking skills in students with learning disabilities: An instructional program. *Journal of Learning Disabilities, 26,* 483–490.

Leslie, C. (1991, February 11). Classrooms of Babel. *Newsweek,* pp. 56–57.

Lester, D. (1990). *Understanding and preventing suicide: New perspectives.* Springfield, IL: Thomas.

Lester, D., & Leenaars, A. A. (1998). Suicide in Canada and the United States: A societal comparison. In A. A. Leenaars, S. Wenckstern, I. Sakinofsky, R. J. Dyck, M. J. Kral, & R. C. Bland (Eds.), *Suicide in Canada* (pp. 108–121). Toronto: University of Toronto Press.*

Leung, K., & Iwawaki, S. (1988). Cultural collectivism and distributive behavior. *Journal of Cross-Cultural Psychology, 19,* 35–49.

Leutwyler, K. (1994, March). Prosthetic vision. *Scientific American,* p. 108.

LeVay, S. (1991). A difference in hypothalamic structure between heterosexual and homosexual men. *Science, 253,* 1034–1037.

LeVay, S. (1993). *The sexual brain.* Cambridge, MA: MIT Press.

Levenson, R. W. (1992). Autonomic nervous system differences among emotions. *Psychological Science, 3,* 23–27.

Levenson, R. W. (1994). The search for autonomic specificity. In P. Ekman, & R. J. Davidson (Eds.), *The nature of emotion:*

Fundamental questions. New York: Oxford University Press.

Levenson, R. W., Ekman, P., & Friesen, W. V. (1990). Voluntary facial expression generates emotion-specific nervous system activity. *Psychophysiology, 27,* 363–384.

Levenson, R. W., Ekman, P., Heider, K., & Friesen, W. V. (1992). Emotion and autonomic nervous system activity in the Minangkabau of West Sumatra. *Journal of Personality and Social Psychology, 62,* 972–988.

Leventhal, H. (1970). Findings and theory in the study of fear communications. In L. Berkowitz (Ed.), *Advances in experimental social psychology* (Vol. 5). New York: Academic Press.

Leventhal, H., Baker, T., Brandon, T., & Fleming, R. (1989). Intervening and preventing cigarette smoking. In R. Ney, & A. Gale (Eds.), *Smoking and human behavior.* Chichester, England: Wiley.

Leventhal, H., & Cleary, P. D. (1980). The smoking problem: A review of the research and theory in behavioral risk modification. *Psychological Bulletin, 88,* 370–405.

Leventhal, H., Nerenz, D., & Leventhal, E. (1985). Feelings of threat and private views of illness: Factors in dehumanization in the medical care system. In A. Baum, & J. E. Singer (Eds.), *Advances in environmental psychology* (Vol. 4). Mahwah, NJ: Erlbaum.

Leventhal, H., & Tomarken, A. J. (1986). Emotion: Today's problems. *Annual Review of Psychology, 37,* 565–610.

Levine, J. M. (1989). Reaction to opinion deviance in small groups. In P. B. Paulus (Ed.), *Psychology of group influence* (2nd ed.). Mahwah, NJ: Erlbaum.

Levine, M. W., & Shefner, J. M. (1991). *Fundamentals of sensation and perception* (2nd ed.). Pacific Grove, CA: Brooks/Cole.

Levine, R. V. (1993, February). Is love a luxury? *American Demographics,* pp. 27–29.

Levinger, G. (1983). Development and change. In H. H. Kelley et al., *Close relationships.* San Francisco: Freeman.

Levinson, D. J. (1986). A conception of adult development. *American Psychologist, 41,* 3–13.

Levinson, D. J. (1990). A theory of life structure development in adulthood. In C. N. Alexander, & E. J. Langer (Eds.), *Higher stages of human development: Perspectives on adult growth.* New York: Oxford University Press.

Levinson, D. J., & Levinson, J. D. (1996). *The seasons of a woman's life.* New York: Knopf.

Levitan, I. B., & Kaczmarek, L. K. (1991). *The neuron: Cell and molecular biology.* New York: Oxford University Press.

Levy, B. (1996). Improving memory in old age through implicit self-stereotyping. *Journal of Personality and Social Psychology, 71,* 1092–1107.

Levy, B. A. (1996). Whole words, segments, and meaning: Approaches to reading education. In R. Klein & P. McMullen (Eds.), *Converging methods for understanding reading and dyslexia.* Mahwah, NJ: Erlbaum.*

Levy, B. A., Campsall, J., Browne, J., Cooper, D., Waterhouse, C., & Wilson, C. (1995). Reading fluency: Episodic integration across texts. *Journal of Experimental Psychology: Learning, Memory and Cognition, 21,* 1169–1185.*

Levy, B. L., & Langer, E. (1994). Aging free from negative stereotypes: Successful memory in China and among the American deaf. *Journal of Personality and Social Psychology, 66,* 989–997.

Levy, D. A. (1997). *Tools of critical thinking: Metathoughts for psychology.* Boston: Allyn & Bacon.

Levy, S. (1997, May 19). Big Blue's hand of God. *Newsweek,* p. 72.

Levy, S., & Fletcher, E. (1998). Kamatsiaqtut, Baffin Crisis Line: Community ownership of support in a small town. In A. A. Leenaars, S. Wenckstern, I. Sakinofsky, R. J. Dyck, M. J. Kral, & R. C. Bland (Eds.), *Suicide in Canada* (pp. 353–366). Toronto: University of Toronto Press.*

Levy, S. M., Lee, J., Bagley, C., & Lippman, M. (1988). Survival hazards analysis in first recurrent breast cancer patients: Seven-year follow-up. *Psychosomatic Medicine, 50,* 520–528.

Lewandowsky, S., Dunn, J. C., & Kirsner, K. (Eds.). (1989). *Implicit memory: Theoretical issues.* Mahwah, NJ: Erlbaum.

Lewis, C., O'Sullivan, C., & Barraclough, J. (1994). *The psychoimmunology of human cancer.* New York: Oxford University Press.

Lewis, C. E. (1994, March). Paper presented at the meeting of the American Heart Association, Tampa, FL.

Lewis, M., & Feinman, S. (Eds.). (1991). *Social influences and socialization in infancy.* New York: Plenum Press.

Lewis, M., Feiring, C., McGuffog, C., & Jaskir, J. (1984). Predicting psychopathology in six-year-olds from early social relations. *Child Development, 55,* 123–136.

Lewis, P. (1987). Therapeutic change in groups: An interactional perspective. *Small Group Behavior, 18,* 548–556.

Lewis-Fernandez, R., & Kleinman, A. (1995). Cultural psychiatry: Theoretical, clinical, and research issues. *Psychiatric Clinics of North America, 18,* 433–448.

Lex, B. W. (1995). Alcohol and other psychoactive substance dependence in women and men. In M. V. Seeman (Ed.), *Gender and psychopathology.* Washington, DC: American Psychiatric Press.

Ley, P., & Spelman, M. S. (1967). *Communicating with the patient.* London: Staples Press.

Li, J. H., & Watanabe, H. (1994). A bayesian study of the correlation between standard scores of twins. *Behaviormetrika, 21,* 121–130.

Li, S. (1995). A comparative study of personality in supernormal children and normal children. *Psychological Science—China, 18,* 184–186.

Lichtenstein, E. (1982). The smoking problem: A behavioral perspective. *Journal of Consulting and Clinical Psychology, 50,* 804–819.

Lichtenstein, E., & Penner, M. D. (1977). Long-term effects of rapid smoking treatment for dependent cigarette smokers. *Addictive Behaviors, 2,* 109–112.

Licinio, J., Wong, M. L., & Gold, P. W. (1996). The hypothalamic-pituitary-adrenal axis in anorexia nervosa. *Psychiatry Research, 62,* 75–83.

Lidz, T. (1973). *The origin and treatment of schizophrenic disorders.* New York: Basic Books.

Lidz, T., & Fleck, S. (1985). *Schizophrenia and the family* (2nd ed.). New York: International Universities Press.

Lieberman, J. A., & Koreen, A. R. (1993). Neurochemistry and neuroendocrinology of schizophrenia: A selective review. *Schizophrenia Bulletin, 19,* 371–429.

Lieberman, M. A. (1982). The effects of social supports on responses to stress. In L. Goldberger, & L. Breznitz (Eds.), *Handbook of stress.* New York: Free Press.

Lieberman, M. A., & Bond, G. R. (1978). Self-help groups: Problems of measuring outcome. *Small Group Behavior, 9,* 222–241.

Liebert, R. M., & Sprafkin, J. (1988). *The early window: Effects of television on children and youth* (3rd ed.). New York: Pergamon.

Lietaer, G. (1984). Unconditional positive regard: A controversial basic attitude in client-centered therapy. In R. F. Levant, & L. M. Shlien (Eds.), *Client-centered therapy and the person-centered approach.* New York: Praeger.

Lim, K. O., Tew, W., Kushner, M., & Chow, K. (1996). Cortical gray matter volume deficit in patients with first-episode schizophrenia. *American Journal of Psychiatry, 153,* 1548–1553.

Lindsay, P. H., & Norman, D. A. (1977). *Human information processing* (2nd ed.). New York: Academic Press.

Linscheid, T. R., Iwata, B. A., Ricketts, R. W., Williams, D. E., & Griffin, J. C. (1990). Clinical evaluation of the self-injurious behavior inhibiting system (SIBIS). *Journal of Applied Behavior Analysis, 23,* 53–78.

Linszen, D. H., Dingemans, P. M., Nugter, M. A., Van der Does, A. J. W., et al. (1997). Patient attributes and expressed emotion as risk factors for psychotic relapse. *Schizophrenia Bulletin, 23,* 119–130.

Linz, D. G., Donnerstein, E., & Penrod, S. (1988). Effects of long-term exposure to violent and sexually degrading depictions of women. *Journal of Personality and Social Psychology, 55,* 758–768.

Lipman, J. (1992, March 10). Surgeon General says it's high time Joe Camel quit. *Wall Street Journal,* pp. B1, B7.

Lipsey, M. W., & Wilson, D. B. (1993). The efficacy of psychological, educational, and behavioral treatment: Confirmation from meta-analysis. *American Psychologist, 48,* 1181–1209.

Lisak, D., & Roth, S. (1988). Motivational factors in nonincarcerated sexually aggressive men. *Journal of Personality and Social Psychology, 55,* 795–802.

Liskin, L. (1985, November–December). Youth in the 1980s: Social and health concerns 4. *Population Reports, 8,* no. 5.

Lister, R. G., & Weingartner, H. J. (Eds.). (1991). *Perspectives on cognitive neuroscience.* New York: Oxford University Press.

Little, T. D., & Lopez, D. F. (1997). Regularities in the development of children's causality beliefs about school performance across six sociocultural contexts. *Developmental Psychology, 33,* 165–175.

Lloyd, J. W., Kameenui, E. J., & Chard, D. (Eds.). (1997). *Issues in educating students with disabilities.* Mahwah, NJ: Erlbaum.

Lobsenz, M. M. (1975). *Sex after sixty-five.* Public Affairs Pamphlet #519, New York Public Affairs Committee.

Locke, D. C. (1992). *Increasing multicultural understanding.* Newbury Park, CA: Sage.

Locke, E. A., & Latham, G. P. (1991). The fallacies of common sense "truths": A reply to Lamal. *Psychological Science, 2,* 131–132.

Loeber, R., & Hay, D. (1997). Key issues in the development of aggression and violence from childhood to early adulthood. *Annual Review of Psychology, 48,* 371–410.

Loehlin, J. C., Willerman, L., & Horn, J. M. (1987). Personality resemblance in adoptive families: A 10-year follow-up. *Journal of Personality and Social Psychology, 53,* 961–969.

Loewenstein, G. (1994). The psychology of curiosity: A review and reinterpretation. *Psychological Bulletin, 116,* 75–98.

Loftus, E. F. (1979). *Eyewitness testimony.* Cambridge: Harvard University Press.

Loftus, E. F. (1993). Psychologists in the eyewitness world. *American Psychologist, 48,* 550–552.

Loftus, E. F. (1997). Memory for a past that never was. Current Directions in *Psychological Science, 6,* 60–65.

Loftus, E. F., & Ketcham, K. (1991). *Witness for the defense: The accused, the eyewitness who puts memory on trial.* New York: St. Martin's.

Loftus, E. F., Loftus, G. R., & Messo, J. (1987). Some facts about "weapon focus." *Law and Human Behavior, 11,* 55–62.

Loftus, E. F., & Palmer, J. C. (1974). Reconstruction of automobile destruction: An example of the interface between language and memory. *Journal of Verbal Learning and Verbal Behavior, 13,* 585–589.

Loftus, E. F., Smith, K. D., Klinger, M. R., & Fiedler, J. (1992). Memory and mismemory for health events. In J. M. Tanur (Ed.), *Questions About Questions: Inquiries into the Cognitive Bases of Surveys.* New York: Russell Sage Foundation.

Logie, R. H. (1995). *Visuo-spatial working memory.* Mahwah, NJ: Erlbaum.

Logothetis, N. K., & Schall, J. D. (1989, August 18). Neuronal correlates of subjective visual perception. *Science, 245,* 761–763.

Logue, A. W. (1991). *The psychology of eating and drinking* (2nd ed.). New York: Freeman.

Lohman, D. F. (1989). Human intelligence: An introduction to advances in theory and research. *Review of Educational Research, 59,* 333–373.

Long, A. (1987, December). What is this thing called sleep? *National Geographic, 172,* 786–821.

Long, B. C., & Flood, K. R. (1993). Coping with work stress: Psychological benefits of exercise. Special Issue: Exercise, stress and health. *Work and Stress, 7,* 109–119.

Long, G. M., & Beaton, R. J. (1982). The case for peripheral persistence: Effects of target and background luminance on a partial-report task. *Journal of Experimental Psychology: Human Perception and Performance, 8,* 383–391.

Lonsway, K. A., & Fitzgerald, L. F. (1995). Attitudinal antecedents of rape myth acceptance: A theoretical and empirical reexamination. *Journal of Personality and Social Psychology, 68,* 704–711.

Loomis, J. M., Golledge, R. G., & Klatzky, R. L. (In press). Navigation system for the blind: Auditory display modes and guidance. Presence: Teleoperators and Virtual Environments.

Loomis, J. M., Klatzky, R. L., Golledge, R. G., Cicinelli, J. G., Pellegrino, J. W., & Fry, P. A. (1993). Nonvisual navigation by blind and sighted: Assessment of path integration ability. *Journal of Experimental Psychology: General, 122,* 73–91.

Looy, H. (1995). Born gay? A critical review of biological research on homosexuality. *Journal of Psychology and Christianity, 14,* 197–214.

LoPiccolo, L. (1980). Low sexual desire. In S. R. Leiblum, & L. A. Pervin (Eds.), *Principles and practice of sex therapy.* New York: Guilford Press.

Lorenz, K. (1966). *On aggression.* New York: Harcourt Brace Jovanovich.

Lorenz, K. (1974). *Civilized man's eight deadly sins.* New York: Harcourt Brace Jovanovich.

Lovaas, O. I., & Koegel, R. (1973). Behavior therapy with autistic children. In C. Thoreson (Ed.), *Behavior modification and education.* Chicago: University of Chicago Press.

Lovallo, W. R. (1997). *Stress and health.* Newburyport, CA: Sage.

Lowe, M. R. (1993). The effects of dieting on eating behavior: A three-factor model. *Psychological Bulletin, 114,* 100–121.

Lowinson, J. H., Ruiz, P., Millman, R. B., & Langrod, J. G. (1992). *Substance abuse: A comprehensive textbook* (2nd ed.). Baltimore: Williams & Wilkins.

Lowinson, J. H., Ruiz, P., Millman, R. B., & Langrod, J. G. (Eds.). (1997). *Substance abuse: A comprehensive textbook* (3rd. ed.). Baltimore, MD: Williams & Wilkins.

Lubart, T. I. (1994). Creativity. In R. J. Sternberg (Ed.), *Thinking and problem-solving.* San Diego, CA: Academic Press.

Lubart, T. I., & Sternberg, R. J. (1995). An investment approach to creativity: Theory and data. In S. M. Smith, T. B. Ward, & R. A. Finke (Eds.), *The creative cognition approach.* Cambridge, MA: MIT Press.

Lubinski, D., & Benbow, C. P. (1992). Gender differences in abilities and preferences among the gifted: Implications for the math-science pipeline. *Current Directions in Psychological Science, 1,* 61–66.

Luborsky, L. (1988). *Who will benefit from psychotherapy?* New York: Basic Books.

Luce, R. D. (1993). *Sound and hearing.* Mahwah, NJ: Erlbaum.

Luchins, A. S. (1946). Classroom experiments on mental set. *American Journal of Psychology, 59,* 295–298.

Lucy, J. A. (1992). *Language diversity and thought: A reformulation of the linguistic relativity hypothesis.* Cambridge, England: Cambridge University Press.

Lucy, J. A. (1996). The scope of linguistic relativity: An analysis and review of empirical research. In J. J. Gumperz, & S. C. Levinson (Eds.), *Rethinking linguistic relativity. Studies in the social and cultural foundations of language,* No. 17. Cambridge, England: Cambridge University Press.

Ludwick-Rosenthal, R., & Neufeld, R. W. J. (1988). Stress management during noxious medical procedures: An evaluative review of outcome studies. *Psychological Bulletin, 104,* 326–342.

Ludwig, A. M. (1969). Altered states of consciousness. In C. T. Tart (Ed.), *Altered states of consciousness.* New York: Wiley.

Ludwig, A. M. (1996, March). Mental disturbances and creative achievement. *The Harvard Mental Health Letter,* pp. 4–6.

Luria, A. R. (1968). *The mind of a mnemonist.* Cambridge, MA: Basic Books.

Lusted, H. S., & Knapp, R. B. (1996, October). Controlling computers with neural signals. *Scientific American,* 82–87.

Lykken, D. T. (1995). *The antisocial personalities.* Mahwah, NJ: Erlbaum.

Lykken, D. T., McGue, M., Tellegen, A., & Bouchard, T. J., Jr. (1993). Emergenesis: Genetic traits that may not run in families. *American Psychologist, 47,* 1565–1577.

Lynch, G., Granger, R., & Staubli, U. (1991). Long-term potentiation and the structure of memory. In W. C. Abraham, M. C. Corballis, & K. G. White (Eds.), *Memory mechanisms: A tribute to G. V. Goddard.* Mahwah, NJ: Erlbaum.

Lynch, J. G., Jr., & Cohen, J. L. (1978). The use of subjective expected utility theory as an aid to understanding variables that influence helping behavior. *Journal of Personality and Social Psychology, 36,* 1138–1151.

Lyness, S. A. (1993). Predictors of differences between Type A and B individuals in heart rate and blood pressure reactivity. *Psychological Bulletin, 114,* 266–295.

Lynn, S. J. (1997, August). *Should hypnosis be used for memory recovery? The answer is no.* Paper presented at the annual meeting of the American Psychological Association, Toronto.

Lynn, S. J., Neufeld, V., Green, J. P., Sandberg, D., et al. (1996). Daydreaming, fantasy, and psychopathology. In R. G. Kunzendorf, N. P. Spanos, & B. Wallace (Eds.), Hypnosis and imagination. Imagery and human development series. Amityville, NY: Baywood.

Lynn, S. J., & Rhue, J. W. (1988). Fantasy-proneness: Hypnosis, developmental antecedents, and psychopathology. *American Psychologist, 43,* 35–44.

Lynn, S. J., Rhue, J. W., & Weekes, J. R. (1990). Hypnotic involuntariness: A social cognitive analysis. *Psychological Review, 97,* 169–184.

Lynn, S. J., & Snodgrass, M. (1987). Goal-directed fantasy, hypnotic susceptibility, and expectancies. *Journal of Personality and Social Psychology, 53,* 933–938.

Lynn, S. J., Weekes, J. R., Neufeld, V., Zivney, O., Brentar, J., & Weiss, F. (1991). Interpersonal climate and hypnotizability level: Effects on hypnotic performance, rapport, and archaic involvement. *Journal of Personality and Social Psychology, 60,* 739–743.

Lytton, H., & Romney, D. M. (1991). Parents' differential socialization of boys and girls: A meta-analysis. *Psychological Bulletin, 109,* 267–296.

Maccoby, E. E. (1992). The role of parents in the socialization of children: An historical overview. *Developmental Psychology, 28,* 1006–1017.

Maccoby, E. E., & Jacklin, C. N. (1974). *The psychology of sex differences.* Stanford, CA: Stanford University Press.

MacCoun, R. J. (1993). Drugs and the law: A psychological analysis of drug prohibition. *Psychological Bulletin, 113,* 497–512.

MacDermid, S. M., Huston, T. L., & McHale, S. M. (1990). Changes in marriage associated with the transition to parenthood: Individual differences as a function of sex-role attitudes and changes in division of labor. *Journal of Marriage and the Family, 52,* 475–486.

MacDonald, T. K., Zanna, M. P., & Fong, G. T. (1996). Why common sense goes out the window: The effects of alcohol on intentions to use condoms. *Personality and Social Psychology Bulletin, 22,* 763–775.*

MacEwen, K. E. (1994). Refining the intergenerational transmission hypothesis. *Journal of Interpersonal Violence, 9,* 350–356.

MacFadyen, J. T. (1987, November). Educated monkeys help the disabled help themselves. *Smithsonian,* pp. 125–133.

Mackay, R., & Myles, L. (1995). A major challenge for the education system: Aboriginal retention and dropout. In M. Battiste & J. Barman (Eds.), *First Nations education in Canada*: The circle unfolds. Vancouver: UBC Press.*

MacKenzie, B. (1984). Explaining race differences in IQ: The logic, the methodology, and the evidence. *American Psychologist, 39,* 1214–1233.

MacKenzie, E. K. R. (1990). *Introduction to time-limited group psychotherapy.* Washington, DC: American Psychiatric Press.

Mackie, D. M. (1987). Systematic and nonsystematic processing of majority and minority persuasive communications. *Journal of Personality and Social Psychology, 53,* 41–52.

Mackie, D. M., & Hamilton, D. L. (1993). *Affect, cognition, and stereotyping: Interactive processes in group perception.* San Diego, CA: Academic Press.

MacLeod, D. I. A., & Willen, J. D. (1995). Is there a visual space? In R. D. Luce, M. D'Zmura, D. D. Hoffman, G. J. Iverson, & A. K. Romney (Eds.), *Papers in honor of Tarow Indow on his 70th birthday.* Mahwah, NJ: Erlbaum.

Macmillan, M. (1991). *Freud evaluated: The competed arc.* Amsterdam: North-Holland.

Macrae, C. N., Stangor, C., & Hewstone, M. (1996). *Stereotypes and stereotyping.* New York: Guilford Press.

Maddi, S. R., Bartone, P. T., & Puccetti, M. C. (1987). Stressful events are indeed a factor in physical illness: Reply to Schroeder and Costa (1984). *Journal of Personality and Social Psychology, 52,* 833–843.

Madon, S., Jussim, L., & Eccles, J. (1997). In search of the powerful self-fulfilling prophecy. *Journal of Personality and Social Psychology, 72,* 791–809.

Maier, S. F., Watkins, L. R., & Fleshner, M. (1994, December). Psychoneuro-immunology: The interface between behavior, brain, and immunity. *Science Watch, 49,* 1004–1017.

Mairs, D. A. E. (1995). Hypnosis and pain in childbirth. *Contemporary Hypnosis, 12,* 111–118.

Major, B. (1993). Gender, entitlement, and the distribution of family labor. *Journal of Social Issues, 49,* 141–159.

Major, B., & Konar, E. (1984). An investigation of sex differences in pay expectations and their possible causes. *Academy of Management Journal, 27,* 777–792.

Malamuth, N. M., Linz, D., Heavey, C. L., & Barnes, G. (1995). Using the confluence model of sexual aggression to predict men's conflict with women: A 10-year follow-up study. *Journal of Personality and Social Psychology, 69,* 353–369.

Malin, J. T. (1979). Information-processing load in problem solving by network search. *Journal of Experimental Psychology: Human Perception and Performance, 5,* 379–390.

Malinowski, C. I., & Smith, C. P. (1985). Moral reasoning and moral conduct: An investigation prompted by Kohlberg's theory. *Journal of Personality and Social Issues, 49,* 1016–1027.

Malott, R. W., Whaley, D. L., & Malott, M. E. (1993). *Elementary principles of behavior* (2nd ed.). Englewood Cliffs, NJ: Prentice Hall.

Mamabolo, L. M. (1996). Group treatment program for sexually and physically assaultive young offenders in a secure custody facility. *Canadian Psychology, 37,* 154–160.*

Mandal, M. K., Asthana, H. S., Pandey, R., & Sarbadhikari, S. (1996). Cerebral laterality in affect and affective illness: A review. *Journal of Psychology, 130,* 447–459.

Mann, D. (1997). *Psychotherapy: An erotic relationship.* New York: Routledge.

Mann, T. (1994). Informed consent for psychological research: Do subjects comprehend consent forms and understand their legal rights? *Psychological Science, 5,* 140–143.

Mansfield, E. D., & McAdams, D. P. (1996). Generativity and themes of agency and communion in adult autobiography. *Personality and Social Psychology Bulletin, 22,* 721–731.

Manstead, A. S. R. (1991). Expressiveness as an individual difference. In R. S. Feldman, & B. Rime (Eds.), *Fundamentals of nonverbal behavior.* Cambridge, England: Cambridge University Press.

Manuck, S., Olsson, G., Hjemdahl, P., & Rehnqvist, N. (1992). Does cardiovascular reactivity to mental stress have prognostic value in postinfarction patients? A pilot study. *Psychosomatic Medicine, 54,* 102–108.

Manz, C. C., & Sims, H. P., Jr. (1992). The potential for "groupthink" in autonomous work groups. In R. Glaser (Ed.), *Classic readings in self-managing teamwork: 20 of the most important articles.* King of Prussia, PA: Organization Design and Development, Inc.

Mapes, G. (1990, April 10). Beating the clock: Was it an accident Chernobyl exploded at 1:23 in the morning? *Wall Street Journal,* pp. A1, A16.

Marco, C. C., McKee, L. J., Bauer, T. L., et al. (1996). Serum immunoreactive-leptin concentrations in normal-weight and obese humans. *New England Journal of Medicine, 334,* 292–295.

Marcus, G. F. (1996). Why do children say "breaked"? *Current Directions in Psychological Science, 5,* 81–85.

Marks, G., & Miller, N. (1987). Ten years of research on the false-consensus effect: An empirical and theoretical review. *Psychological Bulletin, 102,* 72–90.

Markus, H., & Kitayama, S. (1991). Culture and the self: Implications for cognition, emotion, and motivation. *Psychological Review, 98,* 224–253.

Markus, H. R., & Kitayama, S. (1994). A collective fear of the collective: Implications for selves and theories of selves. Special Issue: The self and the collective. *Personality and Social Psychology Bulletin, 20,* 568–579.

Marr, D. C. (1982). *Vision.* New York: Freeman.

Marshall, G., & Zimbardo, P. (1979). The affective consequences of "inadequately explained" physiological arousal. *Journal of Personality and Social Psychology, 37,* 970–988.

Martin, A., Haxby, J. V., Lalonde, F. M., Wiggs, C. L., & Ungerleider, L. G. (1995, October 6). Discrete cortical regions associated with knowledge of color and knowledge of action. *Science, 270,* 102–105.

Martin, C. L. (1987). A ratio measure of sex stereotyping. *Journal of Personality and Social Psychology, 52,* 489–499.

Martin, J. (1993). Episodic memory: A neglected phenomenon in the psychology of education. *Educational Psychologist, 28,* 169–183.

Martin, J. H., Brust, J. C. M., & Hilal, S. (1991). Imaging the living brain. In E. R.

Kandel, J. H. Schwartz, & T. M. Jessell (Eds.), *Principles of neural science* (3rd ed.). New York: Elsevier.

Martin, J. K., & Shehan, C. L. (1989). Education and job satisfaction: The influences of gender, wage earning status, and job values. *Work and Occupations, 16,* 184–199.

Martin, L. (1986). Eskimo words for snow: A case study in the genesis and decay of an anthropological example. *American Anthropologist, 88,* 418–423.

Martin, L., & Pullum, G. K. (1991). *The great Eskimo vocabulary hoax.* Chicago: University of Chicago Press.

Martin, R. A. (1996). Humour as therapeutic play: Stress moderating effects of humour. *Journal of Leisurability, 23,* 8–15.*

Martindale, C. (1981). *Cognition and consciousness.* Homewood, IL: Dorsey.

Martinez, J. L., Jr., & Derrick, B. E. (1996). Long-term potentiation and learning. *Annual Review of Psychology, 47,* 173–203.

Marx, J. (1995, December 22). A new guide to the human genome. *Science, 270,* p. 1919–1920.

Marx, M. B., Garrity, T. F., & Bowers, F. R. (1975). The influence of recent life experience on the health of college freshmen. *Journal of Psychosomatic Research, 19,* 87–98.

Marxsen, D., Yuille, J. C., & Nisbett, M. (1995). The complexities of eliciting and assessing children's statements. *Psychology, Public Policy and the Law, 1,* 450–460.*

Masfield, E. D., & McAdams D. P. (1996, July). Generativity and themes of agency and communion in adult autobiography. *Personality and Social Psychology Bulletin, 22,* 721–731.

Maslow, A. H. (1970). *Motivation and personality* (2nd ed.). New York: Harper & Row.

Maslow, A. H. (1987). *Motivation and personality* (3rd ed.). New York: Harper & Row.

Mason, J. W. (1974). Specificity in the organization of neuroendocrine response profiles. In P. Seeman, and G. M. Brown (Eds.), *Frontiers in neurology and neuroscience research.* First International Symposium of the Neuroscience Institute. Toronto: University of Toronto Press.

Mason, J. W. (1975). A historical view of the stress field. *Journal of Human Stress, 1,* 6–12, 22–37.

Mason, M. (1994). *The making of Victorian sexual attitudes* (Vol. 2). New York: Oxford University Press.

Massaro, D. (1991). Psychology as a cognitive science. *Psychological Science, 2,* 302–306.

Masters, W. H., & Johnson, V. E. (1966). *Human sexual response.* Boston: Little, Brown.

Masters, W. H., & Johnson, V. E. (1979). *Homosexuality in perspective.* Boston: Little, Brown.

Masters, W. H., & Johnson, V. E. (1994). *Heterosexuality.* New York: HarperCollins.

Mastropieri, M. A., & Scruggs, T. (1987). *Effective instruction for special education.* Boston: College-Hill Press/Little, Brown.

Mastropieri, M. A., & Scruggs, T. E. (1991). *Teaching students ways to remember: Strategies for learning mnemonically.* Cambridge, MA: Brookline Books.

Mastropieri, M. A., & Scruggs, T. E. (1992). Science for students with disabilities. *Review of Educational Research, 62,* 377–411.

Matarazzo, J. D. (1992). Psychological testing and assessment in the 21st century. *American Psychologist, 47,* 1007–1018.

Matlin, M. M. (1987). *The psychology of women.* New York: Holt.

Matlin, M. W. (1996). *The psychology of women.* Fort Worth, TX: Harcourt Brace.

Matson, J. L., & Mulick, J. A. (Eds.). (1991). *Handbook of mental retardation* (2nd ed.). New York: Pergamon.

Matsumoto, D. (1987). The role of facial response in the experience of emotion: More methodological problems and a meta-analysis. *Journal of Personality and Social Psychology, 52,* 769–774.

Matsumoto, D. (1990). Cultural similarities and differences in display rules. *Motivation and Emotion, 14,* 195–214.

Matsumoto, D., Kudoh, T., Schjerer, K., & Wallbot, H. G. (1988). Emotion antecedents and reactions in the U.S. and Japan. *Journal of Cross-Cultural Psychology, 19,* 267–286.

Matthews, D. B., Best, P. J., White, A. M., Vandergriff, J. L., & Simson, P. E. (1996). Ethanol impairs spatial cognitive processing: New behavioral and electrophysiological findings. *Current Directions in Psychological Science, 5,* 111–115.

Matthies, H. (1989). Neurobiological aspects of learning and memory. *Annual Review of Psychology, 40,* 381–404.

Matute, H. (1994). Learned helplessness and superstitious behavior as opposite effects of uncontrollable reinforcement in humans. *Learning and Motivation, 25,* 216–232.

Matute, H. (1995). Human reactions to uncontrollable outcomes: Further evidence for superstitions rather than helplessness. *Quarterly Journal of Experimental Psychology Comparative and Physiological Psychology, 48,* 142–157.

Maunsell, J. H. R. (1995, November 3). The brain's visual world: Representation of visual targets in cerebral cortex. *Science, 270,* 764–768.

Maurer, D., & Maurer, C. (1988). *The world of the newborn.* New York: Basic Books.*

Mauro, R., Sato, K., & Tucker, J. (1992). The role of appraisal in human emotions: A cross-cultural study. *Journal of Personality and Social Psychology, 62,* 301–317.

Mawhinney, V. T., Boston, D. E., Loaws, O. R., Blumenfeld, G. T., & Hopkins, B. L. (1971). A comparison of students' studying behavior produced by daily, weekly, and three-week testing schedules. *Journal of Applied Behavior Analysis, 4,* 257–264.

May, R. (1969). *Love and will.* New York: Norton.

May, R. (1990). Will decision and reponsibility. In K. Hoeller (Ed.), *Readings in existential psychology and psychiatry. Studies in existential psychology and psychiatry.*

Seattle, WA: Review of Existential Psychology and Psychiatry.

Mayer, J. D., McCormick, L. J., & Strong, S. E. (1995). Mood-congruent memory and natural mood: New evidence. *Personality and Social Psychology Bulletin, 21,* 736–746.

Mayer, R. E. (1982). Different problem-solving strategies for algebra word and equation problems. *Journal of Experimental Psychology: Learning, Memory, and Cognition, 8,* 448–462.

Mayes, A., & Downes, J. J. (Eds.). (1997). *Theories of amnesia: A special issue of the journal Memory.* Washington, DC: Psychology Press.

Mayford, M., Barzilai, A., Keller, F., Schacher, S., & Kandel, E. R. (1992). Modulation of an NCAM-related adhesion molecule with long-term synaptic plasticity in aplysia. *Science, 256,* 638–644.

Mayr, U., Kliegl, R., & Krampe, R. T. (1996). Sequential and coordinative processing dynamics in figural transformations across the life span. *Cognition, 59,* 61–90.

Mays, V. M., Rubin, J., Sabourin, M., & Walker, L. (1996). Moving toward a global psychology: Changing theories and practice to meet the needs of a changing world. *American Psychologist, 51,* 485–487.

Maziotta, J. (1993, June). *History and goals of the human brain project.* Paper presented at the annual meeting of the American Psychological Society, Chicago.

McAdams, D. P., Diamond, A., de St. Aubin, E., & Mansfield, E. (1997). Stories of commitment: The psychosocial construction of generative lives. *Journal of Personality and Social Psychology, 72,* 678–694.

McAndrews, M. P., & Milner, B. (1991). The frontal cortex and memory for temporal order. *Neuropsychologia, 29(9),* 849–859.*

McCain, N. L., & Smith, J. (1994). Stress and coping in the context of psychoneuroimmunology: A holistic framework for nursing practice and research. *Archives of Psychiatric Nursing, 8,* 221–227.

McCann, C. D., Ostrom, T. M., Tyner, L. K., & Mitchell, M. L. (1985). Person perception in heterogeneous groups. *Journal of Personality and Social Psychology, 49,* 1449–1459.

McCarley, R. W. (1994). Human electrophysiology: Basic cellular mechanisms. In S. C. Yudofsky, & R. E. Hales (Eds.), *Synopsis of neuropsychiatry.* Washington, DC: American Psychiatric Press.

McCarthy, M. J. (1991, March 18). Marketers zero in on their customers. *Wall Street Journal,* p. B1.

McCaul, K. D., Ployhart, R. E., Hinsz, V. B., & McCaul, H. S. (1995). Appraisals of a consistent versus a similar politician: Voter preferences and intuitive judgments. *Journal of Personality and Social Psychology, 68,* 292–299.

McCauley, C. (1989). The nature of social influence in groupthink: Compliance and internalization. *Journal of Personality and Social Psychology, 57,* 250–260.

McCauley, C., & Swann, C. P. (1980). Sex differences in the frequency and functions of fantasies during sexual activity. *Journal of Research in Personality, 14,* 400–411.

McClearn, G. E., Johansson, B., Berg, S., Pedersen, N. L., Ahern, F., Petrill, S. A., & Plomin, R. (1997, June 6). Substantial genetic influence on cognitive abilities in twins 80 or more years old. *Science, 276,* 1560–1583.

McClelland, D. C. (1985). How motives, skills, and values determine what people do. *American Psychologist, 40,* 812–825.

McClelland, D. C. (1993). Intelligence is not the best predictor of job performance. *Current Directions in Psychological Research, 2,* 5–8.

McClelland, D. C., Atkinson, J. W., Clark, R. A., & Lowell, E. L. (1953). *The achievement motive.* New York: Appleton-Century-Crofts.

McClintock, M. K. (1971). Menstrual synchrony and suppression. *Nature, 229,* 244–245.

McClintock, M. K., & Herdt, G. (1996). Rethinking puberty: The development of sexual attraction. *Current Directions in Psychological Science, 5,* 178–183.

McCloskey, M., Wible, C. G., & Cohen, N. J. (1988). Is there a special flashbulb-memory mechanism? *Journal of Experimental Psychology: General, 117,* 171–181.

McClusky, H. Y. (1991). Efficacy of behavioral versus triazolam treatment in persistent sleep-onset insomnia. *American Journal of Psychiatry, 148,* 121–126.

McConaghy, N. (1993). *Sexual behavior: Problems and management.* New York: Plenum.

McConkey, K. M., & Sheehan, P. W. (1995). *Hypnosis, memory, and behavior in criminal investigation.* New York: Guilford Press.

McConnell, A. R., Sherman, S. J., & Hamilton, D. L. (1994). Illusory correlation in the perception of groups: An extension of the distinctiveness-based account. *Journal of Personality and Social Psychology, 67,* 414–429.

McCormick, C. M., & Witelson, S. F. (1994). Functional cerebral asymmetry and sexual orientation in men and women. *Behavioural Neuroscience, 108,* 525–531.*

McCrae, R. R., & Costa, P. T., Jr. (1994). The stability of personality: Observations and evaluations. *Current Directions in Psychological Science, 3,* 173–175.

McCrae, R. R., & Costa, P. T., Jr. (1997). Personality trait structure as a human universal. *American Psychologist, 52,* 509–516.

McCrae, R. R., Yik, M., Trapnell, P. D., Bond, M., & Paulhus, D. L. (1998). Interpreting personality profiles across cultures. *Journal of Personality and Social Psychology, 74,* 1041–1055.

McDaniel, M. A., Riegler, G. L., & Waddill, P. J. (1990). Generation effects in free recall: Further support for a three-factor theory. *Journal of Experimental Psychology: Learning, Memory, and Cognition, 16,* 789.*

McDermott, K. B. (1996). The persistence of false memories in list recall. *Journal of Memory and Language, 35,* 212–230.

McDonald, H. E., & Hirt, E. R. (1997). When expectancy meets desire: Motivational effects in reconstructive memory. *Journal of Personality and Social Psychology, 72,* 5–23.

McDonald, J. L. (1997). Language acquisition: The acquisition of linguistic structure in normal and special populations. *Annual Review of Psychology, 48,* 215–241.

McDonald, S. M. (1989). Sex bias in the representation of male and female characters in children's picture books. *Journal of Genetic Psychology, 150,* 389–402.

McDougall, W. (1908). *Introduction to social psychology.* London: Methuen.

McFadyen, R. G. (1996). Gender, status and "powerless" speech: Interactions of students and lectures. *British Journal of Social Psychology, 35,* 353–367.

McFarland, D. J., Neat, G. W., Read, R. F., & Wolpaw, J. R. (1993). An EEG-based method for graded cursor control. *Psychobiology, 21,* 77–81.

McFarlane, J., Martin, C. L., & Williams, T. M. (1988). Mood fluctuations: Women versus men and menstrual versus other cycles. *Psychology of Women Quarterly, 12,* 201–223.

McGaugh, J. L. (1989). Involvement of hormonal and neuromodulatory systems in the regulation of memory storage. *Annual Review of Neuroscience, 12,* 255–287.

McGaugh, J. L., Weinberger, N. M., & Lynch, G. (Eds.). (1990). *Brain organization and memory: Cells, systems, and circuits.* New York: Oxford University Press.

McGinnis, J. M., & Foege, W. H. (1993, November 10). Actual causes of deaths in the United States. *Journal of the American Medical Association, 270,* 2207–2212.

McGrath, E., Keita, G. P., Strickland, B. R., & Russo, N. F. (Eds.). (1990). *Women and depression: Risk factors and treatment issues.* Washington, DC: American Psychological Association.

McGraw, K. M., & Bloomfield, J. (1987). Social influence on group moral decisions: The interactive effects of moral reasoning and sex-role orientation. *Journal of Personality and Social Psychology, 53,* 1080–1087.

McGuire, A. M. (1994). Helping behaviors in the natural environment: Dimensions and correlates of helping. *Personality and Social Psychology Bulletin, 120,* 45–56.

McGuire, P. K., Shah, G. M. S., & Murray, R. M. (1993, September 18). Increased blood flow in Broca's area during auditory hallucinations in schizophrenia. *Lancet, 342,* 703–706.

McGuire, T. R. (1995). Is homosexuality genetic? A critical review and some suggestions. Special Issue: Sex, cells, and same-sex desire: The biology of sexual preference: I. *Journal of Homosexuality, 28,* 115–145.

McGuire, W. J. (1985). Attitudes and attitude change. In G. Lindzey, & E. Aronson (Eds.),

Handbook of social psychology (Vol. 2, 3rd ed.). New York: Random House.

McGuire, W. J. (1997). Creative hypothesis generating in psychology: Some useful heuristics. *Annual Review of Psychology, 48,* 1–30.

McHugh, P. R. (1993, September). Multiple personality disorder. *Harvard Medical School Letter,* pp. 4–6.

McInerney, D. M., Roche, L. A., McInerney, V., & Marsh, H. W. (1997). Cultural perspectives on school motivation: The relevance and application of goal theory. *American Educational Research Journal, 34,* 207–236.

McIntosh, H. (1994, July/August). Psychologists find way to help blind navigate. *APS Observer,* 22–23.

McIvor, R. J., Davies, R. A., Wieck, A., Marks, M. N., et al. (1996). The growth hormone response to apomorphine at 4 days postpartum in women with a history of major depression. *Journal of Affective Disorders, 40,* 131–136.

McKeever, C. F., Joseph, S., & McCormack, J. (1993). Memory of Northern Irish Catholics and Protestants for violent incidents and their explanations for the 1981 hunger strike. *Psychological Reports, 73,* 463–466.

McKim, M. K., Cramer, K. M., Stuart, B., & O'Conner, D. L. (1999). Infant care decisions and attachment security: The Canadian transition to child care study. *Canadian Journal of Behavioural Science, 31(2),* 92–106.*

McKinley, J. B. (1975). Who is really ignorant —physician or patient? *Journal of Health and Social Behavior, 16,* 3–11.

McLaughlin, S., & Margolskee, R. F. (1994, November–December). The sense of taste. *American Scientist, 82,* 538–545.

McManus, F., & Waller, G. (1995). A functional analysis of binge-eating. *Clinical Psychology Review, 15,* 845–863.

McMillen, L. (1997, January). Linguists find the debate over 'Ebonics' uniformed. *The Chronicle of Higher Education,* A16–A17.

McNally, R. J. (1994). *Panic disorder: A critical analysis.* New York: Guilford Press.

McNeal, E. T., & Cimbolic, P. (1986). Antidepressants and biochemical theories of depression. *Psychological Bulletin, 99,* 361–374.

McRae, R. R., & Costa, P. T., Jr. (1990). *Personality and adulthood.* New York: Guilford.

McWhirter, D. P., Sanders, S., & Reinisch, J. M. (1990). *Homosexuality, heterosexuality: Concepts of sexual orientation.* New York: Oxford University Press.

Mead, M. (1949). *Male and female.* New York: Morrow.

Mearns, D. (1994). *Developing person-centered counselling.* London: Sage.

Mednick, A. (1993). World's women familiar with a day's double shift. *APA Monitor,* p. 32.

Mehler, J., & Dupoux, E. (1994). *What infants know: The new cognitive science of early development.* Cambridge, MA: Blackwell.

Mehren, E. (1996, Oct. 11). Parents want safety, not family values: A survey discovers that moms and dads are far more interested in the practical matters of daily life. (National Parenting Association report). *Los Angeles Times,* p. E1.

Meichenbaum, D. (1977). *Cognitive-behaviour modification: An integrative approach.* New York: Plenum.*

Meichenbaum, D. (1991). Evolution of cognitive behaviour therapy: Origins, tenets and clinical examples. In J. Zeig (Ed.), *The evolution of psychotherapy II.* New York: Brunner/Mazel.*

Meier, R. P., & Willerman, R. (1995). Prelinguistic gesture in deaf and hearing infants. In K. Emmorey, & J. S. Reilly (Eds.), *Language, gesture, and space.* Mahwah, NJ: Erlbaum.

Melamed, T. (1995). Barriers to women's career success: Human capital, career choices, structural determinants, or simply sex discrimination. *Applied Psychology: An International Review, 44,* 295–314.

Melges, F. T., & Bowlby, J. (1969). Types of hopelessness in psychopathological process. *Archives of General Psychiatry, 70,* 690–699.

Mel'nikov, K. S. (1993, October–December). On some aspects of the mechanistic approach to the study of processes of forgetting. *Vestnik Moskovskogo Universiteta Seriya 14 Psikhologiya,* 64–67.

Meloy, J. R., Acklin, M. W., Gacono, C. B., Murray, J. F., & Peterson, C. A. (Eds.). (1997). *Contemporary Rorschach interpretation.* Mahwah, NJ: Erlbaum.

Melton, G. B., & Garrison, E. G. (1987). Fear, prejudice, and neglect: Discrimination against mentally disabled persons. *American Psychologist, 42,* 1007–1026.

Meltzer, H. Y. (1993, August). Clozapine: A major advance in the treatment of schizophrenia. *Harvard Mental Health Letter, 10,* 4–6.

Meltzoff, A. N. (1996). The human infant as imitative generalist: A 20-year progress report on infant imitation with implications for comparative psychology. In C. M. Heyes, & B. G. Galef, Jr. (Eds.), *Social learning in animals: The roots of culture.* San Diego, CA: Academic Press.

Meltzoff, A. N., & Moore, M. K. (1993). Why faces are special to infants: On connecting the attraction of faces and infants' ability for imitation and cross-modal processing. In B. de Boysson-Bardies, S. de Schonen, P. W. Jusczyk, P. McNeilage, & J. Morton (Eds.), *Developmental neurocognition: Speech and face processing in the first year of life. NATO ASI series D: Behavioural and social sciences, Vol. 69.* Dordecht, Netherlands: Kluwer Academic Publishers.

Melzack, R., & Wall, P. D. (1965). Pain mechanisms: A new theory. *Science, 150,* pp. 971–979.

Mendez, F. J., & Garcia, M. J. (1996). Emotive performances: A treatment package for children's phobias. *Child and Family Behavior Therapy, 18,* 19–34.

Mendolia, M., & Kleck, R. E. (1993). Effects of talking about a stressful event on arousal: Does what we talk about make a difference? *Journal of Personality and Social Psychology, 64,* 283–292.

Mendoza, R., & Miller, B. L. (1992, July). Neuropsychiatric disorders associated with cocaine use. *Hospital and Community Psychiatry, 43,* 677–680.

Menella, J. A., & Beauchamp, G. K. (1996). The early development of human flavor preferences. In E. D. Capaldi (Ed.), *Why we eat what we eat: The psychology of eating.* Washington, DC: American Psychological Association.

Mentzer, S. J., & Snyder, M. L. (1982). The doctor and the patient: A psychological perspective. In G. S. Sanders, and J. Suls (Eds.), *Social psychology of health and illness* (pp. 161–181). Mahwah, NJ: Erlbaum.

Merai, A. (Ed.). (1985). *On terrorism and combating terrorism.* College Park, MD: University Publications of America.

Mercer, R. T., Nichols, E. G., & Doyle, G. C. (1989). *Transitions in a woman's life: Major life events in developmental context.* New York: Springer.

Merikle, P. M. (1992). Perception without awareness: Critical issues. *American Psychologist, 47,* 792–795.

Merikle, P. M., & Daneman, M. (1996). Memory for unconsciously perceived events: Evidence from anesthetized patients. *Consciousness and Cognition, 5,* 525–541.*

Merlin, D. (1993). Origins of the modern mind: Three stages in the evolution of culture and cognition. *Behavioral and Brain Sciences, 16,* 737–791.

Merritt, A., & Helmreich, R. (1996). Human factors on the flightdeck: The influence of national culture. *Journal of Cross-Cultural Psychology, 27,* 5–24.

Mesquita, A. M., Bucaretchi, H. A., Castel, S., & deAndrade, A. G. (1995). Estudantes da Faculdade de Medicina da Universidade de Sao Paulo: Uso de substancias psicoativas em 1991. (Medical students of the University of Sao Paulo: Use of alcohol and other drugs in 1991). *Revista ABP-APAL, 17,* 47–54.

Mesquita, B., & Frijda, N. H. (1992). Cultural variations in emotions: A review. *Psychological Bulletin, 112,* 179–204.

Messer, S. B., & Warren, C. S. (1995). *Models of brief psychodynamic therapy: A comparative approach.* New York: Guilford Press.

Messick, D. M., & Brewer, M. B. (1983). Solving social dilemmas: A review. In L. Wheeler, & P. Shaver (Eds.), *Review of personality and social psychology* (Vol. 4). Beverly Hills, CA: Sage.

Messick, S., & Jungeblut, A. (1981). Time and method in coaching for the SAT. *Psychological Bulletin, 89,* 191–216.

Metcalfe, J. (1986). Premonitions of insight predict impending error. *Journal of Experimental Psychology: Learning, Memory, and Cognition, 12,* 623–634.

Metee, D. R., & Aronson, E. (1974). Affective reactions to appraisal from others. In T. L. Huston (Ed.), *Foundations of interpersonal attraction* (pp. 235–283). New York: Academic Press.

Meyer, J. P., & Pepper, S. (1977). Need compatibility and marital adjustment in young married couples. *Journal of Personality and Social Psychology, 35,* 331–342.

Meyer, R. G., & Macciocchi, S. N. (1989). The context of self-disclosure, the polygraph, and deception. *Forensic Reports, 2,* 295–303.

Meyer, R. G., & Osborne, Y. V. H. (1987). *Case studies in abnormal behavior* (2nd ed.). Boston: Allyn & Bacon.

Meyer, R. G., & Parke, A. (1991). Terrorism: Modern trends and issues. *Forensic Reports, 4,* 51–59.

Meyer-Bahlburg, H. F. L., Ehrhardt, A. A., Rosen, L. R., Gruen, R. S., Veridiano, N. P., Vann, F. H., & Neuwalder, H. F. (1995). Prenatal estrogens and the development of homosexual orientation. *Developmental Psychology, 31,* 12–21.

Meyerhoff, M. K., & Whilte, B. L. (1986, September). Making the grade as parents. *Psychology Today,* pp. 38–45.

Michael, R. T., Gagnon, J. H., Laumann, E. O., & Kolata, G. (1994). *Sex in America: A definitive survey.* Boston: Little, Brown.

Middlebrooks, J. C., Clock, A. E., Xu, L., & Green, D. M. (1994, May 6). A panoramic code for sound location by cortical neurons. *Science, 264,* 842–844.

Middlebrooks, J. C., & Green, D. M. (1991). Sound localization by human listeners. *Annual Review of Psychology, 42,* 135–159.

Mikamo, K., Takao, Y., Wakutani, Y., Naishikawa, S. (1994). Effects of mecobalamin injection at acupoints on intractable headaches. *Current Therapeutic Research, 55,* 1477–1485.

Mikhail, A. (1981). Stress: A psychophysiological conception. *Journal of Human Stress, 7,* 9–15.

Miklowitz, D., Velligan, D., Goldstein, M. J., Neuchterlein, K., Gitlin, M., Ranlett, G., Doane, J. (1991). Communication deviance in families of schizophrenic and manic patients. *Journal of Abnormal Psychology, 100,* 163–173.

Milewski, A. E. (1976). Infants' discrimination of internal and external pattern elements. *Journal of Experimental Child Psychology, 22,* 229–246.

Milgram, R. M., Dunn, R. S., & Price, G. E. (Eds.). (1993). *Teaching and counseling gifted and talented adolescents: An international learning style perspective.* Westport, CT: Praeger Publishers/ Greenwood Publishing Group.

Milgram, S. (1974). *Obedience to authority.* New York: Harper & Row.

Millar, W. (1996). Chronic pain. In Statistics Canada, *Health Reports, 7,* (pp. 47–52). Ottawa: Statistics Canada.*

Miller, A. G. (1986). *The obedience experiments: A case study of controversy in social science.* New York: Praeger.

Miller, A. G., Collins, B. E., & Brief, D. E. (1995). Perspectives on obedience to authority: The legacy of the Milgram experiments. *Journal of Social Issues, 51,* 1–19.

Miller, G. A. (1956). The magical number seven, plus or minus two: Some limits on our capacity for processing information. *Psychology Review, 63,* 81–97.

Miller, G. R., & Stiff, J. B. (1992). Applied issues in studying deceptive communication. In R. S. Feldman (Ed.), *Applications of nonverbal behavioral theories and research.* Mahwah, NJ: Erlbaum.

Miller, J. G. (1984). Culture and the development of everyday social explanation. *Journal of Personality and Social Psychology, 46,* 961–978.

Miller, J. G., & Bersoff, D. M. (1992). Culture and moral judgment: How are conflicts between justice and interpersonal responsibilities resolved? *Journal of Personality and Social Psychology, 62,* 541–554.

Miller, J. G., Bersoff, D. M., & Harwood, R. L. (1990). Perceptions of social responsibility in India and in the United States: Moral imperatives or personal decisions? *Journal of Personality and Social Psychology, 58,* 33–47.

Miller, L. T., & Vernon, P. A. (1997). Developmental changes in speed of information processing in young children. *Developmental Psychology, 33,* 549–554.

Miller, M. W. (1986, September 19). Effects of alcohol on the generation and migration of cerebral cortical neurons. *Science, 2133,* 1308–1310.

Miller, M. W. (1994, December 1). Brain surgery is back in a limited way to treat mental ills. *Wall Street Journal,* pp. A1, A12.

Miller, N., & Brewer, M. B. (1984). *Groups in contact: The psychology of desegregation.* New York: Academic Press.

Miller, N. E. (1985a, February). Rx: Biofeedback. *Psychology Today,* pp. 54–59.

Miller, N. E. (1985b). The value of behavioral research on animals. *American Psychologist, 40,* 423–440.

Miller, S. M., Brody, D. S., & Summerton, J. (1988). Styles of coping with threat: Implications for health. *Journal of Personality and Social Psychology, 54,* 142–148.

Miller, S. M., & Mangan, C. E. (1983). Interacting effects of information and coping style in adapting to gynecologic stress: Should the doctor tell all? *Journal of Personality and Social Psychology, 45,* 223–236.

Miller, T. Q., Smith, T. W., Turner, C. W., Guijarro, M. L., & Hallet, A. J. (1996). A meta-analytic review of research on hostility and physical health. *Psychological Bulletin, 119,* 322–348.

Miller-Jones, D. (1989). Culture and testing. *American Psychologist, 44,* 360–366.

Millon, T. (1991). Classification in psychopathology: Rationale, alternatives, and standards. *Journal of Abnormal Psychology, 100,* 245–261.

Millon, T. (Ed.). (1997). *The million inventories: Clinical and personality assessment.* New York: Guilford Press.

Millon, T., & Davis, R. D. (1995). *Disorders of personality: DSM-IV and beyond* (2nd ed.). Somerset, NJ: Wiley.

Milloy, C. (1986, June 22). Crack user's highs, lows. *Washington Post,* p. A-1.

Milner, A. D., & Goodale, M. A. (1995). *The visual brain in action.* Oxford: Oxford University Press.*

Milner, A. D., & Rugg, M. D. (Eds.). (1992). *The neuropsychology of consciousness.* San Diego, CA: Academic Press.

Milner, B. (1966). Amnesia following operation on temporal lobes. In C. W. M. Whitty, & P. Zangwill (Eds.), *Amnesia.* London: Butterworth.*

Milner, B., & Kolb, B. (1985). Performance of complex arm movements and facial-movement sequences after cerebral commissurotomy. *Neuropsychologia, 23(6),* 791–799.*

Milner, P. M. (1996). Neural representations: Some old problems revisited. *Journal of Cognitive Neuroscience, 8,* 69–77.

Mineka, S., & Henderson, R. W. (1985). Controllability and predictability in acquired motivation. *Annual Review of Psychology, 36,* 495–529.

Ministry of the Solicitor General of Canada. Weapons in schools study, 1994-08-23.*

Mintz, J. H., Layne, N., Ladouceur, R., Hazel, J., & Desrosiers, M. (1997). Social advertising and tobacco demand reduction in Canada. In M. E. Goldberg, M. Fishbein, & S. E. Middlestadt (Eds.), *Social Marketing: Theoretical & Practical Perspectives.* New Jersey: Lawrence Erlbaum Associates.*

Minuchin, S. (1974). *Families and family therapy.* Cambridge, MA: Harvard University Press.

Minuchin, S., & Nichols, M. P. (1992). *Family healing.* New York: Free Press.

Miserando, M. (1991). Memory and the seven dwarfs. *Teaching of Psychology, 18,* 169–171.

Misra, R. K., Kharkwal, M., Kilroy, M. A., & Thapa, K. (1997). *Rorschach test: Theory and practice.* Thousand Oaks, CA: Sage.

Misra, S., & Beatty, S. E. (1990). Celebrity spokesperson and brand congruence: An assessment of recall and affect. *Journal of Business Research, 21,* 159–173.

Mistlberger, R. E. (1991). Scheduled daily exercise or feeding alters the phase of photic entrainment in syrian hamsters. *Physiology and Behaviour, 50,* 1257–1260.*

Mitchell, J. V. (Ed.). (1983). *Tests in print III.* Lincoln, NE: Buros Institute of Mental Measurements.

Mitchell, K. J., & Zaragoza, R. (1996). Repeated exposure to suggestion and false memory: The role of contextual variability. *Journal of Memory and Language, 35,* 246–260.

Mitchell, S. A., & Black, M. J. (1996). *Freud and beyond: A history of modern psychoanalytic thought.* New York: HarperCollins.

Mittelstaedt, H., & Glasauer, S. (1993). Crucial effects of weightlessness on human orientation. Special Issue: Space and the Vestibular System. *Journal of Vestibular Research Equilibrium and Orientation, 3,* 307–314.

Mitterer, J., & Begg, I. (1979). Can meaning be extracted from meaningless stimuli? *Canadian Journal of Psychology, 33,* 193–198.*

Mittleman, M. A., Maclure, M., Sherwood, J. B., Mulry, R. P., Tofler, G. H., Jacobs, S. C., Friedman, R., Benson, H., & Muller, J. E. (1995, October 1). Triggering of acute myocardial infarction onset by episodes of anger. *Circulation, 92,* 1720–1725.

Miyake, K., Chen, S., & Campos, J. J. (1985). Infant temperament, mother's mode of interaction, and attachment in Japan: An interim report. *Monographs of the Society for Research in Child Development, 50,* 276–297.

Miyashita, Y. (1995, June 23). How the brain creates imagery: Projection to primary visual cortex. *Science, 268,* 1719–1720.

Mogelonsky, M. (1996, September). Aficionados de cerveza. *American Demographics,* 8.

Moghaddam, F. M., Taylor, D. M., & Wright, S. C. (1993). *Social psychology in cross-cultural perspective.* New York: Freeman.

Moldofsky, H., Gilbert, R., Lue, F. A., & MacLean, A. W. (1995). Sleep-related violence. *Sleep, 18,* 731–739.

Molitor, F., & Hirsch, K. W. (1994). Children's toleration of real-life aggression after exposure to media violence: A replication of the Drabman and Thomas studies. *Child Study Journal, 24,* 191–207.

Molotsky, I. (1984, November 30). Implant to aid the totally deaf is approved. *New York Times,* pp. 1, B-10.

Money, J. (1987). Sin, sickness, or status? Homosexuality, gender identity, and psychoneuroendocrinology. *American Psychologist, 42,* 384–399.

Montemayor, P. (1983). Parents and adolescents in conflict: All families some of the time and some families most of the time. *Journal of Early Adolescence, 3,* 83–103.

Montemayor, R., Adams, G. R., & Gullotta, T. P. (Eds.). (1994). *Personal relationships during adolescence.* Thousand Oaks, CA: Sage.

Montgomery, G., & Kirsch, I. (1996). Mechanisms of placebo pain reduction: An empirical investigation. *Psychological Science, 7,* 174–176. Washington, DC: Center for Media Education.

Montgomery, K. C., & Pasnik, S. (1996). *Web of deception: Threats to children from online marketing.* Washington, DC: Center for Media Education.

Montreal Neurological Institute. (1997). Conference on Neuropsychology Beyond the Millennium (October 16–17, 1997). Speaker profile for Dr. Brenda Milner.*

Moon, C., Cooper, R. P., & Fifer, W. P. (1993). Two-day-olds prefer their native language. *Infant Behavior and Development, 16,* 495–500.

Moore, B. C. J. (Ed.). (1995). *Hearing.* New York: Academic Press.

Moore, B. E., & Fine, B. D. (1990). *Psychoanalytic terms and concepts.* New Haven, CT: Yale University Press.

Moore, D. S., & Erickson, P. I. (1985). Age, gender, and ethnic differences in sexual and contraceptive knowledge, attitudes, and behaviors. *Family and Community Health, 8,* 38–51.

Moore, J. C., & Surber, J. R. (1992). Effects of context and keyword methods on second language vocabulary acquisition. *Contemporary Educational Psychology, 17,* 286–292.

Moore-Ede, M. (1993). *The twenty-four hour society.* Boston: Addison-Wesley.

Moorhead, G., Ference, R., & Neck, C. P. (1991). Group decision fiascoes continue: Space shuttle Challenger and a revised groupthink framework. *Human Relations, 44,* 539–550.

Morell, V. (1996, February 16). Setting a biological stopwatch. *Science, 271,* 905–910.

Morell, V. (1996, April 5). Manic-depression findings spark polarized debate. *Science, 272,* 31–32.

Morgan, M. (1982). Television and adolescents' sex-role stereotypes: A longitudinal study. *Journal of Personality and Social Psychology, 43,* 947–955.

Morgan, P. (1996). *Who needs parents? The effects of childcare and early education on children in Britain and the USA.* London: England: Institute of Economic Affairs.

Morgan, P. M. (1977). *Deterrence: A conceptual analysis.* Beverly Hills, CA: Sage.

Morris, M. W., & Peng, K. (1994). Culture and cause: American and Chinese attributions for social and physical events. *Journal of Personality and Social Psychology, 67,* 949–971.

Morris, R. G. (1994). Working memory in Alzheimer-type dementia. Special Section: Working memory. *Neuropsychology, 8,* 544–554.

Morris, R. J. (1991). Fear reduction methods. In F. H. Kanfer, & A. P. Goldstein (Eds.), *Helping people change: A textbook of methods* (4th ed.). Pergamon general psychology series, Vol. 52. New York: Pergamon.

Morrow, J., & Wolff, R. (1991, May). Wired for a miracle. *Health,* pp. 64–84.

Moscovici, S. (1985). Social influence and conformity. In G. Lindzey, & E. Aronson (Eds.), *Handbook of social psychology* (3rd ed.). New York: Random House.

Moses, L. J., & Chandler, M. J. (1992). Traveler's guide to children's theories of mind. *Psychological Inquiry, 3,* 286–301.

Mosher, D. L., & Anderson, R. D. (1986). Macho personality, sexual aggression, and reactions to guided imagery of realistic rape. *Journal of Research in Personality, 20,* 77–94.

Motley, M. T. (1987, February). What I meant to say. *Psychology Today,* pp. 25–28.

Moutoussis, K., & Zeki, S. (1997). A direct demonstration of perceptual asynchrony in vision. *Proceedings of the Royal Society of London, B., Biological Sciences, 264,* 393–399.

Movshon, J. A., & Newsome, W. T. (1992). Neural foundations of visual motion perception. *Current Directions in Psychological Science, 1,* 35–39.

Mrzljak, L., Bergson, C., Pappy, M., Huff, R., et al. (1996). Localization of dopamine D4 receptors in GABAergic neurons of the primate brain. *Nature, 381,* 245–248.

Mucha, T. F., & Reinhardt, R. F. (1970). Conversion reactions in student aviators. *American Journal of Psychiatry, 127,* 493–497.

Muehlenhard, C. L., & Hollabaugh, L. C. (1988). Do women sometimes say no when they mean yes? The prevalence and correlates of women's token resistance to sex. *Journal of Personality and Social Psychology, 54,* 872–879.

Mueller, E., & Lucas, T. (1975). A developmental analysis of peer interaction among toddlers. In M. Lewis, & L. A. Rosenblum (Eds.), *Friendship and peer relations.* New York: Wiley-Interscience.

Mueser, K. T., Bellack, A. S., Wade, J. H., Sayers, S. L., Tierney, A., & Haag, G. (1993). Expressed emotion, social skill, and response to negative affect in schizophrenia. *Journal of Abnormal Psychology, 102,* 339–351.

Muir, D. (1999). Theories and methods in developmental psychology. In A. Slater and D. Muir (Eds.), *The Blackwell reader in developmental psychology.* Oxford: Blackwell Publishers.*

Muir, D. W., Humphrey, D. E., & Humphrey, G. K. (1994). Pattern and space perception in young infants. *Spatial Vision 8(1),* 141–165.*

Mukerjee, M. (1997, February). Trends in animal research. *Scientific American, 276,* 86–93.

Mullen, M. K., & Yi, S. (1995). The cultural context of talk about the past: Implications for the development of autobiographical memory. *Cognitive Development, 10,* 407–419.

Muller, R. T., & Diamond, T. (1999). Father and mother physical abuse and child aggressive behaviour in two generations. *Canadian Journal of Behavioural Science, 31(4),* 221–228.*

Mumme, D. L., Fernald, A., & Herrera, C. (1996). Infants' responses to facial and vocal emotional signals in a social referencing paradigm. *Child Development, 67,* 3219–3237.

Murphy, S. T., & Zajonc, R. B. (1993). Affect, cognition, and awareness: Affective priming with optimal and suboptimal stimulus exposures. *Journal of Personality and Social Psychology, 64,* 723–739.

Murray, B. (1996, June). Computer addictions entangle students. *APA Monitor,* p. 38–39.

Murray, D. J., Kilgour, A. R., & Wasylkiw, L. (2000). Conflicts and missed signals in psychoanalysis, behaviourism, and Gestalt psychology. *American Psychologist, 55,* 422–426.*

Murray, J. B. (1990). Nicotine as a psychoactive drug. *Journal of Psychology, 125,* 5–25.

Murray, J. B. (1995). Evidence for acupuncture's analgesic effectiveness and proposals for the physiological mechanisms involved. *Journal of Psychology, 129,* 435–461.

Murray, S. L., & Holmes, J. G. (1997). A leap of faith? Positive illusions in romantic relationships. *Personality and Social Psychology Bulletin, 23,* 586–604.

Murray, S. L., Holmes, J. G., & Griffin, D. W. (1996). The self-fulfilling nature of positive illusions in romantic relationships: Love is not blind, but prescient. *Journal of*

Personality and Social Psychology, 71, 1155–1180.

Mussen, P. H., & Jones, M. C. (1957). Self-conceptions, motivations, and interpersonal attitudes of late- and early-maturing boys. *Child Development, 28,* 243–256.

Mustaca, A. E., & Bentosela, M. (1995). Estados psicologicos, salud y enfermedad. Psychological states, health, and disease. Special Issue: Aids and psychology. *Avances en Psicologia Clinica Latinoamericana, 13,* 101–119.

Mutrie, N., & Biddle, S. J. H. (1995). The effects of exercise on mental health in nonclinical populations. In S. J. H. Biddle (Ed.), *European perspectives on exercise and sport psychology.* Champaign, IL: Human Kinetics.

Myerhoff, B. (1982). Rites of passage: Process and paradox. In V. Turner (Ed.), *Celebration: Studies in festivity and ritual.* Washington, DC: Smithsonian Institution Press.

Myers, N. A., Perris, E. E., & Speaker, C. J. (1994). Fifty months of memory: A longitudinal study in early childhood. In R. Fivush (Ed.), *Long-term retention of infant memories. Memory, Vol. 2, No. 4.* Hove, England: Erlbaum.

Nagel, J. (1995). Resource competition theories. *American Behavioral Scientist, 38,* 442–458.

Nahome, L., & Lawton, M. P. (1975). Similarity and propinquity in friendship formation. *Journal of Personality and Social Psychology, 32,* 205–213.

Nakagawa, M., Lamb, M. E., & Miyaki, K. (1992). Antecedents and correlates of the strange situation behavior of Japanese infants. *Journal of Cross-Cultural Psychology, 23,* 300–310.

Naroll, R., Bullough, V. L., & Naroll, F. (1974). *Military deterrence in history: A pilot cross-historical survey.* Albany: State University of New York Press.

Nash, M. (1987). What, if anything, is regressed about hypnotic age regression? A review of the empirical literature. *Psychological Bulletin, 102,* 42–52.

Nathans, J., Davenport, C. M., Maumenee, I. H., Lewis, R. A., Hejtmancik, J. F., Litt, M., Lovrien, E., Weleber, R., Bachynski, B., Zwas, F., Klingaman, R., & Fishman, G. (1989, August 25). Molecular genetics of human blue cone monochromacy. *Science, 245,* 831–838.

Nathans, J., Piantanidu, T. P., Eddy, R. L., Shows, T. B., & Hogness, D. S. (1986, April 11). Molecular genetics of inherited variation in human color vision. *Science, 232,* 203–210.

National Center on Addiction and Substance Abuse. (1996, June). *Substance Abuse and the American Woman.* New York: National Center on Addiction and Substance Abuse.

National Center for Health Statistics. (1991). *Adolescent suicide.* Washington, DC: National Center for Health Statistics.

National Center for Health Statistics. (1994). *Report on obesity in the United States.* Washington, DC: National Center for Health Statistics.

National Institute on Alcohol Abuse and Alcoholism (NIAAA). (1990). *Alcohol and health.* Washington, DC: U.S. Government Printing Office.

National Institute on Drug Abuse. (1991). *National survey results on drug use.* Washington, DC: U.S. Department of Health and Human Services.

National Institutes of Health (NIH). (1996a). Integration of behavioral and relaxation approaches into the treatment of chronic pain and insomnia. NIH Technology Assessment Panel on Integration of Behavioral and Relaxation Approaches into the Treatment of Chronic Pain and Insomnia. *Journal of the American Medical Association, 276,* 313–318

National Institutes of Health (NIH). (1996b). *Statement on behavioral and relaxation approaches for chronic pain and insomnia.* Washington, DC: National Institutes of Health.

National Task Force. (1994). *Suicide in Canada: Update of the report of the task force on suicide in Canada.* Ottawa: Minister of National Health and Welfare.*

Nature (1999, December). The DNA sequence of human chromosome 22, 402, 489–495.

Navon, R., & Proia, R. L. (1989, March 17). The mutations in Ashkenazi Jews with adult G(M2) Gangliosidosis, the adult form of Tay-Sachs disease. *Science, 243,* 1471–1474.

Nay, W. R. (1995). Cognitive-behavioral and short-term interventions for anger and aggression. In L. VandeCreek, S. Knapp, & T. L. Jackson (Eds.), *Innovations in clinical practice: A source book,* Vol. 14. Sarasota, FL: Professional Resource Press/ Professional Resource Exchange, Inc.

Neck, C. P., & Moorhead, G. (1995). Groupthink remodeled: The importance of leadership, time pressure, and methodical decision-making procedures. *Human Relations, 48,* 537–557.

Neely, K. (1990, October 4). Judas Priest gets off the hook. *Rolling Stone,* p. 39.

Negrin, G., & Capute, A. J. (1996). Mental retardation. In R. H. A. Haslam, & P. J. Valletutti (Eds.), *Medical problems in the classroom: The teacher's role in diagnosis and management* (3rd ed.). Austin, TX: PRO-ED, Inc.

Neher, A. (1991). Maslow's theory of motivation: A critique. *Journal of Humanistic Psychology, 31,* 89–112.

Neher, E. (1992, April 24). Ion channels for communication between and within cells. *Science, 256,* 498–502.

Neisser, U. (1982). *Memory observed.* San Francisco: Freeman.

Neisser, U. (1996, April). Intelligence on the rise: Secular changes in IQ and related measures. Conference at Emory University, Atlanta, GA.

Neisser, U., Boodoo, G., Bouchard, T. J., Jr., Boykin, A. W., Brody, N., Ceci, S. J., Halpern, D. F., Loehlin, J. C., Perloff, R., Sternberg, R. J., & Urbina, S. (1996). Intelligence: Knowns and unknowns. *American Psychologist, 51,* 77–101.

Neisser, U., & Harsch, N. (1992). Phantom flashbulbs: False recollections of hearing the news about Challenger. In E. Winograd, & U. Neisser (Eds.), *Affect and accuracy in recall: Studies of "flashbulb" memories.* New York: Cambridge University Press.

Neitz, J., Neitz, M., & Kainz, P. M. (1996, November 1). Visual pigment gene structure and the severity of color vision defects. *Science, 274,* 801–804.

Nelson, G., Prilleltensky, I., Laurendeau, M., & Powell, B. (1996). The prevention of mental health problems in Canada: A survey of provincial policies, structures and programs. *Canadian Psychology, 37,* 161–172.*

Nelson, K. (1993). The psychological and social origins of autobiographical memory. *Psychological Science, 4,* 7–14.

Nelson, M. (1992, February 3). Too tough to die. *People Weekly,* pp. 30–33.

Nelson, R. J., Badura, L. L., & Goldman, B. D. (1990). Mechanisms of seasonal cycles of behavior. *Annual Review of Psychology, 41,* 81–108.

Nemeth, M. (1994, October 31). An alarming trend: Suicide among the young has quadrupled. *Maclean's, 107,* pp. 14–16.*

Néron, S., Lacroix, D., & Chaput, Y. (1995). Group vs. individual cognitive behaviour therapy in panic disorder: An open clinical trial with a six-month follow-up. *Canadian Journal of Behavioural Science, 27,* 379–392.*

New York Times/CBS News Poll. Respondents citing each problem as the most important facing the country. (February 20, 1994). *New York Times,* p. 3E.

New York Times/CBS Public survey. (1997, January 14–17). *New York Times/CBS News.*

Newell, A. (1990). *Unified theories of cognition.* Cambridge, MA: Harvard University Press.

Newman, D. L., Caspi, A., Moffitt, T. E., & Silva, P. A. (1997). Antecedents of adult interpersonal functioning: Effects of individual differences in age 3 temperament. *Developmental Psychology, 33,* 206–217.

Newman, J. P., & Kosson, D. S. (1986). Passive avoidance learning in psychopathic and nonpsychopathic offenders. *Journal of Abnormal Psychology, 95,* 252–256.

NICHD Early Child Care Research Network. (1997). The effects of infant child care on infant-mother attachment security: Results of the NICHD study of early child care. *Child Development, 68,* 860–879.

Nichols, M. (1994, August 8). Questioning Prozac. *Maclean's, 107,* pp. 36–41.*

Nichols, M. P., & Schwartz, R. C. (1995). *Family therapy: Concepts and methods* (3rd ed.). Boston: Longwood.

Nickerson, R. S. (1994). Teaching of thinking and problem-solving. In R. J. Sternberg (Ed.), *Thinking and problem-solving.* San Diego, CA: Academic Press.

Nicol, J., & Nolen, S. (1998, May 11). The curse of casinos. *Maclean's, 111,* pp. 44–47.*

Nicoladis, E., & Genesee, F. (1997). Language development in preschool bilingual children. *Journal of Speech-Language Pathology and Audiology, 21,* 258–270.*

Nierenberg, A. A. (1998, February 17). The physician's perspective. *HealthNews,* pp. 3–4.

Nigg, J. T., & Goldsmith, H. H. (1994). Genetics of personality disorders: Perspectives from personality and psychopathology research. *Psychological Bulletin, 115,* 346–380.

Nisbett, R. (1994, October 31). Blue genes. *New Republic, 211,* 15.

Nisbett, R. E. (1968). Taste, deprivation, and weight determinants of eating behavior. *Journal of Personality and Social Psychology, 10,* 107–116.

Nisbett, R. E. (1972). Hunger, obesity, and the ventromedial hypothalamus. *Psychological Review, 79,* 433–453.

Nisbett, R. E. (1990). Evolutionary psychology, biology, and cultural evolution. Special issue: Symposium on sociobiology. *Motivation and Emotion, 14,* 255–263.

Nisbett, R. E., & Cohen, D. (1996). *Culture of honor: The psychology of violence in the south.* Boulder, CO: Westview Press.

Nisbett, R. E., Krantz, D. H., Jepson, D., & Kunda, Z. (1993). The use of statistical heuristics in everyday reasoning. In R. E. Nisbett (Ed.), *Rules for reasoning.* Mahwah, NJ: Erlbaum.

Noben-Trauth, K., Naggert, J. K., et al. (1996, April 11). A candidate gene for the mouse mutation tubby. *Nature, 380,* p. 534.

Noble, B. P. (1993, June 13). Staying bright-eyed in the wee hours. *New York Times,* p. F11.

Nock, S. L. (1995). A comparison of marriages and cohabiting relationships. *Journal of Family Issues, 16,* 53–76.

Noels, K. A., & Clément, R. (1998). Language in education: Bridging educational policy and social psychological research. In J. Edwards (Ed.), *Language in Canada.* Cambridge: Cambridge University Press.*

Nofzinger, E. A., & Wettstein, R. M. (1995). Homicidal behavior and sleep apnea: A case report and medicolegal discussion. *Sleep, 18,* 776–782.

Nogrady, H., McConkey, K. M., & Perry, C. (1985). Enhancing visual memory: Trying hypnosis, trying imagination, and trying again. *Journal of Abnormal Psychology, 94,* 105–204.

Nolan, M. F. (1997, April 26). Tiger's racial multiplicity. *Boston Globe,* p. A11.

Nolen-Hoeksema, S. (1995). Epidemiology and theories of gender differences in unipolar depression. In M. V. Seeman (Ed.), *Gender and psychopathology.* Washington, DC: American Psychiataric Press.

Nolen-Hoeksema, S., & Girgus, J. S. (1994). The emergence of gender differences in depression during adolescence. *Psychological Bulletin, 115,* 424–443.

North, C. S., Ryall, J. M., Wetzel, R. D., & Ricci, D. A. (1993). *Multiple personalities, multiple disorders.* New York: Oxford University Press.

Novaco, R. W. (1975). *Anger control: The development and evaluation of an experimental treatment.* Lexington, MA: Lexington Books.

Novaco, R. W. (1986). Anger as a clinical and social problem. In R. J. Blanchard, & D. C. Blanchard (Eds.), *Advances in the study of aggression* (Vol. 2). Orlando, FL: Academic Press.

Novak, M. A., & Petto, A. J. (1991). *Through the looking glass: Issues of psychological well-being in captive nonhuman primates.* Washington, DC: American Psychological Association.

Novak, M. A., & Suomi, S. J. (1988). Psychological well-being of primates in captivity. *American Psychologist, 43,* 765–773.

Novy, M., Nelson, D. V., Francis, D. J., & Turk, D. C. (1995). Perspectives of chronic pain: An evaluative comparison of restrictive and comprehensive models. *Psychological Bulletin, 118,* 238–247.

Nowak, R. (1994a, March 4). Chronobiologists out of sync over light therapy patents. *Science, 263,* 1217–1218.

Nowak, R. (1994b, March 18). Nicotine scrutinized as FDA seeks to regulate cigarettes. *Science, 263,* 1555–1556.

Nowak, R. (1994c, July 22). Genetic testing set for takeoff. *Science, 265,* 464–467.

Nowicki, S., & Duke, M. (1978). An examination of counseling variables within a social learning framework. *Journal of Counseling Psychology, 25,* 1–7.

Noyes, R., Kathol, R. G., Fisher, M. M., Phillips, B. M., et al. (1993). The validity of DSM-III-R hypochondriasis. *Archives of General Psychiatry, 50,* 961–970.

Nunn, K. P. (1996). Personal hopefulness: A conceptual review of the relevance of the perceived future to psychiatry. *British Journal of Medical Psychology, 69,* 227–245.

Nyberg, L., & Tulving, E. (1996). Classifying human long-term memory: Evidence from converging dissociations. *European Journal of Cognitive Psychology, 8,* 163–183.

Oatley, K. (1992). *Best laid schemes: The psychology of emotions.* Cambridge, MA: Cambridge University Press.*

Oatley, K., & Duncan, E. (1994). The experience of emotions in everyday life. *Cognition and Emotion, 8,* 369–381.*

Oatley, K., & Jenkins, J. M. (1996). *Understanding emotions.* Oxford, England: Blackwell.*

Oatley, K., & Johnson-Laird, P. N. (1987). Towards a cognitive theory of emotions. *Cognition and Emotion, 1,* 29–50.*

Oberle, I., Rousseau, F., Heitz, D., Kretz, C., Devys, D., Hanauer, A., Boue, J., Bertheas, M. F., & Mandel, J. L. (1991, May 24). Instability of a 550-base pair DNA segment and abnormal methylzatin in fragile X syndrome. *Science, 252,* 1097–1102.

Oblinger, D. G., & Rush, S. C. (Eds.). (1997). *The learning revolution: The challenge of technology in the Academy.* Bolton, MA: Anker.

O'Brien, C. P., Childress, A. R., McLellan, A. T., & Ehrman, R. (1992). Classical conditioning in drug-dependent humans. In P. W. Kalivas, & H. H. Samson (Eds.), *The neurobiology of drug and alcohol addiction. Annals of the New York Academy of Sciences,* Vol. 654. New York: New York Academy of Sciences.

O'Connor, S. C., & Rosenblood, L. K. (1996). Affiliation motivation in everyday experience: A theoretical comparison.

Journal of Personality and Social Psychology, 70, 513–522.

O'Donohue, W. (Ed.). (1997). *Sexual harassment: Theory, research, and treatment.* Boston, MA: Allyn & Bacon.

O'Donohue, W., & Geer, J. H. (Eds.). (1992). *The sexual abuse of children* (Vol. 1). Mahwah, NJ: Erlbaum.

Office of Demographic, Employment, and Educational Research. (1994). *Demographic characteristics of members by type of APA membership.* Washington, DC: American Psychological Association.

Office on Smoking and Health. (1989). *Statistics on quitting smoking.* Atlanta, GA: Centers for Disease Control.

Office of Technology Assessment. (1990). *Unconventional cancer treatments.* Washington, DC: U.S. Government Printing Office.

Ogbu, J. (1992). Understanding cultural diversity and learning. *Educational Researcher, 21,* 5–14.

Ogilvie, R., & Harsh, J. (Eds.). (1994). *Sleep onset: Normal and abnormal processes.* Washington, DC: American Psychological Association.

O'Grady, W. D., & Dobrovolsky, M. (Eds.). (1996). *Contemporary linguistic analysis: An introduction* (3rd ed.). Toronto: Copp Clark Pitman, Ltd.

O'Hara, J. (2000, June 26). Abuse of trust. *Maclean's, 113,* pp. 16–21.*

O'Hare, D., & Roscoe, S. (1990). *Flightdeck performance: The human factor.* Ames: Iowa State University Press.

Ohring, R., Apter, A., Ratzoni, G., Weizman, R., et al. (1996). State and trait anxiety in adolescent suicide attempters. *Journal of the American Academy of Child and Adolescent Psychiatry, 35,* 154–157.

Olanow, C. W., & Lieberman, A. (Eds.). (1992). *Neurodegeneration and neuroprotection in Parkinson's disease.* San Diego: Academic Press.

Olds, J., & Milner, P. (1954). Positive reinforcement produced by electrical stimulation of septal area and other regions of rat brain. *Journal of Comparative and Physiological Psychology, 47,* 411–427.

Olds, M. E., & Fobes, J. L. (1981). The central basis of motivation: Intracranial self-stimulation studies. *Annual Review of Psychology, 32,* 123–129.

O'Leary, D. S., Andreasen, N. C., Hurtig, R. R., Kesler, M. L., et al. (1996). Auditory attentional deficits in patients with schizophrenia: A positron emission tomography study. *Archives of General Psychiatry, 53,* 633–641.

Oliet, S. H. R., Malenka, R. C., & Nicoll, R. A. (1996, March 1). Bidirectional control of quantal size by synaptic activity in the hippocampus. *Science, 271,* 1294–1297.

Oliver, C. (1995). Self-injurious behaviour in children with learning disabilities: Recent advances in assessment and intervention. *Journal of Child Psychology & Psychiatry & Allied Disciplines, 36,* 909–927.

Oliver, M. B., & Hyde, J. S. (1993). Gender differences in sexuality: A meta-analysis. *Psychological Bulletin, 114,* 29–51.

Olshansky, S. J., Carnes, B. A., & Cassel, C. (1990, November 2). In search of Methuselah: Estimating the upper limits to human longevity. *Science, 250,* 634–639.

Olson, R. P., Schwartz, N. M., & Schwartz, M. S. (1995). Definitions of biofeedback and applied psychophysiology. In M. S. Schwartz (Ed.), *Biofeedback: A practitioner's guide* (2nd ed.). New York: Guilford Press.

Omdahl, B. (1995). *Cognitive appraisal, emotion, and empathy.* Mahwah, NJ: Erlbaum.

O'Neil, M. (1990, April 1). Dieters, craving balance, are battling fears of food. *New York Times,* pp. 1, 22.

O'Neill, P. (1998). Negotiating consent in psychotherapy. New York: New York University Press.

Ontario Ministry of Health (1994). Ontario Health Survey: Mental health supplement. Catalogue No. 2224153. Toronto, ON.: Queen's Printer for Ontario.*

Opler, L. A., Kay, S. R., Rosado, V., & Lindenmayer, J. P. (1984). Positive and negative syndromes in chronic schizophrenia in patients. *Journal of Nervous and Mental Disease, 172,* 317–325.

O'Regan, J. K. (1992). Solving the "real" mysteries of visual perception: The world as an outside memory. Special Issue: Object perception and scene analysis. *Canadian Journal of Psychology, 46,* 461–488.

Oren, D. A., & Terman, M. (1998, January 16). Tweaking the human circadian clock with light. *Science, 279,* 333–334.

Orlans, F. B. (Ed.). (1993). *In the name of science: Issues in responsible animal experimentation.* New York: Oxford University Press.

Orne, M. T., Dinges, D. F., & Orne, E. C. (1984). On the differential diagnosis of multiple personality in the forensic context. *International Journal of Clinical and Experimental Hypnosis, 32,* 118–169.

Orne, M. T., & Holland, C. C. (1968). On the ecological validity of laboratory deceptions. *International Journal of Psychiatry, 6,* 282–293.

Ornstein, P. A., & Naus, M. J. (1988). Effects of the knowledge base on children's memory strategies. In H. W. Reese (Ed.), *Advances in child development and behavior* (Vol. 19). New York: Academic Press.

Ornstein, R. E. (1977). *The psychology of consciousness* (2nd ed.). New York: Harcourt Brace Jovanovich.

Orth-Gomer, K., Chesney, M. A., & Wenger, N. K. (Eds.). (1996). *Women, stress and heart disease.* Mahwah, NJ: Erlbaum.

Orth-Gomer, K., & Schneiderman, N. (Eds.). (1995). *Behavioral medicine approaches to cardiovascular disease prevention.* Mahwah, NJ: Erlbaum.

Ortony, A., & Turner, T. J. (1990). What's basic about basic emotions? *Psychological Review, 97,* 315–331.

Orwin, R. G., & Condray, D. S. (1984). Smith and Glass' psychotherapy conclusions need further probing: On Landman and Dawes's re-analysis. *American Psychologist, 39,* 71–72.

Osborne, J. W. (1995). Academics, self-esteem, and race: A look at the underlying assumptions of the disidentification hypothesis. *Personality and Social Psychology Bulletin, 21,* 449–455.

Oskamp, S. (1984). *Applied social psychology.* Englewood Cliffs, NJ: Prentice-Hall.

Osman, A., Bashore, T. R., Coles, M. G. H., Donchin, E., & Meyer, D. E. (1992). On the transmission of partial information: Inferences from movement-related brain potentials. *Journal of Experimental Psychology: Human Perception and Performance, 18,* 217–232.

Osofsky, J. D. (Ed.). (1997). *Children in a violent society.* New York: Guilford Press.

Osofsky, J. D. (1995). The effects of exposure to violence on young children. *American Psychologist, 50,* 782–788.

Oster, M. I. (1994). Psychological preparation for labor and delivery using hypnosis. Annual Scientific Meeting of the American Society of Clinical Hypnosis (1992, Las Vegas, Nevada). *American Journal of Clinical Hypnosis, 37,* 12–21.

Ottoson, D. (Ed.). (1987). *Duality and unity of the brain.* London: Macmillan.

Owen, A. M., Doyon, J., Dagher, A., Sadikot, A., & Evans, A. C. (1998). Abnormal basal ganglia outflow in Parkinson's disease identified with PET: Implications for higher cortical functions. *Brain, 121,* 949–965.*

Owens, J., Bower, G. H., & Black, J. (1979). The "soap opera" effect in story recall. *Memory and Cognition, 7,* 185–191.

Ozeki, M. (1993, February 28). On turning 13: Reports from the front lines. *New York Times,* sec. 4, p. 2.

Paalman, M. (Ed.). (1990). *Promoting safer sex: Prevention of sexual transmission of AIDS and other STD.* Amsterdam: Swets & Zeitlinger.

Pagliaro, L. A. (1995). Adolescent depression and suicide: A review and analysis of the current literature. *Canadian Journal of School Psychology, 11,* 191–201.

Paivio, A. (1971). *Imagery and verbal processes.* New York: Holt, Rinehart & Winston.

Paivio, A. (1975). Perceptual comparison through the mind's eye. *Memory and Cognition, 3,* 635–647.

Pajares, F. (1996). Self-efficacy beliefs in academic settings. *Review of Educational Research, 66,* 543–578.

Palermo, G. B. (1995). Adolescent criminal behaviour: Is TV violence one of the culprits? *International Journal of Offender Therapy and Comparative Criminology, 39,* 11–22.

Palermo, G. B., & Knudten, R. D. (1994). The insanity plea in the case of a serial killer. *International Journal of Offender Therapy and Comparative Criminology, 38,* 3–16.

Palladino, J. J., & Carducci, B. J. (1984). Students' knowledge of sleep and dreams. *Teaching of Psychology, 11,* 189–191.

Palmer, S. F. (1975). The effects of contextual scenes on the identification of objects. *Memory and Cognition, 3,* 519–526.

Paludi, M. A. (Ed.). (1990). *Ivory power: Sexual harassment on campus.* Albany: State University of New York Press.

Paludi, M. A. (Ed.). (1996). *Sexual harassment on college campuses: Abusing the Ivory Power.* Albany: State University of New York Press.

Pancyr, G., & Genest, M. (1993). Cognition and pain experience. In K. S. Dobson, & Philip C. Kendall (Eds.), *Psychopathology and cognition. Personality, psychopathology, and psychotherapy series.* San Diego, CA: Academic Press.

Papalia, D., & Olds, S. (1989). *Human development* (4th ed.). New York: McGraw-Hill.

Papini, M. R., & Bitterman, M. E. (1990). The role of contingency in classical conditioning. *Psychological Review, 97,* 396–403.

Parke, R. D. (1981). *Fathers.* Cambridge, MA: Harvard University Press.

Parke, R. D. (1996). *Fatherhood.* Cambridge, MA: Harvard University Press.

Parkes, C. M., Laungani, P., & Young, B. (Eds.). (1997). *Death and bereavement across cultures.* New York: Routledge.

Parkin, A. J. (1997). *Memory and amnesia: An introduction* (2nd ed.). London: Blackwell.

Parlee, M. B. (1979, October). The friendship bond. *Psychology Today,* pp. 43–45.

Parrott, A. C. (1995). Stress modulation over the day in cigarette smokers. *Addiction, 90,* 233–244.

Parsons, T. (1975). The sick role and the role of the physician reconsidered. *Milbank Memorial Fund Quarterly/Health and Society, 53,* 257–278.

Participant. (1994). *Young lives in the balance.* Washington, DC: Teachers Insurance and Annuity Association.

Pascual-Leone, Alvaro, et al. (1995). Bethesda, MD: National Institutes of Neurological Disorders and Stroke. U.S. Department of Health & Human Services.

Paterson, R. J., & Neufeld, R. W. J. (1987). Clear danger: Situational determinants of the appraisal of threat. *Psychological Bulletin, 101,* 404–416.

Patrick, C. J., & Iacono, W. G. (1991). Validity of the control question polygraph test: The problem of sampling bias. *Journal of Applied Psychology, 76,* 229–238.

Patterson, C. H. (1996). Multicultural counseling: From diversity to universality. *Journal of Counseling and Development, 74,* 227–231.

Patterson, C. J. (1994). Lesbian and gay families. *Current Directions in Psychological Science, 3,* 62–64.

Patzwahl, D. R., Zanker, J. M., & Altenmuller, E. O. (1994). Cortical potentials reflecting motion processing in humans. *Visual Neuroscience, 11,* 1135–1147.

Paulhus, D. L., & Bruce, M. N. (1992). The effects of acquaintanceship on the validity of personality impressions: A longitudinal study. *Journal of Personality and Social Psychology, 63,* (816–824).*

Paulhus, D. L., & Morgan, K. L. (1997). Perceptions of intelligence in leaderless groups: The dynamic effects of shyness and acquaintance. *Journal of Personality and Social Psychology, 72,* 581–591.*

Paunonen, S. V. (1998). Hierarchical organization of personality and prediction of behaviours. *Journal of Personality and Social Psychology, 74,* 538–556.*

Paunonen, S. V., Jackson, D. N., & Keinonen, M. (1990). The structured nonverbal assessment of personality. *Journal of Personality, 58,* 481–502.*

Paunonen, S. V., Jackson, D. M. N., Trzebinski, J., & Forsterling, F. (1992). Personality structure across cultures: A multimethod evaluation. *Journal of Personality and Social Psychology, 62,* 447–456.*

Paunonen, S. V., Keinonen, M., Trzebinski, J., & Forsterling, F., et al. (1996). The structure of personality in six cultures. *Journal of Cross Cultural Psychology, 27,* 339–353.*

Pavlides, C., & Winson, J. (1989). Influences of hippocampal place cell firing in the awake state on the activity of these cells during subsequent sleep episodes. *Journal of Neuroscience, 9,* 2907–2918.

Pavlov, I. P. (1927). *Conditioned reflexes.* London: Oxford University Press.

Pawlik, K., & d'Ydewalle, G. (1996). Psychology and the global commons: Perspectives of international psychology. *American Psychologist, 51,* 488–495.

Payne, D. G. (1986). Hyperamnesia for pictures and words: Testing the recall level hypothesis. *Journal of Experimental Psychology: Learning, Memory, and Cognition, 12,* 16–29.

Payne, D. G., Elie, C. J., Blackwell, J. M., & Neuschatz, J. S. (1996). Memory illusions: Recalling, recognizing, and recollecting events that never occurred. *Journal of Memory and Language, 35,* 261–285.

Payne, D. G., & Wenger, M. J. (1998). *Cognitive psychology.* Boston: Houghton Mifflin.

Peachey, N. S., Arakawa, K., Alexander, K. R., & Marchese, A. L. (1992). Rapid and slow changes in the human cone electroretinogram during light and dark adaptation. *Vision Research, 32,* 2049–2053.

Peacock, E. J., Wong, P. T., & Reker, G. T. (1993). Relations between appraisals and coping schemas: Support for the congruence model. *Canadian Journal of Behavioural Science, 25,* 64–80.

Pearlson, G. D., & Petty, A. Y. (1996). Schizophrenia: A disease of heteromodal association cortex? *Neuropsychopharmacology, 14,* 1–17.

Pederson, D. R., Gleason, K. E., Moran, G., & Bento, S. (1998). Maternal attachment representations, maternal sensitivity, and infant-mother attachment. *Developmental Psychology, 34,* 925–933.*

Pedlow, R., Sanson, A., Prior, M., & Oberklaid, F. (1993). Stability of maternally reported temperament from infancy to 8 years. *Developmental Psychology, 29,* 998–1007.

Peele, S., & Brodsky, A. (1991). *The truth about addiction and recovery.* New York: Simon & Schuster.

Peirce, R. S., Frone, M. R., Russell, M., & Cooper, M. L. (1996). Financial stress, social support, and alcohol involvement: A longitudinal test of the buffering hypothesis

in a general population survey. *Health Psychology, 15,* 38–47.

Pekala, R. J., Kumar, V. K., & Marcano, G. (1995). Hypnotic types: A partial replication concerning phenomenal experience. *Contemporary Hypnosis, 12,* 194–200.

Peled, E., Jaffe, P. G., & Edleson, J. L. (Eds.). (1995). *Ending the cycle of violence: Community responses to children of battered women.* Thousand Oaks, CA: Sage.

Pelleymounter, M. A., Cullen, M. J., Baker, M. B., Hecht, R., Winters, D., Boone, T., & Collins, F. (July 18, 1995). Effects of the obese gene product on body weight regulation in *ob/ob* mice. *Science, 269,* 540–550.

Pelligrini, A. D. (Ed.). (1995). *The future of play theory: A multidisciplinary inquiry into the contributions of Brian Sutton-Smith.* Albany: State University of New York Press.

Penfield, W., & Rasmussen, T. (1950). *The cerebral cortex of man.* New York: Macmillan.

Peng, K., & Nisbett, R. E. (1997). *Cultural differences in preferences for linear vs. non-linear proverbs.* Unpublished manuscript, University of Michigan.

Penn, A., & Snyder, C. (1993, October). *Circulation, 88,* 1820.

Penn, D. L., Corrigan, P. W., Bentall, R. P., Racenstein, J. M., & Newman, L. (1997). Social cognition in schizophrenia. *Psychological Bulletin, 121,* pp. 114–132.

Pennebaker, J., & Roberts, T. A. (1992). Toward a his and hers theory of emotion: Gender differences in visceral perception. *Journal of Social and Clinical Psychology, 11,* 199–212.

Pennebaker, J. W. (1990). *Opening up: The healing power of confiding in others.* New York: Morrow.

Pennebaker, J. W., & Harber, K. D. (1993). A social stage model of collective coping: The Loma Prieta earthquake and the Persian Gulf War. *Journal of Social Issues, 49,* 125–145.

Pennisi, E. (1997, October 24). Enzyme linked to alcohol sensitivity in mice. *Science, 278,* 573.

Peper, R. J., & Mayer, R. E. (1978). Note taking as a generative activity. *Journal of Educational Psychology, 70,* 514–522.

Pepler, D., King, G., Craig, W., Byrd, B., & Bream, L. (1995). The effectiveness of social skills training for aggressive children. *Child and Youth Forum, 24,* 297–313.*

Pepler, D., & Salpy, R. (1994). A developmental perspective on violence and youth. In L. Eron, (Ed.), *Reason to hope: A psychosocial perspective on violence and youth.* (27–58). Washington DC: APA Publications.*

Peplau, L. A., Rubin, Z., & Hill, C. T. (1977). Sexual intimacy in dating relationships. *Journal of Social Issues, 2,* 86–109.

Perdue, C. W., Dovidio, J. F., Gurtman, M. B., & Tyler, R. B. (1990). Us and them: Social categorization and the process of intergroup bias. *Journal of Personality and Social Psychology, 59,* 475–486.

Pereira-Smith, O., Smith, J., et al. (1988, August). Paper presented at the annual

meeting of the International Genetics Congress, Toronto.

Pérez-Peña, R. (1996, February 12). Engineer in fatal train collision had a record of running signals. *New York Times,* pp. A1, B5.

Perkins, D. N. (1983). Why the human perceiver is a bad machine. In J. Beck, B. Hope, & A. Rosenfeld (Eds.), *Human and machine vision.* New York: Academic Press.

Perlmutter, M. (1994). Cognitive skills within the context of adult development and old age. In C. B. Fisher, & R. M. Lerner (Eds.), *Applied developmental psychology.* New York: McGraw-Hill.

Perlmutter, M., & Hall, E. (1992). *Adult development and aging* (2nd ed.). New York: Wiley.

Perlmutter, M., & Mitchell, D. B. (1986). The appearance and disappearance of age differences in adult memory. In I. M. Craik, & S. Trehub (Eds.), *Aging and cognitive processes.* New York: Plenum.

Perloff, R. M. (1993). *The dynamics of persuasion.* Mahwah, NJ: Erlbaum.

Perls, F., Hefferline, R., & Goodman, P. (1994). *Gestalt therapy: Excitement and growth in the human personality* (2nd ed.). New York: New York Journal Press.

Perls, F. S. (1970). *Gestalt therapy now: Therapy, techniques, applications.* Palo Alto, CA: Science and Behavior Books.

Perls, F. S. (1967). Group vs. individual therapy. *ETC: A Review of General Semantics, 34,* 306–312.

Perry-Jenkins, M. (1993). Family roles and responsibilities: What has changed and what has remained the same? In J. Frankel (Ed.), *The employed mother and the family context.* Focus on women series, Vol. 14. New York: Springer.

Pervin, L. A. (Ed.). (1990). *Handbook of personality: Theory and research.* New York: Guilford.

Persons, J. B. (1991). Psychotherapy outcome studies do not accurately represent current models of psychotherapy: A proposed remedy. *American Psychologist, 46,* 99–106.

Petersen, A. C., Compas, B. E., Brooks-Gunn, J., Stemmler, M., Ey, S., & Grant, K. E. (1993). Depression in adolescence. *American Psychologist, 48,* 155–168.

Petersen, A. C., Silbereisen, R. K., & Sorenson, S. (1996). Adolescent development: A global perspective. In K. Hurrelmann, & S. F. Hamilton (Eds.), *Social problems and social contexts in adolescence: Perspectives across boundaries.* New York: Aldine de Gruyter.

Petersen, S. E., & Fiez, J. A. (1993). The processing of single words studied with positron emission tomography. *Annual Review of Neuroscience, 16,* 509–530.

Peterson, A. (1985). Pubertal development as a cause of disturbance: Myths, realities, and unanswered questions. *Genetic, Social, and General Psychology Monographs, 111,* 205–232.

Peterson, A. C. (1988, September). Those gangly years. *Psychology Today,* pp. 28–34.

Peterson, B. E., & Stewart, A. J. (1993). Generativity and social motives in young adults. *Journal of Personality and Social Psychology, 65,* 186–198.

Peterson, C., Maier, S. F., & Seligman, M. E. P. (1993). *Learned helplessness: A theory for the age of personal control.* New York: Oxford University Press.

Peterson, C., & Raps, C. S. (1984). Helplessness and hospitalization: More remarks. *Journal of Personality and Social Psychology, 46,* 82–83.

Peterson, D. R. (1991). Connection and disconnection of research and practice in the education of professional psychologists. *American Psychologist, 46,* 422–429.

Peterson, K. C., Prout, M. F., & Schwarz, R. A. (1991). *Post-traumatic stress disorder: A clinician's guide.* New York: Plenum.

Peterson, L. R., & Peterson, M. J. (1959). Short-term retention of individual items. *Journal of Experimental Psychology, 58,* 193–198.

Peterzell, D. H. (1993). Individual differences in the visual attention of human infants: Further evidence for separate sensitization and habituation processes. *Developmental Psychobiology, 26,* 207–218.

Petri, H. L. (1991). *Motivation: Theory, research, and applications* (3rd ed.). Belmont, CA: Wadsworth.

Petri, H. L. (1996). *Motivation: Theory, research, and applications* (4th ed.). Pacific Grove, CA: Brooks/Cole.

Petrill, S. A., Luo, D., Thompson, L. A., & Detterman, D. K. (1996). The independent prediction of general intelligence by elementary cognitive tasks: Genetic and environmental influences. *Behavior Genetics, 26,* 135–147.

Petronis, A., & Kennedy, J. L. (1995). Unstable genes—unstable mind? *American Journal of Psychiatry, 152,* 164–172.

Pettigrew, T. F. (1997, February). Generalized intergroup contact effects on prejudice. *Personality and Social Psychology Bulletin, 23,* 173–185.

Pettingale, K. W., Morris, T., Greer, S., & Haybittle, J. L. (1985). Mental attitudes to cancer: An additional prognostic factor. *Lancet,* 750.

Pettito, L. A. (1993). On the ontogenetic requirements for early language acquisition. In B. de Boysson-Bardies, S. de Schonen, P. W. Jusczyk, P. McNeilage, & J. Morton (Eds.), *Developmental neurocognition: Speech and face processing in the first year of life. NATO ASI series D: Behavioural and social sciences,* Vol. 69. Dordrecht, Netherlands: Kluwer Academic Publishers.

Pettito, L. A., & Marentette, P. F. (1991, March 22). Babbling in the manual mode: Evidence for the ontogeny of language. *Science, 251,* 1493–1496.

Petty, F. (1996, November). What is the role of GABA in mood disorders. *The Harvard Mental Health Letter,* p. 8.

Petty, R. E. (1994). Two routes to persuasion: State of the art. In G. d'Ydewalle, P. Eelen, & P. Bertelson (Eds.), *International perspectives on psychological science, Vol. 2: The state of the art.* Hove, England: Erlbaum.

Petty, R. E., & Cacioppo, J. T. (1984). The effects of involvement on responses to

argument quantity and quality: Central and peripheral routes to persuasion. *Journal of Personality and Social Psychology, 46,* 69–81.

Petty, R. E., & Cacioppo, J. T. (1986). The elaboration likelihood model of persuasion. In L. Berkowitz (Ed.), *Advances in experimental social psychology* (Vol. 10). New York: Academic Press.

Petty, R. E., Cacioppo, J. T., Strathman, A. J., & Priester, J. R. (1994). To think or not to think: Exploring two routes to persuasion. In S. Savitt, & T. C. Brock (Eds.), *Persuasion: Psychological insights and perspectives.* Boston: Allyn & Bacon.

Petty, R. E., Wegener, D. T., & Fabrigar, L. R. (1997). Attitudes and attitude change. *Annual Review of Psychology, 48,* 609–647.*

Petzold, P. (1992). Context effects in judgments of attributes: An information-integration approach. In H. G. Geissler, S. W. Link, & J. T. Townsend (Eds.), *Cognition, information processing, and psychophysics: Basic issues.* Scientific psychology series. Mahwah, NJ: Erlbaum.

Peyser, M., & Underwood, A. (1997). Shyness, sadness, curiosity, joy: Is it nature or nurture? *Newsweek, 149,* 60–64.

Pezdek, K., & Banks, W. P. (Eds.). (1996). *The recovered memory/false memory debate.* New York: Academic Press.

Phares, V. (1992). Where's poppa? The relative lack of attention to the role of fathers in child and adolescent psychopathology. *American Psychologist, 47,* 656–664.

Philippot, P., Reldman, R. S., & Coats, E. J. (Eds.). *Social context of nonverbal behavior.* Cambridge, England: Cambridge University Press.

Phillips, D., McCartney, K., & Scarr, S. (1987). Child-care quality and children's social development. *Developmental Psychology, 23,* 537–543.

Phillips, R. D., Wagner, S. H., Fells, C. A., & Lynch, M. (1990). Do infants recognize emotion in facial expressions? Categorical and "metaphorical" evidence. *Infant Behavior and Development, 13,* 71–84.

Phillips-Hershey, E. H., & Ridley, L. (1996). Strategies for acceptance of diversity of students with mental retardation. *Elementary School Guidance and Counseling, 30,* 282–291.

Phinney, J. S. (1996). When we talk about American ethnic groups, what do we mean? *American Psychologist, 51,* 918–927.

Piaget, J. (1970). Piaget's theory. In P. H. Mussen (Ed.), *Carmichael's manual of child psychology* (Vol. I, 3rd ed.). New York: Wiley.

Piaget, J., & Inhelder, B. (1958). *The growth of logical thinking from childhood to adolescence* (A. Parsons, & S. Seagrin, Trans.). New York: Basic Books.

Piasecki, T. M., Kenford, S. L., Smith, S. S., Fiore, M. C., & Baker, T. B. (1997). Listening to nicotine: Negative affect and the smoking withdrawal conundrum. *Psychological Science, 8,* 184–189.

Piattelli-Palmarini, M. (1994). *Inevitable illusions: How the mistakes of reason rule our minds.* New York: Wiley.

Pich, E. M., Pagliusi, S. R., Tessari, M., Talabot-Ayer, D., Hooft van Huijsduijnen, R., & Chiamulera, C. (1997, January 3). Common neural substrates for the addictive properties of nicotine and cocaine. *Science, 275,* 83–86.

Pickar, D. (1988). Perspectives on a time-dependent model of neuroleptic action. *Schizophrenia Bulletin, 14,* 255–265.

Pierce, G. R., Sarason, B. R., & Sarason, I. G. (Eds.). (1996). *Handbook of social support and the family.* New York: Plenum.

Piercy, F. P., Sprenkle, D. H., Wetchler, J. L., and Associates. (1996). *Family therapy sourcebook.* New York: Guilford Press.

Pihlgren, E. M., Gidycz, C. A., & Lynn, S. J. (1993). Impact of adulthood and adolescent rape experiences on subsequent sexual fantasies. *Imagination, Cognition and Personality, 12,* 321–339.

Piliavin, J. A., & Piliavin, I. M. (1972). Effect of blood on reactions to a victim. *Journal of Personality and Social Psychology, 23,* 353–362.

Pillard, R. C. (1996). Homosexuality from a familial and genetic perspective. In R. P. Cabaj, & T. S. Stein (Eds.), *Textbook of homosexuality and mental health.* Washington, DC: American Psychiatric Press.

Pillemer, D. B. (1990). Clarifying the flashbulb memory concept: Comment on McCloskey, Wible, and Cohen (1988). *Journal of Experimental Psychology: General, 119,* 92–96.

Pines, M. (1981, April 16). Recession is linked to far-reaching psychological harm. *New York Times,* p. C1.

Pinker, S. (1990). Language acquisition. In D. N. Osherson, & H. Lasnik (Eds.), *Language.* Cambridge, MA: MIT Press.

Pinker, S. (1994). *The language instinct.* New York: William Morrow.

Pion, G. M., Mednick, M. T., Astin, H. S., Hall, C. C. I., Kenkel, M. B., Keita, G. P., Kohout, J. L., & Kelleher, J. C. (1996). The shifting gender composition of psychology: Trends and implications for the discipline. *American Psychologist, 51,* 509–528.

Piotrowski, C., & Keller, J. W. (1989). Psychological testing in outpatient mental health facilities: A national study. *Professional Psychology: Research and Practice, 20,* 423–425.

Pi-Sunyer, F. X. (1987). Exercise effects on caloric intake. In R. Wurtman (Ed.), *Obesity.* New York: New York Academy of Science.

Pledge, D. S. (1992). Marital separation/divorce: A review of individual responses to a major life stressor. *Journal of Divorce and Remarriage, 17,* 151–181.

Plomin, R. (1989). Environment and genes: Determinants of behavior. *American Psychologist, 44,* 105–111.

Plomin, R. (1990, April 13). The role of inheritance in behavior. *Science, 248,* 183–188.

Plomin, R. (1994). *Genetics and experience: The interplay between nature and nurture.* Newbury Park, CA: Sage.

Plomin, R. (1995). Molecular genetics and psychology. *Current Directions in Psychological Science, 4*, 114–117.

Plomin, R., & McClearn, G. E. (Eds.). (1993). *Nature, nurture, and psychology.* Washington, DC: American Psychological Association.

Plomin, R., & Neiderhiser, J. M. (1992). Genetics and experience. *Current Directions in Psychological Science, 1*, 160–163.

Plomin, R., & Petrill, S. A. (1997). Genetics and intelligence: What's new? *Intelligence, 24*, 53–77.

Plous, S. (1988). Disarmament, arms control, and peace in the nuclear age: Political objectives and relevant research. *Journal of Social Issues, 44*, 133–154.

Plous, S. (1991). An attitude survey of animal rights activists. *Psychological Science, 2*, 194–196.

Plous, S. (1996a). Attitudes toward the use of animals in psychological research and education: Results from a national survey of psychologists. *American Psychologist, 51*, 1167–1180.

Plous, S. (1996b). Attitudes toward the use of animals in psychological research and education: Results from a national survey of psychology majors. *Psychological Science, 7*, 352–358.

Plucker, J. A., & McIntire, J. (1996). Academic survivability in high-potential, middle school students. *Gifted Child Quarterly, 40*, 7–14.

Plumert, J. M., Carswell, C., De Vet, K., & Ihrig, D. (1995). The content and organization of communication about object locations. *Journal of Memory and Language, 34*, 477–498.

Plummer, W., & Pick, G. (1996, October 10). Beating the blitz. *People Weekly*, pp. 129–132.

Plutchik, R. (1980). *Emotion, a psychoevolutionary synthesis.* New York: Harper & Row.

Plutchik, R. (1984). Emotion. In K. Scherer, & P. Ekman (Eds.), *Approaches to emotion.* Mahwah, NJ: Erlbaum.

Polivy, J., & Herman, C. P. (1985). Dieting and binging: A causal analysis. *American Psychologist, 40*, 193–201.

Polivy, J., & Herman, C. P. (1991). Good and bad dieters: Self-perception and reaction to a dietary challenge. *International Journal of Eating Disorders, 10*, 91–99.

Polk, N. (1997, March 30). The trouble with school testing systems. *New York Times*, p. CN3.

Pollack, A. (1993, February 9). Computers taking wish as their command. *New York Times*, pp. A1, D2.

Pollock, D. A., Rhodes, P., Boyle, C. A., Decoufle, P., & McGee, D. L. (1990). Estimating the number of suicides among Vietnam veterans. *American Journal of Psychiatry, 147*, 772–776.

Polymeropoulos, M. H., Higgins, J. J., Golbe, L. W., Johnson, W. G., Ide, S. E., Di Iorio, G., Sanges, G., Stenroos, E. S., Pho, L. T., Schaffer, A. A., Lazzarini, A. M., Nussbaum, R. L., & Duvoisin, R. C. (1996, November 15). Mapping of a gene for Parkinson's Disease to chromosome 4q21–q23. *Science, 274*, 1197–1199.

Pomerleau, O. F. (1995). Individual differences in sensitivity to nicotine: Implications of genetic research on nicotine dependence. Special Issue: Genetic, environmental, and situational factors mediating the effects of nicotine. *Behavior Genetics, 25*, 161–177.

Pomerleau, O., Adkins, D., & Pertschuk, M. (1978). Predictors of outcome and recidivism in smoking cessation treatment. *Addictive Behaviors, 3*, 65–70.

Pomerleau, O. F., & Pomerleau, C. S. (1989). A biobehavioral perspective on smoking. In T. Ney, & A. Gale (Eds.), *Smoking and human behavior.* New York: Wiley.

Ponomarev, D. (1993, February 28). On turning 13: Reports from the front lines. *New York Times*, Sec. 4, p. 2.

Pontieri, F. E., Tanda, G., Orzi, F., & Di-Chiara, G. (1996, July 18). Effects of nicotine on the nucleus accumbens and similarity to those of addictive drugs. *Nature, 382*, 255–257.

Porer, S. L., Malpass, R. S., & Koehnken, G. (Eds.). (1996). *Psychological issues in eyewitness identification.* Mahway, NJ: Erlbaum.

Porkka-Heiskanen, T., Strecker, R. E., Thakkar, M., Bjorkum, A. A., Greene, R. W., & McCarley, R. W. (1997, May 23). Adensosine: A mediator of the sleep-inducing effects of prolonged wakefulness. *Science, 276*, 1265–1268.

Porte, H. S., & Hobson, J. A. (1996). Physical motion in dreams: One measure of three theories. *Journal of Abnormal Psychology, 105*, 329–335.

Porter, C. P., Oakley, D., Ronis, O. L., & Neal, R. W. (1996). Pathways of influence on fifth and eighth graders' reports about having had sexual intercourse. *Journal of Research in Nursing and Health, 19*, 193–204.

Porter, R. H., Cernich, J. M., & McLaughlin, F. J. (1983). Maternal recognition of neonates through olfactory cues. *Physiology and Behavior, 30*, 151–154.

Posner, M. I. (1993). Seeing the mind. *Science, 262*, 673–674.

Potheraju, A., & Soper, B. (1995). A comparison of self-reported dream themes for high school and college students. *College Student Journal, 29*, 417–420.

Potter, M. C. (1990). Remembering. In D. N. Osherson, & E. E. Smith (Eds.), *Thinking.* Cambridge, MA: MIT Press.

Pottieger, A. E., Tressell, P. A., Inciardi, J. A., & Rosales, T. A. (1992). Cocaine use patterns and overdose. *Journal of Psychoactive Drugs, 24*, 399–410.

Powell, D. H., & Whitla, D. K. (1994a). *Profiles in cognitive aging.* Cambridge, MA: Cambridge University Press.

Powell, D. H., & Whitla, D. K. (1994b, February). Normal cognitive aging: Toward empirical perspectives. *Current Directions in Psychological Science, 3*, 27–31.

Powell, J. (1996). *AIDS and HIV-related diseases: An educational guide for professionals and the public.* New York: Plenum/Insight Books.

Powell, L. H., Shaker, L. A., & Jones, B. A. (1993). Psychosocial predictors of mortality in 83 women with premature acute myocardial infarction. *Psychosomatic Medicine, 55*, 426–433.

Power, T. (1981). Sex typing in infancy: The role of the father. *Infant Mental Health Journal, 2*, 226–240.

Power, T. G., & Parke, R. D. (1982). Play as a context for early learning: Lab and home analyses. In L. M. Laosa, & I. E. Sigal (Eds.), *The family as a learning environment.* New York: Plenum.

Powers, D. E. (1993). Coaching for the SAT: A summary of the summaries and an update. *Educational Measurement Issues and Practice, 12*, 24–30, 39.

Prado-Alcala, R. A. (1995). Serial and parallel processing during memory consolidation. In J. L. McGaugh, F. Bermudez-Rattoni, & R. A. Prado-Alcala (Eds.), *Plasticity in the central nervous system: Learning and memory.* Mahwah, NJ: Erlbaum.

Pratt, S. I., & Moreland, K. L. (1996). Introduction to treatment outcome: Historical perspectives and current issues. In S. I. Pfeiffer (Ed.), *Outcome assessment in residential treatment.* New York: Haworth Press.

Pressley, M. (1987). Are keyword method effects limited to slow presentation rates? An empirically based reply to Hall and Fuson (1986). *Journal of Educational Psychology, 79*, 333–335.

Pressley, M., & Levin, J. R. (1983). *Cognitive strategy research: Psychological foundations.* New York: Springer-Verlag.

Pressman, M. R., & Orr, W. C. (1997). *Understanding sleep: The evaluation and treatment of sleep disorders.* Washington, DC: American Psychological Association.

Preston, J. M. (1998). From mediated environments to the development of consciousness. In J. Gackenbach (Ed.), *Psychology and the Internet: Intrapersonal, interpersonal, and transpersonal implications.* San Diego: Academic Press.

Pribram, K. H. (1984). Emotion: A neurobehavioral analysis. In K. R. Scherer, & P. Ekman (Eds.), *Approaches to emotion.* Mahwah, NJ: Erlbaum.

Price, R. (1992). Psychosocial impact of job loss on individuals and families. *Current Directions in Psychological Science, 1*, 9–14.

Priester, J. R., & Petty, R. E. (1995). Source attributions and persuasion: Perceived honesty as a determinant of message scrutiny. *Personality and Social Psychology Bulletin, 21*, 637–654.

Prince, R. J., & Guastello, S. J. (1990). The Barnum effect in a computerized Rorschach interpretation system. *Journal of Personality, 124*, 217–222.

Prochaska, J. O. (1995). An eclectic and integrative approach: Transtheoretical therapy. In A. S. Gurman, & S. B. Messer (Eds.), *Essential psychotherapies: Theory and practice.* New York: Guilford Press.

Pruitt, D. G., & Rubin, J. Z. (1986). *Social conflict: Escalation, stalemate, and settlement.* New York: Random House.

Pryor, J. B., & Reeder, G. D. (Eds.). (1993). *The social psychology of HIV infection.* Mahwah, NJ: Erlbaum.

PsychINFO. (1991, January). The PsychINFO Basic Workshop. *Psychological Bulletin, 107,* 210–214.

Pulkkinen, L. (1994). Emootion saately kehityksessa. / Emotion regulation in human development. *Psykologia, 29,* 404–418.

Pulvirenti, L., & Koob, G. F. (1994). Lisuride reduces intravenous cocaine self-administration in rats. *Pharmacology, Biochemistry and Behavior, 47,* 819–822.

Purdy, M. (1994, January 30). Budding scientist's success breaks the mold. *New York Times,* pp. A1, A36.

Purves, D., Augustine, G. J., Fitzpatrick, D., Katz, L. C., LaMantia, A., & McNamara, J. O. (Eds.). (1997). *Neuroscience.* Sunderland, MA: Sinauer.

Purvis, A. (1997, January 6). The global epidemic. *Time,* pp. 76–78.

Putnam, F. W. (1995a). Development of dissociative disorders. In D. Cicchetti, & D. J. Cohen (Eds.), *Developmental psychopathology, Vol. 2: Risk, disorder, and adaptation.* Wiley series on personality processes. New York: Wiley.

Putnam, F. W. (1995b). Traumatic stress and pathological dissociation. In G. P. Chrousos, R. McCarty, K. Pacak, G. Cizza, E. Sternberg, P. W. Gold, & R. Kvetnansky (Eds.), *Stress: Basic mechanisms and clinical implications.* Annals of the New York Academy of Sciences, Vol. 771. New York: New York Academy of Sciences.

Putnam, F. W., Guroff, J. J., Silberman, E. K., Barban, L., et al. (1986). The clinical phenomenology of multiple personality disorder: Review of 100 recent cases. *Journal of Clinical Psychiatry, 47,* 285–293.

Quick, E. K. (1996). *Doing what works in brief therapy: A strategic solution focused approach.* San Diego, CA: Academic Press.

Quinn, M. (1990, January 29). Don't aim that pack at us. *Time,* p. 60.

Quinn, M. J. (1997). *Sexual harassment.* Amherst, MA: University of Massachusetts Office of Equal Opportunity & Diversity.

Quirion, R., Wilson, A., Rowe, W., Aubert, I., et al. (1995). Facilitation of acetylcholine release and cognitive performance by an M_2-muscarinic receptor antagonist in aged memory-impaired rats. *Journal of Neuroscience, 15,* 1455–1462.

Rachman, S., & deSilva, P. (1996). *Panic disorder.* Oxford, England: Oxford University Press.*

Rachman, S., & Hodgson, R. (1980). *Obsessions and compulsions.* Englewood Cliffs, NJ: Prentice-Hall.*

Rachman, S. J. (1990). The determinants of treatment of simple phobias. *Advances in Behaviour Research and Therapy, 12,* 1–30.*

Rachman, S. J. (1991). Neo-conditioning and the classical theory of fear acquisition. *Clinical Psychology Review, 11,* 155–173.*

Rachman, S. J. (1997). A cognitive theory of obsessions. *Behaviour Research and Therapy, 35,* 793–802.*

Racy, J. (1996, August). Combined therapy. *The Harvard Mental Health Letter,* pp. 5, 6.

Raggozzino, M. E., Hellems, K., Lennartz, R. C., & Gold, P. E. (1995). Pyruvate infusions into the septal area attenuate spontaneous alternation impairments induced by intraseptal morphine injections. *Behavioral Neuroscience, 109,* 1074–1080.

Ragland, D. R. (1988, January 14). Type A behavior and mortality from coronary heart disease. *New England Journal of Medicine, 318,* 65.

Ragozin, A. S. (1980). Attachment behavior of day care children: Naturalistic and laboratory observations. *Child Development, 51,* 409–415.

Rahe, R. H., & Arthur, R. J. (1978). Life change and illness studies: Past history and future directions. *Human Stress, 4,* 3–15.

Raichle, M. E. (1994). Images of the mind: Studies with modern imaging techniques. *Annual Review of Psychology, 45,* 333–356.

Raikkonen, K., Keskivaara, P., Keltikangas, J. L., & Butzow, E. (1995). Psychophysiological arousal related to Type A components in adolescent boys. *Scandinavian Journal of Psychology, 36,* 142–152.

Rainville, P., Duncan, G. H., Price, D. D., Carrier, B., & Bushnell, M. C. (1997, August 15). Pain affect encoded in human anterior cingulate but not somatosensory cortex. *Science, 277,* 968–971.

Rajecki, D. W. (1989). *Attitudes* (2nd ed.). Sunderland, MA: Sinauer.

Rakel, R. E. (1993). Insomnia: Concerns of the family physician. *Journal of Family Practice, 36,* 551–558.

Rakoff, V. M. (1995). Trauma and adolescent rites of initiation. In R. C. Marohn, & S. C. Feinstein (Eds.), *Adolescent psychiatry: Developmental and clinical studies,* Vol. 20. Annals of the American Society for Adolescent Psychiatry. Mahwah, NJ: Analytic Press, Inc.

Ralph, M. R., & Lehman, M. N. (1991). Transplantation: A new tool in the analysis of the mammalian hypothalamic circadian pacemaker. *Trends in Neuroscience, 14,* 362–366.*

Ramachandran, V. S. (1992). Filling in gaps in perception: Part 1. *Current Directions in Psychological Science, 1,* 199–205.

Ramachandran, V. S. (1995). Filling in gaps in logic: Reply to Durgin et al. *Perception, 24,* 841–845.

Randolph, C., Tierney, M. C., & Chase, T. N. (1995). Implicit memory in Alzheimer's disease. *Journal of Clinical and Experimental Neuropsychology, 17,* 343–351.

Rankin, C. H., & Wicks, S. R. (2000). Mutations of the Caenorhabditis elegans brain-specific inorganic phosphate transporter eat-4 affect habituation of the tap-withdrawal response without affecting the response itself. *The Journal of Neuroscience, 20,* 4337–4344.*

Raphael, B. (1976). *The thinking computer.* San Francisco: Freeman.

Rapoff, M. A., & Christophersen, E. R. (1982). Improving compliance in pediatric practice. *Pediatric Clinics of North America, 29,* 339–357.

Rappaport, Z. H. (1992). Psychosurgery in the modern era: Therapeutic and ethical aspects. *Medicine and Law, 11,* 449–453.

Raskin, N. J., & Rogers, C. R. (1989). Person-centered therapy. In R. J. Corsini, & D. Wedding (Eds.), *Current psychotherapies* (4th ed.). Itasca, IL: Peacock.

Rasmussen, J. (1981). Models of mental strategies in process control. In J. Rasmussen, & W. Rouse (Eds.), *Human detection and diagnosis of system failures.* New York: Plenum.

Ratcliff, R., & McKoon, G. (1989). Memory models, text processing, and cue-dependent retrieval. In H. L. Roediger, III, & F. I. M. Craik (Eds.), *Varieties of memory and consciousness: Essays in honour of Endel Tulving.* Mahwah, NJ: Erlbaum.

Ratner, H. H., Schell, D. A., Crimmins, A., Mittelman, D., et al. (1987). Changes in adults' prose recall: Aging or cognitive demands? *Developmental Psychology, 23,* 521–525.

Rattermann, M. J. (1992). Developmental trends in similarity as structural alignment: Evidence from children's performance in mapping tasks. *Dissertation Abstracts International, 52,* 6108.

Rau, H., Weitkunat, R., Brody, S., Buhrer, M., et al. (1996). Biofeedback of R-wave to pulse interval produces differential learning of blood pressure control. *Scandinavian Journal of Behaviour Therapy, 25,* 17–25.

Rauch, S. L., & Renshaw, P. F. (1995). Clinical neuroimaging in psychiatry. *Harvard Review of Psychiatry,* 297–312.

Raykov, T. (1995). Multivariate structural modeling of plasticity in fluid intelligence of aged adults. *Multivariate Behavioral Research, 30,* 255–287.

Raymond, J. L., Lisberger, S. G., & Mauk, M. D. (1996, May 24). The cerebellum: A neuronal learning machine? *Science, 272,* 1126–1131.

Read, J. D. (1996). From a passing thought to a false memory in 2 minutes: Confusing real and illusory events. *Psychonomic Bulletin and Review, 3,* 105–111.

Rector, N. A., Segal, Z. V., & Gemar, M. (1998). Schema research in depression: A Canadian perspective. *Canadian Journal of Behavioural Science, 30,* 213–224.*

Redding, G. M., & Hawley, E. (1993). Length illusion in fractional Müller-Lyer stimuli: An object-perception approach. *Perception, 22,* 819–828.

Redmond, R., & Redmond, X. (1994). *Anger kills.* New York: Harper Perennial.

Ree, M. J., & Earles, J. A. (1992). Intelligence is the best predictor of job performance. *Current Directions in Psychological Research, 1,* 86–89.

Reed, D. R., Bartoshuk, L. M., Duffy, V., Marino, S., & Price, R. A. (1995). Propylthiouracil tasting: Determination of underlying threshold distributions using maximum likelihood. *Chemical Senses, 20,* 529–533.

Reed, S. K. (1988). *Cognition: Theories and applications* (2nd ed.). Monterey, CA: Brooks/Cole.

Reed, S. K. (1996). *Cognition: Theory and applications* (4th ed.). Pacific Grove, CA: Brooks/Cole.

Rees, G., Frith, C. D., & Lavie, N. (1997, November 28). Modulating irrelevant motion perception by varying attentional load in an unrelated task. *Science, 278,* 1616–1619.

Reeves, R. A., Baker, G. A., Boyd, J. G., & Cialdini, R. B. (1991). The door-in-the-face technique: Reciprocal concessions vs. self-presentational explanations. *Journal of Social Behavior and Personality, 6,* 545–558.

Regan, D. (Ed.). (1991). *Binocular vision.* New York: Macmillan.*

Register, A. C., Beckham, J. C., May, J. G., & Gustafson, D. F. (1991). Stress inoculation bibliotherapy in the treatment of test anxiety. *Journal of Counseling Psychology, 38,* 115–119.

Reich, C., & Purbhoo, M. (1975). The effect of cross-cultural contact. *Canadian Journal of Behavioural Science, 7,* 313–327.*

Reich, P. A. (1986). *Language development.* Englewood Cliffs, NJ: Prentice-Hall.

Reich, W. (Ed.). (1990). *Origins of terrorism: Psychologies, ideologies, theologies, states of mind.* Mahwah, NJ: Erlbaum.

Reichman, W. E., & Rabins, P. V. (1996). Schizophrenia and other psychotic disorders. In W. E. Reichman, & P. R. Katz (Eds.), *Psychiatric care in the nursing home.* New York: Oxford University Press.

Reinisch, J. M., Rosenblum, L. A., Rubin, D. B., Schulsinger, M. F., et al. (1997). Biological causation: Are gender differences wired into our biology? In M. R. Walsh (Ed.), *Women, men, & gender: Ongoing debates.* New Haven, CT: Yale University Press.

Reis, S. M. (1989). Reflections on policy affecting the education of gifted and talented students. *American Psychologist, 44,* 399–408.

Reisberg, D. (1997). *Cognition: Exploring the science of the mind.* New York: Norton.

Reisenzein, R. (1983). The Schachter theory of emotion: Two decades later. *Psychological Bulletin, 94,* 239–264.

Reiss, B. F. (1980). Psychological tests in homosexuality. In J. Marmor (Ed.), *Homosexual behavior* (pp. 296–311). New York: Basic Books.

Reiss, I. L. (1960). *Premarital sexual standards in America.* New York: Free Press.

Reitman, J. S. (1965). *Cognition and thought.* New York: Wiley.

Report of the Commission on Systemic racism in the Ontario Criminal Justice System, 1995.*

Rescorla, R. A. (1988). Pavlovian conditioning: It's not what you think it is. *American Psychologist, 43,* 151–160.

Resnick, S. M. (1992). Positron emission tomography in psychiatric illness. *Current*

Directions in Psychological Science, 1, 92–98.

Reuman, D. A., Alwin, D. F., & Veroff, J. (1984). Assessing the validity of the achievement motive in the presence of random measurement error. *Journal of Personality and Social Psychology, 47,* 1347–1362.

Reynolds, B. A., & Weiss, S. (1992, March 27). Generations of neurons and astrocytes from isolated cells of the adult mammalian central nervous system. *Science, 255,* 1707–1710.

Reynolds, C. F., III, & Kupfer, D. J. (1994). Sleep disorders. In J. M. Oldham, & M. B. Riba (Eds.), *Review of Psychiatry, 13.* Washington, DC: American Psychiatric Press.

Reynolds, R. I., & Takooshian, H. (1988, January). Where were you August 8, 1985? *Bulletin of the Psychonomic Society, 26,* 23–25.

Rheingold, H. L. (1994). *The psychologist's guide to an academic career.* Washington, DC: American Psychological Association.

Rhodes, N., & Wood, W. (1992). Self-esteem and intelligence affect influenceability: The mediating role of message reception. *Psychological Bulletin, 111,* 156–171.

Rhodewalt, F., & Fairfield, M. (1991). An alternative approach to Type A behavior and health: Psychological reactance and medical noncompliance. In M. J. Strube (Ed.), *Type A behavior.* Newbury Park, CA: Sage.

Rhue, J. W., & Lynn, S. J. (1987). Fantasy-proneness and psychopathology. *Journal of Personality and Social Psychology, 53,* 327–336.

Rhue, J. W., Lynn, S. J., & Kirsch, I. (Eds.). (1993). *Handbook of clinical hypnosis.* Washington, DC: American Psychological Association.

Ricciuti, H. N. (1993). Nutrition and mental development. *Current Directions in Psychological Science, 2,* 43–46.

Rice, A. (1984, May). Imagination to go. *Psychology Today,* pp. 48–52.

Rice, M. L. (1989). Children's language acquisition. *American Psychologist, 44,* 149–156.

Rich, F. (1997, May 1). Harnisch's perfect pitch. *New York Times,* p. A35.

Richards, M., Boxer, A., Petersen, A., & Albrecht, R. (1990). Relation of weight to body image in pubertal girls and boys from two communities. *Developmental Psychology, 26,* 313–321.

Richards, R., Kinney, D. K., Benet, M., & Merzel, A. P. C. (1988). Assessing everyday creativity: Characteristics of the lifetime creativity scales and validation with three large samples. *Journal of Personality and Social Psychology, 54,* 476–485.

Richie, J. (1994, April). Paper presented at the annual meeting of the American Association for Cancer Research, San Francisco.

Richmond, B. J., Optican, L. M., Podell, M., & Spitzer, H. (1987). Temporal encoding of two-dimensional patterns by single units in primate inferior temporal cortex. 1. Response characteristics. *Journal of Neurophysiology, 57,* 132–146.

Ricklefs, R. E., & Finch, C. E. (1995). *Aging: A natural history.* New York: Scientific

American Library/Scientific American Books.

Rieder, R. O., Kaufmann, C. A., & Knowles, J. A. (1996). Genetics. In R. E. Hales, & S. C. Yudofsky (Eds.), *The American Psychiatric Press synopsis of psychiatry.* Washington, DC: American Psychiatric Press.

Riefer, D. M., Keveri, M. K., & Kramer, D. L. F. (1995). Name that tune: Eliciting the tip-of-the-tongue experience using auditory stimuli. *Psychological Reports, 77,* 1379–1390.

Riegel, K. F., & Riegel, R. M. (1972). Development, drop, and death. *Developmental Psychology, 6,* 306–319.

Rierdan, J. (1996). *Adolescent suicide: One response to adversity.* In R. S. Feldman (Ed.), *The psychology of adversity.* Amherst, MA: University of Massachusetts Press.

Riese, M. L. (1990). Neonatal temperament in monozygotic and dizygotic twin pairs. *Child Development, 61,* 1230–1237.

Riggio, R. F., & Porter, L. W. (Eds.). (1996). *Introduction to industrial/organizational psychology* (2nd ed.). New York: HarperCollins.

Riggs, D. S., & Foa, E. B. (1995, April). Post-traumatic stress disorder following assault: Theoretical considerations and empirical findings. *Current Directions in Psychological Science, 4,* 61–65.

Ringold, D. J. (1996). Social criticisms of target marketing: Process or product? In R. P. Hill (Ed.), *Marketing and consumer research in the public interest.* Thousand Oaks, CA: Sage.

Rinn, W. E. (1984). The neuropsychology of facial expression: A review of neurological and psychological mechanisms for producing facial expressions. *Psychological Bulletin, 95,* 52–77.

Rinn, W. E. (1991). Neuropsychology of facial expression. In R. S. Feldman, & B. Rimé (Eds.), *Fundamentals of nonverbal behavior.* Cambridge, England: Cambridge University Press.

Rips, L. J. (1990). Reasoning. *Annual Review of Psychology, 41,* 321–353.

Rips, L. J. (1994a). Deductive reasoning. In R. J. Sternberg (Ed.), *Thinking and problem-solving.* San Diego, CA: Academic Press.

Rips, L. J. (1994b). *The psychology of proof: Deductive reasoning in human thinking.* Cambridge, MA: MIT Press.

Rips, L. J. (1995). Deduction and cognition. In E. E. Smith, & D. N. Osherson (Eds.), *Thinking: An invitation to cognitive science,* Vol. 3 (2nd ed.). Cambridge, MA: MIT Press.

Risch, N., & Merikangas, K. (1996, September 13). The future of genetic studies of complex human diseases. *Science, 273,* 1516–1517.

Ritzler, B., & Rosenbaum, G. (1974). Proprioception in schizophrenics and normals: Effects of stimulus intensity and interstimulus interval. *Journal of Abnormal Psychology, 83,* 106–111.

Rizley, R. C., & Rescorla, R. A. (1972). Associations in higher order conditioning and sensory pre-conditioning. *Journal of*

Comparative and Physiological Psychology, 81, 1–11.

Robbins, M., & Jensen, G. D. (1978). Multiple orgasm in males. *Journal of Sex Research, 14*, 21–26.

Robbins, T. W. (1988). Arresting memory decline. *Nature, 336*, 207–208.

Robbins, W. J. (1929). *Growth*. New Haven, CT: Yale University Press.

Roberts, A. H., Kewman, D. G., Mercier, L., & Hovell, M. (1993). The power of nonspecific effects in healing: Implications for psychosocial and biological treatments. *Clinical Psychology Review, 13*, 375–391.

Roberts, B. W., & Helson, R. (1997). Changes in culture, changes in personality: The influence of individualism in a longitudinal study of women. *Journal of Personality and Social Psychology, 72*, 641–651.

Roberts, L. (1988, January 1). Zeroing in on the sex switch. *Science, 239*, 21–23.

Roberts, S. B., Savage, J., Coward, W. A., Chew, B., & Lucas, A. (1988, February 25). Energy expenditure and intake in infants born to lean and overweight mothers. *New England Journal of Medicine, 318*, 461–466.

Roberts, S. M. (1995). Applicability of the goodness-of-fit hypothesis to coping with daily hassles. *Psychological Reports, 77*, 943–954.

Robertson, J. M. (1994). Tracing ideological perspectives through 100 years of an academic genealogy. *Psychological Reports, 75*, 859–879.

Robinson, B. A. (1998). Female and intersexual genital mutilation in North America and Europe. Available: <http://www.religioustolerance.org/fem_cira.htm>. [March 16, 1998; updated April 13, 2000].

Robinson, D. N. (1995). *An intellectual history of psychology* (3rd ed.). Madison, WI: University of Wisconsin Press.

Robinson, J., & Godbey, G. (1997). *Time for life*. Pennsylvania State University Press.

Robinson, R. J., Keltner, D., & Ross, L. (1991). Misconstruing the views of the "other side": Real and perceived differences in three ideological conflicts. Working Paper No. 18, Stanford Center on Conflict and Negotiation, Stanford University.

Rodin, J. (1981). Current status of the internal-external hypothesis of obesity: What went wrong? *American Psychologist, 34*, 361–372.

Rodin, J. (1985). Insulin levels, hunger, and food intake: An example of feedback loops in body-weight regulation. *Health Psychology, 4*, 1–18.

Rodin, J. (1986, September 19). Aging and health: Effects of the sense of control. *Science, 233*, 1271–1276.

Rodin, J., & Janis, I. L. (1979). The social power of health care practitioners as agents of change. *The Journal of Social Issues, 35*, 60–81.

Roediger, H. L., III. (1990). Implicit memory: Retention without remembering. *American Psychologist, 45*, 1043–1056.

Roediger, H. L., III, & Jacoby, J. D. (1996). Misinformation effects in recall: Creating false memories through repeated retrieval.

Journal of Memory and Language, 35, 300–318.

Roediger, H. L., III, & McDermott, K. B. (1995). Creating false memories: Remembering words not presented in lists. *Journal of Experimental Psychology: Learning, Memory, and Cognition, 21*, 803–814.

Roediger, H. L., Weldon, M. S., & Challis, B. H. (1989). Explaining dissociations between implicit and explicit measures of retention: A processing account. In H. L. Roediger, & F. I. M Craik (Eds.), *Varieties of memory and consciousness: Essays in honour of Endel Tulving*. Mahwah, NJ: Erlbaum.

Rogers, C. R. (1951). *Client-centered therapy*. Boston: Houghton-Mifflin.

Rogers, C. R. (1971). A theory of personality. In S. Maddi (Ed.), *Perspectives on personality*. Boston: Little, Brown.

Rogers, C. R. (1980). *A way of being*. Boston: Houghton Mifflin.

Rogers, M. (1988, February 15). The return of 3-D movies—on TV. *Newsweek*, pp. 60–62.

Rogers, P., & Eftimiades, M. (1995, July 24). *People Weekly*, 42–43.

Rogoff, B. (1990). *Cognitive development in social context*. New York: Oxford University Press.

Rohner-Jeanrenaud, F., & Jeanrenaud, B. (1996). Obesity, leptin, and the brain. *New England Journal of Medicine, 334*, 324–325.

Rokeach, M. (1971). Long-range experimental modification of values, attitudes, and behavior. *American Psychologist, 26*, 453–459.

Rolland, J. S., & Walsh, F. (1996). Family therapy: Systems approaches to assessment and treatment. In R. E. Hales, & S. C. Yudofsky (Eds.), *The American Psychiatric Press synopsis of psychiatry*. Washington, DC: American Psychiatric Press.

Rolls, E. T. (1994). Neural processing related to feeding in primates. In C. R. Legg, & D. A. Booth (Eds.), *Appetite: Neural and behavioural bases*. European Brain & Behaviour Society Publications Series, 1. Oxford, England: Oxford University Press.

Rorschach, H. (1924). *Psychodiagnosis: A diagnostic test based on perception*. New York: Grune and Stratton.

Rosch, E. (1974). Linguistic relativity. In A. Silverstein (Ed.), *Human communication: Theoretical explorations* (pp. 95–121). New York: Halstead Press.

Rose, R. J. (1995). Genes and human behavior. *Annual Review of Psychology, 46*, 625–654.

Rose, R. J., Koskenvuo, M., Kaprio, J., Sarna, S., & Langinvainio, H. (1988). Shared genes, shared experiences, and similarity of personality: Data from 14,288 adult Finnish co-twins. *Journal of Personality and Social Psychology, 54*, 161–171.

Rose-Krasnor, L., Rubin, K. H., Booth, C. L., & Coplan, R. (1996). The relation of maternal directiveness and child attachment security to social competence in preschoolers. *International Journal of Behavioral Development, 19*, 309–325.*

Rosenau, J. N. (1967). Introduction. In J. N. Rosenau (Ed.), *Domestic sources of foreign policy*. New York: Free Press.

Rosenblatt, R. (1996, August 26). New hopes, new dreams. *Time*, p. 40–51.

Rosenfeld, J. P. (1995). Alternative views of Bashore and Rapp's (1993) alternatives to traditional polygraphy: A critique. *Psychological Bulletin, 117*, 159–166.

Rosenhan, D. L. (1973). On being sane in insane places. *Science, 179*, 250–258.

Rosenheck, R., Cramer, J., Xu, W., Thomas, J., Henderson, W., Frisman, L., Oye, C., & Charney, D. (1997). A comparison of clazapine and haloperidol in hospitalized patients with refractory schizophrenia. *New England Journal of Medicine, 337*, 809–815.

Rosenman, R. H. (1990). Type A behavior pattern: A personal overview. *Journal of Social Behavior and Personality, 5*, 1–24.

Rosenman, R. H., Brond, R. J., Sholtz, R. I., & Friedman, M. (1976). Multivariate prediction of coronary heart disease during 8.5 year follow-up in the Western collaborative group study. *American Journal of Cardiology, 37*, 903–910.

Rosenstein, D. S., & Horowitz, H. A. (1996). Adolescent attachment and psychopathology. *Journal of Consulting and Clinical Psychology, 64*, 244–253.

Rosenthal, A. M. (1993, July 27). The torture continues. *New York Times*, p. A13.

Rosenthal, E. (1991, April, 23). Pulses of light give astronauts new rhythms. *New York Times*, pp. C1, C8.

Rosenthal, J. (1997, March 9). The age boom. *New York Times Magazine*, pp. 39–43.

Rosenthal, L. H. (1997). *A new perspective on the relation between fear and persuasion: The application of dual-process models*. Unpublished doctoral dissertation, University of Massachusetts, Amherst.

Rosenthal, R. (1994a). Interpersonal expectancy effects: A 30-year perspective. *Current Directions in Psychological Science, 3*, 176–179.

Rosenthal, R. (1994b). Science and ethics in conducting, analyzing, and reporting psychological research. *Psychological Science, 5*, 127–134.

Rosenthal, T. L., & Steffek, B. D. (1991). Modeling methods. In F. H. Kanfer, & A. P. Goldstein (Eds.), *Helping people change: A textbook of methods* (4th ed.). Pergamon General Psychology Series, Vol. 52. New York: Pergamon Press.

Rosenzweig, M. R. (1992). Psychological science around the world. *American Psychologist, 47*, 718–722.

Rosenzweig, M. R. (1996). Aspects of the search for neural mechanisms of memory. *Annual Review of Psychology, 47*, 1–32.

Rosewicz, B. (1996, September) Here comes the bride . . . for the umpteenth time. *The Wall Street Journal*, p. B1.

Roskos-Ewoldsen, D. R., & Fazio, R. H. (1992). The accessibility of source likability as a determinant of persuasion. *Personality and Social Psychology Bulletin, 18*, 19–25.

Rosnow, R. L., & Rosenthal, R. (1997). *Turn away influences that undermine scientific experiments*. New York: Freeman.

Rosnow, R. L., Rotheram-Borus, M. J., Ceci, S. J., Blanck, P. D., & Koocher, G. P. (1993). The institutional review board as a mirror of scientific and ethical standards. *American Psychologist, 48,* 821–826.

Ross, C. A. (1989). *Multiple personality disorder: Diagnosis, clinical features and treatment.* New York: Wiley.*

Ross, C. A. (1994). *The Osiris complex: Case-studies in multiple personality disorder.* Toronto: University of Toronto Press.*

Ross, C. A. (1996). *Dissociative identity disorder: Diagnosis, clinical features, and treatment of multiple personality.* Somerset, NJ: Wiley.*

Ross, C. A., Miller, S. D., Reagor, P., Bjornson, L., Fraser, G. A., & Anderson, G. (1990). Structured interview data on 102 cases of multiple personality disorder from four centers. *American Journal of Psychiatry, 147,* 596–601.

Ross, D. F., Read, J. D., & Toglia, M. P. (Eds.). (1994). *Adult eyewitness testimony: Current trends and developments.* New York: Cambridge University Press.

Ross, L. (1977). The intuitive psychologist and his shortcomings. Distortions in the attribution process. In L. Berkowitz (Ed.), *Advances in experimental social psychology* (Vol. 10, pp. 174–221). New York: Academic Press.

Ross, L., Greene, D., & House, P. (1977). The false consensus effect: An egocentric bias in social perception and attribution processes. *Journal of Experimental Social Psychology, 13,* 279–301.

Ross, L., & Nisbett, R. E. (1991). *The person and the situation.* New York: McGraw-Hill.

Ross, M., & Newby, I. R. (1996). Distinguishing memory from fantasy. *Psychological Inquiry, 7,* 173–177.

Rossi, P. H., & Freeman, H. E. (1993). *Evaluation* (5th ed.). Newbury Park, CA: Sage.

Roth, A., & Fonagy, P. (1996). *What works for whom? A critical review of psychotherapy research.* New York: Guilford Press.

Rothbart, M. K., Ahadi, S. A., & Hershey, K. L. (1994). Temperament and social behavior in childhood. Special Issue: Children's emotions and social competence. *Merrill Palmer Quarterly, 40,* 21–39.

Rothbaum, B. O., Hodges, L. F., Kooper, R., Opdyke, D., Williford, J. S., & North, M. (1995). Effectiveness of computer-generated (virtual reality) graded exposure in the treatment of acrophobia. *American Journal of Psychiatry, 152,* 626–628.

Rothblum, E. D. (1990). Women and weight: Fad and fiction. *Journal of Psychology, 124,* 5–24.

Rothstein, R. (1998, May). Bilingual education: The controversy. *Phi Delta Kappan,* 672–678.

Roush, W. (1995, September 1). Can "resetting" hormonal rhythms treat illness? *Science, 269,* 1220–1221.

Routtenberg, A., & Lindy, J. (1965). Effects of the availability of rewarding septal and hypothalamic stimulation on bar pressing for food under conditions of deprivation. *Journal of Comparative and Physiological Psychology, 60,* 158–161.

Rovee-Collier, C. (1993). The capacity for long-term memory in infancy. *Current Directions in Psychological Science, 2,* 130–135.

Rovescalli, A., Maderna, A., Gaboli, G., & Conti, A. (1992). Patologia cromosomica e ritardo mentale. Indagine epidemiologica in una popolazione di soggetti istituzionalizzati. (Chromosome aberrations and mental retardation: An epidemiological investigation of a group of institutionalized subjects.) *Giornale di Neuropsichiatria dell'Eta Evolutiva, 12,* 7–14.

Rowe, J. W., & Kahn, R. L. (1987, July 10). Human aging: Usual and successful. *Science, 237,* 143–149.

Roy, A. (1993). Genetic and biologic risk factors for suicide in depressive disorders. *Psychiatric Quarterly, 64,* 345–358.

Royal Commission on Aboriginal Peoples. (1995). *Choosing life: Special report on suicide among aboriginal peoples.* Ottawa: Minister of Supply and Services Canada.*

Royce, J. E., & Scratchley, D. (1996). *Alcoholism and other drug problems.* New York: Free Press.

Royer, J. M., & Feldman, R. S. (1984). *Educational psychology: Applications and theory.* New York: Knopf.

Rozin, P. (1977). The significance of learning mechanisms in food selection: Some biology, psychology, and sociology of science. In L. M. Barker, M. R. Best, & M. Donijan (Eds.), *Learning mechanisms in food selection.* Waco, TX: Baylor University Press.

Rozin, P. (1990). The importance of social factors in understanding the acquisition of food habits. In E. D. Capaldi & T. L. Powley (Eds.), *Taste, experience, and feeding.* Washington, DC: American Psychological Association.

Rubenstein, C. (1982, July). Psychology's fruit flies. *Psychology Today,* pp. 83–84.

Rubin, D. C. (1985, September). The subtle deceiver: Recalling our past. *Psychology Today,* pp. 39–46.

Rubin, D. C. (1995). *Memory in oral traditions.* New York: Oxford University Press.

Rubin, D. C. (Ed.). (1996). *Remembering our past: Studies in autobiographical memory.* New York: Cambridge University Press.

Rubin, J. Z., & Friedland, N. (1986). Theater of terror. *Psychology Today,* pp. 18–19, 22, 24, 26–28.

Rubin, K. H., Stewart, S. L., & Coplan, R. J. (1995). Social withdrawal in childhood: Conceptual and empirical perspectives. *Advances in Clinical Child Psychology, 17,* 157–196.

Rubin, Z. (1970). Measurement of romantic love. *Journal of Personality and Social Psychology, 16,* 265–273.

Rubin, Z. (1973). *Liking and loving.* New York: Holt, Rinehart and Winston.

Ruble, D. N., Fleming, A. S., Hackel, L. S., & Stangor, C. (1988). Changes in the marital relationship during the transition to first-time motherhood: Effects of violated expectations concerning division of household labor. *Journal of Personality and Social Psychology, 55,* 78–87.

Runco, M. A. (1991). *Divergent thinking.* Norwood, NJ: Ablex.

Runco, M. A., & Sakamoto, S. O. (1993). Reaching creatively gifted students through their learning styles. In R. M. Milgram, R. S. Dunn, & G. E. Price (Eds.), *Teaching and counseling gifted and talented adolescents: An international learning style perspective.* Westport, CT: Praeger Publishers/ Greenwood Publishing Group.

Runowicz, C. (1996, October 29). Genetic testing for breast cancer. *HealthNews,* pp. 4–5.

Ruppin, E., Reggia, J. A., & Horn, D. (1996). Pathogenesis of schizophrenic delusions and hallucinations: A neural model. *Schizophrenia Bulletin, 22,* 105–123.

Rushton, J. P., & Ankney, D. (1995). Brain size matters: A reply to Peters. *Canadian Journal of Experimental Psychology, 49*(4).*

Russell, J. A. (1980). A circumplex model of affect. *Journal of Personality and Social Psychology, 39,* 1161–1178.*

Russell, J. A. (1991). Culture and the categorization of emotion. *Psychological Bulletin, 110,* 426–450.*

Russell, J. A. (1991). In defense of a prototype approach to emotion concepts. *Journal of Personality and Social Psychology, 60,* 37–47.*

Russell, J. A., & Fehr, B. (1994). Fuzzy concepts and the perception of emotion in facial expressions. *Social Cognition, 4,* 309–341.*

Russell, J. A., Fernandez-Dols, J. M., & Mandler, G. (1997). *The psychology of facial expressions.* New York: Cambridge University Press.*

Russell, J. A., & Sato, K. (1995). Comparing emotion words between languages. *Journal of Cross Cultural Psychology, 26,* 384–391.*

Russell, M. A. H. (1979). Tobacco dependence: Is nicotine rewarding or aversive? In N. A. Krasnegor (Ed.), *Cigarette smoking as a dependence process* (NIDA Research Monograph No. 23, U.S. Department of Health, Education, and Welfare, Publication No. [ADM] 79–800). Rockville, MD: National Institute on Drug Abuse.*

Russell, M. A. H. (1990). The nicotine addiction trap: A 40-year sentence for four cigarettes. *British Journal of Addiction, 85,* 293–300.

Russo, D. C., Carr, E. G., & Lovaas, O. I. (1980). Self-injury in pediatric populations. *Comprehensive handbook of behavioral medicine* (Vol. 3: Extended applications and issues). Holliswood, NY: Spectrum.

Russo, N. (1981). In L. T. Benjamin, Jr., & K. D. Lowman (Eds.), *Activities handbook for the teaching of psychology.* Washington, DC: American Psychological Association.

Russo, N. F., & Denmark, F. L. (1987). Contribution of women to psychology. *Annual Review of Psychology, 38,* 279–298.

Russo, R., & Parkin, A. J. (1993). Age differences in implicit memory: More apparent than real. *Memory & Cognition, 21,* 73–80.

Rusting, R. L. (1992, December). Why do we age? *Scientific American,* pp. 130–141.

Rutter, M. (1982). Social-emotional consequences of day-care for preschool children. In E. F. Zigler, & E. W. Gordon (Eds.), *Day-care: Scientific and social policy issues.* Boston: Auburn House.

Rutter, M. L. (1997). Nature-nurture integration: The example of antisocial behavior. *American Psychologist, 52,* 390–398.

Ruzgis, P., & Grigorenko, E. L. (1994). Cultural meaning systems, intelligence, and personality. In R. J. Sternberg, & P. Ruzgis (Eds.), *Personality and intelligence.* New York: Cambridge University Press.

Ryan, M. (1991, January 27). *Parade,* p. 14.

Ryan, R. M., & Deci, E. L. (1996). When paradigms clash: Comments on Cameron and Pierce's claim that rewards do not undermine intrinsic motivation. *Review of Educational Research, 66,* 33–38.

Ryan, R. M., & Solky, J. A. (1996). What is supportive about social support? On the psychological needs for autonomy and relatedness. In G. R. Pierce, B. R. Sarason, & I. G. Sarason (Eds.), *Handbook of social support and the family. Plenum series on stress and coping.* New York: Plenum Press.

Rychlak, J. (1997). *In defense of human consciousness.* Washington, DC: American Psychological Association.

Saariluoma, P. (1994). Location coding in chess. *Quarterly Journal of Experimental Psychology, Human Experimental Psychology, 47A,* 607–630.

Sacco, W. P., & Beck, A. T. (1995). Cognitive theory and therapy. In E. E. Beckham, & W. R. Leber (Eds.), *Handbook of depression* (2nd ed.). New York: Guilford Press.

Sack, R. L., Lewy, A. J., White, D. M., Singer, C. M., Fireman, M. J., & Vandiver, R. (1990). Morning vs. evening light treatment for winter depression: Evidence that the therapeutic effects of light are mediated by circadian phase shift. *Archives of General Psychiatry, 47,* 343–351.

Sackett, P. R. (1994). Integrity testing for personnel selection. *Current Directions in Psychological Science, 3,* 73–76.

Sackheim, H. A. (1985, June). The case for E.C.T. *Psychology Today,* pp. 36–40.

Sackheim, H. A., Luber, B., Katzman, G. P., et al. (1996, September). The effects of electroconvulsive therapy on quantitative electroencephalograms. *Archives of General Psychiatry, 53,* 814–824.

Sadava, S. W. (1987). Interactional theory. In H. T. Blane, & K. E. Leonard (Eds.), *Psychological theories of drinking and alcoholism.* New York: Guilford.*

Sadava, S. W., & McCreary, D. R. (1997). *Applied Social Psychology.* Upper Saddle River, New Jersey: Prentice Hall.*

Sadker, M., & Sadker, D. (1994). *Failing at fairness: How America's schools cheat girls.* New York: Scribners.

Saigh, P. A. (1996). Post-traumatic stress disorder among children and adolescents: An introduction. *Journal of School Psychology, 34,* 103–105.

Sajda, P., & Finkel, L. H. (1995). Intermediate-level visual representations and the construction of surface perception. *Journal of Cognitive Neuroscience, 7,* 267–291.

Sakinofsky, I. (1998). The epidemiology of suicide in Canada. In A. A. Leenaars, S. Wenckstern, I Sakinofsky, R. J. Dyck, M. J.

Kral, & R. C. Bland (Eds.), *Suicide in Canada* (pp. 37–66). Toronto: University of Toronto Press.*

Salber, E. J., Freeman, H. E., & Abelin, T. (1968). Needed research on smoking: Lessons from the Newton study. In E. F. Borgatta, & R. R. Evans (Eds.), *Smoking, health, and behavior.* Chicago: Aldine.

Salovey, P., Mayer, J. D., & Rosenhan, D. L. (1991). Mood and helping: Mood as a motivator of helping and helping as a regulator of mood. In M. S. Clark (Ed.), *Prosocial Behavior.* Newbury Park, CA: Sage.

Salthouse, T. A. (1996, July). The processing-speed theory of adult age differences in cognition. *Psychological Review, 103,* 403–428.

Samora, J., Saunders, L., & Larson, R. F. (1961). Medical vocabulary knowledge among hospital patients. *Journal of Health and Social Behavior, 2,* 83–89.

Sandler, B. (1994, January 31). First denial, then a near-suicidal plea: "Mom, I need your help." *People Weekly,* pp. 56–58.

Sanes, J. N., Donoghue, J. P., Thangaraj, V., Edelman, R. R., & Warach, S. (1995, June 23). Shared neural substrates controlling hand movements in human motor cortex. *Science, 268,* 1775–1777.

Sansavini, A., Bertoncini, J., & Giovanelli, G. (1997). Newborns discriminate the rhythm of multisyllabic stressed words. *Developmental Psychology, 33,* 3–11.

Sanson, A. V., Smart, D. F., Prior, M., & Oberklaid, F., et al. (1994). The structure of temperament from age 3 to 7 years: Age, sex, and sociodemographic influences. *Merrill Palmer Quarterly, 40,* 233–252.

Sapolsky, R. M. (1996, August 9). Why stress is bad for your brain. *Science, 273,* 749–750.

Sapsford, R., & Jupp, V. (Eds.). (1996). Data collection and analysis. London: Sage.

Sarafino, E. P. (1990). *Health psychology: Biopsychosocial interactions.* New York: Wiley.

Sarason, B. R., Sarason, I. G., & Pierce, G. R. (1990). *Social support: An interactional view.* New York: Wiley.

Sarason, I. G. (1976). A modeling and informational approach to delinquency. In E. Ribes-Inesta, & A. Bandura (Eds.), *Analysis of delinquency and aggression.* Mahwah, NJ: Erlbaum.

Sarason, S., Johnson, J. H., & Siegel, J. M. (1978). Assessing the impact of life changes: Development of the Life Experiences Survey. *Journal of Consulting and Clinical Psychology, 46,* 932–946.

Sarbin, T. R. (1991). Hypnosis: A fifty year perspective. *Contemporary Hypnosis, 8,* 1–15.

Sarbin, T. R. (1993). Whither hypnosis? A rhetorical analysis. *Contemporary Hypnosis, 10,* 1–9.

Sarter, M., Berntson, G. G., & Cacioppo, J. T. (1996). Brain imaging and cognitive neuroscience: Toward strong inference in attributing function to structure. *American Psychologist, 51,* 13–21.

Sasaki, K., Kyuhou, S., Nambu, A., Matsuzaki, R., et al. (1995). Motor speech

centres in the frontal cortex. *Neuroscience Research, 22,* 245–248.

Sauber, S. R., L'Abate, L., Weeks, G. R., & Buchanan, W. L. (1993). *The dictionary of family psychology and family therapy* (2nd ed.). Newbury Park, CA: Sage.

Saudino, K. J., Pedersen, N. L., Lichtenstein, P., McClearn, G. E., & Plomin, R. (1997). Can personality explain genetic influences on life events? *Journal of Personality and Social Psychology, 72,* 196–206.

Saudino, K. J., & Plomin, R. (1996). Personality and behavioral genetics: Where have we been and where are we going? *Journal of Research in Personality, 30,* 335–347.

Saul, E. V., & Kass, T. S. (1969). Study of anticipated anxiety in a medical school setting. *Journal of Medical Education, 44,* 526.

Savage-Rumbaugh, E. S., Murphy, J., Sevcik, R. A., Williams, S., Brakke, K., & Rumbaugh, D. M. (1993). Language comprehension in ape and child. *Monographs of the Society for Research in Child Development, 58,* nos. 3 & 4.

Savage-Rumbaugh, S. (1987). Communication, symbolic communication, and language: Reply to Seidenberg and Petitto. *Journal of Experimental Psychology: General, 116,* 288–292.

Savage-Rumbaugh, S., & Brakke, K. E. (1996). Animal language: Methodological and interpretive issues. In M. Bekoff, & D. Jamieson (Eds.), *Readings in animal cognition.* Cambridge, MA: MIT Press.

Sawaguchi, T., & Goldman-Rakic, P. S. (1991, February 22). D1 Dopamine receptors in prefrontal cortex: Involvement in working memory. *Science, 251,* 947–950.

Saxe, L. (1994). Detection of deception: Polygraphy and integrity tests. *Current Directions in Psychological Science, 3,* 69–73.

Saxe, L., Dougherty, D., & Cross, T. (1985). The validity of polygraph testing. *American Psychologist, 40,* 355–366.

Sayette, M. A. (1993). An appraisal disruption model of alcohol's effects on stress responses in social drinkers. *Psychological Bulletin, 114,* 459–476.

Saywitz, K., & Goodman, G. (1990). Unpublished study reported in Goleman, D. (1990, November 6). Doubts rise on children as witnesses. *New York Times,* pp. C-1, C-6.

Scarr, S. (1992). Developmental theories for the 1990s: Development and individual differences. Biennial Meetings of the Society for Research in Child Development Presidential Address (1991, Seattle, Washington). *Child Development, 63,* 1–19.

Scarr, S. (1993). Genes, experience, and development. In D. Magnusson, P. Jules, & M. Casaer (Eds.), *Longitudinal research on individual development: Present status and future perspectives. European network on longitudinal studies on individual development, 8.* Cambridge, England: Cambridge University Press.

Scarr, S. (1994). Why developmental research needs evolutionary theory: To ask interesting questions. In P. Bertelson, P. Eelen, & G. d'Ydewalle (Eds.),

International perspectives on psychological science, Vol. 1: Leading themes. Hove, England: Erlbaum.

Scarr, S. (1996). Behavior genetics and socialization theories of intelligence: Truce and reconciliation. In R. J. Sternberg, & E. Grigorenko. (Eds.), *Intelligence, heredity, and environment.* New York: Cambridge University Press.

Scarr, S., & Carter-Saltzman, L. (1982). Genetics and intelligence. In R. J. Sternberg (Ed.), *Handbook of human intelligence* (pp. 792–896). Cambridge, England: Cambridge University Press.

Scarr, S., & Weinberg, R. A. (1976). I.Q. test performance of black children adopted by white families. *American Psychologist, 31,* 726–739.

Schab, F. R. (1990). Odors and the remembrance of things past. *Journal of Experimental Psychology: Learning, Memory, and Cognition, 16,* 648–655.

Schab, F. R. (1991). Odor memory: Taking stock. *Psychological Bulletin, 109,* 242–251.

Schab, F. R., & Crowder, R. G. (Eds.). (1995). *Memory for odors.* Mahwah, NJ: Erlbaum.

Schachter, S. (1971). Some extraordinary facts about obese humans and rats. *American Psychologist, 26,* 129–144.

Schachter, S., Goldman, R., & Gordon, A. (1968). Effects of fear, food deprivation, and obesity on eating. *Journal of Personality and Social Psychology, 10,* 91–97.

Schachter, S., & Singer, J. E. (1962). Cognitive, social, and physiological determinants of emotional state. *Psychological Review, 69,* 379–399.

Schacter, D. (1993). Understanding implicit memory: A cognitive neuroscience approach. In A. F. Collins, S. E. Gathercole, M. A. Conway, & P. E. Morris (Eds.), *Theories of memory.* Mahwah, NJ: Erlbaum.

Schacter, D. (1997). *Searching for memory: The brain, the mind, and the past.* New York: Basic Books.

Schacter, D. L. (1992). Understanding implicit memory. *American Psychologist, 47,* 559–569.

Schacter, D. L. (1994a, May). Harvard conference on false memories. Cambridge, MA.

Schacter, D. L. (1994b). Implicit knowledge: New perspectives on unconscious processes. In O. Sporns, & G. Tononi (Eds.), *Selectionism and the brain. International review of neurobiology, Vol. 37.* San Diego, CA: Academic Press.

Schacter, D. L. (1995). Implicit memory: A new frontier for cognitive neuroscience. In M. S. Gazzaniga (Ed.), *The cognitive neurosciences.* Cambridge, MA: MIT Press.

Schacter, D. L., Chiu, C.-Y. P., & Ochsner, K. N. (1993). Implicit memory: A selective review. *Annual Review of Neuroscience, 16,* 159–182.

Schacter, D. L. (1983). Amnesia observed: Remembering and forgetting in a natural environment. *Journal of Abnormal Psychology, 92,* 236–242.

Schacter, D. L. (1996). Searching for memory: The brain, the mind, and the past. New York: Basic Books.

Schafer, M., & Crichlow, S. (1996). Antecedents of groupthink: A quantitative study. *Journal of Conflict Resolution, 40,* 415–435.

Schaffer, R. H. (1996). *Social development.* Cambridge, MA: Blackwell.

Schaie, K. W. (1991). Developmental designs revisited. In S. H. Cohen, & H. W. Reese (Eds.), *Life-span developmental psychology: Methodological innovations.* Mahwah, NJ: Erlbaum.

Schaie, K. W. (1993). The Seattle longitudinal studies of adult intelligence. *Current Directions in Psychological Science, 2,* 171–175.

Schaie, K. W. (1994). The course of adult intellectual development. *American Psychologist, 49,* 304–313.

Schaller, M., Asp, C. H., Rosell, M. C., & Heim, S. J. (1996). Training in statistical reasoning inhibits the formation of erroneous group stereotypes. *Personality and Social Psychology Bulletin, 22,* 829–844.

Schatz, R. T., & Fiske, S. T. (1992). International reactions to the threat of nuclear war: The rise and fall of concern in the eighties. *Political Psychology, 13,* 1–29.

Schechter, B. (1996, October 18). How the brain gets rhythm. *Science, 274,* 339–340.

Scheff, T. J. (1985). The primacy of affect. *American Psychologist, 40,* 849–850.

Scheier, M. F., & Carver, C. S. (1992). Effects of optimism on psychological and physical well-being: Theoretical overview and empirical update. Special issue: Cognitive perspectives in health psychology. *Cognitive Therapy and Research, 16,* 201–228.

Schellhardt, T. D. (1990, September 19). It still isn't dad at home with sick kids. *Wall Street Journal,* p. B1.

Schelling, T. C. (1992, January 4). Addictive drugs: The cigarette experience. *Science, 255,* 430–433.

Scherer, K. R. (1984). Les motions: Fonctions et composantes. [Emotions: Functions and components.] *Cahiers de psychologie cognitive, 4,* 9–39.

Scherer, K. R. (Ed.). (1988). *Facets of emotion.* Mahwah, NJ: Erlbaum.

Scherer, K. R. (1994). Emotion serves to decouple stimulus and response. In P. Ekman, & R. J. Davidson (Eds.), *The nature of emotion: Fundamental questions.* New York: Oxford.

Scherer, K. R., & Wallbott, H. G. (1994). Evidence for universality and cultural variation of differential emotion response patterning. *Journal of Personality and Social Psychology, 66,* 310–328.

Schickedanz, J. A., Schickedanz, D. I., & Forsyth, P. D. (1982). *Toward understanding children.* Boston: Little, Brown.

Schindehette, S. (1990, February 5). After the verdict, solace for none. *People Weekly,* pp. 76–80.

Schindehette, S. (1994, January 17). High life. *People Weekly,* pp. 57–66.

Schliecker, E., White D. R., & Jacobs, E. (1991). The role of day care quality in the prediction of children's vocabulary. *Canadian Journal of Behavioural Science, 23(1),* 12–24.

Schmeck, H. M., Jr. (1987, December 29). New light on the chemistry of dreams. *New York Times,* pp. C-1, C-2.

Schmidt, F., & Hunter, J. E. (1995). The impact of data-analysis methods on cumulative research knowledge: Statistical significance testing, confidence intervals, and meta-analysis. Special Issue: The meta-analytic revolution in health research: II. *Evaluation and the Health Professions, 18,* 408–427.

Schmidt, L. A., & Fox, N. A. (1994). Patterns of cortical electrophysiology and autonomic activity in adults' shyness and sociability. *Biological Psychology, 38,* 183–198.

Schmidt, L. A., Fox, N. A., Schulkin, J., & Gold, P. W. (1999). Behavioural and psychophysiological correlates of self-presentation in temperamentally shy children. *Developmental Psychobiology, 35,* 119–135.*

Schmidt, U., & Treasure, J. (1993). *Getting better bit(e) by bit(e): A survival kit for sufferers of bulimia nervosa and binge eating disorders.* Mahwah, NJ: Erlbaum.

Schmitz, S., Saudino, K. J., Plomin, R., Fulkner, D. W., et al. (1996). Genetic and environmental influences on temperament in middle childhood: Analyses of teacher and tester ratings. *Child Development, 67,* 409–422.

Schneider, A. M., & Tarshis, B. (1995). *Elements of physiological psychology.* New York: McGraw-Hill.

Schneider, E. L., & Rowe, J. W. (Eds.). (1996). *Handbook of the biology of aging* (4th ed.). San Diego, CA: Academic Press.

Schneider, K. J., & May, R. (1995). *The psychology of existence: An integrative, clinical perspective.* New York: McGraw-Hill.

Schneider, K. S. (1996, June 3). Mission impossible. *People,* pp. 65–74.

Schneider, W., Gruber, H., Gold, A., & Opwis, K. (1993). Chess expertise and memory for chess positions in children and adults. *Journal of Experimental Child Psychology, 56,* 328–349.

Schneiderman, N. (1983). Animal behavior models of coronary heart disease. In D. S. Krantz, A. Baum, & J. E. Singer (Eds.), *Handbook of psychology and health* (Vol. 3). Mahwah, NJ: Erlbaum.

Schneiderman, N., McCabe, P., & Baum, A. (Eds.). (1992). *Stress and disease processes.* Mahwah, NJ: Erlbaum.

Schneidman, E. S. (1987). A psychological approach to suicide. In G. R. VandenBos, & B. K. Bryant (Eds.), *Cataclysms, crises, and catastrophes: Psychology in action.* Washington, DC: American Psychological Association.

Schoen, L. M. (1996). Mnemopoly: Board games and mnemonics. *Teaching of Psychology, 23,* 30–32.

Schofield, W. (1964). *Psychotherapy: The purchase of friendship.* Englewood Cliffs, NJ: Prentice-Hall.

Schofield, W., & Vaughan-Jackson, P. (1913). *What a boy should know.* New York: Cassell.

Schorr, J. A. (1993). Music and pattern change in chronic pain. *Advances in Nursing Science, 15,* 27–36.

Schuler, G. D., Boguski, M. S., Stewart, E. A., Stein, L. D., Gyapay, G., et al. (1996, October 25). A gene map of the human genome. *Science, 274,* 540–545.

Schulman, M. (1991). *The passionate mind: Bringing up an intelligent and creative child.* New York: Free Press.

Schuman, E. M., & Madison, D. V. (1994, January 28). Locally distributed synaptic potentiation in the hippocampus. *Science, 263,* 532–536.

Schuman, H., & Presser, S. (1996). *Questions and answers in attitude surveys: Experiments on question, form, wording and content.* Newbury Park, CA: Sage.

Schuman, S. P. (1996). The role of facilitation in collaborative groups. In C. Huxham (Ed.), *Creating collaborative advantage.* London: Sage.

Schwartz, M. S. (Ed.). (1995). *Biofeedback: A practitioner's guide* (2nd ed.). New York: Guilford Press.

Schwartz, M. S., & Schwartz, N. M. (1993). Biofeedback: Using the body's signals. In D. Goleman, & J. Gurin (Eds.), *Mind-body medicine.* Yonkers, NY: Consumer Reports Books.

Schwartz, S. H., & Inbar-Saban, N. (1988). Value self-confrontation as a method to aid in weight loss. *Journal of Personality and Social Psychology, 54,* 396–404.

Schwartzberg, N. S., & Dytell, R. S. (1996). *Journal of Occupational Health Psychology, 1,* 211–223.

Schwarz, N., Bless, H., Strack, F., Klumpp, G., et al. (1991). Ease of retrieval as information: Another look at the availability heuristic. *Journal of Personality and Social Psychology, 61,* 195–202.

Schwebel, M., Maher, C. A., & Fagley, N. S. (Eds.). (1990). *Promoting cognitive growth over the life span.* Mahwah, NJ: Erlbaum.

Schweitzer, R. D., & Hier, S. J. (1993). Psychological maladjustment among homeless adolescents. *Australian and New Zealand Journal of Psychiatry, 27,* 275–280.

Scott, J. (1994, March 11). Multiple personality cases perplex legal system. *New York Times,* pp. A1, B6.

Scott, J. (1996). Cognitive therapy of affective disorders: A review. *Journal of Affective Disorders, 37,* 1–11.

Seagraves, R. T., & Schoenberg, H. W. (1985). *Diagnosis and treatment of erectile disturbances.* New York: Plenum Press.

Searleman, A., & Herrmann, D. (1994). *Memory from a broader perspective.* New York: McGraw-Hill.

Sears, D. O. (1986). College sophomores in the laboratory: Influences of a narrow data base on social psychology's view of human nature. *Journal of Personality and Social Psychology, 51,* 515–530.

Sears, R. R. (1977). Sources of life satisfaction of the Terman gifted men. *American Psychologist, 32,* 119–128.

Sebel, P. S., Bonke, B., Winograd, E. (Eds.). (1993). *Memory and awareness in anesthesia.* Englewood Cliffs, NJ: Prentice-Hall.

Sedlacek, K., & Taub, E. (1996). Biofeedback treatment of Raynaud's disease.

Professional Psychology Research and Practice, 27, 548–553.

Seeman, P. (1993). Schizophrenia as a brain disease: The dopamine receptor story. *Archives of Neurology, 50,* 1093–1095.

Seeman, P., Guan, H. C., & Van Tol, H. H. (1993). Dopamine D4 receptors elevated in schizophrenia. *Nature, 347,* 441.

Segal, N. L. (1993). Twin, sibling, and adoption methods: Tests of evolutionary hypotheses. *American Psychologist, 48,* 943–956.

Segal, N. L., Topolski, T. D., Wilson, S. M., Brown, K. W., et al. (1995). Twin analysis of odor identification and perception. *Physiology and Behavior, 57,* 605–609.

Segal, N. L., Weisfeld, G. E., & Weisfeld, C. C. (Eds.). (1997). *Uniting psychology and biology: Integrative perspectives on human development.* Mahwah, NJ: Erlbaum.

Segal, Z. V., Gemar, M., Truchon, C., Guirguis, M., & Horowitz, L. M. (1995). A priming methodology for studying self-representation in major depressive disorder. *Journal of Abnormal Psychology, 104,* 205–213.*

Segal, Z. V., & Vella, D. D. (1990). Self-schema in major depression: Replication and extension of a priming methodology. *Cognitive Therapy and Research, 14,* 161–176.*

Segall, M. H. (1988). Cultural roots of aggressive behavior. In M. Bond (Ed.), *The cross-cultural challenge to social psychology.* Newbury Park, CA: Sage.

Segall, M. H., Campbell, D. T., & Herskovits, M. J. (1966). *The influence of culture on visual perception.* New York: Bobbs-Merrill.

Segalowitz, N. (1997). Individual differences in second language acquisition. In A. de Groot & J. Kroll (Eds.), *Tutorials in bilingualism.* Mahwah, NJ: Erlbaum.*

Seidenberg, M. S., & Petitto, L. A. (1987). Communication, symbolic communication, and language: Comment on Savage-Rumbaugh, McDonald, Sevcik, Hopkins, & Rupert (1986). *Journal of Experimental Psychology: General, 116,* 279–287.

Self, D. W., Barnhard, W. J., Lehman, D. A., & Nestler, E. J. (1996, March 15). Opposite modulation of cocaine-seeking behavior by D$_1$- and D$_2$-like dopamine receptor agonists. *Science, 271,* 1586–1589.

Seligman, L. (1995). *Promoting a fighting spirit: Psychotherapy for cancer patients, survivors, and their families.* San Francisco: Jossey-Bass.

Seligman, M. (1994). *What you can change and what you can't.* New York: Knopf.

Seligman, M. E. P. (1975). *Helplessness: On depression, development, and death.* San Francisco: Freeman.

Seligman, M. E. P. (1988, October). Baby boomer blues. *Psychology Today,* p. 54.

Seligman, M. E. P. (1995, December). The effectiveness of psychotherapy: The *Consumer Reports* study. *American Psychologist, 50,* 965–974.

Selgiman, M. E. P. (1996, October). Science as an ally of practice. *American Psychologist, 51,* 1072–1079.

Seligmann, J. (1991, June 17). A light for poor eyes. *Newsweek,* p. 61.

Selikowitz, M. (1997). *Down syndrome: The facts.* (2nd Ed.). New York: Oxford University Press.

Selkoe, D. J. (1997, January 31). Alzheimer's disease: Genotypes, phenotype, and treatments. *Science, 275,* 630–631.

Sells, R. (1994, August). Homosexuality study. Paper presented at the annual meeting of the American Statistical Association, Toronto.

Selman, R. L., Schorin, M. Z., Stone, C. R., & Phelps, E. (1983). A naturalistic study of children's social understanding. *Developmental Psychology, 19,* 82–102.

Selsky, A. (1997, February 16). African males face circumcision rite. *The Boston Globe,* p. C7.

Seltzer, L. (1986). *Paradoxical strategies in psychotherapy.* New York: Wiley.

Selye, H. (1976). *The stress of life.* New York: McGraw-Hill.

Selye, H. (1993). History of the stress concept. In L. Goldberger, & S. Breznitz (Eds.), *Handbook of stress: Theoretical and clinical aspects* (2nd ed.). New York: Free Press.

Seppa, N. (1996, May). A multicultural guide to less spanking and yelling. *APA Monitor,* p. 37.

Seppa, N. (1997, June). Children's TV remains steeped in violence. *APA Monitor,* p. 36.

Serpell, R., & Boykin, A. W. (1994). Cultural dimensions of thinking and problem solving. In R. J. Sternberg (Ed.), *Thinking and problem-solving.* San Diego, CA: Academic Press.

Service, R. F. (1994, October 14). Will a new type of drug make memory-making easier? *Science, 266,* 218–219.

Service, R. F. (1996, June 7). New dynamic duo: PET, MRI, joined for the first time. *Science, 272,* 1423.

Sesser, S. (1993, September 13). Opium war redux. *New Yorker,* pp. 78–89.

Seyfarth, R., & Cheney, D. (1996). Inside the mind of a monkey. In M. Bekoff, & D. Jamieson (Eds.), *Readings in animal cognition.* Cambridge, MA: MIT Press.

Seyfarth, R. M., & Cheney, D. L. (1992, December). Meaning and mind in monkeys (vocalizations and intent). *Scientific American, 267,* 122–128.

Shapiro, A. P. (1996). *Hypertension and stress: A unified concept.* Mahwah, NJ: Erlbaum.

Shapiro, D. A., Rees, A., Barkham, M., et al. (1995). Effects of treatment duration and severity of depression on the maintenance of gains after cognitive-behavioral and psychodynamic-interpersonal psychotherapy. *Journal of Consulting and Clinical Psychology, 63,* 378–387.

Shapiro, E. (1993, April 1). Trend toward quitting smoking slows as discount cigarettes gain popularity. *Wall Street Journal,* pp. B1, B8.

Shapiro, L. (1993, April 19). Rush to judgment. *Newsweek,* pp. 54–60.

Shapiro, T., & Emde, R. N. (Eds.). (1994). *Research in psychoanalysis: Process, development, outcome.* Madison, CT: International Universities Press.

Shapiro, Y., & Gabbard, G. O. (1994). A reconsideration of altruism from an evolutionary and psychodynamic perspective. *Ethics & Behavior, 4,* 23–42.

Sharma, S., Ghosh, S. N., & Spielberger, C. D. (1995). Anxiety, anger expression, and chronic gastric ulcer. *Psychological Studies, 40,* 187–191.

Sharpe, L. T., Fach, C., Nordby, K., & Stockman, A. (1989, April 21). The incremental threshold of the rod visual system and Weber's Law (achromatism). *Science, 244,* 354–356.

Sharps, M. J., Price, J. L., & Williams, J. K. (1994). Spatial cognition and gender: Instructional and stimulus influences on mental image rotation performance. *Psychology of Women Quarterly, 18,* 413–425.

Sharpton, W. R., & West, M. D. (1996). Severe mental retardation. In P. J. McLaughlin, & P. Wehman (Eds.), *Mental retardation and developmental disabilities* (2nd ed.). Austin, TX: PRO-ED, Inc.

Shatz, C. J. (1992, September). The developing brain. *Scientific American, 267,* 60–67.

Shaughnessy, J. J., & Zechmeister, E. B. (1997). *Research methods in psychology* (4th ed.). New York: McGraw-Hill.

Shaw, L. L., Batson, C. D., & Todd, R. M. (1994). Empathy avoidance: Forestalling feeling for another in order to escape the motivational consequences. *Journal of Personality and Social Psychology, 67,* 879–887.

Shawver, L. (1995). *And the flag was still there: Straight people, gay people, and sexuality in the U.S. military.* New York: Harrington Park Press/Haworth Press.

Shaywitz, B. A., Shaywitz, S. E., Pugh, K. R., Constable, R. T., Skudlarski, P., Fulbright, R. K., Bronen, R. A., Fletcher, J. M., Shankweller, D. P., Katz, L., & Gore, J. C. (1995, February 16). Sex differences in the functional organization of the brain for language. *Nature, 373,* 607–609.

Shea, C. (1996a, January 12). New students uncertain about racial preferences. *Chronicle of Higher Education,* p. A33.

Shea, C. (1996b, September 27). Researchers try to understand why people are doing better on IQ tests. *Chronicle of Higher Education,* p. A18.

Shear, J. (Ed.). (1997). *Explaining consciousness: The hard problem.* Cambridge, MA: MIT Press.

Sheehan, S. (1982). *Is there no place on earth for me?* Boston: Houghton Mifflin.

Shepard, R., & Metzler, J. (1971). Mental rotation of three dimensional objects. *Science, 171,* 701–703.

Shepard, R. N., & Cooper, L. A. (1992). Representation of colors in the blind, color-blind, and normally sighted. *Psychological Science, 3,* 97–104.

Shepherd, G. M. (Ed.). (1990). *The synaptic organization of the brain* (3rd ed.). New York: Oxford University Press.

Sherman, J. W. (1996). Development and mental representation of stereotypes. *Journal of Personality and Social Psychology, 70,* 1126–1141.

Sherman, J. W., & Klein, S. B. (1994). Development and representation of

personality impressions. *Journal of Personality and Social Psychology, 67,* 972–983.

Sherry, D. F. (1997). Memories are made of this. *Natural History, 106,* 56–58.*

Sherry, D. F., & Healy, S. D. (1998). Neural mechanisms of spatial representation. In S. D. Healey (Ed.), *Spatial representation in animals* (pp. 133–157). New York: Oxford University Press.*

Sherry, D. F., Jacobs, L. F., & Gaulin, S. J. (1992). Spatial memory and adaptive specialization of the hippocampus. *Trends in Neuroscience, 15,* 298–303.

Shettleworth, S. J., & Hampton, R. R. (1998). Adaptive specialization of spatial cognition in food-storing birds? Approaches to testing a comparative hypothesis. In R. P. Balda, I. M. Pepperberg, & A. C. Kamil (Eds.), *Animal cognition in nature: the convergence of psychology and biology in laboratory and field.* San Diego: Academic Press.*

Shim, S., & Bickle, M. C. (1994). Benefit segments of the female apparel market: Psychographics, shopping orientations, and demographics. *Clothing & Textile Researchers Journal, 12,* 1–12.

Shine, J. (1994, October). Mind games. *Sky,* p. 120–127.

Ship, J. A., & Weiffenbach, J. M. (1993). Age, gender, medical treatment, and medication effects on smell identification. *Journals of Gerontology, 48,* M26–M32.

Shnek, Z. M., Foley, F. W., LaRocca, N. G., Smith, C. R., et al. (1995). Psychological predictors of depression in multiple sclerosis. *Journal of Neurologic Rehabilitation, 9,* 15–23.

Shock, N. W. (1962, January). The physiology of aging. *Scientific American,* pp. 100–110.

Short, R. H., & Hess, G. C. (1995). Fetal alcohol syndrome: Characteristics and remedial implications. *Developmental Disabilities Bulletin, 23,* 12–29.

Short, R. V., & Balaban, E. (Eds.). (1992). *The differences between the sexes.* Cambridge, England: Cambridge University Press.

Shorter, E. (1991). *From paralysis to fatigue: A history of psychosomatic illness in the modern era.* New York: Free Press.*

Shotland, R. L. (1984, March). Paper presented at the Catherine Genovese Memorial Conference on Bad Samaritanism, Fordham University, New York.

Shotland, R. L. (1985, June). When bystanders just stand by. *Psychology Today,* pp. 50–55.

Shotland, R. L. (1992). A theory of the causes of courtship rape: Part 2. *Journal of Social Issues, 48,* 127–143.

Shrique, C. L., & Annable, L. (1995). Tardive dyskinesia. In C. L. Shriqui, & H. A. Nasrallah (Eds.), *Contemporary issues in the treatment of schizophrenia.* Washington, DC: American Psychiatric Press.

Shuchter, S. R., Downs, N., & Zisook, S. (1996). *Biologically informed psychotherapy for depression.* New York: Guilford Press.

Shurkin, J. N. (1992). *Terman's kids: The groundbreaking study of how the gifted grow up.* Boston: Little, Brown.

Shweder, R. A. (1994). "You're not sick, you're just in love": Emotion as an interpretive system. In P. Ekman, & R. J.

Davidson (Eds.), *The nature of emotion: Fundamental questions.* New York: Oxford University Press.

Shweder, R. A., & Sullivan, M. A. (1993). Cultural psychology: Who needs it. *Annual Review of Psychology, 44,* 497–523.

Si, G., Rethorst, S., & Willimczik, K. (1995). Causal attribution perception in sports achievement: A cross-cultural study on attributional concepts in Germany and China. *Journal of Cross Cultural Psychology, 26,* 537–553.

Sibicky, M. E., Schroeder, D. A., & Dovidio, J. F. (1995). Empathy and helping: Considering the consequences of intervention. *Basic and Applied Social Psychology, 16,* 435–453.

Sieber, J. E. (1992). *Planning ethically responsible research.* Newbury Park, CA: Sage.

Sieber, J. E. (1993). Ethical considerations in planning and conducting research on human subjects. *Academic Medicine, 68,* Suppl. S9–S13.

Sieber, W. J., Rodin, J., Larson, L., Ortega, S., et al. (1992). Modulation of human natural killer cell activity by exposure to uncontrollable stress. *Brain, Behavior and Immunity, 6,* 141–156.

Siegel, B. (1996a). Is the emperor wearing clothes? Social policy and the empirical support for full inclusion of children with disabilities in the preschool and early elementary grades. *Social Policy Report, 10,* p. 2–17.

Siegel, B. (1996b). *The world of the autistic child: Understanding and treating autistic spectrum disorders.* New York: Oxford University Press.

Siegel, G. J., Agranoff, B. W., Albers, R. W., & Molinoff, P. B. (Eds.). (1994). *Basic neurochemistry: Molecular, cellular, and medical aspects.* New York: Raven Press.

Siegel, J. M. (1990). Stressful life events and use of physician services among the elderly: The moderating role of pet ownership. *Journal of Personality and Social Psychology, 58,* 1081–1086.

Siegel, J. M. (1993). Companion animals: In sickness and in health. *Journal of Social Issues, 49,* 157–167.

Siegel, J. M., Nienhuis, R., Fahringer, H. M., Paul, R., Shiromani, P., Dement, W. C., Mignot, E., & Chiu, C. (1991, May 31). Neuronal activity in narcolepsy: Identification of cataplexy-related cells in the medial medulla. *Science, 252,* 1315–1318.

Siegel, M., Carrington, J., & Radel, M. (1996). Theory of mind and pragmatic understanding following right hemisphere damage. *Brain and Language, 53,* 40–50.

Siegel, R. K. (1989). *Life in pursuit of artificial paradise.* New York: Dutton.

Siegelbaum, S. A., & Koester, J. (1991). Ion channels. In E. R. Kandel, J. H. Schwartz, & T. M. Jessell (Eds.), *Principles of neural science* (3rd ed.). New York: Elsevier.

Siegler, R. S. (1989). Mechanisms of cognitive development. *Annual Review of Psychology, 40,* 353–379.

Siegler, R. S. (1991). *Children's thinking* (2nd ed.). Englewood Cliffs, NJ: Prentice-Hall.

Siegler, R. S. (1994). Cognitive variability: A key to understanding cognitive development. *Current Directions in Psychological Science, 3,* 1–5.

Siegler, R. S., & Ellis, S. (1996). Piaget on childhood. *Psychological Science, 7,* 211–215.

Siegman, A. W., & Smith, T. W. (Eds.). (1994). *Anger, hostility, and the heart.* Mahwah, NJ: Erlbaum.

Siever, L. J. (1995). Brain structure/function and the dopamine system in schizotypal personality disorder. In A. Raine, T. Lencz, & S. A. Mednick (Eds.), *Schizotypal personality.* New York: Cambridge University Press.

Sigman, M. (1995). Nutrition and child development: More food for thought. *Current Directions in Psychological Science, 4,* 52–55.

Signorielli, N., Gerbner, G., & Morgan, M. (1995). Violence on television: The Cultural Indicators Project. *Journal of Broadcasting and Electronic Media, 39,* 278–283.

Silbereisen, R., Petersen, A., Albrecht, H., & Kracke, B. (1989). Maturational timing and the development of problem behavior: Longitudinal studies in adolescence. *Journal of Early Adolescence, 9,* 247.

Silver, R. L., & Wortman, C. B. (1980). Coping with undesirable life events. In J. Barber, & M. E. P. Seligman (Eds.), *Human helplessness: Theory and application.* New York: Academic Press.

Silverman, K., Evans, S. M., Strain, E. C., & Griffiths, R. R. (1992, October 15). Withdrawal syndrome after the double-blind cessation of caffeine consumption. *New England Journal of Medicine, 327,* 1109–1114.

Silverman, K., Mumford, G. K., & Griffiths, R. R. (1994). Enhancing caffeine reinforcement by behavioral requirements following drug ingestion. *Psychopharmacology, 114,* 424–432.

Silverstein, B., Perdue, L., Peterson, B., Vogel, L., et al. (1986). Possible causes of the thin standard of bodily attractiveness for women. *International Journal of Eating Disorders, 5,* 907–916.

Simmons, R., & Blyth, D. (1987). *Moving into adolescence.* New York: Aldine de Gruyter.

Simon, R. J., & Aaronson, E. E. (1988). *The insanity defense: A critical assessment of law and policy in the post-Hinckley era.* New York: Praeger.

Simonoff, E., Bolton, P., & Rutter, M. (1996). Mental retardation: Genetic findings, clinical implications and research agenda. *Journal of Child Psychology and Psychiatry and Allied Disciplines, 37,* 259–280.

Simons, R. L. (1996). *Understanding differences between divorced and intact families: Stress, interaction, and child outcome.* Thousand Oaks, CA: Sage.

Simonton, D. K. (1994). *Greatness: Who makes history and why.* New York: Guilford.

Simpson, G. E., & Yinger, J. M. (1985). *Racial and cultural minorities: An analysis of prejudice and discrimination* (5th ed.). New York: Harper & Row.

Simpson, J. A. (1987). The dissolution of romantic relationships: Factors involved in relationship stability and emotional distress. *Journal of Personality and Social Psychology, 53,* 683–692.

Simpson, J. A., & Harris, B. A. (1994). Interpersonal attraction. In A. L. Weber, & J. H. Harvey (Eds.), *Perspectives on close relationships.* Boston: Allyn & Bacon.

Sinclair, C. M. (1998). Suicide in First Nation's people. In A. A. Leenaars, S. Wenckstern, I. Sakinofsky, R. J. Dyck, M. J. Kral, & R. C. Bland (Eds.), *Suicide in Canada* (pp. 165–178). Toronto: University of Toronto Press.*

Sinclair, J. D. (1990). Drugs to decrease alcohol drinking. *Annals of Medicine, 22,* 357–362.

Sinclair, R. C., Hoffman, C., Mark, M. M., Martin, L. L., & Pickering, T. L. (1994). Construct accessibility and the misattribution of arousal: Schachter and Singer revisited. *Psychological Science, 5,* 15–19.

Singelis, T., Choo, P., & Hatfield, E. (1995). Love schemas and romantic love. *Journal of Social Behavior & Personality, 10,* 15–36.

Singer, J. L. (1975). *The inner world of daydreaming.* New York: Harper & Row.

Singer, W. (1995, November 3). Development and plasticity of cortical processing architectures. *Science, 270,* 758–764.

Sinnott, J. D. (Ed.). (1989). *Everyday problem solving: Theory and applications.* New York: Praeger.

Sippola, L. K., Bukowski, W. M., & Noll, R. B. (1997). Dimensions of liking and disliking underlying the same-sex preference in early childhood and early adolescence. *Merrill-Palmer Quarterly, 43(4),* 591–609.*

Sisk, J. E., Gorman, S. A., Reisinger, A. L., Glied, S. A., et al. (1996). Evaluation of Medicaid managed care: Satisfaction, access, and use. *Journal of the American Medical Association, 276,* 50–55.

Sizemore, C. C. (1989). *A mind of my own: The woman who was known as Eve tells the story of her triumph over multiple personality disorder.* New York: Morrow.

Skinner, B. F. (1957). *Verbal behavior.* New York: Appleton-Century-Crofts.

Skinner, B. F. (1975). The steep and thorny road to a science of behavior. *American Psychologist, 30,* 42–49.

Skrypnek, B. J., & Snyder, M. (1982). On the self-perpetuating nature of stereotypes about women and men. *Journal of Experimental Social Psychology, 18,* 277–291.

Slater, A. (1996). The organization of visual perception in early infancy. In F. Vital-Durand, J. Atkinson, & O. J. Braddick (Eds.), *Infant vision. The European brain and behaviour society publication series, Vol. 2.* Oxford, England: Oxford University Press.

Slater, A., Mattock, A., & Brown, E. (1990). Size constancy at birth: Newborn infants' responses to retinal and real size. *Journal of Experimental Child Psychology, 49,* 314–322.

Slater, A., & Morison, V. (1991). Visual attention and memory at birth. In M. J. S. Weiss, & P. R. Zelazo (Eds.), *Newborn attention: Biological constraints and the influence of experience.* Norwood, NJ: Ablex.

Slater, E., & Meyer, A. (1959). Contributions to a pathography of the musicians. *Confinia Psychiatrica.* Reprinted in K. R. Jamison, *Touched with fire: Manic-depressive illness and the artistic temperament.* New York: Free Press.

Sleek, S. (1995, November). Online therapy services raise ethical question. *APA Monitor,* p. 9.

Slevin, K. F., & Aday, D. P. (1993). Gender differences in self-evaluations of information about current affairs. *Sex Roles, 29,* 817–828.

Sloan, E. P., Hauri, P., Bootzin, R., Morin, C., et al. (1993). The nuts and bolts of behavioral therapy for insomnia. *Journal of Psychosomatic Research, 37, (Suppl),* 19–37.

Slovic, P., Fischhoff, B., & Lichtenstein, S. (1976). Cognitive processes and societal risk taking. In J. S. Carroll, & J. W. Payne (Eds.), *Cognition and social behavior.* Mahwah, NJ: Erlbaum.

Slusher, M. P., & Anderson, C. A. (1987). When reality monitoring fails: The role of imagination in stereotype maintenance. *Journal of Personality and Social Psychology, 52,* 653–662.

Smith, C. A., & Ellsworth, P. C. (1987). Patterns of appraisal and emotion related to taking an exam. *Journal of Personality and Social Psychology, 52,* 475–488.

Smith, C. A., Haynes, K. N., Lazarus, R. S., & Pope, L. K. (1993). In search of the "hot" cognitions: Attributions, appraisals, and their relation to emotion. *Journal of Personality and Social Psychology, 65,* 916–929.

Smith, D. (1991). *Imagery in sport: An historical and current overview.* New York: Plenum Press.

Smith, E. (1988, May). Fighting cancerous feelings. *Psychology Today,* pp. 22–23.

Smith, E. R. (1984). Attributions and other inferences: Processing information about the self versus others. *Journal of Experimental Social Psychology, 20,* 97–115.

Smith, J. (1990). *Cognitive-behavioral relaxation training.* New York: Springer.

Smith, M., & Lin, K. M. (1996). Gender and ethnic differences in the pharmacogenetics of psychotropics. In M. F. Jensvold, U. Halbreich, & J. A. Hamilton (Eds.), *Psychopharmacology and women: Sex, gender, and hormones.* Washington, DC: American Psychiatric Press.

Smith, M. L., Glass, G. V., & Miller, T. J. (1980). *The benefits of psychotherapy.* Baltimore: Johns Hopkins.

Smith, M. V. (1996). Linguistic relativity: On hypotheses and confusions. *Communication and Cognition, 29,* 65–90.

Smith, R. C., Lyles, J. S., Mettler, J. A., Marshall, A. A., et al. (1995). A strategy for improving patient satisfaction by the intensive training of residents in psychosocial medicine: A controlled, randomized study. *Academic Medicine, 70,* 729–732.

Smith, S. M. (1994). Frustrated feelings of imminent recall: On the tip of the tongue. In

J. Metcalfe, & A. P. Shimamura (Eds.), *Metacognition: Knowing about knowing.* Cambridge, MA: MIT Press.

Smith, S. M., Ward, T. B., & Finke, R. A. (Eds.). (1995). *The creative cognition approach.* Cambridge, MA: MIT Press.

Smith, T. W. (1990, December). Ethnic images. *GSS Topical Report No. 19.* Chicago: National Opinion Research Center.

Smith, T. W. (1991). Adult sexual behavior in 1989: Number of partners, frequency of intercourse, and risk of AIDS. *Family Planning Perspectives, 23,* 102–107.

Snarey, J. R. (1985). Cross-cultural universality of social-moral development: A critical review of Kohlbergian research. *Psychological Bulletin, 97,* 202–232.

Snyder, F. (1970). The phenomenology of dreaming. In L. Madow, & L. H. Snow (Eds.), *The psychodynamic implications of the physiological studies on dreams.* Springfield, IL: Thomas.

Snyder, M., & Cantor, N. (1979). Testing hypotheses about other people: The use of historical knowledge. *Journal of Experimental Social Psychology, 15,* 330–343.

Snyder, R. A., Verderber, K. S., Langmeyer, L., & Myers, M. (1992). A reconsideration of self- and organization-referent attitudes as "causes" of the glass ceiling effect. *Group and Organization Management, 17,* 260–278.

Snyder, S. H. (1978). Dopamine and schizophrenia. In L. C. Wynne, R. L. Cromwell, & S. Matthysse (Eds.), *The nature of schizophrenia: New approaches to research and treatment* (pp. 87–94). New York: Wiley.

Soble, A. (1990). *The structure of love.* New Haven, CT: Yale University Press.

Sohn, D. (1996). Publication bias and the evaluation of psychotherapy efficacy in reviews of the research literature. *Clinical Psychology Review, 16,* 147–156.

Solano, L., Montella, F., Coda, R., Costa, M., et al. (1995). Espressione delle emozioni e situazione immunitaria nell'infezione da HIV-1: studio su 33 soggetti sieropositivi asintomatici. / Expressed emotions and immunological assessment in 33 asymptomatic HIV-1 patients. *Medicina Psicosomatica, 40,* 135–146.

Solcova, I., & Tomanek, P. (1994). Daily stress coping strategies: An effect of hardiness. *Studia Psychologica, 36,* 390–392.

Solms, M. (1996). *The neuropsychology of dreams.* Mahwah, NJ: Erlbaum.

Solomon, C. (1993, December 21). Having nightmares? Chances are, they are about your job. *Wall Street Journal,* pp. A1, A4.

Solomon, J. (1996, May 20). Breaking the silence. *Newsweek,* pp. 20–21.

Solomon, Z. (1995). *Coping with war-induced stress: The Gulf War and Israeli response.* New York: Plenum Press.

Solso, R. L. (1991). *Cognitive psychology* (3rd ed.). Boston: Allyn & Bacon.

Sorenson, S. B., & Siegel, J. M. (1992). Gender, ethnicity, and sexual assault: Findings from a Los Angeles study. *Journal of Social Issues, 48,* 93–104.

Sorrentino, C. (1990). The changing family in international perspective. *Monthly Labor Review, 113,* 41–58.

Sorrentino, R. M., Hewitt, E. C., & Raso-Knott, P. A. (1992). Risk-taking in games of chance and skill: Informational and affective influences on choice behavior. *Journal of Personality and Social Psychology, 62,* 522–533.

Sos-Pena, R., Gabucio, F., & Tejero, P. (1995). El impacto actual de la psicologia de la Gestalt. (The influence of Gestalt psychology in the current social sciences.) *Revista de Psicologia Universitas Tarraconensis, 17,* 73–92.

Southern, W. T., Jones, E. D., & Stanley, J. C. (1993). Acceleration and enrichment: The context and development of program options. In K. A. Heller, F. J. Monks, & A. H. Passow (Eds.), *International handbook of research and development of giftedness and talent.* Oxford, England: Pergamon.

Spangler, W. D. (1992). Validity of questionnaire and TAT measures of need for achievement: Two meta-analyses. *Psychological Bulletin, 112,* 140–154.

Spangler, W. D., & House, R. J. (1991). Presidential effectiveness and the leadership motive profile. *Journal of Personality and Social Psychology, 60,* 439–455.

Spanos, N. P. (1986). Hypnotic behavior: A social psychological interpretation of amnesia, analgesia, and "trance logic." *Behavioral and Brain Science, 9,* 449–467.

Spanos, N. P. (1994). Multiple identity enactments and multiple personality disorder: A sociocognitive perspective. *Psychological Bulletin, 116,* 143–165.

Spanos, N. P. (1996). *Multiple identities and false memories: A sociocognitive perspective.* Washington, D.C.: American Psychological Association Books.

Spanos, N. P., Burgess, C. A., Roncon, V., Wallace-Capretta, S., et al. (1993). Surreptitiously observed hypnotic responding in simulators and in skill-trained and untrained high hypnotizables. *Journal of Personality and Social Psychology, 65,* 391–398.

Spanos, N. P., & Chaves, J. F. (Eds.). (1989). *Hypnosis: The cognitive-behavioral perspective.* Buffalo, NY: Prometheus Books.

Spanos, N. P., Cross, W. P., Menary, E. P., Brett, P. J., & deGroic, M. (1987). Attitudinal and imaginal ability predictors of social cognitive skill-training enhancements in hypnotic susceptibility. *Personality and Social Psychology Bulletin, 13,* 379–398.

Spanos, N. P., Menary, E., Gabora, N. J., DuBreuil, S. C., & Dewhirst, B. (1991). Secondary identity enactments during hypnotic past-life regression: A sociocognitive perspective. *Journal of Personality and Social Psychology, 61,* 308–320.

Spates, C. R., Little, P., Stock, H. V., & Goncalves, J. S. (1990). Intervention in events of terrorism. In L. J. Hertzberg, G. F. Ostrum, & J. R. Field (Eds.), *Violent behavior, Vol. 1: Assessment & intervention.* Costa Mesa, CA: PMA Publishing.

Spearman, C. (1927). *The abilities of man.* London: Macmillan.

Spector, P. E. (1996). *Industrial and organizational psychology: Research and practice.* New York: Wiley.

Spence, J. T. (1985, August). *Achievement American style: The rewards and costs of individualism.* Presidential address. 93rd Annual Convention of the American Psychological Association, Los Angeles.

Spence, M. J., & DeCasper, A. J. (1982, March). Human fetuses perceive maternal speech. Paper presented at the meeting of the International Conference on Infant Studies, Austin, TX.

Spence, M. J., & Freeman, M. S. (1996). Newborn infants prefer the maternal low-pass filtered voice, but not the maternal whispered voice. *Infant Behavior and Development, 19,* 199–212.

Spencer, R. (2000, May 3). "Wanna piece of me?" *The Globe and Mail,* R1.*

Sperling, G. (1960). The information available in brief visual presentation. *Psych Monographs, 74* (whole no. 498).

Sperry, R. (1982). Some effects of disconnecting the cerebral hemispheres. *Science, 217,* 1223–1226.

Spetch, M. L. (1995). Overshadowing in landmark learning: Touch-screen studies with pigeons and humans. *Journal of Experimental Psychology: Animal Behavior Processes, 21,* 166–181.*

Spetch, M. L., Cheng, K., & MacDonald, S. E. (1966). Learning the configuration of a landmark array: Touch-screen studies with pigeons and humans. *Journal of Comparative Psychology, 110,* 55–68.*

Spiegel, D. (1993). Social support: How friends, family, and groups can help. In D. Goleman, & J. Gurin (Eds.), *Mind-body medicine.* Yonkers, NY: Consumer Reports Books.

Spiegel, D. (1995). Commentary. Special Issue: Psychosocial resource variables in cancer studies: Conceptual and measurement issues. *Journal of Psychosocial Oncology, 13,* 115–121.

Spiegel, D. (1996a). Dissociative disorders. In R. E. Hales, & S. C. Yudofsky (Eds.), *The American Psychiatric Press synopsis of psychiatry.* Washington, DC: American Psychiatric Press.

Spiegel, D. (1996b). Hypnosis. In R. E. Hales, & S. C. Yudofsky (Eds.), *The American Psychiatric Press synopsis of psychiatry.* Washington, DC: American Psychiatric Press.

Spiegel, D. (1996c, July). Cancer and depression. *British Journal of Psychiatry, 168,* 109–116.

Spiegel, D. (in press). *Living beyond limits.* New York: Times Books.

Spiegel, D., & Cardena, E. (1991). Disintegrated experience: The dissociative disorders revisited. *Journal of Abnormal Psychology, 100,* 366–378.

Spiegel, D., Bloom, J. R., Kraemer, H. C., & Gottheil, E. (1989, October 14). Effect of psychosocial treatment on survival of patients with metastatic breast cancer. *Lancet, 2,* 888–891.

Spiegel, D., Frischholz, E. J., Fleiss, J. L., & Spiegel, H. (1993). Predictors of smoking abstinence following a single-session restructuring intervention with self-hypnosis. *American Journal of Psychiatry, 150*, 1090–1097.

Spiegel, H. (1987). The answer is: Psychotherapy plus. Special issue: Is hypnotherapy a placebo? *British Journal of Experimental and Clinical Hypnosis, 4*, 163–164.

Spiegel, R. (1989). *Psychopharmacology: An Introduction.* New York: Wiley.

Spielman, D. (1997). Reducing boys' aggression: A basic human needs and skill training approach. Unpublished manuscript, University of Massachusetts.

Spillmann, L., & Werner, J. (Eds.). (1990). *Visual perception: The neurophysiological foundations.* San Diego, CA: Academic Press.

Spira, A., Bajos, N., Bejin, A., & Beltzer, N. (1992). AIDS and sexual behavior in France. *Nature, 360*, 407–409.

Spira, J. (Ed.). (1997). *Group therapy for medically ill patients.* New York: Guilford Press.

Spitz, H. H. (1987). Problem-solving processes in special populations. In J. G. Borkowski, & J. D. Day (Eds.), *Cognition in special children: Comparative approaches to retardation, learning disabilities, and giftedness.* Norwood, NJ: Ablex.

Spitzer, R. L., Skodol, A. E., Gibbon, M., & Williams, J. B. W. (1983). *Psychopathology: A case book.* New York: McGraw-Hill.

Sporer, S. L., Malpass, R. S., & Koehnken, G. (Eds.). (1996). *Psychological issues in eyewitness identification.* Mahway, NJ: Erlbaum.

Sprecher, S., & Hatfield, E. (1996). Premarital sexual standards among U.S. college students: Comparison with Russian and Japanese students. *Archives of Sexual Behavior, 25*, 261–288.

Sprecher, S., & McKinney, K. (1993). *Sexuality.* Newbury Park, CA: Sage.

Sprecher, S., Sullivan, Q., & Hatfield, E. (1994). Mate selection preferences: Gender differences examined in a national sample. *Journal of Personality and Social Psychology, 66*, 1074–1080.

Sprenkle, D. H., & Moon, S. M. (Eds.). (1996). *Research methods in family therapy.* New York: Guilford Press.

Springer, S. P., & Deutsch, G. (1989). *Left brain, right brain* (3rd ed.). New York: Freeman.

Springer, S. P., & Deutsch, G. (1993). *Left brain, right brain* (4th ed.). New York: Freeman.

Squire, L. (1987). *Memory and brain.* New York: Oxford University Press.

Squire, L. R. (1993). The hippocampus and spatial memory. *Trends in Neurosciences, 6*, 56–57.

Squire, L. R. (1995). Biological foundations of accuracy and inaccuracy in memory. In D. L. Schacter (Ed.), *Memory distortions: How minds, brains, and societies reconstruct the past.* Cambridge, MA: Harvard University Press.

Squire, L. R., Knowlton, B., & Musen, G. (1993). The structure and organization of memory. *Annual Review of Psychology, 44*, 453–495.

Sridhar, K. S., Raub, W. A., Weatherby, N. L., & Metsch, L. R., et al. (1994). Possible role of marijuana smoking as a carcinogen in the development of lung cancer at a young age. *Journal of Psychoactive Drugs, 26*, 285–288.

Sroufe, L. A., Fox, N. E., & Pancake, V. R. (1983). Attachment and dependency in a developmental perspective. *Child Development, 54*, 1615–1627.

St. Onge, S. (1995a). Modeling and role-playing. In M. Ballou (Ed.), *Psychological interventions: A guide to strategies.* Westport, CT: Praeger Publishers/ Greenwood Publishing Group, Inc.

St. Onge, S. (1995b). Systematic desensitization. In M. Ballou (Ed.), *Psychological interventions: A guide to strategies.* Westport, CT: Praeger Publishers/Greenwood Publishing Group, Inc.

Staats, A. W. (1975). *Social behaviorism.* Homewood, IL: Dorsey Press.

Stacy, A. W., Newcomb, M. D., & Bentler, P. M. (1991). Social psychological influences on sensation seeking from adolescence to adulthood. *Personality and Social Psychology Bulletin, 17* (6), 701–708.

Stacy, A. W., Sussman, S., Dent, C. W., Burton, D., & Flay, B. R. (1992). Moderators of peer social influence in adolescent smoking. *Personality and Social Psychology Bulletin, 18*, 163–172.

Stahl, L. (1994, February 13). *Sixty Minutes: Changing the odds.* Livingston, NJ: Burrelle's Information Services.

Stairs, A. (1995). Learning processes and teaching roles in Native education: Cultural base and cultural brokerage. In M. Battiste & J. Barman (Eds.), *First Nations education in Canada: The circle unfolds.* Vancouver: UBC Press.*

Stake, R. E. (1995). *The art of case study research.* Newbury Park, CA: Sage.

Stambak, M., & Sinclair, H. (Eds.). (1993). *Pretend play among 3-year-olds.* Mahwah, NJ: Erlbaum.

Stampi, C. (1992). Evolution, chronobiology, and functions of polyphasic and ultrashort sleep: Main issues. In C. Stampi (Ed.), *Why we nap: Evolution, chronobiology, and functions of polyphasic and ultrashort sleep.* Boston, MA: Birkhauser.

Stanley, B. H., & Guido, J. R. (1996). Informed consent: Psychological and empirical issues. In B. H. Stanley, J. E. Sieber, & G. B. Melton (Eds.), *Research ethics: A psychological approach.* Lincoln, NE: University of Nebraska Press.

Stanley, J. C. (1980). On educating the gifted. *Educational Researcher, 9*, 8–12.

Stanley, J. G. (1990). Finding and helping young people with exceptional mathematical reasoning ability. In M. J. A. Howe (Ed.), *Encouraging the development of exceptional skills and talents.* Leicester, England: British Psychological Society.

Stanton, H. E. (1994). Sports imagery and hypnosis: A potent mix. *Australian Journal of Clinical and Experimental Hypnosis, 22*, 119–124.

Staples, E., & Dare, C. (1996). The impact of childhood sexual abuse. In K. Abel, M. Buszewicz, S. Davison, & S. Johnson (Eds.),

Planning community mental health services for women: A multiprofessional handbook. London: Routledge.

Stapp, J., Fulcher, R., & Wicherski, M. (1984). The employment of 1981 and 1982 doctorate recipients in psychology. *American Psychologist, 39*, 1408–1423.

Stark, C. (1998). Ethics in the research context: Misinterpretations and misplaced misgivings. *Canadian Psychology 39(3)*, 202–211.*

Statistics Canada. (1996). 1996 census language statistics.* Available: <http://www.statcan.ca/english/Pgdb/ People/popula.htm#lan>.

Statistics Canada. (1998a). *National public health survey.* Ottawa: Statistics Canada.*

Statistics Canada. (1998b). Suicides, and suicide rate, by sex, by age group.* Available: <http://www.statcan.ca/ ca/english/Pgdb/People/Health/ health01.htm>.

Statistics Canada. (1999a). *Canada yearbook 1999.* Ottawa: Statistics Canada.*

Statistics Canada. (1999b). How healthy are Canadians? A special issue. *Statistics Canada Health Reports, Winter 99, (Vol. 11)*, 3. Ottawa: Statistics Canada.*

Staub, E. (1988). The evolution of caring and nonaggressive persons and societies. *Journal of Social Issues, 44*, 81–100.

Staub, E. (1995). *The caring schools project: A proposal for a program to develop caring, helping, positive self-esteem and nonviolence.* Unpublished manuscript, University of Massachusetts at Amherst.

Staub, E. (1996). Cultural-societal roots of violence. *American Psychologist, 51*, 117–132.

Staub, E. (1996a). Altruism and aggression in children and youth: Origins and cures. In R. Feldman (Ed.), *The psychology of adversity.* Amherst, MA: University of Massachusetts Press.

Staub, E. (1996b). Cultural-societal roots of violence: The examples of genocidal violence and of contemporary youth violence in the United States. *American Psychologist, 51*, 117–132.

Steadman, H., McGreevy, M. A., Morrissey, J. P., et al. (1993). *Before and after Hinckley: Evaluating insanity defense reform.* New York: Guilford Press.

Steblay, N. M. (1992). A meta-analytic review of the weapon focus effect. *Law and Human Behavior, 16*, 413–424.

Steele, C. M. (1992, April). Race and the schooling of Black America. *Atlantic Monthly*, 37–53.

Steele, C. M. (1997). A threat in the air: How stereotypes shape intellectual identity and performance. *American Psychologist, 52*, 613–629.

Steele, C. M., & Aronson, J. (1995). Stereotype threat and the intellectual test performance of African Americans. *Journal of Personality and Social Psychology, 69*, 797–811.

Steele, C. M., & Josephs, R. A. (1990). Alcohol myopia: Its prized and dangerous effects. *American Psychologist, 45*, 921–933.

Steele, C. M., & Southwick, L. (1985). Alcohol and social behavior I: The psychology of drunken excess. *Journal of Personality and Social Psychology, 48,* 18–34.

Steen, R. G. (1996). *DNA and destiny: Nature and nurture in human behavior.* New York: Plenum Press.

Steil, J. M., & Hay, J. L. (1997, April). Social comparison in the workplace: A study of 60 dual-career couples. *Personality and Social Psychology Bulletin, 23,* 427–438.

Stein, J. A., Newcomb, M. D., & Bentler, P. M. (1992). The effect of agency and communality on self-esteem: Gender differences in longitudinal data. *Sex Roles, 26,* 465–483.

Stein, M., & Baum A. (Eds.). (1995). *Chronic diseases.* Mahwah, NJ: Erlbaum.

Stein, N. L., Brainerd, C., Ornstein, P. A., & Tversky, B. (Eds.). (1996). *Memory for everyday and emotional events.* Mahwah, NJ: Erlbaum.

Stein, N. L., Ornstein, P. A., Tversky, B., & Brainerd, C. (Eds.). (1997). *Memory for everyday and emotional events.* Mahwah, NJ: Erlbaum.

Steinberg, L. (1987, September). Bound to bicker. *Psychology Today,* pp. 36–39.

Steinberg, L. (1989). *Adolescence* (2nd ed.). New York: Knopf.

Steinberg, L. (1993). *Adolescence* (3rd ed.). New York: McGraw-Hill.

Steinberg, L., & Dornbusch, S. (1991). Negative correlates of part-time employment during adolescence: Replication and elaboration. *Developmental Psychology, 27,* 304.

Steiner, J. E. (1979). Human facial expressions in response to taste and smell stimulation. In H. Reese, & L. P. Lipsitt (Eds.), *Advances in child development and behavior* (Vol. 13). New York: Academic Press.

Steinmetz, H., Staiger, J. F., Schlaug, G., Huang, Y., et al. (1995). Corpus callosum and brain volume in women and men. *Neuroreport: An International Journal for the Rapid Communication of Research in Neuroscience, 6,* 1002–1004.

Stephens, T. (1998). Population mental health in Canada. Mental Health Promotion Unit. Health Canada.*

Stern, P. C. (1992). What psychology knows about energy conservation. *American Psychologist, 47,* 1224–1232.

Stern, R. M., & Koch, K. L. (1996). Motion sickness and differential susceptibility. *Current Directions in Psychological Science, 5,* 115–120.

Sternbach, R. A. (Ed.). (1987). *The psychology of pain.* New York: Raven Press.

Sternberg, R. (1996). *Successful intelligence: How practical and creative intelligence determine success in life.* New York: Simon & Schuster.

Sternberg, R. J. (1982). Reasoning, problem solving, and intelligence. In R. J. Sternberg (Ed.), *Handbook of human intelligence* (pp. 225–307). Cambridge, MA: Cambridge University Press.

Sternberg, R. J. (1985a). *Beyond IQ: A triarchic theory of human intelligence.* New York: Cambridge University Press.

Sternberg, R. J. (1985b). Implicit theories of intelligence, creativity, and wisdom. *Journal of Personality and Social Psychology, 49,* 607–627.

Sternberg, R. J. (1986). Triangular theory of love. *Psychological Review, 93,* 119–135.

Sternberg, R. J. (1987). Liking versus loving: A comparative evaluation of theories. *Psychological Bulletin, 102,* 331–345.

Sternberg, R. J. (1988a). *The nature of creativity.* Cambridge, England: Cambridge University Press.

Sternberg, R. J. (1988b). Triangulating love. In R. J. Sternberg, & M. J. Barnes (Eds.), *The psychology of love.* New Haven, CT: Yale University Press.

Sternberg, R. J. (1990). *Metaphors of mind: Conceptions of the nature of intelligence.* Cambridge, England: Cambridge University Press.

Sternberg, R. J. (1991). Theory-based testing of intellectual abilities: Rationale for the Sternberg triarchic abilities test. In H. A. H. Rowe (Ed.), *Intelligence: Reconceptualization and measurement.* Mahwah, NJ: Erlbaum.

Sternberg, R. J. (1994). Experimental approaches to human intelligence. *European Journal of Psychological Assessment, 10,* 153–161.

Sternberg, R. J. (1995). Theory and measurement of tacit knowledge as a part of practical intelligence. *Zeitschrift fur Psychologie, 203,* 319–334.

Sternberg, R. J. (1996). Educating intelligence: Infusing the triarchic theory into school instruction. In R. J. Sternberg, & E. Grigorenko (Eds.), *Intelligence, heredity, and environment.* New York: Cambridge University Press.

Sternberg, R. J. (Ed.). (1997). *Career paths in psychology: Where your degree can take you.* Washington, DC: American Psychological Association.

Sternberg, R. J., & Beall, A. E. (1991). How can we know what love is? An epistemological analysis. In G. J. O. Fletcher, & F. D. Fincham (Eds.), *Cognition in close relationships.* Mahwah, NJ: Erlbaum.

Sternberg, R. J., Conway, B. E., Ketron, J. L., & Bernstein, M. (1981). Peoples' conceptions of intelligence. *Journal of Personality and Social Psychology, 41,* 37–55.

Sternberg, R. J., & Davidson, J. E. (Eds.). (1986). *Conceptions of giftedness.* New York: Cambridge University Press.

Sternberg, R. J., & Detterman, D. (1986). *What is intelligence?* Norwood, NJ: Ablex.

Sternberg, R. J., & Frensch, P. A. (1991). *Complex problem solving: Principles and mechanisms.* Mahwah, NJ: Erlbaum.

Sternberg, R. J., & Grigorenko, E. (Eds.). (1996). *Intelligence, heredity, and environment.* New York: Cambridge University Press.

Sternberg, R. J., & Grigorenko, E. L. (1997). Are cognitive styles still in style? *American Psychologist, 52,* 700–712.

Sternberg, R. J., & Lubart, T. I. (1992). Buy low and sell high: An investment approach to creativity. *Current Directions in Psychological Science, 1,* 1–5.

Sternberg, R. J., & Lubart, T. I. (1995). An investment perspective on creative insight. In R. J. Sternberg, & J. E. Davidson (Eds.), *The nature of insight.* Cambridge, MA: MIT Press.

Sternberg, R. J., & Lubart, T. I. (1996). Investing in creativity. *American Psychologist, 51,* 677–688.

Sternberg, R. J., & Wagner, R. K. (Eds.). (1986). *Practical intelligence: Nature and origins of competence in the everyday world.* New York: Cambridge University Press.

Sternberg, R. J., & Wagner, R. K. (1993). The g-ocentric view of intelligence and job performance is wrong. *Current Directions in Psychological Science, 2,* 1–5.

Sternberg, R. J., Wagner, R. K., Williams, W. M., & Horvath, J. A. (1995). Testing common sense. *American Psychologist, 50,* 912–927.

Stevens, C. F. (1979, September). The neuron. *Scientific American,* p. 56.

Stevens, G., & Gardner, S. (1982). *The women of psychology: Pioneers and innovators* (Vol. 1). Cambridge, MA: Schenkman.

Stevens, H. W., Chen, C., & Lee, S. Y. (1993). A comparison of the parent-child relationship in Japan and the United States. In L. L. Roopnarine, & D. B. Carter (Eds.), *Parent-child socialization in diverse cultures.* Norwood, NJ: Ablex.

Stevenson, H. W. (1992, December). Learning from Asian schools. *Scientific American,* pp. 70–75.

Stevenson, H. W. (1995). Mathematics achievement of American students: First in the world in 2000? In C. A. Nelson (Ed.)., *Basic and applied perspectives on learning, cognition, and development.* Minneapolis: University of Minneapolis Press.

Stevenson, H. W. (1997, August). *Bronfenbrenner award address.* Paper presented at the meeting of the American Psychological Association, Chicago.

Stevenson, H. W., Chen, C., & Lee, S. (1993). Motivation and achievement of gifted children in East Asia and the United States. *Journal for the Education of the Gifted, 16,* 223–250.

Stevenson, H. W., Chen, C., & Lee, S. Y. (1992). A comparison of the parent-child relationship in Japan and the United States. In J. L. Roopnarine, & D. B. Carter (Eds.), *Parent-child socialization in diverse cultures.* Norwood, NJ: Ablex.

Stevenson, H. W., & Lee, S. Y. (1990). Contexts of achievement: A study of American, Chinese, and Japanese children. *Monographs of the Society for Research in Child Development, no. 221, 55,* nos. 1–2.

Stevenson, H. W., Lee, S. Y., Chen, C., Lummis, M., Stigler, J., Fan, L., & Ge, F. (1990). Mathematics achievement of children in China and the United States. *Child Development, 61,* 1053–1066.

Stevenson, H. W., & Stigler, J. W. (1992). *The learning gap: Why our schools are failing and what we can learn from Japanese and Chinese education.* New York: Summit.

Steward, E. P. (1995). *Beginning writers in the zone of proximal development.* Mahwah, NJ: Erlbaum.

Stewart, D. W., & Kamins, M. A. (1993). *Secondary research: Information sources and methods* (2nd ed.). Newbury Park, CA: Sage.

Stix, G. (1996, January). Listening to culture. *Scientific American,* pp. 16–17.

Stolberg, S. G. (1997, May 4). Breaks for mental illness: Just what the government ordered. *New York Times,* pp. 4–1, 4–5.

Stoppard, J. M. (1999). Why new perspectives are needed for understanding depression in women. *Canadian Psychology, 40,* 79–90.*

Storandt, M., et al. (1984). Psychometric differentiation of mild senile dementia of the Alzheimer type. *Archives of Neurology, 41,* 497–499.

Straube, E. R., & Oades, R. D. (1992). *Schizophrenia: Empirical research and findings.* San Diego, CA: Academic Press.

Straughan, R. (1994). Why not act on Kohlberg's moral judgments? (Or how to reach stage 6 and remain a bastard). In B. Puka (Ed.), *The great justice debate: Kohlberg criticism. Moral development: A compendium,* Vol. 4. New York: Garland.

Stricker, E. M., & Zigmond, M. J. (1976). Recovery of function after damage to catecholamine-containing neurons: A neurochemical model for hypothalamic syndrome. In J. M. Sprague, & A. N. Epstein (Eds.), *Progress in psychobiology and physiological psychology* (Vol. 6). New York: Academic Press.

Stricker, G., & Gold, J. R. (Eds.). (1993). *Comprehensive handbook of psychotherapy integration.* New York: Plenum.

Strickland, B. R. (1992). Women and depression. *Current Directions in Psychological Science, 1,* 132–135.

Stroebe, M. S., Stroebe, W., & Hansson, R. O. (Eds.). (1993). *Handbook of bereavement: Theory, research, and intervention.* Cambridge, England: Cambridge University Press.

Stroh, L. K., Brett, J. M., & Reilly, A. H. (1996). Family structure, glass ceiling, and traditional explanations for the differential rate of turnover of female and male managers. *Journal of Vocational Behavior, 49,* 99–118.

Strong, L. D. (1978). Alternative marital and family forms: Their relative attractiveness to college students and correlates of willingness to participate in nontraditional forms. *Journal of Marriage and the Family, 40,* 493–503.

Strongman, K. T. (1996). *The psychology of emotion: Theories of emotion in perspective* (4th ed.). Chichester, England: Wiley.

Strube, M. (Ed.). (1990). Type A behavior [Special issue]. *Journal of Social Behavior and Personality, 5.*

Strupp, H. H. (1996, October). The Tripartite model and the *Consumer Reports* study. *American Psychologist, 51,* 1017–1024.

Strupp, H. H., & Binder, J. L. (1992). Current developments in psychotherapy. *The Independent Practitioner, 12,* 119–124.

Studd, M. V. (1996). Sexual harassment. In D. M. Buss, & N. M. Malamuth (Eds.), *Sex,*

power, conflict: Evolutionary and feminist perspectives. New York: Oxford University Press.

Stumpf, H. (1995). Gender differences in performance on tests of cognitive abilities: Experimental design issues and empirical results. Special Issue: Psychological and psychobiological perspectives on sex differences in cognition: I. Theory and research. *Learning and Individual Differences, 7,* 275–287.

Suarez, E. C., & Williams, R. B., Jr. (1992). Interactive models of reactivity: The relationship between hostility and potentially pathogenic physiological responses to social stressors. In N. Schneiderman, P. McCabe, & A. Baum (Eds.), *Stress and disease processes.* Mahwah, NJ: Erlbaum.

Subotnik, R. F., & Arnold, K. D. (1993). Longitudinal studies of giftedness: Investigating the fulfillment of promise. In K. A. Heller, F. J. Monks, & A. H. Passow (Eds.), *International handbook of research and development of giftedness and talent.* Oxford, England: Pergamon.

Subotnik R. F., & Arnold, K. D. (1994). *Beyond Terman: Contemporary longitudinal studies of giftedness and talent.* Norwood, NJ: Ablex.

Suddath, R. L., Christison, G. W., Torrey, E. F., Casanova, M. F., & Weinberger, D. R. (1990, March 22). Anatomical abnormalities in the brains of monozygotic twins discordant for schizophrenia. *New England Journal of Medicine, 322,* 789–794.

Sudsuang, R., Chentanez, V., & Veluvan, K. (1991). Effect of Buddhist meditation on serum cortisol and total protein levels, blood pressure, pulse rate, lung volume and reaction time. *Physiology and Behavior, 50,* 543–548.

Sue, D. (1979). Erotic fantasies of college students during coitus. *Journal of Sex Research, 15,* 299–305.

Sue, D. W. (1981). *Counseling the culturally different: Theory and practice.* New York: Wiley

Sue, D. W., & Sue, D. (1990). *Counseling the culturally different: Theory and practice* (2nd ed.). New York: Wiley.

Sue, D. W., Sue, D., & Sue, S. (1990). *Understanding abnormal behavior* (3rd ed.). Boston: Houghton-Mifflin.

Suedfeld, P. (1992). Bilateral relations between countries and the complexity of newspaper editorials. *Political Psychology, 13,* 601–632.

Suedfeld, P., & Tetlock, P. (1977). Integrative complexity of communications in international crises. *Journal of Conflict Resolution, 21,* 169–184.

Sullivan, B. (1985). *Double standard.* Paper presented at the annual meeting of the Society for the Scientific Study of Sex, San Diego, CA.

Sulzer-Azaroff, B., & Mayer, R. (1991). *Behavior analysis and lasting change.* New York: Holt.

Sundin, O., Ohman, A., Palm, T., & Strom, G. (1995). Cardiovascular reactivity, Type A behavior, and coronary heart disease: Comparisons between myocardial infarction patients and controls during laboratory-

induced stress. *Psychophysiology, 32,* 28–35.

Super, C. M. (1980). Cognitive development: Looking across at growing up. In C. M. Super, & S. Harakness (Eds.), *New directions for child development: Anthropological perspectives on child development* (pp. 59–69). San Francisco: Jossey-Bass.

Suris, O. (1997, February 28). AIDS deaths drop significantly for first time. *Wall Street Journal,* p. B1.

Surra, C. A. (1991). Mate selection and premarital relationships. In A. Booth (Ed.), *Contemporary families.* Minneapolis, MN: National Council on Family Relations.

Sutker, P. B., Uddo, M., Brailey, K., & Allain, A. N., Jr. (1993). War-zone trauma and stress-related symptoms in Operation Desert Shield/Storm (ODS) returnees. *Journal of Social Issues, 49,* 33–49.

Sutton, S. (1992). Shock tactics and the myth of the inverted U. *British Journal of Addiction, 87,* 517–519.

Suzuki, K. (1991). Moon illusion simulated in complete darkness: Planetarium experiment reexamined. *Perception & Psychophysics, 49,* 349–354.

Svarstad, B. (1976). Physician-patient communication and patient conformity with medical advice. In D. Mechanic (Ed.), *The growth of bureaucratic medicine.* New York: Wiley.

Swaab, D. F., & Gofman, M. A. (1995). Sexual differentiation of the human hypothalamus in relation to gender and sexual orientation. *Trends in Neurosciences, 18,* 264–270.

Swanson, J. (Ed.). (1999). *Sleep disorders sourcebook.* New York: Omnigraphics, Inc.

Swede, G. (1993). *Creativity: A new psychology.* Toronto: Wall & Emerson, Inc.

Swerdlow, J. L. (1995, June). Quiet miracles of the brain. *National Geographic,* 2–41.

Swets, J. (1996). *Signal detection theory and ROC analysis in psychology and diagnostics: Collected papers.* Mahwah, NJ: Erlbaum.

Swets, J. A. (1992). The science of choosing the right decision threshold in high-stakes diagnostics. *American Psychologist, 47,* 522–532.

Swets, J. A., & Bjork, R. A. (1990). Enhancing human performance: An evaluation of "new age" techniques considered by the U.S. Army. *Psychological Science, 1,* 85–96.

Sylvain, C., Ladouceur, R., & Boisvert, J. (1997). Cognitive and behavioural treatment of pathological gambling: A controlled study. *Journal of Consulting and Clinical Psychology, 65,* 727–732.*

Symbaluk, D. G., Heth, C. D., Cameron, J., & Pierce, W. D. (1997). Social modeling, monetary incentives, and pain endurance: The role of self-efficacy and pain perception. *Personality and Social Psychology Bulletin, 23,* 258–269.

Szasz, T. (1982). The psychiatric will: A new mechanism for protecting persons against "psychosis" and psychiatry. *American Psychologist, 37,* 762–770.

Szasz, T. S. (1961). *The myth of mental illness.* New York: Harper & Row.

Szasz, T. S. (1994). *Cruel compassion: Psychiatric control of society's unwanted.* New York: Wiley.

Tabakoff, B., & Hoffman, P. L. (1996). Effect of alcohol on neurotransmitters and their receptors and enzymes. In H. Begleiter, & B. Kissin (Eds.), *The pharmacology of alcohol and alcohol dependence. Alcohol and alcoholism, No. 2.* New York: Oxford University Press.

Tafarodi, R. W. (1998). Paradoxical self-esteem and selectivity in the processing of social information. *Journal of Personality and Social Psychology, 74,* 1181–1196.*

Tafarodi, R. W., & Vu, C. (1997). Two-dimensional self-esteem and reactions to success and failure. *Personality and Social Psychology Bulletin, 23,* 626–635.*

Tafti, M., Villemin, E., Carlander, B., & Besset, A., et al. (1992). Sleep in human narcolepsy revisited with special reference to prior wakefulness duration. *Sleep, 15,* 344–351.

Tagiuri, R. (1958). Social preference and its perception. In R. Tagiuri, & L. Petrullo (Eds.), *Person, perception, and interpersonal behavior* (pp. 316–336). Stanford, CA: Stanford University Press.

Tajfel, H. (1982). *Social identity and intergroup relations.* London: Cambridge University Press.

Takami, S., Getchell, M. L., Chen, Y., Monti-Bloch, L., Berliner, D. L., Stensaas, L. J., & Getchell, T. V. (1993). Vomeronasal epithelial cells of the adult human express neuron-specific molecules. *Neuroreport, 4,* 375–378.

Talbot, J. D., Marrett, S., Evans, A. C., Meyer, E., Bushnell, M. C., & Duncan, G. H. (1991, March 15). Multiple representations of pain in human cerebral cortex. *Science, 251,* 1355–1358.

Tamura, T., Nakatani, K., & Yau, K.-W. (1989, August 18). Light adaptation in cat retinal rods. *Science, 245,* 755–758.

Tan, V. L., & Hicks, R. A. (1995). Type A-B behavior and nightmare types among college students. *Perceptual and Motor Skills, 81,* 15–19.

Tandon, R. (1995). Neurobiological substrate of dimensions of schizophrenic illness. *Journal of Psychiatric Research, 29,* 255–260.

Tanford, S., & Penrod, S. (1984). Social influence model: A formal integration of research on majority and minority influence processes. *Psychological Bulletin, 95,* 189–225.

Tanner, J. M. (1978). *Education and physical growth* (2nd ed.). New York: International Universities Press.

Tanner, J. M. (1990). *Foetus into man: Physical growth from conception to maturity, Revised.* Cambridge, MA: Harvard University Press.

Tasker, F., & Golombok, S. (1995). Adults raised as children in lesbian families. *American Journal of Orthopsychiatry, 65,* 203–215.

Tavris, C. (1992). *The mismeasure of woman.* New York: Simon & Schuster.

Taylor, A. (1991, April 8). Can Iacocco fix Chrysler—again? *Fortune,* pp. 50–54.

Taylor, M. (1996). A theory of mind perspective on social cognitive development. In R. Gelman, & T. K-F. Au (Eds.), *Perceptual and cognitive development. Handbook of perception and cognition* (2nd ed.). San Diego, CA: Academic Press.

Taylor, R. J., Chatters, L. M., Tucker, M., & Lewis, E. (1991). Developments in research on Black families. In A. Booth (Ed.), *Contemporary families.* Minneapolis, MN: National Council on Family Relations.

Taylor, S. E. (1982). Hospital patient behavior: Reactance, helplessness, or control. In H. S. Friedman, & M. R. DiMatteo (Eds.), *Interpersonal issues in health care.* New York: Academic Press.

Taylor, S. E., & Aspinwall, L. G. (1996). Mediating and moderating processes in psychosocial stress: Appraisal, coping, resistance, and vulnerability. In H. B. Kaplan (Ed.), *Psychosocial stress: Perspectives on structure, theory, life-course, and methods.* San Diego, CA: Academic Press.

Taylor, S. E., Buunk, B. P., & Aspinwall, L. G. (1990). Social comparison, stress, and coping. *Personality and Social Psychology Bulletin, 16,* 74–89.

Taylor, S. E., Helgeson, V. S., Reed, G. M., & Skokan, L. A. (1991). Self-generated feelings of control and adjustment to physical illness. *Journal of Social Issues, 47,* 91–109.

Taylor, S. L. (1995). Quandary at the crossroads: paternalism versus advocacy surrounding end-of-treatment decisions. *American Journal of Hospital Palliatory Care, 12,* 43–46.

Tellegen, A., Lykken, D. T., Bouchard, T. J., Jr., Wilcox, K. J., Segal, N. L., & Rich, S. (1988). Personality similarity in twins reared apart and together. *Journal of Personality and Social Psychology, 54,* 1031–1039.

Teller, D. Y., & Palmer, J. (1996). Infant color vision: Motion nulls for red/green vs. luminance-modulated stimuli in infants and adults. *Vision Research, 36,* 955–974.

Tepper, E. L. (1994). Immigration policy and multiculturalism. In J. W. Berry & J. A. Laponce (Eds.), *Ethnicity and culture in Canada: The research landscape.* Toronto: University of Toronto Press.*

Tepperman, L., & Curtis, J. (1995). A life satisfaction scale for use with national adult samples from the USA, Canada, and Mexico. *Social Indicators Research, 35,* 255–270.

Terman, L. M., & Oden, M. H. (1947). *Genetic studies of genius, IV: The gifted child grows up.* Stanford, CA: Stanford University Press.

Tesser, A. (1988). Toward a self-evaluation maintenance model of social behavior. In L. Berkowitz (Ed.), *Advances in experimental social psychology* (Vol. 21). New York: Academic Press.

Tesser, A., & Shaffer, D. R. (1990). Attitudes and attitude change. *Annual Review of Psychology, 41,* 479–523.

Tessier-Lavigne, M. (1991). Phototransduction and information processing in the retina. In E. R. Kandel, J. H. Schwartz, & T. M. Jessell (Eds.), *Principles of neural science* (3rd ed.). New York: Elsevier.

Tetlock, P. E. (1988). Monitoring the integrative complexity of American and Soviet policy rhetoric: What can be learned? *Journal of Social Issues, 44,* 101–131.

Tetlock, P. E., Hoffmann, S., Janis, I. L., Stein, J. G., Kressel, N. J., & Cohen, B. C. (1993). The psychology of international conflict. In N. J. Kressel (Ed.), *Political psychology: Classic and contemporary readings.* New York: Paragon House Publishers.

Tetlock, P. E., McGuire, C. B., & Mitchell, G. (1991). Psychological perspectives on nuclear deterrence. In M. R. Rosenzweig, & L. W. Porter (Eds.), *Annual review of psychology, Vol. 42.* Palo Alto, CA: Annual Reviews, Inc.

Tetlock, P. E., Peterson, R. S., McGuire, C., Chang, S., & Feld, P. (1992). Assessing political group dynamics: A test of the groupthink model. *Journal of Personality and Social Psychology, 63,* 403–425.

Thacker, R. A., & Gohmann, S. F. (1996). Emotional and psychological consequences of sexual harassment: A descriptive study. *Journal of Psychology, 130,* 429–446.

Thagard, P. (1996). *Mind: Introduction to cognitive science.* Cambridge, MA: MIT Press.

Tharp, R. G. (1989). Psychocultural variables and constants: Effects on teaching and learning in schools. Special issue: Children and their development: Knowledge base, research agenda, and social policy application. *American Psychologist, 44,* 349–359.

t'Hart, P. (1991). Groupthink, risk-taking and recklessness: Quality of process and outcome in policy decision making. *Politics and the Individual, 1,* 67–90.

Thatcher, R. W., Hallett, M., Zeffiro, T., John, E. R., & Huerta, M. (1994). *Functional neuroimaging.* San Diego: Academic Press.

Thiel, A., Broocks, A., & Schussler, G. (1995). Obsessive-compulsive disorder among patients with anorexia nervosa and bulimia nervosa. *American Journal of Psychiatry, 152,* 72ff.

Thienhaus, O. J., Margletta, S., & Bennett, J. A. (1990). A study of the clinical efficacy of maintenance ECT. *Journal of Clinical Psychiatry, 51,* 141–144.

Thoma, S. J., Rest, J. R., & Davison, M. L. (1991). Describing and testing a moderator of the moral judgment and action relationship. *Journal of Personality and Social Psychology, 61,* 659–669.

Thomas, C. B., Duszynski, K. R., & Schaffer, J. W. (1979). Family attitudes reported in youth as potential predictors of cancer. *Psychosomatic Medicine, 4,* 287–302.

Thomas, E. (1996, April 22). Blood brothers. *Newsweek,* p. 28

Thomas, E. (1997, April 7). Web of death. *Newsweek,* pp. 26–35.

Thompson, A. (2000, April 13). Dallaire's last battle. *The Toronto Star,* A3.*

Thompson, C. P., Skowronski, J. J., Larsen, S. F., & Betz, A. (Eds.). (1996).

Autobiographical memory: Remembering what and remembering when. Mahwah, NJ: Erlbaum.

Thompson, L. (1992, August 14). Fetal transplants show promise. *Science, 257,* 868–870.

Thompson, S. C. (1988, August). *An intervention to increase physician-patient communication.* Paper presented at the annual meeting of the American Psychological Association, Atlanta.

Thompson, S. C., Nanni, C., & Schwankovsky, L. (1990). Patient-oriented interventions to improve communication in a medical office visit. *Health Psychology, 9,* 390–404.

Thompson, V. A. (1996). Reasoning from false premises: The role of soundness in making logical deductions. *Canadian Journal of Experimental Psychology, 50,* 315–319.*

Thompson, W. C. (1996). Research on human judgment and decision making: Implications for informed consent and institutional review. In B. H. Stanley, J. E. Sieber, & G. B. Melton (Eds.), *Research ethics: A psychological approach.* Lincoln, NE: University of Nebraska Press.

Thomson, A. M. (1997, January 10). More than just frequency detectors? *Science, 275,* 179–180.

Thoresen, C. E., & Low, K. G. (1990). Women and the Type A behavior pattern: Review and commentary. *Journal of Social Behavior and Personality, 5,* 117–133.

Thorndike, E. L. (1932). *The fundamentals of learning.* New York: Teachers College.

Thorndike, R. L., Hagan, E., & Sattler, J. (1986). *Stanford-Binet* (4th ed.). Chicago: Riverside.

Tierney, J. (1988, May 15). Wired for stress. *New York Times Magazine,* pp. 49–85.

Time. (1976, September). Svengali squad: L.A. police. *Time,* p. 76.

Time. (1982, October 4). "We're sorry: A case of mistaken identity." *Time,* p. 45.

Time. (1996, Fall Special Issue). The human condition: Pain. *Time,* p. 86.

Timnick, L. (1985, August 25). The *Times* poll: 22% in survey were child abuse victims. *Los Angeles Times,* pp. 1, 34.

Tiunova, A., Anokhin, K., Rose, S. P. R., & Mileusnic, R. (1996). Involvement of glutamate receptors, protein kinases, and protein synthesis in memory for visual discrimination in the young chick. *Neurobiology of Learning and Memory, 65,* 233–243.

Toga, A. W., & Mazziotta, J. C. (Eds.). (1996). *Brain mapping: The methods.* New York: Academic Press.

Tolan, P., Keys, C., Chertok, F., & Jason, L. (1990). *Researching community psychology.* Washington, DC: American Psychological Association.

Tolman, E. C. (1959). Principles of purposive behavior. In S. Koch (Ed.), *Psychology: A study of a science* (Vol. 2). New York: McGraw-Hill.

Tolman, E. C., & Honzik, C. H. (1930). Introduction and removal of reward and maze performance in rats. *University of California Publications in Psychology, 4,* 257–275.

Tomlinson-Keasey, C. (1985). *Child development: Psychological, sociological, and biological factors.* Homewood, IL: Dorsey.

Tomlinson-Keasey, C., Eisert, D. C., Kahle, L. R., Hardy-Brown, K., & Keasey, B. (1979). The structure of concrete operations. *Child Development,* 1153–1163.

Torgersen, S. (1983). Genetic factors in anxiety disorders. *Archives of General Psychiatry, 40,* 1085–1089.

Torrey, E. F. (1996). *Out of the shadows: Confronting America's mental illness crisis.* New York: Wiley.

Torrey, E. F. (1997, June 13). The release of the mentally ill from institutions: A well-intentioned disaster. *Chronicle of Higher Education,* pp. B4–B5.

Toth, J. P., & Reingold, E. M. (1996). *Beyond perception: Conceptual contributions to unconscious influences of memory.* Oxford, England: Oxford University Press.

Toynbee, P. (1977). *Patients.* New York: Harcourt Brace Jovanovich.

Trainor, J., Pomeroy, E., & Pape, B. (Eds.). (1999). *Building a framework for support: A community development approach to mental health policy.* Toronto: Canadian Mental Health Association.*

Trappler, B., & Friedman, S. (1996). Post-traumatic stress disorder in survivors of the Brooklyn Bridge shooting. *American Journal of Psychiatry, 153,* 705–707.

Travis, J. (1992, September 4). Can "hair cells" unlock deafness? *Science, 257,* 1344–1345.

Trehub, S. E., Schneider, B. A., Thorpe, L. A., & Judge, P. (1991). Observational measures of auditory sensitivity in early infancy. *Developmental Psychology, 27,* 40–49.

Treisman, A. (1988). Features and objects: The Fourteenth Bartlett Memorial Lecture. *Quarterly Journal of Experimental Psychology, 40,* 201–237.

Treisman, A. (1993). The perception of features and objects. In A. D. Baddeley, & L. Weiskrantz (Eds.), *Attention: Selection, awareness, and control: A tribute to Donald Broadbent.* Oxford, England: Oxford University Press.

Tremblay, S. (1999). Crime statistics in Canada, 1998. *Juristat 19(9).* Ottawa: Canadian Centre for Justice Statistics, Statistics Canada.*

Triandis, H. C. (1994). *Culture and social behavior.* New York: McGraw-Hill.

Trinder, J. (1988). Subjective insomnia without objective findings: A pseudodiagnostic classification. *Psychological Bulletin, 107,* 87–94.

Tsuang, M. T., & Faraone, S. V. (1996). Epidemiology and behavioral genetics of schizophrenia. In S. J. Watson (Ed.), *Biology of schizophrenia and affective disease.* Washington, DC: American Psychiatric Press.

Tsunoda, T. (1985). *The Japanese brain: Uniqueness and universality.* Tokyo, Japan: Taishukan Publishing.

Tulving, E. (1972). Episodic and semantic memory. In E. Tulving, & W. Donaldson (Eds.), *Organization of memory.* New York: Academic Press.

Tulving, E. (1985). How many memory systems are there? *American Psychologist, 40,* 385–398.

Tulving, E. (1993). What is episodic memory? *Current Directions in Psychological Science, 2,* 67–70.

Tulving, E. (2000). Concepts of memory. In E. Tulving, & F. I. M. Craik (Eds.), *The Oxford handbook of memory,* New York: Oxford University Press.*

Tulving, E., Hayman, C., & McDonald, C. (1991). Long-lasting perceptual and semantic priming in amnesia: A case experiment. *Journal of Experimental Psychology: Learning, Memory, and Cognition, 17,* 595–617.*

Tulving, E., & Psotka, J. (1971). Retroactive inhibition in free recall: Inaccessibility of information available in the memory store. *Journal of Experimental Psychology, 87,* 1–8.*

Tulving, E., & Schacter, D. L. (1990, January 19). Priming and human memory systems. *Science, 247,* 301–306.*

Tulving, E., & Thompson, D. M. (1973). Encoding specificity and retrieval processes in episodic memory. *Psychological Review, 80,* 352–373.*

Turk, D. C. (1994). Perspectives on chronic pain: The role of psychological factors. *Current Directions in Psychological Science, 3,* 45–49.

Turk, D. C., & Melzack, R. (Eds.). (1992). *Handbook of pain assessment.* New York: Guilford Press.

Turk, D. C., & Nash, J. M. (1993). Chronic pain: New ways to cope. In D. Goleman, & J. Guerin (Eds.), *Mind-body medicine: How to use your mind for better health.* Yonkers, NY: Consumer Reports Publications.

Turkewitz, G. (1993). The origins of differential hemispheric strategies for information processing in the relationships between voice and face perception. In B. de Boysson-Bardies, S. de Schonen, P. W. Jusczyk, P. McNeilage, & J. Morton (Eds.), *Developmental neurocognition: Speech and face processing in the first year of life. NATO ASI series D: Behavioural and social sciences, Vol. 69.* Dordrecht, Netherlands: Kluwer Academic Publishers.

Turkington, C. (1987, September). Special talents. *Psychology Today,* pp. 42–46.

Turkington, C. (1992, December). Ruling opens door—a crack—to IQ-testing some Black kids. *APA Monitor,* pp. 28–29.

Turkkan, J. S. (1989). Classical conditioning: The new hegemony. *Behavioral & Brain Sciences, 12,* 121–179.

Turner, J. C. (1987). *Rediscovering the social group: A self-categorization theory.* New York: Blackwell.

Turner, M. E., Pratkanis, A. R., Probasco, P., & Leve, C. (1992). Threat, cohesion, and group effectiveness: Testing a social identity maintenance perspective on groupthink. *Journal of Personality and Social Psychology, 63,* 781–796.

Turner, W. J. (1995). Homosexuality, Type 1: An Xq28 phenomenon. *Archives of Sexual Behavior, 24*, 109–134.

Tuss, P., Zimmer, J., & Ho, H. Z. (1995). Causal attributions of underachieving fourth grade students in China, Japan, and the United States. *Journal of Cross Cultural Psychology, 26*, 408–425.

Tversky, A., & Kahneman, D. (1974). Judgment under uncertainty: Heuristics and biases. *Science, 185*, 1124–1131.

Tversky, A., & Kahneman, D. (1990). Judgment under uncertainty: Heuristics and biases. In P. K. Moser (Ed.), *Rationality in action: Contemporary approaches.* New York: Cambridge University Press.

Tversky, B. (1981). Distortions in memory for maps. *Cognitive Psychology, 13*, 407–433.

Twine, N. & Barraclough, N. (1998). Crisis lines, telephone technology, and confidentiality. In A. A. Leenaars, S. Wenckstern, I. Sakinofsky, R. J. Dyck, M. J. Kral, & R. C. Bland (Eds.), *Suicide in Canada* (pp. 342–352). Toronto: University of Toronto Press.*

Tyler, T. R., & McGraw, K. M. (1983). The threat of nuclear war: Risk interpretation and behavioral response. *Journal of Social Issues, 39*, 25–40.

Tzeng, O. C. S. (Ed.). (1992). *Theories of love development, maintenance, and dissolution: Octagonal cycle and differential perspectives.* New York: Praeger Publishers/ Greenwood Publishing Group.

U.S. Bureau of Census. (1996). *Current projections of the population makeup of the U.S.* Washington, DC: U.S. Bureau of Census.

U.S. Bureau of Labor Statistics. (1988). *Special labor force reports.* Washington, DC: U.S. Government Printing Office.

U.S. Census Bureau. (1988). *Current population reports.* Washington, DC: U.S. Government Printing Office.

U.S. Census Bureau. (1991). Household and family characteristics, March 1990 & 1989. *Current population reports.* Washington, DC: U.S. Census Bureau.

U.S. Census Bureau. (1993). *The top 25 languages.* Washington, DC: U.S. Census Bureau.

U.S. Census Bureau. (1996). *Planning document.* Washington, DC: U.S. Census Bureau.

U.S. Commission on Civil Rights. (1990). *Intimidation and violence: Racial and religious bigotry in America.* Washington, DC: U.S. Commission on Civil Rights Clearinghouse.

U.S. Department of Education. (1993). *Projection of minority students.* U.S. Department of Education. Washington, DC.

U.S. Department of Health and Human Services. (1981). *The health consequences of smoking for women: A report of the Surgeon General.* Washington, DC: Public Health Service.

U.S. Public Health Service. (1992). *Pain control after surgery.* Washington, DC: U.S. Public Health Service.

U.S. Surgeon General. (1988, May). *Report on smoking.* Washington, DC: U.S. Government Printing Office.

Ubell, E. (1993, January 10). Could you use more sleep? *Parade,* pp. 16–18.

Ubell, E. (1996, September 15). Are you at risk? *Parade,* pp. 20–21.

Uchino, B. N., Cacioppo, J. T., & Kiecolt-Glaser, J. K. (1996). *Psychological Bulletin, 119*, 488–531.

Udolf, R. (1981). *Handbook of hypnosis for professionals.* New York: Van Nostrand.

Ullman, L. P., & Krasner, L. (1975). *A psychological approach to abnormal behavior* (2nd ed.). Englewood Cliffs, NJ: Prentice-Hall.

Ullman, S. (1996). *High-level vision: Object recognition and visual cognition.* Cambridge, MA: MIT Press.

Ulrich, R. E. (1991). Animal rights, animal wrongs and the question of balance. *Psychological Science, 2*, 197–201.

Underwood, G. D. M. (Ed.). (1996). *Implicit cognition.* Oxford, England: Oxford University Press.

Unger, R. K., & Crawford, M. E. (1992). *Women and gender: A feminist psychology.* Philadelphia: Temple University Press.

Urberg, K. A., Degirmencioglu, S. M., & Pilgrim, C. (1997). Close friend and group influence on adolescent cigarette smoking and alcohol use. *Developmental Psychology, 33*, 834–844.

Ursano, R. J., Sonnenberg, S. M., & Lazar, S. (1991). *Concise guide to psychodynamic psychotherapy.* Washington, DC: American Psychiatric Press.

Valenstein, E. S. (1986). *Great and desperate cures: The rise and decline of psychosurgery and other radical treatments for mental illness.* New York: Basic Books.

Valente, S. M. (1991). Electroconvulsive therapy. *Archives of Psychiatric Nursing, 5*, 223–228.

Valentiner, D. P., Foa, E. B., Riggs, D. S., & Gershuny, B. S. (1996). Coping strategies and post-traumatic stress disorder in female victims of sexual and nonsexual assault. *Journal of Abnormal Psychology, 105*, 455–458.

Vallis, M. (2000, April 28). Researchers narrow schizophrenia gene link search. *National Post,* A10.*

Van Biema, D. (1996, November 11). Just say life skills. *Time,* p. 70.

Van Ginkel, R. (1990). Fishermen, taboos, and ominous animals: A comparative perspective. *Anthrozoos, 4*, 73–81.

van Goozen, S. H. M., Cohen-Kettenis, P. T., Gooren, L. J. G., Frijda, N. H., et al. (1995). Gender differences in behaviour: Activating effects of cross-sex hormones. *Psychoneuroendocrinology, 20*, 343–363.

van Goozen, S. H. M., Van de Poll, N. E., & Sergeant, J. A. (Eds.). (1994). *Emotions: Essays on emotion theory.* Mahwah, NJ: Erlbaum.

Van Manen, S., & Pietromonaco, P. (1994). *Acquaintance and consistency influence memory from interpersonal information.*

Unpublished manuscript. University of Massachusetts at Amherst.

Vance, E. B., & Wagner, N. W. (1976). Written descriptions of orgasm: A study of sex differences. *Archives of Sexual Behavior, 5*, 87–98.

VanLehn, K. (1996). Cognitive skill acquisition. *Annual Review of Psychology, 47*, 513–539.

Vannatta, R. A. (1996). Risk factors related to suicidal behavior among male and female adolescents. *Journal of Youth and Adolescence, 25*, 149–160.

Varnhagen, C. K., McCallum, M., & Burstow, M. (1997). Is children's spelling naturally stage-like? *Reading and Writing, 9*, 451–481.*

Vassar, R., Chao, S. K., Sitcheran, R., Nunez, J. M., Vosshall, L. B., & Axel, R. (1994). Topographic organization of sensory projections to the olfactory bulb. *Cell, 79*, 981–991.

Veitch, J. A., & Gifford, R. (1997). Editors' introduction to the special issue: Behavioural origins and solutions of environmental problems. *Canadian Journal of Behavioural Science, 29(3)*, 138–144.*

Velichkovsky, B. M., & Rumbaugh, D. M. (Eds.). (1996). *Communicating meaning: The evolution and development of language.* Mahwah, NJ: Erlbaum.

Verdoux, H., Van Os, J., Sham, P., Jones, P., et al. (1996). Does familiarity predispose to both emergence and persistence of psychosis? A follow-up study. *British Journal of Psychiatry, 168*, 620–626.

Verhaeghen, P., Marcoen, A., & Goossens, L. (1992). Improving memory performance in the aged through mnemonic training: A meta-analytic study. *Psychology and Aging, 7*, 242–251.

Vernon, P. A., Jang, K. L., Harris, J. A., & McCarthy, J. M. (1997). Environmental predictors of personality differences: A twin and sibling study. *Journal of Personality and Social Psychology, 72*, 177–183.

Victor, S. B., & Fish, M. C. (1995). Lesbian mothers and the children: A review for school psychologists. *School Psychology Review, 24*, 456–479.

Vihman, M. M. (1996). *Phonological development: The origins of language in the child.* London, England: Blackwell.

Vingerhoets, A. J., Croon, M., Jeninga, A. J., & Menges, L. J. (1990). Personality and health habits. *Psychology and Health, 4*, 333–342.

Vinogradov, S., & Yalom, I. D. (1996). Group therapy. In R. E. Hales, & S. C. Yudofsky (Eds.), *The American Psychiatric Press synopsis of psychiatry.* Washington, DC: American Psychiatric Press.

Vital-Durand, F., Atkinson, J., & Braddick, O. J. (Eds.). (1996). *Infant vision. The European brain and behaviour society publication series, Vol. 2.* Oxford, England: Oxford University Press.

Vlaeyen, J. W. S., Geurts, S. M., KoleSnijders, A. M. J., Schuerman, J. A., Groenman, N. H., & van Eek, H. (1990). What do chronic pain patients think of their pain? Towards a pain cognition questionnaire. *British Journal of Clinical Psychology, 29,* 383–394.

Voeller, B., Reinisch, J. M., & Gottlieb, M. (1991). *AIDS and sex: An integrated biomedical and biobehavioral approach.* New York: Oxford University Press.

Vogt, W. P. (1993). *Dictionary of statistics and methodology: A nontechnical guide for the social sciences.* Newbury Park, CA: Sage.

Volling, B. L., & Feagans, L. V. (1995). Infant day care and children's social competence. *Infant Behavior and Development, 18,* 177–188.

von Restorff, H. (1933). Uber die wirking von bereichsbildungen im Spurenfeld. In W. Kohler, & H. von Restorff, *Analyse von vorgangen in Spurenfeld. 1. Psychologische forschung, 18,* 299–342.

Vonnegut, M. (1975). *The Eden express.* New York: Bantam.

Vroom, V. H., & Yetton, P. W. (1973). *Leadership and decision making.* Pittsburgh, PA: University of Pittsburgh Press.

Vygotsky, L. S. (1926/1997). *Educational psychology.* Delray Beach, FL: St. Lucie Press.

Vygotsky, L. S. (1979). *Mind in society: The development of higher mental processes.* Cambridge, MA: Harvard University Press. (Original works published 1930, 1933, and 1935).

Vyse, S. A. (1994, February 27). Unpublished e-mail message. Connecticut College.

Wachs, T. D. (1993). The nature-nurture gap: What we have here is a failure to collaborate. In R. Plomin, & G. E. McClearn (Eds.), *Nature, nurture, and psychology.* Washington, DC: American Psychological Association.

Wachs, T. D. (1996). Environment and intelligence: Present status, future directions. In D. K. Detterman (Ed.), *Current topics in human intelligence, Volume 5, The environment.* Norwood, NJ: Ablex.

Wachtel, P. L., & Messer, S. B. (Eds.). (1997). *Theories of psychotherapy: Origins and evolution.* Washington, DC: American Psychological Association.

Waddington, J. L. (1990). Sight and insight: Regional cerebral metabolic activity in schizophrenia visualized by positron emission tomography, and competing neurodevelopmental perspectives. *British Journal of Psychiatry, 156,* 615–619.

Wagner, B. M. (1997). Family risk factors for child and adolescent suicidal behavior. *Psychological Bulletin, 121,* 246–298.

Wagner, B. M., Cole, R. E., & Schwartzman, P. (1995). Psychosocial correlates of suicide attempts among junior and senior high school youth. *Suicide and Life Threatening Behavior, 25,* 358–372.

Wagner, D. A. (1981). Culture and memory development. In H. C. Triandis, & A. Heron (Eds.), *Handbook of cross-cultural psychology: Vol. 4. Developmental psychology.* Boston: Allyn & Bacon.

Wagner, R., & Sternberg, R. (1985). Alternate conceptions of intelligence and their implications for education. *Review of Educational Research, 54,* 179–223.

Wagner, R. K. (1997). Intelligence, training, and employment. *American Psychologist, 52,* 1059–1069.

Wagner, R. K., & Sternberg, R. J. (1991). *Tacit knowledge inventory.* San Antonio, TX: The Psychological Corporation.

Wahlsten, D. (1995). Increasing the raw intelligence of a nation is constrained by ignorance, not its citizens' genes. Special Issue: Canadian perspectives on *The Bell Curve. Alberta Journal of Educational Research, 41,* 257–264.*

Wahlsten, D., & Gottlieb, G. (1997). The invalid separation of effects of nature and nurture: Lessons from animal experimentation. In R. J. Sternberg & E. L. Grigorenko (Eds.), *Intelligence, heredity and environment.* Cambridge University Press.*

Waid, W. M., & Orne, M. T. (1982). The physiological detection of deception. *American Scientist, 70,* 402–409.

Waitzkin, H., Stoeckle, J. D., Beller, E., & Mons, C. (1978). The informative process in medical care: A preliminary report with implications for instructional communication. *Instructional Science, 7,* 385–419.

Wald, M. L. (1997). Eye problem cited in '96 train crash. *New York Times,* pp. A1, A22.

Waldorf, D., Reinarman, C., & Murphy, S. (1991). *Cocaine changes: The experience of using and quitting.* Philadelphia: Temple University Press.

Waldrop, M. W. (1989, September 29). NIDA aims to fight drugs with drugs. *Science, 245,* 1443–1444.

Walker, L. J. (1984). Sex differences in the development of moral reasoning: A critical review. *Child Development, 55,* 677–691.*

Walker, L. J., & Hennig, K. H. (1997). Parent/child relationships in single-parent families. *Canadian Journal of Behavioural Science, 29(1),* 63–75.*

Walker, N., & Jones, P. (1983). Encoding processes and the recall of text. *Memory and Cognition, 11,* 275–282.

Walker, W. D., Rowe, R. C., & Quinsey, V. L. (1993). Authoritarianism and sexual aggression. *Journal of Personality and Social Psychology, 65,* 1036–1045.

Wall, P. D., & Melzack, R. (Eds.). (1984). *Textbook of pain.* Edinburgh: Churchill Livingstone.

Wall, P. D., & Melzack, R. (1989). *Textbook of pain* (2nd ed.). New York: Churchill Livingstone.

Wallace, P. (1977). Individual discrimination of humans by odor. *Physiology and Behavior, 19,* 577–579.

Wallace, R. K., & Benson, H. (1972, February). The physiology of meditation. *Scientific American,* pp. 84–90.

Wallerstein, J., & Kelly, J. B. (1996). *Surviving the breakup: How children and parents cope with divorce.* New York: Basic Books.

Wallis, C. (1984, June 11). Unlocking pain's secrets. *Time,* pp. 58–60.

Wallis, C., & Willwerth, J. (1992, July 6). Schizophrenia: A new drug brings patients back to life. *Time,* pp. 52–57.

Walsh, D. M., Liggett, C., Baxter, D., & Allen, J. M. (1995). A double-blind investigation of the hypoalgesic effects of transcutaneous electrical nerve stimulation upon experimentally induced ischaemic pain. *Pain, 61,* 39–45.

Walster, E., & Walster, G. W. (1978). *Love.* Reading, MA: Addison-Wesley.

Walter, H. J., Vaughan, R. D., & Wynder, E. L. (1994). Primary prevention of cancer among children: Changes in cigarette smoking and diet after six years of intervention. In A. Steptoe, & J. Wardle (Eds.), *Psychosocial processes and health: A reader.* Cambridge, England: Cambridge University Press.

Walters, J. M., & Gardner, H. (1986). The theory of multiple intelligences: Some issues and answers. In R. J. Sternberg, & R. K. Wagner (Eds.), *Practical intelligence.* Cambridge, England: Cambridge University Press.

Wang, D., & Arbib, M. A. (1993). Timing and chunking in processing temporal order. *IEEE Transactions on Systems, Man, and Cybernetics, 23,* 993–1009.

Wang, J., & Kaufman, A. S. (1993). Changes in fluid and crystallized intelligence across the 20- to 90-year age range on the K-BIT. *Journal of Psychoeducational Assessment, 11,* 29–37.

Wang, M. C., Reynolds, M. C., & Walberg, H. J. (Eds.). (1996). *Handbook of special and remedial education: Research and practice* (2nd ed.). New York: Pergamon.

Wang, M. Q., Fitzhugh, E. C., Westerfield, R. C., & Eddy, J. M. (1995). Family and peer influences on smoking behavior among American adolescents: An age trend. *Journal of Adolescent Health, 16,* 200–203.

Wang, Z. W., Black, D., Andreasen, N. C., & Crowe, R. R. (1993). A linkage study of chromosome 11q in schizophrenia. *Archives of General Psychiatry, 50,* 212–216.

Ward, K. D., Klesges, R. C., & Halpern, M. T. (1997). Predictors of smoking cessation and state-of-the-art smoking interventions. *Journal of Social Issues, 53,* 129–145.

Ward, T. (1997, April 15). Resolving Gulf War Syndrome. *HealthNews,* p. 4.

Ward, T. B., Smith, S. M., & Vaid, J. (1997). *Creative thought: An investigation of conceptual structures and processes.* Washington, DC: American Psychological Association.

Ward, W. C., Kogan, N., & Pankove, E. (1972). Incentive effects in children's creativity. *Child Development, 43,* 669–677.

Warga, C. (1987, August). Pain's gatekeeper. *Psychology Today,* pp. 51–56.

Wark, G. R., & Krebs, D. L. (1996). Gender and dilemma differences in real-life moral judgement. *Developmental Psychology, 32,* 220–230.

Warner, R. E. (1991). A survey of theoretical orientations of Canadian clinical psychologists. *Canadian Psychology, 32,* 525–528.*

Warshaw, R. (1988). *I never called it rape: The 'Ms.' report on recognizing, fighting, and surviving date and acquaintance rape.* New York: Harper & Row.

Wartner, U. G., Grossman, K., Fremmer-Bombik, E., & Suess, G. (1994). Attachment patterns at age six in south Germany: Predictability from infancy and implications for preschool behavior. *Child Development, 65,* 1014–1027.

Warwick, H. M. C., & Salkovskis, P. M. (1990). Hypochondriasis. *Behaviour Research and Therapy, 28,* 105–117.

Washton, A. M. (Ed.). (1995). *Psychotherapy and substance abuse: A practitioner's handbook.* New York: Guilford Press.

Wasserman, E. A., & Miller, R. R. (1997). What's elementary about associative learning? *Annual Review of Psychology, 48,* 573–607.

Waters, H. F. (1993, July 12). Networks under the gun. *Newsweek,* pp. 64–66.

Waterson, E. J., & Murray-Lyon, I. M. (1990). Preventing alcohol-related birth damage: A review. *Social Science and Medicine, 30,* 349–364.

Watkins, L. R., & Mayer, D. J. (1982). Organization of endogenous opiate and nonopiate pain control systems. *Science, 216,* 1185–1192.

Watson, J. B. (1925). *Behaviorism.* New York: Norton.

Watson, J. B., & Rayner, R. (1920). Conditioned emotional reactions. *Journal of Experimental Psychology, 3,* 1–14.

Watson, T. (1994, August 8). A tissue of promises. *U.S. News & World Report,* pp. 50–51.

Wauquier, A., McGrady, A., Aloe, L., Klausner, T., et al. (1995). Changes in cerebral blood flow velocity associated with biofeedback-assisted relaxation treatment of migraine headaches are specific for the middle cerebral artery. *Headache, 35,* 358–362.

Webb, D. (1990, November 7). Eating well. *New York Times,* p. C3.

Webb, W. B. (1992). *Sleep: The gentle tyrant* (2nd ed.). Boston, MA: Anker.

Webber, B. (1996, February 19). A mean chess-playing computer tears at the meaning of thought. *New York Times,* pp. A1, B6.

Weber, K., & Bennett, S. (1999). Special education in Canadian schools. Thornhill, Ontario: Highland Press.

Weber, R., & Crocker, J. (1983). Cognitive processes in the revision of stereotypic beliefs. *Journal of Personality and Social Psychology, 45,* 961–977.

Webster, R. (1995). *Why Freud was wrong: Sin, science, and psychoanalysis.* New York: Basic Books.

Wechsler, D. (1975). Intelligence defined and undefined. *American Psychologist, 30,* 135–139.

Week, D., & James, J. (1995). Eccentrics: A study of sanity and strangeness. New York: Villard Books.

Wegener, D. T., & Petty, R. E. (1994). Mood management across affective states: The hedonic contingency hypothesis. *Journal of Personality and Social Psychology, 66,* 1034–1048.

Weinberg, M. S., Williams, C. J., & Pryor, D. W. (1991, February 27) Personal communication. Indiana University, Bloomington.

Weinberg, R. A. (1996). Commentary: If the nature-nurture war is over, why do we continue to battle? In D. K. Detterman (Ed.), *Current topics in human intelligence, Volume 5, The environment.* Norwood, NJ: Ablex.

Weiner, B. (1985a). "Spontaneous" causal thinking. *Psychological Bulletin, 97,* 74–84.

Weiner, B. (1985b). *Human motivation.* New York: Springer-Verlag.

Weiner, B. A., & Wettstein, R. (1993). *Legal issues in mental health care.* New York: Plenum Press.

Weiner, I. B. (1994). Rorschach assessment. In M. E. Maruish (Ed.), *The use of psychological tests for treatment planning and outcome assessment.* Mahwah, NJ: Erlbaum.

Weiner, I. B. (1996). Some observations on the validity of the Rorschach Inkblot Method. *Psychological Assessment, 8,* 206–213.

Weiner, R. (1982). Another look at an old controversy. *Contemporary Psychiatry, 1,* 61–62.

Weinshel, E. M., & Renik, O. (1996). Psychoanalytic technique. In E. Nersessian, & R. G. Kopff, Jr. (Eds.), *Textbook of psychoanalysis.* Washington, DC: American Psychiatric Press.

Weinstein, C. E. (1986). Assessment and training of student learning strategies. In R. R. Schmeck (Ed.), *Learning styles and learning strategies.* New York: Plenum Press.

Weintraub, M. (1976). Intelligent noncompliance and capricious compliance. In L. Lasagna (Ed.), *Patient compliance.* Mt. Kisco, NY: Futura.

Weisberg, H. F., Krosnick, J. A., & Bowen, B. D. (1996). *An introduction to survey research, polling, and data analysis.* Newbury Park, CA: Sage.

Weisberg, R. W. (1994, November). Genius and madness? A quasi-experimental test of the hypothesis that manic-depression increases creativity. *Psychological Science, 5,* 361–367.

Weiskrantz, L. (1989). Remembering dissociations. In H. L. Roediger, & F. I. M. Craik (Eds.), *Varieties of memory and consciousness: Essays in honour of Endel Tulving.* Mahwah, NJ: Erlbaum.

Weisman, A., Lopez, S. R., Karno, M., & Jenkins, J. (1993). An attributional analysis of expressed emotion in Mexican-American families with schizophrenia. *Journal of Abnormal Psychology, 102,* 601–606.

Weiss, A. S. (1991). The measurement of self-actualization: The quest for the test may be as challenging as the search for the self. *Journal of Social Behavior and Personality, 6,* 265–290.

Weiss, R. (1990, February 3). Fetal-cell recipient showing improvements. *Science News,* p. 70.

Weiss, R. (1992, April 28). Travel can be sickening; now scientists know why. *New York Times,* pp. C1, C11.

Weiss, R. S. (1994). A different kind of parenting. In G. Handel, & G. G. Whitchurch (Eds.), *The psychosocial interior of the family* (4th ed.). New York: Aldine de Gruyter.

Weissman, M., & the Cross-National Collaborative Group. (1992, December 2). Changing rates of major depression. *Journal of the American Medical Association, 262,* 3098–3105.

Weissman, M. M., Bland, R. C., Canino, G. J., Faravelli, C., Greenwald, S., Hwu, H. G., Joyce, P. R., Karam, E. G., Lee, C. K., Lellouch, J., Lepine, J. P., Newman, S. C., Rubio-Stipec, M., Wells, J. E., Wickramarante, P. J., Wittchen, H., & Yeh, E. K. (1996, July 24–31). Cross-national epidemiology of major depression and bipolar disorder. *Journal of the American Medical Association, 276,* 293–299.

Weissman, M. W., & Olfson, M. (1995, August 11). Depression in women: Implications for health care research. *Science, 269,* 799–801.

Weisz, J. R., Weiss, B., & Donenberg, G. R. (1992). The lab versus the clinic: Effects of child and adolescent psychotherapy. *American Psychologist, 47,* 1578–1585.

Weisz, J. R., Weiss, B., Han, S. S., Granger, D. A., & Morton, T. (1995). Effects of psychotherapy with children and adolescents revisited: A meta-analysis of treatment outcome studies. *Psychological Bulletin, 117,* 450–468.

Weitzenhoffer, A. M. (1989). *The practice of hypnotism.* New York: Wiley.

Weller, E. B., & Weller, R. A. (1991). Mood disorders in children. In G. J. Wiener (Ed.), *Textbook of child and adolescent psychiatry.* Washington, DC: American Psychiatric Press.

Weller, L., & Weller, A. (1995). Menstrual synchrony: Agenda for future research. *Psychoneuroendocrinology, 20,* 377–383.

Wells, E. K. (1997, January/February). New prognosis for HIV. *HIV Frontline,* pp. 4, 6.

Wells, G. L. (1993). What do we know about eyewitness identification? *American Psychologist, 48,* 553–571.

Wells, G. L., Luus, C. A. E., & Windschitl, P. D. (1994). Maximizing the utility of eyewitness identification evidence. *Current Directions in Psychological Science, 3,* 194–197.

Wells, K. (1993, July 30). Night court: Queen is often the subject of subjects' dreams. *Wall Street Journal,* pp. A1, A5.

Wells, R. A., & Giannetti, V. J. (1990). *Handbook of the brief psychotherapies.* New York: Plenum Press.

Werker, J. F. (1989). Becoming a native listener. *American Scientist, 77,* 54–59.*

Wertheimer, M. (1923). Untersuchungen zur Lehre von der Gestalt. II. *Psychol. Forsch., 5,* 301–350. In Beardsley and M. Wertheimer (Eds.) (1958), *Readings in perception.* New York: Van Nostrand.

Wertsch, J. V., & Tulviste, P. (1992). L. S. Vygotsky and contemporary developmental psychology. *Developmental Psychology, 28,* 548–557.

West, R. L. (1995). Compensatory strategies for age-associated memory impairment. In A. D. Baddeley, B. A. Wilson, & F. N. Watts

(Eds.), *Handbook of memory disorders.* Chichester, England: Wiley.

Westen, D. (1990). Psychoanalytic approaches to personality. In L. A. Pervin (Ed.), *Handbook of personality: Theory and research.* New York: Guilford Press.

Westera, D. A., & Bennett, L. R. (1994). Population-focused research: A broad-based survey of teens' attitudes, beliefs, and behaviours. *International Journal of Nursing Studies, 31,* 521–531.

Westover, S. A., & Lanyon, R. I. (1990). The maintenance of weight loss after behavioral treatment: A review. *Behavior Modification, 14,* 123–127.

Wever, R. A. (1989). Light effects on human circadian rhythms: A review of recent experiments. *Journal of Biological Rhythms, 4,* 161–185.

Whimbey, A., & Lochhead, J. (1991). *Problem solving and comprehension* (5th ed.). Mahwah, NJ: Erlbaum.

Whisman, M. A. (1993). Mediators and moderators of change in cognitive therapy of depression. *Psychological Bulletin, 114,* 248–265.

Whitbourne, S. K. (1986). *Adult development* (2nd ed.). New York: Praeger.

Whitbourne, S. K., Zuschlag, M. K., Elliot, L. B., & Waterman, A. S. (1992). Psychosocial development in adulthood: A 22-year sequential study. *Journal of Personality and Social Psychology, 63,* 260–271.

White, A. P., & Liu, W. Z. (1995). Superstitious learning and induction. *Artificial Intelligence Review, 9,* 3–18.

White, J. (1998). Comprehensive youth suicide prevention: A model for understanding. In A. A. Leenaars, S. Wenckstern, I. Sakinofsky, R. J. Dyck, M. J. Kral, & R. C. Bland (Eds.), *Suicide in Canada* (pp. 275–290). Toronto: University of Toronto Press.*

White, P. A. (1992). The anthropomorphic machine: Causal order in nature and the world view of common sense. *British Journal of Psychology, 83,* 61–96.

White, R. (1984). *Fearful warriors: A psychological profile of U.S.-Soviet relations.* New York: Free Press.

Whitehead, B. D. (1993, April). Dan Quayle was right. *Atlantic Monthly,* pp. 47–84.

Whitfield, C. L. (1995). How common is traumatic forgetting? Special Issue: Trusting childhood memories. *Journal of Psychohistory, 23,* 119–130.

Whiting, B. B. (1965). Sex identity conflict and physical violence: A comparative study. *American Anthropologist, 67,* 123–140.

Whorf, B. L. (1956). *Language, thought, and reality.* New York: Wiley.

Wickens, C. D. (1984). *Engineering psychology and human performance.* Columbus, OH: Merrill.

Wickens, C. D. (1991). *Engineering psychology and human performance* (2nd ed.). New York: HarperCollins.

Widiger, T. A., Frances, A. J., Pincus, H. A., & Davis, W. W. (1990). DSM-IV literature reviews: Rationale, process, and limitations.

Journal of Psychopathology and Behavioral Assessment, 12, 189–202.

Widmeyer, W. N., & Loy, J. W. (1988). When you're hot, you're hot! Warm-cold effects in first impressions of persons and teaching effectiveness. *Journal of Educational Psychology, 80,* 118–121.

Widner, H., Tetrud, J., Rehncrona, S., Snow, B., Brundin, P., Gustavii, B., Bjorklund, A., Lindvall, O., & Langston, J. W. (1992, November 26). Bilateral fetal mesencephalic grafting in two patients with Parkinsonism induced by 1-methyl-4-phenyl-1,2,3,6-tetrahydropyridine (MPTP). *New England Journal of Medicine, 327,* 1591–1592.

Widom, C. S. (1989). Does violence beget violence? A critical examination of the literature. *Psychological Bulletin, 106,* 3–28.

Wiebe, D. J. (1991). Hardiness and stress moderation: A test of proposed mechanisms. *Journal of Personality and Social Psychology, 60,* 89–99.

Wiederhold, W. C. (Ed.). (1982). *Neurology for non-neurologists.* New York: Academic Press.

Wiehe, V. R., & Richards, A. L. (1995). *Intimate betrayal: Understanding and responding to the trauma of acquaintance rape.* Thousand Oaks, CA: Sage.

Wiggins, J. G., Jr. (1994). Would you want your child to be a psychologist? *American Psychologist, 49,* 485–492.

Wiggins, J. S. (Ed.). (1996). *The five-factor model of personality: Theoretical perspectives.* New York: Guilford Press.*

Wiggins, J. S. (1997). In defense of traits. In R. Hogan, J. Johnson, & S. Briggs (Eds.), *Handbook of personality psychology.* Orlando, FL: Academic Press.*

Wiggins, J. S., & Pincus, A. L. (1992). Personality: Structure and assessment. In M. R. Rosenzweig & L. W. Porter (Eds.), *Annual review of psychology,* (vol.43). Palo Alto: Annual Reviews Inc.*

Wiggins, J. S., & Trapnell, P. D. (1997). Personality structure: The return of the Big Five. In R. Hogan, J. Johnson, & S. Briggs (Eds.), *Handbook of personality psychology.* Orlando, FL: Academic Press.*

Wilber, D. M. (1993, May/June). H. Ross Perot spurs a polling experiment (unintentionally). *The Public Perspective,* pp. 28–29.

Wilcock, G. K. (1993). Nerve growth factor and other experimental approaches. In R. Levy, R. Howard, & A. Burns (Eds.), *Treatment and care in old age psychiatry.* Petersfield, England: Wrightson Biomedical Publishing.

Wilder, D. A. (1986). Social categorization: Implications for creation and reduction of intergroup bias. In L. Berkowitz (Ed.), *Advances in experimental social psychology* (Vol. 19). San Diego, CA: Academic Press.

Wilder, D. A. (1990). Some determinants of the persuasive power of in-groups and out-groups: Organization of information and attribution of independence. *Journal of Personality and Social Psychology, 59,* 1202–1213.

Wildman, R. W., Wildman, R. W., II, Brown, A., & Trice, C. (1976). Note on males' and females' preference for opposite-sex body

parts, bust sizes, and bust-revealing clothing. *Psychological Reports, 38,* 485–486.

Wileman, R., & Wileman, B. (1995). Towards balancing power in domestic violence relationships. *Australian and New Zealand Journal of Family Therapy, 16,* 165–176.

Wilford, J. N. (1994, March 29). Sexes equal on South Sea isle. *New York Times,* pp. C1, C11.

Wilkerson, I. (1991, December 2). Black-White marriages rise, but couples still face scorn. *New York Times,* p. B6.

Wilkerson, I. (1992, June 21). The tallest fence: Feelings on race in a White neighborhood. *New York Times,* p. A18.

Wilkie, D. M., Carr, J. A. R., Galloway, J., Parker, K. J., & Yamamoto, A. (1997). Conditional time-place learning. *Behavioural Processes, 40,* 165–170.*

Williams, J. E., & Best, D. L. (1990). *Measuring sex stereotypes: A multinational study.* Newbury Park, CA: Sage.

Williams, J. E., Munick, M. L., Saiz, J. L., & FormyDuval, D. L. (1995). Psychological importance of the "Big Five": Impression formation and context effects. *Personality and Social Psychology Bulletin, 21,* 818–826.

Williams, K. (1997). Preventing suicide in young people: What is known and what is needed. *Child: Care, Health & Development, 23,* 173–185.

Williams, R. B. (1993). Hostility and the heart. In D. Goleman, & J. Gurin (Eds.), *Mind-body medicine.* Yonkers, NY: Consumer Reports Books.

Williams, R. B. (1996). Coronary-prone behaviors, hostility, and cardiovascular health: Implications for behavioral and pharmacological interventions. In K. Orth-Gomer, & N. Schneiderman (Eds.), *Behavioral medicine approaches to cardiovascular disease prevention.* Mahwah, NJ: Erlbaum.

Williams, R. B., Jr., Barefoot, J. C., Haney, T. L., Harrell, F. E., Jr., Blumenthal, J. A., Pryor, D. B., & Peterson, B. (1988). Type A behavior and angiographically documented coronary atherosclerosis in a sample of 2,289 patients. *Psychosomatic Medicine, 50,* 139–152.

Williams, S. W., & McCullers, J. C. (1983). Personal factors related to typicalness of career and success in active professional women. *Psychology of Women Quarterly, 7,* 343–357.

Willis, S. L., & Nesselroade, C. S. (1990). Long-term effects of fluid ability training in old-old age. *Developmental Psychology, 26,* 905–910.

Willis, S. L., & Schaie, K. W. (1994). In C. B. Fisher, & R. M. Lerner (Eds.), *Applied developmental psychology.* New York: McGraw-Hill.

Willis, W. D., Jr. (1988). Dorsal horn neurophysiology of pain. *Annals of the New York Academy of Science, 531,* 76–89.

Willson, R. J., & Wilkie, D. M. (1993). Pigeons remember briefly trained spatial location-food associations over extended time periods. *Journal of Experimental Psychology: Animal Behaviour Processes, 19(4),* 373–379.*

Wilson, F. A. W., O Scalaidhe, S. P., & Goldman-Rakic, P. S. (1993, June 25). Dissociation of object and spatial processing domains in primate prefrontal cortex. *Science, 260,* 1955–1958.

Wilson, G. T., & Agras, W. S. (1992). The future of behavior therapy. *Psychotherapy, 29,* 39–43.

Wilson, G. T., Franks, C. M., Kendall, P. C., & Foreyt, J. P. (1987). *Review of behavior therapy: Theory and practice* (Vol. 11). New York: Guilford Press.

Wilson, J. P., & Keane, T. M. (Eds.). (1996). *Assessing psychological trauma and PTSD.* New York: Guilford Press.

Wilson, M. A., & McNaughton, B. L. (1994, July 29). Reactivation of hippocampal ensemble memories during sleep. *Science, 265,* 676–679.

Winch, R. F. (1958). *Mate selection: A study of complementary needs.* New York: Harper & Row.

Windholz, G. (1997, September). Ivan P. Pavlov: An overview of his life and psychological work. *American Psychologist, 52,* 941–946.

Winerip, M. (1993, November 15). No. 2 pencil fades as graduate exam moves to computer. *New York Times,* pp. A1, B9.

Winerip, M. (1994, June 11). S.A.T. increase the average score, by fiat. *New York Times,* pp. A1, A10.

Wink, P., & Helson, R. (1993). Personality change in women and their partners. *Journal of Personality and Social Psychology, 65,* 597–605.

Winkler, K. J. (1997, July 11). Scholars explore the blurred lines of race, gender, and ethnicity. *Chronicle of Higher Education,* pp. A11–A12.

Winner, E. (1997). *Gifted children: Myths and realities.* New York: Basic Books.

Winograd, E., & Neisser, E. (Eds.). (1992). *Affect and accuracy in recall: Studies in "flashbulb memories."* Cambridge, England: Cambridge University Press.

Winograd, E., & Neisser, U. (Eds.). (1993). *Affect and accuracy in recall: Studies of "flashbulb" memories.* New York: Cambridge University Press.

Winson, J. (1990, November). The meaning of dreams. *Scientific American,* pp. 86–96.

Winter, D. G. (1973). *The power motive.* New York: Free Press.

Winter, D. G. (1987). Leader appeal, leader performance, and the motive profile of leaders and followers: A study of American presidents and elections. *Journal of Personality and Social Psychology, 52,* 196–202.

Winter, D. G. (1988). The power motive in women—and men. *Journal of Personality and Social Psychology, 54,* 510–519.

Winters, D., Boone, T., & Collins, F. (1995, July 28). Effects of the *obese* gene product on body weight regulation in *ob/ob* mice. *Science, 269,* 540–543.

Wisniewski, H. M., & Wegiel, J. (1996). The neuropathology of Alzheimer's disease is caused by fibrillisation of ABeta and PHF (tau) proteins. In C. N. Stefanis, & H. Hippius (Eds.), *Neuropsychiatry in old age: An update. Psychiatry in progress series.* Gottingen, Germany: Hogrefe & Huber.

Witelson, S. (1989, March). *Sex differences.* Paper presented at the annual meeting of the New York Academy of Sciences, New York.

Witelson, S. F. (1995). Neuroanatomical bases of hemispheric functional specialization in the human brain: Possible developmental factors. In F. L. Kitterle (Ed.), *Hemispheric communication: Mechanisms and models.* Mahwah, NJ: Erlbaum.

Wixted, J. T., & Ebbeson, E. B. (1991). On the form of forgetting. *Psychological Science, 2,* 409–415.

Wohl, M. (1995). Depression and guilt. In M. Laufer (Ed.), *The suicidal adolescent.* Madison, CT: International Universities Press.

Wolman, B. B., & Stricker, G. (Eds.). (1990). *Depressive disorders: Facts, theories, and treatment methods.* New York: Wiley.

Wolozin, B. L., Pruchnicki, A., Dickson, D. W., & Davies, P. (1986). A neuronal antigen in the brains of Alzheimer patients. *Science, 232,* 648–650.

Wolpaw, J. R., & McFarland, D. J. (1994). Multichannel EEG-based brain-computer communication. *Electroencephalography and Clinical Neurophysiology Evoked Potentials, 90,* 444–449.

Wolpe, J. (1990). *The practice of behavior therapy.* Boston: Allyn & Bacon.

Wolters, G. (1995). Het geheugen. Functie, structuur en processen. (Memory: Its function, structure, and processes.) *Psycholoog, 30,* 369–374.

Women Fight Uphill Battle for Equity. *Science* (1996 October 4); 274 (5284):50 (in Science in Japan: Competition on Campus; News) J. Kinoshita.

Wonderlich, S., Klein, M. H., & Council, J. R. (1996). Relationship of social perceptions and self-concept in bulimia nervosa. *Journal of Consulting and Clinical Psychology, 64,* 1231–1237.

Wong, D. F., Gjedde, A., Wagner, H. M., Jr., Dannals, R. F., Links, J. M., Tune, L. E., & Pearlson, G. D. (1988, February 12). Response to Zeeberg, Gibson, and Reba. *Science, 239,* 790–791.

Wong, D. F., Wagner, H. N., Jr., Tune, L. E., Dannals, R. F., Pearlson, G. D., Links, J. M., Tamminga, C. A., Broussolle, E. P., Ravert, H. T., Wilson, A. A., Toung, T., Malat, J., Williams, J. A., O'Tuama, L. A., Snyder, S. H., Kuhar, M. J., & Gjedde, A. (1986, December 19). Positron emission tomography reveals elevated D2 dopamine receptors in drug-naive schizophrenics. *Science, 234,* 1558–1563.

Wong, M. M., & Csikszentmihalyi, M. (1991). Affiliation motivation and daily experience: Some issues on gender differences. *Journal of Personality and Social Psychology, 60,* 154–164.

Wong, P. T. P. (1989). Personal meaning and successful aging. *Canadian Psychology, 42(9),* 803–804.*

Wood, F. B., Flowers, D. L., & Naylor, C. E. (1991). Cerebral laterality in functional neuroimaging. In F. L. Kitterle (Ed.), *Cerebral laterality: Theory and research.* Mahwah, NJ: Erlbaum.

Wood, J. M., & Bootzin, R. (1990). The prevalence of nightmares and their independence from anxiety. *Journal of Abnormal Psychology, 99,* 64–68.

Wood, J. M., Nezworski, M. T., & Stejskal, W. J. (1996). The comprehensive system for the Rorschach: A critical examination. *Psychological Science, 7,* 3–10.

Wood, W., Lundgren, S., Ouellette, J. A., Busceme, S., & Blackston, T. (1994). Minority influence: A meta-analytic review of social influence processes. *Psychological Bulletin, 115,* 323–345.

Wood, W., & Stagner, B. (1994). Why are some people easier to influence than others? In S. Savitt, & T. C. Brock (Eds.), *Persuasion: Psychological insights and perspectives.* Boston: Allyn & Bacon.

Woolfolk, R. L., & McNulty, T. F. (1983). Relaxation treatment for insomnia: A component analysis. *Journal of Consulting and Clinical Psychology, 4,* 495–503.

Wozniak, R. H., & Fischer, K. W. (Eds.). (1993). *Development in context: Acting and thinking in specific environments.* Mahwah, NJ: Erlbaum.

Wright, J. H., & Beck, A. T. (1996). Cognitive therapy. In R. E. Hales, & S. C. Yudofsky (Eds.), *The American Psychiatric Press synopsis of psychiatry.* Washington, DC: American Psychiatric Press.

Wright, M. J. (1993). Women Groundbreakers in Canadian Psychology: World War II and its aftermath. *Canadian Psychology, 33(4),* 675–682.*

Wright, M. J., & Myers, C. R. (1982). *History of Academic Psychology in Canada.* Toronto: C. J. Hogrefe.*

Wright, R. (1996, March 25). Can machines think? *Time,* pp. 50–56.

Wu, C., & Shaffer, D. R. (1987). Susceptibility to persuasive appeals as a function of source credibility and prior experience with the attitude object. *Journal of Personality and Social Psychology, 52,* 677–688.

Wurtman, R. J., Corkin, S., Growdon, J. J., & Nitsch, R. M. (Eds.). (1996). *The neurobiology of Alzheimer's disease. Annals of the New York Academy of Sciences, Vol. 777.* New York: New York Academy of Sciences.

Wyatt, G. E. (1992). The sociocultural context of African American and White American women's rape. *Journal of Social Issues, 48,* 77–92.

Wyatt, G. E. (1994). The sociocultural relevance of sex research: Challenges for the 1990s and beyond. *American Psychologist, 49,* 748–754.

Wyatt, R. J., Apud, J. A., & Potkin, S. (1996). New directions in the prevention and treatment of schizophrenia: A biological perspective. *Psychiatry, 59,* 357–370.

Wynn, K. (1992, August 27). Addition and subtraction by human infants. *Nature, 358,* 749–750.

Wynn, K. (1993). Evidence against empiricist accounts of the origins of numerical knowledge. In A. I. Goldman (Ed.),

Readings in philosophy and cognitive science. Cambridge, MA: MIT Press.

Wynn, K. (1995). Infants possess a system of numerical knowledge. *Current Directions in Psychological Science, 4,* 172–177.

Wynne, L. C., Singer, M. T., Bartko, J. J., & Toohey, M. L. (1975). *Schizophrenics and their families: Recent research on parental communication.* Psychiatric Research: The Widening Perspective. New York: International Universities Press.

Wyshak, G., & Barsky, A. (1995). Satisfaction with and effectiveness of medical care in relation to anxiety and depression: Patient and physician ratings compared. *General Hospital Psychiatry, 17,* 108–114.

Yalom, I. D. (1995). *The theory and practice of group psychotherapy* (4th ed.). New York: Basic Books.

Yalom, I. D. (1997). *The Yalom reader: On writing, living, and practicing psychotherapy.* New York: Basic Books.

Yamamato, T., Yuyama, N., & Kawamura, Y. (1981). Cortical neurons responding to tactile, thermal and taste stimulations of the rat's tongue. *Brain Research, 22,* 202–206.

Yang, G., & Masland, R. H. (1992, December 18). Direct visualization of the dendritic and receptive fields of directionally selective retinal ganglion cells. *Science, 258,* 1949–1952.

Yee, A. H., Fairchild, H. H., Weizmann, F., & Wyatt, G. E. (1993). Addressing psychology's problem with race. *American Psychologist, 48,* 1132–1140.

Yell, M. L. (1995). The least restrictive environment mandate and the courts: Judicial activism or judicial restraint? *Exceptional Children, 61,* 578–581.

Yenerall, J. D. (1995). College socialization and attitudes of college students toward the elderly. *Gerontology and Geriatrics Education, 15,* 37–48.

Yontef, G. M. (1995). Gestalt therapy. In A. S. Gurman, & S. B. Messer (Eds.), *Essential psychotherapies: Theory and practice.* New York: Guilford Press.

Yost, W. A. (1992). Auditory perception and sound source determination. *Current Directions in Psychological Science, 1,* 179–184.

Youdim, M. B. H., & Riederer, P. (1997, January). Understanding Parkinson's disease. *Scientific American,* pp. 52–59.

Youkilis, H., & Bootzin, R. R. (1981). A psychophysiological perspective on the etiology and treatment of insomnia. In S. M. Haynes, & L. A. Gannon (Eds.), *Psychosomatic disorders: A psychophysiological approach to etiology and treatment.* New York: Praeger.

Young, M. A., Fogg, L. F., Scheftner, W., Fawcett, J., et al. (1996). Stable trait components of hopelessness: Baseline and sensitivity to depression. *Journal of Abnormal Psychology, 105,* 155–165.

Young, W. (1996, July 26). Spinal cord regeneration. *Science, 273,* 451.

Youngman, N. (1992, February). Adapt to diversity or risk irrelevance, field warned. *APA Monitor, 23,* 44.

Yu, S., Pritchard, M., Kremer, E., Lynch, M., Nancarrow, J., Baker, E., Holman, K., Mulley, J. C., Warren, S. T., Schlessinger, D., Sutherland, G. R., & Richards, R. I. (1991, May 24). Fragile X genotype characterized by an unstable region of DNA. *Science, 252,* 1179–1181.

Yuille, J. C. (1988). The systematic assessment of children's testimony. *Canadian Psychology, 29,* 247–262.*

Yuille, J. C. (1997). Interviewing children is a complex task. *Contemporary Psychology, 42,* 803–804.*

Yuille, J. C., & Cutshall, J. L. (1986). A case study of eyewitness memory of a crime. *Journal of Applied Psychology, 71,* 291–301.*

Yuille, J. C., & Tollestrup, P. A. (1992). A model of the diverse effects of emotion on eyewitness memory. In S. A. Christianson (Ed.), *The handbook of emotion and learning: Research and theory.* Hillsdale, NJ: Erlbaum.*

Yurek, D. M., & Sladek, J. R., Jr. (1990). Dopamine cell replacement: Parkinson's disease. *Annual Review of Neuroscience, 13.*

Yuskauskas, A. (1992). Conflict in the developmental disabilities profession: Perspectives on treatment approaches, ethics, and paradigms. *Dissertation Abstracts International, 53,* 1870.

Zaidel, D. W. (1994). Worlds apart: Pictorial semantics in the left and right cerebral hemispheres. *Current Directions in Psychological Science, 3,* 5–8.

Zaidel, E., Aboitiz, F., Clarke, J., Kaiser, D., & Matterson, R. (1995). Sex differences in interhemispheric relations for language. In F. L. Kitterle (Ed.), *Hemispheric communication: Mechanisms and models.* Mahwah, NJ: Erlbaum.

Zajonc, R. B. (1968). The attitudinal effects of mere exposure. *Journal of Personality and Social Psychology, 9,* 1–27.

Zajonc, R. B. (1985). Emotion and facial efference: A theory reclaimed. *Science, 228,* 15–21.

Zajonc, R. B., & McIntosh, D. N. (1992). Emotions research: Some promising questions and some questionable promises. *Psychological Science, 3,* 70–74.

Zamarra, J. W., Schneider, R. H., Besseghini, I., Robinson, D. K., & Salerno, J. W. (1996). Usefulness of the transcendental meditation program in the treatment of patients with coronary artery disease. *American Journal of Cardiology, 77,* 867–870.

Zanna, M. P. (1994). On the nature of prejudice. *Canadian Psychology, 35,* 11–23.*

Zanna, M. P., & Pack, S. J. (1974). On the self-fulfilling nature of apparent sex differences in behavior. *Journal of Experimental Social Psychology, 11,* 583–591.*

Zanna, M. P., & Remple, J. K. (1988). Attitudes: A new look at an old concept. In D. Bar-Tal, & A. W. Kruglanski (Eds.), *Social Psychology of Knowledge* (315–334). New York: Cambridge University Press.*

Zaragoza, M. S., & Mitchell, K. J. (1996). Repeated exposure to suggestion and the creation of false memories. *Psychological Science, 7,* 294–300.

Zaslow, M. J. (1991). Variation in child care quality and its implications for children. *Journal of Social Issues, 47,* 125–138.

Zautra, A. J., Reich, J. W., & Guarnaccia, C. A. (1990). Some everyday life consequences of disability and bereavement for older adults. *Journal of Personality and Social Psychology, 59,* 550–561.

Zebrowitz-McArthur, L. (1988). Person perception in cross-cultural perspective. In M. H. Bond (Ed.), *The cross-cultural challenge to social psychology.* Newbury Park, CA: Sage.

Zeidner, M., & Endler, N. S. (Eds.). (1996). *Handbook of coping: Theory, research, applications.* New York: Wiley.*

Zeidner, M., & Saklofske, D. H. (1996). Adaptive and maladaptive coping. In M. Zeidner & N. S. Endler (Eds.), *Handbook of coping: Theory, research, applications.* New York: Wiley.*

Zeki, S. (1992, September). The visual image in mind and brain. *Scientific American, 267,* 68–76.

Zeki, S. (1993). *A vision of the brain.* Boston: Blackwell Scientific Publications.

Zevon, M., & Corn, B. (1990). Paper presented at the annual meeting of the American Psychological Association, Boston.

Zhang, Y., Proenca, R., Maffei, M., Barone, M., Leopold, L., & Friedman, J. M. (1994, December). Positional cloning of the mouse obese gene and its human homologue. *Nature, 372,* p. 425.

Zhdanova, I., Wurtman, R., & Green, C. H. (1996, June). How does melatonin affect sleep? *The Harvard Mental Health Letter,* 8.

Ziegler, E., & Styfco, S. J. (1993). *Head start and beyond: A national plan for extended childhood intervention.* New Haven, CT: Yale University Press.

Ziegler, S. (1981). The effectiveness of cooperative learning teams for increasing cross-ethnic friendship: Additional evidence. *Human Organization, 40,* 264–267.*

Zigler, E., & Glick, M. (1988). Is paranoid schizophrenia really camouflaged depression? *American Psychologist, 43,* 284–290.

Zigler, E. F., & Lang, M. E. (1991). *Child care choices: Balancing the needs of children, families, and society.* New York: Free Press.

Zika, S., & Chamberlain, K. (1987). Relation of hassles and personality to subjective well-being. *Journal of Personality and Social Psychology, 53,* 155–162.

Zilbergeld, B., & Ellison, C. R. (1980). Desire discrepancies and arousal problems in sex therapy. In S. R. Leiblum, & L. A. Pervin (Eds.), *Principles and practices of sex therapy.* New York: Guilford Press.

Zillman, D. (1978). *Hostility and aggression.* Mahwah, NJ: Erlbaum.

Zillman, D. (1993). Mental control of angry aggression. In D. M. Wegner, & J. W. Pennebaker (Eds.), *Handbook of mental control.* Englewood Cliffs, NJ: Prentice Hall.

Zimmer, J. (1984). Courting the gods of sport: Athletes use superstition to ward off the devils of injury and bad luck. *Psychology Today*, pp. 36–39.

Zimmer, L., & Morgan, J. P. (1997). *Marijuana myths, marijuana fact. A review of the scientific evidence.* New York: Lindesmith Center.

Zimmerman, B. J. (1995). Self-efficacy and educational development. In A. Bandura (Ed.), *Self-efficacy in changing societies.* New York: Cambridge University Press.

Zimmerman, B. J. (1996). Enhancing student academic and health functioning: A self-regulatory perspective. *School Psychology Quarterly, 11,* 47–66.

Zinberg, N. E. (1976). Normal psychology of the aging process, revisited (I): Social learning and self-image in aging. *Journal of Geriatric Psychiatry, 9,* 131–150.

Zito, J. M. (1993). *Psychotherapeutic drug manual* (3rd ed., rev.). New York: Wiley.

Zola-Morgan, S., & Squire, L. R. (1993). The neuroanatomy of memory. *Annual Review of Neuroscience, 16,* 547–563.

Zola-Morgan, S. M., & Squire, L. R. (1990, October 12). The primate hippocampal formation: Evidence for a time-limited role in memory storage. *Science, 250,* 288–290.

Zubin, J., & Spring, B. (1977). Vulnerability: New view of schizophrenia. *Journal of Abnormal Psychology, 86,* 103–126.

Zuckerman, M. (1978). The search for high sensation. *Psychology Today*, pp. 30–46.

Zuckerman, M. (1991). One person's stress is another person's pleasure. In C. D. Spielberger, I. G. Sarason, Z. Kulczar, & G. L. Van Heck (Eds.), *Stress and emotion: Anxiety, anger, and curiosity.* New York: Hemisphere.

Zuckerman, M. (1994). *Behavioral expressions and biosocial bases of sensation seeking.* New York: Cambridge University Press.

Zuckerman, M., Miyake, K., & Elkin, C. S. (1995). Effects of attractiveness and maturity of face and voice on interpersonal impressions. *Journal of Research in Personality, 29,* 253–272.

Zuger, A. (1996, October 8). Home testing for HIV. *Health News*, p. 4.

Acknowledgments

Chapter 1: Figure 1-1 from Office of Demographic, Employment and Educational Research (ODEER). (1994). Major speculate areas within the field of psychology. Washington, DC: American Psychological Association. Copyright © 1994 by the American Psychological Association. Adapted with permission. **Page 27** Drawing by Handelsman; © The New Yorker Magazine.

Chapter 2: Figure 2-2 used with the permission of Carol Donner. **Figure 2-7** from Loftus, E., & Wortmann, C. (1989). *Psychology,* 4th Ed. New York: Knopf. (McGraw-Hill), p. 63. Reproduced with permission of The McGraw-Hill Companies. **Figure 2-11** used with the permission of Carol Donner. **Figure 2-12a** from Schneider, A. M., & Tarshis, B. (1995). *Elements of Physiological Psychology.* New York: McGraw-Hill. Reproduced with permission of The McGraw-Hill Companies. **Figure 2-13b** used with the permission of Carol Donner. **Figure 2-14** from Penfield, W., & Rasmussen, T. (1950). *The cerebral cortex of man.* New York: Macmillan Publishing. **Figure 2-16** Used with the permission of Dr. Peter Fox, Research Imaging Center, University of Texas at San Antonio, Health Science Center; **Figure 2-19** used with permission of Dr. Mark R. Rosenzweig and Dr. Arnold L. Leiman; **Figure 2-20:** reprinted with permission from Psychology Today Magazine, Copyright © 1985 (Sussex Publishers, Inc.).

Chapter 3: Figure 3-5 adapted from *Human Information Processing: An Introduction to Psychology,* Second Edition by Peter H. Lindsay and Donald A. Norman, copyright © 1977 by Harcourt Brace & Company, reproduced by permission of the publisher. **Figure 3-7** used with permission of Michael L. Atkinson from *Psychology: Alternate Edition for Canada* by Camille B. Wortman, Elizabeth F. Loftus, Charles Weaver and Michael L. Atkinson (Toronto: McGraw-Hill Ryerson, 2000). **Figure 3-10** from National Institutes of Health, 1996, Washington, DC. **Figure 3-12** used with permission from Dr. Linda Bartoshuk and Laura Lucchina. **Figure 3-13** from Kinshalo, R. *The skin senses.* (1968). Courtesy of Charles C Thomas, Publisher, Springfield, Illinois. **Figure 3-14c** from *Mind Sights* by Shepard. © 1990 by Roger N. Shepard. Reprinted with permission of W. H. Freeman and Company. **Page 112** (*margin*) © 1996 Ian Falconer originally in The New Yorker. All rights reserved. **Figure 3-16** from *Sensation and Perception* by E. B. Goldstein. Copyright © 1996, 1989, 1984, 1980 Brooks/Cole Publishing Company, Pacific Grove, CA 93950, a division of International Thomson Publishing Inc. By permission of the publisher. **Figure 3-17** from Biederman, I. (1990). Higher level vision. In D. N. Osherson, S. Kosslyn, & J. Hollerbach (Eds.), *An invitation to cognitive science: Visual cognition and action.* Cambridge, MA: MIT Press. **Figure 3-18** Reprinted from *Vision research, 26,* Julesz, B., Stereoscopic vision, pgs 1601–1602. Copyright © 1986 with kind permission from Elsevier Science Ltd, The Boulevard, Langford Lane, Kidlington OX5 1GB, UK. **Figure 3-19** from *Sensation and Perception,* Third Edition by Stanley Coren and Lawrence M. Ward, copyright © 1989 by Harcourt Brace & Company, reproduced by permission. **Figure 3-20** used with permission of Dr. Donald A. Norman and Dr. David

Rumelhart. **Figure 3-21a-d** adapted from *Sensation and Perception,* Second Edition by Stanley Coren, Clare Porac, and Lawrence M. Ward, copyright © 1984 by Harcourt Brace & Company, reproduced by permission of publisher. **Figure 3-22a** adapted from *Sensation and Perception,* Second Edition by Stanley Coren, Clare Porac, and Lawrence M. Ward, copyright © 1984 by Harcourt Brace & Company, reproduced by permission of publisher.

Chapter 4: Figure 4-1 from Palladino, J. J. & Carducci, B. J. (1984). Students knowledge of sleep and dreams. *Teaching of Psychology, 11,* 89–191. Copyright © 1984 Lawrence Erlbaum Associates, Inc. **Figure 4-2** from *Sleep* by Hobson © 1995 by J. Allen Hobson. Used with permission of W. H. Freeman and Company. **Figure 4-3** from Hartmann, E., *The Biology of Dreaming* (1967). Courtesy of Charles C Thomas, Publisher, Springfield, Illinois. **Figure 4-4** from *Secrets of Sleep* by Alexander Borbely. English translation copyright © 1986 by Basic Books, Inc., copyright © 1984 by Deutsche Verlag-Anstalt GmbH, Stuttgart. Reprinted by permission of BasicBooks, a division of HarperCollins Publishers, Inc. **Figure 4-5** used with permission from Dr. Martin Moore-Ede. **Figure 4-6** from Dement, W. C., in D. F. Dinges, & R. J. Broughton, (Eds.) (1989). *Sleep and Alertness: Chronobiological, Behavioral, and Medical Aspects of Napping.* Philadelphia: Lippincott-Raven. **Page 137** THE FAR SIDE © 1983 THE FARWORKS, INC. Used with permission of UNIVERSAL PRESS SYNDICATE. All rights reserved. **Figure 4-7** from Griffith, R. M., Otoya, M., & Tago, A. (1958). The universality of typical dreams: Japanese vs American. *American Anthropologist, 60:6,* pt. 1. 1958. Reproduced by permission of the American Anthropological Association from American Anthropologist 60:6, Pt. 1, 1958. Not for further reproduction. **Page 148** Drawing by Richter; © 1993 The New Yorker Magazine, Inc. **Figure 4-8** from Benson, H., *The Relaxation Response,* Copyright © 1975 William Morrow and Co., Inc., New York. Used by permission of publisher. **Figure 4-10** from The New York Times. (August 7, 1991). Blakeslee. Levels of caffeine in various foods. Copyright © 1991 by The New York Times Company. Reprinted by Permission. **Figure 4-11** Gawin, F. H., & Kleber, H. D. (Mar 29, 1991). Cocaine abstinence phases. *Science.* Copyright © 1991 American Association For the Advancement of Science.

Chapter 5: page 178 Drawing by Cheney; © 1993 The New Yorker Magazine, Inc. **Figure 5-6** from Tolman, E. C., & Honzik, C. H. (1930). Introduction and removal of reward and maze performance in rats. *University of California Publications in Psychology, 4,* 257–275. Used with permission of the University of California Press. Copyright © 1992 Jossey-Bass, Inc., Publishers. **Page 190** Gahan Wilson © 1995 from The New Yorker Collection. All Rights Reserved. **Table 5-2** from Anderson, J. A., & Adams, M. (1992). Acknowledging the learning styles of diverse student populations: Implications for instructional design. *New Directions for Teaching and Learning, 49,* 19–33.

Chapter 6: Figure 6-2 from Atkinson, R. C., & Shiffrin, R. M. (1968). Human memory: A proposed system and its control processes. In K. W. Spence and

J. T. Spence (Eds.), *The psychology of learning and motivation: Advances in research and theory* (Vol. 2, pp. 80–195). New York: Academic Press. **Page 210** Drawing by R. Chast; © 1994 The New Yorker Magazine, Inc. **Figure 6-5** from Gathercole, S. E., & Baddeley, A. D. (1993). *Working memory and language processing.* Hillsdale, NJ: Erlbaum. **Figure 6-7** adapted from Collins, A. M., & Quillian, M. R. (1969). Retrieval times from semantic memory. *Journal of Verbal Learning and Verbal Behavior, 8,* 240–247. Academic Press. **Page 215** © Rob Rogers, reprinted by permission of UFS, Inc. **Figure 6-10** reprinted with permission from *Psychology Today Magazine,* Copyright © 1985 (Sussex Publishers, Inc.). **Figure 6-11** from Allport, G. W., & Postman, L. J. (1958). The basic psychology of rumor. In E. D. Maccoby, T. M. Newcomb, & E. L. Hartley (Eds.), *Readings in social psychology,* (3rd Ed.). New York: Holt.

Chapter 7: Figure 7-1 from Shepard, R., & Metzler, J. (1971). Mental rotation of three dimensional objects. *Science, 171,* 701–703. American Association For the Advancement of Science. Copyright © 1971 American Association For the Advancement of Science. **Table 7-1** from Rosch, E., & Mervis, C. B. (1975). Family resemblances: Studies in the internal structure of categories. *Cognitive Psychology, 7,* 573–605. Academic Press; **Figure 7-5a** from Poncini, M. (1990). *Brain Fitness.* New York: Random House. **Figure 7-5b** from Solso, R. L. *Cognitive psychology,* 3rd ed. Copyright © 1991 by Allyn and Bacon. Reprinted/adapted by permission. **Figure 7-6** used with permission of Dr. Barry F. Anderson. **Page 255** THE FAR SIDE © 1981 THE FARWORKS, INC. Used by permission of UNIVERSAL PRESS SYNDICATE, All Rights Reserved. **Figure 7-10** from Luchins, A. S. (1946). Classroom experiments on mental set. *American Journal of Psychology, 59,* 295–298. University of Illinois Press. **Figure 7-11** courtesy of Drs. Betty Hart and Todd Risley, 1997.

Chapter 8: Figure 8-2: Simulated items similar to those in Wechsler Intelligence Scale for Children: Third Edition. Copyright © 1990 by The Psychological Corporation. Reproduced by permission. All Rights Reserved. "Wechsler Intelligence Scale for Children" and "WISC-III" are registered trademarks of The Psychological Corporation. **Figure 8-3** from The New York Times, Nov. 15, 1994, p. B9. A new approach to test-taking. Copyright © 1994 by The New York Times Company, reprinted with permission. **Figure 8-4** from Walters, J. M., & Gardner, H. (1986). In R. J. Sternberg, (Ed.). *Practical Intelligence.* Excerpt, pp. 167–173. New York: Cambridge University Press. Reprinted with the permission of Cambridge University Press. **Figure 8-5** from Reasoning, problem solving, and intelligence. In R. J. Sternberg (Ed.). *Handbook of human intelligence* (pp. 225–307). New York: Cambridge Univ. Press. Reprinted with the Permission of Cambridge University Press. **Figure 8-6** used with permission of Dr. Robert J. Sternberg. **Figure 8-7** from Sternberg, R. J., & Wagner, R. K. (1993). The *g*-ocentric view of intelligence and job performance is wrong. *Current Directions in Psychological Science, 2,* 1–5. Used with the permission of Cambridge University Press. **Page 288**

THE FAR SIDE © 1982 THE FARWORKS INC. Used by permission OF UNIVERSAL PRESS SYNDICATE. All rights reserved. **Table 8-1** reprinted with permission of Knight-Ridder/Tribune Information Services; **Page 298** Charles Barsotti © 1994 from The New Yorker Collection. All Rights Reserved. **Figure 8-8** abstracted with permission from Bouchard, T. J., & McGue, M. Familial studies of intelligence: A review. *Science, 212*, 1055–1059. Copyright © 1981 American Association for the Advancement of Science. **Figure 8-9** used with permission from Dimitry Schildlovsky.

Chapter 9: Table 9-1 reprinted with permission from *Psychology Today Magazine*, Copyright © 1978 (Sussex Publishers, Inc.). **Figure 9-1** from *Motivation and Personality*, 3rd ed. By Abraham H. Maslow. Copyright 1954, 1987 by Harper & Row Publishers, Inc. Copyright © 1970 by Abraham H. Maslow. Reprinted by permission of Addison-Wesley Educational Publishers Inc. **Figure 9-3** from Fischer, K. W., Shaver, P. R., & Carnochan, P. (1990). How emotions develop and how they organize development. *Cognition and Emotion, 4*, 81–127. Reprinted by permission of Psychology Press Limited, Hove, UK. **Figure 9-5** from George, M. S., Ketter, T. A., Parekh, P. I., Horwitz, B., Herscovitch, P., & Post, R. M. (1995). Brain activity during transient sadness and happiness in healthy women. *American Journal of Psychiatry, 152*, 341–351. **Table 9-2** from Jenkins, C. D., Zyzanski, S. J., & Rosenman, R. H. (1979). Coronary-prone behavior: One pattern or several? *Psychosomatic Medicine, 40*, 25–43. Copyright © 1979 Williams & Wilkins. **Figure 9-6** from Selye, H. (1976). *The stress of life.* New York: McGraw-Hill. Reproduced with permission of The McGraw-Hill Companies. **Figure 9-7 (Hassles)** from Chamberlain, K., & Zika, S. (1990). The minor events approach to stress: Support for the use of daily hassles. *British Journal of Psychology, 81*, 469–481. © The British Psychological Society. **Figure 9-7 (Uplifts)** Kanner, A. D., Coyne, J. C., Schaefer, C., & Lazarus, R. (1981). Comparison of two modes of stress measurement: Daily hassles and uplifts versus major life events. *Journal of Behavioral Medicine, 4*, 14. Reproduced with permission from Plenum Publishing Corporation.

Chapter 10: Figure 10-1 from Shirely, M. M., *The first two years: A study of twenty-five babies*, Vol 2. (University of Minnesota Press, 1933). **Page 374** Drawing by Lorenz; © 1985 The New Yorker Magazine, Inc. **Figure 10-5** from Schickedanz, J. A., Schickedanz, D. I., & Forsyth, P. D. (1982). *Toward understanding children.* Boston: Little, Brown. **Table 10-5** from Kohlberg, L. (1969). Stage and sequence: The cognitive-developmental approach to socialization. In D. Goslin (Ed.), *Handbook of socialization theory and research.* Chicago: Rand McNally. Used with permission of David Goslin, President, American Institutes for Research. **Page 392** Michael Crawford © 1991 from The New Yorker Collection. All Rights Reserved. **Figure 10-6** from Schaie, K. W. (1994). The course of adult intellectual development. *American Psychologist, 49*, 304–313. Copyright © 1994 by the American Psychological Association. Adapted with permission.

Chapter 11: Figure 11-2 from Catell, Eber & Tatsuoka, 1970. *Handbook for the 16PF.* Champaign, IL: Institute for Personality and Ability Testing. **Figure 11-3** from Eysenck, H. J. (1990). Biological dimensions of personality. In L. A. Pervin (Ed.), *Handbook of personality: Theory and research*, p. 246. New York: Guilford. **Table 11-3** from Pervin, L. A., (Ed.). (1990). *Handbook of personality: Theory and research.* New York: Guilford. **Figure 11-4** from Tellegen, A., Lykken, D. T., Bouchard, T. J., Jr., Wilcox, K. J., Segal, N. L., & Rich, S. (1988). Personality similarity in twins reared apart and together. *Journal of Personality and Social Psychology, 54*, 1031–1039. Copyright © 1988 by the American Psychological Association. Adapted with permission. **Page 429** Robert Mankoff © 1991 from The New Yorker Collection. All Rights Reserved. **Figure 11-5** Based on Halgin, R. P., & Whitbourne, S. K. (1994). *Abnormal psychology.* Fort Worth, TX: Harcourt Brace, and Minnesota Multiphasic Personality Inventory 2. University of Minnesota. Reproduced with permission of The McGraw-Hill Companies.

Chapter 12: Figure 12-1 from *Anxiety disorders and phobias* by Aaron T. Beck and Gary Emery, with Ruth L. Greenberg. Copyright © 1985 by Aaron T. Beck, MD & Gary Emery, PhD. Reprinted by permission of BasicBooks, a division of HarperCollins Publishers, Inc. **Figure 12-3** from *The New York Times*. Oct. 10, 1993, p. C8. Mapping madness and genius. Copyright © 1993 by The New York Times Company, reprinted with permission. **Figure 12-5** from *Schizophrenia genesis: The origins of madness* by Gottesman © 1991 by Irving I. Gottesman. Reprinted with permission of W. H. Freeman and Company. **Figure 12-6** used with permission of Dr. Nancy C. Andreasen. **Figure 12-8** Health Canada.

Chapter 13: Table 13-2 used with permission of Dr. Herbert Benson. **Page 491** Donald Reilly © 1994 from The New Yorker Collection. All Rights Reserved. **Figure 13-1** from Smith, M. L., Glass, G. V., & Miller, T. J. *The benefits of psychotherapy*, Copyright © 1980, Johns Hopkins University Press. **Figure 13-2** Copyright 1995 by Consumers Union of U.S., Inc., Yonkers, NY 10703–1057. Reprinted by permission from CONSUMER REPORTS, November 1995. **Page 506** Drawing by Gahan Wilson; © 1994 The New Yorker Magazine, Inc. **Figure 13-3** from Howard, A., Pion, G. M., Gottfredson, G. D., Flattau, P. E., Oskamp, S., Pfafflin, S. M., Bray, D. W., & Burstein, A. D. (1986). The changing face of American psychology: A report from the committee on employment and human resources. *American Psychologist, 41*, 1311–1327. Copyright © 1986 by the American Psychological Association. Adapted with permission.

Chapter 14: Figure 14-4 adapted from Anderson, C. A., Krull, D. S., & Weiner, B. (1996). Explanations: Processes and consequences. In E. T. Higgins & A. W. Kruglanski (Eds.), *Social Psychology: Handbook of basic principles* (pp. 271–296). NY: Guilford Press. **Figure 14-7** reprinted with permission from *Psychology Today Magazine*, Copyright © 1979 (Sussex Publishers, Inc.). **Table 14-2** from Buss, D. L. International preferences in selecting mates: A study of 37 cultures. *Journal of Cross-Cultural Psychology, 21*, 5–47. Copyright © 1990 by Sage Publications. Reprinted by permission of Sage Publications. **Figure 14-8** from Sternberg, R. J. (1986). Triangular theory of love. *Psychological Review, 93*, 119–135. Copyright © 1986 by the American Psychological Association. Adapted with permission. **Figure 14-9** from Duck, S. (Ed.). (1984). *Personal Relationships.* New York: Academic Press. **Table 14-3** from Benjamin, L. T., Jr. (1985, February). Defining aggression: An exercise for classroom discussion. *Teaching of Psychology, 12* (1), 40–42. Copyright © 1985 Lawrence Erlbaum Associates, Inc. **Figure 14-10** from *The Unresponsive Bystander* by Latané/Darley, © 1970. Adapted by permission of Prentice-Hall, Inc. Upper Saddle River, NJ.

Photos

Research by LouAnn Wilson, Lesley Mann, and Elain Freedman

Chapter 1: Opener: Canada Day celebrations at Parliament Hill (July 1, 2000)—CP Picture Archive / Rod MacIvor; **pages 4 & 18:** AP/Wide World Photos; **page 8:** © Beringer/Howard Dratch/The Image Works; **page 15:** (top & bottom) Canadian Psychological Association; **page 16:** Corbis-Bettmann; **page 17:** Culver Pictures Inc.; **page 22:** CP Picture Archive / Marc Gallant; **page 24:** © Robert Brenner/Photo Edit; **page 26:** CP Picture Archive / Fred Chartrand; **page 28:** © Michael Newman/Photo Edit; **page 30:** © James Wilson/ Woodfin Camp; **page 30:** Katherine Unruh, University of Winnipeg; **page 36, 37:** © B. W. Hoffman/ Unicorn Stock Photos

Chapter 2: Opener: © Howard Sochurek/The Stock Market; **page 46:** © Bob Daemmrich/Stock Boston; **page 47** (left and right): © Manfred Kage/Peter Arnold, Inc.; **page 49;** CP Picture Archive / Chuck Stoody; **page 54:** CP Picture Archive / Kevork Djansezian, Associated Press AP; **Figure 2.9a,b** Science Photo Library/Science Source/Photo Researchers, Inc.; **Figure 2.9c** © Scott Camazine/Photo Researchers, Inc.; **Figure 2.9d:** © Dan McCoy/ Rainbow; **Figure 2.9e:** © Hank Morgan/Photo Researchers, Inc.; **page 62:** © Stephen Ferry/Gamma Liaison; **Figure 2.15:** The National History Museum, London; **page 70:** Used with permission from Antonio Damascio in *Science Magazine,* Vol. 264, May 20, 1994. Copyright © 1994 American Association for the Advancement of Science; **Figure 2.16:** Courtesy of Peter T. Fox and Jack L. Lancaster; **page 72:** courtesy Julien Doyon; **Figure 2.17:** © J. C. Mazziota & M. E. Phelps, UCLA School of Medicine/Dan McCoy/Rainbow; **Figure 2.18:** Shaywitz, et al., 1995 NMR Research/Yale Medical School; **page 78:** © James Schnepf/Gamma Liaison

Chapter 3: Opener: © Robert Holmes/Corbis; **page 84:** AP/Wide World Photos; **page 87:** CP Picture Archive / Fred Greenslade; **Figure 3.6a–d:** © Joe Epstein 1988/Design Conceptions; **page 98:** Photo courtesy of Dr. Jack M. Loomis, Dr. Reginald G. Golledge & Dr. Robert L. Klatzky; **page 105:** © Louie Psihoyos/Contact Press Images; **page 109:** courtesy Patrick J. McGrath; **Figure 3.14a:** Courtesy Kaiser-Porcelain Ltd.; **Figure 3.15:** Ronald C. James, from R. G. Carraher and J. B. Thurston, *Optical Illusions in the Visual Arts,* 1966, Van Nostrand Reinhold Press, New York.; **Figure 3.18:** Courtesy of Dr. Bela Julesz, Laboratory of Vision Research, Rutgers University; **Figure 3.21:** © John G. Ross/Photo Researchers, Inc.; **Figure 3.23a,b:** © Innervisions

Chapter 4: Opener: Laurie Rubin/The Image Bank, © 1998; **page 130:** AP/Wide World Photos; **Figure 4.1:** © Ted Spagna/Science Source/Photo Researchers, Inc.; **page 136:** © William McCoy/Rainbow; **page 142:** Divino Mucciante, Brock University; **page 144:** Dick Hemingway / Sleep Disorders Centre of Metropolitan Toronto; **page 146:** © John Ficara/Woodfin Camp; **page 148:** © Deborah Davis/Photo Edit; **page 152:** © Dion Ogust/The Image Works; **page 153:** © Mary Kate Denny/Photo Edit; **page 154:** © Mark C. Burnett/Photo Researchers, Inc.; **page 157:** © Steve Skjold/Photo Edit

Chapter 5: Opener: © Jeff Greenberg/Photo Edit; **page 168:** Heritage Studio; **page 170:** Culver Pictures Inc.; **page 177:** Nina Leen/Life Magazine © Time, Inc.; **page 181:** CP Picture Archive / Fred Chartrand; **page 185:** © Frieda Leinwand/ Monkmeyer; **page 186** (top): courtesy Catharine Rankin; **page 186** (bottom):

© Michael Newman/Photo Edit; **page 191**: The Photo Works/Photo Researchers, Inc.; **page 192**: Gamma Liaison; **page 196**: © Lester Sloan/Woodfin Camp

Chapter 6: Opener: Saskatchewan First Nations Grand Chief Howard Anderson commemorates the Tomb of the Unknown Soldier in Ottawa (May 28, 2000)—CP Picture Archive / Tom Hanson; **page 204**: © Adolphe Pierre-Louis; **page 212**: © Jeffrey Muir Hamilton/Stock Boston; **page 217**: © Tom McCarthy Photos/Index Stock; **page 218**: © Disney Enterprises, Inc.; **page 219**: AP/Wide World Photos; **Figure 6.15**: Courtesy of Dr. Steven E. Peterson, Washington University Medical School; **page 231**: CP Picture Archive / Andrew Vaughan; **page 232**: courtesy Holly Tuokko

Chapter 7: Opener: © Bob Daemmrich/Stock Boston; **page 240**: © Paula Lerner/Woodfin Camp; **Figure 7.2**: Courtesy of Dr. Alvaro Pascual-Leone, M.D., PhD.; **page 244**: © Bob Daemmrich/Stock Boston; **page 246**: © Najlah Reanny/Stock Boston; **page 254**: *The Mentality of Apes,* by Wolfgang Kohler, 1925. Reprinted by permission of Routledge, England; **page 259**: © Michael Schwarz/Gamma Liaison; **page 262**: Courtesy of Dr. Laura Ann Petitto © 1991/photo by Robert LaMarche; **page 263**: Dick Hemingway; **page 265**: © W. & D. McIntyre/Photo Researchers, Inc.; **page 266**: courtesy Fred Genesee

Chapter 8: Opener: © Bill Bachmann/Stock Boston; **page 275** (*top*): © James S. Douglass; **page 274** (*bottom*): © Pat Harbron/Outline/*Newsweek;* **page 275**: © David Hiser/Photographers Aspen; **page 278**: © Suzanne Szasz/Photo Researchers, Inc.; **page 283** (*left*): © Sepp Seitz/Woodfin Camp, **page 285** (*right*): © Bob Daemmrich/The Image Works; **page 286**: © Bill Bachmann/The Image Works; **page 289**: CP Picture Archive / Colin Corneau; **page 291**: © Stephen Frisch/Stock Boston; **page 293**: courtesy Jo-Anne Trigg; **page 296**: © Bob Daemmrich/The Image Works

Chapter 9: Opener: © E. B. Graphics/Liaison International; **page 306**: CP Picture Archive / Kevin Frayer; **page 311**: © Peter Southwick/Stock Boston;

page 315: © Dean Berry/Liaison International; **page 317 & 318**: © Tony Freeman/Photo Edit; **page 320** (*left*): © Chuck O'Rear/Woodfin Camp; **page 320** (*right*): © Bill Bachmann/Stock Boston; **page 323**: CP Picture Archive / Hans Deryk; **Figure 9.2**: Reprinted by permission of the publisher, from Henry A. Murray, *Thematic Apperception Test,* Cambridge, Mass: Harvard University Press, © 1943 by the President & Fellows of Harvard College, © 1971 by Henry A. Murray; **page 328**: Medical Photography, Queen's University; **page 335**: Courtesy of Donald G. Dutton, Ph.D; **Figure 9.5** *American Journal of Psychiatry,* (152); **page 345**, March 1995, American Psychiatric Press Association. Photo courtesy of Dr. Mark S. George. Reprinted by permission; **page 342**: CP Picture Archive / Robert Galbraith

Chapter 10: Opener: © Ed Malisky/Liaison International; **page 354**: © Michael Gallacher/Missoulian/Gamma Liaison; **page 356**: © Peter Byron; **page 360**: CP Picture Archive / Ken Faught; **page 362** (*left*): Lennart Nilsson/Albert BonnierForlag AB, *A Child is Born,* Dell Publishing; **page 362** (*right*): Petit Format/Science Source/Photo Researchers, Inc.; **page 363**: Toronto Board of Health; **Figure 10.3**: From A. N. Meltzoff & M. K. Moore, "Imitations of Facial and Manual Gestures by Human Neonates," *Science* 1997: Vol. 198, pages 75–78; **Figure 10.4**: Harlow Primate Laboratory, University of Wisconsin; **page 371**: The Photo Works/Photo Researchers, Inc.; **page 372**: © Lawrence Migdale/Photo Researchers, Inc.; **page 381**: © M. S. Wexler/Woodfin Camp; **page 385**: © David Young Wolff/Tony Stone; **page 389**: © Catherine Karnow/Woodfin Camp; **page 390**: courtesy Lorrie Sippola; **page 394**: © James Wilson/Woodfin Camp; **page 397**: © Bob Daemmrich/Stock Boston

Chapter 11: Opener: Governor-General Adrienne Clarkson presents the Medal of Bravery to 8-year-old Nick Vezina for rescuing his sister in a house fire (December 3, 1999)—Rideau Hall photo by Sgt. Julien Dupuis / courtesy of the Office of the Governor General; **page 410**: CP Picture Archive / Wayne

Hiebert; **page 413**: © Margaret Miller/Photo Researchers, Inc.; **page 417** (*both*): Photofest; **page 419**: © J. C. Francolon/Gamma Liaison; **page 424**: CP Picture Archive / Ryan Remiorz; **page 427**: © Bob Daemmrich/Stock Boston; **page 433**: Dick Hemingway; **page 434**: Romin Tafarodi

Chapter 12: Opener: © Vanessa Vick/Photo Researchers, Inc.; **page 444** (*left*): © Joseph Sohm/Chromosohm; **page 444** (*right*) CP Picture Archive / Ian Macalpine; **page 445**: Corbis-Bettmann; **page 449**: courtesy Sylvia Geist; **page 460**: ©Frank Micelotta/Outline; **Figure 12.4**: From Dr. Hans Prinzhorn, *The Artistry of the Mentally Ill: A Contribution to Psychopathology of Configuration,* 1995. Reprinted by permission of Springer-Verlag, Vienna; **Figure 12.6a,b:** Nancy Andreasen, University of Iowa Hospitals & Clinics; **Figure 12.7:** Monte S. Buchsbaum, M.D., Mount Sinai Medical Center; **page 471**: © Kal Muller/Woodfin Camp; **page 473**: CP Picture Archive / Jacques Boissinot

Chapter 13: Opener: © Zigy Kaluzny/Tony Stone; **page 480**: © Lynn Johnson/Black Star; **page 485**: © Jonahan Nourok/Photo Edit; **page 486**: © Rick Friedman/Black Star; **page 488**: CP Picture Archive / Jacques Boissinot; **page 490**: © David Young-Wolff/Photo Edit; **page 494**: © Alon Reininger/Contact Press Images; **page 498**: CP Picture Archive / Michael MacDonald; **page 501**: Custom Medical Stock Photo; **page 505**: Joy Cummings, UNB Audio Visual Services

Chapter 14: Opener: Protesters march on the APEC conference in Vancouver (November 23, 1997)—CP Picture Archive / Chuck Stoody; **page 512**: CP Picture Archive / Frank Gunn; **page 515**: © Gilles Mingason/Gamma Liaison; **page 518**: courtesy James Alcock; **page 528**: © Bob Daemmrich/The Image Works; **Figure 14.6a,b:** © 1965 Stanley Milgram, from the film "Obedience" distributed by Pennsylvania State University Media Sales; **page 533**: AP/Wide World Photos; **page 540**: © Esbin-Anderson/The Image Works; **page 545**: CP Picture Archive - Adrian Wyld

Name Index

Note: Page numbers in *italics* indicate illustrations; page numbers followed by *t* indicate tables.

Subject Index

Note: Page numbers in *italics* indicate illustrations; page numbers followed by *t* indicate tables.